McGraw-Hill
PERSONAL COMPUTER PROGRAMMING ENCYCLOPEDIA

LANGUAGES AND OPERATING SYSTEMS

McGraw-Hill
PERSONAL COMPUTER PROGRAMMING ENCYCLOPEDIA

LANGUAGES AND OPERATING SYSTEMS

William J. Birnes, Editor

Nancy Hayfield, Production Editor

McGraw-Hill Book Company

New York   St. Louis   San Francisco

Auckland   Bogota   Guatemala   Hamburg   Johannesburg
Lisbon   London   Madrid   Mexico   Montreal
New Delhi   Panama   Paris   San Juan   Sao Paulo
Singapore   Sydney   Tokyo   Toronto

McGRAW-HILL PERSONAL COMPUTER PROGRAMMING ENCYCLOPEDIA: LANGUAGES AND OPERATING SYSTEMS Copyright © 1985 by McGraw-Hill, Inc. All rights reserved. Printed in the United States of America. Except as permitted under the United States Copyright Act of 1976, no part of this publication may be reproduced or distributed in any form or by any means, or stored in a database or retrieval system, without the prior written permission of the publisher.

2 3 4 5 6 7 8 9 0   DODO   8 9 2 1 0 9 8 7 6

ISBN 0-07-005389-8

Library of Congress Cataloging in Publication Data

McGraw-Hill personal computer programming encyclopedia.

  Includes index.
      1. Microcomputers—Programming. 2. Programming languages (Electronic computers) 3. Operating systems (Computers) I. Birnes, William J. II. McGraw-Hill Book Company.
QA76.6.M414 1985   001.64'2   85-135
ISBN 0-07-005389-8

CONTENTS

8/25/86 MIDWEST 72.00

CONTENTS

CONTENTS

STAFF

Shadow Lawn Press

The Encyclopedia was compiled, typeset, and paged by Shadow Lawn Press, Neshanic Station, New Jersey.

William J. Birnes, President and Project Editor
Nancy Hayfield, Production Editor
Dorothy L. Amsden, Art Director and Illustrator
William Thompkins, Technical Illustrator
Jeanne Neilson, Illustrator
Robin E. Sigmann, Layout
Victoria Boyle, Index

McGraw-Hill

Sybil P. Parker, Editor in Chief
Edward J. Fox, Art and Production Director
Joe Faulk, Editing Manager
Patricia W. Albers, Senior Editing Assistant

CONTRIBUTORS

Jonathan Amsterdam, Artificial Intelligence Laboratory, Massachusetts Institute of Technology.

Henry F. Beechhold, Professor of English and Linguistics, Department of English, Trenton State College.

David Dameo, Director of Computer Operations, RTK Computer Services, Perth Amboy, New Jersey.

Michael Iannone, Chairman, Department of Mathematics and Computer Science, Trenton State College.

CONTRIBUTORS

Claude A. R. Kagan, Research and Development, Western Electric; Operating Systems Standards Committee, IEEE, Princeton.

Guy M. Kelly, Chairman Forth Standards Team, Chairman San Diego Chapter of the Forth Interest Group, La Jolla, California.

Yong M. Lee, Professor of Mathematics, Department of Mathematics and Computer Science, Trenton State College.

David Lewis, Department of Mathematics and Computer Science, Trenton State College.

Len Lindsay, President, COMAL Users Group USA, Ltd., Madison, Wisconsin.

Kenneth Madell, Software Developer and Programmer, Hamburg, New Jersey.

Lawrence Mahon, Software Consultant and Marketing Representative, Computerland, Inc., Somerville, New Jersey.

Gary Markman, Software and Systems Consultant, Yonkers, New York.

Norman Neff, Professor of Mathematics, Department of Mathematics and Computer Science, Trenton State College.

Karl Nicholas, Physical Acoustics Corporation, Princeton, New Jersey.

Ross Overbeek, Research and Development, Argonne National Laboratories, Lisle, Illinois.

Mark J. Robillard, Systems Consultant, Milford, New Hampshire.

Al Rubottom, President, New Technica, Inc., San Diego, California.

Max Schindler, Senior Editor, *Electronic Design;* President, Prime Technology, Inc., Boonton, New Jersey.

Stephen E. Seadler, President, Uniconsult, New York City.

Ernest R. Tello, President, Integral Systems, Santa Cruz, California.

Michael Tilson, Vice President, Human Computing Resources Corporation, Toronto, Ontario.

CONTRIBUTORS

Charles R. Walther, President, New Century Educational Corporation, Piscataway, New Jersey.

Linda Weisner, Research Assistant, Department of English, Trenton State College.

Michael Wetmore, Chief of Engineering, Pierce-Phelps, Inc., Philadelphia, Pennsylvania.

Robert Wharton, Professor of Mathematics, Department of Mathematics and Computer Science, Trenton State College.

William Woodall, Software Specialist, Somerville, New Jersey.

PREFACE

The concept of personal computing had its beginnings in the late 1970s with the assembly of the first microcomputers based on the technology of the integrated circuit. The initial commercial success of the microprocessor-driven units converged with the ongoing development of high-level computer programming languages. The appearance of these languages in the 1950s took programming, once a field open only to the engineers and designers who had originally developed computers, out of the laboratory and into the business marketplace. By the late 1960s there were a number of high-level languages with applications in the sciences, engineering, business, and even elementary and secondary education. When the first BASIC interpreters were bundled with the new "personal computer" packages in the 1970s, the two development streams were officially joined, and the personal computing revolution began.

Over the next eight years, each success in personal computing technology prompted a new surge of development. The machines themselves grew in power and capability from 8-bit 8K PET computers with membrane-type keyboards and onboard cassette recorders to the IBM PC-AT with its 20 megabytes of hard-disk storage and true 16-bit speed. By the end of 1984, the LISA technology developed by Apple for its 32-bit office machines was repackaged to appeal to a home market and quickly caught on as the Macintosh. In a lockstep with the development of new hardware systems was the invention of new software systems and applications programs. The BASICs of the 1960s and 1970s gave birth to more powerful versions that had built-in graphics and music commands and system utilities that allowed even novice programmers a sophistication and efficiency of code that previously could only have been found in assembly language routines. However, beyond BASIC, versions of Pascal, C, and Forth were developed which put enormous programming power into the hands of personal computer users and allowed them to emulate the processing capabilities of large mainframes at their desktop terminals. And this is only the beginning. Languages such as Ada, the Department of Defense's new projected standard information-processing language, and Prolog, which is at the center of artificial intelligence research and development, have recently been implemented on personal computers and will become more popular as succeeding generations of more powerful computers find their way into the home and business markets.

This proliferation of computing language implementations has created a serious need for a single reference volume which not only introduces the various languages and indexes all of their command words and statements, but provides for a cross-referencing of applications and a comparison of the languages' capabilities. This is the purpose of the *Personal Computer Programming Encyclopedia*. The Encyclopedia illustrates the capabilities of each language with overviews of the language's design and architecture, and by comparing the operational differences of each language through sample programs, the Encyclopedia demonstrates the different ways applications can be addressed by programmers working within the different language environments.

The Encyclopedia is divided into two types of sections: the double-column sections which cover the high-level languges, operating system commands, and assembly language commands, and the single-column sections which contain background and introductory material. In the single-column sections, readers will find articles which explain the architecture and design of computer programs, examine the user-oriented issues of software development in business

PREFACE

and education, and explore the newest areas of development in graphics, robotics, and artificial intelligence. In choosing these different types of entries for the Encyclopedia, recognition has been given to the major areas of personal computing that affect users: (1) the need to understand the logic of program design; (2) the current trends and issues in the most important areas of software development; (3) the diversity of languages that are available to personal computer users and the primary applications of these languages; and (4) the relationship of hardware systems to software systems. The result is a volume that addresses the needs of the entire personal computing community from the business user and consumer of professional software products to the home user learning about a type of information technology that promises to transform the ways people organize their lives.

The Encyclopedia provides background histories of the high-level programming languages, operating systems, and applications software cited. It relates the development of these various software tools to the current computing environment as well as to the historical period during which the software was originated and marketed. The result of this approach is a social history of personal computing in which programmers, personal computer users, and general readers will discover the underlying reasons for much of the product development in the marketplace. The Encyclopedia explains the different trends in languages, operating systems, and applications software over the past five to ten years, and the effects of these products on users in different professional fields.

The Encyclopedia contains an index to all of the keywords and statements in the high-level languages that are cited. This index is an important reference tool for programmers and serious users because it provides an immediate cross-reference between the different languages. Programmers seeking to translate source code from one compiler to another or from one dialect of BASIC to COMAL or structured BASIC will find the cross-index a handy tool. General readers interested in the history and intellectual backgrounds of programming languages will find in the cross-index of high-level language keywords a generic approach to the types of commands that are used in programming. Teachers will also find this system a valuable reference tool for use in comparative programming.

The Encyclopedia also examines the different corporate cultures from which the most popular types of personal computers have evolved and evaluates the dynamic relationships between manufacturer and the manufacturer's product history, the hardware system and supporting software, and the user market the computer was targeted to reach. Readers will find an interesting perspective on the current trends of technological development in the areas of hardware, software, and operating environments. There is a capsule summary of the history of personal computers from the first attempts to market basic user-assembled kits to the 32-bit supermicros that will be making their appearance within the next several years. Their history, brief as it is, will provide a needed background to the dynamic microcomputer marketplace and the different products that are announced in the computer magazines and newspapers.

PREFACE

The articles in the *Personal Computer Programming Encyclopedia* are written by individuals from a variety of backgrounds. This diversity of opinion is reflected in the different levels of emphasis within the entries and the broad perspective of the volume in general. In short, the Encyclopedia embraces the types of related informational materials that spread across the traditional boundaries often found in a reference book on science and technology. This is what makes the volume an innovative reference tool.

While a number of computer dictionaries and comparative reference books on programming languages have appeared recently, the *McGraw-Hill Personal Computer Programming Encyclopedia* is the only single-volume reference to provide a comprehensive introduction to the entire personal computing environment both as a science and as a commercial industry. Thus, it will become a valuable reference both for the computer professional and for the novice. Business users, students, teachers, hobbyists, and home users will find this *Encyclopedia* a most useful desktop computer reference.

William J. Birnes
Editor

McGraw-Hill

PERSONAL COMPUTER PROGRAMMING ENCYCLOPEDIA

LANGUAGES AND OPERATING SYSTEMS

How to Begin to Program

DESIGN

CODE

PROGRAM

1
PROGRAM DESIGN AND ARCHITECTURE

As in most creative work, the fundamental aspect of writing good applications and systems programs lies in the preliminary design and architecture. It is on this level that some of the most important thinking takes place. Goals are defined, pathways are mapped out, logical relationships between data types are developed, and the rules that will govern the decisions the machine will make are stipulated. It is here, at the very heart of a well-designed program, that a definition of truth is implemented, and the execution of this program, the processing of line after line of code, is a test for that truth. And as a statement of truth and a test for that truth's existence in the data that flows through it, the computer program takes its place right alongside literature and art as a form of creative expression. There is a practical creativity, to be sure, but a computer program is no less creative and structured in its disciplined expression of truth than a line of poetry by Keats, a portrait by Albrecht Dürer, or a Bach concerto.

What takes place in the design and architecture of a computer program? On the most obvious and visible level, it is a patient sequence of logic that expresses the complexity of human thought in terms of an organized pattern of connected decisions to be implemented ultimately as a series of electronic pulses. On an even more fundamental level, it is nothing less than the definition of the reality that the computer will understand as its truth. The design of a computer program, therefore, is a microcosm of the physical universe, and as an amalgamation of artistic creativity and technical precision, it is the marriage of C. P. Snow's "Two Cultures."

The choice of the actual programming language and the subsequent coding of the program, while important, take place after the logic of the program has been designed. Programming languages by themselves are only forms of machine code generators. By definition, they are a source of code that is either compiled or interpreted by the machine and translated into the sets of instructions that the machine can process. As a source of code, they help the programmer implement a coherent and executable logical design and serve as a matrix for the actual commands. In addition, high-level computing languages provide for the definition of the types of data and, in some cases, particularly COBOL, the specific machine environments. But, while an indicator of program efficiency, the programming language is not, and should not be considered, the ultimate indicator of quality. The best programs are good, not because they are written in C rather than BASIC, or in LISP rather than Pascal, but because they are designed from concept through code to be disciplined and creative tests for validity and truth.

As an implementation of a logical structure, the original programming environments in the early days of digital computing were required to be designed efficiently and completely because they were written on a machine level which was unforgiving of mistakes. High-level languages, which were developed later, were oriented more toward the natural language of speakers than they were toward the opening and closing of electronic circuits. High-level languages addressed compilers and interpreters which in turn generated the machine code. As a result, high-level languages often have built-in mechanisms which, though quick to trap errors in the usage and syntax of source code, can sometimes be quite forgiving of fundamental mistakes in design and logic. And it is these hidden structural mistakes which ultimately surface in the program's execution to make debugging the program a seemingly impossible task. Therefore, all professional computing training curricula, whether on a secondary school, college, or vocational level, usually begin with a unit on program design and architecture.

But program design and architecture begin with an understanding of commonsense sequential logic. In other words, to design a program, an individual need not have the actual high-level language code at his or her fingertips; rather the person must understand fundamentally how the computer of choice will operate and how to define logically the complete task of the program from beginning to end. It is this task definition and the realistic design of an operation from beginning to end that is necessary in order to write a good program. Whether the task is designing an operating system or writing a program to calculate the principal and interest payments on a loan, the programmer begins with a list of items the program must accomplish and ends with a chart showing the order in which the program will do just that. This section will introduce you to the elements of programming design and architecture from a programmer's point of view and will look at the elements of goal-setting, evaluating the programming tools to be used, and the construction of a programming structure.

Principles of Program Design

In principle, designing a program is not different from approaching any other task. We require a goal that is clearly defined because we need to know what we want to accomplish, we require an understanding of our beginning resources, and we must have a thorough understanding of the means we will use to reach the goal. As an example, consider the act of going to work in the morning. The goal is to get to work. The beginning resource is your home. The means to reach the goal is some form of transportation. The only difference between this process and the process of writing a computer program is that there's no need to make any part of the task of getting to work in the morning a conscious, consistent, and repetitive test for truth every day. However, how would these actions appear without a goal? Your normal activities such as waking up at 6:30, getting dressed in work attire, going to the train station, and so on, would seem silly indeed if you performed them on a Sunday morning or a holiday. The point is that most of the things we do need a goal in order for the actions to have any meaning. Designing a program is no exception.

Probably the least practical way to begin writing a computer program is to sit down at your computer and start writing code. Many beginning programmers, eager to see results, will do just that. The result is usually very awkward and inefficient code, poor documentation, and an absolute nightmare when debugging time comes (and it always does).

The three steps named above—goal, beginning resources, and means—are essential in the design of a good program. And the first language any beginning programmer should consider using is not BASIC, Fortran, Pascal, or COBOL, but rather English. Specifically, the way to begin writing a program is to identify in common language the goals, the beginning, and the means. Typically the programmer will be working on part of an overall system which has been defined. However, for purposes of this example, consider that the programmer is also responsible for designing the system. Let's say that the task is to design part of a billing system for a client. If the design steps were identified as in Fig. 1-1, the programmer would have virtually no useful information with which to begin. It

Fig. 1-1

would be like the going-to-work analogy without knowing where you worked. The goal, beginning, and means must be identified as specifically as possible. For example, in Fig. 1-2, the goal is specific, the beginning is defined, and the means (in this case the programming language) is specified. It is also important for the

Fig. 1-2

programmer to know that the BASIC to be used will be compiled, since compiled BASIC runs much faster than interpreted BASIC. This knowledge could influence the programmer's decision on designing the program since speed of execution would become a less important factor. The steps the programmer would take are:

1. Define the goal by designing the actual appearance of the bill.
2. Examine the input that this section of the program will receive.
3. Decide how to operate on that input by formatting the output in BASIC.

Logic of the Flow Chart

In the course of structuring the logic and the flow of control within the actual program, the most important tool is the formal flowchart. A flowchart is a diagram showing the order of the steps of a process. It is particularly useful in the design of computerized systems and programs, but can also be used in noncomputer settings to demonstrate the sequential and logical relationship among different but related elements. For example, a simple flowchart describing the act of getting up and going to work might look like Fig. 1-3. The box symbol in a

Fig. 1-3

flowchart indicates that a command is to be executed. The arrows indicate the order of the steps.

From the point of view of a computer, the above example is lacking many things. Specifically, the computer program will not perform any functions not listed in this sequence because it can only do exactly what it was instructed to do and nothing more. If you were to act just like a computer in following the above steps in the flowchart, you would never wash up, brush your teeth, or eat breakfast. And, if you added those items in the flowchart in proper sequence, you would still have the problem of going to work 7 days a week, 52 weeks a year. What would be missing would be the capacity to decide whether "today" is a workday. To include this, the flowchart might look like the example in Fig. 1-4.

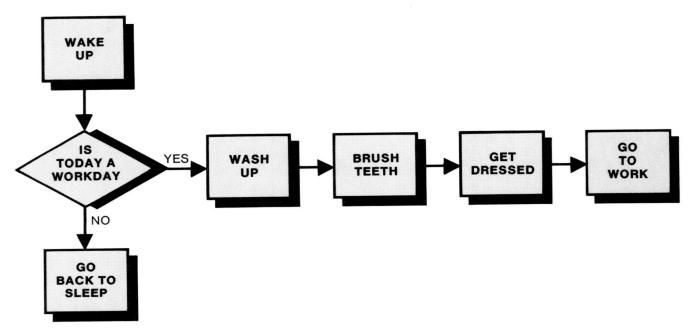

Fig. 1-4

Note here that a diamond symbol in a flowchart indicates that a decision is to be made based on whether the statement in the diamond is true or false. If it's true, the order of steps follows the "yes" arrow; if false, the steps follow the "no" arrow. Similarly, if we were to apply this logical structure to the design of a billing invoice, the flowchart might look like the flowchart shown in Fig. 1-5, while routine 1 might look like the example in Fig. 1-6 and routine 2 might look like Fig. 1-7.

Since flowcharts can become quite complicated, it is customary to divide them into separate routines or subflowcharts. In the above billing example, before a programmer would even be able to design the flowchart, it would be necessary to know what all the possible forms of the input might be. Only then would it be possible to design a response for past-due notices, credit balances, and zero balances, as well as normal balances.

To summarize, a well designed program must include:

1. A specific goal (output).
2. An understanding of the beginning material (input).
3. An understanding of the means of reaching the goal (the capacity of the computer and the programming language).

As mentioned earlier, it is useful to start programming by describing the task in straightforward written English. This step may not be necessary if a pro-

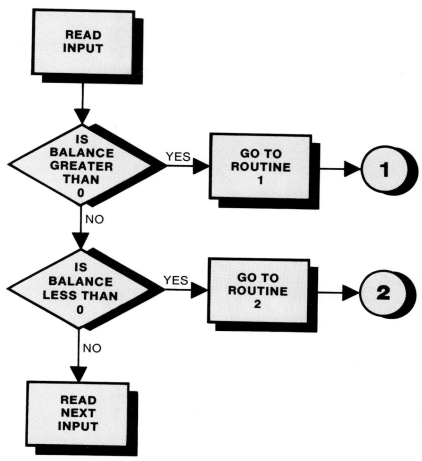

Fig. 1-5

grammer is very familiar with the task; however, it is quite valuable when the task is new to the programmer. In the above example, a programmer might start the process by writing the following:

GOAL: To design the output of a bill.
TASKS:

    A. Design Format
      1. See present manual bill.
    B. Process Input
      1. Obtain record layout.
      2. Identify all types of possible inputs.

The programmer would then go through the above steps and obtain the information needed. For example, a typical record layout, which defined the types of data and allocated memory storage in the system in terms of "bytes" or individual alphanumeric characters, might look like the chart in Fig. 1-8. In the right-hand column, the label "A" stands for alphanumeric, meaning that the characters can be either letters or numbers. The label "N" stands for numeric, meaning that the characters can only be numbers. The above example is structured for only four transactions. In practical application, the number of transactions would be much greater. The programmer would then be concerned with taking each field (specific part of the record) and placing it in the proper format. That is, the programmer may want the customer ID number in the upper left corner, the name and address right-justified, and the billing information centered on

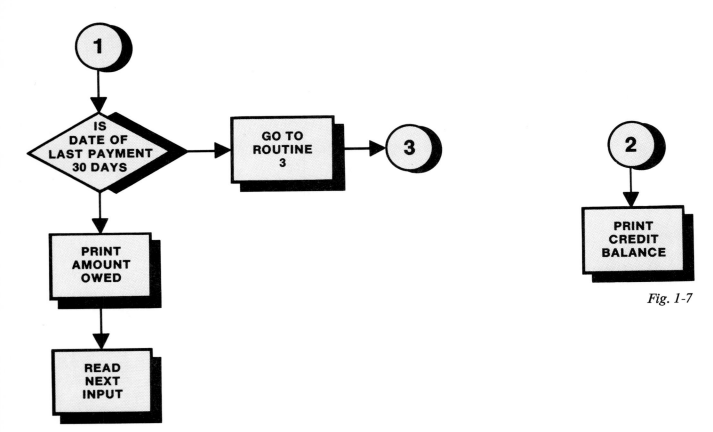

Fig. 1-6

Fig. 1-7

the bill. In addition, the programmer would need to know what kinds of numbers are possible in the Amount Charged and Amount Paid fields. Usually, the programmer would use a formula to produce a balance due on the bill in which the formula would add all the numbers from the Amount Charged fields and subtract all the numbers from the Amount Paid fields, take the result, and add it to the previous balance to get a new balance. Not only would the programmer have to be careful to use the correct fields (most customers would not want the date added to their bill), but as indicated in the flowchart analysis, it would also be necessary to know what kind of number the balance due can be, since a different action may be taken based on the value of the balance due. The source code in BASIC might look like:

```
2000 REM BALANCE DUE PRINT OUT
2050 REM VARIABLE LIST FOLLOWS
2100 REM AC(I)..AMT CHGD; AP(I)..AMT PD: BD..BAL DUE; PB..
     PREV BAL
2110 REM PD(I)..PAY'T DATE
2200 REM TOTAL FOR BAL DUE
2220 BD=0
2240 FOR I=1 TO 4
2260 BD=BD+AC(I)−AP(I)
2280 NEXT I
2300 BD=BD+PB
2320 IF BD<0 THEN GOSUB 3000:REM CREDIT MEMO
2320 IF BD>0 THEN GOSUB 4000:REM BILL FOR BAL DUE
2340 GOTO 1000:REM STORE BAL DUE AND READ NEXT
     CUSTOMER
```

The above routine would represent only a small section of what the programmer would have to do. Before even getting to the code, however, the programmer would have to separate the fields used from the entire record and assign them to the variables.

Documenting the Code

Lines 2000-2110 are notes stating what this section does and defining the variables used.

Lines 2200-2280 produce a balance due figure by adding all the Amount Charged fields and subtracting all the Amount Paid fields.

Line 2300 obtains a balance due by adding the result of the calculations for the current transactions to the previous balance due.

Lines 2320-2340 make a decision based on whether the balance due is 0, positive, or negative. Note that the zero case is not stated explicitly, but if the balance due were 0, the code would "fall through" (give a false reading) in lines 2300 and 2320.

Line 2340 returns program execution to line 1000 (hypothetically), the subroutine which stores the current balance due as the previous balance for the next

Item	Byte Range	# Bytes	Type
Customer ID #	1-9	9	N
Title	10-12	3	A
First Name	13-22	10	A
Last Name	23-37	15	A
Street Address	38-67	30	A
City	68-87	20	A
State Code	88-89	2	A
Zip Code	90-98	9	A
Country	99-108	10	A
Previous Balance	109-115	7	N
Service Date 1	116-121	6	N
Service Code 1	122-123	2	A
Amount Charged 1	124-129	6	A
Amount Paid 1	130-135	6	N
Payment Date 1	136-141	6	N
Service Date 2	142-147	6	N
Service Code 2	148-149	2	A
Amount Charged 2	150-155	6	N
Amount Paid 2	156-161	6	N
Payment Date 2	162-167	6	N
Service Date 3	168-173	6	N
Service Code 3	174-175	2	A
Amount Charged 3	176-181	6	N
Amount Paid 3	182-187	6	N
Payment Date 3	188-193	6	N
Service Date 4	194-199	6	N
Service Code 4	200-201	2	A
Amount Charged 4	202-207	6	N
Amount Paid 4	208-213	6	N
Payment Date 4	214-219	6	N
End of Record Signal	220	1	A

Fig. 1-8

series of transactions and reads in data from the next customer and begins the processing again. Note that program execution will always reach line 2340 regardless of the value of the balance due.

The subroutines at lines 3000 and 4000 would process the bills and print messages based on the value of the balance due.

Testing the Code for Errors

After completion of the code, the debugging process begins. The first step is to make a list of all the possible input values for AC(I), PD(I), AP(I), and BD and then go by hand through the steps which the computer would take. After the subroutine "runs" correctly by hand, the next step is to use sample data and actually run through the routine. One of the potential trouble spots that must be addressed is accounting for a sufficient number of test customers to adequately test the system. The reason is that in some cases the program will run properly for the first X cases but at case X+1 an error will occur. One of the most common reasons for this phenomenon is that the computer system must be told how many customers to expect. This is generally accomplished through the use of a program statement which defines the number of items the program can expect to file under various categories. In BASIC, this is called a DIMension statement. If the program is not told how many customers we expect it to hold, it assumes the number is 10. Were this the case, customer number 11 would produce an error message.

System Design and Architecture

A systems analyst is to a programmer what an architect is to a builder. A builder who constructs a house must rely on the specifications developed and provided by the architect. The architect must: (a) communicate with the client and understand the client's needs and wants; (b) be able to translate those needs and wants into the design of the house. The client will specify those items that are absolutely necessary, such as bathrooms and bedrooms and kitchen, those items that are matters of personal taste such as the floorplans of certain rooms or the types of materials used in surface construction, and, finally, will specify cost. A good architect will arrive at a balance between what the client needs, what the client wants, and what the client can afford to pay.

The systems analyst must do much the same thing. In one sense the systems analyst has more information with which to work than the architect since some system usually will already exist (although not necessarily involving a computer). In another sense the systems analyst has less information to work with than the construction architect since the architect's client is familiar in general with what can and can't be done with the design of a house, but the clients of the systems analyst are often not at all familiar with capacity and power of a business computer system. Thus, the first and most important task of a systems analyst is to interview the client.

When conducting interviews, the systems analyst should have a client intake questionnaire or at least a standard form on which he or she will note the answers to some of the basic questions that all system architects must ask:

1. What tasks will the system perform?
2. What is the volume of information that the system is likely to process?
3. Who will use the system?
4. How many locations will require direct access to the computer?

Since the system will be run by people, the interviews should include all the people who will be involved in dealing with the system, from the person in charge of the company on down to the person inputting the data. One of the most common (and often most costly) mistakes made by businesses installing a system is to neglect having the systems analyst speak with the people who will be responsible for operating it on a daily basis. At the conclusion of the interview process, the analyst should have the information necessary to determine what features the system requires, what features would be desirable but not critical, and what features would be desirable but not needed depending on cost requirements. The trade-off question is almost always a cost-versus-features issue because clients often want less than they really need and more than they can afford. As the concept of the system develops, the system will be modified. Any potential modification must always be categorized as either necessary or desirable. After the analyst has designed a system on paper, he or she then decides on the tools with which to implement the system.

Implementing the System

The first question concerns the applications software, that is, the actual program or programs which will be used to operate the system on a daily basis. It can be either a canned program (a program sold off the shelf) or a program designed from scratch and written specifically for the client. In the industry today, there is an increasing move toward canned software packages which the analyst may then modify to meet the specific needs of the client. The dBASE II and III packages fall into this category because they are actually software implementation systems that come with libraries of ready-to-use routines and utilities that can be programmed to meet a broad range of client-specific tasks.

After the applications software is determined, an operating system must be chosen. The operating system is actually a master program which, quite literally, tells the computer how to behave like a computer and perform the basic chores all computers perform. The operating system tells the computer how to process internal information, where to store certain types of data, what types of disk drives are on the system and how to access them, where the printer is located and what types of data transfer will be executed, and what types of enhancements or peripheral devices will be supported by the computer. Some of the more common operating systems in use today are UNIX, MS-DOS, and CP/M. Each operating system has spawned proprietary operating systems such as PC-DOS and Z-DOS (IBM's and Zenith's versions of MS-DOS), and XENIX (Microsoft's version of UNIX). Only after the applications software and operating system are chosen is a computer selected.

One of the most important decisions in choosing a system concerns the number of concurrent users the system will have to support. In other words, if more than one person will be on the system at one time how will the system support that input and process the information? The system architect will have to decide whether the system needs to be either multiuser or networked. A multiuser system is one in which a number of terminals share one central processing unit, or CPU, in a computer. The primary benefit of this kind of system is that changes can be made to existing data and then displayed instantly at other terminals. This is particularly useful in operations such as sales in department stores when inventory must be constantly updated each time a sale is made. The biggest drawback to a multiuser system is that as the number of terminals on the system increases, the system runs slower. Typically, a system with many terminals operating on one CPU is used on a mini or a mainframe computer system where the internal RAM (memory space available for the terminals) is considerably larger than the RAM available to microcomputers.

A networked system refers to a number of computers or terminals being connected via cable or telephone modem. Multiuser systems are a form of networked system since the terminals are connected to one another and to the host CPU via cable. There is also a network system which is not true multiuser (since each computer has its own CPU), although it simulates the activity of a true multiuser system. These systems have become increasingly popular for two reasons: they do not slow down as more units are added to the system; and a true multiuser system is usually not necessary for most applications. These networked systems consist of a number of microcomputers connected to one another via cable or telephone lines. The network usually includes a large information storage device (such as an 80-megabyte disk drive) and at least one printer (and usually more) which are shared by each computer on the network. Thus, the networked computers have shared access to a large memory storage, but do not share access to a common processing unit. In this way, networked systems offer microcomputer system buyers a flexibility that ordinarily is not available to buyers of multiuser systems. Networked systems operate in this way: each computer has its own independent CPU and can communicate with the other members of the network or operate on a stand-alone basis as if it weren't connected to a network. The trade-offs in a network system in which each unit consists of a computer using its own CPU are cost, since completely independent microcomputers are more expensive than terminals; and the absence of the "instant update" or system-wide immediate display function of the multiuser systems. Even this is changing, however, because there is an increasing body of network software being marketed which very closely emulates a true multiuser environment in terms of access speed.

System Flowcharting

Flowcharting is an integral part in the design of any system. The principles of flowcharting in a system are the same as those in designing programs except that the scope is much broader. An example of a flowchart which might be used in designing the system for client billing is shown in Fig. 1-9. The difference between system and program flowcharting is that in system flowcharting the entire picture is being described, including, in the most complex of system flowcharts, designated output devices and patterns of information flow. In program flowcharting traditionally, only the specific tasks are being described.

Designing Programs to Fit Systems

As indicated earlier, from the point of view of the systems analyst, when the step is reached to choose and/or design the actual software system, the first item to be examined is the applications software, which is actually going to do the jobs the system was installed to do. For example, a systems analyst would not choose a word processing program to perform accounting functions, for it would be the wrong applications program for the job. However, the analyst may choose one accounting program over another to use in a particular system because the package may have more features than others in its price range or because some of the features integrate especially well with the needs of the client. Or in the case in which a program is to be designed from scratch, the choice lies in which language to use in writing the code. If, for example, the systems analyst is designing a multiuser configuration in an insurance claims office in which data has to move around the system very quickly because it will be handled by many people at once, the analyst may choose C because of its multiuser capabilities. The C language was originally designed to write applications for multiuser systems and has many assembly language-like features that allow programmers to address specific parts of the machine to move data into and out of locations quickly and efficiently. If, on the other hand, the analyst is working with many programmers at the same time on different machines, he or she may decide to develop applications programs in CBASIC because it allows different programmers with different programming skills and levels of ability to write various sections of the code and different subroutines that will be integrated with one another by the

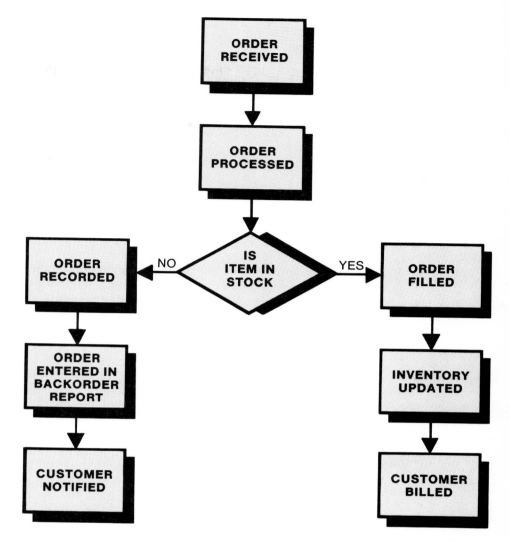

Fig. 1-9

senior programming team. A structured BASIC program lends itself to this type of development and, because it will be compiled before it is implemented, it will run at least ten times faster than an uncompiled BASIC program. Furthermore, since the analyst must consider all aspects of the system design (including costs), he or she may choose an operating system and/or a computer for which a particular applications program or programming language may not be available. From the point of view of the programmer, the analyst's choice may not be the best one. However, since the analyst must take many factors into account, the programmer's choices may not be the ones used. For example, the programmer may love working with the UNIX operating system, but if the computer chosen by the analyst does not support UNIX, the programmer will have to work with a different operating system.

Principal Operating Systems

Three of the major operating systems and their features are:

UNIX and its derivatives
MS-DOS and its derivatives
CP/M and its enhancements

UNIX is extremely flexible. It has a modular design, which permits the programmer to use previously existing libraries of routines or to design her or his own for future use. UNIX requires extensive memory to run and therefore cannot be supported on some microcomputers. Recently, however, with the release of IBM's new AT Personal Computer, the company announced the release of a UNIX look-alike called XENIX that will support networking and multiuser functions on the system. This means that users will be able to network PCs and ATs using XENIX as an extension of DOS 3.0.

MS-DOS has become one of the two industry standards for microcomputer operating systems. MS-DOS supports virtually every programming language available on microcomputers including interpreted and compiled BASIC, C, COMAL, APL, Pascal, Fortran, COBOL, Logo, and Assembler. Because MS-DOS was the operating system selected by IBM for its PC, all software written for the PC and for PC compatibles runs under MS-DOS. This is why it has become the industry standard for all business applications software, largely replacing CP/M.

CP/M, which was one of the first operating systems for microcomputers ever developed, is the other industry standard for microcomputer operating systems. Versions of CP/M are available for both 8-bit and 16-bit microcomputers, and a version of CP/M called concurrent CP/M (available only for 16-bit processors) permits multitasking. Multitasking means that the computer can accomplish up to four different tasks simultaneously, an obvious advantage when moving back and forth between different word processing, accounting, or database search and retrieval operations to prepare a single document. Still another version of CP/M, called MP/M, is used for multiuser environments. CP/M, developed by Digital Research, was one of the earliest operating systems. Written originally for Z80- or 8080-based computers, CP/M, by 1980-1981, had the largest number of business libraries for data processing, word processing, and number crunching. CP/M's strength lay in its very efficient management of all of the microcomputer's functions. Programs that were written under CP/M merely had to access the functions of the system in order to perform their housekeeping chores such as disk access, printing, and addressing information at various memory locations within the computer. CP/M was also a system language in and of itself, and it provided opportunities for system programmers to develop very creative methods for manipulating information at a close-to-assembly-language level without actually having to write in a true Z80 assembler. UNIX, developed in the C language, has borrowed some of these concepts, which is why UNIX-based systems can be very flexible and efficient.

When working with operating systems such as these, the programmer will frequently have to create utility programs. For example, when BASIC is used under MS-DOS, there is a system command which will dynamically renumber lines. The same utility also exists in Atari BASIC. Other utility programs enable programmers to troubleshoot the hardware by checking the system's functions; diskettes can be inspected for damage by writing bits of data to the disk and retrieving it, track by track or sector by sector; printer functions can be tested by sending test data to be printed in a variety of formats. These utilities are often included on the disks which accompany the main operating system disk. And, of course, system programmers can write utility programs that run under any of the major operating systems. UNIX, in particular, has a large library of these. Utility programs are cost-effective devices for system programmers because by creating utility programs, the programmers can add features to an operating system which are not part of the system itself. In this way they are able to customize the system without having to spend large amounts of development time to reinvent the operating system for their clients.

Applications Programs

Applications programs are programs which perform a specific task. Some categories of applications programs are word processors, electronic spreadsheets, graphics drawing packages, and database managers. To reach the largest market possible, software publishers design applications software to be used with the most popular operating systems. Because of this, 8-bit CP/M has a very large base of applications software. With the advent of the 16-bit processors, many of the 8-bit CP/M software packages were revised to run under 16-bit CP/M or MS-DOS. Typically, programs which were revised also added new features to take advantage of the additional power of the 16-bit processors. Two examples of applications programs which were at the top of their respective classes in an 8-bit environment are Wordstar and VisiCalc, the former having been the industry standard in word processors and the latter, the standard in electronic spreadsheets. In both cases, the publishers developed more powerful 16-bit versions which still rank near the top of their respective classes, although both have been challenged by a new wave of software designed exclusively for 16-bit processors. The Word and Multimate have become very popular among the 16-bit word processors, and Lotus 1-2-3 became the most popular electronic spreadsheet program almost overnight.

Lotus 1-2-3 warrants additional comment. It became the most popular of the integrated software packages. Integrated software combines features normally found in more than one software package. In the case of Lotus 1-2-3, spreadsheet, graph generation, and database management features are combined in the one package. More recently, Lotus, Inc. expanded 1-2-3 with Lotus Symphony. Symphony includes word processing and telecommunications in addition to the features of 1-2-3.

Framework, developed by Ashton-Tate, the publishers of dBASE II and III, is another integrated software package which combines database management, electronic spreadsheet, graph generation, and word processing within a modular or framelike structure which allows users to move entire blocks of information around an electronic desktop without having to leave one application and enter another. This is what an integrated functions program is designed to do, and as desktop computers become more powerful, integrated functions software will become more popular. Moreover, with the successful introduction of the Macintosh, integrated packages designed to utilize a system of icons or representational symbols rather than actual commands are now being marketed in large numbers. By moving the cursor or pointer, controlled by a device that moves across a tabletop, the user can physically point to or highlight the function he or she wants to invoke rather than key in a command or series of commands. Although it seems limiting at first, the new system is designed to address a full 32 bits of processing power, and that means, with the necessary onboard RAM available to users, it can successfully carry the overhead of a large, memory-consuming operating system.

As the icon technology begins to predominate and is combined with a complete set of integrated functions, the end user will eventually be able to create documents of any type, combining text, graphics, and charts, using data extracted from a variety of sources, including remote locations (via telephone lines), and then transmit the documents instantly to multiple locations, all without ever leaving the basic system program.

Gary Markman

Program Design Features

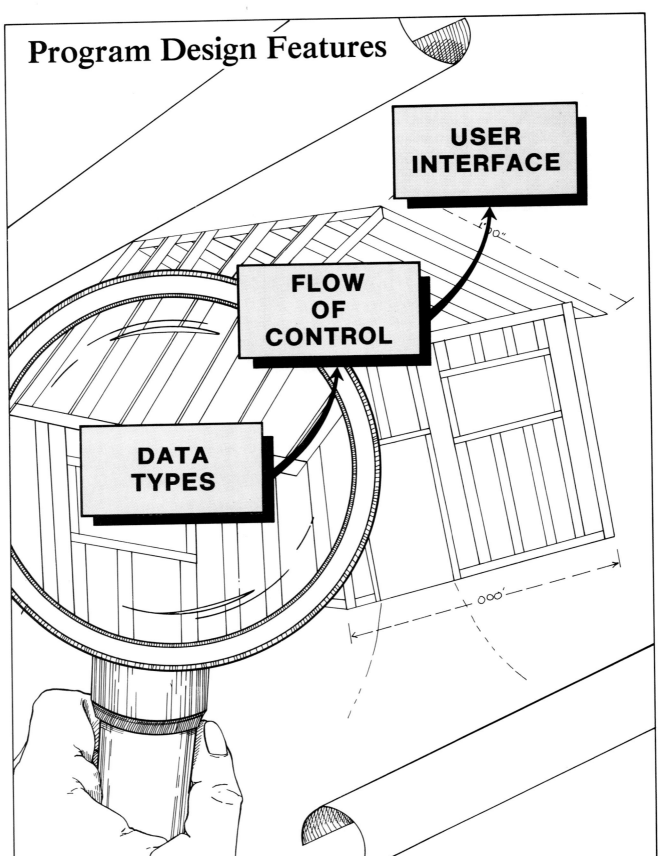

2
PRINCIPLES OF EFFECTIVE PROGRAMMING

Once a programmer has moved beyond the design phases of his or her program and into the actual housekeeping chores of what the logic will accomplish, there are a number of general details that the programmer must consider. For example, if the program will be manipulating records and processing information in and out of files, the programmer must decide early in the design upon the types of files that will be created. Will the program create sequential data files, thereby saving disk space but requiring that End of File flags be set to signal the borders between records? Or will the program create random access files that will be quicker to write to and read from but which will require more disk space and a series of queries to the user that will prompt him or her to predetermine the size of the records that will be stored? How will the program handle text? Will provision be made for editing functions? Will there be screen graphics? Will printer functions be supported in the program? All of these questions and more must be considered after the general logic and architecture of the program has been sketched out.

The programmer who worries about how the program will accomplish its tasks after determining what tasks will be accomplished will have an easier time of it. For example, BASIC allows programmers to achieve primary goals by jumping right in and writing code. This method usually backfires, but it gives programmers the immediate gratification of seeing their source code get results quickly. COBOL, PL/I, and Fortran do not allow this. Programs that will spend time handling assembler functions generally require jumps between assembly language subroutines and high-level source code. C makes these transitions easily and bridges the gap between machine-level functions and high-level types of routines. Programs that require an extensive interaction between user and machine, such as the types of dialogues often found in expert systems, usually have to be written in LISP or Prolog because these languages can update their own databases from user input. BASIC requires extensive secondary routines to emulate this function.

It is obvious, therefore, that there are at least two categories of planning that must take place before any coding can begin. The programmer must look at the way the program will accomplish certain tasks, and the type of high-level language that is best suited for the tasks in question. This section addresses the categories of general tasks that programs handle. Section 5 will examine the high-level languages in detail.

What follows are examples of the types of tasks that programmers look to solve in their work, and the types of situations that make these tasks necessary.

Item	Byte Range	# Bytes	Type
Customer ID #	1-9	9	N
Title	10-12	3	A
First Name	13-22	10	A
Last Name	23-37	15	A
Street Address	38-67	30	A
City	68-87	20	A
State Code	88-89	2	A
Zip Code	90-98	9	A
Country	99-108	10	A
Previous Balance	109-115	7	N
Service Date 1	116-121	6	N
Service Code 1	122-123	2	A
Amount Charged 1	124-129	6	A
Amount Paid 1	130-135	6	N
Payment Date 1	136-141	6	N
Service Date 2	142-147	6	N
Service Code 2	148-149	2	A
Amount Charged 2	150-155	6	N
Amount Paid 2	156-161	6	N
Payment Date 2	162-167	6	N
Service Date 3	168-173	6	N
Service Code 3	174-175	2	A
Amount Charged 3	176-181	6	N
Amount Paid 3	182-187	6	N
Payment Date 3	188-193	6	N
Service Date 4	194-199	6	N
Service Code 4	200-201	2	A
Amount Charged 4	202-207	6	N
Amount Paid 4	208-213	6	N
Payment Date 4	214-219	6	N
End of Record Signal	220	1	A

Fig. 2-1

String Handling

A string is a series of ASCII characters. The characters may be any valid ASCII character including letters, numbers, and nonprinting characters. Figure 2-1 refers to the file input example of Section 1, page 6. The programmer would have to first separate the section of the input file and store them as variables before performing any operations on them.

```
2000 REM BALANCE DUE PRINT OUT
2020 REM INPUT VARIABLE:PB
2040 REM OUTPUT VARIABLES AC(I), AP(I), PB, BD
2060 REM TEMP VARIABLES:I
2100 REM AC(I)..AMT CHGD; AP(I)..AMT PD; BD..BAL DUE; PB..
     PREV BAL
2200 REM TOTAL FOR BAL DUE
2220 BD=0
```

```
2240 FOR I=1 TO 4
2260 BD=BD+AC(I)-AP(I)
2280 NEXT I
2300 BD=BD+PB:PB=BD
2320 IF BD<0 THEN GOSUB 3000:REM CREDIT MEMO
2330 IF BD>0 THEN GOSUB 4000:REM BILL FOR BAL DUE
2340 RETURN:REM TO MAIN PROCESSING
```

The programmer would want to assign sections of the input file to the variables AC(I), AP(I), and PB. Assuming that the entire input file was assigned to a variable A\$, the string assignment might look like this:

```
1500 REM STRING ASSIGNMENTS
1520 REM INPUT VARIABLE A$
1540 REM OUTPUT VARIABLES AC(I), AP(I), PB
1560 REM TEMP VARIABLES I,B$,N
1580 B$=MID$(A$,109,7)
1600 PB=VAL(B$)
1620 N=124
1640 FOR I=1 TO 4
1660 B$=MID$(A$,N,6):REM AM'T CHGD
1680 AC(I)=VAL(B$)
1700 N=N+6
1720 B$=MID$(A$,N,6):REM AM'T PD.
1740 AP(I)=VAL$(B$)
1760 N=N+20
1780 NEXT I
1800 RETURN:REM TO MAIN PROCESSING
```

Note the documentation. The programmer would indicate through REM (non-executing reminder) statements the input variable(s), output variables, and temporary variables.

The MID\$ function is used to extract portions of a string. The format is MID\$(X\$,a,b). It means "take b characters of string X\$ beginning with character #a."

Lines 1580, 1660, and 1720 each take a portion of the incoming record and assign it to variables. Therefore, the temporary variable B\$ is set equal to the portion of variable A\$ (the entire record) starting with character number N and the next 6 characters (including character number N). In line 1620, N is assigned the value 124, so that in line 1660, B\$ is assigned a string 6 characters in length starting with character 124. If you look at the record layout, you'll see that that corresponds to Amount Charged 1.

The VAL command changes the contents of a string to a numerical value. For example, when B\$ = 129.87, the computer does not recognize B\$ as having a numerical value of 129.87. The computer doesn't recognize the contents B\$ as being any different in style from B\$ = "Hi! How are you today?" If you asked the computer to multiply B\$ by 2, thinking you would get "2 times 129.87," the computer would react as if you asked it to multiply "Hi? How are you today?" by 2. It would send an error message. The VAL command causes the computer to recognize the numerical value of the contents of a string. So, in line 1680, the variable AC(I) is assigned the numerical value of B\$. In line 1700, the value of N is increased by 6, so that when the next MID\$ is performed, the starting character is 130. This corresponds to Amount Paid 1 in the record layout.

Lines 1720 and 1740 perform the same functions as lines 1660 and 1680 except that the (new) value of B\$ is assigned to variable AP(I), the amount paid.

In line 1760, the value of N is increased by 20, so that when the next MID$ is encountered, the beginning character is 150. This corresponds to Amount Charged 2 in the record layout. Note that the record layout was designed so that the number of characters between variables is the same. This makes it possible to use the FOR . . NEXT loop in reading and assigning variables.

The process would repeat until the last amount paid was processed, and then execution would transfer to the bill processing section.

Some points which should be emphasized regarding string handling and files are:

1. Assign the file to one or more string variables so that all types of characters can be read into the program from the file. String variables can handle alphabetic characters, numeric characters, and special nonprinting characters the program uses but which does not appear in the output.
2. The record layout should be designed so that recursive techniques can be used to assign variables from the record.

There are a few other string handling commands. RIGHT$(A$,7) takes the rightmost 7 characters of variable A$. E.g., if A$ = "Good Morning," then the above command would give "Morning." LEFT$(A$,7) takes the leftmost 7 characters from A$ for "Good Mo." (Notice that the space between Good and Morning is counted as a character.) STR$(A) converts the numerical value of the variable A to a string. This is the opposite of the VAL command which was discussed earlier. It is important to know that neither VAL nor STR$ actually changes the contents of a variable; they merely change the way the computer will treat the contents of the variable. For example, if A = 129.87 and B$ = STR$(A), B$ would still contain the characters 129.87, but in processing B$ the computer would treat the 129.87 as individual characters and not as a number.

Documentation

The value of good documentation cannot be overstated. A programmer's documentation, because it is a running explanation of the operation of a program and a definition of the data types and variable names, is an invaluable aid both to the programmer who wrote it and to subsequent programmers hired to support the code. Frequently, the person who did a particular section of a program will not be available when changes or corrections need to be made. The person who is then responsible for making the changes in the program will have nightmares for a long time if there is no adequate documentation available.

Documentation can be placed either within the program itself or in separate notes outside the program. When placed within the program, REM statements are used. REM stands for REMark. REM statements are nonexecuting. That is, the computer will ignore anything following a REM statement, but of course the reminder will be printed when the program is listed.

One of the most difficult aspects of debugging a program with poor documentation is tracing variables. It is very difficult to trace the operation of a variable throughout a program without documentation. For each routine and subroutine of a program, the documentation should include:

1. A list of the input variables.
2. A list of the output variables.
3. A list of the temporary variables.

In addition, there should be a section in the program in which all variables are clearly defined. The program which prints the bills is a good example of how documentation should look. Notice that input, output, and temporary variables are listed. Also each routine is preceded by a REM statement describing what is being done in the routine. Some programmers don't use thorough documentation. One reason is that it takes up memory space. However, if RAM space is a problem, it's always possible to write the documentation outside the program, e.g., with a word processor. Another reason for sloppy documentation is that good documentation is time consuming; not however, as time consuming as trying to debug a program with insufficient documentation.

Routines and Subroutines

A routine is a section of a program which performs a particular task. The string assignment program above is an example of a routine. It is also an example of a subroutine (although routines are not necessarily also subroutines). A subroutine is executed as part of a larger routine. For example, if you consider the routine of processing billing statements, the record-read/string assignment portion would be a subroutine.

Subroutines in BASIC are accessed by the GOSUB command, and are exited by the RETURN command.

The way this might look for the bill processing program is as follows:

```
500 REM MAIN PROCESSING ROUTINE
520 GOSUB 800:REM OPEN FILE AND READ RECORD
540 GOSUB 900:REM TEST FOR END OF FILE
560 GOSUB 1500:REM ASSIGN STRING VALUES
580 GOSUB 2000:REM PROCESS BILLS
600 GOTO 520
```

The above section of the program is the main routine, while each of the other sections is a subroutine.

In general, subroutines are used to divide a large program into smaller modules, or when the routine will be accessed by the program more than once. Using subroutines saves memory space since the same code does not have to be repeated a number of times.

Allocation of Memory and RAM Storage

Computers consist of three main parts, the CPU, ROM, and RAM.

CPU: The central processing unit is the command center of the computer. It contains all the instructions for performing all the functions. The CPU is a microchip usually larger than the other chips on the main board. Some of the common CPUs used in computers today are: 6502, Z80, 8080, and 8085 (8-bit processors), and 8086, 8088, 80186, 80286 (16-bit processors), and 68000 (32-bit processor). The CPU is programmed at the machine level in binary or hex code or in an assembly language written specifically for the microprocessor.

ROM: Read-only memory. ROM chips contain code used by the computer to perform different functions. ROM chips cannot be changed by a user. That is, the user cannot "write" (send data to) a ROM chip, hence the name read only. Some examples of ROM chips are the Apple II series computer which contains Applesoft BASIC in ROM, and more recently some of the portable computers have been manufactured containing applications software in ROM. Programs such as word processing and spreadsheets use ROM. The Commodore PET was one of the first business computers to bundle its operations system and major applications on ROM chips.

RAM: Random access memory. RAM consists of a series of chips which can be written to (to which data can be sent) and read from (from which data can be retrieved). RAM is usually volatile, meaning that when the computer power is turned off the contents of RAM are lost. To most users, the amount of RAM available in a computer is considered an important feature in judging a computer for purchase. RAM is measured in kilobytes. A byte is a character of information. Any ASCII character occupies 1 byte of RAM space regardless of whether the character is a number, letter, or nonprinting. A kilobyte is actually 1024 bytes, but most people think of a kilobyte as 1000 bytes since it's easier for calculation purposes. The first microcomputers contained 4K of RAM (4000 characters), the next wave contained 8K, and the Apple II series was the first mass-produced home computer to have 48K of RAM. Although there are many features which must be considered in evaluating a computer, available RAM space is one of the most important, since applications programs require different amounts of RAM to run. For example, Wordstar, for years the industry standard in word processing software, requires 64K (minimum) to run. Lotus 1-2-3, presently the industry standard in spreadsheet programs, requires 192K to run, while Lotus Symphony requires 320K of RAM.

An additional consideration in gauging the available RAM for a system is to find out how much RAM is used by the DOS and any other elements of the system. For example, in the 48K Apple II series, Apple DOS 3.3 used 10K of RAM. In the 192K Zenith Z-100, Z-DOS uses approximately 30K of RAM.

Also of concern to a programmer is the way in which a system allocates available memory (RAM). For example, in the 48K Apple II series, using DOS 3.3, the highest memory location after DOS is loaded is 38,400. However, a portion of that memory space is reserved for graphics and cannot be accessed by Applesoft BASIC (except for graphing). In addition, Applesoft BASIC handles strings in such a way as to cause unused string values to remain stored in memory. This results in the need to remove those string values which are no longer used. Applesoft BASIC does that automatically after a certain point, but when it does, the system operation halts for a few seconds up to a minute (depending on how much "garbage collection" there is). Although this would be a drawback to any system, there are utility programs available which bypass the problem. The point is that a programmer needs to look at how much RAM is advertised with a computer. There's much more to be considered.

Editing

A program editor is an indispensable feature to a programmer. No matter how carefully a program is written, there is almost always going to be some editing involved. If the act of editing is very slow and/or cumbersome, a programmer can waste inordinate amounts of time. The BASICs that exist for 16-bit systems all have editors built in; however, some BASICs for the 8-bit systems do not. As an example, Applesoft BASIC does not have a built-in editor, and editing programs can be excruciating. However, again outside software developers came along and produced excellent program editors. A programmer needs to know the availability of editors and their effectiveness before using a particular system.

Error Messages

When errors in a program exist, interpreted BASIC displays them only when the program is run. For this reason, it's important to design the program in a modular format, so that each module can be tested separately. Modular format in BASIC refers to a program design in which there is one main routine containing a number of references to various subroutines. The subroutines are the modules. Common error messages from Applesoft BASIC are shown in Fig. 2-2.

Error Trapping

Error trapping is a very valuable tool to programmers. Normally, when an error is encountered in an interpreted BASIC program, execution of the program stops. Using error trapping, it is possible to have the program respond to an error and then continue execution. In Applesoft BASIC this is accomplished with the ONERR GOTO command to send program execution to an error-trapping routine. The error-trapping routine can be used to display messages to a user when certain errors occur, and to continue program execution once the errors are corrected.

SYNTAX: A command has not been recognized. This usually is caused by a misspelling or typo.

BAD SUBSCRIPT: An array variable has not been DIMensioned for sufficient space.

OUT OF DATA: A program using a READ DATA command came to the end and tried to continue reading data after the last data item. This can be prevented by using a data signal as the last data entry.

NEXT WITHOUT FOR: During program execution, a NEXT statement has been encountered without a FOR statement as part of the loop.

WRITE PROTECTED: An attempt was made to write to a disk with the write protect tab in place.

FILE NOT FOUND: A file has been requested for reading which does not exist.

END OF DATA: Similar to an OUT OF DATA message, except that this refers to an attempt to read data from a disk file after the last data item has been read. This can be prevented by the use of an END OF DATA signal (see the record layout on page 16.)

Fig. 2-2

Sorting

One of the most frequently used routines in programs is sorting. Data which is input into a file is virtually never in the same order as users want it to be when various reports are generated. As a simple example, let's say a list is compiled of people who have subscribed to a magazine. The orders are entered as they come in, but when a report is produced, the order of the report might be alphabetical by last name or numerical by account number. To accomplish this, a sort subroutine is used.

One of the most common sort routines is the bubble sort, in which the desired values (highest or lowest) "bubble" to the top. Consider the following bubble sort program:

```
1200 REM ALPHA SORT ON LAST NAME
1220 REM INPUT VARIABLES:L$(I),N
1240 REM OUTPUT VARIABLES:L$(I)
1260 REM TEMP VARIABLES:I,S,T$
1300 FOR I=1 TO N-1
1320 S=0
1340 IF L$(I)<=L$(I+1) THEN 1400
1360 T$=L$(I):L$(I)=L$(I+1):L$(I+1)=T$
1380 S=1
1400 NEXT I
1420 IF S=1 THEN 1300
1440 RETURN
```

In the above program L$(I) is the last name, I the subscript, and N the number of people being sorted.

The principle behind this sort routine is to compare last names on the list in pairs and to switch the last names if the first lst name of the pair is alphabetically "greater than" the second lst name in the pair. If the first is alphabetically "less than or equal to" the second, no switch is made.

The terms "alphabetically greater," "less," or "equal to" refer to the ability of the computer to compare the ASCII codes of letters in a string and to make a judgment on which code has a higher value. For example, in comparing last names ALLEN and ALLAN, the computer would judge ALLAN to come first, since the ASCII codes for the first three letters of each would be the same (since the letters are the same), but for the fourth letter, the ASCII code for A (65) would show as less than the ASCII code for E (69).

Line 1320 is a switch signal. That is, the temporary variable is initially set equal to 0. If a switch is made of any pair of last names, S is set equal to 1 in line 1380. In line 1420 the value of S is examined. If S=1 a switch was made, which means that the whole list is not in alphabetical order yet, and the process starts over. If the value of S in line 1420 is 0, it means that no switch was made, which means that the list is in alphabetical order. Execution of the routine then reaches line 1440 which ends the subroutine and sends program execution back to the main routine.

Line 1340 compares a pair of last names, L$(I) being the first and L$(I+1), the next. If the first, L$(I), is less than or equal to the second, L$(I+1), program execution goes to line 1400 which calls in the next pair of last names. If L$(I) is not less than or equal to L$(I+1) (i.e., the first is alphabetically greater than the second), program execution falls to line 1360.

Line 1360 produces the switch in order by using the temporary variable T$. To see the switch, consider the comparison of last names JONES and ALLEN in Fig. 2-3.

Step	L$(I)	L$(I+1)	T$	Command
1	JONES	ALLEN	(empty)	(start)
2	JONES	ALLEN	JONES	T$=L$(I)
3	ALLEN	ALLEN	JONES	L$(I)=L$(I+1)
4	ALLEN	JONES	JONES	L$(I+1)=T$

Fig. 2-3

Note that even though at the conclusion of the switch, T$ contains the string JONES, T$ will be replaced by the next name when the next switch is made.

Line 1380 then sets S=1, indicating that a switch has been made so that at the conclusion of the loop, execution will start over and pairs of last names will continue to be compared.

This process keeps repeating for each alphabetic comparison: L$(I)<=L$(I+1). When this occurs, S would equal 0, the S test in line 1420 would fall through to 1440, and the routine would end. Although the logic of sorting may seem slow and tedious, because of the very high execution speed of the computer the actual sorting is quite fast.

Arrays

In general terms, an array can be thought of as an arrangement of items based on the position (or location) of the item within the group making up the array. The position of the item can be identified with one or more parameters. The number of parameters used is called the dimension of an array. We are quite familiar with two-dimensional arrays. For example, consider a city in which streets and avenues are numbered. The location identified by 7th Street and 2nd

Avenue might be symbolized by (7,2). It would be different from the location identified by (2,7) (2nd Street and 7th Avenue).

Airline pilots are quite familiar with three-dimensional arrays. A plane's location on an air controller's grid would need more than numbers such as (70,20), since certainly altitude is important. A location such as (70,20,2.5) might be grid location (70,20) at an altitude of 2500 feet.

It's even possible to conceptualize a four-dimensional array, where the fourth dimension is time. So a location such as (70,20,2.5,16) might refer to grid location (70,20), altitude 2500 feet, at 1600 hours (4:00 P.M.).

However, it's possible to have arrays with many dimensions, even though there might not be a corresponding analogy in reality to represent the array.

For purposes here, we'll consider two-dimensional arrays. Consider a classroom with students seated as in Fig. 2-4.

| JOE
KATHE
BILL | PETE
GARY
ANDY | SALLY
LESLIE
RON | AL
JOEL
CINDY |

Fig. 2-4

Assume the variable which will store the student's names is N$. Then, N$(2,3) would identify Leslie while N$(3,2) would identify Andy. A common use for two-dimensional arrays is in lists in which two items are related. For example, in using random access disk files, the user would type in the key field information (e.g., a person's ID number), the system would then go directly to the record containing the customer information. However, in order to be able to find the record, a record number must be associated with the customer ID number in an index. Such an index might look like:

```
10001,467
10002,29
10003,211
10004,9
10005,401
```

where the first number is the customer ID sorted numerically, and the second number is the record location of that customer's information. If the variable C(I,J) identifies the entries, then C(4,2) would be 9 (the record location for customer ID 10004).

The DIMension statement for a two-dimensional array looks like:

$$DIM\ C(x,y)$$

where x is the maximum number of entries for the first member of the array, and y the maximum number of entries for the second member. The DIM statement is important because it defines the number of items that will be allowed in the array. In this example, x and y would be equal, since the number of entries has to be the same. But in the former example with the classroom, the x and y values would be different since there were more columns than rows.

Data

Data is basically of two types: text and code. Text consists of data which is visible to the user on the screen, and as mentioned earlier, can be either numeric or alphanumeric. Code is data which is used by the system as a signal to perform certain tasks. As an example, in the file record layout, there is room for an End of Data signal. This signals the program that no more data will be forthcoming for that particular record. In deciding what character should be used for such a signal, a programmer would want to choose a character which would not normally appear anywhere else in the record. This immediately rules out all letters, numbers, punctuation symbols, and special keyboard characters such as &. The reason why none of these should be used as the End of Data signal is that, even for a character such as & which a data entry person might never intentionally enter in a record, typos do occur. This is why nonprinting characters are typically used for signals.

All characters are related in that they are represented in the computer as a numerical code. Although there are other character coding systems, the one most commonly used is ASCII, which stands for the American Standard Code for Information Interchange. ASCII is the industry standard for coding all of the uppercase and lowercase letters of the alphabet as well as special symbols and the numbers from 0 to 9. In ASCII, each character is represented by a number. As an example, A is 65, CTRL-A is 1, and a is 97. Clearly, if a programmer had to choose one of these three characters as an End of Data signal, he'd choose the nonprinting CTRL-A.

Calculations

Calculations are done internally in a computer using the binary number system (base 2), since a bit can be either on (1) or off (0). When a computer is asked to add 7 and 8, the numbers 7 and 8 are first changed to their base 2 equivalents (111 and 1000 respectively).

Calculations are performed in algebraic order rather than in reverse Polish notation (which some calculators use). This means that calculations are entered as they would be algebraically. For example, if you wanted the sum of 7 and 8 raised to the third power, you would write 100 $(7\times8)^\wedge3$. The carat symbol $\wedge$ represents exponentiation.

The algebraic order of operations (the order in which arithmetic operations are performed) is: Parentheses, Powers and Roots, Multiplication and Division, Addition and Subtraction. For example, $6\times5-4$ would give an answer of 26, not 6. To produce an answer of 6, the expression would have to be written $6\times(5-4)$.

Searching

Searching refers to the act of locating one or more characters within the body of text, data, or a program. Although there are many search algorithms, the logic is based on the MID$ string function. Specifically, a search program would query a user on the string to be found. After the user enters the string, the program would search through the data (or program or text) for that particular string. Since interpreted BASIC operates significantly slower that compiled code, BASIC searches are usually written in assembly language subroutines. The logic within a search routine that compares strings is the same as the logic of the sort routine discussed earlier. Searching is a common feature in sophisticated word processing and program editing applications software. Also related to searching is the search and replace feature in which not only is a string found but it is then replaced by another string. For example, if a 200-page book has been written about the life of George Washington and the name "Washington" was mentioned in the text 387 times and was spelled "Washingtun" all 387 times, sophisticated word processing programs will replace "Washingtun" with "Washington" automatically. This is referred to as a global search and replace. In addition, it's also possible to replace a string in some instances and not others. For example, if the word "ton" was spelled "tun," the user would want to make the replacement, but not in a word such as tunnel. Sophisticated word processors permit the user to search for and replace the string "tun" only in whole words. The way this is accomplished is that in addition to comparing strings to see if they're equal (meaning ASCII equal), the string is tested to see if the leading and trailing characters are spaces (ASCII 32), indicating that the string is a separate word. In addition, if the replacement string is longer than the original string, word processors will automatically reformat the text to accommodate the longer word.

Of all the features of program editors and word processors, the ability to search and replace is one of the most time saving and valuable.

Validation

The term validity applied to programming refers to the internal consistency of a program. That is, does the program logic operate properly? Using interpreted BASIC as an example, the program is checked for coding errors (such as SYNTAX and NEXT WITHOUT FOR) but not for validity. The validity of a program must be checked by the programmer. For example, consider the routine discussed earlier which separated the file record into variables and then operated on the variables. Amount Charged 1 was found in characters 124-129 of the record. But if the programmer had made an error in the record handling algorithm so that the program treated characters 130-135 as the Amount Charged field, the customer would then have the date added to the bill. This kind of error will not be detected by the system. It is an example of a program which is not valid.

There is also a way in which a program can be valid, yet wrong. Beginning philosophy students learn that there is a difference between an argument's validity and its truth. Using syllogistic logic as an example, consider:

> Major premise: All men are green.
> Minor premise: Socrates is a man.
> Conclusion: Socrates is green.

The above argument is valid. But it's not true. The reason why it's valid yet false is that the major premise is false. In the same way a program can be valid, yet produce incorrect results. In the above example in which the programmer's algorithm caused the date to be charged to the customer, the problem was one of validity. The program code would have been valid, however, if the programmer intended for the date to be added to the bill (although still wrong). The point is that if one of the concepts of the program is wrong, the coding logic might be valid, yet produce false results.

Debugging

It is often said that there is no such thing as a completely debugged program. As evidence there are COBOL programs which have been debugged and revised and appended and used for nearly a quarter century in which bugs have been found in the original portions of the code still in use.

In the debugging process a program's validity is checked. Each module of a program is checked separately to see if the output is correct based on the processing which has been applied to the input. The entire program in turn is validated in the same way. In BASIC a line number can be used with the RUN command so that portions of a program can be run without running the whole program. This is a useful tool in the debugging process, although the programmer frequently has to make adjustments in the module's input to account for missing operations. As an example, typically DIMension statements are placed at the beginning of a BASIC program while the variables which depend on the DIM statements are used in modules farther along into the program. If the DIM statements are bypassed by using the RUN [LINE NUMBER] technique, the programmer will get a BAD SUBSCRIPT error when the module is tested. There are always ways around this problem, but the point is that when one is testing program modules there may be other problems introduced due to the fact that certain portions of the program are not RUN with those modules.

Fig. 2-5

Defensive Programming

Programs should be planned with ease of correction and error-trapping in mind. Therefore, debugging begins with the concept of defensive programming. In other words, when the program's structure is first laid out and the flow of control is diagrammed, the careful programmer has already made provisions for the types of errors that can creep into the code and the ways that the logical roadmap can lead to a dead end. A checklist of defensive programming tips follows:

- Strange things can happen at the program's boundaries.
  Logic should be carried to illogical conclusions to see if the program structure is valid under all legal conditions.
- Files do not end by themselves.
  Markers must be set at the ends of files, even if they are placed there only for testing purposes and will be removed later. In this way, the program's data handling capabilities can be evaluated properly.
- Output should be easy to read.
  Programs should do all the work of formatting output data for ease of readability and understanding.
- Logic should correct for bad data.
  Mistakes can creep in during input and not all data is perfect. Therefore, the program's logic should be able to evaluate the legality of the data and correct for any reasonable mistakes.
- Subroutines should be tested separately wherever possible.
  This is an important rule for efficiency and correctness when programming in a block-structured language.
- Locate subroutines properly.
  A program should take the most direct route to a subroutine.
- All code should be documented.
  Source code becomes unintelligible once the program is finished. Therefore, documentation must be clear and, most importantly, complete, if the program is to be checked for correctness later.
- All names should be meaningful.
  The names of variable strings should reflect what they will actually represent.
- Calculate memory requirements carefully.
  Know the combined memory requirements for the program, the operating system of the machine, and the data to be input.

As these brief examples indicate, debugging code, and also debugging the logical structure of a program, require special types of expertise. Often, the program designer is not the technician who manages the debugging process because of his or her proximity to the program and to the original logical design that drives the operation. Within a programming department, therefore, junior programmers are often hired to support an ongoing piece of software by testing for bugs and analyzing the code and its accompanying documentation. Debugging existing code helps new programmers learn how software is constructed and adjusted to fit the needs of the specific application. Amateur or novice programmers can learn a lot from the institutionalized structure of some of these programming departments because of the emphasis they place upon the continued evaluation of code and structure. If COBOL and Fortran programs can have a life of twenty-five years based on conscientious support and upgrading, then so can programs written in BASIC that are only two or three years old or applications written in dBASE or Lotus 1-2-3. If programmers keep careful notes, document their structural charts as well as their code, and evaluate how their programs handle specific tasks, debugging will be an easier task, and the program itself will only improve over time.

Gary Markman

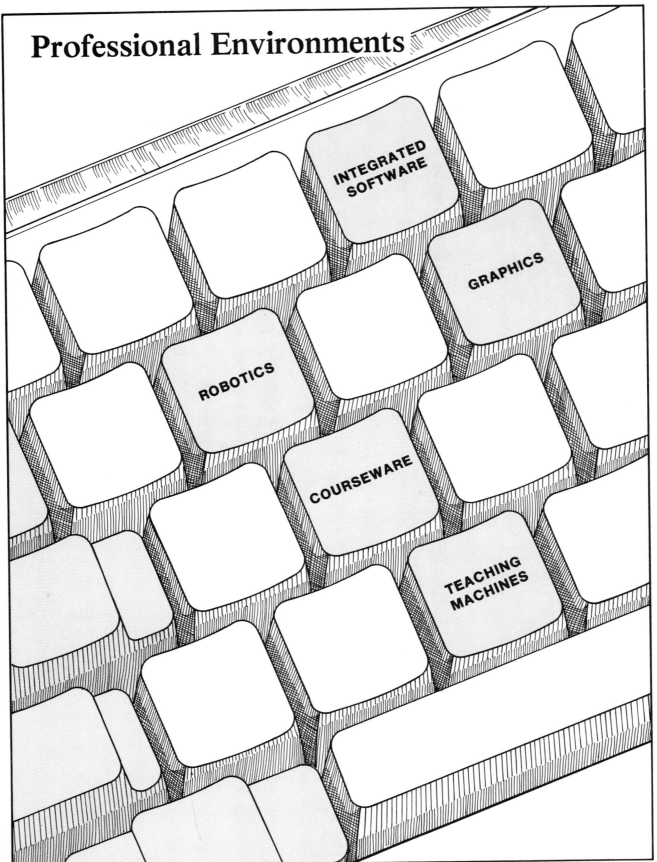

Professional Environments

3
SPECIAL APPLICATIONS SOFTWARE

One of the most instructive ways to understand and appreciate the structure, design, logic, and execution of computer programs is to evaluate the way professional software companies and their programmers adapt their product to the demands of the market and the professional user environment. For example, writing a program in BASIC on a home computer to balance a checkbook probably will not require the extensive error checking, screen prompting, and screen or printer formatting as a similar application written as a component of an off-the-shelf home financial package. Yet in order to understand how a checkbook balancing program should look, it would be better to examine the professional application before writing a home-brewed version. What is true for a checkbook program is even truer for a more comprehensive application, especially now that standard program formats and presentations are starting to emerge. Just as there are standard formulas for success for television shows and movies, there are standard formulas for success in the software marketplace as well.

This section looks at the types of products that are beginning to set standards within their area. It looks at these products, however, not from a user perspective but from a programming perspective. The aim will be to evaluate the products as comprehensive programs within their respective applications marketplaces to see, for example, how the market is defined and how the programs fit into the markets. The software will be examined as examples of programming as well as examples of consumer product that satisfy professional needs within a very tightly defined market. In addition, this section will analyze the professional software typologically because the various categories of product represented here point to the major areas of professional applications. Each application has defined a separate market in today's personal computing environment, and has itself been defined by a definite set of expectations.

This section examines (1) integrated business software, (2) educational software and educational programming in general, (3) graphics programming, (4) artificial intelligence and expert systems software, and (5) robotics. The business programming subsection will look at professional management and administrative software, and spreadsheets and word processors as components of integrated software packages. Evaluating these products from a programmer's perspective, the subsection examines how the disparate functions are unified under a common command structure that offers users a similarity of approach to processing data without limiting his or her ability by a command set that is too restrictive to allow for creative use of the software. It looks at integrated software as an extension of the electronic desktop concept that grew out of the approach to small business computing in the 1960s. By using graphics presentations to emulate desktop functions, today's integrated software products seek to combine the familiarity of typical administrative chores with comprehensive data tracking and manipulation. What problems does this design pose to programmers? The products themselves answer the question by showing how success was achieved.

Educational programming is examined from two perspectives. The first is a historical overview of the goals and achievements of early attempts to bring computers into the classroom. From the teaching-machine concept of the 1950s through the modern computer resource room in today's classroom, the advances in microcomputer technology have presented challenges to educators that have consistently helped them to redefine their perceptions of computer literacy and computer-based educational training. The second perspective looks at educational programming as another attempt to develop a true prescriptive learning program that actually reconfigures the sequence of curriculum to meet the needs of the individual student regardless of his or her background and educational competency. Currently, this is the area of greatest promise because it offers schools an opportunity to filter out the traditional classroom environment and replace it with a workshop or laboratory environment with each student performing tasks at his or her own educational appliance.

The subsection on graphics programming covers the latest developments in the field as well as the types of programming languages that offer users and professional programmers alike a "natural language" shorthand to the kinds of tasks that previously were only accomplished through painstaking bit mapping of separate screens. By examining extensions of BASIC and languages such as C and Forth on the newest compilers, the subsection shows how graphics routines are designed and executed and how they are increasingly forming the central aspect of all types of other applications.

The artificial intelligence (AI) and expert systems subsection first introduces the concepts of these two applications to a new personal computer market. Previously, AI and expert systems were limited to the large mainframe environments because of the memory requirements of the early systems. But recently, both because of the larger onboard memory extensions of PCs and because of the development of subsets of AI languages such as LISP and Prolog, this area of new software technology has become available to PC users. The subsection explains the essential differences between LISP, Prolog, Logo, and Smalltalk—the primary high-level AI programming languages—and procedural or algorithmic languages such as BASIC, PL/I, and Fortran. The subsection also explains how expert system toolkits such as M.1, Expert Advisor, Infoscope, and Expertease work and how they can be used to build functional expert systems and AI diagnostic and dialogue applications on PCs. Artificial intelligence and expert systems programming hold out the promise of beginning a new generation of interactive PC applications because they are configured by the user for the user. The programming design of these packages, and indeed for most AI or expert systems in general, allows the final product to "learn" invisibly from user input so that it becomes more expert as the user applies it to new and different problems or in different situations. AI and expert systems programs are rules based rather than procedures based, and this means that once the rules for decision making are set up by the user, the program can take new information and apply it to the existing structure of rules. Users can query the system to find out which rules are in force at any point in the interaction and why the program is doing what it's doing. This is a very different level of interaction than a user is accustomed to having with programs like Lotus 1-2-3 or dBASE II. Its implications for processing and customizing information are enormous. Essentially, AI and expert systems programming take desktop personal computers, especially desktops that are networked to large, data-heavy mainframes, from the era of strict data processing into the era of "intelligent" and verifiable decision support. This subsection examines these products and these possibilities.

The robotics subsection serves two purposes. First, it introduces PC users and programmers to the newest generation of robotics software and ambulatory hardware. Second, it explains the basic software principles behind the applications of integrated motion, the movement of artificial limbs, voice synthesis and sound recognition, photorecognition, and the processing of sensory input for use by digitalized processing systems. The robotics subsection looks at the promise of translating software commands into the physical manipulation of external objects and the extension of computing power beyond the physical perimeter of the desktop computer. Software that governs the processing of photo or auditory information into human-understandable data allows professional users in all areas of industry and business to create executable procedures that are not inherently computerized. Robotlike devices can deliver mail, retrieve objects, perform telemetric functions in areas where humans cannot go, and provide on-site visual confirmation of events. Today's space program already utilizes an array of robots and robotic devices that perform a variety of tasks in a hostile environment, and the latest trends in computer-assisted manufacturing indicate that there is an important practical future for the technology.

This entire section of the Encyclopedia, therefore, develops the concepts explained in the first two sections and orients them to the practical applications of computer programming, software design, and the architecture of high-level user/programmer-oriented languages. This is a problem-solving section that examines particular task families in the major areas of business, education, science, and design, and shows how programming technologies respond to market needs.

The Electronic Desktop

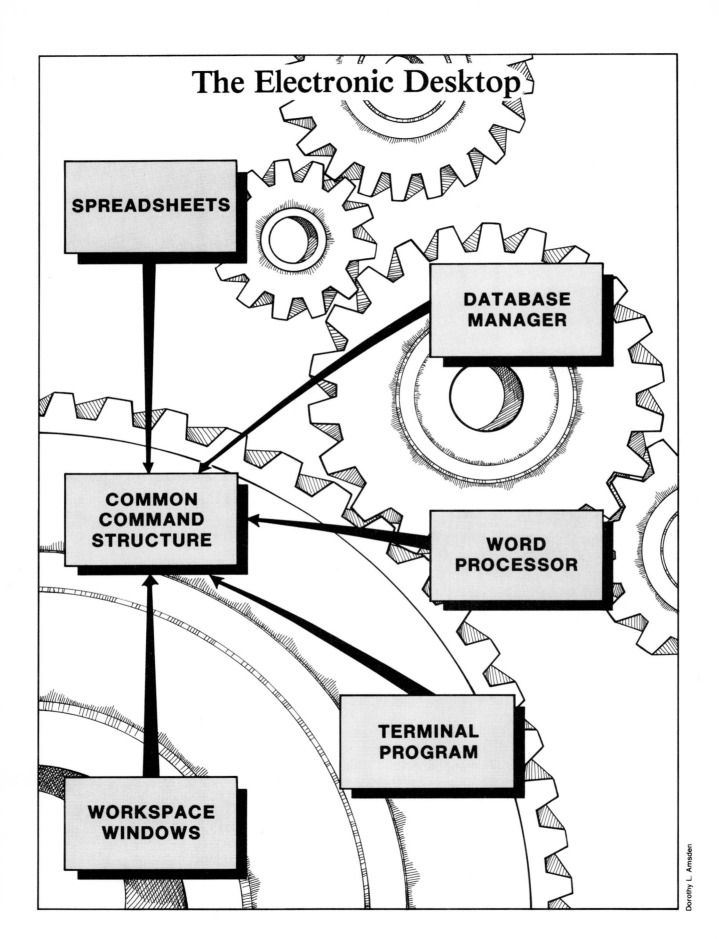

Introduction to Integrated Software

With a variety of integrated software and windowing packages becoming available for the IBM PC and other MS-DOS microcomputers, there is a special need for evaluations that help users make the wisest choice for their needs. It is certainly bad enough to make the wrong choice of a single application program. But with integrated systems that involve so many of the things you will be doing on your machine, and with the resulting higher price tags, there is virtually no margin for error in making product selections. As in most software, there are details about the day-to-day operation of integrated software packages which may turn out to be very important to you, but which you had no way of anticipating. The information provided here is intended to help fill that gap for you.

You will be reading descriptions and evaluations of essentially three types of closely related software: (1) integrated software systems, (2) integrated windowing environments, and (3) multitasking operating systems with windowing and other integrated features. While the technical aspects of these three categories of integrated software can differ widely from one another, for you the user there is one bottom-line issue that all of them have to come to terms with regardless of their ways and means: what helps you get your particular type of work done most easily and efficiently and at what cost? So with this ruler in hand, let's try to get an overview of the three different categories of integrated software and the issues they present.

Integrated Software Systems

Integrated software systems refers to software packages that try to provide many of your software needs by essentially one product that can handle, say, word processing, spreadsheet, and database functions, yet do not necessarily offer windows, ability to run more than one program at once, and mouse control as their main attraction. The advantages here are potentially great. Not only are there common commands that stay the same across several applications so you drastically cut down the learning time, but there are often less obvious redundancies that are eliminated, resulting in time savings for you. For example, it is probably important that you be able to get all of the powerful features of information processing to print on the specific make and model of printer that you have. With five separate products, this usually means five separate installation routines so that you can actually get on paper all the nice things your programs can do. But if an integrated software system is well designed, then you should only have to configure your printer once for a whole set of application programs.

Before we go into the various details of this type of product, it will be worthwhile to have an overview of the main issues that it is important for you to weigh before laying out the cash for an integrated software system. Here is a checklist that summarizes the main things to consider in selecting integrated software systems.

- What are the hardware requirements? system memory? color/graphics card? hard disk?
- Are all of the included applications of high caliber?
- What type of information transfer facilities are there?
- Can you import and export information with other software?
- What output hardware is supported?
- How fast do the applications run?
- How easy is it to go back and forth between applications?
- What operating system, if any, does it use?
- What is the total price, including extra hardware?

Hardware Requirements

Integrated software systems differ widely in regard to what hardware configurations they require to run and are equipped to handle. For example, Ovation requires a hard disk and 512K of memory for operation, whereas Open Access runs with two floppy disk drives and only 192K. If you don't already have the amount of hardware that is needed, the cost of this hardware has to be added to the price of the software as the real price of choosing that system. But naturally, if you already have the required hardware, that is not an issue for you. If you already have a hard disk and plenty of onboard memory, the question becomes which of the software packages makes best use of what you have. For example, although two integrated software systems may both support your hard disk, one may require you to partition the hard disk for it; this means not only that you have to completely reconfigure your hard disk, but also that the integrated software system will sit in its own partition so that integrating with other software will require special procedures, if in fact it is possible at all.

Information Transfer Capabilities

One of most important and complex issues in integrated software systems is how information is shared and transferred between various modules of the system. The range extends from those where information transfer is very limited and difficult to accomplish, to those like Jack-2 and Ovation where integration is so complete that updating one component of the system automatically updates the item for all the others, such as database, calculation sheet, and graphics. It is important to know exactly what information can be shared and transferred between different modules of an integrated system, and how technical and involved the process is. Certainly, at this point in the development of software technology, it is not state of the art to have to go through a lengthy configuration process to transfer information from one module of a system to another.

The two main routes for information transfer are by the 'front door" and by the "back door." The front door transfer is done directly, section by section, through a window or other means of selecting information to be transferred while you see it directly onscreen. The back door transfer is by transferring or reformatting an entire file, which you don't need to be viewing at the time, usually by its file name.

Another aspect of information transfer is the ability of an integrated system to transfer files and information with other popular software such as Wordstar, VisiCalc, dBASE II, and Lotus 1-2-3. Some systems do not offer export and import facilities of this type. Others do, but it is such a technical and tedious process that most users would not consider it "user friendly." The important thing is to know exactly what it is you are getting and to make sure that it is compatible with your needs and abilities.

The User Environment

In most integrated software systems there is the intention to set up an environment in which you are able to move from word processing to spreadsheet to database and graphics, and possibly communications as well, with the least difficulty. With those systems that are designed for use with floppy disks, you will want to know how much disk changing is involved. Things like having to repeatedly change floppy disks may seem like a minor inconvenience, but remember that the less "transparent" the system is and the more demands it makes on you the user, the more your concentration is being diverted from what you are really trying to accomplish in your work.

Another point is just how easy the system is both to learn in the beginning and to use on a daily basis. Integrated software should make it possible that, instead of having to learn five or six separate programs and sets of commands, you really have to learn just one very large one. Just how close does the system you are considering purchasing come to this ideal? One of the important things in making a software system easy to use is the way displays are organized. For ease of use, it is important to be able to orient yourself readily at each stage of your work. It should never be ambiguous just where you are in the program. What you see on the screen not only has to be pleasing to look at for the hours you will be putting in, but has to be designed to give you just the information you need at each step without allowing the screen to get too cluttered.

The System Functions

1. Word Processing. With integrated software systems, it is important to know what role the designers intended the word processing module to have. In some systems, it is minor, to be used mainly as a convenient support utility with the other modules. With others, however, the designers intended to provide a full-fledged word processor with state of the art features. And with still others, the word processing is designed to be powerful in its own right and still designed to be used as a utility in designing the forms for the other parts of the system. To be feasible for this, the system must be designed so that you can move very quickly from the word processor to any other component of the system. Naturally, if the word processor is on a different floppy disk from other parts of the system, it is not terribly convenient to use it for preparing the forms to be used there.

2. Spreadsheet. This is the place to really focus some attention in examining an integrated software system, because there are many areas where power and quality can be lost or sacrificed. One of the first things to consider is speed. Particularly if your needs require extensive and complex calculations, you must make sure that the spreadsheet module is not crippled by poor time performance. The actual power of spreadsheets can differ considerably, so you should spend some time using a spreadsheet to get to know the functions that will be important to you. Another important question is macros, the ability to have frequently repeated keystrokes execute automatically. Lotus 1-2-3 has a particularly powerful array of functions for storing keystrokes as macros. However, no one has found this feature of Lotus especially easy to use. Some integrated systems offer the global capability of having the system remember your keystrokes as you execute them so that you do not have to become an expert at coding to get the benefit of this. All you have to do is execute and the macro is automatically stored. Needless to say, you should investigate whether this is a feature that you will want to have.

Currently, there seems to be a pointless competition among some software developers to see who can claim that their spreadsheet allows the largest number of rows or columns in a single worksheet. One developer claims to have a spreadsheet that can hold a worksheet with up to 10,000 rows. If you have any question whether this is an important feature for a spreadsheet, ask a qualified representative for a product that makes such a claim to create a macro that fills all of the rows automatically, and then to time how long it takes the spreadsheet to perform a recalculation of even one number in each of the rows. Speed is really the more relevant performance criterion, so be sure that you check some objective evaluations or benchmarks for the spreadsheet module in any of the products you are considering.

3. Database. It may seem to inexperienced users that all components whose function is just to hold data are basically the same, since they are essentially empty containers that you can configure however you wish to hold your information. However, there is quite a bit more than this to effective database systems that can mean a great deal in timesaving to you when designing, using, and updating them. The most important difference is between the relational and the nonrelational databases. Briefly, a relational database is one in which whole systems of files are not completely sealed off from one another, but allow you to define relatively permanent relations between them so that they form an integrated system. This is important in distinguishing between a true relational database and those only partly relational. Some databases that are called relational let you create connections between different record systems, but those relations are only temporary. Each time you want to use them in a relational way, you have to redefine the relations all over again. In a true relational database, you can establish relatively permanent connections between record systems that remain there for you to use until such time as you decide to change them. A true relational database allows you to set up a permanent application system that can be called up by a single name, which contains all the file modules needed for the application.

These observations, though far from being complete, give you an idea of what to look for in integrated software systems and in the evaluations of them contained in this book.

Integrated Windowing Environments

A windowing environment is usually presented as something that is supposed to make software easier to operate and more user friendly. Whether this is true in general is still to be determined, and whether it is true for a particular system greatly depends on how well done the system is. Certainly, windows in and of themselves do not guarantee that software will be easier to use. As a matter of fact, windows represent a whole area of additional functionality that is sophisticated and complex, so that a special effort must be made to make sure that they do not make software systems even more difficult to use.

The theory is that windows make software systems easier to use because they emulate objects you are already familiar with in your office environment. Various windows can be layered on top of one another without disturbing their contents, much like pieces of paper on a desk. This means that the user is on familiar ground. The more a software environment is based on analogies to familiar things in a physical office environment, the reasoning goes, the easier it is to learn and the less likely the user is to get lost.

There are several important categories of software that make windowing environments available to the end user. The main distinguishing features are:

1. For specially written software only
2. For use with popular software you may already own
3. For bit-mapped graphics or text only
4. True concurrency or simulated only
5. With or without mouse support
6. Overlapping or tiling windows

1. Windowing for Dedicated Applications. Originally, in the Apple Lisa/Macintosh software systems, windowing environments were made available only with their own special application programs for word processing, graphics, and so on that were written especially for them. In spite of the many advantages to this approach, there are also some disadvantages which led to the development of windowing environments like Desq, Microsoft Windows, Core Executive, and others. The main advantages to windowing environments with specially written applications just for them are very similar to those of integrated software systems. Many of the commands across all of the different applications can be made the same so that they are potentially much easier to learn and less prone to requiring relearning. And generally, since the applications were specifically designed to be used in an integrated windowing environment, things generally go more smoothly.

2. Window Environments for Popular Software Packages. Since only specially written application programs, which sometimes tend to mediocrity, were originally available with windowing environments, some companies developed the strategy to produce window environment software that could be used with the best and most popular packages available like Lotus 1-2-3. What resulted are several windowing environments that can provide most of the same window management functions as the self-contained systems, but you can use them with some of the application programs you already own and have some expertise in using. So the advantages of this approach are quite apparent. The idea is that with this type of software you can have the benefit of integrated window management without having to give up the good application software you already own and without relearning other applications that may not be as suitable to your needs. And with these window management shells, you potentially have a greater selection among each type of application software for those with the most state of the art features, or those that you yourself prefer.

That's the good news. Now we must also speak about the disadvantages of this type of software. First of all, you should be warned that there is no such thing as an integrated windowing environment that can run any and every software package you would like. In many cases the window managers have to be specially configured, either by you or by the software manufacturers, to run each particular application program. In others there are inherent limitations that make it impossible for them to run certain programs. So before running out to purchase one of these programs with the expectation that it will be usable with all your favorite programs, it is absolutely essential to make certain beforehand that it will do what you anticipate.

3. Windows With or Without Graphics. On the IBM PC, as on most microcomputers, there is a sharp difference between the two basic types of display modes: those that are character mapped to produce sharp alphanumeric characters from a fixed character set, and those that are bit mapped to produce pixel-by-pixel graphics and character displays. Without special hardware, you cannot get graphics in text mode of the color/graphics adapter, and the text in the medium-resolution color graphics is only 40 column. This means, of course, that windowing systems such as that on the uNETix operating system, which are only designed for text mode, cannot in principle be used with programs that rely heavily on the graphics mode. However, some software manufacturers have chosen to do everything in the graphics or bit-mapped mode, often with carefully redone character fonts, so that graphics and sharp 80-column character sets can be present together. This is an important matter, because it affects what you will be able to see clearly on any given screen, and it will also be subject to change as better video hardware becomes available at reasonable enough prices to become accepted as standard.

4. True Concurrent Operation or Otherwise. Most of the windowing environments do not offer true concurrent operation, meaning that you cannot have more than one program actually executing in its window at one time. There are some, however, that do allow you to do this, such as Core Executive and the uNETix operating system. You might wonder what the advantage is of windows that do not support multitasking. There are a number of advantages. What these windowing managers offer is a way of dividing the screen into separate, independent viewing areas, each of which can obtain its display from a different application program or file. Also, at any time you may choose any window as the active window and the program will come alive again, picking up right where it left off. This means you have the ability to switch back and forth between programs without separately exiting and rebooting them each time. It also means that you can have a number of screens or subscreens of information from different programs either on the screen now or just a few keystrokes away, rather than having to exit the program you are currently running to get to the information or display. And usually there are provisions for transferring the information to some degree between the various window displays.

On the other hand, the advantages of integrated windowing environments that do support concurrent operation of programs in different windows are not too difficult to see. In the ideal situation, you should be able to do things like ordering a complex search of a database that will output a report to the printer and a complicated spreadsheet recalculation both in the background, while in the foreground you go on editing the final version of a report or cover letter with your word processor. However, you should realize that whether this kind of thing really saves you time depends very much on how good a scheduler has been implemented in the multitasking system.

What is really happening, of course, is that the processor of your PC is being time shared by the different tasks. This almost always means that the various tasks will run slower than they would individually. How much slower depends on how well the software developers did their job. In the worst conceivable case, the concurrent tasks would all be slowed up so much that the process as a whole takes longer than the sequence of each of them running separately. Naturally this would almost never be the case. The other part of it is purely psychological. If the multitasker is too slow, even though it still saves time to do some things concurrently, it may be frustrating for you to have to wait for things to happen in the foreground task when you are used to rapid execution. The comparative evaluations in Fig. 3-1 will offer some objective benchmarks for concurrently operating integrated enviroments.

5. With or Without Mouse Support. At some point you will probably have to decide whether and to what degree you will want to use a mouse device for interacting with your integrated software. Here again, the various products vary considerably in their approach to the issue. Some give you little or no choice: they either are totally mouse oriented or choose not to support the mouse at all. In between the two extremes are those that give you a choice whether, and to what extent, to use the mouse or keyboard. Whether the mouse makes life easier is still a disputed question, and the answer seems to be that it depends on the particular user. Some general rules, however, have emerged.

If you are already very familiar with most of the commands from the keyboard you need in operating a program you are now using, then it will almost never make your life easier to change to a mouse. The reasons for this are (1) you will have to learn a whole new way to use your program, (2) you will have to learn to coordinate using both a mouse and keyboard off and on, and (3) finding commands on a menu system is often much slower than typing in commands you already know from the keyboard.

On the other hand, there are certain situations where the mouse is almost always superior to the keyboard. One of them is in learning an entirely new program which you have had no experience with before. Here, you will see various pop-up or pull-down menus that describe the different things you may want to do in the program. So without any knowledge of the actual command names or keys in the program, you will often be able to select the command option that you need. Another situation where the mouse has superiority is when you have to do a lot of quick moving of the cursor all over the screen. A good example of this is in an interactive graphics paintbox program where you draw directly on the screen with the mouse and choose various options from a menu. The mouse is usually much faster and more appropriate for this kind of operation than a keyboard would be.

Some manufacturers give the impression that if you have a mouse, with their software you can forget about your keyboard. Even if you have had no experience with a mouse, a moment's reflection can tell you that this could not possibly be the case. In almost every application such as word processing, spreadsheet, database, and so on, a substantial part of the work involves entering data and editing it. This of course means entering letter and number characters from the keyboard. Take the case where you may have left out a letter in a word. You could use the mouse to move the cursor to the location of your error. You may also have been able to select the insert function with it. But then how are you going to supply the missing letter without using the keyboard? There is no system that dispenses entirely with the keyboard for entering data and editing it. This may lead to problems for you, because going back and forth between mouse and keyboard may not be your idea of user friendliness.

Some applications seem as though there is no input from the keyboard needed at all. For example, if all of your data and text have already been entered and edited, and now it is a matter of just rearranging blocks of it and moving them from various other files and applications into your current work file, no keyboard seems needed. However, in the course of doing this work, you will have a need to scroll through the various files. The producers of mouse-driven software have usually provided for this. Often there will be a special button on the mouse set aside just for scrolling. But in the opinion of some people, this writer included, moving a mouse back and forth on the table is not a very appropriate and easy way to scroll through the windows. It seems far easier to just press an assigned key of the keyboard and have the window scroll for you. So even here, it is not at all clear that the keyboard can be dispensed with.

These remarks are not intended to be a negative assessment of the mouse as an input device. They are meant to point out that there are very few activities on your PC where you will be able to completely dispense with the keyboard in favor of the mouse. The one exceptional case, as we have mentioned, is when you use the mouse directly to draw images on the screen and to select different functions that are part of the job. That you can do this extremely well without any use of the keyboard whatsoever has been shown conclusively by Bill Atkinson with his MacPaint program for the Apple Macintosh. But with practically any other application, the keyboard cannot be completely eliminated.

Comparison of Integrated Software Packages

PRODUCT	Ashton-Tate Framework	Corporate MBA	Context MBA	Lotus Symphony
Operating system	MS-DOS 2.0	MS-DOS	MS-DOS	MS-DOS
Minimum memory	256K (512K recom.)	320K	256K	320K
Special requirements		color graphics card	color graphics card	
Copy protection	yes	yes	yes	yes
Minimum storage	720K	720K	720K	360K
Hard disk	yes	yes	yes	yes

APPLICATIONS

Wordprocessing	yes	yes	yes	yes
Spreadsheet	yes	yes	yes	yes
Database	yes	yes	yes	yes
Graphics	yes	yes	yes	yes
Programming languages	yes	no	no	no
Telecommunications	yes	yes	yes	yes
Macros	yes	yes	no	yes
3720 Emulation	no	yes	no	no
Forms creation	no	yes	yes	no
Menus	yes	no	no	yes
Commands	yes	yes	yes	yes
Icons	no	no	no	no
Applications in memory simultaneously	yes	yes	yes	yes
Applications accessed from disk	no	no	no	no
Simultaneous access to multiple applications	yes	yes	yes	yes
Access to applications while in program	yes	yes	yes	yes
Data exchange between applications	yes	yes	yes	yes
Data exchange between files	yes	no	no	no
Uniform commands throughout	yes	yes	yes	yes

DISPLAY FEATURES

Maximum # windows	unlimited	4	4	unlimited
Overlapping windows	yes	no	no	yes

USER INTERACTION

Voice	no	no	no	no
Touch	no	yes	yes	yes
Mouse	no	no	no	no
Pulldown menus	yes	no	no	yes
Query language	yes	yes	yes	yes

FILE COMPATIBILITY

ASCII	yes	yes	no	yes
DIF	yes	yes	no	yes

USER SUPPORT

Help menus	yes	yes	yes	yes
Tutorial	yes	yes	yes	yes
Demo disk	no	no	no	no
Phone support	yes	yes	yes	yes
List price	$695	$895	$695	$695

Fig. 3-1

Comparison of Integrated Software Packages (continued)

PRODUCT	Microsoft Windows	Peachtree Peachtext 500	Peachtree Decision Manager	Visicorp VisiOn
Operating system	MS-DOS 2.0	MS-DOS	MS-DOS	MS-DOS
Minimum memory	192K	128K	256K	386K
Special requirements				VisiCorp mouse, pad
Copy protection	yes	no	yes	yes
Minimum storage	2 drives		2-320K drives	360K
Hard disk	yes	yes	yes	yes
APPLICATIONS				
Wordprocessing	yes	yes	yes	yes
Spreadsheet	yes	yes	yes	yes
Database	yes	yes	yes	yes
Graphics	yes	no	yes	no
Programming languages	yes	no	no	no
Telecommunications	yes	no	yes	yes
Macros	yes	no	no	no
3720 Emulation	no	no	no	no
Forms creation	yes	no	no	no
Menus	yes	yes	yes	yes
Commands	no	no	no	no
Icons	yes	no	no	no
Applications in memory simultaneously	NA	no	yes	yes
Applications accessed from disk	yes	yes	no	no
Simultaneous access to multiple applications	yes	yes	yes	yes
Access to applications while in program	yes	yes	yes	yes
Data exchange between applications	yes	yes	yes	yes
Data exchange between files	no	no	no	yes
Uniform commands throughout	NA	yes	yes	yes
DISPLAY FEATURES				
Maximum # windows	32,000	2	10	unlimited
Overlapping windows	no		yes	yes
USER INTERACTION				
Voice	no	no	no	no
Touch	yes	no	no	no
Mouse	yes	no	yes	yes
Pulldown menus	yes	no	no	yes
Query language	yes	yes	yes	no
FILE COMPATIBILITY				
ASCII	NA	yes	yes	yes
DIF	NA	no	yes	yes
USER SUPPORT				
Help menus	no	yes	yes	yes
Tutorial	no	yes	no	yes
Demo disk	no	no	no	no
Phone support	yes	yes	yes	yes
List price	**NA**	$325	$625	$1115

For some users this will not present any problem at all. They will find it perfectly acceptable to be going back and forth between the keyboard and the mouse. They will not feel this process too distracting, or that it requires too much space in their work. But for others, this will not be an acceptable or comfortable way to work. They will feel that if the keyboard is going to have to be used some of the time for most things anyway, then it is easier just to stay with it and not have to spend the extra time and money for the mouse. Which of these two types of users are you? We suggest that you spend some time experimenting before investing time and money in a system that may not turn out to be the right one for you. In the evaluation chart (Fig. 3-1) on page 40, information will be given on the usability of the different systems to aid you in your selection.

6. Overlapping or Tiling Windows. Another interesting difference in some of the main windowing packages involves those which let you pile several windows on top of one another so that some are temporarily either partially or even completely covered, and those which prevent this by adjusting the size of the different windows so that nothing can ever be covered up. Here again, there are two different philosophies of software design which may appeal to two different classes of users. You may belong to the group that likes to store current information in separate overlapping windows that you can then uncover as needed. Or, you may be among those who like to have everything right there in front of them at all times. But these two alternatives are not necessarily exclusive. In the future, there may be products that allow you the option of choosing between these two different modes of window operation.

Integrated Operating Systems

The ability to run multiple tasks in windows or otherwise is a function that is ordinarily associated with operating systems rather than application software. The category of window management software is in an area that does not easily fall into either of these classes of software. One commentator has even suggested that the appearance of this type of software represents the end of operating systems as we know them in favor of "operating environments." It is not surprising, then, that some software developers have chosen to make window management a built-in aspect of their operating systems rather than separate applications.

The Concurrent CP/M operating system from Digital Research has the capability of allowing up to four CP/M-86 programs at once, each in its own separate window. More recently a version called Concurrent DOS has appeared which allows PC-DOS programs to be run as well. The one important limitation is that programs that bypass MS-DOS and address the hardware directly will run only in a "suspend" mode, where the multitasking capability is immediately suspended while that program is running. This is not a trivial condition, because some of the best and most popular programs are precisely the ones in this category. Generally, most of the issues that were discussed in the previous subsection apply to integrated operating systems with window management.

There are, however, some issues to consider that concern operating systems specifically. First is the fact that operating systems are tools not only for application users but for application developers also. A multitasking operating system with window management can potentially be an extremely powerful environment for software development under the right conditions. The second point involves ease of use. As long as a multitasking window manager is designed to run under the operating system, nothing affects how easy the operating system itself is to use unless special provisions have been made for this. But with an operating system that has multitasking, screen management, and windowing features built in, it is important to know whether this makes the operating system an easier one to use or more difficult.

A third issue is whether the operating system really offers true multitasking and/or multiuser capability. This is not always as straight-ahead a question as it might seem. Digital Research, for example, will be offering a configuration option for Concurrent DOS that allows a second user to be connected by way of a serial port on the PC. This could be an important consideration for your application. If it is, make sure that the execution speed lost by the additional user is acceptable to you. A fourth issue is whether the operating system supports hard disks and hierarchical file directories like DOS 2.0. Some operating systems support hard disk but not subdirectories, which is virtually the same as no hard disk support, considering the enormous number of files that a hard disk can hold. Just stop and think what a hard disk would be like with just one huge directory. Therefore, if you have a hard disk but an operating system that will run DOS 1.1 only but not DOS 2.0 programs, your hard disk system will be practically useless because you will not be able to create a tree system of subdirectories. Therefore, it would be best to wait until the subdirectory capability is supported.

Generally, the issues with integrated operating systems are quite a bit more complex than those with other integrated software. As a rule, these systems should not be considered solely for their integrated or windowing capabilities. If there are other reasons why you might want them, such as the ability to concurrently run programs that normally cannot run on a single operating system, then the windowing features are an added consideration that might well make one the right choice.

Ernest R. Tello

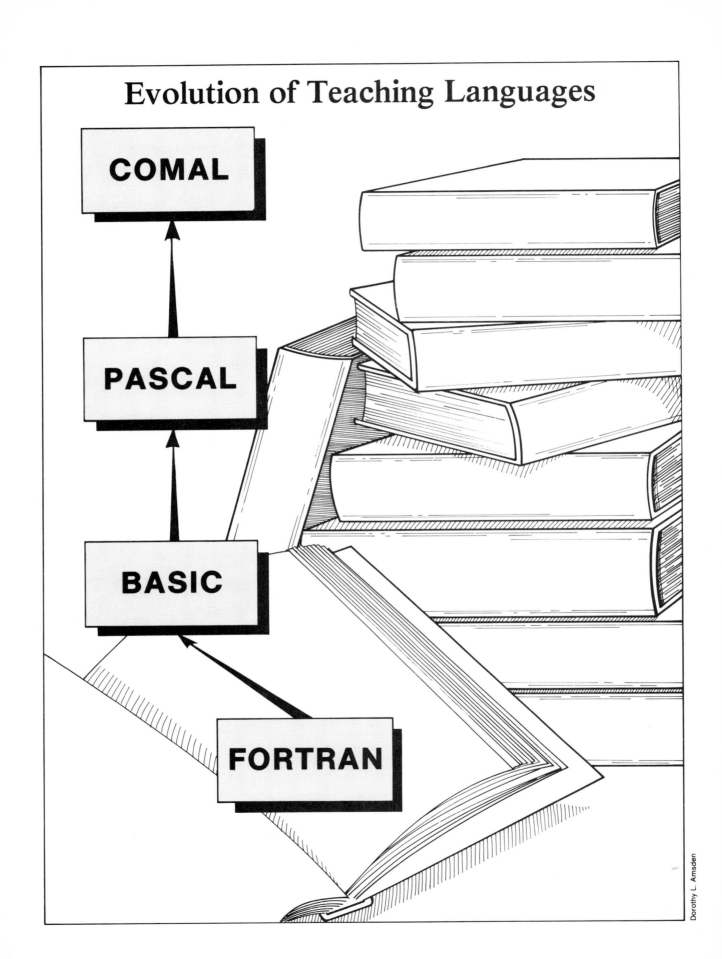

Evolution of Teaching Languages

COMAL

PASCAL

BASIC

FORTRAN

Educational Computing and Computer Programming

Computers have been performing a vital role in American education since the 1950s when the first programming languages made their appearance. Since that time, computers, computer literacy, and computer education have become buzz words for a fundamental shift in the way educational materials are delivered in the classroom and in educational resource facilities. Schools have invested millions of dollars in computers and educational software, and they have created a new job market for computer science teachers and computer curriculum developers. As the demands in business, science, and industry for computer personnel continue to increase, the burden of training new generations of public and private school children in the fundamentals of computing will also increase and place greater pressure on schools and teacher training institutions. Yet, beyond the immediate needs of trained computer resource personnel, the use of computers to teach academic basic skills themselves has created a new market for educational software and related computer materials. The schools, even at the elementary-grade levels, are becoming training grounds for a new type of worker who will enter, process, and retrieve information through a computer terminal. This section examines educational computing and its relationship to computer training, computer education, and programming languages.

From the Beginnings to the Present

The earliest attempts at writing computing or programming languages were made out of a perceived need to teach programming skills to individuals. Fortran, one of the earliest commercial programming languages and a development tool for business, scientific, and mathematics programs, began as an internal project at IBM primarily for educational purposes. Likewise, LISP, Logo, Pascal, Pilot, and of course BASIC all had their beginnings as educational tools designed to teach the concepts of computer programming. The language designers believed that a high-level language which resembled English in its vocabulary and gross syntax and which could eliminate the need for coding at the machine-specific assembly level would be an effective method of teaching the processes of programming. To that end, a variety of languages were developed which addressed a compiler that transformed the source code into a machine code. As new compilers were written for new machines, the high-level languages became more transportable and less dependent upon the type of machine upon which the object code would eventually be run. Thus, in the early years of computer language development, computer education meant, in part, teaching programming. This has remained an important aspect of computer education today, and, indeed, even the Educational Testing Service, the organization which administers the Scholastic Aptitude Test for college admission, has designated Pascal as the language of choice for its Advanced Placement Test in Computer Science.

The Promise of Teaching Machines

There was another concept that was emerging in the 1950s that would prove to have a profound impact on computer education and education in general by the 1980s: the concept of the teaching machine. Promulgated by educational psychologists and behavioral psychologists such as B. F. Skinner, the teaching machine presupposed that children could master specific academic or educational skills without the direct supervision of an instructor. If the scope and sequence of the skills to be mastered were organized correctly, the teaching-machine enthusiasts suggested, students would be motivated by the positive reinforcement of continual success to proceed through each lesson until they had achieved the mastery of the necessary skills. The adherents to the technology of teaching machines argued further that by eliminating the personality interactions between students and their teachers, students might be more effective at the acquisition of specific skills. The early teaching-machine technology lagged far behind the concept. Teaching machines were cumbersome and expensive and, in many cases, were down for repair or maintenance more than they were in use. Also, most teaching machines were beyond the reach of the school budget and lacked the type of product support necessary for the average school. As a result, the early attempts at developing a curriculum centered on teaching machines languished, and the machines became known more as oddities than as valuable resource tools. The development of low-cost microcomputers, however, in the 1970s revived the early arguments in favor of the classroom teaching machine, and the ground that was prepared in the 1950s proved more than fertile for the microcomputer revolution in classrooms in the late 1970s and early 1980s.

Converging Technologies

These three technologies, high-level teaching languages, classroom teaching machines, and low-cost microprocessor based computers, came together in the 1970s and have had a profound effect upon primary and secondary education. First, high-level languages, after they had gained acceptance in the programming and software development communities, demonstrated that they were viable commercial products. The success of Fortran, COBOL, and PL/I showed that there was a ready market for languages that allowed programmers to develop applications software for specific compilers that could be transported to other machines. This, in turn, inspired further development of high-level languages, and over the next ten years, work progressed on the development of teaching languages such as LISP, Pascal, Pilot, BASIC, and eventually Logo.

Each of these languages, as it became implemented in its original versions, gathered around itself its own set of developmental applications that not only helped determine the future course of the language's educational value, but also created a market for the types of applications that could be served by programming in the language. Hence, Logo, although a relatively new language, became popular because of its dictionary capabilities that allowed the language to be transported to non-English-speaking countries where children could substitute words from their native languages as macros or program labels. Likewise Pilot, which was itself an implementation of LISP, quickly became an authoring and course development tool and, therefore, a product in itself.

Of this group of teaching languages, BASIC is certainly the most famous. Because it was almost immediately available when the earliest microcomputers were being developed, and because it was an interpreted language whose actual memory requirements, unlike Fortran, COBOL, or LISP, were rather small, it was adopted as the language of choice by the emerging microcomputer industry. Thus, BASIC, which was not the best of applications programming languages, became an immediate applications development tool and helped to create a generation of instant programmers because of the coincidence of time and place and the emergence of an entirely new technology that placed desktop computing power in the hands of a generation that had grown up on hi-fi's, TV's, stereos, and C.B.'s.

Attributes of Teaching Languages

Each of the teaching languages had key attributes which recommended it as a language upon which to learn the principles of computing, and all of the languages could boast that they were natural language oriented, that is, that they used a standard English vocabulary as a basis for the command set so that users would not have to learn what amounted to a new vocabulary in order to program.

Virtues of Basic

BASIC was a nonstructured language that encouraged a degree of creativity among its users. New programmers who were not used to the requirements of flowcharting and topdown program design would be able to write simple programs, and even simple programs with series of nested subroutines, without having to worry about the block structure of the language. Routines could be called from anywhere in the program, and syntax mistakes or errors in the code would be trapped by the BASIC interpreter without eating up computer time. The language was versatile and could handle a variety of numeric data types as well as character strings. A user could write simple word processors and mini number processors that could be enhanced as the user's knowledge of programming increased. And BASIC had the virtue of being there at the beginning when the first Altair microcomputer was developed. It was then picked up by other newly emerging computer manufacturers and software developers and became an industry standard.

Virtues of Pascal

Pascal, too, emerged as something of a standard even though it was originally conceived of by Nicholas Wirth as a method of teaching logical constructive thought. Pascal, and its offspring, Modula-2, by combining the structural organization of a PL/I with the English-like facility of BASIC, served as a vehicle for teaching professional programming concepts and logical thinking. Pascal is an organizational language for a more formal teaching environment. It fostered in users a respect for the sequential structure of a series of algorithms and the positioning of routines so that control of the logic could be passed from one block or subroutine to the next. Pascal paid due respect to the necessity of managing computer memory as well. Like PL/I, and unlike BASIC, Pascal programs reserved only as much memory as they needed for storage of variables, and at a time when the storage of information meant money this aspect of the language was a valuable commodity.

Virtues of Logo

Only Logo has remained firmly within the domain of a teaching language and has gained its own group of adherents as it has been implemented in a broad spectrum of versions to take advantage of graphics and sound capabilities of its different host microcomputers. An implementation of LISP that was developed at MIT by Seymour Papert, Logo places enormous power in the hands of programmers without requiring learning an entirely new programming language and a set of algorithms. In fact, the language was designed to allow children to create their own algorithms in a sequence that was not defined by the language itself. This meant that a novice programmer could create a sequence, such as a routine for drawing a square, by going up, to the right, down, and to the left, or by going down, to the left, up, and to the right in whatever order he or she wished, name the entire procedure as a block, and invoke the block from memory or from disk and execute it in a variety of ways. Teachers recognized the value of a teaching tool such as Logo and used it, as Papert recommended, as more than a programming language. And while there is still considerable debate among educators about the value of Logo and about what children actually learn from their programming in Logo, the educational and consumer markets have already found in the language a viable product that immediately engages the interest of children. Logo adherents maintain that learning to program in the language provides children with a way of expressing themselves logically and graphically entirely within the framework of a changing technological society. Children become adept at using keyboards and learn the meaning of concepts such as storage devices and printers or plotters. The language takes advantage of the fact that generations of children grow up in cultures in which the television set is taken for granted as an information appliance. By giving to children control over the video display of that appliance and by integrating that control with a method of teaching procedures definition and execution, Logo adherents suggest that the language is a teaching tool very much in tune with today's educational needs. Other educators and administrators take a skeptical view of the language's value. They suggest that what children learn from programming in Logo is, simply, how to program in Logo. This group, and its ranks are growing, maintains that the real value of a computer education is not in learning to program machines, but in understanding what computers can do and how they can be used as appliances and tools rather than as development devices. This is a debate that will not be resolved within the near future because the results of computer curricula will not be available for evaluation until this generation of elementary school children is in high school or college. By then, the hardware and software markets will have changed so drastically that today's debates will most likely be moot.

The debate about the value of teaching Logo is, for the most part, a general debate about the value of teaching any programming language in school. On one side, programming enthusiasts argue that learning computer programming is more than learning to use a language; it is learning to utilize the skills of logical thinking and structural organization. Opponents of formal programming training in schools maintain that the same logical skills could be taught through learning to use real-world applications software that will teach skills in word processing, data processing, and arithmetic as well as keyboarding and computer operation skills. Furthermore, they suggest, learning to program in BASIC or Logo is like learning a trade that will be obsolete by the time students are ready for work. The real professional programming, they suggest, will be done at a systems level rather than at an applications level, and it will be in languages like C, Forth, or Smalltalk that are too difficult to teach in elementary schools.

Early Teaching Machines

One of the first issues to arise in educational computing regarded the teaching of programming and the use of high-level languages which were originally developed as teaching tools and then became viable applications programming languages and educational products in their own right. The second major issue was the use of the computer as a teaching machine and the value that teaching machines held for the student and for the educational institution itself. In part, largely because of the early work of Skinner and other behaviorists, the teaching machine has become something of an ideal concept that would solve a host of problems almost immediately and allow each student to progress through an entire curriculum at his or her own speed without interference from the teacher or educational institution. This has proved to be an elusive dream because the technology simply did not support the ideal.

After the first types of machine-based tutorial devices proved less than viable for large-scale development, attention turned toward the computer terminal as a front end of a centralized teaching machine. Before the advent of microcomputers, a stand-alone computer per teaching station was far too expensive for schools to consider, but the proliferation of the mainframe computer network in the business environment and the development of minicomputers prompted educators to look at remote or "dumb" terminals as an economically feasible point of access to an instructional computing facility. The problem was, of course, software.

Introduction of Plato

Software development costs in the 1960s were very high because the large computer systems were usually time shared and software was written for specific applications for specific customers. Therefore, educational training programs were not generally available to the schools, and those that were available were often too expensive and required too much hardware for a normal school budget. An early potential answer to the software problem, though, was provided by a product called Plato from Control Data Corporation. Plato was originally developed in Minnesota under a federal grant as a method of teaching specific skills through drill and practice and positive reinforcement. It was entirely self-contained and machine based, and because it was a programmed sequence of events, it required no intervention by an instructor. Plato seemed to work. Students could proceed at their own speed, they were not affected by classroom interaction, and they did not receive any negative reinforcement from the educational environment. It was a particularly successful method of skills acquisition and mastery for slow learners who tended to perform poorly in traditional classroom situations.

When the federal funding for the Plato project ran out, it was continued privately by Control Data which ultimately brought Plato to market. Today, Plato is available in a variety of implementations on microcomputers, as disk-based software, and as a downloaded program from a mainframe on a time-sharing basis. Plato programs are also available at Control Data learning centers and to industry and private corporations. The success of Plato as an educational product pointed the way for software developers when microcomputers became available and formed the basis of the first wave of educational software or "courseware." The design of this early educational software was simple and straightforward: the skills to be mastered within a given subject area were organized in ascending order of difficulty with enough repetition of the most important information so that students would learn by encountering the same information over and over again in a variety of contexts. Each series of questions built on the previous series so that skills newly acquired could be carried over to the next group. Incorrect answers routed students back to a previous set of skills through a variety of loops so that reinforcement was constant. This method of learning lent itself to standardized testing; therefore, it was not surprising that students' scores on standardized tests tended to rise as result of this exposure to programmed learning. Teachers were enthusiastic at first, and so were administrators whose performance was measured by the standardized tests, and this encouraged developers to pursue computer-based programmed learning as a viable alternative to a strict classroom-based curriculum. The teaching machine was finally becoming a reality.

The Advent of the Microcomputer

The broad-based implementation of the first microcomputers brought the teaching-machine concept within reach of schools and, at the same time, raised many of the issues which are currently being debated among educators. The early TRS-80 Model I, the Apple, and the Commodore PET enabled local schools to implement desktop computer programs designed to run on 8 to 16K machines. The first cassette storage and retrieval devices that drove these early micros were slow, and they were sometimes unreliable, but they offered a technology that included graphics and text handling, immediate feedback for students, and rudimentary administration of scoring and test reporting. The second wave of devices, which included floppy disk storage, offered even greater power and more advantages such as classroom management packages, word processing, authoring systems in Pilot, Logo, and learning games. As a result of the appearance of microcomputers, the early teaching languages became available to schools on floppy disk or, in the case of BASIC, on ROM chips that were included with the purchase of the machine.

The First Courseware Programs

The first applications for microcomputer-based educational software echoed the programmed learning packages that had been developed in the early 1960s. These "electronic flashcards" were essentially drill and practice sets that were designed to present information and test students on their retention of the material. As flashcards, these applications performed sufficiently. Students could be assigned to a desktop computer workstation to study vocabulary, multiplication, historical facts, or any other subject and return for a test or take a test on the computer. At the same time, applications for microcomputers appeared that were programming language oriented as well as subject oriented. Students could now learn to program in Logo and BASIC on desktop units either as a part of the school curriculum or as a learning enrichment unit within one of the school resource centers.

Between 1979 and 1981, budgets for the acquisition of computers and related software swelled while curriculum directors and administrators sought to find ways of integrating the new material into the existing scope and sequences of the district. It was clear that integrating educational computing materials and courses into an existing curriculum was going to be far more difficult than finding the right machines and software to buy. Teachers complained that the computers could be disruptive and tended to slow down the performance of an entire class. There were also some complaints from teachers that the colorful graphics in the software tended to become more of an entertainment than the actual software. In other words, students were deliberately selecting wrong answers because the screen prompts were amusing, the bright colors on the screen were entertaining, or the beeps and tones from the computer were more rewarding than the screen prompts for a correct answer. By 1982, just as the first wave of computer buying was beginning to slow down, a new generation of educational software was being developed for microcomputers. There was a decreasing emphasis placed on learning programming languages for the sake of programming and a renewed interest in teaching students to use computers through off-the-shelf applications packages such as "Bank Street Writer" or "Easy Calc." At the same time, educational computing companies began to make their appearance by offering complete curricula and resource facilities to schools. The computer manufacturers themselves were active participants in the marketplace, offering price and sales incentives, software packages, and personnel training to sell more units. The manufacturers correctly believed that by offering their products to schools, they were creating an even broader market, and one which would eventually spread into the students' homes.

The Current Environment

By 1983, a number of changes had begun to take place that affected the type of educational programming development and even the school computing environment. Teacher training programs, which during the late 1970s and early 1980s had been suffering because of the lack of jobs, suddenly were inundated with requests for computer resource teachers and math teachers with a specialty in computer science or computer literacy. School districts themselves began listing computer resource personnel slots in hiring budgets, and a new teaching field had emerged: the computer specialist. Armed with a hardware and software budget, the computer resource specialist, by 1984, began to affect the types of educational products the schools purchased. And now, in the present generation of educational computer hardware and software development, distinct trends can be seen that reflect the influence computer resource specialists are having on their local school administrations and school boards.

School software is turning back to reinforcement of some of the basic academic skills that were neglected in the ten-year period from 1969 to 1979. A renewed emphasis on reading and computational skills as well as on reasoning skills is forcing educational development companies to redesign software so that the student can construct a response at the keyboard rather than simply press an A, B, or C. The appearance of 16- and 32-bit microcomputers such as the PCjr and the Macintosh is also beginning to have an effect. Screen displays can be made more sophisticated, and the student can request help from hidden screens and pull-down windows. The added onboard memory and communications ports are making local area networking possible within computer resource centers, even if the networking is only for the purpose of sending scores up to a fileserver terminal for records processing and classroom administration. And finally, the appearance of integrated business software products is influencing educational software developers to create integrated educational products. These products, sometimes marketed as separate modules with menu access from module to module, cover a variety of subjects and provide for a vertical scope and sequence of academic skills.

William J. Birnes

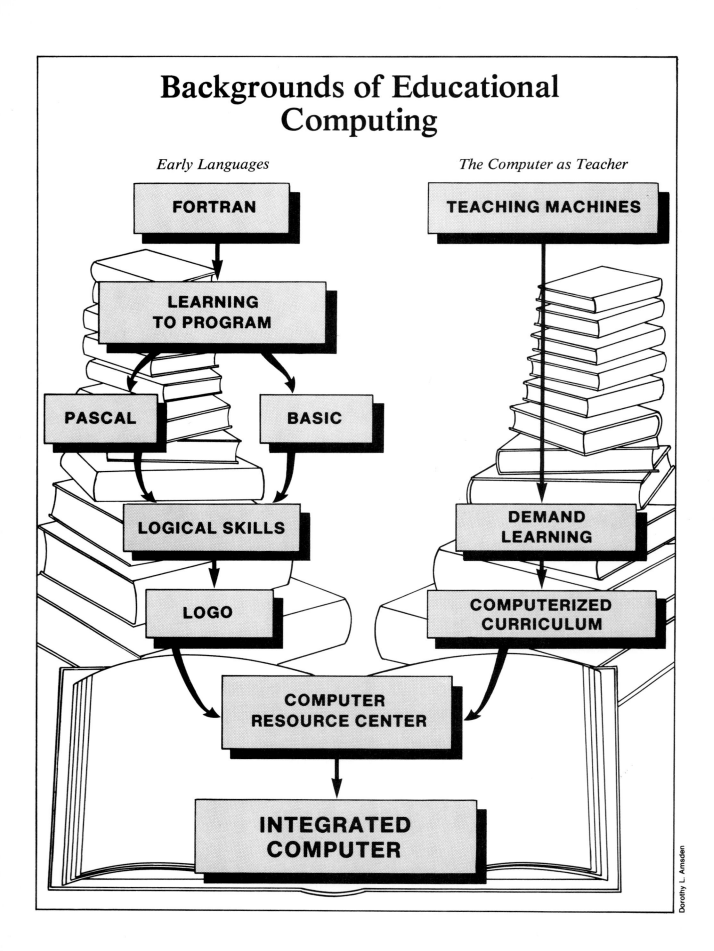

Backgrounds of Educational Computing

Early Languages

The Computer as Teacher

FORTRAN

TEACHING MACHINES

LEARNING TO PROGRAM

PASCAL

BASIC

LOGICAL SKILLS

DEMAND LEARNING

LOGO

COMPUTERIZED CURRICULUM

COMPUTER RESOURCE CENTER

INTEGRATED COMPUTER

Dorothy L. Amsden

Educational Computing Facilities Today

During the past decade, nothing had a greater effect on schools than the microcomputer and the programs to make it go. The dynamic changes that took place in schools during earlier decades—e.g., the formation of national collective bargaining agencies, racial integration, federal assistance for special needs of students—had matured and stabilized by the mid 1970s. Only the microcomputer, and perhaps the establishment of statewide or district competency examinations, make schools in the mid 1980s different from those of the mid 1970s.

Our embrace of the microcomputer for schools is remarkable. In a few years, we have gone from level zero to nearly one hundred percent acceptance of the premise that microcomputers belong in schools, in all schools. This acceptance has been both stimulated and satisfied by the microcomputer industry and by software providers. Look at the forces that have led to this acceptance:

1. We have small machines and large ones; cheap computers and mid-priced ones; packaged systems, custom components, and add-ons. Schools have equipment options—many of them—and with these choices comes competition. With competition come better prices and better service.

2. We have Logo, BASIC, Pascal; word processing, spreadsheet, and database management software (and their several combinations); drill and practice; tutorial authoring programs for teachers; and other software in great quantity. Since 1980 there has been an output of software for school use that is awesome. Certainly, there is criticism of the quality of some of these programs; but most educators would agree that software quality, however defined, improves with each passing month. This observation applies to proprietary and so-called public domain software.

3. There is support from a large and growing subculture for school adoption and use of microcomputers. The personal computer set, those who own or have use of a computer, is an unusually well-educated segment of the United States population. Generally, they have supported the growth of school uses of computers. This almost parallel growth of the numbers of computers in both homes and schools is without precedent. The two markets are also mutually reinforcing as well as complementary.

4. We have journals, newsletters, magazines, research reports, television programs, skilled advertising, and publicity. Both premicro media and new magazines focus on the micro and very often on how it can be used in schools. From a positive view point, no other school-related subject has had the recent media coverage that computers have had.

We have witnessed the formation of a beachhead of change due to increased availability of appropriate hardware, much new educational software, support from powerful public constituencies, and hype made available through large, company advertising budgets and massive media coverage. Where do we go from here?

The Emerging Issues

As in any period of rapid change, new problems and issues soon become apparent. To be expected, as the school marketplace makes its prerequisites known, pragmatic issues replace theoretical ones. It's happened before. Can you remember in the late 1960s the acrimonious debates about the effectiveness of branching versus linear sequences by teaching-machine programmers? The debate went on even as schools put their machines away in closets and janitors' storage rooms. Or, do you recall the university-based advocates of open classrooms extolling the theoretical advantages of such structures just as movable partitions defining a teacher's turf were being put in place?

The school environment, with its traditions, mores, and well-established protocols, provides a challenge for any force for change. And, in the long run, the following are the issues which must be addressed if the microcomputer software beachhead in schools is to remain and expand.

Curriculum Integration. This issue is paramount. Integration can be approached from two different positions: either the software publisher must describe exactly how and where the objectives of the publisher's program correlate with the instructional objectives of the school district, and aid in accomplishing them; or the district must amend or add the instructional objectives of the published software to its own set, and get acceptance of these new objectives throughout the district. Since the latter approach involves the work of professional educators and, often, the acceptance of the new objectives by concerned lay constituencies, this is a far less likely scenario than the first one.

What makes curriculum integration of software particularly difficult is that each district may be guided by differing instructional objectives. Not only do school districts have their own sets of objectives, but most of the standardized tests and state-mandated competency tests have their own as well. These objectives are taken quite seriously by schools, and are frequently correlated with those of the district.

Typically, those in the district who have not supported the purchase of computers begin to ask the familiar questions: Are teachers using micros to accomplish defined tasks? Have scores increased? Have we done a cost-effectiveness study? Has the district prepared a statement of goals for the implementation of Logo? I fear greatly the answers to these questions until we have integrative procedures in place.

Distribution and Management. A related issue is this: How does a school district configure any number of computers—from two to, say, thirty—in a multiclassroom building? This is an issue not only for elementary grades but for all grade levels. It involves antecedent questions of equity of usage, teacher training, and technical competency.

Dr. Inabeth Miller ("How School Becomes Computer Literate," *Popular Computing,* October 1984) describes the five evolutionary stages of school use of computers. Stage One is experimentation. Stage Two involves the introduction of nonintegrated computer literacy software. After Stage Three, in which a school district struggles to make individualized software programs work in multiple classrooms, schools try to group computers into a single location. The same classroom teachers may use the computers in the new center, but rudimentary schedules of student usage evolve. An attempt is made to broaden usage to include many students who were denied access in the earlier micro configuration. Sometimes, hardware and software are purchased to allow networking within this location. (As we will see, "networking" has different meanings for different educators.) Very soon, however, the special, practical concerns of schools take precedent: Who schedules which students? Who's responsible for contacting the manufacturer when micros are down? Who knows about software and hardware compatibility? Who knows about software availability? Does software exist to remedy a specific skill deficiency, so that a classroom teacher can send a student to the facility for that purpose? Usually, the consequence of grouping microcomputers is the assignment, either part-time or full-time, of a teacher to "manage" that special resource. This teacher will have some technical bent, a basic understanding of instructional systems, and a managerial capability, but will be an excellent teacher as well.

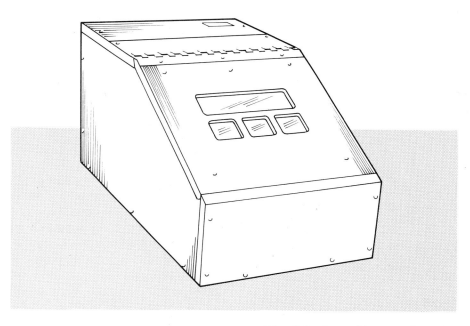

Fig. 3-2. A teaching machine designed to teach basic pattern recognition skills. The figure appears in the top window and the choices appear below.

The single practical alternative to such centralized resources will be provided not by "Gee Whiz" software houses but by old-line publishers of basal textbooks. Software that is coordinated with basal textbooks may be used by individual teachers in individual classrooms with back-of-the-room micros. Textbook publishers have known the importance of integration of their instructional objectives with those of the schools for many years. But even in this case, the picture of a well-managed microcomputer resource center is an attractive alternative. It will become more so as schools acquire more computers.

Learning to Program vs. Nonprogramming Skills. The idea of the computer as an investment on which to learn to program versus the view of a computer as a means to learn a new nonprogramming skill is an issue which will absorb educators for several more years. Given a scarcity of resources, the question is whether to teach all students elementary programming or, instead, to focus on basic skills and software applications. The scales are tipping, at least in elementary and middle schools, toward the latter.

Practical, not theoretical, conditions are again at work. Questions are being asked about the educational benefits of a fundamental computer programming capability versus mastery of word processing or database management applications programs. Alternatively, schools are asking whether mastery of basic skills—reading, math, reasoning, writing—are not of higher general priority than mastery of a computer language. The school universe is one of limited time, limited funds, and limited teacher knowledge of computer programming. The issue will be addressed and solved within these constraints. We may see high schools soon expanding the number of programming courses offered, but as electives and not as required courses.

Teacher Training. Who will train teachers in the new technology and in what depth? The answers are not obvious. But one thing is certain: there will be different levels of training required for certain teachers than for others. A teacher who elects, or is selected, to manage a computer-intensive facility will need to acquire very different new behaviors from those who use the resource from a classroom base. Additionally, school principals will require a related but quite different set of skills from those of either a participating classroom teacher or a resource specialist.

Who will provide these training programs. It is likely that both private and public institutions will have training workshops and seminars, as many do now. But as software products become more integral to the local curriculum, software proprietors will have to become responsible for the cost-effective implementation of their programs. This will mean teacher and administrator training conducted by these vendors. Some of these training programs will be intensive and extensive. In such cases, the specific programs for which effective training is provided will be more likely to survive than the one without such training.

Equal Opportunities. An equal opportunity to use computers in an affluent school district as in a poor one will remain a serious issue for the near future. This concern will not evaporate or be silenced by political rhetoric. It will eventually be resolved by action, at state or federal levels—if only because inequality of access, in the case of computers, is so straightforward and simple to document that a case for remedy can be made to the public at any time. Some states have already addressed this issue. Others are about to do so. If this question is found to require a uniform national solution—unlikely but possible—we will have two very different analyses of the problem, and at least two solutions presented as bills.

Evaluating the Results. Will schools accept "soft" data as the benefit of their computer investment or "hard" results? By what standard will the schools judge the effectiveness of their program? The answers to these questions are complicated by the narrow understanding of a school district's mission by its interested public. Most school districts have a majority of adults who believe that reading and math scores on standardized tests, and good SAT scores are the dominant criteria for evaluating the success of a district. They lack understanding or confidence in other measures, perhaps because other measures are more complicated, or because they have been "burned" by the softer ones of the 1960s. In many school districts, representatives of this position serve on the school board, sometimes even control it. In such instances, the goal of better results on nationally normed tests will turn attention to the computer as a means to achieve that end. Other uses of the computer will take a back seat to its use as an effective tool for teaching or supplementing basic skills.

These are the issues of the day: curriculum integration, in-building computer configuration, using computers to teach programming versus applications or basic skills, teacher training, equal access, and soft versus hard data. To face those questions, educators will need to order, classify, and put in priority certain dynamic properties of computers and software. Unfortunately, the terms and classifications of the recent past will not help them do so.

The Need For New Gateways

Old ways of thinking, categories and classifications which have served us well, often linger well beyond their natural useful life. Instead of being helpful in ordering things, they become insidious handicaps, closing us in and preventing progress. Evaluations and decisions become stilted; worse, they become unreal. We face such problems now in the world of microcomputers and related software. We will examine some of these problems in detail below.

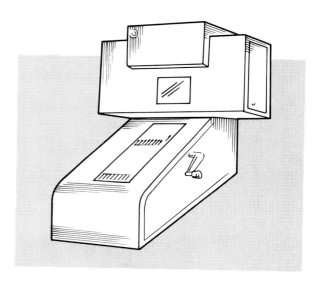

Fig. 3-3. A spelling or math problem is shown in the upper window and the student supplies the missing information by moving the sliders below and turning the crank to lock in the answer.

Types of Educational Software. In the evolution of instructional software, tidy classifications—useful at first—become generally adopted. The distinctions between drill and practice, games, tutorial, and, later, simulations, tools, and even artificial intelligence programs, were accepted as categories having almost mutually exclusive properties. When were these distinctions outdated? Probably the day they were first used by a journalist; certainly by the start of the 1980s.

Very few software programs today are drill and practice in the same sense that they were fifteen years ago. In addition to strengthening existing student behaviors (the old "drill and practice"), the new programs often shape new behaviors, even though the frame formats for both strengthening and shaping behavior can appear identical. In short, identifying a program as "drill and practice" can mask its intent and the actual outcomes. In addition, since drill and practice programs today often get a bad rap, some very good software is being overlooked.

There are other reasons why these old software classifications are no longer useful. As more software becomes available, dynamic characteristics, as well as typological ones from several of the old categories, are often blended into a coherent, instructional whole. A writing program, for example, intended to teach a student the need to describe an object in appropriate and sufficient detail may possess a tutorial aspect, a simulation, a word processing component, and a gamelike conclusion in which another student, selecting from a set of alternative objects, determines whether the first student's description properly communicated the properties of the object. (This program, incidentally, will soon be available.) These old software categories just don't work and, more to the point, they do not need to be replaced. Journalists will not be happy about their demise but educators should be.

Software Evaluation. Are we asking the right questions about software? The answer is "probably not." For the most part, we tend to focus our software evaluations on various instructional characteristics: instructional design, contents, and teaching strategies. This focus is a narrow one. In the context of the broader environment in which the software is to be used, it may lead to poor choices. To be more specific, if a software program is intended for use without the help of a teacher, by a single student in a classroom, and while simultaneous group instruction occurs, one set of evaluative criteria may apply. If the software is to be used in a computer resource or laboratory environment, under management software control, a very different set should be used. For example, whereas the software to be used in a regular classroom is not designed for regular teacher intervention, the program in the computer center may be deliberately designed so that a teacher should check student progress from time to time. Another example: Graphics intended to reinforce a student, when used in a regular classroom, may be desirable for student motivation. But in a computer-managed learning center, where an automatic recording of progress can occur, reinforcing events can be scheduled outside the learning program. Intraprogram reinforcers may be quite undesirable under these conditions, since any interruption that keeps the student from making the fastest possible progress might well become aversive.

An equally serious shortcoming in our software evaluation method is that the process is often controlled by hardware capability rather than being based upon the minimum program features required to reach instructional objectives. The argument goes like this: Branching and color graphics are useful in teaching anything; computers have those capabilities; therefore, computer software should always make use of those capabilities. Yet, while it is certainly true that branching and color graphics can be used to teach certain skills more effectively than traditional means, it does not follow that all skills are better taught by using either color graphics or branching procedures. Subtly, our software evaluation assumptions and procedures have been shaped by what a machine can do, not always by the best and least costly way to accomplish a teaching task.

Networks. As grouping of computers take place, a need will arise to be much more precise about networks than we have been to date. Talk to a half dozen educators about networks and you will find six different perceptions. Clarification is needed.

The first question is this: Is the instructional program to be completely individualized? If the reply is yes, then this network is very different from one in which all students have the same lesson at different terminals.

Here's the second question: Is the instructional program to be computer managed for all students, with permanent student records updated in real time? If this answer is yes, then the network requirements are very different from a down-load-only system.

The third and fourth network questions are these: Will the instructional program have diagnostic and mastery tests? Will computer-generated student prescriptions be used? If the answers are yes, yet another network aspect will be required.

To our great disadvantage, our views about computer networks have come from noncomputer examples. The most common one is the language laboratory, in which a teacher can select and listen to a single student pronouncing something in a second language. If we base our understanding of the potential of computer networks on this thin and limited model, we will make inferior use of networks in the future.

Empirical Evidence. Our resistance to empirical evidence is wasteful and leads to biased choices. How many times have you heard a teacher or administrator say that such-and-such a program, or a particular type of program, is "boring." Or conversely, you hear pronouncements that a program will "engage students and spark their creativity." Gratuitous statements of this type are harmless enough if they are ignored by software purchasers in schools; but all too often, decisions are based upon them.

These statements, and many like them, are subject to empirical tests in the environment in which real students are attempting to learn. In that environment, all such matters are relative. A program thought by an adult to be boring may be the most welcome learning experience of the day for students. Conversely, a program thought to be engaging or challenging may quickly become punishing in a particular classroom or computer center. We must be less inclined to pass our personal appraisals and judgments of software characteristics on to its target users. A program's history of success in learning conditions, similar to the intended one, should be our primary guide to software selection.

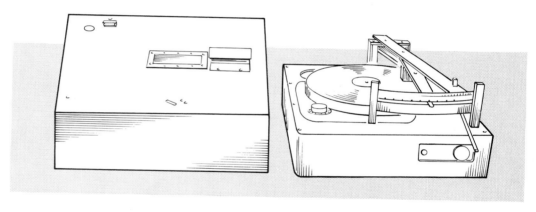

Systems and Their Components. Distinctions between administrative uses of computers, computer-managed instruction through criterion or mastery tests, and instructional software are melting away. They are becoming components of systems packages rather than separate entities. Blendings of diagnostic and mastery testing with computer-controlled instruction, along with administrative by-products, are a natural evolution. It serves little purpose to consider these functions as separate software programs.

The organizing and ordering mechanisms of the past cannot survive if educational software is to become an integral part of the school day. We will need new and more realistic "sorting utilities"—ways of looking at a software program, its instructional objectives, and its history of effectiveness within highly specified environments. We will need to focus on outcomes, not program features. We will need to develop methodologies which ensure that these outcomes—usually new or strengthened student behaviors—are generally accepted by both the school district and by concerned investors at local, state, and federal levels. The same, tired way of evaluating educational software will not provide a gateway to the future. At worst, we may do battle against ourselves, leaving the beachhead as quiet and relatively unchanged as it was after teaching machines, programmed instruction, and television landed on school shores years ago and held out the promise of a demand learning environment.

Fig. 3-4. In this 1957 version of a teaching machine, material was printed on a disk within the larger box. A question appeared in the window, and the student wrote the answer on a strip of paper in the second slot. The phonograph supplied additional auditory stimuli.

The Promise of the Future

There are reasons to be cautiously optimistic about the direction of educational programming. Unlike the response to several technical innovations of the postwar years, educators for the most part did not rush to embrace the microcomputer at its face value. Too many overhead projectors and 8-mm video devices were still in classroom closets or in central audio-visual departments to accept yet another machine in their place. This time, educators wanted software first, not just machines. Their demands were and are being met. Their priorities, in this respect, are right, and the momentum from this way of making decisions will carry us forward. There are examples of real headway:

IBM's "Write to Read." What makes this program an exceptional event is not its specific approach or its outcomes, but the fact that IBM itself is behind the program. Assuming continued corporate support, IBM's reputation for ensuring total user satisfaction and maximum client benefit from each purchase will ensure a successful implementation of this program when applied to the school market. Computer labs with the "Write to Read" program, given IBM's immense financial, marketing, and customer service resources, could change elementary schools forever. If IBM stays committed to the school marketplace, most of the handicaps and issues I have described above are likely to become but minor irritants.

WICAT Experiment. WICAT Systems is currently attempting to market large-scale educational systems to schools. These systems include hardware, basic skills programs, authoring software, and administrative and management components. WICAT also understands the need for teacher and administrator training. Currently, these systems represent the freshest approach to the development of educational software and its implementation in the United States.

However, in spite of a highly successful round of public financing in mid 1983 (successful in the sense of raising funds), one must question whether this company has the resources to "go the course." If they do, and can survive the first waves of resistance, they will have lasting impact on schools.

Diagnostic and Mastery Programs. The quiet growth of computer-managed diagnostic and mastery programs is a healthy indicator. Very little is said in the popular press about the many examples of successful implementation of these programs, particularly computer-based mastery programs. Often, these programs are public domain. Many come from local or regional companies or agencies, and do not provide exciting copy for newspeople. They are, however, widespread. When these programs have been in effect for a few years, they alter the school district's instructional methodology and procedures significantly. Standardized test objectives are correlated with local or state objectives. Then, regular series of tests are computer administered to get periodic "balance sheets" of student progress. Without computers, data management was overburdened. With it, and using micros as test-administering instruments, schools have both a structure and a method to improve themselves. For software developers, the important message here is that it is but a small step from microcomputer as a testing instrument to microcomputer as a teaching instrument.

These are but a few examples of projects and programs acting as change agents or direction setters for educational programming in the future. Many other companies, my own included, are involved in new approaches to software and systems development and will be making these products available soon. Some of us expect the school market to "harden" in the short run. Dissatisfaction with the current state of matters may lead school boards away from new computer and software purchases. (See, for example, the commentary of Douglas D. Noble, "Jumping Off the Computer Bandwagon," *Education Week,* vol. iv, no. 5, October 3, 1984.) A recovery from such reactions will be gradual, but it will occur.

In *Esquire Magazine* ("The Great Reform Hoax," April 1984), George Leonard discusses with his usual brilliance the sorry notions of school improvement and reform which were publicized in 1982 and 1983. He has positive proposals and he offers them for our consideration. Some of those proposals are excellent, some arguable, but each one is thoughtful.

At the end of his article, Leonard describes a fictional high school, Jefferson Interactive Learning School, and the way students learn. Students there master skills and the basics of all academic subjects on an individualized basis. They use computers primarily, but they attend seminars and occasional lectures as well. The building in which these "rational" masteries take place is called the Academic Building. It is complemented by the Human Resources Building. In the latter, students are taught the performing arts, physical dexterities, and interpersonal skills. If there was but one article that those who write software for schools could read, I would point to this one. Jefferson is the most humanistic learning environment ever envisioned. It uses computers as they should be used; and it uses teachers wisely, taking full advantage of their unique capabilities. Educational software developers could do well to consider the many transitional steps leading from today's schools to Jefferson High.

Charles Walther

Computer Generated Images

BIT MAPPING · DIGITIZERS · UTILITIES

Dorothy L. Amsden

Microcomputer Graphics

The screen of a microcomputer is an interactive printed page of text and pictures. Blocks of random access and read-only memory are allotted to hold the data needed to describe a visual image. The screen is drawn by circuitry which scans the memory and outputs a signal synchronized with the raster, the picture-scanning beam of the monitor.

Computer graphics serves the needs of people in business through columnized listings of figures; multiple graphics windows; line, bar and pie graphs; form creation; report formatting; and text processing. Home users can enjoy animated educational programs and games. Teachers can create their own illustrated instructional material. Artists can create kinetic images, draw pictures and alter them interactively, overlay images, and create patterns.

All these applications are available using only two techniques, character graphics and bit mapping. Character graphics is the usual method for displaying text, and bit mapping is the usual method for displaying pictures. However, there is a good deal of overlapping in the two modes' capabilities as we will see. A computer's ability to display text is described in terms of rows and columns; 25 rows by 40 or 80 columns is typical. When one is drawing pictures by bit mapping, the size of a single display dot, called a pixel, is the descriptive unit. Screen resolutions of 160×100 (width $\times$ depth) pixels would be termed medium resolution, while 320×200 is high resolution. About 160×200 is the minimum needed for a natural-looking picture.

One fascination of computer graphics comes from how easily many pleasing and/or useful visual displays can be formed. This discussion will concentrate on the basic theory and practice of personal graphics programming. The aim is to give the computer user an appreciation for the graphics encountered in everyday computing, with programming examples of simple graphics applications to illustrate basic concepts.

The beginning programmer is advised to stick to graphics that can be programmed with high-level language commands. Charts, graphs, reports, character graphics games, and simple shapes and pictures are all in this category. Arcade-type games and animations are generally not basic programming on currently available machines. (SIMON'S BASIC cartridge for the Commodore 64 includes high-level control of sprite graphics for game programming.)

Selecting the language(s) in which to program graphics is important. The scope and ease of your programming depends on how well the language harnesses the graphics ability of your computer. Not all languages support bit-mapped graphics on a particular computer. In some cases, there will be restriction on combining text with bit-mapped pictures.

Many BASICs include bit-mapped drawing commands like LINE, CIRCLE, PAINT, and PLOT. These commands are good for drawing graphs and diagrams. You can even have a bit of creative fun with them. A very good language for creative graphics is turtle graphics, which was designed as a teaching tool for children. Some versions of Pilot, Forth and Pascal support bit mapping.

To produce pictures and embellished graphics, it is a good idea to have available a graphics editor and a sophisticated drawing program preferably operated through a light pen or graphics tablet. The pictures produced by these programs can be saved on a disk. Some drawing programs will include information on using these pictures in your own programs.

Basic Techniques

High-level graphics programming is a lot like pencil-and-paper drafting. The usual set of commands includes those to draw lines, circles, and dots, and to fill in bounded shapes. Drawing with these commands requires making a graph of the picture to be drawn and giving the x,y coordinates of certain points to the computer program. This is a tedious way to draw a picture, but an easy way to create diagrams, charts, and graphs.

Text and pictures cannot be freely mixed on a single screen on some computers. This is because text and pictures have a different internal representation in the computers' memory, and are displayed differently by the graphics system. In others there is no conflict, because text characters are treated like little pictures. Any computer that can draw pictures is capable of combining text and pictures on the screen; however, the high-level software languages may not harness the facility.

A block of memory of from 1 to 16K is commonly allotted for screen data. Each address in memory corresponds to a particular location on the screen. Changing the value in a particular memory address changes what appears on the screen in the corresponding location. The organization of memory to represent the two-dimensional screen is called memory mapping and the contents of memory which represent a screen image is called the memory image of the screen.

In most micros the microprocessor stores values directly into the graphics memory, thus altering the screen image. A second type of graphics system is terminal-type graphics. In this case, the microprocessor sends data sequentially to an output port connected to a graphics terminal. The terminal has an independent graphics memory under the control of a video display chip or other circuitry. Terminal-type systems vary greatly in sophistication depending on the amount of independent graphics processing they can do. In some cases only primitive text positioning can be done by the terminal; in other cases the terminal has its own microprocessor(s) performing complex high-speed graphics functions under the control of programs which reside in the terminal. So far there is no standard for the memory mapping used in microcomputers.

System Graphics Primitives

Most micros have built-in but limited capability to format text. The machine-coded programs for these primitive graphics functions are located in the operating system. Text is stored in the screen memory at consecutive locations beginning at the cursor, which marks the current position. The operating system performs such simple functions as HOMEing the cursor to the top left of the screen, CLEARing or blanking the screen, SCROLLing the screen up from its bottom, positioning the cursor at a desired row and column of the screen, and returning the location of the cursor to a program.

High-level languages have commands for the output of single characters to the cursor location. For example:

> **BASIC:** PRINT CHR$(87)
> **C:** putchar(87)
> **Forth:** 87 EMIT
> **Logo:** CHAR 87

Much of computer graphics can be actualized simply by positioning the cursor at the appropriate screen location and outputting the desired graphics characters. This is done in most high-level languages by commands which direct the formatted printing of data to the screen (screen memory) using the graphics primitive functions of the operating system. Here are examples of simple text printing in four common languages.

in BASIC:

```
PRINT CHR$(26): REM home on some computers
PRINT TAB(7)"WHERE'S THE CURSOR?";TAB(30);"AT 35"
```

in C:

```
cubes()        /* prints 100 cubes with screen scroll */
{
     int i;
     float num;

     for(i=0; i<100; ++i)  {
          num=i;
          printf("\n The cube of %d is %f",i,num*num*num);
     }
}
```

in Logo:

```
CURSOR 10 12
PRINT [THIS LIST IS PRINTED AT COLUMN 10, ROW 12]
```

in Forth:

```
CR ." texting, texting, texting . . . "
```

Text and the Video Matrix

Text and pictures have different internal representations in the computers memory. Similar to a printed page, predefined type is used for text, and an array of dots is used for pictures. For the printing of text, the screen memory is arranged so that consecutive memory locations represent consecutive spaces

Fig. 3-5

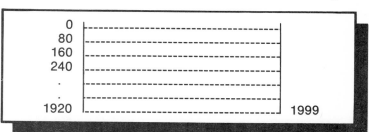

where a piece of type can be placed. For example, 2K of memory can be used to represent an 80 column by 25 row screen as in Fig. 3-5.

We will call each memory location a cell. The screen memory composed of the cells is called the video matrix. The number stored in each cell tells the graphics system which character to display on the screen in the corresponding position. The characters which are available include letters, numbers, symbols, and simple character-sized graphic shapes.

A standard numbering system called ASCII applies to the alphanumeric characters, assuring consistency among most microcomputers. Programs which use ASCII characters only, and which output data to the screen using only operating system primitives, are easily transported from computer to computer.

Bar charts and simple geometric shapes can be made from the character-sized graphics shapes, though the shapes themselves and the numbers used to select them vary from computer to computer.

The operating system primitives are simple routines which store values into the video matrix. Since these routines represent some of the programming concepts used in more sophisticated graphics, let's see how they work by writing equivalent routines in BASIC. We'll be using a 40 × 25 video matrix whose base address (starting address) is 1024 (see Fig. 3-6). The matrix is made of 1000 consecutive memory locations. The graphics system of our computer displays 40 of these locations on each row of the visual screen.

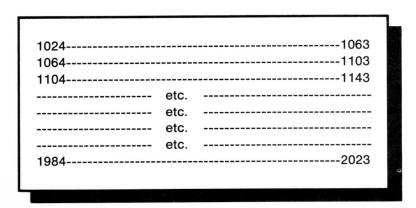

Fig. 3-6

To clear the screen, the number of the blank character is stored into every address in the video matrix.

```
FOR X=1024 TO 1024 + 40*25 -1
POKE X, BLANK
NEXT X
```

Scrolling is a little harder. The value in each column of each row is placed in the same column position one row higher.

```
FOR ROW=0 TO 23
FOR COLUMN=0 TO 39
POKE 1024 + ROW*40+COLUMN PEEK(1024 + (ROW+1)*40+COLUMN)
NEXT COLUMN, ROW
```

To position the cursor at a desired row and column on the screen, the corresponding address in the video matrix is calculated with ADDRESS=ROW*40 + COLUMN + 1024 where row is from 0 to 24 and column 0 to 39.

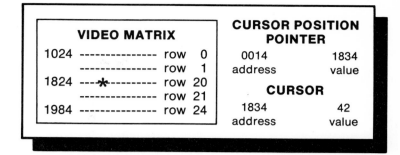

VIDEO MATRIX		CURSOR POSITION POINTER	
1024 -------------- row 0		0014	1834
-------------- row 1		address	value
1824 ----*---------- row 20		**CURSOR**	
-------------- row 21		1834	42
1984 -------------- row 24		address	value

Fig. 3-7

The cursor character number is stored in the memory location ADDRESS. The computer also remembers the value ADDRESS so it can start outputting text there. The value ADDRESS is used as a pointer to the cursor. In Fig. 3-7 the pointer value is shown, stored in address 0014. For the cursor, we are using a star, which is character number 42. The cursor (*) is on row 20 column 10: 1024 + 20*40 + 10 = 1834.

When the computer starts to output text to the screen, it will use the value 1834 in memory location 0014 as the address from which to start storing the output text. As each character is output, the pointer value is incremented by one, maintaining the current cursor position.

Cursor positioning at a specified ROW,COLUMN is not always available from high level. In this case the programmer must home the cursor and PRINT empty lines to the screen until the desired row is reached.

Columnized printing can be done easily in most high-level languages. BASIC has TAB and SPC for moving the cursor to specified columns and sometimes PRINT USING for printing figures in a specified format. Without a command such as PRINT USING, the printing of columnized figures is a small programming chore. For example, to print a right justified number with 2 decimal places in BASIC:

```
100 NUM$ = STR$(INT(NUM*100)) : REM CONVERT DIGITS TO STRING
110 LN = LEN(NUM$) : REM GET LENGTH OF STRING
120 DOLLAR$ = LEFT$(NUM$,LN-2): REM PROCESS THE STRING
130 CENTS$ = "."+RIGHT$(NUM$,2)
140 PRINT TAB(20-LN) DOLLAR$;CENTS$
```

In FORTH:

```
: D.2R  ( d/width --- )
    >R  DUP  ROT ROT  DABS
        <#  # #  ASCII . HOLD  #S  ROT SIGN  #>
    R>  OVER -  SPACES  TYPE ;
```

In C:

```
printf("%16.2f",num);     /* formatted print command */
```

Bar charts can be constructed in character graphics. (Later we'll draw a bar chart with bit mapping for comparison.) Many computers have graphic characters that are filled and partially filled such as these:

162   163   164

Such computers can give more accurate graphs in character graphics mode than those which have only a single full filled box character.

The following is a simple bar chart program written in C. If only the full box character is available, omit the optional (/* opt */) lines. Since only the operating system graphics primitives are involved, this program will work on any computer as long as the constants are appropriately defined.

```
#define    MAXLENGTH            60
#define    BOX                 162
#define    THIRD1              163              /* opt */
#define    THIRD2              164              /* opt */
#define    HOME                 26
#include   "stdio.h"
```

BAR CHART PROGRAM IN C

```
int number[9], unit, maxnum;

main()
{
    int count;

    putchar(HOME);
    puts("This program prints a simple bar chart");
    puts("\nHow many numbers do you have to graph? ( 1-9 )?");
    scanf("%d",&count);
    input_numbers(count);
    scale_line(maximum);
    graph(count);
}

input_numbers(count)
int count;
{
    int i;
    maxnum = 0;
    printf("\nEnter %d numbers to graph",count);
    for( i = 0; i<count; ++i ) {
        printf("\n Number %d ?     ",i); scanf("%d",&number[i]);
        if( number[i] > maxnum ) maxnum = number[i];
    }
    unit = maxnum / MAXLENGTH; if( unit ==0 ) ++unit;
}

graph(count)
int count;
{
    int accum, i, remainder;
    for( i = 0; i<count; ++i ) {
        accum = 0;
        while ( (accum += unit) < number[i] ) putchar(BOX);
        remainder = number[i] - (accum - unit);    /* opt */
        if( remainder > unit*2/3 ) putchar(THIRD1); /* opt */
        else if(remainder>unit/3 ) putchar(THIRD2); /* opt */
        printf(" %d\n\n",number[i]);
    }
}
```

```
scale__line(maxnum)
{
    int i;
    putchar(HOME);
    for( i = 0; i<MAXLENGTH/10; ++i) printf("123456789-");
    printf("\n\nunit = %d \n\n",unit);
}
```

Design Elements in Character Graphics

A variety of graphic design elements are available to the high-level programmer in character graphics mode. Among them are the use of reversed
graphics, intensity and/or color selection, use of a graphics character set, and
programmable characters. The nice thing about these capabilities is that they
can all be printed to the screen like text. These days, most computers include at
least a basic set of graphics characters for composing borders and simple shapes,
and include reverse graphics capabilities.

A well-designed screen can make data entry and review less tiring and
improve operator reliability. In the following BASIC program for the Commodore 64, reverse graphics and color can be selected from within the PRINT
statement. The program could be called as a subroutine in order to create the
screen template. Then data from a disk file would be printed on the screen in the
appropriate locations by using TAB, SPC, or other available cursor control
commands.

Note that information enclosed in the < and > symbols indicates various
<control functions> which are single key presses on the Commodore 64.
For example:

> <revon> is reverse graphics on
> <revoff> is reverse graphics off
> <dn> is cursor down one line
> <up> is cursor up one line

ORDER SCREEN PROGRAM
FOR COMMODORE C 64 IN BASIC

```
100 BCKGND = 53281: BRDR = 53280 : REM color register addresses
110 WHITE = 1
120 POKE BRDR,WHITE: POKE BCKGND,WHITE: REM set to white
130 PRINT"<home>"; : REM clear screen and home cursor
140 PRINT"<red>COMPANY NAME:    "
150 PRINT
160 PRINT" <revon><light blue>
170 PRINT" <revon> ORDER#    DATE    SHIPPED    "
180 PRINT"<dn><dn><dn><blue> <revon> ITEM    DESC
    QTY    NET    "
190 PRINT"<dn><dn><dn><dn><dn><dn><dn>";TAB(21)
    "<revon><green> TOTAL    "
200 PRINT"<lt blue>    :--------------------------------:":REM  C64 HAS
210 PRINT"   :            :    :REM  NICER
220 PRINT"   :            :    :REM  CHARACTERS
230 PRINT"   :            :    :REM  THAN
240 PRINT"   :--------------------------------:    :REM  THESE
250 PRINT"<up><up><up><up>"TAB(6)"<revon> N <revoff>EXT"
    TAB(21)"<revon> A <revoff>DD"
```

```
260 PRINT TAB(21) "<revon> C <revoff>HANGE"
270 PRINT TAB(6) "<revon> P <revoff>REVIOUS" TAB(21) "<revon>
    D <revoff>ELETE"
280 GOTO280
```

A terminal graphics computer may have a variety of character attributes available, such as intensity, underline, and reverse. For instance, the previous order screen program can be revised for a KAYPRO 4-84 by using low and high intensity and reversed attributes, along with direct x,y cursor positioning. On the KAYPRO, a 3-byte code sequence is sent to the terminal to select a graphics attribute or to position the cursor.

ORDER SCREEN PROGRAM FOR KAYPRO 4-84 IN FORTH

```
( screen 1        TERMINAL CONTROL WORDS )
: HOME 26 EMIT ;
: <ESC> 27 EMIT :
: ASCII BL WORD HERE 1+ C@ [COMPILE] LITERAL ; IMMEDIATE
: DIMON <ESC> ASCII B EMIT ASCII 1 EMIT ;
: DIMOFF <ESC> ASCII C EMIT ASCII 1 EMIT ;
: REVON <ESC> ASCII B EMIT ASCII 0 EMIT ;
: REVOFF <ESC> ASCII C EMIT ASCII 0 EMIT ;
: CURSOR ( ROW/COL--- ) <ESC> ASCII = EMIT SWAP
          32+EMIT  32+EMIT;


( screen 2        ORDER SCREEN PROMPTS )

: PRV  ( N--- ) REVON SPACE EMIT SPACE REVOFF ;

: PROMPTS
    DIMOFF 18 4 CURSOR
    ."  ----------------------------------------  " CR
    3 0 DO 4 SPACES
    ."  :                                 :" CR LOOP
    4 SPACES ."  ----------------------------------------  "
    DIMON  19 11 CURSOR  ASCII N PRV ." EXT"
           19 28 CURSOR  ASCII A PRV ." DD"
           20 28 CURSOR  ASCII C PRV ." HANGE"
           21 28 CURSOR  ASCII D PRV ." ELETE"
           21 11 CURSOR  ASCII P PRV ." REVIOUS"
    DIMOFF 2 33 CURSOR ;


( screen 3   ORDERSCREEN FOR KAYPRO-4 )

: CI ." !         !                           !  !            !" CR ;


: ORDERSCREEN
    HOME CR CR REVOFF DIMOFF
    ." COMPANY NAME: ----------------------------------------------------" CR
    CR 4 SPACES REVON DIMON
    ." ORDER #        DATE         SHIPPED  BY        " CR
    REVOFF 4 SPACES REVON
    ."                                          " CR
    CR REVOFF  DIMOFF  SPACE  REVON
    ." ITEM   DESCRIPTION                QTY         NET       " CR
```

```
REVOFF  CI CI CI CI CI CI CI CI CI
."  ----------------------------------------" REVON
."       TOTAL       " REVOFF CR  PROMPTS ;
```

Simple shapes and pictures can be composed with character graphics on most computers. The complexity of the pictures depends on the flexibility of the graphics character set and the number of characters that can fit on the screen. Large-sized letters, logos, figurines, and icons can jazz up most programs.

Some computers allow you to design your own character sets. On such a computer you can compose almost any image, given enough patience. Character graphics shapes can be included in text strings; however, composing PRINT statements for a picture is like typing on a keyboard that has been completely rearranged. The programmer will have to hunt and peck on the keyboard in coordination with a chart showing what keystrokes will access each desired character. Still, high-level PRINTing is usually easier than storing character numbers directly to the video matrix. If you are programming your own graphics character set, have a pencil and graph paper handy, and grab a beer or turn on the radio. The job can be quite rewarding, but takes some time.

Graphics Character Definitions

What actually is a character? How is it displayed, and what is the numbering system used to tell the computer which character is wanted? The description of the characters are stored in a ROM chip. Eight consecutive bytes are typically used to define a character, as shown in Fig. 3-8, with each bit telling the graphics system whether a corresponding pixel will be turned on or off.

A character's number is used as an index by the graphics system to fetch the character definition from the ROM and display it on the screen. For example, if a base address is established in ROM at 53248 = $d000, then Fig. 3-8 represents a possible configuration of data in the ROM.

ROM ADDRESS

CHARACTER	NUMBER	DECIMAL	HEX
D	68	53792	$d220
E	69	53800	$d228
F	70	53808	$d230
G	71	53816	$d238

Fig. 3-8

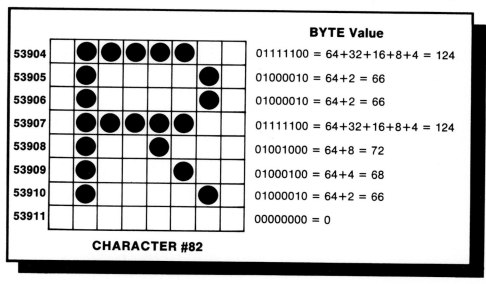

CHARACTER #82

Conventional ASCII definitions are from 0 to 127. Characters from 128 to 255 are usually graphics characters or reversed characters. Interesting in this respect is the blinking cursor which usually shows itself by changing the character at which it is located to reverse graphics and back again. This can usually be done by toggling bit 7 of the character number, thus pointing to a character in the ROM which is 128 higher than the ASCII value.

In character graphics mode, the graphics-generating circuitry has the internal knowledge to organize the 8 consecutive bytes of a character definition into a character image. All of the dots of the character will be displayed in the character-sized area of the screen corresponding to the video matrix cell which contains the character's number. Thus, an 82 in memory location 1160 of the video matrix in Fig. 3-6 puts an R in the third row of the screen in column 16 (1024 + 3*40 + 16 = 1160).

There are three principal reasons why beginning graphics programmers have to take care with character numbers:

1. It is sometimes easier to place graphics characters on the screen by reading their numbers from an array and storing the values directly to the desired video matrix addresses.
2. Not all characters can be typed at the keyboard. To print these characters, use a command like PRINT CHR$(character number).
3. The motion for game graphics can involve direct storage of character numbers to the video matrix. Game programs (and sometimes others) must know what characters are in particular locations on the screen. The values found in the video matrix are the character numbers.

In BASIC now for the Commodore 64 is a short game segment that moves a little "beastie" character around a screen in search of "food."

BEASTIE GAME
FOR COMMODORE C 64 IN BASIC

THE CHARACTERS —	BEASTIE	FOOD	BLANK
number	87	81	32

```
100 POKE 53280,1 : REM SCREEN WHITE
110 POKE 53281,1
120 CS = 13*4096 + 2048: CE = CS + 999 : REM COLOR RAM
130 SS = 1024: SE = SS + 999 : REM VIDEO MATRIX
140 FOOD = 81: BE = 87 : REM CHARACTER NUMBERS
150 PRINT "<home>"
160 BP = 1800 : REM STARTING CELL
170 FOR X = CS TO CE : REM ALL BLUE
180 POKE X,6 : REM 6 IS BLUE
190 NEXT X
200 FOR X = 1 TO 16 : REM SCATTER FOOD
210 POKE SS + RND(X)*999, FOOD
220 NEXT X
230 GET A$ : REM SCAN KEYBOARD
240 IF A$="A" THEN A = 1
250 IF A$="W" THEN A = 2
260 IF A$="S" THEN A = 3
270 IF A$="Z" THEN A = 4
```

```
280 ON A GOSUB 360,370,380,390 : REM MOVE BEASTIE
290 IF BP < SS THEN BP = SS
300 IF BP > SE THEN BP = SE
310 IF PEEK(BP) = FOOD THEN GOSUB 400 : REM EAT IT
320 POKE BP,BE
330 IF SF = 10 THEN PRINT "<home> YUMMY, I'M FULL!": END
340 FOR D = 1 TO 100 : NEXT D
350 GOTO 230
360 POKE BP,32: BP = BP − 1 : RETURN
370 POKE BP,32: BP = BP − 40 : RETURN
380 POKE BP,32: BP = BP + 1 : RETURN
390 POKE BP,32: BP = BP + 40 : RETURN
400 REM YUMMY
410 FOR L = 1 TO 10
420 POKE 53280,L : REM FLASH THE BORDER
430 FOR D = 1 TO 30 : NEXT D
440 NEXT L
450 SF = SF + 1 : REM KEEP SCORE
460 RETURN
```

Sprites

Sprites are a graphics feature particularly suited for, but by no means restricted to, arcade game programming. A sprite is a user-definable graphics object which can be placed anywhere on the screen independent of any character or bit-mapped picture. The programmer defines a sprite in a manner similar to a user-defined character, with the difference that the sprite is bigger and requires more bytes to define. A pointer to the sprite definition in RAM, and the sprite's x,y screen coordinates in pixels are stored in special memory locations for the graphics system. The sprite can be moved by changing its coordinates and will not affect the video RAM in any way. Visually, the sprite will overlay whatever is on the screen. There are only a few high-level implementations which support sprite graphics. Trying to program sprites without such an implementation may be too difficult for beginning programmers. Therefore, keep your reference manual handy.

Bit Mapping

When one is generating graphics by bit mapping, every pixel on the screen is displayed directly from RAM. In a single-color bit map each bit of memory corresponds to one screen pixel. For a screen resolution of 320 × 200 pixels = 64,000 pixels, the RAM required to hold the memory image is about 8K (8K * 1024 bytes/K * 8 bits/byte = 65,536 bits). The mapping of the memory image to the screen image depends on the computer.

All drawing has as its basis the turning on or off of any desired pixel. Therefore, high-level language commands must have as their basis some machine code which translates x,y pixel coordinates into a value to store in the bit map RAM. Let's take a look at the translation problem. Then we will look at some high-level applications.

Our sample screen has a resolution of 300 × 200 pixels requiring 8K of memory to map. The starting address of the bit map is 1024.

BIT MAP FOR 8K OF MEMORY

		COLUMN			
LINE	**0**	**1**	**2**		**39**
0	1024	1032	1040	...	1336
1	1025	1033	1041	...	1337
2	1026	1034	1042	...	1338
3	1027	1035	1043	...	1339
4	1028	1036	1044	...	1340
5	1029	1037	1045	...	1341
6	1030	1038	1046	...	1342
7	1031	1039	1047	...	1343
8	1344	1352	1360	...	1656
9	1345	1353	1361	...	1657
10	1346	1354	1362	...	1658
11	1347	1355	1363	...	1659
.					
.					
199	8711	8719	8727	...	9023

Each byte contains 8 bits displayed on the screen as 8 adjacent pixels in the same line. For a pixel at x,y:

$$\text{ADDRESS} = 1024 + (\text{INT}(Y/8) * 320) + \text{MOD}(Y/8) + \text{INT}(X/8) * 8$$
$$\text{VALUE} = 2\wedge(7 - \text{MOD}(X/8))$$

where INT = integer part and MOD = remainder part. Bit-mapped multicolor pictures introduce another little complication. In order to select the right color for each pixel, more information is needed than just on or off. One possibility is to use 2 bits instead of one for each pixel. Then:

    00 = background (color 0)
    01 = color 1
    10 = color 2
    11 = color 3

$$\text{ADDRESS} = 1024 + (\text{INT}(Y/8) * 320) + \text{MOD}(Y/8) + \text{INT}(X/4) * 8$$
$$\text{VALUE} = \text{COLOR} * (4\wedge(3 - \text{MOD}(X/4)))$$

High-level drawing frees one from the concern about the organization of the bit map. For example, to draw a red circle with its center at x=80,y=100 and with a radius of 20 and then draw its diameter in blue:

```
100 CIRCLE 80,100,20,2 : REM 2 stands for the color red
110 LINE 60,100,100,100,6 : REM 6 stands for the color blue
```

Here is the command syntax for the next two examples in a version of BASIC.

    LINE x1,y1,x2,y2,type
    CIRCLE x,y,xr,yr,type
    ANGL x,y,angle,xr,yr,type
    PAINT xi,yi,type
    CHAR x,y,charnum,type,size

TEXT x,y,"<ctrl A> text",type,size,spacing
HIRES color,color
MULTI color,color,color
where: x1.y1 are starting coordinates of a line
 x2,y2 are ending coordinates of a line
 x,y are the center coordinates of a circle or oval
 xr,yr are the x and y radii of a circle or oval
 xi,yi are a point, somewhere inside a shape to be filled
 color is a color number from 0 to 7
 type selects color (0-3) from available colors
 charnum is a character's number
 size and spacing are print parameters

Bit Map Bar Chart

This bar chart (Fig. 3-9) is similar to the one done in character graphics. It will run on the Commodore 64 with SIMON'S BASIC.

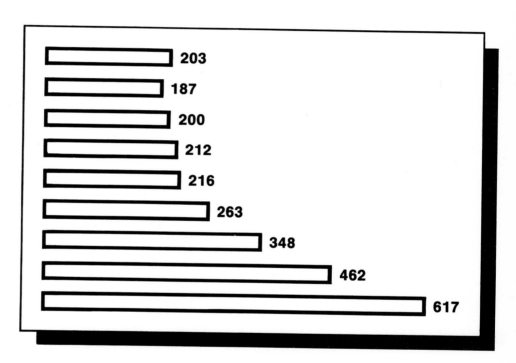

Fig. 3-9

BAR CHART PROGRAM

```
100 PRINT"<home><dn><dn>THIS PROGRAM PRINTS A SIMPLE BAR
    CHART
110 PRINT:PRINT"HOW MANY NUMBERS DO YOU HAVE TO GRAPH?
120 INPUT COUNT
130 FOR X = 1 TO COUNT
140 PRINT"NUMBER";X;" ":INPUT NUM(X)
150 IF NUM(X) > MAXNUM THEN MAXNUM = NUM(X)
160 NEXT X
170 REM
180 UNIT = MAXNUM / 30
190 HIRES 6,14
200 TEXT 14,1,"<ctrl A>123456789-123456789-123456789",1,2,8
210 TEXT 248,8,"<ctrl A>UNIT=",1,1,8
```

```
220 X=0 : NUM(X)=MAXNUM/30 : E=280 : B=6 : GOSUB 340
230 A = 10 : B = 20
240 FOR X = 1 TO COUNT
250 E= A + 8 * NUM(X)/UNIT
260 LINE A,B,A,B+10,1
270 LINE A,B+10,E,B+10,1
280 LINE E,B+10,E,B,1
290 LINE E,B,A,B,1
300 GOSUB 340
310 B = B+20
320 NEXT X
330 GOTO 330
340 N$ = STR$(NUM(X))
350 FOR Y = 1 TO LEN(N$)
360 CP = ASC(MID$(N$,Y,1))
370 CHAR E+8*(Y-1),B+2,CP,1,1
380 NEXT Y
390 RETURN
```

Pie Chart

Drawing a pie chart is easy with an ANGL command at your disposal. The finished graphic should look like Fig. 3-10.

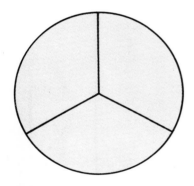

Fig. 3-10

PIE CHART PROGRAM

```
100 PRINT"<home>PLEASE ENTER 3 NUMBERS FOR A PIE CHART
110 INPUT N(1),N(2),N(3)
120 HIRES 0,1 : MULTI 6,7,4
130 CIRCLE 80,100,48,72,1
140 TA = N(1) + N(2) + N(3)
150 UA = 360/TA
155 UT=0
160 FOR X = 1 TO 3
170 ANGL 80,100,UT+N(X)*UA,48,72,1
180 UT = UT+N(X)*UA
190 NEXT X
200 PAINT 81,99,1
210 PAINT 79,99,2
220 GOTO 220
```

In order to create a label for the graph or to color in one or more of the graph's segments, the program must be enhanced with a subroutine to calculate an interior point for each segment of the pie.

Logo

Logo drawing is done by directing the motion of a "turtle," which leaves a trail on the screen as it moves. Turtle commands can be written in an immediate mode in which the turtle will move as soon as the ENTER key is depressed, or in a delayed mode, in which a series of commands are grouped under a procedure name and executed when the procedure is called. The turtle can be turned off with a PENUP command. Here are some basic turtling programs and the designs that result (see Figs. 3-11, 3-12, and 3-13).

```
CLEARSCREEN
HOME
PENDOWN
FORWARD 40
RIGHT 120
FORWARD 40
RIGHT 120
FORWARD 40
```

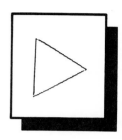

Fig. 3-11

Commands can be combined into named procedures and executed by typing the procedure name. These procedures can be combined to make other procedures.

```
TO TRI
      REPEAT 3 [FORWARD 40 RIGHT 120]
END

TO POLYTRI
      REPEAT 20 [TRI RIGHT 18]
END
```

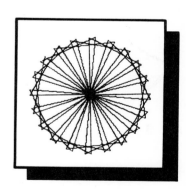

Fig. 3-12

Variables can be passed to procedures. Their values can be altered and the procedure called recursively.

Fig. 3-13

```
TO SQUIRAL : SIDE :ANGLE
    IF :SIDE < 10 STOP
    FORWARD :SIDE
    RIGHT :ANGLE
    SQUIRAL :SIDE - 2 :ANGLE
END
```

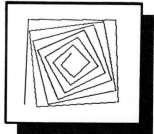

Pictures

Detailed bit-mapped pictures are best made using a program designed to draw pictures and store the data necessary to recreate them. Either the entire memory image of the finished drawing is saved on disk, or the step-by-step coordinates of each operation can be saved and used to recreate the picture later.

Drawing is usually done on a graphics tablet, a two-dimensional peripheral which sends x,y coordinates to the computer. A light pen or a mouse can also be used. Commercial software for drawing includes functions such as:

BRUSH SELECTION for a variety of line textures
LINE DRAWING either independent or connected lines
FREEHAND DRAWING
MIRROR DRAWING for creating symmetric images
CIRCLE and ELLIPSE drawing and repositioning
FRAME and BOX drawing and repositioning
SELECTIVE COPYING of portions of drawings to new locations on the
    same drawing, or to other drawings
TRANSPARENT OVERLAYING of one picture onto another
ERASING
ENLARGING
COLOR ALTERATIONS

One note of caution: You may not be able to use pictures created by a commercial drawing program in your own programs without specific knowledge of your machines graphics hardware and the program's disk files.

Current Developments

As microprocessors continue to become faster number crunchers, they will be able to manipulate very high resolution bit-mapped images using only a portion of their processing time. New graphics co-processor chips will further free the microprocessor from the many detailed calculations needed to draw a bit-mapped picture.

The growing graphics freedom is resulting in new applications and operating systems which introduce new ways for people and computers to communicate. The movement of visual symbols representing items and activities in the physical world can replace verbal commands to the computer.

The Macintosh/LISA graphics engine is so sophisticated, in fact, that its designers created from it an iconographic user interface for the operating system and for all resident software. This represents a quantum jump in user interfaces because it replaces keystrokes with visual graphics displays, such as file folders for file commands and trash cans for discard commands that are highlighted or dragged around the screen. Graphics windows can overlay graphics windows, providing additional areas of work and drawing space that are supported by a range of design tools that can create perfectly straight lines, circles, squares, or rectangles. The Macintosh display screen has become so popular so quickly that software developers have successfully created graphics packages based on a similar iconographic system for other machines. The Apple IIe now supports a version of a Macintosh-type screen called "Mousepaint," and the PC and PCjr have similar products that support a mouse and a screen design space with a variety of painting and drawing utilities.

The Macintosh/LISA graphics operating system has spawned a range of new products that use screen graphics as a way of transmitting data-oriented information. Besides the various "scrapbook" and "clip art" programs, database managers, financial programs, simulation games, and type fonts have all been created specifically for the high-resolution LISA/Macintosh graphics screen. These, combined with Macintosh's resident utilities such as the notepad, calendar, calculator, and alarm clock, point to a new direction in integrated onscreen graphics utilities.

Microcomputer graphics programs are also being developed to support sophisticated computer-aided design, or CAD, functions. AutoCAD, one of the newer software packages, has all the drawing features found in many shape generators as well as a full range of professional utilities that can be used by architects and engineers within a small office environment. AutoCAD is written for the PC and compatibles, and supports a digitizing tablet, mouse, or a lightpen. It also contains a file of graphics templates for applications such as electronic schematics, architectural icons, and mechanical icons. As CAD packages become even more powerful and sophisticated, they bring to the level of the small architectural, design, landscaping, or engineering firm an access to interactive machine-supported design before available only to larger offices.

Microcomputer graphics development will also have a profound effect upon the entire printing and publishing industry in the area of prepress work, page design, and layout. Sophisticated typesetting and layout programs now give small graphics shops the ability to design full pages on the PC screen, save the design as a work file, retrieve it and modify it to a customer's specifications, and print it as a hard copy before actually sending it to the typesetter. The newest of these software products even provide users with the capability of using a shape generator to design their own character sets. When combined with the technology of laser printing, which will have its greatest initial impact in 1985, these graphics programs promise to bring to the small to medium-sized advertising agency or even to the typical business office, all the facilities of a completely automated design and graphics studio. And as laser printing technology reaches an increasingly higher level of dots-per-inch resolution, it will eventually be able to reproduce a production-quality master. When this happens, it will, in effect, bring the print shop into the office and revolutionize the printing industry.

William J. Birnes

The Inference Machine

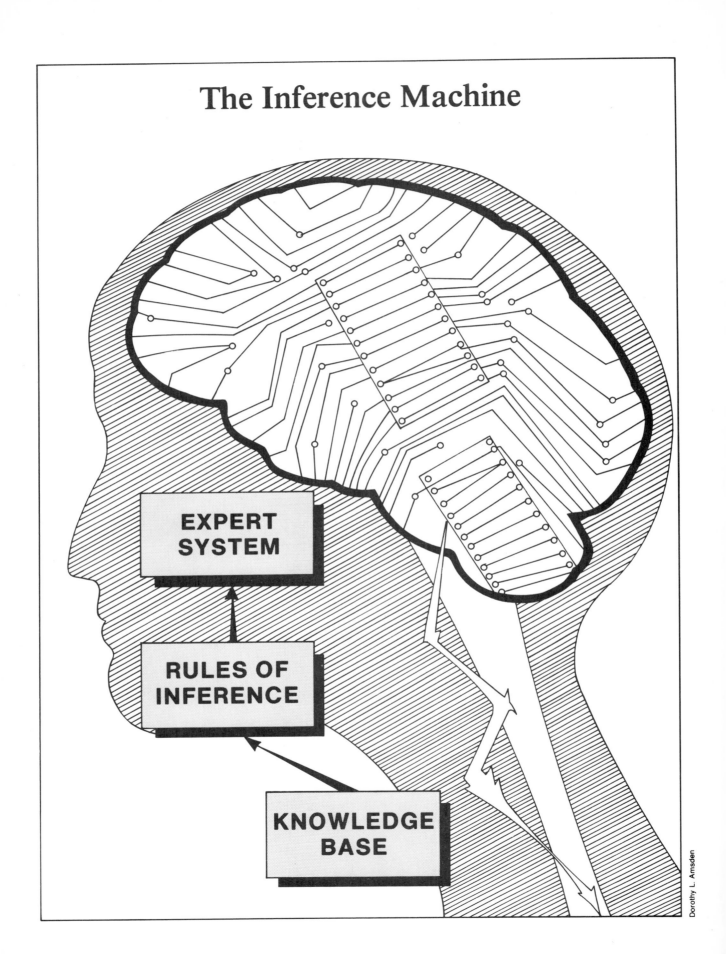

EXPERT SYSTEM

RULES OF INFERENCE

KNOWLEDGE BASE

Dorothy L. Amsden

Artificial Intelligence and Expert Systems

Artificial intelligence is one of the most exciting and quickly expanding areas of one of the most rapidly growing industries. This is due in part to the dropping costs and proliferation of powerful, low-cost hardware. The term artificial intelligence was coined in 1956 by John McCarthy who is the inventor of the LISP programming language, still the primary programming tool in the field. McCarthy is primarily concerned about doing research in those areas that seem to him most critical for true computer intelligence to pass into maturity. While the term he invented has stuck, not all researchers are delighted with its connotations. There may be a need for a less misleading name such as automated intelligence. In this article, the abbreviation AI is used for brevity, without the need to choose between the two designations.

The term personal computer will be understood here to include the category of 32-bit supermicrocomputers that are based on VLSI processors such as the Intel APK 286 and 386, the National Semiconductor 32032, and the Motorola 68020. With the appearance of desktop machines based on these microprocessors and others of comparable power, it is no longer appropriate to regard sophisticated AI technology as having inadequate hardware support on personal computers. With this in mind, the following survey of AI developments and techniques is intended to help bring the personal computer programmer up to date for the next generation of personal computer AI technology.

A Brief History of Early AI Research

It is helpful to divide AI research into three major periods: the early (1950-1965), the middle (1966-1976), and the recent (1976-present). Below is a quick summary of some important developments in the early period. Many of the important developments in subsequent periods will come up under their headings in the thematic sections.

The earliest efforts in AI aimed at developing strategic game-playing programs, particularly chess programs. The basic theory on which most of the subsequent research on chess and other strategy games has been based had already been provided by Alan Turing and Claude Shannon by 1950. They were the first to propose the approach of implementing a search tree composed of all move continuations from any given position to a specified depth, with a numerical rating assigned to the position reached at the end of each continuation. This allowed the adoption of a minimax algorithm by assuming that each opponent would adopt the move leading to the position with the highest rating, so that the minimax optimum could be computed.

Shannon in particular had brought the theory of chess-playing programs to a surprisingly sophisticated level at this early date. Although the position scores were based mainly on just material, piece mobility, and pawn structure, he outlined a procedure for the quiescent search, a method of searching to a more natural stopping point for each continuation, rather than stopping at a fixed depth for each move, and most importantly, he suggested pruning certain weak lines of play out of the search. It was still to be many years, though, before chess-playing programs were produced that could compete with professional level players.

The early period also marked the appearance of two important programs written in collaboration by Allen Newall, J. C. Shaw, and H. A. Simon: the "Logic Theorist" (1956) and the "General Problem Solver" (1957). In the latter, GPS, techniques were developed that even today still exert an influence on AI approaches to problem solving. It is helpful to think of all AI approaches as consisting of one of a few very basic overall strategies, or of combinations of them: (1) bottom-up or forward-moving strategies that work from the tools and facts existing to the final goal; (2) top-down or backward-moving strategies that start with a representation of the final goal and attempt to find or deduce the transformations that can produce it from the initial state; (3) general-purpose systems that are able to choose appropriate subordinate tools and appropriate data to solve as general a group of problems as possible. Clearly, the third strategy reflects the overall goal of AI itself, as well as the intent of the GPS program.

The main achievement of GPS was the development of the technique called means-ends analysis (MEA). This is the implementation of a kind of software feedback mechanism that allows elements of both the forward- and backward-moving strategies to be used together. What is involved is the ability to represent the goal state as well as any current state, and the ability to compute the difference between them. In this way, a method can be formulated of evaluating the degree or lack of progress as well as of the method in use, so that finally the difference between the current state and the goal state becomes as small as required. This general strategy has many different forms in many different application areas, and has become a permanent part of the AI toolkit.

The way GPS actually works can be seen quite easily from this quote from an early paper by Simon and Newall ("Heuristic Problem Solving: The Next Advance in Operations Research," *Operations Research,* vol. 6, January-February 1958, pp. 8ff.):

> I want to take my son to a nursery school. What's the difference between what I have and what I want? One of distance. What changes distance? My automobile. My automobile won't work. What is needed to make it work? A new battery. What has new batteries? An auto repair shop. I want the repair shop to put in a new battery; but the shop doesn't know I need one. What is the difficulty? One of communication. What allows communication? A telephone . . . and so on.

For the most part, efforts in the early period focused on developing and refining heuristic search and problem reduction tools. The table in Fig. 3-14 summarizes important programs in the middle and recent periods.

Heuristic Search

An important way of seeing the AI approach to solving problems is as a heuristic, as opposed to algorithmic, procedure. Basically, an algorithm directly solves a specific problem by implementing the solution in code. The program that results solves only the exact problem it is written to solve, no others, and usually requires specific input without which it cannot proceed. A heuristic approach, on the other hand, is intended to have greater flexibility. It is written so that it can find and then execute the solution to a certain range of problems, sometimes even when all the data is not available. It may be objected that even heuristic programs have to be written using algorithms in some programming language, so that the distinction is really an artificial one. But the difference is this: although algorithms are used to write heuristic programs, the algorithms are not implementations of a problem's solution, but rather algorithms that solve the problem of how to find solutions to certain types of problem.

AI search methods are needed when a search problem cannot be solved by a simple algorithm but must be solved in each case through the application of a strategy. There are two basically different strategies: reasoning forward and reasoning backward. And there are also methods, such as means-end analysis, as we have seen, that use a combination of the two.

New improved techniques continue to emerge for conducting efficient heuristic searches. In 1978 Hans Berliner developed an algorithm for a type of best-first search called the B* Tree Search. Briefly, this algorithm consists of four steps:

1. Find a proof that an arc at the root of a tree is better than any other.
2. Use this to determine the order of node expansions.
3. Provide upper and lower bound for expanded nodes.
4. Where these bounds converge, end the search.

Knowledge Representation

One of the foremost problems in AI research is how knowledge can be most effectively represented. A knowledge representation scheme usually consists of data structures for storing information, and accessing and interpreting methods that allow the knowledge to be put to use. Below, some of the more common knowledge representation schemes will be introduced.

Production Systems. A production system is an AI methodology for producing desired results using a rule base for carrying out its procedures. Most production systems are composed of these parts:

1. A rule base containing the production rules.
2. A data buffer called the Context.
3. An interpreter to handle the execution of the system's functions.

Fig. 3-14

MIDDLE PERIOD	RECENT PERIOD
ELIZA (1966) Weizenbaum	1976: HAPPY MYCIN WHISPER
SIN (1967) Moses	1977: GUS PUFF TEIRESIAS NUDGE
MAC HACK VI (1967) Greenblatt	1978: B* TREE SEARCH
DENDRAL (1967) Feigenbaum	1979: EXPERT PROSPECTOR EMYCIN
SIR (1968) Bertram Raphael	1980: HEARSAY II
STUDENT (1968) Bobrow	1981: ROSIE
MACSYMA (1971) Moses	
SHROLU (1972) Winogrod	
GSP (1973) Ronald Kaplan	
MARGIE (1975) Shank	
SOPHIE (1975) Brown and Burton	

The rule base consists of a list of productions such as in the following example:

P1. If on Context List salads then put on Cold Food List.
P2. If on Context List soups then put on Hot Food List.
P3. If on Context List ice cream put on Frozen Food List.
P4. If on Context List beer put on Beverages List.
P5. If on Context List checks put on Income List.
P6. If on Context List bills put on Expenses List.

In this case, the production rule interpreter might implement the following algorithm:

1. Make applicable all productions whose conditions are true.
2. Delete all duplicate productions.
3. Carry out the applicable productions, lowest number first.
4. Reset production applicabilities and return to #1.

A production system of this type will typically operate in cycles, processing the "applicable productions" once, resetting the status of the production rules, and then repeating the entire sequence.

Since the mid 1970s there have been production system languages in use for implementing and experimenting with production systems. Most of the first expert systems used production systems as the backbone of their inference engines and means of achieving their objectives. They have been used as well in psychological research for modeling human behavior.

One of the advantages of the production system approach is the ease with which the list of production rules can be amended. Another is the uniformity of the coded implementation which increases the readability for other people besides the programmer or knowledge engineer who may have produced it. Production systems also have some important disadvantages, however. One of the main ones is high overhead and low efficiency. Since every production is executed by the matching cycle using the rule base, and conveys information via the context data structure, it is very difficult to make production systems that are responsive and efficient in adjusting to recurring sequences of events or to take large-scale actions when situations demand it. Another point is that although the rule base itself is very transparent, the control algorithm is not as easy to understand, implement, or discover from reading the source code, as is the case with most programming languages. A final disadvantage with production systems is that the larger a system is, the slower its execution speed. Even when the additional productions are not executing, their presence slows down the system, because they are part of the structure that must be scanned before any production is executed. In spite of these limitations, production systems have become one of the standard items in the AI toolkit and are likely to remain so for the foreseeable future.

Logic Programming and Automated Reasoning. Logic programming is one of the expressions of the declarative or descriptive approach to knowledge representation and the solution of AI problems. The idea is that instead of telling the computer what to do, a descriptive programmming language describes the essential features of a problem and the result to be accomplished, without telling the computer a step-by-step list of what instructions to execute. It emphasizes the stable and structural aspects of knowledge: objects, events, facts, and relationships. This approach is suitable when the results that are needed can be put in a form that allows the outcome to be determined through a process of deductive inference. Most theorem-proving programs in AI research, for example, have used this approach. A common technique is known as the resolution method of inference, which is governed by relatively simple heuristic rules. Here, computer science and the discipline of symbolic logic both meet on common ground. The Prolog programming language includes an implementation of a modified predicate calculus, a formal symbolism in which not only can inferences be made about the truth or falsity of propositions, but predicate clauses expressing the properties and relationships of people and things can be deduced, though within very definite limits.

In problems with any degree of realism and complexity, simple resolution runs into the classic problem of the explosive multiplication of possibilities and combinations. For this reason, appropriate methods of controlled resolution have been devised and have led to the successful development of general-purpose automated reasoning programs.

Current practice in automated reasoning using logic programming involves the implementation of a number of inference rules, some of which initiate processes of resolution inference, while others impose restrictions on these resolution procedures. Some of the main procedures currently in use include:

1. Unification
2. Binary resolution
3. UR resolution
4. Hyperresolution
5. Negative hyperresolution
6. Paramodulation
7. Demodulation
8. Subsumption
9. Weighting
10. Factoring

Here are how these main rules of inference and control may be defined, followed by examples of each:

Unification. Unification is the inference rule according to which two formulas are unified to produce a clause by determining that a replacement variable can be found that makes the two identical, with the possible difference only of a sign.

Happy(Henry)   and   Not Happy(x) OR Not Unhappy(x)
yields Not Unhappy(Henry) by unification

Binary resolution. Binary resolution is an inference rule that produces a new clause from two existing clauses by performing a unification on predicates in each that are the same, but of opposite sign.

Not Smiling(x)   OR   Cheerful(x)   plus
Not Cheerful(x)   OR   Not Sad(x)   yields
Not Smiling(x)   OR   Not Sad(x)   by binary resolution

UR resolution. UR resolution is the inference rule that derives a simple or unit clause from a set of clauses, one of which is a compound clause, such that the most general set of values of the variables is satisfied for all of the clauses.

Not Siblings(x,y)   OR   Not Father(z,x)   OR   Father(z,y)   plus
Siblings(Jill, Jack)   and
Not Father(Jim,Jill)   yields
Not Father(Jim,Jack)   by   UR resolution

Hyperresolution. Hyperresolution is an inference rule that can derive a positive nonsimple clause from a set of clauses, where at least one includes a negative formula, so that the most general set of values of the variables allows all expressions to be satisfied. Negative hyperresolution is an inference rule that is identical to hyperresolution, but with the positive and negative reversed.

```
Not Siblings(x,y)   OR   Not Father(z,x)   OR   Father(z,y)        plus
Siblings(Jack,Jill)   OR   Not Brother(Jack, Jill)     and
Father(Jerry,Jack)     yields
Father(Jerry,Jill)   OR   Not Brother(Jack, Jill)
```

Paramodulation. Paramodulation is the inference rule applied to a pair of clauses of which one includes a positive equality predicate, which produces a clause in which the corresponding equality substitution has been made.

```
MALE(Brother(x))     plus
EQUALP(Brother(Jill), Jack)     yields
MALE(Jack)   by   paramodulation
```

Demodulation. Demodulation is the technique, which can be used as an inference rule, of rewriting expressions as equality expressions, where the equality predicate is expressed as a simple clause, and variables are replaced only in the various equality predicates.

```
EQUALP(Daughter(Father(x)),   Sister(x) )   plus
NAME(Daughter(Father(Jack)), Jill )   reduces to
NAME(Sister(Jack), Jill)  by  demodulation
```

Subsumption. Subsumption is the technique, which also can be used as an inference rule, of discarding all clauses that are less general or which duplicate the most general clause available.

```
EQUALP(Daughter(Father(x)), Sister(x) ) would replace
EQUALP(Daughter(Father(Jack)), Sister(Jack) ) by subsumption
```

Weighting. Weighting is the technique of assigning priorities to various elements in a reasoning problem, including its terms, clauses, and concepts. It is a tool that allows a programmer or user to control how they think a program should proceed in solving a problem. By assigning appropriate weights, one can make the program focus in on those aspects which are thought most crucial for the problem's solution.

Factoring. Factoring is an inference rule that operates on a single clause, selecting two formulas with the same predicate, and attempts to produce a clause by unifying them with suitable replacement values.

Automated reasoning programs and logic programming are not suitable only for deductive theorem proving and making inferences on factual premises. There are various "real-world" problems that can be solved by the descriptive and formalistic approach, such as the design of logical circuits, real-time control systems, natural language processors, and expert systems.

To date, there have been two significant programming efforts that have resulted in automated reasoning programs at the Argonne National Laboratory and Northern Illinois University. The first was the development of AURA ("Automated Reasoning Assistant"), over a twelve-year period, a program written in 360/370 Assembly Language, which has been used sucessfully to explore open questions in mathematics and formal logic, to design and validate circuits, and to solve mental problems and puzzles. Second was the development of LMA ("Logic Machine Architecture") and its companion ITP ("Interactive Theorem Prover"), which together form a system coded in 60,000 lines of Pascal. These latter two programs are both in the public domain. Information on how the programs or their user manuals may be obtained is available from National Energy Software Center, Argonne National Laboratory, Argonne, IL 60439.

Frames and Scripts. Among the recent knowledge representation schemes are frames and scripts, closely related to one another, and both developed in the late 1970s. The rationale for these two approaches is to provide a knowledge representation system based on an analogy to the way we typically rely on a large implicit body of background knowledge to interpret common meaningful situations. Frame and script schemes both provide formalized methods for representing knowledge about the typical objects and events normally expected in various situations. The paradigm example usually given is that of being in a restaurant. The "restaurant frame" or "restaurant script" has "slots" or "props" and "characters" built into it for things like "menu," "waitress," "ordering-the-main-course," and "paying-the-check." The following discussion will bring out some of the important differences between these two knowledge representation schemes.

Based on an idea proposed originally by Marvin Minsky of MIT in 1975, frames have become one of most popular knowledge representation schemes in AI. Frames use built-in slots to organize knowledge about various items of the world into context forms based on familiar situations. But a frame is not just an inert holder for properties and associations. It is intended as an element in a dynamic knowledge-based reasoning system. So, like other object-oriented approaches in AI, frames allow slots to be inherited. This means that if "Restaurant" is a specialization of the "Business-Establishment" frame, then it automatically inherits the "Manager," "Employee," and "Customer" slots, just as the "Nautilus Restaurant" frame would inherit the "Menu" and "Chef" slots from the general frame for "Restaurant." This property inheritance hierarchy is very similar to the implementation of the inheritance of the "isa" link in semantic networks. Property inheritance as an actual programming function is one of the most important concepts in the field of general semantics. In its most elementary representation, property inheritance is transferred up the ladder of abstraction from the object itself that is being described to the word that labels the object. General semanticists assert that the properties are transferred from the object to the word which labels the object.

Carrying this a step further, scripts not only provide for slots that hold props, roles, times, and locations, but prescribe event sequences that are expected to occur in a specified order. Returning to the favorite restaurant example, a GOING-OUT-TO-EAT script could be constructed that looks roughly like this:

GOING-OUT-TO-EAT

1. Enter-the-Restaurant
2. Seat-yourself or Wait-to-be-seated
3. Read-menu
4. Give-order
5. Food-served and food-eaten
6. Pay-the-check and give-tip
7. Leave-the-Restaurant

Often scripts of this type will specify a normal or default sequence with provided exceptions and even error conditions.

Not surprisingly, script representations are useful in developing programs that are capable of understanding written stories. In the SAM ("Script Applier Mechanism") program, for example, by Roger Schank and Robert Abelson, scripts, as well as plans, goals, and themes, are constructed from a limited set of semantic primitives. Each script has a script header, which is used to match script templates with sentences and phrases as they are parsed. In addition, each script has a central idea or goal which, in the case of the GOING-OUT-TO-EAT script, is well captured in the title. Once a match has been made between a sentence and a script, the appropriate meanings of words that are used in this context are assigned, where needed. For example, "menu" would be given a different meaning in a Restaurant script than in a Computer Programming script. The generalized representational schema of frames and scripts holds out the promise that wide varieties of events can be categorized into a scenario of sequential subevents.

Natural Language Processing

Programs that can interact with a user in familiar terms without requiring knowledge of technical symbol systems are important because they are one of the primary ways that computer technology can be made accessible to the general public. Although there are many elusive problems involved with developing programs that can use natural languages on the same level as humans do, natural language processing is one of the areas of AI where there are several operational systems available as commercial applications.

The techniques used to accomplish natural language facility are extremely diverse, and the choice of an effective approach is highly dependent on the degree and type of capability desired. Natural language problems include such things as the ability to query a database with sentences in English or other languages, systems that can both interpret and respond in appropriate and grammatical sentences, and machine translation systems for translating one natural language into another. For the most part, machine translation has proven to be a surprisingly difficult problem and has met only very limited success. The difficulty is that few translation tasks can be reduced to simple procedures applying knowledge just about the languages involved. Acceptable translations often involve sophisticated knowledge about the world and their subject matter as well as a fair degree of "common sense."

All languages have two main components, the external or surface structure, and the meaning. Grammar and syntax are concerned with the permissible ways of combining words to produce correct sentences. Semantics is concerned with the meaning of the grammatic structures. Most of the problems connected with producing natural language systems arise from the fact that the relation between these two components of language is not one to one, but is extremely complex. There are usually several different surface structures whose meaning is identical, and often a given sentence can have levels of ambiguity for a machine that it would never have for people.

For example, take the phrase:

Time flies like an arrow.

This is not a particularly ambiguous statement for us, but there are four different ways that a machine could conceivably parse it.

First, there is the obvious way:

NOUN	VERB	PREP	ART	NOUN
Time	flies	like	an	arrow

Second, as a command to use a stopwatch to time houseflies as you would the flight of an arrow:

VERB	NOUN	PREP	ART	NOUN
Time	flies	like	an	arrow

Third, the interpretation could be to time them as an "arrow" would:

VERB	NOUN	PREP	ART	NOUN	VERB
Time	flies	like	an	arrow	(would)

And fourth, as saying that a variety of "time flies" enjoy arrows:

NOUN	NOUN	VERB	ART	NOUN
Time	flies	like	an	arrow

Among other things, this problem brings out the fact that even though a sentence is correct grammatically and the vocabulary words are recognized, ambiguous, silly, or meaningless expressions still can pose problems. Take the example:

The shy dog ate the freshly baked cookies.

How is the computer to be programmed to recognize that the following variations, while grammatically correct, are nonsensical?

The freshly baked dog ate the shy cookies.
The freshly baked cookies ate the shy dog.
The shy cookies ate the freshly baked dog.

The answer to these and other questions requires an understanding of current AI techniques in natural language processing, a number of which will be discussed below.

Template Matching

This was one of the earliest tools used in parsing natural language input and was the technique used in the famous ELIZA program written by Weizenbaum in 1966. ELIZA was written in the SLIP language which was an extension of Fortran equipped with list processing. Since that time, versions have been written in LISP, and various other computer languages, including various diluted versions in BASIC.

ELIZA made considerable impact when it was introduced because it showed how little a program really had to "know" to be able to appear to be carrying on a conversation of sorts. And indirectly it raised the question of to what degree therapists themselves are really heeding or grasping what their patients say to them. To get an idea of how ELIZA works, it is first essential to distinguish the full-strength ELIZA from the many watered-down imitations that are currently in circulation.

As developed by Weizenbaum, ELIZA consists of two main levels, the language analyzer or parser and the script system. The script is actually a set of rules for carrying on a conversation on a particular, though limited, subject. Weizenbaum himself compared the script to a set of premises that might be given to an actor to be used for improvisations on some theme. In this way, theoretically, the program could be given different scripts to allow it to communicate on any one of a variety of topics. DOCTOR, the form under which it was first demonstrated, and the only form that seems to have received interest, is ELIZA when supplied with a script designed to simulate a Rogerian therapist, one who employs the method of repeatedly encouraging the patient to continue speaking about his or her feelings. The following is a portion of an original transcript circulated by Weizenbaum to his classes at MIT (Handout for 6.45 Introduction to Automatic Computation, Fall 1964):

Doctor, I have terrible news . . .
> YOU SAY YOU HAVE TERRIBLE NEWS

Yes. There is a computer program at M.I.T. that'll ruin us.
> WHY DO YOU SAY THAT

I have seen it working . . .
> YOU SAY YOU HAVE SEEN IT WORKING

It's frightening—you must see it . . .
> YOU THINK I MUST SEE IT

It listens to patients chatter just as you and I listen . . .
> YOU THINK I AND YOU LISTEN

No, not usually—no need to get nasty though . . .
> WHY DO YOU SAY THAT

Someone might hear us—don't you care . . .
> YOU THINK I CARE

You sound depressed to me . . .
> IN YOUR PHANTASY—PERHAPS WE SOUND DEPRESSED TO EACH OTHER

Yes—perhaps . . .
> I UNDERSTAND

I do too . . .
> YOU SAY YOU DO TOO

We are both in the same boat with respect to that computer . . .
> LET'S CONTINUE TO TALK ABOUT YOU—SHALL WE

You are a comfort . . .
> WHAT MAKES YOU THINK I AM A COMFORT

At a time like this you want to talk about me . . .
> WHY DO YOU THINK I WANT TO TALK ABOUT YOU

Because you share my feelings about that damned computer . . .
> WHAT DOES THAT SUGGEST TO YOU

That, of course, you hate computers too . . .
> YOU THINK I HATE COMPUTERS TOO

Why not, they're hardly human, are they . . .
> PERHAPS THAT'S WHAT WE'RE HERE TO FIND OUT

No computer can converse as you can, for example . . .
> OH

I can't understand how anyone could be fooled by a mere machine . . .
> CAN'T YOU REALLY

No, after all there is nothing creative about a computer program . . .
> YOU ARE BEING NEGATIVE

I am convinced I am correct . . .
> ARE YOU WORRIED TO HAVE BEEN CONVINCED YOU ARE CORRECT

No, not in the least. Not at all. Not even a little . . .
> YOU ARE BEING NEGATIVE

You said you agreed with me didn't you . . .
> IS THAT WHAT YOU HEARD ME SAY

Why don't you try to dissuade me—computers diddle with numbers, that's all . . .
> YOU WISH ME TO TRY TO DISSUADE YOU

You can't . . .
> YOU THINK I CAN'T

For example, could a computer in a conversation like this raise a new topic . . .
> YOU SEEM TO HAVE AVOIDED SPEAKING OF YOUR
> PARENTS ALTOGETHER

Precisely as you just did . . .
> YOU THINK I JUST DID

Yes, and that's what shows the difference between a man and a computer . . .
> I SEE

How does ELIZA accomplish the illusion? Quite bluntly, by a series of tricks. The overall means used is to make local predictions about sentences and phrases that lead to applying hypotheses about what is being said, in order to generate appropriate responses. For example, if phrases occur in the user's response of the form "everyone . . . me," the assumption implemented in the rule is that this is a latent reference to a recent incident, so that ELIZA's response would be something of the form "Interesting. Who . . . you recently?"

This is accomplished by providing lists of keywords and for each key a set of patterns to match, which in turn are linked to transformations associated with each of the patterns to generate ELIZA's response. So in the case of the above example, the pattern to match might be:

$$(0 \text{ everyone } 0 \text{ me})$$

and the transformation rule for the response could be:

$$(\text{Why do you say everyone } 3 \text{ you})$$

Here the 3 indicates that in forming the response ELIZA must insert the third matching element, which happens to be all the words falling between the key words "everyone" and "me."

Some of the other devices used in ELIZA are: (1) associating key words with certain categories or subject matters and providing sets of appropriate responses for them; (2) having noncommittal responses like "I understand" or "I see" when no key matches have been made; and (3) remembering some key words for insertion in later responses such as "Earlier you mentioned . . ." In the transcript quoted, the way ELIZA could be made to appear to raise a new topic is by providing a response that is triggered by matching on the patterns "new topic" or ". . . talk about something else."

No one was more surprised than Weizenbaum by the enormous response and credulity with which ELIZA was met, since he was one of the very few in AI research to take the position that because the problem of understanding natural language is dependent on reading things in context, it is insoluble. Perhaps the most important conclusion to be drawn from ELIZA is that often useful and important results can be accomplished from the point of view of the interface to the user by methods that are relatively modest from the point of view of the more advanced AI techniques and the ambitious problems it addresses. A secondary conclusion is that the interface itself is the message. In fact, part of ELIZA's mystique has been the machine interface which makes some of ELIZA's stock responses entirely plausible.

Semantic Networks

This structure was used extensively in the 1970s, not only for natural language systems but as a general AI knowledge representation scheme. The structure is really quite simple, consisting of nodes, which are used to represent things like objects, names, concepts, and situations, and arcs or links representing the relations between them. An example would look like Fig. 3-15.

By storing these words in nodes separated by appropriately defined links, it is clear not only how we can avoid nonsense like:

Every leg has four Collies.

but also how it is possible to add knowledge about the world to the knowledge base about words by defining appropriate arc types. Also, by building an inheritance property into the "isa" link, the network will support simple syllogistic inferences such as concluding that IF Lassie is a Collie. and A Collie is a dog. and Dogs have 4 legs. THEN Lassie has 4 legs. While a semantic network is a useful structure for many problems, it cannot be pushed too far in this form to handle the full range of natural language problems. For such things as the tense and mood of verbs, an augmented network approach is more suitable.

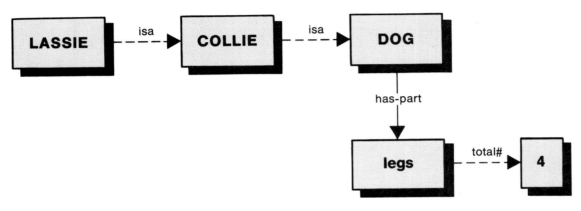

Fig. 3-15

Augmented Transition Networks

To understand what an augmented transition network (ATN) is, it is best to first consider the idea of a simple transition network. If we define the state of a semantic net as a full set of nodes, then this state of nodes can be considered as itself a node with arcs leading to other sets of nodes. For the system to make a transition from the START node at the beginning of a sentence in the input stream, the proper words must be found to allow this transition. Certain states are designated as FINAL states. The system then can be regarded as accepting a sentence of input if it is able to begin at the START state and reach a FINAL state when the end of the input is reached. The machine has to be able to tell whether any given sentence is part of the language it recognizes.

However, a simple transition network such as this is unable to handle the complexities of a natural language. Consider then a recursive transition network (RTN) that has a recursive mechanism to give it considerable added flexibility. In this case, the transition arcs can be driven not only by words, but also by higher-level symbols that stand for subnetworks to which temporary control of the parsing process can be given. These higher-level symbols can be functional units such as a noun, verb, or prepositional phrase. The same principle works for transitions based on these functional units, as for words in the simple transition network. Yet the RTN is still not powerful enough to handle natural language.

An ATN expands on the power of RTNs in three basic ways: (1) It adds a set of "registers" for storing partial derivation trees when it has to jump from one subnetwork to another. (2) Conditional tests are applied to arcs that have to be satisfied before the arc can be traversed. (3) Specific performances can be assigned to arcs that must be carried out on data structures whenever the arc is taken. With these additions, it is thought that ATNs have the potential of forming ideal Turing machines that have the ability of recognizing any known language. The expanded features of ATNs allow them to do sophisticated parsing that keeps track of its own progress and can develop deep structure interpretations of sentences that can be transformed to provide for tenses, moods, and alternative sentences that have the same meaning.

One of the earliest operational uses of an ATN was in the LUNAR program developed by by William Woods for NASA in the early 1970s. This program was able to interact with the user and answer questions in English about rock samples brought back from the moon by astronauts on missions during the Apollo program. Augmented transition networks and augmented transition trees are now one of the standard methods in use for both parsing and generating significant subsets of natural languages. One main advantage of this approach is that the same data structure can often be used for both interpreting and formulating natural language statements.

Semantic Grammar

One promising way for providing a natural language interface to various types of application is by using a semantic or procedural grammar. Many experts in natural language processing are in agreement that the most efficient route is to apply both syntactic and semantic procedures as soon as possible in evaluating input statements.

A very successful use of the semantic grammar approach was in the LIFER system developed by Gary Hendricks while at SRI. There were two main components to LIFER: a set of functions for specifying a language, and a parser to interpret input statements. The basic idea is that for many applications, only a small subset of English, or other natural language, is really needed, which includes a limited set of statement types. These statement forms are defined using the language specifying component with certain plug-in slots for words of a certain type inserted where needed in a sequence of definite words. The parser then reads entire sentences as an interpreter reads commands, with the plug-in words treated as arguments and user-supplied data.

For example, the language specifier could supply the following statement forms for use with a database query system:

How many <attribute> <articles> are there?
How many <attribute> <articles> were <verb> in <year>?
What is the <attribute> of <article>?
What are all the <attribute> <articles>?
Who are the <class> who <verb> <number range>?

The language specifier builds a transition tree which the interpreter searches for matches in the input until it reaches one of the new words, and then attempts to apply one of the rules for higher-level plug-in symbols. These rules can do various things, such as looking the word up in a list, testing to see if it is a number or a string, jump to another transition tree to start interpreting a subclause, and so on. But the main strategy here is that grammar has in a sense been reduced to semantics, because the parser is in effect reading a sentence as a single command with a complex option tree.

The LIFER system showed that a general natural language interface tool can be developed economically that can be used to build a variety of interfaces to a wide selection of application systems without a major development effort. A semantic grammar is a significant shortcut because rather than having to use a complicated grammar, an expandable set of statement types are defined that are really treated semantically as commands to an interpreter.

Semantic Primitives

One of the influential approaches to handling the problem of developing a more sophisticated approach to language, which has grown largely out of independent work by Yorick Wilks and Roger Schank, is based on the strategy of being able to implement a scheme for representing the meaning of language structures, by invoking a limited set of meaning categories in terms of which the various external structures that have the same meaning can be expressed.

Wilks's system is intended for machine translation for generating French from an English text. The basic approach is by using a dictionary that defines words in terms of the semantic primitives grouped into five classes:

1. **Entities:**   e.g., people, things, parts of things
2. **Actions:**   e.g., causes, movements, states of being
3. **Cases:**   e.g., prepositions, expressing state or direction
4. **Qualifiers:** e.g., adjectives
5. **Types:**   e.g., adverbs and categories

In addition to these, there are also subclasses such as "animate" and "physical object" that allow for more specific descriptive definitions. In total, there are about 80 actual primitives in Wilks's system. Although there is no "correct" system of primitives, the only test being what works for a given application, Wilks is confident about his system because there are about 80 similar words that are the most frequently occurring in definitions in *Webster's Dictionary*.

Schank's conceptual dependence approach is considerably more ambitious, intending to be a general-purpose system, independent of any particular application such as machine translation. The approach has been used for translation, but also for paraphrasing, drawing inferences, and answering questions about a body of text. Schank's system employs these eleven primitive ACTs:

Physical Acts

1. **PROPEL:**   to apply a force to a physical thing
2. **MOVE:**   move a part of one's body
3. **INGEST:**   an animate being taking something inside
4. **EXPEL:**   an animate being driving something out from within
5. **GRASP:**   hold onto a physical thing

Acts That Produce a Change of State

6. **PTRANS:**   transport a physical thing to a new place
7. **ATRANS:**   change an abstract relationship

Acts That Are Instrumental to Other Acts

8. **SPEAK:**   utter a meaningful sound
9. **ATTEND:**   focus one of the senses on an object

Acts of the Mind

10. **MTRANS:**   transfer information or ideas
11. **MBUILD:**   form new information from old

As research progresses with the conceptual dependency approach, new concepts are being added to the system. Some of the additions include goals, plans, and themes, as was explained earlier in the context of knowledge representation. This has resulted in four new primitives in the category of Social Acts:

12. **AUTHORIZE:**   allow transfer or information or other ACTs
13. **ORDER:**   require that an ACT be done

14. **DISPUTE:**   negate an ACT of another person or group
15. **PETITION:**   ask that an ACT be performed

Expert Systems

1. Some Historically Important Expert Systems.   Although expert systems are becoming catchwords in the personal computer community and thus have an aura of currency about them, they have actually been in existence for almost fifteen years.

DENDRAL.   DENDRAL is very important in the expert system field because it was the project that spearheaded the knowledge-based approach in AI, and because it was able to actually perform better at its task than all human experts in the same field. DENDRAL is used to determine the most plausible molecular structures of an unknown compound by analyzing chemical data such as that provided by mass spectroscopy and nuclear magnetic resonance measurements. The way DENDRAL does its job is by first generating all of the partial molecular structures that fit the data, next elaborating these in all possible ways to create the complete structures, and then rapidly eliminating all the implausible substructures. Those remaining are thought to be all the plausible complete structures that fit the data. Because it is so systematic in generating all plausible molecular structures, DENDRAL can often provide expert chemists with candidates for the structure of new compounds that may otherwise have been overlooked. Another great plus is that it enables the solution of these problems using relatively low-resolution data available from low-cost instruments.

DENDRAL was developed by the collaboration of Edward F. Feigenbaum and Joshua Lederberg. Since its completion in the late 1960s, it has been on the job in chemical labs in industry and at universities across the globe. The key elements in DENDRAL's design are a production system and a breadth-first search procedure that can choose between expansion and pruning for each node it considers. DENDRAL was a successful implementation of the approach of data-directed search control based upon heuristic rules derived from expert chemists. DENDRAL uses a structure-generating algorithm whose procedures are unavailable to the system itself. Many expert systems to date resemble DENDRAL in being able to make quick large-scale interpretive leaps in ways that are not analyzable and explainable by the system's self-analyzing capabilities.

The knowledge base of DENDRAL does not incorporate any general principles of chemistry. It is confined to a narrow range of specifics that allow it to get the job done. It is implemented primarily in the molecular structure generator and production rules for the data-driven evaluation component. Pruning is introduced early in the generate-and-test cycle.

More recently a support program called META-DENDRAL has been carefully developed that implements automated knowledge acquisition for DENDRAL. Although META-DENDRAL was a success as a research project, it has not been judged to be a more cost-effective means of data acquisition than the manual approach.

PROSPECTOR.   This expert system is important not only for the special things that it accomplishes technically, but because it achieved the largest monetary payoff by far of any expert system to date. Built by knowledge engineers at Stanford Research Institute (SRI), working in cooperation with geologists at the U.S. Geological Survey, it is used as an assistant to a geologist involved in field exploration for mineral deposits. In 1982 PROSPECTOR successfully made predictions that resulted in a find of molybdenum deposits in the Cascade region of Washington State that have been valued at up to $100 million.

PROSPECTOR operates on a considerably different principle than DEN-DRAL by virtue of its use of semantic net models and by a probabilistic evaluation of its soil and geological deposit data. But like DENDRAL it has no general principles of its native science of geology embodied in its knowledge base, but incorporates only very specific information about geographical regions under exploration. Its strong points are its inherent capability of reasoning under conditions of uncertainty, and its ability to provide extensive explanations of its reasoning in obtaining its results.

2. Expert System Components. The minimum components that even the most rudimentary expert system must include are:

1. A domain-specific knowledge base of facts and rules
2. An inference engine for drawing conclusions
3. A way that the user interfaces with these functions

Actual expert systems are usually considerably more complex than this in their architecture, but these three basic functions are always present in one form or another. The user interface, of course, can range anywhere from just the code of the programming language to a sophisticated natural language dialogue system. Naturally, the knowledge base assumes a knowledge representation system. Currently, there is a need at this level for specially trained "knowledge engineers" whose job is to be able to extract expertise from the experts and put it into a form acceptable by the knowledge base. Ultimately, there will be knowledge acquisition systems that can be used directly by the experts that capture their expertise without the need for knowledge engineers. So far, however, it is only in the most rudimentary systems that automated knowledge acquisition from experts has proven to be cost effective.

The inference engine can have the greatest possible variety, depending upon the requirements of the system, and the skill and creativity of the system architects. The most advanced inference engines include a "blackboard" where a record is kept of current hypotheses, decisions, subgoals, and so on. An important factor is the degree to which an expert system has knowledge of its own activities, and can draw conclusions and provide explanations of its own activity and results. Another issue is the means exployed to ensure that the system of subgoals and results will be consistent with itself. Obviously, it is possible to get very elaborate with many of the features and conveniences that can be implemented at this level. But it is usually more important to provide for the system's efficiency by designing an inference engine that can quickly abandon unfruitful possibilities, while at the same time avoiding redundant searches. Finally, there is the whole area of techniques used to draw conclusions when only incomplete or probabilistic information is available.

3. Knowledge Engineering. Development of the knowledge base of an expert system can be so exacting a process that specially trained professionals are often needed in the knowledge acquisition process. A knowledge engineer has the responsibility of putting problem-solving expertise of specialists into a form that can be used in the knowledge base. The expertise is generally a collection of facts, procedures, and "rules of thumb" about a restricted, specialized domain, and typically does not include general principles of the discipline of which the specialty is a branch.

4. The Design of Inference Engines. An inference engine is the active intelligence of an expert system. Whereas the knowledge base is where the expertise is stored, the inference engine is the focus of its intelligent reasoning capabilities. It is the area where the most critical performance is needed and where the most creative design work is often exercised.

The inference engine cannot be implemented independently of a choice of knowledge representation systems. A given system for drawing inferences must be designed to work with a particular formalism for representing the rules and facts about which inferences are to be drawn. Before selecting either, it is indispensable to consider those features that are essential to the application. Here are some of the more relevant features for expert systems that should be decided upon before being committed to a particular system of implementation. Obviously there will have to be some trade-offs, because we are not yet at the point where all these features can be included in a system that still operates efficiently.

- User modifiable
- Explains its results
- Identifies missing information
- Can use probabilistic reasoning
- Accesses its own rules and controls
- Resolves subgoal conflicts
- Processes multiple goals
- Handles data interrupts
- Learns from mistakes
- Keeps expert and performance rules separate
- Has concurrent capability
- Sophisticated programming environment
- Natural language interface
- Knowledge is modular or granular
- Fast execution
- Memory efficient

Microcomputer Expert Systems

There are now a number of software products to assist in the development of expert systems on microcomputers. They range from general-purpose shells for the development of advisory systems, to knowledge engineering tools, to general-purpose inference engines and interaction systems which can be supplied with a variety of knowledge bases. All of those discussed here are for the IBM PC/XT/AT and compatibles.

ESP/Advisor: Expert Systems International. This is a special-purpose shell that is intended for developing advisory systems using a technique called "text animation." There are three parts to it: (1) the knowledge compiler that translates knowledge bases into a compact form used by the system; (2) the consultation shell that allows a user to interact with a completed knowledge base; and (3) the programming interface to Prolog-1, an implementation of Prolog also available from ESI.

The type of advisory expert system that can be developed with ESP/Advisor is particularly suitable for application areas where the procedures, standards, and rules-of-thumb are well defined, but there is a need to have them available on-line for consultation as needed, rather than as part of a reference guide that has to be studied or repeatedly searched by the nonexpert. This applies to various standards, regulations, laws, and technical areas where the material is too technical, voluminous, or complex for most users to be able to absorb in a reasonable time.

The Knowledge Representation Language (KRL) that is used with the system has several powerful features that makes ESP/Advisor stand out from some of the more rudimentary expert development systems. In addition to the facility for displaying large paragraphs of text, KRL allows branching from one section of the knowledge base to others, and includes the XOR operator as a logical keyword that can allow substantial time saving by automatically ruling out alternative possibilities once one has been set, so that further questions during a consultation are eliminated.

The Interface to the Prolog programming language is not a standard feature of ESP/Advisor, but is sold as an additional option. Possible uses for the imbedding of Prolog routines in an expert system would be to access external hardware or software environments, or to invoke imbedded application programs that use ESP as a "front end." Prolog may also be used to add commands to the consultation shell, and facilities of ESP, in turn, are available to Prolog. These features in particular give the system an open-ended architecture that allows the expert programmer to customize it as desired. Because of the limitations of a Prolog-based system in performing heavy numerical processing and in handling many different types of inference, this system is not appropriate for discovery systems or other scientific expert systems that require complicated calculations to produce answers to specific questions. ESP is suitable as an advisory system that can be customized to control additional application programs.

EXSYS: EXSYS Inc. This is an inexpensively priced development package for developing simple rule-based expert systems. It was written in the C language and comes in two formats for either small or large-sized applications. There are basically two parts to the EXSYS package: the knowledge base parser and inference engine for running and testing knowledge systems, and a rule editor for the actual preparation of the rule base files. There are also some utilities for compressing the size of a knowledge base, once it has been completed.

The type of rules that EXSYS can handle are surprisingly flexible for such an inexpensive program. Since a rule consists of two parts, the IF or conditional part and the THEN or consequence, it is useful to be able to have the option of multiple conditions in each of the parts. EXSYS offers this flexibility, with up to 126 conditions in both the IF and THEN sections. Each attribute or qualifier in the IF part of a rule can have up to 31 possible values. This scope is far in excess of what the practical limit ever ought to be. An extraordinary rule that might have greater than 126 conditions should be broken down into a number of shorter rules for the readability and maintainability of the knowledge base.

KES: Software Architecture and Engineering, Inc. KES, which stands for Knowledge Engineering System, is really three systems in one, offering three different types of inference engine and interaction shells for expert systems. The three systems are a production-rule-type inference engine, a frame-oriented knowledge system, and a Bayesian system for handling knowledge in a probability format. KES was adapted from a system developed at the University of Maryland. Originally written in LISP on a VAX minicomputer, it has been ported to the IBM PC running IQLISP. A version of this product was tested by the author and runs satisfactorily on the IBM AT when outfitted with 640K RAM. Although the system will run with 512K, its operation with this amount of memory is repeatedly interrupted by pauses for garbage collection to reclaim more space.

The main data structure used by KES is an "attribute hierarchy." Attributes are the various concepts or parameters that pertain to a specific problem domain. These attributes are, or can be, interrelated to one another in a hierarchy by the "is inferred from" relation. At the apex of the hierarchy is the final goal or goals of the expert system. At the bottom are the attributes whose values are supplied by the user. In defining an expert knowledge base, a value set is associated with each attribute which defines the set of possible values the attribute may assume.

A user interacts with an expert system built under KES by first responding to questions of either a multiple-choice format or those requesting numerical input. The system will ask only those questions which pertain to the solution of the problem at hand, as dictated by the information entered at each step. The same questions are not asked each time an expert system is used, but rather different questions are generated when earlier questions are answered differently.

In addition to the question-and-answer format, KES expert systems can also be command driven by the user to respond to specific requests. Generally commands can be entered as an alternative response when a question is posed by the expert system. By entering "help command," a listing is displayed of all the available user commands. Help is also available individually for each command by entering a help command name. Among the commands available are advanced user commands which allow sophisticated users to control the execution of the expert system. For example, some of the inference engines allow the user to make the request JUSTIFY RESULTS which instructs the system to supply the reasoning on which it bases the result given to the user. This is important in proper use of an expert system because results should not be accepted blindly, but rather taken into consideration and evaluated in the context of the means by which they were obtained.

Other commands available to the user include the FREEZE option which takes a "snapshot" of the expert system in the precise context of when the command is executed and saves it to disk for future consultation. Also, the OBTAIN RESULTS command allows a user to direct the expert system in obtaining an answer to a question in a particular area of interest.

As with some other expert development systems, SAE claims that the KES system allows an expert in a particular field to develop his or her own expert system without the aid of a knowledge engineer. The knowledge representation language in which a knowledge base is prepared is very English-like, and the process of developing a knowledge base involves four steps: (1) analysis, (2) design, (3) implementation, and (4) verification.

The resulting knowledge base can have as many as ten possible types of entry, each declared in its own separate section of the knowledge base. The possible types of entry are:

1. **Certification:** Text displayed to the user concerning knowledge base status.
2. **Attachments:** Text associated with particular rules.
3. **Quotations:** Declaring named string variables.
4. **Instruction:** Text on how to use the system.
5. **References:** Sources used in building the system.
6. **Patterns:** Strings for pattern matching.
7. **Attributes:** Key factors in the problem domain.
8. **Externals:** Operations on files outside the system.
9. **Rules:** Conditions to control reasoning process.
10. **Actions:** Tests for execution of system commands.

The actual implementation of the knowledge base file can be accomplished with an ordinary text editor, and because of the English-like syntax it is relatively straightforward. Knowing what to include in it to make the expert system do as desired is another matter, and must be determined in the analysis and design phases. In the analysis phase, the problem domain is carefully studied to determine what the attribute hierarchy for the expert system will be. Usually a diagram of the hierarchy is drawn with the primary goals of the system at the top and the input attributes for the factor which can then be used to determine the goals at the bottom. As previously mentioned, the hierarchy is created by the ability of some attributes to be inferred from others or combinations of others. The inference engine moves up the hierarchy, attempting to infer the final result from the lower attributes.

In the design phase it is determined what exact results are desired in the expert system and which precise combination of components is necessary to produce that result. To do this, the author of the knowledge base must know how each of the inference engines works in the three subsystems so that the right choice is made. Then, when the appropriate subsystem has been selected, the right entries in the knowledge base must be determined to make sure that the expert system will perform as intended. It is also essential to make sure that the screen and displays seen by the user and the questions the system generates will be understandable by the non-expert. As can be seen from this, there are skills and responsibilities involved in the analysis and design phases of knowledge base development that are normally assigned to the knowledge engineer. There are undoubtedly some experts in many fields who are capable of making their own expertise explicit in the form of an attribute hierarchy and learning the inner workings of KES so that they can design an expert system with it. However, it takes both the time and inclination, as well as some additional expertise, to do this. In this author's estimation, those experts who are determined to develop an expert system without a knowledge engineer should, with reasonable effort, be able to do so. But it should be recognized that some rather substantial knowledge and skill beyond their own expertise may be required.

KES offers some very interesting and powerful features not always found in general-purpose expert system shells. One of these is "calculation attachments," which gives KES the ability to attach mathematical equations to a numerical attribute by which its value may be calculated in terms of other numerical attributes. All of the customary math functions are available for specifying such calculations including exponentiation, log and trig functions, and absolute value. Another nice feature is the ability to make "combine attachments." This applies to string attributes, and gives the ability to form combination strings built from values of other string attributes. If we compare this to a database, then this feature would be parallel to the ability to specify an expression based upon a sequence of character fields which could be filled in differently according to the values currently under consideration. For example, if string attributes are defined corresponding to a person's "first name," "last name," "middle initial," and "title," then they can be combined in different orders to generate expressions used in different contexts.

By far the most interesting and powerful feature, and the one that distinguishes KES from most other expert system shells, is the "external attachments" or "Exits." This is the ability to construct an expert system that can run and access other software external to itself and pass commands and parameters back and forth. And because this naturally includes the subsystems of KES itself, it means that expert systems with complex architectures can be built that are not restricted to just one inference engine or knowledge base, but can include as many as is necessary and feasible to include. Of course it also means that custom routines can be written in LISP, Prolog, or any other programming language and included as part of an expert system's architecture. With this feature, KES becomes, at present, the expert development system with the most open-ended architecture. When the version using the IQLISP Compiler becomes available, the speed and performance limitations of this system may improve appreciably.

Computer-Aided Instruction and Graphics

Computer-aided instruction (CAI) has become a vast field, most of which is no longer associated with AI. Included in the AI branch are those areas of research and application where the computer is programmed to interact in "intelligent" and unanticipated ways with the user to aid not only in the grasp of information and concepts, but also as a means of exploration and discovery. Graphics in AI is not just involved with research toward the development of computer-aided design (CAD) expert systems, but has received considerable attention as a sophisticated tool for instruction and explorative education in mathematics. The research conducted by the Logo Group at the MIT Artificial Intelligence Laboratory since 1970 in connection with turtle geometry is one of the significant contributions in this area. The rest of this discussion will be devoted to providing an overview of turtle geometry. For a more complete survey of the fields of AI graphics and CAI, see the list of recommended reading in the Bibliography.

Turtle Geometry

Turtle graphics is by no means merely a toy for children and hobbyists. As developed by Seymour Papert, Harold Abelson, and others at the MIT Artificial Intelligence Laboratory, the discipline of turtle geometry (TG) is a dynamic and fertile approach to mathematics that studies geometrical objects and shapes, not as static structures, but in terms of the exploratory behavior of mathematical "animals" called turtles. Very simply, a turtle is an active agent whose movements create traces on the screen that can describe any kind of shape or object. The description of these dynamic focal points as turtles was inherited from the work of Grey Walter, a British neurologist who conducted research in the 1960s with small robot creatures he named tortoises.

The main idea behind TG is that it allows spaces and shapes to be studied and represented from the point of view of beings who have a limited viewpoint on them and travel through or over them. For this reason, the features of geometrical objects are approached from their observable local features rather than those that are known to omniscient observers outside them. One of the most important things is to be able to detect global features from those that can be determined locally. From this it can be seen that TG has very tangible applications: it is extremely helpful in understanding how to represent physical space from the point of view of one who needs to navigate through it, and how this can be represented and depicted by a computer.

TG also provides a ready framework in which turtles can be given capabilities that allow them to simulate almost any kind of behavior that affects their patterns of movement in space. For example, one of the first things that can be done is to give "eyes and smell" to the turtle that allow it to avoid obstacles and find food. Then these "senses" can be allowed to interact, and the turtle can take on role of predator with chasing and following behavior.

One of the most dramatic proofs of the success of TG as an educational tool is that a very important algorithm, called the Pledge algorithm, was developed by John Pledge of Exeter, England, at age 12, which allows a turtle to escape from any maze. The algorithm is not trivial because it involves knowledge of the Closed-Path Theorem concerning the total degress of turning allowed for closed figures. This is in fact one of the key issues for understanding how to simulate the navigation of a turtle on unusual surfaces and curved spaces.

In general, any subdiscipline in geometry can be explored with the turtle dynamics approach. The Logo Group at MIT investigated topological surfaces with turtle paths, such as cubes, spheres, and toroids. The most remarkable application of this approach was in the area of exploring curvatures in space, and even in time, as postulated by Einstein in his theory of General Relativity. Devices such as mapping wedges from turtle walks that attempt to reconstruct the curved regions, and postulating regions of curvature within larger normal spaces through which turtles must travel, provide methods for gaining precise, yet qualitative understanding of the principles at work. Finally, an actual simulator of the world of space and time as it is described in the Relativistic scheme has been developed. As can readily be seen, turtle geometry is an excellent tool for people of many age groups and levels of education to find imaginative ways to explore their concepts about the world.

Machine Learning

Certainly one of the most definitive keys to intelligence is the ability to learn. A being or system that is so omniscient to have lost all need and ability to learn anything new would be regarded as having transcended intelligence altogether, with its kind of knowing based on something entirely different. Accordingly, machine learning is one of most important areas of AI. To be more explicit, machine learning involves understanding a program that can introduce something new and valuable in the machine's performance, whether by taking advice from a user, by learning from examples of its own mistakes or shortcomings, by discovering new general rules, by applying analogous rules to new situations, by making important assumptions that provide a breakthrough, or by any other means. In spite of the importance of the concept, there has not been an enormous amount of success in developing programs that can learn, though there are some very promising directions in which research is now moving.

There are two broad types of machine learning: that which aims at the increase of knowledge, and that which aims at the improvement and refinement of skills. Nearly all research to date has been conducted on the first of these because it lends itself to treatment by symbolic processing, whereas the latter has been relegated to the field of adaptive control and largely ignored by the AI community. There are currently four main approaches to learning as knowledge aquisition: (1) empirical induction, (2) discovery systems, (3) analogy, and (4) analytical generalization.

Before going into some of the current avenues of research, it will be helpful to look at some of the conditions for a software system to be capable of learning. One of the basic findings of research is that to be able to learn, a system must possess considerable knowledge initially. The earlier attempts to produce "tabula rasa" systems that start out with nothing and gradually build up knowledge have not proven to be successful. The feeling now is that all learning systems must be knowlege-based to some extent. A certain portion of the initial knowledge base must be self-knowledge about the current state and capabilities of the system. Usually learning will be incremental, progessing in small stages or steps. If the learning process is automated, then it will be necessary for the system to be able to generate and select learning tasks for itself. At any time, such a system should have some way of keeping track of what it currently "knows."

Included in the first type of learning, empirical induction, are both those software systems that can "learn by being told" and those that can "learn from examples." In either case, learning involves the ability to assimilate and apply new concepts to describe new data. For symbolic processing, this means being able to continually accept new terms for use in generating and applying new descriptions. In building up knowledge from specific cases, the system has to have general descriptions that can be scanned for matches. One major approach has been to reduce the process of inductive reasoning to a heuristic search problem in the description space of previously recorded examples.

Discovery systems are basically expert systems whose main task, like DENDRAL and PROSPECTOR, is the discovery of things not already known. A distinction here is between systems that remain substantially unchanged by each discovery, and those that by each new discovery increase their overall ability to make further discoveries. Generally systems that obtain their results by some type of "theorem-proving" process have the advantage that each new discovery is represented as an entry in a deductive system which can be used to generate further theorems. The disadvantage of this type of system is often inefficiency.

An important research project in machine learning has been under way at the SRI Artificial Intelligence Laboratory to learn the conditions for developing a KLAUS (Knowledge Learning and Using System). In the first experimental system, NANOKLAUS, one of the primary considerations was the ability to handle natural language and learn and use new language structures. It was found that the LIFER natural language system was suitable for use as the language interface for NANOKLAUS. This program was able to respond to questions like "What do you know about?" and carry on some useful conversations about its level of knowledge. A more recent project is MICROKLAUS, in which the LIFER natural language processor is replaced by Jane Robinson's DIAGRAM system. Some of the overall objectives of the research on KLAUS systems are to develop systems that can:

1. Hold interactive, mixed initiative dialogue conversations about various domains of interest.
2. Retrieve relevant information that comes up.
3. Apply external software systems for the solution of various problems.

Pattern Recognition

Possibly one of the most underestimated fields of AI research, pattern recognition (PR) is concerned with the detecting, comparing, and classifying of patterns of input. Its scope is considerable, ranging from algorithms for pattern recognition of statistical, linguistic, geometric, graphic, and data structures. It includes recognizable patterns in space, in time, and in pure data and other abstract environments.

Some of the most common application areas of PR are in speech recognition, character recognition, and natural language processing. In the field of data analysis, the task is often like that of the clustering problem: detecting the grouping and clustering of unlabeled and unsorted collections of data. Applications vary according to whether there are predetermined objects that the machine must be programmed to recognize, or whether the patterns and groups are not known in advance, as is the case with raw data analysis.

A variety of classification techniques are in use. Probabilistic classifiaction schemes asssign a pattern to the most probable class, given the detected features. Geometric classifications are based on the computation of a similarity measure. Still other approaches can discriminate according to active functions. The techniques of pattern recognition are applicable in nearly every other field of AI research. In the areas of natural language processing and machine learning, in particular, there is room for important applications of PR technology.

AI and Robotics

Although much of robotics is concerned with relatively routine industrial chores, handled by "pick-and-place" manipulators, there is an important overlap between AI and the development and operation of intelligent robots. This discussion will cover some important concepts and current research in the development of robot intelligence.

The Robot Institute of America provides this definition: "A robot is a re-programmable, multifunctional manipulator designed to move material, parts, tools, or specialized devices through variable programmed motions for the performance of a variety of tasks." It is important to keep in mind the difference between automated manufacturing machinery that is programmable and robots. Generally a robot is a more mobile and general-purpose device, whereas even programmable automated manufacturing machines are generally designed to manufacture particular products. How, then, are intelligent robots defined? As understood here, an intelligent robot is one that (1) has its own onboard memory,

(2) is capable of performing complex tasks and task sequences, and (3) has a sophisticated decision-making capability.

Medium-technology intelligent robots are typically used for tasks like spray painting. The way that such robots are "taught" or programmed to do a specific job is by the "walk-through" method. A skilled human spray painter puts the robot through the exact sequence of movements required for the job, and the sequence is stored on magnetic media to be repeated exactly each time. High-technology intelligent robots are currently used for tasks like spot welding, precision assembly and handling, and testing.

Another important category of intelligent robots is those equipped with vision systems. These robots are used for parts testing and will have an ever-increasing role in handling delicate and precision assembly. Particularly in Japan, this category of intelligent robot has come to have a major role in high-technology manufacturing. NEC has become one of the first to use robots in the assembly of electronic circuit boards. Fujitsu Fanuc operates a factory employing a combination of people, robots, and other automated equipment where one of the products is more robots.

As this is written, a number of other important operational robotics projects are under way. Mitsubishi has developed its Move Master RM-101 robot, which has been successfully programmed to press microcomputer keys with a pencil. Certainly this raises fascinating issues concerning the ability of robots to re-program themselves. Odetics Corporation has produced the Functionoid, a six-legged microprocessor-controlled robot that is six feet tall and weighs in at 370 pounds, and is able to lift a 3000-pound load. In Florence, Kentucky, experts from Yamazaki Machine Works are helping to construct a $15 million machine tool parts plant where a total of only six workers will be needed to tend the master control computer. It is clear that the age of automation is not something in the future.

Automatic Programming

Much of the activity involved in writing programs is in producing and debugging the actual working code, even when the correct algorithms are fully known. The meticulous attention to detail and occasional unpredictable responses of computers have prompted more than one programmer to declare that it is an activity "unfit for humans." For these and other reasons it has been one of the goals of AI research to develop software that can automate the programming process to various degrees, turning over much of the work to the computer itself, for which it is particularly well suited. At this point there have been a number of successful automatic coding systems implemented. The main alternative approaches to automatic programming have been:

1. Deductive
2. Transformational
3. High-level language
4. Knowledge based

The first type, such as the DEDALUS program, derives the main control structures for a program by a deductive process. The second approach operates by transforming existing programs into new programs that perform according to requirements. In the third type, a higher-level language is implemented which is especially suited to writing code in a target language. The SETL language is an example of this approach. Knowledge-based approaches implement what amounts to an expert system that encodes the expertise of the best programmers and uses it to plan and generate code.

The PSI-PECOS system is a knowledge-based approach to writing programs in the INTERLISP dialect of LISP. The PSI system as a whole consists of seven parts:

1. The Parser/Interpreter Expert
2. The Dialog Moderator Expert
3. The Explainer Expert
4. The Example/Trace Expert
5. The Task Domain Expert
6. The Program—Model Builder Expert
7. The Coding and Efficiency Expert(s)

The way these parts function in the system is clear from this outline. The Parser/Interpreter receives input in English from a user concerning the specifications of the program to be generated. It has a very large knowledge base of English grammar, and has an extensive knowledge of technical programming jargon. It parses this input and converts the information into the program net, the internal form in which the knowledge about the program-to-be is stored.

The Dialog Moderator is capable of modeling not only the state of the system but the user and dialogue as well, and uses these models to select various questions and statements to make to the user. Once selected, they are turned over to the Explainer, the expert able to convert the information in the program net into good, understandable English terms and phrases, which generates the actual wording. The Example/Trace Expert is also able to accept traces and examples to help complete the specification.

If the specification is still incomplete, the Task Domain Expert is able to cooperate with the Parser and the Example/Trace Expert to supply missing information through its knowledge of the specific type of application. Then, when the specification is complete, the Model Builder uses knowledge of what constitutes a correct program to convert the program net into a complete and consistent model of the program to be generated. Finally, the Coding and Efficiency Experts use rules for program efficiency and conversion of the model to generate the code of the program in the target language. The success of this project has led to a commercial product in the business sector, the CHI system developed at Kestrel Institute.

These knowledge-based automated programming systems may well be the best examples of both automatic programming and knowledge-based programming, because the developers are themselves the experts who are able to encode their expert knowledge of programming in the rule bases without the need for other experts or knowledge engineers as intermediaries. For these and other reasons, expert program-generating systems will be one of the important areas of AI to watch in the coming years.

AI and Space Technology

According to George von Tiesenhausen, automation team head at the NASA Space Flight Center in Huntsville, Alabama, sometime in 1986 the agency expects to put a robot in orbit via the Space Shuttle. In 1980, the NASA Study Group prepared a report titled "Machine Intelligence and Robotics," which concluded that increased research in automation "will enhance significantly the cost-effectiveness and total information-return from future NASA activities." Shortly after this report appeared, NASA increased its annual budget for artificial intelligence and related activities. One of the recent studies was the ARAMIS project by Marvin Minsky at MIT which investigated the feasibility of automation in the area of satellite repair.

In a summer study group in 1980 at the University of Santa Clara, sponsored by NASA, the theme of self-replicating robots and automated factories was investigated. One of the first steps, it concluded, would be to build a robot which was capable of assembling another robot identical to itself from its components. The final step would be the construction in orbit of a fully self-replicating factory, one that could build other identical automated factories.

The theory of self-reproducing automatons was first provided in 1949 by von Neumann. In his theory, four components are required: Component A, the automated factory which given raw materials can turn them into products according to instructions; Component B, which duplicates the instructions; Component C, a controller connected to both A and B; and Component D, the instruction which allows A to manufacture the complete system, A + B + C. Naturally, the key to the theory is the fantastic device represented as Component A, which is usually called a Replicator.

However, in July 1980, engineering drawings and specifications for a factory built in accordance with von Neumann's theory was produced by George von Tiesenhausen and Wesley Darbro at NASA. The key to the design is the "universal constructor" which can take parts from the production system and turn out complete new factories. The universal constructor is composed of two parts, a stationary module and several mobile robots. The robots are coordinated by a master controller in the center of the universal constructor which supervises the assembly of the new self-replicating automated factory. It is fortunate that at least some of the administrators at NASA are now realizing that one of the greatest application areas for automated intelligence is in space technology, where the costs for maintaining human beings is usually quite exorbitant.

AI and the Creative Arts

Computer art is normally associated with computer-generated graphics and music. One of the few areas where AI has figured into this is in pattern recognition processing. In his highly stimulating book, *Godel, Escher, Bach,* Douglas Hofstadter's dissection of creative work in the areas of metalogic, illusionist art, and masterful musical counterpoint uncovered another area of convergence: recursiveness. In Hofstadter's view, the heart of intelligence lies in the peculiar self-referential recursiveness that he describes as "Strange Loops" and "Twisted Hierarchies," and which he finds in Godel's incompleteness proof, M. C. Escher's woodcuts and lithographs such as "Drawing Hands," Bach's "Musical Offering," and even in some of Magritte's more masterful pictorial illusions. In this, he feels, lies the key to developing intelligent programs, i.e., implementing "Strange Loops involving rules that change themselves directly or indirectly." Hofstadter pointed out that several programs so far appear to come close to making original discoveries, such as Gelehrnter's program which succeeded in independently discovering a geometrical proof originally found in A.D. 300 by Pappus, but points out that this program fails an important test in that its discovery turned out to be a one-time-only affair. No other comparable proofs have been discovered by it.

Another important area where computers appear to be exercising some form of creative originality is in a story-generating program like TALE-SPIN by James Meehan. This program produces a model of a cast of characters and each of their goals and motives. The characters are placed in a set of circumstances, and each allowed to respond and interact as he or she would desire to. The problem-solving component scans the world of each character to determine what he or she would do and why. The system then calls on a text generator which is capable of writing a story from start to finish. If this story can be done, the next step is actually creating the characters by a combination of random choice and selective elimination, so that it would be very difficult to draw the line between original creation and story generation. Still, we can hardly expect that such stories would begin to compare with powerfully moving works of fiction that have been derived from the life experiences of their authors.

There is also some work being done that needs to be mentioned because of its potential importance to the field of AI as a whole. The field of responsive environment design as illustrated in the work of Myron W. Krueger has made very novel uses of AI techniques and developed new computer architecture concepts that are applicable in many areas besides that of creating aesthetic environments. For example, Krueger has been contracted to use the responsive technology methodology to develop a CAD system for electronic circuit design with a natural language interface that uses a model of the user's level of knowledge to adjust its explanations to the level of users as they learn.

The system architecture developed by Krueger for his responsive environments implements multiple levels of functions in a parallel processing environment that mirrors human psychological functioning. For real-time responsiveness there are "reflex processors" on the level just above the sensor input system. On the top level are "cerebral processors" which remain aloof from real-time interactions but are responsible for determining overall choices and fitting the reflex processing toward the primary goals of interactions. Between the cerebral processors and the reflex processors is the staging systems whose responsiblity is to load the modules associated with various contexts so that when context switches occur, information is transferred as rapidly as possible to all affected processors. Although the cerebral processors are not directly involved in real-time operations, they monitor the interactions with the purpose of redirecting them if necessary. While it is obvious that this is an effective system for controlling the direction of aesthetic environments, it is also quite clear that it is a dynamic model of human processes equipped for rapid real-time responses that is of immediate interest for AI applications. As is frequently the case, projects undertaken with the freedom to pursue exciting directions often turn out having the broadest practical importance, as the work conducted at the Xerox PARC facility demonstrates perfectly.

AI and the Future

1. Parallel Architectures. To date, there has been surprisingly little work done in AI research in multiple parallel and distributed processing environments, apart from Defense Department projects and Japan's Fifth Generation project. Most of the current techniques and algorithms in AI research assume a single sequential processor environment. It is clear that this is one of the most important areas where change will be occurring, because the dropping cost of powerful microprocessors is making it feasible to build machines with hardware support for AI objectives never before possible. Some of the new capabilities that will be available for implementation in AI systems with parallel processing hardware will include:

1. Parallel processing of set intersections needed for efficient computation of property inheritances.
2. Application of several inference or production rules simultaneously, rather than backtracking or expanding search trees one node at a time.
3. Separate processor assignment in systems with multiple-component databases.
4. Interaction between several operational AI systems.
5. The implementation of sophisticated real-time AI sytems.

2. Japan's Fifth Generation Project. Kazuhiro Fuchi, the director of ICOT, the institute in Tokyo dedicated to research on Fifth Generation computers, has made it clear that they are thoroughly committed to following through with their highly publicized goal of taking hardware and software beyond its present limits for automated intelligence processing. It is now also apparent that the intention is to do this with personal computers as well as with very large multiprocessing supercomputers. The first prototype is expected to be a personal computer with an unheard-of amount of internal memory, perhaps even as much as 80 megabytes. Then, by the end of the ten-year project, a gigantic supercomputer network is envisioned with as much as 100 gigabytes total memory.

Whether or not these hardware objectives are reached, it is clear that whatever machine ICOT develops will have an extremely advanced architecture and Prolog implemented in microcode as its machine language. Many experienced AI researchers in the United States familiar with the specialized features of Prolog expect that this plan will be abandoned, with the more versatile LISP adopted instead as the target language. However, in the face of this criticism the Japanese have reaffirmed their intentions, but clarifying that it is "prolog" (with a small "p") that they will be implementing as the machine language of their supercomputer. The implication is that the version of Prolog they will implement will not be the conventional Prolog, but rather a Prolog-like language that will be broader, more generic, and presumably more flexible. Even so, it is difficult to envision how this would be superior to a LISP with a Prolog-in-LISP as part of its environmnent, since the system will have the speed advantages of a machine language.

3. Common Sense.   One of the things that will haunt AI researchers of the future, as it does John McCarthy now, is how to provide AI programs with "common sense." McCarthy likes to point out that if you type a statement into the MYCIN medical expert system that you followed the diagnosis it provided and the patient died, the system would not recognize what "died" referred to, and would most likely respond with "input ungrammatical." Another aspect of the "common sense" problem has to do with the conditions under which rules and principles apply. A rule such as "Birds can fly." does not actually hold for birds with injured wings, those still too young to fly, those whose legs are being held, and so on. McCarthy is interested in developing a logic for representing knowledge that could allow you to say things like "Birds can fly except when X conditions prevent them." where you don't have to specify right away or ever fully specify what all the X's are.

Toward this end he has proposed implementing programs that are capable of "circumscription." Circumscription is intended to be a formalized procedure for making reasoned conjectures that can jump to conclusions without being told that objects with certain properties are the only ones that have them. It turns out that doing this involves the ability to make special types of inference not normally a part of standard formalized deductive reasoning systems. The successful implementation of systems with the capability of circumscription would offer a possible solution to the qualification problem discussed earlier, the problem of representing knowledge when it is impractical or impossible to specify all or most of the conditions under which it is valid.

For those like McCarthy who really believe in machine intelligence, it is understandably unsatisfying that expert systems that can often outdo experts in their specialized tasks "know" not only nothing about the general principles of their disciplines, but not even the most rudimentary things about people or the world. Because expert systems behave from within a specific set of rules that are governed by a specific set of inferential relationships, the world as an external universe becomes irrelevant unless made relevant by the knowledge base. In some sense, expert systems are bound by the same limitations of other types of software systems in that they must be fed by an external source or must be able to learn from previous events. They cannot apply general rules of knowledge to a new set of specific circumstances that fall outside their rule-based universe so as to make intuitive inference. The human expert's intuition, which is really not intuition at all, is a type of lopsided inference in which the expert's war chest of knowledge and experience is used as a reference point for combination of specific rules and general rules. The specific rules define the relationship of elements in the expert's database to one another. The general rules, however, allow an expert to make the critical leap over the body of specific rules to a conclusion that might be unsupported but nevertheless correct. Ask an expert to validate his intuition and you might get an unsatisfactory answer. Query an expert system such as MYCIN to validate one of its judgments, and it responds with a rule. MYCIN must operate within a specific universe of rules and data. A human expert can bring to bear upon a problem experience from other problems and other endeavors.

Does this impose a critical limitation to expert systems? Not at all. But this acts as a strong reminder for those who might otherwise put blind faith in computerized expertise. We see then that today's expert systems are still rather easy problems when compared to those still to be solved before computer-based systems can begin to approach true "intelligence."

Ernest R. Tello

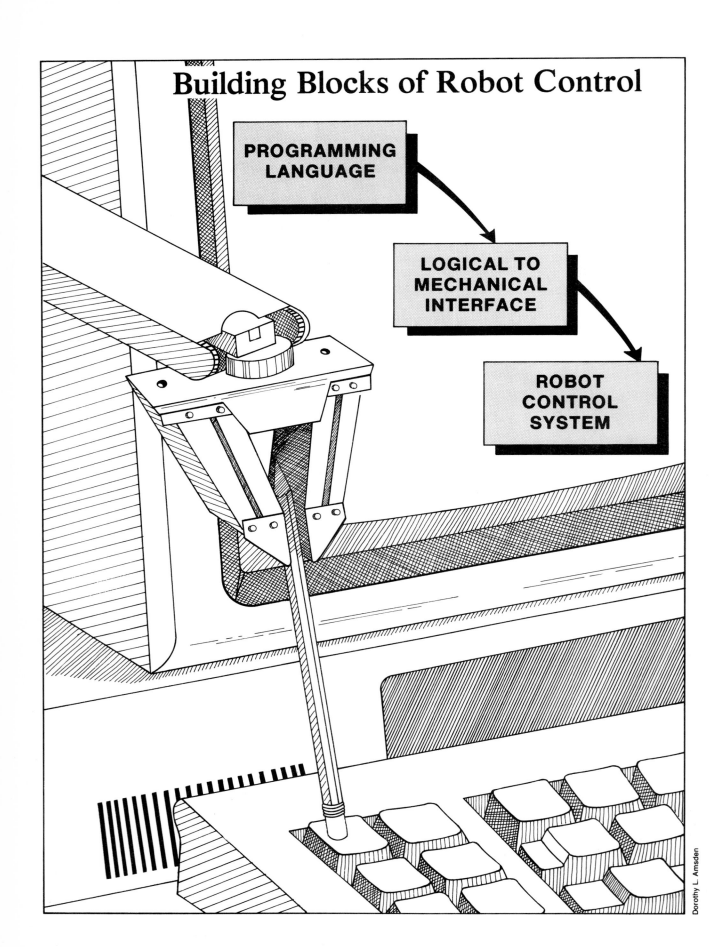

Building Blocks of Robot Control

PROGRAMMING LANGUAGE

LOGICAL TO MECHANICAL INTERFACE

ROBOT CONTROL SYSTEM

Dorothy L. Amsden

Robotics

Robotics is the study of robots, the science of robot design, or the theory of robot-assisted manufacture or industrial fabrication. The word "robotics" was coined by Isaac Asimov over thirty years ago in his *I Robot,* a volume of short stories. Asimov, who has said that science fiction has a disturbing way of being taken too seriously by those who should know better, used the term robotics to describe the rules-governed behavior of automatons, mechanical creatures who were manufactured to serve and protect humankind. Robots were programmed according to the First Laws of Robotics under which no robot was able to harm a human being directly or indirectly or, through its inaction, allow any harm to come to a human being.

Robots were first introduced in a 1936 work of European science fiction called *R.U.R.* (Rossum's Universal Robots), a drama by Czech playwright Karel Capek. The word "robot" itself is Czech and is derived from the word for "forced labor" and "serf." Hence, the concept of the robot had its origins not in science but in science fiction, and that aura of fantasy has lingered on despite the very real and mundane industrial applications that robots have today.

Types of Robots

Currently in the robotics industry, there are two basic classes of robots—industrial robots and personal robots—and a variety of subclasses. Industrial robots, used in factory assembly lines for manufacture or process control, are the first class. Implemented by the Japanese and then by the Europeans, industrial robots are finally making their appearance in American manufacturing facilities where they perform such tasks as automobile assembly, mechanized welding, manipulation of hazardous materials, and telemetry in hostile environments. Industrial robots had their beginnings in the numerical control industry where once-manual tasks were automated through the use of electronic and electromechanical machinery. Characteristics of the industrial robot include its mechanical lift abilities and its large size in relation to the task it performs. By far, the majority of industrial robot applications involve the movement or manipulation of large, heavy objects, and as a result, most industrial robots require a huge power source to operate. Robot devices welded most of the frames of American and Japanese cars built since 1983, and it is a robot spacecraft called *Voyager* that will carry a human message to distant galaxies.

Most personal computer owners, however, are more familiar with the robot-arm kits that can be configured to almost any microcomputer system or with the complete personal mobile robots with their own onboard computer systems. It is these three-wheeled devices which demonstrate some of the most innovative hardware and software packaging taking place in the microcomputer industry today. The personal robot, such as the Heathkit model or the Andro-bot, is typically used around the home as a personal assistant. Such devices, often capable of speech synthesis and, to a limited degree, voice recognition, are mobile gadgets which navigate by a photosensor apparatus and can lift small objects. Because of the mechanical lift requirements, personal robots use considerably less power than industrial robots and can often be powered by an onboard battery for up to twelve hours. Personal robots can be driven by dedicated microprocessors that control the movement of arms, the pattern of voice and light discrimination, and the stored locomotive patterns that enable the robot to navigate around obstacles. Larger 8- or 16-bit computer systems can act as hosts or master control devices, storing more complicated programs that require more memory capacity than the robots have. The programs can be implemented on the host or control computer and then off-loaded to the robot for execution. However, as the microcomputer industry becomes more sophisticated, larger, 32-bit units will drive robots and enable them to function as ambulatory personal computers.

Mechanics of Robots

Size and power supply notwithstanding, there are more similarities between industrial and personal robots than dissimilarities. Most comparisons begin with the analysis of the robot arm: in one form or another the building block of the entire robotics industry. The robot arm is also important as a concept because it illustrates the pragmatic interface between modern electronics theory and classical mechanics through which lift, reach, rotation, and other forms of physical manipulation are executed.

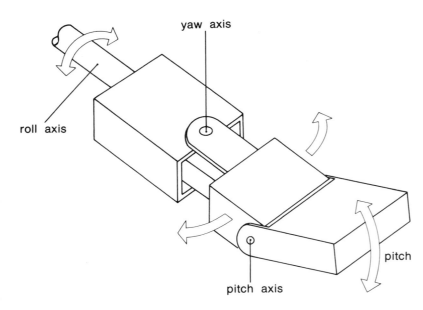

Fig. 3-16

Types of Motion. Figure 3-16 shows the three different motions available to the prototypical robot wrist: (1) roll, which allows the wrist to rotate along the horizontal axis, (2) yaw, which allows the wrist to move its linkages from side to side with a range from 45 to 90 degrees, and (3) pitch, the up-and-down motion at the end of the wrist. These three wrist directions allow the appropriately designed robot arm to have three degrees of freedom beyond a fixed or rigid robot wrist. A degree of freedom is a formal measurement adopted by roboticists that defines the number of linkages existing with a robot arm. Therefore, within the three directions—roll, yaw, and pitch—the completely mobile robot wrist will be able to perform tasks that are three times harder than those that can be performed by the fixed mechanical wrist and will be able to act much like the human wrist in terms of flexibility and maneuverability.

How does the construction of the robot wrist provide for the emulation of humanlike motion? In the case of roll, requiring a horizontal axis rotation, imagine a wooden dowel being moved with the tips of the fingers. When the dowel is turned, it emulates the rotation of the shaft of an electric motor. Thus one way of providing controllable motion to the roll axis is by linking the output shaft of an electric motor to the roll axis shaft of the robot wrist. However, the specifications that exist for most electric motors do not provide the amount of true mechanical power necessary to twist the assembly, especially if there is resistance to the direction of the motion. Moreover, most electric motors turn their shafts much too fast for the assembly to emulate a true wrist. In order to translate the electric power into mechanical power, one must calculate the torque.

Torque. Torque is a force that produces motion and is expressed as the amount of rotational power the shaft of the electric motor can supply to any joint. This calculation is in reality a true ratio of ounce/inches, pound/inches, or foot/pounds. The motion of a motor is normally circular about the armature axis, such as that of the roll axis of the wrist. To determine the torque necessary to lift or move an object, multiply the required force by the distance to be traveled, making sure that the distance is calculated correctly. In a system where the rotational axis is a shoulder mechanism, this principle can be easily explained. For example, if the hand/arm linkage mechanism that is connected to the shoulder weighs 1 pound and an object to be lifted, called a payload, also weighs 1 pound, then the total weight to be lifted at the shoulder pivot point is both weights combined or 2 pounds. If the arm is 18 inches long between the pivot point of the shoulder and the payload center, the torque required of the motor equals 2 pounds times 18 inches (the distance to be traveled) or 36 pound/inches. Figure 3-17 illustrates the calculation of these forces.

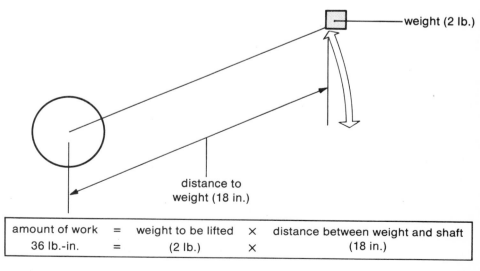

weight (2 lb.)

distance to
weight (18 in.)

amount of work	=	weight to be lifted	×	distance between weight and shaft
36 lb.-in.	=	(2 lb.)	×	(18 in.)

Fig. 3-17

Once the amount of necessary torque has been calculated, one has to determine whether the electric motor has the capability of providing it. Most personal computer robotics enthusiasts who purchase electric motors for their devices can find the torque listing in motor specifications. However, when experimenting with surplus motors or motors removed from other appliances, the torque supplied by the motor must be determined. In order to do this, the experimenter

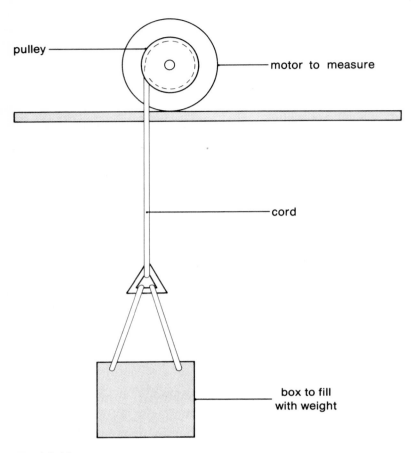

Fig. 3-18

must mount a pulley onto the shaft of the motor to turn it into a winchlike device which will lift a test weight against the pull of gravity. This procedure is illustrated in Fig. 3-18. A small box or pail is attached to the end of a string to carry the test weights. The motor is turned on and additional weights are added until the motor actually stalls. Measure the stall weight of the motor and multiply it by the radius of the pulley. This number is an approximation of the torque of the motor. The next step is to see whether the torque is sufficient to execute a rotation along the horizontal axis.

Power Transmission Trains. For the purposes of argument, assume that the motor does not provide the required torque to rotate the wrist assembly. If so, further steps must be taken to transfer power from the motor to the mechanical device. This is normally accomplished by a system of gear linkages much like the linkage mechanism in a standard automobile transmission or "stick shift." And in an automobile transmission as well as in a robotics experiment, the relationship between gear size, gear type, and number of gear teeth must be understood before any power transmission mechanism can be designed. These relationships, premised on the configuration of the spur gear, are illustrated in Fig. 3-19.

The spur gear, a hub with a toothed circumference, is a basic mechanical device used to drive many different kinds of apparatus, and, consequently, it is commonly used in most types of transmission linkages. The number of teeth on the meshing spur gears determines the reduction ratio from gear to gear. In Fig.

driver spur

20 teeth   15 teeth

Relationship Between Receiver and Driver Spur

$$\frac{20}{15} = 1.333$$

| Receiver Gear | 1.333 times stronger (torque) |
| | 1.333 times slower |

Fig. 3-19

3-19, for example, a driver gear that receives power directly from the motor shaft has 15 mechanical teeth, and the meshing receiver gear has 20. The receiving shaft, that is, the shaft which will be used as the wrist roll driver, is mounted to the receiver gear. Now, power can be transferred from the rotating shaft on the electric motor to the wrist roll driver shaft through the meshing gears at a ratio calculated by dividing the receiver gear by the driver gear. The result, 1.333, is the time differential or reduction ratio between the gears. The receiver gear will travel 1.333 times more slowly than the driver gear and will provide 1.333 times greater torque than the motor shaft. Hence the torque power from the electric motor is increased in indirect proportion to the relative speed of the receiver gear to the drive gear. By increasing the number of teeth on the receiver gear, the force is increased. Hence, because the reduction ratio is a direct result of the relative sizes of the meshing gears, the transfer of power can be easily executed by lining up the correct gear linkages. This basic principle of power transmission determines how electric motors of relatively low torque can drive sophisticated robot devices and apply lifting or rotating forces to objects from the simple robot-arm kits.

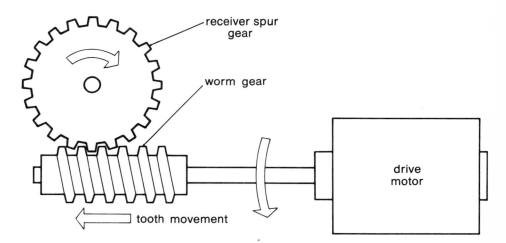

Fig. 3-20

In addition to spur gears, worm gears are used in the construction of robot arms to transfer power from the electrical shaft to a perpendicular receiver gear. As Fig. 3-20 illustrates, by mechanically mounting the roll axis of the wrist to the driven spur gear, one can provide the necessary horizontal-axis movement. The worm gear linkage also provides for the yaw and pitch axes as well. By moving the horizontal rotation perpendicular to that provided for the roll axis, one can assemble the yaw-axis linkage. Arranging the worm gear to spur gear assembly in a different way provides for the pitch axis. In other words, the tabletop experimenter, by moving the same mechanical linkages into different drive positions, can develop a variety of robot mechanisms and transfer power in different directions and at different ratios from the electrical shaft to the robot wrist. Interestingly, the same principles apply to this workshop experiment that apply to the creation of the robot assembly systems that function in America's smokestack industries. The sizes of the gears and the outputs of the power supplies may be different, but the mechanical and electrical principles are essentially the same. Clearly, an understanding of the mechanical principles of personal computer robotics contributes to an understanding of the way robots can transform the industrial environment.

Robot Driver Motor

Industrial and personal robots are also similar in the way they utilize and distribute electric power within their respective systems. Traditionally, power is supplied to a driver motor, thence to the gear linkages. However, the term "motor" can easily be misused. There are actually three types of motors used in the two classes of robots. Personal robots typically use electric motors, which can be subdivided into linear, permanent-magnet motors and stepper motors which provide precise controllable motion. Stepper motors, for example, control the read/write heads in floppy disk drives where precise positioning is essential to the function of the disk drive mechanism. Permanent-magnet motors, on the other hand, turn shafts and provide power to the transmission linkages in the robot limbs.

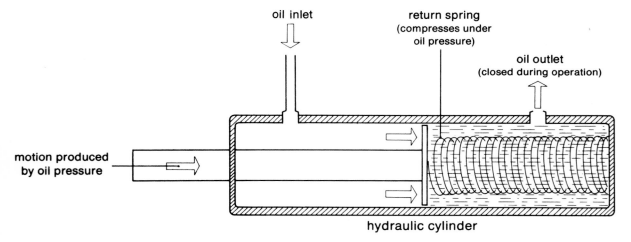

Fig. 3-21

Industrial Robot Motors: Hydraulic. Lightweight industrial robots also use direct-drive electric motors as a source of power. However, the heavy industrial robots utilize a fluid-drive power base that employs a hydraulic or pneumatic mechanism. Thus the third type of motor is the hydraulic motor, commonly found in a basic snowplow assembly, which uses the medium of oil to move mechanical linkages. The oil is packed into a drive system, a cylinder in the case of a snowplow, under pressure. When the pressure is released, the oil moves. As Fig. 3-21 illustrates, the basic principle of the hydraulic piston mechanism is to move a shaft in a linear in/out motion. When oil is allowed to enter the cylinder under pressure, the piston is pushed within the cylinder toward the return spring. This spring then compresses, providing back force when the oil is released. As oil enters the cylinder, the shaft connected to the piston face is moved outward. To provide motion in the opposite direction, the oil inlet connection is mechanically cut off through the use of a valve, and the relief valve is then opened, allowing the oil to escape as the spring action pushes against the other side of the piston, this time toward the oil. The pressure from the oil against the piston is greater than the back pressure that the return spring provides against the oil. Hence, the relief valve is the controlling device in the hydraulic cylinder because it provides for a measured release of pressure. In the snowplow example, the oil under pressure enters the cylinder from the fluid reservoir and pushes against the piston. The rising piston exerts force against a chain which provides the power to lift the heavy metal plow from the ground. The weight of the plow is the counterforce. When the relief valve is opened, the weight of the plow forces the piston down and the oil back into the fluid reservoir.

To calculate the torque or the amount of work provided by the hydraulic cylinder, one must know the pounds of pressure per square inch that the oil exerts against the piston. This is actually the pressure at which the oil is being forced into the cylinder. A 1-inch-diameter cylinder and a 100 pound-per-square inch source of oil provides 100 pounds of force. Similarly a 2-inch cylinder provides two times that force. From these simple calculations, one can see that hydraulic motors and controllable motion elements have a greater capacity to provide power than a typical direct-drive electric motor.

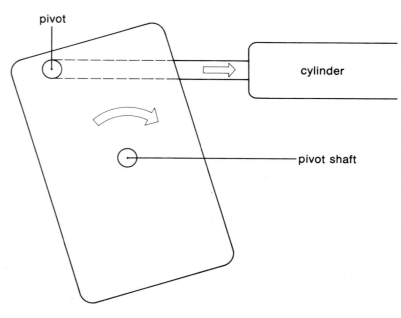

Fig. 3-22

Pneumatics. Pneumatic power drivers, the use of which is increasing among smaller industrial robot manufacturers, work on the same piston-cylinder principle as the hydraulic motor, except that the medium is air rather than oil. Pneumatic cylinder drivers provide less precise control and less power than hydraulic cylinder drivers. However, pneumatic cylinders require less maintenance and are less expensive to manufacture. Therefore, because air is more compressible than oil and, consequently, less able to apply a precise hold-control on the mechanism, pneumatic drivers are often found in lighter industrial applications where the torque requirements are less stringent.

Transferring Power from Cylinder to Gears. Figure 3-22 shows how the in/out linear motions of hydraulic or pneumatic cylinders can be converted into the rotational motion that the electric motor shaft provides. As the piston is driven in or out, power is transferred from a pivot point at the end of the piston shaft across a rectangular plate to a pivot shaft in the center. Hence, the back-

and-forth linear motion is translated into a rotation which is transmitted along a shaft to a series of gear linkages. At this point, the power from the rotational shaft can be reduced or increased according to the corresponding spur or worm gear ratios. The power that the rotational shaft applies to the gears is a direct result of the ratio of the oil or air pressure entering the cylinder to the diameter of cylinder. This acts upon the piston which rotates the transfer plate along the pivot and transfers power to the rotational shaft.

Feedback Loop. In an industrial environment, the torque specifications necessary to lift or move heavy objects are translated into gear ratios, cylinder diameters, oil pumps, air compressors, relief valve controls, and the lengths of shafts or transfer plates. Since stress against metal, fluid, or air can be measured and monitored, computers can regulate the operation of the robot system based upon sensory inputs from the system itself that are compared to stored or programmed instruction sets. In this way, operational feedback from the system is processed by the system's own computers to regulate the system according to changes in the operating environment or the operating conditions. Human intervention is kept to a minimum—it is usually restricted to monitoring display terminals—and the robot systems are left to regulate themselves. This concept is known as a process feedback loop and is becoming a mainstay of the reindustrialization now under way in many manufacturing facilities.

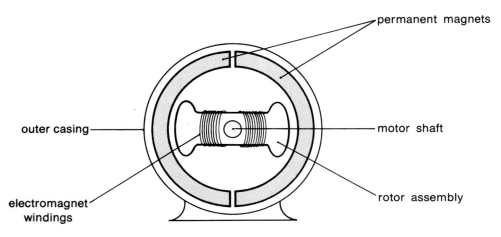

Fig. 3-23

Electromagnetic Principles. The electric motors typically used in personal robots operate on the principle of electromagnetics, where opposite poles of a magnet attract one another. The motor is partitioned into two areas: the outer casing and the internal electromagnetic winding. In the case of the permanent-magnet motor, as illustrated in Fig. 3-23, there is an outer casing of two permanent-magnet poles. Within this casing is an electromagnetic coil wound around the rotor shaft. As the rotor is turned, its electromagnets change fields, so that they attract or repel the permanent magnet enclosed in the casing which is used to shroud the rotor. This electromagnetic attraction and repulsion provides rotational movement along the horizontal axis.

Stepper motors have a different configuration. This type of motor is specifically wound to stop at certain positions along the rotational axis. By exciting different windings within the rotor of the stepper motor, precise movement of the shaft can be controlled. Thus, in applications where very delicate movements of a mechanism are required, such as a disk drive or a hazardous waste manipulation assembly, stepper motors are used almost exclusively.

Robot Control Systems

The microcomputer is among the most recent advances in robot control mechanisms. Previously, robots were controlled by direct intervention from operators or through a series of electromechanical relays. These automatic or semiautomatic switches provide the power gates to turn motors on and off at various intervals. Today's microcomputer control allows a greater degree of flexibility in the initial programming and reprogramming of robot devices because large and complex programs can be stored in a small space and, because of the advances in microcomputer networking capabilities, the informational database sometimes required to feed the entire system can be distributed among various locations for quick access and retrieval by the system's control program. This means that a database-structured robot manufacturing facility need not face the queue bottlenecks that plagued large central computer banks as recently as ten to fifteen years ago.

A typical industrial robot may be programmed to perform a specific repetitive task such as the assembly of a car bumper. When a new model year begins and the production design of the bumper changes, this robot must be reprogrammed to assemble the new bumper. In the early electromechanical control systems, this reprogramming required actual hard rewiring of the device's switching mechanism. After the implementation of the first mainframe-driven robots, the reprogramming was accomplished at a machine-language level by "logically" reconfiguring the device's switching mechanism. The introduction of assembly-language instruction sets made robot reprogramming even easier, although the programmers still sought to remain as close to a machine level as possible because of the need to code very precise motion commands to exacting specifications. Microcomputer circuitry, with plug-in boards and upgradable logic chips, has allowed for a greater standardization in the robotics industry and for a faster and more efficient retooling process. An extension of the industry has found its way into the consumer market with the personal robot.

Basic Control and Logic Concepts. The basic control mechanisms for a robot are very similar to the basic logical processes of the computer itself. As Fig. 3-24 illustrates, the components of the computer—data storage, transient memory or RAM, control program, input and output ports, and other external devices—all emanate from a central processing unit or CPU. In many robot control structures, this complete block diagram can be implemented within the architecture of a single-chip computer. The difference between this implementation and the typical personal computer system used for business software applications is the input and output peripherals. Where an industrial robot may be interfaced to an external storage medium such as a disk drive, it is typically not connected to a data-processing peripheral such as an open input terminal. The peripherals of industrial robots are those controllable motion elements such as motors, hydraulic cylinders, and sensors which provide feedback data to the robot control structure. Thus the input peripheral is actually a part of a closed-end system. Access to the system might be provided through an input terminal to the robot control program, but even these types of configurations are becoming obsolete. However, the typical business data-processing system must allow for open-end access by programmers and nonprogrammers alike. This is a primary difference between the configuration of a business computer system and a robot system.

Closed- and Open-Loop Mechanisms. Robots that are controlled by using the inputs from feedback sensors are called closed-loop mechanisms. Those that simply manipulate controllable devices such as stepper motors without any form of direct feedback information are called open-loop mechanisms. Many open-loop mechanisms operate not within a robotics environment but within the data-

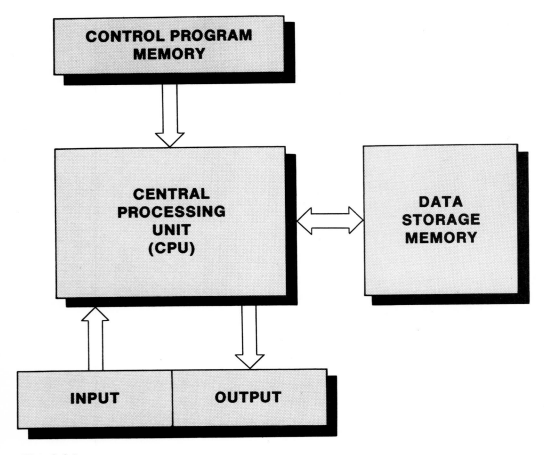

Fig. 3-24

processing organization because of the need for operator and data-entry clerk access. A typical example of an open-loop mechanism is the early version of a standard floppy disk drive. The head mechanism which is used as a medium to read and write on the magnetic surface of the disk must be positioned precisely on a track-by-track basis. The controllable motion element used to position this head is a stepper motor. The stepper motor, through the use of a lead screw assembly, navigates the head in a direct linear motion. Floppy disk control electronics, usually transmitted to the motor through the disk controller card, command the stepper motor to step to a specific track. If, however, the stepper motor does not align the head properly to the correct track, because of a mechanical rather than a logical condition, the computer tends not to return an error message because no fault is recognized.

In contrast, today's Winchester drive mechanisms provide closed-loop systems. A special servo track with positioning telemetry information is usually provided on one of the enclosed magnetic surfaces. This servo or positioning information is consulted automatically by the drive's control program whenever the motor is moved to reposition the head. Thus errors can be detected and corrected from within the system rather than by an external monitoring source. And by extending this simple model to a highly sophisticated robot-controlled and robot-monitored environment, one can see how robot arms or robot instruments use sensors to determine whether their mechanical position conforms to the coordinates of the control program. Hence, the closed-loop system provides for a method of error trapping and consistent monitoring that open-loop systems tend to lack. When combined with a rules-governed expert system that makes "intelligent" control decisions based on a knowledge base, the closed-loop system is an even more powerful industrial tool.

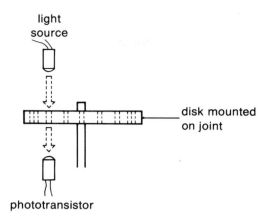

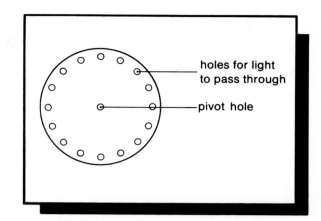

Fig. 3-25

Robot Sensors

These are the mechanical eyes and ears of the feedback loop. One of the most common sensors in this category is the position-sensing element that provides information about rotational position or relative movement. Note that the term "movement" requires a further definition because it refers not only to current movement but to recent movement or to a series of positions occupied by the device within a specific period of time as defined by the programming instructions.

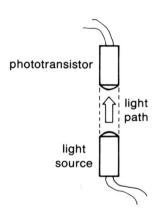

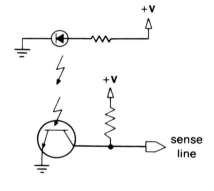

Fig. 3-26

A typical position-motion sensor is illustrated in Fig. 3-25. The sensor, an optoelectronic disk, is used to calibrate position by determining whether a robot arm or other instrument is actually being moved. The position-motion sensor works as follows: A light-emitting diode or even a single lamp is pointed directly at a phototransistor or other light-sensing device. Between the the light source and light sensor is a disk with positional information written to it. When light is allowed to strike the lens surface of the detector, the circuit is completed. In the case of the phototransistor, the output assumes a ground potential (Fig. 3-26). If this beam of light is interrupted, the circuit opens and the switch output voltage rises.

This type of sensor can be be applied to arm movement as well as to arm position. When the disk in Fig. 3-25 is mounted on the pivot shaft of a joint, it rotates as the joint is flexed. The disk can thus generate a stream of on/off pulses as the light stream passing through its positioned series of holes is interrupted. If the pulses are counted by a control program, a relative-motion measurement can be determined from the last count. This device can also indicate actual distances traveled: the distance the joint must move to pass each hole through the light stream is established and multiplied by the number of holes counted.

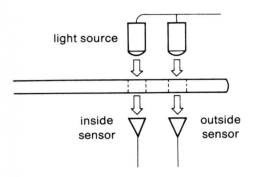

Fig. 3-27

Furthermore, by using two such sensors (Fig. 27), actual direction can also be determined. The first detector to generate a pulse reveals the direction in which the wheel is moving. If the slot configurations were to be altered to allow for the addition of another set of holes on the wheel (Fig. 3-28) and the second

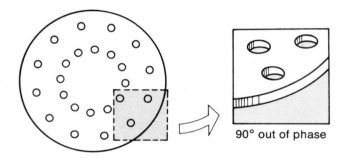

Fig. 3-28

90° out of phase

light sensor, motion can also be detected because the holes on the wheel are 90 degrees out of phase with one another (Fig. 3-29). In this configuration, either light sensor can detect when the arm is in motion.

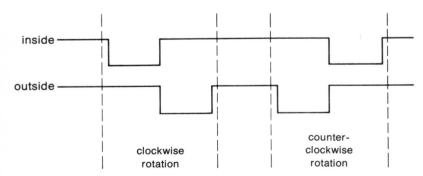

Fig. 3-29

Figure 3-30 illustrates another method of using a phototransmitter and detector to determine position and movement. Here, however, instead of actually interrupting the beam of light by alternating holes and solid areas, the light is bounced off alternating reflective strips on the wheel. This type of sensing device is called a photoreflective detector.

Most robot motion- and position-feedback mechanisms are constructed by using either the photointerrupter or the photoreflector as digital position detectors. They recognize information by counting a stream of on and off signals from a specific source, in this case, the photodetection devices on the wheel. Other position-measuring devices are premised on analog devices in which the motion

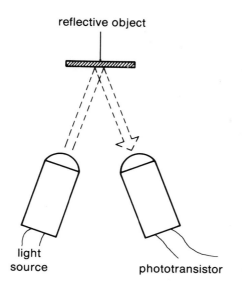

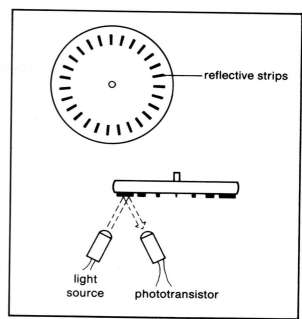

Fig. 3-30

of the entire device actually simulates the motion of the robot. These are called servo systems.

A servo control system is a combination of at least two devices, one that will generate the motion and another that will measure the motion generated. In the case of a simple robot servo system (Fig. 3-31), the motor which moves the limb whose position is to be checked is the motion generator. The shaft of this motor is connected to the shaft of a potentiometer or variable resistor so that any movement in the motor results in a change of resistance of the potentiometer. Thus, mechanical movement is measured by converting it to an equivalent value, in this case electrical resistance. Typically, in a servo mechanism, a form of control circuit is added to the system that allows the motor to rotate until the resistance of the potentiometer equals a preselected value. Voltage is supplied to this control circuit, sometimes called a comparator circuit, through the variable resistor. When the voltage from the potentiometer equals that of an incoming control level, the circuit shuts off the motor. The logic and schematics of this type of servo mechanism are illustrated in Fig. 3-32.

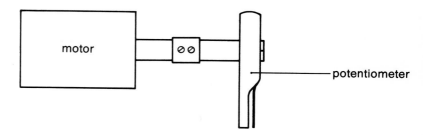

Fig. 3-31

Ultrasonic Measuring Devices

The ability to judge a distance and discriminate between near and far objects is a critical form of sensory input for a mobile robot. Humans approximate distances and discriminate between objects by overlaying the image from one eye upon the image from the other. The brain translates this overlay of optical signals into a perception of depth. An optical-based depth perception system

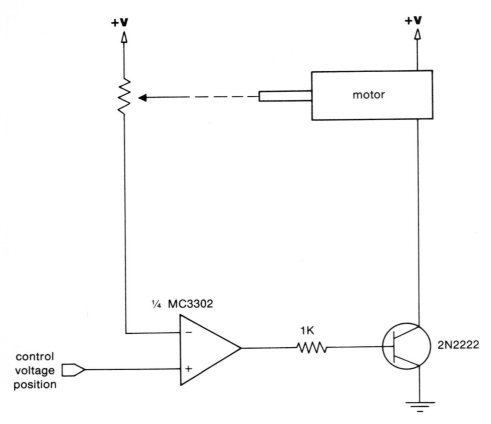

Fig. 3-32

is impractical for small robot systems because it requires an extensive system of cameras and autofocus lenses that feed data to an image analysis program in the controller. This procedure would be cumbersome because the mechanical and electrical overhead required to drive the optical system would be far greater than the benefits derived from the system itself. Instead, robots can use ultrasound.

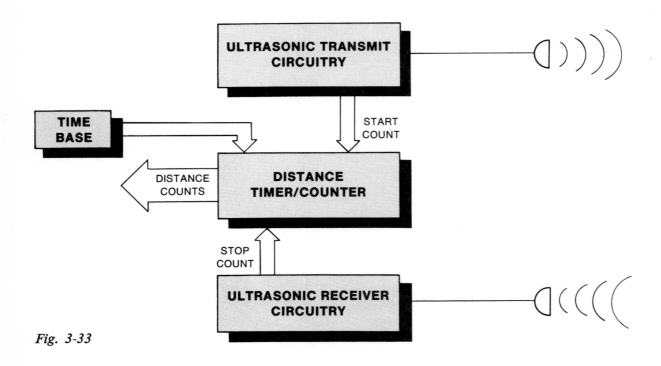

Fig. 3-33

Ultrasonics is the science of inaudible sounds. These sounds are normally generated in short pulses through small speakerlike devices called ultrasonic ceramic transducers driven by conventional oscillators mounted on the printed circuit board of the distance analyzer. Figure 3-33 shows the block diagram of this type of circuit. The short pulses of ultrasound are emitted by the transducer and spread out as they travel through an object-free area. As soon as the first pulse is generated, a discriminator circuit in the robot starts its count. It will continue the count until a stop-count command is generated by the ultrasonic receiver circuit.

When the ultrasonic waves strike an object that has entered the area, they are reflected to the receiving transducer which now acts as a microphone. If these returning sound waves are too weak to be measured, they are amplified by the robot's onboard ultrasonic circuit and sent to a discriminator which then issues the stop-count command to the distance counter. The final value in the counter measures the time it took for the ultrasonic pulses to find the object and return to the robot. By multiplying the number of counts by the speed of sound, the robot can then determine the distance to the object and appropriate control signals can be issued to the robot's master program.

Ultrasonic distance-measurement systems form the basis of many auto-focus cameras on the market today. The ultrasonic pulses are emitted toward the object that is being photographed and bounce back to a receiver circuit in the camera. The distance can then be calculated, and an electric signal automatically adjusts the lens to the proper distance.

Robot Programming

The type of programming used to provide a robot with explicit instruction sets for assembly, control, navigation, or other tasks must rely heavily on position-feedback mechanisms. As a result, sophisticated robot programming languages have finally evolved that can utilize position-feedback signals as a form of direct input from within the system itself. The first robot programming languages, however, lacked such ability.

Robot programming languages were used initially in the United States for the control and guidance of the UNIMATE robot series. This first language enabled the device to move to a specific set of coordinates and perform a specific task. There was no internal feedback mechanism. Upon reaching the specific coordinates, a "record" button was pushed to "memorize" the precise configuration of all of the robot joints at that particular moment in time. The controller program then logged the joint configurations for that specific task with the joint configurations for other tasks. In this way, a master program was constructed, step by step, until the robot "learned" all of the possible joint alignments necessary for its specific tasks. When the learning process was completed, the operator then pushed a "replay" button which would recall each point from the device's memory in the sequence in which it was entered and applied to a motion control element. In this way, human operators were able to train their robot devices to perform specific tasks much like a physical therapist trains a patient to relearn basic motor skills. This type of lead-through instant programming is still in use today in a variety of short-run manufacturing and manipulation applications. The procedure requires almost no programming skills, and the task is completed once the job has been performed. The sequence is then learned until it is erased from memory or updated.

Another form of programming language was developed at Stanford University which enabled a robot arm to sort through blocks of different sizes, pick them up, and stack them according to a predetermined order. This system utilized a logic that performed the following functions: (1) initialize; (2) servo; (3) open; (4) close.

The first command initialized the arm mechanism to a predefined logical state. "Servo" specified the numerical alignment of the joint positions at the six points along the arm. "Open" opened a gripper at the end of the arm and was used in conjunction with the "close" command to retrieve and hold a block. Each of these commands was called by a separate program that operated as if it were a subroutine. Flow of control within the program stopped while the subroutine was operating. When the called function was completed, flow of control resumed and the program's execution continued until its logical termination.

In 1971, a more advanced programming system was developed which enabled an operator to tell the manipulator which object it was to grasp and where it was to place it. The system was intelligent enough to search out the desired object from a group of like objects, determine how best to grasp it to avoid slippage, and move it to the predetermined location. The first phase of this project, which came to be known as the Move Instance System, was implemented using a computer graphics display screen. On the screen, the operator was able to command the simulated arm to move and stack objects. Once the execute command was entered, the mechanical arm performed the task. This early form of CAD/CAM was critical to the later development of visual simulation systems for the design and architecture of robot-controlled manufacturing facilities.

Subsequent robot programming languages had greater success in controlling the real-world mechanical factors, such as gravity, torque, and friction, that had to be calculated in any robotics equations. These languages were able to utilize various types of position-feedback information that were being made available to the mechanical devices by developments in touch- and torque-sensing technology. The WAVE system was one such language. It had two modes of operation. In the planning phase, the operator entered high-level commands that were assembled and stored for later execution in much the same way that an editing program in a BASIC interpreter operates. In the second phase, immediate execution of the commands would take place as soon as the commands themselves were entered. This resembled the Immediate Mode of an APL program in which operations are carried out from the keyboard rather than from within the program. The WAVE language was used with success in controlling two robot manipulators by alternating control from one to the other. In this way, simultaneous movement was emulated; however, it was done inefficiently and with an unacceptably high programming overhead.

Language developers turned to Algol, a popular high-level language, for help in resolving some of the inefficiencies presented by WAVE. The result was a language called AL: a combination of WAVE and Algol that enabled programmers to control the simultaneous motion of the two manipulators. However, the developers found that the command structures of WAVE conflicted with the control logic of an Algol program. As a result, although specific actions could be programmed with greater efficiency in AL than in WAVE, more complex logical procedures that had to be defined became extremely time consuming because of the embryonic block structure of the Algol component of AL. A further development, called PAL, was even more efficient than AL, and overcame many of the shortcomings of both the AL and WAVE implementations by providing a refined manipulator movement and a stronger control structure.

Today, Pascal has become one of the most popular robot programming languages. This descendant of Algol combines a block-structured logic with a natural-language front end that makes it a favorite among personal computer robot hobbyists. New implementations of Pascal that provide for a high level of interactivity and editing are also being introduced as rudimentary artificial intelligence development tools. The resulting combination of personal-computer-level artificial intelligence with personal robotics promises to redefine the area of home- or end-user robots and make available to them a degree of technology that up to now has been restricted to the laboratory or industrial facility.

Moreover, because companies have begun to develop personal robot language systems that are object oriented and rely on natural-language terminology, even novices will be able to program their own robot devices to perform specific meaningful tasks that can enrich the user's lifestyle.

Mark J. Robillard

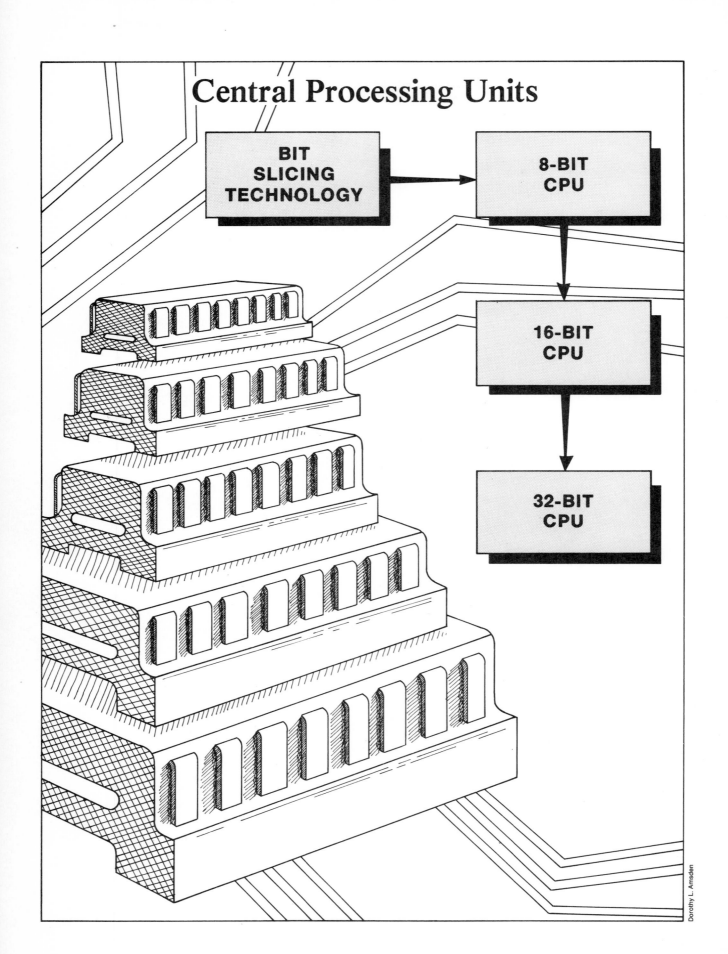

Central Processing Units

BIT SLICING TECHNOLOGY → **8-BIT CPU**

16-BIT CPU

32-BIT CPU

Dorothy L. Amsden

4
MICROPROCESSOR BASICS

Prior to the development of the microprocessor, a single device incorporating a variety of complex circuits, the central processing unit (CPU) of a computer system required many cards densely packed with discrete components, predominant among which were transistors. The transistor, whose primary function in a CPU is that of a switch, continues to predominate, but has been reduced in size to a virtually microscopic component, with many thousands integrated on a piece of specially treated silicon. A discrete transistor—a single, power-hungry, and relatively slow digital switch—was often as large as one of today's microprocessor chips, capable of performing its manifold tasks with great electrical efficiency and at very high speed. Without the microcprocessor, there would be no microcomputer industry, and without the microcomputer, there would be a very different kind of society emerging than is presently the case. One can argue that the microprocessor, and integrated circuits in general, will be looked upon in the future as, in great measure, the author of that future.

As the CPU grew smaller (by several orders of magnitude), the CPU capabilities grew, for circuit integration applied not only to the main processing unit (MPU) but to all of the peripheral circuits, those concerned with memory, input/output, and a variety of digital housekeeping chores. Today, the typical business-oriented microcomputer system can cheaply and easily handle computing applications that the largest of mainframe computers could handle only clumsily and at great cost but a few short years ago. As miniaturization proceeds, the desktop computer will become a formidable device with capabilities even yet not fully appreciated.

The development and production of microprocessor chips is a costly process limited to the few large companies with the financial resources to commit to a task that will not necessarily result in a profit. Like any other product in a competitive marketplace, some make it, some don't. The big successes of the day are Intel (8080 and descendants) and Motorola (6800 and descendants). MOS Technology (6502 family) and Zilog (Z80 and descendants), important as their products have been to the industry, have yet to make a significant dent in the 16-bit microprocessor market.

The term 16-bit microprocessor needs explanation, which will be found under ADDRESSING SPACE in the following general glossary of microprocessor terms designed (1) to acquaint the reader with those terms which have some universality in the microprocessor world and (2) to prepare the reader for a detailed examination of all the major microprocessors. The information for each chip will include all of the relevant terms. Additional terms more specifically related to assembly language programming are treated in a second glossary in which the types of assembly language instructions are defined so that instruction set summaries in the microprocessor directory will have more meaning and readers will be able to compare the different types of CPUs with one another.

Glossary: Basic Microprocessor Terms

ABORT. Cancel current operation abruptly.

ACCESS TIME. In a general sense, the time it takes for an electronic device to respond reliably to a request. The speed rating of a chip (INTEGRATED CIR-CUIT) is a measure of how fast a randomly selected bit can be processed by the chip. A memory chip, for example, rated at 150NS (nanoseconds) will respond twice as fast as one rated at 300NS. One NS is approximately the time it takes light to travel 1 foot. The designers of a computer system must specify support and memory chips of sufficient speed to take advantage of the speed of the MICROPROCESSOR.

ACTIVE HIGH. A positive voltage signal equivalent to a LOGICAL 1. See ACTIVE LOW.

ACTIVE LOW. A negative voltage signal equivalent to a LOGICAL 0. IC pin designations marked with a bar are active-low signals.

ADDRESS. A location in the MEMORY space of the computer. Each location or "mail box" in memory holds 8 BITs (1 BYTE) of DATA.

ADDRESS BUS. The electrical pathway over which address bits travel. There is an address bus inside the microprocessor as well as between the micro-processor and the memory section of the computer.

ADDRESSING MODE. Each microprocessor chip provides several means (modes) of defining an address for a particular operation. These modes—inherent, direct, extended, immediate, indexed, and relative—are explained in the "Addressing Modes and Instructions" subsection. Some microprocessors can expand these basic modes into two dozen or more, providing for the pro-grammer a powerful range of possibilities for program design.

ADDRESSING SPACE. The amount of memory available for use by the mi-croprocessor (and, by extension, the programmer or program). Eight-bit micro-processors (e.g., 8080, 8085, Z80, 6502, 6800) are designed to address 65,536 (64 kilobytes) locations. An 8/16-bit chip (Intel 8088) can address about a megabyte; a true 16-bit chip (Motorola 68000, Zilog Z8000) about 16 mega-bytes. Because the 8-bit chips are designed to manipulate data in 8-bit packages, they lack the processing power of the 8/16- and 16-bit chips. The designation 8/16 means that the chip uses 16-bit registers and moves data internally 2 bytes at a time, but talks to the outside world over an 8-bit data bus. A 16-bit chip has a 16-bit data bus available. The larger the registers and bus, the greater the com-puting power because of (1) increased numeric precision (larger numbers), (2) greater speed and efficiency (fewer machine cycles required for complex opera-tions), and (3) greater memory-addressing capability (larger, more sophisticated programs).

ARCHITECTURE. (1) The type and arrangement of functional elements within an integrated circuit and (2) the type and arrangement of functional elements in a computer system. Each chip and each computer has its own architecture. In some cases, the architecture is simply a minor variation of that of another chip or system, and in some cases it is distinctive—to be admired and copied or to be shunned. A rule of thumb in making such evaluations is to give highest marks to a design that offers the greatest capability with the least complexity, one that achieves elegance in the scientific sense of the word.

ARITHMETIC/LOGIC UNIT (ALU). The part of the microprocessor that performs arithmetic and certain logical operations. Typically, the ALU accepts inputs from two REGISTERS, performs the required operation, and sends the result back to one of the registers.

ASCII. American Standard Code for Information Interchange. In the microcomputer industry, the standard coding system for representing the symbols and alphanumeric characters on a computer keyboard. Thus, the ESCape key will always be interpreted as 00011011 (27 decimal, 1B hex), and uppercase letter B will always be represented by 01000010 (66 decimal, 42 hex). This standard makes possible the transfer of textfiles among different microcomputers of different brands.

ASSEMBLER. A program which converts ASSEMBLY LANGUAGE into MACHINE (OBJECT) CODE for the benefit of the microprocessor, which cannot use assembly language directly.

ASSEMBLY LANGUAGE. A type of programming language in which the INSTRUCTION SET of the microprocessor is represented by MNEMONICS instead of BINARY or HEXADECIMAL digits to ease the task of writing programs. An assembly language is a low-level language, that is, one close to the actual operations of the microprocessor. Pascal, BASIC, and so on, are HIGH-LEVEL languages because they are remote from the microprocessor. A line of code in BASIC written around, for example, the IF-THEN-ELSE statement will take many lines of explicit instructions in an assembly language. But the latter will execute more rapidly and use less memory than the former. To turn an assembly language program into an executable program, it must be assembled by an ASSEMBLER.

BANK. A defined segment of memory. Computers with microprocessors capable of directly addressing 65,536 memory locations can be made to appear to address more than that by a procedure known as bank switching, in which additional memory is switched in and out of the microprocessor's control as needed by the program being run.

BINARY. Base-2, the NUMBER BASE "native" to computers, represented by the digits 1 and 0, which, in digital electronics, are achieved by the two electrical conditions of volts and no-volts. Binary values derive from the powers of two as DECIMAL (base-10) values derive from the powers of ten. Base-10 has ten numerals: 0123456789. Base-2 has two numerals: 01. When we add 1 to 9 in base-10, we move from the units column to the tens column. When we add 1 to 1 in base-2, we move from the ones column to the twos column. The tens column in base-10 uses the same numerals as the units column, but the magnitude has increased by one power of ten. The twos column in base-2 use the same numerals as the ones column, but the magnitude has increased by one power of two. Each succeeding column of any NUMBER BASE increases the magnitude of the number expressed by one power of that base. The third base-10 column is thus equal in numeric weight to $1 \times 10 \times 10$ or 100; hence it is called the hundreds column. In base-2, the third column is equal in numeric weight to $1 \times 2 \times 2$, and is called the fours column. Two to the tenth power comes to 1024, the value of a kilobyte. That's why 64K or 64 kilobytes comes to 65,536 bytes. The binary representation of 1024 is 10000000000 (1 followed by ten zeros). How does one arrive at that? Consider 1 as presence of a positional value and 0 as simply a place holder. The positional values (in decimal) are these:

1024   512   256   128   64   32   16   8   4   2   1

To determine the binary numeral from 1024, we need only place 0 beneath the numbers we don't want and 1 under the number we do want:

1024   512   256   128   64   32   16   8   4   2   1
   1   0   0   0   0   0   0   0   0   0   0

By this means, therefore, the binary representation of, say, 1089, would be 10001000001.

BIT. The smallest unit of data. Logically, a 1 or a 0. Electrically, volts or no-volts.

BUFFER. A circuit for temporarily storing data until it can be used by another circuit. Certain integrated circuits (ICs) are designed specifically to perform the function.

BUS (BUSS). An electrical pathway for either POWER (electricity for running the circuitry) or SIGNALS (data stream). See ADDRESS BUS, CONTROL BUS, DATA BUS, POWER BUS.

BYTE. Eight data bits. In actual operations, a byte is a coherent package or string, not just any 8 bits.

CLOCK. A regular pulse, generated by the microprocessor under control of a highly accurate, crystal oscillator, used to provide the timing signals for the synchronization of all computer operations. The clock pulse is propagated over the CONTROL BUS. Inaccuracies in clocking will cause a variety of computer malfunctions.

CONDITION CODE REGISTER. Also called STATUS REGISTER and FLAG REGISTER, a register usually containing 6 active bits each of which is set or cleared depending on the particular CPU operation. For example, adding the contents of one ACCUMULATOR to the other in the 6800 microprocessor will either set or clear all but one of the bits (FLAGS) in the Condition Code Register. One or more of these bits can then be referenced in other operations as conditional tests, for example "If the Carry Bit is set, then branch to . . . and do the following . . ."

CONTROL. A composite of functions that keep all computer operations synchronized. These functions include CLOCK, HALT, ENABLE, INTERRUPT, READ, WRITE, RESET, STROBE, and SYNC.

CONTROL BUS. That part of the system bus structure that carries the synchronization signals. See CONTROL.

COPROCESSOR. A second CPU that shares the burden of processing activities. The 8087 Numeric Data Processor is a popular "number crunching" coprocessor, one for which provision exists in all of the IBM PC and PC-like computers.

CPU. Central processing unit, a term interchangeable in the microcomputer world with MICROPROCESSOR or MPU (main processing unit).

CRYSTAL. A thin slice of quartz cut to vibrate at a given frequency and used as the reference for the clock oscillator circuit. An oscillator is a circuit that generates a repetitive signal. The output of the oscillator is fed to the clock input of the microprocessor, which in turn generates the CLOCK or TIMING signals for the computer.

CYCLE. A CLOCK or TIMING pulse is a waveform consisting of a RISING EDGE, a plateau, a FALLING EDGE, and a trough. It can be pictured as a squared-off sine wave. One cycle of the pulse consists of the movement of the waveform from the zero point to the next zero point. See MACHINE CYCLE.

DATA. Digital information, bits, the representation in 1's and 0's of program, numeric, and text material. TIMING signals and POWER are not considered data.

DATA BUS. The electrical path for DATA signals or BIT streams.

DECODER. A circuit, usually built around a special-purpose decoder chip, which interprets a given package of signals and causes some action to be performed on the basis of that interpretation. Address decoders are used to assure that the right address is activated for a particular action. If the program means that a byte of data in address X is needed for some operation, the system must be able to reach address X on cue. The decoding system takes care of it.

DIRECT MEMORY ACCESS (DMA). A method of high-speed data transfer in which the data can be moved between system memory and peripheral devices (e.g., disk drives) without the need of CPU intervention and the need, therefore, to use the normal clock cycling time of the system. Transfer speed thus depends mainly on the speed of the memory chips and the peripheral. DMA is managed by a special IC called a Direct Memory Access Controller, of which the Intel 8237 is an example.

ENABLE. A signal that sets a chip to its READY state, or a chip function like READ to its operational state.

ENCODER. A circuit that generates a signal based on two or more input signals. A keyboard encoder, for example, produces a coded signal for each of the keys. The input for each code is derived from the position of the key in an X-Y (row-column) matrix as well as the mode (shifted, unshifted, graphics, control, etc.).

EXECUTE CYCLE. That part of an operational CYCLE when the computer performs an instruction. See FETCH CYCLE.

EXTERNAL STORAGE. Various means of storing data outside of the basic computer system. Currently, cassette and disk systems are the most common means of external storage. Bubble memory, which acts as a disk-drive substitute, is beginning to make its appearance on a commercial scale.

FETCH CYCLE. That part of an operational cycle when the computer gets an instruction from MEMORY. See EXECUTE CYCLE.

FIRMWARE. Program material stored permanently in ROM (read-only memory). Typically, this material includes the startup (boot) routines for the system. In some computers, a programming language may be stored as firmware. Firmware is really software in a chip as opposed to software on tape or disk or entered from the keyboard.

FLAG. STATUS bit. See also CONDITION CODE REGISTER.

GATE. Typically, a digital circuit with two or more inputs and a single output and operating according to the principles of boolean logic. Figure 4-1 is a truth table and a representation for a two-input AND gate and a two-input OR gate. See TRUTH TABLE for the logical configurations of the other gates used in computer design.

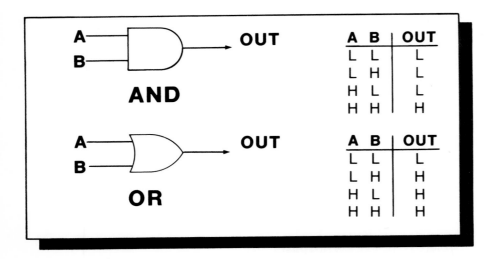

A	B	OUT
L	L	L
L	H	L
H	L	L
H	H	H

AND

A	B	OUT
L	L	L
L	H	H
H	L	H
H	H	H

OR

Fig. 4-1

HALT. One of the microprocessor CONTROL functions. A signal to the HALT input will cause the CPU to finish executing its current INSTRUCTION and then go into a standby condition, with no loss of data.

HANDSHAKING. Control signals that establish agreement between two components so that each can communicate with the other. In practical terms, the handshaking signals indicate that one component is ready to receive data while the other is ready to send data.

HEXADECIMAL. Base-16, a number base derived from the powers of sixteen. The virtual standard numbering system used by assembly language programmers. The hexadecimal ("hex") system uses sixteen digits, six of which are letters understood as numerals:

0 1 2 3 4 5 6 7 8 9 A B C D E F

In decimal terms, A = 10, B = 11, etc. However, 10 hex = 16 decimal. Why? Because we've gone to the second, or sixteens, column. Compare the tens column in decimal and the twos column in BINARY. FF hex = 255 decimal and 11111111 binary. The next hex number beyond FF is 100, which is equal to 256 decimal and 100000000 binary. Computer MEMORY MAPs are almost always numbered in hex.

HIGH-LEVEL LANGUAGE. A programming language like BASIC, Pascal, COMAL, Modula-2, ADA, C, LISP, Prolog, etc., not directly in touch with the CPU, that is, one that requires the programmer to know little or nothing about the machine-level operations of the system. A single statement in a high-level language may take a page of ASSEMBLY LANGUAGE instructions to accomplish, but the high-level-language programmer need know nothing about this. High-level languages are friendlier to use than assembly and machine language, but generally execute more slowly and require more memory. Current technology, however, increasingly trivializes these disadvantages.

HIGH-ORDER BYTE. The most significant byte of a 2-byte (16-bit) number, such as an ADDRESS. The LOW-ORDER BYTE is the least significant byte of that number. "Significance" refers to positional weight, with the leftmost digits having the highest numeric value.

INPUT/OUTPUT (I/O). The movement of data between, say, the microprocessor and the rest of the system. Or between the computer and its peripherals (printer, disk system, display monitor, etc.).

INSTRUCTION. A program step. See INSTRUCTION SET.

INSTRUCTION SET. The programming vocabulary native to a particular CPU; the ASSEMBLY LANGUAGE of the CPU.

INTEGRATED CIRCUIT (IC). A "chip," an ultra-small-scale collection of electronic circuits permanently formed on a substrate (e.g., silicon) and sealed in an enclosure designed for easy insertion into a PRINTED CIRCUIT BOARD (PCB). The enclosure is typically a dual-inline package (DIP), consisting of a body and two parallel rows of insertion pins. ICs may be mounted in sockets or directly on the circuit board. A microprocessor is a particularly complex IC, containing the equivalent of many thousands of transistors and other basic electronic components.

INTERFACE. The hardware (circuitry, cabling, etc.) and the software that provide for the communication between two electronic devices.

INTERRUPT. A break in the current CPU operations called by a program instruction or by a peripheral (e.g., the keyboard) to allow the CPU to tend to the special needs of the program or peripheral. Each CPU allows for several levels of interrupt. See MASKABLE INTERRUPT, NONMASKABLE INTERRUPT.

LABEL. In ASSEMBLY LANGUAGE, a name used to represent an ADDRESS in a particular program. When the program calls the label, the program goes to the address implied and executes the routine that begins at that address. In most computer systems, certain routines have been built into the system MONITOR (FIRMWARE) for use by any program or programmer wishing to use them.

LATCH. A circuit, built around a special IC, that holds data until the receiving circuit for the data is ready to accept it.

LEAST SIGNIFICANT DIGIT (LSD). The digit in the column with the lowest positional value; effectively, the rightmost digit; the least significant bit (LSB) in bitwise (BINARY) calculations. See MOST SIGNIFICANT DIGIT.

LOGIC. With respect to computer operations, logic refers to boolean relationships or "yes/no" logic as originally defined by the Anglo-Irish mathematician George Boole (1815-1864). Computers are more or less multilayered switching systems in which binary digits (BITs) of data move from decision point to decision point, the decisions dependent on the requirements of the operation and the nature of the decision point. These points are called GATEs, each of which is designed to perform a particular boolean function. The basic functions are AND and OR. NAND (Not-AND), NOR (Not-OR), XOR (exclusive-OR), and XNOR (exclusive-not-OR) are variations on the basics to allow for the full range of computer capabilities. See TRUTH TABLES for a picture of the logical inputs and outputs.

LOGICAL HIGH. Electrically, a signal from +2.0V to +5.0V. Such a signal is understood as 1 by digital circuitry.

LOGICAL LOW. Electrically, a signal from 0V to 0.8V. Such a signal is understood as 0 by digital circuitry.

LOW-ORDER BYTE. The least significant byte of a 2-byte (16-bit) number, such as an ADDRESS. See HIGH-ORDER BYTE.

MACHINE CODE. Binary or hexadecimal programming instructions. Strictly speaking, the computer circuitry understands nothing but binary digits (in the form of voltage levels). The first microcomputer was programmed in binary code by toggling rows of switches on the front panel of the machine.

MASK. A programming technique used, for example, to clear certain data bits in a given byte. Assuming that we need to clear (set to zeros) the least significant NYBBLE of the BYTE 10101010, we can write an ASSEMBLY LANGUAGE routine that imposes the bit pattern 11110000 on the byte in question via the AND instruction. Since the TRUTH TABLE for AND says that 1 AND 1 = 1, but 1 AND 0 = 0, the result of the operation will be:

$$10101010 \text{ AND } 11110000$$

$$\overline{}$$

$$10100000$$

The byte has thus been MASKed and the selected nybble cleared. The reason for wanting to do this can be explained only in terms of the program, but it might be necessary in order to perform a certain type of calculation or make a decision. If masking allows, say, a given bit to appear as a 1 rather than a 0, the program flow may need to be interrupted.

MASKABLE INTERRUPT. Certain interrupt requests to the CPU can be masked off via programming techniques as described under MASK. Interrupt masking sets a FLAG that disallows the interrupt. The interrupt request will be honored only after this flag has been reset. See NONMASKABLE INTERRUPT.

MEMORY. That part of a computer system where information (DATA) is stored. Memory may be volatile or permanent. Volatile memory, which is called RAM (random access memory), holds information only as long as the computer is turned on. Permanent memory, either in the form of FIRMWARE or EXTERNAL STORAGE, survives the absence of electrical power.

MEMORY MAP. A guide to the way a manufacturer has allocated the memory usage of a particular computer system. The term also applies to the allocation itself. A memory map specifies, for example, that user memory resides in a certain range of addresses, video memory in another range, system functions in yet another, and so on. The programmer must not try to preempt areas of memory that have been allocated for other than programming uses.

MICROCODE. The programming material built into the CPU that enables it (1) to perform certain internal functions and (2) to respond to the programming instructions that come to it from the outside. Microcode is part of the basic design of the microprocessor.

MICROPROCESSOR (CPU, MPU). The master chip in a microcomputer system. Most operations of the system take place directly under the control of the CPU/MPU (central processing unit or main processing unit). The development of the INTEGRATED CIRCUIT made it possible to package the CPU in a single device.

MNEMONICS. A mnemonic in general is a verbal memory jogger, usually in the form of an abbreviation of the parent word or phrase. In ASSEMBLY LANGUAGE, mnemonics are two- to four-letter abbreviations of OPCODE functions like "jump to a subroutine" (JSR) and "decrement the stack pointer" (DES). The mnemonics differ from microprocessor to microprocessor, though there are obvious similarities. One chip will remove a value from the STACK with a POP, another with a PUL. One will rotate bits to the left with RAL, another with RLA, another with ROL. And so it goes. In some cases the actions performed are identical, in some there are differences in detail if not in principle.

MOST SIGNIFICANT DIGIT (MSD). The high-order (leftmost) digit of a number, representing the greatest positional weight. MSD takes the form of MSB (most significant bit) in bitwise calculations. See LEAST SIGNIFICANT DIGIT.

MULTIPLEXER (MUX). A high-speed switching circuit that accepts data from several sources and combines it into a single bitstream, which ordinarily will be demultiplexed—that is, separated into its original constituents—at its destination. Sending DATA, ADDRESS, and CONTROL information on a single electrical pathway (BUS) exemplifies the practical use of multiplexing in a computer system. The LED (light-emitting diode) display of an electronic calculator is multiplexed, each segment of a number actually being turned on and off very rapidly, with no two segments lighted at the same instant. The effect is of a constantly lighted display. Multiplexing and timesharing are nearly synonymous.

NONMASKABLE INTERRUPT (NMI). A high-priority interrupt which when called cannot be MASKed off or even delayed. When NMI is called in a program, it gets the CPU's full attention. But it differs from the RESET (which is effectively the highest-priority nonmaskable interrupt) in that most of the transient values of the current program are left in place.

NUMBER BASE. The place-value system of numbers. In the decimal or base-10 system, each column to the left of the first number increases in value by a factor of ten. Thus base-10 is based on the powers of ten. Base-2 is based on the powers of two, and base-16 on the powers of sixteen. Adding a new place adds a power of the number base.

NYBBLE (NIBBLE). A half byte or four bits. The nybble is not widely used as a distinctive value, although it does occur in some assembly language programs.

OBJECT CODE. MACHINE CODE or program material in the language of the object, that is, the microprocessor. See SOURCE CODE.

OPCODE. An assemble language instruction. Each opcode consists of two hexadecimal digits and includes the ADDRESSING MODE where appropriate. Thus, the 6809 microprocessor has an instruction called LDA ("load data from memory into Accumulator A"). But this instruction can be carried out in any one of several addressing modes, the choice of which will be reflected in the actual opcode. So depending on whether the programmer desires direct, extended, immediate, or indexed addressing, LDA would be coded as 96, B6, 86, or A6. Since, however, the programmer would probably be using MNEMONICS rather than MACHINE CODE to write a program, the type of addressing will be indicated by another shorthand technique. A "load immediate A" would be achieved by using the mnemonic, a special symbol, and the value to be loaded: LDA #XX (where # indicates immediate addressing and XX is any byte in hexadecimal).

OPERAND. In programming, the datum being manipulated or operated on. The value placed in a register by an INSTRUCTION is the operand of the instruction. See OPERATOR.

OPERATOR. In programming, the manipulator of the OPERAND. In the example under MNEMONICS, LDA is the operator, the value being loaded is the operand.

OSCILLATOR. A circuit designed to generate a particular waveform at a particular frequency (or narrow range of frequencies). In a computer, the oscillator is crystal controlled and used as the reference for the CPU CLOCK.

PAGE. A block of memory addressed as an entity (as opposed to simply addressing individual addresses). Paging is commonly used in multiplaned video display programming.

PARALLEL COMMUNICATION. The transfer of data bytewise, so that 8 bits are sent over eight lines at the same time. This is the normal mode of data transfer within a computer system. It is also used as one means of data transfer between the computer and certain peripherals like printers and plotters. See SERIAL COMMUNICATION.

POINTER. The address of the next available address in memory space. All pointers are automatically updated to reflect memory use. A typical example is on the stack. Another example is the Instruction Pointer which, on an 8-bit chip, points to the next instruction that is to be executed.

POWER BUS. The electrical pathway in a computer over which the electrical power travels. Power should not be confused with signal, even though +5V typically appears on both the power and signal buses. Because signals lack current (amperage), they are incapable of supplying power. Power is a composite of voltage and current, the output of a power supply.

PRINTED CIRCUIT BOARD (PCB). A board made of copper which has been plated onto a substrate material like fiberglass-epoxy and etched according to the design requirements of the circuitry. The etching process removes all of the copper except where connections are needed. The board is drilled to accept electronic components (ICs, sockets, resistors, capacitors, etc.) and printed with parts designations.

QUEUE. A stream of data awaiting some action. Within the microprocessor, for example, there is a temporary storage area, a BUFFER, in which the bytes are formed into a queue to wait for the microprocessor to do something with them. A print queue is the stack of documents being printed.

RAM. Random access memory, the transient memory section of the computer. This section is built of ICs called RAMs, the most commonly used size of which is currently 64K. Since these chips are only 1-bit "wide," eight of them are required for 64 kilobytes (65,536 bytes) of memory. Strictly speaking, all memory in a computer is random access, whether in RAM or ROM. A better term for RAM would be read/write memory, as opposed to read-only memory (ROM). Of the two types of RAM, static (SRAM) and dynamic (DRAM), the latter is the more widely used because of its lower manufacturing cost and its lower power consumption. In order, however, for the DRAM to maintain its memory even while the comptuer is on, it must be constantly REFRESHed or repowered cyclically. A static RAM is fully powered all the time, hence the greater demand for system power. Data is stored in memory chips as minute electrical charges.

READ (RD). The microprocessor signal that specifies that data in memory should be accessed, that is, read.

REFRESH. An action required by DRAMs (see RAM) to maintain the data bits stored therein. The Z80 and Z8000 exemplify microprocessors with built-in refresh functions.

REGISTER. A temporary storage bin or holding tank for data in a microprocessor. In any given microprocessor, the registers go by an assortment of names depending on their function: accumulator, stack pointer, index register, program counter, and so on.

RESET (RST). The "ultimate" INTERRUPT short of turning off the computer. When the CPU's reset function is activated, the system is set to its startup state, zeroing the registers, although the data in memory will be left untouched.

ROM. Read-only memory. ROM chips are factory programmed and will retain their data even when the computer is turned off. ROMs are accessible for READ operations only; they cannot be written to. See FIRMWARE.

SERIAL COMMUNICATION. Data transfer in a stream of single bits. Modems and certain other peripheral devices use serial communication, usually following an interfacing standard called RS-232C. All else being equal, serial data transfer is approximately eight times slower than PARALLEL data transfer. Its advantage lies in the fact that serial interfacing can be accomplished using as few as two wires. Its disadvantage lies in its (relatively) slow speed and in disagreement among manufacturers on how the so-called RS-232C standard should be applied, resulting in many practical interfacing problems.

STACK. A section of memory set aside by the CPU for carrying on various operations. The stack pointer (SP) is a register that keeps track of stack activity. Since stacks usually grow from higher to lower memory, the SP decrements when data is added to the stack and increments when data is removed. One use of a stack is as a storage bin for data in various registers when an INTERRUPT is called. The CPU must make the data registers available for the operations that will go on during the interrupt, but the data that was in those registers must not be lost before the interrupt. Conceptually, a stack is like a pile of trays, with the last tray added being the first removed (LIFO—last-in-first-out). All CPU instruction sets provide for direct programming of the stack through pushes and pops (or pulls): PSH, POP, PUL.

STATUS REGISTER. See CONDITION CODE REGISTER and FLAGS.

STROBE. A HANDSHAKING signal used to indicate that there is valid data on the data bus.

SYNCHRONIZATION. The organization of CPU operations according to a strict TIMING sequence. See CONTROL.

TIMING. See CONTROL.

TRUTH TABLE. A table showing the boolean values of a particular logical pattern or a device. The basic patterns are AND and OR. These are elaborated into NAND, NOR, XOR, and XNOR. See Fig. 4-2 for the truth tables and logical symbols for each. See LOGIC.

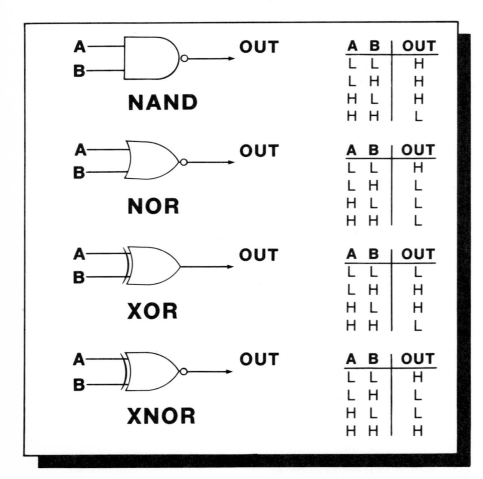

Fig. 4-2

VSLI. Very-large scale integration—the type of circuit integration used to create today's highly complex microprocessors.

WORD (COMPUTER). In the microcomputer world, a word is a coherent data string 16 bits (2 bytes) long. An ADDRESS, for example, is a computer word. A word in a natural language, by contrast, can be many computer words long, for each letter of a language word requires 1 byte of ASCII code.

WRITE (WR). A signal to the microporcessor that data on the bus is to be placed into (written to) memory.

ZERO PAGE. In page-oriented computer architecture, this is the first page. Commonly, this page of memory is reserved for system functions of various kinds.

Addressing Modes and Instructions

The preceding subsection provided a general introduction to the world of microprocessors. This subsection, before consideration of the popular microprocessor chips, will review addressing modes as well as the various categories of programming instructions, such as data movement, data alteration, arithmetic and logical functions, and so on.

The instruction sets provide for commands that move data bit by bit or in some cases two bits at a time in and out of memory and through the different registers in the microprocessor. It will seem as though the entire process is as mechanical as picking up a stick from one pile and putting it in another. This is, in fact, the case and it is what makes assembly language programming so efficient and elegant. It is here on the level of the actual circuitry that some of the most creative programming design can take place.

Microprocessor Instructions

The instruction set of a microprocessor can be categorized as follows, though there is nothing inevitable about the scheme.

1. Instructions that move data. Example (6502): LDA (load accumulator A). This instruction tells the CPU to put a byte of data into the general-purpose register known in this chip as ACCUMULATOR A.

2. Instructions that change data. Example (6800): DECA (decrement accumulator A). Each application of this instruction will subtract one from the number in the accumulator.

3. Instructions that shift and rotate data. Example (Z80): RLC (rotate left). Shift and rotate instructions allow the programmer to examine individual data bits, using any one for a test or flag in a given operation. Shift instructions push the bits one position left or right without regard to the end bit. Rotate instructions move the end bit to the opposite end while shifting the other bits over one to accommodate the move, no bits being "lost" in the process.

4. Arithemtic and logic instructions. Example (8080): SUBB (subtract the contents of the B register from the contents of the A register). Example (8086): ORA (boolean OR 2 bytes, the current byte in register A and the other in memory).

5. Control transfer instructions. Example (68000): BCC (branch if carry clear). Since the instruction will be carried out only if the carry flag has been cleared, this exemplifies a conditional transfer of control. The instructions in this group are designed to move program execution from its current track and transfer control to some other part of the program. And while many instructions depend on various tests, others are unconditional, such as JMP (jump to some other part of the program—no conditions imposed).

6. Status, flag, or condition code instructions. Example (6800): SEI (set interrupt mask). This instruction allows the programmer to prevent the CPU from accepting interrupt requests. The mask bit can be cleared with the CLI instruction.

7. String manipulation instructions. Example (8086/8088): MOVS (move string). The availability of a set of string-handling instructions makes a number of programming tasks a good deal easier than they would otherwise be, for the programmer can deal with blocks of contiguous and related data rather than individual bytes. These kinds of instructions are not found in the the 8-bit microprocessors.

8. Test instructions. Example (6809): TSTA (test the contents of accumulator A to determine if positive, negative, or zero). There are numerous ways to test and compare data in assembly language, but the test instructions allow for quick checks that serve to update the condition code register without changing anything else.

9. Stack pointer and index register instructions. Example (Z80): LDSP (load stack pointer). With this and similar instructions the programmer can use the 16-bit registers in an 8-bit chip in pretty much the same fashion as the normal 8-bit registers.

10. CPU control instructions. Example (8080): HLT (halt current operations). Example (6502): NOP (do nothing for a bit—wait until the next instruction). This group of instructions allows the programmer to exert direct control over the microprocessor, even to the point of resetting the system.

Addressing Modes

A computer program resides in memory and uses areas in memory to perform its activities. Each location in memory has an address and is thus unique. Two different pieces of data cannot occupy the same address at the same time. Nor can the same address exist in different places in the usable memory of a given computer. The way in which memory is managed looms large in the programming process. A particular operation can be addressed in different ways to achieve different results. Some operations allow a considerable variety of addressing techniques; others do not.

To provide a simple conceptual framework for what we mean by addressing mode, consider the difference between sending a package by fourth-class mail and by private delivery service. In both cases the package will get to its destination, but there will be differences in time, condition, and paperwork. Or contrast mailing a letter through normal channels and giving it to a friend to deliver by hand. Or mailing a letter to a person at that person's home address, P.O. box number, and business address. Although the end result will be the same, the actual addresses and route will be be different. One's reasons for picking one approach over another in a given case will also be different.

In computer programming, an address is an identity, a label, a location. In order for data to be read from memory or transferred to memory, or manipulated in any way, it must be addressed; that is, the correct piece of data must be identified—otherwise, chaos. Let's assume that you want to send data to a certain port, or I/O doorway. The data must be addressed as well as the port itself. Addressing errors will result in program errors. Fortunately, the programmer does not have to be concerned with every detail of addressing, as will be seen.

Examination of the instruction set of any microprocessor will reveal that a range of addressing modes is available for a number of the instructions, the actual opcode specifying the addressing method. For example, in the 6809 instruction set, LDD (load accumulator A from memory, 2 bytes) can be represented by any one of four opcodes (DC, FC, CC, or EC) depending on whether the programmer specifies direct, extended, immediate, or indexed addressing for this instruction. Which mode is chosen derives from the nature of the programming task at hand.

At the heart of most lines of assembly language programming code lie the operator (opcode) and the operand. The opcode tells the CPU what to do and the operand tells the CPU where to do it or what to do it to. The operand, sometimes called the argument, identifies the data, registers, and/or locations in memory where the opcode will operate. As it happens, some instructions require no operand, which means that the addressing mode is inherent in the instruction itself. The INC (increment accumulator) instruction is 1-byte long and takes no operand. When INC is executed, no additional addressing information is needed because the instruction carries its own implied or inherent address, namely, that of the accumulator itself. Let's explore these addressing concepts further.

Every instruction must go through two stages, a fetch and an execute. In terms of machine cycles or clock periods, the fetch takes one, and the execute takes one or more. An inherent or implied addressing instruction like INC or HLT (halt) takes a single machine cycle during the execution stage. Why? Because there is no operand, no address added to the opcode. In the case of INC, the accumulator is at once the operator and the operand. In the case of HLT, the CPU HALT line is at once the operator and the operand. Two-byte, and longer, instructions, on the contrary, take two, even three or more machine cycles during the execution stage. The more cycles, obviously, the longer the actual time it takes for an instruction to be carried out. Programmers like to be parsimonious with time, but the more prodigal addressing modes have their advantages in allowing for flexibility in program design.

Inherent or Implied Addressing. CPU action: fetch instruction, decode instruction, execute instruction. Inherent or implied addressing is a 1-byte instruction that may take as few as two machine cycles or as many as twelve or more. Typical inherent-mode instructions (generalized) are: add accumulators, compare accumulators, clear carry bit, clear or set a status bit, decrement a register, halt operations, increment a register, do nothing (no operation, NOP), return from and interrupt, return from a subroutine, subtract one register from another, software interrupt call, move the contents of one register to another, wait for an interrupt.

Register or Accumulator Addressing. This can be thought of as a special case of inherent addressing, the difference being only that the instructions apply to those instructions which transfer, clear, or complement a register. Rotate, shift, push, pop, increment, and decrement are typical accumulator addressing instructions.

Immediate Addressing. CPU action: fetch instruction, decode instruction, get operand, perform specified operation. A 2-byte instruction, typically requiring two machine cycles. What happens here is that the instruction tells the CPU to do something to the data in the memory location that appears as the operand of the instruction. Thus LDA $7F says "load accumulator A with the data at address 7F." The $ indicates immediate-mode addressing, and the instruction jargon is properly "load A immediate." The commonest immediate-mode instructions are those that load the accumulator.

Direct Addressing. At first glance, direct addressing looks like immediate addressing. But it isn't, because the operand in this case is really the address of the operand. CPU action: fetch instruction, decode instruction, get operand address, decode address, get operand, perform specified operation. Direct address opcodes are 2-byte instructions which typically require three machine cycles. A typical instruction might ADD the contents of a location in memory (given by the second byte of the instruction, the "operand" byte) to the contents of an accumulator and put the result of the addition in the accumulator. Where immediate addressing works well with a value that will be used by only one instruction in the program, direct addressing is handy when the same value will be used by various instructions during the course of the program. The value is simply stored somewhere and accessed for manipulation as the program demands. Direct addressing is used with arithmetic and logic instructions, and register loading and storing instructions.

Extended Addressing. Extended address is direct addressing with the whole address space available because the "operand" part of the instruction is 2 bytes long. These bytes are the high and low bytes of a 16-bit slice of memory, in which will be stored the actual operand. Remember that with 16 bits, one has access to the entire addressing capability of the microprocessor, whereas with 8 bits, only 256 locations are accessible. CPU action: fetch instruction, decode instruction, get and decode high-order and low-order address bytes, get operand, perform specified operation. These 3-byte instructions typically require four machine cycles. Extended addressing is used the same way as direct addressing.

Indexed Addressing. Indexing allows the programmer to set up pointers or indexes to various locations in memory such that the index register will take its pointer address and add it to the offset value given in the instruction (as the "operand") to reach a desired memory address, where the data sought will be found. The index register can be used as an incrementing or decrementing counter and repeatedly referenced through a program loop. CPU action: fetch instruction, decode instruction, get address from index register, decode address, get offset, decode offset, get operand, perform operation required. A 2-byte indexed instruction will usually take a minimum of five machine cycles. Any instruction that uses an operand stored in memory can be indexed. And since the index register of, for example, an 8-bit microprocessor is 16 bits wide, it can point to any location in memory. Load, store, add, subtract, and, or, compare, etc., are the types of instructions indexed.

Relative Addressing. If the programmer wants the program to step off to a new location in memory a certain number of addresses from the present location, the instruction can be used in the relative addressing mode, in which the "operand" is an offset of X bytes forward or backward from the present location. When the program gets to where it has been sent by this offset, it continues according to the requirements of the instruction. CPU action: fetch instruction, decode instruction, get displacement value (from -126 bytes to $+129$ bytes), calculate address, go to new address. This 2-byte instruction typically takes four machine cycles. Branch routines (branch if equal, branch if not equal, branch if zero, branch to subroutine, etc.) use relative addressing.

Register Indirect Addressing. Some microprocessors provide for the storage of memory location in a pair of 8-bit registers (to allow for addressing the full 8-bit chip memory addressing capability). The CPU action is similar to that of immediate addressing. The "operand" will be the name of the register pair in which the actual operand will be found, thus LDA BC, where BC designates a pair of 8-bit registers. Load, store, arithmetic, and logic instructions are the common types of instructions used in register indirect addressing.

Other addressing modes exist, but for the most part these are variations on or combinations of those already discussed. The existence of addressing-mode options considerably expands the basic instruction set of a given microprocessor.

Condition (Status) Codes

The condition code or status register in a typical 8-bit microprocessor is an 8-bit register with six meaningful bits. The Motorola 6800 will serve as a representative example (Fig. 4-3).

```
: - : - : H : I : N : Z : V : C : code
: 7 : 6 : 5 : 4 : 3 : 2 : 1 : 0 : bit
```

6800 Condition Code Register

Bit 0   C (Carry, borrow)
Bit 1   V (2's complement overflow)
Bit 2   Z (Zero Indicator)
Bit 3   N (Negative Indicator)
Bit 4   I (Interrupt mask)
Bit 5   H (Half carry)

Fig. 4-3

The terminology is not universal, though the functions are essentially the same from chip to chip. The microprocessor data sheets always include (1) a description of the condition code register and (2) an indication of the effect of each instruction on the condition codes.

These condition code bits act as flags or status indicators, one or more of which are set (1) or cleared (0) according to the particular instruction being executed. For instance, the instruction ABA (add the contents of accumulator B to the contents of accumulator A and place the result in accumulator A) affects the condition code register as follows:

H   Set if carry from bit 3, else cleared.
I   Not affected.
N   Set if most significant bit of result is set, else cleared.
Z   Set if all bits of result are cleared, else cleared.
V   Set if a 2's complement overflow occurred as a result of operation, else cleared.
C   Set if there was a carry from most significant bit of result, else cleared.

The flags keep the CPU informed regarding the state of affairs at any given moment. The programmer can access this information for his or her own purposes, or even change it. All of the 6800 branching instructions hinge on the state of one or more of the condition codes, though the execution of a branch has no effect on the codes. A frequently used branch is BNE (branch if not equal), which looks at the Z bit and will cause the program to branch only if the Z bit is clear (0). The program may need a valid data bit for some operation (perhaps a start bit for a communication interface). If the data required hasn't appeared yet (determined with a test of some sort, perhaps an AND), the Z bit will be clear. Only when it is set can the program continue along its main track.

Hardware and Software Interrelationships

In order for a program to accomplish its purposes, it must "force" the CPU to perform a number of operations. The program is a set of instructions to the CPU, the actions of the CPU are physical (electrical) events. But in order for the software instructions to become hardware operations, they must be understood in hardware terms. So when the user presses a key on the keyboard, the user's intention is manifested first as the mechanical action of a key being depressed. The key is really an electrical switch. The closing of the switch causes the generation of an electrical signal. This signal is routed according to the design of the computer system to that part of the computer circuitry that has been set up to act on the signal. That action depends on information that has been wired into the circuitry in the form of a block of memory containing the 1's and 0's that, when they appear to the CPU as packets of volts/no-volts, it can interpret for its own use. The transmutation of stored data ("switches" set on or off) into electrical signals is made possible by the existence of electrical power, for as soon as the power is discontinued, the stored data returns to its potentially though not actually useful state.

The programmer's ideas are expressed as strings of written instructions, which in turn are converted into electrical signals that cause the CPU to act in certain ways. If, for example, the chip designer has configured the internal circuitry of the CPU to respond to an interrupt request when the IRQ line is pulled low, a programmed request for an interrupt must be converted from its software state to its hardware state (electrical signals) in order for the CPU to act on the request. A software interrupt, then, is no different from a hardware interrupt at the point at which something actually happens. A hardware interrupt is one that might come from a peripheral device like a keyboard. When a key is struck, the first thing that happens is a hardware IRQ from the keyboard logic circuitry. Interrupts can be prioritized so that some will take precedence over others.

On the programming side of the equation, the written instructions become usable machine code through the operation of a program called an assembler, the task of which is to convert or translate the instructions into binary digits (bits) representing the addresses, operators, and operands that constitute meaningful information for the CPU, based on the microcode designed into the microprocessor. On the hardware side, the instructions in their binary form are streams of electrical pulses that activate the microprocessor's internal switches, i.e., the transistors that make up a large part of the CPU circuitry. The system monitor (not the display monitor), found in one or more ROMs on the main computer board, acts in collusion with the CPU and the program being executed, for the monitor contains its own preprogrammed subroutines that the programmer can draw on in the programming efforts. These routines occupy fixed locations in the memory space of the computer and are "on call" at any time. In this sense they are no different from any other material stored in memory. But because they are a permanent part of the system hardware, they do not disappear when the system is turned off.

The relationship between hardware and software is so intimate that at some levels it is difficult to say where one ends and the other begins. By way of illustration, let us briefly consider the interface between the CPU and a peripheral device like a serial printer. A computer with a serial port will have as a part of its hardware a circuit built around an IC called a UART (universal asynchronous receiver/transmitter). This can be thought of as a specialized microprocessor, the primary function of which is to convert the parallel signals that the CPU itself generates into serial signals that the peripheral understands. A small program called a driver suffices to initialize the UART, that is, activate it and set it up for the particular communication protocols required. However, in the absence of a UART, one can create a port with a few inexpensive parts and write a "software UART," an example of which occurs further on in this section. In other words, through certain programming techniques, one can contrive phantom hardware capable of precisely the same things as actual hardware. There is an obvious trade-off: with hardware, very little programming; without hardware, a sizable amount of programming.

Refer to Section 7: Hardware for a more detailed and explicit examination of microcomputer hardware design.

Glossary: Assembly Language Programming Terms

ADDRESS. A location in memory. Part of the memory space of a computer is open for general use, and part is reserved for the computer's own internal operations. Termed a memory map, the partitioning of memory in a given computer is a fixed characterstic of the computer.

ARRAY. A matrix or "map" of similar data ITEMs, such as the telephone numbers for a given city.

ASSEMBLER. A program for converting assembly language SOURCE CODE into executable OBJECT CODE (also called machine code).

CODE. (1) Instructions to the CPU expressed in the conventions of the programming language being used (see SOURCE CODE). (2) Those instructions in the digital form "understood" by the CPU (see MACHINE CODE and OBJECT CODE). Turning a program concept or design into actual lines of assembly language, BASIC, LISP, etc., is called coding. The program designer isn't necessarily the same person as the program coder.

COMMENT. Documentary material written into a program to explain the various operations. Commented code is much easier to debug and modify than uncommented code.

COMPILER. A program for turning high-level-language source code into executable OBJECT CODE. Fortran, Pascal, Modula-2, Ada, and C exemplify compiled languages. Compiled versions of BASIC exist (e.g., CB-80), but BASIC was designed as an interactive or INTERPRETER-based language. Program modifications to a compiled program can be made only by re-editing the source code and re-compiling the program. Program modifications to an interpreted program can be made interactively without the need of the intermediate step(s) necessary in compiling. A compiled program, however, will execute faster than an interpreted one and will use less memory—all else being equal. The trade-off is between ease of coding (interpeted language) and efficiency of execution (compiled languages).

CROSS-ASSEMBLER. A program that can convert the SOURCE CODE written in the instruction set of one microprocessor into the object code of another microprocessor. Thus, one can write an assembly language program in 6800 source code and cross-assemble it to run on a 6502-based computer. Cross-assembled programs may not run very well, or even at all.

DATA. At the CPU level, a datum is a binary digit (1 or 0); data are streams or strings of binary digits. At the programmer's level, data can be typed with respect to real-world values into numeric (integer, real, single-precision or multiple-precision, etc.), boolean (representing tests for "true" or "false"), string (ASCII or alphanumeric), and array (matrix-like patterns of numeric or string data). Structured systems of data constitute most business programming applications. A database management system (DBMS), for example, uses a range of data types. See ARRAY, ITEM, LIST.

DEBUGGER. A program consisting of a number of subprograms for examining MACHINE CODE and modifying it. A typical debugging program will include a dump routine for displaying segments of a program in hexadecidmal digits, which represent the instructions written by the programmer. Any of these digits can then be changed as necessary to correct some error or bug in the program.

DISASSEMBLER. A program for returning MACHINE CODE (OBJECT CODE) to SOURCE CODE. Any executable program can be disassembled into the string of instructions that represent the intention of the programmer, even if the program was not originally written in assembly language. A Pascal program in its compiled (object code) form can be disassembled into assembly language as easily as if it had originally been written in assembly language.

DOCUMENTATION. See COMMENT.

FLOWCHART. A formal schematizing of the logical structure of a program or program segment. Several flowchart formats are in common use, but the programmer can easily contrive his or her own. The programmer should use any format that he or she feels comfortable with.

INTERPRETER. A program that allows one to write immediately executable high-level language code (e.g., BASIC, Forth, Comal). The interpreter, which resides in memory during programming and program execution, converts the program to OBJECT CODE as it is entered and parses each line, checking for SYNTAX (correct spelling and use of the keywords of the language).

ITEM. A single datum in a database management system file. A ZIP code would be considered a data item.

LABEL. In assembly language, the first field in a program line. Labels are optional, but when they are used the assembler replaces the label with the address of the routine introduced by the label. Thus, a routine that the programmer has labelled, say, COUNT, can be called in the program by using COUNT elsewhere as an OPERAND: BRA COUNT (branch to COUNT).

LIFE CYCLE. With repect to programming, the life cycle consist of these stages: (1) recognition and definition of problem for programming; (2) design of program; (3) coding of program; (4) translation (assembly or compilation) of program; (5) testing, debugging, and modification of program; and (6) using and upgrading (maintenance) of program.

LINKER (LINKING LOADER). A program for combining program modules into a monolithic structure. It is convenient to write and assemble subroutines which are later combined into the target program. The linker performs that combination function and allows programs to be written in separate modules, at separate times, and even by separate programmers.

LIST. A one-dimensional ARRAY of DATA items arranged in alphabetic or numeric order.

MACHINE CODE. (1) Binary digits, the only "language" understood by the CPU. (2) Hexadecimal digits, the numeric representations of the instruction set of the microprocessor.

MACRO. A segment of code that can be repeatedly called during the execution of a program. The existence of a library of macros increases the efficiency with which the programmer can write a program.

MACRO-ASSEMBLER. An assembler that includes a "pre-processor" able to assemble MACROs as packaged components within a given program.

MENU. A selection of options offered on the display screen of a computer. Choice of an item often results in the appearance on the screen of a sub-menu, offering a more specialized range of choices than the master menu. A menu-drive program is one in which every option is accessible to the user via item selection from the appropriate menu.

MNEMONIC. In assembly language, a "memory jogger" representing MACHINE CODE. In 6809 assembly language, BSR is the mnemonic for "branch to a subroutine" and stands for the machine code 8D hexadecimal or binary 10001101.

MODULAR PROGRAMMING. A "small-bite" approach to program design—in contrast with the monolithic or "large-hunk" approach. The rationale behind modular programming is the sound notion that one can create and control small segments of a program a lot more easily and more reliably than one can create and control a single large program structure. Certain programming languages (Pascal, Modula-2, and Forth, among others) have been designed with modularity in mind. BASIC, on the other hand, allows for large, unwieldy programs of no easily recognizable structure, although one can with care write a kind of modularized BASIC.

OBJECT CODE. The machine-specific binary code required by the microprocessor. SOURCE CODE is converted to machine code by programs called ASSEMBLERs (for assembly language) and COMPILERs (for high-level languages like Pascal and Fortran).

OPCODE. In assembly language, the instruction, in the form of a MNEMONIC, that tells the CPU to perform some action. DECA tells the CPU to decrement the value in the accumulator. In MACHINE CODE, the opcodes are expressed as hexadecimal digits, which, in turn, represent binary digits.

OPERAND. In assembly language, the information that appears in the operand field of an instruction. When used, this field follows the OPCODE field, and contains the data on which the OPCODE will operate. BRA COUNT (branch to COUNT) uses COUNT (a LABEL elsewhere in the program) as an operand.

OPERATOR. Effectively the same as OPCODE. The operator performs an operation on the OPERAND.

PROGRAMMING. The art of solving computer-soluble problems with sets of instructions to the computer expressed in any one of a number of formalized systems known as programming languages.

PSEUDO CODE. Generalized programming code used as a guide to the logical structure of a program. Pseudo code cannot be run. Rather, it can be thought as of preprogramming, the purpose of which is to sketch in the steps that the program under development should follow. A pseudo-coded program can usually be translated into the true code of a programming language.

PSEUDO INSTRUCTION (PSEUDO OPERATION). In assembly language, an instruction directed to the ASSEMBLER rather than the CPU. EQUate, for example, is a pseudo instruction, telling the assembler that A EQUates to B (where A is typically a LABEL and B is typically a value). ORG (origin), another example of a pseudo operation, tells the assembler the starting address of the program being assembled.

SOURCE CODE. Program code written in the vocabulary of the programming language. In assembly language programming, the source code is written on a text editor like any ordinary ASCII file.

STRUCTURED PROGRAMMING. More of a buzz word than any definable process or set of unambiguously applicable principles. Any program has some sort of structure. What adherents of structured programming attempt to do is to write programs that are modular, clearly documented, and organized as rationally as possible. See MODULAR PROGRAMMING.

SYNTAX. The standardized usage required by each programming language, for example, correct spelling and proper arrangement of keywords.

Microprocessor Programming

A computer program, whether in assembly language or a high-level language, is a formalized, codified representation of the intent of the programmer. This intent presumably arises from the desire to solve a problem of a type that is soluble with a computer. And while higher-level languages are machine independent, that is, transportable with relative ease from computer to computer, each microprocessor has its own instruction set served by its own version of assembly language. Thus, the source code of a program in standard Pascal is, in a certain sense, universal. That is, it can be compiled for virtually any computer. But an assembly language program written for, say, a 6502 is written explicitly in the "native language" (instruction set) of the 6502 and cannot be successfully assembled by the assembler for another microprocessor. There are cross-assemblers available for certain microprocessors that will take the assembly source code of one chip and generate from it the object code of another chip. The results are not always ideal.

Despite the relentless logic of a computer, program design is an art, not a science, and just as there are innumerable ways of representing some bit of reality artistically, there are innumerable solutions to any non-trivial programming problem. It is possible to speak not only of programming technique but of programming style. Each programmer will in time develop a unique style of programming, derivative or original, but distinctive. In the last analysis there are few rules, other than those related to the restrictions of the programming language, that can be laid down as rigid prescriptions, proscriptions, or even invariable guidelines. The good programmer seeks "elegant" solutions to problems, that is, solutions that maximize the resources of the language and minimize memory use and execution time, while fully solving the problem at hand. This solution must include the entire range of activities relevant to the aims of the program realized in ways which minimize user anxiety.

To create a program, the programmer must of course master the assembly language selected. This means that the programmer must know the instruction set—its strengths and limitations—and how to actually set up the program. The first step should be a careful study of a book on the programming of the microprocessor in question.

With a particular problem in mind, the programmer will next write a scenario, a paragraph or two outlining the nature of the problem and a generalized solution based on the programmer's understanding of the topic. For example, if the problem is to write a program that will enable a company that provides armored-car services to keep track of its operations, the programmer will have to learn the nature of these operations and outline a clear picture of the paper content and paper flow which the computer will now be asked to manage. The scenario should cover this information in broad terms.

From the scenario the programmer proceeds to an outline, which is a step-by-step statement of the operations, arranged in meaningful packages—perhaps hourly, daily, weekly, monthly, quarterly, and yearly operations—with their interrelationships and subdivisions indicated. This outline is a kind of informal flowchart.

The outline can now be turned into a master flowchart and a set of subsidiary, more specific, flowcharts. The master flowchart establishes the program framework (see Fig. 4-4), whereas the subsidiary flowcharts specify the logic of each segment of the program. The programmer need not, however, create a formal flowchart. Indeed, some programmers feel that this mechanistic approach to program design detracts from the artistic and intuitive side of programming. But all programmers agree on the need for some kind of paper-and-pencil planning.

Many programmers move from flowcharts to pseudo code, which might be called the script of the program. Pseudo coding allows the programmer to work out the details of the program design without yet having to worry about applying the actual instruction set. It should be remembered that an assembly language program is an explicit set of instructions. Every operation of the CPU must be stated. If one tries to leap from flowcharts directly to assembly language coding, one can get bogged down rather quickly. With pseudo code, the programmer can work in plain language until the fine details of the program are clearly organized. From pseudo code to assembly code is not a large step. Also, the pseudo code provides the basic shape of a program free of the peculiarities of any given language. At some later time, the programmer might decide to rewrite the program in C or Modula-2 or some other high-level language. It's far easier to do this from pseudo code than from assembly code.

To illustrate pseudo code, let us assume that the programmer wishes to prompt the user for a response to items on a menu:

SCREEN DISPLAY

1. Journal
2. General Ledger
3. Accounts Payable
4. Accounts Receivable
5. Inventory

Please select by number.
PROCEDURE: Master-menu choice
IF choice is 1, 2, 3, 4, or 5 THEN
        CALL PROCEDURE Sub-menu

ELSE
    No operation. Wait for proper selection
ENDIF
END Master-menu choice
PROCEDURE: Sub-menu
    .

    .

    .

The advantages of pseudo coding as a technique in program design can easily be seen. These pre-programs serve as informal flowcharts as well as guides to the control structures and other operational details required by the final program.

With the program now pre-coded, the programmer turns to the given instruction set. The task is to translate pseudo code into operational code. Thus, if the pseudo code has specified a delay of some sort, this must now be worked out with an appropriate set of instructions that will provide the delay time needed. One solution might be to lead a register with a value and use a loop to decrement the value to zero. When zero appears in the register, a test routine reports the fact and the loop ends. Or the programmer can increment a register to a specified value, or use NOPs (no operations). There are almost always a number of alternative programming paths to take to a given goal.

By way of summary, here is a list of programming precepts:

1. Identify the problem and establish its limits with respect to (a) computer equipment available, (b) budget (time and money), (c) range of tasks necessary for software to perform, and (d) users. Don't try to design one program to do every possible job. Programming effort increases with the length and complexity of the program.
2. Design the program modularly. Avoid monolithic programming.
3. Pre-program in pseudo code. Pseudo coding should be in plain language and documented in detail. Use standard control structure terms (IF-THEN-ELSE, DO-WHILE, etc.) to universalize the code and make it easy to translate into an actual programming language.
4. Be simple and direct. If a choice must be made between operational efficiency on the one hand and coding simplicity and directness on the other, opt for the latter.
5. Try to avoid unconditional branches and jumps. Placing conditions on branches and jumps helps keep the program from getting lost.
6. Use macros and library functions (pre-packaged routines) to ease the programming task. A variety of programming libraries are available commercially.
7. Test modularly. As each section of the program is written, assemble and test it.
8. Document heavily. Ideally, every line of code should be commented.
9. Design the program to trap the inevitable user errors. Examples: allow the program to accept upper- or lowercase entries. Lock out all but the pertinent keys for a particular kind of input. Allow a program segment to execute only after an "acceptance prompt" ("You have entered $12.95. Is this amount correct? Please type Y to accept or N to change.")
10. Design programs which can be read "narratively" from beginning to end. This is called top-down programming and is one of the major elements of structured programming.

11. Consider every program a draft that needs revision. There are no perfect programs. Every program of appreciable size will reveal its bugs eventually.

12. To get a program to work, violate any programming rule, precept, or principle.

The routine that follows is a software UART for an RS-232 interface. The assumptions are 8-bit data word, 1 start bit, and 1 stop bit. The baud rate is a dummy value. The actual number will depend on the clock speed of the computer. The routine given is meant to receive rather than transmit data.

Software UART (6800 Assembly Language)

Note that all digits are hexadecimal, indicated by the $ symbol. The # symbol represents Immediate Addressing mode. Address operands are dummy values (xxxx). This program runs on any 6800 CPU computer.

SERIAL INTERFACE RECEIVER

```
LDX $xx00
    ;  Load a starting address into Index Register. This address is a
    ;  hex number ending in 00. The last two digits (00) will be tested at
    ;  the end of the program.

START SEI
    ;  Set Interrupt to enable CPU to act on an input from I/O port.

    ;  The start bit (STBIT) routine begins at the STBIT label.

STBIT  LDAA $xxxx
    ;  Load Accumulator A from I/O port. This instruction begins the
    ;  search for a valid start bit (namely, O).

ANDA #$01
    ;  AND the byte in Accumulator A with 1 to determine if we do
    ;  indeed have a valid start bit (0). AND is a boolean operation. If
    ;  we have a 1 in the LSD position, an AND 1 will result in a 1 (1 AND
    ;  1 = 1)—not what we need here. ANDing sets or clears the Z
    ;  bit.

BNE STBIT
    ;  Branch if Not Equal (to 0) to beginning of the STBIT routine.
    ;  BNE actually tests the Z bit of the Condition Code Register. It will
    ;  have been set or cleared as a result of the AND instruction
    ;  above.

BSR HBIT
    ;  Branch to Subroutine named HBIT (half bit), for timing (baud
    ;  rate) purposes. A half bit is half the time value of a full bit. This
    ;  "bit splitting" assures us that the program will count the data
    ;  bits correctly by starting the count in the middle of a pulse
    ;  instead of at the rising or falling edge, which might cause mis-
    ;  timing. Altogether, the program provides for a 1.5-bit-delay
    ;  cycle plus a very brief hesitation (one NOP).
```

LDAA $xxxx
;   Load Accumulator A again. This is a redundant operation just to
;   play it safe.

ANDA #$01
;   Ditto.

BNE STBIT
;   Ditto.

BSR FBIT
;   Branch to Subroutine FBIT (full bit) for the rest of timing re-
;   quired. FBIT provides the value needed for the particular
;   baud rate.

LDAA #$08
;   Load a bit-count value into Accumulator A. Since we are as-
;   suming an 8-bit data word, we want to count down from 8.

PSHA
;   Push this counter value (now in Accumulator A) onto the Stack
;   for use later on.

LDAA #$00
;   Load a number into Accumulator A. We'll need 00 a little later.

PSHA
;   Push the contents of Accumulator A onto the Stack. When we
;   pull the 00 from the Stack, the counter value (8) will appear at
;   the top, ready for use.

;   The routine labeled DATA actually gathers the bytes being
;   input to the computer from an I/O port.

DATA LDAA $xxxx
;   Load Accumulator with the data byte that just came through the
;   I/O port.

ANDA #$01
;   AND 1 with the contents of Accumulator A to set or clear Z bit (as
;   above).

RORA
;   Rotate the bits in Accumulator A to put the first data bit into C of
;   the Condition Code Register. This is the normal effect of a
;   Rotate. It's necessary to Rotate Right in order to move the data
;   bits to their correct final position, with the least significant digit
;   at the right and the most significant digit at the left.

PULA
;   Pull the number on the top of the Stack and put it into Ac-
;   cumulator A. This is the second number that was pushed onto
;   the Stack earlier (00).

RORA
;   Rotate Accumulator A to move bit to MSD position (leftmost).

PULB

; Pull the next number (08, the bit counter) from the Stack and put
; it into Accumulator B.

DECB

Decrement B (by one). This leaves 07 in the Accumulator. When 00
; is reached, the incoming data is complete.

BEQ DONE

; Branch if Equal to subroutine DONE. BEQ tests the Z bit, caus-
; ing the program to branch if the Z bit is set (1). The DEC instruc-
; tion sets or clears the Z bit. The 00 left at last application of DEC
; resulted in the Z bit's being set.

PSHA

; Push the contents of Accumulator A (the full data byte) onto the
; Stack. After DATA has cycled eight times, the incoming data
; byte is complete and must be saved.

BSR FBIT

; Branch to Subroutine FBIT for timing purposes.

LDAA $xxxx

; Load Accumulator A from I/O at address xxxx. (See start of
; program.)

ANDA #$01

; Test for valid stop bit, which should be a 1. (0 to start, 1 to end.)
; This will be the tenth bit in total: 1 start bit, 8 data bits, and 1
; stop bit.

BEQ FMERR

; Branch if Equal to subroutine called FMERR (framing error).
; The AND in the preceding instruction will clear the Z bit (if there
; is a proper stop bit) and set it if not. In pseudo code: IF stop bit =
; 1 THEN set Z bit to 0, ELSE set Z bit to 1 and branch to Fram-
; ing Error.

PSHB

; Push the bit counter value back onto the Stack from Accumu-
; lator B. Ready to count the next data bit.

PSHA

; Push data bit onto Stack from Accumulator A. One more bit on
; the way to eight.

BRA DATA

; Branch to Subroutine DATA, (i.e., this one) to pick up the next
; bit. DATA is a loop routine under the control of the counter.
; When the counter has gone from 8 to 0, the program leaves
; DATA for awhile, to return when the next data byte starts to
; enter.

; Start of Subroutine DONE, which saves the data byte.

DONE   PSHA
        ; Push the data byte now in Accumulator A onto the Stack to
        ; save it.

        PULA
        ; Pull the data byte off the Stack.

        PULA
        ; Two pushes need two pulls — the Stack was pushed in the
        ; DATA routine and it needs a matching pull to clear it.

        STAA X
        ; Store the data byte now in Accumulator A at the address in the
        ; Index Register set at start of program.

        INX
        ; Increment Index Register to next address.

        CPX #$xx00
        ; Compare the contents of the Index Register with the contents of
        ; the last address in the program. This address must always end
        ; in 00. See beginning of program.

        BNE STBIT
        ; Branch if Not Equal to STBIT routine. The preceding instruction
        ; (CPX) will have set or cleared the Z bit and the BNE instruction
        ; will act on the results.

        LDAA #$00
        ; Load Accumulator A with 0's in preparation for the next data
        ; byte.

        RTI
        ; Return from Interrupt. The program is effectively started with
        ; the SEI instruction, allows the CPU to act on the interrupt re-
        ; quest from the I/O port.

        ; The start of the Framing Error Subroutine, the purpose of which
        ; is to stop the program so that whatever is causing the problem
        ; can be fixed.

FMERR   PULA
        ; Clear the Stack.

        BSR CRASH
        ; Branch to Subroutine Crash to let user know that something
        ; has gone wrong. (This subroutine is not included here.)

        RTS
        ; Return from Subroutine.

        ; Start of HBIT (half-bit), part of the timing routine.

HBIT   LDAA #$yy
        ; Load Accumulator A with a number that represents half of the
        ; value used to set the desired baud rate (given here as xx).

```
        BRA DLOOP1
        ;   Branch to Delay Loop 1

        ;   Start of FBIT (full bit), the rest of the timing routine.

FBIT    LDAA #$xx
        ;   Load Accumulator A with a number that represents the baud
        ;   rate.

        ;   Start of Delay Loop 1.

DLOOP 1 LDAB #$0x
        ;   Load Accumulator B with a number representing a 1-bit delay.
        ;   Start of Delay Loop 2.

DLOOP 2 DECB
        ;   Decrement Accumulator B.

        BNE DLOOP2

        ;   Branch if Not Equal to beginning of this loop. When the value in
        ;   Accumulator B is 00, the Z bit will be set, and the BNE test will
        ;   fail, and the loop will end.

        DECA
        ;   Decrement Accumulator A. This was loaded in FBIT.

        NOP
        ;   Waste a little time for good measure. Since NOP takes only two
        ;   machine cycles, it's a very brief delay.

        BNE DLOOP1
        ;   Branch if Not Equal to Delay Loop 1. See comments on earlier
        ;   BNE instruction.

        RTS
        ;   Return from Subroutine.
```

In summary, this program (1) tests the Z bit of the Condition Code Register to determine whether the start bit is valid, (2) accepts each data bit and moves it to the right, (3) counts the bits, (4) provides for the correct timing (baud rate) so that the acceptance rate will be the same as the transmission rate, (5) stores the accepted data bytes in memory, and (6) crashes the program in the event of a bad stop bit (framing error). BNE and BEQ are conditional branches. BSR is a controlled unconditional branch; that is, it is a branch to a subroutine that ends in a RTS (Return from Subroutine), which prevents the branch from falling into oblivion.

The procedures carried out in this little assembly language program are common enough yet complex enough to require a special LSI device called the UART, or Universal Asynchronous Receiver/Transmitter. The UART device will manage the reception operation and transmit the data in parallel along with a DATA READY signal. The UART also accepts parallel data and sends a PERIPHERAL READY signal when it can accept more data. UART chips vary in complexity and in the types of features they can support. Accordingly, UARTS vary in price from $5 for a basic chip with few additional features to $50 for a device that supports full RS-232 compatibility.

The following graphics program was written in 8088 assembly language specifically for the Zenith 150 PC compatible. This routine is called from within a CBASIC 86 program and is used to draw a rectangle on the screen as a border for text. This heavily documented routine was written in assembly language so that it would execute quickly without interfering with the main program's operation. This program demonstrates the way assembly language routines can operate within the matrix of larger high-level language programs.

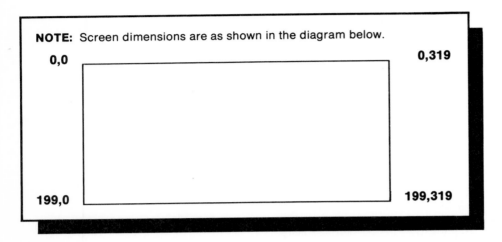

NOTE: Screen dimensions are as shown in the diagram below.

Fig. 4-5

NEW CENTURY BORDER PROGAM
by William Woodall

```
        PUBLIC DRWLIN
        CSEG
            ;   Equates: parameters on stack frame
        row1        equ         10[bp]
            ;   1st
        col1        equ         08[bp]
            ;   2nd
        row2        equ         06[bp]
            ;   3rd
        col2        equ         o4[bp]
            ;   4th
        line color      equ         02[bp]
            ;   5th

            ;   function start:
        DRWLIN:
        1mov      bp,sp
            ;   set stack frame to retrieve parameters
        pushf
            ;   save
        push      si
            ;   registers
        push      di
            ;   used
        push      dx
            ;   by
```

```
        push      cx
              ;   this
        push      bx
              ;   routine

              ;   **************************************************************

              ;   Real work starts here:

              ;   find │ row2-row1 │   −result is delta__y
        mov       ax,row2
              ;   get row2
        sub       ax,row1
              ;   subtract row1
              ;   result in ax

              ;   figure out if delta__y + or −
              ;   si = 1 if + , si = −1 if −
        mov       si,1
              ;   set positive
        jge       STORE__Y
              ;   and go on if positive
        mov       si,−1
              ;   else set negative
        neg       ax
              ;   and perform abs() function
STORE__Y:
        mov       delta__y,ax
              ;   store delta__y value

              ;   find│ col2-col1 │  − result is delta__x
        mov       ax,col2
              ;   get col2
        sub       ax,col1
              ;   subtract col1
              ;   result in ax
              ;   figure out if delta__x + or −
              ;   di = 1 if +, di = −1 if −
        mov       di,1
              ;   set positive
        jge       STORE__X
              ;   and go on if positive
        mov       di,−1
              ;   else set negative
        neg       ax
              ;   and perform abs() function
STORE__X
        mov       delta__x,ax
              ;   store delta__xvalue

              ;   see if slope is greater or less than 1
        mov       ax,delta__x
              ;   get delta__x
        cmp       ax,delta__y
              ;   and compare
        jl      CSTEEP
```

```
                     ;   slope > 1
            call         EASY
                     ;   slope <=1
            jmp          ENDF
                     ;   let's go home!!!!
    CSTEEP:
            call         STEEP
                     ;   slope > 1

    ENDF:
                     ;   end game . . .
            pop      bx
                     ;   restore
            pop      cx
                     ;   previously
            pop      dx
                     ;   saved
            pop      di
                     ;   registers
            pop      si
            popf
            ret      10
                     ;   pump parameters off stack and
                     ;   back to CB86
    EASY:
                     ;   calculate half of delta__x (halfx)
            mov      ax,delta__x
                     ;   get delta__x
            shr      ax,1
                     ;   shift right to divide by 2
            mov      halfx,ax
                     ;   and store result
                     ;   set control values
            mov      cx,col1
                     ;   cx = start column
            mov      dx,row1
                     ;   dx = start row
            mov      bx,0
                     ;   initialize bx (error count)
            mov      ax,delta__x
                     ;   set to count
            mov      count,ax
                     ;   and store
            mov      ax,delta__x
    NEWDOT:
            call     POINT DRAW
                     ;   draw a point
            add      cx,di
                     ;   inc/dec x
            add      bx,delta__y
                     ;   add delta to bx
            cmp      bx,halfx
                     ;   compare to half of delta__x
            jle      DCOUNT
                     ;   don't change y if not enough error
            sub      bx,delta__x
```

```
          ;    subtract from bx
     add       dx,si
          ;    inc/dec y

DCOUNT:
     dec       count
          ;    dec line position counter
     jge       NEWDOT
          ;    and continue till through
     ret
          ;    go back when done
     jge       NEWDOT

          ;    ****************************************************************

STEEP:
          ;    calculate half of delta__y (halfy)
     mov       ax,delta__y
          ;    get delta__y
     shr       ax,1
          ;    shift right to divide by 2
     mov       halfy,ax
          ;    and store result
          ;    set control values
     mov       cx,col1
          ;    cx = start column
     mov       dx,row1
          ;    dx = start column
     mov       bx,0
          ;    initialize bx (error count)
     mov       ax,delta__y
          ;    and store

NEWDOT2:
     call      POINT__DRAW
          ;    draw a point
     add       dx,si
          ;    inc/dec y
     add       bx,delta__x
          ;    and delta to bx
     cmp       bx,halfy
          ;    compare to half of delta__y
     jle       DCOUNT2
          ;    don't change y if not enough error
     sub       bx,delta__y
          ;    subtract from bx
     add       cx,si
          ;    inc/dec x

DCOUNT2:
     dec       count
          ;    dec line position counter
     jge       NEWDOT2
          ;    and continue till through
     ret
          ;    go back when done

          ;    ****************************************************************
```

```
POINT_DRAW:
            ;   save registers and off to the depths of BIOS
    cmp     bx,halfy
    push    bx
            ;   save registers
    push    cx
            ;   from the
    push    dx
            ;   havoc of ROM
    push    si
    push    di
    mov     ax,line_color
            ;   set line_color value
    mov     ah,12
            ;   write point function
    int     10h
            ;   off to ROM
    pop     di
            ;   restore
    pop     si
            ;   registers
    pop     dx
            ;   saved
    pop     cx
    pop     dx
    ret
            ;   next

    ;   ************************************************************
    ;   ************************************************************

    ;   End of code - define data areas:

                            DSEG
    halfx                   dw                  0
    halfy                   dw                  0
    delta_x                 dw                  0
    delta_y                 dw                  0
    count                   dw                  0
```

This routine could have been written entirely in CBASIC or in any other dialect of BASIC using the DRAWTO or PLOT commands that most BASICs support. However, because the real purpose of this program is to draw a series of lines on a screen to act as a frame around lessons that are going to be loaded from disk, the programmers want the program to plug into the high-level language spine of the system as if it were a logical module, but run below the surface as if it were a machine. Writing this in assembly code therefore, is the obvious choice. The assembly language program will operate much faster than a comparable BASIC program because it is functioning at a machine level and it is designed to be recycled into the main program whenever it is needed. Block modules in standard BASIC can get in the way of the main program because the BASIC interpreter will read every line of code when it searches through the program for the subroutine. Assembly language routines are out of sight and out of mind. They can be called into the main program only when needed, and they don't interfere with the speed of the system.

Directory
of Microprocessors

The microcomputer industry owes its start to the Intel Corporation, which in 1972 developed the first functional microprocessor, the 4004, a 4-bit CPU. An 8-bit version, the 8008, soon followed. Neither of these chips carried microcomputing very far, however; rather it was Intel's third design, the 8080 (followed by the identical, but faster, 8080A), that changed the world. The 8080 almost overnight proved to be the foundation stone for an entire industry. And almost overnight, Zilog, Motorola, and MOS Technology (now part of Commodore) brought out their own microprocessors, respectively the Z80, the 6800, and the 6502 (the chip from which the Apple, the Commodore PET, the Ohio Scientific C1P and C4P, the Rockwell AIM, the KIM, the SYM, and the Atari computers all sprang). It was as though an industry were simply waiting to happen.

The technology for integrating more and more circuitry into less and less space has developed with breathtaking rapidity. One can only guess at the wonders of integration that lie ahead. But with each succeeding generation of microprocessors, we see huge advances in the state of the microcomputer art so that today's desktop machines of modest cost are able to far outperform the expensive monsters of but a few years ago.

This directory of currently popular microprocessors will provide the design and hardware characteristics as well as the instruction set of each microprocessor. All commercially available 8-, 8/16-, and 16-bit microprocessors are packaged in DIPs, ranging in pin count from 40 to 64. Further, they contain the following features in common:

1. An instruction set to allow for programming. With few exceptions, each instruction set is unique, but they are all broadly similar.
2. Internal address, data, and control buses.
3. General-purpose registers for manipulating and temporarily storing data. These registers can be categorized into (a) accumulators and (b) data registers. The accumulators are where the operands are held prior to execution of an instruction. After execution, they hold the results. A data register holds such things as an instruction while it is being decoded and can be thought of as the terminus of the data bus. Some microprocessors have sets of general registers that act as accumulators.
4. An arithmetic logic unit (ALU) for performing arithemtic and logical operations on the data sent to it.
5. A program counter (PC) for keeping track of the order of operations. After each operation, the counter increments according to the number of bytes or words required by the instruction just perfomed. The PC always points to the location in memory where the next element of the program resides.
6. An instruction decoder for interpreting the instruction-set codes that it receives.
7. A method of queuing the instructions so they are performed in the correct sequence.
8. A flag, status, or condition code register.
9. A clock for timing and control.
10. Hardware and software interrupt capability.

Most microprocessors are available in one or more variant versions and from several secondary manufacturers who produce the chips under license to the prime manufacturers, an arrangement known as "second sourcing." For most of these chips, the manufacturers also provide various support chips—serial and parallel communication interfaces, bus controllers, video interfaces, and so forth. Except in certain cases, the support chips of one manufacturer can be used with the CPU of another.

The summary of instructions, descriptions of registers, and listings of addressing modes for each of the microprocessors in this section provide an overview of the similarities and differences among the different chips. Detailed descriptions of the complete instruction sets with their precise register operands and binary and hexadecimal equivalents can be found in the specification sheets provided by the manufacturers and in the different microprocessor-specific books cited in the bibliography. Readers who are interested in learning assembly language programming should consult the manufacturer's specification sheets and the many excellent books available on the subject.

8-BIT MICROPROCESSORS

Eight-bit chips are still the basic machines in the home computer industry, even though they have been largely replaced in the business computer market by the 16/8-bit CPUs in the PC and XT or 32/16-bit CPUs in the Macintosh. The 8-bit CPU was a marvel of technology for its time because of its powerful addressing capabilities and its efficient architecture. It lent itself easily to adaptation and improvement.

The basic 8-bit chip consists of the following functional units:

1. The register array and address logic.
2. The arithmetic and logic unit.
3. The instruction decoder and machine control component.
4. Buffers for the data and address bus.

The arithmetic unit consists of the accumulator, the status register, and the ALU or Arithmetic/Logic Unit. This section of the CPU is responsible for performing the logic functions and the basic arithmetic that the chip has to calculate to do its job. The results of this arithmetic are ported over to the accumulator. The accumulator is the register where most of the information resulting from the sequence of instructions will reside. Data will enter the CPU and exit it as well through the accumulator.

In the status register there are specific indicators known as status flags which, as their name implies, flag the results of the instructions that have been executed by the chip. The number and type of status flags vary from chip to chip, with the larger chips, like the 68000, having special flags that flip the CPU back and forth between different modes of instruction.

Like any CPU, the 8-bit chip is really a function of its register sets. These include registers that are used to store data and instructions and registers that are only usable by the internal logic of the chip itself. The latter are sometimes known as hardware registers and are not really addressable by the user. The CPU also uses a register mechanism known as the Program Counter to hold the address of the next instruction. The current stack address of the instruction sequence is held by the stack pointer. Whenever new information is loaded or PUSHed onto the stack the pointer is decremented by two as it moves down the stack.

The following 8-bit microprocessors are covered here: Intel 8080A, Intel 8085A, Z80, NSC800, MC6800, MC6809, and MOS Technology 6502.

Intel 8080A

Even though the Intel 8080 is already ancient history in the compressed time scale of the microprocessor world, the chip is still available and still in fairly wide use. Its biggest current advantages are cost and familiarity to programmers. It is well known and certainly well tested. And for inexpensive microprocessor-controlled products, it shouldn't be sneered at. Furthermore, experience with the 8080 prepares the designer and programmer for the Z80, 8085, 8086, and 8088, all of which are descended by one route or another from the venerable 8080. The first commercially viable microcomputer, the M.I.T.S. Altair, which served the industry as the source of the S-100 bus structure, used the 8080, as did the first 8-bit Heathkit computer, the H8. Other early users of the 8080 include IMSAI and Processor Technology (the SOL). A number of these computers are still in operation, though the manufacturers have either gone out of business or moved to later designs.

Generally compatible with its forerunner the 8080, the 8080A has six 8-bit general-purpose registers in addition to an accumulator. The registers can be addressed individually or in 16-bit pairs, providing programmers with single-precision and double-precision numeric operators. The 8080A's external data stack enables any portion to be used on a last-in first-out basis to store or retrieve that data in the accumulator, the program counter, or the status register. The external stack architecture means that the 8080A can handle interrupts on a multiple-level priority basis.

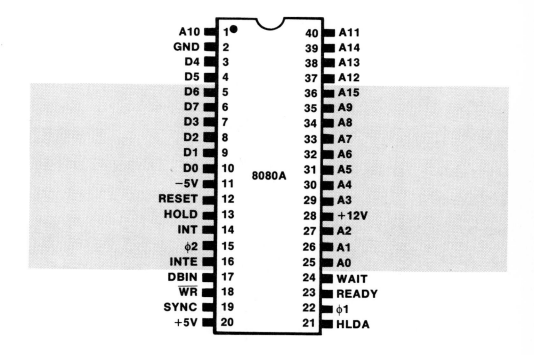

FLAGS

Zero Flag: If the result of an instruction has a 0 value, this flag is set.
Sign Flag: If the most significant bit of the result of an operation has the value of 1, this flag is set.
Parity Flag: If the sum of the bits results in even parity, this flag is set.
Carry Flag: If the instruction resulted in a carry out of or a borrow into the high-order bit, this flag is set.

MULTIPLEXER			

```
              MULTIPLEXER

  R   R    W           (8)   Z           (8)
  E   E    TEMP REG          TEMP REG
  G   G
  I   S    B           (8)   C           (8)
  S   E    REG               REG
  T   L
  E   E    D           (8)   E           (8)
  R   C    REG               REG
      T
           H           (8)   L           (8)
           REG               REG

           STACK   POINTER        (16)

           PROGRAM   COUNTER      (16)

           INCREMENTER/DECREMENTER (16)
           ADDRESS LATCH
```

REGISTER ARRAY

A15   AD
ADDRESS BUS

SUMMARY OF INSTRUCTIONS

Data Transfer Instructions

MOV X,X Move contents from register to register or from register to memory

XCHG Exchange D and E register with H and L register

MVI X,(n) Load designated register X with (n). (n) represents 8 or 16.

MVI M,(8) Load memory with (8)

LXI B,(16) Load B and C registers with (16)

LXI D,(16) Load D and E registers with (16)

LXI H,(16) Load H and L registers with (16)

LXI SP,(16) Load stack pointer with (16)

LDAX B Load A register with memory location defined by B and C

LDAX D Load A register with memory location defined by D and E

LHLD (adr) Load H and L with contents of (adr)

LDA (adr) Load A with contents of (adr)

STAX B Store A register in memory location defined by B and C

STAX C Store A register in memory location defined by D and E

SHLD (adr) Store H and L in (adr)

STA (adr) Store A in (adr)

Arithmetic and Logical instructions

ADD X Add to A register the register defined in X

ADC X Add register defined in X and carry to A register

SUB X Subtract register defined in X from A register

SBB X Subtract register defined in X and borrow from A register

DAD B Add B and C registers to H and L

DAD D Add D and E registers to H and L

DAD SP Add stack pointer to H and L

INR X Increment register defined in X

INX B Increment B and C register pair

INX D Increment D and E register pair

INX H   Increment H and L register pair

INX SP   Increment stack pointer

DCR X   Decrement register defined in X

DCX B   Decrement B and C register pair

DCX D   Decrement D and E register pair

DCX H   Decrement H and L register pair

DCX SP   Decrement stack pointer

DAA   Decimal adjust A

CMA   Complement A register

STC   Set Carry Flag

CMC   Complement Carry Flag

ANA X   AND A register with register defined in X

ANA M   AND A register with contents of memory

XRA X   Exclusive OR A register with register defined in X

ORA X   Logically OR A register with register defined in X

CMP X   Compare register defined in X to A register

ADI (8)   Add (8) to A register

ACI (8)   Add (8) and carry to A register

SUI (8)   Subtract (8) from A register

SBI (8)   Subtract (8) and borrow from A register

ANI (8)   AND (8) with A register

XRI (8)   Exclusive OR (8) with A register

ORI (8)   Logically OR (8) with A register

CPI (8)   Compare (8) with A register

Block Instructions

RLC   Rotate A one bit left

RRC   Rotate A one bit right

RAL   Rotate A left through carry

RAR   Rotate A right through carry

Branch Control Instructions

JMP (adr)   Jump to (adr)

JNZ (adr)   Jump to (adr) if Zero Flag not set

JZ (adr)   Jump to (adr) if Zero Flag set

JNC (adr)   Jump to (adr) if Carry Flag not set

JC (adr)   Jump to (adr) if Carry Flag set

JPO (adr)   Jump to (adr) if parity odd

JPE (adr)   Jump to (adr) if parity even

JP (adr)   Jump to (adr) if positive

JM (adr)   Jump to (adr) if negative

PCHL   Move H and L to program counter

CALL (adr)   Call subroutine at (adr)

CNZ (adr)   Call subroutine at (adr) if Zero Flag not set

CZ (adr)   Call subroutine at (adr) if Zero Flag set

CNC (adr)   Call subroutine at (adr) if Carry Flag not set

CC (adr)   Call subroutine at (adr) if Carry Flag set

CPO (adr)   Call subroutine at (adr) if parity odd

CPE (adr)   Call subroutine at (adr) if parity even

CP (adr)   Call subroutine at (adr) if positive

CM (adr)   Call subroutine at (adr) if negative

RET   Return

RNZ   Return if Zero Flag not set

RZ   Return if Zero Flag set

RNC   Return if Carry Flag not set

RC   Return if Carry Flag set

RPO   Return if parity odd

RPE   Return if parity even

RP   Return if positive

RM   Return if negative

RST n   Restart at n (1 to 7) interrupt location

PUSH B   Place B and C register pair on stack

PUSH D   Place D and E register pair on stack

PUSH H   Place H and L register pair on stack

PUSH PSW   Place flags and A register on stack

POP B   Place current stack in B and C register pair

POP D   Place current stack in D and E register pair

POP H   Place current stack in H and L register pair

POP PSW   Place current stack in flags and A register

XTHL   Exchange current stack with H and L

SPHL   Move H and L to stack pointer

OUT (port)   Output A register to port

IN (port)   Input port to A register

Hardware Instructions

DI   Disable interrupts

EI   Enable interrupts

NOP   No operation

HALT   Halt machine operation

Intel 8085A

The Intel 8085A can be thought of as a hardware-enhanced 8080A. And while it cannot substitute for the 8080 in an existing circuit, it is completely software compatible with the parent chip. Hardware incompatibility arises from differences in pinouts as well as voltage requirements. The 8080 needs +5VDC, −5VDC, and +12VDC, whereas the 8085 needs +5VDC only.

The 8085 was designed to improve the 8080-based machine design by offering computer design manufacturers a higher system speed with a complete software compatibility with the 8080A. The 8085 integrates the functions of the 8224 clock generator and the 8228 system controller that were previously provided as part of the 8080 system. Thus, the 8085 is a more efficient chip than the 8080, and it offers a fully integrated CPU design to system manufacturers. The instruction set compatibility with the 8080 means that system programmers and high-level language compiler and interpreter designers need not rewrite code in order to transport their software to the new chip. The chip's direct accessing capability to a full 64K of memory also speeds up the CPU's control over software run time and consequently, the processing time of the entire computer.

The 8085 adds two new instructions to the 8080 set: SIM and RIM. Both instructions effect the 8085's serial in/serial out port. The RIM instruction reads the serial input; SIM sets the serial output.

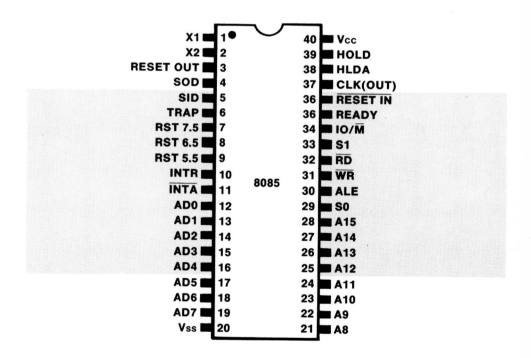

FLAGS

Zero Flag: If the result of an instruction has a 0 value, this flag is set.
Sign Flag: If the most significant bit of the result of an operation has the value of 1, this flag is set.
Parity Flag: If the sum of the bits results in even parity, this flag is set.
Carry Flag: If the instruction resulted in a carry out of or a borrow into the high-order bit, this flag is set.

The structure and instruction set of the 8085 is virtually identical to that of the 8080A (see preceding listing) with the addition of only two instructions:

RIM   Loads accumulator with restart interrupt masks (affects SID, the serial input data line)

SIM   Contents of accumulator used in programming the restart interrupt masks (affects SOD, the serial output data line)

B REG (8)	C REG (8)	
D REG (8)	E REG (8)	
H REG (8)	L REG (8)	**REGISTER ARRAY**
STACK POINTER (16)		
PROGRAM COUNTER (16)		
INCREMENTER/DECREMENTER ADDRESS LATCH (16)		

Zilog Z80

The Zilog Z80, a product of designers who left Intel to start their own company, combines some unique features with certain 8080 and 6800 features. Part of its great success stems from the fact of its compatibility with 8080 code, so that a program written for the 8080 will run on the Z80 without modification. The reverse, however, is not true. The curious but predictable result of this one-way-only compatibility has been that while most of the machines running the CP/M operating system are designed around the Z80, most of the programs written under CP/M are written in 8080 code. Why? Because CP/M was itself written in 8080 code and the earlier CP/M computers were all 8080 machines. TP/M, a CP/M-like operating system written in Z80 code for Z80 programmers, has not been widely used. The Z80 has often been called a second-generation 8080 because of this software compatibility and because some of the same opcodes that are used in the Z80 are used in the 8080. Zilog has managed to produce a CPU with a healthy longevity in an arena highlighted by very short product lives.

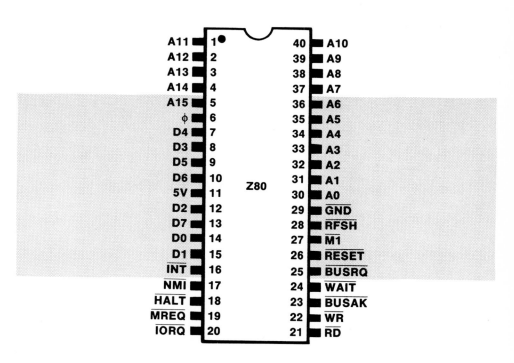

FLAGS

Carry Flag: If the instruction generates a carry or a borrow, this flag is set.

Zero Flag: If the result of the operation is a zero in the accumulator, this flag is set.

Sign Flag: Represents a negative number. If the operation results in a 7-bit high in the accumulator, this flag is set because a 7-bit high is a negative number.

Parity/Overflow Flag: This flag indicates the parity of the result in the accumulator when logical operations are performed. It also indicates overflow.

Half Carry Flag: Used by the DAA instruction for BCD operations.

Add/Subtract Flag: Indicates what type of instruction was performed most recently so that the DAA operation will be correct for either addition or subtraction.

Accumulator   Flags

A	F
B	C
D	E
H	L

8-bits   8-bits

"EXX" instruction

Accumulator   Flags

A'	F'
B'	C'
D'	E'
H'	L'

I	R
Index IX	
Index IY	
Program counter	
Stack pointer	

16-bits

ADDRESSING MODES

Immediate
Immediate Extended
Modified Page Zero Addressing
Relative Addressing
Implied Addressing
Register Indirect Addressing
Bit Addressing

REGISTERS

Program Counter (16 bit): Holds the address of the current instruction retrieved from memory.

Stack Pointer (16 bit): Holds the address of the current top of the stack.

Index Registers 1X and 1Y: Holds the base address used in the index addressing modes.

Interrupt Page Address Register (8-bit): Contains the high-order 8 bits of the indirect address for an interrupt.

Memory Refresh Register (7-bit): A memory refresh counter for use with dynamic memories. This register is not normally used by the programmer.

SUMMARY OF INSTRUCTIONS

Alphabetical Listing of Instructions

ADC A Add with Carry to Accumulator

ADC HL, rp Add Register Pair with Carry to HL

ADD Add

AND Logical AND

BIT Test Bit

CALL addr   Call Subroutine

CALL cond,addr   Call Conditional

CCF   Complement Carry Flag

CP   Compare

CPD,CPDR   Compare, Decrement (Repeating)

CPI,CPIR   Compare, Increment (Repeating)

CPL   Complement Accumulator

DAA   Decimal Adjust Accumulator

DEC   Decrement

DI   Disable Interrupts

DJNZ   Decrement and Jump if Not Zero

EI   Enable Interrupts

EX   Exchange

EXX   Exchange Register Pairs and Alternatives

HALT   Halt

IM n   Set Interrupt Mode

IN   Input

INC   Increment

IND,INDR   Input, Decrement (Repeating)

INI,INIR   Input, Increment (Repeating)

JP addr   Jump

JP cond,addr   Jump Conditional

JR   Jump Relative

JR cond,addr   Jump Relative Conditional

LD reg,(HL)   Load

LD A (addr)   Load Accumulator Direct

LD data   Load Immediate

LD (HL),reg   Store Register

LD(addr),A   Store Accumulator Direct

LD A,I   Load Accumulator with Interrupt Vector Register

LD A,R   Load Accumulator from Refresh Register

LD dst,src   Move Register-to-Register

LD A,(BC) or (DE)   Load Accumulator Secondary

LD HL,(addr)   Load HL direct

LD I,A   Store Accumulator to Interrupt Vector Register

LD R,A   Store Accumulator to Refresh Register

LD reg,(xy+disp)   Load Register Indexed

LD rp,(addr)   Load Register Pair Direct

LD xy,(addr)   Load Index Register Direct

LD (BC) or (DE),A   Store Accumulator Secondary

LD (addr),HL   Store HL Direct

LD (xy+disp),reg   Store Register Indexed

LD (addr),rp   Store Register Pair Direct

LD (addr),xy   Store Index Register Direct

LD (HL),data   Store Immediate to Memory

LD (xy+disp),data   Store Immediate to Memory Indexed

LD SP,HL   Move HL to Stack Pointer

LD SP,xy   Move Index Register to Stack Pointer

LDD,LDDR   Load, Decrement (Repeating)

LDI,LDIR   Load, Increment (Repeating)

NEG   Negate (Twos Complement) Accumulator

NOP   No Operation

OR   Logical OR

OUT   Output

OUTD,OTDR   Output, Decrement (Repeating)

OUTI,OTIR   Output, Increment (Repeating)

POP   Remove from Stack

PUSH   Place onto Stack

RES   Reset Bit

RET   Return from Subroutine

RET cond   Return Conditional

RETI   Return from Interrupt

RETN   Return from Nonmaskable Interrupt

RLA   Rotate Accumulator Left Through Carry

RL   Rotate Left Through Carry

RLC   Rotate Left Circular

RLCA   Rotate Accumulator Left Circular

RRA   Rotate Accumulator Right Through Carry

RR   Rotate Right Through Carry

RRC   Rotate Right Circular

RRCA   Rotate Accumulator Right Circular

RLD   Rotate Accumulator and Memory Left Decimal

RRD   Rotate Accumulator and Memory Right Decimal

RST   Restart

SBC   Subtract with Borrow

SCF   Set Carry Flag

SET   Set Bit

SLA   Shift Left Arithmetic

SRA   Shift Right Arithmetic

SRL   Shift Right Logical

SUB   Subtract

XOR   Logical Exclusive OR

National Semiconductor NSC800

Without being a literal copy of either the 8085 or the Z80, the National Semiconductor NSC800 combines elements of both chips. The result is a powerful 8-bit chip able to run Z80 and 8080A/8085 software. The NSC800 has not enjoyed the degree of acceptance a microprocessor of this power and flexibility would seem to warrant. It is not, however, directly pin compatible with the Z80 or 8080/8085 chips.

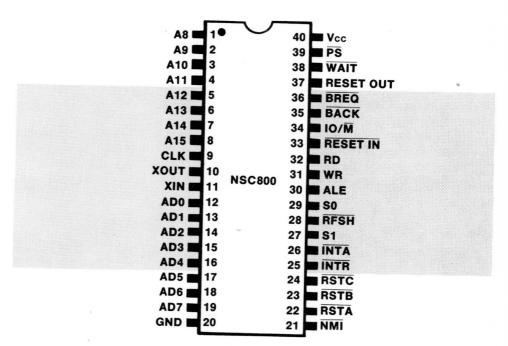

ADDRESSING MODES

Immediate Addressing
Immediate Extended Addressing
Modified Page Zero Addressing
Extended (Direct) Addressing
Relative Addressing
Register Indirect Addressing
Indexed Addressing
Register Addressing
Implied Addressing
Bit Addressing

REGISTERS

Main Working Registers

Accumulator A (8-bit)
Register B (8-bit)
Register C (8-bit)
Register D (8-bit)
Register E (8-bit)
Flags F (8-bit)
Register H (8-bit)
Register L (8-bit)

Alternate Working Registers

Accumulator A′ (8-bit)
Register B′ (8-bit)
Register C′ (8-bit)
Register D′ (8-bit)
Register E′ (8-bit)
Flags F′ (8-bit)
Register H′ (8-bit)
Register L′ (8-bit)

DEDICATED REGISTERS

Program Counter: Contains the 16-bit address of the current instruction being retrieved from memory.

Stack Pointer: Contains the 16-bit address of the current top of a stack located in RAM.

Index Registers (IX and IY):   Contain the 16-bit address used in indexed addressing modes.

Interrupt Page Address Register (I):   Used to store the high-order 8-bits of the address of any memory location in response to a mode 2 interrupt.

Memory Refresh Register (R):   Contains a memory refresh counter which is automatically incremented after each new instruction retrieval. This mode of memory refresh is transparent to the user.

     The NSC800 register set is, of necessity, similar to the register set of the Z80 because the NSC800 executes the Z80's entire instruction set. There are eighteen 8-bit registers, four 16-bit registers, and one write-only register that is 4-bits. Eight of these 8-bit registers form what is known as the NSC800's working register set. These working registers are supported by alternate registers. By flipping the contents of the working and alternate registers, programmers can execute applications that require an almost immediate interrupt.

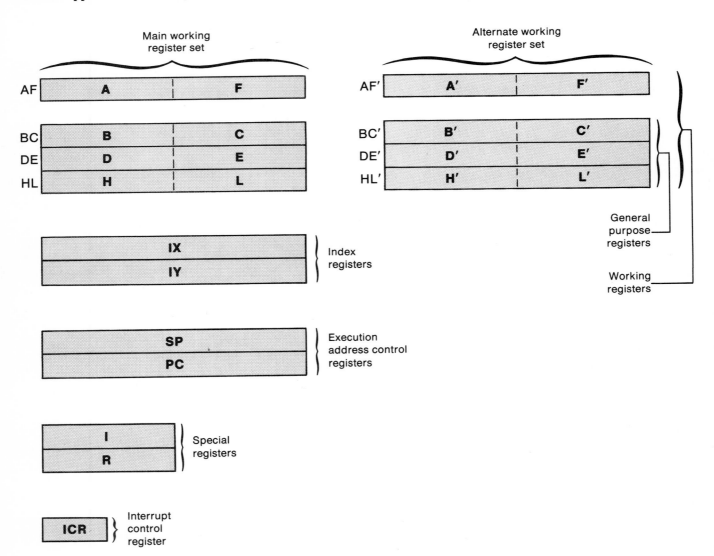

FLAGS

Carry Flag: Set by the carry from the highest-order bit of the accumulator during an add instruction or by a borrow during a subtract.

Zero Flag: Set when a zero is loaded into the accumulator as the result of an operation.

Sign Flag: Stores the sign bit in the accumulator after an arithmetic operation. Flag is used with signed numbers.

Parity/Overflow Flag: Set during logical operations when the parity of the result is even and it is reset when the parity is odd. It signals an overflow when signed twos complement arithmetic operations are performed and the resultant of the operation is out of range.

Half Carry Flag: Indicates a BCD carry or borrow result from the least significant four bits of an operation. On a Decimal Adjust instruction, the flag is used to correct the result of a previously packed decimal add or subtract.

Add/Subtract Flag: Indicates what type of instruction was executed last so that the Decimal Adjust operation will be correct for either addition or subtraction.

SUMMARY OF INSTRUCTIONS

8-Bit Load

LD register to register Load contents of register to register

LD register to memory Load contents of register to memory

LD register with ACC Load register with Accumulator

LD ACC with register Load Accumulator with register

LD data to register Load register with immediate data

LD memory to register Load contents of memory to register

LD data to memory Load memory with immediate data

LD memory from ACC Load memory from Accumulator

LD ACC from memory Load Accumulator from memory

16-Bit Load

LD register with data Load register pairs with immediate data

LD SP,ss Load Stack Pointer with HL, IX, or IY

LD (16-bit binary n),rr Load memory location with 16-bit register pair (BC,DE, HL,SP,IX,IY)

PUSH Place contents of 16-bit register pair onto memory stack

POP Place contents of stack to 16-bit register pair

Arithmetic and Logical Instructions

ADD Add register to Accumulator

ADC Add with carry

ADD A Add number to Accumulator

ADC A Add number to Accumulator with carry

ADD A,m Add memory to Accumulator

ADC A,m Add with carry memory to Accumulator

SUB Subtract contents of register from Accumulator

SBC Subtract with carry

SUB n Subtract number from Accumulator

SBC A,n Subtract number with carry from Accumulator

SUM m   Subtract memory from Accumulator

SBC A,m   Subtract with carry memory from Accumulator

AND   Logic AND register with Accumulator

AND n   AND number with Accumulator

AND m   AND memory with Accumulator

OR   Logic OR register with Accumulator

OR n   OR number with Accumulator

OR m   OR memory with Accumulator

XOR   Exclusive OR contents of register with Accumulator

XOR n   Exclusive OR number with Accumulator

XOR m   Exclusive OR memory with Accumulator

CP   Compare contents of register to Accumulator

CP n   Compare number to Accumulator

CP m   Compare memory with Accumulator

INC   Increment contents of register

INC m   Increment memory

DEC   Decrement contents of register

DEC m   Decrement memory

DAA   Decimal adjust Accumulator

CPL   Complement Accumulator

NEG   Negate Accumulator

CCF   Complement Carry Flag

SCF   Set Carry Flag

SET   Set bit in register or memory

RES   Reset bit in register or memory

BIT   Test bit in register or memory

EX DE,HL   Exchange contents of DE and HL register

EX AF,AF'   Exchange contents of A and F registers with A' and F' registers.

EXX   Exchange contents of BC, DE, and HL registers with corresponding alternate registers

EX (SP)   Exchange top of stack with 16-bit index registers

LDI   Move data from memory location HL to memory location DE, increment memory pointers, and decrement byte counter BC

LDD   Move data from memory location HL to memory location DE and decrement memory pointer and byte counter BC

CPI   Compare data in memory location HL to Accumulator, increment memory pointer, and decrement byte counter BC

CPD   Compare data in memory location HL to Accumulator and decrement memory pointer and decrement byte counter BC

LDIR   Repeat LDI until BC=0

LDDR   Repeat LDD until BC=0

CPIR   Repeat CPI until BC=0 or HL=A

CPDR   Repeat CPD until BC=0 or HL=A

I/O Instructions

IN A,n   Input to Accumulator from I/O device at address n

OUT n,A   Output to I/O device at address n from Accumulator

IN r,C   Input to register from I/O device at address C

OUT C,r   Output to I/O device at address C from register

INI   Input from I/O device at address C to memory location HL, increment pointer, decrement B counter

OUTI   Output to I/O device at address C from memory location HL, increment pointer, and decrement B counter

IND   Input from I/O device at address C to memory location HL and decrement pointer and B counter

OUTD   Output to I/O device at address C from memory location HL and decrement pointer and B counter

INIR   Repeat INI until B=0

OUTIR Repeat OUTI until B=0

INDR Repeat IND until B=0

OUTDR Repeat OUTD until B=0

Hardware Commands

NOP No operation

HALT Halt

DI Disable Interrupts

EI Enable Interrupts

IM 0 Set Interrupt Mode 0

IM 1 Set Interrupt Mode 1

IM 2 Set Interrupt Mode 2

Branching Instructions

JP Jump

JR Unconditional jump to Program Counter + 8-bit signed twos complement displacement

JR cc Conditional jump as above depending upon condition of Zero Flag or Carry Flag

DJNZ Decrement B register and jump to Program Counter + 8-bit signed twos complement displacement if B does not equal zero else continue

CALL nn Unconditional call to subroutine at location nn

CALL cc,nn Conditional call to subroutine at location nn if Zero Flag or Carry Flag is set

RET Unconditional Return from subroutine

RET cc Conditional Return from subroutine if Zero Flag or Carry Flag is set

RETI Return from Interrupt

RETN Return from Nonmaskable Interrupt

RST T Interrupt to location T

Block Instructions

RLC r Rotate register r left circular

RL r Rotate register r left through carry

RRC r Rotate register r right circular

RR r Rotate register r right through carry

SLA r Shift register r left arithmetic

SRA r Shift register r right arithmetic

SRL r Shift register r right logical

RLC m Rotate memory left circular

RL m Rotate memory left through carry

RRC m Rotate memory right circular

RR m Rotate memory right through carry

SLA m Shift memory left arithmetic

SRA m Shift memory right arithmetic

SRL m Shift memory right logical

RLD Rotate digit left and right between Accumulator and memory location HL

RRD Rotate digit right and left between Accumulator and memory location HL

Motorola MC6800

Whereas the 8080A and its progeny are primarily register oriented in their operations, the Motorola 6800 is primarily memory oriented. The result is a chip with fewer register-related instructions than the 8080A group and a greater number of addressing modes, which effectively multiply the modest instruction set several times. The fundamental design difference between the 8080A (and its descendants) and the 6800 (and its descendants) has produced two distinct approaches to programming, each with its own band of dedicated partisans.

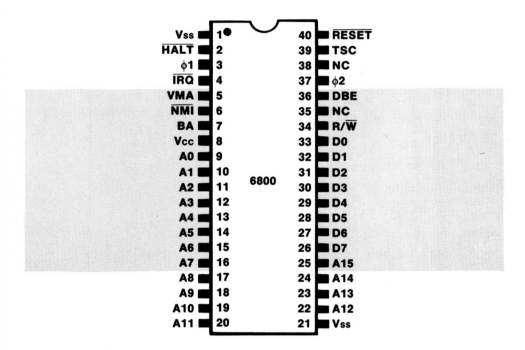

REGISTERS

Program Counter: A 16-bit register that points to the current program address.

Stack Pointer: A 16-bit register that contains the address of the of the next available location on the memory stack in RAM.

Index Register: A 16-bit register used to store data or a 16-bit memory address for the indexed mode of memory addressing.

Accumulators: Two 8-bit accumulators are used to hold operands and results from the Arithmetic/Logic Unit (ALU).

Condition Code Register: An 8-bit register that contains six flags which indicate the results of an ALU operation. The flags and bit definitions are:

Bit	Flag
0	Carry (from bit 7)
1	Overflow
2	Zero
3	Negative
4	Interrupt
5	Half Carry (from bit 3)
6 & 7	Not used

ADDRESSING MODES

Accumulator Addressing (ACC [A] or [B]):   When the accumulator only is addressed, the address must specify either ACCA or ACCB and must be an 8-bit instruction:

Immediate Addressing
Direct Addressing
Extended Addressing
Indexed Addressing
Implied Addressing
Relative Addressing

Program Counter H	Program Counter L
Stack Pointer H	Stack Pointer L
Index Register H	Index Register L
	Accumulator A
Instruction Register	Accumulator B
	Condition Code Register
	ALU

SUMMARY OF INSTRUCTIONS

Arithmetic and Logical Instructions

ADD A   Add to register A

ADD B   Add to register B

ABA   Add register A to B

ADCA   Add with carry to Accumulator A

ADCB   Add with carry to Accumulator B

ANDA   Logical AND with Accumulator A

ANDB   Logical AND with Accumulator B

BITA   Bit test with Accumulator A

BITB   Bit test with Accumulator B

CLR   Set designated location to zero

CLRA   Set Accumulator A to zero

CLRB   Set Accumulator B to zero

CMPA   Compare with Accumulator A

CMPB   Compare with Accumulator B

CBA   Compare Accumulator A with B

COM   Complement of 1 if location specified

COMA   Ones complement of Accumulator A

COMB   Ones complement of Accumulator B

NEG   Twos complement of specified location

NEGA   Twos complement of Accumulator A

NEGB   Twos complement of Accumulator B

ORAA   OR specified location with Accumulator A

ORAB   OR specified location with Accumulator B

DAA   Decimal adjust Accumulator A

DEC   Decrement the specified location

DECA   Decrement Accumulator A

DECB Decrement Accumulator B

EORA Exclusive OR Accumulator A with specified location

EORB Exclusive OR Accumulator B with specified location

INC Increment specified location

INCA Increment Accumulator A

INCB Increment Accumulator B

LDAA Load specified location into Accumulator A

LDAB Load specified location into Accumulator B

Shift and Rotate Instructions

PHSA Place Accumulator A onto stack

PHSB Place Accumulator B onto stack

PULA Pull Accumulator A from stack

PULB Pull Accumulator B from stack

ROL Rotate left through carry

ROLA Rotate Accumulator A left through carry

ROLB Rotate Accumulator B left through carry

ROR Rotate right through carry

ROR Rotate Accumulator A right through carry

RORB Rotate Accumulator B right through carry

ASL Arithmetic shift left of designated location

ASL Arithmetic shift left of Accumulator A

ASLB Arithmetic shift left of Accumulator B

ASR Arithmetic shift right of designated location

ASRA Arithmetic shift right of Accumulator A

ASRB Arithmetic shift right of Accumulator

LSR Logic shift right of designated location

LSRA Logic shift right of Accumulator A

LSRB Logic shift right of Accumulator B

Data Transfer Instructions

STAA Store Accumulator A at designated location

STAB Store Accumulator B at designated location

SBA Subtract Accumulator B from Accumulator A

SBCA Subtract memory and carry from Accumulator A

SBCB Subtract memory and carry from Accumulator B

TAB Transfer Accumulator A to Accumulator B

TBA Transfer Accumulator B to Accumulator A

TST Test memory for zero or minus

CPX Compare index register with memory

DEX Decrement index register

DES Decrement stack pointer

INX Increment index register

INS Increment stack pointer

LDX Load index register

LDS Load stack pointer

STX Store index register

STS Store stack pointer

TXS Move index register -1 to stack

TSX Move stack pointer $+1$ to index register

Hardware and Software Instructions

CLC Clear carry

CLI Clear interrupt mask

CLV Clear overflow

SEC Set carry

SEI Set interrupt mask

SEV Set overflow

TAP Move Accumulator A to condition code register

TPA Move condition code register to Accumulator A

Branch and Jump Instructions

BRA Branch always

BCC Branch if carry clear

BCS Branch if carry set

BEQ Branch if equal to zero

BGE Branch if equal to or greater than zero

BGT Branch if greater than zero

BHI Branch if higher

BLE Branch if zero

BLS Branch if lower or same

BLT Branch if zero

BMI Branch if minus

BNE Branch if not equal to zero

BVC Branch if overflow clear

BVS Branch if overflow set

BPL Branch if plus

BSR Branch to subroutine

JMP Jump

JSR Jump to subroutine

NOP No operation

RTI Return from interrupt

RTS Return from subroutine

SWI Software interrupt

WAI Wait for interrupt

Motorola MC6809

At first glance, the Motorola 6809 instruction set looks like that of the 6800, and there is a degree of similarity as well as source code compatibility. A program assembled into 6800 object code, however, cannot be run by the 6809. Beyond this surface similarity the two chips are very different, the 6809 approaching the computing power of 16-bit designs. Since the Motorola design philosophy is memory oriented, the strength of this chip lies in its enhanced addressing modes. The instruction set is, indeed, fairly small, but when the addressing modes are considered, it turns out that the chip is capable of 1121 distinct operations (59 instructions multiplied by 19 addressing modes). The MC6809 was a revolutionary breakthrough in chip design because it provided programmers with a series of powerful addressing modes.

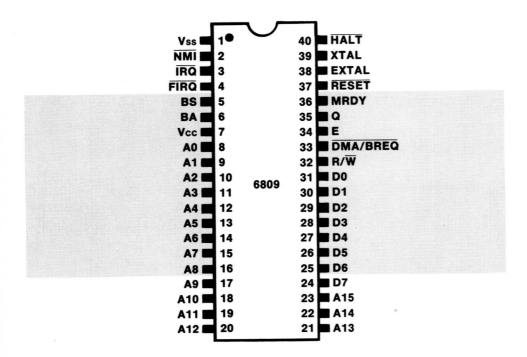

REGISTERS

Accumulator A (8 bits)
Accumulator B (8 bits)
Index Register X (16 bits)
Index Register Y (16 bits)
User Stack Pointer U (16 bits)
Hardware Stack Pointer SP (16 bits)
Program Counter PC (16 bits)
Direct Page Register DP (8 bits)

Condition Code Register (8 bits) containing the following status flags:

Carry/Borrow Flag
Overflow Flag
Zero Flag
Sign Flag
Half-Carry Flag

ADDRESSING MODES

Addressing Modes:
Inherent Addressing
Register Addressing
Immediate Addressing
Base Page Addressing
Extended Direct Addressing
Extended Indirect Addressing
Constant Offset from Base Register Addressing
Indirect with Constant Offset from Base Addressing
Accumulator Offset from Base Register Addressing
Indirect with Accumulator Offset from Base Register Addressing
Autoincrement/Autodecrement Addressing
Program Relative for Branches Addressing

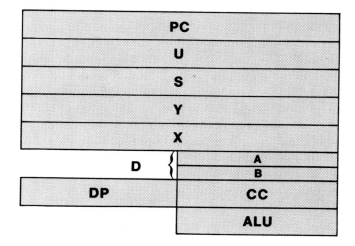

SUMMARY OF INSTRUCTIONS

Alphabetical Listing of Instructions

ABX Add Accumulator B to Index Register X

ADC Add with Carry

ADD Add

AND Logical AND

ANDCC Logical AND Mask with Status Register (Clear Flags)

ASL/LSL Arithmetic (Logical) Shift Left

ASR/LSR Arithmetic (Logical) Shift Right

BCC/BHS Branch if Carry Clear ("Higher or Same")

BCS/BLO Branch if Carry Set ("Lower")

BEQ Branch if Zero Set ("Equal")

BGE Branch if Greater Than or Equal

BGT Branch if Greater Than

BHI Branch if Higher

BIT Bit test (Logical AND)

BLE Branch if Less Than or Equal

BLS Branch if Lower or Same

BLT Branch if Less Than

BMI Branch if Sign (Negative) Set (−)

BNE Branch if Zero Clear

BPL Branch if Sign (Negative) Clear (+)

BRA Branch Always

BRN Branch Never

BSR Branch to Subroutine

BVC Branch if Overflow Clear

BVS Branch if Overflow Set

CLR Clear

CMP Compare

COM Ones Complement

CWAI Clear Condition Code Register Bits and Wait for Interrupt

DAA Decimal Adjust Accumulator A

DEC Decrement by 1

EOR Exclusive OR

EXG Exchange Registers

INC Increment by 1

JMP Jump

JSR Jump to Subroutine

LD Load

LEA Load Effective Address

MUL Multiply

NEG Twos Complement

NOP No Operation

OR Logical OR

ORCC Logical OR Mask with Status Register (Set Flags)

PSH Place Data onto Stack

PUL Pull Data from Stack

ROL Rotate Left

ROR Rotate Right

RTI Return from Interrupt

RTS Return from Subroutine

SBC Subtract with Carry

SEX Sign Extend

ST Store

SUB Subtract

SWI Software Interrupt

SYNC Synchronize with Interrupt Line

TFR Transfer Register-to-Register

TST Test for Zero or Minus

MOS Technology 6502

Developed by former employees of Motorola, the MOS Technology 6502 can be thought of as a lean and highly efficient version of the 6800. Its use in a number of the microcomputers that formed the basis of the modern home-computer industry—Apple, Commodore, KIM, Atari, Ohio Scientific, and others—attests to its special qualities. It has been judged by many as the easiest to program of all microprocessors. Perhaps the greatest single strength of the 6502 lies in its extended set of addressing modes, allowing for capabilities, which, prior to its appearance, were available only in minicomputers and main-frame computers.

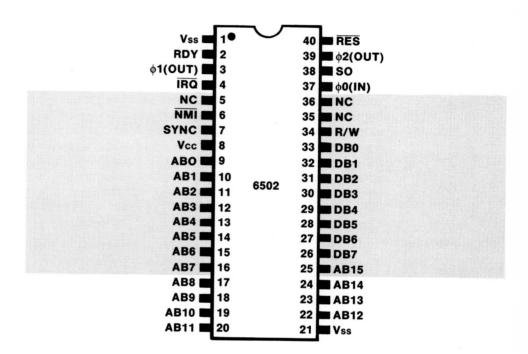

REGISTERS

Accumulator
Program Counter
Zero Page
Stack Pointer
Index X
Index Y
Processor Status Register which contains the following flags:

Carry Flag
Zero Flag
Overflow Flag

Interrupt Disable Flag: Prevents the processor from servicing an interrupt instruction.
Decimal Mode Flag: Changes the mode of the processor from hex to binary-coded decimal.
Break Flag: Set when a BRK is executed.
Negative Flag: Indicates positive or negative results.

ADDRESSING MODES

Implied Addressing
Accumulator Addressing
Immediate Addressing
Relative Addressing
Zero Page Addressing
Zero Page Indexed by X
Zero Page Indexed by Y
Indexed Indirect Addressing
Indirect Indexed Addressing
Absolute Addressing
Absolute Indexed by X
Absolute Indexed by Y
Absolute Indirect Adressing

```
+---------------------+
|     ARITHMETIC      |
|       LOGIC         |
|       UNIT          |
+---------------------+
|    ACCUMULATOR      |
+---------------------+
|       STACK         |
|     POINTER         |
+---------------------+
|     INDEX  X        |
+---------------------+
|     INDEX  Y        |
+---------------------+
```

The 6502 has been called a difficult chip to program because of the complexity of some of the addressing modes. First of all, it is important to point out that almost all of the addressing modes on the 6502 are memory oriented rather than register oriented as they are on the Z80. Data in the 6502 is typically moved from location to location, two locations are compared with a third, and the contents of one memory location are combined with the contents of another. The typical Z80 programs often involve the swapping of data between registers and the flipping between the working register set and an alternate set. This inherent difference beween the chips is manifested in the basic difference between the machines that the chips drive and the software that those machines will eventually run.

SUMMARY OF INSTRUCTIONS

Alphabetical Listing of Instructions

ADC   Add with carry

AND   Logical AND

ASL   Shift memory or Accumulator 1 bit left

BCC   Branch if Carry Clear

BCS   Branch if Carry Flag Set

BEQ   Branch if Zero Flag Set

BIT   Test bit

BMI   Branch if Negative Flag Set (Branch on minus)

BNE   Branch if Zero Flag Clear

BPL   Branch if Negative Flag Clear (Branch on plus)

BRK   Forced break

BVC   Branch if Overflow Flag Clear

BVS   Branch if Overflow Flag Set

CLC   Clear Carry Flag

CLD   Clear the Decimal Flag

CLI   Clear the Interrupt Disable Flag

CLV   Clear the Overflow Flag

CMP   Compare memory to the Accumulator

CPX   Compare memory to X Register

CPY   Compare memory to Y Register

DEC   Decrement specified memory location

DEX   Decrement X Register

DEY   Decrement Y Register

EOR   Logical Exclusive OR memory with Accumulator

INC   Increment specified memory location

INX   Increment X Register

INY   Increment Y Register

JMP   Jump to new address

JSR   Jump to subroutine

LDA   Load Accumulator from memory

LDX   Load X Register from memory

LDY   Load Y Register from memory

LSR   Shift memory or Accumulator right

NOP   No operation

ORA   OR memory with Accumulator

PHA   Place contents of Accumulator onto stack

PLA   Pull contents off stack into Accumulator

PLP   Pull contents off stack into status processor

ROL   Rotate memory or Accumulator left

ROR   Rotate memory or Accumulator right

RTI   Return from interrupt

RTS   Return from subroutine

SBC   Subtract from memory and Carry

SEC   Set Carry Flag

SED   Set Decimal Flag

SEI   Set Interrupt Disable Flag

STA   Store contents of Accumulator in memory

STX   Store contents of X Register in memory

STY   Store contents of Y Register in memory

TAX   Transfer contents of Accumulator to X Register

TAY   Transfer contents of Accumulator to Y Register

TSX   Transfer stack pointer to X Register

TXA   Transfer contents of X Register to Accumulator

TXS   Transfer contents of X Register to stack pointer

TYA   Transfer contents of Y Register to Accumulator

8/16-BIT MICROPROCESSORS

Between the 8-bit microprocessors and the true 16-bit microprocessors exists a group of hybrids that share certain limitations of the former group and certain advantages of the latter. Of the 8/16's, only one, the Intel 8088, has achieved great success in the microcomputer industry. The Texas Instruments 9900 succeeded only to the extent that the now-defunct TI 99/4 series of home computers succeeded. These two will be described in detail here. There are others (e.g., National Semiconductor's INS8900) that are certainly not 8-bit chips but lack a fully developed 16-bit architecture. Because these lesser-known CPUs play no part in today's microcomputers, they have not been included here.

Texas Instruments TMS9900

In some respects, Texas Instruments TMS9900 is a highly sophisticated design, finding its first application in TI's minicomputer line. The first home microcomputer to use something more than an 8-bit chip was the TI 99/4 (later the 99/4A). That chip was the 9900. And while it uses 16-bit architecture and is more a memory-oriented than a register-oriented chip, it can address only 64 kilobytes, no greater than an 8-bit CPU.

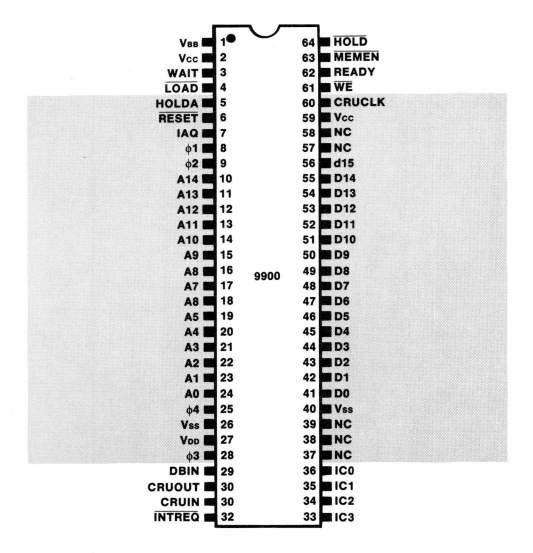

REGISTERS

The 9900 has four internal registers. They are the Program Counter, the Status Register, and the Workspace Register. The Program Counter and the Status Register perform much the same functions that they perform in other chip architectures. Of the three registers, the Workspace Register is unique to the TMS9900. The Workspace is a block of locations which can be used for holding data or used as a register file. The memory locations in the Workspace can be used as accumulators, registers for operands, address registers, and index registers. There is an additional register called the Workspace Pointer which indicates the area of the Workspace that is being addressed. Hardware input/output commands are channeled through the Communications Register Unit (CRU) which is a directly addressable command-driven hardware feature.

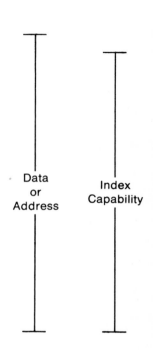

MEMORY ADDRESS	
WP + 00	0
WP + 02	1
WP + 04	2
WP + 06	3
WP + 08	4
WP + 0A	5
WP + 0C	6
WP + 0E	7
WP + 10	8
WP + 12	9
WP + 14	10
WP + 16	11
WP + 18	12
WP + 1A	13
WP + 1C	14
WP + 1E	15

Data or Address

Index Capability

STATUS FLAGS

The 9900 has a 16-bit status register consisting of the following flags:

Interrupt Mask: Identifies the level of interrupt currently enabled.

XOP: A software interrupt flag that is set when a software interrupt is executed.

Equal Flag: Set if a Branch-if-Equal condition exists or if a Control Register Unit bit is to be tested.

Arithmetic Greater Than Flag: Set during an arithmetic move operation.

Logical Greater Than: Set during a logical move operation.

Parity Flag

Overflow Flag

Carry Flag

ADDRESSING MODES

Absolute
Relative
Immediate
Register
Register Indirect
Register Indirect with Autoincrement
Indexed
CRU Bit Addressing

SUMMARY OF INSTRUCTIONS

Data Transfer Instructions

MOV   16-bit move

MOVB   8-bit move

LI (reg)   Load immediate to workspace

SWPB   Swap bytes to and from specified locations

Arithmetic and Logical Instructions

A   16-bit add

AB   8-bit add

S   16-bit subtract

SB   8-bit subtract

C   16-bit compare

CB   8-bit compare

XOR   Exclusive OR with workspace

MPY   Multiply

DIV   Divide

INC   Increment

DEC   Decrement

CLR   Clear

SETTO   Set to FFFF

INV   Ones complement

NEG   Twos complement

ABS   Absolute value

AI   Immediate Add

ANDI   Immediate AND

ORI   Immediate OR

CI   Immediate compare

Bit Set Instructions

SOC   Set bits in 16-bit destination

SOCB   Set bits in 8-bit destination

SZC   Clear bits in 16-bit destination

SZB   Clear bits in 8-bit destination

COC   Compare bits

CZC   Compare bits

Branching Instructions

B   Branch unconditionally

BL   Branch and link

BLWP   Branch and load workspace pointer

JMP   Unconditional jump

JMP (cond)   Conditional jump. Conditions can be arithmetic or logical, carry, no carry, overflow, no overflow, or parity.

Shift and Rotate Instructions

SLA   Arithmetic shift left

SRA   Arithmetic shift right

SRL   Logical shift right

SRC   Rotate right

Control Instructions

XOP   Software interrupt

X src   Execute contents of the source register as an instruction

RTWP   Return from a software interrupt

STST   Store the contents of the status register in the designated register

STWP   Store the contents of the workspace pointer in the designated register

CRU Instructions

LDCR   Load the CRU with a designated number of bits

STCR   Load specified destination from CRU

SBO   Set CRU bit

SBZ   Reset CRU bit

TB   Test CRU bit

Intel 8088

IBM's adoption of the Intel 8088 for the company's entry into the microcomputer market made a great success story of a CPU that otherwise would have in all likelihood passed quickly from the microcomputer scene. Because of its 8-bit external bus, the 8088 can use 8-bit support chips, a fact that adds to its cost effectiveness, a primary consideration in IBM's selection of this chip. The 8088 can be thought of as the IBM chip in more ways than one, for IBM now owns an appreciable share of Intel. The chip's characterization as an 8/16 derives from its 8-bit data bus. The chip has a 20-bit address bus, allowing for an addressing space of 1 megabyte (1,048,576 bytes).

The 8088 is divided into two separate processing units. One unit, called the Execution Unit, carries out all instructions. The other unit, the Bus Interface Unit, fetches instructions and moves data between the 16-bit internal bus and the 8-bit external bus. This enables the 8088, and its full 16-bit cousin, the 8086, to perform its computing functions internally while it is busy fetching and sending data back and forth. In other words, while the 8088 seems otherwise occupied by communicating with its 8-bit external environment, it is still doing its work within the internal 16-bit processor. This means that the 8088 is a faster microprocessor than its great grandfather, the 8080.

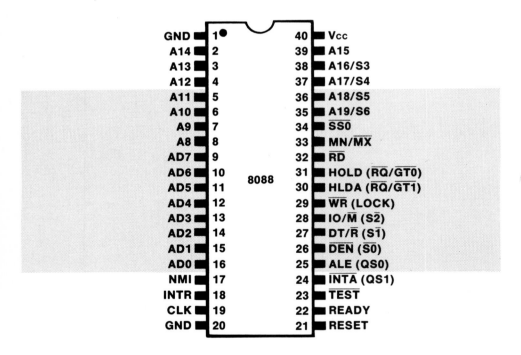

REGISTERS

The 8088 has fourteen 16-bit registers organized as follows:
Four 16-bit general registers which can also be subdivided and addressed separately as eight 8-bit registers.
Four 16-bit pointer and index registers.
One 16-bit status register that contains nine flags.
Four segment registers known as the code segment, data segment, stack segment, and extra segment.
One instruction pointer.

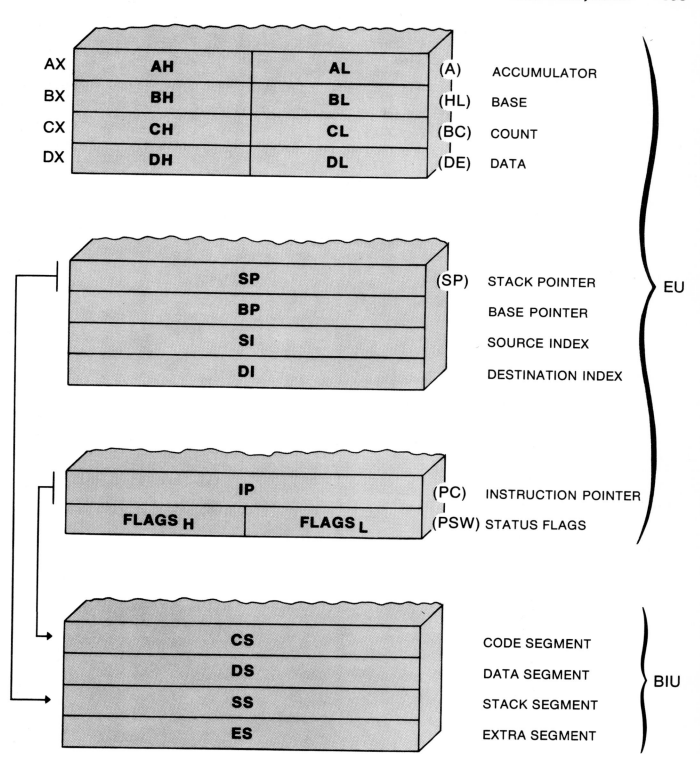

AX	AH	AL	(A)	ACCUMULATOR
BX	BH	BL	(HL)	BASE
CX	CH	CL	(BC)	COUNT
DX	DH	DL	(DE)	DATA

SP — (SP) STACK POINTER
BP — BASE POINTER
SI — SOURCE INDEX
DI — DESTINATION INDEX

IP — (PC) INSTRUCTION POINTER
FLAGS H   FLAGS L — (PSW) STATUS FLAGS

CS — CODE SEGMENT
DS — DATA SEGMENT
SS — STACK SEGMENT
ES — EXTRA SEGMENT

EU

BIU

FLAGS

Zero Flag: Set when the result of an operation is zero.
Sign Flag: Sets sign.
Parity Flag: Set when there is an even number of 1 bits as the result of an operation.

Carry Flag: Indicates when there is a carryover from an addition or a borrow from a subtraction.

Direction Flag: Indicates whether string operations will autoincrement or autodecrement.

Interrupt Flag: Set to enable interrupts.

Trap Flag: Set to cause a software interrupt after the execution of each instruction. Acknowledgement of the interrupt will reset the Trap Flag.

Auxiliary Carry Flag

Overflow Flag

ADDRESSING MODES

Direct Memory Addressing
Implied Memory Addressing
Direct Indexed Addressing
Base Relative Indexed Addressing
Data Memory Base Relative Addressing
Port Addressing
Program Relative Addressing

SUMMARY OF INSTRUCTIONS

In this subsection, "word" refers to 16-bit instructions and "byte" refers to 8-bit instructions.

Data Transfer Instructions

MOV   Move word

MOVB   Move byte

MOVI   Move immediate data

MOVBI   Move immediate data to byte destination

XCHG   Exchange contents of locations (word)

XCHGB   Exchange contents of locations (byte)

PUSH   Place data onto stack

POP   Take data from top of stack

IN   Input 2 bytes to register AX

INB   Input byte to register AL

OUT   Target output from register AX to target location (word)

OUTB   Target output from register AL to target location (byte)

OUT   Output from AX to DX (word)

OUTB   Output from AL to DX (byte)

XLAT   Translate

LEA   Load effective address

LDS   Load DS and register

LES   Load ES and register

Binary Integer Arithmetic Instructions

NEG   Negate contents of specified location (word)

NEGB   Negate in specified location (byte)

ADD   Add (word)

ADDB   Add (byte)

ADDI   Add immediate data to specified location (word)

ADDBI   Add immediate data to specified location (byte)

ADC   Add plus Carry (word)

ADCB   Add plus Carry (byte)

ADCI   Add immediate data plus Carry (word)

ADCBI   Add immediate data plus Carry (byte)

SUB   Subtract (word)

SUBB   Subtract (byte)

SUBI   Subtract immediate data from specified location (word)

SUBBI   Subtract immediate data from specified location (byte)

SBB   Subtract and borrow (word)

SBBB   Subtract and borrow (byte)

SBBI   Subtract and borrow immediate data from specified location (word)

SBBBI   Subtract and borrow immediate data from specified location (byte)

MUL   Unsigned 16-bit multiply

MULB   Unsigned 8-bit multiply

IMUL   Signed 16-bit multiply

IMULB   Signed 8-bit multiply

DIV   Unsigned 16-bit divide

DIVB   Unsigned 8-bit divide

IDIV   Signed 16-bit divide

IDIVB   Signed 8-bit divide

CBW   Convert from byte to word

CWD   Convert from word to double word

INC   Increment (word)

INCB   Increment (byte)

DEC   Decrement (word)

DECB   Decrement (byte)

Logical Operations

NOT   Logical NOT (word)

NOTB   Logical NOT (byte)

AND   Logical AND source location with target location (word)

ANDB   Logical AND source location with target location (byte)

ANDI   Logical AND immediate data with target location (word)

ANDIB   Logical AND immediate data with target location (byte)

OR   Logical OR source location with target location (word)

ORB   Logical OR source location with target location (byte)

ORI   Logical OR immediate data with target location (word)

ORIB   Logical OR immediate data with target location (byte)

XOR   Exclusive OR source location with target location (word)

XORB   Exclusive OR source location with target location (byte)

XORI   Exclusive OR immediate data with target location (word)

XORIB   Exclusive OR immediate data with target location (byte)

Shift and Rotate Instructions

These instructions specify the CL register as one of the operands and direct that the information be shifted or rotated by the number previously loaded into the CL register).

SHL   Logical shift left (word)

SHLB   Logical shift left (byte)

SHR   Logical shift right (word)

SHRB   Logical shift right (byte)

SAL   Arithmetic shift left (word)

SALB   Arithmetic shift left (byte)

SAR   Arithmetic shift right (word)

SARB   Arithmetic shift right (byte)

ROL   Rotate left (word)

ROLB   Rotate left (byte)

ROR   Rotate right (word)

RORB   Rotate right (byte)

RCL   Rotate left through Carry (word)

RCLB   Rotate left through Carry (byte)

RCR   Rotate right through Carry (word)

RCRB   Rotate right through Carry (byte)

Binary Coded Decimal Arithmetic

AAA   ASCII Adjust for Addition

DAA   Decimal Adjust for Addition

DAS   Decimal Adjust for Subtraction

AAM   ASCII Adjust for Multiplication

AAD   ASCII Adjust for Division

String Operation Instructions

REP   Repeat

MOVC   Move string Characters (byte)

MOVW   Move string Words

CMPC   Compare string Characters (byte)

CMPW   Compare string Words

SCAC   Scan string Characters (byte)

SCAW   Scan string Words

LODC   Load string Characters (byte)

LODW   Load string Words

STOC   Store string Characters (byte)

STOW   Store string Words

CLD   Clear Direction Flag

STD   Set Direction Flag

Jump Instructions

JMP   Direct jump

JMPS   Short jump

JMPI   Indirect jump

JMPL   Indirect long jump

JE   Jump if Equal

JZ   Jump if Zero

JNE   Jump if Not Equal

JNZ   Jump if Not Zero

JS   Jump if signed number (negative)

JNS   Jump if not signed number

JP   Jump if Parity (parity must be even)

JNP   Jump if Not Parity (parity must be odd)

JPE   Jump if Parity Even

JPO   Jump if Parity Odd

JL   Jump if Less Than

JNGE   Jump if Not Greater Than or Equal to

JNL   Jump if Not Less Than

JGE   Jump if Greater Than or Equal to

JLE   Jump if Less Than or Equal to

JNG   Jump if Not Greater Than

JNLE   Jump if Not Less Than or Equal to

JG   Jump if Greater Than

JB   Jump if Below

JNAE   Jump if Not Above or Equal to

JNB   Jump if Not Below

JAE   Jump if Above or Equal to

JBE   Jump if Below or Equal to

JNA   Jump if Not Above

JNBE   Jump if Not Below or Equal to

JCXZ   Jump if register CX is Zero

Compare and Test Instructions

CMP   Compare (word)

CMPB Compare (byte)

CMPI Compare against immediate data (word)

CMPBI Compare against immediate data (byte)

TEST Test

TESTB Test (byte)

TESTI Test against immediate data

TESTBI Test against immediate data (byte)

RETS Return from segment

RETS number Return from segment and adjust stack

Hardware and System Instructions

INT Interrupt

INTO Interrupt if Overflow

IRET Interrupt Return

CLI Clear Interrupt Flag

STI Set Interrupt Flag

HLT Halt

WAIT Wait

LOCK Lock

ESC Escape

NOP No Operation

CLC Clear Carry

STC Set Carry

CMC Complement Carry

SAHF Store register AH into Flags

LAHF Load register AH from Flags

PUSHF Push Flags

POPF Pop Flags

Call and Program Loop Instructions

CALL Direct call

CALLI Indirect call

CALLL Indirect long call

LOOP Loop

LOOPZ Loop if Zero

LOOPNZ Loop if Not Zero

LOOPE Loop if Equal

LOOPNE Loop if Not Equal

RET Return

RET number Return and adjust stack

16-BIT MICROPROCESSORS

The following subsections cover four 16-bit microprocessors: Intel 8086, Zilog Z8001, Zilog Z8002, and Motorola 68000 (actually, a 16/32 hybrid).

Intel 8086

The Intel 8086 is a full 16-bit version of the 8088. (The "8" in 88 means 8-bit; the "6" in 86 means 16-bit.) Programmers familiar with Intel's earlier chips will have relatively little difficulty in moving to the 8086.

Programs written for the 8088 and 8086 are mutually compatible. The 8086 has the same architecture, addressing modes, and set of instructions as the 8088 with the exception of the Bus Interface Unit. The 8088 BIU must communicate with an 8-bit external bus and, therefore, must address an 8-bit universe. The 8086 is designed to communicate with a 16-bit external bus and, consequently, it does not have to convert data from 16 to 8 bits.

The internal and external functions on the 8086 enable the chip to perform tasks concurrently that other chips have to perform sequentially. For example, data communication functions on a Z80 require that an interrupt of sorts take place so that the instructions for performing an input or output function can be executed. On the 8086, the input or output function can take place while the chip's internal processor is working away.

The data pipelining method incorporated into the design of the 8086 allows this simulated coprocessing to take place. Data pipelining means that when the external processor of the 8086 fetches an instruction, rather than turning it over immediately to the internal processor, it places it on a special stack of instructions called a queue. The Execution Unit of the 8086 pulls the specific 2-byte instruction off the top of the queue when it is finished executing the previous instruction.

But instructions on the queue can pile up as they are fetched from the external environment by the Bus Interface Unit because they are stacked on a first-

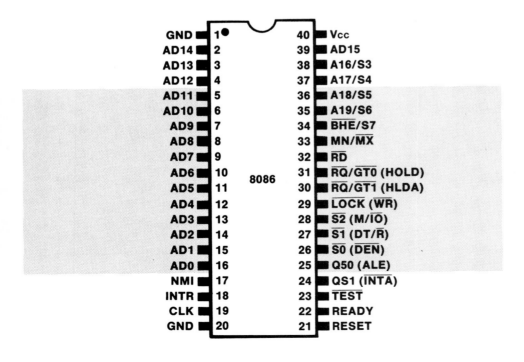

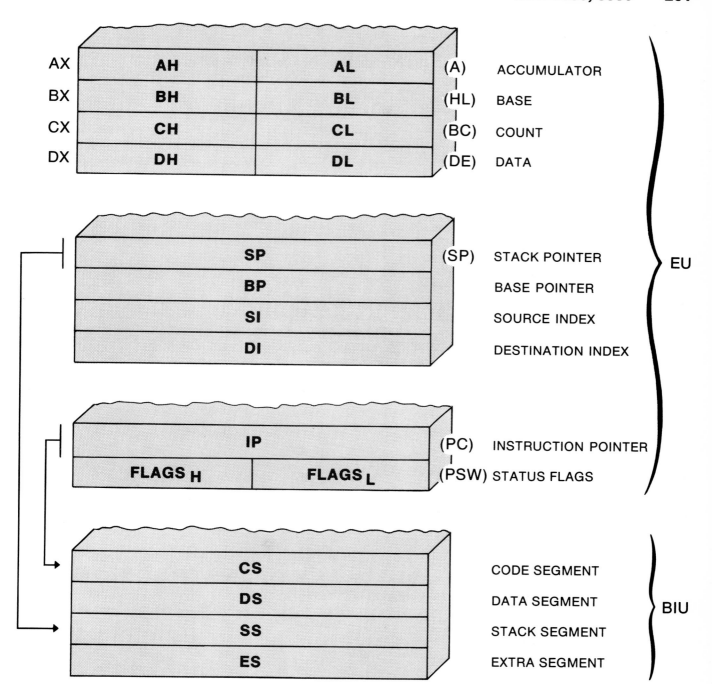

in, first-out basis. This is how the two processors work in tandem and keep from interfering with the activities of the other.

Since the primary task of the 8086 is the internal computing of data, the BIU's interface management and stacking operations free the Execution Unit by performing all of the organizational housekeeping chores necessary to keep the chip in communication with the rest of the system.

REGISTERS

The 8086 has fourteen 16-bit registers organized as follows:
Four 16-bit general registers which can also be subdivided and addressed

separately as eight 8-bit registers.
Four 16-bit pointer and index registers.
One 16-bit status register that contains nine flags.
Four segment registers known as the code segment, data segment, stack segment, and extra segment.
One instruction pointer.

FLAGS

Zero Flag: Set when the result of an operation is zero.
Sign Flag: Sets sign.
Parity Flag: Set when there is an even number of 1 bits as the result of an operation.
Carry Flag: Indicates when there is a carryover from an addition or a borrow from a subtraction.
Direction Flag: Indicates whether string operations will autoincrement or autodecrement.
Interrupt Flag: Set to enable interrupts.
Trap Flag: Set to cause a software interrupt after the execution of each instruction. Acknowledgement of the interrupt will reset the Trap Flag.
Auxiliary Carry Flag
Overflow Flag

ADDRESSING MODES

Direct Memory Addressing
Implied Memory Addressing
Direct Indexed Addressing
Base Relative Indexed Addressing
Data Memory Base Relative Addressing
Port Addressing
Program Relative Addressing

SUMMARY OF INSTRUCTIONS

The instructions are the same as for the preceding Intel 8088 microprocessor.

Zilog Z8000

There are actually two basic versions of the Zilog Z8000, the one of concern here being the Z8001, which can address 8 megabytes. The Z8002 is limited to 64 kilobytes of addressing space. The Z8000 has not found the favor with system designers that is enjoyed by the company's justly popular Z80, nor is there any compatibility between the two chips. One interesting feature of the Z8000 is the use of word-sized (16-bit) instead of byte-sized (8-bit) opcodes.

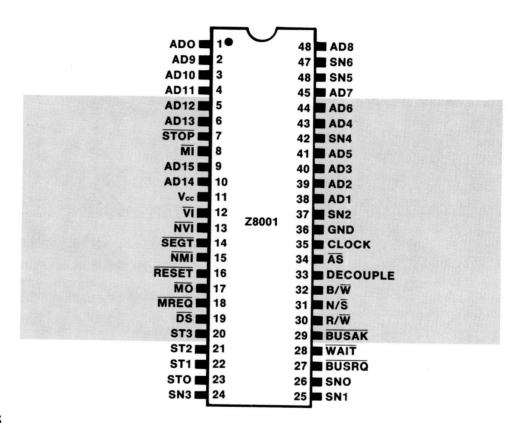

INTERNAL REGISTERS

The Z8000 is actually supplied as two processors: the Z8001 for complex configurations and the Z8002 for simpler configurations. The CPU has 16 general registers, all of which can be used as accumulators and all but one of which can be used as index registers or memory address pointers. The registers can be used as individual 16-bit registers, 32-bit paired registers, or 64-bit quadruple registers. The Z8000 has a memory refresh register, a program counter, and a second offset register. The PSAP, or Program Status Area Pointer, is a 16-bit single register and is associated with a second segment register. The status register, called the Flag and Control Word register on the Z8000, is also a single 16-bit register which controls interrupts and mode switches.

FLAGS

The Flag and Control Word register contains the following status flags:

Parity Flag: Set to 1 for even parity and cleared for odd.
Zero Flag: Set to 1 when the result of an operation is 0.

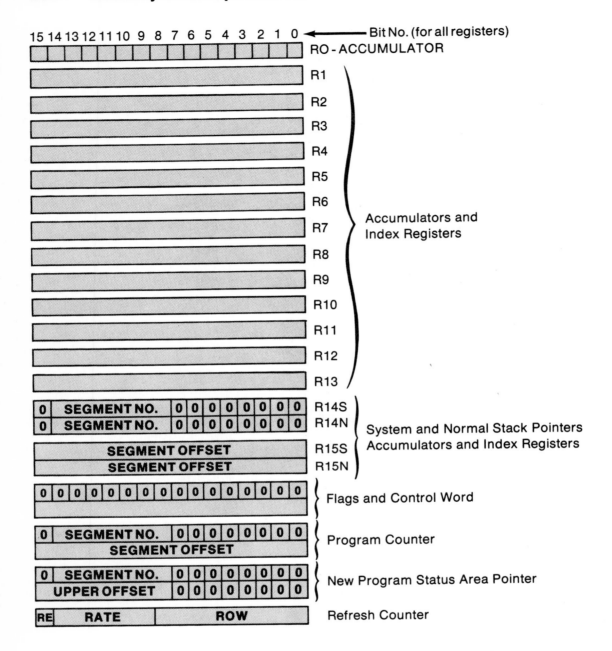

VIE: Enables vectored interrupts.

NVIE: Enables nonvectored interrupts.

System/Normal Mode Status Flag: Used to shift between system and normal mode. On 1, the CPU operates in system mode; on 0 it operates in normal mode.

SEG Status Flag: Used by the Z8001 only. When it is set to 1, the Z8001 operates on segmented mode.

Additional flags are:

Z8000 Carry Flag
Auxiliary Carry Flag
Decimal Adjust Flag
Overflow Flag
Sign Flag

ADDRESSING MODES

Base Address
Implied Memory Addressing
Direct Memory Addressing
Long Segmented Direct Memory Addressing
Short Segmented Direct Memory Addressing
Indexed Addressing
Short Segmented Indexed Addressing
Long Segmented Indexed Addressing
Base Relative Addressing
Implied Indexed Addressing
Short Segmented Base Relative Addressing
Long Segmented Base Relative Addressing
Program Relative Addressing
Indexed Memory Addressing
Autoincrement and Autodecrement

SUMMARY OF INSTRUCTIONS

Input/Output Commands

IN   Input to 16-bit register

INB   Input to 8-bit register

IND   Input and decrement (16-bits)

INDB   Input and decrement (8-bits)

INDR   Repeat IND until 0 (16-bits)

INDRB   Repeat INDB until 0 (8-bits)

INI   Input and increment (16-bits)

INIB   Input and increment (8-bits)

INIR   Repeat INI until 0 (16-bits)

INIRB   Repeat INIR until 0 (16-bits)

OTDR   Output block of words from designated location to specified I/O port and decrement

OTDRB   Output a block of 8-bit bytes and decrement as in previous instruction

OTIR   Repeat OTDR until 0

OTIRB   Repeat OTDRB until 0

OUT   Output (16-bits)

OUTB   Output (8-bits)

OUTD   Output and decrement (16-bits)

OUTDB   Output and decrement (8-bits)

OUTI   Output and increment (16-bits)

OUTIB   Output and increment (8-bits)

SIN   SIN to SOUTIB operate exactly like IN to OUTIB; all input and output is channeled through pins STO-ST3

SINB   Special I/O commands for 16 and 8 bits respectively

SIND   Inputs and decrements

SINDB   Input and decrement (8-bits)

SINDR   Repeat SIND until 0 (16-bits)

SINDRB   Repeat SINDB until 0 (8-bits)

SINI   Input and increment (16-bits)

SINIB   Input and increment (8-bits)

SINIR   Repeat SINI until 0 (16-bits)

SINIRB   Repeat SINIB until 0 (16-bits)

SOTDR   Output block of words from designated location to I/O and decrement

SOTDRB   Output a block of 8-bit bytes and decrement as in previous instruction

SOTIR   Repeat SOTDR until 0

SOTIRB   Repeat SOTDRB until 0

SOUT   Output (16-bits)

SOUTB   Output (8-bits)

SOUTD   Output and decrement (16-bits)

SOUTDB   Output and decrement (8-bits)

SOUTI   Output and increment (16-bits)

SOUTIB   Output and increment (8-bits)

Primary Memory Reference Instructions

LD   16-bit load

LDB   8-bit load

LDL   32-bit load

LDA   Load segmented/nonsegmented/base address/implied/indexed (16- or 32-bits)

LDAR   Load relative segmented/nonsegmented (16- and 32-bits)

LDR   Load program relative addressing (16-bits)

LDRB   Load program relative addressing (8-bits)

LDB   Load base relative addressing/implied, indexed addressing

LDL   Load base relative addressing/implied, indexed addressing (32-bits)

LD   Store data (16-bits)

LDB   Store data (8-bits)

LDL   Store data (32-bits)

LDRL   Load (32-bits) into memory location using program relative addressing

Secondary Memory Reference

ADD   Add (16-bit)

ADDB   Add (8-bit)

ADDL   Add (32-bit)

AND   AND designated register with memory (16-bits)

ANDB   AND designated register with memory (8-bits)

CLR   Clear word in memory

CLRB   Clear byte in memory

COM   Ones complement memory word

COMB   Ones complement memory byte

CP   Compare register and memory location (16-bits)

CPB   Compare register and memory location (8-bits)

CPL   Compare register and memory location (32-bits)

DEC   Subtract immediate value from memory word

DECB   Subtract immediate value from memory byte

DIV   Divide

DIVL   Divide long

EX   Exchange contents of specified registers (16-bits)

EXB   Exchange contents of specified registers (8-bits)

INC   Add the value of the immediate data to the memory word

INCB   Add the value of the immediate data to the memory byte

MULT   Multiply

MULTL   Multiply long

NEG   Replace the contents of the memory word by twos complement

NEGB   Replace the contents of the memory byte by twos complement

OR   Inclusive OR the contents of the specified 16-bit register and the memory word and place the result in the 16-bit register

ORB   Inclusive OR the contents of the specified 8-bit register and the memory byte and place the result in the 8-bit register

SUB   Subtract (16-bits)

SUBB   Subtract (8-bits)

SUBL Subtract (32-bits)

TEST OR the designated memory contents with 0 and set Status Flags (16-bits)

TESTB OR the designated memory contents with 0 and set Status Flags (8-bits)

TESTL OR the designated memory contents with 0 and set Status Flags (32-bits)

TSET Move the significant bit of the memory word to the Sign Flag

TSETB Move the significant bit of the memory byte to the Sign Flag

XOR Exclusive OR the contents of the designated memory location and register and store the result in the register (16-bits)

XORB Exclusive OR the contents of the designated memory location and register and store the result in the register (8-bits)

Instructions for Immediate Data Operations

LD Load 16 bits of immediate data into 16-bit register

LDB Load 8 bits of immediate data into 8-bit register

LDL Load 32 bits of immediate data into 32-bit register

LDK Load the immediate 4-bit value of data into 16-bit register and clear the remaining 12 bits

PUSH Place immediate data on stack

Jump and Call Subroutine Instructions

JP Jump to the designated memory location

JR Jump program relative

LDPS Load program status and jump to designated memory location

CALL Call addressed subroutine

CALR Call program relative

RET Return from subroutine

SC System subroutine call

Instructions for Operations with Immediate Data

ADD Add immediate 16-bit data to designated 16-bit register

ADDB Add immediate 8-bit data to designated 8-bit register

ADDL Add immediate 32-bit data to designated 32-bit register

AND AND immediate 16-bit data to 16-bit register

ANDB AND immediate 8-bit data to 8-bit register

CP Compare immediate 16-bit data with 16-bit register. Save Status Flags.

CPB Compare immediate 8-bit data with 8-bit register. Save Status Flags.

CPL Compare immediate 32-bit data with 32-bit register. Save Status Flags.

DIV Divide

DIVL Divide long

MULT Multiply

MULTL Multiply long

OR OR contents of designated 16-bit register with immediate data word

ORB OR contents of designated 8-bit register with immediate data byte

SUB Subtract immediate 16-bit data from designated 16-bit register

SUBB Subtract immediate 8-bit data from designated 8-bit register

SUBL Subtract immediate 32-bit data from designated 32-bit register

XOR Exclusive OR contents of designated 16-bit register with immediate data word

XORB Exclusive OR contents of designated 8-bit register with immediate data byte

Conditional Branch and Jump Instructions

DJNZ Decrement 16-bit register and Jump if Not Zero

DBJNZ Decrement 8-bit register and Jump if Not Zero

JP Jump to specified location if designated condition code is true

JR Jump program relative if designated condition code is true

Instructions for Register-to-Register Move Operations

EX Exchange contents of designated 16-bit registers

EXB Exchange contents of designated 8-bit registers

LD Move data between any two 16-bit registers

LDB Move data between any two 8-bit registers

LDL Move data between any two 32-bit registers

Block Transfer and Search Operations

CPD Search specified string for designated condition and compare word with next word using implied memory addressing

CPDB Search specified string for designated condition and compare byte with next byte using implied memory addressing

CPDR Repeat CPD until Zero

CPDBR Repeat CPDB until Zero

CPI Perform CPD and increment implied memory address by 2

CPIB Perform CPDB and increment implied memory address by 1

CPIR Repeat CPI until Zero

CPIBR Repeat CPIB until Zero

CPSD Compare two strings for designated condition as follows: Compare word in source string with word in target string. Both strings are addressed in implied memory addressing mode. If condition code is true, Zero Flag is set to 1, else reset to 0. Decrement implied memory address by 2.

CPSDB Compare two strings for designated condition as follows: Compare byte in source string with byte in target string. Both strings are addressed in implied memory addressing mode. If condition code is true, Zero Flag is set to 1, else reset to 0. Decrement implied memory address by 1.

CPSDR Repeat CPSD until 0

CPSDRB Repeat CPSDB until 0

CPSI Perform CPSD and increment implied memory address by 2

CPSIB Perform CPSDB and increment implied memory address by 1

CPSIR Repeat CPSI until 0

CPSIRB Repeat CPSIB until 0

LDD Transfer a word from designated memory location to designated memory location and decrement addresses by 2

LDDB Transfer a byte from designated memory location to designated memory location and decrement addresses by 1

LDDR Repeat LDD until register has decremented to 0

LDDRB Repeat LDDB until register has decremented to 0

LDI Perform LDD but increment by 2

LDIB Perform LDDB but increment by 1

LDIR Repeat LDI until register rw decrements to 0

LDIRB Repeat LDIB until register rw decrements to 0

LDM Move block of memory words from memory to register or register to memory

TRDB Translate memory byte and decrement destination address and byte counter

TRDRB Repeat TRDB until register rw = 0

TRIB Perform TRDB but increment destination address

TRIRB Repeat TRIB until register rw = 0

TRTDB Load a table byte into register RH1 and decrement destination address and byte counter

TRTDRB Repeat TRTDB until 0

TRTIB Perform TRTDB but increment destination address

TRTIRB Repeat TRTIB until 0

Register-to-Register Operations

ADC Add source 16-bit register plus Carry to target 16-bit register

ADCB Add source 8-bit register plus Carry to target 8-bit register

ADD Add source 16-bit register to target 16-bit register

ADDB Add source 8-bit register to target 8-bit register

ADDL Add source 32-bit register to target 32-bit register

AND AND source 16-bit register to target 16-bit register

ANDB AND source 8-bit register to target 8-bit register

ANDL AND source 32-bit register to target 32-bit register

CP Compare 16-bit register contents by subtracting source from target register and set Status Flags

CPB Compare 8-bit register contents by subtracting source from target register and set Status Flags

CPL Compare 32-bit register contents by subtracting source from target register and set Status Flags

DIV Divide

DIVL Divide long

MULT Multiply

MULTL Multiply long

OR OR contents of 16-bit source register with 16-bit target register

ORB OR contents of 8-bit source register with 8-bit target register

RLDB Rotate register left

RRDB Rotate register right

SBC Subtract 16-bit source from 16-bit destination register, using twos complement arithmetic

SBCB Subtract 8-bit source from 8-bit destination register, using twos complement arithmetic

SUB Subract 16-bit source from 16-bit destination register

SUBB Subract 8-bit source from 8-bit destination register

SUBL Subract 32-bit source from 32-bit destination register

XOR Exclusive OR contents of 16-bit source register with 16-bit target register

XORB Exclusive OR contents of 8-bit source register with 8-bit target register

Instructions for Operations within the Register

CLR Clear specified word register

CLRB Clear specified byte register

COM Complement specified word register

COMB Complement specified byte register

DAB Decimal adjust contents of 8-bit register rbd

DEC Subtract an immediate value of 16 times variable number (n) from 16-bit register

DECB Subtract an immediate value of 16 times variable number (n) from 8-bit register

EXTS The sign bit of the low-order word of the register pair is copied into all bits of the high-order word of the register pair

EXTSB The sign bit of the low-order byte of the register is copied into all bits of the high-order byte of the register

EXTSL The sign bit of the low-order register pair of the quadruple register is copied into all bits of the high-order register pair

INC Add an immediate value of 16 times variable number (n) to 16-bit register

INCB Add an immediate value of 16 times variable number (n) to 8-bit register

NEG Replace contents of 16-bit register with twos complement

NEGB Replace contents of 8-bit register with twos complement

RL Left rotate contents of word

RLB Left rotate contents of byte

RLC Left rotate through Carry contents of word

RLCB Left rotate through Carry contents of byte

RR Right rotate contents of word

RRB Right rotate contents of byte

RRC Right rotate through Carry contents of word

RRCB Right rotate through Carry contents of byte

SDA Shift (right or left) the contents of a word

SDAB Shift (right or left) the contents of a byte

SDAL Shift (right or left) the contents of a long word

SDL Shift logical right or shift left the contents of a word

SDLB Shift logical right or shift left the contents of a byte

SDLL Shift logical right or shift left the contents of a long word

SLA Implements SDA with an immediate shift bit count

SLAB Implements SDAB with an immediate shift bit count

SLAL Implements SDAL with an immediate shift bit count

SLL Identical to SDL on left shift, but specifies immediate shift bit count

SLLB Identical to SDLB on left shift, but specifies immediate shift bit count

SLLL Identical to SDLL on left shift, but specifies immediate shift bit count

SRA Identical to SDA on right shift, but specifies immediate shift bit count

SRAB Identical to SDAB on right shift, but specifies immediate shift bit count

SRAL Identical to SDAL on right shift, but specifies immediate shift bit count

SRL Identical to SDL on right shift, but specifies immediate shift bit count

SRLB Identical to SDLB on right shift, but specifies immediate shift bit count

SRLL Identical to SDLL on right shift, but specifies immediate shift bit count

TSET Moves most significant bit of the 16-bit register to Sign and fills register with 1 bit

TSETB Moves most significant bit of the 8-bit register to Sign and fills register with 1 bit

TEST Logical OR contents of specified 16-bit register with 0

TESTB Logical OR contents of specified 8-bit register with 0

TESTL Logical OR contents of specified 32-bit register with 0

Instructions that Manipulate the Stack

LDCTL Transfer data between specified 16-bit register and Z8001 Normal Stack Pointer Segment Address register

POP Pop word from memory and load into 16-bit register or new memory location

POPL Executes POP with 32-bit word

PUSH Push a 16-bit word onto memory stack from register, memory location, or immediate data

PUSHL Executes PUSH with 32-bit word

Bit Manipulation Operations

BIT Set Zero Flag status to complement of specified bit in designated 16-bit register

BITB Set Zero Flag status to complement of specified bit in designated 8-bit register

RES Clear bit in 16-bit register or memory

RESB Clear bit in 8-bit register or memory

SET Sets bit cleared in RES

SETB   Sets bit cleared in RESB

Interrupts

DI   Disable designated interrupt

EI   Enable designated interrupt

IRET   Return from interrupt

LDCTL   Transfers data between Z8001 Program Status Area Pointer Segment register and designated 16-bit general-purpose register

Status Register Instructions

COMFLG   Complement designated flag

LDCTL   Load register FCW or FCW register (16-bit)

LDCTLB   Load byte register FCW or FCW byte register

RESFLG   Reset designated flag

SETFLG   Set designated flag

TCC   Test for cc="true" (16-bits)

TCCB   Test for cc="true" (8-bits)

Processor Control and Hardware Instructions

HALT   Halt operation until reset or interrupt

LDCTL Refresh   Transfer contents between designated 16-bit register and the Dynamic Memory Refresh Control register

MBIT   Set Sign status to 1 if multi-micro input signal is low or reset to 0 if input signal is high

MREQ   Executes a multi-micro bus request

MRES   Resets Sign status to 0 if multi-micro output signal is high

MSET   Sets Sign status to 1 if multi-micro output signal is low

NOP   No operation

Zilog Z8002

Zilog's implementation of the Z8000 is a two-chip solution to the problem of targeting specific applications with a single basic design. The Z8000 addresses the needs of two different types of systems. The latter system is a true microcomputer requiring no chip-resident memory management and an addressing capability of 64K. The Z8002 is a 40-pin device, in contrast to the 48-pin Z8001, that will nonetheless handle the rudimentary demands of certain applications software.

One of the more important features of this member of the Z8000 family, which makes it a markedly more advanced device than its predecessors, is a special software feature which sends the chip into a supervisory mode. The reason for this mode is simple: the Z8000 has a series of input/output operations, hardware control instructions, and interrupt handling instructions which, if misused by a novice programmer, could seriously disrupt the chip's operation in a multiuser environment. The creation of a "privileged mode of use" was designed to prevent the potential of this disruption by elevating the critical input/output and hardware control commands to a supervisory status. In this way, certain critical commands can only be executed when the chip is in the supervisory mode, and this mode that can only be invoked by an external interrupt on the system.

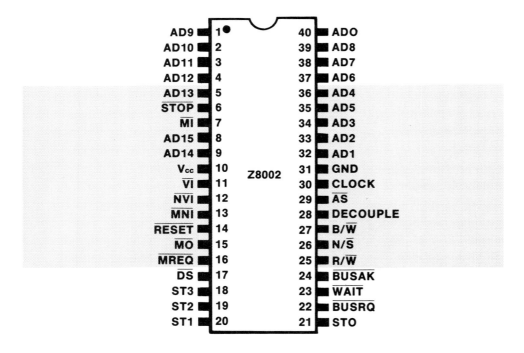

INTERNAL REGISTERS

The Z8000 is actually supplied as two processors: the Z8001 for complex configurations and the Z8002 for simpler configurations. The CPU has 16 general registers, all of which can be used as accumulators and all but one of which can be used as index registers or memory address pointers. The registers can be used as individual 16-bit registers, 32-bit paired registers, or 64-bit quadruple registers. The Z8000 has a memory refresh register, a program counter, and a second offset register. The PSAP, or Program Status Area Pointer, is a 16-bit single register and is associated with a second segment register. The status register, called the Flag and Control Word register on the Z8000, is also a single 16-bit register which controls interrupts and mode switches.

FLAGS

The Flag and Control Word register contains the following status flags:

Parity Flag: Set to 1 for even parity and cleared for odd.
Zero Flag: Set to 1 when the result of an operation is 0.
VIE: Enables vectored interrupts.
NVIE: Enables nonvectored interrupts.
System/Normal Mode Status Flag: Used to shift between system and normal mode. On 1, the CPU operates in system mode; on 0 it operates in normal mode.
Z8000 Carry Flag
Auxiliary Carry Flag
Decimal Adjust Flag
Overflow Flag
Sign Flag

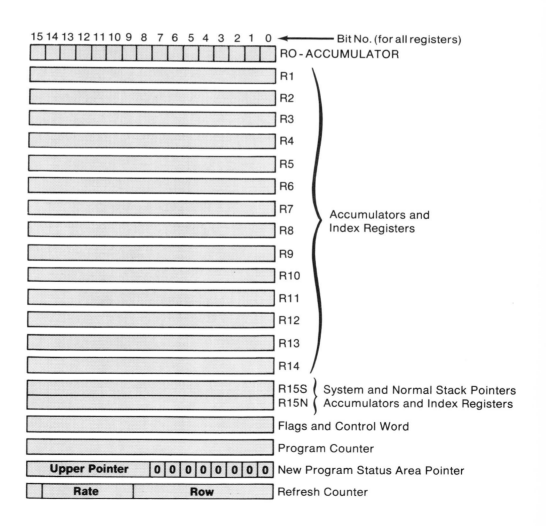

ADDRESSING MODES

Base Address
Implied Memory Addressing
Direct Memory Addressing
Long Segmented Direct Memory Addressing
Short Segmented Direct Memory Addressing
Indexed Addressing
Short Segmented Indexed Addressing
Long Segmented Indexed Addressing
Base Relative Addressing
Implied Indexed Addressing
Short Segmented Base Relative Addressing
Long Segmented Base Relative Addressing
Program Relative Addressing
Indexed Memory Addressing
Autoincrement and Autodecrement

SUMMARY OF INSTRUCTIONS

The instructions are the same as for the preceding Zilog Z8000 micro-processor.

Motorola 68000

The Apple Lisa and Macintosh computers, which make intensive use of graphics, were designed around the Motorola 68000, perhaps the most versatile and powerful of the microprocessors currently available on a production basis. Highly sophisticated memory management techniques and the ability to handle data in segments of 8, 16, and 32 bits make of the 68000 a mainframe-like CPU. Strictly speaking, the 68000 should be categorized as a 16/32 hybrid.

The 68000, like the Z8000, has two modes of operation. On the 68000, these modes are called the Supervisor mode and the User mode, and each has a separate stack pointer for executing instructions. Running in the Supervisor mode, the 68000 can execute certain privileged commands that take priority over User mode instructions. Therefore, in intensive applications such as "MacWrite" and "MacPaint" on Apple's 68000-based Macintosh, system commands that drive the screen and menu overlays can be separated easily from the applications commands. The chip has a 32-bit-wide data and address register structure and a 32-bit program counter.

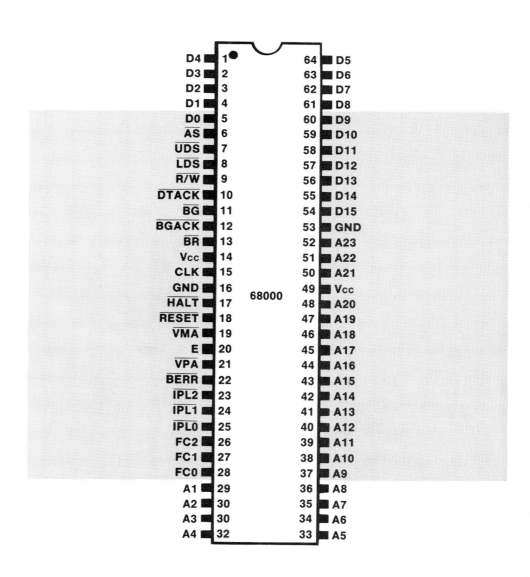

REGISTERS

Data Registers: There are seventeen 32-bit data and address registers and a 16-bit status register. The data registers can also be used as index registers and data counters in addition to their primary function as source and destination registers.

Address Registers: There are also seven general-purpose address registers that can handle words of 16 or 32 bits.

Stack Pointers: There are two stack pointers on the 68000, one for the Supervisor mode and one for the User mode. Mode switching is accomplished by setting the S-bit in the status register. Usually, the Supervisor mode is used only for system commands which will take priority over applications commands. Setting the S-bit to move from mode to mode allows system commands to be always accessible to the user, even from within applications because once the S-bit is set to a particular mode, only that mode's stack pointer is enabled.

Status Register: There is a 16-bit status register which is divided into two 8-bit bytes: the System byte and the User byte. The System byte of the register contains status information that is related to the operation of the system such as the Trace Mode Flag, the S-bit select, and the Interrupt Mask. Bits in the System byte of the 68000 can only be altered when the chip is operating in the Supervisor mode. The status flags in the User byte indicate condition code status such as Carry, Overflow, Negative, and Zero. They are program related and indicate the results of an instruction in a program.

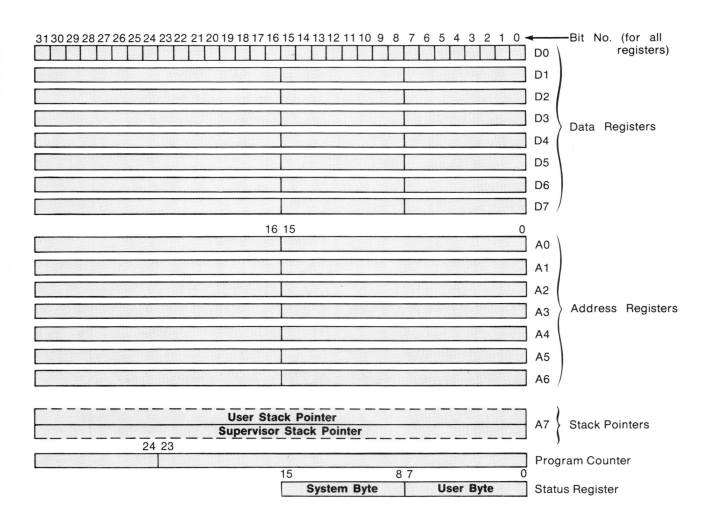

FLAGS

The 68000 status register contains the following flags:

Carry Flag: Set on a carry or borrow from the most significant bit during addition or subtraction.

Overflow Flag: When set, signifies a magnitude overflow.

Zero Flag: Set whenever the result of an operation is 0.

Negative Flag: Equal to the value of the most significant result bit following an arithmetic calculation.

Extend Flag: Set to the same state as the Carry Flag and used in multiprecision arithmetic calculations.

Interrupt Mask: Indicates the seven levels of interrupt.

S-bit: Indicates whether the chip is in the Supervisor or the User mode. When the bit is set to 1, the chip is in the Supervisor mode.

Trace Mode Flag: When set, puts the chip into a single step mode. This effectively opens a trap after each instruction so that the execution of each instruction can be monitored.

ADDRESSING MODES

Register Direct Addressing: Includes Data Register Direct and Address Register Direct.

Register Indirect Addressing: Includes Register Indirect, Postincrement Register Indirect, Postdecrement Register Indirect, Register Indirect with Offset, Indexed Register Indirect with Offset.

Absolute Addressing: Includes Absolute Short and Absolute Long.

Program Counter Relative Addressing: Includes Relative with Offset and Relative with Index and Offset.

Immediate Data Addressing: Includes Immediate and Quick Immediate.

Implied Register Addressing

Unlike the Z8000 and the 8086, the 68000 has a 64-pin configuration. This means that there is no need for multiplexing and demultiplexing information that has to share the same pin with another signal. The 68000 eliminates the need for this because each type of message is confined to its own chip.

The 68000 forms the third element of a family of 16- and 32 × 16-bit chips that began with the Intel 8086 and includes the Z8000. All three chips try to address the problem of combining the attributes of a simple system configuration with the power of a complex system configuration. The former mode is an easy-to-program mode of operation that places no real demands upon the design of the microprocessor. The latter mode points not in the direction of desktop personal computers but to the environment of the minicomputer with its multitasking capabilities and concurrent applications. It is to this environment that the 68000 is directed.

How the three chips satisfy the demands of both types of environments is an illustration of their design features. The 8086 combines both modes of operation in a single device by utilizing a series of dual function pins which carry more than one type of signal. The pins effectively serve the demands of a simple system with one function and the demands of a more complex system with another function. The signals on the pin are multiplexed on output and demultiplexed by the system so that the signals do not mix. The Z8000 solves the problem of addressing two modes of operation because it is supplied in two different hardware configurations.

SUMMARY OF INSTRUCTIONS

Input/Output
Primary Memory Reference Instructions

LEA   Load effective address into designated address register

MOVE.B   Store or load byte to data register or memory location from specified memory location

MOVE.W   Store or load word to data register or memory location from specified memory location

MOVE.L   Store or load long word to data register or memory location from specified memory location

MOVEM.W   Store or load multiple words to data registers or memory locations with postincrement or predecrement specified memory locations or registers

MOVEM.L   Perform MOVEM.W with long words and move all 32-bits of the registers

MOVEP.W   Store or load peripheral data bytes from alternate memory locations to data register word or from data register long to alternate memory locations

MOVEP.L   Store or load peripheral data bytes from alternate memory locations to data register long or from data register long to alternate memory locations

Arithmetic and Logical Instructions

ABCD   Add decimal memory byte to memory byte with carry

ADD.B   Add byte (data register from memory location*memory location from data register)

ADD.W   Add word (data register from memory location*memory location from data register)

ADD.L   Add long word (data register from memory location*memory location from data register*address register from memory location)

ADDX.B   Add memory byte to memory byte with carry

ADDX.W   Add memory word to memory word with carry

ADDX.L   Add memory long word to memory long word with carry

AND.B   AND byte (data register from memory location*memory location from data register)

AND.W   AND word (data register from memory location*memory location from data register)

AND.L   AND long word (data register from memory location*memory location from data register)

CLR.B   Clear memory byte to zeroes

CLR.W   Clear memory word to zeroes

CLR.L   Clear memory long word to zeroes

CMP.B   Compare data register byte with memory byte and set condition codes

CMP.W   Compare (data*address) register word with memory word and set condition codes

CMP.L   Compare (data*address) register long word with memory long word and set condition codes

CMPM.B   Compare memory bytes and set condition codes

CMPM.W   Compare memory words and set condition codes

CMPM.L   Compare memory long words and set condition codes

DIVS   Divide signed numbers

DIVU   Divide unsigned numbers

EOR.B   Exclusive OR byte to memory location from data ragister

EOR.W   Exclusive OR word to memory location from data register

EOR.L   Exclusive OR long word to memory location from data register

MULS   Multiply two signed 16-bit numbers to yield a 32-bit signed product

MULU   Multiply two unsigned 16-bit numbers to yield a 32-bit unsigned product

NBCD   Negate decimal memory byte

NEG.B   Negate memory byte

NEG.W   Negate memory word

NEG.L   Negate memory long word

NEGX.B   Negate memory byte with extend bit

NEGX.W   Negate memory word with extend bit

NEGX.L   Negate memory long word with extend bit

NOT.B   Ones complement memory byte

NOT.W   Ones complement memory word

NOT.L   Ones complement memory long word

OR.B   OR byte (data register from memory location*-memory location from data register)

OR.W   OR word (data register from memory location*memory location from data register)

OR.L   OR long word (data register from memory location*memory location from data register)

SBCD   Subtract decimal memory byte from memory byte with carry

SCC   Set status in memory byte

SUB.B   Subtract byte (memory from data register*data register from memory)

SUB.W   Subtract word (memory from data register*data register from memory*memory from address register)

SUB.L   Subtract long word (memory from data register*data register from memory*memory from address register)

SUBX.B   Subtract memory byte from memory byte with borrow

SUBX.W   Subtract memory word from memory word with borrow

SUBX.L   Subtract memory long word from memory long word with borrow

TAS   Test status of memory byte and set high-order bit to 1

TST.B   Test status of memory byte and byte value remains unchanged

TST.W   Test status of memory word and word value remains unchanged

TST.L   Test status of memory long word and long word value remains unchanged

Immediate Operation Instructions

MOVEQ   Load immediate data byte to data register

MOVE.B   Load immediate data byte (data register*-memory location)

MOVE.W   Load immediate data word (data register*address register*memory location)

MOVE.L   Load immediate data long word (data register*address register* memory location)

Arithmetic and Instructions

ADD.B   Add immediate data byte to (data register*-memory location)

ADD.W   Add immediate data word to (data or address register*memory location)

ADD.L   Add immediate data long word to (data or address register*memory location)

ADDQ.B   Add immediate three bits to (data register*-memory location) byte

ADDQ.W   Add immediate three bits to (data or address register*memory location) word

ADDQ.L   Add immediate three bits to (data or address register*memory location) long word

AND.B   AND immediate data byte to (data register*-memory location) byte

AND.W   AND immediate data word to (data register*memory location) word

AND.L   AND immediate data long word to (data register*memory location) long word

CMP.B   Compare (data register*memory byte with immediate memory byte) and set condition codes

CMP.W   Compare (data or address register*memory word with immediate memory word) and set condition codes

CMP.L   Compare (data or address register*memory long word with immediate memory long word) and set condition codes

DIVS   Divide signed numbers

DIVU   Divide unsigned numbers

EOR.B Exclusive OR data byte to (data register*-memory location)

EOR.W Exclusive OR data word to (data register*-memory location)

EOR.L Exclusive OR data long word to (data register*memory location)

MULS Multiply two 16-bit signed numbers

MULU Multiply two 16-bit unsigned numbers

OR.B OR immediate data byte to (data register*-memory byte)

OR.W OR immediate data word to (data register*-memory location)

OR.L OR immediate data long word to (data register*memory location)

SUB.B Subtract immediate data byte from (data register*memory byte)

SUB.W Subtract immediate data word from (data or address register* memory word)

SUB.L Subtract immediate data long word from (data or address register* memory long word)

SUBQ.B Subtract immediate three bits from (data register*memory byte)

SUBQ.W Subtract immediate three bits from (data or address register* memory word)

SUB.L Subtract immediate three bits from (data or address register* memory long word)

Jump and Branch Instructions

BRA Unconditional short branch

JMP Unconditional jump

BSR Branch to subroutine

JSR Jump to subroutine

RTS Return from subroutine

RTR Restore condition codes and return from subroutine

Bcc Branch on condition

DBcc Test condition, decrement, and branch until the specified condition is satisfied or until the loop counter has completed its count.

Register-to-Register Instructions

MOVE.B Move one byte of data from any data register to any other data register

MOVE.W Move one word of data from any data or address register to any other data or address register

MOVE.L Move the contents of any data or address register to any other data or address register

Arithmetic and Logical Instructions

ABCD Add decimal source data register byte to data register byte with carry

ADD.B Add byte from data register to data register

ADD.W Add word from (source*address) register to (data*address) register

ADD.L Add long word from source register to (data* address) register

ADDX.B Add byte register to register with carry

ADDX.W Add word register to register with carry

ADDX.L Add long word register to register with carry

AND.B AND byte from data register to data register

AND.W AND word from data register to data register

AND.L AND long word from data register to data register

CMP.B Compare data register bytes and set condition codes

CMP.W Compare register (data*address) words and set condition codes

CMP.L Compare register (data*address) long words and set condition codes

DIVS Divide by signed numbers

DIVU Divide by unsigned numbers

EOR.B Exclusive OR byte from data register to data register

EOR.W Exclusive OR word from data register to data register

EOR.L Exclusive OR long word from data register to data register

EXG Exchange contents of two registers

MULS Multiply two signed 16-bit numbers

MULU Multiply two unsigned 16-bit numbers

OR.B OR byte from data register to data register

OR.W OR word from data register to data register

OR.L OR long word from data register to data register

SUB.B Subtract data register bytes

SUB.W Subtract register words (data or address register)

SUB.L Subtract register long words (data or address register)

SUBX.B Subtract data register bytes with borrow

SUBX.W Subtract register words (data or address register) with borrow

SUBX.L Subtract register long words (data or address register) with borrow

CLR.B Clear data register byte to zeroes

CLR.W Clear data register word to zeroes

CLR.L Clear data register long word to zeroes

EXT.W Extend sign bit of data byte to data word size

EXT.L Extend sign bit of data word to data long word size

NBCD Negate decimal register byte

NEG.B Negate register byte

NEG.W Negate register word

NEG.L Negate register long word

NOT.B Ones complement of data register byte

NOT.W Ones complement of data register word

NOT.L Ones complement of data register long word

Scc Set status in data register byte

SWAP Exchange two 16-bit halves of data register

TAS Test status of data register byte and set bit 7 to 1

TST.B Test status of data register byte without changing contents of register

TST.W Test status of data register word without changing contents of register

TST.L Test status of data register long word without changing contents of register

Shift and Rotate Instructions

ASL Arithmetic shift left one bit of memory word

ASL.B Arithmetic shift left data register byte

ASL.W Arithmetic shift left data register word

ASL.L Arithmetic shift left entire data register

ASR Arithmetic shift right one bit of memory word

ASR.B Arithmetic shift right data register byte

ASR.W Arithmetic shift right data register word

ASR.L Arithmetic shift right entire data register

LSL Logical shift left one bit of memory word

LSL.B Logical shift left data register byte

LSL.W Logical shift left data register word

LSL.L Logical shift left entire data register

LSR Logical shift right one bit of memory word

LSR.B Logical shift right data register byte

LSR.W Logical shift right data register word

LSR.L Logical shift right entire data register

ROL Rotate left one bit of memory word

ROL.B Rotate left data register byte

ROL.W Rotate left data register word

ROL.L   Rotate left entire data register

ROR   Rotate right one bit of memory word

ROR.B   Rotate right data register byte

ROR.W   Rotate right data register word

ROR.L   Rotate right entire data register

ROXL   Rotate left one bit of memory word and extend one bit

ROXL.B   Rotate left data register byte with extend

ROXL.W   Rotate left data register word with extend.

ROXL.L   Rotate left entire data register with extend.

ROXR   Rotate right one bit of memory word with extend.

ROXR.B   Rotate right data register byte with extend.

ROXR.W   Rotate right data register word with extend.

ROXR.L   Rotate right entire data register with extend.

Bit Manipulation Instructions

BTST   Test bit

BSET   Test and set bit

BCLR   Text and clear bit

BCHG   Text and complement specified bit

Stack Manipulation Instructions

MOVE   Move contents (address register to User Stack Pointer*User Stack Pointer to address register)

LINK   Save contents of specified address register on stack and load the current Stack Pointer to the specified address register and set the Stack Pointer to point beyond the temporary stack storage area

PEA   Compute long word address and push address onto stack

UWLK   Store contents of specified address register to Stack Pointer and load specified address register from stack

Instructions to Set and Check Interrupts and Traps

CHK   Set Check Interrupt Processing if register word is out of bounds

TRAP   Set Trap mode on specified vector

RTE   Return from Trap mode (exception)

Status Register Instructions

MOVE   Move (status and immediate status data or status register from memory locations and registers to condition codes or status register*status register to memory location)

AND.B   AND immediate data byte to low-order status register byte

AND.W   AND immediate data to status register

EOR.B   Exclusive OR immediate data byte to low-order status register byte

EOR.W   Exclusive OR immediate data to status register

OR.B   OR immediate data byte to low-order status register byte

OR.W   OR immediate data with status register

Hardware Control Instructions

NOP   No operation

RESET   Reset

STOP   Stop processor

The Supermicros

Beyond the 68000 CPU, we leave the realm of the "traditional" microcomputer and enter that of the minicomputer. Here the definitions become fuzzy. Is AT&T's 3B2 system, based on the 32-bit WE32000 from Bell Research Laboratories, a minicomputer or a super microcomputer? Because the 3B2 was designed to be part of an integrated UNIX-based system, it should be categorized as a minicomputer. Yet, because of efficient and elegant single-chip technology, it falls into the category of supermicro. At this state of computer development, the distinction really has no significance.

The power of the 3B2 derives in large measure from its CPU. Designed originally to manage the automated switching and high-speed voice and data transfer requirements of modern telecommunications systems, the WE32000 was the natural choice for AT&T's entry into the business computing environment. The chip's assembler is written in C, a language developed at Bell Laboratories that is designed to handle both machine-level and high-level programming. The microprocessor allows for a high degree of unity between the assembler, the operating system, and the applications programming language, all of which are C-based. This makes applications development very straightforward and efficient, and on WE32000 machines it reduces the system overhead considerably.

Minicomputers and mainframes use the bit-slice technology in which processing and addressing functions are managed by different chips acting as separate components of a larger system. Neither the Z80 nor the 8088 is a "computer-on-a-chip." Both are microprocessors—a big difference. The individual chips on the board of a bit-slice mini or mainframe work in consort. This "bee colony" effect of many chips assuming different aspects of the total processing operation promises to give way to a single chip technology as the size and processing capabilities of new chips increase. When that happens, the distinction between microcomputer, super microcomputer, minicomputer, and mainframe will blur even more and perhaps even disappear.

Beyond Assembly Language

Just as assembly language, with its system of mnemonics, freed programmers from writing out instructions in binary code, high-level language compilers free programmers from having to write assembly language code for specific machines. Assembly language, as evidenced by the discussions of the microprocessors in this section and the accompanying sample program, allows programmers to directly control the operation of the CPU. Data can be manipulated as single bits, bytes, or 16-bit clusters. But assembly language programming can be a complicated process. Program utilities help, of course, but the process is still time consuming.

The earliest high-level compilers brought computer programming into the realm of the non-computer specialist. The first Fortran programmers were engineers and mathematicians who were less concerned with the techniques of programming a specific computer than they were about solving a number of problems quickly and parsimoniously. Compiled and interpreted languages are generally not only closer to plain English than assembly language, but have provisions for trapping errors and, on costly timesharing systems, for saving the programmer money by running the high-level code through the compiler before running it on the machine. In this way, serious errors can be quickly flagged.

As high-level languages like Fortran, PL/I, and COBOL became the rule rather than the exception in applications development, the trend was to make the code as portable and as modular as possible so that other programmers could support the system, and the program itself could be easily upgraded. Thus new languages were developed that offered both abstraction and ease of interpretation.

Another trend in programming is the prepackaged library of assembly language utilities, which allows the programmer to incorporate routines written for applications such as managing screen displays or driving an I/O port into the high-level language source code. Assembly language routines can be purchased on disk; they can be copied from the various "bluebooks" of assembly language currently on the market; and they can be downloaded from user-supported bulletin boards. Many self-contained assembly language utilities are available as pieces of copyright-free or public domain software.

Once these utilities are loaded into user files, they can be called from within the source code to perform their chores with a minimum of programming overhead and then return control to the main program. As programming functions become more and more stereotyped and as screen displays and input/output functions gradually evolve into a hardware and software standard, the assembly language routines that drive them will also evolve into a set of CPU- and system-specific standards.

Many of these standards already exist in the PC and Apple environments and will soon exist in the Macintosh environment. Of course, standards have existed for many years in the mainframe and minicomputer environments. At some point in the very near future, it is even likely that high-level code, especially code written in BASIC and Pascal, might only be used to define program functions, establish data types and string definitions, create the relevant file structures, and of course, implement the sequential or procedural logic of the program. All of the busy work and housekeeping chores of the program can then be relegated to a series of assembly language subroutines that have been organized separately and stored in either function-specific or high-level language-specific cubby holes for easy access. The programmer who seeks to reduce overhead can even use the line editor functions of the computer to create and store the different types of calls and naming routines so that programs can easily be pieced together quickly from a variety of sources.

Prepackaged subroutines can be found in a variety of C language and Forth guides and directories. In addition, within the Forth community, many machine-level-routines are easily obtained from public domain bulletin boards. This trend in packaging the low-level functions of high-level programming languages also promises to influence the future of programming in these hybrid languages and make them more accessible to novice users.

Trends in programming, however, are leading away from the generalized high-level languages and pointing again to the power and control offered by assembly-level operations. The languages that support this concept—C, Forth, and Structured BASIC—are finding their way into more and more applications programs as the program developers attempt to fully exploit the relatively limited memories of microcomputers. Forth and C are closely akin to assembly language in certain ways, but offer various "friendly" features of high-level languages. Forth is well suited for industrial and scientific process control, while C, with its stress on controlling the flow of data within a larger system, is well suited for networking.

Henry F. Beechhold

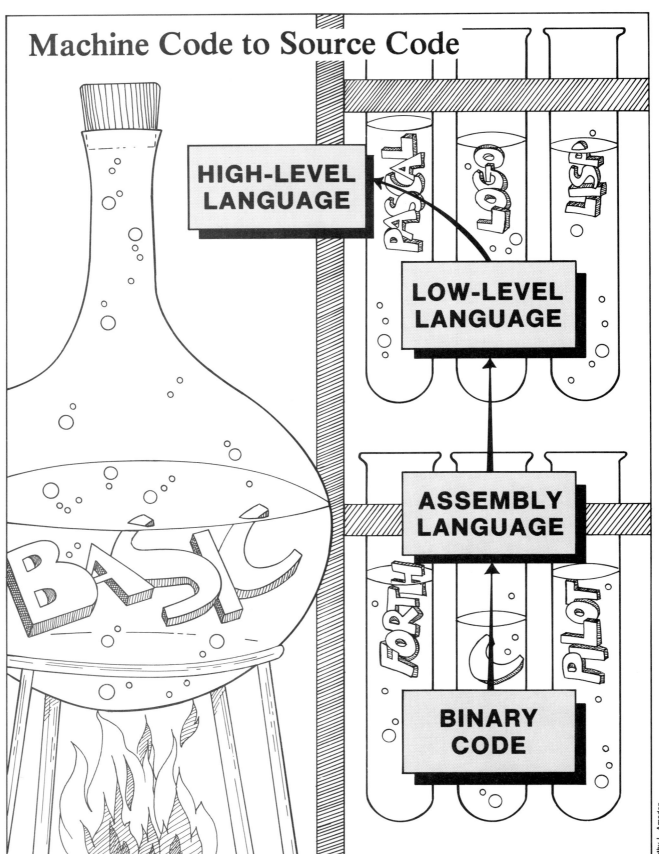

Machine Code to Source Code

Dorothy L. Amsden

5

HIGH-LEVEL PROGRAMMING LANGUAGES

Some of the basic concepts that defined the nature of high-level programming languages have evolved considerably since the early 1950s when Fortran first made its appearance internally at IBM. Concurrent with this evolution, and indeed, spurring it along, has been the evolution of the digital computer itself. Originally the tool of a technological elite, the digital computer has been redefined again and again, and with each new definition the computer has emerged in a different version. The computer centers of the 1950s and 1960s, with their cubbyholes overflowing with punchcards, were transformed by the early 1970s into computer laboratories subdivided into carrels housing the slave terminals. Moreover, by the middle to late 1960s computers were no longer confined to the government and university computer centers and central data processing facilities of large corporations. The minicomputers had appeared and promised to alter the way small to mid-sized businesses processed their data and organized their clientele records.

By the late 1960s to the early 1970s not only had the language of computers and computer programming begun to change, but the basic concept of the computer as a business machine had changed as well. Hardware stores and beverage distributors, independent insurance agencies and import/export merchants, and even municipal and local government offices had implemented small one-to-three-terminal business computers within their office environments. Administrators and clerical assistants discovered that computers could process text as well as grind out the solutions to prime number problems. And as the acceptance of computers on the local business level grew, the computer manufacturers and independent software companies produced the applications programs to serve the new markets.

All of this, however, was only a prologue to the growth and consumer acceptance of the personal computer as an appliance as much at home in the American family setting as the second television set. The hardware developments contributing to this event have been well documented. Transistor technology was introduced in 1947. The 1960s saw the development of the integrated circuit, which combined the functions of several semiconductor devices onto one silicon sliver. By 1971 the 4004 microprocessor was a marketable reality, and by early 1973 the PL/I computing language had been written to program it and an early operating system, a prototype of CP/M, was developed to manage the microprocessor's functions. By the end of 1973, engineers who supported the idea of a microprocessor-based personal computer were becoming frustrated at the lack of support the minicomputer manufacturers were providing. Independently, engineers began to form another stream of concurrent technological development that, by the end of 1974, began to provide marketable product. When the January 1975 issue of *Popular Electronics* heralded the birth of the Altair computer, many imaginations were fired by the possibilities.

But the technological hardware development by itself would have had only a limited impact without the concurrent development of a high-level language technology that eventually made computer programming in BASIC or Logo into a family activity. It was the development of languages and software systems that took the early Altair—a bare-bones kit that could be programmed only by throwing a series of switches on the front panel—from the hobbyist's workbench to an honored place alongside the business telephone. How did high-level languages evolve from a virtual experimental training program at IBM to a consumer product that can be purchased on cartridge, tape cassette, or floppy diskette from stores in shopping malls from coast to coast? The answer lies not only in the history of computer programming languages themselves, but in the history of computer applications. As computing technology was brought to bear on new areas of desktop word processing, personal financial planning, and, of course, games and graphics, a hungry market sought new products. The early products generated a fascination with microcomputing technology that continues unabated. And, fortunately for the newly emerged microcomputer in the early 1970s, BASIC, which had only been developed five years earlier at Dartmouth, was looking for a home. And when MicroSoft was founded in December 1975, that home was found.

While much has been written about the technical strengths and weaknesses of BASIC as a programming language, two principal factors contributed to its almost universal acceptance as the early standard high-level language of microcomputing. First, it was undeniably easy to learn and provided immediate positive feedback to new programmers. The language allowed novice programmers to retrofit routines and learn structured programming as they improved their logical thinking skills. And BASIC, as opposed to a language like COBOL, required almost no preprogramming operations such as declarations of data types and identification of the hardware environment. It was, in this regard, a true beginners' symbolic language. Second, BASIC happened to be in the right place at the right time. It is a highly portable language that is easily adaptable to different hardware environments, and this portability lent itself very quickly to a growth market in microcomputers in which different manufacturers needed a low-overhead programming language to bundle with their systems.

BASIC is also a malleable language which can be tailored to fit different microcomputers. It has a ready assembly language interface to enable programmers to write quick machine-level routines. It can comfortably reside on a disk or on a chip. In larger microcomputers, it can be tucked neatly away in the operating system where it can be called, as if it were a subroutine, from the batch-load program of an applications package written in BASIC that needs the language to be resident in memory before it can run.

In part, the malleability of BASIC resulted from its early history. BASIC was popular because it was so easy to learn and use and required no special symbology. Unlike APL that was directly interactive with mainframes and had its own character set, BASIC was programmable apart from any machine environment. And unlike Fortran or COBOL, BASIC did not have to have its instruction set preexecuted on a compiler before the actual run-time program could begin. This made it inexpensive as well as independent. Finally, because of BASIC's beginnings as a teaching tool, the language was almost immediately placed into the hands of creative electronics and engineering students who were able to adapt it to what was to become its primary market.

In summary, the input streams which resulted in the current personal computer market comprised the development of the digital computer itself, the invention of the concept of a high-level programming language, and the invention and immediate marketability of the personal computer. Of these streams, only the second requires further explanation to set the stage for this high-level language section of the Encyclopedia.

Initially, as the history of Fortran has documented, there was a very negative reaction from the formal computer programming community toward the concept of high-level language programming in general and to Fortran and its derivatives in particular. This opposition was in part a function of the machine environment and in part a skeptical reaction to any programming operation that required the generation of an intermediate set of codes before the machine itself could do its job. In the environments of expensive, energy-consuming mainframe computers, efficiency and speed of performance were paramount. Low-level programming operations that directly addressed the machine's memory registers and spoke to the central processing unit in its own language of opening and closing circuit gates were the most efficient. To the EDP departments of large corporations and government bureaus, computer time was money and the less time a program spent on the system, the more time was available to run additional programs. It was as simple as that. Why worry about the advantages of high-level language portability, it was argued, when corporations only had one computer anyway, and that computer already had a data processing department whose job was to support the software and maintain the data processing functions of the organization.

High-level language programming offered advantages besides software portability, although portability, the computer market of the 1980s would demonstrate, is a powerful advantage over low-level programming. High-level programming in general, and programming in the early Fortran in particular, was a point of entry into the mainframe systems for individuals whose primary expertise was not programming or computer design, but other branches of engineering. Rather than have their instruction sets interpreted by human programmers who coded them into machine-level commands, many engineers believed that the machine itself could handle those functions more efficiently and less expensively. Hence, compilers and subsequently interpreters could replace human encoders and be more responsive to the requirements of the abstract instruction set. This allowed engineers and eventually other interested professionals to concentrate on the abstract or symbolic nature of the computer program rather than on the specific machine-level coding requirements. This is not to say that the compilers did all the coding and abstract programmers did all the thinking. It only means that a subtle shift in emphasis ould take place during the late 1950s and early 1960s from worrying about the specific requirements of a machine's environment and its demands to the process of translating human thought to an abstract series of steps that could implement that thought. And once the symbolic cat was let out of the bag, development in symbolic high-level languages began in earnest.

The major computer manufacturing companies also realized the tremendous market potential of high-level language programming. Software did not have to be "reinvented" in order to be implemented on additional machines with slightly different features. Compilers could be modified to change the machine-code instruction sets, and this reduced the software development overhead. Business and scientific software packages could be developed more abstractly in a natural language than in a machine environment. The natural language instruction sets were more easily convertible into Fortran statements than into machine codes. This enlarged the programming development pool and allowed independent software companies to emerge in the growing computer market. The marketing force provided the economic impetus to pursue development of high-level computing languages. With the appearance of COBOL, in which the central data processing program was enveloped within a machine identification program and a data declaration program, business-oriented high-level language programming became a professional occupation. The high portability of CO-BOL routines, the abundant documentation provided by the program itself, its natural language interface, and, accordingly, the ease of software support, all combined to make the language a near-perfect general business programming tool. This accounts for COBOL's thirty-year history as a feature of the business machine marketplace and its reemergence with a new life as a microcomputer programming language.

With the market forces both within and outside of the computer manufacturing and programming communities now supporting the concept of high-level language programming, development money began to flow. This, in turn, stimulated research into more abstract forms of high-level languages that could teach the symbolic logic required to make the machines emulate human thought patterns even closer. An early result of this experimentation and research at MIT was LISP, the second oldest high-level programming language. Despite LISP's age, the language never became petrified at a level of development and is only now beginning to find its true implementation in the areas of artificial intelligence and expert systems programming. LISP is a strictly symbolic language which, because it is premised on the recursive features of human language, emulates natural human thought processes much more closely than Fortran or COBOL. And because recursive or nested thought patterns are one of the absolute bases of rule-ordered, syllogistic behavior, LISP seemed to emulate human thought. Hence, its role as an artificial intelligence tool.

The invention of LISP started a new development stream that resulted in such implementations of the language as Logo and Prolog. Logo, developed by Seymour Papert at MIT, also was designed to teach symbolic thought and help orient children to what Papert saw as a "QWERTY" or keyboard environment in which much of what was traditionally accomplished with paper and pencil would be executed through a hardware/software system. Much of what Papert saw has come to pass, but Logo has gone beyond the learning laboratories and computer resource rooms at schools to become a consumer item all by itself. Because the language is, like its parent LISP, a recursive system in which entire processes can be defined, repackaged within a larger process, and defined again, children using Logo learn how to build executable programs from abstract blocks that can be modified, expanded, improved, or simply altered independently of the main program. Also, because Logo is not statement heavy, as is COBOL or Fortran, and because, like Forth, one point of Logo is to define new items for a personalized programming dictionary, Logo can easily be implemented in non-English-speaking environments. Words like "casa" or lexical items from Bantu or Japanese suddenly become valid programmable Logo definitions that are initiated by the child at the keyboard rather than the software engineer in a laboratory. Logo programming, consequently, is taking place in schools throughout the Third World as an entire generation of elementary school children learn to implement their thought patterns, as Papert predicted, at the computer keyboard.

Prolog, another LISP derivative, has been adopted by the Japanese for their Fifth Generation project as an expert systems tool, and Prolog "kits" for CP/M and MS-DOS machines in the United States are growing in popularity. Because of the fascination with "expert" simulation programs written in other languages, Prolog, which was designed to write such programs, will have a profound impact on a software hungry population that has been prepared for it by the magic of electronic spreadsheets and simple database managers.

Forth, although structurally different from LISP, Logo, and Prolog, shares with them one important conceptual tool and, hence, can rightly be included in this group of vanguard languages. Forth, like LISP, is a type of list processor, although data stack processor is perhaps a better term. This means that new Forth terms can be defined and placed upon the program stack to be executed as routines by themselves or as routines that call other routines. Hand-held calculators, for example, are pocket-sized Forth machines in which numbers are swapped in and out of memory and incrementing or decrementing routines (and sometimes entire formulas) churn their way through a stack of numbers, swapping or replacing like a chemical drain cleaner at work. New Forth implementations, specifically for microcomputers, are, in fact, types of dictionaries that mesh with the operating system to call subroutines and address machine functions. Forth is a creative language and finds its home on machines like the Macintosh where it can simulate a form of concurrent applications by drawing overlapping series of pull-down menus that fill the screen with what seem to be parallel operations.

There are many other languages that represent different conceptual approaches to computer programming. The group of languages that includes PL/I, Pascal, Modula-2, C, and COMAL, for example, features a block-structured approach to the design of logical sequences in which machine functions are managed efficiently, low-level operations can be carried out, in the case of C by the language itself, and data can be transferred from one major suboperation to another without losing its identity to the programmer. These types of languages also foster the concurrent development of programs in different modules that can be combined by a system manager into a coherent, system-wide implementation. C, developed at AT&T to facilitate system development and process control, promises to have a future not unlike Fortran or COBOL. Pascal and Modula-2, because of their heavily block-structured approach to independent but related program components that exchange data with one another without pausing to redefine or redeclare it, are easily implementable on robotics devices.

This quasi-historical approach to high-level languages demonstrates the final aspect of what has taken the computer from the college laboratory of the 1950s to the family living room or den of the 1980s. Programming language as a concept has become more friendly, and more usable by a consumer public that has grown up in an era of button-pushing. C-programmed desk telephones manage the functions of the spinning roll-file; Forth-programmed calculators appear just as dramatically in the hands of adversarial negotiators as rapiers did in the hands of sixteenth-century duelists on the streets of Paris or Florence; LISP- or Prolog-programmed expert systems dialogue routines advise, counsel, and prompt the solemn decision-makers of the 1980s as, Sophocles tells us, the Oracle at Delphi counseled the troubled decision-makers of the ancient Hellenes; and, finally, the Smalltalk-generated representational icons that are dragged about and clicked open and closed on the screens of the Macintosh or the Lisa are, conceptually at least, remarkably close to humankind's first attempts at symbolic communication. Cave artists painted images of wild animals on the stone walls of their shelters, the ancient Egyptians and Chinese developed entire writing systems out of an organized series of representational icons, and even the nonverbal child can communicate with a parent by moving physical objects in an organized sequence. All that this demonstrates is that computing languages work because they emulate, not machine thinking, but human thinking.

In this section of computing languages, each entry is focused on the human and communications aspects of the technology. The language is introduced, its historical background is discussed, and its features are demonstrated and documented. A glossary of each language follows in which the programming statements are defined and used in a line of code as an example of the way they are executed. By comparing the different functions, as they are defined, from language to language, readers will be able to find how some of the languages take strikingly similar or strikingly contrasting approaches to solving problems or structuring routines. Readers will find that the languages resolve into basic groupings: procedural languages such as BASIC, Fortran, or COBOL; block-structured modular languages such as PL/I, Pascal, Modula-2, or C; and non-procedural, list-based, or rule-ordered languages such as LISP, Logo, Prolog, and Forth. Readers will also find that many of the most visible software applications packages are in fact a subset or an implementation of high-level languages. That is why dBASE II and the electronic spreadsheet applications have been included in this section along with the more formal languages. These software applications have a command language and query structure that is as formalized and structured as any programming language, and today's microcomputer marketplace can rightly be considered that of high-level language systems.

Beyond the query language of today's applications software lie additional realms of human-to-machine interface that are just now beginning to make their appearance on the personal computer level. The first type of interface is iconographic: the representation of commands and options as graphics designs. First implemented on the Xerox office computer, then on the LISA, and most recently on the Macintosh, this Smalltalk-based query system communicates ideas rather than specific lexical items as command options. The theory underlying iconographic systems is as old as the first cave drawings in northern Europe and the hieroglyphics on Egyptian tablets. Simply stated, the theory is that the idea of command need not be expressed in a specific word; it only need be expressed as a concept. The user can supply the word. For example, the hieroglyph of a half sun sliced by a straight line at the bottom can represent either a rising sun or a setting sun depending on the context of the image. If there are other "morning" ideas conveyed in the inscription, then the half sun represents sunrise. These are stylized drawings in that there is no attempt to depict the object as realistically accurate. The hieroglyph stands for the idea of the rising or setting sun.

Similarly, in the MacPaint application for Apple's Macintosh, the images of the HAND and the LASSO represent very similar concepts. In both cases the HAND and the LASSO are used to move images around the screen. The LASSO, however, is used to isolate the part of the image that is going to be moved, while the HAND actually moves the entire screen as if it were a decal for a plastic model that was being lifted off its backing sheet in a pan of water. Both of these commands, although similar, are used for very different purposes, but neither of these commands need have an exact lexical representation for the user. The LASSO can be translated into English as "just move a part of the drawing" while the HAND can be translated as "move the entire screen around." Icons such as BRICKS or DOTS represent different background designs, while the screen design for NOTEPAD is a true icon. It is exactly what it looks like. Why bother to display the image of a notepad for writing notes that can be lifted off, flipped or paged through, or dumped to the printer without having to leave the specific application? Why not simply open up a portion of the screen, call it "Notepad" and let the user figure out what to do in the same way?

"Sidekick" and other electronic desktop software packages accomplish the same task. The answer, according to the people at Apple, is that other software packages require that volumes of information be understood by the user before the package can be loaded and run. Macintosh applications are self-explanatory because they convey meaning iconographically. Whether this is actually true or not is not the point: what is the point is that the Macintosh/LISA operating system communicates the idea to the user through an image or icon and lets the user supply the specific lexical items. The interface, therefore, is representational, allowing users to supply for themselves the actual command language keywords and their meanings.

This a very important direction in query language systems because it replaces specific command words with command concepts: to copy a file from disk to disk is not to type "copy A: FILENAME B:", as it is in MS-DOS; it is to move the mouse pointer to the file folder that is to be copied on the area representing the source disk, click the mouse to grab the folder, drag the folder by holding the mouse button down and moving the mouse across the tabletop to the area representing the destination disk, and then releasing the mouse button, as it is on the Macintosh. The Macintosh, once the file folder has been physically dragged, then begins its actual copying procedure. The machine commands which execute this are invisible to the user unless the user wants to see them. Only the graphic representation is immediately visible.

Command and query systems like this encourage the user not to think in terms of specific codes, but in computer concepts such as file creation and storage, data retrieval, data transfer, and electronic editing. The MacPaint and now the MacDraw utilities contain icons which, when clicked, give users the ability to draw straight lines automatically or radiate perfectly round circles out from a given point; stretch, rotate, duplicate, or flip shapes on a screen; and combine different prepackaged images with one another to create a completely new design. Most of this can be accomplished with a mouse and an array of iconographically represented options on the screen. The user need not know or memorize any specific command keyword sequences in order to execute these instructions. This is certainly an important new direction in the evolution of computing languages.

The other new direction in command and query languages is called the "natural language interface." Used largely in artificial intelligence applications, the natural language interface program operates from a database of lexical items and syntactic frames. Subsets of these natural language generators are easy enough to construct in BASIC, and many of the demonstration dialogue programs, such as ELIZA II, that are found in computer magazines, begin by building such a natural language generator. Once the defined set of lexical items has been loaded, each item can be categorized by storing it within a syntactic frame. The frames may use such standard syntactic descriptors as "verb," "noun," "pronoun," or any other terminology that the programmer decides. It is only important that the syntactic frames in the program match the syntactic frames in English and that words that are used as verbs or nouns or pronouns really are verbs, or nouns, or pronouns. Once the right words are in the right syntactic frames, the program can be told to look for certain input signals or query signals from the user and to respond by building the syntactic frames and loading the words from each category into them.

This, at its most elementary level, can be thought of as the beginning of a natural language generator. There is no artificial intelligence here, although the program behaves as if it is carrying on a rudimentary dialogue. However, even the most cursory glance indicates that this type of little program seems to be hopelessly random. How does the program know, for example, which words from the same category to insert into a specific syntactic frame? How does it know if it is responding correctly to a user input? The answer is, of course, that it doesn't. It doesn't know whether the words it is inserting into the syntactic frames are semantically correct, it only knows that it is going to the correct stack and inserting either the next word, if it has been told to increment the stack counter by one, or another word if there is a random number generator at work. Because the English language is a syntax-based language, any word inserted into its correct syntactic frame will look as though it should be making sense to the listener or the reader, especially if that word is framed by the correct articles, correctly inflected verb, and correctly placed qualifier. In other words, if there is a word that looks like in a noun in a spot where a noun is supposed to be, the normal English speaker will interpret that sentence as grammatically correct, even if the meaning of the word is not clear.

Thus, it is not difficult, even in BASIC, to build a language model that looks as though it is generating correct sentences. If the word set in the program's memory, also called a lexicon, is very small and care is taken to interact with the program using only those words, it is even possible for the program to interpret user input correctly even when the user generates it. With this interpreter feature added to our little BASIC natural language generator, the program is upgraded to a natural language interpreter. This is the jumping-off point for what will become an important level of query and command interface in the next generation of computer software: the natural language interface. The natural language interface, currently used by such programs as Infoscope, allows users to construct whatever queries they want, and, working on the basis of a key word in context, can interpret the user's query and retrieve the specified data. Thus, the user does not have to interface with the machine through a specific series of commands or through a paradigm of nested menu screens. All the user has to do is make sure that, first, a workable personal dictionary or personal lexicon has been built into the natural language interpreter component of the query program and, second, that communication with the program is through that lexicon.

Building the personal lexicon is not unlike building a personal dictionary in many of the proofreading and spelling checker programs currently on the market. In fact, it is entirely possible that the current generation of disk-based spelling dictionary kits can become the basis of a personal lexicon kit for use with a variety of data-intensive search, retrieval, and indexing programs. When combined with an icon-driven electronic desktop as a front end screen and an automatic phone directory and terminal program, our new user interface becomes a PC user environment in and of itself. It can mediate with other programs through the natural language translator, manage all file handling and subroutine calls through the icon screen, and communicate with the rest of the world through its terminal program. With the addition of a printer driver and a password access entry system, the natural language-based, icon-driven program we have described here is a model for the type of non-query language program that allows users to communicate with the software without having to learn a specialized artificial language.

It should be clear, therefore, from this section that even as new products develop, our conception of what computers do and what the languages that program them are supposed to do is undergoing an evolutionary development with each business quarter. If, in the twentieth century, the marketplace is sometimes the progenitor of invention, then, indeed, there is much more invention to come. That is, in part, one of the underlying reasons for the structure and content of this section of the Encyclopedia. How better to understand what we will be able to do with computers in the future than to begin with a thorough grounding in those languages that make possible what computers can do?

Ada

The U.S. Department of Defense (DoD) is the world's biggest buyer of computer hardware and software. Recognizing that use of a single standard programming and development language could save the DoD as much as $24 billion by 1999, DoD software experts began searching over ten years ago for a general-purpose language to replace the more than 450 different computer languages and incompatible dialects in use within the military. This formerly impossible goal—a single standard system for software development—was achieved through international efforts and joint cooperation among domestic and foreign military and industrial organizations and universities. After years of clarification by over 100 experts in fifteen countries, a design competition was held in 1978. Seventeen companies entered, four semifinalists were finally selected, and the winning entry was Cii-Honeywell Bull's team led by Jean Ichbiah, who designed the computer language LIS and now heads Alsys, a company making Ada products. All of the semifinal entrants based their design on Pascal, a procedural language renowned for its high-order semantic constructs. The winning language was named Ada.

Ada is the first computer language that really supports the dream of using standardized building blocks to make complete programs. Because Ada is so large, so complex, and so full of features, it is far more than just another language: it is a complete software development system with the avowed goals of efficiency, programming as a human activity, and simplified program reliability and maintenance.

Although the initial motive was economic, Ada reflects the desire to have a good programming language that addresses the most important, widely recognized problems in software development: simplicity and completeness, program reliability, correctness, maintainability and portability, the development of large programs, real-time programming, and error handling. Ada also reflects the trend away from large computers and toward multicomputer architecture, that is, several different computers without a shared memory that communicate with each other by sending messages. The DoD requirements also demanded concurrent programming, i.e., the ability to write a program whose components can be executed on different computers in parallel or on the same computer by interleaved execution.

Advantages of Ada

For years experts have predicted that software would someday be made better and cheaper by using software packaged into components, just as electronic hardware is now assembled from standardized boards, component subassemblies, and integrated circuits. These software counterparts of manufacturer's chips will be sold as off-the-shelf components and assembled as needed for each application. Because past attempts to in-

troduce a standard language, like IBM's PL/I, have been more than a little disappointing, this current trend toward component software is promising.

Ada seems destined to succeed for several reasons, primarily because no language has ever been so thoroughly designed, documented, tested, and standardized before being put into use. Ada will help ease a programmer shortage that is already critical and getting acutely worse each year. No other language has the guaranteed market position or the approval of the DoD: not only is the DoD the number one buyer globally, it also owns and licenses the use of the Ada trademark through its rigorous validation of the compilers needed to implement Ada. Most importantly, Ada represents the state of the art in software design, comprising a virtual encyclopedia of all the features needed but never before combined into one effective system: real-time tasking, strong data typing, generics, modularity, information hiding, structured programming, data abstraction, and top-down programming. No other language has all the features of Ada.

Because it is so comprehensive, Ada is not easy to master. As a result, many professional programmers are reluctant to learn a new language as complex as Ada, even if the promised gains in efficiency and savings in cost are real. In addition, Ada compilers—the software that translates the high-level instructions into the machine code needed to run the computer—are both complex and expensive. Despite these drawbacks, Ada is being used more widely each year in both commercial and military applications.

Ada is big enough to span applications ranging from programming a small microprocessor that runs a specialized servomotor to the real-time processing of a large mainframe computer for air traffic control. These "embedded" (i.e., dedicated) computers already account for 70-90% of all DoD needs, and are on the increase in the civilian world as well. The DoD expects to spend $37 billion on embedded systems by 1990. Although much of the civilian demand for software will be general-purpose applications like paycheck writing for some years (usually performed by COBOL, a twenty-five-year-old warhorse), accounting needs are not expanding as rapidly as the special-purpose implementations that require embedded systems. Ada supporters predict that more code will be written in Ada than in any other language within just a few years.

Ada products and services already constitute a $150 million market that will reach at least $1 billion by 1986. Ada development systems, including hardware, the all-important compilers, and other program-support tools, will account for $600 million of this quantum leap. The DoD announced in 1983 that new code for its "mission-critical" (weaponry, not payroll) embedded systems must be written in Ada by January 1984 for systems entering the advanced design stage and by July 1984 for the full-scale engineering phase. From now on, defense contractors must use Ada or explain why not. Contractors must choose Ada compilers from a very select club, those vendors who have received validation of their compilers from the Ada Validation Office, the DoD's agency for administering an extensive suite of tests to candidates. To pass, a compiler must satisfy fully 100% of more than 2000 tests.

So far there are only a few validated compilers on the market, each with its unique requirements and advantages. Different compilers run more or less efficiently in execution, of course, and these differences make for intense competition between vendors. While validation is an important milestone for any vendor, production quality, portability, and program support tools rank as major issues as well.

Ada is designed to be portable, in order to be implemented across the various computers used in embedded systems. Portability requires that Ada compilers segregate the characteristics that must be specified for each different target computer in the machine-dependent "back end" (i.e., the machine code generator) of the compiler. A machine-independent "front end" contains the components that can be used in common on all the computers used for program development. This segmented design is the approach taken by many of the leading producers of Ada products.

Programs are usually developed on larger, far more flexible multi-user computers, typically 32-bit superminicomputers like the DEC VAX and IBM 370 computer families. These "host" computers are the ideal hardware both for the development of Ada software and for compilers to generate code for the smaller target systems, such as those embedded in special applications like navigation systems. Thus, to the extent that a compiler is "rehostable," transferable from one host to another, it offers more advantages than a compiler that can be used only on one host.

Most military programming to date has been done in assembly language, the number and symbol code understood directly by microprocessors. Ada's high-order syntax is more like English, but has the flexibility and self-correcting restrictions to be even more efficient in the long run than assembly language programs. Much of that power is due to the "housekeeping" duties that an Ada compiler performs beyond its primary task of translating source code (Ada) into object code (machine language). An Ada compiler not only translates the high-order instructions through intermediate steps into machine code, but also provides Ada's wide array of powerful tools. Compilers check for errors, print out diagnostics, manage the computer's time and storage space, and arrange for information to be passed from one subprogram to another.

Packaged, Readable, Reusable Code

The most exciting concept in Ada is the package. Packaging allows programmers to combine existing data objects into powerful programs with a minimum of coding effort and time. Packages include not only subroutines, but data, types, and other subprogram units. A package's body contains private information and the specification public information, thus preventing all parts of a program from accessing any other data object,

as conventional software too easily allows. This hiding or encapsulation of data cuts the spread of errors, and hence reduces debugging and maintenance, two of the most difficult and costly software needs.

Ada's multi-tasking feature allows separate parts of a program to run simultaneously, in one computer or on coprocessors, and the information can be passed between these tasks as needed by Ada's rendezvous facility. Exceptions, which are unexpected events like division by zero or uncertain events like the end of a tape, are handled by routines that tell the program just what to do in each case. Generics permit "cloning" of a program unit so that it can be reused like a template, needing only to be repeated and filled in with the applicable parameters for each use. A single statement can change 16-bit to 32-bit integers, or floating-point to integer or character types, without rewriting the entire procedure. All of these features promote more productive coding and enforce error correction during programming and compilation better than most other languages.

Although Ada requires more time to design a program initially, this expense will be repaid over the long run through much reduced maintenance costs. While it is the least glamorous aspect of programming, maintenance is the most overlooked and expensive part of the software life cycle. Maintenance accounts for at least 50% of the entire life cycle cost, and many estimates run as high as 60 to 80%. The Pentagon spends over $6 billion a year on program maintenance alone on its accumulated $25 billion worth of software.

Maintenance includes simple correction of errors, which are often not detected until late in the life cycle; adaptive changes, like new data; and requested changes in program features. In other words, whatever the original software developer does not do first will end up being done later as "maintenance." The later in the software life cycle that such fixing and improving occur, the more expensive and difficult the process will inevitably be. Often the only programmers who can maintain a complex program are the ones who originally wrote it, with the result that customers like the DoD have been "locked in" to long-term maintenance contracts, with little negotiating power during the product's life cycle. Ada promises to make maintenance both less expensive and less frequent a requirement, by its demand that programmers check and correct errors at every step of software design, development, and compilation.

One of Ada's primary design goals was to improve program reliability and to simplify program maintenance by emphasizing readability rather than writability. To programmers familiar with more concise and often cryptic languages, Ada is much more like English. Ada permits a later programmer to decipher, update, change, or correct a program much more easily than the more densely packed syntax of other high-order languages like COBOL and Fortran. Ada proponents claim that Ada is easier to program in than Fortran, while at the same time, it is more efficient because it is harder to make errors in. In addition, Ada supports structured programming, the team approach preferred in today's complex software development.

Ada forces programmers to write more reliable, readable, portable, modular, maintainable, efficient code—all qualities of a good program. Ada requires a programmer to declare all data objects, to use objects in a manner consistent with their types, and to access objects only according to Ada's visibility rules. Programmers will appreciate this strictness, when Ada's restrictions and strict checking both detect more errors early and automatically, and help the programmer to write good programs.

Wherefore Ada?

The name Ada was taken from Lady Augusta Ada Byron, Countess of Lovelace and daughter of the English poet Byron. Lady Ada has been called the first computer programmer because of her work on Charles Babbage's Analytical Engine, a calculating machine which she programmed to compute the Bernoulli numbers. She programmed the engine using punched cards to "weave algebraic patterns just as the Jacquard loom weaves flowers and leaves." Publishing under her initials to avoid criticism of this unladylike pastime, she predicted winners at the race track using her programmed calculations. She died in 1852 at the age of 36, an outcast from her family. In 1977, the year that the Department of Defense announced its design competitions for a standard computer language, a new biography of Lady Ada appeared that revealed many new details of her unappreciated genius. The ANSI Standard Reference Manual for the Ada language is known as MIL-STD-1815, in honor of her birth year.

Ada products, such as compilers, program support tools, and some package software components, are available now from a number of vendors. A partial list follows:

Alsys, Inc.; Amdahl Corp.; Bell Labs; Bolt, Beranek, and Newman; Burroughs Federal and Special Systems; Carnegie-Mellon University; Control Data Corp.; Data General Corp. with ROLM Corp.; Digicomp Research Corp.; Digital Equipment Corp.; Florida State University; Gensoft Corp.; Honeywell Office Management Systems Division; Intel Corp.; Intermetrics, Inc.; Mills International; New York University; NuSoft; ROLM Corp.; RR Software; Science Applications, Inc.; SofTech, Inc.; Stanford University; TeleSoft, Inc.; Univac Defense Systems Division; USAF Armament Lab; USC-ISI.

Training in Ada is and will increasingly be a critical need. Some vendors, like TeleSoft and Alsys, already offer general and specialized training as well as on-site assistance for users. Many vendors are already accumulating libraries of tested software products that are sold as program components off the shelf. To meet the emerging microcomputer market demand, TeleSoft offers an IBM PC-based subset of their Ada compiler that enables smaller-budget users to enter the Ada development field. Accordingly, there are more and more organizations that conduct in-depth training sessions in the language. A partial list of the companies offering training courses in Ada follows:

Alsys; CACI Inc.; CAP Ltd. UK; Computer Thought Corp.; Control Data Corp.; Data General; DigiComp; EVB Consulting; Gould; PIM; Pragmatics Inc.; ROLM; Saib Seminars; Telesoft.

SAMPLE ADA PACKAGE PROGRAM

```
with SAMS__IO__PACKAGE, MIKES__IO__
    PACKAGE;
use SAMS__IO__PACKAGE, MIKES__IO__
    PACKAGE;
procedure ALS__PROGRAM is

procedure P1 is use SAMS__INTEGER__IO
  begin
  put (1+1);--Sam's "put"
  end P1

procedure P2 is use MIKES__INTEGER__10
  begin
  put (2+2);--Mike's "put"
  end P2

end ALS__PROGRAM
```

GENERICS, OR PACKAGE CLONING

```
generic -- specification
  type T is ( )
  function SUM (X, Y, Z: T);

  function SUM (X, Y, Z: T) return T is
  begin -- body
  return X+Y+Z;
  end SUM
```

This reproduction process can be repeated as often as needed, thus generating libraries of software from only a few original routines:

```
FUNCTION SUM__FLO is new SUM (float)
FUNCTION SUM__INT is new SUM
```

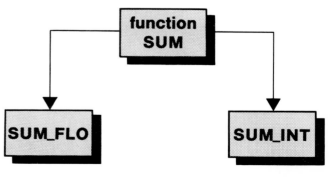

Al Rubottom

ADA GLOSSARY

Unlike some of the more traditional languages such as Fortran, COBOL, and BASIC which share a set of fundamental language descriptors and concepts, Ada has its own set of descriptors and concepts. Because of the complexity of Ada's applications and the broad scope of what will be Ada's full implementation, a highly specialized vocabulary has grown up around the language as it continues to be developed. The following glossary of specialized Ada terminology has been assembled by New Technica to introduce those unfamiliar with Ada to the highly specialized Ada environment. The vocabulary focuses on defining basic concepts in Ada as well as the specialized way that Ada categorizes its instruction sets and data types. What this vocabulary shows is that ADA is emerging as more than a high-level language; it is its own discrete environment that provides ease of portability in its own program structures, programming utilities and tools, and code implementation.

ACCEPT STATEMENT. A statement which specifies the actions to be performed when an ENTRY is called.

ACCESS TYPE. A pointer which designates an object with a value. The designated object can be read and updated via the access value. The type of several designated objects can be composite. Also see ALLOCATOR and COLLECTION.

ACTUAL PARAMETER. The particular entity associated with the corresponding formal parameter in a subprogram call, entry call, or generic instantiation. Also see PARAMETER.

AGGREGATE. An operation that combines component values into a value of an array or record type. The values of the aggregates are specified using positional ASSOCIATION and named associations.

ALLOCATOR. An instruction which creates an object of an appropriate type, and provides an access value that designates the object. For example, the storage allocator, which is called "new," is used to create dynamic objects.

ANCESTOR COMPILATION UNIT. A unit related to a compilation unit (CU) currently being compiled, made visible to the CU during compilation. Ancestor compilation units are one of the following categories:

1. A unit mentioned in a WITH clause of the current CU.
2. An outer textually nested unit containing the current CU, if the CU is a subunit.
3. The specification portion of a subprogram or package body currently being compiled.
4. One of the units mentioned in the WITH clause(s) of the ancestor CU defined in categories 1 and 2 above.
5. Package STANDARD.

ARRAY TYPE. A value which designates a set of components which are all the same type or subtype. A component of an array value or array object has a sequence of one or more indices that uniquely determines the component of the array. Each index is a value of a discrete type.

ASSIGNMENT. The operation that replaces the current value in a variable by a new value. An assignment statement explicitly specifies a variable, and assigns an EXPRESSION whose value is to replace the current value in the variable.

ASSOCIATION. A named property of nodes with values that are collections of pointers to other nodes.

ATTRIBUTE. An operation that yields a predefined characteristic of a named entity. Some attributes are functions.

BLOCK STATEMENT. A single statement that contains a sequence of statements. It may also include a declarative part, an exception handler, or both. These parts are local to the block statement.

BODY. That part of a PACKAGE that defines the execution of a subprogram, package, or task. A body stub is a form of body that indicates that this execution is defined in a separately compiled subunit.

CHARACTER. A symbol located in the program text, consisting of a letter, digit, space, special character (i.e., comma or equals sign), or a format effector such as carriage return or line feed.

COLLECTION. The entire set of objects obtained by executing allocators of an access type.

COMPILATION. (1) An execution consisting of zero or more compilation units submitted to the compiler. (2) The translation of a compilation into instruction for the target machine.

COMPILATION UNIT. A declaration or a body of a program unit, presented for compilation as an independent text. As such, the CU is the smallest unit of Ada text that may be submitted for compilation. The compilation units of a program are said to belong to a program "library." A compilation unit defines either a library unit or a secondary unit.

COMPLETE PROGRAM. A program with no unresolved external references.

COMPONENT. A value that is a part of a larger value, or an object that is part of a larger object.

COMPUTER PROGRAM COMPONENT. A functionally or logically distinct part of a computer program configuration item. The computer program component is distinguished to help design complex computer program configuration items.

COMPUTER PROGRAM CONFIGURATION ITEM. A portion of the computer program which is part of a configuration item. The configuration item is an aggregation of hardware and software, or any of its discrete portions which satisfies an end use.

CONSTANT. An OBJECT whose value cannot be changed. The reserved word "constant" appears in the object declaration. The value of the constant cannot be modified after initialization. Constants also consist of formal parameters of mode in subprograms, entries, and generic units. A subcomponent or slice of a constant is also a constant.

CONSTRAINT. Any limitation that determines a subset of values of a type. A value in that subset satisfies the constraint.

CONTEXT CLAUSE. A statement or series of statements optionally used to precede a COMPILATION UNIT naming other compilation units upon which the original compilation unit depends.

DECLARATION. A statement that associates an identifier with an entity. At certain places the identifier can be used as a simple name for the associated entity. Varieties of declarations include: record type declarations, renaming declarations, generic parameter declaration, program unit declaration, or entry declaration. A declaration is terminated by a semicolon.

DECLARATIVE PART. A sequence of declarations and related information such as subprogram bodies and representation clauses that apply over a region of program text.

DENOTE. To name an associated entity by a DECLARATION name.

DEPENDENCE RELATION. The relationship among compilation units; indicates the order of compilation.

DERIVED TYPE. A type whose operation and values are taken ("derived") from those of an existing type. The existing type is called the PARENT TYPE of the derived type.

DESIGNATE. To point out how an ACCESS TYPE assigns an object with a value.

DIRECTORY NODE. A node used to name and group other nodes. Nodes are created within a directory node.

These nodes are sometimes referred to as the "offspring" of the directory node.

DISCRETE TYPE. A type which has an ordered set of distinct values. Discrete types are used for indexing and iteration, and for choices in case statement and record variants.

DISCRIMINANT. A syntactically distinguished component of a record value or record object. The value of the discriminant may govern the presence of some record components, or the size of array components.

ENTITY. Anything that can be named or designated in a program. Includes objects, types, values, and program units.

ENTRY. A unique kind of statement used for communication between tasks. Externally, an entry is called in the same manner as a subprogram; its internal behavior is specified by one or more ACCEPT STATEMENTs. Also see RENDEZVOUS.

ENUMERATING TYPE. A discrete type whose values are represented by enumeration literals. These values are given explicitly in the type declaration, and are either identifiers or character literals.

EXCEPTION. An event that causes suspension of normal program execution. Bringing an exception to attention is called "raising" the exception. An exception handler is a piece of program text specifying a response to the exception. Execution of such a program text is called "handling" the exception.

EXPANDED NAME. A selected component of which the prefix denotes a program unit, BLOCK STATEMENT, loop statement, or ACCEPT STATEMENT. An expanded name denotes an entity declared immediately with the construct denoted by the prefix.

EXPRESSION. A portion of a program that computes a value.

FILE NODE. A node which contains a data portion that may be read or written via the INPUT__OUTPUT and TEXT__IO packages. As is common practice, the data portion of the file nodes does not have a type. Ada programs interpret the data as a sequence of values of some type when an Ada (internal) file is associated with the file node.

FORMAL PARAMETER. An identifier used to denote the PARAMETER within the body of a subprogram, entry, or generic unit.

FOSTER PARENT. A directory node or variation set which relates to a node by sharing a node.

FUNCTION. One of two types of SUBPROGRAMs.

GENERIC UNIT. A template either for a set of subprograms or for a set of packages. A generic unit is written as a subprogram or package but with the specification prefixed by a general formal part (which optionally contains declarations of generic formal parameters).

HANDLER. A portion of program text specifying a response to the exception. Same as EXCEPTION handler.

HOST. A computer system upon which an Ada Program Support Environment resides, executes, and supports Ada software development and maintenance.

IDENTIFIER. A lexical element consisting of a letter, optionally followed by one or more letters, digits, or underline character (but not ending with an underline character).

INCOMPLETE PROGRAM. A program in which some external references are unresolved.

INDEX. An instruction used to distinguish an ARRAY TYPE. An index designates or accesses an element or group of elements in an array.

INDEX CONSTRAINT. A portion of an ARRAY TYPE which gives a range constraint for every index of the type, and thus determines the subset of values of the array type. Each index of each value satisfies the corresponding range constraint.

INDEXED COMPONENT. A name denoting a component in an array or an entry in the entry family.

INTEROPERABILITY. The ability of Ada Program Support Environments to exchange database objects and their relationships in forms usable by tools and user programs without conversion.

INSTANCE. A subprogram created using GENERIC UNIT.

INTEGER TYPE. A discrete type whose values represent all integer numbers between two limits.

JOB. The total computational activity performed on behalf of a user from the time of login through logout.

LEXICAL UNIT. One of the basic syntactic elements making up a program, including an identifier, a literal, a delimiter, or a comment.

LIBRARY SUBPROGRAM BODY. The body of a subprogram which is not a subunit.

LIMITED TYPE. A type whose type definition does not implicitly declare either ASSIGNMENT or an equality operator. All task types, for example, are limited. A private type can be defined to be limited.

LITERAL. A representation which denotes an explicit value of a given type; the value is one of a number (numeric literal), an enumeration value (enumeration literal), a character (character literal), or a string (string literal).

LOCATOR. A short name for any node by which its physical storage may be found. At any instant, a locator uniquely identifies a single node. When a node is destroyed, its locator may be recycled and used later for a newly created node.

LOGGED PROGRAM. An executable program for which derivation information is kept and given to created files.

LOGGED SEQUENCE. A subtree of executing programs for which the root is a logged program, and for which the parent of the root is not a logged program.

MAIN PROGRAM. The subprogram which initially receives control at execution time.

MODE. The characteristic of a formal PARAMETER which specifies whether the associated actual parameter supplies a value for the formal parameter, or the formal supplies a value for the actual parameter, or both.

MODE ANCESTORS. The ancestors of a node. Mode ancestors are its true and foster parents plus the ancestors of these parents. The root node has no ancestors.

MODEL NUMBER. An exactly representable value of a real type. Operations of a real type are defined in terms of operations on the model number of the type. The properties of the model numbers and of their operations are the minimal properties preserved by all implementations of the real type.

MODULE. An independently compilable software component. Modules comprise one or more procedures.

NAME. A construct that stands for an entity.

NAMED ASSOCIATION. An association between arguments and their corresponding parameters. The named association specifies the association of an item with one or more positions in a list, by naming the positions.

OBJECT. Anything which contains a value. A program creates an object either by elaborating an object declaration or by executing an ALLOCATOR. The allocator or declaration gives a type for the object; the object can only contain values of that type. An object whose value can be changed is a variable.

OPERATION. An elementary action associated with one or more types. It is either implicitly declared by the declaration of the type, or it is a subprogram that has a parameter or result of the type.

OPERATOR A function with one or two parameters, for which the call is usually written without enclosing the parameters in parentheses, and for an operator with two parameters written with the name of the operator between the parameters. This notation is not allowed for other function calls.

ORIGINAL CONTAINER. A container that is produced by a compiler, assembler, or importer and contains only one COMPILATION UNIT.

OVERLOADING. The property of aggregates, allocators, identifiers, literals, and operators that can have several alternative meanings with the same scope. For example, an overloaded enumeration literal is a literal that appears in two or more enumeration types.

PACKAGE One of four forms of program units of which programs can be composed. The other forms are subprograms, tasks units, and generic units. A package specifies a COLLECTION of related events, such as types, variables of those types, and subprograms with parameters of those types. A type is written as a package declaration and a package body. The visible part of the package contains the declarations of the entities that can be explicitly used outside the package. The private part of the package contains structural details that are irrelevant to the use of the package, but that completes the specification of the visible entities. The body of a package contains implementations of subroutines or tasks and possibly other packages specified in the visible part.

PARAMETER. One of the named entities associated with a subprogram entry or generic unit and used to communicate with the corresponding subprogram body, task body, or generic body.

PARENT TYPE. An existing type having a DERIVED TYPE.

POSITIONAL ASSOCIATION. An association which specifies the association of an item with a position in a list, by using the same position in the text to specify the item.

PRAGMA. An instruction which conveys information to the compiler. For example, PRAGMA OPTIMIZE( ); will try to optimize for space in the program compilation.

PARENT NODE. A directory node or a variation header node that contains a separate node.

PREFIX. A function call or a name. A prefix is used as the first part of certain kinds of names.

PRIVATE PART. The portion of a PACKAGE which contains structural details.

PRIVATE TYPE. A type whose structure and set of values are clearly defined, but not directly available to the user of the type. A private type is known only by its discriminants and by the set of operations defined for it. A private type and its applicable operation are defined in the visible part of a package. Assignment, equality, and inequality are also defined for private types, unless the private type is marked as a limited type.

PROCEDURE CALL. A statement which invokes a PROCEDURE. Also see SUBPROGRAM.

PROGRAM. A collection of one or more compilation units which have all been compiled separately. One of the subprograms is designated to be the main program. Program units may be subprograms, packages, tasks, or generic units. Each unit normally consists of two parts: a specification, containing the information that must be visible to other units, and a body, containing the implementation details which do not have to be visible to other units.

PROGRAM LIBRARY. A collection of compilation units of which a program is composed.

QUALIFIED EXPRESSION. An EXPRESSION qualified by the name of a type or subtype. It can be used to state the type or subtype of an expression.

RANGE. A contiguous set of values of a scalar type. A range is specified by giving the lower and upper bounds for the values. A value in the range is said to belong to the range.

RANGE CONSTRAINT. A portion of a type which gives a range, and selects the subset of the values of the type that are in the range.

REAL TYPE. A scalar type whose values represent numbers with a fractional part.

RECORD TYPE. A value which comprises a set of components. The components are usually different types or subtypes. For each component of a record value or record object, the type definition gives an identifier that uniquely determines the component within the record.

REHOSTABILITY. The ability for an Ada Program Support Environment to be installed on a different host.

RENDEZVOUS. The interaction that occurs between two parallel tasks when one task has called an entry of the other task, and a corresponding ACCEPT STATEMENT is being executed by the other task on behalf of the calling task.

REPRESENTATION CLAUSE. A statement or series of statements that specify the mapping of a type, an object, or a task onto features of the underlying machine that executes a program. In some cases, representation clauses completely specify the mapping; in other cases, they provide criteria for choosing a mapping.

RETARGETABILITY. The ability of a target-sensitive Ada Program Support Environment tool to accomplish the same function for another target.

REUSABILITY. The ability of a program unit to be employed in the design, documentation, and construction of new programs.

REVISION. An instance of a file node; each revision supersedes all previous ones.

REVISION SET. The collected revisions of a file node viewed as a single set of file nodes.

SCALAR TYPE. Either a discrete type or a real type. The values of a scalar type are arranged in a predefined order. An object or value of a scalar type does not have components.

SCOPE. The portion of a DECLARATION wherein the identifier given in the declaration is a simple name for the associated entity.

SELECTED COMPONENT. A name consisting of an identifier called the selector, and a prefix. Selected components are used to denote record components, entries, and objects designated by access values. Selected components are also used as expanded names.

SELECTOR. One of two portions of a SELECTED COMPONENT.

SERIAL NUMBER. A short name by which a node may be unambiguously identified. At the time of creation, each node is assigned a unique serial number. Unlike locators, serial numbers are never recycled.

SIMPLE NAME. The identifier denoting the associated entry in the immediate scope of a DECLARATION. Both the entity and the declaration define a meaning of the simple name.

SLICE. A portion of a one-dimensional array formed by a sequence of one or more consecutive components selected from that one-dimensional array.

SNAPSHOT CONTAINER. A view of the state of a container during the execution of a tool. The snapshot container includes both permanent and temporary information and can be used to restart the tool at the point of the snapshot or as input to Maintenance Aids. A snapshot container is not part of a program library.

STATEMENT. Anything which specifies one or more actions to be performed during execution of the program.

STRING. A sequence of characters.

SUBCOMPONENT. Either a component, or a component of another subcomponent.

SUBPROGRAM. One of four forms of program units, of which programs can be composed. The other forms are packages, task units, and generic units. A subprogram is written as a subprogram declaration and a subprogram body. The declaration specifies the name of the subprogram and any formal parameters, while the body specifies the execution of the subprogram. A subprogram call gives actual parameters for the formal parameters of a subprogram, and invokes execution of the body of the subprogram. A subprogram is either a procedure or a function. A procedure specifies only a sequence of actions. A procedure call is one of the kinds of statement. A function additionally returns a value called the result of the function. A function call is one of the kinds of EXPRESSION.

SUBTYPE. A description of a type which has a subset of the values of the type. The subset is determined by a constraint on the type. Each value in the set of values of a subtype belongs to the subtype and satisfies the constraint determining the subtype.

SUBUNIT. A separate compilation that defines the execution portion of a BODY.

TARGET. A computer system upon which Ada programs execute.

TASK. A program unit that may operate in parallel with other program units. A task specification establishes the name of the task and the names and parameters of its entries; a task body defines its execution. A task type is a specification that permits the subsequent declaration of any number of similar tasks.

TRANSPORTABILITY. The ability of an Ada Program Support Environment tool to be installed on a different KAPSE. The tool must perform with the same functionality in both installations. Transportability is measured in the degree to which this installation can be accomplished without reprogramming. Portability and transferability are commonly used synonyms.

TRUE PARENT. The directory node or variation set in which a NODE is created. The term is relative to the node.

TYPE. A class of values that characterizes a set of values and a set of operations applicable to those values. A type definition is a language construct that introduces a type. A type declaration associates a name with a type introduced by a type definition. A particular type is either an access type, an array type, a private type, a record type, a scalar type, or a task type.

USABLE CONTAINER. A container which can be used as input to any tools. An unusable container can only be used as input to the maintenance aids.

USE CLAUSE. A clause which opens the visibility to declarations given in the visible part of a package.

VARIABLE. An OBJECT that is not a constant. The object declared by an object declaration that does not include the reserved word CONSTANT is a variable.

VARIANT. An element in a variation set.

VARIATION SET. A set of incarnations of an object; each element co-exists with the others.

VISIBILITY. The state of a declaration of an entity with a certain identifier if the entity is an acceptable meaning for an occurrence at that point of the identifier.

VISIBLE PART. The portion of a PACKAGE which contains the declarations of the entities that can be explicitly used outside the package.

WITH CLAUSE. A clause in the context clause of a compilation unit which includes the name of another compilation unit. The "with" clause make the name of that other compilation unit visible in the current compilation unit.

Algol

Algol is one of the oldest and least used computer programming languages. Algol is an algorithmic language, designed for general-purpose problem solving. Originally developed in 1958 as a means of communicating programming theories and concepts, Algol was implemented as an actual programming language in 1960.

Algol 60 was a scientific language, supporting many advanced mathematical concepts, but without character string handling facilities. The current "standard" version of the language, Algol 68, corrects many of the deficiencies of Algol 60. The language has been stable since that time, although implementation differences do exist. Algol is quite popular in Europe, but never quite caught on in the United States. Burroughs is the major supporter of Algol in the United States, with a continuously updated compiler. A limited version of Algol 68 is available for CP/M computers from the CP/M Users Group.

Algol is a structured programming language. Line numbers are not used, and programs are formed by defining procedures and calling them from the main program. It is easy to write complete programs without ever directly referencing a location within the program; however, labels are definable for a goto statement (usually used to abort program execution safely in case of error). Loops and decision statements usually define flow of control.

Strong data typing is included in the language, as well as multilevel pointer control. The common types of data are used are int and real for numeric data, and char for character strings. A boolean-data-type bool is supported. Data of type bool occupy a single bit of storage, and have two possible values: true and false. Integer-type data can be short (usually two bytes) or long (four bytes). Real data can also be of the short (single precision) or long (double precision). Pointers are defined by prefacing a type reference with ref, and pointers to pointers by ref ref.

Variables and identifiers (used to name a procedure or define a label) can be composed of any combination of letters and numbers, always with a letter as the first character of an identifier. Identifiers cannot contain special characters or embedded spaces, or any of the reserved words of the language. Thus, a, algol68, and algorithmiclanguage1968 are all legal identifiers. Practically, individual compilers may place a limit on the length of an identifier.

Program lines in Algol are ended with the semicolon, but lines can be of any length. All variables must be declared as to type before usage in a program or procedure. Also, programs and procedures must be explicitly defined with begin and end. The following is a complete Algol program, to illustrate simple typing and declaration of variables, and program structure.

```
begin
    int x=1;
    int y=2;
```

```
    int z=x+y;
    print(("the sum of",x,"and",y,"is",z))
end
```

In this program is an important construct (int z=x+y;), showing that a variable declaration can be dependent on the value(s) of previously defined variables. The print function called by this program does not make use of any formatting instructions. This program constitutes a "serial clause": a sequential series of steps to solve a particular problem. The individual declarations of the program are "unitary clauses"—the most basic programming unit of an Algol program.

Input/output in Algol is implementation dependent; each compiler will have its own rules on filenames, device names, etc. Generally speaking, each compiler recognizes that the print function sends output to the local list device (or file), and that read gathers input from the local read device (or file). "Open", "close", etc. are dependent largely on the local implementation for syntax, and are generally called as functions. Printed output can be formatted using format statements. File input/output can be controlled via format statements, or by the use of structured variables. For example:

```
struct ([1:3] char month, int day, int year) date=
    ("Mar",31,1984)
```

defines the structure of a date record (and in this example, also defines a date). The char declaration of month signifies a single element character string three characters in length. The structure above may be referred to as "date", in which case the entire date will be returned, or by any of the date's component parts; i.e., "year of date" is 1984, "day of date" is 31, and "month of date" is "Mar". Substrings in Algol can be referenced directly:

```
(month of date)[1:2]
```

returns "Ma", letters 1 and 2 of "Mar".

Data values in Algol are normally stored in a last-in first-out stack. The compiler automatically maintains the stack. As an example, the identifier j is initially declared as int j=2. At a later stage in the program, j is redefined as int j=3. The original value of j is removed from the stack and the new value added. Stack storage is used for efficiency. However, there may be the need to always preserve the value of an identifier. Thus the identifier may be declared as part of the heap. Storage on the heap, once allocated, is never removed. Excessive use of heap storage can cause a program to run out of free memory for intermediate results; the stack can be compressed dynamically at runtime, the heap, never. Stack storage (the default mode) can also be expressly declared, as loc.

Procedures are the building blocks of large Algol programs. A procedure may itself consist of other procedures and/or clauses. A procedure to return the number of days in a month is defined below:

```
proc daysinamonth = (int monthnumber, bool
    leapyear)int:
```

```
begin
   case monthnumber
       in31,   (leapyear  |   29  |   28),31,30,
           31,30,31,31,
           30,31,30,31
       out 0
   esac
end
```

The procedure is named "daysinamonth". Two parameters are required by the procedure: the "monthnumber" expressed as an integer, and "leapyear" expressed as true or false. The case operator acts to force a selection of one of the values "in" the list; a value of 1 returns 31, a value of 11 returns 30. A value outside the range of 1 to 12 returns 0, as evidenced by the out 0. A short logical statement selects the value returned if "monthnumber" = 2. The logical statement takes the value of "leapyear" and if true returns 29, if false returns 28. A fuller version of the expression "(leapyear | 29 | 28)" can be written as:

```
if leapyear then daysinamonth := 29 else
    daysinamonth := 28 ;
```

Note that in a logical statement := is used to test for equality. This logical statement tests for the boolean value of "leapyear". Logical statements can also directly compare the values of identifiers, such as x > y, x < y, etc. Expressions can be evaluated by logical statements, as in:

```
if (bankbalance minusab value of check)< 0 then
    check bounced
```

This is not truly an executable statement. Note that the operator minusab reads "minus and becomes", so that "bankbalance" is altered by this statement. There are also operators divab, multab, and plusab.

Loops in Algol are controlled by for statements and while statements. The for statement requires a counter; while does not. The for statement generally takes the form of:

```
for i from 1 to 10 by 2 do x=x+1 od
```

"i" is the counter, running from 1 to 10 in steps of 2. The controlled clause is "x=x+1", enclosed by do and od. The from can be left out, in which case the loop is started at 1; the by can also be omitted and the step will default to 1.

The while loop is used when the value of a variable is to control the loop; i.e., the number of iterations through the loop is dependent on the value of the control variable:

```
while x < 3 do x=x+0.25 od
```

This loop will execute until the value of "x" equals or exceeds 3. Should "x" already be greater than or equal to

3 when the loop is encountered, no execution of the loop will take place.

The overall structure of an Algol program is:

```
begin
   co This is acomments line co
   co variable declarations go here co

   co procedure definitions usually come next co

   co main program after procedures are defined co

end
```

In addition to the features mentioned previously, most implementations of Algol have defined trig functions, square root and exponentiation functions, logarithmic functions, and various input/output file and device handlers. Algol implements most of these features through a system library, which the compiler automatically searches. This allows each implementation to best use the resources available.

Strengths of Algol are:

- Strong and flexible data typing.
- Support of modular program construction through use of separately definable procedures.
- A wide variety of loop controls and logical statements.

Unfortunately, Algol does suffer from one weakness—a lack of support for the language in the United States. Except for Burroughs, no new development is being made in the language.

The joys of programming in ALGOL will make up for the deficiency in available support, however. As one progresses in the language and begins to learn its intricacies, certain advantages emerge. Entire procedures can be manipulated as simple variables, and restructuring a complex program is made easy. Thus the level of complexity may range from an eggshell to a skyscraper, and the programmer is in total control each step of the way. For further information on programming in Algol, see the Algol section in the bibliography.

William Woodall

ALGOL GLOSSARY

The following Algol glossary is a working vocabulary of statements and function words for the implementation of the language designed to run under CP/M.

BEGIN Statement indicating the start of a program or procedure. Required as first statement of a program or first statement of procedure after procedure declaration.
   begin

BIT   Data-type declaration. Declares data to be a word length of individual bits (which is also bool type). Implementation dependent as to number of bits available. Bits are not individually addressable.
    bit a = 1 true

BOOL   Data-type declaration. Declares data to be bool type, that is, a single bit that is either true or false.
    bool leapyear = true

BY   Used as part of for statement. Indicates increment for counter.
    for i to 10 by 3

BYTE   Data-type declaration. Declares data to be a word-length of characters, stored as individual bytes. Implementation dependent as to number of bytes available. Bytes are not individually addressable.
    byte = "test"

CASE   Multiple-choice logical test. Uses integer value as entry to choose from available choices. Works in conjunction with in and out statements.
    case a
        in 1,2,3
        out 0
    esac

CHAR   Data-type declaration. Declares data to be of character type. Brackets [ ] denote number of elements and maximum length of string.
    [1:6] char guitarstring = "ABCDEF"

CO   Comment statement. Any text inside matched pair of co is taken to be a comment. Non-executable.
    co This is a comment co

DIVAB   Arithmetic operator. Meaning is "divide and become". Performs division by argument with result replacing original value of preceding variable.
    j divab 5

DO   Indicates controlled clause in loop. All code inside matched pair of do and od is executed for each iteration of loop.
    do x=x+1 od

ELSE   Used in logical if to indicate alternate path if test fails.
    else j = 27

END   End of program or procedure.
    end

ESAC   End of case logical test.
    esac

FALSE   Boolean data value. The actual value of false is implementation dependent. Usually used to initialize boolean variables.
    bool testval = false

FOR   Loop control statement. Used for loops that require a definite number of iterations.
    for i to 10

FORMAT   Output control statement. Used to define a mask for printed output. Precise details of format masks is implementation dependent.
    format (format mask)

FROM   Used in loop control. Initializes counter value in a for statement.
    for i from 3 to 10

GOTO   Flow of control statement. Directly transfers program control to labeled location.
    goto abort

HEAP   Data declaration. Places declared variable value in a preserved area of memory. The heap functions somewhat similar to the COMMON statement in Fortran.
    ref int = heap int j := 33

IF   Logical test statement. Tests for truth of expression, then branches to then clause. If the expression is false, control passes to the else clause.
    if x > y

IN   Part of case statement. Starts the group of choices offered by the case statement.
    in 1,2,3

INT   Data declaration. Declares data to be of integer type. No decimal point values are accepted. Integer values default to a range of $-32768 < i < 32767$.
    int j = 1

LABEL   Defines a location in a program or procedure. Labels can be used for convenience, or as the target of a goto statement. The word label is not required.
    label: co come here to abort program co

LOC   Data declaration. Places declared variable on last-in first-out stack. This is the default for variable declaration.
    loc int j = 1

LONG   Data declaration. Denotes double-sized form of declared variable. Actual length increase is implementation dependent.
    long int j = 123456

MINUSAB   Arithmetic operator. Meaning is "subtract and become". Performs subtraction of argument with result replacing original value of preceding variable.
    j minusab 5

MULTAB   Arithmetic operator. Meaning is "multiply and become". Performs multiplication by argument with result replacing original value of preceding variable.
    j multab 5

OD   Indicates end of controlled clause in loop. All code inside matched pair of do and od is executed for each iteration of loop.

do x=x+1 od

OF   Data reference. Refers to subpart of a structured data type.

month of date

OUT   Part of case statement. Ends the group of choices offered by the case statement, and optionally defines a default choice if the entry value is out of range.

out 0

PLUSAB   Arithmetic operator. Meaning is "add and become". Performs addition of argument with result replacing original value of preceding variable.

j plusab 5

PRINT   Output function. The print function calling syntax is implementation dependent.

print (("output data goes here"))

PROC   Procedure definition. Used to define a procedure; must be used with type declaration(s) for input parameter(s) and output value(s).

proc sum2integers = (int arg1, int arg2)int:

READ   Input function. Implementation dependent for source of data being input.

read a;

REAL   Data declaration. Declares data to be of real number type (floating point). Implementation dependent.

real x = 12.357

REF   Data declaration. Declares data to be a pointer to the address where a variable is stored.

ref int j = 5

SHORT   Data declaration. Denotes short-sized form of declared variable. Actual length is implementation dependent.

short int j = 1234

STRUCT   Data declaration. Declares data to be a structure formed from listed components.

struct ([1:20] char lastname,[1:20] char firstname)

THEN   Used in logical if to indicate main path if test is true.

then j = 24

TRUE   Boolean data value. The actual value of true is implementation dependent. Usually used to initialize boolean variables.

bool testval = true

WHILE   Loop control function. Used to make a loop where number of iterations of loop is dependent upon entry value of a variable.

while x < 3 do x = x+1 od

APL

APL, an acronym for A Programming Language, was developed by Kenneth Iverson of IBM in 1962. It is considered a general-purpose algebraic language and is ideally suited for physical scientists and engineers. It was developed to be implemented on the IBM 360 series originally to solve problems in the areas of Fourier analysis, least-squares method, numerical integration, solution of Laplace equations by numerical methods, eigenvalue problems, and mathematical physics. It uses an immediate mode unless a function is being defined: as the user types in a single statement, it is immediately executed.

APL is clearly different from the more traditional computer languages. It needs a special keyboard for input. The character set consists of the 26 uppercase alphabetic characters, the 10 digits, and the 52-special-character set displayed below:

$$+ \quad - \quad \times \quad \div \quad * \quad < \quad \leq \quad = \quad \geq \quad > \quad \neq \quad \bar{\ }$$
$$. \quad : \quad , \quad ; \quad \cdot\cdot \quad (\quad) \quad [\quad] \quad ? \quad ' \quad \circ$$
$$\vee \quad \wedge \quad \div \quad \uparrow \quad \rightarrow \quad \downarrow \quad \backslash \quad /$$
$$\top \quad \bot \quad | \quad \cap \quad \cup \quad \supset \quad \subset$$
$$\Gamma \quad L \quad \sim \quad \Delta \quad \nabla \quad \circ \quad \Box$$
$$\alpha \quad \omega \quad \varepsilon \quad \rho \quad \iota$$

Some of the special characters require overstriking. To differentiate between the computer's typing and the user's typing, APL utilizes the convention that computer typing starts at the left margin, while what the user types is indented six spaces.

The first group of special characters are the standard five arithmetic operators of addition, subtraction, multiplication, division, and exponentiation ($+ \quad - \quad \times \quad \div \quad *$). These operators can be used with real numbers either in conventional decimal form or in exponential notation. Another major difference in the language is that the evaluation of mathematical expressions does not follow the normal arithmetic precedence rules. In APL, mathematical expressions are evaluated from right to left within symbols of grouping. For example, A $\times$ B + C is evaluated as A$\times$(B+C).

An important feature of APL is that unlike some languages, when in the immediate mode, variables can be assigned values, and these values will be retained in memory and can be recalled later at the same session. Variable names are given by the standard convention where a name can be any string of alphabetic or numeric characters beginning with a letter of the alphabet. Literal expressions are enclosed within quotation marks. Below is an example of the use of a variable in the immediate mode:

```
     5×6
30
```

When typed by the user, this action results in a 30 being typed by the computer.

$$A \longleftarrow 5 \times 6$$

When typed by the user, the value 30 is assigned to A.

```
     A
30
```

When the user types A, the value stored in A is typed by the computer. This procedure, in which the user types in a single statement that is immediately executed by the computer, is the typical method of interaction with APL.

Another strength of the language is its ability to handle vectors and matrices. Assignment statements are used to define these arrays. For example:

$$x \longleftarrow 2\ 4\ 7\ 9\ 5$$

assigns the vector <2,4,7,9,5> to x, while

$$m \longleftarrow 2\ 3\ \rho\ 1\ 2\ 3\ 4\ 5\ 6$$

assigns the matrix $\begin{bmatrix} 1 & 2 & 3 \\ 4 & 5 & 6 \end{bmatrix}$ to m.

When the user types the variable names x and m, APL types the array as shown:

```
          x
2  4  7  9  5
          m
1  2  3
4  5  6
```

The symbol ρ is an example of a scalar function. APL contains a large number of built-in functions which are denoted by special characters within the character set used for APL. These functions and their definitions appear in the glossary. Many of these functions have both unary and binary definitions and are referred to as monadic and dyadic in this language. For example, when ρ is used to structure a matrix, it is being used in its dyadic form. However, when the same symbol is used in conjunction with a single vector V in its monadic form, ρV returns the number of components in V, called the dimension of V.

Many applications in science and engineering require more than using only the immediate mode. Whenever the same sequence of instructions needs to be repeated, it is generally efficient to enter the function definition mode which permits the user to define a function and proceed in a "program-like" fashion. The character ∇ causes the computer to switch from the execution mode to the definition mode. This permits the user to enter a sequence of commands that will not be executed when the RETURN key is pressed. When the user types ∇ again after computing the definition of the function, the computer reverts to its execution mode.

Every user-defined function begins with a header which defines the syntax of the function. It always contains a name for the function and may indicate the arguments of the function. If there is one argument, it appears on the right of the function names as with the built-in monadic of the function. If there are two arguments, the arguments straddle the function name. When no arguments appear, the arguments of the function are considered to be constants, and in this case, all of the variables appearing in the function definition will have to be assigned values prior to calling the function. These user-defined functions can be used in the same way that a primitive (built-in) function is used in that:

1. The result may be typed as output.
2. The function may be used as part of a more complex expression.
3. The result may be used to assign a value to a variable as part of an assignment statement.

Thus a user-defined function may or may not give an explicit result, and since a user-defined function can have 0, 1, or 2 arguments and either 0 or 1 explicit results, there are six different forms for headers.

1. ∇ NAME
2. ∇ NAME A
3. ∇ A NAME B
4. ∇ Z ⟵ NAME
5. ∇ Z ⟵ NAME A
6. ∇ Z ⟵ A NAME B

Forms 2 and 5 define monadic functions, and 3 and 6 define dyadic functions, while 1 and 4 have no specific arguments. Functions of the form 1, 2, and 3 must appear by themselves in a statement, while those of the form 4, 5, and 6 may be used as arguments within statements. For example, consider the function defined below for converting Fahrenheit temperatures to Celsius.

```
     ∇  C ⟵TEMP F
[1]     C ⟵ (F−32)×5÷9
     ∇

     TEMP 77
45
```

Since TEMP has a single result, it can also be used in an expression such as 20 + TEMP 77. However, if the header ∇ TEMP F had been used, that same expression would result in an error message. Thus to execute a user-defined function is analogous to executing a primitive function provided the proper header has been used.

In defining functions the user is required to perform function editing. After the user initially types the header, the computer will respond with:

[1]

which is a statement number and the user enters the first command. Once that command is entered, a new statement number appears in sequential integer order:

[2]

As indicated, the user continues typing the definition, using another ∇ to end the definition. If alterations or deletions are necessary, the user can first display the function definition by typing:

∇ NAME [□] ∇

which gives a listing of the statements in the function. To make an insertion, the user types:

∇ NAME [1:5]

which will insert a statement between [1] and [2]. The computer will respond with a .1 increment:

[1.6]

Another statement could then be entered, or the user can override the computer by typing a different statement number. A statement can also be deleted by striking the ATTN key after the statement number. If alterations to a statement need to be accomplished, the user simply retypes the statement number of the statement to be changed, then types the new statement, and this overrides the previous statement. More sophisticated editing techniques are also available.

Branching is also available in APL by use of the monadic primitive function ⟶ . It has the general form ⟶ S, where S is any APL expression. It is executed as follows:

1. If the value of the expression is a statement number in the user-defined function, that statement is executed next.
2. If the value is not one of the statement numbers in the function, the function terminates.

Here are some examples of user-defined functions. Note that comments are accomplished by making the first character of a statement the character formed by overstriking the character above the C on the APL keyboard (∩) with the small circle above the J (•).

```
           ∇ T ⟵ RECT A; X; Y; Z
[1] ⍝   THE FUNCTION RECT CONVERTS A GIVEN
[2] ⍝   SET OF SPHERICAL COORDINATES
[3] ⍝   (R,∝, ω) TO THE EQUIVALENT
[4] ⍝   CARTESIAN COORDINATES (X, Y, Z)
[5] ⍝   ANGLES ∝, ω MUST BE GIVEN IN RADIANS
[6] X  ⟵A[1]×(1 ○ A[2])×2 ○ A[3]
[7] Y ⟵ A[1]×(1 ○ A[2])×1   A[3]
[8] Z⟵ A[1]×(2 ○ A[2])
[9] T⟵X,Y,Z
```

```
           ∇TRIANGLE S;A;B;C
[1] ⍝   THIS PROGRAM PRINTS THE SINE, COSINE,
[2] ⍝   AND TANGENT OF EACH ANGLE OF A
```

[3] ⋔ TRIANGLE ABC GIVEN THE LENGTHS OF
[4] ⋔ THE THREE SIDES, AS WELL AS THE
[5] ⋔ ANGLES IN DEGREES AND THE AREA OF
[6] ⋔ THE TRIANGLE S IS A VECTOR WITH
[7] ⋔ THREE COMPONENTS DENOTING THE
[8] ⋔ LENGTH OF THE THREE SIDES.
[9] A ⟵ −2 o ((S[1]*2)−(S[2]*2)+(S[3]*))÷−2×
        S[2]×S[3]
[10] B ⟵ −2 o ((S[2]*2)−(S[1]*2)+(S[3]*))÷−2×
        S[1]×S[3]
[11] C ⟵ (o 1)−A+B
[12] 'ANGLES A, B, AND C IN DEGREES'
[13] (A,B,C)×(180÷ o 1)
[14] 'SINES OF ANGLES A, B, C'
[15] 10(A,B,C)
[16] 'COSINES OF ANGLES A, B, C'
[17] 20(A,B,C)
[18] 'TANGENTS OF ANGLES A, B, C'
[19] 30(A,B,C)
[20] 'AREA OF TRIANGLE'
[21] 0.5×S[2]×S[3]×1 o A

This function returns all the prime numbers between 2 and N inclusively. Note the use of the branching function.

```
          ∇ D ⟵ PRIMES N;X
[1] D ⟵ 2,X ⟵ 3
[2] ⟶ (N < X ⟵ X+2)/0
[3] ⟶ (V/0=D | X)/2
[4] D ⟵ D,X
[5] ⟶ 2
```

Michael Iannone

APL GLOSSARY

The APL operators in this glossary are organized in a sequence that novices would encounter in a typical mathematical learning progression. Generally speaking, APL requires a large amount of memory for its compiler. Most professional implementations of the language, therefore, are on mainframe computers. However, in schools and colleges, APL is downloaded to a PC terminal from a central network.

⟵ Assignment operator. For example:
        A ⟵ 3×4
assigns 12 to A.

Arithmetic Operators

+ (Dyadic) addition operator. For example:
        4+5
9

− (Dyadic) subtraction operator. For example:
        18−23
⁻5

× (Dyadic) multiplication operator. For example:
        15×20
300

÷ (Dyadic) division operator. For example:
        28÷7
4

* (Dyadic) exponentiation operator. A*B returns A raised to the B power. For example:
        2*3
8

+ (Monadic) addition with a left argument of zero understood.

− (Monadic) subtraction with a left argument of zero understood. Thus −8 means 0−8 = ⁻8

× (Monadic). This operator is called the signum function. For any scalar A:
×A equals   1 if A > 0
              0 if A = 0
             ⁻1 if A < 0

For example:
        A ⟵ −8
        *A
⁻1

÷ (Monadic). ÷ A returns the reciprocal of A.
        A ⟵ 4
        ÷A
.2500000000

Relational Operators

= Equal To

> Greater Than

< Less Than

≥ Greater Than or Equal To

≤ Less Than or Equal To

≠ Not Equal To

Each of these is a dyadic operation which returns a 1 if the relation is true and a 0 if it is not. For example:

        5 = 3 + 2
1
        7 + 1   8
1
        5 + 4 ÷ 2 < 6
0

Boolean Operators

The boolean operators are given below and conform to the usual rules of boolean algebra.

∨   or

∧   and

~   not

=   equal

≠   not equal

⩑   not and (nand)

⩒   not or (nor)

Mathematical Functions

*   Monadic Exponential (base e). *A returns the value of e raised to the A power. For example:

```
      *(.5)
1.648721271
```

*   Dyadic Power. A*B returns the value of A raised to the B power. For example:

```
      A  ←  .5
      B  ←  2
      B * A
1.414213562
```

⊛   Monadic Natural Logarithm. The character ⊛ is formed by overstriking the O and * characters. ⊛ A returns the value of $\log_e$ A (i.e., the logarithm of A to the base e).

```
      ⊛10
7.2
```

⊛   Dyadic Logarithm to a Base. A ⊛ B returns the logarithm of B to the base A (i.e., $\log_A$ B). For example:

```
      A ← 10
      B ← 1000
      A ⊛  B
3
```

L   Monadic Floor.   LA returns the greatest integer less than or equal to A.

```
      L3.14
3
```

L   Dyadic Minimum.   A L B returns the minimum of A and B.

```
      3 L 4
3
```

⌈   Monadic Ceiling.   ⌈A returns the smallest integer greater than or equal to A.

```
      ⌈3.14
4
```

⌈   Dyadic Ceiling.   A⌈B returns the maximum of A and B.

```
      3 ⌈ 4
4
```

| Monadic Absolute Value. |A returns the absolute value of A.

```
      |−3.5
3.5
```

| Dyadic Residue. A | B returns the remainder when B is devided by A.

```
      16.82 | 75.1
7.82
```


Trignometric and Inverse Trignometric Functions

○   Monadic Times π.   ○A returns the product of π and A.

```
      ○1
3.141592654
```

○   Dyadic Trignometric Functions. I ○ A with an integer between −7 and 7 inclusive and A an argument in the domain of the functions selected by I returns the value of the function as defined in a chart. For example:

```
      A ← 1
      1 ○ A
.8414709848
      3 ○ A
1.557407725
```

! Monadic Factorial. !A returns A factorial.

```
      !6
720
```

! Dyadic Combinational. A!B returns the number of combinations of B things taken A at a time.

```
      3!6
10
```

? Monadic Roll. ?A returns a random integer from the set 1,2,. _ ,A.

```
      ?30
5
```

Array (Vector and Matrix) Operators

ρ   **Dyadic Restructure.** This function has the general form m n ρ(list of components). It generates a matrix with m rows and n columns using the given list. For example:

```
        3  2  ρ  1  2  3  4
1   2
3   4
1   2
```

Note: The first two digits are reused.

ρ Monadic Dimension. ρ R returns the dimension of the array R. For example:

```
     N ←── 4 6 7 2 9
     ρN
5
```

ι   **Monadic Index Generator.** ιN returns a vector whose components are the integers 1 through N inclusive.

```
      ι 5
1 2 3 4 5
```

ι   **Dyadic Index Of.** This function has the general form V ιR where V is a vector and R is an array. It returns an array S whose components are the indices in V of the corresponding components of R.

```
     A ←── 4.6    6.7    3.8    2.1    6.25
     A ι 2.1
4
     A ←── 7.3    8.257    3    7
     B ←── 8.257    7
     A ιB
2   4
```

[ ] Dyadic Indexing. A [list of indices] returns the components of A which correspond to the indices in the given list. For example:

```
     A ←── 4 5 6 7 8
     A [3 4]
6   7
     m ←── 2 3 ρ ι 6
     m
1 2 3
4 5 6
     m [2;3]
6
```

,   **Monadic Ravel.** , R is used to convert an array R into a vector.

```
     A ←── 2  3  ρ  1  2  5
     A
```

```
1 2 5
1 2 5
     , A
1 2 5 1 2 5
```

, **Dyadic Catenate.** V_1 ,V_2 chains vector V_2 to vector V_1

```
     A ←── 1 3 5 8
     B ←── 9 12
     A,B
1   3   5   8   9   12
```

/ Dyadic Reduction. f /V where f is a permissible dyadic function and V is a vector returns V [1] f   V[2] f ... f V [n].

```
     A ←── 4    5    6    9
     +/A
24
```

Note: +/A is equivalent to Σ A.

```
     ×/A
1080
```

Note: ×/A is equivalent to π A.

The reduction operator / can also be used on matrices. The reduction takes place over each row in the matrix and the result is a vector.

```
     M ←── 3×3 ? ρι9
     M
2 3 2
2 4 6
3 7 8
     T ←── +/M
     T
7   12   18
```

⊞   **Monadic-Matrix Inverse.** This character is formed by overstriking the quad character with the division sign. It has the general form ⊞ M and returns the inverse of a matrix M provided the inverse exists. For example:

```
       M         3  3  ρ 1  1  1  0  2  1  1  0  1
       m
1   1   1
0   2   1
1   0   1
         ⊞M
2.00000000    −1.000000000    −1.000000000
1.000000000    0              −1.000000000
−2.000000000   1.000000000    2.000000000
```

⊞   **Dyadic-Matrix Division.** This function has the general form V ⊞ M and returns the matrix (inner) product of the inverse of M (provided it exists) and M. It is generally used to solve systems of equations. For example, to solve the system:

$$3x + 2y + 3z = 16$$
$$2x - y + 5z = 15$$
$$x + y + 2z = 9$$

proceed as follows:

```
M ←— 3 3 ρ 3 2 3 2 ¯1 5 1 1 2
V ←— 16 15 9
V ⊞ M
1 2 3
```

+.× Dyadic Matrix Multiplication.

A+.×B returns the matrix product of A and B provided the matrix product exists. For example:

```
A ←— 3 2 ρ 1 2 3 0 ¯1 2
B ←— 2 4 ρ 1 0 1 2 ¯1 3 0 2
A+.×B
¯1   6   1   6
 3   0   3   6
¯3   6  ¯1   2
```

Matrix multiplication is a special case of the generalized inner product operation which has the general form Af.dB where f and d are usually one of the primary arithmatic operators. The character . denotes an inner product operation. The function on the right of the . is executed on a component by component basis by using the ith row of A and the jth column of B to determine the corresponding entry in the inner product matrix.

o.x Dyadic Outer Product.

An o.x returns an array C C by multiplying each component of the vector B by each component of A. Note that ρC is equal to (ρA),ρB. For example:

```
A ←— ι3
B ←— ι5
Ao.xB
1 2 3 4 5
2 4 6 8 10
3 6 9 12 15
```

Sorting Functions

⍋ Monadic Grade Up.

The character ⍋ is formed by overstriking the characters Δ and |. It has the general form ⍋ V and returns a vector of indices which orders V in ascending order. For example:

```
T ←— 45.5  34.1  49.5  22.7  15.3
⍋ T
5 4 2 1 3
```

This function is often used to place an array in ascending order as shown:

```
T[⍋T]
15.3  22.7  34.1  45.5  49.5
```

⍒ Monadic Grade Down.

This function works analogous to ⍋ except that it sorts in descending order.

↑ Dyadic Take.

This function has the general form K ↑ V where V is a vector and K is an integer such that |K is less than or equal to ρV. It returns the first K or last K elements of V depending on whether K is positive or negative. For example:

```
V ←— 5 6 2 7 8 3
¯2 ↑ V
8   3
3 ↑ V
5   6   2
```

This function can be used to select the K smallest or K largest elements in a vector V. K ↑ V[⍋ V] would yield the K smallest elements.

↓ Dyadic Drop.

This function works like the Take function except that elements are dropped rather than taken. For example:

```
V ←— 2 5 11 8
2 ↓ V
11   8
```

Permutation Functions

⍉ Monadic Transpose.

This character is formed by overstriking the O with the backslash \. It has the general form ⍉ R where R is an array. When R is a matrix, ⍉ R returns a matrix with the rows and columns of R interchanged.

```
M ←— 3 2 ρ ι6
M
1 2
3 4
5 6
⍉ M
1 3 5
2 4 6
```

⍉ Dyadic Transpose.

This function has the general form V ⍉ R where V is a permutation vector and R is an array of rank 1 or greater. A necessary condition is that ρV equals ρ (ρR). V ⍉ R returns an array.

⌽ Monadic Reversal.

⌽ V returns the elements of a vector in their reverse order.

```
V ←— 7 4 2 3
⌽V
3 2 4 7
```

If M is a matrix, ⌽ M reverses the order of the rows of the matrix.

```
M ←— 2 3 ρ ι6
⌽ M
3 2 1
6 5 4
```

⌽ Dyadic Rotate.

This function has the general form N ⌽ V where N is an integer and V is a vector. It returns a vector which is a cyclic rotation of n placed in a counterclockwise direction if n is positive and n places in a clockwise direction if n is negative. For example:

```
V ← 4 6 7 1 3 8
  3 Φ V
1 3 8 4 6 7
```

Set Operation Functions

/ Dyadic Compress. L/W where L is a scalar or a logical vector of the same dimension as W returns a vector consisting of the components of W corresponding to the components of L which are equal to 1.

```
      W ← 6 8 3 7
      T ← 1 1 0 1/W
      T
6 8 7
      Z ← 58  79  63  112  42
      T ← (Z<60)/Z
      T
58 42
```

When W is a matrix, L/W will compress along columns while L/[1]W will compress along rows. For example:

```
      W ← 3 4 ρ ι 12
      T ← 1 0 0 1/W
      W
1   2   3   4
5   6   7   8
9  10  11  12
      T
1   4
5   8
9  12
```

\ Dyadic Expand. The form of this function is similar to the compress function, the difference being that this function expands a vector by filling in a numeric vector with zeros. For example:

```
      X ← 1 9 8 4
      U ← 1 0 1 0 0 1 0 0 0 1
      U\X
1 0 9 0 0 8 0 0 0 4
```

This function, too, can be extended as the following example shows:

```
      M ← 3 3 ρ ι 9
      U ← 1 0 1 0 1
      M
1 2 3
4 5 6
7 8 9
```

```
      U \[1]M
1 2 3
0 0 0
4 5 6
0 0 0
7 8 9
```

ε Dyadic Membership. This function has the general form R ε U where R and U are arrays of arbitrary rank. It returns a logical array of the same dimension as R, so that each entry is 1 or 0 depending upon whether the corresponding element of R is an element of U. For example:

```
      R ← ι 6
      U ← 3 7 2 4
      R ε U
0 1 1 1 0 0
```

? Dyadic Deal. M ? N returns M integers selected randomly from the set 1,2,...,N. For example:

```
      5?100
21  37  78  45  9
```

Decode and Encode Functions

⊥ Dyadic Decode. The decode function is useful in conversion problems from one system to another such as from binary to decimal and for evaluating polynomials. If V and T are vectors of the same dimension, V⊥T is defined as the scalar S where S ← +/U×T and is a vector such that U [ρ V] = 1 and U[I] is equal to V[I]x U[I] for I equal 1 to T equal to (ρ V)−1. Fortunately, it is relatively simple to use for polynomials. Given the polynomial function $f(x) = x^5 + 3x^4 - 2x^3 + 3x + 1$ to evaluate at x=2, the user simply proceeds as follows:

```
      C ← 1 3 ‾2 0 3 1
      V ← ι
      V⊥C
68
```

⊤ Dyadic Encode. The encode function, which is the inverse of the decode function, can also be used for conversion problems. V ⊤ Z is defined as in the decode function to be the scalar S where S ← +/Z×U and U is as defined in that function. It is generally used to convert from one base to another. For example, to change 1367 to a base 8 number the user proceeds as follows:

```
      S ← 1367
      V ← 8 8 8 8
      V⊤S
2 5 2 7
```

BASIC

The acronym BASIC stands for Beginners All-Purpose Symbolic Instruction Code. BASIC is the most commonly used high-level language for microcomputers; often, it is included with the microcomputer at point of purchase either on the system disk, as in IBM PC computers, or on a ROM chip that is plugged into the computer's motherboard, as in Commodore computers. BASIC was developed at Dartmouth University in 1964 exclusively for use on timesharing mainframe systems and was intended to be a general-purpose language able to handle business, scientific, and professional applications. BASIC quickly became the language of choice for microcomputers, however, for two primary reasons.

First, it was there at the right time when the early micros were being developed as experimental machines. Second, and more important, BASIC lent itself very easily to the new microchip technology. BASIC is an interpreter; it processes only one line of code at a time. Compiled languages, such as Fortran and COBOL, process entire programs at a time. Interpreters have smaller memory requirements than compilers and thus were crucial to the early memory-starved microcomputers. Hence, BASIC solved one of the more crucial problems facing microcomputer technology: it was able to fit in the allotted space.

Since its introduction, many different dialects of BASIC have been developed and circulated. The most popular, and the one currently in use on most micros, was developed by Microsoft, Inc. and is known as Microsoft BASIC. Versions of it appear for the IBM PC and PCjr, Apple, Radio Shack, and Commodore computers.

BASIC carries out the principal functions of any programming language: inputting information, arithmetic computation, string processing, outputting information, and branching to different sections of the program. Constants can be represented in BASIC as decimal numbers having seven significant digits (with single precision) or sixteen significant digits (with double precision). Memory locations can be identified by variable names to represent numerical or string quantities; a suffix character ($) denotes a string variable.

Arithmetic expressions can be constructed by combining constants and variables using the operation symbols (+) addition, (−) subtraction, (*) multiplication, (/) division, and (**) exponentiation. The numerical value of these expressions can then be stored under a particular variable name using an arithmetic assignment statement which has the form:

VARIABLE NAME = ARITHMETIC EXPRESSION

Or, for example, A = (6+3)−(4/8). Both numeric and string quantities can be input using either an INPUT statement or a READ/DATA statement, both of which are exemplified in the sample program below. The INPUT statement interacts with the user in the form of a dialogue because it requires that data be entered only when the program is executed or RUN. The READ/DATA statement, on the other hand, requires that the data be included in the program itself. The content of both numeric and string variables can be output using the PRINT statement or the more versatile PRINT USING statement. Additional literal information can be output to the screen or printer by enclosing it in quotation marks in the PRINT list. Also statement numbers in a BASIC program are required for editing and sequencing operations.

SAMPLE PROGRAM

```
100  READ A$
110  PRINT"ENTER:EXPERIMENT NUMBER AND
     DEGREES IN CENTIGRADE"
120  INPUT N$,C
130  F=(9/5)*C+32
140  PRINT A$;N$
150  PRINT C;"DEGREES CENTIGRADE
     EQUALS";F;"DEGREES FAHRENHEIT"
160  DATA EXPERIMENT
170  END
```

In the following description of the program's execution, ONE, 0 is user-supplied information, [RUN] is a system command and not an instruction in BASIC; and the question mark is a standard prompt:

```
[RUN]
ENTER: EXPERIMENT NUMBER AND DEGREES
IN CENTIGRADE
? ONE, 0
EXPERIMENT ONE
0 DEGREES CENTIGRADE EQUALS 32
DEGREES FAHRENHEIT
```

This sample program is a straightforward set of input and computation instructions. More complicated operations, however, often require logical operators such as "If X = Y, then perform Z" or, more likely, "If X conditions apply, then perform Z operations." These are called branching operations and they allow programmers to alter the natural sequence in which instructions would be executed within a program. The two most common branching or control instructions used in BASIC are the GOTO statement, which causes unconditional branching to a statement having the statement number following the GOTO, and the IF...THEN statement which allows conditional execution of a BASIC instruction. The actual conditions under which the statements are executed are based on a logical expression following the word IF; for example: "IF N$=3 THEN PRINT N$." Other standard branching statements which permit a more structured program development are: ON GOTO and IF...THEN...ELSE. Branching statements can be used to construct loops or repetitive actions within a program, although FOR...NEXT statements are more commonly used for this purpose. In FOR...NEXT loops, every instruction in the program between the related FOR and NEXT structure will be executed for each value of an index which is incremented between specified starting and stopping values.

In other words, in a loop defined by the values 1 to 10, one can specify particular increments for which an instruction or set of instructions will take place. Similarly, loops can define decrements, or decreasing values, for which a set of instructions will take place. FOR...NEXT statements are particularly convenient for use with subscripted variables which can be defined by the use of the DIM (dimension) statement. This is used to construct an array or a set of pigeon holes for organizing data that the program will manipulate in some way. The following example program illustrates the use of a FOR...NEXT loop in a program which constructs an array. The program reads a list of names into a string array denoted N$, searches the array for the name which appears "first" alphabetically, stores this name in F$, and prints out this name. There is a 10-item array in the DIM statement and line 120 sets the loop counter to increment to 10, and increments the counter by one step at each cycle of the loop.

ALPHABETIZING PROGRAM

```
100 REM***THE FOLLOWING PROGRAM FINDS
    THE FIRST IN A LIST OF NAMES
110 DIM N$(10)
120 FOR I=1 TO 10
130 READ N$(I)
140 NEXT I
150 F$=N$(1)
160 FOR J=1 TO 10
170 IF F$ > N$(J) THEN F$=N$(J)
180 NEXT J
190 PRINT "THE FIRST NAME IN ALPHABETI-
    CAL ORDER IS";F$
200 DATA SMITH, JONES, BROWN, MARTIN,
    MAGEE, HARRIS, BENSON, AARON,
    GREGORY, REILLY
210 END
```

On the monitor, the execution of the program looks like this:

```
[RUN]
THE FIRST NAME IN ALPHABETICAL ORDER IS
AARON
```

More advanced BASIC capabilities include use of library functions for such procedures as square roots and trigonometric functions (SIN, COS, TAN) as well as the ability to develop one's own functions and subroutines through the use of DEF (define a mathematical function) and GOSUB (go to a defined subroutine, perform it, and return to the next line in the program) instructions.

Different computers also have different built-in graphics capabilities such as LINE, CIRCLE, DRAW, PAINT,

GET, and PUT. The LINE and CIRCLE statements allow the construction of lines and circles, respectively, and the DRAW statement employs a special graphics routine to draw combinations of lines and points. The GET and PUT statements are associated with the color graphics capabilities of different computers. New dialects of BASIC are currently being introduced into the home computer market which allow users to add music, sound effects, and voice synthesis to their programs, but these are more clearly defined by the computer's own hardware and firmware than by the actual rules of BASIC themselves. Newer introductions of structured BASIC, such as those found on the Acorn computer, emulate the features of Pascal more than those of traditional BASIC.

As users become adept at addressing the capabilities of not only their own computers but of computer systems in general, more structured languages such as Pascal and C are becoming increasingly popular. However, BASIC is still by far the most commonly used language for microcomputers.

BASIC GLOSSARY

The following glossary of BASIC reserved words, functions, commands and statements represents a full implementation of the industry-standard version of the language. Different microcomputer implementations of BASIC contain different sets of reserved words, especially the additional commands for graphics, music, and voice synthesis. With the exception of these accessory-specific commands, this glossary contains commands from most of the major microcomputer BASIC dialects such as TRS-80 BASIC, Applesoft BASIC, Atari BASIC, Commodore BASIC, TI BASIC, and Microsoft BASIC.

The BASIC commands are cross-referenced extensively so that readers will be able to find similar terms in the different versions of the language. Readers will find very little difference between the 8-bit versions of the language in this glossary and the 16-bit versions of MBASIC and ZBASIC in the next two glossaries.

ABS(n) (ANSI) Determines the absolute value of a specified number or numerical value. Absolute value is the value of a number without a plus or minus sign, i.e., +10 and −10 both have an absolute value of 10. The ABS function gives the absolute value of numbers as large or small as your computer's interpreter can handle. Many interpreters also allow for the use of ABS in those arithmetic operations in which the absolute values of numbers are required. To perform ABS in these cases, the whole operation must be enclosed in parentheses following ABS. Some computers such as the TRS-80 (in Level 1 BASIC) use the spelling A for ABS.

ACS(n) Computes the ARCCOS in radians. The ARCCOS is the angle formed by the intersection of the hypotenuse of a right triangle and the side adjacent to the

angle. A radian equals about 57 degress. The Sinclair ZX80 uses the spelling ARCOS instead of ACS. The Sharp 1211 uses AC. Some computers calculate the ARCCOS in degrees (ACDS) or in grads. 100 grads = 90 degrees. If your computer does not calculate in degrees, multiply the radians by 57.29578. To convert degrees to radians, multiply by .0174533.
See: ASN, ATN, SQR, SIN, TAN, COS

AND A logical math operator with IF-THEN statements. AND allows the IF-THEN statements to have two qualifiers instead of one. AND is also used by some computers to logically compare strings or to determine whether the IF-THEN conditions are met in two operations. In some computers, AND is also used as an operator in boolean algebra to test the truth of statements or to compute the logical AND of two numbers. The WANG 2200B uses AND as a statement to compute the binary logical AND of two hexadecimal values or two character strings.
See: OR, XOR, NOT, *, +, =, <, >

APPEND To add a program from an externally stored disk or tape to a program already in memory. The lines of the external program are APPENDed to the lines of the resident program. Therefore, the first line number of the outside program must be higher that the last line number of the program in memory to which it will be added. APPEND is often used to add subroutines to stored programs or to load stored data files. Some computers use the spellings TAPPEND, MERGE, and WEAVE.
See: PEEK, POKE, CLOAD, CSAV, DATA

ASC(n) Converts characters of string variables to their ASC decimal number. Some computers use the spelling ASCII instead of ASC. ASCII stands for American Standard Code for Information Interchange, a code which assigns binary computer numbers to stand for letters, decimals, numbers, and other characters. The ASCII characters represented by numbers are not 100 percent uniform. Consult an ASCII number chart and check your computer to see which characters it assigns for decimal code numbers. Some computers can accept character strings which are longer than one number, but the ASC function often converts only the first character to the ASCII code. Check your computer's string limit. MAXIBASIC uses ASC (A$,x) to print the ASCII code for the first x characters in A$. ASC can be used with POKE to POKE a value directly into screen memory.
See: CHR$, CODE

ASCII American Standard Code for Information Interchange is a code developed to represent the letters, numbers, characters, and functions commonly used in programming. Typically, the ASCII code has a range from 0 to 127. ASCII codes vary from computer to computer. Check the codes of different computers when translating programs. Many computers have an extend-ed ASCII with a range from 0 to 255 which enables the code to accommodate special functions and graphic characters.

ASN(n) Computes ARCSIN of the ratio in radians (a radian=57 degrees) by the Tektronics 4050 BASIC. Sinclair ZX80 uses ARCSIN in place of the ASN spelling. ARCSIN (the opposite of SINE) is the angle created by length on the side opposite to the length of the hypotenuse in right triangles. ARCSIN finds the value of the angle when the ratio of two of the sides is known. Some computers which calculate the ASN in degrees or grads (100 grads=90 degrees) use the function ASND or ASNG respectively. The Sinclair ZX80 and others use ARCIN instead of ASN. To convert degrees to radians, multiply the degrees by .0174533. To convert radians to degrees, multiply by 57.29578.
See: ACS, ATN, COS, SIN, SQR, TAN

AT Used after a PRINT to specify a PRINT STATEMENT location in TRS-80 Level 1 BASIC, Applesoft, and Integer BASIC. The AT value can be a number, numeric variable, or a mathematical operation. The AT value must be followed by a comma or a semicolon. TRS-80 Level II, Level III, Disk BASIC, and others use the @ operator for the AT function. Tiny BASIC uses A. for AT. The TRS-80 will PRINT AT 1024 locations if an AT value above 1023 or below 0 is entered. The computer will automatically assign an AT value by finding the difference between the inappropriate number and 1023, i.e., if the AT value is entered as 1033, the computer will then PRINT on line 9, 1033−1024=9, since 0 is a location.
See: @, PRINT, TAB, HLIN, VLIN, DRAW, XDRAW

ATN(n) To compute ARCTANGENT of the ratio n. Most computers give the result in radians. The ARCTANGENT is the angle determined by a given ratio of the length of the side opposite the angle to the side adjacent to it or the angle of the tangent. Computers which calculate the ARCTANGENT in degrees use ATND, and those computing in grads (100 grads=90 degrees) may use ACTNT. Multiply the angle by 57.29578 (180/π) to convert radians to degrees. To convert degrees to radians, multiply by .0174533. ATN is used in Applesoft, PET BASIC, and Level II BASIC (TRS-80). Some computers use the spelling ATAN for the ARCTANGENT. Others, including the Sinclair ZX80, use ARCTAN. ATN is the only inverse trigonometric function in many computers and must be used to calculate all angles.
See: TAN, ASN, SIN, COS, ACS

AUTO To provide program line numbers automatically. The computer automatically sets the starting line number at 10 and goes on to set line numbers at increments of 10 unless the starting line and line increments are specified. For example: AUTO 1000, 20 would instruct the computer to start on line 1000 and increase by the number 20 for each new line. Some computers signal when a line that is added is already in use. An asterisk appears before the line to prevent the user from automatically erasing the existing line by entering new information on it. This feature can be turned off by one of two ways, depending on the computer: either by pressing the BREAK key or by typing Control C. Out-of-sequence lines may be entered after the BREAK key has been pressed to stop AUTO. AUTO instructions should be entered again with an asterisk next to the line in which data is already stored. Press ENTER to erase and go on, or press BREAK to save the existing information.

See: BREAK, LIST, MAN

BASE (ANSI)   To define the lowest variable array element as 0 or 1 in some computers (with Control Data version 3) BASE enables the automatically established array elements (0-10) set by most computers to be changed to one to ten elements, enabling the computer to go from the normal eleven elements to ten and back again. Although a few computers allow more than one BASE statement, there is usually only one per program and it must be executed before Dimensioning and before the array variables are manipulated. MAXBASIC allows any integer to be defined as a BASE value and it allows more than one BASE statement in a program. The American National Standards Institute (ANSI) BASIC includes OPTION in their BASE statements, i.e., OPTION BASE.

See: DIM, OPTION

BREAK   To stop program execution. This statement is similar to STOP. BREAK puts the computer in the monitor or immediate mode (used by the Harris BASIC-V). Stops program execution of any lines entered after BREAK, i.e., to continue the program after BREAK use the computer's continue command (CO CONT etc.). BREAK ALL can stop execution of a range of lines if a dash is entered between the first and last line numbers in the range. BREAK ALL will stop execution at the beginning of each line. All variables remain stored while BREAK statement are executed.

See: STOP, CONT, END

BYE   To exit from BASIC. BYE (or GOODBYE) is usually associated with large computer time-sharing systems. BYE is the user's signoff. Some small computers like Sol and Atari use BYE to enter the monitor level. Processor Technology's extended BASIC includes BYE as a program statement.

See: SYSTEM

CALL   To transfer program control from BASIC to a machine language program located at a specific entry point in memory. The machine language program may be from the computer's systems software or it may be user written. Some BASICs use the CALL statement to jump

to a specific BASIC subroutines. In these cases a specific subroutine name is called instead of a line number.

See: USR, POKE, SYSTEM, GOSUB, RETURN

CDBL(n)   Changes single-precision numbers containing six significant digits into double-precision numbers which contain seventeen significant digits (sixteen only are actually printed). Numbers used to generate a result must be double precision if the answer is to be given in double-precision numbers. An answer changed at the end of a process will be distorted. Variables which are used with CDBL return to single-precision numbers when used again without CDBL.

See: DEFDBL, DEFSNG, DEFINT, CSNG, #, !, "/", CINT

CH(n)   A nonstandard function used by the Acorn Atom computer from Britain to give the ASCII numbers for the first characters of a string.

See: ASC, CODE, CHR$, ASCII

CHAIN   To load a new program into the computer memory from a disk, tape, or other external device and execute the program without further commands. CHAINing is often used in large systems in which there are sizable common DATA files stored on rapidly accessible disks. Some BASICs (i.e., Micro BASIC 5.0) are able to pass variables from the starting program to programs in the CHAIN. A program may CHAIN to another program and back again using the starting program as a "menu". Microcomputers can use floppy disks or cassettes to CHAIN.

See: CLOAD, CSAVE, COMMON, RUN

CHANGE(n)   Changes character strings into their ASCII numbers and back again. The ASCII numbers are stored in an array. If your computer does not accept CHANGE, it can be duplicated using LEN, ASC, CHR$, or DIM.

See: LEN, ASC, MID$, DIM, ASCII

**CHR$**   To convert an ASCII code into a character. This function enables the computer to print characters which are not usually accessible from the keyboard. Some BASICs use different spellings for CHR$, i.e., Micropolis BASIC uses CHAR$, SOL and SWTP use CHR, and MAXBASIC uses CHAR. BASICS using the CHR$ include PET BASIC and Level II BASIC (TRS-80). The Swedish ABC 80 uses a slightly different function, CHR (⌧) to convert up to four ASCII numbers at a time into characters.

See: ASC, STRINGS, ASCII

CINT(n)   Converts numbers into their integer values. Variables used in CINT cannot be smaller than −32768 or larger than +32767. The numbers assigned to CIN return to their original values when they are used again without CINT. The CINT function rounds numbers to the nearest smaller whole number.

See: DEFINT, INT, DEFDBL, CDBL, CSNC, !, #, "/"

CLEAR Used by many computers to reset all variables to zero and to erase all data being held by string variables. Some computers use CLEAR to erase the resident program. CLEAR followed by an argument is used by some computers to set aside bytes in memory storage when more than the automatic reserve of bytes (often 50) is required. Integer BASIC (Apple) and PET BASIC both use the shortened CLR for CLEAR. CLEAR is used by TRS-80 to clear the display after SHIFT. Some computers use CLEAR to clear terminal input.
See: FRE(A$), COMMON, NEW, ERASE, SCRATCH

CLG Used by the Honeywell Series 60 BASIC to compute the common logarithms of any number greater than 0. Some computers use CLOG. A common log can be converted to a natural log by multiplying the common log by 2.302585. The natural log value times .4342945 will equal the common log.
See: LOG10, LOG

**CLK$** Used to print in the Texas Instrument 990 BASIC and the DEC BASIC PLUS to indicate the time in hours, minutes, and seconds. PRINT CLK$ will give the current time in six digits, i.e., 11:10:18 equals 11:10 a.m. Sperry Univac System 19 uses the CLK spelling.
See: TIME, TIM$

CLOAD Used as a command to load a program from a cassette into computer memory. Some computers such as PET and Apple use the LOAD spelling. CLOAD can be used as a program statement along with an array name (CLOAD*) to load array data while a program is being executed.
See: CSAVE, LIST, CHAIN, RECALL, APPEND, VERIFY

CLRDOT(L,R) Turns off a graphics block on the display by Sweden's ABC 80. CLRDOT(L,R) indicates the line and row of the block coordinates.
See: RESET, SETDOT, SET, ⌧

CLS Used as a command to clear the video screen in a way similar to the CLEAR key. CLS may also be used as a program statement to clear the screen for a new graphics display or fresh information. CLS is often used in games. CLS is used by the TRS-80 Color Computer to clear the screen and set background color. Apple computers use ESC with SHIFT@ or the GR graphics command to clear the screen. The TRS-80 uses CLS(n) to clear the screen and to return the video screen to the 64 character per line mode after using CHR$ (32 characters per line mode).
See: CHR$, ASCII

CODE(n) Used by the Sinclair ZX80 to convert a character to its special code number. Sinclair does not use ASCII.
See: ASC, CHR$

COLOR Used as a command for a special feature which specifies the color to be displayed on the screen when using graphics statements, PLOT, HLIN-AT, and VLIN-AT. COLOR is used by Apple's Applesoft and Integer BASIC. To change the color on the screen, the COLOR statement is used along with one of the sixteen numbers assigned to the available colors, i.e., COLOR = 4 will change the screen color to dark green. However, the TRS-80 color computer and the Atari computers have COLOR as key words.
See: GR, PLOT, HLIN-AT, VLIN-AT

COMMON Used in some computers to transfer variable values from one program to another when the programs are being CHAINed. All the current values being stored in variables which are common to the two programs will be available to the new program. The Wang 2200 uses the COM spelling and is also able to use the COM statement to specify the length of string variables.
See: CHAIN, DIM

CONT To continue program execution after an interruption by STOP, or use of the BREAK key. CONT contains the program at the line after the break, unlike RUN which starts the program from the beginning. Some computers use the CON, C, or CO spellings.
See: STOP, END, RUN

COS(n) Computes the COSINE of the angle when the angle is measured in radians. The cosine (COS) is the ratio of the length of the adjacent side of a right triangle to the length of the hypotenuse. Some computers will find the cosine of an angle entered in degrees (COSD) or grads (COSG). A very few computers will convert all measurements to degrees automatically. To convert radians to degrees, multiply radians by 57.29578. To convert from degrees to radians, multiply degrees by .0174533.
See: SIN, ASN, ATN, TAN, ACS, COSH, SINH, TANH

COSH(n) Calculates the hypotenuse cosine of a number. The hyperbolic functions express numerical relationships based on a hyperbola. The argument in the COSH function can be any real positive number greater than or equal to 1. Harris BASIC-V uses the CSH spelling for the hyperbolic cosine function.
See: SINH, TANH, EXP

COUNT Used by the British Acorn Atom to count the number of characters printed since the last carriage return.
See: POS

CSAVE To record a program in the computer's memory onto a cassette. After the program is transferred to cassette and cleared from memory, the recorded program can be loaded back into the computer using CLOAD. Microsoft BASIC 5.0 uses CSAVE* to save

the value of a numeric array on tape. Some computers (Applesoft and Integer BASIC) use SAVE.
See: CLOAD, LIST, STORE

CUR   Used by ABC 80 computer along with a PRINT statement to position the next character at a desired print location.
See: PRINT AT, @, LOCATE

D   Used with scientific notation to identify a variable as a double-precision number. Single-precision numbers are identified by the letter "E".
See: E, #, !, DEFDBL, DEFSNG

DATA   (ANSI) To contain data elements to be read by a READ statement. Each of the data values in a DATA statement must be separated by a comma, except at the ends of lines. Most computers accept strings in DATA statements but computers differ on the method of entry. Some require the strings to be placed in quotes. Check your computer's requirements. The spelling D is used in Level I BASIC (TRS-80) and the Tiny BASIC. DAT is used by PDP-8E.
See: READ, RESTORE

DEF   (ANSI) To define new functions which can then be used in the same way as built-in functions. The new function is represented by FN followed by a variable name, i.e., FNX. The variable in the new function is placed in parentheses after the function, i.e., FNX(n). Some computers allow more than one variable in the DEF function, in which case the variables are listed in the parentheses. When you are storing a new function, the variables used in the parentheses must be the same as those used in the defined expression. For instance, when you are storing FNX(N)=N−6*3, N must be the dummy variable on both sides of the equal sign.
See: FN, FNEND, GOSUB, RETURN

DEFDBL   To define a variable as a double-precision number. Double-precision numbers are accurate to seventeen places (only sixteen are printed). Many computers allow more than one variable to be declared a double-precision number in one statement, i.e., DEFDBL X,X,Z. Double-precision numbers take up more memory than single-precision numbers and should only be used when needed.
See: DEFSNG, DEFINT, #, "/", !, CDBL, CSNG, CINT, D, E

DEFINT   To define variables as integers (whole numbers). DEFINT enables the computer to use less space since integers require less memory than noninteger values. DEFINT must be executed before number values are assigned to the variables in a DEFINT statement. The use of DEFINT is limited by the fact that many interpreters can only process numbers from −32767 to +32767. Users should be aware that some interpreters have declarative characters which override DEFINT statements. For instance, if any declarative character # has been assigned to any number in the DEFINT statement in order to define it as a double-precision number,

this declarative character will keep the number from being converted to an integer by DEFINT.
See: INT, #, DEFDBL, CINT, SCNG, CDBL, "/", !

DEFSNG   To define variables as single-precision numbers. Single-precision numbers are accurate to seven places, six of which are printed. DEFSNG is usually used to redefine numbers after they have been previously defined as double-precision numbers (accurate to seventeen places) by DEFDBL or as integers by DEFINT. Most computers automatically treat variables as single-precision numbers unless they are redefined. Most computers allow more than one variable or a range of variables in a DEFSNG statement. In most computers, DEFSNG statement must be executed before variables used in the DEFSNG statement are given number values.
See: DEFINT, #, DEFDBL, !, CSNG, CDBL, CINT, "/"

DEFSTR   To define variables as string variables. More than one variable may be used in a DEFSTR statement if they are separated by commas. The DEFSTR statemnent must be executed before specific variables are given by string notation. The variables in a DEFSTR statement are treated by a $. Some interpreters make it necessary to reserve space in memory for string variables bu using DIM or CLEAR. When you are using DEFSTR and DIM statements in the same program in Level II BASIC, always use the DEFSTR statement first because DEFSTR resets the array depth to 10 automatically. Interpreters with declarative characters will allow such characters (#, !, or %) to override DEFSTR statements.
See: DEFDBL, DEFINT, DEFSNG, DIM, CLEAR, $, D, E, "/", #, !

DEG   Used by a few computers as a command to execute trigonometric functions in degrees. Most computers execute trig functions in radians. A degree equals approximately .02 radian. Chromenco 16K Extended BASIC uses the DEG command. MAXBASIC uses DEG as a built-in function to convert expressed values from radians to degrees. The TRS-80 Pocket Computer uses DEG to convert from the degree, minute, second form to degrees and decimal fractions. Some computers use the spelling DEGREE.
See: SIN, COS, TAN, ATN, RAD, ASN, ACS

DELETE   To erase specific program lines or groups of lines from the computer memory. Some computers allow single lines and groups of lines to be erased in the same DELETE (DELETE 30, 60-90). Others allow the user to delete a specific line and everything after it (DELETE 70-). Some computers, including the Apple and DEC 10, use DEL spelling. The Apple also uses a different notation for the line numbers, substituting a comma for a dash in deleting groups of lines. DELETE 40,60 means

erase lines 40 to 60. DELETE line 40 is entered as DE-LETE 40,40. DELETE minus a line number is used in some computers to erase everything in a program up to the specified line (DELETE −60).
See: NEW, LIST, SCRATCH

DET Used as a determinant function to calculate the single numeric value associated with a square matrix. A square matrix is a two-dimensional array having the same number of rows as columns. Some interpreters give DET only if MAT INV (inverse of the matrix) has been calculated first.
See: MAT INV, DIM

DIGITS Used by TSC Extended BASIC to specify the maximum number of digits to be printed by a PRINT statement. If the actual value to be printed is too big for the number of digits allowed, the value is given in exponential form. PERCOM Super BASIC uses DIGITS to specify only the number of digits to be printed after the decimal point.
See: PRECISION, PRINT USING, IMAGE, FMT, INT

DIM Used as a dimension statement to establish (AN-SI) the number of elements in a numeric string or array. DIM is followed by the array name which is followed by the array size. DIM A (30) indicates that array A will use array elements 0 to 30. Some computers set the lowest array element at 0, others set it at 1. A few computers allow the lowest array number to be set at either 0 or 1 through the use of the BASE statement. Most computers allow the use of 0 through 10 elements for arrays automatically. The DIM statement is used when more than 0-10 elements are needed. A few computers do not need dimensioning since their array sizes are only limited by the amount of unused memory available. Some computers with two-dimensional array capability also use DIM to specify the maximum element size for arrays.
See: CLEAR, MAT INPUT, MAT READ

DOT Used by the ABC 80 to show whether or not a specified graphics block on the screen is turned on. Line and column coordinates are used to specify the graphic block in question.
See: POINT, SETDOT, CLRDOT

DPS Used by Apple II Basic to display specific variables and their values each time the variables are given new values. DPS also shows the line number of the variables. NO DPS or TROFF is used to stop the DPS process.
See: TRON, TRACE

DRAW Used by some computers, including Apple II, to draw a defined shape (loaded by cassette) at a specified location. Also used by the Sinclair ZX80 to draw a line from one specified position to another. DRAW TO is Atari's statement which draws a line from the current location to a specified position.
See: PLOT, XDRAW

E To indicate that numbers will be expressed in exponential notation.
See: D, !, #, DEFSNG, DEFDBL, CSNG, CDBL

EDIT Used by Microsoft BASIC to allow editing of a program line specified in the EDIT command. Some computers automatically use the first line number of a program in the EDIT command if no line number is specified. Some computers use EDIT to call up the editor. Other computers, especially multilanguage machines, require several commands to allow editing.

ELSE Used after IF-THEN statement to direct the program to the appropriate line when the IF condition is not met. Without an ELSE statement, the program continues at the next line when the IF condition is not met. Using ELSE often saves memory space.
See: IF-THEN, GOTO

END (ANSI) To end the execution of the program without printing the last line. Some computers require END to come at the highest numbered line of the program. E. is used for the END by Tiny BASIC. To avoid confusion between STOP and END, get to know how your machine uses these commands.
See: STOP

EQ Used by a few computers for equal (=) when equal is used as a relational operator. EQ is not interchangeable with = when used to assign a variable.
See: =, <>, IF-THEN, GE, GT, LE, LT, NE, <, >, <=, >=

ERASE Used as a command to erase a program from memory. Some computers use NEW or SCRATCH instead. Some interpreters, including the BASIC-80, use ERASE as a statement to erase an array from the program to free storage space. In some cases, ERASE can be used to redimension an array while the program is running.
See: NEW, SCRATCH, DIM, LIST

ERL Used with the ON-ERROR statement to identify the last line in which an error has occurred. Whenever an error is made, ERL gives the number of the line where the error can be found. The ERL spelling is used by Hewlett-Packard's 35, 45, and 85 computers.
See: ERROR, ON-ERROR-GOTO, RESUME

ERR Used by Microsoft BASIC to identify the error code of the last error made in a program. The error code changes each time a different type of error occurs, helping the user to identify the error and correct it. Check your computer manual for its particular error codes. ERRN is the spelling used by Hewlett-Packard's 35, 45, and 85 computers.
See: ERL, ON-ERROR, RESUME, DIM, CLEAR

ERROR To simulate a program error. The computer's error code is used to specify the kind of error to be caused.

The ERROR statement is usually used to execute error trapping routines in programs. It is also used to print error messages. Check your computer manual for specific error codes and error statements.
See: ON-ERROR-GOTO, RESUME, ERR, ERL

EXAM   To read the contents of specified addresses in the computer's memory. The contents are given in the form of a decimal between 0 and 255, this being the range of values storable in an 8-bit memory byte. When used with FILL (or POKE or STUFF in some computers) EXAM reads what FILL has stored in the memory.
See: FILL, POKE, PEEK, USR, SYSTEM, STUFF, FETCH

EXCHANGE   To switch the values of of two variables or array elements in a few BASICs, including TDL BASIC. EXCHANGE X,Y would cause the value in X to be placed in Y and the Y value to be switched to X. MAXBASIC uses = = to switch the values of variables. Some computers, including COMPUCORP, INTELLEC, and SWTP, use the SWAP statement to exchange variables.
See: SWAP

EXIT   Used in some BASICs to transfer execution of the program out of FOR-NEXT loop before the loop has completed its specified number of cycles. The EXIT statement transfers execution to a designated line and continues from then, cancelling the FOR-NEXT loop. The loop counter value remains in effect for use in the rest of the program.
See: FOR, NEXT, GOTO

EXP   (ANSI) To compute the natural logarithm's base value (2.178289) raised to the power n in EXP(n). EXP is the opposite of LOG.
See: LOG, LOG 10, CLG

FETCH   To read the contents of specified memory addresses in Digital's Group Opus 1 and Opus 2 BASIC. The contents will be given as a number between 0 and 255 (the range of values storable in an 8-bit memory byte). Used with STUFF, FETCH will read what STUFF has stored.
See: EXAM, FILL, PEEK, POKE, STUFF, SYSTEM, USR

FILL   Used by North Star BASIC, MAXBASIC, and others to assign values from 0 to 255 into specified bytes in the computer's memory (255 is the maximum 8-bit value). For instance, FILL 4000, 20 puts the decimal number 20 into memory address 4000. The information placed in the computer by FILL can be inspected using EXAM (some computers use PEEK or FETCH). Check the amount of memory and the number of memory addresses available before using FILL so that memory dedicated to other purposes will not be erased by the FILL statement.
See: EXAM, FETCH, PEEK, POKE, STUFF, SYSTEM, USR

FIX   To remove all numbers to the right of the decimal point. FIX is like INT except that it does not round negative numbers. FIX will work with any number within the limitations of your interpreters.
See: INT, ABS, SGN

FLASH   Used by the Apple II as a statement or command which causes the output on the screen to flash. The characters on the screen flash alternately from black on white to white on black. The NORMAL command returns the screen to a non-flashing mode.

FLOW   Used in Micropolis BASIC as a troubleshooting command which prints the line numbers of each program line as it is executed by the computer. NOFLOW is used to turn off the FLOW command. FLOW can also be used as a statement with the NOFLOW command to print program lines in only one part of a program.
See: NOFLOW, TRACE, TRACE ON, TRON

FMT   Used by some BASICs, including Micropolis BASIC, as a function for formatting the output of PRINT statements. FMC sets the format of the values to be printed in a string expressions using a particular set of valid characters (9, Z, V, $, *, period, comma). The string expression must be enclosed in quotes. Any string which cannot be interpreted by the computer's valid characters is printed as text. Honeywell uses FMT as a statement to format a print line. This FMT statement is similar to the IMAGE statement. The PRINT statement to be formatted using the FMT statement must contain the line number of the FMT statement as the first item after the word PRINT.
See: PRINT USING, IMAGE

FN   To allow user-defined functions to be used like intrinsic functions. FN is followed by the new functions name and one or more values, i.e., FNA(X,N). The DEF statement is used with FN to set up the new function and define it so it can be executed when FN is used later. Some BASICs, including DEC BASIC PLUS, allow the FN function to work with strings to cause them to have specified lengths by adding leading blanks.
See: DEF, FNEND

FNEND   To end the defining process in computers which has the capability to define and redefine functions during a program using the DEF statement. Every DEF statement longer than one line must be followed by a FNEND statement. Otherwise, the computer cannot branch out of the DEF statement.
See: DEF, FN

FOR   Used with a FOR-TO-NEXT statement to assign numbers to numeric variables within a specified range. The number after FOR is increased by one each time its corresponding NEXT statement is executed. When the number after TO is exceeded, the program continues at the line following the NEXT statement. Some computers can increment FOR-TO-NEXT by

more than 1 by using the STEP statement. STEP may also allow the numbers to change in descending order (decrement). Acorn and TRS-80, Level I, use F instead of FOR.
See: NEXT, STEP

FRAC Used by some BASICs, including Micropolis BASIC, to give the fractional part of a number with its proper sign, i.e., 20 F=FRAC(−72.0863) gives F= −0.0863.
See: INT, FIX

FRE(n) A function that reveals the number of free (unused) bytes of allocated string space in the computer's memory. Any character or variable can be used with the FRE function. The character or variable must be enclosed in parentheses, such as FRE(C$). Most computers with the FRE function automatically reserve 50 bytes of string space. Some computers use the FRE function with the numbers or numeric values to determine the amount of total memory remaining (not just memory allocated to strings). Some BASICs, including Processor Technology and North Star, use FREE(0)to report the amount of total unused memory.
See: CLEAR MEM, NEW, $

GE Used as an abbreviation for "greater than or equal to" by some computers, including the TI990. GE compares two numeric values in IF-THEN statements.
See: >, =, IF-THEN

GET Used by some computers, including Apple II and PET, to accent a single character from the keyboard without displaying it and without waiting for the RE-TURN key to be pressed. GET is similar to INKEYS$. GET accepts only numeric values when used with a numeric variable. When used with a string variable, GET will accept any key input except STOP. Apple II's GET statement causes program execution to pause until a key is pressed. PET, on the other hand, stores a null character if no key is pressed and proceeds with the program. GET# is used by many computers to read a record from a tape or disk. GET@ is used to store information found on one section of the screen by some BASICs, including TRS-80, Extended Color BASIC, NEC's N-BASIC, and Microsoft Level III BASIC. Hewlett-Packard uses GET to load a disk or data file from disk to tape. GET can also be used like APPEND to add part of a program to an existing program. For example, GET "SUB1", 300 would add SUB2 program to the existing program at line 300. The SUB2 program will be numbered starting with 300.
See: APPEN, INKEY$, KEY$, PUT, #

GO Used with other BASIC words in statements such as GOTO and GOSUB. GO is also used as an abbreviation of GOTO by DATAPOINT which also uses GO as a command to restart the program at a specific line, i.e., GOTO 30.
See: GOTO, GOSUB, GOTO-OF, GOSUB-OF, IF-GOTO, ON-GOTO, ON-GOSUB, CONT GOSUB

GOSUB To branch out of the main program into a subroutine. GOSUB must be followed by the first line number of the subroutine to be executed. The RETURN statement must be used to return control to the main program after the subroutine is executed. Some computers, including the Sinclair ZX-80 and the British Acorn Atom, allow the use of variable expressions in GOSUB statements. Some Tiny BASICS use the GOS spelling of GOSUB.
See: IF-GOSUB, ON-GOSUB, RETURN

GOSUB-OF Used for multiple subroutine branching by Hewlett-Packard and Tektronix computers. The statement GOSUB X OF 100,200 indicates that the computer should branch to line 100 if X equals 1 and to 200 if X equals 2.
See: IF-GOSUB, ON-GOSUB, RETURN

GOTO To transfer program execution to a specific line. Many computers accept GO TO for GOTO. Others will not allow a space between the two words. Some computers, including the Sinclair ZX-80, Acorn Atom, and computers using Micropolis BASIC, allow the use of variable expressions in GOTO statements. GOTO can also be used in combination with key words. Some computers use the abbreviated spelling GOT or GT.
See: IF-GOTO, ON-GOTO, GOTO-OF

GOTO-OF Used for multiple branching to include a number of IF-THEN trials in one statement. GOTO X OF 1000,2000,3000 causes the computer to go to line 1000 if X=1, line 2000 if X=2, and line 3000 if X=3. The possible values of X must correspond with the number of branches in the statement. Otherwise, the program will move on to the next line. For instance, in the example above, an X= would default the statement's execution.
See: ON-GOTO, GOSUB-OF, ON-GOSUB, IF-THEN, INT

GR Used as both a command and a program statement in the Apple II BASIC to switch the computer's operation from the TEXT mode to the graphics mode. GR must be used before the graphics statement, PLOT, HLIN-AT, and VLIN. GR is also used to erase the screen before a new graphics display is started.
See: COLOR, CLS, HLIN-AT, PLOT, TEXT, VLIN-AT

GRAD Used by a few computers, including the Sharp/ TRS-80 Pocket Computer and Tektronix 4050 Series, to calculate in GRADs instead of radians (100 grads=90 degrees). Most computers calculate in the radian mode but some are capable of calculating trigonometric functions in degrees. Few computers can use grads.
See: ACS, ASN, ATN, COS, RAD, SIN, TAN

GT Used as a "greater than" instead of >. GT is a relational operator which compares numeric values or strings in IF-THEN statements.
See: >, IF-THEN, >=, <, <=, <>, EQ, GE, LE, LT, NE

HLIN-AT   Used by the Apple II BASIC to display a horizontal line at a specified row on the screen. HLIN-AT is followed by two numbers which determine the length of the line by identifying the starting and ending points, i.e., HLIN 20,30 at 35 will tell the computer to draw a line from column 20 to column 30 at row 35. The numbers range from 0 to 39. The GR (graphics) statement must be executed before HLIN-AT or any other graphics statement can be used. The color of the line is governed by the color statement.
See: COLOR, GR, PLOT, TEXT, VLIN-AT

HOME   Used as a command to clear the screen and put the cursor at the top left corner of the screen. Some computers use CLS to do a similar task. HOME is also a statement used to clear the screen before a new graphics display.
See: CLS

IF   (ANSI) Used in conditioned branching statements such as IF-THEN, IF-GOTO, IF-GOSUB, and IF-LET. IF tests variable values using the relational operators =, >, <, <>, <=. The next program line to be executed depends on the results of the IF statement. For instance, IF X 5 THEN 50 indicates that line 50 will be executed if X is 6 or more. If X is less than 5, the next program line after the IF-THEN will be executed. Therefore, the IF-THEN must be the last line of any multiple statement lines so that the next line will be appropriate when the IF condition is not met. Some BASICs, including DEC BASIC PLUS 2, use IF as a modifier of most other statements.
See: IF-THEN, IF-GOTO, IF-LET, ELSE

IF-LET   Used as a conditional statement which uses the relational operators =, <>, <, >, <=, >=, to determine the condition under which the computer will assign a value to the variable after LET. For instance, IF X= 30LET X=5 will instruct the computer to assign the value 5 to any variable under 30. Many computers allow LET to be omitted from this type of statement. THEN is often used instead of LET as are PRINT, INPUT, GOSUB, etc.
See: IF, IF-THEN, LET

IF-THEN   (ANSI) Used as a conditional branching statement which employs one of the relational operators: =, <>, <, >, <=, >=. When the IF condition is met, the program control is transferred to the line number after THEN. For instance, IF X = 20 THEN 2000 will tell the computer to branch to line 2000 if x + 2. When the condition is not met, the program continues at the next line after the IF-THEN statement. Some computers will permit mathematical operations to be done if the IF-THEN condition is met. Some interpreters will allow the computer to branch to any operating statement if the IF-THEN condition is met. For example, IF X 0, THEN END. Whenever the IF-THEN condition is not met, the program "falls through" to the next numbered line. Therefore, it is important to remember that no statement should follow the IF-THEN statement on the same line because most computers will not execute such a statement. Some computers use abbreviated spellings for IF-THEN such as IF-THE (PDP-8E) or IF-T (TRS-80 Level I).
See: ELSE, END, GOTO, GOSUB, IF, IF-GOTO, IF-LET, STOP

IMAGE   Used by some computers, including Hewlett-Packard, as a print formatting statement in conjunction with PRINT USING. IMAGE uses format characters (A, D, E, S, X, period, comma, slash, O, +, −, #) to specify the form in which output should be printed. String constants (in quotes) can be used anywhere in an HP IMAGE line.
See: FMT, :, PRINT USING

INDEX(str,str)   Reports the starting position of the first character in a string; part of a larger string. The computer counts positions starting at the left. For instance, INDEX("XYZX","XY")=2. INDEX is similar to INSTR, a function used on some small computers. INDEX is equal to zero when the small string in question is not a part of the larger string.
See: INSTR, POS

**INKEY$**   To read a character from the keyboard without stopping execution of the program. Instead of waiting for the ENTER key to be pressed, INKEY$ scans the keyboard until it receives a message. If no key is pressed or if the wrong key is pressed, the program just loops back and keeps scanning the keyboard until a proper character is entered.
See: GET, IF-THEN, INPUT$, INPUT

INP   To read the value of a byte of information in decimals from a specific port. The decimal value can be any number from 0 to 255. INP is a useful monitoring device for checking regularly updated information. The PDP-8 uses INP as a short form of INPUT.
See: INPUT, OUT, PEEK, PIN, POKE

INPUT   (ANSI) To enter a numeric or string variable from the keyboard. Execution halts and a question mark appears on the screen until a value is assigned to the variable. The ENTER key or RETURN key must be pressed to complete the INPUT statement. An input statement can ask for more than one response from a user. Each INPUT demand must be separated by a comma. The short spelling IN is used for INPUT by Acorn and many Tiny BASICs. The I. spelling is allowed in TRS-80 Level 1. Some PDP-8's allow the INP spelling. Many microcomputer interpreters permit INPUT to fulfill both PRINT and INPUT statements in the interest of saving space.
See: INKEY$, INPUT1, INP, INPUT$, INPUTLINE, LINEINPUT, PIN

INPUTLINE Used in TSC Extended BASIC and PRIME BASIC/VM to INPUT a whole line of characters and assign it to one string variable. The line may include special characters like commas but does not need to be in quotes. The computer asks for input to the INPUTLINE statement by displaying an exclamation point (!). The statement LINEINPUT is like INPUTLINE except that no user's prompt (!) is given in LINEINPUT.
See: INPUT, LINEPUT

**INPUT$** Used to read a specified number of characters from the keyboard without displaying them. INPUT$ is a function of Microsoft BASIC. It is not necessary to press the ENTER or RETURN keys to complete the entry, but a specified number of characters must be entered to signal the program to resume. For instance, A$=INPUT#(7) will cause the program to pause until seven characters are entered.
See: GET, INKEY$, INPUT, KEY$

INPUT1 Used like INPUT except that INPUT1 stops the feed line and carriage return as soon as the entered data has been assigned to a variable. INPUT1 is only used by a few computers, including MaxiBASIC Digitals and the North Star.
See: INP, INPUT, INPUTLINE, LINEINPUT, PIN

INSTR To report the starting positions of a string which is part of a larger string. For instance, the computer looks for the starting position of C$ within B$. INSTR=0 if C$ is not contained in B$. INSTR is similar to POS and INDEX.
See: INDEX, POS, LEN, MID$

INT(n) (ANSI) Finds the integer or whole number value of a number. INT removes everything from the right side of the decimal point. Numbers are always rounded down including negative numbers, i.e., $-6.47 = -7$. Most computers limit the size of the numbers which can be used with the INT function. Microcomputers often limit INT to numbers between -32768 and 32767. Most Tiny BASICs use the short spelling I.
See: CINT, FIX, "/"

INVERSE Used by the Apple II to change the screen output to black on white instead of the normal white on black. The NORMAL command is used to return the display to the white-on-black mode.
See: FLASH, NORMAL

KEY$(n) Inputs a character without displaying it in APF Imagination Machine BASIC. KEY$(n) allows only three possible values for N, one of which reads the keyboard (0). One reads the right-hand game control (1). And the last reads the left-hand game control (2). The spelling KEY is used by the Texas Instrument TI99/4 to read the keyboard in the CALL statement, CALL KEY, same as KEY$(0).
See: GET, INKEY$, INPUT, PDL

LE Used by some computers, including the TI990, as a short form of "less than or equal to" ($<=$).
See: $=$, $<>$, $<$, $>$, $<=$, $>=$, EQ, GE, GT, LT, NE, IF-THEN

LEFT$(str,n) Removes part of a string for use elsewhere. LEFT$("string",number) starts at the left side of the string. The string must be in quotes unless it is listed as a string variable. The number of characters can be entered as a number, a variable, or an arithmetic operation. Decimal numbers will be converted to integers automatically. The spelling LEFT (string,n) is used in some BASICs, including DEC BASIC PLUS and MAXBASIC.
See: CHR$, DEFSTR, INKEY, INSTR, PRINT, RIGHT$, SEG$, SPACE$, STR$, STRING$, MID$, POS

LEN(str) Measures the length of strings by counting the number of characters in the string variables. Blanks and nonprintable characters are also counted. LEN can also be used to count characters enclosed in quotes. The Acorn Atom uses the short spelling L. for LEN.
See: ASC, FRE, LEFT$, MID$, RIGHT$, SEG$, VAL

LET (ANSI) To assign numeric values to variables. LET is optional on many computers. When LET is optional, LET X=Y will achieve the same results as X=Y. Sometimes LET is used optionally to signal a change in a variable value.

LIN To signal the computer to skip a specified number of lines on a CRT or printer before the next line is printed. LIN is used in Digital Group Opus 1 and 2 BASIC and Hewlett-Packard 2000 BASIC.
See: PRINT, VTAB

LINEINPUT To accept a whole line of characters and assign it to one string variable. LINEINPUT will accept up to 254 characters. No user prompt is automatically given by LINEINPUT. Special characters such as commas need not be enclosed in quotes. The shorter spelling LINPUT is used by some computers.
See: INPUT, INPUTLINE

LIST To display a program listing starting with the lowest program line number. The computer will usually scroll through the whole program unless it is stopped using a key function such as shift @ or Control C. Some computers will stop listing at intervals to wait for the ↑ or ↓ keys to be pressed. Many computers allow the list command to include specified line limits for the list, i.e., LIST 50-100 will cause the computer to display lines 50 to 100. Some computers accept LIST as a program statement. TRS-80 Level I BASIC uses the abbreviated spelling L.
See: LLIST

LLIST To list a program which is currently in memory on a printer. LLIST is used by Microsoft BASIC as a command and sometimes as a program statement. The program being listed on a printer will continue printing until it is stopped by pressing an appropriate key such as BREAK or RESET. The printer must be connected and ready before the LLIST command is given. Otherwise, the program may be lost.

See: LIST, LPRINT

LOAD To load a program into the computer from a disk or tape. The program which has been saved on the tape or disk may have been named, in which case the program name should be entered after LOAD so that the computer will load the specified program and ignore any other on the disk or tape, i.e., LOAD "SCORES". After loading a program, check that it has been transferred accurately by listing it on the screen before running it.

See: CLOAD, CSAVE, LIST, NEW, SAVE

LOG(n) (ANSI) Computes the natural logarithm of any specified number greater than 0. To compute common logs from natural logs, multiply .434295 times the natural log. The common log times 2.3026 equals the natural log. LOG is used by a very few computers, including the IMSAI 4K, to compute the common log. Some computers use the LN or LOGE spellings for LOG.

See: CLG, LOG10

LOG 10(n) Computes the common logarithm (base 10) of any specified number greater than zero. Several alternate spellings of LOG 10 are used by various computers, including LGT, CLG, and CLOG. To compute common logs from natural logs, multiply the natural log by .434295. The common log times 2.3026 equals the natural log.

See: CLG, LOG

LPRINT Used by Microsoft BASIC to have a PRINT statement carried out on a printer rather than on the video screen. LPRINT can be used as a command or a program statement. LPRINT can be used with TAB and USING. Zone printing with commas and close printing with semicolons are also possible with LPRINT. The printer must be connected to the computer and ready to print before LPRINT is run. Otherwise the program may be lost.

See: LLIST, PRINT, PRINT USING, TAB, comma, semicolon

LT Used as "less than" instead of <. LT is a relational operator which compares numeric values or strings in IF-THEN statements.

See: <, IF-THEN, =, <=, >, >=, EQ, GE, LE, LT, NE

MAN To allow the user to insert lines manually in Apple II BASIC. When the computer is in the automatic line numbering mode (AUTO), the user must press control X (CTRL X), then the MAN command, and then RETURN in order to enter lines manually.

See: AUTO

MAT CON To fix the value of each element in an array to a constant, usually number 1. The array may also be redimensioned by CON if the number of cells in the array is equal to or less than the number of cells reserved by the original DIM statement.

See: DIM, FOR, NEXT, MAT, IDN, MAT ZER

MAT IDN To form the identity matrix of a square matrix. The identity matrix is a matrix with 0's in each cell except the main diagonal, i.e.:

100
010
001

IDN can be used to redimension the matrix if the number of cells in the matrix is equal to or less than the number reserved by the original DIM statement.

See: DIM, FOR, NEXT

MAT INPUT To assign values to each array element using the keyboard. The number of array elements that may be given values is determined by a DIM statement. Most computers allow the array size to be set by MAT INPUT unless the array is larger than ten elements, in which case it must be dimensioned. When MAT INPUT is executed, the computer prompts the user with a question mark (?) signaling that it is ready to accept the first array element value. MAT INPUT assigns values to all of the vertical columns in the first row of a two-dimensional array before filling in the next horizontal row.

See: DIM, FOR, INPUT NUM, MAT PRINT, MAT, READ

MAT INV(mat) Forms the inverse of a specified square matrix. A square matrix is a two-dimensional matrix with the same number of rows as columns. The inverse matrix is that matrix which when multiplied by the original matrix equals the identity matrix, i.e., MAT B= INV(A) if MAT B × MAT A = MAT IDN. Some computers calculate the determinant function of a matrix at the same time as the inverse in order to test whether a true inverse exists. If the determinant (DET) is 0, the matrix has no inverse.

See: DET, DIM, FOR, MAT, MAT IDN, MAT READ, MAT PRINT, MAT*

MAT PRINT To print the values stored in specific array elements. The number of values printed is set by the Dimension statement (DIM). Most computers with MAT PRINT will allow some zone printing with a comma and close printing with a semicolon. The MAT PRINT statement can be used to print the contents of arrays with more than one dimension. The DIM statement establishes the number of dimensions in the array and names the array, i.e., DIM B(3,4). MAT PRINT B then tells the computer to print a matrix with three rows and four columns. A few computers use MAT PRINT USING to format the printing arrays.

See: DIM, FOR, MAT INPUT, MAT READ, PRINT, PRINT USING, comma, semicolon

MAT READ   To read values from a DATA statement and assign them to an array. The array size is established by a DIM statement. MAT READ assigns values to all of the vertical columns in the first row of a two-dimensional array before assigning values to the next row. Most computers allow the array size to be set by the MAT INPUT statement as long as the array has less than 10 elements. If the array is larger than 10 elements, it must be dimensioned (DIM).
   See: DATA, DIM, FOR, MAT INPUT,
         MAT PRINT, READ

MAT TRN(mat)   Develops the transpose of a matrix. A matrix is a two-dimensional array. The transpose of a matrix changes the rows of the matrix to columns and the columns to rows. For instance, if matrix A is an X*Y array, then its transpose, matrix T, is an Y*X array. The first row of matrix A becomes the first column of matrix T.

MAT ZER   To set the value of each array element at 0. Most computers with MAT ZER allow the array size to be redimensioned by MAT ZER as long as the number of cells in the redimensioned array is equal to or less than the number set by the original dimension statement (DIM).
   See: DIM, FOR, NEXT, MAT CON, MAT IDN

MAT=   To assign the stored values in one array to the corresponding cells of a second array. Most computers with MAT= will dimension the second array to the same dimension as the first, as long as enough space has been provided by the original dimension statement (DIM). The word MAT may be optional on some computers.
   See: DATA, DIM, MAT PRINT, MAT READ,
         NEXT, PRINT, READ

MAT+   To add the values in one array to the corresponding values in a second array and to store the sums in a third array. All three arrays must have the same dimensions. The word MAT may be optional on some computers.
   See: DIM, FOR, MAT−, MAT*, MAT PRINT,
         MAT, READ, NEXT

MAT−   To subtract the values in one array from the corresponding values in another array of equal dimensions and store the results in a third array of the same size. The word MAT may be optional in some computers.
   See: DIM, FOR, MAT=, MAT*, MAT READ,
         MAT, PRINT, NEXT

MAT*   To multiply each value stored in a matrix by a single value (scalar multiplication) or to multiply one matrix by another (matrix multiplication). To multiply matrix A by 5, use the form B=(5)*A. Each element in the array will then be multiplied by 5 and the result will be stored in matrix B. The form A=(5)*A will tell the computer to store the results in matrix A, erasing the original element values. To do matrix multiplication, the second dimension of matrix A must be equal to the first dimension of matrix B, i.e., MAT A=X*Y and MAT B= Y*Z. (C=A*B is not interchangeable with C=B*A.) The results of MAT C=A*B will be stored in a matrix with dimensions Y*X, i.e., MAT C=Y*Z. The word MAT is optional in some computers.
   See: DIM, FOR, MAT=, MAT PRINT,
        MAT READ, NEXT

MAX(n,n)   Tells which of two values is larger. For instance, P=X MAX 10 assigns P the value of X if it is larger than 10. If P < = 10, it becomes 10. Some computers use the form MAX (A,B). MAX is used by Micropolis BASIC to compare the alphabetical order of two strings and choose the one that would come later in alphabetical order. A few computers use MAX to find the largest value in an array, i.e., 20 M=MAX(X).
   See: ABS, MIN, > =

MEM   Used with the PRINT command to display the number of unused bytes left in the computer's memory. MEM is sometimes used as a program statement or subroutine. The MEM statement helps to keep track of remaining memory in longer programs.
   See: CLEAR, FRE

MID$(str,n,n)   Extracts a specific number of characters (NL) from the middle of a string starting with a character that is a certain number of places (nP) left of the beginning of the string. MID$("CHARACTER",5,7) would instruct the computer to print ACT. The string must be enclosed in quotes unless it is assigned to a string variable. The string and the numbers must be separated by commas. The number of characters to be extracted and the starting position can be given as variables, numbers or arithmetic operations. Decimal values will be converted to integers automatically. Some interpreters use MID$ to change the contents of a string variable. For instance, MID$ (X$,6,2)=Y$ instructs the computer to replace six characters of X$ with the first six from Y$, starting at the second character from the left of X$. MID is used instead of MID$ by some computers, including Harris BASIC-V.
   See: CHR$, INKEY$, LEFT, PRINT, RIGHT$,
         SEG$, SPACE, STR$, STRING$

MIN(a,b)   Tells which of two values is smaller. For instance, P=X MIN 10 assigns P the value of X, if X is smaller than 10; if not, P=10. The form MIN (A,B) is used by some computers to do the same thing. MIN is used by Micropolis BASIC to compare two strings and give the one which comes earlier in alphabetical order. The smallest value in an array can be identified using MIN by some computers, i.e., M=MIN(A).
   See: ABS, MAX, L=

MOD   To compute the remainder in A MOD B when A is divided by B. MOD is only used by some computers, including Apple, COMPAL, HP 3000, and Harris. For instance, PRINT 9 MOD 2 instructs the computer to print 1 which is the remainder of 9÷2. The MOD value is

automatically converted to an integer. The Harris BASIC-V and others used the form MOD(A,B).
See: FIX, INT

NE   Used as a short form of the NEW command by a few computers including the TI 990. NE is also used in place of "not equal" or < > as a relational operator. NE is recognized as an operator when used as a program statement.
See: <>, >, <, =, >=, <=, EQ, GE, GT, LE, LT, IF-THEN

NEW   To erase the resident BASIC program from memory. NEW erases all program lines as well as variables but not the interpreter. NEW is usually used before entering a new program. The TRS-80 accepts the spelling N. for NEW. A few other computers use NE. SCRATCH or SCR may be used instead of NEW in some computers. The Sinclair ZX80 and others use use NEWn to erase the program and set the amount of memory available for BASIC simultaneously. This enables the user to set aside memory space for any machine language program to be stored in memory along with BASIC programs.
See: CLEAR, SCRATCH

NEXT   (ANSI) To return execution to the first statement of a FOR NEXT loop. When the loop value is higher than the specified limit, the loop teminates and program control is transferred to the statement following NEXT. NEXT statements with variables return only to FOR statements using the same variable. Many computers allow NEXT statements to contain no variables, in which case the computer returns to the preceding FOR statement until the specified limit is reached. Some computers allow more than one variable in a NEXT statement. NEX and N. (TRS-80 Level I BASIC) are spellings used by some computers.
See: FOR

NOFLOW   Used in Microsoft BASIC to stop the FLOW or tracing function. FLOW displays the program lines as they are executed. NO FLOW can also be used as a program statement to interrupt FLOW at specified points in the program.
See: FLOW, NOTRACE, TRACE OFF, TROFF

NORMAL   To return the screen to its normal display mode (white on black). NORMAL turns off both the FLASH and INVERSE commands. INVERSE changes the display to alternate rapidly between white on black and black on white.
See: FLASH, INVERSE

NOT   Used as a logical operator to reverse the condition in IF-THEN statements. IF NOT A<=8 THEN 50 indicates that the computer should GOTO 50 if the value in A is not less than or equal to 8. Some computers use NOT to compare strings. For instance, IF NOT A$="PASS" or A$=FAIL THEN 80 tell the computer to continue execution at line 80 if string A is neither a PASS or FAIL. Some computers use NOT to compare the binary com-

plement of a number. In this case, the NOT operator changes all 0's to 1's and all 1's to 0's, changing each bit in the binary representation of a number.
See: AND, IF-THEN, OR, XOR

NOTRACE   Used by the Apple II to stop the TRACE function which displays program lines as they are executed. NOTRACE can also be used as a program statement to turn off the TRACE function at specified intervals during the program. NOTRACE is similar to TROFF (TRS-80 Level II) and NOFLOW (Microsoft).
See: TRACE, NOFLOW, TRACE OFF, TROFF

NUM   Used in some BASICs, including Digital Group BASIC, to convert a numeric string into its numeric value. The string of digits including decimals is changed into the number it represents. Numeric strings cannot be used for computation until converted to the numbers they represent. Computers with MAT INPUT can use NUM to find out how many items have been typed into a list.
See: MAT INPUT, VAL

NUM$ To convert numeric expresions into a string of numbers. Numeric values need to be converted into a numeric string in order for string function to be applied.
See: ASC, CHR$, VAL

ON-ERROR-GOTO   To branch to an error subroutine when an error is encountered during execution. ON-ERROR-GOTO does not stop program execution. To stop execution and print the error message, execute ON-ERROR-GOTO 0 during the ON-ERROR-GOTO subroutine. The edit feature can be triggered on some computers when a syntax error is encountered. The computer will go into the EDIT mode after the error is printed and the ON-ERROR-GOTO statement has been executed and the program is stopped. The RESUME statement returns program control to the main program after an ON-ERROR-GOTO subroutine. Applesoft and others use the shorter spelling ON ERR GOTO.
See: ERL, ERR, ERROR, RESUME

ON-GOSUB   Used as a multiple-branching statement to evaluate the expression after ON in order to direct program control to one of the subroutines specified by the line numbers following GOSUB. ON GOSUB combines several IF-GOSUB tests in one statement. For instance, ON A GOSUB 50,100,150 tells the computer to branch to 50, 100, or 150 depending on whether A is equal to 1, 2, or 3. Any other values of A cause the test to be invalid, and the computer either continues on the next program line or the program "crashes" and the computer prints an error message.
See: GOTO-OF, GOSUB-OF, GOSUB, ON-GOTO, ON-ERROR-GOTO

ON-GOTO   Used as a multiple-branching statement to combine a number of IF-THEN test in one statement. For instance, ON A GOTO 100,150,200 tells the computer to branch to line 100, 150, or 200 depending on whether the value of A is 1, 2, or 3. Any other value for A will cause the test to fail, and the program execution will resume on the next program line or the program will "crash." Different interpreters set various limits on the number of branching options available. If the value of A is a decimal, it will be integered automatically. A few computers use short spellings such as PDP-8E's ON X GOT or the ON XG used by some Tiny BASICs. When the value of A is not 1, 2, or 3, the base can be shifted to make ON GOTO usable for more numbers. ON A-100 GOTO 100,150,200 will direct the computer to accommodate A values of 101, 102, or 103. ON GOTO can be used with other key words in such statements as ON END GOTO or ON ERROR GOTO. This enables the computer to branch to another part of the program under certain conditions.

See: GOTO, GOTO-OF, GOSUB-OF, ON-GOSUB, ON-ERROR

OPTION   (ANSI) Used by Harris BASIC-V with the BASE statement to identify the BASE or lowest array element as an integer value from 1 to 10. For instance, 10 OPTION BASE=6 20 DIM X(10) identifies the number of elements in this array to be 6, that is, A(6) to A(10). The computer assumes the OPTION BASE value to be 0 unless it has been specified otherwise. An equals sign is not required after BASE in ANSI Standard BASIC since ANSI specifies only 0 and 1 as OPTION BASE values.

See: BASE

OR   Used with an IF-THEN statement to set up a logical math operator for testing multiple conditions. For instance, IF x>2 OR y<10 THEN 100 directs the computer to go to line 100 if variable x is greater than 2 or y is less than 10, or both. A few computers use OR to do multiple tests on literal strings. For instance, IF A$="U" or A$="UP" THEN 150 tells the computer to go to 150 if the string variable contains "U" or "UP" or both. Some computers accept + rather than OR. OR is used by some computers to see if the conditions are met in either of two logical operators. If the conditions are met, the computer gives the answer True (−1). If neither condition is met, the answer False (0) is given. A few computers use the OR as in boolean algebra to compute the binary logical OR of two numbers. In this operation, the binary forms of two numbers are compared bit by bit. If either bit is 1, the computer outputs 0. The result of the OR comparison is a third binary number, i.e., 01101 or 00110 = 01111. The OR operator in the form OR(X$,Y$) is used to modify strings by doing the OR operation on each character. OR(X$,Y$) is used by the WANG 2200B to do the OR operation on a string (X$) and a hex constant (Y).

See: AND, XOR, NOT, =, *

OUT   To send a byte value (number) to a specified output port. The format for this statement is OUT port number, byte number. For instance, OUT 255,5 sends the binary equivalent of 5 to port number 255. The port and byte numbers must be positive integers within the range from 0 to 255. The OUT statement is often used in control operations such as sound generation.

See: INP, PIN, PEEK, POKE

PAUSE   Used by the Sharp RTS-80 Pocket Computer to cause the data to be displayed in the window for 0.85 second before the program resumes. PAUSE is like PRINT except that PRINT stops the program until the enter key is pressed. PAUSE can be used with PRINT USING to format output. Processor Tech and a few other BASICs use PAUSEn to tell the computer to pause for a specified number of seconds(n) before resuming the program execution.

See: PRINT, PRINT USING

PDL   Used with game paddles to set the two game control units. The control units are called paddle 0 and paddle 1, identified as PDL(0) and PDL(1).

See: COLOR, GR, KEY$, PLOT

PEEK   To read the contents of a specific memory address. A = PEEK(15238) gives the value stored in memory address 15238 to A. The value in the memory address will be expressed as a number from 0 to 255 (the range storable in an 8-bit memory cell). PEEK is sometimes used to check on what number was POKEd into a memory address. Before using POKE and PEEK, make sure to avoid POKEing data into memory addresses which have been reserved for normal operations. See your computer manual for memory address maps. PEEK and POKE are often used with USR(x) to start a machine language subroutine.

See: EXAM, FETCH, FILL, POKE, STUFF SYSTEM, USR(x)

PI   To represent the value 3.14159265 or π which is used in numeric operations. The Harris BASIC-V uses PI(x) to compute π*x.

PINT   To read the decimal value of a byte of information at a specific port by Heath Benton Harbor BASIC and a few other interpreters. The byte value must be a positive interger from 0 to 255 (the range of numbers storable in an 8-byte memory cell). The word INP is used by some computers to do the same function as PINT.

See: INPUT, PEEK, OUT, USR

PLOT   To "turn on" a color graphics block on the computer screen. The block to be lit up is identified by two numbers, i.e., PLOT 14,7 which represents the column and row numbers. 0,0 represents the top left block on the screen. The number of both columns and rows can go from 0 to 39. Eight rows on the screen are reserved for text. The COLOR of the graphics display is determined by the COLOR statement. Coloring the screen black (COLOR 0) or executing a GR statement will erase the screen.

See: COLOR, GR, TEXT, HLIN AT, VLIN AT, SET, RESET, POINT, DRAW

POINT   Used by TRS-80 Level I and Level II BASICs to check whether or not a specific graphics block is "turned on" or lit up. The block is specified by its column and row numbers, i.e., POINT (20,10). If the block is on, the computer returns 1 (Level I) or −1 (Level II). If the block is off, a zero is returned.
  See: CLS, DOT, RESET, SET

POKE   To store values from 0 to 255 in specific memory locations. POKE 13725,70 tells the computer to store the ASCII code for 70, (F), in memory address 13725.
  See: EXAM, FETCH, FILL, PEEK, STUFF

POP   To remove one address from a memory stack. POP allows the computer to branch to a newly specified line in the program after a GOSUB statement instead of branching to the line previously specified by the program. In effect the POP command simply removes one memory address from an address stack, called a pushdown stack, in which the GOSUB addresses have been stored. The RETURN statement reads the top address on a stack to see where to return program control after the GOSUB has been executed. POP removes the top address, causing the RETURN statement to go to the next address down to continue program execution. POP is used when an error or a specific result indicates that the program should branch to a location other than the one originally specified.

POS   Used as a string function to locate the first occurrence of a string X$ in string Y$. POS(Y$,X$) tells the computer to look for the string X$ in the string Y$ starting at the first character of Y$. POS(5Y$,X$) will tell the computer to start looking at line 5. If X$ is not found in Y$, POS will equal 0. POS(n) is used by some interpreters, including those using Microsoft BASIC, to give the next position available to print a character, i.e., the position of the cursor in the print line. The value is a dummy number. Any number can be used. POS is the same as INSTR.
  See: INSTR, INDEX

PRECISION   Used with a PRINT statement to set the maximum number of digits to be printed to the right of the decimal point. For instance, 100 PRECISION 2 will instruct the computer to round numbers to two decimal points. This statement would be used when printing values in dollars and cents.
  See: DIGITS, FMT, IMAGE, INT, PRINT USING

PRINT   Used in various ways to PRINT numbers, strings, or letters on the screen. PRINT A tells the computer to print the value of the variable A. PRINT "A" tells the computer to print the values in string A$. Used as a command, PRINT can direct the computer to give the result of an arithmetic function. PRINT 6*2 will cause the computer to print 12.
  The use of commas with a PRINT statement will space the printed output into horizontal zones. Semicolons can be used in PRINT statements to leave out spaces between letters or words, i.e., PRINT "G";"O"

prints GO. TAB is used with PRINT to tell the computer to leave a specific number of spaces before starting to print. PRINT by itself will cause an empty line to be left in the program. PRINT USING is used to specify a particular format for printing strings. PRINT AT is used in TRS-80 Level I BASIC to tell the computer where to start printing. North Star and some other BASICs include the formatting directions in the PRINT statement immediately after the word PRINT. For instance, PRINT CZ,X will tell the computer to print X, inserting commas at three-digit intervals (C) and dropping trailing zeros. 5078.5670 would be printed 5,078,567. The TRS-80 Level I BASIC uses PRINT# to store data on tape. Some computers use PRINT# to store data in "files" on external disks or cassette tapes. Several alternate spellings of print are accepted by different computers such as P. used by some Tiny BASICs or PRI used by PDP-80. Microsoft BASIC uses the single-character substitute ?, and DEC BASIC Plus uses &.
  See: AT, CUR, LIN, L PRINT, MAT, PRINT, PRINT USING, @, #, comma, semicolon, "/", ?, &, !

PRINT AT   Used by TRS-80 Level I BASIC to specify the starting location of a numeric value or string to be printed on the screen. For instance, PRINT AT 20, "NICK" will tell the computer to print NICK at location 20. A comma must be inserted between the location and the string. There are 16 rows of 64 horizontal addresses equaling 1024 possible screen locations. TRS-80 Level II uses Print @. Tiny BASICs allow P.A. for PRINT AT.
  See: AT, @, PRINT, TAB

PRINT USING   To format the printed output to be displayed on the screen. The sign for number (#) is used to reserve a position for each digit to be printed. The double asterisk (**) is used to tell the computer to fill all unused spaces left of the decimal point. For instance, PRINT USING "**##,##";25.54 will tell the computer to print **25.54. A double dollar sign ($$) before the number signs (#) will tell the computer to print the output in dollars, i.e., PRINT USING "$$##.##"; 25.54 prints $25.54. Inserting commas at one or more places between #'s in the print statement will cause commas to be inserted at three digit intervals in the output regardless of where the commas occur in the print statement. PRINT USING:

  "####,#"; 25.000
  "##,###; 25000
  "###,##"; 25,000

will all yield 25,000. PRINT USING can be used to format for plus (+) and minus (−) signs and exponential notation. It can be used to print only certain characters in a word or string. Consult your manual for your computer's specific PRINT USING capabilities.
  See: DIGITS, FMT, IMAGE, PRINT, #, **. !, ↑ , +, −, "/", backslash (\), $, &, :

RAD   Used by the Cromemco 16K Extended BASIC and others to signal the computer to perform trigonometric functions using radians. Most computers do this automatically, but some have a DEG statement to switch the calculations of trig functions into degrees. The RAD command is used to return these computers to the normal radian mode. A radian is equal to 57 degrees. Some computers such as the Sharp/TRS-80 Pocket use RAD as a statement that tells the computer to calculate in radians. MAXBASIC and a few others use RAD(n) as a function to change values from degrees to radians.

See: ACS, ASN, ATN, COS, DEG, GRAD, SIN, TAN

RANDOMIZE   (ANSI) To instruct the computer to provide a new set of random numbers for the RND function each time it is used. The new set of numbers is selected randomly from a group of numbers stored in the computer. Some BASICs, including BASIC-80, require a number to be included in the RANDOMIZE statement, i.e., RANDOMIZE 12379. This number, called a seed number, will be shuffled to provide the random set of numbers. Some computers use the shortened spellings RANDOM (TRS-80 Level II BASIC) or RAN (PDP-8E).

See: RND

READ   (ANSI) To read numeric or string data from data lines and to assign that data to variables. When the READ statement is executed on a line of data, the pointer moves to the next line and waits for another READ statement. When all of the data is read, the pointer must be reset by means of a RESTORE statement or an OUT OF DATA ERROR will occur. More than one variable may be placed in the same READ statement. Each variable should be separated by a comma. Most computers read strings from DATA statements. Each string read from a DATA statement must have a corresponding string variable in a READ statement. Alternate spellings of READ such as REA. and REA are accepted by a few computers.

See: DATA, RESTORE, comma

RECALL   To load an array of numeric values back into the computer after it has been stored on a tape. For instance, RECALL A loads array A into the computer memory. The array to be reloaded must have been dimensioned properly.

See: CLOAD, DIM, STORE

REM   Used before any lines that constitute notes or remarks on the program. These lines are not executed and they are ignored by the computer. They are for users to mark subroutines or identify specific parts of the program, etc. Some computers accept REMARK or REM.

See: apostrophe, !

RENUMBER   Used by some computers, including the Cremenco 16K Extended BASIC, to renumber program lines. If no line numbers are specified in the RENUMBER command, the computer will renumber all the line numbers starting at 10. The line numbers used in the pro-

grams GOTO, GOSUB, IF-THEN, ON-GOSUB, and ON-GOTO statements are changed to be constant with the original branching scheme. Some computers use the shorter spellings RENUM or REN. RESEQUENCE is used by DEC computers. TRS-80 Disk BASIC uses the word NAME instead of RENUMBER.

See: IF-THEN, GOSUB, GOTO, ON-GOSUB, ON-GOTO, LIST

**REPEAT$**   To generate a character string by repeating a given set of characters a number of times. For instance, REPEAT$ ("GIMME,3) creates the phrase GIMMEGIMMEGIMMME. REPEAT$("!",5) creates !!!!!

See: STRING$

RESET   Used by TRS-80 to "turn-off" a graphics block on the screen which has been previously lit by a SET command. The block is identified by its column and row numbers. RESET (7,9) turns off the block located at the seventh column and the ninth row of the graphics grids. Tiny BASIC uses the R. abbreviation for RESET.

See: CLS, CLRDOT, POINT, SET

RESTORE   (ANSI) To restore all the data in the DATA statement and to reset the pointer to the first piece of data in the first data line. This makes it possible for the DATA staements to be used again when the next READ statement comes along in the program. In this way the computer can use data stored in the DATA statement more than once. The shorter REST. is used by the TRS-80 Level I BASIC. The DEC-8E allows RES. Some computers can reset data on a specific line without resetting the other data lines. The line number to be reset is entered after the RESTORE statement. The DEC 10 and some other computers can RESTORE string data and numeric data separately, using RESTORE and RESTORE* respectively.

See: DATA, READ

RESUME   Used at the end of an ON-ERROR-GOTO statement to tell the computer to continue program execution at a specific line, i.e., RESUME 40 means continue at line 40. RESUME NEXT tells the computer to resume in the next line after the line in which the error occurred. RESUME (with no line number) or RESUME 0 are used to send program control back to the line in which the error occurred.

See: ERL, ERR, ON-ERROR-GOTO

RETURN   (ANSI) Used at the end of a subroutine to tell the computer to return program execution to the line following the GOSUB statement. Some computers use the abbreviated spellings RET., RET, or T.

See: GOSUB, GOSUB-OF, IF-GOSUB, ON-GOSUB

**RIGHT$**   Used to isolate a specified number of characters from a string, counting the characters from right to left. For instance, PRINT RIGHT$ ("BASIC",3) prints SIC. MAXBASIC uses the spelling RIGHT. Some BA-

SICs use RIGHT$ to isolate characters from a string by starting at a position counted fron the left and isolating it plus everything to the right of it. RIGHT$ ("COMPUTER" 4) would print PUTER because P is in the fourth position.

See: CHR$, INKEY$, INSTRA, LEFT$, MD$, PRINT, SEG$, STR, STRING$, SPACE

RND To generate random numbers. RND is used by virtually all computers with wide variation in usage. ANSI rules require that RND be used by itself or with a RANDOMIZE statement. However, most computers use the form RND(n) to generate a random decimal number between 0 and 1. Other computers use RND(N) to generate a random integer number from a certain range depending on the minimum and maximum numbers possible or a particular machine (usually −32768 to +32767). To avoid confusion, check your computer manual to see how your computer uses RND.

See: RANDOMIZE

RUN Used as a command to execute any program or command programs in the computer's memory starting with the lowest program line number unless another specific line number is specified. A few computers allow RUN as a program statement. RUN is allowed as a form of CHAIN statement by Microsoft Disk BASIC. The shortened spelling R. is used in Tiny Basic and RU. is used by the TI 990 and others.

See: CHAIN

SAVE To save programs by transferring them from memory onto cassette tape. SAVE is used by the Apple II and the Commander PET. Many computers used the CSAVE command instead. After a program has been SAVEd on cassette, list it to check that the saved program is identical to the one in the memory. Then erase the program from memory by using NEW (or another appropiate word). To load the program back into the computer, use LOAD. Some computers with disk storage use SAVE with a disk file number to save programs in disk memory.

See: CLOAD, CSAVE, LIST, LOAD

SCRATCH Used as a command to erase a program from memory to reset the variables to zero. Some computers use NEW instead of SCRATCH. SCRATCH is used as a statement by some computers, including the DEC-10, to clear a disk file before entering new data. Micropolis BASIC and others use SCRATCH followed by a file name as a command to exclude files from a disk directory. The short spelling SCR is allowed by some computers.

See: CLEAR, ERASE, NEW

SCRN Used by Apple II BASIC and Applesoft to reveal the color of a specified graphics block on the screen. The computer is capable of displaying sixteen colors, each of which has a code number. The graphics block is identified by its column and row numbers. SCRN(5,10)=4 indicates that the color of the graphics block at column 5, row 10 is dark green (4).

See: COLOR, GR, PLOT, POINT

**SEG$** To isolate a part of a string from a string variable. SEG$ is followed by the string variable, the starting point of the string to be isolated, and the number of characters to be extracted. For instance, if A$="PRINTOUT" then PRINT SEG$ (A$,6,3,) returns OUT. SEG$ can be used in place of RIGHT$ or LEFT$. A few computers use the spelling SEG.

See: DIM, MID$, LEFT$, RIGHT$

SET Used by the TRS-80 to turn on a graphics block. The block must be specified after SET by its column and row numbers. SET (7,18) tells the computer to light up the block at column 7, row 18. RESET is used to turn off graphics blocks. TRS-80 Level I allows the spelling S.

See: RESET, SETDOT

SETDOT Used by the ABC 80 to turn on a graphics block. The block must be specified after SETDOT by its line and column numbers. SETDOT 10,20 tells the computer to light up the graphics block at the tenth row and twentieth column counting from the left corner. CLRDOT is used to turn off a graphics block.

See: CLRDOT, RESET, ⌷

SGN To tell whether a number's sign is positive or negative. If a number is negative, the computer gives a −1. If it is positive, the computer returns a 1. If the number in question is zero, a 0 is returned.

See: ABS

SIN (ANSI) To calculate the angle formed by the ratio of the hypotenuse of a right triangle to the side opposite the angle being measured. The angle is given in radians. One radian equals approximately 57 degrees. The opposite of SIN is ARCSIN. Some computers calculate the angle in degrees (SIND) or grads (SING). 100 grads = 90 degrees. To convert degrees to radians, multiply the degrees by .0174533. To convert radians to degrees, multiply the radians by 57.29578. A very few computers convert radians and grads to degrees automatically.

See: ACS, ASN, COS, SINH, TAN

SINH To calculate the hyperbolic sine of a number. SINH(N) gives the sine of any real number based on its relationship to a hyperbola. The Harris BASIC-V uses the spelling SNH for the same function.

See: COSH, EXP, TANH

SLEEP To delay a program for a specified number of tenths of second by the Harris BASIC-V. For instance, SLEEP500 causes the program to pause for 50 seconds before continuing.

See: WAIT

SKIPF Used by the Sharp/TRS-80 Pocket Computer and others to skip a file by advancing the cassette tape to the end of a file. If no particular file is specified, SKIPF will skip the current file and stop. If a file is specified, the

computer will search for that file and stop at the end of it.
See: CLOAD, CSAVE

**SPACE$**   To insert spaces before a printed number or string. PRINT SPACE$ (10); "NAMES" prints 10 spaces and the word NAMES. Most computers allow up to 256 spaces. The Apple and the PET use the spelling SPC. MAXBASIC uses SPACE and Hewlett-Packard 2000 uses SPA. TAB is used by TRS-80.
See: STRING$, TAB

SQR   (ANSI) To calculate the square root of a positive number. The DEC-10 and North Star use SQRT.

STEP   Used with a FOR-NEXT statement to indicate the size of the step increment. The STEP value can be a positive or negative integer or decimal. If a STEP value is not specified, the STEP increment is automatically given a value of +1. Some computers allow a variable STEP value. The TI 990 uses ST for STEP and the TI 990 uses the ST spelling. STE is used by the PDP-8E.
See: FOR, NEXT

STOP   (ANSI) To stop program execution. Many computers print the line at which execution stopped. STOP can be used anywhere in a program. Some computers jump to the line where the END statement occurs when a STOP statement is executed. Computers which print the line number where the execution stops usually allow the program to continue with a CONT (Continue) command. To avoid confusing STOP and END, check your manual to see how they can be used on your computer. STO (PDP-8E and Tektronix 4050 series) and S.and ST. (TRS-80 Level I) are alternate spellings for STOP.
See: CONT, END, GO

STORE   Used by the Apple II to save a numeric array on tape. The array can be put onto a tape under program control and be recalled by the same program or by another program via a RECALL command. For instance, 200 DIM X(4,4,4) and 210 STORE X will store 125 (5*5*5) values on tape to be recalled for later use.
See: CSAVE, DIM, RECALL

**STRING$**   Used with a PRINT statement to print a specified ASCII code character a certain number of times. The information used is STRING$ (number, ASCII code). STRING$ (5,35) prints ##### (# = ASCII code 35). String characters or string variables are accepted in the STRING$ function by the TRS-80 and some other computers. Some computers allow the STR and STRING spellings.
See: ASC, CHR$, LEFT$, LEN, MID$,
   PRINT, RIGHT$, STR$, VAL

**STR$**   To change a numeric value into a string so that string functions like RIGHT$, LEFT$, and MID$ can operate on it.
See: ASC, CHR$, LEN, LEFT$, MID$, RIGHT$,
   STRING$, VAL, NUMS

STUFF   Used by Digital Group Opus 1 and 2 to place integer values from 0 to 255 in specified memory locations. STUFF 2155, 83 puts decimal value 83 into memory address 2155. FETCH can be used to verify the number put into memory by STUFF. Before STUFFing data, be sure of which memory locations are free, non-critical locations.
See: EXAM, FETCH, FILL, PEEK, POKE

SWAP   To switch the value of two variables or array elements. SWAP is used by SWTP, COMPUCORP, INTELLEC, and others. SWAP is just like the EXCHANGE statement used by some computers.
See: EXCHANGE

SYSTEM   Used as a command to transfer machine language data from a cassette or tape into the computer. SYSTEM may also be used as a program statement. When the SYSTEM statement is executed, the computer gives a sign (*?) that the computer is ready to receive the data from the disk or tape. SYSTEM is similar to the ESC key on many computers. SYS is a spelling used by some computers, including the DEC-10 and the Sperry Univac System 9.
See: PEEK, POKE

TAB   Used with a PRINT statement to insert a specified number of spaces before the characters to be printed. The TAB value is always positive and less than the number of spaces on a line. T. is accepted by Tiny BASIC.
See: PRINT, PRINT AT, PRINT USING,
   SPACE$, comma, semicolon

TAN   (ANSI) To compute the tangent of a specific angle in radians. The tangent of an angle equals the ratio of the opposite side to the adjacent side. ARCTAN is the opposite of TAN. Some computers measure the tangent in degrees (TAND) and others use grads (TANG). A few interpreters change all angle measurements to degrees automatically. To change degrees to radians, multiply the radians by 57.29578.
See: ACS, ASN, ATN, SIN, TANH

TANH   To calculate the hyperbolic tangent of a number. TANH(X) expresses the relationship of X to the hyperbola, but it is not a measurement. X can be any real positive or negative number. TANH(X) is always be-

tween −1 and 1. The spelling TNH. is used by Harris BASIC-V.
See: COSH, EXP, SINH

TAPPEND   Used by some interpreters, including Percom, to add a program from an externally stored cassette to a program already in memory. The lines of the stored program are added to the lines of the resident program. Therefore, the first line of the outside program must be higher than the last line of the program in memory.

TEXT   Used by the Apple II to return to normal text mode after using the graphics mode. The text mode allows 24 lines of 40 characters each. TEXT is used in MAXBASIC to designate variables such as string variables.
See: DEFSTRA, GRA, $

THEN   (ANSI) Used in IF-THEN to tell the computer which line to execute when the IF conditions is met. TRS-80 Level I BASIC accepts T as well as THEN. The PDP-8E accepts THE.
See: IF-THEN

TIME   Used as a function to tell how much time has elapsed since the computer was turned on. Time-sharing computers usually tell time around the clock. Some computers tell the time in seconds; others show fractions of seconds. The DEC BASIC PLUS 2 updates the time every second. The PET updates 60 times a second and the computers using MAXBASIC increment time 1000 times per second. Some computers use the spellings TIM (DEC-10) and TI (PET). TIME is used as a command by the Hewlett-Packard 2000F TIME-SHARED BASIC to log terminal time.
See: CLK$, TIME$

**TIME$**   Used by the PET and the DEC BASIC PLUS 2 to tell the time in six-digit numbers. TIME$ runs on a 24 hour format. For instance, TIME$="203011" means that the time is 20 hours (8 p.m.), 30 minutes, and 11 seconds. The time is updated every second from the time the computer is turned on or the time is reset. The DEC BASIC PLUS 2 prints the time in hours and minutes using the statement PRINT TIME$(n), which prints the number of (n) minutes before midnight.
See: CLK$, TIME

TLOAD   Used by PERCOM to load a program from a cassette tape into the computer.
See: CLOAD, LIST, NEW, SCRATCH, TSAVE

TOP   To locate the first unused byte of available memory in the Acorn Atom.
See: FRE(0), MEM

TRACE   Used by the Apple II as a command to print all program lines as they are executed. TRACE is often used to help in program debugging. The NOTRACE command must be given to deactivate the TRACE feature. (TRACE will not be turned off by CLEAR, DEL, NEW, or RESET.) TRACE can also be used as a statement to instruct the computer to print selected parts of a program as they are executed.
See: FLOW, NOTRACE, TRACE ON, TRON

TRACE OFF   Used with Motorola BASIC as a command to turn off the TRACE feature. The TRACE feature prints program lines as they are executed. TRACE OFF can also be used as a statement to discontinue a TRACE at certain parts of a program.
See: NOFLOW, NOTRACE, TRACE ON, TROFF

TRACE ON   Used with Motorola BASIC to print line numbers as they are executed. TRACE ON is helpful in debugging programs. TRACE OFF is used to turn off TRACE ON. TRACE OFF can also be used as a statement to trace certain parts of a program as they are executed.
See: FLOW, TRACE OFF, TRON

TROFF   Used as a command to turn off the TRON (trace on) feature which "traces" program lines as they are executed. TROFF can also be used as a program statement to turn off a TRON (trace on) statement which is used to trace certain parts of a program.
See: NOFLOW, NOTRACE, TRACEOFF, TRON

TRON   Used as a command by the TRS-80 and others to print program lines as they are executed. TRON is helpful for debugging programs. TRON is turned off by TROFF. TRON can also be used as a program statement to print certain parts of a program as they are executed.
See: FLOW, NEW, TRACE, TRACEON, TROFF

TSAVE   Used by Percom BASIC to transfer a program from the computer memory onto cassette tape. After the program is recorded on tape, it can be erased from the memory. The program should also be listed to check that it has been transferred accurately.
See: CSAVE, LIST, NEW, SAVE, SCRATCH, TLOAD

UNTIL   Used by the DEC PDP-11 and others as a type of FOR statement. For instance, FOR A=1 STEP 5 UNTIL A>50+17*6. The UNTIL statement does not end until the specified condition is met.

USR   To call up a machine language subroutine from the computer's memory and to execute it. Machine language programs are loaded into the memory by using the POKE statement from the keyboard or the SYSTEM command when loading from a disk or tape. USR can also be used to execute a machine language program which specifies the value to be used in a machine language subroutine. Some computers use the spelling USER.

VAL   To change string values into numeric values.

For instance:
```
100 x$ = "70"
110 PRINT VAL(X$)
```

will print the number 70. Some computers will not print a numeric value if spaces, plus or minus signs, or a letter precedes the numbers in a string. Some computers will print a numeric value for such strings if the numbers come first in the string. For instance, PRINT VAL ("785XYZ") will give the number 785.
  See: ASC, CHR$, LEFT$, LEN, MID$, RIGHT$, STRING$, STR$

VARPTR   To point out the memory address of a specified variable (VARiable PoinTeR). P=VARPTR(X) gives the address P to the first memory cell in which X is stored. To print the address, use PRINT PEEK(P). If X is an integer variable, the variable address location P will contain the least significant byte, or LSB, of the X value. Location P+1 will contain the most significant byte, or MSB. VARPTR can be used with string variables. In this case, the variable address location P contains the length of the string. P=1 and P+2 contain the LSB and the MSB of the starting address for the string. VARPTR can be used to exchange the contents of two different strings. VARPTR can also make strings available for USR subroutines. The most common use for VARPTR is to find the address of a variable which will then be transferred to a machine language routine.

VLIN-AT   Used by Apple II BASIC to display a vertical line at a specified column on the screen. VLIN-AT is followed by two numbers which determine the length of the line by identifying the starting and ending points. For instance, VLIN-AT 20,30 at 35 will tell the computer to draw a line from row 20 to row 30 at column 35. The GR (graphics) statement must be executed before VLIN-AT or any other graphic statement can be used. The color of the line is governed by the COLOR statement.
  See: COLOR, HLIN-AT, GR, PLOT,TEXT

VTAB   Used by Apple II BASIC to specify the vertical screen location for a PRINT statement. There are twenty-four vertical screen lines. VTAB 10 specifies line 10 as the starting line for a PRINT statement.
  See: ASC, CHR$, HOME, LIN, PRINT, PRINT AT, TAB

WAIT   To suspend program execution for a specified length of time. WAIT can be used by some computers such as those using MAXBASIC to wait a given number of seconds, i.e., WAIT 20 tells the computer to wait 20 seconds before continuing. Some computers will wait up to 10 seconds (Varian 620). Others such as those using ADDS BASIC will wait up to 1000 seconds. In Microsoft BASIC, WAIT is used to cause the computer to wait until the byte value at a specified computer port fulfils the conditions set by two byte values listed after WAIT. Each value in a WAIT statement must fall between 0 and 265, which is the range of values storable in an 8-bit memory cell. In Processor Technology Extended Cas-

sette BASIC and others, WAIT will stop execution until the byte value at a certain port ANDed with a second byte value equals a third byte value. Some computers use WAIT as a command. Check your manual to see how WAIT is used by your computer.
  See: AND, FOR, INP, NEXT, XOR

WHILE   To cause a series of lines to be executed over and over again until a certain condition is not met. WHILE begins a loop which must be closed by another statement such as WEND, ENDLOOP, or THEN. For instance:
```
50 WHILE X ≥ 10
60 INPUT X
70 Y=Y+X
80 ENDLOOP
90 PRINT "SUM=";Y
```

Lines 60 and 70 will be repeated as long as X is greater than or equal to 10. When a number less than 10 is entered, the computer will go to line 90. WHILE can also be used by some BASICs to form conditional loops with DO. In these cases the loop is ended with DOEND. DEC BASIC PLUS and others use WHILE as a modifier to make statements conditional. The statement is only executed in those instances when a certain condition exists. For instance:
```
50 X=5
60 X=X+1 WHILE X<25
70 PRINT X
99 END
```

The computer will add 1 to X until X equals 24.
  See: FOR, IF, UNTIL

XDRAW   Used by the Apple II to erase a shape which has been drawn on the screen or to draw a shape onto the screen. When XDRAW is used to draw a shape, XDRAW can be used a second time to erase the drawing without erasing the background. Shapes are drawn using a code from the user's shape table plus the coordinates of the starting location.
  See: DRAW

" (quotation mark)   (ANSI) To signal the computer to print the actual numbers, letters, or characters enclosed in the quotation marks instead of their variable values. For instance, 100 PRINT"70"will tell the computer to print the number 70. Quotes are also used in many of the newer computers to let the INPUT statement act as a PRINT statement as well. Quotes are required around strings in DATA statements by some computers while others require quotes only when the string follows, encloses, or precedes a blank, comma, or colon. Check your manual for details. Quotes are also used in Microsoft BASIC to indicate the name of programs which are saved on cassette tapes. The program name can then be used to load or save the program using CLOAD, or

CSAVE, i.e., CLOAD "T". Quotes are used in TRS-80 Level 1 BASIC with the PRINT# statement to record data onto cassette tape.

See: CLOAD, CSAVE, DATA, PRINT, TAB, comma, semicolon

, (comma)   Used in many ways, most commonly as a zoning device in PRINT statements. For instance, PRINT 5,10,15,20 tells the computer to print each number on a seperate screen zone. Each zone allows up to sixteen characters. The number of zones per line depends on the screen printer width. Another common use of the comma is to separate elements in an array field, i.e., X(A,B,C) indicates that A, B, and C are individual elements in a three-dimensional array. The comma is also used in DATA, DIM, INPUT, ON-GOTO, and READ statements to separate data items. See these statements for examples. Some computers, including those using Palo Alto Tiny BASIC, use the comma in LET statements instead of the colon.

See: AT, DATA, DIM, INPUT, ON-GOTO, PRINT USING, READ, @

. (period)   (ANSI) Used as a decimal point except by computers having only integer BASIC. Microsoft BASIC uses a period to tell the computer to EDIT or LIST the last program line which has been entered or one which has an error on it. Some computers using Tiny BASIC use the period in word abbreviations such as P. for PRINT or R. for RUN.

See: EDIT, INPUT, INT, LIST

; (semicolon)   (ANSI) To join characters or sections together on one line of a PRINT statement, i.e., PRINT "G";"O" prints GO. This is called concatenating the printed characters or strings. Spaces may be inserted automatically before and after any number values separated by semicolons to make room for + or − signs and to allow for spaces between numbers. Check your manual to see if your computer inserts spaces in order to avoid any formatting difficulties that these spaces might cause.

See: PRINT USING, TAB, comma

: (colon)   To allow the printing of more than one statement on a program line. For instance, 20 LET X = Y + 10:IF = Y 150 GOTO 40. LET and IF GOTO are both on line 20. Care must be taken to put branching statements at the end of multiple-statement lines so that no statement will be lost. For instance, in the statement 20 LET X = Y + 10: IF = Y 150 GOTO 40:PRINT"SHORT-FALL", the computer will leave line 20 before executing the PRINT statement. Different computers vary in the way they handle IF-THEN statements which occur on multiple-statement lines. In Microsoft BASIC, the IF-THEN will only be executed when the IF condition is true. North Star BASIC will execute the next statement on the line after an IF-THEN statement even if the condition is not met. Most computers will not accept DATA statements on multiple-statement lines. Some computers use a back-slash (\) instead of a colon to write more than one statement on a line. the DEC-10 computer uses the colon as the first character of the image line to be used with a PRINT USING statement. For instance, 40: #,#,###,## is used before PRINT USING 40,14000 to format 14000.

See: GOTO, IF-GOTO, ON-GOTO, IF-THEN, IMAGE, PRINT USING

() (parentheses)   (ANSI) To specify the order in which math operations are performed. Those operations in parentheses are performed first. If the operations in parentheses are contained in other operations in parentheses, the computer selects the innermost parentheses and does the operation enclosed there first. When two or more operations in parentheses occur in sequence, the one to the left is performed first.

<= (less than or equal to sign)   (ANSI) Used as a relational operator with the IF-THEN statements to find those values which are less than or equal to one another. For instance, IF X <= Y THEN 90 tells the computer to go to 90 if the X value is less than or equal to the Y value. Most computers will permit the <= sign to compare the ASCII codes of strings. However, some computers will only compare a limited number of characters in each string. Some computers use the =< or ≤ signs instead of <=.

See: EQ, GE, GT, IF-THEN, LE, LT, NE, <, =, > =, <>, $

>= (greater than or equal to sign)   (ANSI) Used as a relational operator to compare two numbers or numeric values to find those which are greater than or equal to another. For instance, IF X>=Y THEN 100 tells the computer to go to 100 if the X value is greater than or equal to the Y value. Most computers allow the >= sign to compare the ASCII codes of strings. However, some computers will only compare a limited number of characters in each string. Some computers use the => or ≥ signs instead of >=.

See: EQ, GE, IF-THEN, LE, LT, NE

& (ampersand)   Used by some computers to add or concatenate two strings together. The concatenated strings are then stored in one string. Some computers, including the DEC-10, use the ampersand to indicate that the PRINT USING statement has an inadequate field. For instance, PRINT USING "####";13579 will print &13579. A few computers use & to signal that a statement which is too long for one line will be finished on the next line. In MAXBASIC, however, the & is to signal that a statement is too long for one line and will be finished on the next. Some computers with MAT INPUT, including the DEC-10, use the & to signal that additional input will be entered on the next line. In MAXBASIC, however, the & is used to signal the end of a list of values being entered following a MAT INPUT statement. Some computers use & as a prefix indicating that a number represents a machine address or hexadecimal number. For a few computers, & is a substitute for PRINT. Applesoft BASIC does not make the amper-

sand available to the user. However, it is used internally by Applesoft. Take care not to use & with Applesoft BASIC or the computer may go out of control.
    See: MAT INPUT, PRINT, PRINT USING, $, +, "/"

ƛ (sol)   Used as a substitute for $ by the Swedish ABC 80 to form strings or to be part of string functions, i.e., CHR is substituted for CHR$ in the ABC 80.
    See: CHR$, LEFT$, MID$, RIGHT$, SPACE$, STRING$, NUM$

?   Used by Microsoft BASIC as a substitute for PRINT. However, PRINT is usually used when a program is listed. Some computers use ? with CLOAD to check a computer program stored on a cassette against a program stored in memory.
    See: CLOAD, INPUT, LIST, PRINT, #, !

\ (backslash)   Used by a few computers to permit more than one statement on a single program line. The backslash is used by some computers to specify how many characters of a string should be printed. PRINT USING "\− −\"; "STUDENTS" will print STUD as indicated by the sum of the two backslashes plus the space between.
    See: PRINT USING, :

**** (double asterisk)**   To compute the value of a base number to a specified power by some computers, including the HP 3000, DEC-10, DEC BASIC PLUS 2, and computers using MAXIBASIC. For instance, 5**3 stands for 5 cubed or 5^3. Microsoft BASIC uses the double asterisk with PRINT USING to indicate that the computer should fill in unused spaces with asterisks. For instance, for printing a check for $219.56 the PRINT USING statement would be PRINT USING "**###.##". The check would read $*****219.56.
    See: PRINT USING, ↑, !

+ (plus sign)   (ANSI) Used most commonly as a sign for arithmetic addition. Some computers use + with the IF-THEN statement as a logical OR. For instance, 10 IF (Y=6)+(X=6) THEN 100 means that if X=6 or IF Y=6 the condition is met and the computer goes to 100. The use of parentheses indicates that the + in this case is being used like OR. The plus sign is also used by many computers to add or concatenate strings. PRINT "U" + "P" adds the two and print UP.
    See: AND, PRINT USING, OR, *, $, &

− (minus sign)   (ANSI) Used most commonly as a minus sign to find the arithmetic difference between two numbers or numeric variables. PRINT X−Y will print the difference between X values and Y values. The minus sign is also used to change a number's sign. This process is called negation. For instance, PRINT −(6−10) causes the computer to subtract 10 from 6, giving −4 and to change the minus to a plus by negating the result of the problem in parentheses. The final result is 4. Some com-

puters use − with a PRINT USING statement to print a − after a negative number which is being printed.
    See: PRINT USING, +

$$X=((4÷2)+6)*8)=7$$
$$X=((2+6)*8)+7$$
$$X=(8*8)+7$$
$$X=64+7$$
$$X=71$$

Parentheses are used in Tiny BASIC with logical math operators to enclose two statements which are being compared, i.e., IF (X=10)*(Y=7) THEN 100. Parentheses also enclose array variables and elements in DIM statements. Characters to be manipulated by built-in computer functions are also put in parentheses, i.e., TR.(25).
    See: AND, DIM, OR, *, +

@ operator   Used by some computers, including the TRS-80 Level II, to identify the starting screen location for a print statement. @ values range from 0 to 1023 and must be followed by a comma. For instance, PRINT @842,"TEST5" prints TEST 5 at grid 842 on the screen. The North Star computer and others use @ to erase the last line displayed on a screen and to cause carriage return. The ExaTRON Stringy Floppy System uses @ as a prefix to its command.
    See: AT, DELETE, PRINT, PRINT AT

 # operator   To identify specified variables as double-precision numbers, i.e., A# identifies A as a double-precision variable. Numbers are accurate to seventeen digits (sixteen of which are printed). The # sign must be used with a number each time it appears in a program if its double-precision status is to be maintained. The # sign will temporarily override a DEFSNG or DEFINT statement within a program to make a variable double precision. Some computers, including Digital Group's Maxi-BASIC, use # as an abbreviation for the print statement. The # is used by most computers with the PRINT USING statement to format the position of digits and spaces in a printed number or numeric value. For instance, 100 PRINT USING "#,####.##":1426 will print 14,260.00. See PRINT USING for more information. A few computers use # as a substitute for the "not-equal-to" sign (<>). File-handling computers use # to indicate a disk or tape number or name for storing and loading data from external memory in statements such as INPUT #, READ #, or CLOSE #.
    See: DFFDBL, DEFINT, DEFSNG, PRINT, PRINT USING, READ, REM, !, "/", <>

/ (division sign)   (ANSI) Used like the ÷ sign to divide one number or numeric value into another. Some interpreters which use only integers use the / sign, but the quotient returned will always be an integer, i.e., PRINT 17/8 will yield 2.

*** (asterisk)**   (ANSI) Used most commonly in the same way as the X to multiply two numbers or numeric values.

PRINT X*10 will multiply X values by 10. The asterisk is also used by some computers to represent the logical math operator AND in IF-THEN statements. When the asterisk is used this way, the values to be ANDed are enclosed in parentheses. For example IF (X=6)*(X=$) THEN 200 means that if X is 6 and 4 is 4 then the IF condition is met and the computer goes to 200. The asterisk can also be used in formatting with a PRINT USING statement.

See: AND, PRINT USING, OR +., 88

= (equal sign) Used most commonly as an assignment operator to assign values to variables, i.e., X=7+2 assigns the value 9 to X. The equal sign can also be used as a relational operator to test whether two values are equal. Most computers also allow strings to be compared in the same manner to see if they are equal. For instance, IF X$="SAME" THEN 90 tells the computer to branch to 90 when the ASCII characters in X's are the same as those in "SAME". The equal sign can also be used to represent "greater than or equal to" (>=) and "less than or equal to" (<=). The length of the character strings which can be compared with =, >=, or <= depends on your interpreter.

See: EQ, GE, GT, LT, NE, <,>,<>,<=, >=, $

↑ (up-arrow) (ANSI) Used as an exponential notation to compute the value of a base number to a certain power. 4 ↑ 3 is the same as 4 cubed or 4^3. Some computers use a ∧ sign or ** instead of ↑ for exponentiation. The ↑ is also used in finding the root value of a number. 4 ↑ ½ is the same as the square root of 4 or $\sqrt{4}$. Four up-arrows can also be used with PRINT USING to print the exponential form of a number. For instance, PRINT USING "##,###"; 75,684 prints 75,684 E+03.

See: EXP, LOG, PRINT USING, **

< (less than sign) (ANSI) Used as a relational operator to compare two numbers or numeric values in IF-THEN statements to see if one is less than another. For instance, IF X<Y THEN 60 tells the computer to go to 60 if the X value is less than the Y value. Most computers allow strings to be compared with < by comparing their ASCII codes, but some computers will only compare a limited number of characters in each string. When combined with the = sign, < can be used to compare values to see if they are less than or equal to (<=) another.

See: EQ, GE, GT, IF-THEN, LE, LT, NE, >, <>, =, $, <=, >=

> (greater than sign) (ANSI) Used as a relational operator to compare two numbers or numerical values in IF-THEN statements to see if one value is less than another. For instance, if X>Y THEN 70 tells the computer to go to 70 if the X value is greater than the Y value. Most computers can compare strings with > by using the ASCII codes. However, some computers will only compare a limited number of characters in each string. The > sign is often used with the = sign to make the relational operator greater than or equal to (>=).

See:EQ, GE, GT, IF-THEN, LE, LT. NE, <, <>, = , <=, <.>=

<> (not equal sign) Used as relational operator to compare two numbers or numeric values and to find those which are not equal. For instance, IF X<>Y THEN 80 tells the computer to go to 80 if the X value does not equal the Y value. Most computers will permit the <> sign to compare the ASCII codes of two strings. However, some computers will only compare a limited number of characters in each string. Some computers use the X or ≠ signs instead of <>.

See: EQ, GE, GT, IF-THEN, LE, LT, NE, #, <, >, =, <=, >=, $

$ (dollar sign) Used following a variable to define it as a string variable. For instance: A$="SPEAK". The quotation marks are usually used to enclose those letters, numbers, or numeric values which are being declared string variables (except when an INPUT statement is used to assign the contents of a string variable). The numbers of characters which can be assigned to a string depends on your computer's interpreter. Some computers accept as many as 255 characters in a string. The Hewlett-Packard Computer, among others, requires a DIM statement to reserve memory space for each string. Intrinsic function or statement names cannot be used as string variables, i.e., "READ" would not be an acceptable string variable. Most computers which can handle strings allow string comparision by means of relational operators. In these operations, strings or string variables can be compared character by character. The strings to be compared to a string variable must be enclosed in quotes. Some computers, including the Apple II, use $ to identify a machine address or a hexadecimal number. The Acorn uses $ before a string variable instead of after, i.e., $A identifies A as a string variable.

See: CHR$, CLEAR, DATA, DEFSTR, DIM, FRE, INKEY, LEFT$, LEN, LET, MID$, READ, RIGHT$, STR$, STRING$, TEXT, ☒ , &

! operator To identify a variable as a single-precision number. Single-precision numbers are accurate to seven places (six of which are printed). The ! operator is used to return numbers to their usual single-precision status after they have been defined as double-precision numbers by DEFDBL or #. Microsoft BASIC and others use the ! with a PRINT USING statement to print only the first character on the left in a string. For instance, PRINT USING "!"; "PASSED" prints the letter P. North Star BASIC uses ! as an abbreviation for PRINT. COMPUMAX BASIC uses ! as a substitute for REM.

See: CDBI, CINT, CSNG, DEFDBL, DEFINT, DEFSING, PRINT, PRINT USING, #, "/"

% operator Used in Microsoft BASIC to define variables as integers. After the % is placed after the variable, it can only store integers. Some computers use % with a PRINT USING statement to specify how many characters of a string should be printed. PRINT USING "%....%"; "RESULTS" will cause six characters starting from the left to be printed, i.e., "RESULT". The number of characters is specified by the two % places plus the number of spaces between. Some computers print % to signify that a number is too big for its specified field. For instance, PRINT USING "##.#"; 732.2 will print %732.2.

See: CDBL, CINT, CSNG, DEFDBL, DEFINT, DEFSNG, FORMAT, IMAGE, INT, FORMAT, PRINT USING, !, &, #, \

MBASIC 86

Microsoft BASIC 86 is an extended version of Microsoft BASIC 80. MBASIC 80 was written for 8-bit processors, while MBASIC 86 is an extension of MBASIC 80 for 16-bit processors. MBASIC 86 is an interpreted BASIC, meaning that each line of code is interpreted by the computer before it is executed. However, a compiler is available for MBASIC 86. The compiler takes the source code written in MBASIC 86 and creates object code or machine language from it. The benefit is that compiled code runs considerably faster than interpreted code. A drawback to using a compiler is that the object code created occupies considerably more disk space than the source code from which it was created.

MBASIC 86 does not contain graphics commands, nor does it contain commands which utilize function keys on computers. However, there are two popular dialects of MBASIC which add these commands. One is ABASIC written for the IBM PC and the IBM clones, and the other is ZBASIC written for the Zenith Z-100.

In the listing of key words which follows, almost all commands can be used in the command mode (i.e., without line numbers) or in execution mode (i.e., as statements in the body of a program).

MBASIC GLOSSARY

The following glossary represents the most recent implementation of MBASIC 86. This dialect is immediately commmpatible with all MS-DOS machines.

ABS   Gives the absolute value of x.
   ABS(x)

AND   The boolean operator for the conjunction. If A>B AND C>D THEN . . .
   AND

ASC   Gives the ASCII code of the first character of the string M$.
   ASC(M$)

ATN   Gives the Arctangent of x in radians.
   ATN(x)

AUTO   Sets automatic line numbering beginning with line x and incrementing by y units.
   AUTO x,y

CALL   Calls an assembly language subroutine.

CDBL   Converts x to double precision.
   CDBL(x)

CHAIN   Calls a program from a storage device and passes variables to it from the program presently in memory.

**CHR$**   PRINT CHR$(n) prints the character whose ASCII value is n. Example: PRINT CHR$(65) will display A.
   CHR$(n)

CINT   Rounds x to the nearest integer.
   CINT(x)

CLOAD   Loads file "f" from cassette tape.
   CLOAD f

CLOAD ?   Verifies file "f" on casette tape by comparing it with the file in memory.
   CLOAD ?f

CLOAD *   Loads a numeric array "n" from cassette tape.
   CLOAD* n

CLOSE   Closes all open files.

CLS   Erases the screen.

COMMON   Passes variables A, B, and C to a chained program. Must be used with the CHAIN command.
   COMMON A, B, C

CONT   Continues program execution after Ctrl-C has been typed or a STOP or END statement has been encountered.

COS   Gives the Cosine of x in radians.
   COS(x)

CSAVE   Saves the program in memory to cassette tape using the first letter of X$ as the file name.
   CSAVE X$

CSAVE *   Saves the value of numeric array "n" on cassette tape.
   CSAVE* n

CSNG   Converts n to a single-precision number.
   CSNG(n)

CVD   Converts N$ to a double-precision number. N$ must consist of 8 bytes.
   CVD(N$)

CVI   Converts N$ to a single-precision number. N$ must consist of 4 bytes.
   CVI(N)$

CVS   Converts N$ to an integer. N$ must consist of 2 bytes.
   CVS(N)$

DATA   Stores numeric and/or string constants used by READ statements.

DEF FN   Defines the function X.
   DEF FN X

DEFDBL   Defines variables beginning with the letters C-E as double-precision.
   DEFDBL C-E

DEFINT   Defines variables beginning with the letters C-E as integer variables.
   DEFINT C-E

DEFSNG   Defines variables beginning with the letters C-E as single-precision.
   DEFSNG C-E

DEFSTR   Defines variables beginning with the letters C-E as string variables.
   DEFSTR C-E

DEF USR   Specifies starting address of an assembly language subroutine. Example: DEF USR 2=2000 assigns a starting address of 2000 (decimal) user-defined function number 2. (n must be between 0 and 9.)
   DEF USR n

DELETE   Deletes line numbers m through n.
   DELETE m-n

DIM   Specifies that the subscripted variable A will have no more than n+1 values.
   DIM A(n)

EDIT   Displays line n for editing.
   EDIT n

END   Stops program execution, closes all files, and returns to command mode.

EOF   Gives a value of −1 if the end of a file (sequential or random access) has been encountered.

ERASE   Eliminates arrays A and B. Used to clear memory space.
   ERASE A.B

ERL   N=ERL assigns the line number at which an error occurred to the variable N.
   ERL

ERR   X=ERR assigns error code of an encountered error to the variable X.
   ERR

ERROR   Displays the error message for error code x.
   ERROR x

EXP   Gives the value of e to the x power.
   EXP(x)

FIELD   Gets data out of a random buffer after a GET and before a PUT statement has been executed.

FILES   Displays the disk directory.

FIX   Gives the integer value of n.
   FIX(n)

FOR..NEXT   Creates a loop for repetitive execution. Example: FOR J=1 TO 20: PRINT J:NEXT J will print numbers from 1 to 20.

FRE   Gives the number of bytes of memory available in RAM.
   FRE(0)

GET   Reads a record from random disk file number f into a buffer.
   GET #f

GOSUB   Program execution branches to subroutine located at line number n.
   GOSUB n

GOTO   Program execution jumps to line number n.
   GOTO n

HEX   N$ gives the hexadecimal value of the decimal value of .A
   N$=HEX$(A)

IF C,THEN D,ELSE E   If condition C is true, program execution is transferred to condition D. If C is false, execution is transferred to condition E. D and E may be either statements or line numbers. Example: 100 IF A>=B THEN PRINT A ELSE 200. This will print the value of A if A is greater than or equal to B. If A is less than B, program execution will jump unconditionally to line 200.

**INKEY$**   A$ is a character read from the keyboard.
   A$=INKEY$

INP   Gives the byte read from port N.
   INP (N)

INPUT   Allows input from the keyboard during program execution. In the format INPUT "message", a message is printed prompting the user how to respond.

INPUT# n,A$,B$ Reads data item from file number n, and assigns the first data item to variable A$ and the next data item to variable B$.

**INPUT$** Gives a string of n characters from file #x. INPUT$ n gives the first n characters typed in from the keyboard.
   INPUT$n,#x

INSTR Gives the starting position of string B$ in the string A$. If A$="HELLO" and B$="EL" then IN-STR A$,B$ = 2.
   INSTR A$,B$

INT Gives the largest integer less than or equal to X.
   INT (X)

KILL Deletes file named "abcd" from disk.
   KILL abcd

**LEFT$** Gives a string consisting of the leftmost n characters of A$.
   LEFT$(A$,n)

LEN Gives the number of characters in the string A$.
   LEN (A$)

LET Used to assign a value to a variable. Example: LET A=7. LET is an optional command. Example: A=7 gives the same program instruction as LET A=7.

LINE INPUT Used to input an entire line of up to 255 characters to a string variable. String input is terminated when a RETURN is encountered.
   LINE INPUT A$

LINE INPUT# Same as LINE INPUT except it's used to read an entire line (up to 255 characters) from a sequential file. Example: LINE INPUT #1, A$ reads a string from file 1 into variable A$.

LIST Displays the entire program presently in memory. LIST a-b lists only the numbers a-b.

LLIST Same as LIST except program is displayed via the printer.

LOAD Loads file "abcd" from disk into memory.
   LOAD abcd

LOC Gives the record number just read from random access file number n, or just written from a GET or PUT command.
   LOC n

LOF Gives the length of file number n in bytes.
   LOF n

LOG Gives the natural logarithm of x.
   LOG(x)

LPOS Gives the present position of the line printer print head within the print buffer. The variable x is a dummy argument.
   LPOS(x)

LPRINT Prints succeeding characters via the line printer.

LPRINT USING Same as PRINT USING except display is via line printer.

LSET Moves data from memory to a random file buffer and stores A$ in the string B$. Characters are left justified, and if necessary, spaces are used as pad characters.
   LSET A$=B$

MERGE Merges disk file "abcd" into memory. If line numbers are the same in "abcd" as in the program in memory, the lines from "abcd" will replace the lines in memory.
   MERGE abcd

**MID$** Gives a substring y characters in length from string A$ starting with the xth character.
   MID$(A$,x,y)

MKD$ Converts numerical expression X to a string. X must be a double-precision number.
   MKD$(X)

**MKI$** Same as MKD$ except X must be an integer expression.
   MKI$(X)

**MKS$** Same as MKD$ except X must be a single-precision number.
   MKS$(X)

MOD Gives the value of the number n in modulo x. Example: 7MOD4 would give the number 3.
   nMODx

NAME Changes the name of disk file "ab" to "cd".
   NAME ab AS cd

NEW Deletes program from memory and clears all variables.

NEXT See FOR..NEXT

NULL Prints x null characters at the end of each line where x must be between 0 and 255.
   NULL x

**OCT$** Gives a string representing the octal value of decimal number X. Example: OCT$(10) would give 12.

ON ERROR GO TO n Transfers program execution to line number n when an error is encountered.

ON x GOSUB a,b,c,d Transfers program execution to a subroutine starting at one of line numbers a, b, c, or d depending on whether the value of x is 1, 2, 3, or 4.

ON x GOTO a,b,c,d Same as ON x GOSUB.. except that program execution is transferred (unconditionally) to line number a, b, c, or d.

OPEN "M",n,"abcd" Opens a file called "abcd" on I/O unit 2. M must be enclosed in quotes and must be one of the following: O, I, R. Where O represents output to a sequential file, I represents input from a sequential file, and R represents either input or output to or from a random access file.

OPTION BASE n Establishes the minimum value of a subscript for an array variable. n must be 0 or 1. Default value is 0.

OR The boolean operator. The form is: IF A>B OR C>D THEN...

OUT Sends integer expression X to output port n.
OUT n,X

PEEK Gives the decimal contents from memory location n.
PEEK (n)

POKE Places decimal expression "a" into memory location "n".
POKE n,a

POS Gives the current horizontal cursor position. N is a dummy argument.
POS (N)

PRINT Prints the variables A and B on the CRT. Also used to print literal expressions. Example: PRINT "Hello". The punctuation separating variables or literals in a PRINT statement determines the spacing between the items printed. A semicolon results in items printing next to one another, not separated by spaces, while a comma results in items being printed in separate screen fields.
PRINT A:B

PRINT USING, E E specifies the format to be used in printing. The formats available are:

> ! Results in only the first character of the string being printed.
> "\n\" Results in 2+n characters from the string being printed. Some number of spaces (or none) must be placed between the two backslash figures. If no spaces are placed, then 2 characters will be printed. If one space is placed between the backslash figures, then 3 characters will be printed; etc.
> & Results in the string being printed exactly as is.
> # For numeric fields, specifies that a digit is to be

printed in each place. If the number has fewer digits than are specified, the number will be right justified.
> . A decimal point may be placed at any point in the field. Example: PRINT USING"###.##";103,2.8,5.895 results in output of 103   2.80   5.89.
> + Placed either at the beginning (or end) of the format string, results in the sign of the number being printed at the beginning (or end) of the number. Example: PRINT USING "+##"; 23 results in output of +23, while PRINT USING"##+";23 results in output of 23+.
> — Placed at the end of the format field, results in negative numbers being printed with a trailing —.
> ** Results in leading spaces in the numeric field being filled with asterisks. Also counts as 2 print positions.
> $$ Results in a dollar sign being printed at the left of the output. Also counts as 2 print positions, one of which is the dollar sign.
> **$ Results in a combination of the preceding two conditions. Example: PRINT USING "**$.##"; 2.34 results in an output of ***$2.34.
> , Placed to the left of the decimal point, the comma results in the printing of a comma to the left of every third digit to the left of the decimal point. Example: PRINT USING "####,.#"; 1557.82 results in output of 1,557.8.
> ^^^^ placed after the last digit position character to specify exponential format. The 4 carat symbols allow space for E+xx to be printed. Example: PRINT USING "###.##"^^^; 1557.82 results in output of 1.56+03.
> __ The underline character results in the next character being printed as a literal. Example: PRINT USING "__!####.##"; 1557.82 results in output of !1557.82.

NOTE: In any of the above formats, if the number to be printed is larger than the specified field, a percent sign is printed in front of the number. Example: PRINT USING"##.##"; 398.743 results in output of %398.74.

PRINT #n,USING E; F Same as PRINT USING statement except that output is sent to disk file number "n". E represents any of the PRINT USING formats. F represents any combination of literals or variables which will have the format(s) specified.

RANDOMIZE Reseeds the random number generator. N must be in the range −32768 to 32767.

READ Reads data placed in data statements. Assigns the first data item to variable A, the second to B, and the third to C. A DATA statement must be used in conjunction with READ.
READ A,B,C

REM The REMark statement is used to place nonexecutable comments in a program. Example: 10 PRINT C$; S$: REM City and State.

RENUM Renumbers a program where y is the line number in the existing program where renumbering will begin, x is the new line number to replace y, and z is the increment. Example: RENUM 100,30,20 will start at line number 30 of the old program, change it to line number

100, and number consecutively in increments of 20.
RENUM x,y,z

RESET   Closes all disk files and writes the directory to the disk. RESET should always be used before removing a disk from the drive.

RESTORE   Allows DATA statements to be reread.

RESUME   Continues program execution after an error trapping procedure has been executed. Program execution is continued at at the statement which caused the error.

RESUME 0   Same as RESUME.

RESUME NEXT   Same as RESUME except that program execution is resumed at the statement following the one which caused the error.

RESUME n   Same as RESUME except that program execution is resumed at the line number "n".

**RIGHT$**   Gives the rightmost n characters of A$. Example: If A$="ABCDEF" then RIGHT$(A$,2) gives EF.
RIGHT$(A$,n)

RND   Gives a random number between 0 and 1. For any value of X, the same random number sequence is generated. Also see RANDOMIZE.
RND(X)

RSET   Same as LSET except characters are right justified with characters truncated from the left if necessary.
RSET A$=B$

RUN   Executes the program currently in memory.

RUN n   Same as RUN except execution begins at line number n.

SAVE   The program named "f" is saved on the disk in compressed binary format.
SAVE f

SAVE f,A   Same as SAVE except the program is saved in ASCII format.

SAVE f,P   Same as SAVE except the program is saved in encoded binary format. In this format, the program can be LOADed or RUN, but cannot be LISTed or EDITed.

SGN   Gives the sign of the value of X. If X>0 then SGN(X) gives 1. If X=0 then SGN(X) gives 0. If X<0 then SGN(X) gives −1.

SIN   Gives the SIN of angle X in radian measure.
SIN(X)

SPACES$ Gives a string of spaces of length n. n must be between 0 and 255.
SPACES$(n)

SPC   Same as SPACES$ except must be used with either a PRINT or a LPRINT statement.
SPC(n)

SQR   Gives the square root of n. If n<0 an error message will be displayed.
SQR(n)

STEP   Optionally used with FOR..NEXT statements. Example: FOR R=1 TO 100 STEP 5: PRINT R:NEXT will produce the output 1 6 11 16...96
STEP n

STOP   Halts program execution and returns to the command mode.

STR$ Converts N to string format. Example:

```
100 N=5
120 B$="The number is "+STR$(N)
140 PRINT B$
```

The above will produce the output "The number is 5".

STRING$**   Gives a string of length n whose characters each have the ASCII value t. Example: STRING$(4,42) gives output **.
STRING$ (n,t)

STRING$(n,A$)   Same as above except the ASCII value used is the first character of the string A$. In the above example, if A$="*HELLO", then STRING$ (4,A$) would produce the same output.

SWAP   Exchanges the contents of variables A$ and B$. Example: If A$="Hello" and B$="Goodbye" then SWAP A$,B$ results in A$="Goodbye" and B$="Hello". Note: any types of variables may be SWAPped, but they must be of the same type.
SWAP A$,B$

SYSTEM   Exits BASIC and returns to the system.

TAB   Begins printing at horizontal position n. TAB must be used in a PRINT or LPRINT statement.
TAB(n)

TAN   Gives the Tangent of angle X in radian measure.
TAN(X)

TROFF   Turns trace mode off.

TRON Turns trace mode on. This causes each line executed to be displayed as a program is executed. It is a debugging tool.

USR Calls a user-defined subroutine defined with the integer n and containing the argument A.
USR n,(A)

VAL Gives the numerical value of the string Z$.
VAL(Z$)

VARPTR Gives the address of the first byte of data identified by the variable name X.
VARPTR X

VARPTR #n Gives the address of the first byte of data from the disk I/O buffer identified by the sequential file n.

WAIT Program execution is suspended while port n is monitored for data input containing a specific bit pattern. The data is combined with "b" via the boolean exclusive OR and then combined with "a" via the boolean AND. If a non-zero value is obtained, program execution continues. If a zero value is obtained, the program loops back and continues reading the port. Note: an infinite loop is possible in which case the computer will have to be manually re-booted.
WAIT n,a,b

WHILE X..WEND Used in loops to repeat the loop as long as X is true. When X is false, execution continues with the statement following the WEND statement. This is particularly useful when doing sorts. Example:

```
100  S=1:REM SIGNAL FOR WHILE TEST
120  WHILE S
140  S=0:REM SET FOR NO REPEAT
160  FOR I = 1 TO 9
180  IF D$(I)>D$(I+1) THEN SWAP D$(I),D$
     (I+1):S=1
200  NEXT I
220  WEND
```

The WEND statement will only be encountered when no swapping has occurred, i.e., when all the D$(I)s are in the correct order.

WIDTH LPRINT n Sets the width of the printed line to n for the line printer.

WRITE Prints A$, B, and C separated by a comma. Literals and strings are printed with quotation marks. Example:

```
100  A$="HELLO":B=9:C=82
120  WRITE A$,B,C
```

The output would be: "HELLO", 9, 82
WRITE A$,B,C

WRITE #n Same as WRITE; output goes to file n.

ZBASIC

ZBASIC is a specific implementation of Microsoft BASIC for the Zenith 100 and 150. The dialect differs from the standard PC implementation of Microsoft BASIC only in those features that are specific to the Zenith such as the enhanced screen graphics and sound applications that require their own specific addresses.

ZBASIC GLOSSARY

The following glossary represents the most recent implementation of MBASIC 86 with extensions specifically for the Z100 and Z150.

ABS   Gives the absolute value of x.
   ABS(x)

AND   The boolean operator for conjunction. IF A>B AND C>D THEN...
   AND

ASC   Gives the ASCII code of the first character of the string M$.
   ASC(M$)

ATN   Gives the Arctangent of x in radians.
   ATN(x)

AUTO   Sets automatic line numbering beginning with line x and incrementing by y units.
   AUTO x,y

BEEP   Sounds speaker at 800 Hz for .25 second. Same as PRINT CHR$(7).

BLOAD   Loads the binary file "f" into memory.
   BLOAD f

BSAVE   Saves the binary file "f" to a specific device.
   BSAVE f

CALL   Calls an assembly language subroutine.

CDBL   Converts x to double-precision.
   CDBL (x)

CHAIN   Calls a program from a storage device and passes variables to it from the program presently in memory.

**CHR$**   PRINT CHR$(n) prints the character whose ASCII value is n. Example: PRINT CHR$(65) will display A.
   CHR$(n)

CINT   Rounds x to the nearest integer.
   CINT(x)

CIRCLE   Draws an ellipse with center x,y and radius r.
   CIRCLE X,Y,R

CLEAR   Sets all numeric values to 0 and all string variables to null.

CLOSE   Closes all open files.

CLS   Erases the screen.

COLOR   Sets the foreground color to a and the background color to b.
   COLOR a,b

COMMON   Passes variables A, B, and C to a chained program. Must be used with the CHAIN command.
   COMMON A,B,C

CONT   Continues program execution after Ctrl-C has been typed or a STOP or END statement has been encountered.

COS   Gives the Cosine of x in radians.
   COS(x)

CSNG   Converts n to a single-precision number.
   CSNG(n)

CSRLIN   Gives the current row in which the cursor is located. Example: X=CSRLIN will store 10 in the variable X (if the cursor is in the tenth horizontal position).
   CSRLIN

CVD   Converts N$ to a double-precision number. N$ must consist of 8 bytes.
   CVD(N$)

CVI   Converts N$ to a single-precision number. N$ must consist of 4 bytes.
   CVI(N$)

CVS   Converts N$ to an integer. N$ must consist of 2 bytes.
   CVS(N$)

DATA   Stores numeric and/or string constants used by READ statements.

**DATE$**   Used to assign or retrieve the current date. Example: DATE$="05-10-84" for May 10, 1984.
   DATE$

DEFDBL   Defines variables beginning with the letters C-E as double-precision.
   DEFDBL C-C

DEF FN   Defines the function X.
   DEF FN X

DEFINT   Defines variables beginning with the letters C-E as integer variables.
DEFINT C-E

DEFSEG   Assigns the address "n" to be used by a BLOAD, BSAVE, PEEK, POKE, CALL, OR user-defined function.
DEFSEG n

DEFSNG   Defines variables beginning with the letters C-E as single-precision.
DEFSNG C-E

DEFSTR   Defines variables beginning with the letters C-E as string variables.
DEFSTR C-E

DEF USR   Specifies starting address of an assembly language subroutine. Example: DEF USR 2=2000 assigns a starting address of 2000 (decimal) user-defined function number 2. (n must be between 0 and 9.)
DEF USR n

DELETE   Deletes line numbers m through n.
DELETE m-n

DIM   Specifies that the subscripted variable A will have no more than n+1 values.
DIM A(n)

DRAW   Enters Graphic Macro Language function.

EDIT   Displays line n for editing.
EDIT n

END   Stops program execution, closes all files, and returns to command mode.

EOF   Gives a value of -1 if the end of a file (sequential or random access) has been encountered.

ERASE   Eliminates arrays A and B. Used to clear memory space.
ERASE A,B

ERL   N=ERL assigns the line number at which an error occurred to the variable N.
ERL

ERR   X=ERR assigns error code of an encountered error to the variable X.
ERR

ERROR   Displays the error message for error code x.
ERROR x

EXP   Gives the value of e to the x power.
EXP(x)

FIELD   Gets data out of a random buffer after a GET and before a PUT statement has been executed.

FILES   Displays the disk directory.

FIX   Gives the integer value of n.
FIX (n)

FOR..NEXT   Creates a loop for repetitive execution. Example: FOR J=1 TO 20: PRINT J: NEXT J will print numbers from 1 to 20.

FRE   Gives the number of bytes of memory available in RAM.
FRE(0)

GET   Reads a record from random disk file Number f into a buffer.
GET #f

GET   Transfers screen image bounded by coordinates (x,y) and (a,b) into an array.
GET(x,y)−(z,b)

GOSUB   Program execution branches to subroutine located at line number n.
GOSUB n

GOTO   Program execution jumps to line number n.
GOTO n

HEX   N$ gives the hexadecimal value of the decimal value of .A
N$=HEX$(A)

IF C,THEN D,ELSE E   If condition C is true, program execution is transferred to condition D. If C is false, execution is transferred to condition E. D and E may be either statements or line numbers. Example: 100 IF A>=B THEN PRINT A ELSE 200. This will print the value of A if A is greater than or equal to B. If A is less than B, program execution will jump unconditionally to line 200.

**INKEY$**   A$ is a character read from the keyboard.
A$=INKEY$

INP   Gives the byte read from port N.
INP (N)

INPUT   Allows input from the keyboard during program execution. In the format INPUT "message", a message is printed prompting the user how to respond.

INPUT # n,A$,B$ Reads data item from file number n, and assigns the first data item to variable A$ and the next data item to variable B$.

**INPUT$**   Gives a string of n characters from file #x. INPUT$ n gives the first n characters typed in from the keyboard.
   INPUT$n,#x

INSTR   Gives the starting position of string B$ in the string A$. If A$="HELLO" and B$="EL" then IN-STR A$,B$ = 2.
   INSTR A$,B$

INT   Gives the largest integer less than or equal to X.
   INT (X)

KEY   Programs any of the 12 function keys with any string expression. N must be in range 1-12. Example: KEY 5, "FILES"+CHR$(13).
   KEY N,A$

KEY OFF   Turns off display of function keys.

KEY ON   Turns on display of function keys.

KILL   Deletes file named "abcd" from disk.
   KILL a,b,c,d

**LEFT$**   Gives a string consisting of the leftmost n characters of A$.
   LEFT$(A$,n)

LEN   Gives the number of characters in the string A$. LET Assigns a value to a variable. Example: LET A=7. LET is an optional command. Example: A=7 gives the same program instruction as LET A=7.
   LEN(A$)

LINE (a,b)-(c,d)   Draws a line from coordinates (a,b) to coordinates (c,d).

LINE INPUT   Inputs an entire line of up to 255 characters to a string variable. String input is terminated when a RETURN is encountered.
   LINE INPUT A$

LINE INPUT #   Same as LINE INPUT except it's used to read an entire line (up to 255 characters) from a sequential file. Example: LINE INPUT #1, A$ reads a string from file 1 into variable A$.

LIST   Displays the entire program presently in memory. LIST a-b lists only line numbers a-b.

LLIST   Same as LIST except program is displayed via the printer.

LOAD   Loads file "abcd" from disk into memory.
   LOAD abcd

LOC   Gives the record number just read from random access file number n, or just written from a GET or PUT command.
   LOC n

LOCATE   Moves the cursor to row number a and column number b. "a" must be 1-25, and "b" 1-40. "c" determines whether the cursor is visible: 0 indicates not visible; non-zero indicates visible.
   LOCATE a,b,c

LOF   Gives the length of file number n in bytes.
   LOF n

LOG   Gives the natural logarithm of x.
   LOG(x)

LPOS   Gives the present position of the line printer print head within the print buffer. The x is a dummy argument.
   LPOS (x)

LPRINT   Prints succeeding characters via the line printer.

LPRINT USING   Same as PRINT USING except display is via line printer.

LSET LSET   Moves data from memory to a random file buffer and stores A$ in the string B$. Characters are left justified, and if necessary, spaces are used as pad characters.
   LSET A$=B$

MERGE   Merges disk file "abcd" into memory. If line numbers are the same in "abcd" as in the program in memory, the lines from "abcd" will replace the lines in memory.
   MERGE abcd

**MID$**   Gives a substring y characters in length from string A$ starting with the xth character.
   MID$(A$,x,y)

MKD$ Converts numerical expression X to a string. X must be a double-precision number.
   MKD$(X)

**MKI$**   Same as MKD$ except X must be an integer expression.
   MKI$(X)

**MKS$**   Same as MKD$ except X must be a single-precision number.
   MKS$(X)

MOD   Gives the value of the number n in modulo x. Example: 7MOD4 would give the number 3.
   nMODx

NAME   Changes the name of disk file "ab" to "cd".
   NAME ab AS cd

NEXT   See FOR..NEXT.

NEW Deletes program from memory and clears all variables.

NULL Prints x null characters at the end of each line. X must be between 0 and 255.
NULL x

**OCT$** Gives a string representing the octal value of decimal number X. Example: OCT$(10) would give 12.
OCT$(X)

ON ERROR GO TO n Transfers program execution to line number n when an error is encountered.

ON x GOSUB a,b,c,d Transfers program execution to a subroutine starting at one of line numbers a, b, c, or d depending on whether the value of x is 1, 2, 3, or 4.

ON x GOTO a,b,c,d Same as ON x GOSUB.. except that program execution is transferred (unconditionally) to line number a, b, c, or d.

OPEN"M",n,"abcd" Opens a file called "abcd" on I/O unit 2. M must be enclosed in quotes and must be one of the following: O, I, R. Where O represents output to a sequential file, I represents input from a sequential file, and R represents either input or output to or from a random access file.

OPTION BASE n Establishes the minimum value of a subscript for an array variable. n must be 0 or 1. Default value is 0.

OR The boolean operator, which states IF A>B OR C>D THEN...

OUT Sends integer expression X to output port n.
OUT n,X

PAINT (x,y),a,b Fills graphics figure beginning with coordinates (x,y). Border is filled with color b and figure is filled with color a. Process must begin on a non-border point or PAINT will have no effect.

PEEK Gives the decimal contents from memory location n.
PEEK (n)

POINT Gives the color code of screen location (x,y).
POINT (x,y)

POKE Places decimal expression "a" into memory location "n".
POKE n,a

POS Gives the current horizontal cursor position. N is a dummy argument.
POS (N)

PRESET (x,y),n Sets point (x,y) to color n.

PRINT Prints the variables A and B on the CRT. Also used to print literal expressions. Example: PRINT "Hello". The punctuation separating variables or literals in a PRINT statement determines the spacing between the items printed. A semicolon results in items printing next to one another not separated by spaces, while a comma results in items being printed into separate and distinct screen fields.
PRINT A;B
PRINT "DATA"
PRINT A,B
PRINT N$
PRINT N$,A,B

PRINT USING, E E specifies the format to be used in printing. The formats available are:
> ! Results in only the first character of the string being printed.
> "\n\" Results in 2+n characters from the string being printed. Some number of spaces (or none) must be placed between the two backslash figures. If no spaces are placed, then 2 characters will be printed. If one space is placed between the backslash figures, then 3 characters will be printed; etc.
> & Results in the string being printed exactly as is.
> # For numeric fields, specifies that a digit is to be printed in each place. If the number has fewer digits than are specified, the number will be right justified.
> . A decimal point may be placed at any point in the field. Example: PRINT USING"###.##";103,2.8,5.865 results in output of 103 2.80 5.89.
> + Placed either at the beginning (or end) of the format string, results in the sign of the number being printed at the beginning (or end) of the number. Example: PRINT USING "+##"; 23 results in output of +23, while PRINT USING "##+";23 results in output of 23+.
> − Placed at the end of the format field, results in negative numbers being printed with a trailing −.
> ** Results in leading spaces in the numeric field being filled with asterisks. Also counts as 2 print positions.
> $$ Results in a dollar sign being printed at the left of the output. Also counts as 2 print positions, one of which is the dollar sign.
> **$ Results in a combination of the preceding two conditions. Example: PRINT USING "**$.##"; 2.36 results in output of ***$2.36.
> , Placed to the left of the decimal point, the comma results in the printing of a comma to the left of every third digit to the left of the decimal point. Example: PRINT USING "####,.#"; 1557.82 will result in an output of 1,557.8.
> ∧∧∧∧ Placed after the last digit position character to specify exponential format. The 4 carat symbols allow space for E+xx to be printed. Example: PRINT USING "###.##" ∧∧∧∧ ; 1557.82 will result in an output of 1.56+03.
> __ The underline character results in the next character being printed as a literal. Example: PRINT USING "__!####.##"; 1557.82 results in output of !1557.82.
NOTE: In any of the above formats, if the number to be printed is larger than the specified field, a per-

cent sign is printed in front of the number. Example: PRINT USING "##.##"; 398.743 results in output of %398.74.

PRINT #n,USING E; F   Same as PRINT USING statement except that output is sent to disk file number "n". E represents any of the PRINT USING formats. F represents any combination of literals or variables which will have the format(s) specified.

PSET (x,y),n   Turns on the point at coordinates (x,y) in color n.

PUT   Writes record number "r" to random access disk file "n".
   PUT #n,r

RANDOMIZE   Reseeds the random number generator. N must be in the range −32768 to 32767.
   RANDOMIZE N

READ   Reads data placed in data statements. Assigns the first data item to variable A, the second to B, and the third to C. A DATA statement must be used in conjunction with READ.
   READ A,B,C

REM   The REMark statement is used to place non-executable comments in a program. For example: 10 PRINT C$; S$:REM City and State.

RENUM   Renumbers a program where y is the line number in the existing program where renumbering will begin, x is the new line number to replace y, and z is the increment. Example: RENUM 100,30,20 will start at line number 30 of the old program, change it to line number 100, and number consecutively in increments of 20.
   RENUM x,y,z

RESET   Closes all disk files and writes the directory to the disk. RESET should always be used before removing a disk from the drive.

RESTORE   Allows DATA statements to be reread.

RESUME   Continues program execution after an error trapping procedure has been executed. Program execution is continued at at the statement which caused the error.

RESUME 0   Same as RESUME.

RESUME NEXT   Same as RESUME except that program execution is resumed at the statement following the one which caused the error.

RESUME n   Same as RESUME except that program execution is resumed at the line number "n".

**RIGHT$**   Gives the rightmost n characters of A$. Example: If A$="ABCDEF" then RIGHT$(A$,2) gives EF.
   RIGHT$(A$,n)

RND   Gives a random number between 0 and 1. For any value of X, the same random number sequence is generated. Also see RANDOMIZE.
   RND (X)

RSET   Same as LSET except characters are right justified with characters truncated from the left if necessary.
   RSET A$=B$

RUN   Executes the program currently in memory.

RUN n   Same as RUN except execution begins at line number n.

SAVE   The program named "f" is saved on the disk in compressed binary format.
   SAVE f

SAVE f,A   Same as SAVE except the program is saved in ASCII format.

SAVE f,P   Same as SAVE except the program is saved in encoded binary format. In this format, the program can be LOADed or RUN, but cannot be LISTed or EDITed.

SCREEN g,r   In a format in which no variable is used, the screen command sets the graphics and/or inverse video mode. The modes are as follows: g: 0 disables graphics mode, 1 enables graphics mode, and any other number causes an error. R: 0 sets normal screen display, 1 sets inverse video, and any other number causes an error. Example: 100 SCREEN 1,0 sets the graphic mode on and produces normal screen display.

SCREEN (x,y),z   If the z value is 0 or not indicated, then the ASCII value of the character at screen position (x,y) is obtained. If the value of z is non-zero, then the color code at screen position (x,y) is obtained. Example: N=SCREEN (12,8) will store 68 in the variable N if the character at screen position (12,8) is the letter D. (The ASCII value of D is 68). N=SCREEN (12,8),9 will store 4 in the variable N if the color at screen position (12,8) is red.

SGN   Gives the sign of the value of X. If X>0 then SGN(X) gives 1. If X=0 then SGN(X) gives 0. If X<0 then SGN(X) gives −1.
   SGN(X)

SIN   Gives the SIN of angle X in radian measure.
   SIN(X)

SPACES\$ Gives a string of spaces of length n. n must be between 0 and 255.
SPACES\$(n)

SPC Same as SPACES\$ except must be used with either a PRINT or a LPRINT statement.
SPC(n)

SQR Gives the square root of n. If n<0 an error message will be displayed.
SQR(n)

STEP Optionally used with FOR..NEXT statements. Example: FOR R=1 TO 100 STEP 5: PRINT R:NEXT will produce the output 1 6 11 16...96.
STEP n

STOP Halts program execution and returns to the command mode.

STR\$ Converts N to string format. Example:

```
100 N=5
120 B$="The number is "+STR$(N)
140 PRINT B$
```

The above will produce the output "The number is 5".
SRT\$(n)

STRING\$ Gives a string of length n whose characters each have the ASCII value t. Example: STRING\$(4,42) gives output ****.
STRING\$(n,t)

STRING\$(n,A\$) Same as above except the ASCII value used is the first character of the string A\$. Example: In the above example if A\$="*HELLO", then STRING\$(4,A\$) would produce the same output.

SWAP Exchanges the contents of variables A\$ and B\$. Example: If A\$="Hello" and B\$="Goodbye", then SWAP A\$,B\$ results in A\$="Goodbye" and B\$="Hello". Note: any types of variables may be SWAPped, but they must be of the same type.
SWAP A\$,B\$

SYSTEM Exits BASIC and returns to the system.

TAB Begins printing at horizontal position n. TAB must be used in a PRINT or LPRINT statement.
TAB (n)

TAN Gives the Tangent of angle X in radian measure.
TAN(X)

TIME\$ Sets or retrieves the current time. Example: PRINT TIME\$ will give 12:43:00. TIME\$="12:43: 00" will set the time at 12:43.

TROFF Turns trace mode off.

TRON Turns trace mode on. This causes each line executed to be displayed as a program is executed. It is a debugging tool.

USR Calls a user-defined subroutine defined with the integer n and containing the argument A.
USR n,(A)

VAL Gives the numerical value of the string Z\$.
VAL(Z\$)

VARPTR Gives the address of the first byte of data identified by the variable name X.
VARPTR X

VARPTR #n Gives the address of the first byte of data from the disk I/O buffer identified by the sequential file n.

WAIT Program execution is suspended while port n is monitored for data input containing a specific bit pattern. The data is combined with "b" via the boolean exclusive OR and then combined with "a" via the boolean AND. If a non-zero value is obtained, program execution continues. If a zero value is obtained, the program loops back and continues reading the port. Note: an infinite loop is possible in which case the computer will have to be manually re-booted.
WAIT n,a,b

WHILE X..WEND Used in loops to repeat the loop as long as X is true. When X is false, execution continues with the statement following the WEND statement. This is particularly useful when doing sorts. Example:

```
100 S=1:REM SIGNAL FOR WHILE TEST
120 WHILE S
140 S=0:REM SET FOR NO REPEAT
160 FOR I = 1 TO 9
180 IF D$(I)>D$(I+1) THEN SWAP
    D$(I),D$(I+1):S=1
200 NEXT I
220 WEND
```

The WEND statement will only be encountered when no swapping has occurred, i.e., when all the D\$(I)s are in the correct order.

WIDTH LPRINT n Sets the width of the printed line to n for the line printer.

WRITE Prints A\$, B, and C separated by a comma. Literals and strings are printed with quotation marks. Example:
```
100 A$="HELLO":B=9:C=82
120 WRITE A$,B,C
```
The output would be: "HELLO", 9, 82

WRITE #n Same as WRITE except output goes to file n.

Compiled BASIC

CBASIC is an implementation of BASIC that is gaining greater popularity among formal programmers because it is a more structured and disciplined form of the language. Essentially, CBASIC is a compiled version of BASIC that offers a compromise between the normal slow-running implementation of the language and the faster-running compiled languages. Compilers act as a mediating element between the high-level source code and the machine-level operating code. Compilers become translators, converting the more user-oriented high-level language to a machine-level intermediate code. The intermediate files are then executed by an interpreter.

Unlike its noncompiled sibling, CBASIC contains structured statements that are closer to Fortran in concept than they are to BASIC. These structures allow for parameter passing, local and global variables, and chaining between programs. CBASIC allows for a free use of commas in the program. Moreover, it does not require line numbers, so that the statement labels do not have to be sequential, and the interpreter, unlike regular MBASIC, does not reorder the lines on the basis of line numbers. Hence the program:

```
5 PRINT "THIS IS A PROGRAM"
1 PRINT "WITH NON SEQUENTIAL LINE
     NUMBERS"
0 GO TO 5
```

will not be reordered by the compiler. The compiler actually reads the numbers preceding statements not as numbers but as character strings. Therefore a statement label of 5.0 is distinct from 5 through the eyes of the CBASIC compiler, whereas through the eyes of the MBASIC interpreter 5.0 and 5 would be read as identical line numbers.

There are three principal data structures in CBASIC: strings, integers, and real numbers. These different structures are signaled by identifiers that are different for all three data types. The identifier for a string must end with a $, the identifier for an integer must end with a %, and the identifier that ends in neither $ or % is used to indicate a real number. For example, NAME$ is a string identifier, NUMBER% identifies an integer, and PAYROLL identifies a real number.

String constants must fit on a single line of code and be delimited by quotation marks. A string cannot contain control characters, but these can be embedded in string expressions or string functions. Number constants in CBASIC can be integers or real depending upon whether they contain an embedded decimal point, are in exponential notation, or range from -32768 to $+32767$. Numeric constants that do not contain an embedded decimal point and are not in exponential notation are integers. Integers can also be expressed as hexadecimal or binary constants. Real numbers contain

decimals and can be rewritten in exponential notation. Thus, -32000 is an integer; $1.5E+2$ is a real number.

Programming in CBASIC is a two-stage process. First, the actual code is keyed in as if it were a standard BASIC program. It is stored to disk as a .BAS file. Then the compiler is invoked by typing CBAS and the file name of the program. The compiler compiles the source code into an intermediate machine code and creates a file for it. Finally the program is run through the interpreter and executed. The creation of intermediate or .INT files on the source code disk can present disk storage problems, especially on older machines such as the H89 with hard sector floppy disks, but these can be managed by leaving enough space on the disk for storing the .INT intermediate code files for the interpreter.

CBASIC GLOSSARY

The following glossary represents the full implementation of CBASIC from Digital Research, to run under CP/M, Concurrent CP/M and CP/M 86.

ABS Returns the absolute value of an expression.
ABS (numeric expression).

ASC Returns the ASCII decimal value of the first character in the string.
1ASC (string expression).

ATN Returns the arc tangent of a numeric expression.
ATN (numeric expression)

CALL Links a machine language subroutine to the program. The statement actually calls a specific machine language address specified by the program.
CALL (numeric expression)

CHAIN Transfers control of the program to another program by calling a program from the storage device and passing the variables to it from the program currently in memory.
CHAIN (file name)

CHR$ Returns the character whose ASCII value is specified in the accompanying numeric expression.
CHR$ (numeric expression)

CLOSE Close opens files and releases the file number. The CLOSE statement also reallocates the buffer memory area used by the file for new information.
CLOSE(file number)

COMMAND$ Returns a string containing the parameters from the command line that started the program.
x$=COMMAND$

COMMON This statement specifies the variables that are shared by the main program and all programs CALLed with CHAIN statements. The COMMON statement must be used with a CHAIN command so that the variables can be passed between the CHAINed programs.

COMMON (variable, variable, variable)

CONCHAR% Stands for console character; the function reads one character from the keyboard or console device.

x%=CONCHAR%

CONSOLE This statement restores output to the console.

CONSOLE

CONSTAT% Returns the console status in terms of a boolean integer. That is, if the console status, which can either be ready or not ready, is ready, a −1 is returned. If the status is not ready, a 0 is returned.

x%=CONSTAT%

COS Returns the cosine of the numeric expression in radians.

COS (x)

CREATE This statement creates files on a selected disk drive. The statement must specify the length of the records in the created file as well as the number of sectors and the size of the record.

CREATE (file name) RECL (record length) AS (file number) BUFF (number of sectors) RECS (size of sector)

DATA This statement stores numeric and/or string constants used by the READ statements.

DATA (constant)

DEF Defines single and multiple statement functions.

DEF FN (function name)

DELETE Deletes files from their directories.

DELETE (file number)

DIM This statement designates the spaces in memory for an array. The DIMension statement acts as an allocator, setting aside the necessary storage for the array.

DIM A (x)

END ENDS a source code program and tells the compiler to ignore any statements that follow.

END

EXP Gives the value of the constant e to the x power.

EXP(x)

FEND Terminates a user-defined function.

FEND

FILE Opens a file for reading or updating. If the file does not exist, then the statement creates the file that is to be read.

FILE (file name)

FLOAT Converts a numeric expression to a real number.

FLOAT (x%)

FOR...NEXT This statement creates a loop for a repetitive execution of a program function.

FOR X=1 TO 20:PRINT X:NEXT X

FRE Displays the number of bytes of memory available in RAM.

x=FRE

GOSUB Branches the execution of the program to a subroutine indicated in the GOSUB statement.

GOSUB (statement identifier)

GOTO Jumps the execution of the program to a statement identifier indicated in the GOTO.

GOTO (statement identifier)

IF A logical condition statement that evaluates whether a given condition is true or false.

IF (x) THEN (statement)

IF END Enables the program to process an end-of-file condition on an active file.

IF END (file number) THEN (statement number)

INITIALIZE Can initialize disks inserted during the execution of a program.

INITIALIZE

INP Returns the value input from an I/O port specified in the program.

xINP (numeric expression)

INPUT Allows data to be input from the keyboard during the program execution.

INPUT (variable)

INT Returns the largest integer of a numeric expression.

INT (x)

INT% Converts the numeric expression to an integer.

INT%(x)

LEFT$ Returns the leftmost character in a string.

LEFT$(x)

LEN Gives the number of characters in a string.

LEN(x$)

LET   Assigns a value to a variable.
LET variable=value

LOG   Returns the natural logarithm of a number.
LOG(x)

LPRINTER   Sends program output to the printer.
LPRINTER (WIDTH number)

MATCH   Returns the first position in x$ in y$ that is indicated by the number in the third parameter of the statement.
MATCH(x$,y$,number)

MID$ Returns a substring of the first string consisting of the number of characters in the third parameter starting at the character indicated by the second parameter.
MID$(any$,x,y)

ON   Transfers the execution of the program to another statement label.
ON (number) STATEMENT (statement number)

OPEN   Opens a file.
OPEN (file name)

OUT   Sends an integer to an output port.
OUT number, port

PEEK   Gives the contents of the memory location indicated by the address.
PEEK (memory location)

POKE   Stores a byte of a variable into a specific memory location indicated by the address.
POKE variable, memory location

POS   Returns the next horizontal cursor position on the console or printer.
POS

PRINT   Prints the value of the expression to the console.
PRINT expression

PRINT #   Outputs data to a disk file.
PRINT # file name, variable

PRINT USING   Formats printed output using a format string.
PRINT USING, format string

PRINT USING #   Formats printed output to a disk file.
PRINT USING #, format string, file name

RANDOMIZE   Initializes CBASIC's built-in random number generator.
RANDOMIZE

READ   Reads the data placed in DATA statements.
READ x,y

READ #   Reads data sequentially from files or from disk files.
READ # file name; x,y

REM   REMark statements are used to document or explain a line of code or insert comments into the program.
REM

RENAME   Changes the name of a file in the second parameter to the name specified in the first parameter.
RENAME (new file name, old file name)

RESTORE   Repositions the pointer in the DATA statement to the beginning of the data.
RESTORE

RETURN   Returns control of the program from a subroutine to the main program.
RETURN

RIGHT$ Returns a substring consisting of the rightmost characters of a string designated by the first parameter.
RIGHT$ (anystring, n characters)

RND   Gives a random number between 0 and 1.
RND (x)

SADD   Gives the address of a string assigned to x$.
SADD(x$)

SAVEMEM   Reserves memory space for a machine language subroutine and loads that specific routine during the execution of the program.
SAVEMEM number of bytes reserved for machine language subroutine, file name ws

SGN   Gives the algebraic sign of the numeric argument. If the number is less than zero, SGN returns a −1, if it is greater than zero, SGN returns a +1, and a 0 if the number equals zero.
SGN(numeric expression)

SIN   Gives the sine of an angle in radians.
SIN(angle x)

SIZE   Gives the size in 1K blocks of a file identified by x$. This function is used to see if there is enough room either on disk or in a program for a file to fit. The SIZE function only inspects the amount of space reserved for a file rather than the amount of data in the file.
SIZE(x$)
SIZE(file name)

SQR   Gives the square root of the numeric argument.
SQR(numeric argument)

STOP   Stops the execution of a program.
STOP

STR$ Converts a number to a string format.
STR$(number)

TAB   Used only in PRINT statements, the TAB function causes the cursor or the printer head to position itself on the column number specified by the expression.
TAB(numeric expression for column number)

TAN   Gives the tangent in radians of an angle specified in the numeric expression.
TAN(angle x)

UCASE$ Translates lowercase characters to uppercase.
UCASE$(lower case character string)

VAL   Gives the numerical value of a string.
VAL(x$)

VARPTR   Gives the memory address of the first byte of data of a variable.
VARPTR(variable)

WEND   Signals the end of a WHILE-governed loop.
WHILE (x expression).....WEND

WHILE   Executes a loop as long as the value of an expression is not zero.

S-BASIC

S-BASIC is a highly specific dialect of BASIC that is currently implemented only on the Kaypro 8-bit personal computer, running under the CP/M operating system. S-BASIC stands for structured BASIC and, to someone familiar with standard MicroSoft BASIC, this hybrid version of the language looks more like a COMAL or a Pascal with BASIC keywords than a real BASIC. Like Digital's CBASIC, S-BASIC is a true compiler. The source code, rather than being interpreted upon the execution of every line, is compiled into a machine language object code during a separate procedure subsequent to the actual programming. Once compiled, the object code will run many times faster than a traditional BASIC source code program that must be reinterpreted every time the program is executed. Unlike CBASIC, however, S-BASIC has source line information and program trace control procedures to make the debugging easier. These mechanisms, similar to the MON command in Applesoft, trace the flow of control in a program from line to line.

S-BASIC behaves more like PL/I or Pascal than a traditional BASIC because it makes formal use of such structured programming concepts as: procedures, functions, logical blocks, and local variables. In other words, S-BASIC allows programmers to construct modular or block-structured programs within a traditional BASIC syntax. This is the major difference between S-BASIC and its cousin, MicroSoft BASIC.

There are other significant differences between the languages. S-BASIC does not require line numbers at every line of code. Like its ancestor, Fortran, S-BASIC requires line numbers at only those lines that are pointed to by GOTO and GOSUB statements. Also, S-BASIC variables must be formally declared in a program with a VAR statement, a requirement that makes the language resemble PL/I.

There are six data types in S-BASIC: real single- and real double-precision, floating-point numbers, fixed decimals, integers, strings, and characters. The first two data types, the binary and the floating-point numbers, provide programmers with six digits of accuracy as real single-precision numbers and twelve digits of accuracy as real double-precision numbers. For programmers developing business applications in which a greater degree of accuracy is required, the third data type, fixed decimals, provides an 11-digit format of decimal math. There is no rounding-off problem with fixed decimal numbers as there normally is with floating points so that for the types of long, number-crunching operations that typically occur in business applications, fixed-decimal data types are preferred. Integers, the fourth data type, are stored as a data word in 2's complement form. In other words, in a binary representation of a decimal number, all of the 1's, in 2's complement, become 0's and the 0's become 1's. There is no rounding off of integer numbers, as there is with floating-point numbers, and S-BASIC makes no check for an overflow. String vari-ables, the fifth data type, can contain any ASCII character except for a null. They can range in length from 0 to 255 characters. The maximum length of the string is assigned in the VAR statement, the formal declaration program variables. For example:

```
VAR
            ; this is a comment line that
    NAME
            ; acts like a REM in M-BASIC but
      TOWN
            ; uses an assembly language format
=STRING:45
            ; instead
REM rems can also be used in S-BASIC
```

If the length is not assigned, then S-BASIC automatically defaults the string to 80 characters, the length of a single line of text. The final data type is the character or CHAR, a single ASCII character that can assume any 8-bit value the programmer assigns to it.

The formal structured nature of S-BASIC allows the programmer a considerable amount of flexibility in the use of data types and variables. For example, variables can share a common storage area in memory, they can be designated as global for the entire program, or global for the main program only. Because an S-BASIC program can be developed in modules and linked together at a later date, variables can be declared which can be passed to different modules without being altered. Moreover, variables that are allocated to a common storage area can be used by other S-BASIC programs that are linked to the original program through a CHAIN statement. This is a powerful feature of S-BASIC that reduces programming overhead and increases the efficiency of individual programmers because variables assigned to a common storage area do not have to be redeclared in order to be reused.

Local variables can be declared within an area of an S-BASIC program called a block structure, a discrete group of statements that behave as if they were one logical statement. Once declared within the block, the variables are considered local and the name and memory allocation are valid only for that particular block. At the end of the block, the compiler will no longer recognize the variable and will reallocate the same data storage areas for the variables in the next block. This feature, one of the more powerful aspects of any structured program, resembles PL/I in that it allows the same area of RAM to be used over and over again without destroying the existing variables. When the flow of control passes to a particular block structure, the variables in that structure are assigned memory locations and used within the program. When the flow of control passes to a new block structure, the same memory area is reallocated. This type of memory management is well suited to the limited capacities of 8-bit machines and makes it possible for programmers to develop more sophisticated and efficient applications. Block structures are usually defined by a BEGIN and END statement which sets them off from the main program and signals the compiler to reallocate memory as necessary. Block structures are also automatically recursive. In other words, blocks can be nested within blocks to any depth, and they are limited only by the availability of memory. Variables declared within the specific block are considered by the program to be local to the block. Variables declared outside any block area are considered global. For example, the following program diagram illustrates the way variables can be redeclared with the same names in different blocks and the way that blocks can be nested within one another:

```
1)  VAR A=INTEGER
        ;   this is the first variable
 2)  BEGIN
        ;   block structure 1 begins here
 3)  VAR B=STRING:30
        ;   this variable is local to
 4)  [PROGRAM STATEMENTS]
        ;   this block structure
 5)  BEGIN
        ;   nested block structure 2
    6)  VAR C=FIXED
        ;   begins here and has two new
    7)  VAR D=CHAR
        ;   variables local only to it
    8)  [PROGRAM STATEMENTS]
        ;   block 2's variables cease to
 9)  END
        ;   exist at this line
10)  VAR C=FIXED
        ;   C can be reused here because
11)  [PROGRAM STATEMENTS]
        ;   it is in block 1
12)  END
        ;   B and C cease to exist
13)  VAR B,C=INTEGER
        ;   B and C redeclared as part of
14)  [PROGRAM STATEMENTS]
        ;   main program
```

In line 1, the first variable, A, is declared as an INTEGER type with a VAR statement. Line 2 begins a block structure that contines to line 12 and contains within it a nested block structure. The variable declared in the first block structure, B, will be considered local to the first block but global to the second block. Hence, it cannot be used again in the nested block, but it will cease to exist when the first block is ended. At line 5, a second block begins that is nested within the first block, runs to line 9, and contains two variables. When the second block ends, the S-BASIC compiler removes the identities of variables C and D and reallocates the memory storage that it had assigned to them. Therefore, when the first block assumes control of program at line 10, C can be redefined with an entirely new identity. C is dismissed from the program again at line 12, when the first block ends, but is redefined as a global in line 13. This type of block-within-block structure is well suited to heavy analytical and recursive number-crunching programs such as those often required by business applications. Like a

traditional BASIC, S-BASIC transfers control to different sections of the program through GOTO and GOSUB statements. Within these sections, FOR...NEXT, IF...THEN, REPEAT...UNTIL, and WHILE...DO statements can be used as subroutines, followed by a RETURN or another GOTO which passes control back to the main program. For example:

```
REPEAT
            ;   loop starts here
    BEGIN
            ;   creates a block structure
        PRINT "NUMBER IS"
            ;   command to be executed
        X=X+1
            ;   X is incremented
    END
            ;   block ends
UNTIL X=10
            ;   until parameter established
RETURN
            ;   returns to main program
```

Conditional branching routines can be structured with IF...THEN...ELSE statements and then control can be transferred back to the main program.

```
IF X > Y THEN
    BEGIN
        PRINT X
    END
ELSE
    BEGIN
        PRINT Y
    END
GOTO 2500
```

S-BASIC also gives programmers access to the compilation procedure from within the source code. These special compilation commands, called $statements, can be used to trace the execution of the program at run time so that errors can be trapped. In addition, these commands allow the programmer to access files from a preexisting program already compiled on disk, or to list source code from the compiler during the compilation, or to relocate the compiled code to a different section of memory. Many of the compiler control commands are software toggles that can be turned off and on again while the compiler is generating code. There is also a panic-button option. This function is a Control C entered at the keyboard on a compiler error message that returns control of the program from the compiler to the system so that the source code can be debugged on the spot before compiling is resumed. Once compiled, the resulting code can run on any CP/M machine. Thus, S-BASIC is also a program development tool for professional-level applications programmers because it provides a structured environment for generating assembly-level object code through a high-level language compiler with the syntactic flexibility and source code simplicity that is typical of any dialect of BASIC. S-BASIC combines the ease of programming in BASIC with an underlying logical structure and the professional tools of program developers.

S-BASIC GLOSSARY

The following glossary contains only those statements and keywords particular to the S-BASIC dialect. Keywords such as GOSUB and RESTORE which are used in traditional BASIC are not defined here, but can be found in the M-BASIC glossary. This dialect of S-BASIC can be implemented on any CP/M machine, and it is the language delivered with the 8-bit Kaypro portable computer.

BASED   Declares variables that are assigned no storage or location. Variables that are base located have their storage allocated to them by S-BASIC and not by the user. BASED can be used in place of a VAR statement.
    BASED A,B=INTEGER

BEGIN   Begins a block procedure or program module which can be executed as if it were one logical statement. Variables can be declared within the block structure that are local only to the block and are wiped out when the block terminates at the END command.
    BEGIN
    [DECLARATION OF LOCAL VARIABLES]
    [PROGRAM STATEMENTS]
    END

CASE   A conditional operative statement that selects a single statement or block structure for execution from among many. CASE is used in logical operations to evaluate a condition and select from alternate branches. CASE is also used to establish a truth test and evaluate a series of statements for a match. When it finds a match, it executes the statement or the block procedure that takes the place of the statement.
    CASE [EXPRESSION] OF
    X:BEGIN
        [X BRANCH OF PROGRAM STATE-
        MENTS]
    END
        Y:[Y BRANCH OF PROGRAM STATE-
        MENTS]
    END
        Z:[Z BRANCH OF PROGRAM STATE-
        MENTS]
    END

CHAR   A variable that is a single ASCII character that may assume any ASCII or 8-bit value assigned to it.
    VAR X=CHAR

COMMENT   A REMark statement for multiple lines of commentary. COMMENT is used in place of REM statements on every line of source code. Because REM and COMMENT statements are ignored by the compiler, COMMENT statements can be as short or long as necessary.
    COMMENT
        ; These are a series of comments that can
        ; be inserted into the program at any
        ; point and will not be turned into object
        ; code by the compiler. Any characters
        ; can be used and the comments or doc-
        ; umentation can be as long as neces-
        ; sary. The comment block will ter-
        ; minate with an END statement.
    END

COM   Allocates variables to the common storage area for chained programs. It is analogous to the COMMON statement in M-BASIC.
    COM X=STRING:45

CONSOLE   Sets the console as the printer device and directs all output to the console.
    CONSOLE [integer constant]

CREATE   A disk drive command that creates an entry in the directory.
    CREATE [filename]

DO   The second half of a WHILE...DO statement. Like its counterparts in Fortran and PL/I, the WHILE...DO statement establishes a condition in which WHILE true, will cause DO to be executed.
    WHILE X > 10 DO
    BEGIN
        PRINT X
    END

ECHO   Similar to the ECHO statement in MS-DOS, this command acts as a software toggle that turns on or off the screen echo of keyboarded input.
    ECHO ON/OFF

ELSE   Analogous to ELSE statements in Fortran, PL/I, and other high-level languages, ELSE establishes an alternative branch if the first test condition is not met.
    IF [CONDITION] THEN [STATEMENT] ELSE
        [STATMENT]
    IF X>1 PRINT "OK" ELSE PRINT "TRY
        AGAIN"

EQV   A logical operator that represents an Equivalent Function. If both values on either side of the EQV operator are either true or false, the EQV is true.

    IF X = T AND Y = T THEN X EQV Y = T
    IF X = F AND Y = F THEN X EQV Y = T
    IF X = F AND Y = T THEN X EQV Y = F
    IF X = T AND Y = F THEN X EQV Y = F

The EQV operator is best used in place of an assembly language call to test, for example, whether two given lines on an RS232-C are carrying the same signal. If T is set to a logical high, or 1, and F is set to a logical low, or 0, and both lines are carrying the same signal, then EQV = T and data can be transmitted via the RS232-C line. If the lines are carrying different signals and the EQV is false, then a message can be echoed to the console that the RS232 port is inactive.

EXECUTE   Loads and executes a .COM file from within an S-BASIC program and then regains control of the system from the program.
    EXECUTE "FILENAME.COM"

FFIX   Returns the integer portion of the fixed type expression.
    FFIX [FIXED EXPRESSION]

FINT   Returns the next lowest integer of the fixed type expression.
    FINT [FIXED EXPRESSION]

IMP   A logical operator that is false only if the first of its arguments is true and the second is false.
    X IMP Y

LOCATE...AT   Places an array at an integer expression.
    LOCATE [NAME OF AN ARRAY] AT
        [INTEGER EXPRESSION]

LOCATION   Sets an integer variable to the memory location of the based located variable or to the location of a file buffer.
    LOCATION VAR/ARRAY/FILE [INTEGER
        VARIABLE] = NAME

LPRINTER   Causes the default print device to be changed to #1, a device other than the console, if an integer constant is not present.
    LPRINTER [INTEGER CONSTANT]

**NUM$**   Returns a string composed of characters that represent the value of the coefficient real number. In the following line, NUM$ returns the characters representing the value of a real number.
    NUM$/STR$(REAL NUMBER)

PROCEDURE   Declares a subroutine that can have variables passed to it when it is called from the main program or from other blocks. Procedures can call themselves without destroying their own local data structures.
    PROCEDURE [NAME] [DEFINED
        VARIABLES]
    [PROGRAM STATEMENTS]
    END

REPEAT...UNTIL   Repeats a statement until an expression is true.
    REPEAT
        BEGIN

            PRINT X
        END
    UNTIL X = 0

SIZE   Returns the size of a disk file in blocks.
    SIZE [DISK FILENAME]

STEP   The value of an increment or decrement in a FOR...NEXT...STEP loop.
    FOR [VARIABLE] TO [EXPRESSION] STEP
        [EXPRESSION]
    [PROGRAM STATEMENTS OR PROGRAM
        BLOCKS]
    NEXT

TEXT   Used to send large blocks of text to a device without having to use a PRINT statement at every line.
    TEXT [INTEGER CONSTANT],[TEXT FRAME]
        [TEXT FILE] [TEXT FRAME]

VAR   Declares a variable type and size.
    VAR A = STRING;25

XOR   The logical exclusive OR of two variables. XOR is true if either one of the values in the following example is either true or false, but false if both are true or false.
    X XOR Y.

$CONSTANT   Compile time command used to define an integer symbolic constant.
    $CONSTANT [NAME] = [INTEGER VALUE]

$INCLUDE   A compile time command used to access another file or a library file.
    $INCLUDE [FILENAME]

$LINES   A compile time software toggle that disables or enables the compiler's line numbering operation.
    $LINES

$LIST   A compile time software toggles that disables or enables the compiler's listing of included program source.
    $LIST (ON) (OFF)

$LOADPT   A compile time command that changes the location of the compiled code in memory.
    $LOADPT [MEMORY LOCATION]

$PAGE   Sends an ASCII form feed to the listing device causing a page to be skipped during a printing operation.
    $PAGE

$STACK   When the location of the data stack must be set by the programmer, the $STACK command is used. $STACK is used with an integer constant that represents the location of the stack in memory.
    $STACK [INTEGER CONSTANT]

$TRACE   Traces the flow of the program by printing the lines of code that are executed every time they are used. This command is used to trace the flow of a subroutine or a conditional branch to see if the correct lines of code were executed.

This command works with the $LINES command by echoing the line numbers on the console. $TRACE prints a number reference for every statement in the source code. If there are line numbers called or pointed to within the source code, the $TRACE will print a number for that line as well. In this way, the compiler can trace not only the direct execution of the program, but the internal flow of logic and the nesting of instructions within subroutines as well. For example, on an IF...THEN... ELSE instruction, the $TRACE command can monitor whether and where control was transferred and which of the elements in the statement was TRUE.

The $TRACE command, like the $LINES command, acts as a software toggle in that each occurrence of the statement in the source code turns the toggle on or off.

$TRACE

Applesoft BASIC

The following glossary of BASIC keywords represents the reserved statements in the Applesoft extension of the BASIC language. Applesoft is an implementation of MicroSoft BASIC with added keywords for high- and low-resolution graphics commands, plot commands, and screen color commands. Applesoft BASIC runs on all Apple II, II+, IIe, and IIc machines.

APPLESOFT GLOSSARY

ATN(num)   Angle whose tangent is num, in radians.

CHR$(num)   Character value of "num."

CLEAR   Clear strings to null and variables to zero.

CONT   Continue after STOP, END or | C.

COS(angle)   Cosine of angle (radians), in radians.

DATA   Store items into memory table.

DEF FN   Create function variable using argument in exponent.

DIM   Define array(s).

DRAW   Draw shape "defno" (0-255) at point "x,y".

EXP(num)   Inverse LOG of num.

FLASH   Set video output mode to flash characters.

FN   User function result. Variable defined in DEF FN statement.

FRE(0)   Number of available bytes in memory.

GET   Assign value of next key pressed to "var".

GOSUB   Perform routine at "line" until RETURN.

GOTO   Branch to "line".

HCOLOR   Set graphics color to "num" (0-7).

HGR   Set high-res mode (280 × 160). Display page 1 (8K-16K).

HGR2   Set high-res mode (280 × 192). Display page 2 (16K-24K).

HIMEM   Establishes high memory address for BASIC.

HOME   Clear window and move cursor to upper left.

HPLOT   Plot point(s) with current color.

HTAB   Tab cursor 1-256 positions from start of current line. (0=256)

IF THEN   Do action(s) based on cond(s).

IF THEN GOTO   Branch to "line" based on cond(s).

INPUT   Prompt for and read keyed response.

INT   Largest whole number not exceeding num. (2.5 = 2) (−2.5 = 3)

INVERSE   Set video output mode to inverse characters.

LEFT$ Substring of "num" chars from left side of string.

LOG   Natural logarithm of "num."

LOMEM   Establish low memory address for BASIC.

MID$ Substring of "str" at "start" position; length "len".

NEXT   Indicate end of FOR loop.

NORMAL   Set video input mode to normal.

ON GOSUB   Perform return "num" in "line" list.

ON GOTO   Branch to return "num" in "line" list.

ONERR GOTO   If error occurs, branch to "line".

POS(0)   Current horizontal position of cursor.

READ   Read items into var(s) from DATA table.

RECALL   Read numeric array from tape into array "var".

RESTORE   Reset pointer to start of DATA table.

RESUME   End err-routine and return to statement in error.

RIGHT$ Substring of "num" chars from right side of string.

ROT   Set angle of shape to DRAW XDRAW. (0-255). 0=normal, 16=90, 32=180, 48=270, 64=360.

SCALE   Set scale size of shape. (0-255). 1=normal, 0=maximum.

SHLOAD   Load shape table into memory from cassette. (If on disk, BLOAD shape table and POKE low/hi address.)

SIN   Sine of angle (radians), in radians.

SPEED   Set input/output speed. (0-255)

SQR   Square root of "num".

STOP   Interrupt program execution until CONT entered.

STORE   Write numeric array "var" to tape.

STR$ Character string of a number, including sign.

TAB(0)   Tab cursor to position 256 (PRINT statement only).

TAB   Tab cursor to position "num" (PRINT statement only).

TAN   Tangent of angle (radians), in radians.

USR   Pass argument to machine language routine.

VAL   Number extracted from character string.

WAIT   Pause until bit compares are satisfied.

XDRAW   At x,y erase shape "defno" (0-255) at point "x,y".

Atari BASIC

The following glossary of BASIC keywords represents the reserved statements in Atari's extension of the language. The implementation of Atari BASIC covers the Atari graphic commands such as DRAWTO and LOCATE and the command BYE, which is comparable to the PC's SYSTEM exit from BASIC. Atari BASIC is a cartridge-based option that runs on the Atari 400 and 800 computers.

ATARI GLOSSARY

The Atari version of BASIC is an extension of the language that includes a variety of graphics and screen color commands as well as commands that allow direct user control over the variety of input devices that Atari supports. There are commands for game paddles and joysticks as well as for screen graphics displays.

ADR(var$)   Memory address of string variable.

BYE   Exit BASIC, enter MEMOPAD mode.

CLOG(num)   Logarithm of num to the base 10.

CLR   Reset all vars, DIMs, and DATA pointer.

COM   Define numeric array/matrix table.

COM   Define string variable length array.

DEG   Forces trig function use of degrees.

DRAWTO   Draw line from last PLOT to col,row using char or color specified by COLOR reg.

ENTER   Merge LISTed program into memory from tape or disk.

INT(RND(1)* (range) + bottom   Random whole number between bottom munus one and bottom plus range.
INT(RND(1) * 100) + 30 = Number 30 to 129.

LIST "P:"   BASIC lines n1 thru n2 on printer.

LIST "filespec"   Save BASIC lines n1 thru n2 on device.

LIST   Display BASIC lines n1 thru n2.

LOCATE   Load screen data at col,row into numvar.

LPRINT   Print items on printer.

NEXT   Indicate end of FOR loop.

OPEN   Open a file for access. Code = 4 (input only), 8 (output only), 12 (input and output), 6 (disk directory input), 9 (output write to the back of the file).

PADDLE(num 0-7)   Position of paddle; 0 counter-clockwise to 128.

POINT   Position disk to NOTEd position.

POP   Clear top of stack. (Use if no RETURN or NEXT after GOSUB or FOR).

POSITION   Move invisible cursor to col,row on screen.

POSITION x,y   Move invisible cursor to point x,y on screen.

PTRIG(num 0-7)   0 = Paddle trigger pressed. 1 = no press.

RAD   Forces trig function use of radians (default).

REM   Remarks following are ignored by the computer. Can also be shown with a period and a space.

SAVE   Save BASIC program from memory to tape or disk.

SETCOLOR   Load color reg (0-4) with color (0-15) and lum or brightness (0-15).

STATUS   Puts device status code into numvar.

STICK(joy-num 0-3)   Position of joystick 1-4. 14 = North, 13 = South, 7 = East, 11 = West, 6 = NE, 10 = NW, 5 = SE, 9 = SW, 15 = Center.

STRIG(joy-num 0-3)   0 = Joystick trigger pressed. 1 = No press.

TRAP   Goto line number if error occurs.

XIO 18   Fill with color from last PLOT POSITION to DRAWTO lines. COLOR = POKE 765, regno(1-3).

XIO 254   Clear and initalize disk.

XIO 35   Install file write-protect.

XIO 36   Remove file write-protect.

XIO   Clear and initialize disk.

TI Extended BASIC

The following glossary of BASIC keywords represents the reserved statements in the TI version of BASIC and TI Extended BASIC. The implementation of BASIC and Extended BASIC for the Texas Instruments 99/4A covers TI's particular file procedures, graphics commands, and machine language calls. TI BASIC is included in ROM on the TI 99/4A, and Extended Basic is a cartridge-based option.

TI GLOSSARY

TI has added a variety of extensions for graphics, sound, and line editing to the traditional core of BASIC commands statements.

! Use this in place of REM to indicate comments.

:: Used between multiple statements on same line.

100 shift E Edit line 100.

100 shift X Edit line 100.

ACCEPT Read keyed response into variable from screen location row and column, accepting only data as specified by data type. Issue a BEEP if requested and clear screen if ERASE ALL is specified. Limit the length of the response to num characters. Row = 1-24, col = 1-28, datatype = UALPHA (uppercase alpha only), DIGIT (0-9), NUMERIC (0 through 9, period, plus, minus, "E"), or a string ("xyz") with desired characters only. If SIZE is omitted or variable is a positive number, the field is blanked before input. If SIZE is a negative number, field is not blanked.
[AT (row,col] [VALIDATE (datatype)] [BEEP] [ERASE ALL] [SIZE (num)] :]

AND If both expressions are true, result is true.
(IF exp AND exp)

CALL progname Transfer call to user-written subprogram.
[(options)]

CALL CHARPAT Return pattern of codes for char n into var$.
(n,var$)

CALL CHARSET Restore standard chars and colors to codes 32-95.

CALL COINC Return 0 if sprites do not overlap, or −1 if they do. #s1 and #s2 are the sprite numbers (the # is required). tol = number of dots allowed between sprites before overlap is considered effective.
(#s1, #s2, tol, var)

CALL COINC Same as above, only results are re-

turned based upon sprite's overlap of a particular screen dot.
(#s1,row,col,tol,var)

CALL COINC Same as above, only results are returned based upon sprite contact without tolerance.
(ALL,var)

CALL COLOR Set sprite #s1 to color fnum.
(#s1,fnum)

CALL DELSPRITE Delete sprite(s) indicated.
(#s1 [,#s2 [,...]]

CALL DELSPRITE Delete all sprites.
(ALL)

CALL DISTANCE Returns square of the distance (in dots) between the upper left corners of sprites #s1 and #s2 into var.
(#s1,#s2,var)

CALL DISTANCE Returns square of the distance (in dots) between the upper left corner of the sprite and the position specified into var. Default = 32767 if too large.
(#s1,row,col,var)

CALL ERR Error-code (var1), Error-code (var2), severity (var3), and line-number (var4).
(var1,var2, [,var3,var4])

CALL FILES(2) Specify 2 as max number of files which can be open at any one time (default = 3). This should not be used within a program. After it is entered, the NEW command should be entered. This is available with the Disk Manager Command Module.

CALL INIT Prepare computer to run machine language programs using the memory expansion feature. Invoke before LINK, LOAD, PEEK.

CALL LINK Pass control and args from BASIC program to subprogram already placed into MEMORY EXPANSION using CALL LOAD.
(subprog [,arg [,arg...])

CALL LOAD Load object program (or bytes specified into addresses) into Memory Expansion to be executed later by CALL LINK.
("filename" [,addr,byte [,sep,addr,byte,...] [,"fil...])

CALL LOCATE Move sprite #s1 to row and col specified.
(#s1,row,col)

CALL MAGNIFY Specify sprite size and type. 1 = one screen dot per single-code sprite bit. 2 = four screen dots per single-code sprite bit. 3 = one screen dot per quadruple-code sprite bit. 4 = four screen dots per quadruple-code sprite bit.

CALL MOTION Move sprite #s1 at speed and direction specified. (−128 to 127). 0 = no motion. Positive number is down(vert) or right(horiz). Negative number is up(vert) or left(horiz). When both are used, direction is angular. The smaller the number, the slower the sprite.
(#s1,vert,horiz [,...]

CALL PATTERN Change char value (32-143) of sprite #s1. All sprite attributes remain unchanged.
(#s1,value [,...]

CALL PEEK Decimal value(s) of byte(s) at loc. addr.
(addr,var [,var...])

CALL POSITION Return screen position of sprite #s1 into var1 (row) and var2 (col).
(#s1,var1,var2 [,...]

CALL SAY Speak word from list of speech words (wordstr) or from SPGET value (dirstr) using the Speech Synthesizer. The wordstr and dirstr entries must alternate, so to SAY two words, not using dirstr data, enter: CALL,SAY(wordstr,,wordstr) ...etc.
(wordstr [,dirstr [,wordstr [,dir...]

CALL SPGET Capture word from list of speech words into var for later use with CALL SAY. Var may be altered to add ING, S or ED to it.
(wordstr,var)

CALL SPRITE Create sprite #s1 (1-28), assign it to value (32-143), color (1-16) at positions row (1-256), at vert and horiz speed and directions (−128 to 127) specified. (Visible row positions are 1-192). See CALL MOTION for vert and horiz explanation.
(#s1,value,color,row,col [,vert,horiz] [...]

CALL VERSION Version of BASIC being used. (Extended BASIC = 100)
(var)

COMMAND ILLEGAL IN PROGRAM Command-only used as statement.

DISPLAY Display var(s) at row and col, blanking num positions before display. BEEP when displaying when desired. ERASE ALL clears screen before display. SIZE clears num positions before display, and when omitted clears rest of the line.
[AT (row,col) [BEEP] [ERASE ALL] [SIZE (num)] :] var,var,...

DISPLAY USING (lineno) Display var(s) using IMAGE at lineno as screen edit pattern. Options = same as DISPLAY [AT, etc...

DISPLAY USING (str) Display var(s) using str pattern to edit the data onto screen. Options = same as DISPLAY [AT, etc...

FOR-NEXT NESTING Next without FOR or FOR without NEXT.

I/O ERROR Not enough memory to list program, data error, or hardware error.

IF cond THEN statement1 If cond true then execute statement1, otherwise execute statement2.
[ELSE statement2]

ILLEGAL AFTER SUBPROGRAM SUBEND not followed by END, REM, or SUB, but something else.

IMAGE ERROR USING or IMAGE, usage or format error.

IMAGE pattern Create USING patter for PRINT and DISPLAY. Char max = 254, and this must be the only statement on the line.

IMPROPERLY USED NAME Invalid usage of varname, reserved word, subscript or string in FOR, array, dimensions, or redefining DIM, or using same var twice in sub.

INCORRECT ARGUMENT LIST CALL/SUB argument mismatch.

LET var,var,var... = value Assign a value to multiple variables.

LINE NOT FOUND References non-existent line number.

LINPUT strvar Reads raw data from keyboard into string variable.

LINPUT strvar Reads file record into string variable.

MAX (num1,num2) Larger of the two numbers.

MERGE "DSK1.INV" MERGE DSK1.INV program into memory program. Disk program must have been SAVEd with MERGE option. New lines replace old lines. Other lines merge in.

MIN (num1,num2) Smaller of the two numbers.

MISSING SUBEND SUBEND not at end of subprogram.

MUST BE IN SUBPROGRAM SUBEND or SUBEXIT not in subprogram.

NAME TOO LONG Var or subprogram name length is 15 max.

NEXT WITHOUT FOR Or FOR without NEXT, or nexting/GOTO err.

NO PROGRAM PRESENT   Program specified is missing.

NOT   Reverse of true/false result. IF NOT A = B

NUMERIC OVERFLOW   Result too small or large for limits.

OLD "DSK1.INV"   Load program INV to memory from disk drive 1.

OLD DSK.VOL1.PAYR   Load program PAYR to memory from disk named VOL1.

ON BREAK NEXT   Go to next program line when breakpoint encountered. Shift C will not stop program when this is used. When this is not used, program stops at breakpoint.

ON BREAK STOP   Stop program when breakpoint encountered.

ON ERROR lineno   Go to routine at lineno which has RETURN at its end if error occurs during program execution.

ON ERROR STOP   Stop program when error occurs. (Default)

ON GOSUB   Perform routine at nth lineno until RETURN encountered.

ON GOTO   Go to routine at nth lineno.

ON WARNING NEXT   Go to next line if warning error occurs.

ON WARNING PRINT   Print error msg if warning error occurs. (Default)

ON WARNING STOP   Stop program if warning error occurs.

ONLY LEGAL IN PROGRAM   Statement-only used as command.

OPTION BASE ERROR   Used twice, or 0, or 1 not specified.

OR   If one or both expressions are true, result is true. (IF exp OR exp)

PRINT #filenum USING lineno   Write data using edit pattern from IMAGE statement at line lineno.

PRINT #filenum USING pattern   Write data using edit pattern.

PRINT USING pattern   Print data using edit pattern.

PRINT USING lineno   Print data using edit pattern from IMAGE statement at lineno.

PROTECTION VIOLATION   Tried to access protected program.

REC   Number of next PRINT, INPUT or LINPUT record.

RECURSIVE SUBPROGRAM CALL   Subprogram called itself.

RETURN   RETURN to line lineno from ON ERROR.

RETURN NEXT   RETURN to line after error-line from ON ERROR.

RETURN WITHOUT GOSUB   Or, ON ERROR out of sync with error.

RPT $(str,num)   String of number repetition of string.

RUN "DSK1.AP"   Load program AP from DSK1 to memory and execute it.

SAVE DSK1.AR   Save AR program from memory to disk drive 1. (Also clears any program breakpoints.)

SAVE DSK1.AR,MERGE   Save AR program as a MERGEable program on disk drive 1.

SAVE DSK1.AR,PROTECTED   Save AR program so it can only be loaded using OLD.

SIZE   Amount of remaining available memory.

SPEECH STRING TOO LONG   255 character maximum (SPGET).

STACK OVERFLOW   Too many parens, memory exhausted, or may be violating nesting or GOSUB rules.

STRING TRUNCATED   String automatically shortened because it exceeded the maximum length.

SUB   First statement in a subprogram, separates code from rest of program and names it subpgm, with variables (when desired) used for arguments to subpgm. Last statement in subpgm must be SUBEND or SUBEXIT (cannot leave a subpgm any other way). Subpgm is invoked by CALL subpgm statement.

SUBEND   Last statement in a subprogram. Returns control to statement after the one which CALLed the subprogram.

SUBEXIT   Returns control to statement after one which CALLed the subprogram. May be placed anywhere in subprogram.

SUBPROGRAM NOT FOUND Does not exist, or program not LINKed.

SYNTAX ERROR Spelling, punctuation, etc.

UNMATCHED QUOTES Must always be a pair of quotation marks.

UNRECOGNIZED CHARACTER String character not enclosed in quotes, or bad object data during LOAD.

XOR If one expression is true, and one false, result is true.

C Language

The C Language was designed by Dennis M. Ritchie in 1972 and was described by him in the *C Reference Manual* published by Bell Laboratories in January 1974. It has recently become very popular on a variety of different microprocessors because the design of C allows for a high transportability. Programmers attempting to reach a large audience must be able to program in a language that allows source code to be used easily on as many of the available processors as possible: this is one of C's greatest strengths, and the use of the language is spreading. In late 1983 and early 1984, the development and release of compilers for the language were announced by MicroSoft and Digital Research. They joined the list of C compilers now available for most popular microprocessors. Both companies have also announced that C is their language of choice for all software development.

C is a powerful language which allows programmers to construct complicated operations with a minimum of commands. It is also used—and this is unusual in a compiler—for writing systems programs, the programs which are at the heart of a computer operating system. Spreadsheets, database managers, and word processors are programs which have requirements similar to those of systems programs, and C is similarly suited to these applications.

This suitability is the birthright of C; it was written at Bell Laboratories as a tool to aid in the development of UNIX, an operating system originally designed for the DEC PDP-11 minicomputer. Rewriting the original assembler code in C enabled the operating system to be easily transported to other computers, once a C compiler for the target processor had been written.

C has the singular quality of combining different levels of programming abstraction from the machine code level to the highest level of applications processing. Computer languages all offer a level of abstraction above the actual machine code of 1's and 0's which operate a digital logic device. On the earliest digital computers, the instruction sets were literally wired directly in, using patch boards and wire connectors, and the programmer had to reduce every instruction to be executed to an expression stated in 1's and 0's. Very little programming is done today at this level.

Assembler language abstracts the programmer one step from the binary instructions and supplies simple mnemonics for the computer which take care of the bits, allowing the programmer to devote more time to the problem at hand. But the assembler programmer remains concerned with the details of the register management of the processor, and the resulting program is inherently nonportable because all processors are different at this level.

A high-level language offers a further abstraction from the processor. The programmer is no longer concerned with any details of the variable storage or how to perform complex arithmetic on a microprocessor lacking the instruction to multiply the contents of two of its registers. Most of the programmer's time may be spent on the actual problem. In return for this ease of use, one loses efficiency. The code generated by a high-level compiler will be several times larger than that required by an assembler program to produce the same result. Efficiency is sacrificed as the actual processor moves further away from the user. It is sacrificed even more in an actual applications program. This is a very highly abstracted set of instructions, and it is the most inefficient in terms of code use. Consider, for example, the coding overhead required to add two numbers in a spreadsheet program such as VisiCalc: @SUM(C4...C25). But when we consider the ease of use of the entire applications program, the program's built-in editor, and the file-handling and system utility features, the coding overhead ceases to be an issue. However, usually lost in a high-level language, not to mention an applications program, is the ability to do low-level operations, which system programs require for speed and efficiency. Most compilers cannot manipulate individual bits, and files cannot be operated on in amounts smaller than fields.

A C compiler, however, has all of these capabilities. In addition, numeric values can be input and output in hexadecimal or octal bases as well as the usual decimal; there are operators available to increment directly, to shift, to refer to the address of a variable, to refer to the contents of an address, to "and" or to "or" either logically or bit by bit. The language is rich in data types, supporting long and short, signed or unsigned integers, real numbers of two levels of precision, floating point variables, functions, and characters. C is in actuality a compromise between the low-level, "hands-on" characteristics of a nonportable assembler and the ease and portability of a high-level language. It operates as close as possible to the processor on which it is implemented. Its many operators do allow a programmer to define exactly what needs to be done. The operators can be mapped directly to the op-codes of the processor by the compiler, thus leading to efficient code generation. C supports pointers to all of its variable types, and pointers to variables are efficient users of memory.

C is a structured language. The syntax encourages a program to consist of stand-alone functions, which are called as required by the main program, and by other functions. There are few keywords; the strength of the language is found in its functions. Several standard functions are supplied with a compiler, and a programmer will, in a short time, have built a library of functions by using code on new projects that was written for previous projects or by purchasing libraries of C functions, which are becoming available as support for the language increases.

A C function has a simple structure. The function name is followed by a list of parameters in parentheses; the parentheses are required even if there are no parameters. Immediately after the parentheses are the declarations of the paremeters, and these declarations are followed by the function statements in braces. The first statements in the braces declare any variables used within the function. For example:

```
#define EOF −1
main()
        /*a program to copy input to output*/
{
  int c;
        /*a variable declaration*/
  c = getchar();
        /*get input character into c*/
  while (c != EOF) {
        /*while c is not end-of-file marker*/
    putchar (c);
        /*output c*/
    c = getchar ();
        /*get the next character*/
  }
}
```

As the comments (surrounded by /* and */) state, this program copies characters from input to output until the end of file is detected. The "#define" statement is a preprocessor macro which substitutes "−1" wherever "EOF" is found in the first pass of the compiler. The use of the macro makes the code more understandable, and there are no parameters to the function "main()". Accordingly, the parentheses are empty. Had there been parameters, they would be located within the parentheses, and the declarations would precede the brace that opens the function itself.

The variable is declared: "int c;". Although the program handles characters, c is declared to be "int", to enable it to hold the value of −1 which will be returned by "getchar()" when the end of the input is reached. The first character is input, and it is tested against the value EOF. The character is put to the output, a new character is retrieved, and the program runs while c is not equal, "!=", to EOF. The brace after the test "(c != EOF)" and its mate on the second-to-last line group enclose the two statements within them so they become a block of statements controlled by the "while" loop. The other pair of braces defines the bounds of "main()", and thus the bounds of the program. A C program itself is called "main()". This function calls other functions, and the program terminates when "main" has run to its end.

The C Language is unusual among programming languages in the breadth of its possible applications. Its abilities to perform lower-level functions more easily than other languages has led to its wide usage for applications that had previously been attempted only in assembler. The growing market for C is causing a growth in support for the language. This is especially the case after 1983, the year in which the support spiral for C became large enough to sustain sizable groups of new C programmers.

C GLOSSARY

addition operator +   Returns the sum of two expressions.
   expression + expression
      a = 10 + (x+y)

address operator &   Returns the address of an object in memory.
   & identifier
      pd = &pay;

ALLOC function   Dynamically allocates space and returns its address to the specified identifier.
   char * pi
   p = alloc (size);
      int size;

AND &&   Returns the logical conjunction of two boolean operands.
   expression && expression
      if (stack[i]!=n&&top!=0)
   i++;

a.out   An executable file that receives the object code produced by the compilation of source code.

array declaration   Defines an array.
   type identifier[integer expression]
      int stack[20];

ATOF function   Converts its parameter to a double-precision floating-point expression.
   atof(x)
      return(atof(x));

ATOI function   Converts a string of digits to a numeric value.
   atoi(x)
      y = 100 * atoi(amount);

binary search function   Returns the position of x in array y, if not found binary returns −1.
   binary(x,y,n)
      binary(tues,week,n);

bit count function   Returns the number of 1 bits in an integer expression.
   bitcount(x)
      y = bitcount(x);

bitwise AND &   Used to set the specified bits to zero.
   expression & expression
   x = y & z;

bitwise inclusive OR |
   Sets the specified bits to one.
   expression | expression
      x = x | mask;

break   Causes an immediate exit from a do, while, for, or switch structure.
   break;
      if (x == y)
         break;

%c   Used to format output as character in the printf statement.
   printf("%c", letter);

CASE   The case statement is a multiple decision operator which uses the value of an expression to select one statement from a group of statements to be executed.
   case constant expression:
      if ((x=y) && (y !=z))
         switch(y) {
         case '1': printf("a")
         case '2': printf("b")
         default: break;
      }

cfree function   Releases previously allocated storage that is referenced by a pointer.
   cfree(p)
      cfree(ptr);

char   Predefined type which represents a character used for communication between the computer and the operator.
   char identifier
      char wspace[512];

close   Closes opened files.
   close(file identifier)
      close(payroll)

copy function   Duplicates the specified line.
   copy(x,y)
      copy(chin,chout);

create   Creates a file and labels it with the specified identifier.
   create(file identifier)
      x = create(payrol);

%d   Used to format output as decimal in the printf statement.
   printf("%d", digit);

decrement operator --   Prefix or postfix operator which decrements the named identifier by 1.
   identifier-- or --identifier
      if done
      --x;

division operator /   Returns the integer part of division.
   expression / expression
      c = x / (4*y);

do   Forces execution of a statement until some condition becomes false.
   do statement while(expression)
      do x++ while(x<19);

equality operator ==   Tests for equality between two expressions.

expression == expression
   if (c == d)
      fsize(buf);

extern   Specifies that a local variable from an outside procedure may be accessed by another procedure.
   extern type identifier
      extern int stack

exit   Terminates program execution.
   exit;
      if done
         exit;

%f   Used to format output as floating point in the printf statement.
   printf("%f",num);

fclose   Releases the file pointer from pointing to the indicated file.
   fclose(pointer)
      fclose(ptr);

float   Defines an identifier as a 32-bit numeric field.
   float identifier
      float x,y,z;

fopen   Returns a file pointer for use in accessing a file.
   fopen(file identifier)
      ptr = fopen(payroll);

for statement   Used to repetitively execute a statement or group of statements a predetermined number of times.

   for expression statement
      for (stack=0; stack=stack+3)
         push(ch);

fprintf   Performs the same function as the printf function with the stipulation that the first argument is a file pointer and the second specifies the control string.
   fprintf(pointer,control string)
      fprintf(ptr,"%d");

fputs   Writes a string to a file.
   fputs(line,file pointer)
      fputs("this is the end",ptr);

free   Releases previously allocated storage.
   free(pointer)
      free(ptr);

fscanf   Performs the same task as the scanf function with the stipulation that the first argument is a file pointer and the second specifies the control string.
   fscanf(pointer,control string)
      fscanf(ptr,"%d");

getbits function Returns a bit field of size n, starting at position p in x.
getbits(x,p,n)
getbits(x,2,5);

getc Returns the next character from a file.
getc(file pointer)
ch = getc(ptr);

getch Accepts the next input character from a pre-defined work space.
getch()
ch = getch();

getchar Accepts input data from an input device such as the keyboard.
getchar()
while (bufffer != full)
getchar();

getint Converts a string of characters into integer values.
getint(&identifier)
getint(ptr);

getop Reads data, in the form of digits, until no more data is found, storing only those digits that will fit in the field.
getop(x,y)
if overflow
getop(x,y);

goto Unconditionally transfers control to the specified point.
goto identifier
if (c<d)
goto step2;

greater than operator > Tests whether the first expression is of greater magnitude than the second.
expression > expression
if (c > d)
fsize(buf);

greater than or equal to operator Tests whether the first expression is of greater magnitude or equal to the second.
expression >= expression
if (c >= d)
fsize(buf);

if statement Allows conditional execution of a statement or statements.
if (condition)
statement;

if (c<d)
c++;

if-else construct Tests for conditional execution of

a statement or statements, and if false then execution of the statements following the else keyword takes place.
if (condition)
statement
else
statement
if (c == d)
c++
else
c--

increment operator Prefix or postfix operator which increments the named identifier by 1.
identifier++ or ++identifier
if done
++y;

index function Returns the position in string x where string y begins.
index(x,y)
i = index(namelist,name);

indirection operator * Assigns the contents of memory, referenced by the specified pointer, to an expression.
*pointer expression
node = *treeptr;

inequality operator != Tests for inequality between two expressions.
expression != expression
if (c != d)
fsize(buf);

install Determines whether a character string already exists in a text table.
install(s,t)
install(name,namelist);

int Predefined type which specifies an identifier to be of type integer.
int identifier list
int x,y,z;

itoa Converts a number to an alphanumeric string.
itoa(x,y)
if (isalpha(p))
itoa(p,n);

label Defines an identifier as a label.
identifier:
if done
goto out;
...............;
...............;
out;
...............;

%ld Used to format output as long-integer in the printf statement.
printf("%ld",digit);

left shift operator <<   Shifts the first operand's bits to the left by the specified number of bit positions in the second operand, replacing the right-hand end with zeros.

```
expression << expression
   a << 4;
```

less than operator <   Tests whether the first expression is of less magnitude than the second.
```
expression < expression
   if (c < d)
      fsize(buf);
```

less than or equal to operator <=   Tests whether the first expression is of less magnitude or equal to the second.
```
expression <= expression
   if (c <= d)
      fsize(buf);
```

logical negation operator !   Performs inverse conversions on binary digits.
```
! expression
   if (!inweek)
      return(a);
```

logical OR operator| | Returns the logical disjunction of two boolean operators.
```
expression| | expression
   if (stack[i] !=n| | top !=0)
      i = I--;
```

long   Predefined type which specifies an identifier to be of type long.
```
long identifier list
   long x,y,z;
```

lookup function   Returns a pointer to its parameter if that parameter is found in the table.
```
lookup(x)
   if yes
      lookup(x);
```

lower function   Returns the lower case of its parameter.
```
lower(x)
   lower("D");
```

macros   Standard C provides for several types of macros which perform character tests and conversions. These are as follows:

```
isalpha(x)
   Returns 0 if x is not alphabetic.

isupper(x)
   Returns 0 if x is not uppercase.
```

```
islower(x)
   Returns 0 if x is not lowercase.

isdigit(x)
   Returns 0 if x is not a digit.

isspace(x)
   Returns 0 if x is not a blank, tab, or new line.

toupper(x)
   Converts x to an uppercase character.

tolower(x)
   Converts x to an lowercase character.
```

main function   The point in the program in which execution begins.
```
main()
   main()
   {
         printf("hello");
   }
```

modulus operator %   Computes the remainder of division.
```
expression % expression
   c = x % (4*y);
```

month day function   Returns the month and day of the year.
```
month day(parameter list)
   month day(year,day);
```

morecore function   Reserves main storage for later use.
```
morecore(x)
   static sharp *morecore(x)
   unsigned x;
```

multiplication operator *   Returns the product of two expressions.
```
expression * expression
   d = 45 * x;
```

null   Used to assign to a pointer the value of null.
```
null
   return(null);
```

numcmp function   Compares two strings numerically.
```
numcmp(x,y)
   numcmp(x1,x2)
   char *x1,*x2;
```

%o   Used to format output as octal in the printf statement.
```
printf("%o",digit);
```

one's complement operator Returns the one's complement of an integer expression.
   expression
      y = q & ~)[{{⟩

open Returns a file descrptor to the specified file.
   open(file)
      x =1 open(payroll);

printf Formats and prints its arguments.
   printf(control, arg1, arg2, ...)
      printf("%o", digit);

putc Writes its parameter to the specified file.
   putc(identifier, file)
      putc("a",name);

putchar Writes its parameter to an output device.
   putchar(x)
      putchar(c);

return Returns control to the calling statement.
   return;
     if done
        return(x);

reverse Returns a string with its characters in reverse order.
   reverse(x)
     if done
      reverse(numstring);

right shift operator >> Shifts the first operand's bits to the right by the specified number of bit positions in the second operand, replacing the left-hand end with zeros.
   expression >> expression
      a >> (x−2);

%s Used to format output as character string in the printf statement.

   printf("%s", string);

scanf Reads from an input device in the same manner as the printf writes to an output device.
   scanf(control, arg1, arg2, ...)
      scanf("%s",string);

SCANF function Searches a line for input.
   scanf(identifier list)
     if (scanf(name) != EOF)
        printf ("searching");

sprintf Performs the same function as printf, with its operand being a string.
   sprintf(string, control, arg1, arg2, ...)
      sprintf(name,"%s",ch);

squeeze Removes all occurrences of the specified character from the specified string.
   squeeze(s,x)
      squeeze(name,"d");

sscanf Performs the same function as scanf with its operand being a string.
   sscanf(string, control, arg1, arg2, ...)
      sscanf(name,"%s", ch);

static Defines an identifier to be of a fixed memory location.
   static type identifier
      static int stack;

strcat Appends its two operands.
   strcat(op1,op2)
      strcat(first,last);

strcmp Compares two character strings.
   strcmp(s,t)
      strcmp(in1,in2);

strcpy Copies a string.
   strcpy(s,t)
      strcpy(receive,original);

strlen Returns the length of a string.
   strlen(x)
     while (x != strlen(y))
        z++;

strsave Copies a string to memory and returns a pointer to its location.
   strsave(x)
     if done
        strsave(name);

structure pointer operator −> Specifies the named identifier to a particular member of a structure.
   expression −> identifier
      struc week *pw;
      pd −> tues;

subtraction operator − Returns the difference of two expressions.
   expression − expression

switch Tests an expression for equality with a predefined constant.
   switch(expression)
     switch(x) {
     case '0':
     case '1':
     case '2':
       break;
     default :
       y++;
     }

typedef Permits the programmer to define new data types.
  typedef declarator
    typedef int maxsize;

while Executes the statements contained within the while construct until the specified condition becomes false.

while (condition)
    statements
        while (x == ")
           getc(x);

%x Used to format output as hexadecimal in the printf statement.
  printf("%x",digit);

COBOL

COBOL, which stands for COmputer Business Oriented Language, is the most widely used programming language for business applications. COBOL was created in 1959 by the Conference on Data Systems and Languages, a committee representing business, government, academic, and computer interests. The language was officially defined in 1968 and again in 1974 by the American National Standards Institute. Today, anywhere from 60 to 75 percent of all new applications code produced is written in COBOL, including an ever-increasing body of business programming for microcomputers.

COBOL has traditionally been the programming language of choice for the business community whenever the application calls for general-purpose data processing. Created to perform specific business, text manipulation, database, financial processing, and general administrative tasks, it is a specialized, noninteractive, relatively unstructured procedural language that is machine independent but entirely business oriented. COBOL fulfills its primary mission by having the capabilities for extensive file handling and manipulation. It can read and write data records simply and can create both direct or random access as well as sequential files. The sequential files, primarily for tape retrieval, store data files one after the other. In order for the program to retrieve record C, for example, it must scan records A and B. Random access files allow the program to go directly to the file in question by scanning the disk or mass storage directory and locating the file by the pointers in the directory map. Sequential record keeping usually involves a longer access time than random access files, but it is a more effective storage management procedure because only the storage necessary for the particular record is utilized. Random access files allocate blocks of storage for each record regardless of whether the storage is used or not.

Business programs also require a sophisticated string handling and manipulation as well as an easy method of data entry and keyboard processing. Most importantly, however, a general-purpose business language must be able to handle dollars and cents amounts accurately in large numbers. Therefore floating point arithmetic is not an acceptable feature. COBOL fulfills all of these requirements, and even though it is not an adequate language for complex number crunching, it is an exact language for simple arithmetic, and this is important for the type of environments in which COBOL is typically used.

COBOL has a rigidly defined structure that is made up of four divisions: identification, environment, data, and procedure. Most general-purpose languages need only have a data division and a procedure division. The data division contains the data areas that the program will process, and the procedure division enumerates the procedures that the program must follow as flow of control passes from procedure to procedure. In other words,

the data division declares all of the variables, and the procedure division executes what has to be done with them. In a COBOL program, however, there is an identification division which contains storage for the name of the program or job, the name of the author, the date of the job or program, and the accompanying documentation. The environment division contains information on the host computer and whatever external files are applicable to the job. The consolidation of the environment division into a program section was one of the features which made COBOL a language of choice for business buyers. Most languages before COBOL required that only a specific type of computer be used. COBOL, however, was portable and was able to be configured to a specific system easily by the programmer who simply set the parameters in the environment division. Thus a typical COBOL program would be:

```
0001  IDENTIFICATION DIVISION.
0002  PROGRAM IDENCYCLOPEDIA COBOL
         EXAMPLE.
0003  ENVIRONMENT DIVISION.
0004  CONFIGURATION SECTION.
0005  SOURCE-COMPUTERCBM SUPER PET
         9000.
0006  OBJECT-COMPUTERIBM PC WITH
         CP/M-86.
0007  DATA DIVISION.
0008  WORKING STORAGE SECTION.
0009  77 A PICTURE IS X.
0010  PROCEDURE DIVISION.
0011  BEGIN.
0012         DISPLAY"WELCOME TO COBOL!".
0013         ACCEPT A.
0014         STOP RUN.
0015  END PROGRAM ENCYCLOPEDIA.
```

All of the independent variables in COBOL are stored in the working storage section of the data divison and are identified by a data level number. In this example, the number 77 identifies the data type "independent variable." The name of the variable is A which is described, or "pictured," by the alphanumeric character X, a one-character-wide descriptor. The DISPLAY statement in 0012 prints the "WELCOME TO COBOL!" to the screen, and the BEGIN, STOP RUN, and END PROGRAM statements are self explanatory.

The way data is represented in COBOL differs from the way it is represented in most other languages. COBOL has alphanumeric, alphabetic, and numeric data types. Alphabetic data is strictly limited to the letters of the alphabet and the space bar, numbers are arithmetic decimal numbers, not floating-point numbers, and alphanumeric data is similar to a character string in a language like BASIC. The PICTURE statement defines the data types in the data division: A PICTURE represents alphabetic data, PICTURE X represents alphanumeric data, and PICTURE plus places holders for numbers, S for sign, 9 for a digit, and V for decimal point placeholder, identifies numeric data. Thus, an identifier for numeric data in COBOL is PICTURE IS S99V99 for a number type of −23.56.

COBOL is not a concise language. There is a large code overhead, much of it involved in data identification and file handling. What is important about the language, however, is its ability to manipulate data in a variety of forms and to identify that data in a separate data division of the program. This makes it a language of choice for the data processing industry because most professional data processing divisions process by committee or piece out the programming job so that any number of individuals might be working on a large application. COBOL's structure allows for this by requiring separate divisions that identify the type of program, the person responsible for the job, and the data that will be included. COBOL also has explicit rather than algebraic computational expressions requiring that a simple equation such as:

IF Y < (B*C)

might have to be expressed as:

MULTIPLY B BY C GIVING X.
IF Y < [VARIABLE NAME]

COBOL's future offers a great promise for the new multitasking networked microcomputing community. COBOL's precision and its ability to handle large numbers still make it a language of choice for most general-purpose business applications, and its availability on PC's and 8-bit systems make it a highly transportable language.

COBOL GLOSSARY

The following glossary represents the full set of ANSI standard COBOL keywords and commands. COBOL compilers, while not expensive, are generally available for a variety of systems running CP/M and MS-DOS.

ACCEPT   Obtains data from an input file.
  ACCEPT identifier [from mnemonic name]
  ACCEPT input-data FROM keyboard.

ADD   Adds the contents of the given identifier list and places the result in the specified identifier-m.
  ADD/identifier1/literal1/,/identifier2/literal2/
  [,/identifier3/literal3/...
    GIVING identifier-m [ROUNDED] [,identifier-n
    [ROUNDED]]...
    [; ON SIZE ERROR imperative statement].
      ADD check-amount, withdrawals
        GIVING debits.

ALL   Repetitively assigns a string to a field. See UN-STRING
  05 ZERO-STRING pic X(4) value all '0'

ALTER   Used to ALTER unconditional GOTO statements.
  ALTER procedure name1 TO procedure name2
    [,procedure name3 TO [PROCEED TO]
    procedure name4]...
      A005-output-report
        GOTO A006-prepare-output.
        ALTER A005-output-report
        TO PROCEED TO b015-subroutine.

AND   When used in the IF statement the word ADD specifies that two conditions must be met before execution of the imperative statement.
  IF condition AND condition
    imperative statement.
      IF flag AND done
        PERFORM A005-output-report.

ASSIGN   Used to ASSIGN a file to an output device.
  See ENVIRONMENT DIVISION.

AT END   Tests for the end of a file.
  AT END
    READ input-data
      AT END
        MOVE 'no' TO any-more-records.

AUTHOR   An option within the IDENTIFICATION DIVISION to specify the programmer.
  See IDENTIFICATION DIVISION.

BLANK   Causes the blanking of a field when a value of zero is obtained.
  03 amount-input PIC 9(7) BLANK WHEN ZERO.

CLOSE   Closes the specified file list.
  CLOSE file name1 [WITH LOCK] [,file name2
  [WITH LOCK]]...
    CLOSE payroll.

COMMA   When used in the PICTURE clause, placing a comma in the field definition will cause a comma to be printed on output.
  03 amount-out PIC 99,999.

COMPUTATIONAL(COMP)   Specifies binary storage for numeric data.
  See USAGE.

COMPUTATIONAL-3 (COMP-3)   Specifies internal decimal format for the given data.
  See Usage.

COMPUTE Allows for arithmetic operations to be specified.
> COMPUTE identifier1 [ROUNDED] [,identifier2 [ROUNDED]]...
>> = arithmetic expression [;ON SIZE ERROR imperative statement].
>>> COMPUTE new = sales − expenses.

CONFIGURATION SECTION Specifies the computer being used to compile and execute the program.
> See ENVIRONMENTAL DIVISION.

CORRESPONDING(CORR) References all fields with common data names.
> MOVE CORRESPONDING identifier1 to identifier2.
> MOVE CORR new-input TO master-file.

DATA DIVISION Describes the files to be used by the program.
> DATA DIVISION
> [FILE SECTION.
> [FD file name
>> [;RECORD CONTAINS [integer TO integer CHARACTERS]
>> ; LABEL/RECORD IS // STANDARD/ OMITTED // RECORDS ARE / STANDARD / / OMITTED
>> [;DATA/RECORD IS/RECORDS ARE/ data name [,data name]...]
> [record-description-entry]...]...]]

> DATA DIVISION

> FILE SECTION.
> FD check-data-input.
>> RECORD CONTAINS 80 CHARACTERS
>> LABEL RECORDS ARE OMITTED
>> DATA RECORD IS check-data-record.
> 01 check-data-record.
>> 03 pay-to-input PIC X(25).
>> 03 amount-input PIC 9(5).
>> 03 date-input PIC 9(6).
>> 03 FILLER PIC X(44).

DATE-COMPILED An option within the IDENTIFICATION DIVISION to specify the compilation date.
> See IDENTIFICATION DIVISION.

DATE-WRITTEN An option within the IDENTIFICATION DIVISION to specify the date on which the program was written.
> See IDENTIFICATION DIVISION.

DATE References the operating system to obtain the current date.
> MOVE CURRENT-DATE TO date-output.

DELIMITED Specifies that the current action is to continue until the first character, indicated by the DELIMITED statement, is found.
> See STRING.

DEPENDING Specifies unconditional branch DEPENDING on the value of an identifier.
> GOTO procedure name1 [,procedure name2... procedure name5]
>> DEPENDING ON identifier.
> GOTO output1, output2, output3, output4, output5
>> DEPENDING ON input-index.

DISPLAY Writes the indicated message out to the printer.
> DISPLAY identifier1/literal1 [,identifier2/literal2]... [UPON mnemonic name]
>> DISPLAY 'entering subprogram'.

DIVIDE Returns the quotient of two numeric data items.
> DIVIDE /identifier1/literal1/ BY /identifier2/ literal2/
>> GIVING identifier3 [ROUNDED] [, identifier4 [ROUNDED]]...
>> [;ON SIZE ERROR imperative statement].
> DIVIDE amount BY months-input
>> GIVING monthly-output ROUNDED.

ELSE Forces execution of one or more statements when the condition is returned false within the IF construct.
> See IF.

ENVIRONMENT DIVISION Identifies the computer on which the program was executed on and specifies files for input and output. These are defined in the CONFIGURATION SECTION and the INPUT-OUTPUT SECTION, respectively.
> ENVIRONMENTAL DIVISION.

> CONFIGURATION SECTION.

> SOURCE-COMPUTER. computer name.
> OBJECT-COMPUTER. computer name.
> [SPECIAL-NAMES. [,implementor IS mnemonic]].

> INPUT-OUTPUT SECTION.

> FILE CONTROL.
>> SELECT [OPTIONAL] file name
>>> ASSIGN TO implementor1 [,implementor2]...
>>> [;RESERVE integer1 [AREA/AREAS]]
>>> [;ORGANIZATION IS SEQUENTIAL]
>>> [;ACCESS MODE IS SEQUENTIAL]
>>> [;FILE STATUS IS data name1].

> ENVIRONMENTAL DIVISION.

> CONFIGURATION SECTION.

> SOURCE COMPUTER. IBM-PC.
> OBJECT COMPUTER. IBM-PC.

INPUT-OUTPUT SECTION.
FILE-CONTROL.
    SELECT input-file
    ASSIGN TO sys007.

EXIT   Returns control to the calling PERFORM statement.
    EXIT.

FD   The File Description statement is used to describe each file within DATA DIVISION.
    See DATA DIVISION.

FILE CONTROL   Names the files to be processed.
    See ENVIRONMENT DIVISION.

FILLER   Used to fill spaces when defining fields within records.
    See DATA DIVISION.

FROM   Indicates the location of the desired data.
    See WRITE.

GIVING   Specifies the identifier that will receive an arithmetic result.
    See DIVIDE, MULTIPLY, ADD, SUBTRACT.

GOTO   Passes control to the specified paragraph.
    GOTO [procedure name].
        IF amount = 0.00
            GOTO A005-zero-balance.

GREATER   Tests for a GREATER value between two operands.
    See IF.

GROUP INDICATE   Specifies that data is printed for only the first record in a group. Used to prevent repetitive printing of the same data.

HEADING   Used to define the information in the heading line that is to be printed.
    01 HEADING
        03 FILLER PIC X(INTEGER) VALUE
        'heading'...

    01 OUTPUT-HEADER
        03 FILLER PIC X(6) VALUE ' NAME '.
        03 FILLER PIC X(4) VALUE SPACES.

HIGH-VALUES   Used to assign the highest value of the collating sequence to a field.
    MOVE HIGH VALUES TO high-field.

IDENTIFICATION DIVISION   Specifies information to identify and document the program.
    IDENTIFICATION DIVISION

    PROGRAM-ID. program name.
    [AUTHOR. comment entry.]

[INSTALLATION. comment entry.]
[DATE-WRITTEN. comment entry.]
[DATE-COMPILED. comment entry.]
[SECURITY. comment entry.]

    IDENTIFICATION DIVISION

    PROGRAM-ID example.
    [AUTHOR. Ben Goldstein.
    [INSTALLATION. N.Y., N.Y.
    [DATE WRITTEN. 03/23/81.
    [DATE COMPILED. 04/01/81.
    [SECURITY. classified.

IF   Allows conditional execution of a statement or statements.
    IF condition/statement1/NEXT SENTENCE/ELSE
    /statement2/NEXT SENTENCE/.
        if AMOUNT-IN is greater than 1000
            MOVE amount-in TO large-amt
        ELSE
            MOVE amount-in to amount.

INDEX   Specifies a fields USAGE is for table lookup operations.
    See USAGE.

INDICATE   Used in conjunction with the GROUP statement.
    See GROUP.

INPUT-OUTPUT SECTION   Specifies the input and output devices that the files are to use.
    See ENVIRONMENTAL DIVISION.

INSPECT   Examines fields and counts the number of occurrences of a specified character and/or replaces specified characters of the field with other characters.
    INSPECT identifier1 TALLYING
        identifier2 FOR, /ALL/LEADING/
        CHARACTERS/ identifier3
            [BEFORE/AFTER/INITIAL/
            identifier4]
        REPLACING
            CHARACTERS BY identifier6 [BEFORE/
            AFTER/INITIAL/ identifier7]
            /ALL/LEADING/CHARACTERS/
            identifier5 BY identifier6
            [/BEFORE/AFTER/INITIAL/ identifier8]

    INSPECT amount
        REPLACING LEADING ' ' BY '*'.

INSTALLATION   An option within the IDENTIFICATION DIVISION to specify the place where the program is to be INSTALLED.
    See IDENTIFICATION DIVISION.

INTO   Specifies the receiving device or field.
    See READ.

JUSTIFIED (JUST) Causes right justification of alphabetic data.
  ; JUSTIFIED RIGHT.
      05 amount-output pic x(10) JUST RIGHT.

LABEL Specifies whether records are standard, nonstandard, or not used.
  ;LABEL /RECORD IS/RECORDS ARE /
STANDARD//OMITTED/.
See DATA DIVISION.

LOW-VALUES Used to assign the lowest value of the collating sequence to a field.
  MOVE LOW-VALUES TO low-field.

MOVE Specifies that data is to be moved from one field to another.
  MOVE/identifier1/literal/ TO identifier2
[,identifier3]...
      MOVE SPACES TO outputline.

MULTIPLY Finds the product of two numeric data items and stores the result in a third numeric data item.
  MULTIPLY /identifier1/literal1/ BY /identifier2/
literal2/
    GIVING identifier3 [ROUNDED] [,identifier4
[ROUNDED]]...
    [;ON SIZE ERROR imperative statement].
note: giving is not required.

    MULTIPLY principal BY interest-input
      GIVING total-due.

NEXT SENTENCE Used to indicate that upon a condition, execution of the NEXT SENTENCE (the next line of code) is to begin.

NUMERIC LITERAL A number used for arithmetic operations.

OBJECT-COMPUTER Specifies the computer used to compile the program.
See ENVIRONMENTAL DIVISION.

OCCURS Allows for the repetition of fields.
  OCCURS integer TIMES
    01 calendar
      03 day pic x (7) OCCURS 31 TIMES.

OMITTED Used within DATA DIVISION to describe files.

OPEN Prepares files for processing.
  OPEN/INPUT/OUTPUT/I-O/ file name1
[,file name2]...
    OPEN INPUT payroll.

OR Used in the IF statement to specify that only one condition need be true for execution of the imperative statement.
  IF condition OR condition
  imperative statement.
    IF done OR test
      PERFORM B007-report-printing.

ORGANIZATION Specifies the ORGANIZATION of the file.
  ENVIRONMENT DIVISION.

PAGE-COUNTER Used to count the number of pages of text and to supply page numbers.
  01 Page-data.
    05 page-counter PIC S999 VALUE +1.

PERFORM Transfers control to the named paragraph.
  PERFORM procedure name1 [THRU procedure
name2]
    UNTIL condition.

    PERFORM A125-report-printing
      UNTIL any-more-records = 'no'.

PICTURE (PIC) Specifies the characteristics of a field.
See DATA DIVISION.

PLUS (+) Used in editing to indicate where a plus sign is to appear on output.
  AMOUNT-OUT PIC +999.

PROCEDURE DIVISION Defines the procedures used by a specific program to achieve the desired results.
  PROCEDURE DIVISION. A001-compute-total-hours.
    OPEN INPUT employee-data-input-file.
    OUTPUT employee-check-record.
  READ employee-data-input-file
    AT END
      MOVE 'no' TO any-more-records.
  ....
  ....
  ....
  STOP RUN.

PROGRAM-ID Must be contained within the IDENTIFICATION DIVISION to identify the program.
See IDENTIFICATION DIVISION.

READ Reads a logical record from an input file.
  READ file name RECORD [INTO identifier]
    [AT END imperative statement].

    READ payroll
      AT END MOVE 'yes' TO any-more-records.

RECORD   Used to specify the attributes of a logical record.
See DATA DIVISION.

REDEFINES   Used to redefine an area of storage with respect to an identifier name and/or the specified area's attributes.
```
05 day-table
   10 day-constants.
      15 FILLER PIC X(3) VALUE 'MON'.
      15 FILLER PIC X(3) VALUE 'TUE'.
      15 FILLER PIC X(3) VALUE 'WED'.
      15 FILLER PIC X(3) VALUE 'THR'.
      15 FILLER PIC X(3) VALUE 'FRI'.
10 day-table REDEFINES day-constants
il3PIC X3 OCCURS 5 TIMES.
```

REMAINDER   Used in conjunction with the DIVIDE statement, REMAINDER computes the remainder of division and assigns the obtained value to a given identifier.
```
DIVIDE identifier1/literal1/ BY /identifier2/literal2/
GIVING identifier3
   REMAINDER identifier4 [; ON SIZE ERROR
imperative statement].

   DIVIDE amount BY payments GIVING monthly-output
      REMAINDER monthly-fraction-output.
```

RENAMES   Used to rename fields.
```
data name1 ; RENAMES data name2 [THRU data name3].
   year-output RENAMES jan-input THRU
   dec-input.
```

RETURN   Returns control to the calling statement.
See EXIT.

ROUNDED   May be used in any arithmetic operation, causing rounding up when the last digit in a numeric field is greater than or equal to 5.
See DIVIDE.

SEARCH ALL   Performs a binary search.
```
SEARCH ALL identifier1 [;AT END imperative
statement]
   WHEN /data name IS = identifier2/condition/
   [AND /data name IS = identifier3/condition]
   imperative statement/NEXT SENTENCE/.

   SEARCH ALL PAGES
      WHEN page-indicator = 'on'.
```

SEARCH   Performs a sequential search.
```
SEARCH identifier1 [VARYING /identifier2/index
name/]
```

```
[AT END imperative statement]
WHEN /condition/imperative statement/
NEXT SENTENCE/
[WHEN condition2/imperative statement2/NEXT
SENTENCE2/...

SET text-condition TO 1.
SEARCH text
   WHEN done
      MOVE '0' TO text-condition.
```

SECURITY   An option within the IDENTIFICATION DIVISION to specify the program's SECURITY clearance.
See IDENTIFICATION DIVISION.

SELECT   Used to name the files.
See ENVIRONMENT DIVISION.

SET   Used in conjunction with the SEARCH statement, SET assigns the index an initial value.
See SEARCH

SIGN   Used in the PICTURE clause to indicate sign dependency upon arithmetic operations.
No syntax available.

SIZE-ERROR   Tests the size of the obtained value determining whether the result will fit in the receiving field.
See SUBTRACT.

SOURCE-COMPUTER   Identifies the computer that was implemented when the SOURCE code was keyed in.
See ENVIRONMENTAL DIVISION.

SPACES   Used to assign blanks to a field.
See HEADING.

SPACES   Represents a string of blanks.
See HEADING.

STANDARD   Used within the DATA DIVISION to describe files.
See DATA DIVISION.

STOP   Terminates program execution and transfers control to the operating system.
```
STOP/RUN/literal/
   STOP RUN.
```

STRING   Copies two or more fields into one field.
```
STRING identifier1 [,identifier2]...
delimited by identifier3
   [,identifier4] [,identifier5]... DELIMITED BY
   identifier6
   INTO identifier7 [WITH POINTER identifier8]
   [;ON OVERFLOW imperative statement].

   STRING car-type DELIMITED BY ';'
```

car-year DELIMITED BY ';'
INTO car-data.

SUBTRACT Subtracts the sum of a given list of numeric data items from a specified item and assigns the obtain value to one or more data items.
SUBTRACT/identifier1/literal1
[,identifier2/literal2/]...
FROM /identifier-m/literal-m/
GIVING identifier-n [ROUNDED]
[,identifier-o [ROUNDED]]...
[;ON SIZE ERROR imperative statement].
note: giving is not required.

SUBTRACT expense1-input, expense2-input
FROM gross-input

SYNCHRONIZED (SYNC) Aligns binary numeric fields on the appropriate boundaries.

UNSTRING Assigns a single field into two or more fields.
UNSTRING identifier1
[DELIMITED BY [ALL] identifier2 [OR[ALL] identifier3]]
INTO identifier4 [,DELIMITER IN identifier5]
[,COUNT IN identifier6]
[,identifier7 [,DELIMITER IN identifier8]
[,COUNT IN ident9]]...
[WITH POINTER identifier10]
[TALLYING IN identifier11]
[;ON OVERFLOW imperative statement].

UNSTRING phone-number DELIMITED BY '-'
INTO area-code
number.

UNTIL Specifies continued execution of a group of statements UNTIL some condition.
See PERFORM.

USAGE Defines the format for which data is to be stored.
[;USAGE [IS] /COMPUTATIONAL/COMP/
DISPLAY/
/INDEX/COMPUTATIONAL-3/COMP-3/]

03 DATA-CONSTANT PIC XX/XX/XX
VALUE IS 03/02/62.

VALUE Used to assign values to fields.
See HEADING.

VARYING Used to compute the sum of a series of fields.
See SEARCH.

WHEN Used in a variety of statements to indicate conditional terms.
See SEARCH.

WORKING-STORAGE SECTION The WORKING-STORAGE SECTION is a part of the DATA-DIVISION SECTION that is used to define data other than that found in the INPUT and OUTPUT sections.
[WORKING-STORAGE SECTION.
[record-description-entry]] WORKING-
STORAGE SECTION. 01
PROGRAM INDICATORS.
03 any-more-records PIC X(3) VALUE 'yes'.

WRITE Causes output to the printer.
WRITE record name [FROM identifier1]
[/before/after/ADVANCING/identifier2/integer/
[LINES].
WRITE payroll.

ZERO Used with the VALUE statement, causing the value of zero to be placed in a field.
05 amount-input PIC 9(5) VALUE ZERO.

COMAL

COMAL-80 is a high-level language, originating in Denmark, which combines the features of BASIC with the more powerful features of Pascal. It was originally proposed by Borge Christensen, Principal Lecturer in Mathematics and Computer Science at the College of Higher Education in Tonder, Denmark. Benedict Lofsted assisted him in its original design, and in June 1974 the design and specifications for COMAL were complete. The language was first implemented on the Data General Nova 1200 minicomputer. By 1978, COMAL had become a very popular language in Danish schools, and implementations for other computers were launched. Subsequently, in an attempt to keep all implementations of COMAL as compatible with each other as possible, a working group was formed in 1979 with members from the Technical University of Copenhagen, the University of Roskilde, and representatives from several Danish manufacturers of microcomputers. The group formalized a new definition of COMAL, COmmon Algorithmic Language, now officially named COMAL-80.

In May 1982, the definition of the COMAL language was further refined and improved, with the objective of true standardization. It is referred to as the COMAL KERNEL, and it is printed in full in Appendix H of the *COMAL Handbook*. This new definition, although very similar to the original definition, contained improved implementations of the user-defined function of the language and the substring specifications. The COMAL KERNEL was reaffirmed by the working group in March 1983 and, again, in December. COMAL is now implemented on several computers, with more implementations under way. The most popular versions of the language are for Commodore microcomputers, including the PET series (the 8032 and 4032) and the Commodore 64. It is also available for the RC700 and the ICL Comet as well as any CP/M system including the Apple II+ and IIe series running under CP/M. Implementations are available for the MS-DOS systems, including the IBM PC and PCjr.

As it was originally conceived, COMAL was designed to replace BASIC as the programming language for schools and home microcomputers. The popularity of BASIC—it is easy to learn, short programs can be written easily, and it has a loose structure that is forgiving to beginning programmers—does not mask the inherent shortcomings in the language. Though the language works perfectly adequately at first for new students, as their short programs grow longer and more ambitious, programming errors become more fequent, and it subsequently takes a long time to find out where students have made their mistakes. The student programs in BASIC are also hard to read, and the discovery of programming errors usually happens during the execution phase of the program. Even the construction of the program and the execution of its logic soon become too difficult for students in BASIC because the BASIC variable names are too short to relay meaningful information

about what they are to represent, and the many GOTO's make it hard to identify the program's tasks. The IF...THEN statement is a primary offender in this area of branching logic because when an IF is true, one often has to look somewhere else in the program to follow the logic, rather than immediately executing the statements at the IF...THEN point. However, the designers of COMAL also wanted to retain BASIC's strongest features: it is highly interactive with the user, it has good editing capabilities, and it is easy to use input/output statements. The designers opted for keeping these features relatively intact while searching for a language that presented a more highly defined structure and allowed for the use of longer variable names. Pascal became the language of choice, and the combination of Pascal and BASIC resulted in COMAL: a language which features both introductory simplicity for beginning students and the power and structured architecture of Pascal. The IBM PC and Commodore 64 implementations of COMAL even have the turtle graphics capabilities of Logo.

COMAL is inherently a friendly language. Many COMAL statements and commands may be executed immediately as they are entered. When preceded with a line number, they will be incorporated into a program. Each line is checked for correct syntax by the language's editor as it is entered, because COMAL will not accept an incorrect line. If it finds an error, an understandable error message is displayed below the line and the cursor is placed at the point of error. Once the error is corrected, the error message is removed from the screen and the original contents are redisplayed. The error message is nondestructive. This is an invaluable feature for beginners because the language's editing functions will keep novice programmers from making syntax errors without interrupting the programming activity.

Line numbers are used by COMAL programs only to allow easy reference by the programmer. The programs themselves do not reference line numbers. For example, there is no GOTO (line number) as in BASIC. Automatic line numbering is provided by COMAL for ease of entering programs. The RENUM command allows lines to be renumbered at any time.

A COMAL program listing is easy to read. Modular structures are emphasized with their statements automatically indented. This feature is often referred to as "pretty print." While Pascal has the same structures, it does not provide the automatic indenting of program listings. COMAL allows long variable names, with each character significant up to 78 characters' length in some implementations. Thus, a variable can have a descriptive name like TOTAL or PLAYER'NAME$ rather than just T or PN$. The combinations of indented structures with long variable names provide an easy-to-follow program.

Modular programming is easy in COMAL. Multiline procedures and functions are named and allow parameter passing as well as both LOCAL and GLOBAL variables. Parameters may be passed by value on input only or in reference on input and output. A procedure or function may be called from anywhere in the program or even in direct mode, and they can call other procedures and functions, or they can even call themselves. This is known as recursion and is especially important because it mimics one of the most powerful features of natural languages: recursive nesting of phrases.

Advanced string handling in COMAL allows any substring to be used or even changed without affecting the rest of the string. COMAL also allows arrays of any dimension within memory limitations. Array indices do not have to begin at 0 or 1, but may begin at any integer. Other features include advanced file handling with sequential and random access files, either in ASCII or in binary. COMAL also automatically detects the End Of File when reading a sequential file, and relays the information to the user via the EOF flag. COMAL can read data from DATA statements and sets an EOD (End Of Data) system flag when the last data item is read.

Output can be directed to either the screen or printer with a SELECT OUTPUT statement. PRINT statements may include PRINT USING for formatted output as well as TAB to skip to any position on the line. Tab position intervals, or ZONEs, may be set at any interval. Most BASICs use a nonchangeable interval of 10. Output to the printer is the same as output to the screen.

The modular structure of COMAL and its similarity to Pascal are evident in this sample program listing which creates a True/False arithmetic test.

```
0010  // TRUE OR FALSE
0020  WRONG:=FALSE
```

```
0030  TRY:=0
0040  WHILE NOT WRONG DO
0050      TRY:+1
0060      FIRST:=RND(1,9)
0070      SECOND:=RND(1,9)
0080      PRINT TRY,"> WHAT IS";FIRST;
          "PLUS";SECOND;
0090      INPUT "===>": ANSWER;
0100      IF ANSWER=FIRST+SECOND THEN
0110          PRINT "YES"
0120      ELSE
0130          PRINT "NO"
0140          WRONG:=TRUE
0150      ENDIF
0160  ENDWHILE
0170  PRINT "NO WRONG ANSWERS UP TO
      PROBLEM";TRY
```

```
[RUN]
    1> WHAT IS 5 PLUS 1 ===> 6 YES
    2> WHAT IS 6 PLUS 9 ===> 15 YES
    3> WHAT IS 1 PLUS 4 ===> 6 NO
    NO WRONG ANSWERS UP TO PROBLEM 3
```

The power of the language can be seen here in the simplicity and relative ease of structuring this quiz. The blocking-out of procedures produces an elementary branching operation with a relatively small amount of code. This illustrates one of the original design features of COMAL for the instruction of program design and the geometry of logic.

COMAL GLOSSARY

ABS   Returns the absolute value of its parameter.
  ABS(x)
    if ABS(x−y) < quest then print x−y

AND   Returns the logical conjunction of two boolean factors.
  if (condition) AND (condition) then imperative statement
    if not(p<>ret AND t=0) then print"goto next page"

ATN   Returns the value of an angle whose tangent is equal to the parameter of the function.
  ATN(expression)
    print ATN(65)

CASE   The CASE statement is a multiple decision operator which uses the value of an expression to select one statement from a group of statements to be executed. The selection of statements must be enclosed between the CASE statement and the ENDCASE statement. The OTHERWISE block is optional.
  CASE expression OF
  WHEN expression
    statements
  WHEN expression
    statements
  OTHERWISE
    statements
  ENDCASE
        CASE amount OF
        WHEN 1
            print"please pay $10.00"
        WHEN 2
            print"please pay $20.00"
        OTHERWISE
            print"you owe nothing"
        ENDCASE

CAT   Shows a catalog of the disk.

CHAIN   Causes the loading and execution of the named program.
  CHAIN filename.

CHR$ Returns the character corresponding to a given ASCII number.
  CHR(integer expression)
    print CHR$(65); CHR$(67)

CLOSED   Preceded by the PROC or FUNC statement, defines all variables within the procedure or function local.
  PROC name(variable list)CLOSED
    statements
  ENDPROC name
        PROC BOX (length)CLOSED
            FOR slides := 1 to 4 DO
                FORWARD length
                LEFT 90
            NEXT slides
        ENDPROC box

CON   Causes the CONtinuation of execution after an interrupt was encountered.
  CON

COS   Real function that returns the cosine of its parameter.
  COS(expression)
    print"the cosine of 100 degrees is"
    print COS(100)

DATA   Allows information to be stored in a program.
  DATA "string",numerical expression
  Note: any combination of strings or digits may be used.
    DATA 65,66,67,"a","b","c"

DIM   Dimensions an array or string.
  DIM string name OF integer
  DIM array name (index)
  DIM string array (index) OF integer
  DIM name$ of 25

ELIF Standing for ELSE IF, causes one section of the structure to close while testing for a true result of some condition in order to open a second section of the structure.
```
IF condition THEN
   statements
ELIF condition THEN
   statements
ENDIF
      IF test>59 THEN
          print "results show you have passed"
      ELIF test>90 THEN
          print "results show you have scored an
          A"
      ENDIF
```

ELSE As part of the IF statment, ELSE forces execution of a statement or statements on a false condition.
```
IF expression THEN
   statements
ELSE
   statements
ENDIF
IF wrong ≠0 THEN
   PRINT "perfect"
ELSE
   PRINT "practice more"
ENDIF
```

ENDCASE Used in conjunction with the CASE statement as a terminator of a body or block of code.
See CASE.

ENDIF Used in conjunction with the IF statement as a terminator of a block of code.
See IF.

ENDPROC Used in conjunction with the PROC statement as a terminator of a procedure.
See PROC.

EXEC Executes a named procedure, then returns control to the statement following the EXEC command.
```
EXEC procedure name
   EXEC new page
```

EXP Returns e to the power of the parameter.
```
EXP(expression)
   EXP(10)
```

FOR Used when a statement or group of statements is to be repeated a predefined number of times.
```
FOR identifier := integer expression to integer expression do
   statements
NEXT identifier
      FOR x := 1 to 10 do
          print x
      NEXT x
```

GOTO Transfers control to a stated point in the program.
```
GOTO label
   GOTO quick exit
```

IF Allows conditional execution of a statement or statements. Additional conditions are optional using ELIF. The ELSE section which is optional allows statements to be executed only when the conditions are not met.
```
IF condition THEN
   statements
ELIF condition THEN
   statements
ELSE
   statements
ENDIF
      IF baudrate = 300 THEN
          set 300
      ELIF baudrate = 1200 THEN
          set 1200
      ELSE
          PRINT "wrong baudrate"
      ENDIF
```

IN Automatically searches a string for any substring.
```
expression IN expression
   if mon$ INweek$ then imperative statement
```

INPUT Allows input from the keyboard much like the READ statement takes data from a DATA statement.
```
INPUT variable
   INPUT "enter your name :": name$
```

INT Returns the integer part of an expression.
```
INT(expression)
   INT(243+ret)
```

LEN Returns the number of characters in a string.
```
LEN(string or string variable)
   print(LEN(day$))
```

LOG   Returns the logarithm of its parameter.
  LOG(expression)
    expr := 20*LOG(lg)

MOD   Computes the remainder of division.
  variable := numeric expression MOD numeric
  expression
    color: = number MOD 16

NOT   Logical math operator reverses the TRUE/
FALSE evaluation of the numeric expression.
  NOT condition
  WHILE NOT EOD DO data'in

OPEN   Prepares a file to be used.
  OPEN channel number, "file name", mode of access
    OPEN 2, "my file", write

OR   Returns the logical disjunction of two boolean
factors.
  IF (string) = (condition) OR (string) = (condition2)
    THEN imperative statement
  IF trys >3 or reply$ = "?" THEN give hint

ORD   Returns the ordinal value of the character string
(similar to ASC in BASIC).
  ORD(string expression)
    PRINT ORD(c$)

OTHERWISE   See CASE.

PRINT   Prints specified message on CRT or other device.
  PRINT"sting variable" or PRINT variable
    PRINT"the number of children born each day is
    1234"

PROC   Used in conjunction with ENDPROC to de-
fine a group of statements as a procedure.
  PROC name (parameters) CLOSED
    statements
  ENDPROC name
    PROC refund(name$, amount)
      PRINT name$, "refund due"
      PRINT USING "$###.##": amount
      check (name$, amount)
    ENDPROC refund

RANDOMIZE   Eliminates the possibility of a program generating the same sequence of numbers when
repetitive use of the program or segment is required.
  Place the word RANDOMIZE once near the beginning of the program.

READ   Assigns the value of elements of a DATA line
to variables.
  READ variable, variable , variable, etc...
    READ cards,suit

REPEAT   Permits repeated execution of a statement
or statements with a condition as the parameter determining when to terminate repetition.
  REPEAT
    statements
  UNTIL condition
    REPEAT
      INPUT "How old are you?": age
    UNTIL age >0 and AGE <150

RND   Returns a pseudo-random integer between two
specified numbers.
  RND(x,y)
    PRINT CHR$(RND(65,68))

SELECT OUTPUT   Used to redirect output of text.
Output locations may include printer, screen, or disk
file.
  SELECT OUTPUT string expression
    SELECT OUTPUT loc$

SIN   Returns the sine of the parameter in radians.
  SIN(expression)
    SIN(89)

STEP   Used to specify the incrementation to take
place during loop execution.
  for variable := integer to integer STEP real
  expression do
    for x := 50 to 12 step −0.5 do

SQR   Returns the square root of the parameter.
  SQR(expression)
    SQR(25)

TAB   Positions the cursor to a specified column position.
  TAB(integer)
    PRINT TAB(32), "hello"

TAN   Returns the tangent of the parameter in radians.
   TAN(expression)
     TAN(64)

UNTIL   See REPEAT.

WHEN   See CASE.

WHILE   Loop control forcing execution of statements
until boolean expression false.
   WHILE not EOF (infile) DO
     READ FILE infile: text$
       PRINT text$
     ENDWHILE

ZONE   Splits the print line into user-defined fields or
zones.

Forth

Forth is more than a programming language. It is a programming environment which is extensible both outwardly and inwardly. Outward extension is accomplished by using Forth to add an application language layer onto Forth and then using that new application language to add further applications layers. Inward extensibility is accomplished by modifying the structure, capabilities, and features of Forth—a process called meta-compilation, i.e., letting Forth recompile a new version of Forth. This is a simple task since most of Forth is written in high-level Forth and the remainder is written using the Forth assembler.

All programming environments are based on a series of design decisions concerning the interactions between the programmer and the computer. A unique set of decisions, made principally by Charles H. Moore, the inventor of Forth, have created the programming environment which is Forth. Some of the decisions were:

- Keep it simple—Forth is understandable and modifiable by one person.
- Keep it small—Forth can reside in under 16K of computer memory (although it usually doesn't these days).
- Keep it fast—provide an "interactive compiler" and an integrated, structured, conditional macro assembler.
- Make it transportable—Forth is written in Forth and has been implemented on almost every computer known.

Forth is:

- an operating system
- an editor
- an assembler
- an interpreter
- a compiler
- a high-level language
- a set of development tools
- a stack machine, traditionally 16 bits wide

It has simple virtual memory management, and many versions include real-time multitasking. Forth has been used to write: BASIC, Pascal, LISP, Logo, COBOL, and Forth, as well as database systems, expert systems, and control systems. Forth is best known for its use at astronomical observatories and in process control and laboratory instrumentation. It has also been used to write a variety of business applications and as a systems implementation language.

The article "An Architectural Trail to Threaded-Code Systems" by Peter M. Kogge, IBM Federal Systems Division (*IEEE Computer,* March 1982, pp. 22-32), provides a logical picture of a Forth system and contains one minor understatement, "Threaded-code systems should find a secure niche where small-to-moderate specialized interactive application packages, real-time control of external devices and sensors, and engineering-type throw-away code dominate." A variety of institutions with 2000-screen (Megabytes of source code) and larger scientific and business applications have gone well beyond the limits mentioned in this article.

Origins

The best source of information on the origins of Forth is contained in *Forth Dimensions,* vol. 1, no. 6, pp. 60-75. The article "FORTH, the Last Ten Years and the Next Two Weeks" is a printed version of a speech given at the October 1979 Forth Convention in San Francisco. The speech was given by Charles H. Moore.

In brief, Moore in the early 1960s became dissatisfied with the available programming systems and began experimenting with a variety of aspects of the programming environment. By about 1969 he had put together most of the elements of what is now Forth. He states (p. 72), "My original goal was to write more than 40 programs in my life. I think that I have increased my throughput by a factor of 10. I don't think that throughput is program-language limited any longer so I have accomplished what I set out to do."

Having designed the software environment he wanted, Moore stated at the 1980 Forth Convention, "Hardware today is in the same shape that software was 20 years ago. There is no point in trying to optimize software any further until we have taken the first crack at optimizing the hardware." Moore has since designed a Forth chip and expects to see the first commercial silicon implementation of the chip within a few years.

The name Forth was chosen by Moore to indicate a "fourth" generation language running on the then "third" generation hardware. It was spelled FORTH because the file system would allow a maximum of five characters in a name and because, as is true in most file systems, case was disregarded. Modern usage is that Forth is the name of the environment, while FORTH is a Forth word (the name of a Forth vocabulary).

History

Forth has followed several somewhat parallel paths to reach the present.

A. Starting at the National Radio Astronomy Observatory, in about 1971, Forth spread to Kitt Peak Observatory, and from there throughout the world of astronomy until, in 1976, it was made a standard language for the International Astronomical Union.

B. In approximately 1973, Charles H. Moore and Elizabeth Rather started FORTH, Inc., which produced MiniFORTH, then microFORTH, and eventually the modern versions, polyFORTH and polyFORTH II.

C. Dr. Hans Nieuwenhuijzen and others at the state university at Utrecht in the Netherlands learned of

Forth. They produced a variety of enhancements and applications and helped organize the European Forth Users Group.

D. Bill Ragsdale and others in the San Francisco Bay Area became involved in Forth and formed the Forth Interest Group (FIG) in 1978. They produced a Forth newsletter named *Forth Dimensions* and then a set of public domain versions of Forth for five different microcomputers and for the DEC PDP11. *Forth Dimensions,* vol. 5, no. 6, pp. 20–25, details the formation and activities of FIG.

E. FORTH, Inc., the European group, and the astronomical users joined to form the Forth International Standards Team and produced a 1977 set of standard Forth words. FIG became involved in 1978, and an updated set of standard words was produced that year. The astronomical users then dropped out of the standardization efforts. In 1979 a charter was proposed, and the group was renamed the Forth Standards Team. A 1979 Standard for Forth was developed to include the "new" 8-bit machines. The European group then dropped out of the standards work, and a group of Forth vendors joined the efforts. This changed the makeup of the group from predominantly users to a more equal mix of users and vendors. In 1982, meetings of the Forth Standards Team were conducted to update the 1979 Standard. The updates were so comprehensive that in 1983 a new standard was released. The 1983 Standard is scheduled for update in 1988, at which time the 32-bit versions of Forth are expected to be included.

F. Around 1978, several vendors licensed micro-FORTH from FORTH, Inc., and started selling their own versions. Later, in about 1978–1979 (after the release of the public domain FIG-Forth), a variety of vendors sprang up selling enhanced versions of FIG-Forth and then 79 Standard versions and now 83 Standard versions.

Forth as an Environment

Forth traditionally includes its own operating system, although versions are available which emulate standard operating systems, reside within other operating systems, use standard named file systems, support calls to and from other programming languages, and have all the other "normal" attributes of the classical programming languages.

Even though there has been a recent strong trend toward combining the programming language aspects of Forth with other operating systems, we will characterize the different environment in which the traditional Forth programmer works. Some of the elements of the environment are similar to those of the interactive languages such as APL, BASIC, or LISP. There are fewer similarities with the "batch" languages such as Ada, ASSEMBLER, C, Fortran, or Pascal.

Editing

In a "batch" environment we must invoke the operating system, have it load the editor, and open the ap-

propriate text file for editing. If the file is a large one and we want only to change a single character somewhere in the source file, we must process the whole file to modify that character.

In the traditional Forth environment the editor is on-line as part of that environment, so we select the 1K block of text the offending character is in, edit that block, and save the modified copy back onto the original. What are the trade-offs? The "batch" method is simple and slow, while the Forth method is fast but requires that the programmer know which 1K block of disk storage the character resides upon. This may seem strange, but is little more onerous than knowing where in the source listing the character is (also a requirement for the "batch" mode).

Compiling

Again, in "batch" mode, the operating system loads the compiler, and points it to the program source-code. The compiler will process the source-code and produce an object-code file and a printed listing or a list-file.

In the traditional Forth environment the compilers are on-line (as well as the interpreters and the assembler) so we need only type n LOAD (where n is the starting number of a set of 1K block of source-code on the disk). Except for a few tracks of self-booting object-code, the whole Forth disk contains nothing but source-code. There are no .COM files, no .EXE files, no .REL files, no .TXT files, etc. There are, in fact, no files at all, just numbered 1K blocks of disk storage which normally contain Forth source-code modules, but can contain anything that the programmer desires.

The trade-offs: in the "batch" environment, the compiler will grind through the whole source-file independently of the number of errors encountered, trying to do something—anything!—until it reaches an "end" statement.

Forth, on the other hand, will terminate compilation on the first error encountered, flag the error, and wait for the programmer to fix the problem. The programmer can then either interactively debug the code successfully compiled up to the point at which the error was encountered, or more probably, correct the error and continue the compilation process from that point. It is not necessary to start the whole process again from the beginning. The result is that the correction process incurs almost no lost time.

Linking

In the "batch" environment, we again return to the operating system, use it to load the linker, point the linker at the relocatable object-file, etc., another time-consuming process. The traditional Forth environment does not involve these processes. The source-code is available and Forth uses it. Forth will typically compile source-code modules as fast as most linkers will link relocatable object modules, hence no relocatable object files are necessary (they are, however, easily supported if desired).

Debugging

Once more we return to the operating system to load the debugger, so that the debugger will load the object-code so that we can finally start testing our program. How do we perform the debugging process? How do we provide data, parameters, and other information to the various program modules and subroutines? Until we have a significant part of the program running, we have to use the debugger to load registers, set breakpoints, etc., because the program either will not have an interactive (console) capability or will not have yet been debugged to that point.

Forth is its own debugger. Parameter passing is uniformly done via a parameter stack (which is separate and distinct from the return stack!) or via named global variables. Symbolic debugging has always been a natural part of the Forth environment. The smallest of program modules or procedures have names and can be tested individually and interactively without having any of the other modules present or working. Of course, if testing a module which requires that some complex data structure exists, you must be able to create and inspect that data structure. Forth allows you to do just that; in fact, Forth supports the creation of any data type you can imagine, by providing the capability of building custom compilers and defining words, which are then used to create exactly the data types required.

Recapitulation

We stated that we should be able to iterate the edit-debug loop as rapidly as possible so that our attention could be kept on the programming problem and not on the mechanics of using the operating system and the various separate files (editor, compiler, linker, debugger) which have to be loaded and used to create a variety of other files (THING.SRC, THING.BAK, THING.REL, THING.OBJ, THING2.OBJ, THING.BAT). The time required to go through the complete loop and to manage the process can take from minutes to hours. The equivalent process in Forth takes from seconds to minutes. It's not that Forth doesn't have the same loop (editor, compiler, debugger)—it does. It's just that the steps are done much faster, and consequently much more often. Less time between iterations means much less loss of concentration and much more productive use of programming time.

Another consequence of the rapidity and ease of the process is that a programmer is much more willing to try various possibilities, to investigate a wider variety of possible data structure, and to more carefully design and debug each of the modules because the programmer can do so easily and quickly. In fact, such experimental programming is so efficient it can become a part of the design process.

Numbers

The complete source-code for the Forth operating system, the editor, assembler, debug utilities, and the in-terpreter and compilers (about 130K of text, usually available as part of a Forth package) can be compiled in less than 3 minutes.

Caveats

There are a number of trade-offs made to give the Forth environment its characteristics. From the point of view of an operating system, Forth is primitive but powerful. It has no named files, hence the burden of the management of the 1K disk storage blocks is placed upon the programmer. Most programmers provide a simple block management system to aid in the process. Forth does not impose a particular scheme upon anyone; you are free to use none or to pick the optimum file management method for your purposes. As a language, Forth is compact, modular, structured, transportable, and extensible; incorporates an interpreter, assembler and compilers; supports any data types; has virtual memory, batch and autoexecute modules, vectored I/O (I/O redirection), real-time processing; and many versions are multitasking. Almost all of the facilities incorporated into Forth are available as primitive functions—simple but powerful general-purpose procedures which are used to build more complex and powerful operations.

Forth words (procedures) usually pass all parameters via a parameter stack. This provides a uniform method of parameter passing and allows reentrant procedures, but requires that the programmer manage the parameter stack. Consequently the programmer is burdened with a task normally managed internally by other high-level languages, and as a result a variety of low-level stack operations are found embedded in much of the high-level Forth code. This accounts, to a great extent, for the reputation of Forth as being a "write-only" language. It also indicates the necessity of providing parameter-stack "picture" comments for each Forth word. A variety of papers have been published in the Forth community addressing the problem of embedded stack operators and one of the recent trends has been toward the use of "named local stack variables."

Since there are, at present, no commercially available native Forth machines, almost all versions of Forth run on either a 16-bit or a 32-bit stack-oriented virtual machine, implemented via a set of fast and compact machine-code routines. Consequently, high-level Forth on many processors runs about 5 to 10 times slower than assembler speed and about 10 to 100 times as fast as most high-level interpreters. Forth assembler words run, of course, at machine speed, but because of the extensive use of the parameter stack for communications between words and because of the overhead of the virtual machine in threading from word to word, many machines run Forth assembler code at about one-half the speed of equivalent modules written using a standard assembler and running in a nonstack (register-oriented) environment.

When Forth was originally developed, minicomputer hardware was expensive and had limited amounts of memory. Because of this and because Forth was originally designed for real-time control and data handling, the typical Forth environment had, and still has, very little built-in protection. It is quite possible for a programmer to crash the system with a keystroke. The Forth programmer is given total access to the hardware and, in exchange for this freedom, has total responsibility for system protection. This is not at all equivalent to saying that an application written using Forth as the programming language is crashable. Indeed, a running Forth application is fully as robust as any other application program. In fact, because Forth modules normally lack undesired coupling and because thoroughly testing each of the modules is so easy, a typical application is quite robust.

Other concerns in a Forth programming environment are documentation and programming team support. Forth has peculiar requirements which must be considered if successful documentation and project control are to be maintained. These have been addressed in the literature and if properly handled are as successful as the techniques used with other languages. Also, because of the simple and effective parameter passing scheme and because of the low coupling between modules, each member of the programming team can do an immense amount of productive work before system integration. System integration is simpler and requires much less time than is normally required in other high-level language environments.

Finale

The trade-offs made in designing Forth have produced a unique and powerful environment which has a particular mix of high-level and low-level features, many of which may seem strange and puzzling when first encountered. There were, however, reasons behind the choices. Further, because Forth is evolving, due to its extensibility and the ease with which it can be internally modified, these reasons are continually being challenged, tested, and either reaffirmed or abandoned. In fact, Forth can, and should, be exactly what is required by your own needs and circumstances.

Forth as a Programming Language

"The reason Forth is among the most misunderstood of programming languages is that it realy isn't a language at all. Forth is a programming tool, one step removed from a language. It is a metalanguage, a language for writing other languages" (from Richard Milewski, "Forth Is Not a Language," *Infoworld,* October 11, 1982). Learning a programming language involves the study of the syntax and grammar of that language. Examples of the use of the features of the language are also studied, and carefully selected problems are addressed. The whole emphasis is on learning the available features of the language and techniques for using them to solve a variety of programming problems. Some problems will be trivial, others will make the programmer wish that a different language were available.

Taking this approach with Forth will yield no better (nor any worse) result. While it is still necessary to understand the syntax, grammar, and features of Forth,

the radical difference is in the application of these features. They are meant to be extended/modified to produce a language specifically tailored to the problem at hand. The problem is then quickly solved using that language.

One of the greatest strengths of Forth is that it can be transformed into the ideal language for solving a specific problem. That capability is also one of its greatest weaknesses. Unless the programmer producing the new application language does a superb job of defining, implementing, and documenting it, the new language will only be useful to that programmer and for that specific task.

Used at its greatest potential, Forth is not a language for the average programmer. However, given an excellent programmer using Forth to produce a new application language, the productivity of other programmers using that language to solve the problems it was tailored to solve can be enormously enhanced.

Forth allows the creation of an incredibly powerful set of programming environments for use in a whole spectrum of applications or your very own tower of Babel.

Simple Introduction to Using Forth

Forth consists of a set of Forth words. (These examples use a public domain 83 Standard version.)
- A Forth program is constructed by using and extending this set of Forth words.
- All words (instructions, commands, data, etc.) must be separated by one or more delimiting characters—normally space(s).
- All parameters (addresses, data, etc.) must be available before an action can be performed upon them. (Parameters first, operations next.)
- Words are arranged in a dictionary. The dictionary is subdivided into vocabularies. The vocabularies are named. Entering the name of a vocabulary will cause it to be available to be searched.
- Forth interprets a word by looking up the definition of that word in its dictionary and then executing the word's definition.
- Forth attempts to look up anything separated by delimiters. If it can't find the thing in its dictionary, Forth then attempts to convert it as a number. If the thing won't convert, Forth then gives up and echoes the offensive thing followed by a ?.
- Things that are converted to numbers are put onto a parameter stack.
- Forth works in any number base from 2 thru 72, and is normally used in base 10.
- When loaded, Forth is in the interpret mode, and will accept and execute words input via the keyboard.

For example, if we type:

VOCS <enter>

Forth will look for the word VOCS in its dictionary. If VOCS is found it will then be executed. The function of

VOCS is to output the names of all the vocabularies available in the dictionary. If we type:

WORDS <enter>

this word will cause Forth to start listing all the words in the currently active vocabulary. If we type:

ORDER <enter>

this word will output the list of all the vocabularies to be searched and the order in which they will be searched. If we type:

EDITOR <enter>

this word will select the editor vocabulary and cause it to be the first vocabulary to be searched. If we type:

7 −5 + . <enter>   (note the "notorious" reverse Polish notation)

Forth will start interpreting the sequence of characters: 7 −5 + . (from left to right). The sequence of actions will be to try to find 7 in the dictionary and fail, then try to convert 7 as a number and succeed, then put the converted number onto the parameter stack. Next, the −5 receives the same treatment and also is placed on the parameter stack. Then the + is looked for and found, so it is executed. Its function is to take the top two numbers off the parameter stack, to add them together, and then to place the resulting sum back onto the parameter stack. Finally the . is looked for and found (it's also a word in Forth and is called "dot"). The function of the . is to remove the top stack item, to convert it to an ASCII string, and to send it to the display. The answer 2 will be displayed.

Forth normally treats numbers as single precision integer (15-bit precision, 1-bit sign) and an overflow gives NO warning message. Double-precision integers (31-bit precision, 1-bit sign) are also usually available. Forth will stay in the interpret mode until it encounters a word which causes it to leave the interpret mode and enter the compile mode. It then stays in the compile mode until it encounters a word which will switch it back to the interpret mode.

The Forth word : will change the mode from interpret to compile (and will also start to enter a new word definition into the dictionary). The Forth word ; will change the mode from compile to interpret and thereby terminate the process of entering a new word definition into the dictionary. The words : and ; are normally used in matched pairs for exactly this purpose. Example:

: DO-NOTHING ; <ENTER>

This will cause a new word to be added to the dictionary, named DO-NOTHING, which will be a null operation. We can now type:

DO-NOTHING <enter>

The answer would be: ok.

Now, consider something a little more useful, the Forth definition:

: 2X (n -- 2n) DUP + ; <enter>

This is interpreted as follows:

:   enter compile mode and start a new definition
2X   give it the name 2X
(start a comment (in this case the comment is a stack picture)
n   represents a signed number on the stack before using 2X
--   separates the before and after stack entries
2n   the number on the stack after using 2X
)   end a comment
DUP   a Forth word which duplicates the top stack entry
+   a Forth word which adds the n and the copy made by the DUP
;   end the definition and return to interpret mode

We have added a new word, named 2X, to the dictionary. The new word functions by duplicating whatever is on the parameter stack and then adding the duplicate to the original, leaving the results on the parameter stack (a method of multiplying a value by 2). The dictionary entry for 2X is, in essence, made up of the name of the word and the equivalent of two calls, one to the execution time procedure of DUP and the other to + . To use 2X, one might type:

3 2X . <enter>

and receive the answer: 6 ok. The word 2X is an example of adding a high-level definition to the dictionary. We can just as easily add an assembly-level word. For example:

```
CODE 2*  ( n -- 2n )   S ) ASL, ( shift top of stack left )

        NEXT, ( terminate code routine)
        END-CODE( end the definition)
```

The word 2* performs the same function as 2X, but executes much faster. The ability to simply define assembler definitions, pass parameters to them, and use them in high-level definitions, makes access to the hardware, for both use and interactive testing, extremely convenient. This capability alone makes Forth desirable in many systems.

Programming in Forth is simply the process of adding words to the dictionary. As each new word is added to the dictionary, it becomes a part of Forth. The new word is then available to be used to add other new words to the Forth dictionary. This process continues until an application has been completely defined. The application words will be defined in terms of the original Forth words and the newly added application words. The last word added to the dictionary is usually the name of the application. The application is then run by entering the name of that word. To illustrate this, we examine such a word:

```
: VOICE-RESPONSE SYSTEM            ( —— )
              ( application program name )
                    ( start loop construct )  BEGIN
HANG-UP            ( initialize system )
                    ( start a nested loop )  BEGIN
RING?             ( if ring exit loop )  UNTIL
GO-OFF-HOOK       ( pick-up phone )
OUTPUT-SIGN-ON-MESSAGE
                  ( note meaningfull name )
START-TIME-OUT      ( for no input )
                    ( another loop )  BEGIN

RECEIVE-TONE? IF
RESET-TIMER         ( true phrase )
PROCESS-TONE        ( do next level )
DONE?        ELSE   ( until done )
```

```
TIME-OUT?     THEN   ( or time up )  UNTIL
            ( non-terminating loop )  AGAIN ;
```

This illustrates not only the use of some of Forth's structure operators, but also the use of previously defined custom application words to construct the top most definition in an application program. (The reverse indentation used to indicate the nesting of the structure operators, though not common, is meaningful in that the operators require a parameter before execution, not after.)

And lastly, Forth is an excellent first language to use in an introductory computer science course. It not only is a modern, structured language, but also can be used to illustrate the entire spectrum of language features—from pure machine code and the direct access to the computer hardware, through assembler, interpreter, compiler, editor, operating system, to high-level language. The more advanced topics such as data structures, metacompiling, and real-time multitasking can also be advantageously illustrated in Forth.

FORTH GLOSSARY

The following is the Forth-83 Standard required word set of the Forth Standards Team. It must be included as a subset of the glossary of a version of Forth claiming to comply with the Forth-83 Standard.

!   16b addr --
16b is stored at addr.

+d1 -- +d2
The remainder of +d1 divided by the value of BASE is converted to an ASCII character and appended to the output string toward lower memory addresses. +d2 is the quotient and is maintained for further processing. Typically used between <# and #>.

#>   32b -- addr +n
Pictured numeric output conversion is ended dropping 32b. addr is the address of the resulting output string. +n is the number of characters in the output string. addr and +n together are suitable for TYPE.

#S   +d -- 0 0
+d is converted appending each resultant character into the pictured numeric output string until the quotient (see "#") is zero. A single zero is added to the output string if the number was initially zero. Typically used between <# and #>.

#TIB   -- addr
The address of a variable containing the number of bytes in the text input buffer. #TIB is accessed by WORD when BLK is zero. {{..capacity of TIB}}.

'   -- addr
Used in the form: '<name>. addr is the compilation address of <name>. An error condition exists if <name> is not found in the current active search order.

(--
     -- (compiling)
Used in the form: (ccc). The characters ccc delimited by) [closing parenthesis] are considered comments. Comments are not otherwise processed. The blank following (is not part of ccc. (may be freely used while interpreting or compiling. The number of characters in ccc may be from zero to the number of characters remaining in the input stream up to the closing parenthesis.

*   w1 w2 -- w3
w3 is the least significant 16 bits of the arithmetic product of w1 times w2.

*/   n1 n2 n3 -- n4
n1 is first multiplied by n2, producing an intermediate 32-bit result. n4 is the floor of the quotient of the intermediate 32-bit result divided by the divisor n3. The product of n1 times n2 is maintained as an intermediate 32-bit result for greater precision than the otherwise equivalent sequence: n1 n2 * n3 / . An error condition results if the divisor is zero or if the quotient falls outside of the range {-32,768..32,767}.

*/MOD   n1 n2 n3 -- n4 n5
n1 is first multiplied by n2 producing an intermediate 32-bit result. n4 is the remainder and n5 is the floor of the quotient of the intermediate 32-bit result divided by the divisor n3. A 32-bit intermediate product is used as for */. n4 has the same sign as n3 or is zero. An error condition results if the divisor is zero or if the quotient falls outside of the range {-32,768..32,767}.

+   w1 w2 -- w3
w3 is the arithmetic sum of w1 plus w2.

+!   w1 addr --
w1 is added to the w value at addr using the convention for + . This sum replaces the original value at addr.

+LOOP   n --
     sys -- (compiling)
n is added to the loop index. If the new index was incremented across the boundary between limit-1 and limit, then the loop is terminated and loop control parameters are discarded. When the loop is not terminated, execution continues to just after the corresponding DO. sys is balanced with its corresponding DO . See DO.

,   16b --
Allot space for 16b then store 16b at HERE 2-.

-   w1 w2 -- w3
w3 is the result of subtracting w2 from w1.

-TRAILING   addr +n1 -- addr +n2
The character count +n1 of a text string beginning at addr is adjusted to exclude training spaces. If +n1 is zero, then +n2 is also zero. If the entire string consists of spaces, then +n2 is zero.

.   n --
The absolute value of n is displayed in a free field format with a leading minus sign if n is negative.

."   --
     -- (compiling)
Used in the form: ." ccc" Later execution will display the characters ccc up to but not including the delimiting " (close-quote). The blank following ." is not part of ccc.

.(--
     -- (compiling)
Used in the form: .(ccc) The characters ccc up to but not including the delimiting) [closing parenthesis] are displayed. The blank following .(is not part of ccc.

/   n1 n2 -- n3
n3 is the floor of the quotient of n1 divided by the divisor n2. An error condition results if the the divisor is zero or if the quotient falls outside of the range {-32, 768..32,767}.

/MOD   n1 n2 -- n3 n4

n3 is the remainder and n4 the floor of the quotient of n1 divided by the divisor n2. n3 has the same sign as n2 or is zero. An error condition results if the divisor is zero or if the quotient falls outside of the range {−32,768.. 32,767}.

0<   n -- flag

Flag is true if n is less than zero (negative).

0=   w -- flag

Flag is true if w is zero.

0>   n -- flag

Flag is true if n is greater than zero.

1+   w1 -- w2

w2 is the result of adding 1 to w1 according to the operation of + .

1−   w1 -- w2

w2 is the result of subtracting 1 from w1 according to the operation of − .

2+   w1 -- w2

w2 is the result of adding 2 to w1 according to the operation of + .

2−   w1 -- w2

w2 is the result of subtracting 2 from w1 according to the operation of − .

2/   n1 -- n2

n2 is the result of arithmetically shifting n1 right 1 bit. The sign is included in the shift and remains unchanged.

:   -- sys

A defining word executed in the form: : <name> ... ; Create a word definition for <name> in the compilation vocabulary and set compilation state. The search order is changed so that the first vocabulary in the search order is replaced by the compilation vocabulary. The compilation vocabulary is unchanged. The text from the input stream is subsequently compiled. <name> is called a "colon definition". The newly created word definition for <name> cannot be found in the dictionary until the corresponding ; or ;CODE is successfully processed.

An error condition exists if a word is not found and cannot be converted to a number or if, during compilation from mass storage, the input stream is exhausted before encountering ; or ;CODE. sys is balanced with its corresponding ; .

;   -- sys
-- (compiling)

Stops compilation of a colon definition, allows the <name> of this colon definition to be found in the dictionary, sets interpret state, and compiles EXIT (or a system-dependent word which performs an equivalent function. sys is balanced with its corresponding : . See EXIT, ":".

<   n1 n2 -- flag

Flag is true if n1 is less than n2.

> −32768 32767 < must return true
> −32768 0 < must return true

<#   --

Initialize pictured numeric output conversion. The words:

$$ \# \ \#> \ \#S \ <\# \ HOLD \ SIGN $$

can be used to specify the conversion of a double number into an ASCII text string stored in right-to-left order.

=   w1 w2 -- flag

Flag is true if w1 is equal to w2.

>   n1 n2 -- flag

Flag is true if n1 is greater than n2.

> −32768 32767 > must return false
> −32768 0 > must return false

>BODY   addr1 -- addr2

addr2 is the parameter field address corresponding to the compilation address addr1.

>IN   --addr

The address of a variable which contains the present character offset within the input stream {{0..the number of characters in the input stream}}. See WORD.

>R   16b --

Transfers 16b to the return stack.

?DUP   16b -- 16b 16b
or 0 -- 0

Duplicate 16b if it is nonzero.

@   addr -- 16b

16b is the value at addr.

ABORT   Clears the data stack and performs the function of QUIT. No message is displayed.

ABORT"   flag --
--(compiling)

Used in the form:

> flag ABORT" ccc"

When later executed, if flag is true the characters ccc, delimited by " (close-quote), are displayed and then a system-dependent error abort sequence, including the function of ABORT, is performed. If flag is false, the flag is dropped and execution continues. The blank following ABORT" is not part of ccc.

ABS   n -- u

u is the absolute value of n. If n is −32,768 then u is the same value.

ALLOT   w --
Allocates w bytes in the dictionary. The address of the next available dictionary location is updated accordingly.

AND   16b1 16b2 -- 16b3
16b3 is the bit-by-bit logical "and" of 16b1 with 16b2.

BASE   -- addr
The address of a variable containing the current numeric conversion radix. {{2..72}}.

BEGIN   --
                     -- sys (compiling)
Used in the form:

> BEGIN ... flag UNTIL

or

> BEGIN ... flag WHILE ... REPEAT

BEGIN marks the start of a word sequence for repetitive execution. A BEGIN-UNTIL loop will be repeated until flag is true. A BEGIN-WHILE-REPEAT loop will be repeated until flag is false. The words after UNTIL or REPEAT will be executed when either loop is finished. sys is balanced with its corresponding UNTIL or WHILE.

BLK   -- addr
The address of a variable containing the number of the mass storage block being interpreted as the input stream If the value of BLK is zero, the input stream is taken from the text input buffer. {{0..the number of blocks available −1}}. See TIB.

BLOCK   u -- addr
addr is the address of the assigned buffer of the first byte of block u. If the block occupying that buffer is not block u and has been UPDATEd, it is transferred to mass storage before assigning the buffer. If block u is not already in memory, it is transferred from mass storage into an assigned block buffer. A block may not be assigned to more than one buffer. If u is not an available block number, an error condition exists. Only data within the last buffer referenced by BLOCK or BUFFER is valid. The contents of a block buffer must not be changed unless the change may be transferred to mass storage.

BUFFER   u -- addr
Assigns a block buffer to block u. addr is the address of the first byte of the block within its buffer. This function is fully specified by the definition for BLOCK except that if the block is not already in memory it might not be transferred from mass storage. The contents of the block buffer assigned to block u by BUFFER are unspecified.

C!   16b addr --
The least significant 8 bits of 16b are stored into the byte at addr.

C@   addr -- 8b
8b is the contents of the byte at addr.

CMOVE   addr1 addr2 u --
Move u bytes beginning at address addr1 to addr2. The byte at addr1 is moved first, proceeding toward high memory. If u is zero, nothing is moved.

CMOVE>   addr1 addr2 u --
Move the u bytes at address addr1 to addr2. The move begins by moving the byte at (addr1 plus u minus 1) to (addr2 plus u minus 1) and proceeds to successively lower addresses for u bytes. If u is zero, nothing is moved. (Useful for sliding a string toward higher addresses.)

COMPILE   --
Typically used in the form:

> : <name> ... COMPILE <namex> ... ;

When <name> is executed, the compilation address compiled for <namex> is compiled and not executed. <name> is typically immediate and <namex> is typically not immediate.

CONSTANT   16b --
A defining word executed in the form:

> 16b CONSTANT <name>

Creates a dictionary entry for <name> so that when <name> is later executed, 16b will be left on the stack.

CONVERT   +d1 addr1 -- +d2 addr2
+d2 is the result of converting the characters within the text beginning at addr1 + 1 into digits, using the value of BASE, and accumulating each into +d1 after multiplying +d1 by the value of BASE. Conversion continues until an unconvertible character is encountered. addr2 is the location of the first unconvertible character.

COUNT   addr1 -- addr2 +n
addr2 is addr1 + 1 and +n is the length of the counted string at addr1. The byte at addr1 contains the byte count +n. Range of +n is {0..255}.

CR   --
Displays a carriage-return and line-feed or equivalent operation.

CREATE   --
A defining word executed in the form:

> CREATE <name>

Creates a dictionary entry for <name>. After <name> is created, the next available dictionary location is the first byte of <name>'s parameter field. When <name> is subsequently executed, the address of the first byte of <name>'s parameter field is left on the stack. CREATE does not allocate space in name>'s parameter field.

D+ wd1 wd2 -- wd3
wd3 is the arithmetic sum of wd1 plus wd2.

D< d1 d2 --flag
Flag is true if d1 is less than d2 according to the operation of < except extended to 32 bits.

DECIMAL --
Sets the input-output numeric conversion base to 10.

DEFINITIONS --
The compilation vocabulary is changed to be the same as the first vocabulary in the search order.

DEPTH -- +n
+n is the number of 16-bit values contained in the data stack before +n was placed on the stack.

DNEGATE d1 -- d2
d2 is the two's complement of d1.

DO w1 w2 --
　　 -- sys (compiling)
Used in the form:

　　　　　　DO ... LOOP
or
　　　　　　DO ... +LOOP

Begins a loop which terminates based on control parameters. The loop index begins at w2, and terminates based on the limit w1. See LOOP and +LOOP for details on how the loop is terminated. The loop is always executed at least once. For example, w DUP DO ... LOOP executes 65,536 times. sys is balanced with its corresponding LOOP or +LOOP.

　　An error condition exists if insufficient space is available for at least three nesting levels.

DOES> -- addr
　　 -- (compiling)
Defines the execution-time action of a word created by a high-level defining word. Used in the form:

　　 : <namex> ... <create> ... DOES> ... ;
and then
　　　　<namex> <name>

where <create> is CREATE or any user-defined word which executes CREATE.

　　Marks the termination of the defining part of the defining word <namex> and then begins the definition of the execution-time action for words that will later be defined by <namex>. When <name> is later executed, the address of <name>'s parameter field is placed on the stack and then the sequence of words between DOES> and ; are executed.

DROP 16b --
16b is removed from the stack.

DUP 16b -- 16b 16b
Duplicate 16b.

ELSE --
　　 sys1 -- sys2 (compiling)
Used in the form:

　　　　flag IF ... ELSE ... THEN

ELSE executes after the true part following IF . ELSE forces execution to continue at just after THEN . sys1 is balanced with its corresponding IF . sys2 is balanced with its corresponding THEN . See IF THEN.

EMIT 16b --
The least significant 7-bit ASCII character is displayed.

EXECUTE addr --
The word definition indicated by addr is executed. An error condition exists if addr is not a compilation address.

EXIT --
Compiled with a colon definition so that, when executed, that colon definition returns control to the definition that passes control to it by returning control to the return point on the top of the return stack. An error condition exists if the top of the stack does not contain a valid return point. May not be used within a do-loop. See ";".

EXPECT addr +n --
Receive characters and store each into memory. The transfer begins at addr proceeding toward higher addresses 1 byte per character either until a "return" is received or until +n characters have been transferred. No more than +n characters will be stored. The "return" is not stored into memory. No characters are received or transferred if +n is zero. All characters actually received and stored into memory will be displayed, with the "return" displaying as a space. See SPAN.

FILL addr u 8b --
u bytes of memory beginning at addr are set to 8b. No action is taken if u is zero.

FIND addr1 -- addr2 n
addr1 is the address of a counted string. The string contains a word name to be located in the currently active search order. If the word is not found, addr2 is the string address addr1, and n is zero. If the word is found, addr2 is the compilation address and n is set to one of two nonzero values. If the word found has the immediate attribute, n is set to 1. If the word is nonimmediate, n is set to −1 (true).

FLUSH --
Performs the function of SAVE-BUFFERS, then unassigns all block buffers. (This may be useful for mounting or changing mass storage media.)

FORGET --
Used in the form:

FORGET <name>

If <name> is found in the compilation vocabulary, delete <name> from the dictionary and all words added to the dictionary after <name> regardless of their vocabulary. Failure to find <name> is an error condition. An error condition also exists if the compilation vocabulary is deleted.

FORTH --
The name of the primary vocabulary. Execution replaces the first vocabulary in the search order with FORTH. FORTH is initially the compilation vocabulary and the first vocabulary in the search order. New definitions become part of the FORTH vocabulary until a different compilation vocabulary is established. See VOCABULARY.

FORTH-83 --
Assures that a FORTH-83 standard system is available, otherwise an error condition exists.

HERE -- addr
The address of the next available dictionary location.

HOLD char --
char is inserted into a pictured numeric output string. Typically used between <# and #> .

I -- w
w is a copy of the loop index. May only be used in the form:

DO ... I ... LOOP

or

DO ... I ... +LOOP

IF flag --
-- sys (compiling)
Used in the form:

flag IF ... ELSE ... THEN

or

flag IF ... THEN

If flag is true, the words following IF are executed and the words following ELSE until just after THEN are skipped. The ELSE part is optional.

If flag is false, words from IF through ELSE , or from IF through THEN (when no ELSE is used), are skipped. sys is balanced with its corresponding ELSE or THEN.

IMMEDIATE --
Marks the most recently created dictionary entry as a word which will be executed when encountered during compilation rather than compiled.

J -- w
w is a copy of the index of the next outer loop. May only

be used within a nested DO-LOOP or DO-+LOOP in the form, for example:

DO ... DO ... J ... LOOP ... +LOOP

KEY -- 16b
The least significant 7 bits of 16b is the next ASCII character received. All valid ASCII characters can be received. Control characters are not processed by the system for any editing purpose. Characters received by KEY will not be displayed.

LEAVE --
-- (compiling)
Transfers execution to just beyond the next LOOP or LOOP+ . The loop is terminated and loop control parameters are discarded. May only be used in the form:

DO ... LEAVE ... LOOP

or

DO ... LEAVE ... +LOOP

LEAVE may appear within other control structures which are nested within the do-loop structure. More than one LEAVE may appear with a do-loop.

LITERAL -- 16b
16b -- (compiling)
Typically used in the form:

[16b] LITERAL

Compiles a system-dependent operation so that, when later executed, 16b will be left on the stack.

LOAD u --
The contents of >IN and BLK , which locate the current input stream, are saved. The input stream is then redirected to the beginning of screen u by setting >IN to zero and BLK to u. The screen is then interpreted. If interpretation from screen u is not terminated explicitly, it will be terminated when the input stream is exhausted and then the contents of >IN and BLK will be restored. An error condition exists if u is zero. See >IN; BLK; BLOCK.

LOOP --
sys -- (compiling)
Increments the DO-LOOP index by one. If the new index was incremented across the boundary between limit-1 and limit, the loop is terminated and loop control parameters are discarded. When the loop is not terminated, execution continues to just after the corresponding DO . sys is balanced with its corresponding DO . See DO.

MAX n1 n2 -- n3
n3 is the greater of n1 and n2 according to the operation of > .

MIN n1 n2 -- n3
n3 is the lesser of n1 and n2 according to the operation of < .

MOD   n1 n2 -- n3
n2 is the remainder after dividing n1 by the divisor n2. n3 has the same sign as n2 or is zero. An error condition results if the divisor is zero or if the quotient falls outside of the range {-32,768..32767}.

NEGATE   n1 -- n2
n2 is the two's complement of n1, i.e., the difference of zero less n1.

NOT   16b1 -- 16b2
16b2 is the one's complement of 16b1.

OR   16b1 16b2 -- 16b3
16b3 is the bit-by-bit inclusive-or of 16b1 with 16b2.

OVER   16b1 16b2 -- 16b1 16b2 16b3
16b3 is a copy of 16b1.

PAD   -- addr
The lower address of a scratch area used to hold data for intermediate processing. The address or contents of PAD may change and the data lost if the address of the next available dictionary location is changed. The minimum capacity of PAD is 84 characters.

PICK   +n -- 16b
16b is a copy of the +nth stack value, not counting +n itself. {0..the number of elements on stack-1}.

> 0 PICK is equivalent to DUP
> 1 PICK is equivalent to OVER

QUIT   --
Clears the return stack, sets interpret state, accepts new input from the current input device, and begins text interpretation. No message is displayed.

R>   -- 16b
16b is removed from the return stack and transferred to the data stack.

R@   -- 16b
16b is a copy of the top of the return stack.

REPEAT   --
        sys -- (compiling)
Used in the form:

> BEGIN ... flag WHILE ... REPEAT

At execution time, REPEAT continues execution to just after the corresponding BEGIN . sys is balanced with its corresponding WHILE . See BEGIN.

ROLL   +n --
The +nth stack value, not counting +n itself, is first removed and then transferred to the top of the stack, moving the remaining values into the vacated position. {0..the number of elements on the stack-1}.

> 2 ROLL is the equivalent to ROT
> 0 ROLL is a null operation

ROT   16b1 16b2 16b3 -- 16b2 16b3 16b1
The top three stack entries are rotated, bringing the deepest to the top.

SAVE-BUFFERS   --
The contents of all block buffers marked as UPDATEd are written to their corresponding mass storage blocks. All buffers are marked as no longer being modified, but may remain assigned.

SIGN   n --
If n is negative, an ASCII "-" (minus sign) is appended to the pictured numeric output string. Typically used between <# and #>.

SPACE   --
Displays an ASCII space.

SPACES   +n --
Displays +n ASCII spaces. Nothing is displayed if +n is zero.

SPAN   -- addr
The address of a variable containing the count of characters actually received and stored by the last execution of EXPECT . See EXPECT.

STATE   -- addr
The address of a variable containing the compilation state. A nonzero content indicates compilation is occurring, but the value itself is system dependent. A Standard Program may not modify this variable.

SWAP   16b1 16b2 -- 16b2 16b1
The top two stack entries are exchanged.

THEN   --
        sys -- (compiling)
Used in the form:

> flag IF ... ELSE ... THEN

or

> flag IF ... THEN

THEN is the point where execution continues after ELSE, or IF when no ELSE is present.   sys is balanced with its corresponding IF or ELSE .

TIB   -- addr
The address of the text input buffer. This buffer is used to hold characters when the input stream is coming from the current input device. The minimum capacity of TIB is 80 characters.

TYPE   addr +n --
+n characters are displayed from memory beginning with the character at addr and continuing through consecutive addresses. Nothing is displayed if +n is zero.

U. u --
u is displayed as an unsigned number in a free-field format.

U< u1 u2 -- flag
Flag is true if u1 is less than u2.

UM* u1 u2 -- ud
ud is the unsigned product of u1 times u2. All values and arithmetic are unsigned.

UM/MOD ud u1 -- u2 u3
u2 is the remainder and u3 is the floor of the quotient after dividing ud by the divisor u1. All values are arithmetic are unsigned. An error condition results if the divisor is zero or if the quotient lies outside the range {0..65,535}.

UNTIL flag --
         sys -- (compiling)
Used in the form:

         BEGIN ... flag UNTIL

Marks the end of a BEGIN-UNTIL loop which will terminate based on flag. If flag is true, the loop is terminated. If flag is false, execution continues to just after the corresponding BEGIN . sys is balanced with its corresponding BEGIN . See BEGIN.

UPDATE --
The currently valid block buffer is marked as modified. Blocks marked as modified will subsequently be automatically transferred to mass storage should its memory buffer be needed for storage of a different block or upon execution of FLUSH or SAVE-BUFFERS.

VARIABLE --
A defining word executed in the form:

         VARIABLE <name>

A dictionary entry for <name> is created and 2 bytes are ALLOTted in its parameter field. This parameter field is to be used for contents of the variable. The application is responsible for initializing the contents of the variable which it creates. When <name> is later executed, the address of its parameter field is placed on the stack.

VOCABULARY --
A defining word executed in the form:

         VOCABULARY <name>

A dictionary entry for <name> is created which specifies a new ordered list of word definitions. Subsequent execution of <name> replaces the first vocabulary in the search order with <name>. When <name> becomes the compilation vocabulary, new definitions will be appended to <name>'s list. See DEFINITIONS.

WHILE flag --
         sys1 --- sys2 (compiling)

Used in the form:

         BEGIN ... flag WHILE ... REPEAT

Selects conditional execution based on flag. When flag is true, execution continues to just after the WHILE through to the REPEAT which then continues execution back to just after the BEGIN. When flag is false, execution continues.

WORD char -- addr
Generates a counted string by nondestructively accepting characters from the input stream until the delimiting character char is encountered or the input stream is exhausted. Leading delimiters are ignored. The entire character string is stored in memory beginning at addr as a sequence of bytes. The string is followed by a blank which is not included in the count. The first byte of the string is the number of characters {0..255}. If the string is longer than 255 characters, the count is unspecified. If the input stream is already exhausted as WORD is called, then a zero length character string will result.

If the delimiter is not found, the value of >IN is the size of the input stream. If the delimiter is found, >IN is adjusted to indicate the offset to the character following the delimiter. #TIB is unmodified.

The counted string returned by WORD may reside in the "free" dictionary area at HERE or above. Note that the text interpreter may also use this area.

XOR 16b1 16b2 -- 16b3
16b3 is the bit-by-bit exclusive-or of 16b1 with 16b2.

[--
     -- (compiling)
Sets the interpret state. The text from the input stream is subsequently interpreted. For typical usage see LITERAL. See "]".

['] --
       addr -- (compiling)
Used in the form:

         ['] <name>

Compiles the compilation address addr of <name> as a literal. When the colon definition is later executed, addr is left on the stack. An error condition exists if <name> is not found in the currently active search order. See LITERAL.

[COMPILE] --
           -- (compiling)
Used in the form:
         [COMPILE] <name>

Forces compilation of the following word <name>. This allows compilation of an immediate word when it would otherwise have been executed.

] --
Sets compilation state. The text from the input stream is subsequently compiled. For typical usage see LITERAL. See "[".

PC Forth

Whereas the Forth-83 Standard was designed to offer a small but complete set of Forth words to be used, on any hardware, to write transportable code, PC Forth was written specifically for the PC and as a super-set of the Forth-83 Standard. PC Forth includes the necessary hardware-specific function to be able to run on any 8086/8088 compatible machine which follows the PC ROM interrupt conventions and has memory mapped video at the standard addresses. It contains many low-level words which provide the interface between the hardware on which it is meant to run, and the Forth virtual machine which it emulates. These low level words and those implementing the Forth virtual machine are, of course, not transportable to a different machine type. However, all of the higher level words, which form the majority of the words available in this version of Forth, are transportable and are written in Forth. PC-Forth contains all of the Forth-83 Standard words, including the required, the double number extension, the assembler extension, and the system extension word sets; as well as the controlled reference words, the words of the experimental proposals, and selected words from the uncontrolled reference words. It also, as is typical of complete Forth packages, contains an editor, a conditional macro-assembler, and a variety of other extensions. This implementation (placed in the public domain by its author) was influenced by the work of the authors of another public domain version known as F-83, and by the efforts of the San Diego Forth Interest Group Language Implementation Team. It is available from the San Diego Forth Interest Group.

PC FORTH GLOSSARY

The following glossary represents a specific extension of Forth for the IBM PC and PC compatibles. This Forth glossary is organized according to language function. PC Forth has been designed specifically to address the system and chip capabilities of the PC and is not directly transportable to any machine other than those most closely compatible with the PC.

STACK NOMENCLATURE

flag boolean
0=false, else=true
16 bits

true boolean
−1 (as a result)
16 bits

false boolean
0
16 bits

b bit
range {0..1}
1 bit

char character
range {1..127}
7 bits

8b 8 arbitrary bits (byte)
not applicable
8 bits

16b 16 arbitrary bits
not applicable
16 bits

n number (weighted bits)
range {−32,768..32,767}
16 bits

+n positive number
range {0..32,767}
16 bits

u unsigned number
range {0..65,535}
16 bits

w unspecified weighted number (n or u)
range {−32,768..65,535}
16 bits

addr address (same as u)
range {0..65,535}
16 bits

32b 32 arbitrary bits
not applicable
32 bits

d double number
range {−2,147,483,648..2,147,483,647}
32 bits

+d positive double number
range {0..2,147,483,647}
32 bits

ud unsigned double number
range {0..4,294,967,295}
32 bits

wdun specified weighted double number (d or ud)
range {−2,147,483,648..4,294,967,295}
32 bits

sys 0, 1, or more system-dependent stack entries
range
no. of bits not applicable

STACK MANIPULATION WORDS

−ROT 16b1 16b216b3 --16b3 16b1 16b2
Rotate 16b3 to "bottom".

?DUP 16b -- 16b 16b
or
0 -- 0
Duplicate 16b if not 0.

2DROP 32b --
Remove 32b from stack.

2DUP 32b -- 32b 32b
Duplicate 32b.

2OVER 32b1 32b2 -- 32b132b2 32b3
32b3 is a copy of 32b1.

2ROT 32b1 32b232b3 -- 32b2 32b3 32b1
32b1 rotated to top.

2SWAP 32b1 32b2 -- 32b2 32b1
32b1 exchange top two 32b's.

3DUP 48b -- 48b 48b
Duplicate 48b.

>R 16b --
Transfer 16b to return stack.

DEPTH -- n
Depth of stack before n.

DROP 16b --
Remove 16b from stack.

DUP 16b -- 16b 16b
Duplicate 16b.

OVER 16b1 16b2 -- 16b1 16b2 16b3
16b3 is a copy of 16b1.

PICK ..16b..+n -- ..16b..16b
Copy +nth item to top.

R@ -- 16b
Copy top of return stack.

R> -- 16b
Remove top of return stack.

ROLL ..16b..+n -- 16b
Rotate +nth item to top.

ROT 16b1 16b216b3 -- 16b2 16b3 16b1
Rotate 16b1to top.

SWAP 16b1 16b2 -- 16b2 16b1
Exchange top two 16b's.

STACK UTILITIES

.S --
Nondestructive display of parameter stack contents.

DEPTH --n
Depth of parameter stack, not including n.

RP! addr --
Store addr into return stack register.

RP0 -- addr
Initial user-return-stack addr.

RP@ -- addr
Fetch contents of return stack register.

SP! addr --
Store addr into parameter stack register.

SP0 -- addr
Initial user-parameter-stack addr.

SP@ -- addr
Fetch contents of parameter stack register.

ARITHMETIC OPERATIONS

* n1 n2 -- n3
n3=n1*n2.

*/ n1 n2 n3 -- n4
n4=n1*n2/n3.

*/MOD n1 n2 n3 -- n4 n5
n1*n2/n3, where n5=quotient and n4=remainder.

+ n1 n2 -- n3
n3=n1+n2.

− n1 n2 -- n3
n3=n1−n2.

/ n1 n2 -- n3
n3=n1/n2.

/MOD n1 n2 -- n3 n4
n1/n2, where n4=quotient and n3=remainder.

1+ w1 -- w2
Add 1 to w1.

1- w1 -- w2
Subtract 1 from w1.

2+ w1 -- w2
Add 2 to w1.

2- w1 -- w2
Subtract 2 from w1.

2* n1 -- n2
Arithmetic shift left 1 bit.

2/ n1 -- n2
Arithmetic shift right 1 bit.

ABS n -- u
Convert n to absolute value.

D2/ d1 -- d2
Arithmetic shift right 1 bit.

D+ d1 d2 -- d3
d3=d1+d2.

D- d1 d2 -- d3
d3=d1-d2.

DABS d -- ud
Convert d to absolute value.

DMAX d1 d2 -- d3
d3 greater of d1 and d2.

DNEGATE d1 -- d2
d2=-d1.

DMIN d1 d2 -- d3
d3 lesser of d1 and d2.

M* n1 n2 -- d
d=n1*n1.

M/MOD d1 n1 -- n2 d2
d1/n1, where d2=quotient and n2=remainder.

MAX 2n1 n2 -- n3
n3 greater of n1 and n.

MIN n1 n2 -- n3
n3 lesser of n1 and n2.

MOD n1 n2 -- n3
n3=remainder of n1/n2.

NEGATE n1 -- n2
n2=-n1.

S>D n -- d
Convert n to d.

SM/MOD dn1 -- n2 n3
d/n1, where n3=quotient and n2=remainder.

UM* u1 u2 -- ud
ud=u1*u2.

UM/MOD ud u1 -- u2 u3
ud/u1, where u3=quotient and u2=remainder.

LOGICAL OPERATORS

AND 16b1 16b2-- 16b3
16b3 is bit by bit logical-and.

NOT 16b1 -- 16b2
6b2 is 1's complement of 16b1.

OR 16b1 16b2 -- 16b3
16b3 is bit by bit logical-or.

XOR 16b1 16b2 -- 16b3
16b3 is bit by bit logical-xor.

COMPARISON OPERATORS

0< n -- flag
Flag is true if n <0.

0<> n -- flag
Flag is true if n not = 0.

0= w -- flag
Flag is true if n =0.

0> n -- flag
Flag is true if n >0.

< n1 n2 -- flag
Flag is true if n1 < n2.
  -32768 32767 < is true.
  -32768   0 < is true.

= w1 w2 -- flag
Flag is true if w1 = w2.

> n1 n2 -- flag
Flag is true if n1 > n2.
  -32768 32767 > is false.
  -32768   0 > is false.

DO=   d -- flag
Flag is true if d =0.

D<   d1 d2 -- flag
Flag is true if d1 < d2.

D=   wd1 wd2 -- flag
Flag is true if wd1 = wd2.

D>   d1 d2 -- flag
Flag is true if d1 > d2.

DU<   ud1 ud2 -- flag
Flag is true if ud1< ud2.

U<   u1 u2 -- flag
Flag is true if u1 < u2.

U>   u1 u2 -- flag
Flag is true if u1 > u2.

NUMERIC FORMATTING WORDS

+d1 -- +d2
Remainder of +d1/BASE is converted to ASCII number.

#>   32b -- addr +n
End conversion, drop 32b addr & count of converted #.

#S   +d -- 0 0
Do # until +d=0.

<#   --
Initialize numeric conversion.

HOLD   char --
Insert char into numeric conversion.

SIGN   n --
If n negative append ASCII − to numeric string being built.

NUMBER BASE OPERATORS

BINARY   --
Set base to binary.

DECIMAL   --
Set base to decimal.

HEX   --
Set base to hexadecimal.

OCTAL   --
Set base to octal.

NUMERIC OUTPUT WORDS

.   n --
Output n using current number base.

.R   +n n --
Output n right aligned in a field of width +n.

D.   d --
Output the signed double number.

D.R   +n d --
Output d right aligned in a field of width +n.

H.   n --
Output n using base 16.

U.   u --
Output u using current base.

U.R   +n u --
As .R except for unsigned number.

UD.   ud --
As U. except for 32b number ud.

UD.R   +n ud --
As U.R except for 32b number ud.

NUMERIC CONVERSION WORDS

CONVERT   +d1 addr1-- +d2 addr2
+d2 is result of converting ASCII char in string after multiplying +d1 by BASE.

DIGIT   char base -- +n flag
Convert char to n using base.

NUMBER   addr -- d
Convert the counted string at addr to d, if error abort.

NUMBER?   addr -- d flag
Convert the counted string at addr to d, if error flag=0.

MEMORY OPERATORS
(BYTE and WORD)

!   16b addr --
Store 16b into addr.

!L   16b offset-addr seg-addr --
Store 16b into long addr.

+!   16b addr --
Add 16b to contents of addr.

2!   32b addr --
Store 32b into addr.

2@   addr -- 32b
Fetch 32b from addr.

@   addr -- 16b
Fetch 16b from addr.

@L   offset-addr seg-addr -- 16b
Fetch 16b from long addr.

C!   16b addr --
Least significant 8b into addr.

C!L   16b offset-addr seg-addr --
Least significant 8b into long.

C@   addr -- 8b
8b is contents of byte at addr.

C@L   offset-addr seg-addr -- 8b
As C@ except long fetch.

CRESET   16b addr --
All least significant 8b of16b which are 1's set same bits at addr to 0's.

CSET   16b addr --
Set selected bits at addr to 1.

CTOGGLE   16b addr --
XOR selected bits at addr.

OFF   addr --
Set 16b = 0 at addr.

ON   addr --
Set 16b = 1 at addr.

MEMORY OPERATORS
(STRINGS)

−TRAILING   addr +n1 -- addr +n2
Remove trailing blanks from string at addr, reduce count.

BLANK   addr u --
u bytes, starting at addr set to ASCII character value of space.

CMOVE   addr1 addr2 u --
u bytes moved from addr 1 to 2 if addr1 > addr2 no contention.

CMOVE>   addr1 addr2 u --
As CMOVE but addr1 < addr2.

CMOVEL   offset-addr1 seg-addr1 offset-addr2 seg-addr2 count −-
Move count bytes from addr1 −>2.

COMPARE   addr1 addr2 +n -- flag
+n bytes at addr1 compared at addr2, flag =0 for match.

COUNT   addr1 -- addr 1+1 +n
Get count byte +n from addr1.

ERASE   addr u --
u bytes starting at addr set=0.

FILL   addr u 8b --
u bytes starting at addr set=8b.

MOVE   addr1 addr2 u --
Move u bytes from addr 1 to 2 uses CMOVE or CMOVE>.

TIB   -- addr
Terminal Input Buffer addr.

PAD   -- addr
addr of a scratch-pad area just above end of dictionary.

HIGH-LEVEL I/O WORDS
CHARACTER AND STRING INPUT

?KEY   -- flag
True if key pressed.

EXPECT   addr +n --
Store-addr for up to +n char.

KEY   -- 16b
Least significant ASCII char input.

CHARACTER AND STRING OUTPUT

CR --
Send CR-LF.

EMIT 16b --
Display least significant ASCII char.

SPACE --
Send 1 ASCII space char.

SPACES +n --
Send +n ASCII spaces.

TYPE addr +n --
Display +n chars from addr.

VIRTUAL MEMORY DISK I/O

--> --
Continue onto next block.

A: --
Select floppy drive A.

B: --
Select floppy drive B.

BLOCK u -- addr
u=block number, addr=buffer into which contents of u put.

BUFFER u -- addr
Assign buffer for block u.

DISCARD --
Unassign current buffer.

EMPTY-BUFFERS --
Empty and unassign all buffers.

ESTABLISH u --
Assign current buffer to u.

FLUSH --
Save any updated buffers, then empty and unassign all.

LINELOAD +n u --
Start interpreting at line +n of block u.

LOAD u --
Make sure a buffer contains u; start interpreting contents of u.

SAVE-BUFFERS --
Save contents of any updated buffers.

UPDATE --
Mark current buffer as updated.

CHARACTER, STRING, AND BLOCK DISPLAY WORDS

" -- addr count
Compile string into definition, string addr & count returned :... " string" ... ;.

." --
Compile string into definition, displayed when definition used :... ." string" ... ;.

.(--
Display string immediately (string).

ABORT" flag --
Compile string into definition, if flag not true when definition used, output string & abort:...ABORT" string" ... ;.

DIR --
Display disk table-of-contents.

DUMP addr count
Display count memory bytes from addr upward.

INDEX u1 u2 --
Display 1st lines of screens u1 through u2.

LIST u --
List the contents of screen u.

MOUNT --
Display diskette volume number; update user variable VOLUME.

SHOW u1 u2 --
List all triads which include u1 through u2.

TRIAD u --
List the 3 screens which include screen u.

VIEW --
Display the source code for <name> from diskette: VIEW <name>.

CONTROL-STRUCTURE WORDS

+LOOP n --
Add to index, goto ?DO (or DO).

?DO   w1 w2 --
w1 = limit, w2 = index ?DO...LOOP or ?DO ...
+LOOP.

?LEAVE   flag --
Exit current loop if flag not 0.

AGAIN   --
Go to BEGIN.

BEGIN   --
BEGIN...WHILE...REPEAT
  BEGIN...UNTIL
  BEGIN...AGAIN.

DO   w1 w2 --
w1 = limit, w2 = index DO...LOOP or DO...
+LOOP.

ELSE   --
See IF.

EXIT   --
Terminate current : definition.

I   -- w
Current inner loop index.

IF   flag --
IF...THEN
  IF...ELSE...THEN.

J   -- w
Current middle loop index.

K   --
Current outer loop index.

LEAVE   --
Exit current loop.

LOOP   --
Go to ?DO (or DO).

THEN   --
See IF.

REPEAT   --
Go to BEGIN, see BEGIN.

UNTIL   flag --
Go to BEGIN terminate if true.

WHILE   flag --
Go to BEGIN terminate if false.

DICTIONARY RELATED FUNCTIONS

'   -- addr count
Search dictionary for the compilation addr of
<name> ' <name>.

,   16b --
Append 16b to dictionary.

−ALSO   --
Pop search-order stack.

−DEFINITIONS   --
Make compilation vocabulary also 1st searched vocabulary.

ALLOT   w --
Allocate w bytes to end of dictionary.

ALSO   --
Push search-order stack.

C,   16b --
Append least significant 8b to dictionary.

DEFINITIONS   --
Make 1st searched vocabulary also compilation vocabulary.

ASSEMBLER   --
Make 1st searched vocabulary ASSEMBLER.

EDITOR   --
Make 1st searched vocabulary EDITOR.

FIND   addr1 -- addr2 n
Counted string at addr1 looked for in dictionary, if n = 0
not found & addr2 = addr1 else addr2 = dictionary location n <>0.

FORGET   --
Forget <name> and all later words.
  FORGET <name>.

FORTH   --
Make 1st searched vocabulary FORTH.

HERE   -- addr
Address of end of dictionary.

ORDER   --
Display current search-order and compilation vocabulary name.

VOCS   --
List names of all vocabularies.

WORDS --
Display names of words in 1st searched vocabulary.

SOURCE TEXT PROCESSING

(--
Skip all following chars to next).

.ENDIF --
An immediate no-op.

.IF flag --
If flag not=0, interpret words between .IF and .ENDIF else skip them.
 ... .IF ... >ENDIF.

.INDF --
If <name> is in searched vocabularies, process words between <name> and .ENDIF else skip them.
 ... .IFDF <name> .... .ENDIF.

.IFNDF --
If <name> is not in searched vocabularies, do as .IFDF.

EXECUTION CONTROL

+ORIGIN rel-addr -- abs-addr
Convert load-rel-addr to offset.

EXECUTE addr --
Execute word definition at addr=cfa.

GO addr --
Jump to object code at addr.

IS addr --
Change deferred word or constant.
 ' <name-to-exec> IS <name>.
 16b IS <name-of-constant>.

PERFORM addr --
Equivalent to @ EXECUTE.

COMPILER DIRECTIVES

83-STD --
Mark latest word as 83 Standard.

COMPILE --
Compile addr of <name>.
 : ...COMPILE <name> ...;.

COMPILE-ONLY --
Mark latest word compile-only.

DLITERAL 32b --
Compile 32b literal.

HIDE --
Mark latest word as invisible.

IMMEDIATE --
Mark latest word as immediate.

LATEST -- addr
addr of latest word compiled.

LITERAL 16b --
Compile 16b literal.

RE- --
Suppress redefinition warning for next definition.

RECURSE --
Compile the addr of the word being compiled.

REVEAL --
Mark latest word as visible.

[--
Set interpret state.

['] --
Compile compilation addr of <name> as a literal.
 :...['] <name>... ;.

[COMPILE] --
Force compilation of <name>.
 :...[COMPILE] <name>...;.
 Set compile state.

] --
Set compile state.

STATE-SMART WORDS

ASCII --
(Compiling) compile the ASCII value of char.

ASCII --
(Interpreting) return the ASCII value of char syntax: ASCII char.

CONTROL --
(Compiling) compile a control char.

CONTROL -- char
(Interpreting) return a control character syntax: CONTROL char.

DEFINING WORDS

The following defining words use names from the input stream, denoted by <name>. The stack pictures are for the execution of <name>. The syntax for using a defining word is given below the word's explanation.

2CONSTANT -- 32b
Define a constant =32b.
  32b 2CONSTANT <name>.

2VARIABLE -- addr
Define a variable of 32b.
  2VARIABLE <name>.

: --
Start a : (colon) definition.
  : <name> ... ;.

; --
Terminate a: definition.

;CODE --
Adds code procedure to a defining word.

CASE: +n1 --
Start a case statement w/ +n2 cases numbered 0 through +n2.
  CASE: <name> ... ;.

CREATE --
Add a header to the dictionary.
  CREATE <name>.

CODE --
Start a code definition.
  CODE <name>... NEXT, END-CODE.

CONSTANT -- 16b
Define a constant =16b.
  16b CONSTANT <name>.

DEFER --
Define an execution vector.
  DEFER <name> (create name).
  ' <name1> IS <name> (load).

DOES> -- addr
addr of <name>'s parameter field adds a : procedure to a defining word.

END-CODE --
Terminate a code definition.

USER -- addr
Define a user-variable.
  +nUSER <name>.

VARIABLE -- addr
Define a variable.
  VARIABLE <name>.

VOCABULARY --
Adds a vocabulary to dictionary.
  VOCABULARY <name>.

SYSTEM WORDS

ctrl-break --
Use keyboard interrupt to force a soft reset (an escape from recoverable hang-ups).

ABORT --
Reset parameter stack & QUIT.

COLD --
Reset boot-on parameters.

FORTH-83 --
Reset search order, output message.

INTERPRET --
Begin interpreting at current input stream.

QUERY --
Get character input.

QUIT --
Clear return stack and restart interpreter.

SET-VOLUME --
Prompt for diskette volume number and update it on diskette.

WARM --
Do ABORT "Warm start".

WORD char -- addr
Use char as delimiter, put count & delimited string at addr.

GLOBAL CONSTANTS

#BUFFERS -- u
Number block buffers available.

#DRIVES -- u
Number of floppy drives assigned.

#SIDES -- u
Number of sides per floppy drive.

#VOCS -- u
Maximum number of vocabularies in vocabulary stack.

0 -- 0
A named constant of value 0.

1 -- 1
A named constant of value 1.

B/BUF -- 1024
Bytes-per-buffer.

BELL -- char
An ASCII BEL.

BL -- char
An ASCII blank.

BLK/SIDE -- u
Number of blocks per floppy side.

BS -- char
System backspace character.

FALSE -- 0
A named constant of value 0.

FIRST -- addr
Starting addr of block buffers.

LIMIT -- addr
Ending addr of block buffers.

MAX-BUFS -- u
Maximum number of block buffers.

TRUE -- −1
A named constant of value −1.

GLOBAL VARIABLES

ATTRIBUTE -- addr
Contains current CRT attribute.

BACKGROUND -- addr
Contains current CRT background color.

CAPS -- addr
If non-0, convert lower to uppercase for dictionary search.

COMM -- addr
Contains identification of resource owner.

COMM# -- addr
Contains number of serial port used by serial I/O primitives.

CRT-MODE -- addr
Contains current CRT mode number.

DISK -- addr
Contains identification of resource owner.

DISK-ERROR -- addr
Contains error-code of latest disk error.

FOREGROUND -- addr
Contains current CRT foreground color.

PRINTER -- addr
Contains identification number of resource owner.

PRINTER# -- addr
Contains number of printer port used by printer I/O primitives.

VOLUME -- addr
Contains volume number of diskette currently "mounted".

USER VARIABLES

#LINE -- addr
Current line number.

#OUT -- addr
Current character output count.

#PAGE -- addr
Current page number.

#TIB -- addr
Number of bytes in text-input-buffer.

>IN -- addr
Index into current text buffer.

BASE -- addr
Contains current number base.

BLK -- addr
If contents=0, interpret from TIB else from contents=block#.

CONTEXT -- addr
Contains addr of search-vocabulary stack.

CURRENT --addr
Contains addr of compile vocabulary.

DP -- addr
Contains addr of end of dictionary.

DPL -- addr
Contains numeric conversion flags.

END? -- addr
Contains flag to signal end of text buffer reached.

ENTRY -- addr
Reserved.

FENCE -- addr
Contains address not to forget below.

HLD --addr
Contents point to numeric string being built by <#
etc.

LINK -- addr
Reserved.

mode -- addr
Contains bits used by Assembler.

OFFSET -- addr
Contains offset to add to block number to go from relative to absolute.

PRINTING -- addr
If non-0 output also goes to printer.

R# -- addr
Contains current relative character location for editor.

RP0 -- addr
Contains init addr return-stack.

SP0 -- addr
Contains init addr parameter-stack.

SCR -- addr
Contains screen number of last screen listed or edited.

STANDARD -- addr
If contents not=0, warn if using non-83-STD words
in definition.

span -- addr
Internal use.

SPAN -- addr
Contains actual count of characters eceived by last
EXPECT.

STATE -- addr
If contents=0, interpreting, if non-0, compiling.

TIB0 -- addr
Contains addr Terminal Input Buffer.

TOS -- addr
Reserved.

VOC-LINK -- addr
Contains pointer to vocabulary chain.

WARNING -- addr
If non-0, warn if definition given duplicate name.

LOW-LEVEL I/O OPERATIONS
PORT I/O

P! 16b addr --
Write 16b to output port "addr".

P@ addr -- 16b
Read 16b from input port "addr".

PC! 16b addr --
Write least significant 8b.

PC@ addr -- 8b
Read 8b from input port "addr".

CRT OUTPUT FUNCTIONS

CLEARSCREEN --
Clear CRT, cursor to top left.

CRT-MODE! 16b --
Truncate 16b to 3b, set mode.

CRT-MODE? -- 3b
Return current CRT mode.

CRT-TTY char --
Send char to CRT using TTY mode.

PARALLEL (PRINTER) PORT I/O

PRINTER-INIT --
Initialize printer port.

PRINTER-OUT 16b --
Write bottom 8b to printer port.

PRINTER-STATUS? -- 8b
Return printer status.

SERIAL (PRINTER) PORT I/O

SERIAL-IN -- 8b
Read serial port (version dependent).

SERIAL-INIT --
Initialize serial port.

SERIAL-OUT   16b --
Write bottom 8b to serial port.

SERIAL-STATUS   -- 16b
Return serial port status.

FLOPPY DISK I/O

This version of FORTH treats disks as eight sectors per track and ignores a ninth sector if it is present. This means that there are four blocks per track and that

BLOCK-I/O reads a sector pair at a time to access one block per read or write operation. Hence, a sector pair specifier must be odd and in the range 1 through 7 (i.e., 1, 3, 5, or 7).

BLOCK-R/W   --flag   (cmd: 0=reset,   1=status, 2=read, 3=write, 4=verify)
Do specified operation for pair of sectors (sect-pair =odd).
   Command head and drive track sect-pair.

DISK-RESET
Reset floppy controller.

Fortran

Fortran, whose name is derived from "Formula Translating," was the first high-level computing language to become widely used in the data processing community, and it is the oldest high-level computing language still in use today. Currently, because of its implementation on microcomputers and because of the new hardware systems that allow stand-alone microcomputers to act as desktop front ends to large mainframe systems, Fortran is enjoying a mini-renaissance. The language was originally developed at IBM for solving the types of large-scale numerical problems that occur in mathematical, scientific, and engineering applications. Since the 1960s, the use of the language has been extended to include text processing applications, and consequently Fortran has become a standard business programming language. It is used as a development language for database systems, for business financial packages, and for report generators and query systems as well as for engineering programs.

Fortran grew up in the 1950s and matured in an environment defined by the economics of large, mainframe computers and very large-scale data processing requirements. The high costs of these mainframes, the salaries of large data processing staffs, and the general administrative overhead required to manage a company-wide electronic data processing operation necessitated an efficient, high-speed, high-throughput, and high-volume operation. Great stress was placed upon developing efficient programs: programs that did the task quickly and got off the machine so that many jobs could be processed in as little computer time as possible. Efficient programs, therefore, saved computer time and money. Early programmers, working within the constraints of this environment, wrote assembly-level code that could be executed efficiently and directly. They worked for computer customers who, in many cases, time-shared the resources of mainframes with other users and were able to realize savings only if the run-time costs were managed effectively. This need for efficient code dominated the early developmental thinking surrounding Fortran.

When Fortran was developed at IBM, the first task in selling customers on the concept was to convince two communities that the high-level compiler was a cost-effective program development tool. Programmers were the first group to raise doubts about the efficiency of Fortran. Schooled in assembly-level programming, they doubted the ability of a compiled high-level language to execute code as efficiently as an assembly-level program. Customers were concerned that programs written in Fortran would take more computer time and consequently be more expensive. For these reasons, even from its earliest implementations Fortran was designed to provide programmers with efficiency of execution. And this has remained the prime directive of Fortran's development throughout its major revisions.

The first reference to Fortran occurred in 1954 in a report issued by the Programming Research Group, Applied Science Division of IBM. The Fortran system mentioned in the group's report was to have been a large set of programs to enable the IBM 704 to accept problems in terms of strict mathematical notation rather than in assembly language. It took two and a half years to develop the system, and in early 1957 Fortran for the IBM 704 was released. Because of initial resistance to the concept of high-level languages that might require more computer time than assembly programs to execute applications, it took a major IBM sales campaign to stress the advantages of English-like programming languages. The campaign helped convince users that the major decrease in software development time more than offset any imagined increase in computer run time when the programs were executed. Historically, IBM's campaign to sell Fortran was very important to the commercial development of computers and computing languages. The successful marketing of Fortran pointed to a commercial future for high-level languages and created a community of buyers and users. This spurred other computer manufacturers to enter the market, and for the next four years there was an intense development of Fortran compilers. FORTRAN II was released in 1958 for the IBM 704, and versions of the language were introduced for the 709 and 650 as well. Finally, in 1962, FORTRAN IV was introduced for the IBM 7030, a mainframe used primarily for scientific and engineering purposes.

The scientific and mathematical applications of Fortran contributed to the basic structure of the language itself. Engineers found it easy to use the language, because a similarity already existed between the terminology of science and engineering and Fortran itself; engineers and scientists found it possible to program their own problems directly without having to work through assembly language programmers. Throughout the 1960s there was a significant increase in the use of Fortran within the scientific community, and the number of different Fortran compilers, each with its own dialect of Fortran, proliferated. This resulted in a need to standardize the language.

Standardization began in 1966 when an American Standard Fortran was officially adapted by the American Standards Association Committee. The new standard, FORTRAN IV, remained in place until 1978 when the American National Standards Institute (ANSI), the new standards committee, designated FORTRAN 77 to be the official industry standard of the language. Still, every manufacturer implements Fortran in a slightly different way. It is not uncommon, for example, to have several different versions of Fortran running on the same computer. Generally, however, the differences between the versions of the language are actually extensions of FORTRAN 77. One of the more popular of these extensions used in educational institutions is WATFIV, a successor to Waterloo FORTRAN (WATFOR) which was developed at the University of Waterloo in Canada primarily for student use.

The design of Fortran reflects its primary mission: efficiency of execution. It was created to satisfy a main frame computing community by providing an ease of development with an English-like language environment while at the same time not using up valuable computer time in the running of the program. A Fortran program is really a main program linked to a set of subprograms. The main programs and subprograms are compiled separately from one another and linked to one another by the computer only during loading. Likewise, the focus of FORTRAN 77 reflects its origins in the mathematics and scientific communities. The language provides for sophisticated mathematical functions, hence its long history as a language of choice for number-crunching operations and operations involving extensive financial calculations. This capacity to perform extensive mathematical calculation is what made Fortran an easy language to adapt to business applications.

Fortran provides for numeric, character, and logical data types. Numeric data falls into three categories: integer, real, and complex. Real numbers may be written in standard decimal form such as −125.89 or in exponential form such as −1.2589 E2. Complex numbers take the form a+bi and are written in ordinal pair notation such as (3,2.1) for 3+2.1i. Character data is any string of characters composed of letters, digits, and certain special characters. Character strings are set off by single quotes. Logical data types consist of the values .TRUE. or .FALSE. Every variable in a Fortran program must be one of these data types.

Fortran also has restrictions that apply to the naming of variables. For example, the only characters permitted are the letters A through Z and the digits 0 through 9. The first character of a variable must be a letter, and the actual number of characters in the name cannot exceed six. Variables can be declared to be a specific type, or else Fortran will assign them to be either integers or reals. Variables beginning with the letters I, J, K, L, M or N will be designated as integer variables by default in Fortran, while all other letters will be designated to be real variables. Hence, variables must be declared and named in the Fortran program so that the computer can allocate the necessary storage before the program is executed. If the programmer does not declare data types, Fortran will automatically implement the default values so that it can allocate the storage requirements of the program. This is an important feature of Fortran that allows it to run efficiently within the restraints imposed by the hardware system.

There are two methods for processing Fortran programs. The older method, which is still in existence, is referred to as batch processing. In this mode, the programmer must first keypunch the program onto statement cards and feed the batch of cards into a card reader. After a time delay, which might be considerable, depending upon the utilization of the computer, the program and program's results are printed out on a line printer. This is tedious because if the programmer has made a mistake or if a card is damaged, the card which caused the error must be repunched and inserted into the deck, and the program must be resubmitted to the card readers. In large computing facilities where there is a data processing queue, there can be a considerable wait before the final output is ready. A second method of pro-

cessing is referred to as interactive processing, in which a programmer keys the program into a terminal, if the terminal is the front end of a mainframe or time-sharing workstation, or into a stand-alone microcomputer. The advantages of this method over the traditional batch method are obvious. As a front end to a mainframe, the individual terminal has access to the processing and storage capabilities of an entire system. Hence, programming errors can be trapped and results can be recovered as soon as the computer processes the data. On large mainframe systems, the network management software itself will establish a processing queue based upon password access codes, priority access commands, or simply on a first-in-first-out basis. However, there is usually considerably less waiting time than in a traditional batch processing mode. Batch processing has also come to mean a method of entering a program into the computer for later execution. This batch-entry input can also be found in many microcomputer programs that allocate a buffer memory for data input, that is, a physical holding area in the computer's memory, and load the data into the actual data fields after the input has been completed. This is a very efficient method of data entry that can save time as well as money.

The simplest way to demonstrate the INPUT/OUTPUT functions of programming in the batch mode is to create a simple routine that contains unformatted READ* and PRINT* instructions. The following example declares two integers, reads the integers into the computer, and prints them out in reverse order:

```
PROGRAM REVERSE
INTEGER VAR1, VAR2
READ* VAR1, VAR2
PRINT* VAR2, VAR1
STOP
END
```

When the user types 7,9 after the program is run, the program will read 7 and 9 and print out 9, 7, reversing the numbers it has read.

While the input and output of data is an important feature of programming, the processing of data is the key to applications. Typically, processing in Fortran involves assignment statements which utilize arithmetic functions. In the sample program below which converts degrees from Fahrenheit to Celsius, it is the assignment statement which does the real data processing of the program:

```
  PROGRAM CONVERT
C THIS PROGRAM INPUTS A NUMBER IN
  DEGREES
  C FAHRENHEIT AND OUTPUTS THE
  EQUIVALENT
  C NUMBER IN DEGREES CELSIUS
  REAL C,F
  READ*, F
  C=(5.0/9.0)*(F−32.0)
```

```
PRINT*,'THE DEGREES FAHRENHEIT
         GIVEN IS',F
PRINT*'      '
PRINT*,'THE EQUIVALENT DEGREES
         CELSIUS IS',C
STOP
END
```

The statement $C=(5.0/9.0)*(F-32.0)$ is an assignment statement, and at execution of the program the value of the expression on the right of the = symbol is determined and stored in the location C. C has been initialized as a real number, as is F, and set to the value determined by the assignment statement. The value for F, the degrees Fahrenheit that will be converted by the program, is input by the user directly. The top three lines in the program are comment statements that function just like REMs in BASIC. The program first declares the data types C and F to be real numbers, reads the value of F which is input by the user, processes F to determine the value of C, prints out F for the user's benefit, skips a line, and prints out the calculated value of C, the degrees Celsius. The program CONVERT ends with the END statement.

Fortran's ability to handle numerical operations efficiently made it a handy programming language for statisticians and accountants. The following example demonstrates how two simple routines in a program create an average for a group of positive numbers and check for a negative number input which automatically terminates the the input and prints out the average.

```
        PROGRAM AVERAGE
C  THIS PROGRAM READS AN UNSPECIFIED
   NUMBER OF POSITIVE
C  NUMBERS AND CALCULATES THE AVERAGE
   OF THE NUMBERS
C  READ. THE PROCESSING STOPS ONCE A
   NEGATIVE NUMBER
C  HAS BEEN READ INTO VARIABLE
   "NUMBER"
C
        INTEGER COUNT
        REAL NUMBER,SUM,AVE
        COUNT=0
        SUM=0.0
100  READ*,(NUMBER.LT.0) GOTO 200
SUM=SUM+NUMBER
COUNT=COUNT+1
GOTO 100
200  AVE=SUM/COUNT
PRINT*,'THE AVERAGE OF THE NUMBERS READ
      IS',AVE
STOP
END
```

The program begins by declaring the data types and intializing their values. COUNT is an integer, initialized at 1; NUMBER, SUM and AVE are real numbers, and the value of SUM is set to 0.0. COUNT is the aggregate number of NUMBERs input by the user. The first routine reads a number that is inputted by the user. If the number is negative (NUMBER LESS THAN 0), the program transfers the user to the next routine which computes the final average (AVE equals SUM divided by COUNT), prints it, and terminates the program. If the number input by the user is positive, the program adds it to SUM and increments COUNT by 1. As long as the user keeps inputting positive numbers, the program will keep adding 1 to COUNT and the NUMBER to SUM. When the user wants to terminate the program, the user simply keys in a NUMBER LESS THAN 0. This acts as an end-of-data indicator and tells the program to calculate AVE.

Even a casual reading of a Fortran program reveals the influence that the language had upon the development of BASIC. Both languages have a straightforward notation, both have an English-like command structure, and both rely heavily upon subroutines to handle confined logical operations. Both share some of the same weaknesses as well. It is often difficult, for example, to follow the flow of control within a Fortran or BASIC program because of the heavy use of GOTOs and, in BASIC, GOSUBs. Unlike Fortran, however, BASIC is an interpreted language. This means that although it runs slower and is less efficient, errors are trapped immediately upon execution of a line rather than upon compiling of the entire program.

Fortran is still taught in formal computer science and programming courses because of its wide variety of applications, its influence upon the history and science of computer programming, and its inherent strengths as a tool for designing mathematical or scientific operations as well as business applications. It remains to be seen whether Fortran will enjoy a renaissance as a programming language of choice now that the formal distinction between stand-alone microcomputer and front-end terminal has been blurred by the new 16- and 32-bit hardware products released by IBM and the terminal emulation software introduced by both IBM and AT&T. The stress on multiuser systems and coprocessing of applications in this current generation of computer applications, and on artificial intelligence, process control, and natural language interfaces in the coming generation of computer programming seems to point to a very different environment from the one that spawned Fortran and its offspring.

FORTRAN GLOSSARY

The following glossary represents the set of keywords for FORTRAN 77, the ANSI standard implementation of the language. This version of Fortran is implemented on virtually every mainframe and mini computer as well as on PC compatible microcomputers. In addition, most Fortran compilers run under MS-DOS as well as CP/M.

ASSIGN   A statement used to assign a statement number to a variable.
ASSIGN 500 TO N

Assigned GOTO   A statement of the form GOTO N (N1, N2,...NI) in which the GOTO transfers control to the statement number NI corresponding to N. For example, GOTO N (10,20,30,40,50) will transfer control to one of the five statements depending upon the value assigned to N.
GOTO N (N1,N2,N3,N4,N5)

BACKSPACE   A statement that causes the record pointer of a data file to backspace one record.
BACKSPACE

CALL   A statement used to call a subroutine and, in so doing, pass control of the program to the operation of that subroutine.
CALL [name of subroutine]

CHARACTER   A nonexecutable statement used to declare a variable to be a character variable. For example, CHARACTER* 10 NAME, TOWN declares both NAME and TOWN to be character variables of length 10 characters.
CHARACTER* [number] [name of variable]

CLOSE   A statement used to close a data file.
CLOSE [name of data file]

COMMON   A nonexecutable statement used to set aside a block of memory to be shared in common by the main program and any subprograms. COMMON allows for efficient run-time processing because a common storage area can be declared at the outset of the program and used by all of the subprograms. This also has the effect of declaring a global variable.
COMMON/BLK/[variable]/[variable]

COMPLEX   A nonexecutable statement used to declare a variable to be a complex variable. For example: COMPLEX A,ROOT,C declares A, ROOT, and C to be complex variables.
COMPLEX[variable],[variable]

CONTINUE   A statement used at the end of a DO loop to serve as a reference point.
DO 20 I=1,5 . . . 20 CONTINUE

DATA   A nonexecutable statement that is used to assign initial values to a list of variables.
DATA A,B,C,/Value1, Value2, Value3/

DIMENSION   A nonexecutable statement used to declare subscripted arrays.
DIMENSION X(n)

DO   A statement used as a counter-controlled looping procedure. The DO statement includes a loop counter to count the number of repetitions of the loop, its initial value, its final value, and its increment as well as a statement number to indicate the end of the DO loop. For example, DO 100 I=1,11,2 controls a loop of statements ending at statement 100 where I, the loop counter, starts at 1, is incremented by 2 each time it is passed through the loop, and ends after completing the loop for the value 11.
DO n X=n,n,n

DOUBLE PRECISION   A nonexecutable statement used to declare a variable to have twice as many significant digits as usual.
DOUBLE PRECISION x

END   A statement used to conclude the main program and any subroutines.
END [name]

ENDFILE   A statement which causes the insertion of a special character called the end-of-file (EOF) symbol at the end of all records contained in a given data file.
ENDFILE

ENDWHILE   A statement used to end a WHILE loop.
ENDWHILE

ENTRY   A statement used to enter a subprogram at an alternate point.
ENTRY

EQUIVALENCE   A nonexecutable statement that shares the same memory location between two or more variables in the same program. It is used to conserve memory.
EQUIVALENCE (A,B,C)

FORMAT   A nonexecutable statement used in conjunction with a READ or PRINT statement to specify how data is to be input or output. For example, READ 100,N,M, and 100 FORMAT (I3,1X,I2) causes the data in columns 1-3 to be assigned to N and the data in 5-6 to be assigned to M.
FORMAT (vXv)

FUNCTION   A nonexecutable statement used to declare the name and parameters of a function which is to be defined later in the program.
FUNCTION function name (x,y,z)

GOTO   A statement used to transfer control to a statement with a specified statement number.
GOTO [statement number]

IF <condition> THEN <set of commands>   A statement used to tell the computer to execute a set of commands provided that the given condition is true.
IF A > B THEN PRINT A

IF < > THEN < > ELSE <command or set of commands> A statement used to tell the computer to execute the commands included with the THEN statement if the condition is true or the commands included within the ELSE structure if the condition is false.
IF A = B THEN PRINT ELSE GOTO [ ]

IMPLICIT A nonexecutable statement which identifies a group of variable names to be a certain type depending upon which letter of the alphabet begins the variable name.
IMPLICIT INTEGER (A,B,C)

INTEGER A nonexecutable statement used to declare a variable to be an integer.
INTEGER A,B,C

LOGICAL A nonexecutable statement used to declare a variable to be a logical variable.
LOGICAL NAME, XNAME

Logical IF A statement similar to the IF THEN statement except that the THEN is omitted and no ENDIF is required. The logical IF executes the statement if the logical expression is true; if it is false, then the next statement is executed.
IF [logical expression] statement

LOGICAL OPERATORS:
.AND.
.NOT.
.OR.
.EQ. Equal to
.NE. Not equal to
.GT. Greater than
.LT. Less than
.GE. Greater than or equal to
.LE. Less than or equal to

OPEN A statement used to prepare a data file for either input or output. A statement which opens a file for activity.
OPEN [file name]

PARAMETER A nonexecutable statement used to assign a constant value to a symbolic name. For example, PARAMETER (pi=3.14) causes the program replace pi with 3.14 every time pi is used in the program.
PARAMETER (name=value)

PAUSE Halts the program temporarily.
PAUSE

PRINT Prints the content of a specified memory location. For example, PRINT A,B causes the values of A and B to be printed.
PRINT [memory location]

READ A statement used to input data into a specified variable location. For example, READ*,A,B will search for two data entries and input the first into A and the second into B.
READ*,[variables]

REAL A nonexecutable statement used to declare a variable to be a real variable.
REAL X,Y,Z

RETURN A statement used to return control to the main program from a function or a subroutine or a subprogram. RETURN signals the end of a subroutine or subprogram.
RETURN

REWIND A statement used to position a data file at its starting point.
REWIND

STOP A statement used to terminate the execution of a program and indicate the logical conclusion.
STOP

SUBROUTINE A nonexecutable statement which declares the name and parameters of a subroutine to be called by the main program. For example, SUBROUTINE ROOT (A,B) names a subroutine which passes information to the subroutine through A and B and then returns information to the main program through A and B.
SUBROUTINE [name] (x,y)

WHILE <condition> DO A statement that provides for the processing of a structure while the stated condition is true. The program will execute commands repeatedly between the WHILE-DO and a concluding ENDWHILE statement as long as the condition is satisfied.
WHILE <logical condition> DO

WRITE Similar to the PRINT statement, WRITE is used to create output to devices other than printers or terminals.
WRITE [output device, statement] (x,y)

= This is an operator used in assignment statements to assign an arithmetic expression on the right of the equals sign to the variable on the left.
A=B+C

+,−,*,/,** Arithmetic operators which indicate addition, subtraction, multiplication, division and exponentiation, respectively.

LISP

LISP is one of the oldest computer languages still in use, standing second only to the old workhorse Fortran. But in spite of its advanced age, LISP is surprisingly modern because it has been able to be responsive and keep evolving by continually incorporating the most up-to-date ideas. LISP is an acronym for List Processing, or List Programming. From the outset, it has been the language par excellence for artificial intelligence programming.

Although LISP has not become a major production language for commercial programming, it is not true that LISP is suitable only for artificial intelligence research. It has been used successfully for projects other than AI, the best known being the EMACS editor, of which there are several versions written entirely in LISP. While LISP is a high-level language, surprisingly it can also be used for systems programming. LISP machines are desktop computers that are workstations with optimized environments for programming in LISP. On most LISP machines, the operating system, interpreters, compilers, editors, and utilities are all written exclusively in LISP.

As might be expected, several different dialects of the language have emerged over the years. The most popular are MACLISP, INTERLISP, FRANZ LISP, UCI LISP, and ZETALISP. In spite of this diversity, after considerable effort, the standard LISP for apparently some time to come has been established. Common LISP, which was developed through the cooperation of most of the major artificial intelligence laboratories in the United States, is not a minimal standard but a fully configured and highly current definition of the language, and every indication is that it has succeeded in becoming very widely accepted.

In John McCarthy's estimation, there are six features that distinguish LISP among programming languages:

1. Its ability to compute symbolic expressions instead of just numbers, taking advantage of the fact that bit patterns may be defined to stand for any symbol.
2. Its capability of list processing where linked lists on the machine level are used to store data that signifies multilevel lists on the level of interpretation.
3. Its extensibility, or the capacity to compose complex functions interactively out of simple ones, so that any LISP function at all can be redefined at any time.
4. Its powerful use of recursion on all levels.
5. The representation of LISP code itself as linked lists on the machine level and structured lists on the interpretive level, so that the format is identical for both code and data.
6. The EVAL function, written in LISP, which serves as the core of the LISP interpreter and one of the key features of the definition of the language and its dialects.

More than any other thing, it is the capacity for symbolic processing that gives LISP its unique power for AI applications. What it means to the programmer is that terms specific to a given application can be entered right from the outset without any initial declarations or development of data structures. It is the ever-present list data structure inherent to LISP that gives the language this powerful symbol-handling capability. Where symbols are represented as string variables and string arrays, storage must be allocated each time a new symbol is used. And when it comes time for rearranging or editing the list of symbols stored sequentially, the actual contents in memory must usually be moved and shifted. But with linked list structures, the contents in memory do not move, only the pointers are reassigned. The speed and facility with which the pointers can be manipulated makes possible the extensive arsenal of functions present in LISP for the rapid processing of complex, structured lists.

The feature that makes LISP unique among programming languages is that both data and LISP code are represented in identical formats as structured lists. Even LISP programs are just lists of lists. The results of this are extremely far reaching. First, it means that programs can be written that exactly mirror data, talking to it, literally, in its own language. It also means that the functions for manipulating lists can be used for manipulating programs or data of any data type, as desired. One consequence of this is that LISP functions can be passed to other functions as arguments by the same means that parameters are. And most importantly of all, it means that programs can be considered as data to be manipulated by other programs. It is possible to write programs, for example, that consider themselves as data to be manipulated, or that write other programs. While it is possible to do these things with difficulty in other programming languages, the uniform syntax of LISP is especially convenient for this type of processing.

The main syntactical device that LISP uses for representing structured lists are its nested parentheses. Many people who are not experienced with LISP cite this as one of the weaknesses, complaining that it makes the language extremely hard to read. Actually, for a LISP programmer who is used to them, the parentheses are a very valuable aid in displaying a program's structure, especially when the code is well formatted. In the case of large applications where there can be a very large number of nested parentheses, there are utilities that aid in avoiding syntax errors involving them.

For example, the following are all valid ways of entering data in LISP:

```
( ASIA EUROPE AMERICA AFRICA AUSTRALIA )
         ( 1 4 9 16 25 36 49 )
    ( ( 21 Barleycorn Lane) ( Altoona, Michigan) )
( NATION ( STATE ( COUNTY ( CITY ( DISTRICT
          (STREET ))))))
```

Unfortunately, though, if lists of data are just entered this way, there is no way of singling them out to be processed or retrieved. In LISP, the process of giving a label to a list is known as variable binding. The special form

SETQ is one of the ways used to assign a label to a list. The list is then the value of the variable designated as the label. To bind the first list above to a variable name the syntax would be:

(SETQ CONTINENTS (QUOTE (ASIA EUROPE AMERICA AFRICA AUSTRALIA)))

or more simply:

(SETQ CONTINENTS '(ASIA EUROPE AMERICA AFRICA AUSTRALIA))

Here the ' symbol is substituted for QUOTE and reduces the levels of parentheses by one. The QUOTE or corresponding symbol is used to indicate that the expression itself rather than its value is to be operated upon.

As mentioned earlier, LISP computes symbols, not just numbers. This means that symbolic, or S, expressions are usually evaluated by a LISP interpreter and their value returned. For this reason, LISP is often described as a functional language because, like mathematical functions, its procedures act upon their arguments and produce a value from them. For example, when the above variable binding is entered in the LISP interpreter, the original list

(ASIA EUROPE AMERICA AFRICA AUSTRALIA)

is returned as the result or value arrived at by evaluating the expression. This same list is returned as a value now whenever its name CONTINENTS' is entered in response to the LISP prompt. When there is no value, or the value is the empty list (), LISP returns NIL.

To get a better idea of how LISP really works, it is helpful to focus in on how list structures are actually represented and manipulated. If we were to make the following variable bindings:

(SETQA '(WHAT GOES ON))
(SETQB '(IN YOUR HEART))

the list cells and pointers would be set up as represented in cons-cell or "cell block" notation in Fig. 5-2. What goes on in LISP when lists are entered is that cells are removed from the free storage list and the entered data is stored in them, and the pointers are set as required by the designated structure? What happens when operations are performed on these lists? If our two lists are to be joined together, the APPEND function can be used in this manner with the subsequent value returned:

* (SETQ AB (APPEND A B))
(WHAT GOES ON IN YOUR HEART)

This conjoined list is implemented as indicated in Fig. 5-3, not as in Fig. 5-4, the reason being that otherwise the binding of variable A would be destroyed by AB, which is not what was called for. In the version

(SET QA '(WHAT GOES ON))

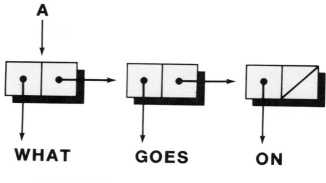

(SET QB '(IN YOUR HEART))

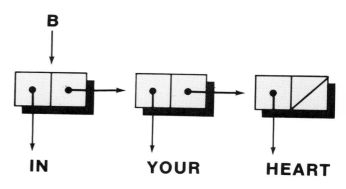

Fig. 5-2

shown in Fig. 5-4, variable A would then have the same value as variable AB. The way APPEND works, then, to avoid destroying the binding of one of the lists it joins together, is first to make a copy of that list and set the end pointer of the copy as Fig. 5-4 would have done on the original. Naturally it is only the structure of pointers that is copied. There still remains only one copy of the text characters stored in memory.

The two most basic list selector functions in LISP are CAR and CDR (pronounced "cutter"). CAR selects and returns the first element of a list only, and CDR selects and returns a list composed of all the members of a list except the first. So for example:

* (CAR (WHAT GOES ON))
(WHAT)
and

* (CDR (WHAT GOES ON))
(GOES ON)

By successive applications of CDR and/or CAR a whole repertoire of functions can be implemented that provide ways of accessing various members of lists. The terminology convention has become standard to use the name CxxxR for these functions where each x can stand for either a D or R. The series of D's and R's represents a sequence of CDRs and CARs respectively. For example, the following statement:

* (CDDR (WHAT GOES ON))

returns

(ON)

because it performs two successive CDR operations. Returning to the example, we can now make two additional bindings:

* (SETQ C '(IN YOUR MIND))
(IN YOUR MIND)

* (SETQ D '(HEAVEN IS))
(HEAVEN IS)

(SET Q AB (APPEND AB))

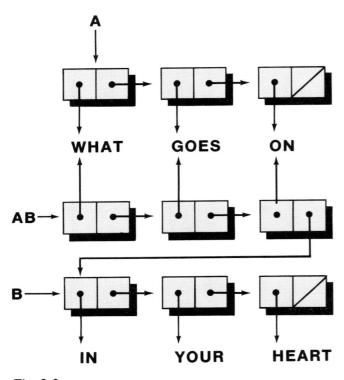

Fig. 5-3

If we want to "cut and paste" various lists to produce different combinations, there are various other functions for manipulating lists. For example, the SUBST function allows one expression to be substituted for another in a list, as follows:

* (SETQ AC (SUBST C B AB))
(WHAT GOES ON IN YOUR MIND)

This declares the label AC and assigns it to the list constructed by substituting C (IN YOUR MIND) for B (IN YOUR HEART) in list AB (WHAT GOES ON IN YOUR HEART). Another way to cut and paste list elements that is convenient for splicing or replacing items toward the front of lists is demonstrated by:

* (SETQ DC (APPEND D (CDDDR AC)))
(HEAVEN IS IN YOUR MIND)

A frequently encountered list structure is the nested list or dotted pair of the form ((A)B). The function used in LISP to create structures of this type is CONS. For example:

* (CONS X Y)
((X) Y)

or, with the labels as they have been defined:

* (CONS A B)
((WHAT GOES ON) IN YOUR HEART)

If we want to cut and paste with structures of this type, there are the destructive replace functions RPLACA and RPLACD which are abbreviations for REPLACe cAr and REPLACe cDr. In this case, we could interact with the system as follows:

* (SETQ AC (RPLACD AB C))
((WHAT GOES ON) IN YOUR MIND)

and

* (SETQ DC (RPLACA AC D))
((HEAVEN IS) IN YOUR MIND)

Fig. 5-4

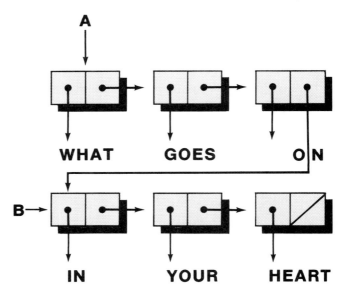

Where LISP really comes into its own is with programs that can create or modify other programs, even programs that can modify themselves. As a simple example, here is the short program called METAMORPHOSIS, which begins responding as a caterpillar, but once the word FLY is entered, from that point on it responds as a butterfly, never to return to its former caterpillar lifestyle. This short routine demonstrates the way that a LISP program can have a built-in method of altering itself that is dependent upon the internal mechanism of the program.

```
(DEFUN METAMORPHOSIS()
        (PROG (WAYS CHANGE)
  LOOP (SETQ WAYS (READ))
        (COND ((EQ WAYS (QUOTE DIES))
                (RETURN (QUOTE (THE END OF OUR
                        FRIEND))))
                (CHANGE (GO MATURE))
                (EQ WAYS (QUOTE FLY))
                (GO CHRYSALIS)) )
                (CATERPILLAR WAYS) (GO LOOP)
  CHRYSALIS (SETQ CHANGE T)
  MATURE
        (BUTTERFLY WAYS) (GO LOOP) ))

(DEFUN CATERPILLAR (WAYS)
        (PRINT (CONS WAYS (QUOTE (IS WHAT
        CATERPILLARS DO)))))

(DEFUN BUTTERFLY (WAYS)
        (PRINT (CONS WAYS (QUOTE (IS WHAT
        BUTTERFLIES DO)))))
```

Here is a sample session using this program:

* (METAMORPHOSIS)

CRAWL MUNCH DEVOUR FLY MUNCH FLUTTER
        SWARM DIES (Sample Data)

(CRAWL IS WHAT CATERPILLARS DO)
(MUNCH IS WHAT CATERPILLARS DO)
(DEVOUR IS WHAT CATERPILLARS DO)
(FLY IS WHAT BUTTERFLIES DO)
(MUNCH IS WHAT BUTTERFLIES DO)
(FLUTTER IS WHAT BUTTERFLIES DO)
(SWARM IS WHAT BUTTERFLIES DO)
(THE END OF OUR FRIEND)

Although at first LISP may seem to be a complicated language, it is essentially very simple. The LISP kernel consists of just seven functions—CAR, CDR, CONS, ATOM, EQ, COND and DEFUN—from which all the others may be derived. In practical LISP systems many more than these seven are written in assembly language, of course, for speed and efficiency. But, in principle, it would be possible to develop a complete system from just this very small core.

For example, the function can be defined as follows:

```
(DEFUN EQUAL (EXP1 EXP2)
  (OR (EQ EXP1 EXP2)
        AND (EQUAL (CAR EXP1) (CAR EXP2))
                (EQUAL (CDR EXP1) (CDR EXP2)))))
```

Once EQUAL has been defined, then the function SUBST, introduced earlier, could be defined:

```
(DEFUN SUBST (EXP1 EXP2 LIST)
  (IF (ATOM LIST)
        (IF (EQUAL EXP2 LIST)
                EXP1
                LIST )
        (CONS (SUBST EXP1 EXP2 (CAR LIST))
                (SUBST EXP1 EXP2 (CDR LIST)))))
```

Both of these definitions are excellent examples of the power of the recursive function definition in LISP. This recursive or nesting feature emulates one of the most powerful structural features of human language: the ability to redefine words or ideas. Therefore LISP, like human language, can extend itself through definition and recursion, with meaning being passed from one nested substructure to the next and back again to the matrix program.

You may have noticed that the two forms OR and IF were used in these definitions. For completeness, here are ways these could be implemented from the core primitives:

```
(DEFUN OR (EXP1 EXP2)
  (COND EXP1 T)
        (EXP2 T)
        (T NIL)))

(DEFUN IF MACRO (X)
  (LIST 'COND (LIST (CADR X) (CADDR X))
  (LIST T (AND (CDDDR X) (CADDDR X)))))
(DEFUN LIST (EXP1 EXP2)
  (CONS EXP1 (CONS EXP2 () )))

(DEFUN AND (EXP1 EXP2)
  (COND (EXP1 (COND (EXP2 T)))))
```

Although it is inherently a very simple language, many subtle and powerful features have been added as part of the LISP repertoire of procedures and utilities during its evolution. Today LISP is frequently used in AI as a systems language for developing still higher-level languages suited for certain types of artificial intelligence application. This practice has become so prevalent that it has exerted a strong influence over the new, and in some ways, transformed standard, Common LISP. Below is a glossary of many of the characteristic functions in the Common LISP definition of the language.

Ernest R. Tello

LISP GLOSSARY

The following LISP glossary represents the complete set of primitives for Common LISP, the generally recognized and accepted standard LISP. This version of the language handles all standard LISP functions and expression types and will run under MS-DOS.

APPEND   Joins two or more lists into one larger list.
(APPEND 'list-1 'list-2 ... 'list-n)

APPLY   Applies a function in turn to each item in a list of data.
(APPLY 'function 'arg &rest 'more-args)

ARRAY   type: integer 1-5; up to 32 bound arguments. Array types: (1) byte, (2) integer, (3) sh. float, (4) lg. float, (5) pointer.
(ARRAY 'type 'bound-1 'bound-2 ... 'bound-n)

ASSOC   Searches the top level of list for a unit whose CAR is EQ to item, and returns it. NIL if list = atom.
(ASSOC 'item 'list)

ATOM   Returns T if obj is an atom, NIL if it is not.
(ATOM 'obj)

BOUNDP   Returns T if variable 'symbol' has a value, else NIL.
(BOUNDP symbol)

CAR   Returns first item in cons-cell.
(CAR 'cell)

CATCH   Special form that acts as a branching target for THROW.
(CATCH tag [form])

CDR   Returns cell minus first item.
(CDR 'cell)

CLOSE   Closes only disk files if open.
(CLOSE 'file)

CONCAT   Returns string chain.
(CONCAT 'string-1 'string-2 ... 'string-n)

COND   clause = test + action. Executes first action whose test succeeds.
(COND clause-1 clause-2 ... claus-n)

CONS   Constructs cons-cell of obj 1 and 2.
(CONS 'obj1 'obj2)

DEFMACRO   Construct that defines macros called by 'name'.
(DEFMACRO name lambda-list [decl] [form])

DEFSTRUCT   Macro that creates data structures with named elements.
(DEFSTRUCT name-and-options [string] [slot])

DEFUN   Defines 'name' as a global function specified by 'lambda-list'.
(DEFUN name lambda-list [decl] [form])

DO   Special form for creating iteration loops.
([var [init [step]]]) (end-test[result])[tag]

EQL   Returns T only if objects are identical.
(EQL 'obj1 'obj2)

EQUAL   Returns T if values are equal.
(EQUAL 'obj1 'obj2)

EVAL   Evaluates the evaluation of the expression.
(EVAL 'expr)

FUNCALL   Evaluates function and applies result to each argument.
FUNCALL function arg-1 arg-2 ... arg-n

GENSYM   Invents a print name and a new symbol of that name.
(GENSYM &optional x)

GET   Returns value of 'propname' if it is found on property list of 'ident'.
(GET 'ident 'propname)

GETD   Returns function definition named by 'ident'.
(GETD 'ident)

GO   Allows PROG to be evaluated only if atom EQ to 'label' is found by evaluation of 'label' until it is an atom.
(GO label)

IF   Control loop for conditional tests.
IF test then [else]

LAMBDA   param-spec = ident. Specifies ident or list of idents for defined function and binds it to a value.
(LAMBDA param-spec action-1 ...action-n)

LAST   Returns the last cons-cell at the top level of 'list'.
(LAST 'list)

LENGTH   Returns the number of elements in 'sequence'.
(LENGTH sequence)

LET   LET ((var-1 value-1) (var-2 value-2) ... (var-n value-n)

LIST   Builds a list of its objects.
(LIST 'obj-1 'obj-2 ...'obj-n)

LISTP   Returns T if object is a list, else NIL.
(LISTP obj)

MAP Applies func to each list and successively to the CDR of each, and the CDR of that, until an atom is reached. Always returns NIL.
(MAP   'func 'list-1 ...'list-n)

MAPCAR Like MAP but applies function to CAR of lists.
(MAPCAR function list &rest more-lists

MEMBER Returns tail of list beginning with first element that matches 'item'.
(MEMBER item list)

MINUSP Returns T if number < 0, else NIL.
(MINUSP number)

NCONC Joins lists into one. Like APPEND, but does not preserve integrity of original lists.
(NCONC &rest lists)

NTH Returns the n-th item in list (CAR = 0).
(NTH n list)

NULL Returns T if object is (), else NIL.
(NULL obj)

NUMBERP Returns T if object is any number, else NIL.
(NUMBERP obj)

PLUSP T if expr is a number and > 0.
(PLUSP 'expr)

PRIN1 Prints expr at current position and includes backslashes and string quotes to allow it to be reread.
(PRIN   'expr 'file)

PRINT Performs TERPRI, PRIN, and then a space.
(PRINT 'expr 'file)

PROG Program-executing function declaring local-args and forms.
(PROG 'local-args expr-1 ... expr-n)

PROGNA A special form that takes a number of forms and evaluates them for their side effects, returning the value of only the last form.
(PROGN [form])

PROG1 Similar to PROGN but returns the value of the first form.

PROPS Returns property list of 'ident.
(PROPS 'ident)

PUT Associates val with prop name on the property list of ident and returns val.
(PUT 'ident 'val 'propname)

QUOTE Prevents evaluation of obj and returns just obj.
(QUOTE obj)

READ Reads one full expression from file and returns it.
(READ 'file)

REMPROP Removes 'indicator' from property list of 'symbol'.
(REMPROP symbol indicator)

REST SAME as CDR.
(REST list)

REVERSE Returns 'sequence' with the same elements but in reverse order.
(REVERSE sequence)

RPLACA Replaces car of cons-cell with obj and returns it.
(RPLACA 'cell 'obj)

RPLACD Replaces cdr with obj.
(RPLACD 'cell 'obj)

RPLACP Replaces property list of ident with list.
(RPLACP 'ident 'list)

SET Evaluates both and stores val as value of ident.
(SET 'ident 'val)

SETF A generalized update function for all variable declarations.
(SETF place new value)

SETQ Evaluates val only and stores as value of ident.
(SETQ ident 'val)

SOME Applies func to lists till not NIL.
(SOME 'func 'list-1...'list-n)

STORE Stores value as arrayref array element.
(STORE arrayref 'value)

STRINGP Returns T if obj a string, otherwise NIL.
(STRINGP 'obj)

SUBSET Applies func and lists non-NIL.
(SUBSET 'func 'list-1...list-n)

SUBST Substitutes exp1 for exp2 on list.
(SUBST exp1 exp2 list)

SUBSTRING Extracts substring.
(SUBSTRING 'string 'start-pos 'end-pos)

TERPRI Prints expr on a new line.
(TERPRI 'expr 'file)

THROW Provides a way to exit a process and return an exp to be evaluated by a matching 'catch' in a nonlocal manner.
(THROW exp form)

Logo

Logo is a very high-level list processing language that is, in actuality, a special version of LISP. Like LISP, Logo was developed at the Massachusetts Institute of Technology in response to a perceived need for a language that relied less upon a strict, fixed vocabulary and highly ordered syntax and more upon a need to construct logical procedures from elements already in the language. Logo and LISP are very similar in design, even though the apparent simplicity of the former is often deceiving to first-time users. Logo was designed to be an educational language, a role that it enjoys today not only in American schools but in schools throughout the world and especially in Third World countries, where the simple vocabulary and the ability to create new function words can incorporate lexical items from the native language. Educational specialists are particularly enthusiastic about the universal applicability of Logo to specialized environments. And because of its graphics utility, called turtle graphics, the language contains what educators recognize as an immediate feedback mechanism which not only provides positive reinforcement to children learning a new technology, but stimulates the same fascination with structures and designs that building toys did for earlier generations.

Although early implementations of Logo were restricted to mainframe computers, largely because of the severe memory requirements, the subsequent development of full Logo on low-cost micros in the 1980s, nearly fifteen years after its creation, has made it a language of choice both for schools and for home users. There are dialects of the language for the Apple, the TI 99/4A, the Commodore 64, the Atari, and the IBM PC. The original micro version of Logo, known as Terrapin Logo, was closest to the MIT original; later versions of the language, however, have been developed to utilize such features as sound and music synthesis, color and sprite graphics commands, and even forms of speech generation. Logo is under constant development and new implementations appear. It is this property of Logo, its adaptability to the hardware capabilities of succeeding generations of microcomputers, that continues to account for the language's popularity as a software product.

Logo began as an educational experiment, funded in part by the National Science Foundation, and developed into a full-blown computing language with applications far beyond the classroom. The idea of a language that could teach the concept of computing to children through a series of simple program operations and procedures and with a limited vocabulary that could be expanded from within the language itself had its origins at the MIT Artificial Intelligence Laboratory in the late 1960s. There, Seymour Papert sought to redefine the concept of computer education and the traditional methodologies of instruction in computer skills. Rather than emphasize the vocational aspects of computer education or develop flashcard-like computer-based delivery of material, Papert focused on the intellectual skills that could be developed by learning computer programming. However, traditional computer programming, with it heavy reliance on code and syntax, did not offer the immediate feedback necessary to engage elementary school children. Therefore, the MIT Logo Group developed a language which, like its ancestor LISP, had a small discrete vocabulary of primitive function words that allowed student programmers to build their own programming vocabulary. Children can define other primitives with only one command. The new primitive will operate exactly like the other primitives already present in the language. Therefore, students using Logo for the first time are able to construct programs, define new procedures, and create and store elaborate routines that can be recalled and built into other programs.

At the center of Logo-based curriculums is the belief that by programming in the language children develop reasoning and problem solving skills. Indeed, Logo forces users to be creative because it is nonrestrictive. For example, in order to create a user-defined procedure, a student will type TO and the name to be assigned to the procedure. To define a procedure called HELLO, the student will type:

TO HELLO

Logo responds with the > prompt. The student can then input the procedures that will be defined by HELLO.

```
TO HELLO
>PRINT [HELLO]
>PRINT [WELCOME TO LOGO]
>END
```

Logo will respond with:

```
HELLO DEFINED
?
```

Whenever the student types HELLO after the question mark prompt, the computer responds with:

```
HELLO
WELCOME TO LOGO
```

This is far more interactive and has less programming overhead than a comparable BASIC program which cannot be defined by a procedure name, cannot be called from within another program, and cannot be differentiated from any other BASIC program.

```
10 PRINT "HELLO"
20 PRINT "WELCOME TO LOGO"
30 END


RUN
HELLO
WELCOME TO LOGO
```

In order to display the Logo program HELLO more than once, the student need only type:

    REPEAT 2 [HELLO]

And the language prints:

    HELLO
    WELCOME TO LOGO

    HELLO
    WELCOME TO LOGO

But perhaps the most fascinating aspect of Logo for children is turtle graphics. The name turtle refers to the original MIT turtle which was a round robot, resembling an actual turtle, with an ink pen that could be raised [PENUP] or lowered [PENDOWN] by command. The turtle robot had wheels and could be controlled by the user with commands to move forward, backward, right, or left. By moving the turtle with the pen down, the device would draw a line on the floor. In current implementations of Logo, the turtle is a cursor-like graphic on the computer screen designed to show what direction it is pointing. Apple Logo, for example, uses an arrowhead. Using the command DRAW, in most micro versions, clears the screen and causes the turtle to appear. After that, the turtle simply obeys the user input commands. FORWARD 50—the number is arbitrary—moves the turtle fifty units forward; LEFT points it to the left; RIGHT points it to the right, and BACK causes it to move backward without actually changing the turtle's position. For example:

    FORWARD 10
    RIGHT 90
    FORWARD 10

creates a right angle.

    FORWARD 10
    RIGHT 90
    FORWARD 10
    RIGHT 90
    FORWARD 10
    RIGHT 90
    FORWARD 10
    RIGHT 90

creates a square and points the turtle back in its initial direction. We can define the entire procedure as SQUARE by typing:

    TO SQUARE
    >FORWARD 10 RIGHT 90
    >FORWARD 10 RIGHT 90
    >FORWARD 10 RIGHT 90
    >FORWARD 10 RIGHT 90
    >END

Logo will respond with SQUARE DEFINED. At this point, in order to see the turtle draw a square, the user need only type SQUARE, and the turtle will create the square on the screen.

The language also uses primitives for defining arithmetic procedures and defining variables and character strings as well. The developers of Logo, by building in a comprehensive list of plain English primitives and by allowing for the one-step creation of new primitive functions, have created a language that serves the needs of novices and accomplished programmers alike. Most important, however, the user's perception of the sophistication of Logo can increase with the skill of the user, and this will make it one of the primary tools of modern computer education.

LOGO GLOSSARY

This following Logo glossary represents the basic MIT standard of the language as currently implemented on the Apple II series. Logo has been implemented on virtually every type of PC currently on the market, with specific extensions of the basic keywords designed to call upon the hardware, graphics, sound, and music functions of the specific machines. The MIT version of Logo is the recognized basic standard from which all other extensions have developed.

Logo is a highly structured computer language which is primarily identified with its graphics capabilities. Although Logo's graphics capabilities are considerable, it offers much more, including text and file manipulation. There are a number of versions of Logo on the market today. For the Apple computer, there are two versions of Logo which are quite popular: one developed by MIT, known as *Terrapin/Krell Logo,* and the other marketed by Apple Computer, Inc.

The commands listed below correspond to Terrapin/Krell Logo. However, command structure in Apple and other versions of Logo is quite similar. In the following entries, the command is followed by the common abbreviation in parenthesis, and an example of the command in syntax is given at the end of the listing.

* Multiplication. Example: PRINT 20 * 8 will display 160.

+ Addition. Example: PRINT 20 + 10 will display 30.

− Subtraction. Example: PRINT 20 − 8 will display 12.

.DEPOSIT .DEPOSIT A n places decimal number n in memory location A.

/ Division. Example: PRINT 20 / 4 will display 5.

<   A < n means A is less than n.

=   A = n means A is equal to n.

>   A > n means A is greater than n.

ALLOF   Used with IF. Displays "TRUE" if all conditions are true; displays "FALSE" if any (one or more) conditions are false. Example: IF ALLOF: (A = 0)(B < 7) will display TRUE if A = 0 and B is less than 7.

ANYOF   Used with IF. Displays "TRUE" if any condition is true; displays "FALSE" only if all condition are false. Example: IF ANYOF: (A = 0)(B < 7) will display TRUE if either A = 0.

BACK (BK)   Draws line by moving turtle n screen units backward.
   BK n

BACKGROUND (BG)   Sets background color. Color codes are same as for PENCOLOR.
   BG n

BUTFIRST (BF)   Same as FIRST except everything but the first character is printed. Example: PRINT BUTFIRST "APPLE will give the display PPLE.

BUTLAST (BL)   Same as LAST except that everything but the last character is printed. Example: PRINT BUTLAST "APPLE will display APPL.

CATALOG   Displays all files from the Logo work disk.

CLEARSCREEN (CS)   Clears the screen and leaves turtle where it was.

CLEARTEXT   Clears the text screen and moves the cursor to the top.

DRAW   Blanks screen and displays turtle at center.

EDIT (ED)   Enters EDIT mode and displays procedure N.
   ED n

END   Ends the procedure.

ERASE (ER)   Erases procedure named N from memory (not disk).
   ER n

ERASEFILE   ERASEFILE "N" will erase the file named "N" from the Logo work disk.

ERASEPICT   ERASEPICT "N" erases the picture named "N" from a disk file.

FIRST   PRINT FIRST A displays the first character of word A. Example: PRINT FIRST "APPLE will display A.

FORWARD (FD)   Draws line by moving turtle n screen units forward.
   FD n

FULLSCREEN (∧F)   Displays full graphics screen without text.

HEADING   PRINT HEADING gives the turtle's present HEADING.

HIDETURTLE (HT)   Removes turtle from screen. This causes drawings to be done faster.
   HT

HOME   Sends turtle to the center of the screen pointing up.

IF   IF: A < n B. When A is less than n command, B will be executed. When A is not less than n, command B will not be executed and the next command line will be executed.

IFFALSE (IFF)   Must be used with the TEST command. Example: IFF PRINT "HI will display HI if the condition TESTed is false. If the condition is true, execution continues with the next line.

IFTRUE (IFT)   Must be used with the TEST command. Example: IFT PRINT "HI will display HI is the condition TESTed is true. If the condition is false, execution continues with the next line.

LAST   Same as FIRST except the last character is printed.

LEFT (LT)   Rotates turtle counterclockwise by d degrees.
   LT d

MAKE   MAKE A B gives procedure A value B. Example: MAKE BOX 50 assigns the value 50 to the procedure BOX.

NODRAW   Removes turtle from screen and prepares screen for text.

NOT   IF NOT A > n B will execute B when A is not greater than n.

NOTRACE   Turns off the TRACE command.

NOWRAP   Prevents drawing beyond screen boundaries. Causes an error message if screen boundaries are exceeded.

OUTDEV Will send display to a printer in slot N. When N is 0, display is sent to the screen.
  OUTDEV N

OUTPUT (OP) Assigns an output. Example: OP "FALSE will display FALSE.

PADDLE 0 Displays a number 0-255 representing the position of Apple paddle 0.

PADDLE 1 Displays a number 0-255 representing the position of Apple paddle 1.

PADDLEBUTTON 0 Displays "TRUE" if paddle button is pressed, "FALSE" if otherwise.

PADDLEBUTTON 1 Displays "TRUE" if paddle button is pressed, "FALSE" otherwise.

PENCOLOR(PC) Sets color for lines to code n. (0 = black; 1 = white; 2 = green; 3 = violet; 4 = orange; 5 = blue.).
  PCn

PENUP (PU) Prevents turtle from drawing when it moves.

PENDOWN (PD) Causes turtle to draw when it moves.

PRINT (PR) The expression N will be printed on the screen. N must be in [].
  PR []

PRINT1 PRINT1 N is the same as PRINT except that the cursor remains on the same line.
  PRINT1 []

PRINTOUT (PO) Prints the procedure N on the screen.
  POn

PRINTOUT TITLES (POTS) Prints names of all user procedures.

RANDOM PRINT RANDOM n will randomly display a number between 0 and n−1.

RANDOMIZE Causes the Apple to select new random numbers.

RC? Displays "TRUE" if a character has been typed, "FALSE" if no character has been typed.

READ Reads all procedures from the disk file named "N" into memory.
  READ "n"

READCHARACTER (RC) Same as REQUEST except input is one character.

READPICT READPICT "N" reads the picture named "N" from a disk file and draws it on the screen.

REMAINDER REMAINDER n a displays the remainder when n is divided by a. Example: PRINT REMAINDER 30 4 will display 2.

REPEAT REPEAT n A will repeat procedure A n times.

REQUEST (RQ) Waits for user input, then displays the input on the screen.

RIGHT (RT) Rotates turtle clockwise by d degrees.
  Rt d

SAVE Saves all procedures presently in memory in a disk file named "N". "N" must be in quotes.
  SAVE "N"

SAVEPICT SAVEPICT "N" will save the picture named "N" to a disk file.

SENTENCE (SE) PRINT SE A B combines words (or lists) A and B into one larger list.

SETHEADING (SETH) Sets turtle's direction to d degrees.
  SETH d

SETX SETX a Same as SETXY but for horizontal only.
  SETX a

SETXY SETXY a b Sets turtle's position to a horizontal units to right of center and b vertical units above center. For negative values, the direction becomes left and below, respectively.
  SETXY a b

SETY SETY b Same as SETXY but for vertical only.
  SETY b

SHOWTURTLE (ST) Displays turtle on screen.

SPLITSCREEN (∧S) Displays graphics with four lines of text at bottom of screen.

SQRT SQRT n displays the positive square root of n. Thus, PRINT SQRT 25 will execute the procedure for square root and the screen will display 5.

STOP Unconditionally halts execution.

TEST TEST B will produce "TRUE" if B is true and "FALSE" otherwise. Example: TEST: A > 8 will display TRUE if A is greater than 8 and FALSE if A is less than or equal to 8.

TEXTSCREEN (∧T) Displays full procedure text without any drawing. Used to see complete procedure at once.

THING PRINT THING A will output the value associated with A.

TO Used when defining user procedures. N is the name of a procedure.
  TO N

TOPLEVEL Halts all procedures and causes the user to type from the keyboard to resume execution.

TRACE Causes execution to occur one command at a time. The return key must be pressed to continue command execution.

TURTLESTATE (TS) Gives the output of A B n m where A and B are either "TRUE" or "FALSE" and where n and m are real numbers from 0 to 5. A gives the PEN condition (TRUE = DOWN, FALSE = UP). B tells whether or not the turtle is visible (TRUE = VISIBLE).

WRAP Permits drawing beyond screen boundaries.

XCOR PRINT XCOR gives the turtle's present X position.

YCOR PRINT YCOR gives the turtle's present Y position.

Modula-2

Niklaus Wirth, designer of Modula-2 and Pascal, describes Modula-2 as "a descendant of its ancestors Pascal and Modula." Pascal, introduced in 1970, was originally intended to be used in teaching concepts of computer science, but has become a general purpose language used for programming everything from operating systems to databases. Modula (sometimes called Modula-1), on the other hand, is little-known outside the Swiss Federal Institute of Technology (Institut für Informatik, ETH Zürich). Modula was developed in 1977 for the special purpose of multiprogramming.

Modula-2, born in 1980, was designed to relieve many of Pascal's shortcomings. It inherits its basic syntax and emphasis on data type from Pascal, and its separate compilation of program modules, multiprogramming capabilities, and low-level access to the computer from Modula.

Syntax

Modula-2 programs are very readable, especially to those familiar with Pascal. Every program (known as a program module) begins with the keyword MODULE and the name of the program, and ends with the keyword END, the name of the program, and a period. Procedures within the module begin with the keyword PROCEDURE and the procedure name, and end with an END and the procedure name once again. Statements within a module or procedure are separated by semicolons:

```
MODULE Example ;
FROM Terminal IMPORT WriteString ;
```

```
PROCEDURE WriteIt ;
BEGIN
  WriteString ("Hello, world") ;
END WriteIt ;

BEGIN (* main program *)
  WriteIt ;
END Example.
```

Notice that the body of a procedure or module is delimited by BEGIN and END statements, and that comments are enclosed within parentheses and asterisks.

Modula-2 provides WHILE, FOR, REPEAT-UNTIL, and LOOP-EXIT statements to control statement iteration, and IF-THEN-ELSIF-ELSE and CASE statements to control conditional execution. The only other Modula-2 statements are variable assignment, procedure call, procedure return, and record field reference (WITH statement).

One syntactic difference between Pascal and Modula-2 is that Modula-2 does not require a separate BEGIN for a statement sequence within WHILE, FOR, REPEAT, and IF statements:

```
FOR index := 65 TO 99 DO
  array [index] := index ;
  Write (CHR (index)) ;
END ;
```

Pascal would require a BEGIN after the DO in the FOR statement, since there is more than one statement in the body of the FOR loop.

Data Types

Modula-2, like Pascal, is a strongly-typed language. Each data element has a data type associated with it, and the programmer must declare the data type of all variables:

```
VAR letter  : CHAR ;
    number  : INTEGER ;
```

The fundamental data types are: INTEGER, CARDINAL, REAL, BOOLEAN, and CHAR. Set, record, and array types can be created from any other type, and new types can be declared as enumerations or subranges of other types:

```
TYPE Department =
        (mfg, eng, prod, sales) ;
TYPE Employee =
    RECORD
        Name: ARRAY[0..40] OF CHAR ;
        dept: Department ;
    END ;
```

Pointers to elements of any data type can also be declared.

The Modula-2 compiler checks to see that data elements are used consistently: that data elements in arithmetic expressions are of the same type, and data passed to procedures as parameters are of the type expected by the procedure. For example, if a procedure expects a CARDINAL parameter, all parameters passed to the procedure must be CARDINALs:

```
MODULE ParameterType ;
VAR counter : CARDINAL ;

PROCEDURE Dummy (value: CARDINAL) ;
END Dummy ;

BEGIN
  FOR counter := 1 TO 10 DO
    Dummy (counter) ;
  END ;
END ParameterType.
```

It is possible, when necessary, to relax Modula-2's strong type checking by the use of type transfer functions. Any variable can be made compatible with any data type occupying the same amount of memory.

```
addressVar := ADDRESS (cardinalVar) ;
```

Separate Compilation

Perhaps the most powerful feature of Modula-2 is its support of separate compilation of modules with strong type checking across module boundaries. Procedures, data types, constants and variables can be exported from one module to another, so that the same constructs need not be programmed repeatedly. Separate compilation also allows a large program to be divided into pieces that can be easily programmed, tested, and maintained.

Modules that export objects are called library modules. Library modules have two parts, a definition module and an implementation module. The definition module defines how exported objects appear to modules that import the objects; the implementation module defines the details of the object's structure. In the case of a procedure, the definition module gives the procedure's name, and the number and type of parameters expected by the procedure. The implementation module contains the statements that are executed when the procedure is called:

```
DEFINITION MODULE Example ;

EXPORT QUALIFIED Even ;

  PROCEDURE Even (num: CARDINAL): BOOLEAN ;

  END Example.

  IMPLEMENTATION MODULE Example ;

  PROCEDURE Even
      (num: CARDINAL): BOOLEAN ;
```

```
BEGIN
  IF num MOD 2 = 0 THEN
    RETURN TRUE
  ELSE
    RETURN FALSE
  END ;
END Even ;

END Example.
```

To use procedure Even, a program module simply imports it and calls it like a locally defined procedure:

```
MODULE EvenDigits ;
FROM Example IMPORT Even ;
FROM Terminal IMPORT WriteString ;
VAR digit : CARDINAL ;
BEGIN
  FOR digit := 0 TO 9 DO
    IF Even(digit) THEN
      WriteString ("even")
    END ;
  END ;
END EvenDigits.
```

Notice that the procedure WriteString is imported from a library module called Terminal. Modula-2 does not have any I/O statements or mathematical functions; every implementation of Modula-2 must provide library modules for file and terminal I/O, trigonometric functions, etc.

Modula-2's separate compilation feature makes the language especially well-suited for large programming projects, since the programmer or programming team can divide the project into modules, define the interfaces between the modules, then attack the project one piece at a time. When program changes are required, whether during program development, debugging, or maintenance, only the implementation module affected need be recompiled, as long as the interface between the modules is not changed.

Multiprogramming

Modula-2 does not have a built-in mechanism for establishing and scheduling coroutines, but provides the primitives for transferring between coroutines. These primitives can be used for creating process schedulers for runtime systems. Procedures can be established as coroutines; control can be passed between coroutines, and coroutine variables can be declared, assigned, and compared.

Although the system programmer is forced into dealing with coroutines on a low level, the ability to do so allows the flexibility and control needed when creating multiprocessing algorithms.

Low-Level Access

Unlike Pascal, Modula-2 allows low-level access to the computer hardware. Variables can be assigned to a specific memory address at declaration, and the memory address of variables can be obtained. The program can also determine the number of memory words occupied by a variable, and the number of memory words occupied by a variable of a specified type. These capabilities can be used to increase the portability of programs; programs can access the low-level facilities of the computer without becoming bound to the architecture of a particular machine.

Individual bits of the computer can also be checked, set, or cleared, using variables of type BITSET.

Morgan B. Adair

MODULA-2 GLOSSARY

The following glossary contains a brief definition of each of the reserved words and standard identifiers of Modula-2. Although there is no standard implementation of the language, existing implementations treat these words and identifiers in a consistent manner.

ABS Returns the absolute value of its parameter.
  IF ABS (integerVar) > max THEN

AND Conjunction of two boolean factors.
  IF (X < 10) AND (area > 100) THEN

ARRAY Structured type consisting of a fixed number of elements of the same type.
  VAR vector : ARRAY [1..20] OF INTEGER ;

BEGIN Marks the beginning of a module or procedure block.

BITSET A set of integers from zero to the wordlength of the computer minus one. BITSET values are used to reference individual bits of a computer's memory.

BOOLEAN A data type consisting of the values TRUE and FALSE.

BY Used in the FOR statement to indicate the incrementation size for each iteration (see FOR).

CAP Returns the capital of a CHAR parameter.
  IF CAP (response) = "Y" THEN

CARDINAL A data type consisting of non-negative integers.

CASE Statement controlling conditional execution. One of several branches is taken, depending on the value of a variable or expression.
  CASE dept OF
        mfg   : salary   :=   18000 ;
    | eng   : salary   :=   25000 ;
    | prod   : salary   :=   17000 ;
    | sales : salary   :=   20000 ;
  END ;

CHAR A data type consisting of alphanumeric and control characters.

CHR Returns the character whose ordinal number (ASCII value) is given.
  ESC := CHR (27) ;

CONST Used for declaring constant values in a module or procedure.
  CONST pi = 3.141593

DEC Decrements a variable by a specified value (or one if no value is specified).
  DEC (index, 2) ;

DEFINITION The part of a module containing a list of exported objects and their declarations.

DISPOSE Deallocates a block of dynamically-allocated memory.
  VAR p: POINTER TO CARDINAL ;
  BEGIN
    NEW (p) ;
    p ↑ := 100 ;
    DISPOSE (p) ;

DIV Arithmetic operator that computes the quotient of two INTEGER or CARDINAL expressions.

DO Marks the beginning of a group of statements to be executed as part of a FOR, WHILE, or WITH statement (see FOR).

ELSE Designates the statements to be executed if the condition in an IF statement is not met (see IF).

ELSIF Designates statements to be executed if the expression in an IF statement is not met, and a specified condition is met (see IF).

END Marks the end of a declaration or block of code.

EXCL Excludes an element from a set.
  IF y IN set1 THEN EXCL (set1, y) ;

EXIT Causes an exit from a LOOP statement.

EXPORT Specifies the identifiers declared within a module that can be accessed outside the module.

FALSE The negative BOOLEAN value.

FLOAT Returns the REAL equivalent of an INTEGER or CARDINAL value.
  integerVar := FLOAT (realVar) ;

FOR A statement used to execute a group of statements a specified number of times.
  FOR index := 2 TO 100 BY 2 DO

FROM Designates the module from which to import an identifier.
  FROM Terminal IMPORT WriteString, WriteLn ;

HALT Terminates the executing program.
  IF denom = 0 THEN
    WriteString ("division by zero") ;
    HALT
  END ;

HIGH   Returns the high index of an array. Used to determine the size of an array parameter.
```
PROCEDURE Size (array: ARRAY OF CHAR) ;
BEGIN
 arraySize := HIGH (array) + 1 ;
END Size ;
```

IF   A statement controlling conditional execution of a group of statements.
```
IF x = 3 THEN WriteString ("3") ;
ELSIF x = 6 THEN WriteString ("6") ;
ELSE WriteString ("other") ;
END ;
```

IMPLEMENTATION   The part of a module that contains the details of a module's operation.

IMPORT   Specifies the identifiers declared outside a module that can be accessed within the module.
```
FROM MathLib IMPORT sqrt ;
```

IN   Tests for membership of an element within a set.
```
IF carry IN flagset THEN
 WriteString ("overflow")
END ;
```

INC   Increments a variable by a specified value.
```
INC (index, 10) ;
```

INCL   Includes an element in a set.
```
INCL (flagset, carry) ;
```

INTEGER   A data type consisting of signed whole numbers.

LOOP   Designates a group of statements to be executed repeatedly until an EXIT statement is reached.
```
LOOP
 Read (character) ;
 IF character = "q" THEN EXIT END ;
END ;
```

MOD   Returns the remainder after division of two CARDINAL or INTEGER values.

MODULE   A sequence of declarations and instructions to carry out a task; a program.

NEW   Dynamically allocates a block of memory.
```
VAR p: POINTER TO CARDINAL ;
BEGIN
 NEW (p) ;
 p ↑ := 100 ;
```

NIL   Pointer value that indicates the pointer points to no object.

NOT   Complement of a BOOLEAN expression.

ODD   Returns true if an INTEGER or CARDINAL value is odd.
```
IF ODD (x) THEN WriteString("next") ;
```

OF   Qualifier in a CASE statement, or array or set declaration.

OR   Disjunction of a BOOLEAN expression.
```
IF (x<3) OR (x=999) THEN
```

ORD   Returns the ordinal value of the parameter within its type. For example, ORD ("A") is 65 because A is the 65th value in type CHAR.
```
cardinalVar := (ORD (numericChar) - 48)
```

POINTER   A data type consisting of pointers to other data objects.

PROC   A data type consisting of parameterless procedures.

PROCEDURE   A group of statements that can be called from a program.

QUALIFIED   Used in an export statement to indicate that modules that reference the exported identifiers must name the module from which the identifiers are import.
```
MODULE Counter ;
EXPORT QUALIFIED Count ;

FROM Counter IMPORT Count ;
```

REAL   A data type consisting of signed floating point values.

RECORD   A data structure combining several fields, not necessarily of the same type.
```
TYPE Employee =
    RECORD
        number : CARDINAL ;
        name: ARRAY [0..40] OF
CHAR ;
    END ;
```

REPEAT   Statement that causes a group of statements to be executed until a specified condition is attained.
```
REPEAT
 Read (character) ;
UNTIL character = "q" ;
```

RETURN   Returns control from a procedure to the point the procedure was called.

SET   A data type consisting of an unordered group of elements of another data type.

THEN   Indicates the statements to be executed in a FOR or IF statement (see FOR, IF).

TO Designates the terminating condition in a FOR statement (see FOR).

TRUE The positive BOOLEAN value.

TRUNC Returns a CARDINAL or INTEGER value equal to the integral part of a REAL value.
  integervar := TRUNC (realvar) ;

TYPE Declaration of a data type.
  TYPE tree = POINTER TO branch ;

UNTIL Designates the terminating condition of a REPEAT statement (see REPEAT).

VAL Returns the value of an ordinal number in a specified type. For example, VAL (65, CHAR) is A, because A is the 65th value of type CHAR.
  TYPE color = (red, orange, green, blue) ;
  VAR hue : color ;

  BEGIN
    hue := VAL (color, 2) ;
    (* hue now equals orange *)

VAR Declaration of data elements and their types.
  VAR ch: CHAR ;
    done: BOOLEAN ;

WHILE Statement causing the execution of a group of statements as long as a specified condition is met.
  WHILE total < 1000 DO

WITH Statement indicating that a group of statements are to act on the fields of a specified record.
  WITH EmployeeRecord DO
    name := "N. Wirth" ;
    salary := 45000 ;
  END ;

Pascal

Pascal is a highly structured language that is organized into paragraphs or blocks of code. Each block contains a specific amount of information or set of instructions to make it self-contained within the larger program sequence. These compartments, which are assigned names within the program, are easier to debug and troubleshoot than unstructured languages like BASIC which define lines only by numbers. Pascal was developed in the early 1970s by Niklaus Wirth, and it was intended to serve as a language for teaching computer programming as a systematic, highly organized and structured discipline. The design of Pascal encourages structured coding as well as a careful consideration and analysis of data types.

The highly structured nature of Pascal and its relative simplicity allowed the language to be implemented on a wide variety of machines, and because of its compartmentlike design, the programs could be modified easily for different system environments. In fact, Niklaus Wirth believed that simplicity was itself a virtue in a language for teaching. Pascal was enthusiastically accepted as an instructional language. As the advantages of structured programming became more widely known, the language was introduced to the professional programming world outside of academia as a software development tool. With the advent of microcomputers, Pascal was seen as a sophisticated language that could be fully implemented on moderately powerful micros as well as on mainframes. Hence, a program written for an institutional IBM could also be implemented on an Apple after adjustments had been made for memory size. After the development of an intermediate compiler for the language at the University of California at San Diego, Pascal became highly transportable from microcomputer system to microcomputer system. However, as new implementations were introduced, extensions of the language were also introduced to correct omissions in the standard Pascal. At present, unfortunately, these extensions differ from one implementation to the next and have resulted in different versions of the language such as the UCSD standard, Apple Pascal, KMMM Pascal, Turbo Pascal, and the like.

Besides allowing users to define their own data types and even create new types of variables to fit their own needs, Pascal is also quite rich in control statements. In the sample program listing below, there are "FOR" loops with index variable testing and incrementing, a "WHILE" loop with expression testing, and an "IF...THEN...ELSE..." structure. Also "BEGIN...END" pairs serve as statement parentheses to enable nesting of any block of statements as a clause within any control structure.

A Pascal program may contain the following components:

program heading

label declarations

const declarations

type declarations

var declarations

procedure and function definitions

begin main body end

All components are optional except for the program heading and the final component containing one or more executable statements within the main body.

The sample program below, which was produced on an Apple II+, prints a list of all possible subsets of a given size from a universe set of a specified size. For example, for the input line 2 3, the subset size is 2, the universe is the set of three letters (a,b,c), and the output consists of ab, ac, and bc on separate printed lines. The sample program contains type declarations for the two data types "elementtype" and "settype". "Elementtype" is declared as the set of characters that are alphabetical. Thus, in the definition of procedure "showsubsets", the declaration "var element:elementtype" means that "element" is expected to take as its value some alphabetical character. Similarly, in procedure "main", the variable U is expected to have as its value some set of alphabetical characters. Pascal is distinguished by its capability to define and redefine data structures of complex types.

Procedure and function definitions, except for the headings, are identical in form to complete programs. Flow of control starts at the first statement in the main body component of the program. In the sample program, the main body is the single statement "main" on the next-to-last line. This statement activates, or calls, the defined "procedure main", which then activates procedures "obtain" and "showsubsets". Note that "showsubsets" recursively activates itself. In most Pascal implementations on small machines, a statement may not refer to a procedure defined later in the source code unless an awkward "forward directive" is supplied. For this reason, procedure definitions appear in the program text before the appearance of statements activating them.

SAMPLE PROGRAM

(Comments enclosed in parentheses and asterisks are REMark statements.)

```
program subsets(input,output);

    (*Prints all subsets of a specified size of a
    universe set U.
    Flow of control starts below at main *)

type
    elementtype='a'..'z';
    settype=set of elementtype;

procedure showsubsets (A,B : settype; r: integer);
```

(*Assumes set A is a subset of set B. Prints every subset of B that contains all elements of A and also r elements that are members of B but not of A.*)

var

   element: elementtype;

```
begin
   if r = 0 then
      begin (* print set A *)
      writeln;
      for element := 'a' to 'z' do
         if element in A then write
         (element)
      end (* print *)
   else if not (B = A) then
      begin
      element := 'a' ; (* pick an element of B − A
      *)
      while not (element in B − A) do
         element := succ(element);
      (* print subsets containing element,
         then print subsets not containing
         element *)
      showsubsets ( A + [element], B, r−1 );
      showsubsets ( A, B − [element], r )
      end

end (* showsubsets *)

procedure obtain(var U: settype; var subsetsize:
integer);
```

(* Reads sizes of subsets and U. Generates U using letters. *)

```
var
   usetsize, counter: 0..25 ;
   letter: elementtype;

begin
   readln (subsetsize,usetsize);
   U:= [];
   letter := 'a';
   for counter := 1 to usetsize do
      begin
      U:= U + [letter];
      letter := succ(letter)
      end
end (* obtain *) ;

procedure main;

var
   subsetsize: integer;
   U: settype;
```

```
begin
   obtain( U , subsetsize );
   showsubsets( [], U, subsetsize )

begin
   min
end.
```

PASCAL GLOSSARY

The following glossary represents the complete standard implementation of Pascal. Pascal is currently available in a number of different implementations and subsets for a variety of computers. Among the most well known are Turbo Pascal for the PC and PC compatibles and KMMM Pascal or Baby Pascal for the Commodore PET, the SuperPET, and the smaller Commodore 64 computers.

The format below lists the reserved word, gives its definition, uses it as a command in syntax, and gives an example of its place in a programming statement.

ABS   Returns the absolute value of its parameter.

   ABS(x)
      writeln('the absolute value of the number',x,'is', ABS(x));

AND   Returns the logical conjunction of two boolean factors.
   if (condition) AND (condition) then imperative statement
      if (r=6) AND (c>4) then writeln('r+c>10);

ARCTAN   Returns the value of an angle whose tangent is equal to the parameter of the function.
   ARCTAN(real or integer expression)
      writeln(arctan(65));

ARRAY   Structured type of a fixed number all of elements of the same type.
   ARRAY [ordinal type] of type
   var num: ARRAY[1..50] of integer;
   BEGIN
      for x := 1 to 50 do
         num[x] := x;
   END

BEGIN   Used in conjunction with END to outline a body or block of code.
   BEGIN
      statements;
   END.
      BEGIN
         readln(x,y,z);
         d := x+y*z;
         writeln(d);
   END.

CASE   The case statement uses the value of an ordinal expression to select one statement from a group of statements to be executed.
    CASE ordinal expression ...
        CASE x of
            su: write('sunday')

CHAR   Predefined ordinal type which represents characters used for communications between the computer and the operator.
    identifier : CHAR;
        letter, string : CHAR;

CHR   Returns the character whose ordinal number is given.
    CHR(integer expression)
        VAR m:integer;
        BEGIN
            writeln('enter two digit);
            readln(m);
            writeln('the coesponding character is',
            CHR(m));
        END.

CONST   Constants are unchanging data items whose value is determined at compile time.
    CONST identifier = constant;
        CONST
            pi = 3.1415926;
            max = 12456

COS   Real function that returns the cosine of its parameter.
    COS(real expression)
        writeln('the cosine of 100 degrees is',COS(100));

DISPOSE   Allows dynamically defined memory to be freed for later use.
    DISPOSE(pointer identifier);
        DISPOSE(treeptr);

DIV   Used to compute the quotient of two integer expressions.
    variable := integer expression DIV integer expression
        m := a DIV z

DOWNTO   Loop control used to decrement the loop parameter.
    for identifier := integer expression DOWNTO integer expression do
        for polls := 50 DOWNTO 1 do

ELSE   As part of the IF statement, ELSE forces execution of a statement on a false condition.
    if expression then statement ELSE statement
        if (r=6) then write('correct') ELSE write('wrong')

END   Used in conjunction with the BEGIN statement as a terminator of a body or block of code.
    (See: BEGIN)

FILE   A sequence of data items all of the same type.
    FILE of type identifier
        FILE of integer

FOR   Used when a statement or group of statements is to be repeated a predefined number of times.
    FOR identifier := integer expression to integer expression do
        FOR x := 1 to 10 do

FUNCTION   A group of statements to which a name is assigned that performs a specific task. Functions are used to avoid repetition of identical blocks of code.
    FUNCTION identifier(parameter list);
        statements;
    end;
        FUNCTION x(y:real):real;
            var... begin
                statements...
            end;
        end; (*x*)

GET   Reads a record from a specified file.
    GET(file variable);
        GET(filea)

GOTO   Transfers control to a stated point in the program.
    GOTO label
        GOTO exit

IF   Allows conditional execution of a statement or statements.
    IF expression then imperative statement.
        IF (r=1) then imperative statement

IN   Tests for membership of a predefined set for a stated identifier.
    expression IN expression
        if d IN lset then imperative statement

INPUT   A predeclared file associated with an input device such as a keyboard or disk file, usually used with the READ or READLN statements.
    program name (input);
        program comp(INPUT,output);

INTEGER   Defines an identifier's internal representation as an integer type.
    identifier : INTEGER
        x,y,z : INTEGER

LN   Returns the natural logarithm of its parameter.
    LN(real or integer expression)
        writeln('the logarithm of',x,'is',LN(x));

MAXINT Integer constant defining the range of correct integer math.
  Integer Constant Identifier
    writeln('the range of correct integer math is',MAXINT);

MOD Computes the remainder of division.
  variable := integer expression MOD integer expression;
    n := a MOD z;
    m := a DIV z;
    writeln(a,'divided by',z,'=',m,n);

NEW Allocates space for a dynamic variable.
  NEW(pointer variable);
    NEW(treeptr);

NIL Used when a pointer does not reference a dynamic variable.
  pointer variable := NIL;
    treeptr := NIL;

NOT A boolean operator used to obtain the complement of a second boolean expression.
  if NOT (condition) then imperative statement
    if NOT (x=y) then imperative statement

ODD Returns the value TRUE when the value being tested has an odd integer value.
  ODD(integer expression);
    if ODD(n) then imperative statement

OF Used as a qualifier in various declarations.
  identifier or structured type OF type
    array[0..12] OF integer;

OR Returns the logical disjunction of two boolean factors.
  if (condition) OR (condition) then imperative statement;
    if (i=6) OR (y=2) then imperative statement

ORD Returns an integer value equal to the ordinal number of the parameter within the given range of values the parameter can take.
  ORD(ordinal expression)
    writeln('ordinal number',ORD(x));

OUTPUT Declares that a program will perform data transmission from memory to an output device.
  program name(OUTPUT);
    program flag(OUTPUT);

PACK Transfers data from an ordinary array to a packed array.
  PACK(array identifier,integer expession,packed array identifier)
    PACK(l,5,m)

PACKED Declares internal representation of a specified variable is in packed decimal format.
  identifier = file of PACKED array[ordinal type] of type
    paper = file of PACKED array[1..10] of char;

PAGE Causes the print device to skip to the top of the next page or a display device to be cleared.
  PAGE(file variable)
    PAGE(f)

PRED Returns the value preceding a given value in the set of all values an ordinal type can take.
  PRED(ordinal expression)
    writeln('the character preceding',x,'is',PRED(w))

READ Assigns the value of elements of a file to variables.
  READ(file variable,variable)
    READ(cards,suit)

PROCEDURE A group of statements which compose an algorithm.
  PROCEDURE identifier(formal parameter list);
    PROCEDURE treesearch(list,w,p);

REPEAT Permits repeated execution of a statement or statements with a boolean expression as a parameter determining number of repetitions.
  REPEAT statement(s) until boolean expression
    REPEAT
      writeln('hi');
    until i

SUCC A standard ordinal function that returns the next value within a given range that the original ordinal type can take.
  SUCC(ordinal expression)
    writeln (SUCC(val))

TYPE Identifies the internal representation of data.
  TYPE identifier = type;
    TYPE elem = integer;

WHILE Loop control forcing execution of statements until boolean expression false.
  WHILE boolean expression do
    WHILE not eof do
      read(let);
    end

WRITE Standard procedure to append values to a file.
  WRITE(file, identifier)
    WRITE(text,x,y)

Pilot

Pilot, which stands for "Programmed Inquiry, Learning Or Teaching," was created by John A. Starkweather at the University of California at San Francisco Medical Center in 1968 as a special-purpose language for the development of CAI, or Computer Aided Instruction, materials. The language was originally conceived of as an elementary authoring system; that is, it was created to be a language that teachers, writers, students, or other non-programmers could use to develop instructional materials and the administration of student testing and lesson sequences. Pilot was one of the early attempts at combining lesson presentation, testing, and interactive response within a single system that educational specialists and curriculum development personnel could use without extensive special instruction and without having to rely upon the services of a professional programmer or coder. In this respect, it had beginnings much like Fortran, which was initially developed to eliminate the need for assembly language programmers, thereby putting the actual computing language directly into the hands of the content specialists.

Because it was originally designed for the non-programmer, Pilot is a very simple language with relatively few commands when compared to a language such as COBOL, which is command heavy, or to Smalltalk, which is category and statement class heavy. Even the commands themselves, MATCH, USE, and TYPE, for example, are straightforward and familiar to course specialists because they were created partially out of the language of curriculum development and educational planning. This makes Pilot a developmental tool that paved the way for the current interest in natural-language authoring systems and code generators.

Because Pilot was originally conceived as a special-purpose language, its strength lies in its ease of use and in its nontechnical appearance. Its weaknesses reside in its inability to drive sophisticated file-handling routines or to do numerical computation of any significance. Pilot is primarily a presentation language that makes it easy for users to create screen displays and the types of rudimentary branching operations, such as True or False or Right or Wrong, that are routinely used in lessons, drills, and tests. Once the matrix logic is created other data entry people can keyboard the questions and answers.

Pilot is an interpreted language which evaluates each line of source code immediately upon execution and translates it into machine code. This makes it a slow-running language, but the speed does not impede its primary application of authoring and presentation. Pilot is also a highly transportable language with implementations on all of the major personal computer operating systems. Later versions of the language, especially versions for the Apple II family, the VIC 20 and Commodore 64, the Atari, even the MS-DOS compatibles, have added graphics and sound commands that weren't included in the original implementation.

There are two basic types of data in Pilot: character strings and integers. Pilot supports both constants and variables. Variables do not have to be declared as a data type in Pilot, unlike PL/I or Fortran, and are represented by a single letter preceded by the #. Thus #X and #Z are valid names for variables in Pilot. Unless assigned a value by the program, all integer variables are initialized automatically at zero. They can be reset to zero within the program by the VNEW:# command. String variable names have a limit of ten characters and are preceded by the $, the reverse notation of BASIC. Thus $PHONE represents a string variable in Pilot, whereas in BASIC the same variable will be represented by PHONE$. String variables can be reset or initialized to zero by the VNEW:$ command or the VNEW: command. The latter command initializes all variables, integer as well as string, and can be used in a program to reset all data types to zero.

The simplest of Pilot programs consists, as in BASIC, of (TYPE), print, and remark statements:

```
R:THIS IS AN ELEMENTARY PILOT PROGRAM
R:IT CONSISTS OF REMARK STATEMENTS
R:AND TYPE STATEMENTS
T:THIS IS AN EXAMPLE OF A TYPE STATE-
   MENT
R:THAT WAS AN EXAMPLE OF A TYPE STATE-
   MENT
```

Running this program through a Pilot interpreter would produce:

```
THIS IS AN EXAMPLE OF A TYPE STATEMENT
```

Print statements can be directed to the printer rather than to the screen with the TYPE PRINTER statement:

```
R:THIS PROGRAM DISPLAYS THE
   DIFFERENCES
R:BETWEEN T AND TP STATEMENTS
T:THIS SENDS A MESSAGE TO THE SCREEN
TP:THIS SENDS A MESSAGE TO THE PRINTER
```

Pilot's keyboard input is expressed by the ACCEPT or A: statement. The ACCEPT statement, often used in conjunction with a TH, or TYPE HANG, statement that keeps the cursor at the end of the line and does not send an automatic line feed to the screen, forms the basis of interactive programs with students. For example:

```
TH:TYPE IN YOUR NAME PLEASE
A:$NAME
TH:TYPE IN YOUR CLASS SECTION PLEASE
A:$CLASS
T:GOOD MORNING $NAME OF $CLASS
T:LET'S BEGIN TODAY'S LESSON
```

The ACCEPT statement has two primary functions in elementary CAI programs. First, as the above example demonstrates, it can be used to read values into a variable. In this way, it performs like the INPUT statement in BASIC. ACCEPT also reserves a memory location or a buffer that can be used to store the ACCEPT input until another ACCEPT statement sends new data to the buffer. Once in the ACCEPT buffer, the number or string can be compared or MATCHed with other values. In this way, an ACCEPT...MATCH routine forms the elementary procedure of a simple short-answer quiz.

```
R:THIS IS A SHORT ANSWER QUIZ
R:IT IS CREATED WITH AN ACCEPT/MATCH
   ROUTINE
CH:
R:CH:IS THE CLEARSCREEN COMMAND IN
   PILOT
R:IT OPERATES LIKE THE CLS IN MS-BASIC
   OR
R:THE HOME COMMAND ON THE APPLE
T:THE DECLARATION OF INDEPENDENCE WAS
   SIGNED IN
T:      A. 1492
T:      B. 1944
T:      C. 1776
TH:TYPE A B OR C FOR THE CORRECT
   ANSWER
A:
M:C, 1776
T:
R:THE T:STATEMENT ABOVE SKIPS A LINE
   JUST LIKE A
R:PRINT STATEMENT IN BASIC
TY:GOOD! YOUR ANSWER IS CORRECT
TN:INCORRECT! PLEASE REREAD CHAPTER 4
E:
```

This shows how easy it is to write programmed learning materials in Pilot. Most of the logical branching is done for the user by the language itself. For example, the TY and TN statements set YES and NO flags, respectively. If there is a match between the student's input in the ACCEPT statement and the answer stored in the MATCH statement, the TY flag is set and the program prints the TY statement to the screen. If there is no match between the ACCEPT and MATCH statements, the TN flag is set and the TN statement is printed on the screen. In this way, ACCEPT and MATCH and TY and TN do all of the IF...THEN or IF...THEN...ELSE work of a BASIC or Fortran program. The MATCH statement is a powerful command that compares the value in the ACCEPT buffer with the value stored under MATCH. The MATCH statement then sets the two flags.

Numerical computation in Pilot is established through the COMPUTE or C: statement. C: also assigns a numerical value to a variable. For example, when C: $\#X = 3 + 4$, T:$\#X$ in the next line will return 7. The COMPUTE statement can also keep track of student scores when it is used in conjunction with the MATCH statement to set yes and no flags. Thus, if the answer in the ACCEPT buffer is correct, a CY:$\#N = N + 1$ will increment the student's score by one.

The unique Pilot construction TY, TN, CY, or CN, in which there is a basic TRUE/FALSE logical condition expressed between the command statement and the colon, is also extended to more elaborate logical conditions

such as EQUAL, GREATER THAN, LESS THAN, AND, NOT, and OR. For example, in the line T($\#X < 7$): the TYPE command is executed only if the value of the variable X is less than 7. If it is 7 or greater than 7, the command is not executed. This is another built-in shorthand feature which allows educational developers to create interactive instructional programs based on student performance during an actual lesson or test. The TYPE WHEN (X) LOGICAL CONDITION IS IN EFFECT statement allows teachers to program a response to student performance based on a counter set within the program to monitor the student score. Therefore, when the counter set by the CY: $\#N = N + 1$ statement reaches a preset number, a T($\#N >$number): statement prints the program's response to the screen.

The flow of control within a Pilot program is altered by the JUMP and the USE statements. JUMP is similar to a GOTO in BASIC or Fortran; it transfers the control of the program to a specified statement indicated by a label. USE is similar to a GOSUB in BASIC; it calls a subroutine that is terminated with an END statement that is equivalent to a RETURN in BASIC.

The JUMP statement, when an ACCEPT...MATCH sets the TRUE/FALSE flag, is often used to create a logical branching lesson or test. For example:

```
T:MATH QUIZ #1
T:TYPE IN THE CORRECT ANSWER
*START TH:DIVIDE 6 BY 3
A:
M:2
T:
TN:THAT IS INCORRECT, TRY AGAIN
JN:*START
TY:GOOD WORK
E:
```

In this program, the JN: or JUMP on NO flag reset the program to the *START statement and brought the problem back to the screen for the student to answer it again. It is an effective shortcut to test creation and lesson branching. Similarly, a JY: statement can be used to branch the student to a more difficult problem or to a different part of the lesson.

Variations of the JN: and JY statements, such as the JUMP MATCH, the JUMP to the PREVIOUS ACCEPT, and the JUMP to the NEXT MATCH, allow the test designer to move the student to a previous question if he or she misses an answer, jump the student to a more difficult question if he or she answers correctly, or recycle the same question with a message that the student's answer was incorrect for the following reason. For example:

```
T:ALBANY IS THE CAPITAL OF WHICH STATE?
T:      A. MAINE
T:      B. NEW YORK
T:      C. NEW HAMPSHIRE
TH:TYPE A, B, OR C FOR YOUR CHOICE
A:
M:B
TY:NEW YORK IS CORRECT. NEXT QUESTION
```

```
JY: @P
M:A
JN: @M
T:MAINE IS INCORRECT. TRY ANOTHER
  STATE
J: @A
M:C
TY:NEW HAMPSHIRE IS INCORRECT. TRY
    ANOTHER STATE
JY: @A
T:ONCE MORE, SELECT FROM A, B, OR C
J: @A
PR:
T:TRENTON IS THE CAPITAL OF WHICH
  STATE?
T:      A. NEW MEXICO
T:      B. PENNSYLVANIA
T:      C. NEW JERSEY
TH:TYPE A, B, OR C
A:
M:C
JN: @M
TY:CORRECT, TRENTON IS IN MERCER
    COUNTY, NEW JERSEY
JY: *END
M:A
TY:NEW MEXICO IS INCORRECT. TRY
    ANOTHER STATE
JY: @A
M:B
TY:PENNSYLVANIA IS INCORRECT. TRY
    ANOTHER STATE
JY: @A
*END E:
```

In this program, the correct answer in the first question jumps the student to a new question, while incorrect answers branch him or her back to the previous accept. When all the choices are exhausted, the student is told to answer the question again. The student is cycled back through the same type of loop in the second question. However, when he or she answers the question correctly, the program jumps to the *END label which exits the student from the test. A more complicated version of this program can have the CY: statement incrementing the student's score by a specified number of points as each question is answered correctly, and at a certain score the T(#N>x): statement can return a congratulatory message to the screen or it can branch to another section of the program which flags the teacher to perform a task such as the assigning of a specific lesson.

Subroutines in Pilot are created with the USE statement and terminated with an END. In educational programs, USE statements are included to append instructional HELP subroutines to the end of examinations or to build in a mandatory explanation when a student fails to answer the same type of question two or three times in a row. For example, rather than simply JUMP the student on NO to the previous ACCEPT statement, the program can transfer control to a USE routine keyed to a particular set of questions that advises the student to study a particular section of the book or to take more care when using a specific math function. The USE subroutine is also valuable in CAI programming because it provides teachers with another built-in utility that branches the student to a different mode of instruction based on the student's response to test or lesson material.

Pilot also can be used to create and administer student files and to direct disk-storage operations. More advanced implementations of Pilot, especially for the Apple II series and the Commodore PET and 64 computers, allow for turtle graphics, colors, and sound. These implementations of the language have direct machine-level address capabilities which can turn on colors, set the graphics screens, and access sound and music chips. As further extensions of Pilot become more machine specific and are enhanced by more complete graphics and sound capabilities, teachers will be able to build into their presentation material a fuller range of visual stimulii.

It remains to be seen how much effect the Pilot language will have on educational computing. Applications programs that have made their appearance in recent years provide schools with much of the same material they would have had to program themselves, and code generators and authoring systems are able to help educational curriculum developers bypass the coding process altogether. Pilot will still be used in industrial education as a method of training sales or service personnel and for training line managers in new procedures. It is a very facile language and allows even novice programmers to write competent routines without having to construct intricate, logic-dependent loops. Pilot is also a good training language in computer science courses at the secondary school and college levels. It is an especially strong language in a Logo, Pilot, BASIC sequence because its routine-oriented structure provides a strong transition to BASIC while its built-in logic functions echo the built-in routines of Logo.

PILOT GLOSSARY

The following glossary of Pilot represents a basic microcomputer implementation of the language for the Commodore PET called Vanilla Pilot. There are no machine-specific commands for graphics creation or for music or sound generation in this implementation beyond the basic BEEP command. The graphics statement is a toggle that turns on the host machine's graphics mode and it operates much like SHOW TURTLE in Logo or HGR in Applesoft BASIC.

Programs written in Pilot using the glossary included here are highly transportable and can be run using any machine-specific implementation. All of the Pilot statements have been alphabetized and because of the language's simplicity, have not been further divided into statement types. Beneath each statement's definition there is an example line which demonstrates syntax and usage.

ACCEPT Creates buffer to hold user input.
A:

ACCEPT # Accepts a number from −999 to +999.
A#:

ACCEPT #X Accepts a number and assigns it to a variable.
A#X:

ACCEPT S Accepts a single character from the keyboard.
AS:

APPEND Writes data to the end of a file without updating the file itself by overlaying or overwriting new information to it.
APPEND:

BEEP Implemented only in those versions of Pilot with sound and music capabilities, this command accesses the sound or music chips on the host computer.
B:

CLEAR HOME Clears the screen and sends the cursor to the HOME position in the upper lefthand corner of the screen.
CH:

CLOSEFILE Closes a file.
CLOSEF: file name

COMPUTE Executes a variety of mathematical operations and is for internal program control as well.
C:

CREATEFILE Creates a program or disk file for data.
CREATEF: file name.file subscript

END Terminates the program.
E:

EOF End of file message.
EOF:

GRAPHICS On those implementations of Pilot for microcomputers with built-in graphics capabilities, the GRAPHICS command turns on the host computer's graphics generator.
G:

HALT Stops the execution of a program to allow the code to be examined. The program can be restarted with a CONTINUE command.
H:

JUMP Transfers control of the program to a specified statement identified by a label.
J: (label)

KILLFILE Deletes a file from the disk.
KILLF: file name

MATCH Matches the contents of the answer field with the data specified in the statement. The MATCH command is used to set the Y/N flags for branching, response, and scoring mechanisms.
M: answer

OPENFILE Opens a file for data.
OPENF: file name

PAUSE Delays the execution of a program for a specific period of time.
P: n seconds

PROBLEM Initializes next test question.
PR:

READ Reads a line of text from a file to the accept buffer.
READ:

REMARK A comment line within the program.
R:

REMARK WRITE Behaves just like the T: command, but writes to the disk file rather than to the screen.
RW:

REWIND Repositions the file to its beginning. Allows the user to write data into a file and read it back again without having to close the file and open it again.
REWIND: file name

TYPE Prints to the screen. Similar to the PRINT command in other computing languages.
T:

TYPE HANG Used before an ACCEPT statement, the TYPE HANG command pauses the cursor at the end of the T: line to allow the user to answer the question.
TH:

TYPE PRINTER Sends the output to the printer.
TP:

USE Transfers control of a program to a subroutine.
U:

WAIT Pauses until the next keystroke from the keyboard before executing the next line.
W:

WRITE Writes contents of the accept buffer to a file.
W:

PL/I

Almost twenty years old, the language PL/I was originally suggested by an Ad Hoc Committee of SHARE (an IBM computer user group) in 1963. The group sought to develop an advanced high-level programming language for both commercial and scientific usage. An early version of PL/I was introduced in 1966 on the IBM 360, and many mainframe versions followed, including ones from other vendors such as Honeywell, Control Data, Burroughs, and Univac. The first implementation on a microcomputer, Subset G, was in 1980 by Digital Research for CP/M operating systems. Since then PL/I has been implemented on a variety of microcomputer architectures and operating system environments including the IBM PC running under PC-DOS.

A PL/I program consists of one or more blocks of statements. Each block is a collection of statements in which one can declare variables. This feature characterizes PL/I as a block-structured language and allows efficient memory management of the storage space at run time, an especially powerful feature for microcomputers whose already limited available memory capacity is reduced even further by the operating system. PL/I offers users the ability to declare variables within blocks in such a way that the memory space for the variables can be allocated and freed automatically, depending upon whether the block is active or not.

The most prevalent form of block is procedure. Procedures may call other procedures, and they may be compiled separately or nested within the calling procedure and compiled together. A procedure block has the format:

```
name:procedure statement;
    statement-1
    . . . .
    statement-n
    end name;
```

Every statement in a PL/I program is either a structural statement, having to do the architecture of the program itself; a declarative statement, which initializes strings and their values; or an executable statement, which, in effect, constructs the activity. One of PL/I's more powerful features is that it allows programmers many different choices of structural statements, different data types, character strings, pointers, labels, and even various data structures. Unlike BASIC, which imposes real limitations upon programmers developing an interlocked series of executions, PL/I offers a wide variety of structural and data choices that make business and scientific programming easier and more efficient. For example, PL/I's string handling capabilities allow for sophisticated editing of data both within the program itself and as an output function.

Another widely publicized feature of the language is the large range of primitive operations that are actually built into it. There are program and data editing operations, for example, that relieve programmers of the task of writing many housekeeping routines, and there are other operations that allow programmers to maximize the capabilities of their individual microcomputer systems. The most important feature is the block-allocate operation with which a programmer can create storage space or free it within the actual program.

In its native mainframe environment, PL/I has file-handling capabilities equivalent to COBOL, one of the standard business and database programming languages, and a numeric task-handling capability equivalent to Fortran, still a language of choice for scientific and mathematical applications and general "number crunching." Much of this power has been retained in its adopted microcomputer environment, although with allowances for file handling. On a microcomputer, COBOL exercises a bit more power. However, for character-string handling capabilities, PL/I is a powerful equivalent to both COBOL and Fortran, as the sample program below will illustrate.

The sample program presents a practical application of string processing. Given a line of text, such as "Pick up each word separately," the program will return each word or "token" separately as:

```
'Pick'
'up'
'each'
'word'
'separately'
```

The procedure block named "scanner" is the main program. Hence, it is called "options (main)," which is the procedure block to which the control is given initially. The procedure block named "get_token" is an internal procedure, a procedure block nested within the calling procedure. The flow of control in the program itself actually starts at the main program "call get_token" statement. The procedure "get_token" asks for a line of text from the user and identifies individual "tokens." When control of the logic returns to procedure "scanner," "scanner" prints each token on the terminal and then returns to "get_token" procedure to receive, or "get," the next line which it identifies as a variable string of eighty characters.

SAMPLE PROGRAM

```
scanner: procedure options (main);
  %replace
            /*initialize variable true*/
    true by '1'b;
  declare
            /*this begins a*/
            /*declarative block*/
    token character(80) varying
    static initial(' ');
```

```
do while (true);
          /*main program repetition unit*/
          /*starts here*/

    call get_ token;
          /*implements*/
          /*get_token procedure*/

    put edit(""""!!token!!"""") (skip,a);
end;
          /*main program repetition unit*/
          /*ends here*/

get_ token: procedure;
    declare
        i fixed,
        line character(80) varying
        static initial (' ');
                            ///
    line = substr(line,length(token)+1);
    do while(true);
        if line = ' '
        then
        get edit(line) (a);
    i = verify(line,' ');
          /*if user returns blank*/
    if i = 0
          /*then neglect the line*/
    then line = ' ';
    else do;
          /*snap shot: i∧=0 and*/
          /*points to first nonblank*/
          /*character*/
        line = substr(line,i);
          /*snap shot: first character*/
          /*of line is nonblank*/
        i = index(line,' ');
          /*find the blank position*/
    if i = 0 & length(line)∧= 0
    then
        token = line
          /*if no blank then take line*/
          /*as token*/
    else
        token = substr(line,1,i-1);
    return;
    end;
  end;
end get_ token;
end scanner;
```

As the comment lines indicate, the program's routines interact with each other as the program interacts with the user. A PL/I program, while it can be tricky to write because of all of the built-in routines that execute themselves automatically, is actually much easier to write to a specific system because it allows the user to utilize memory effectively. In this program, the nesting of routines within routines and the turning on and off of procedures from the procedures themselves provide an effective and efficient way to manage the flow of logic and the manipulation of data input. The sample program illustrates that PL/I, even in its microcomputer habitat, is still a powerful string- and file-handling language.

PL/I GLOSSARY

The following glossary represents the ANSI standard version of PL/I. PL/I compilers are currently available for both CP/M and MS-DOS machines, as well as on the Commodore SuperPET.

ABS Returns the absolute value of its parameter.
  ABS(x)
    z=ABS(−64);

ACOS Returns the arc cosine of its parameter in radians.
  ACOS(x)
    z=ACOS(.65);

ADDR Returns the value of a pointer for subsequent use by the program.
  ADDR(x)
    p = ADDR(treeptr)

ALLOCATE Reserves main storage area for a specified data variable.
  ALLOCATE variable SET(pointer variable);
    declare
        name character(16) based(ptr),
        ptr pointer;
    ALLOCATE name SET(ptr);

ASCII Returns the character that corresponds to a given code.
  ASCII(x)
    ASCII(65);

ASIN Returns the arc sine of its parameter in radians.
  ASIN(x)
    a =ASIN(6);

ATAN Returns the arc tangent of its parameter.
  ATAN(x)
    ATAN(.7323)

ATAND Returns the arc tangent of its parameter in degrees.
  ATAND(x)
    y = ATAND(.7321)

AUTO   Specifies storage for a variable upon execution of the block containing that variable.
    declare variable name AUTO;
        declare tree fixed binary AUTO;

BASED   Specifies storage for a variable, referenced by a pointer.
    declare data type BASED pointer variable;
        declare x (50) fixed binary BASED (ptr);

BEGIN   Used in conjunction with END to outline a body or block of code.
    BEGIN
        statements;
    END.
        BEGIN
        declare r fixed binary(15);
            r=24*wt−wt/2;
            d=x+y*z;
        END.

BINARY (data attribute)   Defines a variable BINARY with storage space of (p + 1) bits.
    declare variable fixed/float BINARY(p);
        declare x fixed BINARY(8);

BINARY (function)   Converts its parameter to an arithmetic BINARY value.
    BINARY(x[,p])
        BINARY(21.32,15)

BIT (data attribute)   Declares a bit string with length X. Where x <=16.
    declare variable name BIT(x);
        declare color BIT(15);

BIT (function)   Converts x to a bit string of length y.
    BIT(x[,y])
        BIT(4,8) returns 00000100

BOOL   Assumes x,y are bit string of length 1 and Z of length 4. Returns the bit value of Z at location 'xy' interpreted as binary integer.
    b = bool(x,y,'0011'b);

BUILTIN   Allows function names to be defined as PL/I built-in function.
    declare function name BUILTIN;
        declare ceil BUILTIN;

CALL   Passes control to the named subroutine.
    CALL proc name (argument list);
        CALL generate(n,ptr);

CEIL   Returns the smallest integer greater than or equal to its parameter.
    CEIL(x)
        num=CEIL(3.2)

CHARACTER (data attribute)   Specifies a character string x characters long, x<=254.
    declare variable name CHARACTER(x);
        declare atlanta CHARACTER(123);

CHARACTER (function)   Converts x to a character string of length y.
    CHARACTER(x[,y])
        CHARACTER(x[,10])

CLOSE   Closes the indicated file.
    CLOSE FILE(file identifier);
        CLOSE FILE(x:payroll.dat);

COLLATE   Returns a string of ASCII characters in ascending order.
    COLLATE()
        Note: no parameters are used.

COPY   Returns a string composed of t copies of x.
    COPY(x,t)
        COPY('*',40)

COS   Returns the cosine of its parameter in radians.
    COS(x)
        c = COS(3.6)

COSD   Returns the cosine of its parameter in degrees.
    COS(x)
        c = COS(3.6)

COSH   Returns the hyperbolic of its parameter.
    COSH(x)
        c = COSH(3.6)

DATE   Returns the current date in the format YYMMDD.
    DATE()
        Note: no parameters are used.

DECLARE   States attributes for identifiers.
    (scalar variables)
        DECLARE name [attribute list];
        DECLARE counter fixed binary(12);
        (array variables)
        DECLARE name (bound pair)[attribute list];
            DECLARE carparts (10:30) character(25)
            varying;
        (structure variables)
        DECLARE [level] name [attribute list] [,[level] name
            [attribute list]];
        DECLARE 1 person
            2 name character(20),
            2 age fixed binary(15);
    (entry data)
        DECLARE proc name [(bound pair]
        [ENTRY(parameter list)]
            [EXTERNAL] [VARIABLE] [RETURNS
            (return-att)];
    (file data)
        DECLARE file id FILE [variable];
            DECLARE fnote file;

DECIMAL   Converts its parameter to a decimal number with precision p and scale factor q.
    DECIMAL(x[,p[,q]])
        d = DECIMAL(62,4,2);

DIMENSION Returns the extent of ith index of an array x.
    DIMENSION (x, i)
        stack = DIMENSION(x,4);

DIVIDE   Used to compute the quotient of two numerical expressions where p and q are optional and are defined as precision and scale factor, respectively.
    DIVIDE(x,y,p,q)
        rat = DIVIDE(11,5,4,3);

DO   Used in conjunction with the END statement to form a DO group.
    DO[control variable] do-specification;
        DO while (x<>0); DO x=1 to 5;   DO;
        ....;   ....;   ....;
        ....;   ....;   ....;
        END;   END;   END;

END   Used in conjunction with the begin statement as a terminator of a body or block of code.
    (See: BEGIN; DO; PROCEDURE)

ENTRY   Defines entry values.
    declare variable name ENTRY;
    declare x ENTRY;

ENVIRONMENT Establishes various options in file declaration, for example, fixed/variable length records.
    declare file identifier FILE ENVIRONMENT (options);
        declare payroll FILE ENVIRONMENT (password(d));

EXP   Returns e(2.71828) to the value of its parameter.
    EXP(x)
        t = EXP(6.24);

EXTERNAL   Defines a variable globally.
    declare variable name [type] EXTERNAL;
        declare per fixed binary EXTERNAL;

FILE   Specifies the name of a PL/I file
    declare file name FILE;
        declare F FILE;

FIXED (data attribute)   Specifies fixed-point arithmetic data with precision p and scale factor q.
    declare identifier FIXED[(p[,q])];
        declare num FIXED decimal(7,2);

FIXED (function)   Converts x to a fixed arithmetic number with precision p and scale factor q.
    FIXED(x[,p[,q]])
        a = FIXED(x,4);

FLOAT (data attribute)   Specifies floating-point data of precision p.
    declare variable name FLOAT type;
        declare gasamt FLOAT binary;

FLOAT (function)   Converts its parameter to a floating-point arithmetic number of precision p.
    FLOAT(x[,p])
        a = FLOAT(231);

FLOOR   Returns the largest integer less than or equal to its parameter.
    FLOOR(x)
        a = FLOOR(6.2);

FORMAT   Specification of remote format list.
    label: FORMAT(format list);
        exit: FORMAT(5 A(3));

FREE   Releases previously allocated storage.
    FREE ⟶ based-variable;
        FREE ptr ⟶A;

GET EDIT   Specifies an input operation on a stream file with format list.
    GET [FILE (file-id)] EDIT (input list) (format list);
    GET EDIT (a,b,c) (3F(3));

GOTO   Transfers control to a stated point in the program.
    GOTO label;
        GOTO exit;

HBOUND   Returns the current upper boundry of the N-th dimension of the array x.
    HBOUND(x,n)
        a = HBOUND(abc,2);

IF   Allows conditional execution of a statement or statements.
    IF expression then imperative statement [ELSE imperative statement2].
        IF r=1 then free r else free ptr;

%INCLUDE   Comands an external file to be included during a preprocessor scan.
    %INCLUDE 'filespec';
        %INCLUDE 'payroll.dat';

INDEX   Specifies the location of the leftmost occurrence of string y in string x scanning from a starting point of i.
    INDEX(x,y[,i])
        id = INDEX(loft, of,2);

INITIAL   Directs the compiler to assign variable values prior to execution of the program.
    declare variable name type static INITIAL (value list);
        declare perf character(6) static INITIAL('   ');

LABEL   Specifies a LABEL variable.
declare variable name LABEL;
   declare exit LABEL;

LBOUND   Returns the current lower boundry of the N-th dimension of the array x.
LBOUND(x,n)
   a = LBOUND(amt,2);

LENGTH   Returns the number of characters in any string that is designated as x.
LENGTH(x)
   l = LENGTH(name);

LINENO   Returns the current line number of the print file referenced by x.
LINENO(x)
   ln = LINENO(pay);

LOCK   A boolean function which locks the record in file f indicated by i preventing access by other users.
LOCK(f,i)
   LOCK(pay,maint);

LOG   Returns the natural logarithm of its parameter.
LOG(real or integer expression)
   a = LOG(234);

LOG2   Returns the logarithm of its parameter in radix 2.
LOG2(real or integer expression)
   b = LOG2(234);

LOG10   Returns the logarithm of its parameter in radix 10.
LOG10(real or integer expression)
   c = LOG10(234);

MAX   Compares x with y and returns the greater value.
MAX(x,y)
   a = MAX(23,34);

MIN   Compares x with y and returns the lower value.
MIN(x,y)
   a = MIN(23,34);

MOD   Computes the remainder of division.
MOD(x,y)
   a = MOD(10,4);

NULL   Used to make a pointer value empty.
pointer variable = Null;
   treeptr = Null;

ON   Specifies the on-unit is to be executed when the named condition occurs.
ON condition name ON unit
   ON error put list(oncode());

ONCODE   Returns the number of the error subcode of the latest signaled condition.
ONCODE()
   Note: no parameters are used.
   a = ONCODE( );

ONFILE   Returns the file name for which the latest ENDPAGE or ENDFILE condition was signaled.
ONFILE()
   Note: no parameters are used.
   a = ONFILE( );

ONKEY   Returns the value of the key for the record that signaled an input/output or conversion condition.
ONKEY()
   Note: no parameters are used.
   a = ONKEY( );

OPEN   Opens a file to be processed.
OPEN FILE(file id)
              [file attributes];
   OPEN FILE(pay) output;

PAGENO   Returns the page number of the print file indicated by x.
PAGENO(F)
   a = PAGENO(FV);

POINTER   Specifies a pointer variable.
declare (variable name) POINTER;
   declare (treeptr,nodeptr) POINTER;

PROCEDURE   Specifies the beginning of a procedure block.
proc name: PROCEDURE[(parameter list)];
   ipl: PROCEDURE(dds);

RANK   Returns the ASCII code that corrresponds to its parameter.
RANK(x)
   a = RANK('f');
   b = RANK('3');

READ   Reads a file into main storage.
READ [FILE(file id)] INTO(x);
   READ FILE(f) INTO buffer;

%REPLACE   Replaces a variable with a constant.
%REPLACE identifier BY constant;
   %REPLACE okid BY '4'b;

RETURN   Returns control to the point of invocation.
RETURN;
   RETURN;

REVERSE   Returns string x in reverse order.
REVERSE(x);
   a = REVERSE('pump');

ROUND   Returns the first parameter rounded to N places to the right of the decimal point.
ROUND(x,y)
    a = ROUND(c,3);

SEARCH   Specifies the location of the first character in string x that equals a character in string y, if no match is found then SEARCH returns a zero.
SEARCH(x,y)
    a = SEARCH('567', '0123456789');

SIGN   Specifies the sign of its parameter by returning a −1, 0, or 1.
SIGN(x)
    a = SIGN(num);

SIGNAL   Simulates the stated condition.
SIGNAL condition;
    SIGNAL overflow;

SIN   Returns the sine of its parameter in radians.
SIN(x)
    a = SIN(5);

SIND   Returns the sine of its parameter in degrees.
SIND(x)
    a = SIND(5);

SINH   Returns the hyperbolic sine of its parameter.
SINH(x)
    a = SINH(5);

STATIC   Allocates storage prior to program execution and releases it postexecution.
declare identifier STATIC [attribute list] [initial (value)];
    declare q fixed binary(15) STATIC initial (0);

STOP   Stops program execution.
STOP;
    STOP;

SQRT   Returns the square root of its parameter.
SQRT(x)
    a = SQRT(4);

SUBSTR   Returns a duplicate string to string x starting at the I-th character and of length J.
SUBSTR(x,i[,j])
    a = SUBSTR(x,1,3);

TAN   Returns the tangent of its parameter in radians.
TAN(x);
    a = TAN(5);

TAND   Returns the tangent of its parameter in degrees.
TAND(x)
    a = TAND(5);

TANH   Returns the hyperbolic tangent of its parameter.
TANH(x)
    a = TANH(5);

TIME   Returns the current time in the format HHMM SStttt, where tttt is microseconds.
TIME
    t = TIME( );

TRANSLATE   String y is padded to the right if its length is shorter than string z. Any character in z and in x is replaced by the character in y corresponding to that position in z.
TRANSLATE(x,y,z)
    a = TRANSLATE('123','abc','123');

TRIM   Returns a character string equal to its parameter less any leading or trailing blanks. TRIM(a,b,c) returns a character string equal to string a less any leading characters that appear in b and any trailing characters that appear in c.
TRIM(a,[b,c])
    a = TRIM(string1, string2, string3);

TRUNC   Returns the integer part of an expression.
TRUNC(x)
    a = TRUNC(3.45);

UNLOCK   A boolean function which unlocks the ith record indicated allowing access by other users.
UNLOCK FILE(file identifier, i)
    UNLOCK FILE(payroll, i);

UNSPEC   Returns the elements of the storage area occupied by its parameter, i.e., bit representation.
UNSPEC(x)
    aa = UNSPEC(a);

VARIABLE   Redifines a constant as a variable.
declare (ENTRY, FILE, or LABEL) VARIABLE
    declare payroll FILE VARIABLE;

VARYING   Defines a string to be of varying length.
declare identifier VARYING
    declare abc char(50) VARYING;

VERIFY   Compares string a to string b and specifies the location of the leftmost character of a that differs from its corresponding position in b, otherwise a zero is returned.
syntax not standard
    if VERIFY(a, '12345') = 1 then unlock
    file(payroll,i);

WRITE   Standard procedure to append values to a file.
WRITE FILE(file identifier) FROM(a)
    WRITE FILE(text) FROM(a);

Prolog

Prolog is a very high-level language based on the idea of using logic itself as a programming language. The first implementation of Prolog was in 1972 by Alain Colmerauer and Philippe Roussel in Marseilles, France. The beauty and elegance of the language became apparent to a number of European computer scientists who rapidly produced a number of improved implementations. A major advance occurred when David Warren of Edinburgh, Scotland, produced a compiler for Prolog that achieved efficiency levels comparable to LISP. At this point, people began to consider seriously Prolog as a useful language for artificial intelligence operations: a direct competitor of LISP. In fact, some of the most recent experiments at implementing both LISP and Prolog for microcomputers have attempted to combine the two languages.

A large amount of interest has been generated recently in the area of expert systems, which perform tasks normally performed by human experts. For example, impressive results have been obtained with systems that perform medical diagnosis, aid in locating mineral deposits, and guide maintenance on telephone trunk lines. Most of the current expert systems are coded in LISP. However, there is a growing perception that Prolog may be extremely well suited for coding expert systems. It contains a number of features that make it an attractive alternative to LISP, particularly its ability to posit rules directly as logical relationships rather than actually build the logical relationships from a series of lists imbedded within other lists. Where LISP must evolve new expressions from sets of primitives, Prolog, which operates at higher level, can focus directly upon the logical relationships without having to create them from something else. Hence Prolog is oriented to the way humans think and speak rather than to the way machines operate. Prolog is emerging as a knowledge systems tool that interacts with users through a natural language command structure that simulates human speech rather than through the type of code we find in C or in BASIC.

In 1981, the Fifth Generation Computer Systems Project was started in Japan. The project was created to produce a computer system that would be particularly suited for the implementation of expert systems by 1990. Prolog was selected as the main language for use in the project, and this action has caused a wave of new interest in the language. A number of researchers around the world now believe that Prolog does in fact offer a notation that effectively integrates notions from artificial intelligence and database systems. It may well be widely used in the emerging field of knowledge engineering.

Microprolog was created as an implementation of Prolog for small microcomputers. It has been used as a vehicle for teaching concepts of applied logic to school children, as well as a tool for implementing modest expert systems. Microprolog is a remarkably powerful implementation for use on either Z80-based CP/M machines or the IBM PC. It includes an implementation of a dialect that is particularly friendly for people who are not used to working with languages like Prolog.

The utility of Prolog can be clarified by some simple examples. A program in Prolog consists of two types of statements: those that assert specific facts and those that give rules that relate facts. In the following sample program, for example, we see how a family relationship database is constructed. It is constructed by a system of rules rather than by a system of procedures that tell the computer how to compare variable to variable to arrive at a match. This type of applications program in BASIC would require a very extensive array of different variables nested within fields. Where Prolog defines variables and establishes the relationships among them with single statements for each entity, a similar BASIC program requires a higher code overhead that implements a series of algorithms or procedures to match what is stored in the computer's memory with what the user is asking for.

FAMILY DATABASE

FEMALE(JAN)
FEMALE(SALLY)
FEMALE(LINDA)
FEMALE(CAROL)
FEMALE(JENNY)
FEMALE(GAIL)
FEMALE(MARY)
MALE(TOM)
MALE(BOB)
MALE(JIM)
MALE(DICK)
MALE(EARL)
MALE(JOHN)

JAN IS-A-PARENT-OF BOB
TOM IS-A-PARENT-OF BOB
JAN IS-A-PARENT-OF JIM
TOM IS-A-PARENT-OF JIM
JAN IS-A-PARENT-OF CAROL
TOM IS-A-PARENT-OF CAROL
SALLY IS-A-PARENT-OF DICK
BOB IS-A-PARENT-OF DICK
SALLY IS-A-PARENT-OF LINDA
BOB IS-A-PARENT-OF LINDA
EARL IS-A-PARENT-OF JOHN
MARY IS-A-PARENT-OF JOHN
CAROL IS-A-PARENT-OF JENNY
JOHN IS-A-PARENT-OF JENNY
CAROL IS-A-PARENT-OF GAIL
JOHN IS-A-PARENT-OF GAIL

X IS-A-GRANDPARENT-OF Y IF X IS-A-PARENT-OF Z AND Z IS-A-PARENT-OF Y

X IS-A-GRANDMOTHER-OF Y IF X IS-A-GRANDPARENT-OF Y AND FEMALE(X)

The first few lines illustrate how to assert facts about single objects or entities. That is:

FEMALE(JAN)

is how one would state the fact that "Jan is a female." Then there are a number of statements which assert facts about how two different entities relate. For example:

JAN IS-A-PARENT-OF BOB

states that "Jan is the parent of Bob." Finally, there are some rules that specify how to reason about the information contained in the facts. That is:

X IS-A-GRANDPARENT-OF Y IF X IS-A-PARENT-OF Z AND Z IS-A-PARENT-OF Y

X IS-A-GRANDMOTHER-OF Y IF X IS-A-GRANDPARENT-OF Y AND FEMALE(X)

represent rules, not facts. In these rules, the symbols X, Y, and Z are called variables, because they can be thought of as representing any specific entity. The first of these rules should be read as: "To show that X is a grandparent of Y, first show that X is a parent of Z, and then show that Z is a parent of Y." This rules define the relation IS-A-GRANDPARENT-OF in terms of the relation IS-A-PARENT-OF. The second rule should be read as: "To show that X is a grandmother of Y, first show that X is a grandparent of Y, and then show that X is a female."

Some of the syntactical and language constructs for Microprolog become clear even from these short examples. First, the concept of "variable" is significantly different than in most programming languages. It does not represent a memory location, but rather an arbitrary complex entity. In the previous examples, the entities were just names; in more complex examples, these entities can be repesented by arbitrarily complex structures. This alone can illustrate how powerful the language can be if entire structures can be manipulated as if they were variables. Furthermore, a rule for performing a computation is formulated in what might be called "goal/subgoal notation." That is, the basic outlook is, first, to achieve the goal of performing a desired computation and, second, to solve the following set of subgoals in order. The idea has been to leave the language as declarative as possible. Procedural languages such as Pascal and BASIC tend to include substantially more details about exactly how a program should execute a computation. In this sense, Prolog is a substantially higher-level language than most commonly used programming languages.

Another example of the concise logical nature of Microprolog can be seen from an attempt to define family relationships in terms of a sequential program. In order to define "niece," one has to construct a two-generation set of family relationships and then check for gender. Microprolog defines niece in this way:

X IS-A-SIBLING-OF Y IF Z IS-A-PARENT-OF X AND Z IS-A-PARENT-OF Y

X IS-A-NIECE-OF Y IF Z IS-A-SIBLING-OF Y AND Z IS-A-PARENT-OF X AND FEMALE(X)

One notices not only how briefly and concisely the logical relationships are expressed, but also that the second program declaration builds upon a logical construct formulated immediately in the first declaration. This formulation of variable entities in terms of expressions of relationshps that can be expanded from one declarative statement to the next illustrates how interactive expert systems are constructed. It also illustrates an important principle of artificial intelligence: the program, because logical relationships can be "carried over" from declarative statement to declarative statement without having to be redefined in many lines of code, can seem almost to "learn" from user input and construct from that input a formulation that the user did not explicitly have to devise. In order to understand this important aspect of the high-level nature of Microprolog, one should imagine trying to define complex family relationships in BASIC or even in Pascal.

The Microprolog interactive environment is, necessarily, quite unlike the normal programming environment. The following interactive session will serve to illustrate the many basic Microprolog commands and the dialog that a user can have with the language. Comments and a description of the activity appear in brackets:

```
&.Add(female(Linda))
     [adds the clause to the current program]
&.Add(female(Carol))
        .
        .
        .
&.Add(Jan is-a-parent-of Bob)
&.Add(Tom is-a-parent-of Bob)
        .
        .
&.Add(x is-a-grandmother-of y if
x is-a-grandparent-of y and female(x))
&.List All
     [lists all clauses in the current program]
        .
        .
        .
&.Does(x is-a-grandmother-of Gail)
     [asks whether such an x exists]
YES
&.Does(Sally is-a-grandmother-of x)
NO
&.One(x x is-a-grandmother-of Gail)
     [asks for one such x]
Answer is Jan. C
     [C means look for next such x]
```

Answer is Mary. C
No (more) answers
&. Which(x Jan is-a-grandparent-of x)
  [asks for all such x]
  Answer is Dick
Answer is Linda
No (more) answers
&. Delete is-a-parent-of 1
    [delete Jan is-a-parent-of Bob]
&. Which(x Jan is-a-grandparent-of x)
No (more) answers

    [the next query asks for all x and y such that two
    conditions are both true]
&. Which((x y) Jan is-a-parent-of x
and y is-a-parent-of x)
Answer is (Jim Tom)
Answer is (Carol Tom)
No (more) answers
&. QT.

The example dialog illustrates a number of features of the Microprolog environment. It also serves to demonstrate the ways in which databases can be constructed so that meaningful searches, in the form of queries, can be set in motion. Obviously the size of the database and the extent of the logical relationships among the database items are limited by the size of the machine's memory.

1. One can add new clauses using the Add command even though in this sample dialog, all of the Add commands were not actually displayed. It is assumed that all of the clauses in the sample dialog were added previous to the interaction.
2. One can delete a specific clause with the Delete command.
3. The Does command asks whether or not a given goal can be solved. It will cause a simple YES or NO answer.
4. The One command asks for one solution of a given goal. The user can then ask for more, or just terminate the search for more solutions.
5. The Which command is used to obtain the entire set of solutions to a given goal. Note the last use of Which that asks for all values of (x y) that cause two distinct conditions to be true.

The gross differences between Prolog and Microprolog are mostly concerned with the differences between the mainframe and microcomputer operating environments. What is important, however, is not the differences themselves but the power of the Microprolog implementation of Prolog to construct expert programs even within the limited memory capabilities of the microcomputer. The language offers students of programming and novice programmers the power to construct interactive expert systems while still learning the rudiments of programming and applied logic. As a vehicle for logical thinking, database technology, and automated reasoning programs, it is a remarkably advanced language.

PROLOG GLOSSARY

The microcomputer implementation of Prolog, also called Microprolog, has a limited vocabulary. Prolog relies heavily on an operator precedence grammar which defines the syntax of the language. However, these built-in grammars are normally only found in mainframe implementations of Prolog because of the extensive memory requirements. Microprolog, on the other hand, has a basic syntax that is modeled on LISP, its parent language, or on extensions of the basic syntax that are included as part of a Microprolog package.

There are other extensions of Microprolog as well, distributed by language development companies in much the same way that Forth companies include dictionaries with their proprietary implementations of the language and C companies sell libraries of C routines to support their compilers. This glossary of Microprolog cites only the "vanilla" commands common to most microcomputer implementations of the language. This glossary is divided into basic program development commands, which perform just like LISP or Logo primitives; data queries, which are used to seek information about specific items of data on the stack; arithmetic functions, which, besides performing the basic arithmetic operations on both floating points and integers, compare numbers within a routine; and file commands, which behave just like the file commands in any standard operating system or programming language system like Logo or BASIC.

PROGRAM DEVELOPMENT COMMANDS

add Adds a sentence, which must be enclosed in brackets, to the workspace.
  add (<sentence>)
  &.add (john likes jane)
  &.

delete Deletes a clause from the program. This command can be used in two ways. It can delete an entire sentence, or it can delete a relation name within a specified sentence.
  delete (<sentence>)
  delete <relation name> p
    (p is the position of the sentence in which the relation name is to be deleted).
  &.delete (John likes Jane)
  &.
  &.delete likes 2

list Lists the program on the monitor or on the printer. List can also be used to list relationships or list the dictionary of relationships defined in the current program. In the CP/M implementation of Microprolog, a listing is sent to the printer by first toggling on the printer with a CTRL P (P) command before typing the list command. When the program listing is complete, type   P again to turn off the printer and return to the program status before listing. This is similar to the PR#1 CAT-ALOG command sequence in Apple DOS 3.3.

list all
list <relation name>
list dict
&.list all
John likes Jane
Mary likes Bob
Joan loves Don
&.
&.list loves
Joan loves Don
&.
&.list dict
likes
loves
&.

kill   Deletes an entire relation, an entire program in the workspace, or a Microprolog module.

kill <relation name>
    Deletes an entire relation.
kill all
    Deletes an entire program from the workspace
kill <module name-XXX>
    Deletes a Microprolog module from the working implementation currently in memory.
&.kill loves
&.
&.kill all

QUERY COMMANDS

?   ? is the basic query command that asks Microprolog if a request can be solved. The ? does not display the solution; it merely asks whether a solution exists. If a solution exists to the query, Microprolog responds with a & prompt. If a solution does not exist or if the query has failed, Microprolog responds with a return query or ?. In order to print a response to a successful query on the monitor, an additional side command is required which establishes the format of the response. This side command, expressed as PP, is also used elsewhere in Microprolog to format output data to the printer. The query command has other uses as well. In addition to its basic function, the ? can identify the position in the database at which additional clauses can be added or current clauses deleted. In this mode, the query command is used in conjunction with the ADDCL primitive to add a clause after the first clause of the argument.

? (<query>)
&.(friend x Mary)
&.
    The query has succeeded and a friend or friends of Mary have been found.
&.? (friend x Mary)
?

    The query has failed because no friend or list of friends of Mary have been found.
&. ? ((friend x Mary)(PP The friend of Mary is x))
The friend of Mary is John
&.

does   The does command asks a yes/no question of the program. The query asks whether a specific condition does exist, and the program responds with a yes or no.

does (<condition>)
&.does (John likes Jane)
YES
&.
&.does(SUM (5 5 x) & x LESS 10)
    This query finds all answers to a specified condition within a specified form. In the syntax of the command:

$$\text{which (<term> <condition>)}$$

term   represents the form of the answer required, and the condition is the query itself that "which" will search for.

&.which(x likes Jane)
Answer is John
No (more) answers
&.
&.which(xSUM(6 6X))
Answer is 12
No (more) answers

one   Like the which query, one finds an answer to a specified condition of a specified form. However, unlike "which," "one" only finds one answer instead of all answers and prompts the user to continue the search. Responding with a "c"or continue instructs "one" to seek the next solution. Any other character terminates the search.

&.one(x x likes Jane)
Answer is John. c
Answer is Michael.t
No (more) answers
&.

ARITHMETIC FUNCTIONS

sum   Sum both adds and subtracts depending upon the syntax of the argument. The basic SUM equation is:

$$\text{(SUM a b c)}$$

which represents $[a+b=c]$. This equation can be used to check a sum, when all three values are given, for example:

$$\text{(SUM 5 5 10)}$$

is evaluated as true. The equation can be used to add two numbers to one another if the first two numbers are known and the third is an unknown variable. For example:

$$(SUM\ 6\ 2\ x)$$

will return an 8 while

$$(SUM\ 6\ -2\ x)$$

will return a 4. SUM will subtract two numbers if the third number in the equation is known and either of the first two are unknown variables. For example:

$$(SUM\ 5\ x\ 10)$$

returns 5, and

$$(SUM\ x\ 6\ 10)$$

returns a 4.

TIMES TIMES can be used to multiply or divide, depending upon the syntax of the statement. The basic TIMES equation is:

(:

$$(TIMES\ a\ b\ c)$$

where [a*b=c]. If all three numbers are known, then the statement

$$(TIMES\ 2\ 5\ 10)$$

is true. In this way TIMES evaluates an equation to test for truth. TIMES multiplies when the first two numbers are known and the third number is an unknown variable. For example:

$$(TIMES\ 2\ 5\ x)$$

returns a 10. TIMES is used to divide two numbers when either of the first two is an unknown variable and the third is a known. For example:

$$(TIMES\ x\ 5\ 10)$$

returns a 2.

FILE COMMANDS

load This command is used to load a file into the workspace memory from disk.
load <file name>

save This command is used to save a file currently in the workspace memory to disk.
save <file name>
The commands list and kill also serve as file commands as well as program development commands.

RPG

The computer language RPG was created by IBM and encompasses three versions. The now extinct original version, called RPG (there never was an official designation RPG I), was neither announced nor sold as such, but was simply made available to customers on the IBM 1401 beginning in January 1961. In that version it served as a batch- and business-oriented Report Program Generator; hence its name.

The language was subsequently upgraded, officially announced as RPG II, and made available for the IBM System/3 in 1969, with first deliveries in 1970. During the 1970s it evolved further as it became the primary language for the new IBM System/32 and the later System 34, together with an extensive Operation Control Language (OCL) to interface with the operating system. The System/34 version has gone through many releases and developed RPG II into what it is today: a very popular high-level, highly flexible, powerful, compact, convenient, symbolic computer language for writing applications programs and systems that meet small- and large-scale, common and sophisticated, business-oriented data processing, analysis, query, and reporting requirements.

RPG II has been further enhanced by a wide range of IBM's and other vendors' utilities and applications packages. Communications capabilities together with language and systems upgrades have further transformed RPG II into a multiuser, multitasking, fully interactive language in addition to its enhanced batch capabilities.

OCL for RPG II is analogous to JCL for COBOL, but whereas JCL is essentially for I/O functions, OCL is an extensive programming language in itself. RPG II programs are embedded in OCL programs, called procedures, and the streams of interconnected and interrelated procedures constitute the applications system.

In 1983 IBM announced its new System/36 mini, with further and especially user-friendly RPG II control-language and control-commands enhancements. RPG II is also available on mainframes, such as the IBM 370 Series (the 370, 43xx, and 30xx) as well as on other manufacturer's systems. Hewlett-Packard, for instance, provides the HP Transform/3000 to migrate RPG II programs from the System/34 to its HP 3000 mini.

In October 1978 IBM introduced the System/38, a supermini with radically new and extraordinarily powerful architecture. This development included major extensions of RPG II—so major as to constitute a new version of the language, RPG III, together with a correspondingly new control language, CL. The control language interfaces with the control program facility, CPF, which constitutes the operating system. The fact that IBM has chosen this route for its new architecture, which industry analysts predict will spread to other IBM computers in the future, may be taken as a portent of the future of RPG.

Inasmuch as RPG II is the prevailing RPG language version, the detailed treatment of this article deals entirely with this version. However, the nature and some of the salient features of RPG III will be sketched in a concluding section.

Recent developments in terminal emulation as well as communications have brought the foregoing RPG developments into the world of micro/mini/mainframe links and networking, and thereby have brought personal computers into RPG's present and future.

RPG II: Structure, Principles, and Specifications

RPG II comprises a high-level, symbolic, fixed-format, program-cycle language and compiler program. The compiler program diagnoses the source program that has been coded and entered. If it finds no terminal errors, it then translates the source program into an executable object program that provides the logical framework for program execution. If the compiler program finds errors that it considers terminal, it issues diagnostic messages keyed to the program lines on the source printout and does not compile the program.

The language is fixed-format in that it must be coded on, or in accordance with, standard eighty-column coding forms, called specifications sheets. Early machines provided punched-card source entry, but today entry is almost entirely through video display stations (VDTs), for which utilities provide appropriately formatted lines and many conveniences. Experienced RPG II programmers remember most of the common column entries and rules, and write programs on ordinary paper for subsequent screen (VDT) entry. Some dispense with manual writing, and "write" code directly onto the screen. For special needs, techniques, and subtleties, they refer to the rack of vendor-supplied language and utilities manuals, which should be available at every installation.

The language is program-cycle in that it is provided with the standard RPG II program logic that is generated by the RPG II compiler. This logic is embedded in a program by means of program controls that effect a fixed sequence of operations to be performed for each record read. That is, the same general cycle of operations is performed for each input record, and this cycle constitutes the standard program cycle. The three basic logic steps—input, processing, and output—are divided into numerous substeps. The primary sequence of substeps is readily learned and is conveniently provided in flowchart form on folded, pocket-size debugging templates, which provide the columnar formats and their key entries for all specifications sheets, spaced so that the templates may be set exactly across a source program printout. For sophisticated applications it is sometimes necessary to know some aspects of the program cycle (logic flow) in greater detail, and this is provided in RPG II reference manuals.

RPG II logic flow removes from the programmer the burden of designing and coding a great deal of program logic. At the same time, the language provides a substantial repertoire of numeric and alphameric indicators so that the programmer can easily control program functions in great detail within the normal RPG logic flow. In addition, operation codes are provided with which to modify the logic flow. All told, it is possible to program logics of very great complexity, merely by appropriate placement of appropriate indicators on the screen specifications sheet formats.

There are seven basic RPG II specifications forms. In two cases two forms are printed on one sheet, resulting in five specifications sheets. In addition, there are, and continue to evolve, special specifications forms, for example, those for telecommunications and utilities for such uses as sorting and screen design. Each form has a standard single-letter designation which is printed on every printout program line pertaining to that form. Not every column or field of a given form is coded on a given line or in a given program. In fact, often only a small number of the available columns and fields are used on a given line and in a given program. For some columns and fields the system supplies default values; for others the available options are simply not exercised.

The RPG II program cycle requires that all lines of a given form be entered together and that all forms be entered in a specified order. The natures of these forms are briefly described below in their required program order, and will be referred to by their designated code letters, given in parentheses. Coded samples are discussed below.

Control Specifications (H). This form provides the compiler with information about the program and the system being used, such as storage size needed to execute, date format, whether certain special RPG II functions are being used, whether disk files may be shared, and the number of screen formats that are linked to the program. This type of control specifications form provides the the RPG compiler with information about the program and the system being used. In this way, the specification form is much like the identification section of a Cobol program.

The H-Spec is always a single line. The coding shown specifies that the date provided by the UDATE operation code (op code, for short) appears in Year/Month/Day format, that a blank separates the date field, and that the program does not halt if a hexadecimal character value is formed during calculations that is not in the system character set but, instead, is replaced by a blank. Among the defaults provided are storage size to compile 14K, size to execute 14K , and that all disk files use a separate I/O area. The line also specifies that there are twelve individual screen formats in the screen format load member that is linked to this program (by adding FM to the program name).

File Description Specifications (F). The F-Spec provides for all files used by the program specification such as the name, type, and organization of each file, how the file is used, the I/O device used for it, blocking, and location of key field if any.

The sample specifies that the program file name for the Account Master is ACCTMSTR; that it is an input

file and a primary file; that the stored physical record size (256 bytes) is four times the logical record size (64 bytes), i.e., the blocking factor is 4; that it is an indexed file with a key field length of 8 bytes beginning in position 1 in zoned decimal format; and that it is stored on disk. It also specifies that a workstation file is attached to this program and that the length of the longest workstation input or output record is 198 bytes. Further workstation specifications would be provided on succeeding lines.

RPG II supports a considerable range of file types, organizations, and functions. File type can be input, output, update, and combined (both input and output). File designations can be primary, secondary, chained, record address, table, array, and demand. Mode of processing can be consecutive, sequential by key, sequential within key limits, and random by relative record number, key addrout (address output: a record address file produced by the Sort utility), and against a direct file (random) load. File organizations can be indexed, direct (records are assigned specific disk positions regardless of the order in which they were loaded), and addrout. In database terms, the basic file structure is the flat file, that is, two-dimensional tablelike structures where record fields correspond to column headings and a record corresponds to a line in the table, the line being an n-tuple in database terminology, with "n" the number of fields across the table. Inasmuch as a given file can contain a variety of record types (not in the above file sense, but in the sense of generic and species variants), record type may be considered a third dimension of file structure. With appropriate combinations of keys, pointers, and programming techniques, hierarchical (tree) and network (plex) database schema can be constructed. Extensive Bill of Materials hierarchical structures have long been implemented in RPG II. Furthermore, inasmuch as relational databases are based on flat files, it should be possible to build at least quasi-relational databases in RPG II systems. It is also likely that the relational operators select, join, and project can be coded in RPG II as callable subroutines, as well as other elements of relational algebra, thus producing a basic relational information system. These points remain to be explored.

Extension Specifications (E). This form is used to specify all record address, table, and array files used in the program, including file name, number of entries in a table or array input record, number of entries in a table or array, and length of table or array. Tables and arrays may be single or alternating (related), where elements of one table (or array) reference elements of another table (or array).

Arrays are one of the most commonly used non-primitive data structures, are extremely powerful, are rarely defined in or related properly to the larger context of mathematics and science, and are rarely distinguished in terms of the particular meaning attached to the term in a particular language or system. This situation can lead to considerable confusion in interdisciplinary applications design, especially as business applications move rapidly from data processing to highly sophisticated analyses and decision support systems. The fol-

RPG CONTROL AND FILE DESCRIPTION SPECIFICATIONS

IBM International Business Machines Corporation

GX21-9092-5 UM/050
Printed in U.S.A.

Program	
Programmer	Date

Punching Instruction	Graphic		Punch	

Card Electro Number

75 76 77 78 79 80
Program Identification: S A M P L E

Page: 1 2 — Ø 1 of ___

Control Specifications

Refer to the specific System Reference Library manual for actual entries.

Line	Form Type	Size to Compile			Object Output	Listing Options	Size to Execute			Debug	MFCM Stacking Sequence		Date Format	Date Edit	Inverted Print	360/20 2501 Buffer	Number Of Print Positions			Alternate Collating Sequence	Address to Start				Work Tapes	Overlay Open	Overlap Printer	Binary Search	Tape Error	2152 Checking	Inquiry	Read/Write/Compute	Keyboard Output	Sign Handling	1P Forms Position	Indicator Setting	File Translation	Punch MFCU Zeros	Nonprint Characters	Table Load Halt	Shared I/O	Field Print	Formatted Dump	RPG to RPG II Conversion	Number of Formats																			
3 4	5 6	7 8 9			10	11	12 13 14			15	16 17		18 19	20	21	22	23 24 25			26	27 28 29 30				31	32	33	34	35	36	37	38	39	40	41	42	43	44	45 46	47	48	49	50	51	52 53 54	55 56 57 58 59 60 61 62 63 64 65 66 67 68 69 70 71 72 73 74
0 1	H												Y	&																								1						1 2	

Model 20

393A

File Description Specifications

Line	Form Type	Filename	I/O/U/C/D (15)	P/S/C/R/T/D/F (16)	F/V/S/M/D (19)	Block Length	Record Length	Length of Key Field (29-30)	A/P/I/K (31)	T/X/D/T/R or 2 (32)	Key Field Starting Location (38)	Device
02	F	WK	C	P	F		198					WORKSTN
03	F	ACCTMSTR	I	C	F	256	64	8	A	I	1	DISK
04	F											
05	F											
06	F											
07	F											
08	F											
09	F											
10	F											

393B

RPG EXTENSION AND LINE COUNTER SPECIFICATIONS

IBM International Business Machine Corporation

Program		Punching Instruction	Graphic			Card Electro Number
Programmer	Date		Punch			

Page Φ2 of ___

Extension Specifications

Line	Form Type	From Filename	To Filename	Table or Array Name	Number of Entries Per Record	Number of Entries Per Table or Array	Length of Entry	P/B/L/R	Decimal Positions	Sequence (A/D)	Table or Array Name (Alternating Format)	Length of Entry	P/B/L/R	Decimal Positions	Sequence (A/D)	Comments
01	E	DISKFIL1		AR1	17	394	7			A						
02	E															
03	E															
04	E															
05	E															
06	E															
07	E															
08	E															

Line Counter Specifications

Line	Form Type	Filename	1 Line Number	1 FL or Channel Number	2 Line Number	2 OL or Channel Number	3 Line Number	3 Channel Number	4 Line Number	4 Channel Number	5 Line Number	5 Channel Number	6 Line Number	6 Channel Number	7 Line Number	7 Channel Number	8 Line Number	8 Channel Number	9 Line Number	9 Channel Number	10 Line Number	10 Channel Number	11 Line Number	11 Channel Number	12 Line Number	12 Channel Number
1	L																									
2	L																									

393C

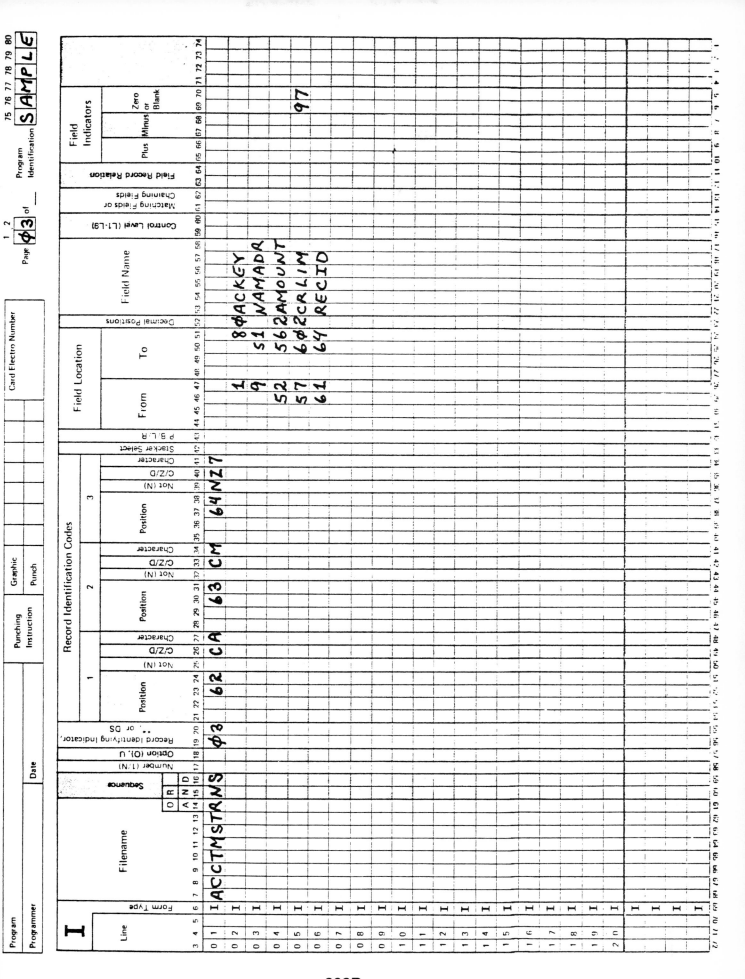

RPG CALCULATION SPECIFICATIONS

IBM — International Business Machines Corporation

Program | Programmer | Date
Punching Instruction — Graphic / Punch
Card Electro Number
Page 04 of —
Program Identification: SAMPLE (75 76 77 78 79 80)
GX21-9093-2 UM/050* Printed in U.S.A. *No. of forms per pad may vary slightly

Line	Form Type	Control Level (L0-L9, LR, SR, AN/OR)	Indicators Not	Indicators	Factor 1	Operation	Factor 2	Result Field Name	Length	Decimal Positions	Half Adjust (H)	Resulting Indicators	Comments
01	C			97		EXSR	NOAMT						
02	C	OR		97		GOTO	END						
03	C			03	AMOUNT	MULT	1	AMOUNT	9	2			
04	C			04	AMOUNT	COMP	CRLIM					474847	
05	C			47		GOTO	OVRLIM						
06	C			48	AMOUNT	MULT	INTPER	FINCHG	6	2			
07	C			48	AMOUNT	DIV	60	PERAMT	8	2			
08	C			48	PERAMT	ADD	FINCHG	BILAMT	8	2	H		
09	C			48		EXSR	BILLL						TREATS = 8 >
10	C												
11	C												
12	C												
13	C												
14	C												
15	C												
16	C												
17	C												
18	C												
19	C												
20	C												

393E

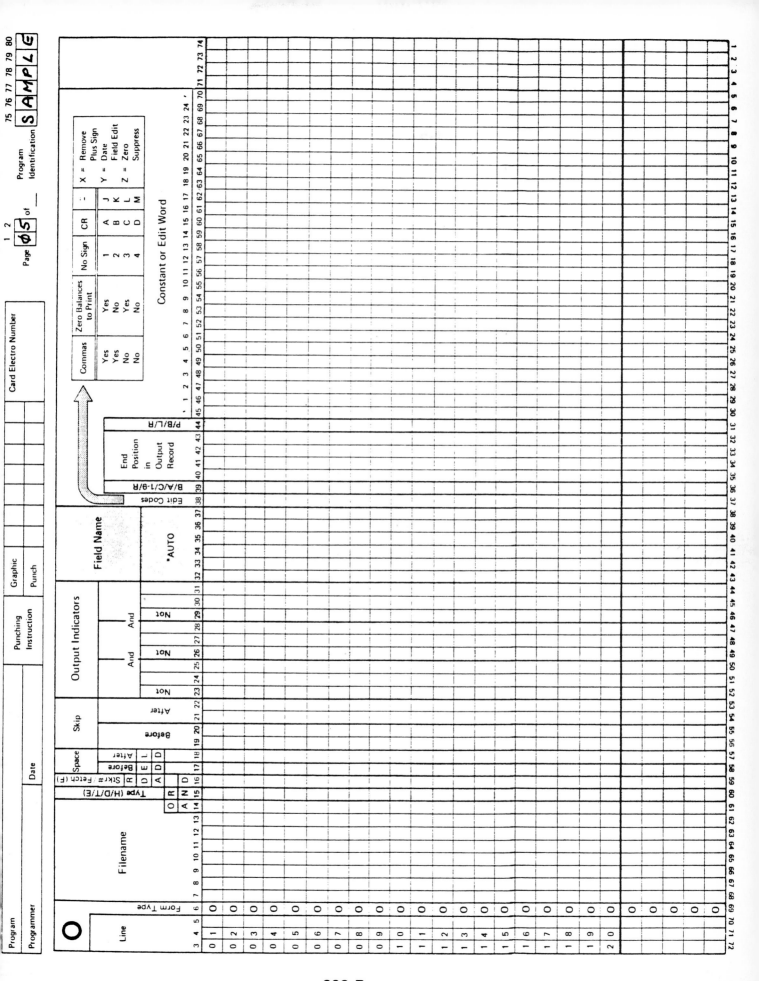

lowing paragraph seeks to repair matters in at least summary fashion and to provide background for discussion of RPG II array capabilities.

In fundamental mathematical terms, an array is simply an arrangement of a collection or set of elements in some geometric pattern, whereby elements are meant quantities, variables, words, expressions, or the like. A system of "mn" elements arranged in a rectangular array of "m" rows and "n" columns is called a matrix. Indexing of matrix elements is implicit where not explicitly provided; e.g., the element "e" at the intersection of the i-th row and j-th column is denoted eij. A scalar quantity, or scalar, has magnitude only; a vector quantity, or vector, has both magnitude and direction. In computer science, however, a vector has come to mean simply a one-dimensional array, that is, a vector array: a linear sequence of elements, with subscripts at least implied. In RPG II the term array is used to mean vector array.

RPG II provides a considerable range of table and array types and features, including the ability to compile them into a program, to read them from auxiliary storage for use in a program, and to generate and use them during execution of a program. Also, it is possible to construct matrices by stacking identically dimensioned and formatted arrays, each with its own name.

The coding sheets designated Extension Specifications describe a preexecution time array named AR1 that is stored in a file named DISKFIL1 and contains 394 alphameric elements (entries) contained in twenty-four records of seventeen 7-byte elements per record, except for the last record, which holds only three elements, arranged in ascending order.

Line Counter Specifications (L).   These forms indicate at what print line the programmer wants overflow to the next page to occur, and the length of the paper or form being used on the printer. They will not be discussed further here.

Input Specifications (I).   Input Specifications further describe the input files that have been specified in the File Specifications, detailing the records and fields within records used from those files. The information provided includes file name, sequence of record types within files, record-identifying indicators, record-identifying codes used to set on those indicators, data structures created for purposes of the given program, detail for locating and processing particular fields, and indicators for control breaks, records matching, and field testing (for plus, minus, and zero or blank).

The sample describes one of the records that will be used from the Account Master file that was previously described by the File Specifications coding. Account Master is a multirecord-type file in a private aircraft manufacturer's accounting system. Those records in the file with the characters A in position 62, M in position 63, and not a 7 in position 64 will be processed in special ways. Therefore, each such record read is to set on a record-identifying indicator, say, 03. The locations of fields that are to be used in subsequent processing are

specified, given names, and further specified as necessary. The Amount field is in packed decimal format (P), and if it is zero or blank, field indicator 97 is to turn on. Indicators 03 and 97 will be used to control subsequent processing; that is, they provide conditions for use in constructing program logic. The order in which the records are read is not significant in this case (NS). Workstation formats and fields used in the program would also be specified on this form.

Calculation Specifications (C).   "Calculation" in RPG II means far more than quantitative calculation and corresponds, rather, to the broader dictionary meaning, "to determine by reasoning, . . . make suitable or fit for a purpose, adapt." In brief, it means a very wide range of processing: alphabetic, string, numeric, and symbolic—all logically controlled by means of indicators. The Calculation Specifications specify the processing to be performed; the order in which and conditions under which they are to be performed; the fields, constants, literals, and variables to be used; and the resulting indicators that are to be set on or off by an operation to control other operations. They also formulate subroutines, generate execution time tables and arrays, control certain input and output operations, and much else.

RPG II logic, both that built into the RPG II program cycle and that provided by the programmer, is constructed by means of indicators: two-character numeric and alphameric fields that are set on and off by the program cycle in some cases and by the programmer's coded conditions in other cases. The programmer takes both the program and program cycle indicator settings into account in constructing the full application logic. The programmer can also combine indicators into simple or complex AND/OR compound logics to control a single program line, and do so also for many program lines by using a combination of GOTO and TAG op codes. Thus, by simply coding indicators in conjunction with op codes and fields on the fixed-format specifications sheets, all programming logic is constructed, and complicated nested and wordy If/Then/Else constructs are avoided.

For numeric calculation, RPG II provides built-in arithmetic ($+$, $-$, $\times$, $\div$), square root, and rounding operators, and column-specific conditionals ($+$, $-$, and 0 for arithmetic; $>$, $<$, and $=$ for comparisons; and high, low, and equal for lookups). Integral exponents can be obtained by simple loops. Functions can be defined as subroutines. Advanced RPG II, comprising exponentiation (that is, fractional as well as integral exponents), and log and antilog functions, has been developed and programmed in RPG II as callable subroutines (Stephen E. Seadler, UNICONSULT, New York City), thus making a wide range of advanced computations and decision support available in both RPG II and RPG III.

The coding guidelines included in the Calculations Specifications sheets allow for coding computations to be made for two record types in the Account Master program described earlier: records that set on record identifying indicators 03 (described earlier) and 04. If any record sets on indicator 97, the program executes subroutine NOAMT and returns to the next line. Otherwise it performs the next line and drops straight through the rest of the sample coding until it finds a logic condition that is true (the specified indicators are on or not on as specified).

Since AMOUNT was stored in packed form and the system unpacks it into zoned decimal form for processing, its unpacked length, including the desired number of decimal positions, is defined next by the simple maneuver of multiplying it by 1 and defining the Result field. AMOUNT is then compared with the account's credit limit (defined on some prior line), and if less than the limit, indicator 48 is set on; otherwise 47 is set on. If 47 is on, the program completely bypasses the rest of the sample coding and goes to a segment of calculations identified by a TAG labeled OVRLIM. If 48 is on, AMOUNT (account balance) is multiplied by the interest per period (month here), resulting in the finance charge, and divided by the running number of payment periods (60 in this case) in this manufacturer's revolving credit system, resulting in period amount. FINCHG and PERAMT are then added, giving the billing amount. Program control then executes the first of several billing subroutines, and returns to the next program line (not described).

Output Specifications (O). It is in the Output Specifications stage of programming that the extraordinary power of RPG II for report generation becomes clearest. This form is used to describe the records and fields to be outputted, when and under what conditions, the format, headings, subheadings, subtotals, totals, and editing. It is also used to specify outputs to workstation files, including names of formats (screen displays), fields within formats, output conditions, and editing.

The Output Specifications chapter of RPG II reference manuals provide an exhaustive table of edit words, together with examples, for specification in the form's Constant or Edit Word space. Edit words are symbolic templates and include, for instance, fixed and floating $ signs, asterisk-fill or blanks-fill for all or a specified number of leading zeros, positioning of dimensional terms such as HRS, MINS, NET, GROSS, CR, CR GROSS, + and − signs, and so on.

Almost any conceivable label, form, letter, and report formatting can be programmed, for any length and width within printer constraints, including repeated, nonrepeated, and variable page headings; automatic pagination and dating; handling of page overflow; variable indentation within page titles and subtitles; totals and subtotals labeling; special occurrence labeling and flagging; and much more, all with relative ease.

Other Specifications. As RPG II and RPG-II-supporting systems and compilers evolve, new specifications sheets evolve. Among these are the Sort, Display Screen Format, and Telecommunications specifications. The Sort utility provides a very simple, powerful, and flexible means of selecting and sorting records, together with additional options such as inserting characters in the records and totaling fields. As new utilities become available, they provide new entries to link to existing specifications, while dispensing with specifications sheets by providing convenient interactive on-line specifications facilities, such as the Screen Design Aid, Data File utility, and Workstation utility, as well as the Sort utility. Generally, all specifications sheets become available on screen. Also included on some systems is the Auto Report function—a special set of codes that provide greatly simplified report generation using the standard specifications forms.

Documentation. Within-program documentation is amply provided for. Although the specifications sheets span 80 bytes, the full source program line is 96 bytes, and the remaining spaces can be used for entering line-by-line documentation. Also, regular coding space, that is, entire coding lines, can be used for documentation in paragraph format by placing asterisks in a designated column. Special and complex algorithms, however, are more conveniently documented in algorithmic language on paper, although they too can be done within the program, e.g., by combining less-than symbols with dashes to form arrows for assignment symbols.

RPG III

RPG III constitutes a major version of RPG and continues to evolve, having gone through seven releases since its introduction in October 1978, the latest being June 1984 (as of this writing). Implementation is presently confined to the IBM System/38, whose operating system, comprising the control program facility (CPF), is accessed via the new control language, CL. Among the RPG III enhancements are the following:

- Calls: RPG III programs can call other RPG programs and also CL programs; and then the called programs can themselves call other programs, and those programs can ultimately return at the end.

- Externally Described Data: File fields are described to the CPF through Data Description Specifications (DDS), which are designated as A-Specs, and thus need to be described only once rather than in each program that will be using the files. However, there are certain DDS definitions that may be overridden and modified in the program I-Specs. A similar procudure is followed for changes in the file descriptions. This results in a logical database containing only logical files—in addition to the physical database. Or, the system can be considered to house a single database comprising all stored objects: programs, logical files, physical files, and device files.

- Device files describe I/O devices. Together, these files comprise the device files database.

- Extensive database functions include, for example, reading backwards through a file.

- Program structure can consist of any group of RPG III specs that can exist by themselves.

- New operation codes promote structured programming, such as conditional selection of subroutine execution in one code; DO loops, including While and Until; and IFxx/ELSE conditional execution of a group of calculations without branching or indicator control.

- Creation of an access path is possible for each member of the database by either of two types: arrival sequence or keyed sequence.

- Composite key and subkey naming is used so that a composite key or its parts may be specified by a single name.

- Debug features are considerably enhanced.

Conclusion

RPG, as RPG II and III in conjunction with OCL, CL, and new facilities and utilities, has developed far beyond its inception as a relatively simple batch-oriented report program generator. It has become a powerful high-level, multifaceted, multiuser, multitasking, interactive, database- and communications-oriented, business-oriented, symbolic computer language whose basic implementations are easy to learn, yet whose full instructions set is enormously rich and offers many advanced functions for experienced programmers and sophisticated systems. RPG compilers have also progressed, and generate highly efficient machine code for fast execution.

When efficiency and cost effectiveness are properly taken to include applications development and maintenance as well as execution, RPG should be seriously considered for production as well as query, analysis, and on-line applications—on mainframes as well as minicomputers. Now, by means of terminal emulation and telecommunications links, the RPG world has also become accessible to, and potentially an integral part of, the personal computer world.

Stephen E. Seadler

RPG GLOSSARY

The following glossary represents recent implementations of RPG II. The language is currently available on many minis and mainframes or as a downloaded system on any personal computer. As a downloaded system, the delivery of RPG II effectively turns the personal computer into a front end for a true RPG-based mainframe network with all the memory capability this implies.

Abbreviations used in the following:

op code   operations code (on Calculations Specifications sheet)

specs   specifications

X-specs   specifications sheet designated by the letter X

*PLACE   Special word used on O-Specs to repeat output of some field(s) by defining only the end position of the repeat.

/COPY   Special word entered on I-Specs to invoke the copy function. Used to include in a program any valid RPG II source specifications residing as a library member on a disk.

/EJECT   Specifications following this entry begin a new page of the compiler listing. Common to all specifications sheets.

/SPACEn   Next specification line of compiler listing will be printed after n blank lines, where n = 1, 2, or 3. Common to all specification sheets.

ACQ   Op code (acquire) used to attach the device specified in factor 1 to the program.

ADD   Arithmetic op code for addition.

ALTSEQ   Special word (alternate sequence) used at the beginning of a specially formatted record to be entered and compiled with a program in order to alter the normal collating sequence.

AN   Short form of AND used on C-Specs to combine the indicators.

AND   Logical conjunction for combining indicator conditions.

BSCA   Device name used on F-Specs to allow an RPG II program to transmit and receive binary synchronous data via data communications network. Each BSCA file defined on the F-Specs must have a corresponding entry on the RPG Telecommunications Specifications sheet.

BEGSR   Op code (begin subroutine) used to mark the beginning of the subroutine named in factor 1.

BITOF   Op code (bit off) for creating and manipulating program bit switches. Causes the 1 to 8 bits identified by a numeric literal or 1-byte field in factor 2 to be turned off in the 1-byte field named as the result field. Fields may be specified 1-byte array elements. Bits that are on in factor-2 field are turned off in result field.
  See also TESTB.

BITON Op code (bit on) for creating and manipulating program bit switches. Causes the 1 to 8 bits identified by a numeric literal or 1-byte field in factor 2 to be turned on in the 1-byte field named as result field. Fields may be specified 1-byte array elements. Bits that are on in factor-2 are turned on in result field.
  See also TESTB.

CHAIN Op code used with input, output, and update files to read a record identified by record key from an indexed file, or by a relative record number from a sequential or direct file. Also used to load a direct file by relative record number.

COMP Op code (compare) used to compare factor 1 with factor 2. Indicators specified in designated columns turn on according to whether factor 1 is greater than, less than, or equal to factor 2.

CONSOLE An input-only device name used with a record address or input data file in order to enter data records directly from a display station to an executing program. System provides simple screen format, obviating need to design, code, and compile a screen format member.

CRT Device name to use the full screen as an output device for any alphameric normal or exceptional output. Display lines move on to screen from bottom to top. Spacing, skipping, edit words, edit codes, and output indicators can be specified.

DEBUG Op code used to invoke the RPG II DEBUG fuction. Can be specified repeatedly throughout the C-Specs. Depending on coding, it prints either one or two lines for each line at which it is encountered during an executing program. First print line lists all indicators that are on at the time of encounter. Second print line, if specified, shows contents of the result field on the encountered program line.

DISK Device name that allows program to process data stored on disk.

DIV Arithmetic op code for division.

ENDSR Op code (end subroutine) used to specify the end of a subroutine.

ERASE Entered in the result field in order to blank the entire buffer for the CONSOLE file named in factor 2 at the beginning of the next program cycle.

EXCPT Op code (exceptional output) that allows records to be written during calculations. Used primarily in loops to write a variable number of similar or identical records. Also used to output data as needed prior to program cycle output phase.

EXIT Op code used at a point in calculations when control is to be transferred from RPG II to assembler language subroutine.

EXSR Op code (execute subroutine) used to branch to the subroutine named in factor 2. When subroutine has been completed, program execution returns to the line following the EXSR specification.

FORCE Op code used to override the multifile processing method by which the program cycle normally selects records for input. Next record read (at start of next cycle) will be from the file identified in factor 2. Can be used with primary or secondary input and update files, but not KEYBORD or WORKSTN files. If used in a count loop, it will successively read records from factor-2 file until count is satisfied.
  See also READ.

GOTO Op code used to branch to a previous or succeeding spec line whose TAG label in factor 1 is identical to the label named in factor 2 of the GOTO.

KEY Op code used to cause a pause in calculations during which the operator can enter data from the keyboard. Can be used only with KEYBORD file. Can be and is normally used in conjunction with the SET operation. I-Specs are not used for KEYBORD FILES; the input data are defined in the KEY or SET/KEY operation itself.

KEYBORD Device named for use with KEY or SET operations. CONSOLE and KEYBORD refer to the same physical unit (display station).

LOKUP Op code (look up) used to search the table or array named in factor 2 for the search word specified in factor 1. The search word can be an alphameric or numeric constant, a field name, an array element, or a table name. The type of search is specified by assigning resulting indicators to equal, high, low, high and equal, or low and equal columns. For other than equal-only, the table or array must be in sequence. When high-and-equal or low-and-equal columns are specified, equal is given preference. If no equal is found, nearest higher or nearest lower is selected. In table searches, the result (contents) of a successful search is accesible via the result field name. In successful array searches, the number (not contents) of the found array element is placed in the field that has been named as the array index. Contents of the element are then accessed in subsequent array operations using that index.

MHHZO Op code (move high to high zone) used to move the zone from the leftmost position of factor 2 to the zone of the leftmost position of the result field. Both fields must be alphameric.

MHLZO Op code (move high to low zone) used to move the zone from the leftmost position of factor 2 to the zone of the rightmost position of the result field. Factor 2 must be alphameric; result field can be alphameric or numeric.

MLHZO   Op code (move low to high zone) used to move the zone from the rightmost position of factor 2 to the leftmost position of the result field. Factor 2 can be alphameric or numeric; result field must be alphameric.

MLLZO   Op code (move low to low zone) used to move the zone from the rightmost position of factor 2 to the rightmost position of the result field. Each field can be either alphameric or numeric.

MOVE   Op code used to transfer characters from the rightmost positions of factor 2 to the rightmost positions of the result field.

MOVEA   Op code (move array) used to transfer characters from the leftmost positions of factor 2 to the leftmost positions of the result field (both cannot reference the same array). All arrays and fields specified by MOVEA must be alphameric. Movement starts with the first element of an array unless a start element is specified by an index. Makes it possible to move contiguous array elements to a single field, move a single field to contiguous array elements, and move contiguous elements of one array to contiguous elements of another array.

MULT   Arithmetic op code for multiplication.

MVR   Op code (move reminder) used to move the remainder from an immediately preceding divide operation into the result field.

NEXT   Op code used to force the next input to the program to come from the display station identified in factor 1 to the WORKSTN file named in factor 2.

OR   Logical inclusive disjunction for combining indicator conditions. Means "A or B or both."

PAGE   When entered on O-Specs, automatically causes pagination beginning with 0001, unless otherwise specified on I-Specs by means of a PAGE field in an input record. Can be restarted at any point in a job.

PAGEn   Provides seven additional Page entries (n = 1,2,...,7) for numbering different page types in the output or for numbering pages for different printer files.

PRINTER   Device name for each of up to eight printer files per program, each of which is assigned a unique file name using the PRINTER OCL statement.

READ   Opcode used to call for immediate input from the demand file named in factor 2, including WORKSTN files, during the calculations phase of the program cycles. Differs from FORCE, which calls for certain input on the next program cycle, not the present one.

REL   Op code (release) used to release the device specified in factor 1. The device is released when REL is encountered during calculations unless the device is the requester of a single requester program, in which case it is released at end of job.

RELABL   Op code (RPG II label) used to allow the assembler subroutine specified in the immediately preceding EXIT operation to reference a field, data structure, table, array, or indicator defined in the RPG II program and named in the result field of the RLABL operation. An indicator is named as INxx, where xx is the indicator.

SET   Op code (set command keys) used with input files assigned to the KEYBORD device. Operations are directed to the display station that loaded the program or has been assigned to the program by the WORKSTN OCL statement. Enables one or more of the following: specification of command keys the operator is allowed to press at this point in the program; display of the field, literal, table, or array element specified in factor 1; display of user messages identified in SETnn and KEYnn; blanking of the CONSOLE buffer if ERASE is specified in the result field. In addition, SET and KEY operations can be combined in programming so that an operator can press all command keys enabled by the SET operation, key a field specified in the KEY operation, and then press an entry function key only once.

SETLL   Op code (set lower limits) used in conjunction with an immediately succeeding READ operation to allow the lower limits for an indexed demand file being processed sequentially to be set during calculations. If the READ operation is performed prior to the SETLL operation, the record with the lowest key in the file is selected.

SETOF   Op code used to turn off specified indicators.

SETON   Op code used to turn on specified indicators.

SHTDN   Op code (shutdown) sets on a specified indicator when the system operator has requested shutdown. Indicator can then be used to condition program termination in ways desired for the application, such as printing or outputting of files to certain fields whose end-of-job or end-of-day contents or status are wanted.

SPECIAL   Device name used for files using devices not directly supported by RPG II. User must supply an assembler subroutine to perform I/O operations required to transfer data between the SPECIAL device and main storage. Subroutine name is entered on same line of F-Specs as SPECIAL.

SQRT   Op code for taking the square root of the field name in factor 2. An entire array can be used in this operation if factor 2 and the result field contain array names.

SUB Arithmetic op code used for subtraction.

SUBRxx Name used for assembler language (external) subroutine. Is placed in factor 2 and used in conjunction with the EXIT and RLABL operations to provide linkage to the RPG II program. In a typical system, characters xx must be alphabetic for user-written subroutines, while numeric characters are reserved for machine-vendor-supplied subroutines, and both types of subroutines are stored in the system library, not the RPG II source library.

TAG Op code used to label the destination of GOTO operation. Factor 1 contains the label which was used in factor 2 of the GOTO.

TESTB Op code (test bit) used to compare the 1 to 8 bits identified by a literal or 1-byte field in factor 2 with the corresponding bits in the 1-byte field named in the result field. Specified indicators in designating columns turn on for on/off, mixed, and on/on comparisons.

TESTZ Op code (test zone) used to test the zone of the leftmost character in the result field, which must be alphameric. The resulting plus indicator turns on for & and A through I zones, minus indicator for − (minus) and J through R zones, and zero indicator for all other zones.

TIME Op code used to access the 12-byte system time and date field derived from entries made during IPL. Either time or time and date may be accessed depending on how the result field is defined. If both are accessed, they can be separated into distinct fields by means of MOVE and MOVEL operations. The system date obtained here is not the same field as UDATE and may or may not be the same value.

UDATE A special 6-byte numeric field used on O-Specs to have the date printed on report or program listing. Contains the program (job step) date. The program date may be the same as or different from the system and session date depending on the used and placement of the DATE OCL statement and DATE procedure. If neither the statement nor the procedure has been used since IPL, the system, session, and program dates are identical. (A procedure is set of related OCL statements, and possibly utility control statements, that interface with the operating system and cause functions to be performed.) Neither UDATE, UMONTH, UYEAR can be changed by operations specified in a program. However, they may be used in compare and test operations.

UDAY A 2-byte subfield of UDATE used to print the day only.

UMONTH A 2-byte subfield of UPDATE used to print the month only.

UYEAR A 2-byte subfield of UDATE used to print the year only.

WORKSTN Device name used on F-Specs to allow an RPG II program to communicate with one or more display stations.

XFOOT Op code (crossfoot) used to add together all elements of an array named in factor 2 and place the sum in the result field.

Z-ADD Op code (zero and add) used to set the result field to zeros and then add to it the contents of the field name or numeric literal in factor 2.

Z-SUB Op code (zero and subtract) used to set the result field to zeros and then subtract from it the contents of the field name or numeric literal in factor 2. The result is simply the negative of factor 2.

SAM76

The SAM76 language is a list and string processor that is uniquely suited for a variety of interactive and user-directed applications, including artificial intelligence programming, and permits a high portability from machine to machine. SAM76 shares certain features in common with the LISP and Forth programming languages and, pointing to the future of multiuser or concurrent systems operation, with the SHELL programming language of the UNIX operating system.

SAM76 had its intellectual origins at Bell Laboratories in 1971. There, Claude Kagan, the language's developer, sought to combine, within a single interpretive processor, the characteristics of two different string and general-purpose macro generators and the provisions to embed multiple infix operator mathematical systems. It is the macro generators which provide one of the keys to understanding the principles behind the development of SAM76. A macro is a code word that can be defined by the user to invoke a specific set of instructions to perform a routine within the program. A user will define a macro to execute a set of instructions, usually in either machine language or assembly language, and insert the macro into a program. In this way, a user need only define a routine once and then when that particular operation is required, the user can substitute the macro. This is a highly efficient method of programming, and languages that can generate macros can be used to create applications of enormous complexity and sophistication. Macros, once generated, can also be stored and inserted into other programs where they are capable of modification to perform different tasks. Most personal computer users are familiar with the macrolike capabilities of Logo or commonly used word processors that enable typists to define an entire procedure with one or two characters.

The SAM76 language follows a well-defined syntax which is both easy to learn and easy to read. It relies heavily, however, on a system of symbols to replace the pseudo English words of BASIC and Pascal. The language is also interpretive, which means that when a string is evaluated and an expression found to contain an instruction or command, the prescribed action is immediately performed and the resulting value, as in the case of a mathematical operation, replaces that expression in the string. The SAM76 interpreter also provides for a highly reactive and interactive language that can almost converse with the user from task to task. Consequently, the language has the capability of performing complex operations in program control, text editing and manipulation, gaming, simulation, and mathematics. Because it has features similar to LISP, Forth, and other list processors, SAM76 also has the capability of functioning as a query language, providing powerful human-machine interaction that uses keyboard data from an interaction to modify and shape further responses.

The language is also capable of growing by extension. Because, like LISP and Logo, there is almost no difference between procedures and data structures, procedures can be treated as data and be acted upon by other procedures, even procedures defined by different users. The new procedures that are mapped or created behave as if they were language primitives or inherent functions of the language. Like Logo, this means that new users can create their own separate vocabularies which can be saved and executed, adding to the language vocabulary and providing for individual customization.

Like LISP, all commands and data objects in SAM76 are represented by lists, or strings of characters. However, in the latter language, syntax plays a vital role in identifying those characters which, because of their position in a given expression, have an additional meaning. The characters are called warning characters and, used initially, represent the following concepts:

%	start symbol for an active expression
&	start symbol for a neutral expression
!	start symbol for a protected string
/	end symbol for all types of expressions
#	alternate start of expression
:	end of active alternate expression
;	end of neutral alternate expression
,	argument separator symbol
( )	string protection pair
< >	alternate string protection pair
@	single-character protection code
∕	single-character ignore code
[ ]	boundaries of a math expression

A legal SAM76 expression is bounded at its left by one of the start symbols and at its right by one of the appropriate types of end symbols. Elements of the expression are separated from each other by the argument separator (,). The first argument is always a command or the name of a user-defined string, expression, or procedure. Subsequent arguments (1, 2, 3, . . . N) are treated as required by the command or as macros which will be plugged into the proper places of the named user-defined string. For example, this sequence demonstrates the creation of user-defined functions. First, the program defines a "text" named "square" to be a procedure which will multiply some value "x" by "x":

%dt,square,!%mu,x,x///=

One can see immediately that the actual multiplication expression (mu) has been protected by the pair of warning characters (!/), and the act of defining with the function (dt) simply creates a data object called "square" but returns no real value.

The next step is to convert the characters "x" into partitions (macro positions) of value 1 using the "partition text" command:

%pt,square,x/=

Now, by examining the object named "square" with a SAM76 function called "view texts," whose mnemonic is "vt," one can see:

```
%vt,square/=
%mu,[1],[1]/
```

We can make use of this new function to square numbers. For example:

```
%square,5/=25
```

Or, using the mnemonic "ad" for addition:

```
%square,%ad,3,2//=25
```

The next sample program illustrates the capabilities of SAM76 to use partitions to assign numbers to words in two different languages in such a way that the correspondence of partition numbers effectively translates the text from one language to another.

```
%dt,text,
the dog and the cat and the horse/=
%pt,text,the,dog,and,cat,horse/=
%text,le,chien,et,chat,cheval/=
le chien et le chat et le cheval
```

The first line of the program shows the definition of a text named "text" to contain the phrase "the dog and the cat and the horse". The second line uses the "partition text" function to convert each of the words in "text" to partitions whose numeric value will correspond to the position in the "pt" expression of the words being matched. The last line above shows the invocation of the partitioned text using a list of French words as the source of data to fill the partitions with words whose positions correspond to the value of the partitions. Use of the "view texts" function to examine the text "t" reveals the partitions as follows:

```
%vt,t/=
[1] [2] [3] [1] [4] [3] [1] [5]
```

Notice that this is not an "intelligent" translation of the English into the French because any words can be inserted into the partition frames for the conversion process to work. All that is happening here is that an input string is partitioned and a new string, corresponding to the existing partitions, is imposed upon the program.

It is evident from these examples that syntax plays a vital role in SAM76, defining the sequence of operations within each string. Use of mnemonics reduces the overhead which, unlike BASIC, allows complicated programs to be written without an overabundance of code. For example, this program illustrates the construction of a password checking system with an automatic exit if either an incorrect password is entered or there is no action after a given time.

```
%dt,password,!%ca,%xc,0D//%os,
Enter password followed by "return" ?- /%iw,100/
%dt,x,&is//%ig,%crd,x/,,!%gotinput//,
!%os,TIMEOUT/%ex///////=
```

Translated, the instruction set reads: Define a text (dt) named 'password' to be a procedure, indicated by the first exclamation point. This procedure will first change the activator (ca) to be that character which results from the 'X' base (x) to character (c) conversion of HEX 0D (a carriage return).

Next this procedure will output the string (os) as follows:

'[carriage return, line feed] Enter password followed by "return" ?-'

After this prompt, the procedure will set the input-wait (iw) timing function to 100 units. An 'ignore symbol' follows which permits the use of a carriage return and line feed code that the program will not evaluate. Next, the procedure will define a text (dt) named 'x' which will contain any material that is entered from the keyboard. The termination of the input will either be the carriage return, specified by the change activator (ca, xc, 0D) command in the first line of the program or the time out feature which set the input wait function (iw) at 100 units. After the program recognizes that input has been terminated, the procedure then implements a conditional test. It looks for a number of characters greater than zero in the set defined by 'x' (dt,x). If the procedure finds a 'null string' or zero characters (,,), it will output the string (os) 'TIME OUT' and exit (ex) the user to the system.

However, if the procedure finds that there are characters in the set (x), then the following routine applies:

```
%dt,gotinput,!%ii,&ft,x/,SAM76,!%os,
YOU GOT IT RIGHT/%ri/,!%os,
WRONG - TRY AGAIN/%password//////=
```

Translated, this second procedure reads: Define a text (dt) named gotinput to be a procedure that will test to determine if the contents of 'x' are identical to the string 'SAM76'. If it is identical, then output the string (os): '[carriage return, line feed] YOU GOT IT RIGHT' and return the user to the initialized condition (ri). If the user input string is not identical to 'SAM76', then output the string (os): '[carriage return, line feed] WRONG' and return the user to the procedure defined (dt) 'password'.

These examples indicate that SAM76, which is a relatively new language, offers interesting possibilities to programmers because its structure resembles the structuring of logical or procedural thought very closely, and its system of ready-to-hand mnemonics can eliminate much of the coding overhead associated with BASIC. Currently, SAM76 enjoys implementation on most CP/M systems including the Apple II+ and IIe, MSX-DOS and DEC SYSTEM 10.

SAM76 GLOSSARY

The following glossary of SAM76 represents the most recent update of the language. SAM76 is available for the Apple under DOS 3.3 and CP/M computers. It will become quite evident from even a cursory inspection of the SAM76 glossary that the language operates on both a high and a low level at the same time. Hence, the identification with the UNIX shell and the microprocessor support features of Forth.

This glossary is organized by functional category; an arbitrary serial number also shown, has been assigned to each function. These functions consist of not less than two and no more than three alphabetic characters that operate much like the mnemonics in a microprocessor's assembly language.

Abbreviations Used in the List of Functions

% function,arguments,...
Active expression

& function,arguments,...
Neutral expression

x,x1,... "x" base (binary, octal, hex) numbers

d,d1,... decimal base numbers

n,n1... "n" base (arithmetic) numbers

s0 prefixing string (as in lists)

s,s1,... character strings

f file name

t text name

vz default value

v−,v+,v0 conditional value

vt,vf true/false value

sub indicates subfunctions—using "lf,s0" as subfunction gives list.

TEXT FUNCTIONS

103 **%dt,t,s,d1,d2/** Define Text

104 **%et,t1,t2,...,t/** Erase Text

105 **%lt,s0/** List Text

114 **%ht,t/** Hide Text

118 **%vt,t1,t1,...,t/** View Text

132 **%ct,t1,t2,t3,...t/** Combine Text

206 **%ea/** Erase All

TEXT DIVISION

137 **%fc,t,vz/** Fetch Character

138 **%fdc,t,d,vz/** Fetch "D" Characters

139 **%fde,t,d,vz/** Fetch "D" Elements

140 **%fdm,t,d,s,vz/** Fetch "D" Matches

141 **%fe,t,vz/** Fetch Element

142 **%ff,t,d,vz/** Fetch Field

143 **%fl,t,s,vz/** Fetch Left match

144 **%fr,t,s,vz/** Fetch Right match

145 **%fp,t,x1,x2,...,x/** Fetch Partition

146 **%md,t,d/** Move Divider to position "d"

      &md,t,d/ Move Divider "d" positions

147 **%crd,t/** Characters Right of Divider

148 **%cld,t/** Characters Left of Divider

197 **%qld,t/** Query Left of Divider

198 **%qrd,t/** Query Right of Divider

207 **%ed,t,d1,d2,vz/** Extract "D" characters

210 **%ftb,t,s,vz/** Fetch To Break character

211 **%fts,t,s,vz/** Fetch To Span character

STRING FUNCTIONS

150 **%hm,t,s/** How many Matches

160 **%ai,s0,s1,s2,...,s/** Alphabetic Insertion

161 **%as,s0,s1,s2,...,s/** Alphabetic Sort

162 **%ps,d,s1,s2/** Pad String

163 **%rs,s/** Reverse String

164 **%ds,d,s/** Duplicate String

168 **%tr,t,s/** Trim

209 **%nu,s1,s2,...,s/** Null

212	**%hc,s/** How many Characters
214	**%lw,s0,s1,s2,...,s/** List Where
215	**%ra,d,s1,s2,s3,...,s/** Return Argument
247	**%rj,d,s1/** Return Justified lines
248	**%rp,c,d,s1/** Return Padded lines

BRANCH FUNCTIONS

111	**%ni,vt,vf/** Neutral Implied
126	**%yt,t,s,vt,vf/** Ys There
127	**%tb,t,vt,vf/** Text Branch
135	**%ii,s1,s2,vt,vf,.../** If Identical
136	**%ig,d1,d2,vt,vf,.../** If Greater
159	**%ab,s1,s2,vt,vf/** Alphabetic Branch
226	**%fb,f,vt,vf/** File Branch

MATHEMATICAL FUNCTIONS

128	**%ad,n1,n2,n3,...,n/** Add
129	**%su,n1,n2,...,n/** Subtract
130	**%di,n1,n2,vz/** Divide
131	**%mu,n1,n2,vz/** Multiply

LOGICAL

186	**%or,x1,x2/** Or the bits
187	**%and,x1,x2/** And the bits
188	**%not,x/** Not (complement) the bits
189	**%rot,d,x/** Rotate the bits
190	**%sh,d,x/** Shift the bits

PARTITION FUNCTIONS

107	**%pt,t,s1,s2,...,s/** Partition Text
108	**%pc,d/** Partition Character
109	**%mt,t,s1,s2,...s/** Multipart Text
110	**%mc,d/** Multipart Character
149	**%hp,t,d/** How many Partitions
151	**%ep,t,p1,p2,...,p/** Erase Partitions
167	**%qp,t/** Query Partition

I/O FUNCTIONS

101	**%os,s/** Output String
102	**%is/** Input String
115	**%ic/** Input Character
116	**%id,d/** Input "D" characters
117	**%im,s1,s2,...,s/** Input to Match
213	**%iw,n/** Input Wait
241	**%lic,s0/** List Input Channels
242	**%loc,s0/** List Output Channels
245	**%sic,sym/** Select Input Channel
246	**%soc,sym/** Select Output Channel
264	**%qio/** Query I/O assignments
265	**%sio,iobyte** Set I/O byte

STORAGE FUNCTIONS

216	**%lf,s0/** List Files
217	**%qfs,filename/** Query File Size
219	**%qfe/** Query File Extension
220	**%bf,f/** Bring File
221	**%sfe,extension/** Set File Extension
223	**%sdu,dir/** Select Directory Unit
224	**%ef,f/** Erase File
225	**%qdu/** Query Directory Unit
233	**%dif,filename/** Designate Input Filename
234	**%dof,filename/** Designate Output Filename
235	**%rfr/** Read File Record
236	**%wfr,s/** Write File Record
243	**%rf,filename/** Read File
244	**%wf,filename,s/** Write File

RANDOM NUMBER

252   **%rn,n/**   Random Number

253   **%srn,n/**   Seed Random Number

CONVERSION

170   **%xc,x1,x2,...,x/**   X to Character

171   **%cx,s0,s/**   Character to X

172   **%xd,x/**   X to Decimal

173   **%dx,d/**   Decimal to X

GRAPHICS

174   **%pl,sub,s1,...,s/**   Plot

175   **%wi,xn1,yn1/**   Write Initialize

176   **%wx/**   Write X displacement

177   **%wy/**   Write Y displacement

178   **%wr**   Width Right

179   **%wl/**   Width Left

180   **%ws,xn1,ynl,...,xn,yn/**   Write Straight lines

ARRAY

182   **%zd,r,v−,v0,v+/**   "Z" register Decrement and branch

183   **%zi,r,v−,v0,v+/**   "Z" register Increment and branch

184   **%zq,r/**   "Z" register Query

185   **%zs,r,n/**   "Z" register Set

TRACE MODES

124   **%tma/**   Trace Mode All deactivated

     &tma/   Trace Mode All activated

125   **%tm/**   Trace Mode activated

     &tm/   Trace Mode deactivated

CONTROL FUNCTION

113   **%ca,s/**   Change Activator

133   **%cnb,d/**   Change Number Base

134   **%qnb/**   Query Number Base

157   **%sfd,fun,dev/**   Specify Function Device

158   **%sar/**   Set Auto Return on Line Feed

169   **%ut,cc/**   User Trap

191   **%cll,d/**   Change Line Length

192   **%qll/**   Query Line Length

193   **%cin,t1,d1,...,t,d/**   Change Id Number

194   **%qin/**   Query Id Number

195   **%cfc,d1,s/**   Change Fill Character Schema

196   **%qfc,s0/**   Query Fill Character Schema

199   **%sem,dev/**   Set "Echoplex" Mode

200   **%cxb,d/**   Change X Base

201   **%qxb**   Query X Base

202   **%qof/**   Query Overflow Functions

203   **%cro,s1/**   Change Rub Out character schema

204   **%qro/**   Query Rub Out character schema

205   **%qta/**   Query Text Area

227   **%qcs/**   Query Command String

237   **%@t/**   wh@ is processor Title

238   **%@f,s0/**   wh@ are Functions

239   **%@n/**   wh@ is processor verification Number

240   **%@cn,current,new/**   Change function Name

250   **%cwc,s1/**   Change Warning Characters

251   **%qwc/**   Query Warning Characters

261   **%cws,d/**   Change Work Space

262   **%qws/**   Query Work Space

266   **%cpc,x1,t1,...tn/**   Change Protection Class

267   **%qpc,s0,t1,t2,...t/**   Query Protection Class

MISCELLANEOUS FUNCTIONS

112   **%ex,f/**   Exit

155   **%xll,s0/**   eXamine Label List

156   **%xal,label,x/**   eXamine Address of Label

165   **%rr,s1/**   Return to Restart

166   **%ri/**   Restart Initialized

228   **%lff,s0/**   List File Function

231   **%sw,s1,s2,s3,...s/**   Switches

232   **%sy,s1,s2,...s/**   Systems functions

257   **%ti,s0/**   Time

258   **%sti,hh,mm,ss/**   Set Time

259   **%da,s0/**   Date

260   **%sda,da,mo,yr/**   Set Date

268   **%nud,func,arguments/**   Null   Display mode

MONITOR FUNCTIONS

119   **%xr,x/**   eXamine Register

120   **%xw,x1,x2/**   eXperimental   Write   in Register

122   **%xwp,x1,x2/**   eXperimental   Write   in Register Pair

123   **%xj,x/**   eXperimental Jump

254   **%xqs,s0/**   X Query Work Space

255   **%xi,port/**   eXperimental Input

256   **%xo,x,port/**   eXperimental Output

269   **%xrs,unit,trk,sec,s0/**   X Read Sector

270   **%xws,unit,trk,sec,X/**   X Write Sector

271   **%xu,sub,arguments**   eXperimental User

272   **%xqf,s/**   eXperimental Query Function

273   **%xcf,s,x/**   eXperimental Change Function

Claude A. R. Kagan, Karl Nicholas

Smalltalk

Smalltalk is a high-level programming language based on the metaphor of objects sending messages to one another. It was developed at Xerox's Palo Alto Research Center (PARC) over a period of 10 years, passing through several incarnations in that time. Smalltalk-72 was the first, followed by Smalltalk-76. The current version of the language, and the one PARC chose to release to the outside world, is Smalltalk-80. Before 1980, the language was implemented only on Xerox personal workstation computers. In 1980, Xerox began working with selected outside groups on implementing Smalltalk for other machines. The publication of the book *Smalltalk: The Language and Its Implementation* in 1983 marked the release of Smalltalk to the rest of the outside world. Smalltalk has been implemented on DEC VAXes and 2020's, a Tektronix 68000-based computer, and the Apple Lisa, but as of this writing (September 1984), no complete Smalltalk implementations are being marketed for microcomputers. However, this situation can be expected to change in the near future, as microcomputers become more powerful and Smalltalk implementations become more efficient.

Smalltalk is an object-oriented language. An object-oriented language describes computations as objects which communicate by sending messages to one another. For example, in Smalltalk the expression "5 + 3" is viewed as sending the "+" message with an argument of 3 to the object 5. In traditional languages, the same expression would be viewed as applying an operation, +, to two numbers, or calling the + function with two arguments.

At the implementation level, objects may, like Pascal record and arrays for example, be merely contiguous regions of memory. Similarly, messages may be implemented as function calls. But Smalltalk objects are distinguished from objects in traditional programming languages because the internal state of an object is hidden to all other objects and is accessible only by sending a message to the object. This property, called abstraction, makes it impossible to corrupt inadvertently the internal state of an object, as can be done in many conventional programming languages. For example, say that we wish to implement a stack in Pascal. We may choose to represent the stack as an array with an integer variable which acts as an indication of the top of the stack. We then write push and pop procedures for the stack. As long as the programmer confines use of the stack to the push and pop operations, no danger can result, but nothing prevents the programmer from changing the stack structure by directly modifying the array or the integer variable. If we were to implement stacks in Smalltalk, we would choose to represent the stack as a single object which would respond to two messages, push and pop. The stack could be implemented internally by an array and an integer, as in Pascal. We should say in Smalltalk jargon that a stack object has two instance variables, an array and an integer. As in Pascal, we would write push

and pop operations, called methods in Smalltalk. In Smalltalk, however, no part of the program except the push and pop methods would have access to the internal representation of the stack, so bugs in which the contents of the stack are inadvertently changed cannot occur. This behavior arises from the fact that an object can handle only those methods which are written for it, and no others. If only push and pop are written for stacks, then stacks will accept only those messages. In particular, stacks will not accept messages which request access to the array or integer they contain.

The abstraction property has been shown to be extremely important to the development of large, bug-free software systems. As a result, many recent programming languages incorporate it, including Ada and Modula-2. Smalltalk goes beyond these languages in that all data structures have this property; Ada and Modula-2 still permit data structures of the Pascal variety to exist. But should the Smalltalk programmer really want an object's internals to be visible, nothing prevents him or her from supplying methods which allow modification of its internal structure. In addition to abstraction, Smalltalk's object-oriented metaphor also contains the idea of inheritance. Objects are grouped into classes, which correspond roughly to the types of traditional languages like Pascal. For instance, the Smalltalk implementation of stacks would consist of a class, Stack, which described the instance variables of a stack object and contained the methods push and pop. Here is part of what such a class might look like:

```
class name            Stack
instance variable names         array, topIndex
instance methods

 push:value
    array at:topIndex put:value.
    topIndex <- topIndex + 1.

 pop
    topIndex <-topIndex −1.
    ↑ array at: topIndex.
```

The leftarrow (<-) is used for variable assignment, and the uparrow (↑) indicates that the value of the expression should be returned from the message sent. To use a stack, we would first create an instance of the Stack class by using the new message and then send push and pop message to it. The pop messages would return the top value of the stack:

```
myStack <- Stack new.
myStack push: 1.
myStack push: 2.
myStack pop.
   2
myStack pop.
   1
```

Now let us suppose we wish to implement a more general data structure, a dequeue, which allows pushes and pops from the top as well as the bottom of the array. Stack already contains much of what we need: the array and the index to its top, and the methods for push and pop. To make the new class, Dequeue, share these features of Stack, we make Dequeue a subclass of Stack or to put it another way, we make Stack the superclass of Dequeue. A class inherits its superclass's methods and instance variables. That is, any instance variable of the superclass are also instance variables of the subclass. So Dequeue would automatically have the array and top-of-stack index of Stack, as well as its push and pop methods. All we would have to add would be an index to the bottom of the array, and the methods bPush and bPop for pushing and popping from the bottom of the array. Depending on how we chose to implement a dequeue, we might not have to change the push and pop methods we wrote for Stack: they will be called automatically when we send a push or pop message to an object of class Dequeue, by virtue of the fact that Dequeue is a subclass of Stack. Inheritance extends the traditional notion of data type in a very powerful way, because it allows the programmer to view his or her objects as having many properties in common, and frees him or her from the need to reimplement identical operations for a variety of data types. Another example should demonstrate how useful this feature can be. Let us consider writing an adventure-style computer game, a la Zork. Object-oriented languages are ideal for this task because adventure games are concerned with the movement and change of objects like the adventurer, monsters, weapons, treasures, and so on. If we were to implement an adventure game in Smalltalk, we would want each type of object to be a class. We might begin by having a class AdventureObject, since certain things will be common to all our objects; for instance, they will all have some location, so AdventureObject would have an instance variable called location. Furthermore, one would wish to allow the player to examine any object in the game, even though many may be uninteresting. We could define a method "examine" for AdventureObject which should simply print on the screen, "I see nothing interesting about that." This would act as the default for all subclasses of AdventureObject. If we wish to override that method for some class, we need merely redefine it in that class. For example, examining a room should produce a description of the room, which is the text string associated with each room. So in the Room class, we would write a method called examine which would print out this string. When a room receives an examine message, it will use its own method for examine rather that the one in AdventureObject; another subclass of AdventureObject would use the method in AdventureObject, unless it, too, explicitly overrode the method. It is important to note that nowhere in the code do we need to check the type of an object and call the appropriate code, as we might have to do in, say, a Pascal version of the game. In Smalltalk, inheritance takes care of this automatically: we need merely send the object an examine message, and the right code will be executed. To continue with our adventure game example, the AdventureObject class could have

AnimateObject and InanimateObject as subclasses. Among the subclasses of the former would be Adventurer and Monster, while Room and Treasure would be subclasses of the latter. We might wish to further subdivide Monster into the various species of monster the game contains. This class hierarchy simplifies the programming of the game, since when writing the code for a particular type of object, we need only worry about what can happen to that object.

Smalltalk is actually much more than a programming language. It is an entire environment, including editor, compiler, debugger, and many other tools to aid in software development. Smalltalk's user interface is in the mouse-and-windows style of the Apple Lisa and Macintosh—indeed, Smalltalk was the inspiration for the Apple machines' user interface. And as the Macintosh and Lisa environments are extended to encompass more types of software, a new standard will emerge which will be characterized by the visual display characteristics of both the Macintosh and its predecessor, the Lisa. This standard is already evident in current releases of Macintosh software which utilize the most visual elements of the Smalltalk environment.

Smalltalk's major strengths are: an excellent user interface, a powerful programming development environment, and a single, powerful computational metaphor: the sending of messages to objects. The metaphor is powerful because it is both simple and general. It can represent any computation and is not tied to the serial, von Neumann architecture of present-day computers. In addition, Smalltalk uses a clean embodiment of abstraction in the concept of object. Abstraction allows for safer, less buggy, more robust software. Smalltalk has a powerful type of system using inheritance which allows many types of objects to share the same methods and instance variables. Smalltalk's only serious weakness is that it demands a fast processor and a great deal of memory in order to run at reasonable speeds. Thus an efficient implementation of Smalltalk on a microcomputer is a very difficult undertaking. This and the relative youth of the language are the reasons no microcomputer implementation has yet appeared. But the fact that Apple has Smalltalk running on the Lisa indicates that a Smalltalk implementation for microcomputers will not long be absent from the market.

For more information: The group at Xerox PARC which designed Smalltalk has written three books on the language, all published by Addison-Wesley, Reading, Massachusetts. *Smalltalk-80: The Language and Its Implementation,* by Adele Goldberg and David Robson (1983), provides complete details on implementing the language. *Smalltalk-80: The Interactive Programming Environment,* by Adele Goldberg (1984), discusses the Smalltalk environment, including the compiler, editor, and debugger. *Smalltalk-80: Bits of History, Words of Advice,* by Glenn Krasner (1983), describes the implementations of Smalltalk by four selected groups outside of Xerox. It provides invaluable hints on optimizing the language for particular computing environments. A fourth book, *Smalltalk-80: Creating a User Interface and Graphical Applications,* is in press.

SMALLTALK GLOSSARY

Unlike most programming languages which have a few simple statements and constructs like IF...THEN or WHILE...DO, the basic Smalltalk system contains some sixty classes and hundreds of messages. For a complete list see the 700-page book *Smalltalk-80: The Language and Its Implementation*. We provide here only the most important of the classes and messages.

Block Context.

Blocks represent pieces of Smalltalk code. Blocks are not actual Smalltalk objects, however; when code containing a block is compiled, an instance of this class is created which contains the code for the block along with other information (such as the method in which the block occurred). Block contexts accept several messages which make them useful in implementing a variety of control structures, including loops and concurrent processes.

value.   The receiver evaluates itself (in other words, the block context's code is executed) and its value is returned.

value: anObject.   This type of value message is used for blocks with one argument. Similar messages exist for blocks with more than one argument.

WhileTrue: aBlock.   The receiver sends itself a value message. If the result is true, it sends the argument a value message and begins again. If false, it returns. For example, we could implement the factorial function n*(n−1)*(n−2)*...*1 in Smalltalk as follows:
```
answer <-1.
count <-n.
[count > 1] while True:
   [answer <- answer*count.
   count <- count -1].
     answer.
```

whileFalse: aBlock.   The receiver sends itself a value message. If the result is false, it sends the argument a value message and begins again. If true, it returns.

fork.   Creates a new process and schedules it. The process will run the receiver's code. For example, to sort a list as a separate process, we could say: [newlist <- list sort] fork.

newProcess.   Creates a new process without scheduling it.

newProcessWith: argumentArray.   Like newProcess, but for blocks which take arguments.

forkAt: priority.   Like fork, but sets the priority level of the process.

Boolean.

This class contains two subclasses, True and False. The IF...THEN statement of many computer languages is implemented in Smalltalk by the following messages, which are sent to instances of Boolean.

ifTrue: aBlock.   If an instance of class True receives this message, it will evaluate the block (by sending it a value message). If an instance of class False receives it, it does nothing. For example, x > 0 ifTrue. [x <- x + 1]. When the value of the variable x (which in this case should be a number) gets the > message with the argument zero, it returns an instance of class True or False, depending on whether it is greater or less than zero. The returned object is then sent the ifTrue: message.

ifFalse: aBlock.   If an instance of class False receives this message, it will evaluate the block (by sending it a value message). If an instance of class True receives it, it does nothing.

ifTrue: Block1 ifFalse: Block2.   Like an IF...THEN...ELSE construct. If the receiver is an instance of class True it sends a value message to Block1 and ignores Block2. If the receiver is an instance of class False it sends a value message to Block2 and ignores Block1.

ifFalse: Block1 ifTrue: Block2.   As above, with the order reversed.

and: aBlock.   If the receiver is true (i.e., of class True) it returns the value of the block; if false, it returns false immediately.

or: aBlock.   If the receiver is true, it returns true immediately. If false, it returns the value of the block.

Boolean also supports common logical operators:

& aBoolean.   Returns true if both the receiver or the argument are true; otherwise, returns false.

| aBoolean.   Returns true if either the receiver or the argument is true; otherwise, returns false.

not.   If the receiver is true, it returns false; if false, it returns true.

eqv: aBoolean.   Returns true if the receiver and the argument are both true, or both false; if they differ, returns false.

xor: aBoolean.   Returns true if either the receiver is true or the argument is true, but not both; otherwise, returns false.

Character.

This class is used to represent ASCII characters. A character can be written literally by preceding it with a dollar sign: $X represents the character X.

asciivalue.   Returns an integer which is the ASCII value of the receiver.

digitValue.   Returns the number corresponding to the receiver, where 0 corresponds to the character $0, 1 to $1, and so on up to 35 for $Z.

isAlphaNumeric.   Returns true if the receiver is a letter or a number.

isDigit.   Returns true if the receiver is a digit.

isLetter.   Returns true if the receiver is a letter.

isLowerCase.   Returns true if the receiver a lowercase letter.

isUpperCase.   Returns true if the receiver is an uppercase letter.

isSeparator.   Returns true if the receiver is a separator, character space, tab, form feed or line feed.

isVowel.   Returns true if the receiver is a vowel (a, e, i, o, or u)

Class, ClassDescription, and Behavior.

Classes are objects, too, and are instances of class Class. Class is a subclass of ClassDescription, which is a subclass of Behavior. These three classes support several important messages. Behavior supplies a minimum description of classes and supports the Smalltalk compiler.

methodDictionary: aDictionary.   Makes the argument the method dictionary (the association of methods with messages) of the receiver.

addSelector: selector withMethod: compiledMethod.   Adds the message selector and the method to the receiver's method dictionary.

compile: code.   code may be either a string or a stream. The compiler is called on the string and if successful, a compiled method is returned.

compile: code notifying: requestor.   Like compile, but notifies requestor if an error occurs.

recompile: selector.   Compiles the method associated in the method dictionary with selector.

decompile: selector.   Decompiles the method associated with selector into a string, which is the source code.

compileAll.   Compiles all the methods in the method dictionary of the receiver.

compileAllSubclasses.   Compiles all the methods in the dictionaries of the receiver's subclasses.

new.   Creates an instance of the receiver. For example, if there is a class Monster, then joe<- Monster new creates a new instance of that class and assigns it to the variable joe.

basicNew.   Like new, but cannot be overridden by other classes.

new: anInteger.   Creates an instance of the receiver and allocates anInteger spaces for instance variables. This form of new is used for objects that use indexed instance variables, such as arrays and strings.

basicNew: anInteger.   Like new: anInteger except that it cannot be overridden.

superclass: aClass.   Makes the argument the superclass of the receiver.

addSubclass: aClass.   Makes the argument a subclass of the receiver.

remove Subclass: aClass.   Removes the argument from the subclasses of the receiver.

selectors.   Returns a set of all the message selectors in the receiver.

allSelectors.   Returns a set of all the message selectors the receiver can understand. This includes all its own selectors, plus all the selectors of its superclasses.

compiledMethodAt: selector.   Returns the compiled method associated with the selector.

sourceCodeAt: selector.   Returns the source code associated with the selector.

allInstances.   Returns a set of the instances of the receiver.

someInstance.   Returns some single instance of the receiver.

instanceCount.   Returns the number of instances of the receiver which currently exist.

instVarNames.   Returns an array of the names of the receiver's instance variables.

subclassInstVarNames.   Returns a set of the instance variable names of the receiver's subclasses.

allInstVarNames.   Returns an array of the instance variable names of the receiver and all its superclasses.

classVarNames.   Returns a set of the receiver's class variable names.

allClassVarNames.   Returns a set of the receiver's class variable names, and all those of its superclasses.

sharedPools.   Returns a set of the names of the pool dictionaries of the receiver.

allSharedPools.   Returns a set of the names of the receiver's and its superclasses' pool dictionaries.

subclasses.   Returns a set with the immediate subclasses of the receiver.

allSubclasses.   Returns a set with the subclasses of the receiver, and the subclasses of its subclasses, and so on.

withAllSubclasses.   Returns a set of the receiver and all its subclasses.

superclass.   Returns the receiver's superclass.

allSuperclasses.   Returns all the superclasses of the receiver.

hasmethods.   Returns true if there are any methods in the receiver's method dictionary.

includesSelector: selector.   Returns true if the method with the given selector is in the receiver's method dictionary.

canUnderstand: selector. Returns true if the receiver can respond to the message selector given.

whichClassIncludesSelector: selector.   Returns the first class on the receiver's superclass chain which contains the selector in its method dictionary. Returns nil if there is no such class.

whichSelectorsAccess: instVarName.   Returns a set of the message selectors which mention the instance variable name.

whichSelectorsReferTo: anObject.   Returns a set of those selectors which refer to the given object.

inheritsFrom: aClass.   Returns true if receiver is a subclass of the given class.

allSubclassesDo: aBlock.   Evaluates the block for each of the subclasses of the receiver.

allSuperclassesDo: aBlock.   Evaluates the block for each of the superclasses of the receiver.

allInstancesDo: aBlock.   Evaluates the block for all of the instances of the receiver.

allSubInstancesDo: aBlock.   Evaluates the block for all of the instances of the receiver's subclasses.

selectSubIcasses: aBlock.   Returns a set of those subclasses for which the block evaluates to true.

selectSuperclasses: aBlock.   Returns a set of those superclasses for which the block evaluates to true.

ClassDescription.

Class ClassDescription supplies the following additional messages:

name.   Returns a string which is the name of the receiver.

comment.   Returns a string which is the comment for the receiver.

comment: aString.   Sets the receiver's comment to the argument.

addInstVarName: aString.   Adds the string to the list of instance variable names of the receiver.

removeInstVarName: aString.   Removes the string from the list of instance variable names of the receiver.

category.   Returns the system organization category of the receiver.

category: aString.   Sets the category of the receiver to the string.

removeCategory: aString.   Removes each of the messages in the category, then removes the category itself.

whichCategoryIncludesSelector: selector.   Returns the name of the category, of the selector, or nil if not found.

fileOutOn: aFileStream.   Writes a description of the receiver onto the file specified by the stream.

fileOutChangedMessages: setOfChanges on: aFileStream. Writes onto the file messages in the set.

Class ClassDescription supplies the following additional messages:

addClassVarName: aString.   Adds the argument to the list of the receiver's class variables.

removeClassVarName: aString. Removes the argument from the list of the receiver's class variables. Signals an error if it is not the name of a class variable or if the variable is still being used by one of the receiver's methods.

addSharedPool: aDictionary. Adds the argument as a pool of shared variables.

removeSharedPool: aDictionary. Removes the argument from the receivers shared variable pools.

classPool. Returns the dictionary of the receiver's class variables.

initialize. Initializes the receivers class variables.

subclass: classNameString
instanceVariableNames: stringInstVarNames
classVariableNames: stringOfClassVarNames
poolDictionaries: stringOfPoolNames
category: categoryNameString. Creates a subclass of the receiver. The arguments supply the appropriate values for the various components of the newly created subclass.

Collection.

This class and its many subclasses deal with groups of objects. Many common data structures are provided as subclasses of Collection. LinkedList, Array, String, Set, Bag (like a set, but allowing more than one occurrence of an element) and Dictionary (a hash table) are all subclasses of Collection. Some less common data structures which are provided are Bitmap, Text (a string with associated font and formatting information), SortedCollection (a list that maintains its elements in sorted order) and Interval (a finite sequence of integers). Nearly all subclasses of Collection respond to the following messages:

add newObject. Adds the object to the receiver. For example, if s is a set, we could add the element 3 by saying s add: 3.

addAll: aCollection. Adds all the elements of the argument to the receiver.

remove: oldObject. Removes the object from the collection. Reports an error if the collection did not contain the object. Returns oldObject. For example, if 3 is in the set s, then s remove 3 will remove it from the set and return 3.

remove: oldObject if Absent: anExceptionBlock. Like remove, but instead of reporting an error evaluates the block and returns its value. For example, if in-

stead of causing an error you wished to return nil, you could send the collection the message: remove: oldObject ifAbsent: [nil].

removeAll: aCollection. Removes all the elements in the argument from the receiver.

includes: anObject. Returns true if the argument is in the collection.

isEmpty. Returns true if the collection contains no objects.

occurrencesOf: anObject. Returns the number of times the object occurs in the receiver.

do: aBlock. Evaluates the block for each element of the receiver. do can often be used where a loop would be needed in another programming language. For example, to print out all the elements of an array A on a stream S (the stream could be a file or the screen) all one needs to write is A do: [:element| element printOn: S]. If one wishes to write a FOR loop as in Pascal or BASIC, one can send an interval a do message. Explicit creation of the interval is not even necessary, since integers themselves respond to the appropriate messages. For example, the statement 2 to: 100 by: 2 do: [i| i printOn: S] will print all the even numbers between 2 and 100 on the stream S.

select: aBlock. Evaluates the block for each element of the receiver and creates a new collection which contains only those elements for which the block evaluates to true. For example, if we had a set s of integers and we wanted a new set which contained only those elements of s which were even and divisible by 3, we could get that with: s select: [:element| (element even) and:[element //3) = 0]].

reject: aBlock. This is similar to select, except only those elements are chosen for which the block evaluates to false.

collect: aBlock. Returns a new collection which contains the value of the block on each element of the old collection. For example, say we had a string (which is a kind of collection) called s, and a method encode for class Character which returned some encoding of the character. Then to produce a new string which is the encoding of the old, we need merely say: s collect: [:char| char encode]. As another example, say we had an array a of integers and we wanted a similar array which contained the squares of the integers. We could write: a collect: [:num | num squared].

detect: aBlock. Returns the first element found in the receiver for which the block evaluates to true. If it is false for all the elements, reports an error. For example, to see if a set s contains the number 5, we could do s detect: [:element| element = 5].

detect: aBlock ifNone: exceptionBlock.   Like detect:, but instead of reporting an error evaluates exceptionBlock and returns its value. For example, if we wished to return the first element in array a which was less than zero, and zero if there is no such element, we could write: a detect: [:element | element<0] ifNone [0].

inject: thisValue into: binaryBlock.   binaryBlock takes two arguments. It is evaluated for each element of the receiver as the second argument. The first argument is the previous value of the block. The starting first argument is thisValue. For example, to take the sum of an array a of numbers, we could write a inject: 0 into: [:oldValue :element| oldvalue + element]. If we wished to take the product of all the even elements, we could write a inject: 1 into: [:oldValue :element| element even ifTrue: [oldValue * element] ifFalse: [oldvalue]].

asBag.   Returns a bag with the same elements as the receiver. This allows conversion between different kinds of collections.

asSet.   Returns a set with the same elements as the receiver.

asOrderedCollection.   Returns an ordered collection with the same elements as the receiver.

asSortedCollection.   Returns a sorted collection with the same elements as the receiver. The function used for sorting is < = (less than or equal to).

asSortedCollection: aBlock.   Returns a sorted collection with the same elements as the receiver. The functions used for sorting are described by the block.

Dictionary.

The subclasses Dictionary and IdentityDictionary are used to represent associations between pairs of items, usually called keys, and their values. The only difference between the two is that the former uses the = message for comparing keys, while the latter uses = =.

at: key.   Returns the value associated with the given key in the receiver. Reports an error if the key is not found. For example, if we had a dictionary spouses associating wives and husbands, and we had previously done spouses at: #Sheila put: #Bob, then spouses at: #Sheila would return #Bob. (The pound sign # before the names indicates that they are Smalltalk symbols, that is, unique strings.)

at: key ifAbsent: aBlock.   Like at: but instead of reporting an error evaluates the block and returns its value.

at: key put: value.   Associates the value with the key and stores it in the receiver.

associationAt: key.   Returns the association (an object consisting of both the key and its value). If the key is not found reports an error.

associationAt: key ifAbsent: aBlock.   Like associationAT: but instead of reporting an error evaluates aBlock and returns its value.

keyAtValue: value.   Returns the key corresponding to the first value found which equals value. Returns nil if no value found. For example, spouses keyAtValue: #Bob would return #Sheila if that corresponded to the first occurrence of #Bob in the dictionary.

keyAtValue: value ifAbsent: aBlock.   Like keyAtValue but instead of returning nil it evaluates the block and returns its value.

keys.   Returns a set of all the receiver's keys.

values.   Returns a bag containing all the receiver's values.

includesAssociation: anAssociation.   Returns true if the association is present in the receiver.

includesKey: key.   Returns true if the receiver has that key.

removeAssociation: anAssociation.   Removes the association from the receiver and returns it.

removeKey: key.   Removes the key and its associated value from the receiver. If key is not present, reports an error.

removeKey: key ifAbsent: aBlock.   Like removeKey: but instead of reporting an error evaluates the block and returns its value.

associationsDo: aBlock.   Evaluates the block for each association in the receiver.

keysdo: a Block.   Evaluates the block for each key in the receiver. For example, if we had two dictionaries d1 and d2 and we wanted to remove all the associations in d2 that were also in d1, we could say d1 keysDo: [key| d2 removeKey: key ifAbsent: []]. The empty block indicates that we wish to do nothing if d2 does not contain the key. We could also have written this as: d1 associationsDo: [:assoc| d2 removeAssociation: assoc].

Sequenceable Collection.

The subclass SequenceableCollection, which includes arrays, responds to these messages in addition to those defined for all collections.

at anIndex. Returns the object stored at that position of the receiver. For example, if s is an instance of SequenceableCollection, and we had previously done a at: 5 put: true then a at: 5 would return true.

at: anIndex put: anObject. Stores the object at the given position in the receiver.

atAll: aCollection put: anObject. Associates the object with each element of the collection in the receiver. For example, if s is a set containing 1, 3, and 5 and sc is a sequence collection, then sc atAll: s put: true would put the value true in sc an indexes 1, 3, and 5.

atAllPut: anObject. Puts the argument in all the positions of the receiver.

first. Returns the first element of the receiver.

last. Returns the last element of the receiver.

indexOf: anElement. Returns the index of the given element in the receiver. Returns 0 if the element is not found.

indexOf: anElement ifAbsent: aBlock. Like indexOf:,but if the element is not found evaluates the block and returns its value.

indexOf SubCollection a SubCollection startingAt: anIndex. If the elements of the subcollection appear in order in the receiver, returns the index of the first element that matches. If nothing matches, returns 0. Starts the search at the given index. For example, given two sequenceable collections sc1 which contain the characters $a, $b, $c and $d and indexes 1, 2, 3, and 4 respectively, and sc2 which contains the characters $b and $c at indexes 1 and 2, then sc1 indexOfSubCollection sc2 startingAt: 1 would return 2, since a match occurs at index 2, but sc1 indexOfSubCollection sc2 startingAt: 3 would return 0.

indexOfSubCollection: aSubCollection startingAT:anIndex ifAbsent: aBlock. As above, but instead of returning 0, this command evaluates the block and then returns its value.

replaceFrom: start to: stop with: replacementCollection. Replaces the elements of the receiver starting at index start and ending at indexstop with the elements of replacementCollection. For example, given sc1 and sc2 as defined above, sc1 replaceFrom: 1 to: with sc2 would change sc1 to have the characters $b, $c, $c, $d.

replaceFrom: start to: stop with: replacementCollection startingAt: repstart. As above, but starts at the element of the replacement collection whose index is repstart.

aSequenceableCollection. Concatenation. Returns a copy of the receiver with the elements of the argument added at the end.

copyFrom: start to: stop. Returns a new sequenceable collection whose first element is at index start of the receiver and whose last is at index stop.

copyReplaceAll: oldSubCollection with: newSubCollection. Returns a copy of the receiver in which all occurrences of the first argument have been replaced by the second.

copyReplaceFrom: start to: stop with: replacementCollection. Returns a copy of the receiver with the elements between indexed start and stop replaced by the collection given.

copyWith: newElement. Returns a copy of the receiver with the argument added at the end.

copyWithout: oldElement. Returns a copy of the receiver with oldElement deleted.

findFirst: aBlock. Returns the index of the first element of the receiver for which the block returns true.

findLast: aBlock. Returns the index of the last element of the receiver for which the block returns true.

reverseDo: aBlock. Evaluates the block for each element of the receiver, starting at the last and moving in order to the first.

with: aSequenceableCollection do: aBlock. Evaluates the block for each element of the receiver and the corresponding element of the argument. For example, say we had two sequenceable collections sc1 and sc2 of the same length, and we wished to add the corresponding elements of the collections to a dictionary d as keys and values. We could do this with: sc1 with: sc2 do: [:key :value| d at: key put :value].

String.

String is a subclass of SequenceableCollection which responds to the following additional messages:

< aString. Returns true if the receiver is lexicographically less than the argument. Case of alphabetic characters is ignored.

<= aString. Returns true if the receiver is lexicographically less than or equal to the argument. Case of alphabetic characters is ignored.

> aString. Returns true if the receiver is lexicographically greater than the argument. Case of alphabetic characters is ignored.

>= aString. Returns true if the receiver is lexicographically greater than or equal to the argument. Case of alphabetic characters is ignored.

match: aString. The receiver is treated as a pattern. Two "wildcard characters," # and *, have special meanings: the first matches any single character in the argument, the second any sequence of zero or more characters. Returns true if the string matches the receiver. For example, '*ous*' match: 'houses' returns true.

Object.

This class is at the top of the Smalltalk class hierarchy. Every Smalltalk object inherits the methods defined in Object, so the messages it defines are of a very general nature.

class. Returns the class of the receiver. For example, 12 class returns the class SmallInteger.

isKindOf: aClass: Returns true if the receiver's class is a subclass of the argument. For example, 3isKindOf: Object is true (because everything is a kind of object).

isMemberOf: aClass. Returns true if the receiver is actually an instance of the argument.

respondsTo: aSymbol. Returns true if aSymbol is the name of a message to which the receiver can respond.

== anObject. Returns true if the argument is the same object as the receiver. For example, x <- Monster new. y <- x. x == y would return true. However, x <- Monster new. x == Monster new returns false, because the two Monster objects are distinct.

= anObject. The implementation of = depends on the subclass that wishes to use it. For numbers, = would mean numerical equality; for arrays, it would mean equality of corresponding components.

--anObject. This is the negation of ==.

-=anObject. This is the negation of =.

copy. Returns another object just like the receiver. Defaults to shallowCopy, but may be redefined by subclasses.

shallowCopy. Just copies the object itself, not its instance variables. After a shallowCopy, the new object shares the same instance variables with the old.

deepCopy. Copies the object and all its instance variables.

at: index. If the object has indexed instance variables, returns the value of the variable at index. If it does not, or if index is greater than the number of instance variables, then indicates an error.

at: index put: anObject. Makes the argument anObject be the value of the index<u>th</u> indexed instance variable of the receiver.

basicAt: index. Like at: index, but cannot be overridden by any subclass.

basicAt: index put: anObject. Same as at:put:, but cannot be overridden by any subclass.

size. Returns the number of indexed instance variables of the receiver.

basicSize. Like size, but cannot be overridden by any subclass.

printString. Returns a string which is the printed representation of the receiver.

printOn: aStream. Prints a representation of the object on the stream given.

storeString. Returns a string which is a representation of the receiver which allows the reconstruction of the receiver.

storeOn: aStream. Like storeString, but prints the value on the stream given as argument. The difference between the storing and printing operations are as follows: the printing operations attempt to provide a simple view of the object. For instance, a set with the elements 1, 2, and 3 might print our as set(1 2 3). The store operations are used when it will be necessary to reconstruct the object exactly. These print out actual Smalltalk code which, when executed, will create the object. The above set might be displayed by a store message as: (Set new add: 1, add: 2, add: 3).

error: aString. Tells the user an error occurred, and prints the string.

isNil. Returns false.

notNil. Returns true.

Number.

This is the class of all numbers. Its subclasses include Float, Fraction, Integer and SmallInteger. All numbers respond to the following kinds of messages: the usual numeric operations +, −, * and /, comparison operators such as =, >, <, and ≠ (not equal); and some others.

// aNumber. Returns the interger quotient of the receiver divided by the argument. (e.g., 14 // 4 will return the integer 3.)

\\aNumber Returns the remainder gotten by dividing the receiver by the argument. (e.g., 14\\ returns 2.)

abs. Returns the absolute value of the receiver.

negated. Returns the negation of the receiver.

reciprocal. Returns 1 divided by the receiver.

exp. Returns the exponential of the receiver (e^x).

ln. Returns the natural logarithm of the receiver.

log: aNumber. Returns the logarithm to the base aNumber of the receiver. (e.g., 100 log: 10 returns 2.)

raisedTo: aNumber. Returns the receiver raised to the given power.

raisedToInteger: anInteger. As above, but the argument must be an integer. (e.g., 3 raisedToInteger 4 returns 81.)

sqrt. Returns the square root of the receiver.

squared. Returns the square of the receiver.

even. Returns true if the number is even, otherwise false.

odd. Opposite of the above.

negative. Returns true if the receiver is negative (<0), otherwise false.

positive. Returns true if the receiver is positive (>0) or zero, otherwise false.

strictlyPositive. Returns true if the receiver is greater than zero, otherwise false.

sign. Returns 1 if the receiver is greater than zero, −1 if it is less, and zero if it equals zero.

ceiling. Returns the smallest integer greater than the receiver.

floor. Returns the largest integer less than the receiver.

truncated. Returns the number truncated toward zero.

truncateTo: aNumber. Returns the nearest multiple of the argument to the receiver, toward zero.

rounded. Rounds the receiver to the nearest integer.

roundTo: aNumber. Returns a nearest multiple of the argument to the receiver.

degreesToRadians. Converts the receiver, assumed to be degrees, to radians.

radiansToDegrees. Converts the receiver, assumed to be radians, to degrees.

Integer.

Integer has some additional messages defined. Some of these messages make it possible to treat the integer as a string of bits.

timesRepeat: aBlock. Does the block the number of times of the receiver. This is useful for simple loops. For example, 10 timesRepeat: [x <- x squared] will square the value in x ten times.

factorial. Computes the factorial function, n*(n−1) *...1, of the receiver.

gcd: anInteger. Returns the greatest common divisor of the receiver and the argument. (e.g., 55 gcd 30 returns 5.)

lcm: anInteger. Returns the least common multiple of the receiver and the argument.

allMask: anInteger. Treats the argument as a bit mask. Returns true if all the bits which are 1 in the argument are 1 in the receiver.

anyMask: anInteger. Treats the argument as a bit mask. returns true if any bits which are 1 in the argument are 1 in the receiver.

noMask: anInteger. Treats the argument as a bit mask. Returns true if none of the bits which are 1 in the argument are 1 in the receiver.

bitAnd: anInteger. Returns the bitwise logical and of the receiver and the argument.

bitOr: anInteger. Returns the bitwise logical or of the receiver and the argument.

bitXor: anInteger. Returns the bitwise logical exclusive or of the receiver and the argument.

bitAt: index.   Returns the value of the bit at the position index in the receiver.

highBit.   Returns the index of the high-order bit of the receiver. This allows the programmer to determine the number of bits being used to represent integers.

bitInvert.   Returns the bitwise complement of the receiver.

bitShift: an Integer.   Returns the value of the receiver shifted by the number of the bits that it has received.

SOFTWARE COMMAND LANGUAGES

The following subsection examines the query languages and user interfaces of some of the more popular microcomputer business applications packages. These command-driven software systems have often been described as programming languages themselves because they function both as user-oriented direct input languages and as internal code generators. Accordingly, they represent an intermediate step between the personal computer user who can structure his or her personal or business database or financial evaluator and the final object code for the particular computer which generates a highly formatted output framework for the user's data.

Command-driven query systems are not a new phenomenon. From the first implementations of business and professional computer systems, programmers wrote user or operator interfaces and query protocols which were designed to facilitate efficient data entry and structured or formatted retrieval. And the computer vendors themselves often supplied software packages tailored to individual business office and data processing applications. These self-contained business packages helped to transform the business computer from the hardware-intensive number-crunching mainframe of large corporations and university research facilities into the efficient operator-oriented information processing tool that it is in most small and intermediate business environments today.

By the end of the 1970s, the emergence of the desktop personal computer as a potential business machine established a third tier in professional applications computing. All that was needed to integrate the personal computer completely into the business and office environment was a software concept which would allow the independent processing of information to take place without the necessity of an operator's having to learn a structured programming language. That software concept was the "off-the-shelf" or "canned" business applications package which combined ease of learning and operation with a powerful processing and output capability. In today's business environment, these types of packages—dBASE, VisiCalc, SuperCalc, MultiPlan, Lotus 1-2-3, Symphony, and Framework—are really command query systems themselves. They have their own command structures and mini operating systems which allow their operators to program complex data processing and retrieval routines with a series of keystrokes that represent hundreds of lines of code. In fact, these software packages have now become a subset of programming languages, and as such they represent an important milestone in the evolution of computer language systems. It can even be argued that what today's business software represents is a higher-level programming language, a real-world user interface that is oriented more to specific techniques of data manipulation than to driving a compiler or interpreter.

This subsection evaluates the major business database and financial applications packages as query systems. It discusses dBASE II, VisiCalc, SuperCalc, MultiPlan, Lotus 1-2-3, Symphony, and Framework from a command and operating perspective against the background of high-level programming languages. Each entry discusses the design and structure of the software, explains the command and query language that the software presents to the user, shows how the product is used within the professional environment, and, for the electronic spreadsheets, compares the products with one another along an evolutionary scale of development.

Each entry also contains a glossary of the command language and an explanation of the way that the command or query language operates as a type of high-level language. What will be evident, for example, even from the most cursory examination of dBase II, Lotus 1-2-3, VisiCalc, SuperCalc, Symphony, and Framework, is that the command and query languages in these applications software packages provide users with a type of programming environment. The programming environment, although rudimentary in VisiCalc and sophisticated in dBase and Framework, allows users to create their own designs for database and financial management.

The command and query languages occupy an interesting position in the universe of programming languages. First, they qualify as types of high-level languages because they behave as if they high-level languages: they define data types, they can assign values to variables, they can define logical branching operations, they address the operating system directly, and they also can be used to drive peripherals. Some, like Symphony and Framework include separate modules for telecommunications and file transfers between external databases and mainframe implementations and the data files that are managed by the software.

In both dBase and Framework, the high-level language facilities are extensive. Similarly, in Symphony, the facilities of a high-level language are translated into a sophisticated set of spreadsheet formulas with which users can create powerful financial models with logical branching capability. In other words, like the minicomputer business software of the 1960s, the language has become a system which can make the desktop computer a dedicated number cruncher, database manager, or word processor. On the one hand, the computer loses its identity as a personal computer but becomes, in return, a terminal that is driven by a business management program.

In fact, packages such as VisiCalc, SuperCalc, dBase II, Lotus, Symphony, and Framework have become so popular within their respective environments that they have almost become more important than the hardware itself and are considered to be one of the primary reasons that the personal computer has been accepted into the business environment.

After the introduction of VisiCalc in 1980, traditional electronic data processing managers began to feel the pressure of the personal computer's ability to access and sort quickly large blocks of data and present a user-defined set of financial models. VisiCalc and the other spreadsheet packages allowed users this capability because they used a command system that was very close to natural mathematical formulas.

COBOL, on the other hand, required that programmers maintain a strict syntactic approach to numerical calculation that was very difficult to change on demand. Also, the standard user interface of VisiCalc or SuperCalc was suited to the individual user who would query his or her system on a need-to-know basis. Software written in the traditional data processing languages such as COBOL and PL/I was structured so that reports and summaries were automated and accessible only through a highly defined system of passwords and query codes.

Yet both the financial spreadsheets and database managers and the mainframe system software sought to accomplish very similar goals: the processing of large amounts of data quickly and accurately and the translation of that data into a highly usable format.

The next generation of personal computer business software sought to model itself on the large mainframe packages without sacrificing transportability and ease of use. Lotus, Symphony, and Framework all provide the type of logical branching and conditional execution of calculations that exist in the data processing environment. However, in order to use these software features users have to become quasi programmers, working in a type of high-level language.

In this subsection, the entries and glossaries to the major business software will illustrate this hybrid quality of the command languages and show that these languages can be adapted to individual needs.

dBASE II

In 1981, Ashton-Tate released its dBASE II database management system, and since that time, dBASE has emerged as the yardstick against which all other microcomputer database systems are measured. The impressive list of functions can handle nearly any data file operation, from sorting on multiple keys to creating and printing customized reports to file structure modifications. Its built-in command programming language, once mastered, allows the user to create, in program files, entire menu-driven systems to facilitate database manipulation, report generation, file updating, and a host of other activities. For those with no time to learn the language, many companies offer dBASE-related products such as program generators and run-time applications software written in dBASE II.

The original version of dBASE II (there never was a dBASE I) was written for 8-bit computers running under the CP/M operating system. The updated 2.4 version can be run on 16-bit computers using PC- or MS-DOS, and is a more powerful programming and management tool than its predecessor. The dBASE system itself is made up of three separate files: DBASE.COM (32K), its overlay file DBASEOVR.COM (37K), and the help text file DBASEMSG.TXT.

There are some serious size constraints (65,535 records per file, 2 files open at a time, 64 memory variables in use at a time) which limit dBASE to small- to medium-sized operations, but they can be overcome through creative programming techniques. Users can create several different types of files: data files, which contain data in ASCII format; command files, or program files, made up of dBASE commands and remarks; index files, which contain information to make a database appear in a certain order for displays or reports; memory files, made up of user-defined variables; report form files, which contain the format for customized report forms; and text files, which are filled with ASCII character information. The programmer is most concerned with command, index, and data files.

dBASE II is a relational database system, which means it uses so-called flat files. These are files made up of individual records, which are in turn made up of data fields. In a relational system, the records are stored in the file sequentially, as if the file were a two-dimensional accountant's table. Each record would fill a column, and each entry in the column would be a field. File input/output is very simple: the USE command both opens and closes a file. Other I/O statements are generally simple one-line commands which can perform very powerful operations on the database in relatively short time. An index file contains pointers which point to the associated database and cause it to appear in a certain order. A special command, FIND, locates records in the database through the index file in a matter of one or two seconds, even in files with thousands of records. In this way, a sequential file can take on some of the benefits of a random access file. Other one-line commands allow updating from a second file, global data field replacements, and report generation.

File creation is fast and easy with dBASE. With the CREATE command, the user can build a file's structure in a few minutes, or in a few seconds by copying the format of another file. Writing command files is also relatively simple, with the somewhat awkward phrase MODIFY COMMAND allowing the user to both create and edit a program. To execute a program, simply type DO followed by the name of the program. The query language is easy for nonprogrammers to use, though some amount of dedication must be taken to learn all the commands and functions. As a bonus to those with an aversion to typing, dBASE needs only the first four letters of a command phrase to understand it. For example, instead of typing MODIFY COMMAND to edit a program, the programmer need only type MODI COMM. There is an error-handling dialog in version 2.4 which saves the user the time of reentering an entire line if a mistake is made in typing. The system redisplays the incorrect line, with a marker at the part in question, and allows the user to change all or part of the line, or abort completely. One negative aspect to the dBASE II package is the documentation. It is confusing to the novice, and frustrating to the experienced programmer because it does not convey the true power of many of the commands. While the 2.4 manual is an improvement over the earlier edition, it is nonetheless an inadequate guide to an excellent program.

The dBASE II programming language uses English-like commands similar to those in C, Pascal, and PL/I (IF...ELSE...ENDIF), and is relatively easy for the experienced programmer to learn, and the novice can pick it up after some practice. dBASE does allow programs to be called from within programs, in effect creating subroutines, and variables are passed between them. Like C, the language upon which dBASE II is based, commands are entered one to a line and logic "flows" from the top down to the bottom, or the end of the program. This makes the programs easy to write and easier to trace and debug than a language such as BASIC, where multiple statements are often crunched on a line to conserve disk space and speed run time.

While dBASE does not use line numbers, there are several ways to control program flow. The first is with the conditional IF...ELSE...ENDIF structure, common to many programming languages in one form or another. Quite simply, the program evaluates the expression stated after the word IF, and if it is true, then the following statement is executed. If it is false, the program falls through to the ELSE statement (if present) and continues execution. There must be a matching ENDIF for every IF, and IFs may be nested inside each other. The following simple example demonstrates the use of the IF statement. The program looks to see if the account number, stored in the variable ACCT:NO, is a 1000 or a 2000. If this condition is true, the amount in the account will be added to the running total and the error flag will be set to indicate no error. If the account number is any number other than 1000 or 2000, an error message is printed on the screen, and an error flag is set.

```
IF ACCT:NO="1000" .OR. ACCT:NO="2000"
  STORE TOTAL+AMOUNT TO TOTAL
  STORE "NO" TO ERRORELSE
  ? "ERROR! Invalid Account Number"
  STORE "YES" TO ERROR
ENDIF
```

The DO CASE structure is really a variation of the IF statement. But instead of evaluating only one expression, it will evaluate any number of expressions. Here's how it works: the program continues to evaluate each CASE until it finds a true one. The commands with that CASE are then executed, and control resumes after the ENDCASE statement. Like the IF command, the DO CASE must end with an ENDCASE, and may be nested according to standard logical rules. The OTHERWISE phrase performs like the ELSE does above. An example follows:

```
DO CASE
  CASE ACCT:NO="1000" .OR. ACCT:NO="2000"
    STORE 100 TO AMOUNT
  CASE ACCT:NO="3000"
    STORE 150 TO AMOUNT
  CASE ACCT:NO="4000"
    STORE 225 TO AMOUNT
  OTHERWISE
    ? "ERROR! INVALID ACCOUNT NUMBER"
    STORE "YES" TO ERROR
ENDCASE
```

The third program control structure is the iterative DO WHILE statement. This command is used to perform tasks until a certain condition is met. It is similar to the WHILE...WEND command in BASIC, or the WHILE...DO command in Pascal. dBASE permits unconditional looping within the DO WHILE through the LOOP command to retest the original condition before the ENDDO is reached. An example follows:

```
STORE 0 TO TOTAL,ERRORCOUNT
          (This initializes the variables to zero.)
DO WHILE TOTAL__5000
  SKIP
          (This advances to the next record in
          the file.)
  DO CASE
    CASE ACCT:NO="1000" .OR.
    ACCT:NO="2000"
    STORE 100 TO AMOUNT
  CASE ACCT:NO="3000"
    STORE 200 TO AMOUNT
  OTHERWISE
    ? "ERROR! INVALID ACCT:NO"+ACCT:NO
    STORE ERRORCOUNT+1 TO ERRORCOUNT
    LOOP
          (This causes the program to return to
          the DO WHILE.)
```

```
  ENDCASE
  STORE TOTAL+AMOUNT TO TOTAL
ENDDO
? "The Total for all Accounts is shown below"
? TOTAL
```

In the direct command mode, the cursor moves down one line after a command is entered, or information is displayed on the screen. A command is provided which allows the user control over the placement of the cursor and items to be printed on the screen, but is really only useful in the indirect (command file) mode. Its syntax is: @ x,y SAY variable/expression/constant, where x is any row between 0 and 23 (the 25th row is unavailable in version 2.4), and y is any column between 0 and 79. What follows the SAY can be a defined variable, a calculation of variables, or a letter, number, or any other ASCII character. When in the print mode, the @ ... SAY can be used to position output to the printer, including most escape or control codes. A complementary command is the GET, which is used to input operator-supplied information to a stored memory variable or a data field. It syntax is similar and in fact can be a part of the @ ... SAY itself. Information is read into the variable or field with the READ statement:

```
@ 5,22 SAY "Enter the part number code "
GET PART:NOREAD
@ 10,22 SAY "Part number selected is "+PART:NO
```

These two powerful commands allow the user to generate custom screens for any type of data entry or display. Version 2.4 also gives the programmer the added ability to use the computer's color capabilities to their fullest extent. The SET COLOR TO command will print all further output to the screen in the specified color, including underlining and reverse video on monochrome displays, and all foreground and background colors on color displays. One final screen formatting command should be mentioned—ERASE. This command simply clears the screen in a split second, similar to CLS in BASIC or DOS.

The language also provides for the logical operators AND, OR, and NOT, as well as the obligatory arithmetic and relational operators ($<$, $>$, $=$, etc.). In addition, dBASE supplies a number of string- and number-handling functions such as substring, instring, concatenation, string-to-numeric, and numeric-to-string operations. Three types of variables are allowed: character, numeric, and logical (true/false), and are easily created (STORE "Dana" TO NAME) and removed (RELEASE NAME). Memory variables can be saved to disk in memory files with the command SAVE TO <file name>, then recalled with RESTORE FROM <file name>. Output can be redirected to the printer (SET FORMAT TO PRINT, SET PRINT ON), or to a diskette file (SET ALTERNATE TO <file name>). The default disk drive may be changed, but path names are not allowed when specifying a file. Also, the system date may be changed, but dBASE does not access the system clock. Several debugging commands of limited use are provided: SET ECHO ON, which displays command file statements and their output on the screen; SET STEP ON, for stopping program execution after each command; and SET DEBUG ON, which prints the output of the previous two commands to the printer instead of cluttering up your screen.

Assembly language routines may be accessed through the CALL statement, as in many other languages, and memory locations can be manipulated with the POKE and PEEK commands as well. Some operating system-type functions can be performed from within dBASE, such as renaming files, deleting files, and pulling a directory of all or selected files.

The final aspect to the programming language which has not been covered is the use of macros, a tool whose true power is only vaguely hinted at in the manual. A macro is a character memory variable which can be recalled by placing an ampersand immediately before the variable name. When dBASE sees a macro anywhere in a program, it replaces the variable name in the program with the actual contents of that variable. The versatility of macros becomes more apparent after the programmer becomes familiar with them. A frequent use is in programs which must be used on different machines, and therefore must operate with different parameters. The configuration may be hard-coded into macros in the beginning lines of the program, or the macros may be interactively user-supplied at the start of the program run. For example, suppose that in a particular program, the diskette is to be inserted into the "C" drive and the data diskette is to be placed in the "A" drive:

```
STORE "C" TO DR1
STORE "A" TO DR2
          (These get stored at the beginning of the
          initial program.)
USE &DR2.ARMASTER
          (Opens the master A/R file
          ARMASTER.DBF on drive "A".)
DO &DR1.ARUPDATE
          (Executes the command file
          ARUPDATE.PRG on drive "C".)
```

A brief description of the nearly eighty commands is included below; the sixteen string and numeric functions are not discussed. Ashton-Tate offers a sample diskette with the dBASE II package which allows buyers to try out the features of dBASE on a limited basis. If the user is not satisfied, he or she need only return the sealed master diskette for a full refund. Along with the program itself, a dBASE II customer may use the services of the Ashton-Tate technical staff through their "Technical Hotline" phone number for any questions regarding dBASE and related products.

dBASE II was begun around 1978 by Wayne Ratliff, a former systems designer working at the Jet Propulsion Laboratory in California. The project started out as Vulcan, a primitive version of dBASE written for the early CP/M micros. It had some of the now-familiar phrases such as EDIT, APPEND, and LIST. Ratliff's sales of Vulcan were less than inspirational, but he kept improving the program anyway, convinced he had a good product. He programmed in straight 8080 assembler code to keep the program as fast as possible, and to conserve precious memory. In 1980, George Tate and Hal Lashlee discovered Vulcan, rechristened it dBASE II, and set out to sell the new product with an aggressive marketing campaign. The latest version, 2.4, came out in 1983 with improvements aimed at capturing a larger share of the market. The fact that it was written for 16-bit MS-DOS computers as well as the CP/M ones seemed to ensure its success. This version accessed some of the 16-bit machine's capabilities, but still left much to be desired. The arrival of the redesigned dBASE III in the middle of 1984 suddenly made dBASE a tool which could be used by large-scale operations.

dBASE GLOSSARY

What follows is a listing of all the dBASE II commands. For some commands, the syntax may be too complex to discuss briefly, or there may be many more combinations of options possible than are shown. In the interest of brevity, only the more common or important uses are shown. All commands work the same under both version 2.3 and 2.4, except where noted. Optional parameters are indicated inside by [] and certain expressions are denoted by < >. A sample use of each command follows its description, along with notes written in lowercase wherever necessary.

? Displays to screen or printer the value of the expression or, if the expression is in quotes, the actual expression. With no expression after it, the ? issues a carriage return/line feed sequence. The double question mark (??) is similar, but does not issue a line feed before printing.
Example: ? "The discounted price plus 6% sales tax is $"
?? ((NET:PRICE * QTY) − DISCOUNT) * .06

@ x,y Erases the display on the screen on the row stated starting at the specified column, where x is the row and y is the column.
Example: @ 12,30 (Erases row 12 from column 30 to 79.)

x,y SAY <expression> [USING <format specification>] Displays to the screen or printer the value of the expression, or the memory variable, etc. at the screen or printer location specified. The optional USING phrase specifies how the data is to be displayed. In addition, the GET option may be used after the SAY to place data into a memory variable or a data field.

Example: @ 10,27 SAY "The total cost per square foot is :"
@ 10,63 SAY COST:SQ:FT USING "$99,999.99"

@ x,y GET <variable or field> [PICTURE <format specification>]

Displays the current value of a memory variable or data field, at the row and column specified. If a READ statement is subsequently issued, the cursor moves to the row and column and allows modification of the variable. The PICTURE phrase performs some validation of data entered, such as allowing only numerals in a character variable. dBASE permits up to 64 GETs to be pending (no READ statement yet issued). The SAY and GET phrases may be combined into one command.

Example: @ 17,5 GET ORDER:NUM PICTURE "A999-99"
@ 20,0 SAY "How many widgets do you want? "
GET QTY
READ

(Gets the two variables ORDER:NUM and QTY from the user on the screen. The PICTURE phrase ensures that the first character of ORDER:NUM will be alpha and the next five will be numeric, separated by a hyphen.)

ACCEPT ["<character string>"] TO <memory variable>

Places character data entered by operator into a memory variable without the need for quote marks as delimiters. An optional message may be displayed to prompt user for information.

Example: ACCEPT "What is your name?" TO NAME

1) APPEND
2) APPEND BLANK
3) APPEND FROM <file name> [FOR <expression>] [WHILE <expression>] [DELIMITED]

Adds records to the end of the database. The first form is used in direct mode as it prompts the user for all the record data. When the last field has been entered, a new record appears on screen and the user either may continue entering new records or may end the append.

Example: USE MYFILE
APPEND

(Adds one record to the end of MYFILE.DBF and fills in fields with values supplied by user through keyboard.)

This second form adds a record to a database but leaves all the fields empty. It does not display anything on the screen, but rather performs this action internally. This is useful in the programming mode, since the program can prompt the operator for the desired information in a customized format on the screen and then store the inputted values to memory variables. Next, it will RE-PLACE the appropriate fields with the entered information.

Example: USE MYFILE
APPEND BLANK (Adds a blank record to the file MYFILE.DBF.)

In the third form, the file in use takes records from the file name specified and adds them to itself. Unqualified, it appends all records form the file. The optional FOR or WHILE phrase is used to define criteria for appending. With the optional DELIMITED clause, dBASE assumes the source file is an ASCII file delimited with quote marks and commas, and accordingly strips these characters before appending. If the index file is in use, dBASE will automatically reindex, except when APPENDing BLANKs.

Example: USE MYFILE
APPEND FROM INSTOCK FOR LOCATION = "NJ" .AND. ON:HAND > 0

(Will only add those items to MYFILE.DBF from INSTOCK.DBF whose on-hand quantity is 50 and are located in New Jersey.)

BROWSE

Allows editing a number of records at a time from a database. The screen acts like a window to the database, and records can be scrolled vertically and horizontally to view the desired fields. Not useful for extensive file modifications.

Example: USE MYFILE
BROWSE

CANCEL

Ends the execution of all command files immediately and returns control to the dBASE II direct command mode.

Example: CANCEL

CHANGE FIELD <list> [FOR <condition>]

Permits changes to the database fields listed in the <list>, and prompts the user for changes, modifications, or deletions.

Example: USE MYFILE
CHANGE FIELD PART:NO,PRICE FOR PART:NO < "5000"

(Allows user to enter new values for part number and price for all records with a part number less than 5000 in MYFILE.DBF.)

CLEAR

Restores the dBASE environment to its original state. All memory variables are released, files are closed, and any GETs not yet read are cleared.

Example: CLEAR

CLEAR GETS

Releases all pending GET statements, meaning that the associated variables may not be modified unless another GET command is issued for that variable. Other commands which will also clear the GETs are CLEAR and ERASE. Since dBASE II allows 64 GETs to be active at any one time, this command need only be used occasionally. (An ERASE does not always clear a GET.)

Example: CLEAR GETS

CONTINUE This command is used with the LO-CATE statement. Once a record has been found, this command continues the search for the specified item at the point left off by the first search.
Example: USE MYFILE
LOCATE FOR NAME = "Smith"
(If this is not the correct Smith, you can keep searching.)
CONTINUE

COPY TO <file name> There are many options on this command, which basically copies records or certain fields within a record from the file in use to the database named, subject to conditions specified optionally. A delimited format is allowed.
Example: USE MYFILE
COPY TO YOURFILE
(Copies all records in MYFILE.DBF to YOURFILE.)
Example: COPY TO YOURFILE FOR STATE = "VT" .AND. INCOME > = 30000
(Copies those records in MYFILE.DBF from Vermont with an income of $30,000 or more to the file YOURFILE.DBF.)
Example: COPY TO HISFILE DELIMITED WITH

(Copies to the text file HISFILE.DBF, omitting the dBASE II structure of the file in use, and delimiting fields with a backslash '\'.)

COPY TO <file name> STRUCTURE or COPY STRUCTURE TO <file name> Copies the structure of the database file in use to the file named; no records are copied. An error results if the target file already exists.
Example: USE MYFILE
COPY STRUCTURE TO YOURFILE

COUNT Counts the records in the database in use. Optional clauses allow conditions to be specified, in which case only records which meet those conditions will be included in the count.
Example: USE YOURFILE
COUNT FOR STATE <> "NY" .AND. STATE <> "AZ"
(Counts how many records are not from either Arizona or New York.)

CREATE <filename> Forms a new dBASE II data file. The structure of the new file may be copied from another data file with the FROM clause, otherwise the user is prompted to fill in field names, types, and lengths. The new file is saved with a .DBF extension, unless otherwise stated at time of creation.
Example: CREATE HERFILE
Example: CREATE ANYFILE.XYZ

DELETE Marks records for deletion in the database in use subject to any conditions stated with the optional FOR or WHILE clause. The records remain in the data file, but may be removed with the PACK command. Records marked for deletion will not be read by subsequent file operations and may be restored to nondeleted (normal) status through the RECALL statement.
Example: USE HISFILE
GO BOTTOM
DELETE
(Deletes the last record in the file.)
Example: USE MYFILE
DELETE 10
(Deletes record number 10.)
Example: USE MYFILE
DELETE ALL
(Deletes all records in the file.)
Example: USE HERFILE
DELETE ALL FOR # > 1599
(Deletes all records in the file after record number 1599. The record number function is #.)

DELETE FILE <file name> Erases the specified diskette file.
Example: DELETE FILE B:OLDFILE.ASM

DISPLAY Similar to the PRINT statement in BASIC, this versatile command can be used to display the contents of memory variables, or specific field variables from the file in use. As with many other dBASE commands, limitations may be placed upon the items to be displayed. For example, the FIELDS clause allows the user to specify which data fields are to be displayed. Normally, dBASE will show the record number along with the file data; the OFF clause suppresses this number. Almost identical to the LIST command.
Example: USE MYFILE
DISPLAY
(Lists all data in the file on the screen.)
Example: USE MYFILE
DISPLAY ALL FIELDS LASTNAME,AGE,SS: NO FOR AGE > 29

1) DISPLAY STRUCTURE
2) DISPLAY STATUS
3) DISPLAY MEMORY
4) DISPLAY FILES [LIKE <format>] [ON <drive spec>] The DISPLAY command, when used in these expressions, performs much differently than described above. The first phrase shows on screen the physical structure of the file in use (field names, types, and lengths). The second statement lists the status of the various dBASE parameters which can be changed by the user with the SET command, as well as reporting on any open files. DISPLAY MEMORY simply shows all defined variables and their values, types, and lengths. The final command pulls a directory of all data files and some relevant information (number of records, etc.), like the DIR command in DOS, or the PIP command in CP/M. The word DISPLAY may be replaced with LIST with the same results.
Example: USE YOURFILE
DISPLAY STRUCTURE

Example: DISPLAY STATUS
Example: DISPLAY MEMORY
Example: DISPLAY FILES LIKE *.PRG ON A:

DO <program name>   Executes the dBASE command file named. If there is no extension stated, .PRG is assumed for DOS systems, and .CMD is assumed for CP/M systems.
   Example: DO THE RIGHT FILE

DO CASE   Structured programming command allowing several conditions to be evaluated with instructions. Described in more detail above. DO CASEs may be nested up to 16 levels deep, and must always contain a matching ENDCASE.
   Example: DO CASE
      CASE BALANCE < 0
        (Processing for negative balance.)
      CASE BALANCE = 0
        (Processing for zero balance.)
      OTHERWISE
        (Processing for positive balance.)
      ENDCASE

DO WHILE   Iterative command which executes statements repeatedly until the original condition becomes false. Processing then continues after the ENDDO These may also be nested up to 16 levels deep. Described in further detail above.
   Example: DO WHILE COUNTER < 101
      STORE COUNTER + 1 TO COUNTER
      ENDDO
      (A simple time delay which loops until the counter reaches 100.)

EDIT [<record number>]   Command permitting the user to go into the database and modify the contents of the file record by record. The fields will be displayed with their current contents on the screen. The cursor keys are used to move from field to field to change data. Pressing control-Q ends the edit without saving the changes; control-W ends editing with the changes saved to diskette.
   Example: USE ANYFILE
      EDIT 996
      (Brings up record number 996 for editing.)

EJECT   Sends a form feed to the printer when in the SET PRINT ON or SET FORMAT TO PRINT modes.
   Example: EJECT

ERASE   Clears the screen and puts the cursor in the "home" position in the upper left corner; also clears any pending GETs. An undocumented syntax of this command clears a portion of the screen from a specified row and column and places the cursor at those x,y coordinates: @ x,y ERASE.
   Example: ERASE
   Example: @ 11,40 ERASE
      (Clears the screen from line 11 down starting at column 40.)

FIND <character string>   Searches the opened index file(s) of the file in use for the first occurrence of the string named. The result is the number of the record which contains the character string. If no match is found, dBASE returns a value of zero and replies NO FIND. The character string may be a literal string or a macro character variable.
   Example: USE MYFILE INDEX MYINDEX
      STORE "GODOT" TO KEY
      FIND &KEY
   Example: USE MYFILE INDEX MYINDEX
      FIND GODOT

GO RECORD <record number>

GOTO RECORD <record number>   Places the dBASE II pointer at the position specified. The position may be a number, variable, macro, or one of two special commands: TOP or BOTTOM. The word GO or GOTO may be omitted entirely and just the record number specified.
   Example: GOTO RECORD 5
      (Places the pointer at record 5.)
   Example: GOTO 5
      (Does the same thing.)
   Example: GO 5
      (Same thing.)
   Example: 5
      (Same thing.)
   Example: GO TOP or GO BOTTOM
      (Places pointer at first or last record.)

HELP <command>   Provides access to dBASE II's on-line help text file DBASEMSG.TXT. The file gives a short description and syntax of the command in question.
   Example: HELP REPLACE
      (Gives information about the command REPLACE.)

IF <expression>   Structured programming command which performs operations based on the outcome of a given expression. Most used in a dBASE command file, but may be used interactively through the keyboard. There is no limit to how deep IFs may be nested; however, each IF must, of course, have a matching ENDIF. This command is further explained above.
   Example: IF ACCIDENTS > 0
      STORE PREMIUM + 250 TO PREMIUM
      DO PROGRAM2
      ELSE
      IF AGE > 24

```
        STORE PREMIUM - 200 TO PREMIUM
        ELSE
        STORE PREMIUM + 100 TO PREMIUM
    ENDIF
    DO PROGRAM3
    ENDIF
```

INDEX ON <expression> TO <index file> Creates an index file keyed to the variables in the expression from the file in use. The index file contains pointers to the records in the database file, not actual data, which is beneficial for two reasons. The first is that disk space is conserved; since it contains only pointers, the index file for even very large files is just a fraction of the size of the original file. The second and even more obvious (to the user) advantage is that records can be found very quickly, regardless of the size of the database. With the FIND command, a specific record can be found in two seconds or so. If records are added to or deleted from a database, or a key field is modified, while the index is set on, dBASE automatically updates the index file. The index is keyed on one or more fields, subject to a limitation of 100 total characters in the key. Changes made to a database without the index set on will not be reflected in the index file. Updating may be done on a file in use with the commands SET INDEX TO index file name, and REINDEX.

Example: USE CUSTLIST
  INDEX ON STATE + CUST:CODE + STATUS TO CUSTLOC
    (Creates the index file CUSTLOC.NDX in ascending order based on state, then customer code number, then status.)

INDEX This command will take the record positioned at the record pointer and insert it into the index file(s) in use. This is used for creating an index which contains only some of the records from the database file.

Example: USE MYFILE INDEX MYINDEX1, MYINDEX2
  GO 159
  INDEX
    (Indexes record 159 to both the MYINDEX1 and MYINDEX2 files.)

INPUT TO <variable name> Accepts keyboard input to a variable whose type (logical, numeric, etc.) is determined by the data entered. Character input must be delimited with either single or double quotes. An optional message may be displayed as a prompt.

Example: INPUT "Are reports to be printed? (Y/N)" TO ANSWER
  INSERT BEFORE BLANK

This command inserts records into the database in use. Without parameters, it prompts the user for the field values and places the new record into the database at the current pointer position. The BEFORE clause will put this record immediately before the pointer. The BLANK phrase inserts a record filled with blank fields, without the on-screen prompts, which is useful in command files. The fields may then be filled in via the REPLACE statement.

Example: USE YOURHEAD
    (The pointer is set to 1.)
  SKIP 49
    (The pointer is set to record 49.)
  INSERT
    (A new record 50 is inserted with prompts.)
Example: USE CASHFLOW LOCATE FOR INVOICE:NO = "B2017"
  INSERT BLANK
    (Inserts a blank record after the one with invoice number B2017.)

JOIN TO <file name> FOR <condition> This statement combines two databases, subject to the conditions stated, to form a third file. While this may seem like a way to get around the dBASE II limit of 32 fields per record or 65,535 records per file, it does not; the JOINed file is still subject to the same laws as all other dBASE files. This command is also very slow, especially if the databases are large. The fields to be joined may be stated optionally.

Example: SELECT PRIMARY
  USE CUSTLIST
  SELECT SECONDARY
  USE BILLING
  SELECT PRIMARY
  JOIN TO CREDHOLD FOR S.OVERDUE > 45 .AND. S.AMT:OVER > 100 ; .AND.
    (P.STATE = "ME" .OR. P.STATE = "NH" .OR. P.STATE = "VT")
    (This creates, from the billing and customer files, a file called CREDHOLD.DBF which contains all the Maine, New Hampshire, and Vermont customers who are more than two months overdue with balances over 100 dollars.)

LIST There are many options on this command, which is nearly identical to the DISPLAY command mentioned above. The major difference is that while DISPLAY pauses after 15 records on screen displays, LIST displays all records without pausing to the end of the file, or until the optional condition is met. Refer to the DISPLAY command for an explanantion of the various functions.

Example: LIST
    (Displays the current record on the screen.)
Example: LIST ALL
    (Displays all records in the file in use without pausing.)
Example: USE INVMAST
  LIST NEXT 50 FOR INVOICETOT > = 500
    (Displays records with an invoice total of 500 dollars or over for the next 50 records in the file INVMAST.DBF.)
Example: LIST STRUCTURE
    (Same as DISPLAY STRUCTURE.)
Example: LIST STATUS

(Same as DISPLAY STATUS.)
Example: LIST MEMORY
(Same as DISPLAY MEMORY.)
Example: LIST FILES LIKE *.NDX ON C:
(Displays all files with an .NDX extension on the C: drive. Same as DISPLAY FILES.)

LOCATE FOR <condition>   Searches the database in use until the condition is satisfied. If a match is found, dBASE II returns the record number. If no match is found, the end of file function (EOF) will yield a true (.T.) answer, and a message appears. This function finds records slower than the FIND command, since it is not operating on an index. The command is useful when searching for a particular field which is not a part of any index key. If the record found is not the desired one, the CONTINUE statement resumes the locating process until the condition is met again or the end of file is reached.
Example: USE DEMOGRFX
LOCATE FOR INCOME < 25000 .AND. SEX = "F"
(This will search for any female earning less than $25,000.)
Example: CONTINUE
(The first result was not satisfactory; keep looking.)

LOOP   Used in a DO WHILE/ENDDO structure to retest the original condition. Refer to the discussion of the DO WHILE statement above.
Example: DO WHILE .NOT. EOF
(Repeat until end of file is reached.)
<More dBASE commands.>
IF ERRORSW = T
(If an error swich has been set,)
GO BOTTOM
(skip to the last record in the file.)
SKIP
(This makes the EOF function be true.)
LOOP
(Retest the condition: .NOT. EOF.)
ENDIF
<More dBASE commands.>
ENDDO

MODIFY STRUCTURE   Allows the user to change the structure of a dBASE II database file. All existing records in the file are destroyed upon execution of this command, so it should only be done on empty files. If a file needs modification, the usual process is to copy the records to a temporary file, change the structure of the original file, then copy the records back to the modified file.
Example: USE MYFILE
COPY TO TEMP
(Copy records to temporary file.)
MODIFY STRUCTURE
(Make changes; control-W to exit MODIFY.)

APPEND FROM TEMP
(Copy records back from temp file.)
USE
(Close MYFILE.DBF file.)
DELETE FILE TEMP.DBF
(Remove temporary file.)

MODIFY COMMAND <file name>   The most frequent command a dBASE programmer will ever use, MODI COMM, as it is generally entered, is the way to create and change a dBASE II command (program) file. Since the command file is written and stored in ASCII, it can also be written with an ordinary text editor, which may be preferable due to the scarcity of text-editing features in the dBASE system. If the file named does not exist on the default drive, a new one is created. Users have the option of exiting the modify with or without saving any changes. When the file is saved, the original is saved with a .BAK extension and the updated file is given the extension .PRG (for MS-DOS systems) or .CMD (for CP/M-86).
Example: MODIFY COMMAND NEWPROG

NOTE or *   Used to place comments in a command file and not echoed during the execution of the program.
Example: NOTE This part of the program checks the date entered.
Example: * Modified 5/7/85 by IPC

PACK   Removes all records marked for deletion with the DELETE command from the file in use. Records cannot be recovered after this process. If the index is set on, the system will automatically reindex after PACKing. (Disk space freed by this procedure is not released to the operating system, resulting in files being padded with useless space. Since this may become a problem in larger databases, the solution is to copy the data to a new file name, delete the old file, then rename the new file with the old name. Deleted files are not copied, so the new file will be smaller than the old one.)
Example: USE CUSTFILE
DELETE ALL FOR STATUS = "EXPIRED"
PACK
USE

QUIT   Exits the dBASE II operating system. Any open files are closed. In CP/M systems, the option exists to QUIT TO a file or system command.
Example: QUIT
(Ends dBASE II session; only version allowed in MS-DOS.)
Example: QUIT TO "DIR B:*.CMD','DBASE START"
(Ends dBASE, pulls a directory of all command files on the B: drive, then returns to dBASE and immediately runs START.CMD.)

READ   Accepts user input from the keyboard to memory and field variables placed on the screen through the GET phrase. The cursor can be moved from one GET to the next via the cursor keys and values may be changed, if desired. The READ is terminated when the last GET on the screen has been entered. Normally, if an index file is in use, any change made to a key field will cause a reindex. The NOUPDATE option overrides this process.

Example: READ
Example: READ NOUPDATE

RECALL <conditions> Removes a record's deletion flag that was set by the DELETE statement. When a record is DELETEd, dBASE marks that record for deletion with an internal flag. The RECALL merely resets that flag.

Example: RECALL
(Recalls current record if deleted.)
Example: RECALL ALL
(Recalls all deleted records.)
Example: RECALL ALL FOR STATE = "CA"
(Recalls all deleted records from California.)

REINDEX After any modifications to an indexed file which will alter the order of the index, such as an added record or an altered key field, this command updates the index file to reflect these changes.

Example: USE TARIFFS INDEX RATEZONE
REINDEX

RELEASE Removes all or some variables from the computer's memory. No error is generated if a specified variables does not exist. This command is useful in command files when the number of variables approaches the 64 dBASE limit.

Example: RELEASE PART:NO,COST,QTY
(Removes the three variables.)
Example: RELEASE ALL
(Removes every variable in memory.)
Example: RELEASE ALL LIKE TAX*
(Removes every variable that begins with "TAX", for example, TAXRATE, TAXABLE, etc. The asterisk acts like a wild card.)
Example: RELEASE ALL EXCEPT TAX
(Removes all variables except the one specified. The asterisk syntax may be used to specify similarly named variables.)

REMARK Similar to the ? statement in that anything following the command is output to the standard device, usually the screen or printer.

Example: REMARK This is a test. This is only a test.

RENAME <file name> TO <file name> Changes the name of any file in the default drive's directory. The file must, of course, exist or an error message is displayed. The default extension for file names is .DBF. The disk drive may be specified.

Example: RENAME OLDPROG.PRG TO
NEWPROG.PRG

REPLACE Allows the user to change the value of specified data fields for one or more records at a time from the file in use. It can REPLACE a field with the value of another field of a matching type in the same or an alternate file, or the field may be replaced with a literal character string, a numeric amount, or a mathematical expression. Unless otherwise specified, only the current record will be changed. If the source data resides in another data file, that file must be opened along with the target file. If the change is made to a key field in an indexed file with the index in use, then dBASE will reposition the record as appropriate in the index.

Example: USE AUTOLOAN
REPLACE ALL CAR:PYMT WITH CAR:PYMT * 1.25 FOR AGE < 25
(Goes through the file AUOTLOAN.DBF and increases the car payment amount by 25 percent for everyone under 25.)
Example: SELECT SECONDARY
USE UPDATE
SELECT PRIMARY
USE AUTOLOAN
REPLACE ALL P.CAR:PYMT WITH P.CAR:PYMT + S.SURCHARGE,; P.PREMIUM WITH S.INCREASE
(Goes through AUTOLOAN and adds the surcharge from the UPDATE.DBF file to every car payment amount and replaces the premium with the amount INCREASE from the secondary file.)

REPORT Used for creating report form files which are used to display information from databases in a user-defined format. When the command is first invoked with a new report form name, dBASE prompts the user on-screen for such information as page headings, margin sizes, and whether or not totals are to be computed. The results are stored in a .FRM file saved to disk, where it may be accessed later to avoid redefining the report format. After all the questions have been answered, the report is then displayed on screen. If the TO PRINT option is specified, the report is sent to the printer also. This command is adequate for the novice user who does not desire customized reports. The experienced dBASE programmer will, however, pass up this feature for the added flexibility and versatility of building his or her own command file in the SET FORMAT TO PRINT mode, filled with @ SAYs.

Example: USE TRANFILE INDEX
ITEMS REPORT FORM SALESREG TO PRINT FOR PURCH:AMT > 0
(Creates the sales register report form file SALESREG.FRM., then prints out the report using all records from TRANFILE.DBF with a purchase price above 0.)
Example: USE WISHLIST GO 150 REPORT NEXT 50 FORM IWANT
(Generates a report of 50 records from the WISHLIST file starting at record number 150 using the format of IWANT.FRM.)

RESET Used to reset the operating system bit map after a diskette swap. The drive specification may be added; otherwise the entire system is reinitialized. After issuing this command, dBASE II makes sure that no files are open on the drive specified in order to avoid read/write errors. This command has no effect if there is no diskette swap.

Example: RESET B:

RESTORE FROM <memory file name>   Places into memory the contents of the memory file, which is made up of variable names and their values stored on the diskette with the SAVE command. Unless the phrase ADDITIVE is specified, all existing variables will be released from memory.

Example: RESTORE FROM LASTCKNO ADDITIVE
> (Merges the variable(s) from the file LASTCKNO.MEM with currently defined variables.)

RETURN   Unconditionally ends execution of a command file and returns control to either the operating system or, if called from another command file, the calling program. All variables remain in memory, all files in use remain open, and all SET commands are unchanged. Reaching the end of the file performs the same function if no RETURN statement is issued.

Example: RETURN

SAVE TO <file name>   Saves all currently defined variables to a memory file on diskette. If only some variables are to be saved, the ALL LIKE <format> option will store only those variables which follow a certain format. If, for instance, all the variables defined in a particular subroutine are to be saved, then the programmer should name them with a common unique format, such as ZTOTAL, ZPART:CODE, ZSTATE, etc.; then save all variables which start with the letter "Z" to the memory file. Memory variables are recalled from the memfile with the RESTORE command.

Example: SAVE TO INVMEM
> (Saves every variable to the memory file INVMEM.MEM.)

Example: SAVE ALL LIKE SS:NO TO SOCSEC
> (Saves only the variable SS:NO to the file SOCSEC.MEM.)

Example: SAVE ALL LIKE Z* TO AMOUNTS
> (Saves all variables which begin with the letter Z.)

Example: SAVE ALL LIKE A??OLD TO SERNUM.OLD
> (Saves to SERNUM.OLD all variables which begin with "A" and have "OLD" as their fourth, fifth, and sixth letters, such as A59OLD and AXXOLD, but not AXOLD or AXXXOLD.)

SELECT PRIMARY or SELECT SECONDARY   Allows user to alternate between two open files, performing operations on one without affecting the other, yet at the same time being able to access the data fields in either file. When dBASE starts up, the PRIMARY area is active. To reference a field variable from one area while in another area, it is necessary to prefix the variable name with either P. or S., depending on which area the field resides, primary or secondary.

Example: SELECT PRIMARY
> USE PRODCODE INDEX PRODCODE
> (Both the data file and the index can have the same name.)
> FIND ABC123
> (Locate the record with a CODE of ABC123.)
> SELECT SECONDARY
> USE UPDATE
> LOCATE FOR S.CODE = "ABC123"
> (Position the pointer at the ABC123 record in the second file.)
> IF S.STATUS = "INACTIVE"
> REPLACE P.PRICE WITH S.PRICE
> REPLACE P.STATUS WITH "I"
> ENDIF
> (These lines will change the PRICE field in the PRIMARY use file to the value of the PRICE field in the secondary file, and replace the primary file field variable STATUS with "I" on the condition that the status of product ABC123 is inactive.)

SET   Allows the user to alter the dBASE II operating environment. There are over twenty-seven different SET commands, seven of which toggle an ON/OFF status bit. A listing of these parameters follows, with default settings written in capital letters.

SET ALTERNATE TO <file name>   Creates and opens a diskette file into which all further screen output will be echoed. This includes all keyboard inputs, as well as output from dBASE II commands.

SET ALTERNATE on   Begins echo of output to alternate file.

SET ALTERNATE OFF   Ends echo of output to alternate file.

SET BELL ON   Computer's bell sounds when the full length of a data field or variable has been reached while entering on screen.

SET BELL OFF   Suppresses bell.

SET CARRY on   The previous record's data will be carried over when appending records on screen.

SET CARRY OFF   Does not carry data from previous record.

SET COLON ON   Begins and ends on screen GETs with a colon.

SET COLON off   Suppresses colons in GETs.

SET COLOR TO <f,n>   Changes the display color of all subsequent screen output. The first number is the code for full-screen operations, such as GETs and EDITs; the second is for normal display output. Available only in version 2.4.

SET CONFIRM on   The system will not allow cursor to advance to next field or GET without pressing the return key, even if the field is full.

SET CONFIRM OFF   dBASE automatically skips to next GET or field whenever the field length has been exceeded.

SET CONSOLE ON   Output is echoed to the screen.

SET CONSOLE off   Output to the screen is suppressed.

SET DATE TO <date>   Sets or resets the system date. This date is valid only during the current dBASE session.

SET DEBUG on   Output from the ECHO and STEP commands is sent to the printer, instead of the screen.

SET DEBUG OFF   No printer output during ECHO and STEP.

SET DEFAULT TO <drive specification>   Changes the current default disk drive.

SET DELETED on   Records flagged for deletion will be skipped over in any FIND statement and any command which uses NEXT, such as DISPLAY, LOCATE, COPY, etc.

SET DELETED OFF   Deleted records may be processed.

SET ECHO on   Displays on the screen all commands in a command file, along with any regular output.

SET ECHO OFF   The echo feature is suppressed.

SET EJECT ON   When the PRINT or FORMAT is set to print, or a REPORT command is given, the printer will do a form feed.

SET EJECT off   Suppresses the eject function.

SET ESCAPE ON   Allows a program or dBASE process to be aborted with the escape key.

SET ESCAPE off   Disables the escape key while in dBASE.

SET EXACT on   All character strings must match exactly in order to be considered equal in any comparison.

SET EXACT OFF   Comparisons will be made according to the length of the second string.

SET FORMAT TO SCREEN/PRINT/<format file name>   For use with the @ SAY command. The first two parameters determine where to display the output. The third option specifies from which format file to READ the @ SAY commands.

SET HEADING TO <character string heading>   Stores the specified string in memory for use as a report heading, subject to a maximum of 60 characters.

SET INDEX TO <index file>, <index file>, ...   Opens the index file(s) named for use with the currently open data file. With no index stated, it closes all indexes associated with the file in use.

SET INTENSITY ON   Reverse video (white or green on black) is displayed for all GETs and field variables when in the full-screen mode.

SET INTENSITY off   Disables the full screen reverse video feature.

SET LINKAGE on   Increments the pointers simultaneously for both files in use during any sequential command, such as LIST. The PRIMARY and SECONDARY files must already be open.

SET LINKAGE OFF   Pointers are moved independently.

SET MARGIN TO <number>   In a report, the left margin will be offset the indicated number of spaces.

SET PRINT on   Output is echoed to the printer.

SET PRINT OFF   Turns off the echo feature.

SET RAW on   Does not insert spaces between field values when LISTing or DISPLAYing the contents of a file.

SET RAW OFF   Puts a space between each field variable.

SET SCREEN ON   Puts dBASE into full-screen editing mode when given a CREATE, EDIT, INSERT, or APPEND command.

SET SCREEN off   Disables the full-screen mode.

SET STEP on   A debugging tool which halts execution of a command file after each statement, then prompts the user to either enter a keyboard command, allow the next statement to be executed, or abort the program.

SET STEP OFF   Disables the STEP function.

SET TALK ON   Results of all dBASE II commands are displayed on the screen.

SET TALK off   Suppresses the output of dBASE commands.

SKIP   Moves the pointer the indicated number of records forward or backward in the file in use. If the index is set on, then the pointer is moved in the index file. The pointer will not move past the end of the file.
>   Example: SKIP 10 or SKIP +10
>   (Advances the record pointer 10 records from its current position.)
>   Example: SKIP −6
>   (Moves the record pointer 6 records back.)

SORT ON <field name> TO <file name> [AS-CENDING/DESCENDING]   Creates a file with the same structure as the file in use that is sorted on the field specified. The original file remains intact. The sort is based on the ASCII value of the characters in the field. The sort may be in ascending or descending order; ascending is assumed if none is specified.
>   Example: USE THISFILE
>   SORT ON NAME TO THATFILE

STORE <expression> TO <variable name(s)>   Assigns the value of the expression to the variable(s) named and places this information in memory. If more than one variable is indicated, all will have the value of the expression.
>   Example: STORE "Los Angeles" TO CITY
>   Example: STORE "55390" TO PART:NO
>   STORE "R" TO SUFFIX STORE PART:NO + SUFFIX TO PROD:CODE
>   (The product code will be 55390R.)
>   Example: STORE (SUB:TOTAL + FREIGHT − DISCOUNT) * 1.06 TO PURCH:PR

SUM <field name> [<conditions>]   Gives the sum of all the fields indicated which match the condition(s) expressed and optionally stores this amount to a variable. The fields, of course, must be numeric and must be present in the file in use or an error will result. Unless otherwise specified, the command will go through all records in the database. The process can be time-consuming, especially in larger files. The maximum number of fields which can be SUMmed is five.
>   Example: USE SALES86
>   SUM GROSS:SLS,TAX,DISCOUNTS TO NET:SLS FOR PRODUCT = "WIDGETS"
>   (Will add up the gross sales, tax, and discounts in the file SALES86.DBF for all Widgets sold and place the total in NET:SLS.)

TEXT   This command echoes everything following it to the output device named in a previous set statement. The ENDTEXT statement terminates the echo. This is generally used to display large blocks of text from within a command file without the need for numerous @ SAY or ? commands. This function is only available to version 2.4 users.
>   Example: TEXT
>   (Anything that goes here will be printed out on the screen or printer.)
>   ENDTEXT

TOTAL   The totals of the numeric fields from the file in use are computed and placed in a data file in the order of the field indicated. If the target file does not exist, a new one will be created based on the structure of the source file. The FIELDS phrase will copy only those fields named to the new file.
>   Example: USE STOCKS
>   TOTAL ON CO:NAME TO GAINS FOR CAP:GAIN > 0
>   (Places the totals of all numeric fields from STOCKS.DBF into the file GAINS.DBF using those records with a showing a capital gain of more than zero. The new file will be in company name order.)

UPDATE   Briefly, this powerful command will modify the file in use by using data from a second database. There are many possibilities in this command: updated fields can be summed or replaced completely; only certain fields may be specified for modification; or all fields can be updated. The process can take a long time to complete, especially on larger-sized databases.
>   Example: USE THISFILE INDEX THISINDX
>   UPDATE ON CODE:NO TO THATFILE REPLACE DIVISION WITH NEW:DIV,; BUDGET WITH BUDGET
>   (Uses the information in THATFILE.DBF to update the indexed file THISFILE.DBF. The fields DIVISION and BUDGET from the target file are to be replaced with the values of the NEW:DIV and BUDGET fields in the source (update) file.)

USE   If followed by a file name, USE opens the indicated file in the present data area, PRIMARY or SECONDARY, while it closes out any file which may be already open in that area. If no file name is specified, it closes out any open file in the data area in use. Optionally, an index file may be opened at the same time with the INDEX phrase. It is extremely important to USE a file after a disk write has been performed on it, to force the contents of the buffer into the file. If this is not done, the user runs the risk of having dBASE scatter the buffer's contents at random over the diskette. This is not as rare an occurrence as it sounds. Many a database has been destroyed by not using USE after modifying.

Example: USE ANYFILE
(Opens the file.)

Example: USE THISFILE INDEX THISNDX
(Opens the file and its index.)

Example: USE
(Closes an open file, if one exists.)

WAIT   Suspends program operation until any key is struck on the keyboard. The message "WAITING" appears, to prompt the user for a response, unless the console has been SET off. The input character may be stored to a variable for future reference or processing with the TO phrase.

Example: WAIT

Example: WAIT TO ANSWER.

VisiCalc

It has been said that the desktop business computer revolution began with the introduction of VisiCalc, the first electronic spreadsheet program to become available for microcomputers. VisiCalc is a historic product because, for a time during the early stages of the business microcomputer market, it was one of the only professionally oriented programs available. Launched as a VISUAL CALCULATOR shortly before the Apple II had come to market, it was the first product to give business professionals a practical reason to use personal computers in an office environment. VisiCalc, by recreating an accountant's spreadsheet on the computer screen and by putting a a series of easy-to-enter arithmetic and logical formulas into the hands of management thinkers, created a market for desktop personal computers at precisely the right moment when desktop computers were being developed for business.

VisiCalc made financial analysis into a form of computer game or interoffice competition and enabled the senior administrative manager to gain an entry into a field dominated by the data processing professional. Consequently, VisiCalc helped to revolutionize financial management. Financial analysis, which had hitherto been in the private domain of mainframes and minicomputers, was never really accessible to most office managers or accountants. This was because of the typical backlog of work that most central office computers had to process and because of the demands that this type of customized processing would have placed upon the traditional data processing manager within a corporate environment. The types of quick access to financial data and the types of calculations necessary to prepare short reports or make projected financial models were just the types of jobs that often interfered with the ongoing processing work of the data processing manager. Consequently, a market existed for a mathematical calculator which could process company financial data quickly and selectively. With the introduction of VisiCalc, not only could the average manager do the task, but the results were almost instantaneous. This ready access to data and the ease of making recalculations by changing one or more of the variables led to what has become the "what if" scenario now practiced by almost every business manager. Projections, budgets, analyses, all of these former drudgeries were now handled with relative ease and a significant savings of time.

Today VisiCalc runs on just about every commercial computer available. In fact, it is said by industry specialists that if a computer does not have VisiCalc available for it, it is not a business computer. It quickly became an industry standard in an environment looking for a standard. Its advantages included the rather small amount of memory required to run it, the lack of a specific hardware configuration needed to implement it, and the wide portability of the program. With a minimum of 64K, a single disk drive, any one of the many operating systems, and any type of video monitor, one

then has the tools necessary to run the program.

VisiCalc met with an unprecedented initial success, and accordingly imitators were quick to follow in its path. These first imitation spreadsheet programs were called VisiClones by market commentators. But, by capitalizing upon some of the drawbacks that VisiCalc had, one of the "clones" quickly managed to achieve some success of its own. This product was called SuperCalc. Developed by Sorcim—"micros" spelled backward—it overcame some of the idiosyncrasies of VisiCalc, and of course was less expensive. SuperCalc improved those areas in which VisiCalc was weakest, but it did not radically change the genre. Therefore they shall be discussed together as if they were one system.

Following the standard format of an accountant's columnar pad, columns were bisected by rows to form individual blocks for entries. The columns in this software version were labeled by letters, the rows by numbers, and the entry blocks were called cells. The first square for entry was A1 (the first column, first row), below it was A2, to A1's right was B1, and so on. Also on the computer display were three lines (at the top in VisiCalc, on the bottom in SuperCalc) that were used to show the address of the cell (called the active cell) in which the cursor was placed, the format indication (how entries in that cell would appear), the actual entry made in that cell, and the command line. The command line was the most important because it echoed the keystroke commands enterd by the user. By pressing the slash key (/) the commands are recognized by the program; and pressing the mnemonic first letter of the command, for example, B for BLANK, invoked it, and returned the prompt of any variation that was selected.

In the cells the user can enter numbers or alphabet labels; the numbers are displayed flush against the right margin of the cell and the alphabet labels are flush with the left margin. To calculate a formulation in the program, for example, one enters the first variable in one cell, the second variable in another, and in the third cell a formula that operates upon the variables in the first two cells. The formula does not specify the two numbers by value, but rather by their respective cell addresses. For example:

```
            A       B        C
    -------------------------------------
    1       2       4        A1+B1
    2
    3
```

The answer here is obvious: 6. However, the fact to remember is that the formula does not calculate $2 + 4$, but rather $A1 + B1$. As these two addresses change in value during a series of financial models and calculations, so does the result found in C1. And the recalculation in C1 is instantaneous. This recalculation can then be duplicated and reported to subsequent cells by the program's COPY command, where the same arithmetic is performed serially at the new locations. The VisiCalc and SuperCalc command structure makes this process simple.

The command line or menu of both programs is similar in design and function. Both programs rely upon a series of mnemonics such as G for GLOBAL, B for BLANK, and P for PRINT to help users master the query language. However, some of the spreadsheet jargon is tricky for first-time users to learn immediately, and they are well advised not to rely too heavily upon the documentation manuals for assistance. The limited "help" features built into both programs (/H) is more direct and useful. In addition to the commands are functions. Functions are preprogrammed, built-in calculations, such as SUM, which allow for arguments or parameters enclosed in parentheses to be added, giving them an application relative to specific areas or ranges, for instance, SUM(A1..A20). In other words, by using a function, a user can bring the full calculating power of the program to bear directly upon an entire range of figures across a column or a row. By copying these functions into other cells, calculations can be made relative to variables not yet added. Hence, both VisiCalc and Super-Calc allowed users to write financial programs that would encompass variables to be added at a later date. Financial models could be updated to cover changing conditions, business reports could be updated to include new data, and the financial processing programs could be created that would change relative to the data without having to be rewritten. The functions in both programs cover several areas, including mathematical, trigonometric, statistical, and logical calculations. There are approximately 25 functions built into both VisiCalc and SuperCalc which span all of these categories.

The command structure of both programs is the same in appearance but not in function. Pressing the slash key returns prompts of /BCLSO and so forth, which represent the user commands directly available. Both programs' command structures cover the same basic operations: erasing of cell entries, erasing of work-sheets, deleting/inserting of columns/rows, formatting cell entries for specific appearance, loading/saving worksheets, printing out worksheets, freezing titles, and creating window-type displays. Though both programs are very useful, they present limitations with regard to the size of the worksheet (63 columns by 255 rows) and to specific cursor movement. Both allow for limited cursor pointing in commands like MOVE in which the user is prompted for a range to move from. The user can point to this range, identify it, and specify a range to move to, but cannot move blocks of entries at one time. The limitations have led to a rash of upgrades and new versions that offer specific enhancements over the older products or implementations that take advantage of the increased memory capability and processing speed of newer microcomputers. SuperCalc running on an IBM PC, for example, offers SuperCalc 1/2/3 or 3 Revised, while VisiCalc offers Visi 1 or Advanced VisiCalc. All of these versions, and the flocks of others on a variety of machines, have been designed to keep pace with the changing software market, correct the bugs of the older products, maintain consumer interest in a genre fading under the pressure of the new, integrated packages, and show the corporate flag by keeping the company logo before the public. It would be less than accurate to compare the different features of all the versions as if they were implemented on the same hardware system; the versions of electronic spreadsheet packages vary from machine type to machine type. However, it is safe to say that as new products were introduced to the market by new software companies, the older products were improved to keep pace.

In conclusion, although VisiCalc and SuperCalc are programmable in the sense that the user starts with a blank spreadsheet and creates from it a working financial model, the user does not have direct control of how the program operates and cannot automate the procedures that follow. As stand-alone operations, therefore, both are powerful albeit dated, and as critical components of an automated system both have their intrinsic advantages and drawbacks.

VISICALC GLOSSARY

The following glossary contains all of the command words for VisiCalc on the Apple, 8-bit CP/M computers, and the Commodore PET and 8000 series.

GOTO>   Moves the cursor to any set of coordinates on the spreadsheet. This command provides a fast way to move around the spreadsheet without having to cursor over formulas and previous entries.

LABEL ENTRY "   Any alphanumeric characters can be entered as a label. Alphabetic characters are automatically evaluated as labels and not calculated. Numbers are evaluated as labels when they are preceded by quotation marks. The quotation marks signal VisiCalc that the following number is not a number to be calculated or part of a formula. Blank spaces can also be entered as labels after quotation marks.

VALUE ENTRY   Any number that is not entered as a label after quotation marks is considered to be a value by VisiCalc. VisiCalc also considers mathematical operators such as + and − to be values as well as (. # @.

@SUM(LIST)   Adds the values of all the cells on the list.

@MAX(LIST)   Chooses the largest value on the list of cells.

@MIN(LIST)   Chooses the smallest value on the list of cells.

@COUNT(LIST)   Returns the number of nonblank entries on the list of cells.

@AVERAGE(LIST)   @SUM(LIST) divided by @COUNT(LIST) which returns the average number from the list of cells.

@ABS(n)   Returns the absolute value of n.

@INT(n)   Returns the integer portion of n.

@SQRT(n)   Returns the square root of n.

@EXP(n)   Returns e (2.71828) to the nth power.

@LOG10(n)   Returns the base 10 logarithm of n.

@LN(n)   Returns the natural log (base e) of n.

@SIN(n)   Returns the Sine of n in radians.

@COS(n)   Returns the Cosine of n in radians.

@TAN(n)   Returns the tangent of n in radians.

@ASIN(n)   Returns the Arc Sine of n in radians.

@ACOS(n)   Returns the Arc Cosine of n in radians.

@ATAN(n)   Returns the Arc Tangent of n in radians.

@NPV   Calculates the net present values of its second parameter discounted by the rate in its first parameter.

@NA   Returns a NA comment when evaluated as part of a formula. The NA is used when a spreadsheet is set up before data is available so that an ERROR will not be returned.

@ERROR   Returned when there is division or multiplication by zero.

@PI   Returns the value of 3.1415926536.

@LOOKUP(v,range)   Looks up the value of a number across a range or list and finds the value that corresponds to it.

/B   Blanks out a cell and erases all data.

/C   Clears all entry positions to blank. When /C is entered, VisiCalc looks for a Y to confirm the blanking out of all cells.

/D   Deletes all the data in an R, row, or C, column. When the /D is entered at the keyboard, VisiCalc looks for an R or a C. Upon entering an R or C, the entire row or column is deleted.

/F   Formats the contents of a cell to left or right justify the display, display the contents as integers, display the contents as dollars and cents, and display the integer values as stars for bar graphs.

/G   The Global command allows users to change the column width for all of the columns specified, recalculate by specified rows, recalculate by specified columns, recalculate automatically over the entire spreadsheet, recalculate manually only in the highlighted cells, and change all formats to the specialized format.

I   Insert column or row. Once a column or row is inserted, all of the rows or columns are pushed down or to the right by the row or column that was inserted. All of the value references that are in cells that were moved are changed to reflect the new positions.

/M   Block moves an entire row or column to a new position pointed to by the cursor.

/P   Prints the entire spreadsheet or the spreadsheet cells defined by the cursor to a disk file or to a printer.

/R   Replicate is one of the most important and utilitarian commands in VisiCalc. Replicate allows users to copy the contents of any entry position including all labels, values, formats, formulas, and blanks to any new entry position. Entire rows, columns, ranges of columns or rows, or selected cells may be copied from a source position to a target position. When copying formulas from one position to another, VisiCalc will ask whether the formulas will be made relative to the new position or not. A relative change means that if the formula in E3, @SUM(A3...D3), is copied to the cell E4, the formula that is copied will be made relative to E4 by changing it to @SUM(A4...D4). No change would copy the result of @SUM(A3...D3) to E4.

/S　The storage command is used to save the current VisiCalc sheet in memory to disk (/S S), load saved sheets from the disk drive into memory (/S L), delete a file from the disk (/S D), load or save DIF files (/S #), quit VisiCalc (/S Q), and initialize the disk in the drive (/S I). The initialize command is particularly dangerous, especially on the Commodore PET and 8000 series computers because VisiCalc will begin at once to initialize the disk in the target drive after the disk specifications are displayed. The Initialize command will erase all current files on the disk. Both the Delete and Quit commands require a Y to confirm and execute immediately thereafter.

/T　Title fixes the titles across the rows and columns as on the borders of the screen so that they remain constantly on the screen even though the rest of the spreadsheet may scroll beneath them. The Title command was created so that at any point in the spreadsheet, users would not lose the identity of the horizontal and vertical lines of titles. /T H fixes the horizontal titles, /T V fixes the vertical titles, /T B fixes both horizontal and vertical titles, and /T N negates all the fixing.

/V　Displays the current version of VisiCalc. This buyer information is important for obtaining help regarding the current implementation of VisiCalc.

/W　Window splits the screen into component windows for the purpose of viewing separate sections of the spreadsheet comparatively. The Window command can split the screen vertically at the cursor, horizontally at the cursor, expand a window at the cursor, and toggle synchronized scrolling on and off. It was, in part, the windowing capabilities of the early VisiCalc and the synchronized scrolling of two separate windows that made the program one of the first best-selling software packages and created the market for electronic spreadsheet software. The synchronized scrolling capability also indicated to the early creators of spreadsheet templates how formulas comparing values in different cells across the spreadsheet were to be assigned.

/-　Repeats a single entry in one cell across the entire cell. Using the Replicate command in conjunction with Repeat will copy the cell data across several cells, a complete row, or a complete column.

SuperCalc

The real design of an effective spreadsheet financial begins before the spreadsheet is actually on the screen. While both SuperCalc and VisiCalc provide users extraordinary flexibility in manipulating the data in columns and rows and in changing and recalculating formulas, it is still important to remember that neither spreadsheet program is a word processor, and one of the important presentation virtues in any financial model is the cleanness and formatting of the text.

Thus, it is best to plan out the financial spreadsheet carefully, on graph paper if possible, so that there will be no last minute surprises concerning the screen formats. SuperCalc users should also know in advance what type of printer that they will be using. What will fit on a 130-column letter quality printer such as the Diablo, NEC, or DaisyWriter, will absolutely not fit on an 80-column Okidata. Also, planning the sheet in advance makes it possible to guarantee that numbers that readers will need to compare will be near each other when the sheet is printed. This is espcially the case when vertical and horizontal window commands will be used to bring related columns and rows onto the same screen page.

There are a number of ways to move around the worksheet once SuperCalc has been loaded and is on the screen. The four arrow cursors are the most direct form of cursor movement. So is the GO TO command, which directly addresses the worksheet to send the cursor to a new active cell. Moving between windows is a bit more complicated. The ";" command must be used to jump the cursor from one split window to the other window.

Once the beginning of a command or data has been entered into an active cell, the four cursor arrow keys no longer move the cursor around the worksheet. Instead, they can only edit the data that is being entered into the cell. After entry is completed, the /E command allows an edit of the cell, and the contents can be changed even after the entry has been committed to the worksheet. Data entry in SuperCalc, as it is in VisiCalc, is interpretive. In other words, once the slash character and first letter have been entered, the program will interpret the rest of the command and fill it in. Thus, entering /G for the beginning of a Global function signals SuperCalc to enter the rest of the command. Although the user does not have to enter the rest of the word, SuperCalc reads the first letter and interprets the rest. Once the command has been entered, all the options that are available from that command are displayed on the prompt line. Thus /W, the window command, brings five options to the prompt line: H for a horizontal split, V for a vertical split, C to remove the windows by making the upper screen the primary screen for the entire display, S to synchronize the scrolling in the two separate window areas so that the correct data goes in the right direction when the screens are scrolled through, and U to unsynchronize the two windows and allow the different portions of the screen to scroll independently. Once the Window option is entered, the screen splits and data can be entered independently to both portions of the spreadsheet. One of the most powerful features not only of SuperCalc but of any comprehensive spreadsheet program is its relative recalculation ability. In other words, if cells or blocks of cells are replicated to a new location, the program, in order not to lose the user, must be able to "read" the new location and offer the user a choice between adjustment of the formulas and leaving the formulas exactly as they are on the screen. Thus if Cell D25 which contains the formula SUM(D1:D14) is copied to T25, a new location, the column identifiers are no longer valid. The user can always go back and retype the formulas into the new locations, but with complicated formulas, that is not always possible.

Therefore, SuperCalc, like VisiCalc, provides an automatic adjustment to the new set of coordinates. In this case, the formula SUM(D1:D14) will be changed automatically to SUM(T1:T14). This is an important feature of SuperCalc because it is not always obvious that a formula must be changed when copying cells to new locations. Other commands in SuperCalc allow users to move formulas without adjustment, and still other commands make a formal query to the user for formula adjustment information. This is expecially true with /R, Replicate, where entire lines or blocks of spreadsheet can be duplicated in another portion of the screen. Unless the old formulas that are being transferred are made relative to the coordinates, the entire spreadsheet may break down. Because the software will not recognize automatically the applicability of replicated data and formulas to their new locations, this places the onus of logical construction squarely upon the user's shoulders.

The final apect of using SuperCalc concerns memory management. SuperCalc was designed for CP/M machines which did not always include large reserves of memory for applications programs and data. Moreover, CP/M requires a significant amount of memory to operate as does SuperCalc.

Therefore, the amount of memory available to data entry and the spreadsheet formatting is, in some cases, severely limited. For this reason, care should be taken not to waste valuable machine memory. Memory can be wasted by blanking out cells that are not going to be used instead of leaving them empty. When cells are empty, there is absolutely no coding overhead that takes place when the spreadsheet is loaded and processed. However, for cells that are blanked, SuperCalc allocates a stubs of memory just to manage the cell. This is a part of the SuperCalc overhead that is automatically loaded whenever the program is being run. Thus, if cells are blanked out indiscriminately, the memory required to perform the task of managing empty cells begins to accrue in significant amounts. Too much memory overhead and the program will run out of usable memory before any meaningful computations have been made. Therefore users should be very aware of actual memory in use and they should find ways of conserving it whenever possible.

SUPERCALC GLOSSARY

The following glossary of SuperCalc contains many of the same commands found in VisiCalc with the addition of relational operators, logical functions, and program functions that support the locking and unlocking of data cells. This SuperCalc glossary is for version 1.0 of the software as it was first implemented on 8-bit CP/M machines.

Formulas and Functions

Formulas specify the types of calculations and comparisons that can be made with SuperCalc. Formulas use values in other cells, numeric constants, and built-in arithmetic and mathematical and logical functions.

+   Addition.

−   Subtraction.

*   Multiplication.

/   Division.

∧   Exponentiation.

=   Equal to.

<>   Not equal to.

<   Less than.

<=   Less than or equal to.

>   Greater than.

>=   Greater than or equal to.

ABS   Absolute value.

AVERAGE   Arithmetic mean of the non-blank values in a range of numbers.

COUNT   The number of non-blank entries in a list.

ERROR, NA   Display or answer is not available for the cell having this formula or for a cell referring to a cell with missing information.

EXP   Raises a number by the exponent operand.

OR(N1,N2)   A logical OR that results in a TRUE if either expression is true or a FALSE if either or both expressions are false.

AND   Results in a TRUE if both expressions are true or a FALSE if either or both expressions are false.

NOT   Logical NOT.

IF   A conditional that can be combined with AND, OR, and NOT.

INT   The integer portion of a value.

LOOKUP   Searches a range for the value less than or

Worksheet Adjustment Commands

/D   Deletes a column or row.

/I   Inserts a column or row.

/M   Moves a column or row to a new location.

Data Assembly Commands

/C   Copies the contents of a cell, partial column, or partial row, or block of the spreadsheet to a new location. Copy command allows formula adjustment or a copy of only the absolute cell values.

/R   Replicate makes one to many copies of a cell to a group of cells, a partial column to a group of partial columns, or a partial row to a group of rows.

Data Protection Commands

/P   Protects a cell, a partial column, partial row, or a block from any formatting changes. Data cannot be entered or edited in a protected cell and all copy and replicate commands bypass cells that have been locked with a protect command.

/U   Unlocks a protected cell by removing the protection from it.

File Commands

/L   Loads the worksheet from a disk file. An entire worksheet can be loaded or only a portion of it can be loaded according to the location coordinates that are entered in response to the P(artial) prompt.

/S   Saves the worksheet as a disk file.

Final Commands

/G Global sets global function for commands that affect the entire spreadsheet.

/Q Quit SuperCalc.

/Z Zap clears the entire worksheet.

Display Commands

/T Locks the worksheet title and the titles of all rows or columns so that the titles remain on the screen while the worksheet scrolls underneath.

/W Windows the screen into vertical or horizontal sections. Also used to set synchronized scroll.

/O Outputs the worksheet to the printer.

MultiPlan

MicroSoft, the software development corporation responsible for the first microcomputer language, BASIC, and the IBM PC operating system, is the inventor of this second-generation spreadsheet and their first applications program.

Using the fundamental design (63 columns by 255 rows, yielding 16,065 cells) and operation of VisiCalc they have introduced new and exciting functions to the spreadsheet genre. MultiPlan operates on virtually every computer: either 8-, 16-, and now 32-bit processors will drive the program (allowing for CP/M, Xenix/Unix, and MS-DOS operating systems). Only 64K of RAM (which leaves 15K available) is needed, and either RGB, TTY monochrome (as in IBM's), or composite displays of 40 or 80 columns are required. Regardless of the amount of memory in your computer, MultiPlan is diskette-based and must retrieve portions of the program when functions are called for. This is what allows the program to run on systems with little RAM, but slows the operating functions. Though this slows the operation, the program's calculation speed is adequate.

While the experienced spreadsheeter may be excited by the new features, he or she will be, at the outset, confused by the conventions Microsoft has used. Rows are defined by the prefix R followed by a number, 1-255. Columns are defined by the prefix C followed also by a number, 11-63. Therefore the uppermost left hand corner is R1C1. This is a logical format, and one that can be easily gotten used to; however, it does not hold the clarity of the A1 designation found in programs like VisiCalc, SuperCalc, and Lotus 1-2-3.

The command structure or menu is always displayed. This has advantages and disadvantages. On the upside, one can always see the possible command options. The downside is that those who have used other spreadsheets will want to press the backslash key, and it clutters the lower portion of the screen, making it difficult to see the status line. Accessing the commands may be done either by pressing the space bar, moving the cursor from one command to another, or typing the first letter of the command.

Below the command menu is the status line where information about the spreadsheet appears. The current cell is indicated in the lower left-hand corner, followed by the amount of memory available, and the name of the active file. One line above these messages MultiPlan displays special messages about the cells, such as "Is the protection feature on?" To move about the spreadsheet itself is a straightforward and varied task. The cursor may be moved one cell or screen up, down, left, and right. The cursor may be homed, returned to the uppermost left-hand corner of a screen or worksheet, and the end key of the IBM keyboard will place you at the bottom of your worksheet.

Cursor movement may be executed through the directional keys of the computer keyboard themselves or through the CTRL (control) key. The escape key will cancel any function being performed; however, this action does not step back one level of the command and allow for a retry at the function but rather cancels it altogether so that long command sequences then have to be reentered.

There are twenty main commands on the menu. Some of these call up subcommands where further choices are made and acted upon. The following glossary will examine these commands and their subcommands in detail.

Overall, the MultiPlan program offers many useful and innovative features to spreadsheets. It has power, overall flexibility, and adapts well to a wide variety of hardware configurations. Its main weakness lies in a confusing and poorly organized command structure with commands that are very different compared with those of other spreadsheet programs.

Even so, it must be noted that many of the complexities of the MultiPlan command structure and nested command sequences have been simplified in the Macintosh implementation of the program. The use of the pulldown menus and windows lend themselves very handily to the simple organization of the program's commands.

Not only for the convenience of previous spreadsheet users, who will have a less turbulent transition from one spreadsheet program to the next, but because in many cases the earlier conventions show greater clarity and directness (DELETE and INSERT come to mind immediately.) The use of the TAB key to transfer from one option to another in a subcommand is inconvenient to the inexperienced user who will find it difficult not to hit the RETURN key instead. To the new user, MultiPlan will be a bit clumsy at first, but after adjusting to the new commands, the user will find MultiPlan to be a worthwhile program for spreadsheet calculations.

MULTIPLAN GLOSSARY

In addition to the 20 main commands on the menu, listed below, there are several built-in calculation features to MultiPlan. Much like the # functions of VisiCalc, MultiPlan offers automatic mathematic functions covering logical, statistical, data, tables, and algebraic/trigonometric functions. The ability to test for logic, values, and validity is a carry over from previous spreadsheets, but MultiPlan can use either text or numbers to check for value.

ALPHA   When highlighted and selected or A is chosen, allows for the entry of characters without the addition of quote marks to differentiate from number/formula entries. It is important to select the ALPHA function first, because if one were to begin typing the entry at once,

MultiPlan would interpret any appropriate letters as command selections. This may leave the user stranded in the middle of a function with no idea how he or she entered it. For example, the entry "GROSS REVENUE" would select the command "GOTO, ROW" and enter as a cell address: "oss Revenue."

BLANK Returns the prompt of "CELLS to BLANK" followed by the cell address that the cursor is currently in. This cell may be moved freely or, to include that area as a starting location, may be expanded by entering a colon followed by pointing the cursor to the last cell to include in the blank.

COPY Offers to the user three options: RIGHT, DOWN and FROM. Selecting the RIGHT or DOWN options will duplicate in those directions. The prompt asks: "COPY RIGHT/DOWN how many cells ?" and a number entry is then allowed (the default is 1) to copy that many cells to the right. The second half of the prompt is: "STARTING at ?" followed by the current active cell (this may be freely changed or an area may be redefined). To move from one prompt to another in these two-step commands it is necessary to press the TAB key. This is an unfortunate feature since many users will be accustomed to pressing the RETURN key to enter selections and will therefore get no performance from that function. These two commands will not allow for copies to be made to the left or down. To perform that function, use the FROM option. FROM is more like the standard copy commands found in other programs. It allows for an area/cell to be defined as the range to copy from, and an area/cell to be copied to, allowing for wide ranges to be duplicated.

DELETE Removes either ROWS or COLUMNS and moves the remainder of the entries either up rows or columns left. It is unusual how these sections are defined. When the DELETE function is selected, the user has the choice of either ROW or COLUMN. When COLUMN is selected, there are the following prompts:

DELETE COLUMN:
# of columns:
starting at:
between rows:
and:

The number of columns to delete is defaulted at 1. The user may enter any NUMBER from 1-63; the starting column is the one currently active and may be changed; the rows to delete are set starting at row 1 and ending at row 255 although the user may define the number of rows. If other rows are selected as a range, the remainder will be raised and the columns will be moved to the left, leaving a potentially inaccurate worksheet. This command should never be used as replacement for the BLANK command as it has disastrous potential. The DELETE ROW command operates in the same manner. Although MultiPlan breaks down the function into four separate sections there is very little warning of its effect on the worksheet.

EDIT Allows for changes to be made to a cell entry. When selecting this function, the cursor need not already be on the cell to edit—it may be moved with the directional arrows. EDIT brings down to the working line the cell entry. The user should be careful when moving the changing cursor position because if the directional arrows are pressed, the cursor selects a new cell to edit (the one in the direction pressed). The user should use the special keys defined (on the IBM version they are the F9/left and F10/right function keys). As edits are made in a formula any dependent numbers are changed also.

FORMAT Returns several options. They are CELLS, DEFAULT OPTIONS, and WIDTH. DEFAULTs may be set of the entire worksheet, and these global commands may be overwritten with the CELL option. They cover the areas of the CELL command as well as global column width (from 1-32 characters long).

CELL returns subcommands for which cell(s) to format. These are selected as acting on a cell/area, and govern the alignment of the entries (default, centered, left-justified, and right-justified). Numbers as well as text entries may be aligned allowing for attractive positioning. Format codes may also be selected. These apply almost exclusively to numbers with the exception of CONTINUOUS which will allow text entries to overlap their cells if the entry is longer than the width. This option requires that the cell adjacent to it be blank and also formatted to CONTINUOUS. Other format codes may be for scientific notation, fixed-decimal values, integer, currency display, percent and the default selection.

The next option, # of DECIMALS, applies only to fixed, percent, and expotential formats. OPTIONS allows for the insertion of commas, number entries, and formulas to be displayed as either the values that they return or as the actual formula used.

WIDTH allows for columns to be shrunk or expanded in character size, the default to be used, and the starting and ending columns to be used.

GOTO Moves the cursor to one of three options: a range-named area, a particular cell, or a particular window and cell (see the WINDOW command).

HELP Accessible through the command menu; presents the user with instructions on how to use the help menus and options to continue pages at a time (backward and forward) or move to common areas of interest/ help. Of better use is its invocation while within a command structure. Regardless of the command entered, pressing the (in the IBM version) ALT + H keys will present the user with useful information on how to operate that function. This is both more flexible than the HELP command on the main menu and much more direct.

INSERT   Performs the same functions as the DELETE command with the reverse results.

LOCK   Sets to either LOCK/UNLOCK the entries of a cell/area. CELL will LOCK all of the entries for specified areas and turn the protection feature on or off. FORMULAS will lock globally the text/formulas of the entire worksheet (the FORMULAS option is also called GLOBAL LOCK).

MOVE   Works with either ROW or COLUMN, much the same as the INSERT and DELETE features. MOVE follows with the prompt MOVE ROW/COLUMN and allows the following options: from row/column, before row/to left of column, or # of rows/columns. Entering answers to these prompts will replace the entries the prescribed number of spaces/directions. This, also like INSERT and DELETE, shifts the entire worksheet display and can have poor effects when used incorrectly. There is no option for moving an individual cell to another location.

NAME   Allows for a cell/area to be referred to by a string of text and to have that name be used interchangeably in any command function. For example, if a long column of numbers is named "sales" you may then include the whole area in a calculation by using its name rather than pointing to its cells every time needed. This can make large worksheets much easier to work with.

OPTIONS   Has three system defaults that may be set. The MUTE function will turn off the beep that sounds when a calculation is entered incorrectly or during other error-trapping instances. RECALC is the option to have the worksheet recalculated every time an entry is made. This may be turned off so that when the user is entering large amounts of data the spreadsheet does not hold up operation due to excessive recalculation. With the RECALC function in manual mode, a special function key will allow recalculation when called for. ITERATION allows for the complete calculation of all formulas to one/one-thousandth decimal value (0.001). This may cause problems if a circular reference occurs (when a cell contains a formula depending on itself). ITERATION may be stopped by pressing the ESC/escape key. The

prompt "completion test at:" is used to indicate a cell where values are being tested for validity (true/false tests).

PRINT   Brings up a series of options which allow the worksheet to be printed either to a printer device or to a file on disk. Without specifying otherwise, the entire worksheet is printed. MARGIN lets the user specify the number of printable lines and columns on a page. OPTIONS will let the user specify only portions of the worksheet to be printed, special codes to be sent to the printer (to access features of that device), formulas to be printed rather than their values, and the column/row borders to be included.

QUIT   Command is confirmed by answering YES, saving accidental erasure of files intended to be saved.

SORT   Another of the innovations of MultiPlan. It allows for areas to be manipulated in ascending or descending order. A primary key is set by specifying the column on which to act and the rows involved. Note: entire rows are sorted. If a worksheet is divided by two sections horizontally, both sections will be sorted and empty cells in the sorted row will be ignored. However, any entries in the other columns of that row are reassigned to either the top or bottom of the heap (ascending or descending order). This is very unfortunate in the case of titles explaining the entries below them.

TRANSFER   Used for the file operations of MultiPlan, it provides subcommands for LOAD, SAVE, CLEAR, DELETE, OPTIONS, and RENAME. This is the most straightforward of MultiPlan's commands. LOAD requires that you place a drive specifier (i.e., B:) for other than the default drive. However, this does provide the convenience of showing a directory of that disk (by pressing any of the directional arrows) and letting the user highlight the file wanted by pressing the return key to load that file. This procedure holds true for the DELETE command as well by confirming the operation before the command is carried out. CLEAR will blank the current worksheet and also requires confirmation of the action. The OPTIONS command allows for different file types to be specified. The default is NORMAL or MultiPlan format. SYMBOLIC is the MultiPlan format to allow for data exchange with other programs (the SYLK file format), and OTHER will load VisiCalc files (this will allow Visi files to be brought into MultiPlan, but not MultiPlan files to be sent out in Visi format). RENAME and SAVE let a user change the name of the active worksheet or file the current one to diskette.

VALUE   The formula/number equivalent of ALPHA, letting the user enter in nontext entries.

WINDOW   Splits the display of a worksheet into several sections, and has a number of options. SPLIT will divide the display into different sections HORIZON-TALLY, VERTICALLY, or specify TITLES that should always be displayed when scrolling. The HORIZON-TAL/VERTICAL splits may be synchronized to scroll both windows in the same direction or left to move independently of each other. MultiPlan will support up to eight separate windows on the screen (given the limits of most computer screens to display 80 columns by 25 lines, this seems to be more than needed). To make the display of these windows easier to see, the program offers the BORDER command to surround each window with equal signs or the PAINT command to specify colors to be set for the individual windows and their contents (provided that the computer has a color monitor). The PAINT option can be used to good effect when designing a model to be used by other persons. The designer of the model may set different colors to draw attention to areas that will make it easier for the user to locate certain sections. LINK will set scrolling for separate windows on the display; for instance: windows one and three may be set to scroll together while window two remains in the same portion. CLOSE will remove a window from the display.

eXTERNAL   Information in one cell of one worksheet may be linked to a cell in another worksheet, updating the second worksheet's calculations to provide accurate information based on variables. This operation brings to a spreadsheet the powers of programs like relational databases where data may be shared by several dependent files. The subcommands of eXTERNAL set the cell to COPY to other worksheets and selects the LINK option (automatic sharing or relative). The COPY function copies not only the value of a formula, not the formula itself. LIST will provide a listing of those worksheets that are dependent to the active worksheet. USE sets a substitute name for a worksheet.

Lotus 1-2-3

The introduction of Lotus 1-2-3 in 1983 by Lotus Development Corporation of Boston was one of the most successful introductions of a program ever achieved by a software company in the short history of microcomputers. This popular electronic spreadsheet package was partially the result of its developer's earlier work on a VisiCalc utility. The company's founder, Mitch Kapor, had previously written a program to reproduce graphics from a VisiCalc file; it was called Visi-Trend/Plot. The contract that Kapor had won from Visicorp seeded the research and development of 1-2-3.

The numbers in Lotus 1-2-3's name indicate the three components of the package: electronic spreadsheet, business graphics, and database management. These features, all of which were programs in themselves, had previously not been combined into one system. Thus, the combination of these features into Lotus made it the first truly integrated program and one of the finest of its kind produced to date. It was also the first program specifically developed to run on the IBM PC and other MS-DOS machines. Consequently, Lotus was able to take advantage of every feature that the PC had to offer, including the microprocessor and the amount of memory that could be accessed. Indeed, every key of the keyboard was used to the program's advantage, and the software even overcame some weaknesses of the keyboard such as the confusing and often tricky CAPS LOCK and NUM LOCK indicators.

Lotus 1-2-3 was also one of the earliest programs to contain a utility that allowed users to install the program specifically for the hardware configuration they had and to take advantage of the MS-DOS date and time prompts at program startup. 1-2-3 also allowed users the very critical ability to port their data files over from other spreadsheet and database programs. This was called the TRANSLATE feature, which converted file types. This TRANSLATE feature allowed VisiCalc files to be used in Lotus and for DBF files, such as those created in dBASE II, to be brought into 1-2-3 or a Lotus file to be sent to a DBF file. The TRANSLATE feature also allowed the exchange of DIF (data interchange files) between programs.

Unlike some of its competitors, the entire working Lotus program loads into active memory after startup. This is a key feature of the software because the resulting speed of processing improves the overall operation of the program, and, consequently, has been one of the contributing factors to 1-2-3's continuing success. The spreadsheet appearence itself is rather similar to most Calc-type software, with columns labled and rows numbered. There is a cell address indicator in the top left-hand corner of the screen and a mode indicator in the right-hand side. Two blank lines follow, which are used as a display area for work in progress or for performing edits, and for the two command lines. The specifications

of Lotus indicate the first difference between this program and the rest of the spreadsheet genre. There are 256 columns and 2048 rows, making Lotus, with over 524,000 cells for entry, over 32 times larger than Visi/SuperCalc and MultiPlan. The bottom row of the display is reserved for indicator lights like CAPS, NUM, CIRC(ular reference), SCROLL, and CALC.

Moving around the worksheet is very simple. Up, down, left, and right are controlled by the directional arrow keys. Page Up and Page Down move the spreadsheet 20 rows at a time, and HOME returns the cursor to the home postion in cell A1. The TAB key moves the display one page to the right horizontally at default settings of 8 columns, and SHIFT and TAB move to the left horizontally. The last directional key to be used is the END key, a key which brings an END indicator. When another directional is pressed in conjunction with the END key, the cursor moves to the last cell in that direction with an entry. For example, consider a table of numbers 55 rows long. To get to the bottom row and total them, the user would press END and the DOWN to have the cursor placed in row 55. This represents a huge time savings and convienience when moving around the large worksheet, but it can be confusing to the first-time user when he or she is suddenly in row 2048 after just having begun to enter data in the cells.

The command menu is accessed in the manner of other Calc programs: through the SLASH (/) key. The choices that then confront the user are not abbreviations but full words that are meaningful and straightforward. The first of the two command lines displays the main choices; on the second line are the subcommands which are associated with the main command. The second-line choices change as the cursor is moved to highlight the next main command. For example, if the command WORKSHEET is selected, the options are Global, Insert, Delete, Column-Width, Erase, Titles, and Windows. When the RANGE command is highlighted, they change to Format, Label-Prefix, and so on. Formulas are entered in the program by preceding them with a PLUS (+) sign, causing the mode indicator in the top right-hand corner to change from the READY state to the VALUE mode. Unlike its predecessors, 1-2-3 does not require that you type a special character or make a command choice to enter a number or text-label. Instead, a PLUS sign is used if a formula is to follow.

The use of the cursor for defining areas is unique in 1-2-3. To specify a cell or range, one only has to move the cursor to that spot with the directional arrows. However, unlike SuperCalc, which also has that feature, the cursor may be expanded to show the entire area needed, not just the top left-hand and bottom right-hand corners. This expanding cursor feature, known as range painting, makes operation smoother and easier for the beginner to understand, and it provides a human interface that is simple and effective. And the results of Kapor's work proved to be one of the most successful software programs ever developed for microcomputers. Lotus 1-2-3 built upon the earlier success of electronic spreadsheets, database managers, and business graphics software.

LOTUS 1-2-3 GLOSSARY

Like some other spreadsheets, 1-2-3 takes advantage of function keys. Those keys may change in number and location from computer to computer, but they have essentially the same functions. The function keys operate as follows:

F1   HELP   Invokes the online help feature

F2   EDIT   Allows changes to be made to entries

F3   NAME   Displays range names

F4   ABS   Turns relatives to absolutes in formulas

F5   GOTO   Moves cursor to specified cell

F6   WINDOW   Moves cursor from active window to other

F7   QUERY   Repeats the last data query function

F8   TABLE   Reproduces data tables from last command

F9   CALC   Recalculates worksheet when in manual mode

F10   GRAPH   Plots last graph selected with current data

The use of function keys not only makes the user comfortable but keeps the command line from becoming cluttered with more options. An interesting function is the combination of GOTO NAME, which moves the cursor to the first active cell of a specified range name. This is a very fast method of locating specific types of label information and marks the beginnings of a natural-language interface for data-heavy processing programs.

What follows is a brief overview of the Lotus 1-2-3 command structure.

WORKSHEET   Comprises the commands that affect the entire spreadsheet and are further organized by subcommands. INSERT adds blank columns or rows to the spreadsheet at any specified area for any duration; the opposite of this is DELETE. GLOBAL controls overriding functions like the FORMAT of cell, how text is displayed (LABEL PREFIX), the width of all columns (COLUMN WIDTH), the manner of RECALCULATION (automatic, manual, rowwise, iteration, columnwise, natural), enabling and disabling the PROTECTION of worksheet entries, and DEFAULT options that contain configuration information.

RANGE   Covers all the commands that affect only portions of the worksheet; these are areas defined with the range-painting feature or expanding cursor. Subcommands include FORMAT, one of the most advanced formatting features available on the market. Formats may be selected to include dollar symbols with embedded commas and two decimal places (CURRENCY), only decimal places (FIXED), decimals and commas with negative parentheses as in accounting notation, exponential notation (SCIENTIFIC), display of formulas rather than the value returned (TEXT), and others. All of these are also found in the WORKSHEET FORMAT command, but operate on a global level. RANGE also comprises other functions similar to WORKSHEET, including PROTECT and UNPROTECT to enable/disable protection on portions of the worksheet, INPUT to input information repeatedly into one or more unprotected cells in a protected worksheet, and LABEL-PREFIX to format text (left/right-justified or centered). Another text feature is RANGE JUSTIFY to input text into a single cell and then to move it to several cells of varying width. This command may be used for quick text entry or short reports in a spreadsheet. As a replacement for a word processor, it is certainly not sophisticated. For example, entered into cell A1 is the following line: Now is the time for all good men to rally to the aid of their flag.

The RANGE JUSTIFY command specified to columns A and B would display:

Now is the time
for all good men
to rally to the aid of their flag

RANGE ERASE   Deletes entries from a specified cell or range of cells; it uses the range-painting convention and is similar to Visi/SuperCalc's BLANK command. The last RANGE command is NAME, one of the carryovers from MultiPlan. A RANGE NAME is given to a portion of a worksheet; this name is now synonymous with the cell range and may be included in all formulas and commands as a replacement. An example is the area of A1 thru A55 containing sales figures: if the range name is defined as SALES, you can issue the command RANGE ERASE SALES and the entire column area is blanked. The range-naming feature not only is convienient but allows for easy programming with macros.

COPY and MOVE   Use the range-painting feature to operate straightforwardly, without confusing the user. After selecting one of these commands, the prompt is returned:

Range to copy/move from: A1..B5

followed by

Range to copy/move to: C20..D25.

This is simple, easy, and virtually foolproof if one is paying proper attention to the display.

FILE Controls the functions relating to file manipulation, and no other program has as many or useful file options as 1-2-3. They include RETRIEVE for the loading of previously created worksheets. A listing of all the files on that disk or directory is produced, and any file may be retrieved by highlighting it and pressing the return key. This has the directness that would have been desirable in MultiPlan (much better than TRANSFER LOAD B: and an arrow key, then return) and follows the design of Visi/SuperCalc but allows for loading from the listing. Other FILE operations are as follows: SAVE, if the file has been retrieved, remembers the file name and displays it automatically; if you press the return key, you are prompted with:

THAT FILE ALREADY EXISTS
REPLACE IT WITH THE NEW DATA
cancel
or
replace.

The FILE ERASE command operates in much the same manner, forcing the user to specify a yes/no answer for the operation to continue. COMBINE overlays parts or all of a file onto the current one. FILE COMBINE, very useful when doing a year-end summary, takes the monthly worksheets and lays them atop each other; the FILE COMBINE ADD command automatically performs addition on all the number entries. FILE COMBINE may be specified for an ENTIRE file or a NAMED-RANGE of a file. The IMPORT command allows for direct inclusion of foriegn files, like WordStar .prn files. EXTRACT will pull either the formulas or values (entries) of files to be included in the current worksheet. LIST produces a listing of the file names on a disk/directory for either a PRINT, WORKSHEET, or GRAPH file type. DIRECTORY lets the user override the WORKSHEET GLOBAL DEFAULT DIRECTORY command and switch drives/directories for file operations.

PRINT These commands are some of the most flexible of all the Calc programs and produce fine reports. PRINT returns the option first of FILE or PRINTER for output destination; the next options are the same in either case. RANGE is returned to specify the area for printing (convenient because it does not print the whole worksheet all the time like some other programs do). CLEAR resets any or all of the specified options that have been selected. LINE and PAGE advance the paper in the printer, a valuable command if the printer is not next to the computer. OPTIONS gives choices to declare MARGINS, HEADER, and/or FOOTER layouts which may be automatically "stamped" with page numbers, date, text messages, or all three. SETUP codes specify the particular print styles your printer may be capable of generating, a particularly useful feature for some of the newer IBM compatible graphics printers. PAGE-

LENGTH and the printing of BORDERS may be specified, as well as the way that formatted entries should be printed using the OTHER command. The following two commands work in tandem: ALIGN resets any of the buffers 1-2-3 uses to track the number of lines per page; before each seperate printing, the ALIGN command should be given followed by GO to execute the print.

GRAPH A function not found in many spreadsheets, returns several options for the creation and storage of visual representations of the worksheet data. The first choice that the user is presented with is TYPE, asking for the style of graph (PIE, XY, BAR, STACKED-BAR, LINE) followed by an X range. The X range is for the selection of titles to be displayed across the bottom line of the graph (usually time periods, persons' names, places, and so forth). There is no need to select a Y axis range; it will be automatically selected by 1-2-3 based on the next set of ranges. The options that follow are labeled A through F; these are the individual items to be compared. After specifying these ranges, selecting the VIEW command will replace the worksheet display and show the appropriate graph with cross-hatching to represent different areas (if there are two monitors attached, one TTY and the other RGB, the graph will show on the RGB while the worksheet will remain on the TTY). Within the OPTIONS command are selections for TITLES (two on the top line, one each on the X and Y axes), LEGEND for the A through F ranges, FORMAT for the display of numbers (same as in RANGE and WORKSHEET), and GRID to display lines bisecting horizontally, vertically, or both. DATA-LABELS may also be set to show titles within the X/Y graph section. COLOR or black-and-white selections may also be made (colors and cross-hatchings are automatically selected). The last of the GRAPH OPTIONS commands is SCALE. The X and Y axis scales are automatically set by 1-2-3, but can be overwritten with this command. If the SCALE is set to MANUAL, an UPPER and LOWER limit must be chosen as well as format or layout for the display. An addition to the SCALE command is SKIP, applied only to the X axis. Since the X axis can accommodate only 40 columns of text (medium resolution on the RGB screen), it may be necessary to display only part of the titles. SKIP will alternate the specified number of spaces. An example is the 12 months of the year; all cannot fit on the screen at the same time, therefore a SKIP SCALE of 2 would show Jan., Mar., May, July, and so on.

DATA Controls some of the most interesting of the 1-2-3 functions. DATA is broken into five selections: SORT, TABLE, DISTRIBUTION, FILL, and QUERY. DATA SORT returns prompts for the data range, which is highlighted by the range-painting convention; it show the area on which to act—this may be a small block of the worksheet or entire combinations of columns and rows. Unlike MultiPlan, 1-2-3 acts only on the specified area, and nothing else is affected. A PRIMARY-KEY is chosen by showing the first entry found in the column selected (the key-field), then specifying the sort as ascending or descending (A or D). The same applies to the SECONDARY-KEY, which is used as a tie breaker when there is no unique case found in the PRIMARY-KEY.

Selecting the GO command will sort the data; if the order is desired at a very rapid rate, after a quick flicker of the screen the data is in new order. It is important to remember that all of the associated information of a data range should be included. Otherwise when the SORT command activates, it will only act on the selected portion of the data, leaving the user with a mess. DATA QUERY allows the user [after selecting the INPUT range where the data, including the column titles, is found, copying the titles to and specifying a CRITERION (the titles and one blank line for user input) and OUTPUT range] to ask a question and have returned all records that match the given criterion. An example is an inventory: A user enters in the blank line beneath the CRITERION range formula to show the first entry in the Quantity column (A5) greater than 25 (the formula would be +A5>25). A 1 or a 0 will display in the cell after pressing the return key; this signifies that either the first record matches the criterion (1) or it does not (0). When the command EXTRACT is issued, a list of all the matching records is copied to the output range.

CRITERIONs may include the addition of ADD or OR statements. If an OR statement is included in the CRITERION formula, then either of two values must be met; AND will test for two valid answers. This, known as compound boolean logic, makes the rather simple data commands of 1-2-3 much more sophisticated than logical commands in other spreadsheets. If the FIND command is issued, the cursor expands to cover the width of the data range and jump the first matching record; pressing the down arrow keys moves the highlight to the next match, and so on, until a beep is issued signifying the last match. If the UNIQUE command is selected, it disallows all duplicates that may be found in the database. DELETE finds the matches based on the specified criterion and removes it from the database, thereby shortening the data range and the resulting program work load. RESET disallows all ranges set to the worksheet regarding the DATA QUERY commands.

Other builti-in functions of 1-2-3 include @ formulas. These prewritten formulas are found in virtually all Calc software, but none is as extensive as 1-2-3. These functions cover statistical, mathematic/algebraic, trigonometric, database statistical, logical, financial, and date arithmetic. Date math is one of the innovations of 1-2-3, using the Julian calendar to calculate every day assigned a number. Issuing the @TODAY formula will have 1-2-3 take the DOS date/time stamp and convert it to the Julian value. Using the RANGE FORMAT DATE command offers the user several display options for that date. With this option, aging of an accounts receivable becomes easy, as does tracking of due dates.

In the area of financial calculation, 1-2-3 offers Net Present Value, Future Value, Payment, Internal Rate of Return, and others. Statistical functions cover Average, Sum, Minimum, Maximum, Count of entries, and Standard Deviation (this is a significant advance in electronic spreadsheet technology). Logical functions cover True and False tests, If statements, And/Or, and other tests of validity. Lookups, both horizontal and vertical, are supported as well as Integer and Round statements.

Given these varied commands and functions, the user/programmer can begin to see possibilities and applications that were heretofore not possible without the ability to automate them. This automation is accomplished through Macros, or the "typing alternative" as it is called in the manual. Macros allow for a series of commands and entries that can be recalled and repeated when needed. Macros are entered into an empty portion of the worksheet and are signified with the RANGE NAME CREATE command. To differentiate a macro from a named range, macros are preceded by the BACKSLASH (\) symbol and named by one letter only. When executing a macro, however, the user holds down the ALT (on some computers it is the SHIFT and CTRL keys) and depresses the letter key.

There obviously can only be 26 macros per worksheet, but there is no limitation to their size or scope. Since no command line has an option that begins with the same letter, macro writing is similar to shorthand, requiring typing the first letter of every choice. A macro to move the cursor to cell A1 and enter the value of 100, then formatted to show dollar signs, is:

$$\text{\&home*100\textasciitilde/rfc2\textasciitilde\textasciitilde.}$$

Notice the directional statement HOME; in Lotus 1-2-3's macros you have full command of the action; the tilde (~) represents the return key. Notice that in the macro there are no prompts; therefore the macroprogrammer should be familiar with the program and do paper runthroughs before entering the data. These simple functions, although they were available in a severely limited capacity in older spreadsheet programs, are utilized by 1-2-3 in a more comprehensive implementation.

X macro commands are the features that make simple command processing more like programming, and suggest an interesting interface between the role of the 1-2-3 user and the 1-2-3 applications programmer. They offer uses that cover conditional execution XI, continuance at other locations XL, user menus XM, and several others that make 1-2-3's programming similiar in nature to BASIC (XI is equal to IF THAN, XL to GOSUB, and so forth). With the combination of predefined functions and menus in a worksheet, any and all of its uses may be automated, making this an efficient model to be used by anyone familiar or unfamiliar with spreadsheets in general or 1-2-3 in particular. As with all other forms of programming, macros can be tedious, long, and complex, and the slightest mistaken entry can crash the whole program's execution. Careful groundwork should be done first.

Though many of the features of Lotus Development Corporation's 1-2-3 have been offered before, they have never been so handily "under one roof." Nor is it that the individual pieces are so valuable to the programmer as stand-alone entities; it is simply that the sum of the whole is greater than the parts. In a smooth, elegant, logical, Englishlike, and straightforward manner, Lotus 1-2-3 offers features and functions that both the beginner and experienced user can benefit from. The first-time spreadsheet user will be able to set up a financial model easily without having to worry about complicated formats or formulas, and the experienced user will be able to utilize Lotus 1-2-3's branching and conditional logic features and its wide range of statistical calculation features as well.

This, as most Lotus users report, was one of the most attractive features of the software. Because it placed so much computational power at the fingertips of even the most novice spreadsheet users, it actually helped to create a generation of power users who could apply some of the sophisticated modeling techniques they had learned in their accounting and statistics courses to real business cases without having to use the facilities of electronic data processing departments or a mainframe-based query language.

Symphony

The latest product from the makers of 1-2-3 is an upgraded extension called Symphony. This unique program builds upon 1-2-3 but includes further functions and improvements on past features. Symphony is, as of late 1984, only available on the IBM PC/XT/AT, the Compaq Portable/Plus/and DeskPro, the ITT XTRA, and several other compatible computers. It requires a truly significant amount of RAM, a minimum of 320K (more is recommended). The reason for this high amount is the torque packed into Symphony's components: spreadsheet, database/forms-filer, graphics, word processor, communications, and macro programming. These features are all present at the press of a button and require a good deal of room in active memory to operate at their best. Several other features have been added to the basic spreadsheet. Windows permit one or more operations to be displayed on the screen at the same time. This "windowing" capability had been heralded in 1983 as the coming wave of software technology, but not many real benefits are derived from it and not all people with Symphony will use it. Symphony also is open ended, meaning that other applications may be run within Symphony's environment. This ability to run other programs and DOS routines with Symphony makes data transfer and exchange much more efficient, especially on a "memory-conscious" microcomputer.

In many ways, Symphony is really a powerful extension of an already powerful program, and because the command structures of the two packages are so similar we have elected not to include a full glossary of Symphony in this entry. Rather, we will point to some of the basic differences in command key functions between Symphony and 1-2-3 and direct the reader to Lotus' own clear explanations of the Symphony commands.

There is much to learn in Symphony, and this may be intimidating to the first-time user. Its size (now 256 columns by 8192 rows) and sophisticated design do complicate matters for novices, but these are easily surmounted. Keys have been moved around to accommodate the new plethora of commands. Most directly affected are the function keys. The main menu is no longer brought to life with the SLASH (/) key but rather the F10 function key (the slash still works in the spreadsheet for convenience). Depressing the ALT and F10 key allows the user to switch the work environment to the other functions (SHEET for the spreadsheet, DOC for word processing, FORM for database, GRAPH, and COMM-

unications). The F10 or MENU key is related to the type of environment that is active. To access the functions which are constant like FILE, use the F9 or SERVICES key. These SERVICES are like global commands in that they control overall operation, including the SETTINGS sheet. The SETTINGS sheet is a new convention from Lotus Development; it contains all of the range/configuration information about a given command/operation. There is a SETTINGS sheet for GRAPHS, COMM, PRINTING, and more. Everything gets its own settings sheet.

The spreadsheet command line has been streamlined very well. No longer are frequently used commands hidden like INSERT/DELETE, COLUMN WIDTH, ERASE, and FORMAT. This should make things easier for the beginner, as the somewhat less used commands are found on the F9 key away from harm. This, however, may aggravate for a short while the 1-2-3 user who automatically types in a command, thinking that everything follows the familiar. This is an incorrect assumption because, for example /FILE RETRIEVE is now {F10} FORMAT BEEP, and other examples abound. Just a little unlearning is necessary before 1-2-3 users are as much at home with Symphony as they are with the orignal program. Symphony is an interesting program because there are virtually no operations that cannot be performed. The tools are all present.

The macro commands in Symphony have been expanded to include many more operators than before. Now, much like the BASIC programming language, macros may perform subroutines even while executing a main macro. With new commands to control everything from the disabling of the ESCape/BREAK keys to suppression of the command line when executing, Symphony becomes an applications programmer's heaven. True automation is now possible for spreadsheet number crunchers for the first time at a desktop level. In addition, security may be set on a worksheet so that unauthorized personnel cannot snoop at templates, and hidden cells may be specified so that certain entries are suppressed. Macros have been simplified by the inclusion of new key representations; in 1-2-3 there was no page-down macro command, now there is {bigdown} or {down 20}. Now there is the ability to repeat automatically; instead of {right}{right}{right}, there is {right 3}.

On the software best-sellers list, Symphony has packed power, functions, features, and enough capabilities to provide even the most ambitious financial modeler with the tools to create a self-generating business plan. Symphony will indeed herald a new type of integrated functions software package.

Framework

In addition to the release of Lotus Corporation's long-awaited Symphony, 1984 also saw the release of Aston-Tate's Framework, a program that its developers heralded as software that operates the way people think. The premise of Framework is that all work performed in any of the programs's components—word processing, database management, electronic spreadsheet calculations, business graphs, outlining of thoughts and ideas, and telecommunications—is performed within a series of modules that appear as three-dimensional frames on the screen.

Frames can be opened, nested one within the other, expanded or contracted, and located anywhere on the screen. The Framework frames are data containers or cubbyholes in which word processing workspaces can be opened up, spreadsheets can be constructed, databases can be designed, graphs drawn, and outlines developed that will help users structure their data. One of the most interesting features of Framework is the basic recursive structure of the software. Frames can be stored within frames as if they were Chinese boxes. Once a frame is stored in this way, a formal logical relationship is established between it and its related frames in such a way that commands affecting one frame can affect the data in all the related frames nested within each other. The important fact to remember about the frames in Framework is that frames are not separate screen windows, as they are in some of the popular "windowing" programs such as "Sidekick" or on the Macintosh screen. The frames are actually independent or logically related workspaces which are defined both by the type of information they contain and by the relationship they have to other frames. Therefore, a frame's function may be only to contain another frame, and that frame may in turn contain an additional frame. This is how to construct an outline in framework so that when one frame is moved, all the related modules of information in the other enclosed frames are moved as well.

Framework Desktop

Framework's user interface is an electronic desktop with command and menu options for the different types of frames displayed across the top. The menus are:

Disk Contains commands for saving and retrieving files, closing all frames on the desktop, entering DOS through Framework and quitting the program.

Create Contains commands for creating new frames or adding columns and rows to spreadsheet frames and database frames.

Edit Contains commands to undo the previous command and remove columns and rows from spreadsheets and databases. Edit also contains commands to lock titles in spreadsheets and databases and to prevent changes to frames. There is also an insert-overwrite toggle as well as a toggle to display hidden characters in the word processor frames.

Locate Contains the commands for search, sort, and replace.

Frames Contains commands for opening, closing, enlarging, and blanking several frames at the same time, arranging frames in a document, and controlling the appearance of the information on the frames' border.

Words Contains commands that control the style and alignment of text, the margin settings, the tab settings, and the depth of paragraph indentations.

Numbers Contains commands that control the format and alignment of numbers and the recalculation of formulas.

Graphs Contains commands that create and style the graphs of spreadsheet and database output.

Print Contains commands that drive the print output. Part of the ease of working with Framework is the on-screen pull-down menus that contain options for each of Framework's components and the online Help instructions that are invoked by depressing the F1 key. The Help instructions are keyed to the particular module or command that is active at the time F1 is depressed. Once in the online Help screen, users can page forward or back to view the particular instructions in a larger context.

Outline Component

Outlining is the most basic function of Framework. New outlines are created by selecting the Outline option from the create menu and determining the labels for the frames within frames that will form the different levels of the outline. Each line in the outline labels a frame that will contain the information specified in the label, and each frame might contain a different Framework module. Thus, in a frame labeled "Sales Report," line 1.1 might be "Major Cities" and be designated as a word processing frame; line 1.2 might be "1984 Figures" and be designated as a spreadsheet frame; and line 1.3 might be "Directory of Products Sold" and be designated as a database frame. Each frame under "Sales Report" is a subordinate frame which can be moved around within the outline. When the frame is moved, all of the information contained in the frame is moved as well. Thus, if in rearranging the outline for "Sales Report" the writer placed 1.2 after 1.3, the spreadsheet would be repositioned after the database. Using this type of structure, the cutting and pasting operation, which is a feature in most integrated packages, is eliminated.

Using the outline function of Framework to organize work also provides a quick method of moving from section to section within a particularly long document. Rather than scroll or page as with a typical word processor, one simply has to view the entire work in its outline format and move from level to level using the arrow, control arrow keys, or page up and down. In addition, movement among different parts of the outline at the same level is allowed. The function keys allow the user to rearrange the outline and copy material from one frame to another.

Using the F6 Extend Select key with the Locate menu allows the outline sections in the frames to be sorted either on the same or different levels. Finally, once the contents of the frames labeled by the outline have been formed into a single document, the outline itself can be turned into a table of contents by the "View Page Numbers" command in the Frames menu. "View Page Numbers" calculates the page number on which each section of the former outline starts and displays the outline as a table of contents. This is a very powerful option for the preparation of any document which contains multiple sections of different types of material.

Word Processor

Framework's word processor is a menu-driven program that displays the page format on the screen exactly as it will appear in print. The word processor is invoked through the Create menu exactly as if an empty frame were being created to hold subframes or an outline. In this instance, however, once text is typed into the empty frame, it automatically becomes a word processing workspace. Cursor movement within the workspace or word processing frame is possible by character, as it is all other word processors; and by word, sentence, line, paragraph, or frame or, like Wordstar, directly to the beginning or to the end of a document. If typing within the frame is too restrictive, and this is the case for long documents, the F9 Zoom feature can be moved to extend the frame to cover the entire screen. Like Wordstar and other full-featured word processors, Framework allows printing in bold and underlined text. However, because the Framework software geneates its own character set in the graphics mode, bold and underline appear on the screen as boldface type and underlined type. This is a feature not found in any program that uses the standard IBM character set. Moreover, Framework has an italics option on the Words menu that appears as an italic on any PC using a graphics card. For PCs that do not have a graphics card, the italics text appears as underlined on the screen but as italics on a dot matrix printout. The Words menu also has choices for a standard left-aligned page, centered text, and left-to-right margin justification. However, the Words menu also has a Flush Right option, not found many word processors, that sets text flush against the right margin with a ragged left margin. This feature is often used in business letters and reports when text such as page numbers or the name and address of a recepient must be on the right-hand side of the page. Finally, the Words menu contains commands for search and replace, search and replace across frames, and block movement of text within the frame.

Printer output is supported by an extensive menu and printer control commands. Most notably, Frame-work supports a concurrent interface of two printers, typically a dot matrix for drafts and a letter-quality for final copy, and a plotter. Because of the interrelationship of frames to other frames and to different types of data, the print output options in Framework support such professional-level data processing features as spooling, job queueing, and batch printing from the label level of the highest frame. In other words, entire documents can be chained together by their frame levels in either the Outline View or Frame View mode and printed without the user's having to retrieve the specific data and send it to the printer on a frame by frame basis. This print-by-outline feature is similar to a global print capability found in many word processors that support the printing of a number of linked documents directly from a file directory. Framework, however, allows the printing of word processed text, spreadsheets, database reports, and graphs with one series of commands that format the entire document.

Spreadsheet

In its spreadsheet mode Framework performs much like SuperCalc. It supports expandable columns, a text number option that allows numbers to be entered as if they were text characters that will not be calculated, and natural languages references for each cell in addition to the standard A6 or D14 cell descriptors. Movement around the spreadsheet is controlled by the same series of cursor movement keys that control the movement within a word processed document. The Home and End keys shuttle back and forth between the first and last column of the sheet, Control Home and Control End between the beginning and end of the spreadsheet, and Control Page Up and Control Page Down between entire rows. Movement from cell to cell is controlled by the up, down, right, and left cursor arrow keys.

FRED Programming Language

Formulas for calculating results can be entered directly into the cells or entered via the F2 Formula Edit key. The formulas used by the spreadsheet component of Framework are all part of the FRED programming language that is included with the Framework package. FRED contains standard formulas such as @SUM, addition, subtraction, multiplication, and division, as well as algebraic, statistical, and trigonometric functions. The FRED language, while most immediate to the mathematical functions supporting the spreadsheet cells, also contains the print format commands and commands to generate calculations through a series of spreadsheet and database frames. It is this use of an auxiliary programming langauge that operates within the Framework desktop environment of related workspaces that allows users to manipulate data from file to file and throughout a number of frames.

In theory, the logical architecture of Framework is much like the logical architecture of a standard block-structured language like Pascal, PL/I, or S-BASIC. The individual frames are separate program modules that are linked by common series of commands to a matrix program. The frames can be chained or conjoined to one another as if they were independent clauses in a sentence, or they can be nested within one another just like the nested blocks of S-BASIC or Pascal. Data can be passed from frame to frame, variables can be shared, and formulas can be extended through frames to perform global calculations through a document. Framework, in fact, is a hybrid creation, standing halfway between a high-level programming language and an applications program with a query or command language. Used in a query or command mode, FRED behaves just as if it were Visi-Calc, SuperCalc, or any word processing or database management program.

As a simple applications package, the commands or queries entered by the user are directly interactive with the software. Entering @SUM(A3:D3) into cell D5 yields the sum of the numbers in cells A3 through D3 in cell D5 while the FRED statement @CHR(@INT("X")) yields the string X as its ASCII value. There are FRED formulas for IF...THEN types of logical branching, for DO...WHILE types of Framework function executions, and for a range of statistical formulas. In fact, it is entirely possible to program in FRED within the Framework environment in much the same way that one can program in Pascal within the environment of a Pascal compiler.

Programming in FRED, however, allows the user to confine his or her work to one or more frames while using additional frames to perform other types of applications tasks without having to leave the electronic desktop. In fact, because the user has complete access to the operating system through the Disk menu, the contents of one frame can be stored as a DOS file while the contents of other frames are still on the screen and while the contents of still other linked or chained frames are being spooled to the printer. All of this requires voluminous amounts of memory, however, and the program slows down to a snail's pace as more tasks are piled into memory. In fact, for serious number crunching, it is recommended that users consider the 8087 math coprocessor chip as an option to enhance the program's numeric calculation speed. Nevertheless, the developers of Framework have managed successfully to combine a directly interactive applications program with a highly utilitarian programming language without sacrificing any of the advantages either one can offer independently.

Framework Database

Databases are created from the Create menu and are organized into rows, called "records," and columns, called "fields," much like the information in the spreadsheet. Also, like the spreadsheet, users determine the amount of fields and records in the same way that they determine the amount of columns and rows. The standard database display, called Table View, resembles the spreadsheet display. Table View shows multiple records, each occupying one line on the screen. Forms View, entered with the F10 View function key, shows only a single record at a time in greater depth, and is used to design forms.

Framework supports an entire range of formulas that can be used to define the relationship among records and among the different fields of a single record. Formulas are used to calculate specific fields automatically or to isolate formulas that meet specific logical conditions. These are the same types of formulas that are supported by most database managers. Formulas that define entire fields of data are entered at the label for the field; formulas that are used only within a particular record and are not general are entered at the specific field within which they will operate; and formulas that act as logical operators or filters for the entire database are entered at the border of the database frame. In this way, the same set of commands can be entered in different areas to perform different tasks. For example, to define a standard 10 percent agency commission for the value of each contract signed by a company, the user need only establish a field labeled "Commission" and use the @SET (FIELD, OPERANDS) formula to establish the numeric calculation. Thus, in a database which contains fields for Contract, Buyer, Gross, and Commission, the user need only type @SET(COMMISSION, GROSS * 10%) to calculate automatically the agency commission for each gross figure. If the gross figure changes, the commission changes accordingly in exactly the same way as if the two fields were cells on a spreadsheet.

The Framework database supports general searches for specific records, searches for specific characters or groups of characters, a search and replace feature, a general record sort feature that reorganizes records according to preset parameters, and a logical sort feature, called a "Filter" in Framework, that identifies records according to a series of logical qualifiers. The filter formulas are premised upon the logical operators:

>   Greater than

<   Less than

=   Equal

>=   Greater than or equal to

<=   Less than or equal to

<>   Not equal to

@AND   Logical AND

@OR   Logical OR

@NOT   Logical NOT.

Records can also be sorted by the name of a field category as well as a logical operator for the purposes of search and retrieval. Thus a user can search for all occurrences of BUYER = "SMITH" @AND(GROSS >=20000) to isolate all records in which Smith was the buyer and the contract gross figure was greater than or equal to $20,000.

Graphing and Plotting Data

Framework's Graphs menu utilizes data from databases or spreadsheets that are already on the desktop and within which a range of values or data has already been selected. Once the data type and data range have been selected, the "Draw New Graph" commands on the edit of the Framework frame do the rest of the work. Graphs can be drawn in empty frames or overlaid upon existing graphs using the "Add to Existing Graph" command. Users can draw standard bar graphs, stacked bar graphs in which the bars are stacked on top of each other, pie charts, plotted line graphs in which the points are connected by a continuous line, market points in which there is no continuous line connecting the different dots, and X-Y graphs which show the trend of one value upon another. Graphs are always drawn in monochrome, but they can be drawn in color by using the F9 Zoom key as a toggle. Color graphs can then be printed through the "Plotter" option on Framework's Print menu. Like Lotus 1-2-3 and Symphony, Framework has a powerful keyboard macro capability that can generate a string of characters formatted to the ALT and any other key. The macro function and the key redefinition are established through the FRED statements @PERFORMKEYS and @SETMACRO respectively. Framework includes a library of macro functions and utilities that can be invoked from disk and can be used as a kernel for other macros.

Framework's final feature is a telecommunications utility that includes MITE, a terminal program that can be used from within a frame to establish or send or load data to and from a remote location. Framework includes protocols to communicate with a remote mainframe computer, online networks, and other Framework users. Framework also allows users to load information directly from online networks such as Dow Jones directly into frames.

FRED GLOSSARY

The following glossary represents the full implementation of FRED, the Frames Editor language of Framework, organized by function category. FRED has the same syntax as any spreadsheet language, but it can be used in frames other than the spreadsheet to create formulas, establish logical branches, and execute printing and other functions according to conditions set from within any one or more frames.

Program Control Functions

@EXECUTE   Puts a formula inside of a frame and executes it

@GETENV   Gets an environmental variable

@GETFORMULA   Retrieves a formula from another source

@LIST   Organizes expressions by unit

@MEMAVAIL   Returns the amount of RAM space available

@PRINTRETURN   Exits immediately from printing

@RESULT   Returns the value of a formula

@RUN   Runs a program from disk

@SELECT   Executes an expression by index

@SET   Assigns a value to a variable or to an entire frame

@SETDIRECTORY   Sets a default directory

@SETDRIVE   Sets a default drive

@SETFORMULA   Replaces a formula in a frame.

@TRACE   Establishes a trace stream and records the execution of a FRED program in much the same way that $TRACE establishes a trace stream for the compiler in S-BASIC

@WHILE   Perform a loop function while X condition is true

@WRITETEXTFILE   Create a DOS text file

Date and Time Functions

@DATE   Enter or use the system date

@DATE1   Displays date as Mon DD YYYY

@DATE2   Displays date as Mon YYYY

@DATE3   Displays date as Mon DD

@DATE4   Displays date as Month DD YYYY

@DATETIME Enters date and time

@DIFFDATE Finds the days between two dates

@SUMDATE Adds or subtracts days to or from entered date

@TIME Enters or uses the system time from the clock

@TIME1 Displays time as HH:MM XM

@TIME2 Displays time as HH:MM

@TIME3 Displays time as HH:MM:SS.hh

@TODAY Reads the date from the system dBASE Interface

@DBASEFILTER Brings a dBASE II or III file to the desktop

Financial Functions

@FV Future value

@IRR Internal rate of return

@MIRR Modified internal rate of return

@NPV Net present value

@PMT Payment

@PV Present value

Function Builders

@ITEM 1...@ITEM16; Value of a parameter

@ITEM Single value of a parameter

@ITEMCOUNT Number of parameter items

@LOCAL Defines local variables

@RETURN Exits a formula and returns the formula value

Graphing Commands

@DRAW Draws a line or shape

@DRAWGRAPH Draws an entire graph

Logical Functions

@AND Checks whether all parameters are true

@IF Evaluates a predetermined condition

@ISNA Checks the availability of a parameter

@ISERR Checks the error condition of a parameter

@ISABEND Checks for the abnormal end of a parameter

@ISALPHA@ Checks to see whether a parameter is alphabetical

@ISNUMERIC Checks to see whether a parameter is numeric

@NOT Checks to see whether a parameter is not true

@OR Checks to see whether any parameter is true

Macro Functions

@ECHO Echoes keystrokes back to the screen in the same way that the ECHO command DOS echoes keystrokes to the screen.

@KEY Identifies value of most reccent keystroke

@KEYFILTER Traps keystrokes

@KEYNAME Converts a key name to a character string

@NEXTKEY Interrupts until next keystroke.

@PERFORMKEYS Defines a number of keystrokes to a single key

@SETMACRO Assigns a macro key to a frame

@SETSELECTION Selects and points to a frame

Numeric Functions

@ABS Returns the absolute value

@ACOS Returns the Arc Cosine value

@ASIN Returns the Arc Sine Value

@ATAN Returns the Arc Tangent value

@ATAN2 Returns the "4 Quadrant" Arc Tangent

@CEILING   Rounds upward to the ceiling value of a parameter

@COS   Returns the Cosine value

@EXP   Raises a number to a power

@FLOOR   Rounds downward to the lowest value of a parameter

@INT   Calculates the integer portion of a parameter and discards the fraction

@LOG   Returns the base 10 logarithm

@MOD   Calculates the modulus of the first parameter divided by the second parameter

@PI   Returns the value of Pi to 15 places

@RAND   Generates a random number to 15 places

@ROUND   Rounds off the first parameter to the number of decimal places specified in the second parameter

@SIGN   Returns the sign of the parameter

@SIN   Returns the value of the Sine

@SQRT   Calculates the square root of a parameter

@TAN   Returns the tangent of a value

Printer Control Functions

@BM   Sets the bottom page margin

@LL   Sets the line length of a page

@PL   Sets the page length

@PO   Sets indents from left margin

@PR   Establishes a group of print functions

@PRINT   Prints a frame

@ST   Sets up the printer

@TM   Sets the top page margin

Header Commands

@HC   Centered header line

@HF   Start header or footers

@HL   Sets a left flush header line

@HP   Sets the number of lines from the top of the page at which the printing of the header will start

@HR   Sets a right flush header line

Footer Commands

@FC   Centered footer line

@HF   Start header or footers

@FL   Sets a left flush footer line

@FP   Sets the number of lines from the bottom of the page at which the printing of the footer will start

@FR   Sets a right flush footer line

Page Commands

@KP   Starts a frame on a new page if part of the frame begins on one page and runs over to the next page

@NP   Starts a new page

@PN   Sets page number

Line Spacing Commands

@SK   Skips a line or the number of lines set in the parameter

@SP   Sets line spacing

Functions Controlling Movement Within Regions

@CHOOSE   Chooses an item from a list

@FILL   Fills cells or database fields with a particular value

@GET   Returns the value of a current region

@HLOOKUP   Lookup a row value and move to the right by the number of rows specified in the third parameter

@NEXT   Move to the next region element and return the value

@PUT   Place the value in the next region element

@RESET Reset the first element to the value of the current element

@VLOOKUP Lookup a column value and move to the number of columns down defined by the third parameter

Sound Control

@BEEP Sounds a tone

Statistical Functions

@AVG Calculates the average of a group of numbers in a list of parameters

@COUNT Counts the number of items in a list of parameters

@MAX Returns the maximum value of a list of parameters

@MIN Returns the mininum value of a list of parameters

@STD Calculates a standard deviation for a list of parameters

@SUM Computes the sum of a list of parameters from Cell XX to Cell YY

@VAR Calculates the variance of numbers in a list of parameters

String Functions

@BUSINESS Rounds the first parameter to the number of decimal places specified by the second parameter, formats it as a business number, and converts it to a text string

@CHR Converts a number into a character

@CURRENCY Rounds off a number, converts it to a currency format, and converts it to a text string

@DECIMAL Rounds off a decimal and converts it to a string

@INTEGER Rounds off an integer and converts it to a string

@LEN Calculates the length in characters of its parameter much like the LEN$ command in BASIC

@MID Extracts a portion of a string much like the MID$ in BASIC

@REPT Repeats the first parameter the number of times specified by the second parameter

@SCIENTIFIC Rounds of a number, formats it according to scientific notation, and converts it to a string

@VALUE Converts a string to a numeric value

Functions that Tailor the Number Formatting

@DOLLAR Displays numbers in dollar format

@MILLI Displays numbers in milli format

@NATIONALIZE Nationalizes the currency value for a frame

@POUND Displays numbers in pound sterling format

@THOUSANDS Displays numbers in a thousands format

@UNIT Define a new unit of currency

@YEN Displays numbers in yen format

User Interface Functions

@DISPLAY Display a frame

@ERASEPROMPT Erase message area

@HIDE Remove frame from desktop and hide

@INPUTLINE Get input from user

@MENU Display a menu

@PROMPT Display a string in a message area

@QUITMENU Exit the user menu

@UNHIDE Reveal a previously hidden frame

DOS Commands

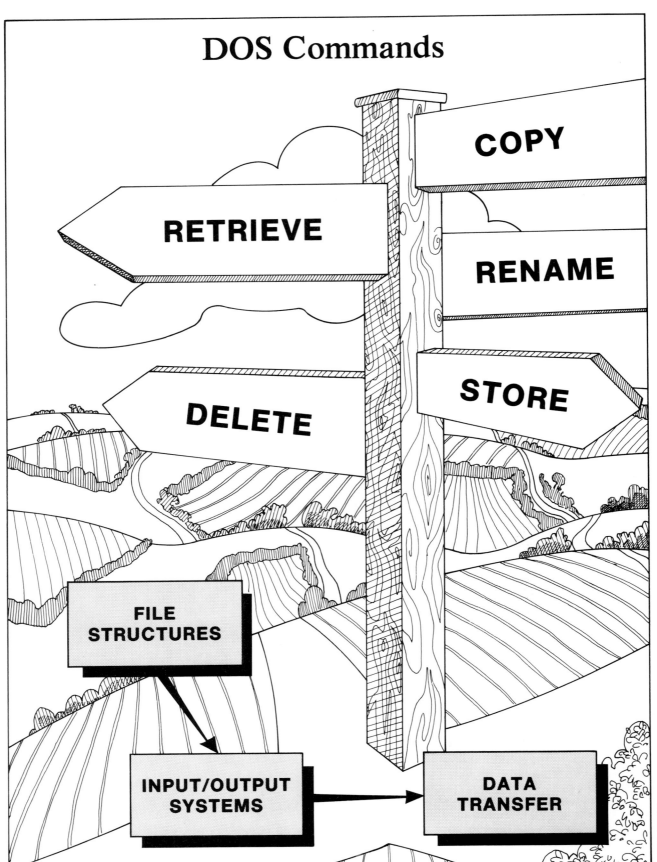

Dorothy L. Amsden

6

OPERATING SYSTEMS DIRECTORY

An operating system contains the information that tells the computer how to handle its basic functions such as receiving information, displaying information, storing and retrieving information, and printing the information or sending over a telephone line. All operating systems do this whether they are loaded from disk (hence the term DOS, or disk operating system), tape cassettes, or a plug-in integrated circuit called a ROM (read-only memory). ROM-based operating systems are common on smaller machines such as the Commodores and on lap computers. ROM-based operating systems take up very little of the computer's random access memory, because they are already stored within the machine's circuitry and can be addressed at a machine level. Tape cassette-based operating systems were common in the early days of personal computers, and the cassette units themselves are still set as the default devices on some of the smaller machines such as the Commodore, the Radio Shack color computers and some of the older Model 3's, and the Atari.

Tape operating systems were slow and sometimes unreliable because of the technology of reading and writing digital data to tape and because cassette-based storage files were sequential rather than random access. In order for the computer to read the operating system's commands, it had to read all the data files preceding the operating system until it found the right location. This is similar to scanning a video tape in the CUE or QUICK modes to find the TV show or the particular play in a taped football game. There is no way to jump right to the spot; you have to look at each scene, determine whether it is the one you want, and then move on to the next until the right one comes up. Although this technology was fine for some of the earlier applications that only occupied 1 or 2K of storage, larger programs took too long to load and too long to find. It was difficult to use tape cassettes with word processing files, for example, and almost impossible to use with any workable database manager. And even games, as they became more sophisticated and required the transportation of data back and forth from a storage device, became unmanagable on tape cassettes.

Disk-based systems offered a more powerful way to move data back and forth from a storage device to the computer and a quicker access to files. Disks, unlike tape cassettes, used both sequential and random access file structures. Sequential files saved disk space, while random access files allowed the computer to find the file almost immediately by reading the disk directory map and following the pointers which told the computer where on the disk the actual file was located. Disk-based storage systems had been in operation for about ten years before the first personal computer disk drives appeared, but they were expensive and bulky. It wasn't until the first mini drives began to appear that disk operating systems became a consumer item.

Most personal computers today are configured to use a disk operating system because the technology has become inexpensive enough to allow even the smaller machines to package a disk drive and a DOS along with the basic unit. Apple was among the first consumer personal computers to use a disk operating system. Business computer users on the early machines such as the Heath/Zenith 89, the Altos, the North Star, and others used CP/M from Digital Research, one of the first disk operating systems capable of sophisticated file handling, data manipulation, printing, and hardware configuration. Where the early versions of Apple DOS were strictly machine specific, CP/M was highly portable and read a universal 8-inch IBM compatible format as well as a growing standard of 5-1/4-inch formats, the 10-sector disk being one of them.

CP/M is still considered one of the industry standards, although it has been largely replaced by MS-DOS, MicroSoft's version of PC-DOS, the operating system created for the IBM PC. MS-DOS-compatible has become a watchword of the business software industry that has produced applications programs for the 16-bit PC and PC look-alikes. CP/M and MS-DOS behave very similarly, and CP/M users often find the transition to MS-DOS not at all jarring. Apple DOS also looks like MS-DOS in certain respects, a similarity that reveals its early origins. Now, however, the common Apple DOS 3.3 is being replaced by a new operating system called ProDOS that has been designed to run on the Apple IIe and the IIc. ProDOS resembles MS-DOS in its ability to support file paths and subdirectories which make data storage and retrieval on multimegabyte hard drives more efficient. ProDOS was originally created to access the Apple III Profile, a 5-megabyte hard drive that was marketed by Apple. Later versions of MS-DOS that were written for IBM XT also supported file paths and subdirectories because of the ease of locating and retrieving information from a large fixed drive.

The future of operating systems, especially within a business environment, is linked to the future of UNIX and its look-alikes. Originally developed at Bell Laboratories for internal use, UNIX provides for multiuser, multiterminal applications as well as concurrent processing of different applications on the same system. UNIX and its look-alikes such as XENIX have already had an impact upon the business community. The 32-bit machines that support multitasking and networking generally are UNIX driven. The UNIX system itself supports many operations that are traditionally confined to applications programs, such as word processing, screen formatting, terminal-to-terminal communication, and even typesetting. While UNIX, like C, the language in which it was developed, is essentially a programmer's tool that does not provide easy access even to sophisticated users, it does have "shells" or communities of commands that allow users to detour around the core command structure of the system and avail themselves of subsets of routines that accomplish a specific series of procedures.

Because of the large library of both UNIX applications for larger machines and MS-DOS applications for 16-bit PCs and PC look-alikes, the market is pushing the two operating systems together. In fact, MS-DOS 3.0, the latest release of DOS for the IBM AT, makes use of a UNIX-like structure for its own projected multiuser mininetwork, and third-party software developers are offering UNIX-to-MS-DOS or XENIX-to-MS-DOS bridges.

A very different future is looming on the horizon for users of Apple's LISA and Macintosh computers as well as for users of the Xerox Star, an icon-based machine. The operating system for these types of machines, while it performs many of the same functions as a traditional DOS, is expressed in terms of graphic images rather than command statements. Placing the cursor over one of the images and pressing return is equivalent to keying in the command associated with that icon, and it executes the system procedure. The Macintosh operating system goes beyond the command structure of the Xerox Star and the LISA. The Macintosh is almost entirely icon based and requires the user to follow a strict sequence of moving icons around the screen and clicking the cursor on the mouse in exactly the right spot in order to access system functions. The applications software for the Macintosh addresses this iconographic system, and even word processing software requires the manipulation of the mouse to select type font, size, and style.

Operating systems are in the process of evolution as their designers build in more applications functions and submerge the system control and monitoring functions beneath user-oriented command shells. Also, as the hardware systems continue to deliver greater onboard memories and more sophisticated addressing capabilities, the operating systems designers can allocate greater portions of the software to housekeeping functions directly under the user's control. The result will be a merging of today's single-applications program into a coordinated and integrated operating systems menu, similar to the Topview program recently released by IBM, which monitors access and execution of integrated software applications while it directs system functions.

UNIX

The UNIX operating system is an operating system for use with computers ranging from the more powerful microcomputers up to mainframe processors. The system has recently attained widespread commercial and academic use, and it has been very influential in the design of other systems.

The UNIX operating system was developed by Ken Thompson and Dennis Ritchie of AT&T Bell Laboratories in the mid 1970s as a personal tool for program development using only the most limited hardware environment. The system was a synthesis of many existing good ideas and a few new ones. Because the basic conception was the product of only two minds, the early UNIX system was especially elegant and exhibited a unity of design rarely found in larger-scale systems.

Features

There are three important characteristics of the UNIX system: simplicity of design, a software tool approach, and a minimal distinction between "system" and "user" programs.

In many cases UNIX features have simple programmer or user interfaces, and yet are extremely general. The approach is to provide a small set of features or primitives which are sufficiently powerful to allow other features to be constructed as needed.

For example, the UNIX file system allows characters to be written to a file, and then allows exactly those characters to be read back, sequentially or randomly, without modification. There is only one file type—an unstructured array of bytes that may hold any data type without regard to blocking or alignment considerations. Files are referenced using a very general tree-structured naming convention.

Surprisingly often, other systems are unable to simply store data and later retrieve the data unchanged. Many other systems insist on adding byte counts, padding records with nulls, rounding to physical track sizes, inserting carriage returns, etc. UNIX files allow any desired record structure to be constructed, without preordaining one particular style. UNIX does not directly provide features such as indexed (ISAM) files, but applications programs can implement any desired indexing structure on top of the underlying file system. This results in considerable freedom for the applications software developer.

Another important concept is the "software tool" or "software component" approach, which is pervasive throughout the system. Most commands are designed to perform only a single function. The output of one command is usually a stream of text lines which can be displayed to the user or reused as the input to another command. More complex functions are constructed in this way by connecting commands together via "pipes" (se-

quential data streams between programs) and by using the features of the "shell" command interpreter, which is also a full programming language in its own right.

UNIX minimizes the distinction between "system" and "user" programs. For example, the UNIX command interpreter uses no privileged functions (in marked contrast to many other commercial systems). Users are able to write their own command language if they wish. The interface to the UNIX monitor or executive (the "kernel") is narrow and free from hardware dependencies, providing an abstract "UNIX machine" as an environment for the user applications. The kernel supports process management, file and I/O management, and enforcement of protection. Nearly all other functions execute as user-level applications.

In addition to its general characteristics, the system has other more specific advantages which explain its popularity:

Multiprocessing capability. UNIX supports multiple independent processes (tasks) with greater ease than most other systems. Some systems view a process as a very special item; UNIX views a process as something that may reasonably be created simply to print the time of day.

Multiuser capability. UNIX has been designed since the beginning to support multiple users. This includes protection and accounting. Even single-user machines benefit, since different users may access the same machine at different times.

Portability. The UNIX system is highly (although not perfectly) portable. It is written almost entirely in the high-level C programming language. UNIX implementations exist on a multitude of machines with varying architecture.

Span of usability. This is related to portability. A UNIX programmer can use anything from an inexpensive desktop micro to a supercomputer. To a large extent, the procedures used by the UNIX programmer will be exactly identical on each machine. The same applications programs can be used.

Highly productive software development environment. UNIX was originally designed by programmers for programmers. While this does not ensure the usability of the system for end users, it does make it quite easy to produce software under UNIX. It is common for companies to use UNIX as a development tool, even for applications software products targeted to other environments.

Completeness. There are hundreds of utility programs as a standard part of the system. These range from file manipulation tools to compilers or text processing programs.

Proven operation. UNIX is now a decade old. It is proven in thousands of commercial applications.

Near-universal acceptance in education. At the university level, UNIX is a standard system for teaching and research. This produces a ready supply of programmers, and also of research developments which turn into future UNIX-based software products.

It is important to recognize that UNIX does not satisfy all requirements. The system lacks some commercial features. There are certain capabilities which were not important in the program development environment, but which are important in the commercial environment. Commonly cited failings are the lack of a standard naive-user interface or a real-time capability.

In recent years the system has been growing in complexity as its usage expands into more areas. The system also has growing inconsistency. The original unified design is now somewhat strained. For example, many programs do text pattern matching. However, the pattern matching syntax varies widely from program to program, for no good reason except that the programs were written at different times by different programmers. There are also few standards for command options, error messages, etc.

Despite the drawbacks, UNIX is rapidly becoming a standard vehicle for applications software, a kind of "software bus" spanning a wide variety of machine architectures.

History

The UNIX system was first used internally at Bell Labs, and was gradually improved. It came to the attention of the academic community, and was released at no charge and totally without support for educational purposes. The first release that had any significant distribution was the Fifth Edition, now known as Version 5. (At that time, there were no UNIX versions. Instead, the Programmer's Manual was updated with a new edition as the system changed. With each new edition of the manual, a tape copy of the research computer system disk was made. This essentially became the distribution tape.)

By the time of the first release outside AT&T, the system had been coded in the C programming language, but it ran only on the DEC PDP-11 processor.

The Sixth Edition (Version 6) had a fuller set of functions. It still ran on the PDP-11, and only a limited number of configurations were supported. Version 6 spread rapidly in some academic circles, and began to be used in commercial and government projects. AT&T also used Version 6 as a base for other UNIX derivatives, such as the "Programmers Workbench."

Version 7 of UNIX provided a fuller set of features. In addition, much of the system had been redesigned to allow portability. Internally within Bell Labs the system had been readapted ("ported") to other computer types. AT&T realized that the system had commercial potential, and allowed for binary redistribution of the system by independent vendors at a lower price. Version 7 was the basis of all of the early commercial versions of UNIX. The system was ported to various microprocessor types by a number of companies, and offered with commercial support in binary form.

UNIX spread rapidly in the academic world. The system was intellectually elegant, easy to use for research purposes, supplied free of charge for noncommercial use, and available in source code form so that

changes needed for computer science research purposes could be accommodated. Most universities had UNIX machines, which were typically run by student labor. A high level of development activity began, which continues unabated to this day. This activity has resulted in a number of variations, changes, and improvements in the system.

The University of California at Berkeley produced the most notable academic variants of the UNIX system. A series of UNIX releases, called "Berkeley Software Distributions," were intended to provide increased performance, greater hardware support (especially for DEC Vax series processors), demand-paging virtual memory, networking and advanced interprocess communications, and a myriad of additions, new options, experimental ideas, and simply gratuitous changes. Release numbers are in the form "4.xBSD."

In parallel with the university activities, AT&T continued its own developments. The introduction of UNIX System III provided lower binary pricing and a number of programmer-productivity features. Both the PDP-11 and Vax were supported. AT&T started to actively market the system. System V followed System III. With System V, AT&T brought the outside world up to date with its own internal version. (System IV was skipped.) A number of system problems were resolved, and the documentation was improved. Certain Berkeley features were added, and performance issues were addressed. Other new features were added, including an interprocess communication capability using shared memory, semaphores, and message queues.

System V was largely upward compatible with System III. Each previous release had been incompatible in important ways with its predecessor. System V Release 2 in turn represented an evolutionary upward-compatible addition to System V.

Today, there are a variety of commercial UNIX systems offered under a variety of tradenames. Most commercial vendors are moving toward System V. However, successive releases, hybrids, upgrades, offspring, proprietary enhancements, and vendor subsetting have resulted in a situation today in which end users are sometimes unsure about what they are purchasing when they buy UNIX. However, despite the variations, it is important to remember that all of the systems remain recognizably UNIX.

The history of multiple UNIX versions has created an industry demand for standardization. Industry groups are actively working to standardize essential UNIX features.

Comparison with Other Systems

UNIX stands between large, complex mainframe operating systems and small, primitive microcomputer operating systems.

Traditional mainframe operating systems have attempted to meet almost all user needs. These systems are highly optimized for particular hardware architectures. They have been developed by thousands of programmers over many years of effort. As a result, these systems have many features built in which are not present as a standard part of UNIX. On the other hand, these systems tend to be complex and unwieldy in comparison to UNIX, and they are tied to individual proprietary machine architectures.

In the microcomputer world, UNIX systems compete with other generic systems such as MS-DOS. Here UNIX has a more advanced set of features, such as multiuser support, while MS-DOS is somewhat simpler in conception and resource requirements, which makes it more suitable for the lowest-priced mass-market microcomputers. MS-DOS is "portable" to various machines, but all of these share the Intel machine architecture. UNIX is portable across architectures, which allows it to run on all of the major microprocessor chips, as well as minis and mainframes.

The UCSD P-System provides another popular comparison. The P-System is highly portable, and in fact can be brought up on a new architecture with less effort than UNIX. Again, the P-System is aimed at low-cost single-user environments, while UNIX spans a range up to supercomputers.

Both the P-System and MS-DOS are optimized for the single-user environment. As a consequence, they generally provide a higher degree of responsiveness, with many commands that repaint a bitmap raster graphics display in real time in response to individual keystrokes. An individual application (e.g., a game program) can take complete control of the machine. UNIX systems are generally optimized for multiuser (or multiple activity) environments, with a modest number of users. While UNIX is highly interactive and applications can respond to individual keystrokes, the system will timeshare the machine among the activities or users. Therefore, no one application can reliably command the entire machine resources on behalf of one user. Mainframe systems are optimized for a very large number (hundreds) of users and activities. Here user interaction is usually batched into "transactions," in which a user interacts with a local editing terminal, than transmits an entire screen of information and awaits a response.

UNIX systems require certain hardware capabilities. A minimum UNIX-capable system has perhaps 256 Kilobytes of main memory, memory management and protection, the ability to execute programs of at least 128 Kilobytes in total size, and 10 Megabytes of disk storage. At present, this makes UNIX unsuitable for the lowest-cost personal computers, which are supplied only with low-capacity floppy-disk storage. The IBM PC-XT is an example of the smallest system that can reasonably run a general-purpose UNIX environment. The XT is marginal, since it lacks memory protection, but it can still be used successfully in single-user applications. A more typical UNIX system would use an IBM PC-AT or a 32-bit virtual memory microprocessor.

In order to move UNIX to a new machine architecture, it is necessary to construct a compiler for the C programming language. Portions of the kernel must be rewritten to account for variations in the handling of memory management and input/output. Finally, the subroutines and utility programs must be recompiled for the new system. Although this "porting" process is simple in principle, it can require considerable time, since the UNIX system involves large amounts of software and there are many important details.

Impact

The character of the market for UNIX is changing rapidly. The system is moving from specialized uses to general uses, from rarity to commodity, from academia to commerce, from programmers to users, and from an end in itself to an applications delivery vehicle. Numerous market analysts have made projections of the potential UNIX market. While estimates vary, all agree that there will be very rapid growth in UNIX usage over the next few years.

In addition to AT&T, North American UNIX systems software vendors include MicroSoft, Interactive Systems, Human Computing Resources, Unisoft, Wollongong Group, Venturcom, Santa Cruz Operation, and Digital Research. Outside North America, major software companies such as Logica are supporting the system. The vast majority of hardware companies now offer UNIX systems on one machine or another. There are no exceptions among the major computer companies.

AT&T and the microcomputer chip makers have cooperated to produce so-called "generic versions" of UNIX for Intel, Motorola, National, and Zilog microprocessor chips.

Unix has been influential in the design of other operating systems. Many systems are now being provided with UNIX-like features. For example, the latest version of MS-DOS includes a number of UNIX-derived features. UNIX capabilities are being designed into larger mini and mainframe systems. The UNIX system shows every sign of becoming an industry standard which will be widely applied.

Michael Tilson

UNIX GLOSSARY

UNIX is the operating system designed at Bell Labs in the late 1960s. It has long been very popular among mainframe and minicomputer users, and recently, with the added processing power of micros, is gaining popularity in the micro environment. The most attractive aspects of UNIX are its portability and its ability to easily support a multiuser environment. Portability refers to the fact that applications created in UNIX using one hardware system can be easily transferred to run on other hardware systems using UNIX. The portability aspect of UNIX also means that applications can be downloaded from larger to smaller systems. For example, a company with UNIX applications operating on their mainframe computer can transfer applications and data to their microcomputer network. The information listed below pertains to UNIX System V.

UNIX DIRECTORIES

UNIX offers multiple-directory capability. Individual files can be accessed by more than one name on a directory and in more than one directory. The different UNIX directories are:

/bin	UNIX utilities
/dev	Files for I/O devices
/etc	Administrative programs
/lib	Library files
/tmp	Temporary files
/usr/adm	Administrative commands
/usr/bin	Overflow from /bin
/usr/games	Game programs
/usr/include	Files used by UNIX language processors
/usr/lib	Archive files and text processing
/usr/mail	Mail files
/usr/news	News files
/usr/spool/	Spooling files for printing
/usr/src/	Source files
/usr/tmp	Temporary files

UNIX file management commands are:

acctcom   Searches/prints accounting files

adb   Absolute debugger

admin   Administers SCCS files

ar   Maintains portable archives

as   Assembler

asa   Interprets ASA control characters

awk   Pattern processing language

banner   Creates banners

basename   Outputs name of file from a path name

bc   Calculator with programming

bdiff   Compares two large files

bs   A compiler/interpreter

cal   Outputs a calendar

cancel   Cancels spooling

cat   Concatenates files

cb   Formats programs written in C

cc   C compiler

cd   Changes current directory

cdc   Changes comments for an SCCS delta

cflow   Produces flow graphs

chgrp   Change file's group ownership

chmod   Change file access permissions

chown   Change file's ownership

cmp   Compare two files

col   Filters out reverse line feeds

comb   Combines SCCS deltas

comm   Chooses or rejects lines common to two sorted files

convert   Converts formats of archive and object files

cp   Copies files

cpio   Copies files archives

cpp   C language preprocessor

crypt   File encoder/decoder

csplit   Splits files according to matching patterns

ct   Sends a getty process to remote terminal

cu   Calls another UNIX system

cut   Chooses columns from table file

cw   Prepares width text for troff

cxref   Produces C cross reference

date   Sets and displays the date

dc   Desktop calculator

dd   Generates file transformations

delta   Changes an SCCS file

deroff   Deletes format commands from a file

df   Displays number of available blocks

diff   Compares two files

diff3   Compares three files

diffmk   Indicates differences between files

dircmp   Compares directories

dirname   Displays the path associated with a path name

disable   Stops printer spooling

du   Displays disk usage

dump   Dumps sections of an object file

echo   Displays arguments

ed   Line based text editor

efl   An extended Fortran compiler

enable   Sets environment for command execution

eqn   Formats mathematical equations

expr   Evaluates expressions

f77   A Fortran compiler

factor   Factors a number

false   Returns a false value from an argument

file   Displays file type

find   Searches for a given file

fsplit   Splits Fortran source code files

gath   Collects files for RJE execution

ged   Graphics editor

get   Gets a version of a SCCS file

getopt   Parses command options

graph   Generates a graph

graphics   Accesses graph commands

grep   Displays file lines according to pattern matching

gutil   Graph utilities

help   Accesses help feature

hyphen   Displays hyphenated words

id   Displays user and group identification and names

ipcrm   Deletes shared memory and semaphores

ipcs   Displays status of interprocess communication

join   Combines two tabular data files

kill   Terminates process

ld   Link editor

lex   Generates lexical analysis routines

line   Copies line from standard input to output

lint   C syntax checker

ln   Links files

login   Admits authorized user to system

logname   Outputs the user's login name

lorder   Displays order relation for object library

lp   Line printer spooler

lpr   Line printer spooler

lpstat   Displays spooling status

ls   Lists contents of directories

m4   Macro processor

mail   Sends and receives UNIX mail

make   Regenerates groups of programs

makekey   Produces an encryption key

man   Prints online manual entries

mesg   Permits or denies messages

mkdir   Creates a directory

mm   Text formatting macros

mmt   Typesetting macros

mv   Moves files

newform   Reformats lines in text file

newgrp   Changes group membership

news   Displays news items

nice   Runs a program at lower priority

nl   Line number filter

nm   Prints names from a common object file

nohup   Runs program without hangups or quits

nroff   Text formatter

od   Sends an octal dump to a file

pack   Packs files

passwd   Changes user password

paste   Merges file lines

pcat   Concatenates packed files

pcc   Portable C compiler

pr   Prints files

prof   Displays execution profile data

prs   Prints an SCCS file

ps   Displays process status

ptx   Produces a permuted index

pwd   Prints name of current directory

ratfor   Compiler for a Fortran dialect

regcmp   Regular expression compiler

rjestat   Displays RJE status

rm   Deletes files

rmdel   Deletes an SCCS delta

rmdir   Deletes directories

rsh   Restricted UNIX shell

sact   Displays current SCCS edit activity

sadp   Displays disk access data

sag   Displays system activity graph

sar   Displays system activity report

scat   Concatenates and prints files

sccsdiff   Compares two versions of an SCCS file

sdb   Symbolic debugger

sdiff   Compares two files

se   Screen editor

sed   Stream editor

send   Submits RJE jobs for execution

sh   The UNIX shell size displays size of object files

sleep   Halts execution for a specified interval

sno   SNOBOL interpreter

sort   Sorts and merges files

spell   Spelling checker

spline   Interpolates curves

split   Splits a file

stat   Statistical network for graphics

strip   Deletes symbol table data from object file

stty   Sets terminal configuration

su   Temporarily changes user identification

sum   Outputs checksum and block count

sync   Writes buffers to disk

tabs   Sets terminal tabs

tail   Outputs last part of file

tar   Archives tape files

tbl   Table formatter

tee   Pipe fitter

test   Evaluates conditions

time   Times command execution

timex   Times command execution

toc   Produces graphic table of contents

touch   Updates times when file is changed

tplot   Graphic filters

tr   Character translation filter

troff   Text formatter for phototypesetting

tru   Gives true value

tsort   Topological sort

tty   Displays name of terminal

umask: Sets file creation mode mask

uname   Displays name of current UNIX system

unget   Ungets a SCCS file

uniq   Outputs a file with unique lines

units   Does unit conversions

unpack   Unpacks packed files

uucp   Copies files from one UNIX system to another

uulog   Displays uucp log data

uuname   Displays uucp names of known systems

uupick   Selects uucp files for processing

uustat   Displays uucp status data

uuto   Copies files from one UNIX system to another

uux   Executes commands on a remote UNIX system.

val   Validates SCCS files

vc   Version control

wait   Pauses until background process is complete

wc   Prints line, word, and character counts to a file

what   Identifies SCCS files

who   Displays data on current users

write   Sends messages to another user

xargs   Produce a list of arguments and executes a command

yacc   A compiler tool

The following are a list of system calls from UNIX System V:

access   Get file access permissions

acct   Toggle (enable/disable) accounting

alarm   Set process alarm clock

brk   Request additional main memory

chmod   Change file access permissions

chndir   Change current directory

chown   Change file owner

chroot   Changes to different root directory

close   Closes a file

creat   Creates new file

dup   Duplicates file description

exec   Execute a new program

exit   End process

fcntl   File control operations

fork   Begin a child process

fstat   Gets file status data

getegid   Get effective group identification number

geteuid   Get effective user identification number

getgid   Get group identification number

getpgrp   Get process group identification number

getpid   Get process identification number

getppid   Get parent process identification number

getuid   Get user identification number

ioctl   Device control operations

kill   End a process

link   Create new link to file

lseek   Moves file pointer

maus   Access shared memory

mknod   Creates new directory

mount   Mount a file system

msgctl   Control a message buffer

msgget   Open message buffer

msgop   Send or receive messages through buffer

nice   Change process priority

open   Opens a file

paus   Halt process and wait for signal

pipe   Create a pipe

plock   Lock a process in main memory

profil   Toggle (enable/disable) executing profiling

ptrace   Trace execution of child process

read   Read data from a file

semctl   Control a semaphore

semget   Open a set of semaphores

semop   Operate on a semaphore

setgid   Set group identification number

setpgrp   Set process group identification number

setuid   Set user identification number

shmctl   Control shared memory

shmget   Open shared memory

shmop   Attach to shared memory

signal   Specify action in response to signal

stat   Get file status

stime   Set time and date

sync   Flush kernel file buffers

time   Get time of day

times   Get process execution time information

ulimit   Get and set process limits

uname   Get name of current UNIX system

unlink   Remove a link to file

unmask   Set (get) file creation mask

unmount   Unmount a file system

ustat   Get file statistics

utime   Change file modification times

MS-DOS

MS-DOS is the operating system originally developed by MicroSoft for the 8088-based IBM PC. When implemented on the IBM, the operating system is called PC-DOS or just DOS. When implemented on other PC compatibles, the operating system is called MS-DOS. MS-DOS was released in versions 1.0 for the original PC, 2.0 for the XT, 2.1 for the PCjr, and now 3.0 for the AT. Each update of MS-DOS added extensions and new commands to the operating system while retaining the commands of the previous version. The version MS-DOS used in this glossary is 2.1, which includes all the commands available on the XT and the Junior. New 3.0 commands for the AT have been compiled separately in an additional section at the end of the glossary. The commands listed below are for version 2.1 of the MS-DOS operating system. These commands drive not only the IBM PC, XT, and PCjr, but all of the compatibles such as the Compaq, the Zenith 150, and the TI Professional.

MS-DOS GLOSSARY

ASSIGN   Changes the drive letter of drive d1 to f.
ASSIGN d1 = f

BREAK   Causes MS-DOS to check to see if the BREAK key has been pressed. MS-DOS does check normally during program execution, but BREAK ON causes the system to check more often.
BREAK ON

BREAK OFF   Restores the BREAK key checking feature to its normal frequency.

CD   Change directory.

CHKDSK   Verifies the disk integrity for drive d.
CHKDSK d

CLS   Clears the screen of all text.

COMMAND   Causes the batch file named f to be executed from within an existing batch file.
COMMAND /Cf

COPY d1:f=d2:g   Copies file f from drive d1 and writes it on drive d2 with the name g. If g is omitted, the file on drive 2 will have the same name as the file on drive 1.

COPY d1:f+g+h=d2:k   Appends files f, g, and h from drive 1 and writes the combined file with the name k to drive 2.

CTTY   Causes the system to obtain input from auxiliary port p rather than from the keyboard.
CTTY p

DATE   Prompts the user to enter the date which is used as reference when a file is written to disk.

DATE mm/dd/yy   Sets the date to month mm, day dd, and year yy.

DEBUG   A utility for debugging files. Output is displayed in hexadecimal code.

DEBUG f   Load file f for the DEBUG utility.

DEL   Deletes file f from the disk directory.
DEL f

DIR   Displays the directory of the disk.

DIR d1:sd   Displays the subdirectory named sd on drive d1.

ECHO   Causes batch file commands to be displayed on the screen as the file is executed.
ECHO ON

ECHO OFF   Stops command display during batch file execution.

EDLIN   Loads text file f for use by the text line editor.
EDLIN f

ERASE   Same as DEL.
ERASE f

EXE2BIN d1:f   Converts .EXE file f on drive d1 to binary format.

FIND "st" f1,f2,...   Finds all occurrences of string "st" in files f1, f2, etc.

FIND/V "st" f1,f2,...   Same as FIND except all lines not containing the string are displayed.

FIND/C"st" f1,f2,...   Displays the total number of lines found containing the string "st".

FOR %%x IN (d1:d2:d3) DO yx   Used within a batch file, executes command y on drives d1:d2:d3. For example: FOR %%x IN (A:B:C:) DO DIR %%x, will list the directories for drives A, B, and C.

FORMAT   Formats the disk in drive d1.
FORMAT d1:

FORMAT d1:/s   Also copies the system onto the formatted disk.

FORMAT d1:/v   Also verifies the sectors on the formatted disk and prevents bad sectors from being used.

GOTO   Used within a batch file to send execution to label L.
GOTO L

IF   If condition a is true, statement b will be executed within a batch file.
If a b

LINK   A utility which combines object files into a RUN file.

MKDIR   Adds the subdirectory sd to the current sub-directory on drive d1.
MD d 1:sd

MORE   Types a file on the screen one screen at a time and waits for a user response before continuing.
MORE f

PATH d1:p1;p2;p3   Tells MS-DOS to search paths p1, p2, and p3 for executable programs if they're not found on the current path. If the paths are on other disk drives, the disk drive letters can also be added.

PAUSE   Halts execution of a BATCH file and waits for user to press a key to resume.

PRINT   Causes ASCII file f to be printed at the currently active PRN device.
PRINT f

PROMPT   Changes the MS-DOS prompt to special character sc (no $) or string sc ($ present). Some special characters and their representations are:

b: Vertical bar.

d: Displays current date.

e: Escape character.

g: > character.

h: Backspace. Last character is erased.

I: < character.

n: Displays default drive.

p: Current path and drive.

q: = character.

t: Current time.

v: MS-DOS version number.

$: $ character.

-:   Carriage return and line feed.

RECOVER   Will recover file f where f has some data in bad sectors. It will not recover data from the bad sectors, however.
RECOVER f

REM   Used to place remarks in a BATCH file.

RENAME   Renames file f with the name g.
RENAME f g

RMDIR   Removes subdirectory sd from drive d1.
RD d1: sd

SET   Defines A$ with the string s and stores in memory with MS-DOS.
SET A$=s

SHIFT   Moves all arguments in batch file down one number.

SORT   Sorts file f in ASCII order.
SORT < f

SORT/R <f   Sorts in reverse ASCII order.

SORT/+n <f   Sorts beginning with column n.

SYS: Copies the system from the default drive to drive d1.
SYS d1

TIME   Displays the time and prompts the user to change it.

TIME hh:mm:ss   Enters the time as hh hours, mm minutes, and ss seconds.

TYPE   Displays the contents of ASCII file f.
TYPE f

VER   Lists the version of MS-DOS being used.

VERIFY   Causes MS-DOS to check data it has written to a disk and compare the data for accuracy to what was in memory.
VERIFY ON

VERIFY OFF   Turns the VERIFY function off.

VOL   Displays the volume label of disk d1.
VOL d1:

MS-DOS 3.0

The following commands represent the most recent additions and enhancements to MS-DOS, known as DOS 3.0 for the PC AT and compatibles.

MS-DOS GLOSSARY

ATTRIB Marks a file as read-only. The file can be read but it cannot be written to.
ATTRIB +r filename.ext

LABEL Names an entire disk for identification purposes. The LABEL command is used to add, change, or delete a volume label which is displayed when the directory of a disk is listed.
LABEL d:label name

LASTDRIVE Installed during the DEVICE configuration program. LASTDRIVE sets the maximum number of drives that can be accessed by telling DOS the last valid drive letter that DOS may accept. This command is included in the CONFIG.SYS file.
LASTDRIVE =1 x

SELECT Selects the keyboard layout and the date and time to be used. This command is used to configure the keyboard layout to the date, time, decimal separator, and currency conventions of different countries. The keyboard and country codes are:

UNITED STATES 001
US

FRANCE 033
FR

SPAIN 034
SP

ITALY 039
IT

UNITED KINGDOM 044
UK

GERMANY 049
GR

SELECT makes a copy of the DOS diskette that includes a CONFIG.SYS file with COUNTRY command and an AUTOEXEC.BAT file that contains the keyboard code. To select a keyboard, date, and time layout for France, type: A> SELECT 033 FR.
SELECT nnn xx

SHARE Installs file-sharing support. If files are going to be shared by a number of users, file-sharing codes have to be established so that all subsequent read and write requests are valid. SHARE allocates the file space in bytes for the area used for recording the file-sharing information and allocates space for the number of locks to be set for the file. Once loaded, SHARE performs all subsequent validation functions.
'filename SHARE/F:filespace in bytes/L:number of locks

VDISK.SYS Installed during the DEVICE configuration program, VDISK allocates a portion of the computer's memory for use as a simulated disk drive called virtual disks. Virtual disk access is faster than access to a traditional disk drive because the virtual disks are actually in memory. Once the virtual disk has been created, that portion of computer memory is treated as if it were a disk drive. Files can be written to it and read from it, and all other DOS commands can be performed. Each virtual disk is assigned an amount of memory to be allocated for its use, the sector size, and the number of directory entries it will contain as well volume label to identify it. Because the virtual disk is actually a portion of RAM, the contents of the virtual disk will be lost if the system is restarted. The files in a virtual disk should be backed up on the external disk drives. VDISK is installed as a command during the DEVICE command.

PC-DOS

PC-DOS was first released as version 1.0 for the PC with floppy disk drives and 64K of memory. Version 2.0 contained commands for the hard-drive PC XT, and Version 2.1 was released for the PCjr. PC-DOS 3.0 was released for the AT. The commands listed are for PC-DOS version 2.1.

PC-DOS GLOSSARY

ASSIGN   Changes the drive letter of drive d1 to f.
   ASSIGN d1 = f

BACKUP   Creates a floppy-disk backup of the hard disk. BACKUP also prompts the user to insert additional floppy disks when they are filled. The BACKUP procedure uses a disk encryption algorithm which does not permit the floppy-disk backups to be read normally. The RESTORE command must be used to transfer the data back to the hard disk.

BREAK   Causes MS-DOS to check whether the BREAK key has been pressed. MS-DOS does check normally during program execution, but BREAK ON causes the system to check more often.
   BREAK ON

BREAK OFF   Restores the BREAK key checking feature to its normal frequency.

CD   Change directory.

CHKDSK   Verifies the disk integrity for drive d.
   CHKDSK d

CLS   Clears the screen of all text.

COMMAND   Causes the batch file named f to be executed from within an existing batch file.
   COMMAND /Cf

COMP   Compares files f and g and displays differences.
   COMP f,g

COPY d1:f=d2:g   Copies file f from drive d1 and writes it on drive d2 with the name g. If g is omitted, the file on drive 2 will have the same name as the file on drive 1.

COPY d1:f+g+h=d2:k   Appends files f, g, and h from drive 1 and writes the combined file with the name k to drive 2.

CTTY   Causes the system to obtain input from auxiliary port p rather than from the keyboard.
   CTTY p

DATE   Prompts the user to enter the date which is used as reference when a file is written to disk.

DATE mm/dd/yy   Sets the date to month mm, day dd, and year yy.

DEBUG   A utility for debugging files. Output is displayed in hexadecimal code.

DEBUG f   Load file f for the DEBUG utility.

DIR   Displays the directory of the disk.

DIR d1:sd   Displays the subdirectory named sd on drive d1.

DISKCOPY d1:d2   Copies contents of disk in drive d1 to disk in drive d2 and first formats disk in d2.

DISKCOMP d1:d2   Compares disks and reports discrepancies by side and track.

ECHO   Causes batch file commands to be displayed on the screen as the file is executed.
   ECHO ON

ECHO OFF   Stops command display during batch file execution.

EDLIN   Loads text file f for use by the text line editor.
   EDLIN f

ERASE   Deletes file f from the disk directory.
   ERASE f

EXE2BIN d1:f   Converts .EXE file f on drive d1 to binary format.

FDISK   A partition utility used to install PC-DOS on a hard-disk partition.

FIND "st" f1,f2,...   Finds all occurrences of string "st" in files f1, f2, etc.

FIND/V "st" f1,f2,...   Same as FIND except all lines not containing the string are displayed.

FIND/C "st" f1,f2,...   Displays the total number of lines found containing the string "st".

FOR %%x IN (d1:d2:d3) DO yx   Used within a batch file, executes command y on drives d1:d2:d3. For example: FOR %%x IN (A:B:C:) DO DIR %%x, will list the directories for drives A, B, and C.

FORMAT: Formats the disk in drive d1.
  FORMAT D1

FORMAT d1:/s Also copies the system onto the formatted disk.

FORMAT d1:/v Also verifies the sectors on the formatted disk and prevents bad sectors from being used.

GOTO Used within a batch file to send execution to label L.
  GOTO L

GRAPHICS Loads a screen dump utility into memory so that the PRTSC key will cause a screen dump to the printer.

IF If condition a is true, statement b will be executed within a batch file.
  If a b

LINK A utility which combines object files into a RUN file.

MKDIR Adds the subdirectory sd to the current subdirectory on drive d1.
  MD d :sd

MODE Sets communications protocols from the PC to peripherals. For example, MODE LPT2: 132,8 sets line printer 2 to a length of 132 characters per line and 8 lines per inch.

MORE Types a file on the screen one screen at a time and waits for a user response before continuing.
  MORE f

PATH d1:p1;p2;p3 Tells MS-DOS to search paths p1, p2, and p3 for executable programs if they're not found on the current path. If the paths are on other disk drives, the disk drive letters can also be added.

PAUSE Halts execution of a BATCH file and waits for user to press a key to resume.

PRINT Causes ASCII file f to be printed at the currently active PRN device.
  PRINT f

PROMPT Changes the MS-DOS prompt to special character sc(PROMPT) or string sc(PROMPT$sc). Some special characters and their representations are:

b: Vertical bar.

d: Displays current date.

e: Escape character.

g: > character.

h: Backspace. Last character is erased.

l: < character.

n: Displays default drive.

p: Current path and drive.

q: = character.

t: Current time.

v: MS-DOS version number.

$: $ character.

—: Carriage return and line feed.

RECOVER Will recover file f where f has some data in bad sectors. It will not recover data from the bad sectors, however.
  RECOVER f

REM Used to place remarks in a BATCH file.

RENAME Renames file f with the name g.
  RENAME f g

RESTORE Takes data which has been copied to floppy disks using BACKUP and transfers it to the hard disk.

RMDIR Removes subdirectory sd from drive d1.
  RD d1: sd

SET Defines A$ with the string s and stores in memory with MS-DOS.
  SET A$=s

SHIFT Moves all arguments in batch file down one number.

SORT Sorts file f in ASCII order.
  SORT < f

SORT/R <f Sorts in reverse ASCII order.

SORT/+n <f Sorts beginning with column n.

SYS Copies the system from the default drive to drive d1.
  SYS d1:

TIME Displays the time and prompts the user to change it.

TIME hh:mm:ss Enters the time as hh hours, mm minutes, and ss seconds.

TREE Displays all subdirectories on drive d1.
  TREE d1:

TREE d1:/f Also displays all files on the subdirectories, which are normally invisible to a DIRECTORY command addressed to the root directory.

TYPE Displays the contents of ASCII file f.

VER Lists the version of MS-DOS being used.
  TYPE f

VERIFY Causes MS-DOS to check data it has written to a disk and compare it for accuracy to what was in memory.
  VERIFY ON

VERIFY OFF Turns the VERIFY function off.

VOL Displays the volume label of disk d1.
  VOL d1:

Z-DOS

The commands that are listed below are from version 1.25 of Z-DOS. At this writing (late 1984), Zenith Data Systems was about to release its version 2.0, which will be very similar to MS-DOS version 2. Z-DOS is the proprietary operating system created by Zenith Data Systems for their Z-100 series of computers. Z-DOS is a variation of MS-DOS, the DOS written by MicroSoft, Inc.

Z-DOS GLOSSARY

CHKDSK Verifies the disk integrity for drive d.
CHKDSK d

CONFIGUR Prepares the I/O system for the appropriate peripherals. For example, CONFIGUR tells the system whether a serial or a parallel printer is interfaced with the system.

COPY d1:f=d2:g Copies file f from drive d1 and writes it on drive d2 with the name g. If g is omitted, the file on drive 2 will have the same name as the file on drive 1.

COPY d1:f+g+h=d2:k Appends files f, g, and h from drive 1 and writes the combined file with the name k to drive 2.

CREF Creates an alphabetical cross reference listing of symbols from a cross reference file.

DATE Prompts the user to enter the date which is used as reference when a file is written to disk.

DATE mm/dd/yy Sets the date to month mm, day dd, and year yy.

DEBUG A utility for debugging files. Output is displayed in hexadecimal code.

DEBUG f Load file f for the DEBUG utility.

DEL Deletes file f from the disk directory.
DEL f

DIR Displays the directory of the disk.

DSKCOMP Compares disks in drives d1 and d2 on a track by track basis to see if they're identical.
DSKCOMP d1:d2:

DSKCOPY Copies the contents of the disk in drive d1 to the disk in drive d2 but first formats the disk in drive d2.
DSKCOPY d1:d2

EDLIN Loads text file f for use by the text line editor.
EDLIN f

EXE2BIN d1:f Converts .EXE file f on drive d1 to binary format.

FILCOM A utility which compares the contents of 2 source code files and creates list of their differences.

FORMAT Formats the disk in drive d1.
FORMAT d1:

FORMAT d1:/s Also copies the system onto the formatted disk.

FORMAT d1:/v Also verifies the sectors on the formatted disk and prevents bad sectors from being used.

LIB A utility which creates a file of code modules from a master source file.

LINK A utility which combines object files into a RUN file.

MAKE A utility which prompts the user to create backup copies of Zenith proprietary software. MAKE contains a wide variety of backup options depending on the software being copied.

MAP Used to reassign disk drive names and types.
MAP ?

MASM Assembles macrocode source files into a file which can be loaded by the LINK utility to create an executable file.

PAUSE Halts execution of a BATCH file and waits for user to press a key to resume.

PRINT Causes ASCII file f to be printed at the currently active PRN device.
PRINT f

RDCPM Reads a CPM file and saves it as a Z-DOS file.

REM Used to place remarks in a BATCH file.

REN Renames file f with the name g.
REN f g

SYS Copies the system from the default drive to drive d1.
SYS d1:

Commodore DOS

Commodore's DOS is a hybrid system, and unlike CP/M, MS-DOS, or Apple DOS in which BASIC must be loaded as if it were a program file. Because BASIC always exists in ROM on a Commodore machine, BASIC as well as the DOS is always present and does not have to be loaded as a separate operation. Therefore, many of Commodore's operating system commands are actually BASIC language commands. Commodore's operating system is also different in that it is implemented on an IEEE bus. This means that all components of a Commodore computer behave as if they are separate devices, assigned device numbers by the system, which are linked to one another through bus signals and system commands. The Commodore's standard device numbers are:

Primary tape cassette: 1
Secondary tape cassette: 2
Printer: 4
Modem: 5
Disk drive: 8
Fixed disk: 9

The following glossary is the most complete implementation of Commodore's disk operating system for the C64. The system commands, however, are common to all of the machines Commodore has produced including the VIC 20, the PET and the CBM 4000 and 8000 series. In Commodore DOS, some of the DOS commands are accessed through BASIC, and some are accessed through the system. The commands which are assessed through BASIC are indicated with a {B}.

COMMODORE GLOSSARY

CLOSE {B} Removes the device numbered n from the DOS and frees the buffer space which had been allocated to n through the OPEN command.
   CLOSE n

CMD {B} Causes the computer to send all output to the device identified by n. The device must be OPENed first.
   CMD n

COPY Copies file f and names the copied file g. Copying must be on the same disk drive.
   COPY d:f=d:g

GET# {B} Reads data from the file identified by N and stores the next character from the file in variable A$.
   GET#N, A$

INITIALIZE Initializes the disk drive to the bootup condition. The #15 causes the output to go to the drive.
   PRINT#15,"I"

INPUT# {B} Reads the file identified by N and stores the next field in the variable A$.
   INPUT#N, A$

LOAD {B} Loads the program named "pn" into memory from cassette (if D=1) or from disk (if D=8).
   LOAD "pn",D

NEW Establishes the directory on the disk in drive 0 and gives it the name nm (16 character maximum). Each file on the disk is subsequently tagged with the identification id (two character maximum).
   NEW O:nm,id

OPEN {B} Opens data file N on device D. To access the disk drive, D must be 8. For the cassette recorder, D is 1.
   OPEN N,D

PRINT# {B} Writes the data stored in variable A$ to the disk file identified by N.
   PRINT#N, A$

RENAME Changes the name of old file "of" to nf in the directory on drive 0.
   RENAME 0:nf=of

RUN Causes the program in memory to execute.

RUN n Causes the program in memory to execute starting at line number n.

SAVE {B} Saves the program named "pn" to disk in drive 0. The syntax requires the use of the @ symbol.
   SAVE "@0:pn",8

SCRATCH Deletes file f from the disk directory on drive 0.
   SCRATCH 0:f

VALIDATE Reorganizes the sectors on a disk so they are able to be accessed more efficiently.
   PRINT#15,"V"

VERIFY {B} Compares the program named "pn" in memory with the version last saved to device D (cassette if D=1, disk if D=8). If the programs do not match, an error message is displayed.
   VERIFY "pn",D

XENIX

XENIX is a subset of the UNIX VII operating system developed by MicroSoft specifically for the more advanced microcomputers. In particular, XENIX has been designed to operate with microcomputers using the 8086, Z8000, or M68000 processors. More recently, XENIX has been adapted to work with Altos, Tandy (Model 16 or 12), IBM PC, and the Apple Lisa and now the Macintosh XL systems. The following are XENIX commands for TRS-XENIX running on the TRS-80 Model 16.

XENIX GLOSSARY

XENIX, like UNIX, offers multiple directory capability. Individual files can be accessed by more than one name on a directory, and in more than one directory.

XENIX DIRECTORIES
Some frequently used XENIX directories are:

/bin   XENIX utilities

/dev   Files for I/O devices

/etc   System maintenance programs

/lib   Library files

/tmp   Temporary files

/usr   Overflow from /bin

TRSSHELL

The XENIX command level using TRSSHELL is a subshell of TRS-80 XENIX which is designed to make the transition from regular TRS-DOS to XENIX more comfortable for TRS-DOS users. The TRSSHELL subsystem is accessed by typing tsh. TRSSHELL can be exited either by typing D (CTRL-D) or exit. The TRSSHELL commands are:

auto   Creates or removes an automatic command.

chdir d   Changes the current directory to directory d.

cls   Clears the screen and moves the cursor to the home position.

copy f1 f2   Copies the file named f1 to the file named f2.

dir d filenames   Lists all files specified on directory d.

Options available with the dir command are:

-a   Lists files beginning with . in addition to other files.

-b   Prints invisible characters as /nnn (octal).

-c   Sorts or prints during file creation time.

-d   Lists directory name but not contents.

-g   Gives group, rather than owner, ID in listing.

-r   Sorts in chronological order.

-s   Gives size in blocks for each entry.

-t   Sorts by time.

-u   Uses last access time for sorting or printing.

-R   Lists contents of all subdirectories.

dismount:d   Removes the file system on drive d.

display   Displays a screenful of text.

Options available with display are:

-n   (Where n is an integer). Displays n lines of text.

-s   Deletes multiple blank lines when printing.

-r   Displays control characters as K where K is any control character.

-w   Causes system to wait for a key to be pressed to exit the system when the end of the input is reached.

do f   Executes the commands stored in filename f.

files   Lists all files from the specified directory in column format.

Options used with files are:

-a   Lists files beginning with . in addition to other files.

-b   Prints invisible characters as /nnn (octal).

-c   Sorts or prints during file creation time.

-d   Lists directory name but not contents.

-g   Gives group, rather than owner, ID in listing.

-r   Sorts in chronological order.

-s Gives size in blocks for each entry.

-t Sorts by time.

-u Uses last access time for sorting or printing.

-R Lists contents of all subdirectories.

-x Forces printing to be done in columns.

-l Cause output to be printed one entry per line.

-C Causes output to be printed in multicolumn format.

free Displays number of free blocks.

help x Displays help information on subject x.

help * Displays subjects for which help is available.

kill f Removes the entry for the files named from the directory.

kill -r Deletes the contents of the directory and also the directory itself.

lib Displays list of TRSSHELL commands.

mount d Informs system that a file system exists on drive d.

move f1 f2 d Copies file f1 to file f2 on directory d.

move -i... Lets user know if destination file already exists and prompts for overwrite decision.

print Causes files named to be readied for printing at the line printer.

Options available with print are:

-r Removes the file after printing.

-c Copies the file before printing.

-m Reports by mail when printing is done.

-n Does not report by mail (default).

rename old.f1 new.f2 Changes the name of file f1 to f2.

restore reads files that have been saved on a floppy disk and restores them to where they were saved from.

save :d Saves files or directories to the floppy in drive d.

Options available with save are:

-ss Used if destination floppy is single sided.

-ds Used if destination floppy is double sided.

set Allows the user to change TRSSHELL's internal option settings.

Options available with set are:

verbose (on/off) Informs the user (or not) of a command's success or failure.

retry (on/off) Causes TRSSHELL to convert the command line to lower case if a command was unable to be executed.

prompt S Sets the TRSSHELL prompt to string S.

showdir Prints the pathname of the current directory.

time Displays current date and time.

version Displays the name and current version of the shell.

Some TRS-XENIX commands are:

cat f1 Displays contents of file f1.

cd Changes working directory.

chdir d Changes working directory to d.

chmod Change mode.

Options available with chmod are:

u Change user permission.

g Change group permission.

o Change other permission.

a Change all permissions.

+ Add permission.

− Remove permission.

= Set permission.

r Read permission.

w Write permission.

x   Execute permission.

cp f   Copies file f.

cron   Causes command files to be executed at pre-set times.

df   Displays the number of free blocks on a disk.

diskutil   Formats or copies disks.

disable t1   Disables terminal 1. This must be done prior to disconnecting it.

du   Displays number of blocks used by files, directories, and subdirectories.

ed f   Brings up filename f for the editor.

enable t1   Informs the system that terminal t1 is on line. This must be done prior to using the terminal.

firsttime   Copies contents from floppy disks to the hard disk on initial boot.

fsck   Checks file systems for errors.

haltsys   Causes normal shutdown of the XENIX system.

hdinit   Boots from the floppy disk and initializes the hard disk.

install   Installs applications programs for individual users.

lc   Lists contents of current directory.

mkdir d   Creates a director named d.

mkfs   Prepares a disk to accept the XENIX file system.

mkuser   Permits entry of a new user on the XENIX system.

motd   Creates a general "message of the day" which is displayed to each user upon logging in.

passwd   Creates a password.

pwd   Displays the working directory.

quot   Displays the number of blocks on a disk allocated to each user.

rm f   Removes the file named f.

rmdir d   Removes the directory named d.

rmuser   Removes a user from the system.

shutdown   Unmounts all file systems at once.

sysadmin   Used for system level backup.

tar   Copies files or directories from a hard disk to a floppy.

tx   Transfers files from a disk formatted in TRS-DOS II to a disk formatted in TRS-XENIX.

update   Automatically writes contents of RAM to disk every 30 seconds.

wall   Sets up immediate communications with all users on the system.

who   Displays names of users who are currently using the system.

CP/M

Digital Research's CP/M was one of the first complete operating systems developed for the microcomputer. Written for 8080-based systems, CP/M provided an environment for file management and basic input/output operations that was standard from machine to machine. This allowed independent computer manufacturers to develop new hardware systems without having to worry about developing a proprietary operating system as well. By developing CP/M machines, independent companies were able to sell to a common marketplace. So successful was CP/M that by 1981-1982, it had become the standard operating environment for all business personal computer software. This glossary represents the most complete implementation of CP/M version 3.0 (also known as CP/M+) and includes those commands used in version 2.2 as well. This version of CP/M will operate on all 8080/Z80-based machines, including the Heath/Zenith, Kaypro, Osborne, and the TRS-80 Model 4.

CP/M GLOSSARY

COPYSYS (See SYSGEN.)

DATE Displays date continuously until a key is pressed.
 DATE C

DATE mm/dd/yy Sets date to month mm, day dd, and year yy.

DEVICE Used to display status and set peripheral devices.

DIR Displays the directory of drive d1.
 DIR d1:

DIR opt Displays disk directory of user files and includes options (opt). The options are:

 ATT Also displays the user-definable attributes. (See SET.)

 DATE Displays date and time stamps for files.

 DRIVE=d1,d2 Displays files on drives d1, d2, etc.

 DRIVE=ALL Displays files on all system drives.

 EXCLUDE f Lists all files except file type f.

 FF Sends form feed character to the printer before printing directory.

 FULL Displays all information about files.

 LENGTH=n Displays n lines before inserting a new heading. Default is 24.

 MESSAGE Displays names of specified drives and user numbers being searched.

 NOPAGE Displays directory continuously. Does not wait when screen-full condition exists.

 NOSORT Displays file names as found (i.e., non-alphabetical).

 RO Displays files with the read-only attribute.

 RW Displays files with the read/write attribute.

 SIZE Displays file size (in addition to file name).

 SYS Same as DIRSYS.

 USER=ALL Displays files from all user areas.

 USER=n1,n2 Displays files from user areas n1 and n2 (where the n values must be between 1 and 15).

DIRSYS Displays directory of system files.

DISKCOPY A utility which prompts the user to copy the contents of one disk to another by first formatting the destination disk.

DUMP Displays file contents in hexadecimal form (CP/M 80), and in both hexadecimal and ASCII (CP/M+).
 DUMP f

ED Accesses the text file editor.

ERASE Erase file f.
 ERA f

FORMAT Prepares disk for subsequent writing. Format program prompts the user for the name of the drive where the disk is to be formatted.

GENCOM Produces a COM-type file from an RSX-type file.

GET Takes subsequent input from disk file f.
 GET FILE f

HELP Displays help menu for CP/M+ commands.

HELP com Displays help information for command com.

HEXCOM Generates a COM file from a hexadecimal file created using ASM or MAC.

INITDIR Prepares disk directory to accept date and time stamps.

LIB A utility by which library files can be created or modified.

LINK Takes ouput code created by MAC or RMAC and produces a COM file. Also combines relocatable code file to produce a single COM file.

MAC A macro assembler which works with 8080 instructions and also allows Z80 mnemonics.

MOVCPM Makes use of all existing RAM space. Some versions of CP/M are set expecting a certain maximum RAM space. If this is less than the actual system, the MOVCPM command will adjust the system to seek the actual available RAM space.

PATCH Takes file f, extension e and adds machine language patch number n.
    PATCH f. e n

PIP Copies old file "of" from drive d2 to drive d1 and gives the file the name nf. (Warning: the PIP convention is the opposite of the MS-DOS "COPY" command. If PIP is used in the same manner as MS-DOS copy, it is possible to overwrite the wrong file.)
    PIP d1:nf=d2:of

PUT Same as GET except output is sent to a disk file.

REN Takes old file "of" on drive d2 and renames it nf.
    REN d1:nf=of

RENAME Same as REN.

RMAC A relocating macro asssembler. (See MAC.)

SAVE nn d1: f.e Saves program f (with extension e) from memory to the disk in d1. nn represents the number of 256 byte blocks of memory to be stored.

SET Takes all files on drive d1 and SETs them with the indicated option(s) opt.
    SET d1: opt

The possible options are:

DIR Sets attributes to user files.

SYS Sets attributes for system files.

RO Read-only files.

RW Read and write files.

ARCHIVE=k k is ON or OFF. When the ARCHIVE bit is ON, the file has not been modified since the last copy. When the ARCHIVE bit is OFF, the file has not been copied since last modified.

SETDEF Causes the system to search for files on the indicated disk drives, d1,d2, etc.
    SETDEF d1,d2,..

SHOW Causes the files on drive d1 to be displayed with options opt.
    SHOW d1: opt

The possible options are:

SPACE Displays drive name, access status, and space remaining.

LABEL Displays the directory name, whether passwords are required, whether the date stamp is on, and when the label was created and updated last.

USERS Displays current user number and all users on the disk. Also displays number of free directory entries.

DIR Displays number of available directory entries on the disk.

SID A debug utility used on machine language programs.

STAT (n/a on CP/M+) For CP/M+ equivalents, see SHOW and DIR options. STAT gives statistics on the disk files.

STAT d1:$xx Displays the files on drive d1 with attributes xx.

The attributes available are:

R/O Read-only files.

R/W Read and write files.

DIR User files.

SYS System files.

STAT Reports the following:

RECS The number of 128 byte records in a file.

BYTES The length of the file in K bytes.

EX The number of physical extents in the file.

ACC   The file access attribute (R/W or R/O).

d1:f.e   d1 is the drive; f, the filename; and e, the extension.

SUBMIT   A batch utility which will execute a series of CP/M commands.

SYSGEN   A utility to copy the CP/M system from one disk to another. The utility prompts the user.

TYPE   Displays contents of ASCII file f on screen.
TYPE f

USER   Sets user area to n. ($1 <= n <= 15$.)
USER n

XREF   Creates a cross-reference file of variables used within a program which has been created with MAC or RMAC.

Applesoft DOS 3.3

The development of Apple's disk operating system was an important event in the history of the microcomputer as a consumer electronics product. Apple's DOS was one of the first software systems that put into the user's hands an inexpensive yet powerful way to create, process, and retrieve mass-storage-based record, data, and program files.

The availability of a disk operating system for the Apple, at a time when the early Radio Shack and Commodore PET computers were still using tape cassettes as a program and data storage and retrieval mechanism, made the Apple one of the early best-selling computers. It also spurred the development of disk-based software and helped to create an entire industry. Apple DOS, unlike CP/M, is a user-oriented proprietary operating system that is designed to make system access straightforward, especially for the novice computer owner.

CP/M is a professional-level operating system that does all of the housekeeping and I/O chores for such file-intensive programs as Wordstar and dBASE II. Apple's DOS, on the other hand, was written to simplify the complex process of file creation and access. By any standard of judgment, Apple's ability to structure an operating system that brought disk file management capability to the level of the elementary school pupil at home and in the classroom was nothing less than remarkable. And although Apple's DOS has now been largely replaced by ProDOS on the IIc and IIe, its contribution to the personal computer industry still remains.

The following DOS commands represent Apple DOS 3.3, the most recent version of the operating system before the implementation of ProDOS. Although it is not available for the Apple IIc, DOS 3.3 is still available for the Apple II+ and Apple IIe computers.

APPLESOFT GLOSSARY

APPEND Adds characters to a sequential text file, called f.
   Append f

B See READ and WRITE.

BLOAD Loads a binary file whose file name is f.
   BLOAD f

BRUN Runs a binary file whose file name is f.
   BRUN f

BSAVE Saves a binary file whose file name is f.
   BSAVE f

C See MON and NOMON.

CALL Inserts a machine language subroutine from memory location n into an executing program.
   CALL n

CATALOG Displays the directory of the disk.

CHAIN In Integer BASIC only, causes program f to be run immediately after the presently executing program. All variables from the first program are passed on to f.
   CHAIN f

CLOSE Closes file f. Without specifying f, all files will be closed.
   CLOSE f

DELETE Deletes file f from the disk directory.
   DELETE f

EXEC Causes a sequential file f to be executed as an executable program.
   EXEC f

FP Returns to Applesoft BASIC from Integer BASIC.

GET Reads one character from an open file and stores it in variable A$.
   GET A$

HIMEM Sets the highest memory location to be accessed by an executing program.
   HIMEM n

IN Takes input from slot number n.
   IN #n

INIT Formats a disk with auto-boot greeting program f.
   INIT f

INPUT Reads a field from an open file and stores the field's characters in variable A$.
   INPUT A$

LOAD Executable BASIC file f is loaded into memory from disk.
   LOAD f

LOCK Prevents disk file f from being changed.
   LOCK f

MAXFILES Sets the maximum number of files that can be open at one time. The value of n must be between 1 and 16, and default is 3.
   MAXFILES n

MON Causes system commands to be displayed on screen as they are executed.

MON C   Only commands sent to the disk are displayed.

MON I   Only input commands from the disk are displayed.

MON O   Only output commands to the disk are displayed.

NOMON   Turns off the corresponding MON command.

OPEN   Opens file f for subsequent READing or WRITEing.
  OPEN f

POSITION   Causes READing or WRITEing from file f to occur at a field which is n fields from the current field.
  POSITION f,n

PR   Sends output to slot number n.
  PR #n

RWTS   A DOS subroutine used to access disk locations directly from machine language.

READ   Causes input to come from disk file f.
  READ f

RENAME   Changes name of file f to g.
  RENAME f,g

RUN   Causes the BASIC program currently in memory to be executed.

RUN   LOADs and executes BASIC program f.

SAVE   Stores the BASIC program currently in memory as file f.
  SAVE f

TRACE   Causes line numbers to be displayed as a program is executing.

UNLOCK   Cancels a LOCK command. Permits changes to file f.
  UNLOCK f

VERIFY   Tests file f for internal consistency.
  VERIFY f

WRITE   Causes output to go to disk file f.
  WRITE f

ProDOS

ProDOS (Professional Disk Operating System) is an operating system developed by Apple Computer. The main difference between ProDOS and Apple DOS 3.3 is that ProDOS contains the ability to handle hard disks as well as standard floppies. ProDOS resembles Micro-Soft's MS-DOS 2.0 and later versions in its UNIX-like file handling and directory/subdirectory abilities. ProDOS is unique as an operating system in that much of it is menu driven rather than command driven.

ProDOS GLOSSARY

The ProDOS file commands are displayed in the file commands menu and are accessed by striking the appropriate key indicated on the menu display.

List ProDOS Directory   Lists all files in the named directory.

Copy Files   Copies files.

Delete Files   Deletes files from the file's directory.

Compare Files   Gives a byte by byte comparison of two files. This is particularly useful for file verification after copying.

Alter Write protection   Permits locking/unlocking of individual files.

Rename Files   Renames a file in the directory.

Make Directory   Creates subdirectories.

Set Prefix   Permits designation of a prefix as a path-name so it is not necessary to type the entire path name.

A volume refers to either an entire floppy disk or to a section of a hard disk. A particular volume of data on the disk might refer to, say, business correspondence or to an accounting program. The ProDOS volume commands are displayed in the volume commands menu. They are accessed by striking the appropriate key indicated on the menu display.

Format   Prepares the disk surface to receive information.

Copy   Copies volumes (from one disk to another or from one section of the hard disk to a floppy).

List   Lists the volumes currently on the system.

Rename   Renames a volume.

Detect Bad Blocks   Indicates the location of "bad" blocks (i.e., sectors of the disk which can not store and/or retrieve information).

Block Allocation   Indicates the current usage of blocks in a volume.

Compare Volumes   Compares volumes on a byte by byte basis. This is particularly useful as a means of verifying a copy of a volume.

The term configuration refers to the way in which a system is set up. For example, one configuration might have one hard disk and one floppy disk and a monochrome monitor. Another configuration might have two floppy disks and a color monitor. Details of a particular system's configuration must be keyed into the configuration menu. The configuration menu also contains default values which are the standard values expected by the ProDOS system unless otherwise indicated by the user. The configuration options are listed below.

SELECT DEFAULTS

Source Slot (default is 6)   ProDOS will look to this slot for copy operations.

Destination Slot (default is 6)   ProDOS will look to this slot for copy operations.

Source drive (default is 1)   ProDOS will look to this drive for copy operations.

Destination drive (default is 2)   ProDOS will look to this drive for copy operations.

OUTPUT DEVICE

Output Device Monitor Only   Output will be displayed only on the screen or monitor. This is the default command.

Printer and Monitor   In this case, output will be both printed out as a hard copy and displayed simultaneously on the monitor.

RESTORE DEFAULTS

This command restores the configuration parameters to the default values after they've been changed. ProDOS has the ability to convert DOS 3.3 files to the ProDOS format and also to convert ProDOS files to the DOS 3.3 format. These conversions are done through the convert menu. The convert commands are listed below.

Reverse Direction of Transfer Establishes transfer from ProDOS to DOS 3.3. or back again.

Change DOS 3.3 Slot/Drive Use this selection only if the DOS 3.3 files are not on the displayed slot and drive.

Set ProDOS Date Set the date with which to mark the ProDOS files.

Set ProDOS Prefix A ProDOS prefix must be selected before files can be transferred.

Transfer or List Files Use this command to begin the file transfer process or to list the files from which the files to be transferred will be chosen.

TRS-DOS

TRS-DOS, like Apple's DOS and CP/M, was one of the first operating systems available for microcomputers. Although TRS-DOS is Radio Shack's proprietary disk operating system for its TRS-80, it nevertheless shares many of the same features and command structures found in the Apple operating system and CP/M. Versions of TRS-DOS were implemented for the early Model I's, the II's, the Model 3, and the present Model 4. The commands which follow are the DOS commands for TRS-DOS operating on the TRS-80 Model II. One important note regarding TRS-DOS: there is a difference between uppercase and lowercase letters in system commands (unlike MS-DOS and CP/M, where the operating system treats upper- and lowercase the same). For example, if a user wants to use the APPEND command but instead types "Append", the system will not recognize the command.

TRS-DOS GLOSSARY

AGAIN Repeats last command.

ANALYZE Displays the way in which disk tracks are allocated between system and user files.
   ANALYZE f

APPEND f TO g Combines file f to file g sequentially. Files f and g must be of the same type and the same length.

ATTRIB f ACC = p1, UPD = p2, PROT = aa
Changes the password of file f from p1 to p2, and establishes access aa. (See also UPD and PROT.) For example, ATTRIB PROCESS/BAS ACC = OKGY, UPD = ABCD, PROT = READ changes the password "OKGY" for the BASIC file PROCESS to "ABCD". The PROT command sets the access level to read only, so no one would be able to write to the file. Access levels are:

EXEC File can only be executed.

KILL Complete access allowed.

NONE No access allowed.

READ File can be read and executed.

RENAME File can be read, written to, executed, and renamed.

WRITE File can be read, written to, and executed.

AUTO Causes system command c to be executed upon bootup. BASIC programs can be used with AUTO as follows: AUTO BASIC f (where f is the name of the basic program).
   AUTO c

BACKUP Copies the TRS-DOS diskette from drive 0 to drive 1.
   BACKUP 0 TO 1

BUILD Used to create or edit an AUTO file.

CLEAR Clears user memory.

CLOCK Turns on clock display in upper right corner of screen.

CLOCK OFF Turns off clock display.

CLS Clears the screen.

COPY d1 f TO d2 g Copies file f from drive d1 to drive d2 and names the copied file g.

CREATE f NGRANS = x1, NRECS = x2, LRL = x3, TYPE = x4 CREATE is used to name and file and then reserve space for future use. f represents the name of the file. NGRANS sets the number of granules allowed for the file. If no number is given for NGRANS, it is calculated by the information for NRECS (number of records) and LRL (length of the record). TYPE can be F (fixed-length record) or V (variable-length).

DATE Sets time and date display.

DATE mm/dd/yyyy Sets the date to month mm, day dd, and year yyyy. (The year is set in four digits, e.g., 1985.)

DEBUG Allows the user to enter and change machine language programs. It is also used to permit data transmission from an external source to the system.

DIR Displays the file directory of user files on drive d1.
   DIR :d1

DIR :d1 {SYS} Displays directory of user and system files.

DIR :d1 {SYS,PRT} Displays directory of user and system files on the line printer.

DO Executes files created with the BUILD command.
   DO f

DUAL Causes output to be sent simultaneously to the CRT and line printer.

DUMP f START=add1, END=add2, TRA=add3, RELO=add4, RORT=ltr DUMP copies a machine language file from memory to disk. START=add1 sets the beginning address. END=add2 sends the ending address. TRA=add3 sets the address at which execution begins when the program is executed. RELO=add4 sets the starting address for reloading the file back into memory. If RELO is omitted, add1 is the default. RORT=ltr is an indication to TRS-DOS whether the file can be executed directly from the system or whether it can only be LOADed from TRS-DOS but not executed. If ltr="R" then TRS-DOS can load but not execute. If "T" is specified, then TRS-DOS will also execute the file. T is the default.

ECHO Permits the user to display text on the screen which TRS-DOS does not interpret as a command. The BREAK key turns ECHO off.

ERROR Displays the error message associated with error code n.
    ERROR n

FORMAT Formats disk in drive d1.
    FORMAT :d1

FORMS p=sz, L=kk, W=xx, C=yy FORMS initializes the printer settings. p gives the total number of lines per page, default is 66. L=kk specifies the maximum number of lines printed before a form feed; default is 60. W=xx specifies the maximum number of characters per line. Default is 132. C=yy sends a hexadecimal code to the printer indicating that the FORMS specifications have been completed.

FREE Displays the disk allocation map in granules (units of 1.28K bytes).
    FREE :d1

HELP Displays the TRS-DOS help menus.

HELP c Displays the specific help menu for command c.

HOST Causes input to be accepted from the RS-232 port.
    HOST ON

HOST OFF Causes input to be accepted from the keyboard.

I Causes TRS-DOS to read the disk identification on each active drive. I is used when disks are swapped.

KILL Deletes file f from the disk directory.
    KILL f

LIB Lists all library commands.

LIST Lists the hexadecimal and ASCII codes of file f. (ASCII values not in the range 32-127 will cause a period to be displayed.)
    LIST f

LOAD Loads a machine language program into memory. (Note: BASIC programs cannot be loaded with this command.)
    LOAD f

MOVE MOVE is used to send a group of files to a specified disk drive. f represents the file name or extension (e.g., /BAS for BASIC files). d1 specifies the destination drive. ABS is a parameter which causes TRS-DOS to overwrite a file on the destination drive if it has the same file name as the file being MOVEd. Without the ABS parameter, the user will be prompted before files are overwritten. The PROMPT parameter causes TRS-DOS to display each file before copying with the prompt: Y/N/S/Q.
    MOVE f TO d1 ABS,PROMPT

Y Copy.

N Don't copy.

S Stop prompting and copy everything.

Q Stop the MOVE (and stop copying).

PAUSE Causes execution of a DO file to stop until the enter key is pressed. msg can be any message.
    PAUSE msg

PRINT Prints text file f at the printer. If no printer is present on the system, a FORMS D command must be executed for print to be sent to the CRT. Without FORMS D the system will hang.
    PRINT f

PROT (See ATTRIB.) In addition to the parameters specified with ATTRIB, PROT can be used to change the master password of a disk. For example, PROT: d1 OLD=op, NEW=np, will change the master password of the disk from op to np.

PURGE Causes the system to ask the user whether to delete files of type f. Queries the user one file at a time.
    PURGE: d1 f

RECEIVE Used to receive object code into RAM from an external device. The SETCOM command must be used first to initialize the serial port.

RENAME f TO g Changes the name of file f to g.

RESET Produces the same effect as pressing the RESET key.

SCREEN Dumps the contents of the screen to the printer. This is not, however, a screen dump as only text is output. Graphics characters are output as periods.

SETCOM Initializes the RS-232 interface.

SPOOL Allows the computer to be used while printing is in progress.

STATUS Displays the status of all TRS-DOS functions.

T Causes the paper in the printer to advance to the top-of-form position.

TIME Used to display the current time or set the new time.

VERIFY Causes TRS-DOS to check whether any data written to the disk can be read.
  VERIFY ON

VERIFY OFF Halts the verify function.

TRS-DOS 6.0

Known as either L-DOS or TRS-DOS 6.0, Tandy's latest version of its TRS-80 disk operating system gives the user a greater access to disk files, the parameters of disk files, and the control the system exerts over files. L-DOS represents Radio Shack's serious attempt to penetrate the business desktop computer market by providing a more thorough mechanism of password levels to govern disk and file access than had previously been available not only in the earlier versions of TRS-DOS but also in CP/M and MS-DOS. The commands which follow are the DOS commands for TRS-DOS 6.0 operating on the TRS-80 Model IV.

TRS-DOS 6.0 GLOSSARY

APPEND f TO g   Combines file f to file g sequentially. Files f and g must be of the same type and the same length, and must be in ASCII format.

ATTRIB   The following are file options available with ATTRIB.
   ATTRIB f (options)

   USER = "pwd"   Sets the user password to "pwd".

   OWNER = "pwd"   Sets the owner password to "pwd".

   PROT = (option)   Sets the protection level for the user password.

The possible levels of user password are:

   EXEC   File can only be executed.

   READ   File can be read and executed.

   UPDATE   Allows update, read, and execute.

   WRITE   Allows read, write, update, and execute.

   RENAME   File can be read, written to, executed, and renamed.

   REMOVE   Total access is allowed except that attributes cannot be changed.

   FULL   Allows complete access.

   VIS   File is visible in directory.

   INV   File is invisible in directory.

Levels of protection can be abbreviated to their first two letters (except that RENAME is RN and REMOVE is RM).

The following commands are the disk options available with ATTRIB.

   ATTRIB :d1 (options)   Gives disk drive d1 the specified options.

   LOCK   Sets the password for all unprotected visible files to the disk master password.

   UNLOCK   Removes user and owner passwords from visible files if they are the same as the master password.

   MPW ="password"   Gives the disk's master password.

   NAME ="dn"   Changes disk name to "dn".

   PW='dp'   Changes the disk master password to "dp".

AUTO   Causes system command c to be executed upon bootup. BASIC programs can be used with AUTO as follows: AUTO BASIC f (where f is the name of the basic program).
   AUTO c

BACKUP f:d1 TO d2 (opt)   Duplicates files specified by f from drive d1 to drive d2 with options opt.

The possible options are:

   MPW="pwd"   Specifies source disk master password.

   SYS   Copies system as well as visible files.

   MOD   Copies files which have been changed since last copy.

   QUERY=YES   Causes system to query the user about each file before any copy is made.

   OLD   Copies only those files which already exist on the destination disk.

   NEW   Copies only those files which do not exist on the destination disk.

   X   Permits copying with no system disk in drive 0.

   DATE = m1/d1/y1-m2/d2/y2   Copies files which have been modified between the two dates.

DATE = m1/d1/y1   Copies files which have been modified on the indicated date.

DATE> = m1/d1/y1   Copies files which have been modified on or before the indicated date.

DATE< = m1/d1/y1   Copies files which have been modified on or after the indicated date.

BOOT   Resets TRS-DOS. Same as warm boot.

BUILD   Creates data file f containing commands and permits the execution of f using DO, KSM/FLT, or PATCH. The default extension is /JCL.
  BUILD f (opt)

The options are:

HEX   Data must be in hexadecimal code.

APPEND   Appends f to the end of an existing file.

CLEAR   Clears user memory.

CLOCK   Turns on clock display in upper right corner of screen.

CLOCK OFF   Turns off clock display.

CLS   Clears the screen.

COMM   Permits two computers to exchange data via device d (usually the RS-232 port).
  COMM d

CONV f:d1 d2: (opt)   Transfers files defined by f from TRS-DOS 1.3 format (Radio Shack Model III) on drive d1: to TRS-DOS 6.0 (L-DOS) format for Radio Shack Model IV on drive d2.

The available options are:

SYS   Copies system as well as visible files.

MOD   Copies files which have been changed since last copy.

QUERY=YES   Causes system to query the user about each file before any copy is made.

OLD   Copies only those files which already exist on the destination disk.

NEW   Copies only those files which do not exist on the destination disk.

VIS   File is visible in directory.

INV   File is invisible in directory.

DIR   Displays short directory of TRS-DOS 1.3 disk.

CPY f TO d2 (opt)   Copies f from current drive to drive d2. f can be a file or a device specification.

Available options are:

LRL=nnn   Specifies record length at destination. Default is source record length.

CLONE=NO   Destination disk will not have same attributes as source.

ECHO   All characters from a device specification are displayed on the screen.

X   Copy occurs using one disk drive.

CREATE f (opt)   CREATE is used to name a file and reserve space for future use. f represesents the name of the file.

Available options are:

LRN=n   Sets record length to n. (n is between 1 and 256 and default is 256.)

REC=n   Sets number of fixed-length records to n.

SIZE=n   Sets allocated disk space to n kilobytes.

DATE   Sets time and date display.

DATE mm/dd/yyyy   Sets the date to month mm, day dd, and year yyyy. (The year is set in four digits, e.g., 1985.)

DEBUG   Allows the user to enter and change machine language programs. Also used to permit data transmission from an external source to the system.

DEVICE   Displays system status for drives and devices.
  DEVICE

DIR   Displays the file directory of user files on drive d1.
  DIR :d1 (opt)

Available options are:

ALL   Displays all information for the files specified.

INV   Displays nonsystem invisible files and visible files.

MOD   Displays only files changed since last copy.

NON   Sets nonstop display.

PRT   Sends directory output to printer.

SYS   Displays system files and visible files.

SORT=NO   Produces nonalphabetical display.

DATE = m1/d1/y1-m2/d2/y2   Displays files which have been modified between the two dates.

DATE = m1/d1/y1   Displays files which have been modified on the indicated date.

DATE_ = m1/d1/y1   Displays files which have been modified on or before the indicated date.

DATE< = m1/d1/y1   Displays files which have been modified on or after the indicated date.

DO   Executes files created with the BUILD command. A DO file is a JCL file containing a series of TRS-DOS 6.0 library commands.
   DO f

DUMP   DUMP copies a machine language file from memory to disk.
   DUMP f (opt)

Available options are:

START=add1   Sets the beginning address.

END=Add2   Sets the ending address.

TRA=add3   Sets the address at which execution begins when the program is executed.

ASCII   Sends dump to ASCII file.

ETX=n   Specifies character at end of ASCII file has ASCII value n.

ECHO   Permits the user to display text on the screen which TRS-DOS does not interpret as a command. The BREAK key turns ECHO off.

ERROR   Displays the error message associated with error code n.
   ERROR n

FILTER d USING f   Changes data as it is sent to device d from device f.

FORMAT   Formats disk in drive d1.
   FORMAT :d1

FORMS   FORMS initializes the printer settings.
   FORMS (opt)

The available options are:

DEFAULT   Sets all parameters to startup values.

ADDLF   Sends line feed after each return.

FFHARD   Sends top-of-form character.

INDENT=n   n is number of spaces a line is to be indented.

LINES=n   Sets number of lines per page to n. Default is 66.

MARGIN=n   Sets left margin to n.

PAGE=n   Sets page size to n lines. Default is 66.

QUERY   Sets user prompt for each parameter.

TAB   Causes TAB character to be interpreted as a number of spaces.

XLATE=X ab   Causes one character (a) in hex format to be translated to b via the filter.

FREE   Displays the disk allocation map in granules (units of 1.28K bytes).
   FREE :d1

KILL   Deletes file f from the disk directory.
   KILL f

LIB   Lists all library commands.

LINK dv1 TO dv2   Connects two logical devices, for example, a printer and the screen display. RESET aborts LINK.

LIST   Lists the contents of file f.
   LIST f (opt)

Available options are:

ASCII8   Displays graphics and special characters along with text.

NUM   Numbers the lines in ASCII text files.

HEX   Sets format to hexadecimal.

TAB=n   Sets tab stops at n.

P   Sends output to printer.

LINE=n   Sets starting line number to n.

REC=n   Sets starting record number to n. Default is 0. REC can only be used with HEX.

LRL=n Sets record length to n.

LOAD Loads a machine language program into memory. (Note: BASIC programs cannot be loaded with this command.)
  LOAD f

MEMORY Reserves a portion of memory or changes current memory settings.
  MEMORY (opt)

Available options are:

  CLEAR=n Fills memory from locations 2600h to HIGH$ with hex character n. default is 00h (NULL).

  HIGH=n Sets HIGH$ to hex value n.

  LOW=n Sets LOW$ to hex value n.

  ADD=wd Displays the word at wd and displays the address of WORD and BYTE.

  WORD=wd Changes contents of ADD and ADD+1 to wd.

  BYTE=bt Changes contents of ADD to bt.

  GO=nn Transfers control to address nnh.

PATCH A utility used to make changes in any disk file either by typing in the patch code directly or by creating an ASCII file containing the patch codes.

PRINT Prints text file f at the printer. If no printer is present on the system, a FORMS D command must be executed for print to be sent to the CRT. Without FORMS D the system will hang.
  PRINT f

PURGE :d1 f (opt) Deletes files of type f from drive d1.

Available options are:

  MPW="pwd" Specifies source disk master password.

  SYS Deletes system as well as visible files.

  QUERY=NO Deletes files automatically without pausing to query the user.

  INV Deletes invisible and visible files.

  DATE = m1/d1/y1-m2/d2/y2 Deletes files which have been modified between the two dates.

DATE = m1/d1/y1 Deletes files which have been modified on the indicated date.

DATE< = m1/d1/y1 Deletes files which have been modified on or before the indicated date.

DATE> = m1/d1/y1 Deletes files which have been modified on or after the indicated date.

REMOVE Deletes file f from the directory and frees the space allocated to it.
  REMOVE f

RENAME f TO g Changes the name of file f to g.

RESET Returns device dvc to its startup condition.
  RESET dvc

ROUTE dv1 TO dv2 Routes data from device dv1 to device dv2.

RUN Loads program f into memory and executes it. f must have extension CMD.
  RUN f

SET A utility used to set a driver or a filter program to a particular device.

SETCOM Used to adjust the parameters of the RS-232 interface.

SETKI Used to set keyboard delay and repeat parameters.

SPOOL Allows the computer to be used while printing is in progress.

SYSGEN Creates a configuration file to be used as bootup configuration. Any system device can be configured this way.

SYSTEM Displays current configuration for all system devices.

TAPE100 f1 TO f2 Permits the system to read a tape file and write it to a disk file or read a disk file and write it to a tape file.

TIME Used to display the current time or set the new time.

VERIFY Causes TRS-DOS to check to see that any data written to the disk can be read.
  VERIFY ON

VERIFY OFF Halts the verify function.

Macintosh Operating System

The Macintosh/LISA operating system is driven by graphic designs on the screen that stand for specific items called icons and by menus that are pulled down from the top of the screen. The icons and menus are accessed by an arrow cursor that is controlled by moving a device called a mouse across a table top. The forward and backward motion of the mouse moves the pointer in exactly the same way. When the the mouse is moved forward, the pointer travels up to the top of the screen, and when the mouse is dragged backwards toward the user, the pointer moves down toward the bottom of the screen. Left and right on the table top are analagous to left and right on the screen.

The icons and windows form a workspace or desktop on the screen on which the user can access a variety of system or applications options. Certain options, accessible through the apple icon, are always available to the user. Different applications, however, add different menus to the top and left side of the screen, and different icons as well, which can be accessed by moving the pointer to the icon or menu and clicking or holding down the mousebutton.

The Macintosh operating system, which originally appeared on the LISA in 1983, utilizes the advantages of the automatic interrupt capability of the Supervisor mode of instructions on the 68000 chip and the modularity of the Smalltalk programming language developed at the Xerox research center in Palo Alto to offer the user a wide variety of system options. In addition to the standard file handling capabilities of the Macintosh Finder, which acts as a temporary storage location for individual files that are moved from disk to disk and as pointer for files that have been placed in temporary holding areas to make room for additional disk data, the Macintosh system also supports utilities such as a calculator, a note pad, an alarm clock, a calendar, and a variety of fonts. The entire Macintosh desktop can be modified by the user to display a different background graphic, a louder or softer beep, and an automatic touch control.

The following glossary identifies the basic icons and menus and their meanings within the Macintosh system. In addition, the glossary also identifies the major menu items and icons in MacPaint and MacWrite.

Although they are two different application programs for the Macintosh, both MacPaint and MacWrite are bundled with the system by Apple and are considered to be system functions. They will be treated as system components for the purposes of this glossary.

MACINTOSH GLOSSARY

Pointer This is the mouse's cursor that moves across the screen as the mouse moves across the table. The cursor in the system mode is normally a pointer; in MacWrite, it is a narrow line crossed at the top and bottom like an I-beam that is used in construction. In MacPaint, this cursor takes the form of the specific utility. It can be a pencil, an eraser, a paint brush, a spray can, a hand, or a lasso.

Pulled-Down Menu These are the menus at the top of the Macintosh screen that are opened by dragging the pointer over to them, until their titles are highlighted, and depressing and holding the mousebutton. When the title is highlighted and the mousebutton depressed, the menu opens up and reveals the

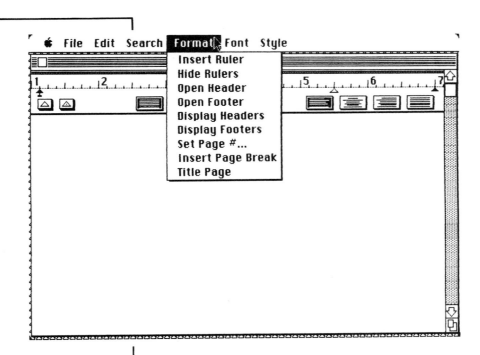

Disk Copy

options that are available. Then, by actually pulling the mouse pointer down across the menu, a different option in that menu is highlighted in black. If the mousebutton is released at that line, then that option will be accessed. If the pointer is dragged off the menu and the mousebutton released, the menu snaps up to the top of the screen. If the menu is pulled down and the mousebutton held, the menu stays in the open position to allow the user to examine the options available.

Active Window   The active window is the frontmost window on the desktop. It is the window in which the next activity will take place unless another window is made active by clicking the cursor in the window's lined menu bar. The contents of a directory are in the active window and they are displayed by icon, by name, by date, by size, and by kind. These options are contained in the View Menu.

Disk Icon   Whenever a disk is loaded into the Macintosh's internal or external disk drive, a disk icon appears on the desktop with its own identification label underneath. In order to load a program from the disk, a user first has to activate it by moving the pointer over to the icon and clicking it twice. Once the disk is activated, it is displayed on the screen as an active window. Programs or data can be loaded from it. More than one disk can be loaded at the same time, and more than one disk icon can appear on the Macintosh screen at any one time. Once a disk is loaded and ejected, its phantom image appears on the screen. If the disk is clicked open to activate it and it is not in the disk drive, the user will be prompted to insert the requested disk in the drive. If the disk is in the drive, then the window will be activated.

Other Disk Icons   The other disk icons will remain inactive unless they are clicked open and inserted into the disk drive. The Macintosh does not actually "know" which disk is in the system until an attempt is made to retrieve data. When the command is registered, the Macintosh operating system searches the drive, looks for the disk identification information that should correspond to the disk label that appears on the screen, and if there is match it can open the active window for that particular disk and display the disk directory on the screen.

Trash   This is the repository of all discarded data files and programs. Unlike the ERASE, DELETE, or SCRATCH commands in other language-based operating systems, Macintosh's delete sequence consists of moving the pointer over to the item that is to be deleted, depressing and holding the mousebutton, dragging the icon from the area on the disk active window to the trash area, and depositing it in the trash by releasing the button.

System Icon   This screen on the system disk of the Macintosh represents the commands the machine uses to manage its internal affairs. When preparing new disks or when preparing disks for special applications, it is usually necessary to copy the system file onto the new disk so that the new disk will contain all the necessary information to run the Macintosh without the necessity to load the system disk first. This is very similar to PC software that is packaged with startup instructions for moving portions of the PC's operating system from the DOS disk to the new applications disk. Once this is is done and an AUTO-EXEC file has been written to boot the PC up from a cold start, the applications software disk can be loaded and run by simply inserting it in the disk drive and turning on the PC. This is the same task users will have to perform when they are making new data or applications disks for their own files. Also, because the Macintosh is only a single-drive computer, it is usually more efficient to copy all the files that will be needed onto a single disk which will remain in the disk drive throughout.

Finder Icon   Although visible on the system disk, the Finder is actually an invisible piece of software that is always available on the desktop. The Finder is the Macintosh's disk and file manager. It is the program that matches the disk icon with the disk in the drive, prompts the user to insert the correct disk, and searches for the identification information to match the correct disk with correct request for information. The Finder program also keeps track where program files are moved, whether they are being moved to locations where they will no longer be active, or whether the user understands that once a particular program file is removed from a disk, the disk will not contain all the information it needs to drive the user's application or manage the user's data.

Warning Prompt   Because moving information from disk to disk, dumping information in the trash, and copying entire disks is so easy on the Macintosh, very inexperienced users can sometimes make what on most computers might be called "fatal" errors. The Macintosh, however, provides warnings and prompts when a fatal mistake is about to occur.

Trash

System disk

Finder

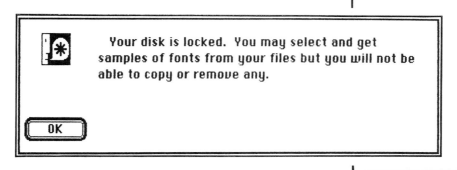

Your disk is locked. You may select and get samples of fonts from your files but you will not be able to copy or remove any.

OK

Fonts

Imagewriter

MACPAINT

body

System Folder

Empty Folder

Fonts Icon   The Fonts icon represents Macintosh's font management system. Because the machine supports eleven fonts on line, there is a sophisticated software component in the operating system that generates font commands and makes the different fonts available to the applications software. A large measure of user enthusiasm for the Macintosh is the result of the availability of the fonts to a variety of applications software including MacWrite, MacPaint, MacDraw, and MultiPlan.

Clipboard File Icon   The clipboard is a section of memory that acts as a temporary holding area for material that was most recently cut or copied from a document.

Imagewriter Icon   Represents the driver programs for the Imagewriter printer. The Imagewriter handles all of Macintosh's graphics and character sets in draft, correspondence, and very high resolution modes. The Imagewriter is interfaced through the Macintosh's serial printer port, as it is to the Apple IIc, and interfaces to the older Apple II series through the Super Serial card that adapts the standard Apple parallel data communication protocols to the serial port of the Macintosh.

Applications Icon   The applications icons, MacWrite, MacPaint, MacDraw, MultiPlan, Macmanager, and others are displayed in the disk's directory window. Software can be backed up or copied from disk to disk by dragging the applications software's icon with the pointer to the target location and releasing the mousebutton. That signals the disk copy program in the Macintosh system to copy the file to the new disk. When the pointer is used to drag an icon in this way, a phantom image is pulled out of the original icon and does not resolve itself into a new icon until the copying is completed.

Document Icon   The document is a user-created file. It can be a MacWrite document, a MacPaint document, or any other file that was created through one of the Macintosh applications programs. When a file is saved, either through the Save command on the Edit menu or as a step that the Macintosh makes automatically when it is printing a final copy of a document, the file is assigned an icon by the operating system. The next time the disk is accessed, the user document will appear as an icon with text for a word processed document or an icon with a paint brush for a MacPaint document. Both MacPaint and MacWrite have the same shape of icons as well.

System Folder Icon   The System Folder that appears on applications programs contains all the system-related files for startup, disk and file management, and font drivers. The System Folder is a handy way to store all the system-related information, and when new user-created disks are assembled with some applications software and some user files, it is usually a good idea to copy the System Folder onto the disk for good measure. With the System Folder on the disk, an applications program, and user files, the Macintosh becomes a turnkey system when booted up, ready to run applications.

Empty Folder Icon   Empty folders are document management tools that should be used to bundle together similar documents. There are usually one or more empty folders on a disk. As new documents, either word processed files or graphics files, are created and saved, they will begin to clutter up the disk window and will occupy more space in the disk directory than they have to. Macintosh's solution to this is to provide users with a folder that can store documents under one icon. Folders can be moved from disk to disk as easily as documents or programs can. However, when a folder is copied from a source to a destination disk, all the information inside the folder is copied as well. In this way, the Macintosh's folder system for organizing files or documents is similar to the outline frame system that is found in Framework. In both systems, similar or logically related documents are nested within one another and when the container is moved, all the contents are moved at the same time. The folder is also functionally similar to the subdirectory in MS-DOS. However, in DOS, the subdirectory must be created with an MD, or make directory, command and then the DOS directory pointer has to be reset with a CD, or change directory, command so that the disk will open to that directory whenever it is set as the logged drive.

Macintosh provides the same subdirectory capability with its folder organization, but makes the folders directly available without having to make or change directories. In order to move documents from the directory to folders, the arrow pointer is brought to the document icon, the mousebutton is depressed and held down, and the document icon is dragged across the screen to the folder.

When the mousebutton is released, the document icon disappears from the directory. It has now been transferred to the folder. When the folder icon is double-clicked open and its active window directory appears on the screen, the icon for the document that had been transferred to the folder now appears in the folder's active window. To remove the document from the folder, the edge of the disk window must be dragged out from behind the folder window, the folder window reactivated, the document dragged from the folder window to the disk window, and the folder window deactivated.

At this point, the document icon appears on the disk directory again, and the folder window collapses into the folder icon on the disk directory. The folder can expand to fill the available space on a disk, or space can be allotted per folder to allow a number of folders on the same disk. Folders can also be titled, for the same reasons that subdirectories are titled, so that the folder's contents, while not visible on the disk directory, are indicated by the title of the folder.

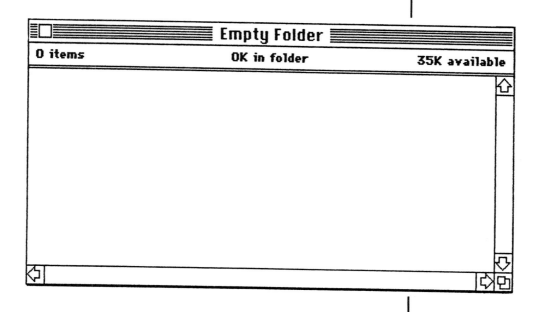

MacPaint Icons

MacPaint is considered to be a part of the basic Macintosh system. This glossary, therefore, includes the MacPaint icons and menus as part of the Macintosh operating system. Users will find that the MacPaint desktop icons are briefly described in the on-screen introduction from the Goodies menu in MacPaint.

Lasso   Used to select an object in a drawing window and drag or move the object to a different screen location. The Lasso is typically used to move a design that is on the screen to another screen location. It is also used to move an object that will become a part of a larger design, but has not yet been attached. Unlike the Grabber, which slides the entire screen underneath the viewing window, the Lasso only moves objects on the screen. The Lasso is often used to construct designs or move designs around prior to a rotation, expansion, or contraction.

Selection Rectangle   Used to isolate and select a rectangular portion of the drawing window. The Selection Rectangle can designate an entire object that will be operated upon, moved, or duplicated.

Grabber   Used to slide the entire screen back and forth beneath the viewing window. The Grabber is used to bring a different portion of a screen into view, and it is used in conjunction with Fat Bits to slide a section of a drawing into the viewer's working area to be cleaned up. And, when only small objects are on the screen, it can be used to move different objects into view.

Spray Can   This sprays a swath of the current pattern wherever the cursor indicates. Spray Can is used for freehand drawing or design, fingerpainting, or for screen art. The different border and background patterns at the bottom of the MacPaint screen can be used for a variety of effects including patchwork, brickwork, lattice, or polka dots.

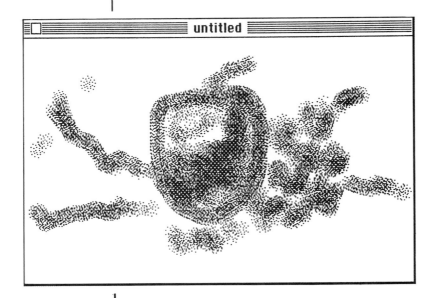

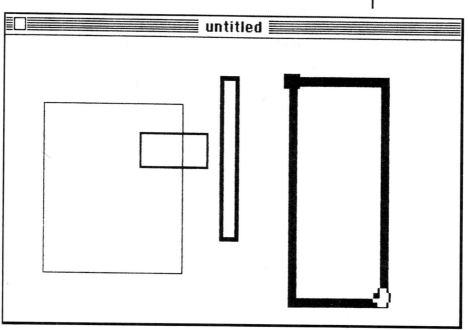

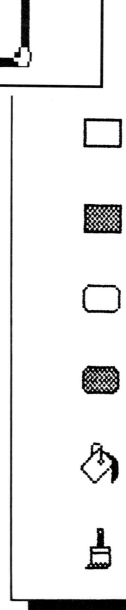

Hollow Rectangle   A utility that draws perfectly squared-off rectangles on the screen. The user starts at one of the right or left hand corners of the rectangle that will be drawn, presses the mousebutton, and extends the rectangle in the direction he or she wants it to go. As it extends, the lines remain straight and the angles perfectly square. When the user is satisfied with the size and dimension of the rectangle, the design can be locked in by releasing the mousebutton. Clicking the mousebutton on the screen, however, will cause the rectangle to disappear.

Filled Rectangle   Performs just like the Hollow Rectangle option, but instead draws rectangles that are filled with the current pattern. These utilities can be mixed and combined in different ways to create right-angled shapes of different configurations and dimensions.

Hollow Rounded-Corner Rectangle   Same as the square-cornered, hollow-rectangle. This utility draws rectangle shapes.

Filled Rounded-Corner Rectangle   Draws a rounded-corner rectangle that is filled with the current screen pattern.

Paint Can   The Paint Can fills an entire region with whatever the current pattern is as if it were pouring on a flow of paint. The region to be filled must be enclosed with a border created with one of the border shapes such as square, rectangle, or circle, or freehand with pencil. The Paint Can operates in much the same way that the Fill command operates in the Koala Pad software.

Paint Brush   This option allows freehand drawing in a variety of brush shapes selected from the options at the lower left of the screen and in a variety of patterns, using the current pattern or a pattern from the selection at the bottom of the screen. The Brush option provides a drawing cursor with a different texture than the Spray Can cursor.

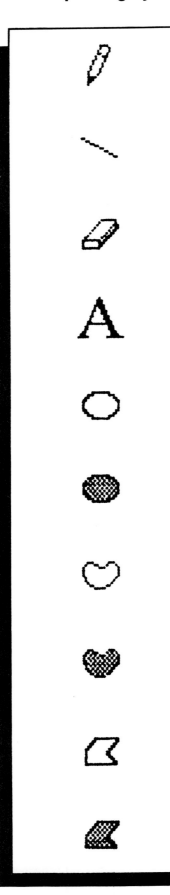

Pencil   Draws a black line on a white screen or a white line on a black screen. This drawing cursor replaces the pointer with a pencil icon and is used for fine line drawing. There are different pencil points which can be used with the Pencil cursor that range from a dotted line to an extra bold point. In the Fat Bits mode, the pencil is used to drop a dot at a time or, when placed over an existing dot and clicked on with the mousebutton, it erases a dot. In this way, the Pencil is a favorite tool for cleaning up drawings in the Fat Bits mode.

Line   A straight line drawing utility. Just like the straight line utilities in Koala Pad, this tool starts at one point and extends a line until it is straight to another point. Once locked in with the mousebutton, the line is fixed.

Eraser   Erases all lines from the screen. The eraser is passed over the lines to be removed. The eraser is a gross tool, however, and often erases more than it is supposed to. Therefore, the work area may also be cleaned up with the Pencil eraser in the Fat Bits mode to make sure that too much of the drawing was not deleted.

Text   This command switches the cursor from the drawing cursor to the I-Beam cursor for text entry. Switching to text mode brings the online fonts, the style, and the size parameters into operation and lets users combine text with graphics for integrated screen displays.

Hollow Oval   Draws hollow circles and oval shapes. The cross-hairs pointer is located at a particular spot on the Macintosh screen and as the mousebutton is held down, the circle or oval is pulled out with the pointer from the outward edge of the figure's circumference. As the cross-hairs pointer moves back and forth over its own path, the circle changes into an oval and back again.

Filled Oval   Draws a rounded figure from a perfect circle to an oval filled with the current screen pattern.

Hollow Free-Form Shape   Draws a free-form line that follows the path of the cursor. The thickness of the line can be set by selecting one of the drawing points at the bottom left of the screen. When a new thickness is selected, the cross-hairs cursor changes to the new weight of the line. By lining up the cursor in the direction to be plotted, the line can be drawn accurately.

Filled Free-Form Shape   Like the hollow shape, this is a line that can be drawn from the cross-hairs cursor in any direction on the screen. However, when the mousebutton is released, the line automatically completes a free-form enclosed shape by drawing a line between the two closest points. Then the free-form shape is filled in with the current screen pattern.

Hollow Irregular Shape   Extends a continuous line from where the mouse-button is first clicked until the mousebutton is clicked again. At that point, a new line is started until the next point where the mousebutton is clicked. This utility draws a series of straight but ragged lines across the screen.

Filled Irregular Shape   Draws a series of lines from mousebutton click to mousebutton click, but when the mousebutton is clicked twice, the line stops and a new line is drawn between the two closest points. The line forms an enclosure which is immediately filled by the current screen pattern. Both the hollow free-form and the filled-in free-form use the weight of the pencil lines at the bottom left of the screen for the weight of the cross-hairs cursor.

Pull-Down Menus

Finder Menus

The Finder contains five pull-down menus: Apple, File, Edit, View, and Special. Each menu has a particular function both in the Macintosh Finder and in Macintosh applications programs.

Apple Menu Contains information about the version of the Finder that is implemented on the Macintosh, opens the scrapbook, displays the alarm clock and opens the time and date module, displays the note pad, displays the calculator, displays the keycaps, displays the user-configurable control panel, displays a word puzzle. Of all the options in the Apple Menu, only the scrapbook requires further explanation. The scrapbook is like a folder in that both graphics and text can be stored there for use in any application. Scrapbook folders can be duplicated and stored on different disks, but the scrapbook itself is always available to the user. Portions of text, once placed in the scrapbook, can be recalled and inserted in any document. Similarly, any graphics display or combined graphics and text screen can be maintained in the scrapbook for use in any program. Many of the Macintosh "clip art" programs are designed to be loaded into the Finder scrapbook and from there into any application that requires a professionally prepared graphic.

File Menu Contains options for opening and closing files, retrieving data from a disk, putting data back to its source, closing a highlighted file or disk, closing all files or disks, immediate print, disk eject.

View Menu Allows files in the active window to be displayed in a variety of formats. By Icon is the default display parameter. In this mode the icons representing each file or document appear in the active window. The By Name option highlights the name of each document; the By Date option highlights the date each document was created; the By Kind option organizes the contents of the disk by file type, and the By Size option reports the amount of memory each document has used.

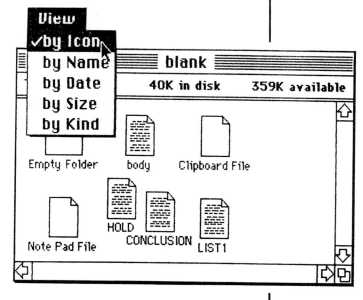

Edit Menu   Allows an immediate Undo of the last command, a cut and paste option which utilizes the clipboard as a transfer point, a copy feature that places the copy of the data on the clipboard, a clear command, and a command that removes information without placing it on the clipboard, a Select All option that opens all icons in the active window, and a Show Clipboard option that displays whatever was cut or copied to the clipboard.

Special Menu   Contains options for cleaning up the desktop or the active window by rearranging the incons into neat rows, an option for taking the accumulated data from the trash can holding area and erasing it from the system's memory, erasing the active disk, and resetting the startup protocols for the Macintosh to boot directly from a user-created disk.

MacWrite Menus

MacWrite contains all the standard features of a prototypical word processor. In addition to the Finder program in the Apple menu, MacWrite has the following pull-down menus:

File   Supports file opening and closing procedures, save commands, save with different file name, procedures to set up special page format parameters, a variety of printing options, and a quit MacWrite command.

Edit   Contains an Undo feature that reverses the previous command; cut, copy, and paste features that utilize the clipboard as a transfer point, and a show clipboard command that allows users to monitor what is being placed on and removed from the clipboard.

Format   Contains commands for inserting and hiding the page ruler and for opening header and footer windows to create the format and the contents of header and footer lines. In addition, the format commands display and remove the header and entry lines, set the page number, force a page ending, and set up a title page by turning off the header and footer protocols.

Style   Contains commands for plain, bold, italic, and other types of highlighted text as well as options for size from 9 through 24 point.

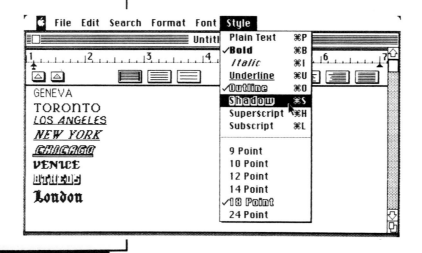

Font Contains all the fonts currently on line and supported by the Macintosh for use in the document to be created. Macintosh fonts are interchangable with one another and new fonts can be placed into service with the font mover. Currently, there are whole families of foreign language and technical fonts including Hebrew, Cyrillic, Greek, and Arabic, and mathematics and electrical schematics. There is even a pseudo-hieroglyphic font for design and purposes. New fonts are selected for the MacWrite document by pulling down the Font menu, moving the pointer to the designated font and clicking the mousebutton. The new text to be typed will appear in the new font. Previous text can be changed to the new font by using the highlight and change commands.

Search Contains standard search and replace commands.

MacPaint Menus

File Contains the file opening and closing, printing, saving, and quitting options that are in File menu for other Macintosh applications. In addition, the File menu contains a Print Catalog option that prints the disk directory to show what types of graphics documents are stored in the file.

Edit Besides containing the cut and paste options, the Edit menu contains commands that can invert the drawing on the screen, fill the drawing with one of the patterns from the bottom of the screen, trace the edges of the drawing, and rotate the drawing, flip it vertically, and flip it horizontally. These features provide interesting effects for standard drawings or portions of standard drawings that have been isolated with the lasso.

Goodies Contains commands for showing the screen grid, expanding the screen with Fat Bits to allow for detailed editing and cleaning up of a drawing, displaying the entire graphics page to illustrate a different perspective of the design, editing the standard patterns at the bottom of the screen or creating new ones to replace existing ones, changing the shape of the paint brush for freehand drawing, selecting a brush mirror for concurrent reverse image drawing, introducing the drawing tools available to MacPaint users, and displaying the keystroke shortcuts for many of the drawing and tool options.

Font Contains the list of the fonts available for the text component of Mac-Paint. These fonts can be changed with the font mover utilities on the system disk to prepare special MacPaint applications with different fonts. The font mover, file folder, and scrapbook utilities enable Macintosh users to prepare special MacPaint disks containing not only the user-created documents, but user modified versions of MacPaint preset to specific default parameters along with a particular group of fonts. Thus one application can become an infinite number of applications through the creative use of Macintosh's system utilities and support features.

FontSize Contains the options which designate the point size of the type that will be used.

Style Contains all of the options for type style and page alignment of text.

Font

New York
Toronto
San Francisco
Los Angeles
Cairo
Chicago
✓Geneva
Monaco
Venice
London
Athens

Goodies

Grid
FatBits
Show Page
Edit Pattern
Brush Shape
Brush Mirrors
Introduction
Short Cuts

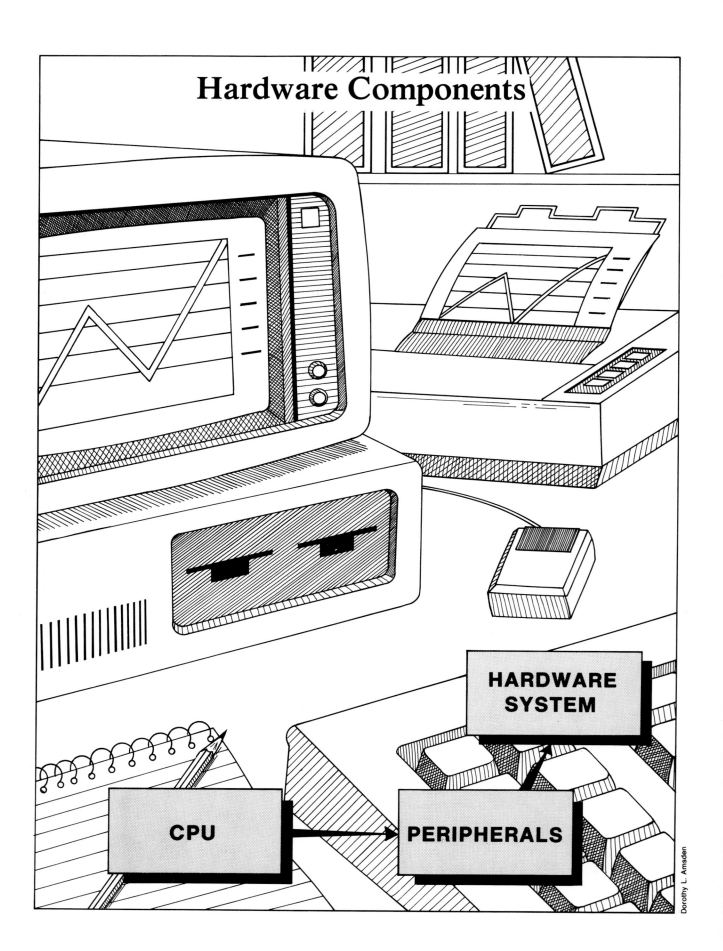

Hardware Components

HARDWARE SYSTEM

CPU → **PERIPHERALS**

Dorothy L. Amsden

7
MICROCOMPUTER SYSTEMS HARDWARE

A traditional view of humans sees the individual as a duality: body and mind. This is probably too simple a picture. But as a description of computers, it works well, for a computer is clearly a two-part system: a body (hardware) and a mind (software). The fact that certain hardware elements are preprogrammed, that is, contain software material as "native" to the computer, shouldn't mislead us. A computer is no more than a collection of manufactured parts integrated into an electromechanical system and controlled by "thoughts" that are electrical patterns programmed either at the factory or from some input device like a keyboard or a disk drive. Thus, the 'thinking" done by a computer is no more than the predetermined manipulation of information already in place or entered during the time the computer is in use. In this section we will look at the parts that constitute the computer's "body."

The external forms that microcomputers take are often simply a matter of human convenience, but the essential computer certainly need not reside in the familiar beige box. From a functional point of view, it could just as easily be mounted in a desk drawer or behind a wall. In many industrial applications, the computer is little more than a single integrated circuit (e.g., 8051) buried somewhere in a piece of manufacturing equipment. Many modern automobiles have one or more microcomputers stashed here and there beyond the user's direct awareness or control.

A Typical Microcomputer

From the least expensive microcomputer system to the most expensive, there is virtually no difference in basic design. Figure 7-1 illustrates a block diagram of a typical microcomputer showing the essential components in any system.

Such microcomputer applications have been a part of the industrial landscape for the past ten years, certainly before the personal computer revolution intruded upon the national consciousness. Now, however, that microprocessor controlled devices have advanced to the forefront of industrial visibility, the actual hardware identity of the typical computer system holds a new interest for the professional user.

Most personal computers consist of a single large circuit board, sometimes called a motherboard, with all of the essential subsystem components wired, soldered, or socketed in place. In addition to the printed circuit board, there are

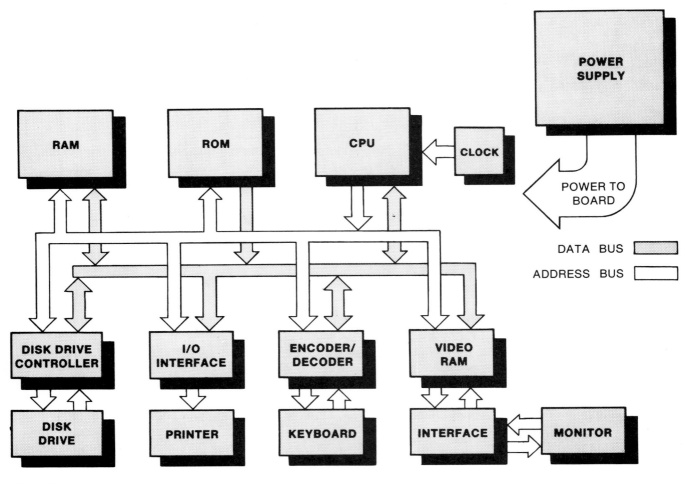

Fig. 7-1

input devices (keyboard, number pad, or mouse), a display component (almost always a video monitor or television set), a power supply, and a variety of input/output connectors to disk drives, printers, tape cassette storage devices, backup mass storage and telecommunications apparatus.

The monitor or television set can be interfaced to the area of random access memory dedicated to supporting the video display in a variety of ways. However, the specific configuration is important because it is contingent upon the type of the application the entire system is designed to fill. Home computers can generally be interfaced to either a dedicated monochrome or color monitor or to a standard television set. More elaborate video displays in which high resolution text and color are important may require different types of signal controllers. For computers that drive large screen slide and presentation graphics applications, an even more precise interface is usually needed to control the resolution of the video signal within the wide-screen matrix.

The external input device is generally a keyboard. However, even the early home computers sported joysticks and game paddles as input devices in addition to or in place of keyboards. By 1983 a simple and inexpensive digitizing pad became available for the home computer. The mouse appeared at about the same time, and is now in wide use. Touch screens and light pens enjoy a limited popularity. The latter is practical mainly in CAD/CAM systems.

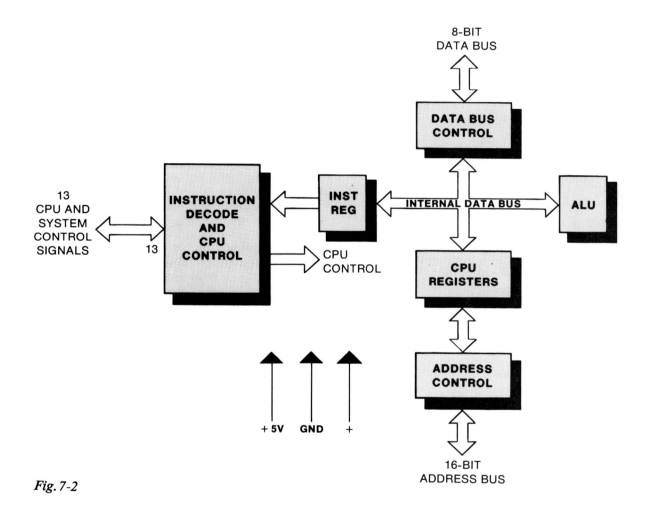

Fig. 7-2

The actual memory section of the block diagram is divided into random access memory, or RAM, and read only memory, or ROM. The RAM section is a block of chips that retain information stored there for as long as power is supplied to the system. RAM is also called transient memory because the data is only temporarily stored there. The size of random access memories has increased dramatically in the typical personal computer configuration as more sophisticated and larger CPUs have been introduced into the market.

The earliest 8-bit systems were typically delivered with only 8 or 16K of RAM. But the public was memory hungry and it wasn't long before 32K and 64K systems were the rule. Read only memory or ROM is a special area of memory that contains programming instructions that cannot be written over in normal use unless someone actually erases and reprograms one of the chips. The information stored in ROM can be used, but it cannot be modified. One of the ROM chips usually contains a monitor or executive program that understands what the user wants the computer to do and translates those instructions into instructions that the CPU can interpret. Some executive programs can be displayed as they execute other programs. In this mode, a programmer can literally monitor the operation of his or her code as the code is executed by the computer. Other types of information sometimes included in a computer's ROM package are a programming language, a form of word processor or text editor, and perhaps a rudimentary electronic spreadsheet. Many portable or lap computers such as the Tandy and the Epson include programming languages and software on ROM, and the Commodore PET series has always packaged BASIC in ROM.

The circuit board is also populated with a variety of support chips that handle many of the electrical and logical housekeeping functions of the system. There is a video interface chip and perhaps a sound or music synthesizor chip. The Commodore 64, for example, is heavily dependent upon the features or functions which are bundled into its support chips. Some of these features even allow elementary programmers to write entertaining graphics and music applications without having to rely on special software utilities. Other types of support chips can be used to handle concurrent processing operations or can be used to speed up the functioning of the entire system.

Microprocessor (CPU, MPU). The central or main processing unit manipulates data according to its instruction set and coordinates computer operations. Commonly, the CPU is housed in a 40-pin dual-inline package (DIP), requires a 5-volt electrical supply, and runs at a clock frequency between 1 and 8 MHz. A typical microprocessor is the Z80 in Fig. 7-2. A number of microprocessors are now being manufactured in CMOS (complementary metal-oxide semiconductor) versions, the big advantage of which is very low power consumption. The availability of CMOS CPUs, memory, and support chips makes the lap or briefcase computer feasible.

The CPU is really the organizer of computing activities and despite its size, the actual "chip" itself if smaller than a fingernail. Most of the surface area of the CPU is taken up with leads and pins. The chip itself, which is a sliver of silicon composed of thousands of electrical components and connections, is sitting at the center of the CPU. In the chip is the ALU, the place where the arithmetic calculations are carried out.

To handle interrupts in an orderly, prioritized fashion, an IC like the Motorola 6828 Priority Interrupt Controller (PIC) will be designed into the computer. In some systems, interrupts are handled by the CPU itself.

Clock. The timing system that all parts of the computer rely on for the orderly sequencing of events, the clock typically operates as a cooperative venture between the clock circuitry of the CPU itself and an external crystal-controlled oscillator. There are variations on the theme, but an oscillator and a method of using the output of the oscillator are the basic requirements. The characteristic clock signal is a pulse train and operations are designed on the rising or falling edge of a given pulse (Fig. 7-3). This triggering is possible because the chips involved are designed to be "edge sensitive," that is, able to detect a rising or falling edge and to act on this perception.

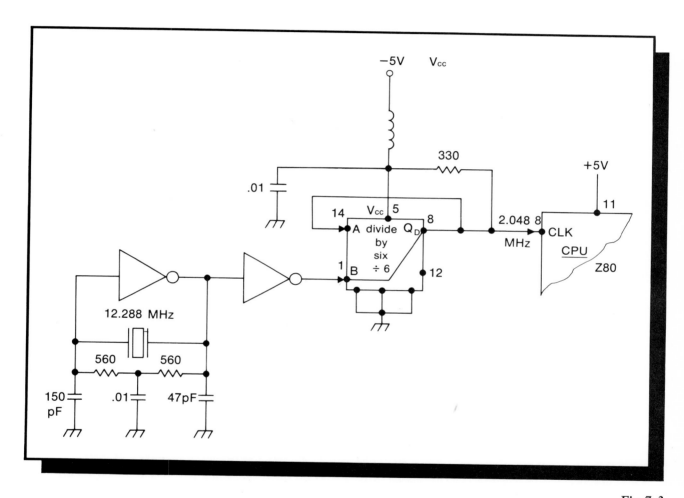

Fig. 7-3

The clock oscillator is a simple circuit, adjustable within fairly narrow limits, that produces a fixed-frequency signal keyed to the operating speed of the CPU. It's possible to speed up a computer by changing the crystal used to control the oscillator frequency. An increase in the clock frequency will force an increase in all the operations controlled by the CPU. It is possible for a CPU performing at, say, 2 MHz to be pushed to perform at 4 MHz. However, if the memory and support chips are not designed for high-speed operation, the system will be overdriven, and chaos will result because the slower chips will force everything out of synchronization.

I/O Ports. The computer's visible ports are those terminated in a connector of some sort—perhaps a 25-pin plug or socket used to attach a modem or printer. But within the computer are the I/O ports necessary for the movement of signals between the CPU and the rest of the circuitry. These are "doorways" or signal pathways into and out of the chip.

The I/O ports communicate through various types of I/O circuits, which are built around complex ICs like the PIA (peripheral interface adapter), USART (universal synchronous/asynchronous receiver/transmitter), and ACIA (asynchronous communication interface adapter).

It's convenient to resolve I/O into three categories: (1) internal or system I/O (example: disk drive or cassette interface), (2) user and peripheral I/O (examples: keyboard, video display, printer), and (3) analog or communication I/O (examples: modems, burglar alarms, fire detectors).

ROM. ROMs (read-only memory) are used to store program material necessary to the operation of the computer. This material includes a "monitor" program that acts as a software interface between the computer user and the CPU. In some computers, the ROM section also contains a programming language (e.g., BASIC-in-ROM). The "read-only" designation of this type of memory derives from the fact that the memory space occupied by ROM is inviolable, that is, cannot be written into. Because the data stored in ROM is permanent, it is called firmware.

ROMs in common use have capacities between 16 and 64 kilobytes. Some ROMs are user programmable. The EPROM (erasable, programmable, read-only memory) exemplifies this type. To program an EPROM requires either a stand-alone PROM burner or a dependent PROM programmer interfaced to a computer. The program, written in machine code, is stored on the EPROM in a manner analogous to storing programs in any storage medium. An EPROM must be erased with ultraviolet light. A small transparent window is provided in the IC for this purpose. An EEPROM (electrically erasable, programmable, read-only memory) needs only an electric current for erasure.

RAM. Random access memory (RAM) should be called read-write memory to distinguish it from read-only memory because access to both kinds of memory is exactly the same. At any rate, RAM is available for transient programs, whether those entered by the user from the keyboard or loaded through a peripheral device like a disk drive or cassette recorder. When a computer is described as having, for example, 128K of memory, it means that the computer has 128 kilobytes of RAM or empty memory space.

There are two types of RAM, static and dynamic, both performing the same function but in distinctly different ways. In dynamic RAM, a given bit (1 or 0) is held as a charge in an electrical storage device known as a capacitor. The storage area allotted to each bit is, of course, extremely small and as a result incapable of holding the charge for very long. In order to maintain the integrity of the stored charge, the RAM memory circuitry must be refreshed regularly. The term dynamic derives from this constant cycling of the special refresh signal. In contrast, a given bit in a static RAM will remain in place until it is changed deliberately or the computer is turned off. Instead of "leaky" capacitors, static RAMs use more elaborate circuitry—in fact, a bistable latch or "flip-flop." But because dynamic RAMs use considerably less power, bit for bit, than static RAMs, and are cheaper to manufacture, most popular microcomputers today use dynamic RAMs.

The progression of RAM capacity in recent years has been from 16 to 64 kilobits per chip. Delivery in quantity of 256-kilobit RAMs is now in full swing, and megabit (and even larger) RAMs are under intensive development. The architecture of all of these chips is such that eight of them are needed to provide the designated number in kilobytes. Thus, a computer with 256 kilobytes memory in 256K chips contains eight of these chips, plus one additional one for error ("parity") checking.

Some computer designs use a memory-management technique called DMA (direct-memory access), whereby the CPU is bypassed for certain operations. Such systems commonly contain a DMAC (direct-memory access controller), actually a slave processor chip, that acts as the executive for direct-memory data transfers.

Bus. The bus is a complex of electrical pathways—inside of the CPU as well as between the CPU and the rest of the computer circuitry—that carry the various signals necessary to computer operation. These signals (hence, their buses) are classified into data, address, and control. In addition, there is a power bus, which carries the computer's electrical power.

In a computer with a backplane (essentially a set of expansion slots), the bus system can be seen as a number of parallel traces, running beneath the slots so that a given trace will connect a given pin number in each slot. In other computers, the physical structure of the bus is less obvious, but it is there nevertheless. The address bus, for example, can be defined simply by following the address lines from their source at the appropriate pins of the CPU.

Bus design includes bus drivers and bus receivers, part of the operational overhead necessary to make the system work. Bus drivers are amplifiers that maintain the address, data, and control signals at usable levels. Bus receivers can be thought of as line conditioners, minimizing the various kinds of electrical noise and interference to which the long bus lines are prey.

As most CPUs are incapable of generating all of the control (clock and status) signals needed for proper operation of a computer system, a bus controller like the Intel 8228 (used in conjunction with, for example, the Intel 8080A) must be included in the design of the computer.

The core of a computer system thus consists of a CPU, timing circuitry, memory, a variety of support chips, and a four-part bus structure. To turn this core into an actual desktop (home or personal) computer, it must be packaged and provided with user-interface hardware and storage hardware. User-interface hardware includes (a) data-entry devices (keyboard, touch screen, joystick, mouse, digitizing pad, lightpen, speech recognition) and (b) data-display devices (video display, printer, plotter, speech synthesis), and (c) communication devices (modems). Storage hardware includes (a) disk drive (floppy disk, cartridge disk, fixed disk), (b) tape drive (cassette), (c) RAM disk, (d) bubble memory, and (e) ROM cartridge. For each type of device, the computer must provide interface circuitry. This circuitry takes a number of forms depending on the nature of the device(s) being interfaced. A floppy-disk drive, for example, requires a complex circuit built around a floppy-disk controller (FDC), a specialized microprocessor chip. The FDC circuit often resides on its own board. In contrast, a barebones interface for running a serial (RS-232) printer can be designed with a few basic electronic parts. The methods by which information is passed from one device to another is treated later: "Data-Transfer Methods and Interfaces."

Data-entry Devices. Seven data-entry devices are described below.

1. KEYBOARD. A keyboard is a set of switches, the closing of any one of which causes a unique code to be generated. All microcomputer manufacturers use some form of the American Standard Code for Information Interchange (ASCII). This code includes all of the numerals, the upper- and lowercase letters, the punctuation marks, and a group of control codes such as those for backspace (BS), linefeed (LF), carriage return (CR), and escape (ESC). In a 7-

bit configuration, ASCII allows for 128 codes; in an 8-bit configuration it allows for 256. In theory, a file-saved ASCII format can be "understood" by any computer.

The common standard in keyboard layout is the QWERTY section, that is, the letter keys, which are arranged to match those of an office typewriter. Function keys, control keys, editing keys, and even numeral keys follow various patterns, although among computers meant for use in office environments, some of these keys (e.g., the numerals) have been standardized for location. Many computers today allow for alternate key designations, which means that the QWERTY layout can be replaced via software with any layout one desires. The most popular of the alternates is the Dvorak or "rational" keyboard, designed for maximum typing efficiency.

Most office microcomputer keyboards include a keypad, invariably located on the right-hand of the keyboard, as a high-speed number-entry facility, as well as cursor-movement keys, often as part of the keypad arrangement.

Ergonomic (literally, "work measuring") studies suggest that a movable (detached) keyboard enhances keyboarding. A second advantage of the detached keyboard is ease of replacement in case the unit needs repair or in case a more desirable keyboard becomes available. Desirability here may refer to layout, selection of secondary keys (function keys and the like), and touch. Every keyboard has a distinctive touch, with a wide range of options: flat membrane, calculatorlike, typewriterlike (full travel); stiff, soft, spongy; mechanical or electronic tactility. Membrane keys are the least tactile, hence least appealing, to a touch typist, but have the advantage of being "user and environment proof." In harsh (damp and dusty) conditions, the membrane keyboard is perhaps the best choice. Tactility can be emulated by a mechanical "clicker" that provides a definite sense of key pressure (e.g., Texas Instruments Professional Computer) or by a "beeper" that sounds when each key is struck (e.g., the Zenith Z100 series). The latter feature can be turned off if desired.

Fig. 7-4

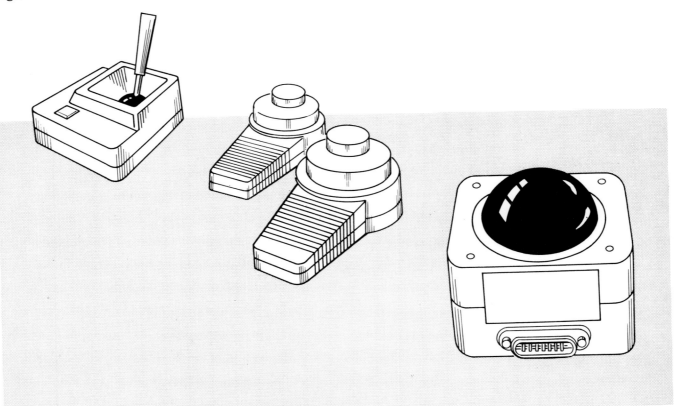

Detached keyboards are of three types: (a) the computer is housed in the keyboard enclosure (e.g., Commodore 64); (b) the keyboard is connected to the computer via a cable (e.g., Compaq): and (c) the keyboard is connected to the computer via an infrared transmitter/receiver (e.g., IBM PCjr). Each type is a given of the computer design and, with the exception of the infrared arrangement, cannot be changed. IBM provides a cable connection for the PCjr.

The purpose of the alternative data-entry methods is to simplify computer use. The joystick, for example, reduces the actions required of the user in manipulating a handle and pressing a "fire" button or trigger. The mouse causes a small arrow (or other simple icon) to move around on the screen for the purpose of selecting the actions the computer is to take. Indeed, these various keyboard substitutes are basically pointers, with the accompanying software taking over many, if not always all, of the inputs formerly demanded of the keyboarder.

2. JOYSTICK. Many computers include one or more "game ports" to which joysticks and similar devices (including game paddle and Trackball) can be attached. The various analog motions of the joystick, paddle, or Trackball (Fig. 7-4) are interpreted by the interface as digital values and accepted by the computer as data entries equivalent to those normally received from the keyboard. In some cases, the keyboard can be programmed to emulate the joystick. In other cases, the action causes an image to move on the screen to a menu of choices, which may be icons in addition to text.

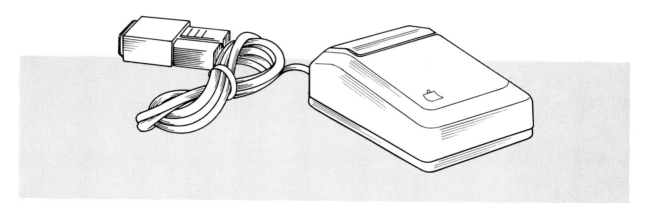

Fig. 7-5

3. MOUSE. The mouse (Fig. 7-5) can be thought of as a version of the Trackball. In this case, the rolling element (ball or otherwise) is hidden from the user and moved as a result of pushing the mouse shell over a surface. The purpose of the mouse is to allow the user to move a pointer on the screen to choices presented and to select or deselect a choice by pressing a button on the top surface of the mouse. Virtually all desktop professional computers can be fitted with a mouse port, and most integrated productivity software supports the mouse. Because the mouse requires a flat, empty surface as large as the computer display screen, computer users with crowded desks may not find the mouse convenient.

4. DIGITIZING PAD. Although all digitizing pads provide the computer with the same kind of information, namely, data representing the location of a pointing device, there are different routes to this result. Some pads are constructed with a touch-sensitive matrix beneath the working surface as in Fig. 7-6. Pressure on a particular point effectively "closes a switch," the result not unlike

Fig. 7-6

that of pressing a key on a keyboard. The switch-closing effect is commonly caused by a change in the electrical value at the pressure point. Another technique is the use of a movable arm, the X-Y location of which is signaled by values of variable resistors to which the arm is attached. A third approach is to move a mouselike pointer across the surface of the pad. The physical movement of this pointer is reproduced on the display screen. Selections (of graphic points, for example) are made by pressing a button on the pointer/mouse. Digitizing pads are usually interfaced through an existing communication port like that used for a printer. The digitizing pad offers the quickest and easiest means of using the computer as a drawing tablet.

5. LIGHTPEN. Although called a "pen," the lightpen doesn't really write—it reads. The lightpen is a sensing device, the location of which on the screen is interpreted by the computer (Fig. 7-7). Thus, when the user points at a block representing a choice, the computer determines the X-Y location of the block and performs according to the choice the pen has read. A considerable amount

Fig. 7-7

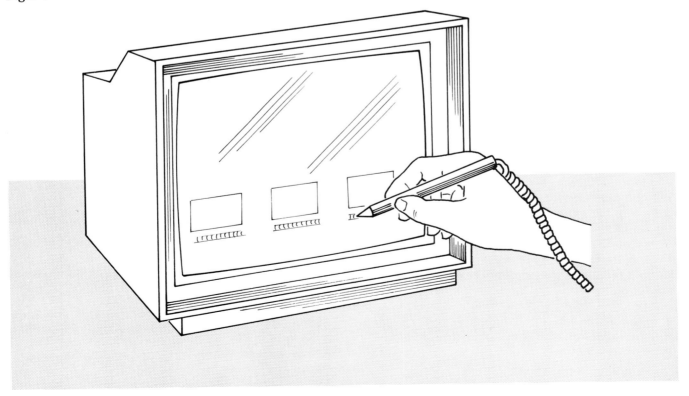

of software support is necessary for all but the simplest of lightpen activities. Where the pen seems to be actually drawing on the screen, it really isn't. The computer is putting dots of light on the screen in response to the position that the pen already determined. For most lightpen software, the color, size, and texture of the lines are the result of touching the pen to the desired choices. The need to constantly reach up to the screen makes the use of the lightpen an awkward and uncomfortable way to work for long periods.

6. TOUCH SCREEN. In this case, the user's finger acts effectively like a lightpen. Generally, however, the purpose of the touch-screen entry technique is merely to offer the user a menu of choices. Touching a selection block displayed on the screen results in the computer's performing the desired action. The screen is made touch sensitive by an electrically active overlay forming a matrix of pressure-responsive points or by an array of "electric eyes," actually light-emitting diodes (LEDs) and photodiodes, installed around the perimeter of the screen. The X-Y position of the finger pressure or light interruption is calculated by the computer. As in the case of the lightpen, using the touch screen more than occasionally is ergonomically questionable. In addition to the potential discomfort of constant screen touching, there is problem of faulty input because of the screen's misreading of the exact point of touch. If the touch areas displayed on the screen are large enough to allow for some degree of imprecision on the part of the user, then this problem will be minimized.

7. SPEECH RECOGNITION. Because speech is the characteristic mode of human communications, data entry via speech recognition systems constitutes

Fig. 7-8

the most "natural" of all the ways to communicate with a computer. The more advanced microcomputers have sufficient processing speed and memory to support fairly sophisticated VDE (voice data entry) technology. Generally, these microcomputer-based VDE systems must be trained by the operator to accept in the operator's voice a list of words and phrases representing the vocabulary of the particular software. In an electronic spreadsheet program, for example, the vocabulary would include the key command words of the program itself as well as the numbers and symbols commonly used in the creation of a spreadsheet. The vocabulary not provided for is entered in the usual way, that is, via the keyboard. In some VDE systems, the "window of acceptance" may be widened to allow input from a variety of speakers.

The electronics of speech recognition is complex in the very high-quality microcomputer-based systems often costing as much as the host computer. In essence, the speech-recognition circuitry must turn the multilayered, continually changing waveforms of speech into digital patterns that match stored patterns usable by the computer and meaningful to the software being run. As microcomputers approach mainframe capability, it is anticipated that VDE systems will be able to handle virtually all data entry, not merely a relatively small list of commands. Thus, with the VDE word processor of the not-too-distant future the operator will be able to dictate entire documents—no keyboarding required.

VDE system interfacing is through an expansion slot or a printer port. In the former case, the speech system is contained on an expansion circuit board. In the latter case, the system is packaged in its own enclosure. A microphone (or headset, in the case of a speech-recognition/speech-synthesis unit) and software complete the system (Fig. 7-8).

Data-Display Devices. These include video-display, printer, plotter, and speech-synthesis systems.

1. VIDEO DISPLAY. The video display—also called CRT (cathode-ray tube), VDT (video display tube), and monitor—is similar to a television set, though lacking a tuner section and offering marginally better to vastly better image quality. The monitors used in computers range from a diagonal measurement of 5 inches (Osborne I) upward. The single-user office computer monitor has been standardized to 12 inches. Larger screen sizes are appropriate for multiviewer stations such as those in airline terminals, but are not ergonomically sound for long-term viewing at the short distances common for a typical computer workstation. Nine-inch screens seem to be acceptable for extended viewing.

Black-and-white has been largely superseded by green, amber, or full-color. Ergonomic studies in Europe suggest that amber (also called European orange) is the easiest on the eyes. Full-color displays, however, are becoming increasingly common. A high-resolution color monitor is generally several times more expensive than an equivalent-quality monochrome monitor. Color displays can, of course, emulate monochrome displays, either through a keyboard command or with a hardware switch on the monitor itself. Lower-resolution color monitors use a composite video signal containing all of the color information. The monitor decodes the signal into the three basic video colors (red, green, and blue). Where a television set acts as the monitor, composite video is the type of signal produced by the computer, but in order for the TV set to use this signal, it must be made to emulate the signal normally received at the antenna—hence the need for a video modulator, which adds to the composite video signal an envelope of varying frequency representing the video information being "transmitted" by the computer. Higher-resolution video requires separate color signals and a monitor capable of accepting them.

In a general sense, resolution refers to the number of dots (pixels, i.e., picture elements) that the monitor is capable of displaying. The smaller the dot, the more can be displayed. The more dots, the finer the visual detail. Special CAD (computer-assisted design) monitors can reproduce images with clarity and sharpness approaching that of high-quality photographs. The IBM PC in monochrome configuration offers a screen resolution of 640 horizontal pixels by 200 vertical pixels, or 128,000 in total. In four-color configuration, this number drops to 64,000. Some CAD displays resolve a million pixels or more.

The number of horizontal lines a monitor can resolve is termed its vertical resolution; the number of vertical lines, its horizontal resolution. The perceived resolution is thus a grid of dots or pixels. In order to achieve sufficient resolution to display, let us say, 80 characters across the screen, both the transmitted and received video bandwidth must be sufficiently large to carry all of the necessary information. The more dots needed to make up a character, the more bandwidth is required to resolve those dots. The average color TV set may have an effective bandwidth of under 4 MHz. A high-quality RGB monitor may exceed 30 MHz. To calculate horizontal resolution (taken as the number of dots that can be clearly displayed across the screen), multiply the video bandwidth by two; then multiply this by the scan rate, a value in microseconds, with 40 microseconds a typical value.

Characters on a display screen can be produced as prepackaged blocks or memory-mapped (pixel-by-pixel) video data. In the former, each character is fetched from the character generator ROM (firmware on board the computer) and placed in video memory as a fully defined entity. None of the values within a given character block can be changed. Hence the character shapes are fixed. The only way to produce different characters is to replace the character generator ROM with one containing a different font. When characters are defined pixel by pixel, it means that each dot making up the character is accessible to the programmer, a fact allowing for software generation of characters and shapes of any kind within the resolving power of the display.

The most common display technology is built around the cathode-ray tube ("picture tube"). And while the technology is antiquated by high-tech standards, it offers reliability, good—even superb—image quality, and relatively low cost. Other technologies beginning to appear as real competition are liquid crystal (both monochrome and color), and plasma or electroluminescent. Both have the advantage of being compact, flat-panel displays, but the former has not yet been maximized for speed and resolution, and the latter has not yet been minimized for power consumption and cost.

In some computers, the keyboard and monitor are part of a single piece of hardware known as a terminal or console. The term console, however, is ambiguous, because it can also mean the the combination of keyboard and CRT, even when they are not packaged as a unit. Terminal can likewise mean any computer system endpoint for data entry or retrieval regardless of whether the device involved is an actual terminal or a full computer. At any rate, the classic terminal is basically a keyboard and display, possibly containing some degree of "intelligence," that is, editing, character-generation, and communication facilities. A "smart terminal" has its own microprocessor and memory, but cannot be considered a full computer because its computerized operations are limited to display and communications functions. To turn a terminal into a full computer, it is necessary to add a CPU, memory, and storage (e.g., one or more disk drives).

2. PRINTER. Printers are two general types: formed character and dot-matrix. The formed-character printer produces hardcopy indistinguishable from that produced by an office typewriter. The characters are created with typing elements of three common configurations: the ball element (e.g., Selectric), daisy wheel (e.g., Diablo), and thimble (e.g., Spinwriter). The character being printed is hammered against the ribbon in essentially the same fashion as it would be on a typewriter. The dot-matrix character is built up on the paper with a precisely coordinated series of dots. These dots may be formed with hammered wires, heated wires (thermal printers), ink droplets (ink-jet printers), or laser beams (laser printers). Some dot-matrix printers are capable of producing full-color images.

The fully formed character printer is desirable for formal correspondence and reports. Certain simple enhancements like boldface are possible and add to the "printshop" appearance of documents produced by these printers, for which a wide range of type styles (fonts) are available. The principal disadvantages are slow speed and limited graphics and printing enhancements.

The dot-matrix printer has evolved rapidly into a highly sophisticated printing machine, capable of emulating the typewriterlike appearance of the fully formed character printer and, because the dot-matrix printer page can be addressed dot by dot like a video display screen, this type of printer can reproduce any image that the screen can display. Software is available which can turn an inexpensive dot-matrix printer into a typesetter by allowing the user to generate virtually any style and size of type desired. In the lower-quality "draft mode," many dot-matrix printers will print at speeds in excess of 150 characters per second.

3. PLOTTER. Plotters, which are specialized printers and interfaced through printer ports, come in single-pen or multiple-pen versions, using either a flat-bed or a drum platen (Fig. 7-9). The principal application of the plotter is in printing graphics materials—architectural and CAD renderings, statistical charts, and the like. The high quality of the images results from the fact that they are produced as solid lines rather than as superimposed dots. High-speed plotters can even be used as printers.

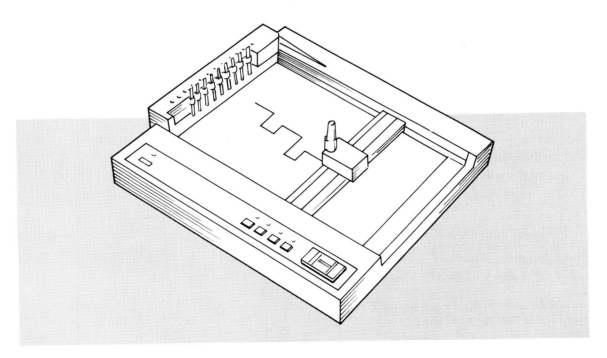

Fig. 7-9

4. SPEECH SYNTHESIS SYSTEMS. These systems do not demand the technological sophistication of voice-recognition systems. Indeed, speech synthesis of remarkably high quality can be added to even the least expensive of home computers at very low cost. In some cases, the "synthesizer" is nothing more than a piece of software that makes use of the computer's sound-generating circuitry. In other cases, the speech synthesizer is a piece of hardware (and associated software) interfaced through an I/O bus port. In most cases, synthesized speech cannot be confused with natural speech, though in the elaborate, business-oriented synthesizers, such as that included in Texas Instruments' Speech Command System, synthesized speech is virtually indistinguishable from tape-recorded speech.

Some synthesizers are designed to generate speech from individual speech sounds (phonemes). Such a system is the Votrax "Type 'N Talk," capable of saying words from letters entered via the keyboard. Because human speech can be analyzed into segmental phonemes (individual speech sounds like /b/, /p/, etc.) as well as intonational features (e.g., pitch and loudness levels), synthesizers provide some means for adding these features, thus avoiding, at least to some degree, the metallic monotone of earlier technology.

The TI Speech Command System synthesizes speech by digitally coding the operator's voice; hence, the natural sound of the "playback." The success of this method depends in large measure on the rate at which the voice being reproduced is sampled—the same issue facing the makers of digital recordings. The greater the number of voice (or music) samples, the greater the accuracy of the synthesized version. But the greater the sampling rate, the greater the complexity of design and the higher the cost. Fortunately, speech synthesis of so-called telephone-line quality can be accomplished at relatively low sampling rates, much lower than would be tolerated for music reproduction.

Data-Storage Devices. These include disk systems, tape systems, bubble memory, RAM disks, and ROM cartridges.

1. DISK SYSTEMS. Floppy-disk and hard-disk (Winchester) systems are currently the most popular means of storing software permanently (or semipermanently). Floppy disks and hard disks both use magnetic-recording technology that in principle is little different from that used in audio tapes. A recording/playback/erase head (called a read/write head in computer usage) causes changes in the magnetically sensitive coating of the disk. In a floppy-disk system, the head bears physically on the surface of the disk, just as it does on a recording tape. In hard-disk systems, the head "flies" just slightly above the disk. Hence, the floppy-disk read/write method eventually wears both the disk and the head. Theoretically, if a hard disk is kept free of contaminants, neither the head nor the platter will ever wear out.

Three sizes of floppy disks are now in common use: 8-inch, 5-1/4-inch, and 3-1/2-inch, with 5-1/4-inch disks by far the most numerous, despite the fact that the only disk-recording format that has become a virtual standard is the IBM 3740 format for 8-inch disks. The advent of the IBM PC and its dominance in the microcomputer marketplace seems to be resulting in its 5-1/4-inch format becoming a de facto standard. Despite the advantage of the 3-1/2-inch disk (size, ruggedness, and recording density), it has not yet captured an appreciable segment of the market. Furthermore, at least two other sizes in the 3-inch range are competing for the buyers' attention.

Floppy-disk drives are either single sided or double sided, which means that they have either a single read/write head or a pair of them. The recording density is a function of the floppy-disk controller (FDC) circuitry and the head design. A drive that is rated at 40 tracks (or 48 track per inch) cannot record as densely as a drive rated at 80 tracks (or 96 t.p.i.). The double-sided 40-track drive is the most widely used in the personal computer; with the appropriate FDC and software, this drive can record as much as 400 kilobytes of data per side. At the other extreme from double-sided, quadruple-density recording

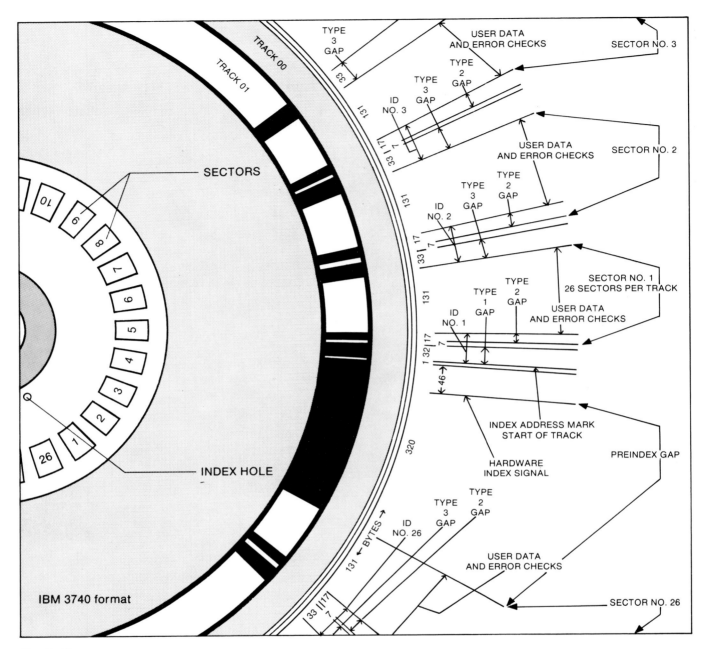

Fig. 7-10

stands single-sided, single-density, at about 100 kilobytes. Eight-inch disks have capacities from rather less than 300 kilobytes (single-sided, single-density) to about 2.5 megabytes (double-sided, quadruple-density). The greater the density, the greater the opportunity for read/write errors. This is another way of saying that alignment tolerances grow increasingly stringent as the density increases. The 80-track drives are the most sensitive to misalignment.

Before a disk can be used for the storage and retrieval of information (programs, data, word-processing files, etc.), it must be formatted, a procedure managed by the formatting program that comes with the disk-operating system (DOS). The purpose of this procedure is to turn a totally blank disk into one that has been digitally compartmentalized and provided with the digital guideposts that allow the DOS to read from and write to the disk in an orderly fashion. The tracks are defined and segmented into sectors which, in turn, are segmented into pointers ("headers" and "footers") and open areas for program material. The formatter also writes a directory onto the disk, and, optionally, an image of the operating system, which will allow the disk to be used for "booting." A formatted disk can be thought of as a newly constructed apartment house awaiting its tenants. The directory lists the tenants and provides push-buttons for contacting them. If the directory has been damaged, there is no way for the DOS to find a given tenant. Since the formatting information (Fig. 7-10) uses part of the disk's storage capacity, the capacity available for storage will be less than the raw capacity of the disk—hence the designations "unformatted capacity" and "formatted capacity."

The disk itself is made of a substrate of Mylar plastic that has been coated with magnetically sensitive material (primarily a highly refined form of iron oxide). The disk is then permanently sealed inside of an envelope, the inner surface of which is coated with a silky, fibrous material designed to help maintain the high polish of the disk and to catch bits of dust and oxide that flake off. Read/write slots in the disk allow contact with the read/write head. The envelope is notched for write protection: in a 5-1/4-inch disk the notch is covered for write protection; in an 8-inch disk it is covered to allow writing. The small hole in the permanent envelope is to allow sensing of the index hole by the disk drive (Fig. 7-11). This hole provides the "home-base" reference for the operating system, which needs an invariable starting point in order to function correctly.

Because Mylar is sensitive to changes in temperature and humidity, and because the recording surfaces of floppy disks are easily damaged by contaminants—dust, smoke, fingerprints, and the like—floppy disks require careful storage and handling. Furthermore, the fact that they are subject to physical wear as a result of the recording technology (i.e., direct head-to-disk contact) means that backup copies of all valuable material should be made regularly, and old disks should be discarded. The "shelf-life" of a disk in storage is said to be about 5 years. The reliable working life of a disk may be no more than a year.

A floppy-disk drive, of whatever size, is an electromechanical device consisting of a drive motor, a stepper motor (for moving the read/write head), one or two read/write heads, a solenoid for bringing the head mechanism into contact with the disk, sensors for reading the index hole and the read/write status of the disk, a chassis containing all the hardware necessary for head and disk movement and disk placement, and one or two circuit boards to manage the various activities of the drive. One of these activities is control of the disk spin rate, which is 300 rpm for 5-1/4-inch drives and 360 rpm for 8-inch drives.

Among the disk-drive parameters controlled by the disk-drive logic board(s) are (a) spin rate or rotational speed, (b) step-rate or access time, (c) transfer rate, (d) latency, and (e) head-load time. The spin rate of 5-1/4-inch drives is 300 rpm; of 8-inch drives, 360 rpm. Step rate is a measure of the time it takes to move from track to track. Many drives are rated at 6 milliseconds. Some DOS-configuration routines allow the user to set the step rate to the speed that best suits the operational characteristics of the particular drives. Transfer rate refers to the speed with which data is transferred to and from the disk, a measurement given in kilobytes per second (Kb/s), with 125 to 250 Kb/s a typical range for 5-1/4-inch drives. The time it takes for a particular segment of data to appear under the head once the head has reached the appropriate track is called latency (or rotational latency). It is measured in milliseconds. Head-load time measures the time required to pull the head down to the surface of the disk in preparation for reading or writing.

Although 8-inch and 3-1/2-inch hard disks exist, the 5-1/2-inch size predominates. Initially, the 5-megabyte capacity enjoyed some popularity, but now 10-megabyte systems are the most common. Generally, a hard disk unit contains two or more platters, each served by its own read/write head. These

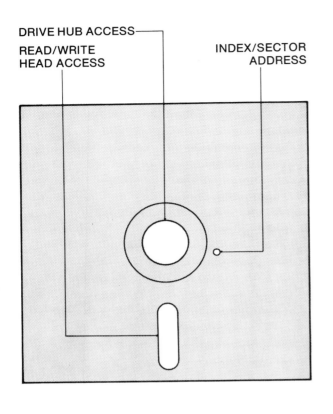

DRIVE HUB ACCESS

READ/WRITE
HEAD ACCESS

INDEX/SECTOR
ADDRESS

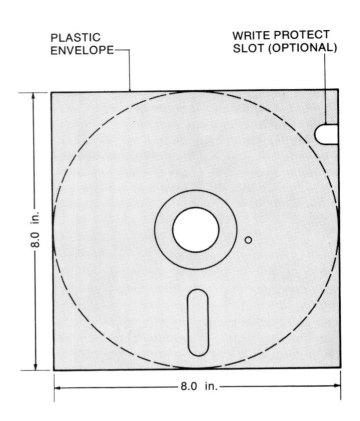

PLASTIC
ENVELOPE

WRITE PROTECT
SLOT (OPTIONAL)

8.0 in.

8.0 in.

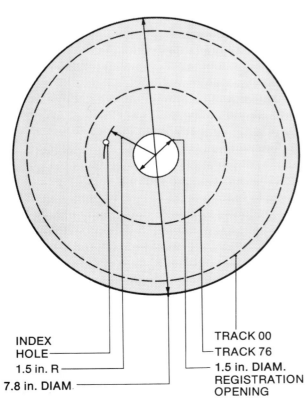

INDEX
HOLE

1.5 in. R

7.8 in. DIAM.

TRACK 00

TRACK 76

1.5 in. DIAM.
REGISTRATION
OPENING

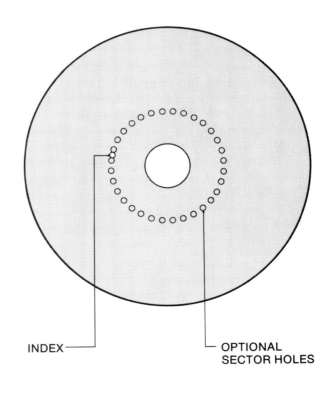

INDEX

OPTIONAL
SECTOR HOLES

Fig. 7-11

platters are made of metal (or glass), the surfaces of which are machined (or formed) to extraordinarily fine tolerances and plated with a recording medium similar to that used for floppies and tape. The heads are provided with small "wings" to enable them to fly at a precise distance from the surface of a platter in the specially filtered air of the enclosed Winchester environment. Because hard disks spin ten times as fast as floppies, access time, latency, and transfer rate values are considerably enhanced, with performance increasing in some cases by eight to ten times, or better.

The inaccessibility of the recording surfaces of hard disks means that they are safe from external contaminants. The heads, however, are free floating and easily bounced on the disks. Where they bounce, they cause damage. To avoid this, the user either must avoid moving a hard disk once it has been set up for use, or run must a small program (called "Ship" in some versions of MS-DOS) that moves the heads to a safe region where, if they do bounce, no data will be lost. Despite this precaution, hard-disk drives should be handled with great care.

The fact that hard disks cannot be removed in the manner of floppies has led to the development of the cartridge disk (Fig. 7-12), a removable hard disk offering the advantages of both the fixed disk (speed, high storage density) and the floppy (interchangeability). Although the cartridge disk is sealed in a hard plastic case it is more likely to be damaged by contaminants than the fixed disk. Among the disk types, the hard-disk cartridge may be the ideal storage medium.

Fig. 7-12

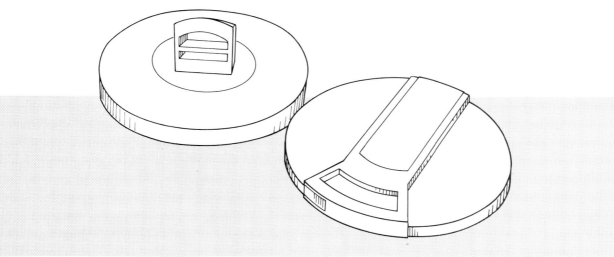

2. TAPE SYSTEMS. The ordinary audio-cassette recorder is the most familiar of the computer tape systems. In the early days of the home-microcomputer boom, the cassette recorder was the predominant storage device. Its major advantage is low cost, but "glacially" slow data transfer rate and unreliability make it the least desirable of all storage systems. However, if a computer has both disk-drive and cassette interfaces, the cassette is useful for making archival copies of data and text files.

Tape is not inherently unreliable, of course, as demonstrated by the various streaming-tape backup systems widely used today in business environments. Most of these units use special tape cartridges that are larger than the standard audio cassette and built to more rigid specifications. Commonly used to back up hard disks, they operate at high speed and store data in megabyte quantities. A popular way to package a backup-tape unit is as part of a hard-disk subsystem, as shown (Fig. 7-13).

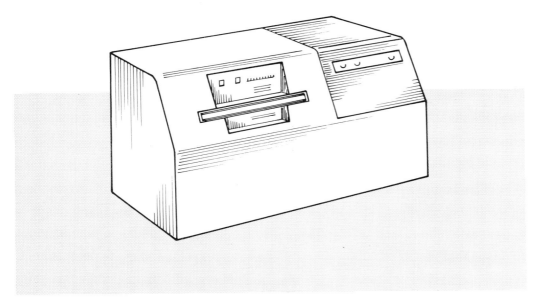

Fig. 7-13

Several companies have developed "wafertape" units, essentially small-scale streaming-tape systems. The "Stringy Floppy," for example, stood midway between cassette recorder and disk drive in both cost and capability. Lack of standardization as well as the rapid decline in the cost of disk drives combined to quickly render these home-computer types of tape systems pointless.

3. BUBBLE MEMORY. Ideally, storage should be as purely electronic as the computer itself—not electromechanical like a disk or tape drive. Mechanical parts are prone to early and frequent failure as a result of heat, friction, and other kinds of physical stress; tape and disks are prone to mechanical as well as magnetic damage. Furthermore, the fact that there are motors and heads causes operational rates to be relatively slow, even with state-of-the-art hard disks. Bubble memory offers at least an interim answer, for in this technology there are no moving parts. Operational speed does not reach that of RAM, but is nevertheless much faster than in the electromechanical media. An average access time for a high-quality hard drive is in the neighborhood of 40 milliseconds; for bubble memory this drops to 4 milliseconds.

Bubble memory operates by generating (writing) small magnetic domains called "bubbles" in a thin magnetic medium that has been deposited on a substrate, usually a type of synthetic garnet. These bubbles represent data bits, which then are detected (read) or destroyed (erased) as required.

Since bubble technology is purely electronic, bubble devices can be mounted on circuit boards for insertion into expansion slots. This method emulates a hard disk, that is, the "disk" becomes a permanent part of the computer system. Another approach, one that emulates removable media, is the bubble cartridge, which looks like a large ROM pack and is as easily transportable as a disk cartridge. The bubble-cartridge receptacle contains electronics analogous to those needed to control a disk drive. To the DOS, a bubble device appears simply as one or more disk drives.

4. RAM DISKS. A RAM disk is nothing more than a block of RAM treated by the operating system as though it were a disk drive, but offering the high-speed operation of RAM. RAM disks cannot be considered storage unless they are provided with a means of holding data after the computer has been turned off. This is not what happens in the case of software designed to temporarily assign a section of memory to function as a RAM disk. There are, however, battery-powered RAM-disk boards available that will maintain data at least semi-permanently. At least one company claims a 14-year RAM-disk storage life.

5. ROM CARTRIDGES. Anyone who has played games on a home computer is acquainted with the ROM cartridge, a storage device for read-only operations. The cartridge offer permanent storage exactly in the manner of the ROMs in the computer itself. The program material is immediately and rapidly accessible, but the user cannot change it or use the cartridge for storing new material. Interfacing a ROM cartridge involves no more than plugging the cartridge into a slot provided. Typically, this slot communicates directly with the CPU.

Data Communication Devices. Data communication here refers to the transfer of data between the computer and the outside world, involving conversion of signals from digital to analog, analog to digital, or both.

Digital signals are defined as voltages representing binary digits (0 and 1) regardless of what information the streams of 0's and 1's actually stand for. Analog signals are defined as voltage values varying analogously with the changing conditions being rendered electrically, such as temperatures, sound levels, and moisture levels. Since a computer is a digital device, it cannot deal directly with analog signals. And since the telephone is an analog device, it cannot deal directly with digital signals. In both instances, conversions are required. These conversions are made through integrated circuits called ADCs (analog-to-digital converters) and DACs (digital-to-analog converters). Thus a fluctuation in voltage arising from the action of a temperature sensor will be periodically sampled by the ADC, each sample being assigned binary values. The stream of binary values can then be used by the computer (and its software) to do whatever is desired, such as sending messages, turning on the fire alarm, or whatever.

1. TELECOMMUNICATIONS SYSTEMS. The two major categories of data communication devices are telecommunication systems and sensing systems. For one computer to communicate with another device (computer, terminal, printer, etc.) over a telephone line requires a modem (modulator/demodulator) at each terminal. The modem may be housed inside the computer on its own circuit board or it may be housed in a separate enclosure. An inboard modem will be able to access the telephone line directly (direct-dial), whereas the discrete modem may be of the direct-dial type or the acoustic-coupler type. A direct-dial modem can be told—via the communication software needed to run any modem—to dial the telephone number of the answering computer, and it will do so without benefit of an actual telephone. The user of an acoustically coupled modem must physically dial the telephone and when the answering computer responds (with a special tone or carrier), the handset of the telephone must be placed in the acoustic-coupler receptacle (a pair of foam or rubber cups) mounted on top of the modem enclosure. From this point on, the operation of the two types of modems is the same.

Because the modem is a serial or sequential-bit communication device, it requires a serial port for operation. The expansion board type of modem includes a telephone line port as part of the circuitry. The external modem needs to be connected to a serial port. If the computer doesn't provide one, it must be added before the modem can be used.

Although very high rates of data transfer are possible, these require special ("dedicated") data lines and special equipment like repeaters or optical modems (see below). Microcomputers generally communicate over ordinary telephone lines at either 300 bits per second (i.e., 300 baud) or 1200 bps. The least expensive modems can operate only at 300 bps. The more costly ones offer both rates. The higher the rate of data transfer, obviously, the less time any transfer will take. Since connect time must be paid for, the greater initial cost of the 1200-baud modem will soon be negated by savings in connect time, assuming a reasonable amount of use. The 2400-band modem has recently appeared in the marketplace, and those using even higher speeds are on the way.

The data to be communicated starts out in digital form inside the computer. The communication software sees to it that the data gets sent to the correct output port, whence it goes to the modem. The modem converts the digital information into analog information in the form of standardized tones, representing the binary digits (1 and 0). The tones are then sent over the telephone line in a bitwise sequence (one tone following the other, that is, tonal 1's and 0's in a single stream). The modem at the receiving end converts the tones back into digital pulses and ships them to the correct input port. From there they enter the computer system and are acted on as appropriate. Perhaps the incoming material will be sent out to a printer, or it will appear on the display screen, or be saved on disk—or all three.

For communication to take place, one of the two modems in a communicating pair must be set up as the originate unit and one as the answer unit. Normally, the originate unit initiates the contact, though it can be done the other way around. The answer unit replies to the call with a special tone called a carrier, which the originate unit is programmed to detect. When this signal is detected, the originate modem is said to be on line and ready for "conversation." From this point, data can move in either direction, even though the answer and originate status of each modem remains unchanged. In fact, if either one were switched to the other mode, communication would cease.

A line-carrier modem (LCM) allows computer-peripheral connections to be made at remote locations within the office electrical wiring system. The communicating device (computer or peripheral) is connected via a standard serial connector to the LCM, which is simply plugged into an electrical outlet. This method of data transfer allows for a high baud rate (typically 9600 baud) at distances up to about 800 feet.

The optical modem uses optical-fiber technology to permit transmission rates as high as 100,000 bps over distances of a mile or greater, using standard RS-232-C interfacing, but requiring optical-fiber cabling. In addition to high-speed data-transfer rates, optical transmission systems are tap-proof and offer immunity from electrical interference.

Where two computers (or other devices) are in close proximity, data can be exchanged between the two via a direct hookup using a simple device called a null modem, which is essentially a specially wired cable. No data conversion is required because the transfer is directly between two digital devices. But some type of communication software is needed—normally the same as used for remote modem operation.

Where it is necessary in null-modem operation to run relatively long transmission lines, a signal amplifier or repeater can be used. The transmission-cable connectors plug into the repeater, which is powered from an electrical outlet.

2. SENSORY SYSTEMS. A great variety of "real-world" sensory apparatus has been developed for use with microcomputers, allowing for digital response to nearly any kind of activity from manufacturing processes to fire detection. In principle, a sensor kind generates varying voltages relative to the nature of its sensitivity (temperature, strain, humidity, light, sound, etc.). These voltages are detected by an analog-to-digital conversion device and sent as digital signal to the computer. The software controlling the particular sensing system then interprets the signals, and the computer is made to respond in an appropriate way. All of the sensory systems listed are currently available for most microcomputers:

- Ambient condition sensing (temperature and moisture)
- Light-level detection (brightness, opacity, turbidity)
- Vision systems (for digital "photographing")
- Sound-level detection (amplitude and frequency)
- Ranging systems (sonar detection and distance measurement)
- Strain measurement (torsion, compression, flection, ductility)
- Electrical measurement (voltage, current, power, resistance)
- Density and thickness measurement
- Flow measurement
- Measurements of every imaginable kind, taken through a wide variety of laboratory instruments

In brief, the microcomputer can be interfaced with any kind of sensory apparatus and, as desired, can be used to generate statistical profiles, cause changes in the operation of various pieces of equipment (including environmental systems), dial the telephone and transmit information, and so on. When a computer operates in this way, it might properly be called a robot. Conversely, a robot can be thought of as a computer specialized for one or more functions formerly carried out by other means that usually required human intervention.

Data-Transfer Methods and Interfaces

A computer can be thought of as a bit-stream transportation system, wherein groupings of binary digits are moved from place to place, undergoing the various changes necessary for a particular application, until they exit the system as displayed or printed information and/or as actions performed. In order for bits to move, they must have pathways. Within the computer, even within the microprocessor itself, there is a multipartite bus structure for the purpose. Between the computer and its peripherals are extensions of parts of this structure that are mediated by interfaces of several kinds.

Broadly speaking, data can be moved serially (sequentially) or in parallel, that is, bitwise or bytewise. Bitwise transfer proceeds one bit at a time—"all in a row"—on a single wire. Bytewise transfer is the simultaneous movement of 8 bits on eight wires. In fact, even wider parallel buses exist (for example, in the Motorola 68000), but for the purpose of this discussion, the byte-wide structure will serve to illustrate the principle. Furthermore, the focus in this section is on inter- not intracommunication, that is, on communication between the computer and its peripherals, not on the internal systems, which have already been examined in Section 4: Microprocessors.

Unfortunately, the microcomputer industry has few standards and, with rare exceptions, the ones it uses are "interpreted" by each manufacturer, thus vitiating the standards. Nevertheless, the Electronic Industries Association (EIA) RS-232-C serial standard, the Institute of Electrical and Electronics Engineers (IEEE) 488 parallel standard, and the Centronics parallel format (a de facto, not "official" standard) represent such data-transfer standards as exist and provide the basis of this outline.

Parallel Data Transfer. Within the microprocessor and the basic computer circuitry, data moves in parallel, 8 (or more) bits at a time, the byte-wide bus thus serving as the fundamental structure for data transfer. No formal standard exists for this internal parallelism. In a manner of speaking, it is a self-defining system. Eight data lines are eight data lines. And while the control signals have different names from microprocessor to microprocessor, they all behave in similar ways. In any case, this part of the data-transfer process is an inherent part of the computer and not directly under the control of the user.

On the other hand, when it comes to connecting a piece of equipment to the computer, the user must see to it that the computer and peripheral can communicate according to expectations. There is, for example, no direct way to connect an IEEE-488-configured printer to an RS-232-C serial port or even to a Centronics parallel port. The printer in question can be interfaced, but only through a special, user-supplied interface.

1. IEEE-488. Also known as the GPIB (General Purpose Interface Bus) and HPIB (Hewlett-Packard Interface Bus), this is actually a complete bus structure, not just an interface standard. It was developed by Hewlett-Packard for use as an instrumentation-interface system and is still principally used for this purpose. Among the general-purpose computer manufacturers, only Hewlett-Packard and Commodore used the IEEE-488 bus, and Commodore's implementation (in the PET and CBM series of computers) was shy of the standard by one line.

Fig. 7-14

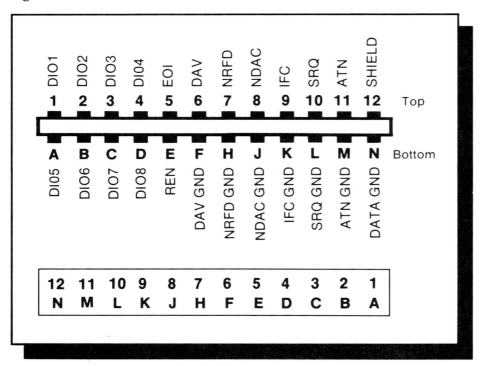

The usual IEEE-488 system (Fig. 7-14) comprises a host computer and a daisy chain of devices, each with some degree of "intelligence" and not entirely dependent on the host. Thus with a single I/O port, a computer can host a full complement of peripherals: disk drives, printer, plotter, and laboratory instruments. Devices can be set up to "talk," "listen," talk and listen, and/or control the bus. Normally, an instrument, say, a voltmeter, will be a talker; a printer a listener; and the computer a talker, a listener, and a bus controller at one time or another. To keep things organized, each device has it own "address" or device number for each of its capabilities and will respond accordingly when thus addressed. All the devices can be addressed more or less simultaneously, the operations being handled by an interface manager in the GPIB.

The bus itself consists of eight bidirectional data lines (DIO, data input/output), five bus-management lines, and three handshaking lines. The cable-end connectors are "stackable," that is, they have both a male and a female face, allowing for either an in-line (daisy chain) configuration or a start configuration, wherein all the peripheral connectors are stacked on the host connector.

PIN	RETURN-PIN	SIGNAL	SOURCE
1	19	Strobe	computer
2	29	Data 1	computer
3	21	Data 2	computer
4	22	Data 3	computer
5	23	Data 4	computer
6	24	Data 5	computer
7	25	Data 6	computer
8	26	Data 7	computer
9	27	Data 8	computer
10	28	ACK	printer
11	29	Busy	printer
12	30	Paper Out	printer
13		Slct	printer
14		Auto Feed	computer
15		NC	
16		Signal Gnd	
17		Chassis Gnd	
18		NC	
31		Init	computer
32		Error	printer
33		Gnd	
34		NC	
35		+5 Volts	printer
36		Slct In	computer

Fig. 7-15

2. CENTRONICS. The Centronics parallel configuration was developed by the Centronics Data Computer Corporation, a printer manufacturer. Because of its early appearance in the marketplace and its usefulness, it soon became a de facto interfacing standard. The Centronics interface pinout is shown in Fig. 7-15. Almost without exception, a parallel interface in a microcomputer printer will be a Centronics interface.

Some minor variations of this interface will be found, but despite the fact that no official agency has specified the Centronics standard, it requires no more of the user than "plug and go." Parallel computer ports talk to Centronics-interface printers without hesitation.

This interface uses three handshaking lines: DATA STROBE, ACKnowledge, and BUSY. Controlled by the computer, the data-strobe signal tells the printer that valid data is flowing on the data lines and should be accepted by the printer. With the ACK signal, the printer tells the computer that it is aware of and able to accept incoming data, and with the busy signal that the computer must halt transmission until the printer buffer has room to accept more data. The buffer is a block of RAM in the printer which acts as a temporary storage area for data. The larger the buffer, the more data the printer can accept before activating the busy signal. The printer requires a buffer because the print mechanism can operate at only a fraction of the speed of parallel data transmission, and if there were no way to temporarily store incoming data, the printer would either lock up or simply lose part of each transmission. External printer buffers allow for transitory storage of as much data as the computer's memory can handle.

Eight data and eight return lines constitute the actual communication segment of the Centronics system. Because data is transmitted a byte rather than a bit at a time, there is no need for either start and stop bits or baud-rate settings. Each byte is defined automatically by virtue of its packetlike transfer. Transfer rate is governed by the handshaking arrangement and data validity is assured by the strobe signal. Presently, this system represents the fastest and most efficient way to move data from computer to peripheral. A disadvantage to parallel data transfer is the fact that parallel cables longer than about 10 feet tend to be sufficiently sensitive to electrical noise or interference that data can be corrupted. Where really long cabling lines are required, some form of serial interfacing is generally used.

Serial Data Transfer. This discussion covers RS-232-C interfacing and telephony.

1. RS-232-C SERIAL. Printers and various other peripherals can be designed for either parallel or serial interfacing, but modems are strictly serial devices. Although practical serial interfacing can be achieved with only two lines, the EIA RS-232 (presently RS-232-C) standard is complex.

Fundamental to the understanding the RS-232-C standard is the distinction between data terminal equipment (DTE) and data communication equipment (DCE). The communication source and the communication destination—typically, computer or terminal A and computer or terminal B—are considered data terminal equipment. The devices required to facilitate the communication process—modem A and modem B—constitute the data communication equipment. Thus, certain RS-232 signals have their source in a DTE and certain ones in a DCE, a circumstance which makes literal compatibility between two of the same types of equipment impossible.

A typical RS-232-C cable uses a male DB-25 connector at one end and a female DB-25 connector at the other, thus the key lines in an RS-232-C circuit are TX (transmitted data), RX (received data), and GND (signal or common ground—the signal return line) as in Fig. 7-16. Since TX moves from a DTE to a DCE and RX moves from a DCE to a DTE, it is clear that attempting to directly mate two DTEs or two DCEs will result in data going nowhere. But a computer and a printer are both by convention DTE devices. How can they be interfaced? Two methods are used. In one, the printer port of the computer is configured as a DCE. In the other, a special cable is made in which the TX and RX lines are crossed, so that TX communicates with RX and vice versa. This crossover configuration is called a null modem, that is, a modem eliminator, which works perfectly well between two pieces of digital equipment. Of course, if the aim is data communications from computer to computer over a telephone line, then a null modem will not work because digital-to-analog and analog-to-digital signal covnersion is necessary for telecommunications.

The RS-232 control and timing signals are likewise defined as originating at either the DTE or DCE device and will not operate "head on." Thus, a common handshaking configuration crosses data set ready (DSR, line 6) with data terminal ready (DTR, line 20) to make a "matched set" between two DTE devices. From DTE to DCE, of course, straight cabling (no crossovers) is all that is needed. However, without a breakout box or other special equipment, this can be a particularly difficult task.

PIN	NAME	TYPE	FROM-TO
1	Chassis GND	Ground	
2	XMIT Data (TD)	Data	DTE-DCE
3	Receive Data (RD)	Data	DCE-DTE
4	Request to Send (RTS)	Control	DTE-DCE
5	Clear to Send (CTS)	Control	DCE-DTE
6	Data Set Ready (DSR)	Control	DCE-DTE
7	Signal Return	Ground	
8	Data Carrier Detect (DCD)	Control	DCE-DTE
9	Open (custom application)		
10	Open (custom application)		
11	Open (custom application)		
12	Secondary DCD	Control	DCE-DTE
13	Secondary CTS	Control	DCE-DTE
14	Secondary TD	Data	DTE-DCE
15	Transmitter Clock	Timing	DCE-DTE
16	Secondary RD	Data	DCE-DTE
17	Receiver Clock	Timing	DCE-DTE
18	Open (custom application)		
19	Secondary RTS	Control	DTE-DCE
20	Data Terminal Ready (DTR)	Control	DTE-DCE
21	Signal Quality Detector	Control	DCE-DTE
22	Ring Indicator	Control	DCE-DTE
23	Data Signal Rate Select	Control	DTE-DCE
24	Ext. Transmitter Clock	Timing	DTE-DCE
25	Open (custom application)		

Fig. 7-16

Several RS-232-C signals are explicitly concerned with modems, though not all of these are necessarily used by any particular modem. The more special features that a modem offers, the more of these special DCE lines are required. A device on either end of the RS-232 may be looking for an handshake signal.

The secondary lines allow for a second channel of communication operating on a common cable. Some manufacturers, however, use one or more of these secondary lines as the primary lines for their particular RS-232 implementation. The availability of so many possible data, control, and timing lines in a single interface standard allows for great variability in actual interface design. This is unfortunate for the user who wants simply to plug printer into computer and get predictable results. The claim of RS-232 compatibility may mean very little in practical terms, for while the various signals meet the requirements of the standard, the "compatible" device may not operate until the user or technician has spent a considerable amount of time trying to establish a reliable communicating relationship between computer and peripheral, the main difficulties almost always arising from the handshaking signals.

To expedite matters, the technician uses a breakout box, a device that allows the signals to be routed at will until the right combination has been found. Status lights apprise the user of the operation of each line in question. When a working pattern has been found, a permanent cable will be made that duplicates the pattern determined with the breakout box. In most cases, the system will be found to work with as few as four or five lines: TX, RX, two handshaking lines, and signal ground. If communication will be taking place at no higher than 300 baud, then the handshaking lines probably won't be needed. But with many printers (of the dot-matrix type) able to operate at 9600 baud, it would be pointless to run them at anything lower. The old Teletype printers operated at 110 baud and required nothing but a data line and a return line. That type of communication is irrelevant in the world of the modern microcomputer and high-speed printer.

Inherent in the EIA RS-232-C standard are certain electrical characteristics—generally adhered to by manufacturers, but not always. Thus, if both the computer manufacturer and the printer manufacturer have followed the electrical standard, the interface will function correctly as soon as the correct cable configuration has been established. But some of the home computers claim to offer an "RS-232" port, which is, in fact, a serial port containing a few lines labeled with RS-232 designations but lacking the voltage values (swings between 5 and 15 volts) to be directly comparable with a true RS-232-C device. These computers require a special interface circuit between the so-called RS-232 port and the genuine RS-232 peripheral.

In fact, the UART (universal asynchronous receiver transmitter), USART (universal synchronous/asynchronous receiver transmitter), or ACIA (asynchronous communications interface adapter) are the common interface ICs used in RS-232-C port design. Being programmable, these chips resemble microprocessors. Note, however, there are eight parallel data lines from the computer circuitry (D0-D7), and two serial data lines out to the port (TX, RX). Parallel data from the computer is thus converted to serial data out (TX), and serial data in (RX) is converted to parallel data to the computer.

The terms asynchronous and synchronous refer to methods whereby the data stream is organized to ensure that data transfer proceeds in an orderly way. Most micrcomputers use an asynchronous pattern, in which the data bytes are framed (see below). Asynchronous here means "nontimed," that is, data moves at the convenience of the system, timing of concern only with respect to the transfer rate of any given burst of data. Synchronous data transfer, on the other hand, requires that data move on a preset schedule, the data bytes being identified by synchronization of timing pulses between the sender and the receiver.

In order to assure the quality (integrity) of asynchronous data transfer in a serial system, certain protocols are required. These protocols, furthermore, must be matched at both the transmitting end and the receiving end, and consist of (a) baud rate, (b) start and stop bits (framing bits), and (c) word length. Word length is not a parameter peculiar to serial transmission. In fact, it is ultimately a hardware-settable feature associated primarily with printers. Thus a printer can be set, usually by a switch selection, to accept characters of a given word length. But the computer software must be set to match. Parity, another communications parameter not limited to but widely used in serial interfacing, will be explained below.

Baud rate: This is the rate at which bits are transmitted, measured in bits per second. Most interface ICs (UART, etc.) allow for a range of baud rates from 75 to 19,200. A typical modem operates at a baud rate of 300 or 1200. Most dot-matrix printers and computer terminals can run at 9600 baud. The baud rate is usually set from the software's configuration routines to allow the user to communicate directly with a printer.

Framing bits: In order for the various parts of the communicating system to know where each valid segment of data (say, a byte) begins and ends, there must be a means of signaling the system to this effect. Serial communication, therefore, provides for marker or framing bits (one or more start bits and one or more stop bits) that act as boundary lines between the pieces of valid data. A bit stream will thus consist of data bytes, each framed by these markers (Fig. 7-17).

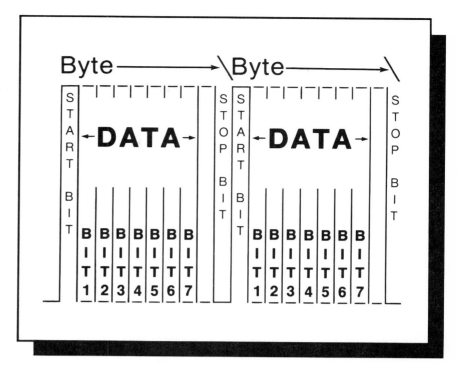

Fig. 7-17

Word length: A standard ASCII character consists of seven data bits. This "package" is termed a data word. In the typical microcomputer system, 7-bit or 8-bit data words are used. For straight text (the full ASCII character and control set), the 7-bit word is adequate, but for special extensions (primarily graphics) 8-bit words are required. Software making use of the dot-addressable graphics capabilities of dot-matrix printers inevitably demands the full 8 bits. Word length is not a feature peculiar to serial data transmission.

Parity: A parity bit is an optional test bit that used to assure that each data byte has reached its destination intact. As an example, assume that the system is transmitting 7-bit ASCII characters, some of which contain an odd number of 1's (high bits) and some of which contain an even number. If odd parity has been decided on, a 1 will be added to each character containing an even number of 1's. At the receiving end, each character will be tested for odd parity, that is, for an odd number of 1's. If a character comes through with an even number, a transmission error is presumed to have taken place. The two other parity options are even parity and no parity ("don't care"). In the case of no parity, of course, no actual test is made. But if a spurious bit appears, the transmission will be garbled.

2. TELEPHONY. This is the classic common-carrier two-wire communications link exemplified by the ordinary telephone line. Presently, microcomputers communicate over telephone lines with modems operating at either 300 baud (Bell 103J compatible) or 1200 baud (Bell 212A compatible). Higher baud rates are possible, though with an ordinary telephone line unacceptably high rates of data loss can be expected. High-speed telecommunication requires a special data line (dedicated line)—expensive to install and to lease—as well as expensive operating equipment.

Basic to telephone-line communication is "plexing," in the form of simplex, half-duplex, and duplex protocols.

Simplex (SX): In simplex data transfer, one side sends a stream of data on the data wire while the other side receives. Since there is a one-way track, movement can occur only in one direction. Every communication will travel in the same direction. A news-service receive-only teletype operates in this fashion.

Half-duplex (HDX): In this case, the same transmission wire can be used for two-way traffic, though only one data stream can travel at a given moment. While A talks, B listens; while B talks, A listens.

Full-duplex (FDX): In order for simultaneous two-way data transfer, either a second two-wire telephone line or some type of data-multiplexing ('timesharing") is required. In an FDX computer link, everything entered at computer A/ modem A will be sent to modem B/computer B, and that same data will be returned to modem A/computer A to appear on computer A's display screen.

Nonstandard serial interfacing must also be mentioned. The serial ports in home computers like the Commodore Vic-20 and Commodore 64 are representative of nonstandard serial interfaces. As was pointed out above, the fundamental discrepancy between RS-232 serial and "proprietary" serial interfacing lies in the voltage values. Furthermore, it has become conventional in RS-232-C interfacing to use DB-25 connectors. The proprietary interfaces generally use DIN (Deutsche Industrie Normenausschus, German Industry Standard) connectors.

Hybrid (Serial/Parallel) Data Transfer. With the few exceptions, microcomputer disk-drive interfaces use a combination of serial and parallel communication, in which the read/write lines operate serially but the various control lines operate in parallel. The predominance of microcomputer manufacturers follow the 5-1/4-inch disk-drive interface pattern (the "Shugart standard"). A similar "standard" exists for 8-inch and Winchester (hard-disk) drives.

The reason for this hybridization stems from the fact that with present technology, data must be streamed to the disk sectors a bit at a time and, of course, retrieved the same way. The problems that would arise from byte-wide sectoring would be difficult to overcome and not worth the manufacturing or maintenance costs. On the other hand, disk-control signals can be easily managed on a parallel basis. The extremely slow transfer rate imposed by straight serial interfacing of disk drives provides the primary reason for the general acceptance of a serial/parallel technique.

NETWORKS. A network is a way of allowing two or more computers (or terminals) to share one or more common resources like a central processor, a large-capacity disk system, a printer, whatever other peripherals are needed. A fully developed network is both multiuser and multitasking, that is, several operators can perform several different tasks simultaneously. But there are networks which will support only a single operator, but several different tasks can be carried on simultaneously. The concurrency of these operations is apparent rather than real, for the various components are managed on a timesharing or multiplexing basis, whereby each request for action is placed in a queue, or segments of a number of actions (e.g., the printing of textfiles from several word processors) are parceled out to the appropriate devices in an "interleaved" fashion. The speed of operations in a well-designed network leads the observer to assume that things are happening "all at once."

Several networking methods have been developed for microcomputers, the most basic of which, perhaps, is the modem-accessed online service. An online service allows the microcomputer user to tap one or more databases and/

or other remote utilities (buying services, directory services, etc.) simply by using a modem and telecommunications software. For a given user, this type of network can be considered an ad hoc arrangement, the "network" essentially vanishing when the connection is broken.

The online network exists at scattered locations in the common-carrier telephone system, with the network control computer acting as a central switchboard as well as data processor. But there are other networks that are essentially private systems set up for operations within a particular organization. Large companies, for example, have their own telecommunications networks that may link all divisions of the company regardless of their physical location, using such transmission media as coaxial cable and telecommunications satellites. Normally, these networks are inaccessible to the general public. High-performance mini- or mainframe computers service these systems.

Local area networks (LANs) can be configured for large-scale business operations as well as small-scale operations of various kinds. The large-scale LAN is exemplified by Ethernet, a comprehensive system designed to integrate all of the office equipment normally used in a typical large business environment: terminals, word processors, copiers, printers, and so on. The Ethernet type of network uses a baseband system, in which signals are "broadcast" over coaxial cable from node to node at low voltage and low frequency. Each node (i.e., device such as a printer) is aware when another node is active and refrains from attempting to communicate until the path is clear. The path may be designed as a ring, star, or bus. Each configuration has its advantages and disadvantages. In the ring configuration, signals—maintained by amplifiers placed throughout the ring—travel circularly from node to node. The amplifiers or "repeaters" assure that valid data moves through the system, but if one node fails, the circuit is broken and communication fails. The star configuration uses a central processor from which the nodes radiate like spokes in a wheel or, more to the point, like a switchboard and its satellite telephones. If a node fails, the system continues to function. If the central processor fails, the system fails. The bus or "daisy chain" links everything in a single complex pathway to which additional nodes can be easily added. The failure of one or more nodes has no effect on the overall operation.

The low-frequency operation of baseband systems is adequate for relatively short transmission lines. But for longer lines (as in the case of cable television), broadband or high-frequency transmission is necessary. Baseband operates at computer frequencies, which don't usually exceed about 8 MHz. Broadband, however, is propagated at frequencies as high as 100 MHz. At high frequencies, line loss (signal degradation) is low enough for reliable data transfer.

The typical small-system microcomputer networking arrangement emulates the larger systems in general design, tying two or more computers to one or more common elements (as mentioned earlier) and allowing for communication from computer to computer as well as between the computer and the shared resource(s). A variety of proprietary LAN devices (e.g., Applenet, C-Net, ARCnet, Omninet, and others) have been announced or are on the market, but no standard yet exists. The uncertain state of the microcomputer industry leaves the question of an industry-wide standard open. This uncertainty extends to the software necessary for controlling a multiuser and/or multitasking network. MP/M and TurboDOS typify the currently available network operating systems. But in software as well as hardware, no standard exists.

Part of the reason for the lack of hardware and software standards is the variety of methodologies and technologies available for managing network functions. Already, AT&T and IBM, the acknowledged leaders in the communications and computer industries, have adopted different approaches to the problems of multiuser networks. Both companies are beginning to release their products to the market, and both companies have invested the vast amount of research and development time and money that are always necessary to support such a product. Other major companies, such as Wang and Litton, are in the arena as well and are contending with a host of smaller companies who see network technology as one of the most important areas of development.

One of the essential requirements for local area network developers is the need to develop an architecture which will not become obsolete by the time the network is fully implemented. This is not as farfetched as it seems because network technology is evolving at a very rapid pace and will soon be able to offer a complete integration of all types of data. Current office network technology does not yet provide for a complete integration of data, in part because the demand for it has not fully materialized. Voice data, video data, and digital information each has its own communications technology, and the three have yet to be fully integrated under one intelligent, fully automated system. This integration, however, is at the center of much of the current development in network technology.

Current network implementations offer what are known as distributed communications links, much like the internal data bus of a microcomputer, which allow for only the transmission of standard digital data. Like the internal data bus, data is broadcast along discrete paths and whatever controller software there is keeps collisions between bundles of data from taking place. Most local area networks in today's offices do not offer any intelligent network control functions, relegating such tasks to the host computers to manage from either end of the communications line. There is also no real standard protocol which supports products from different vendors and which can integrate the functions of desktop computers, access to remote mainframes, mass storage facilities, different types of printers and plotters, and even a typesetter or photocopier. There is a serious need for this type of technology because in most professional office environments the different devices and computers have gradually accumulated over a period of time and were obtained not for the purposes of immediate data sharing but because each device was capable of performing a specific task to the needs of the office. The market, therefore, would more readily support a networking technology which integrated existing devices and peripherals rather than a networking technology which required a wholesale replacement of all existing computers, printers, monitors, storage devices, and other peripherals in an office environment.

Finally, one of the ultimate goals of any networking technology is the complete integration of voice, video, and digital information into one high-speed network. This would have the effect of transforming desktop computers into real information appliances which could deliver spoken messages, images and television-like communications, and videotext information through the same set of wires on the same video display terminal.

Information transmitted along such a network can even be displayed in a screen window format, allowing the user to manage different data formats at the same time. The obvious advantage of this type of area network is that for the first time users will have the capability of managing a fully interactive set of integrated data. The desktop computer will become less of a computing device and more of a communications device that will perform computing functions when necessary. Specific local area networks can also be networked to one another by management software that looks at each LAN as if were a discrete point on a point-to-point communications link. In this way, networks can be expanded as if they were embedded or nested structures within the larger architecture of a complete system. By using a cluster switching technology, similar to the technology used to manage long distance telephone transmissions, nodal points on the larger network can be treated as if they were telephone exchanges. Entire network systems could be reconfigured from a single console, and even this could be managed automatically by the system itself. Thus, in the event of line or hardware failure, the area of the failure can be identified and isolated before secondary problems arise.

The hardware and software components that will drive the completely integrated network are currently being brought to market. As the evolution of the marketplace produces new hardware and software communication standards, the disparate products will begin to amalgamate into protonetworks and finally into full-fledged integrated communications networks. The profound effects of this technology will radically change the way most people will do business and will probably not be fully realized until the end of this century at the earliest.

The hardware cost of a network (exclusive of the computer, terminals, printers, etc.) can run from a few hundred dollars to several thousands. The actual networking hardware consists of the cabling—as complex as coaxial or as simple as a twisted pair—and the interface unit(s). These units are basically input-output managers (serial or parallel interfaces, multiplexers, amplifier/repeaters). They may also be complete microcomputer subsystems that include RAM and disk-drive storage. In the last analysis, the prospective network purchaser must expect to spend a fair amount of time reviewing the systems available for the buyer's hardware, intended applications, and budget, and to seek guidance from knowledgable users.

Henry F. Beechhold

System Configurations

IBM

IBM-PC and Compatibles

The IBM Personal Computer (and its many imitators) are based on 16-bit processor technology. The following memory map and information tables are for the IBM PC-XT; however, all machines that are compatible with the IBM PC follow the same memory ~~~~~~~~~~ similar features.

COMMODORE

COMMODORE VIC-20 AND C-64 SPECIFICATIONS

CPU (Microprocessor)   6502A

TIMING CYCLE   1.02 MHz

RAM (Min/Max)   5K/16K (VIC-20)
64K (C-64)

Mass Storage   Commodore cassette recorder
5-1/4-inch floppy diskette, 170K/disk

DOS   Commodore DOS 1.0 to 4.0

Peripheral Support   Commodore expansion bus
IEEE-488 I/O port
ROM Cartridge slot

APPLE

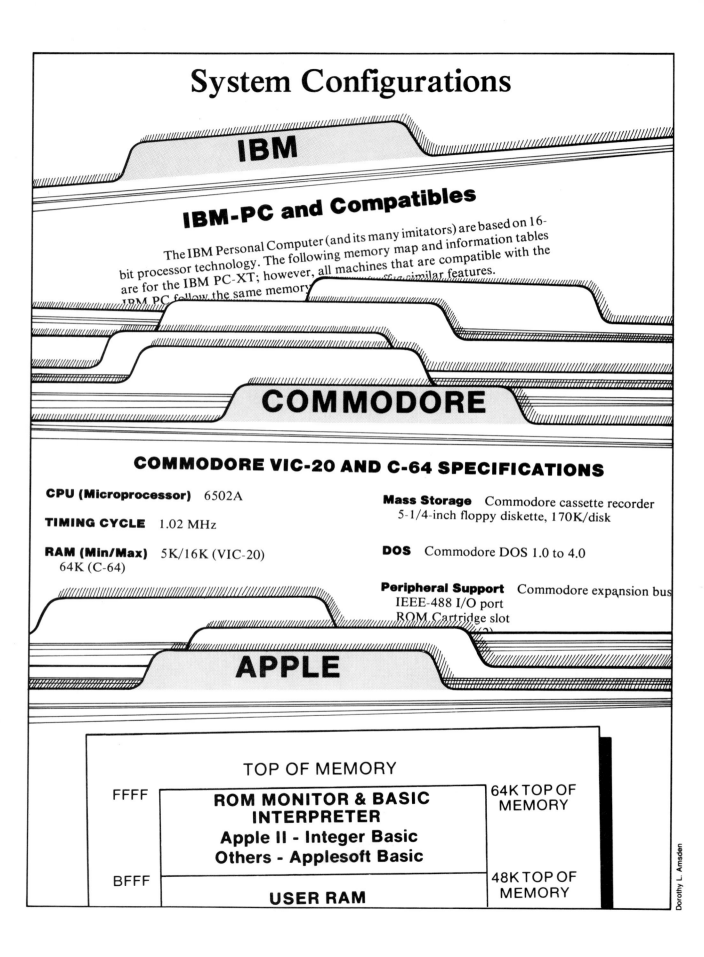

	TOP OF MEMORY	
FFFF	**ROM MONITOR & BASIC INTERPRETER** **Apple II - Integer Basic** **Others - Applesoft Basic**	64K TOP OF MEMORY
BFFF	**USER RAM**	48K TOP OF MEMORY

MAJOR PC PRODUCTS: MARKETS AND SPECS

After seven years of consistent growth that was restricted only by the availability of capital and the aggressive development of new products, the personal computer industry is finally structuring itself into traditional categories. If it is true that after a time products eventually reflect their primary markets, then the stabilization taking place in the personal computing industry now is following a historical trend. IBM and its industry counterparts, Apple and its counterparts, and the other major computer manufacturers have turned to servicing their primary markets with product and product support. At the same time, however, the products that the major computer companies are selling still reflect the basic cultures of the individual corporations and the forces that propelled them into the marketplace. It is also interesting to observe the types of third-party manufactured products that have orbited around the different personal computer systems. These product types, influenced by the consumer market and socioeconomic orientation of the personal computer systems, reflect the cultures of the products themselves, even when the same third-party software producer develops products for more than one system.

For example, it is easier to identify a MicroSoft product by the computer it was developed for than by a generic MicroSoft culture. And as the hardware market becomes increasingly saturated by compatibles and clones and "perform-alikes," it will be the software market that will carry the different banners of the corporate cultures behind the major personal computer systems.

This section provides some technical specifications and system maps for the major hardware microcomputer systems. The introduction below evaluates the major personal computer products and their components in terms of their technology, and their technology in terms of their markets—and the effects on the industry.

Background of the Personal Computing Industry

As most histories of the personal computer report, the gateway toward today's products was opened when the semiconductor was perfected in the late 1940s. In 1977, a momentous year for personal computing, Apple introduced the Apple II, Commodore introduced the PET, Radio Shack introduced the TRS-80, the first ComputerLand store was opened, and the first issue of *Personal Computing* was published. Two years later, Apple was selling the first disk operating system for its II, MicroPro had introduced WordStar, VisiCalc was introduced by Personal Software, and the research for what would eventually become the Macintosh was begun under the name of the LISA project. In 1980, MicroSoft, which had only come into existence five years earlier with the first implementation of BASIC on the Altair, signed a historic consulting agreement with IBM to produce an operating system for the PC. The result was MS-DOS, now in its 3.1 version, which has become one of the industry standards for microcomputer disk operating systems. As any history of the personal computer industry will show, the events have overtaken each other like breaking waves, changing the shoreline with each swing of the tides.

Definition of the Market

And now, ten years after MicroSoft introduced the first BASIC and the first issue of *Byte* was published, a shape and substance to the personal computer environment has become clear. First, as in most industries, the major producers of equipment have remained largely within their corporate cultures. Even when companies such as IBM and Apple sought to go beyond what seemed to be their particular culture, they quickly redefined it in terms of their own history and corporate methodology. When IBM, for example, made its foray into what in 1981 was a wild and wooly personal computing environment, it was widely heralded as a large company acting like a startup. And, indeed, for all the world, they behaved just like one of the puppy companies in a golden industry. Yet to veteran IBM watchers and computer market analysts, IBM was doing what IBM had always done: it waited, it planned, it made sure that the ground under its corporate foot was bedrock solid, it lined up its suppliers, and, in a final logistical adjustment, brought its most considerable marketing expertise to bear on a safe and reliable product with which to break into the field. Once that was accomplished, IBM poured more and more product into the breach until, today, it dominates the personal computer marketplace as it has dominated the office systems marketplace—a marketplace that IBM literally invented—for the past twenty years.

At the other end of the personal computer spectrum is Radio Shack, a chain of electronics stores that was purchased by Tandy in 1962. Radio Shack, as its name implies, was fed by the huge consumer interest in electronics, high-fidelity audio equipment, and citizens band radio equipment in the late 1950s. The Texas-based Tandy company produced a very successful line of arts and crafts supplies for the consumer and educational markets. It was only natural that Tandy purchase the chain of electronics stores at a time when electronics equipment was catching the interest of a new generation of amateur tinkerer.

It was just as natural that the Tandy company introduce a small, cassette-based home computer through its own outlets in 1977, thereby taking advantage at what it correctly perceived was going to be a considerable consumer interest in microprocessor technology. Tandy also correctly perceived that the secret to computer sales was software and not hardware. Therefore, it quickly assembled its own line of software marketed through its own retail outlets and, by 1980, had become one of the dominant forces in the lucrative educational computing market.

Tandy was one of the first companies to announce a personal computer network, one of the first companies to bring to market a 16-bit business machine, and one of the first companies to intoduce hard disk technology to the personal computer industry. Yet, the TRS-80 is still perceived as the hobbyist's computer with a loyal following of computer users whose primary source of product and product support is the Radio Shack Computer Center.

The personal computer market has been shaped by the different corporate cultures that have produced the hardware and software. At the same time, it has been a corporate culture which has largely determined which level of technology the hardware would utilize. For example, the earliest commercial microcomputers and computer kits like the H-8 from Heath used the first 8-bit processors available: the 8080 and 8080A. These devices sold so rapidly and generated such enthusiasm at a consumer level that other manufacturers seized on the product and utilized improved versions of these chips, like the Z80, which were easier to program and offered more system capability. The venerable Z80 is still in use at a commercial level, driving phototypesetting and digital typesetting devices, driving dedicated word processors, and driving some 8-bit personal computers. The register flipping capability of the Z80 made it an ideal CPU for business operations that required various levels of interrupts and the ability to switch back and forth between different operations without loss of data. The Z80, at the close of the 1970s, therefore, was a machine waiting to happen. It only needed a professional entree into the marketplace, and that took place because of three pieces of software: CP/M, WordStar, and VisiCalc. Taking advantage of the Z80's register capabilities, CP/M, WordStar, and VisiCalc created an environment for professional business desktop computing. And computer startup companies seized the moment and projected themselves into the market.

It was the Z80, therefore, and the first applications packages that created not only the technology of professional business computing, but the need for more powerful professional business software. At the home computer end of the spectrum, Apple's entry into the market took advantage of the memory-oriented 6502. The types of color graphics applications for the Apple and the simplicity of Applesoft BASIC made it an immediate candidate for educational implementations. Mathematics teachers who taught sequential logic and who had taken high-level programming courses in college became the first wave of the cottage educational software industry as they adapted their courses to include computer-based material. Where the Z80 machines were sold to businesses and small offices, the 6502-based Apples found an immediate home in classrooms and computer curriculum resource centers. The entire culture surrounding the Apple computer helped to reinforce this product design and implementation.

Apple was the product of a do-it-yourself industry; the company was founded in a garage, and the company was founded by members of a postwar generation that had no immediate ties to the corporate data processing environment that had dominated automated business systems since the 1950s. In short, the Apple computer represented a new type of product for a new consumer generation.

Apple continued to illustrate its aggressiveness in product development with the implementation of the LISA, a machine based on the icon-driven Xerox office system that made its appearance in the early 1980s. Apple saw in the icon system a workable alternative to the command language or menu-driven hardware and software that requires all users to learn a form of code before processing any data. Although the LISA failed to make the impact in the office market that Apple had hoped it would, it nevertheless reflected a certain nontraditional approach to microcomputers that Apple evidenced from its earliest days as a company. It is interesting to note that Apple's one traditional foray into the business market with the Apple III was an absolute failure, and the machine was eventually withdrawn.

However, when Apple seized upon the 68000 chip with its sophisticated architecture and 64 pin set that enabled individual signals to be carried by individual lines, it developed a product that started another fire under the rest of the industry. Now, with similar Macintosh look-alike software packages being released for PC compatibles and with Digital Research's release of its Graphics Management Environment system, the Apple Macintosh venture will have been proven to be successful. It is also to Apple's credit that its 8-bit Apple II line continues as a strong seller in the home computer market.

The hobbyist end of the spectrum was represented by Radio Shack, which utilized the Z80 chip to assemble a low-level, cassette-driven, Model I computer. The TRS-80 Model I, however, was also seized upon by a computer-hungry market and quickly made its entry into the classroom without the software support that Apple enjoyed. And although the TRS-80 computer market flourished rapidly and expanded into some of the business sector, it still largely remained a hobbyist's market, and continues to this day to be an alternative to higher-priced business systems.

When the definitive history of personal computing is finally written, IBM will be given much of the credit for helping to stabilize a highly unstable market in the early 1980s. In fact, the credit belongs to IBM's conservative approach to business more than it does to IBM's aggressiveness in new product development. At the time when IBM was designing the architecture for the PC, it had a choice to make between the full 16-bit 8086 CPU and the 16- by 8-bit 8088 CPU. Although IBM was immediately chastised for selecting the 8088, it was a typically conservative and intelligent IBM decision that ultimately proved to be correct. Simply stated, IBM was taking a 16-bit architecture into an 8-bit world of personal computing. The 16-bit external support simply was not available for IBM to make the type of marketing dent it needed to compete effectively with the low-overhead startup companies already selling to the business community. Also, and this was a powerful consideration, the existing software on the market was written for an 8-bit system, not a full 16-bit system. The easier it would be to modify the 8-bit software, IBM reasoned, the easier it would be to sell IBM PCs. A third consideration was the level of 16-bit support in the component and microchip market. Because IBM had spent over fifty years in the business machine market, it learned never to rely on one or two small suppliers for the beating heart of any system. Therefore, because there were more suppliers of 8-bit support chips than there were 16-bit support chips, the ever wary IBM selected the 8088 and in so doing brought its PC to market without having to rely on a substantial change in the chip support or software support for its computer. By the time other manufacturers, including AT&T, were bringing to market a full 16-bit personal computer, IBM had leapfrogged ahead and developed the even more powerful and faster 16-bit 80286-based PC AT, and the distinction between the personal computer and business minicomputer began to fade away.

Each type of system has found its own market, and each market reflects not only the predilections of the buyers but also the translation of the manufacturer's corporate culture into product. The IBM PC has become a business standard for hardware and software. It has become one of the largest-selling personal computer families and owns the greatest share of the professional market. Apple has survived what industry analysts predicted would be its downfall with the Apple III and has made a success of a machine that some analysts predicted was only a folly. The Macintosh has set a different type of standard in software and has managed to hold down one of the markets. Radio Shack, too, has managed successfully to compete in the computer market with a very secure retail base.

TRS-80 Model I and III

The TRS-80 Model I and Model III computers from Radio Shack are quite similar in design and operation. The Model I was Tandy's first computer; the Model III was the replacement for the Model I. Neither machine is currently in production.

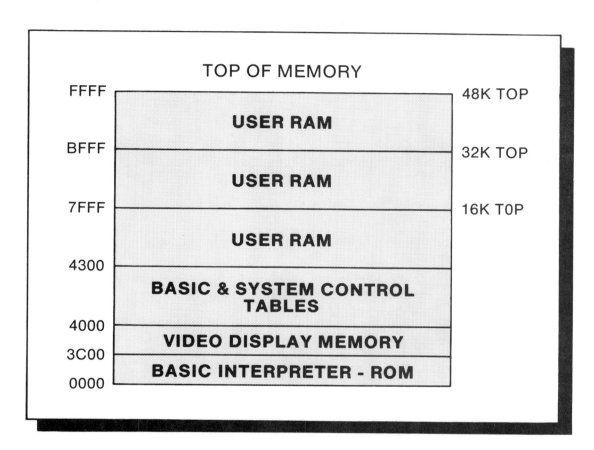

TRS-80 SPECIFICATIONS

CPU (Microprocessor) Z80

TIMING CYCLE 1.77 MHz

RAM (Min/Max) 4K/48K

Display 16 × 64 text, 48 × 128 graphics (b/w)

Languages BASIC in ROM, Fortran, Pilot, assembler

Disk Storage (5-1/4-inch floppy diskette) Model I—88K/disk, 4 drives maximum

Model III—180K/disk, 4 drives maximum

DOS TRS-DOS (proprietary) LDOS (proprietary)

Peripheral Support RS-232 serial port, parallel printer port, bus expansion slot.

Both machines are also available in a 4K RAM cassette-based version. CP/M has been transported to both machines, and both enjoy the availability of several additional disk operating systems.

TRS-80 Model II and 12

The TRS-80 Model II and the Model 12, its replacement, are high-performance Z80A-based machines targeted for the small business market. Both machines are totally RAM based, with only a boot ROM. Radio Shack has offered several different versions of DOS for these machines, as well as CP/M. See the maps for CP/M and TRS-80 Model I for details as to usage of memory in these machines. The Model I memory allocation for the ROM-based BASIC is quite similar to the RAM-based BASIC in the Model II and 12.

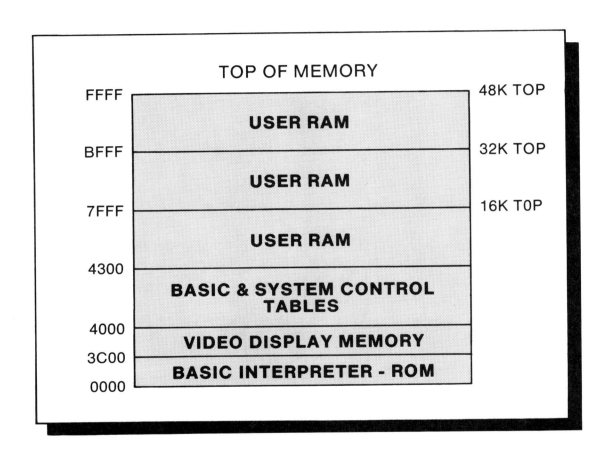

TOP OF MEMORY

FFFF	48K TOP
USER RAM	
BFFF	32K TOP
USER RAM	
7FFF	16K TOP
USER RAM	
4300	
BASIC & SYSTEM CONTROL TABLES	
4000	
VIDEO DISPLAY MEMORY	
3C00	
BASIC INTERPRETER - ROM	
0000	

TRS-80 (Model II and 12) SPECIFICATIONS

CPU (Microprocessor)   Z80A

TIMING CYCLE   4 MHz

RAM (Min/Max)   32K/128K

Display   25 × 80 text, graphics optional

Languages   BASIC, COBOL, Fortran, assembler

Disk Storage   (8-inch floppy diskette)
Model II—500 KB/disk, 1 drive included, 3 more optional

Model 12—1.2 MB/disk, 1 drive included, 3 more optional

DOS   TRS-DOS, CP/M 3.0 (for Model 12)

Peripheral Support   2 RS-232 serial ports, parallel printer port, expansion card cage (for hard disk, graphics upgrades)

TRS-80 Model 4

The TRS-80 Model 4 is the current production model of a series which started with the Model I. The Model 4 is available in a cassette-based version or with disks and a transportable edition. The Model 4 is a RAM-based system, but it can emulate the Model III by switching in a ROM. See the map for the TRS-80 Model I for memory usage in emulation mode, and the map for CP/M for usage in CP/M mode.

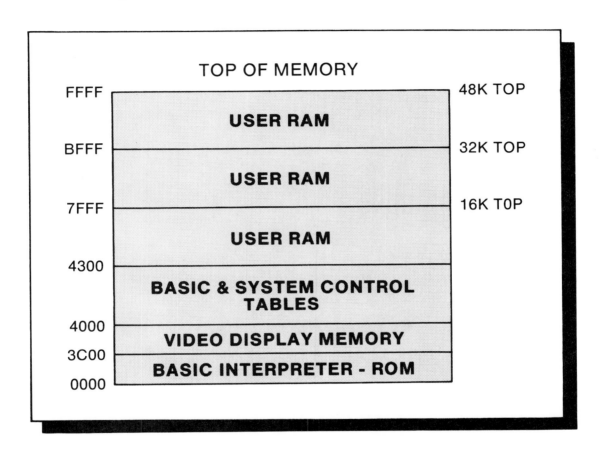

TRS-80 (Model 4) SPECIFICATIONS

CPU (Microprocessor)   Z80A

TIMING CYCLE   4 MHz

RAM (Min/Max)   6K/128K

Display   24 × 80 text, graphics optional

Languages   BASIC, COBOL, Fortran, assembler (TRS-DOS), CP/M languages

Disk Storage   (5-1/4-inch floppy diskette) 180K/disk, 4 drives maximum

DOS   TRS-DOS, LDOS, CP/M 3.0

Peripheral Support   2 RS-232 serial ports, parallel printer port, modem (in transportable 4P)

CP/M Computers

CP/M (Control Program/Microcomputers) is the most popular DOS for use on 8-bit microcomputers. Many vendors have adopted the CP/M standard. The map below shows memory usage for the Kaypro2, a popular CP/M-based transportable system. Memory usage for other CP/M systems is similar, although specific addresses may differ slightly for BIOS, BDOS, and CCP start.

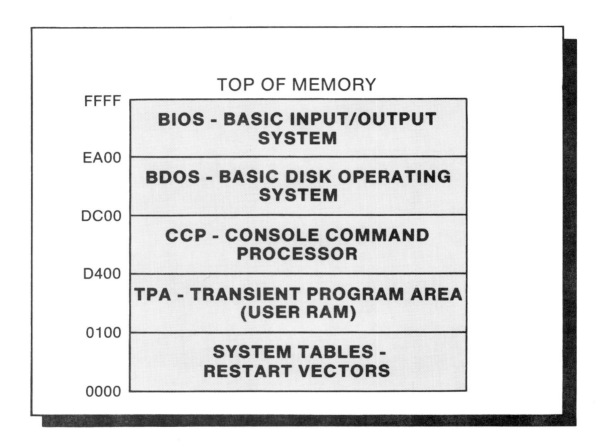

CP/M SPECIFICATIONS

Systems using the CP/M operating system come in virtually every imaginable configuration. Typical configurations include a Z80 CPU, 64K RAM, one or more disk drives (5-1/4-inch or 8-inch), a display, keyboard, one or more serial ports, and a parallel printer port. Many CP/M systems, such as the Kaypro 10 or the Televideo 803H, include 10-MB hard disk systems.

Also part of the CP/M family of computers are the multiuser systems using MP/M-II, a version of CP/M. Systems such as the Altos, North Star Horizon, and Televideo 806 support several users.

Virtually all high-level languages have been transported to the CP/M operating environment. However, the system supports only the 8080 family of microprocessors, so assemblers are limited to those for the 8080, 8085, and Z80.

Vendors providing CP/M systems include: Kaypro, Morrow, CompuPro, North Star, Altos, Televideo, Vector Graphic, Cromenco, Radio Shack, and Heath/Zenith.

IBM-PC and Compatibles

The IBM Personal Computer (and its many imitators) are based on 16-bit processor technology. The following memory map and information tables are for the IBM PC-XT; however, all machines that are compatible with the IBM PC follow the same memory usage and offer similar features.

```
                    TOP OF MEMORY
FFFFF  +---------------------------------------+
       |              ROM BIOS                 |
E0000  +---------------------------------------+
       |        EXPANSION CARD ROM             |
       |         (2K INCREMENTS)               |
C8000  +---------------------------------------+
       |       COLOR GRAPHICS ADAPTER          |
       |           DISPLAY RAM                 |
B8000  +---------------------------------------+
       |       MONOCHROME ADAPTER              |
       |           DISPLAY RAM                 |
B0000  +---------------------------------------+
       |          RESERVED AREA                |
A0000  +---------------------------------------+
       |            USER RAM                   |
00500  +---------------------------------------+
       |      BIOS & DOS SYSTEM DATA           |
00400  +---------------------------------------+
       |        INTERRUPT VECTORS              |
0000   +---------------------------------------+
```

IBM-PC SPECIFICATIONS

CPU (Microprocessor)   8080

TIMING CYCLE   4.77 MHz

RAM (Min/Max)   28K/640K

Display   25 × 80 text, b/w or color

Languages   APL, BASIC, C, COBOL, Fortran, assembler and others

Disk Storage   (5-1/4-inch floppy diskette) 360K/disk, 1 drive in XT 10-MB hard disk in XT

DOS   PC-DOS, CP/M-86, Concurrent CP/M-86, Concurrent PC-DOS, Topview

Peripheral Support   2 RS-232 serial port. Other peripherals add controllers to 8-slot expansion bus.

Commodore PET/PET 2001/CBM

The PET was Commodore's initial entry into the personal computer market. The original PET was upgraded into the PET 2001, and then business versions were released as the CBM 8032 and CBM 8096. All three machines share a similar architecture.

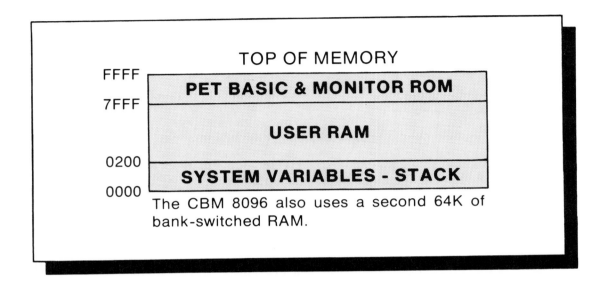

COMMODORE PET SPECIFICATIONS

CPU (Microprocessor) 6502

TIMING CYCLE 1.02 MHz

RAM (Min/Max) 8K (PET)/96K (CBM 8096)

Display 40 × 25 (PET), 80 × 25 (CBM)

Languages BASIC in ROM, assembler

Mass Storage Commodore cassette recorder 5-1/4-inch floppy diskette, 170K/disk

DOS Commodore DOS 1.0 to 4.0

Peripheral Support Commodore expansion bus, IEEE-488 I/O port

Commodore VIC-20 and C-64

The VIC-20 and C-64 are Commodore's second-generation home computers. The VIC and C-64 have color display capability through a television set, and they share a common programming language. The VIC-20 differs from the C-64 mainly in terms of user RAM available. Both machines use the proprietary Commodore peripheral bus. Most peripherals for the older PET and CBM series machines are usable with the VIC-20 and C-64.

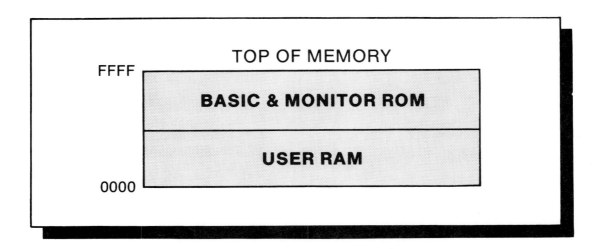

COMMODORE VIC-20 AND C-64 SPECIFICATIONS

CPU (Microprocessor)   6502A

TIMING CYCLE   1.02 MHz

RAM (Min/Max)   5K/16K (VIC-20)
64K (C-64)

Display   20 × 25 (VIC-20), 40 × 25 (C-64)

Languages   BASIC in ROM, assembler

Mass Storage   Commodore cassette recorder
5-1/4-inch floppy diskette, 170K/disk

DOS   Commodore DOS 1.0 to 4.0

Peripheral Support   Commodore expansion bus
IEEE-488 I/O port
cartridge ROM slot
joystick ports (2)

TRS-80 Color Computer

The TRS-80 Color Computer is Tandy's entry into the home computer arena. The Color Computer uses a proprietary programming system (BASIC language and DOS), but can use industry standard peripherals.

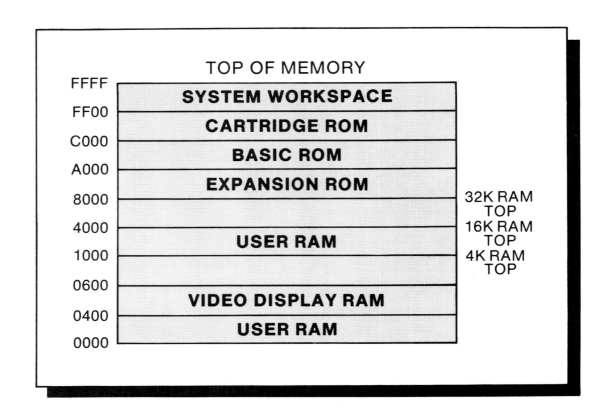

TRS-80 COLOR SPECIFICATIONS

CPU (Microprocessor) 6809

TIMING CYCLE 1 MHz

RAM (Min/Max) 4K/32K

Display 32 × 16 text (8 colors)
Graphics 256 × 192, 128 × 192

Languages BASIC in ROM, assembler

Mass Storage Cassette
5-1/4-inch floppy diskette (180K/disk)

DOS DOS-9 (proprietary)

Peripheral Support RS-232 serial port
expansion bus
cartridge ROM slot
joystick port

Apple II Family

The Apple II family of computers encompasses four different models. All models are software compatible, and three of the models are hardware compatible as well. The Apple II was the first Apple computer to see wide distribution since the earlier Apple I was not produced in quantity and was replaced by the Apple II+. Current production machines are the Apple IIe and the Apple IIc.

```
                        TOP OF MEMORY

FFFF    ┌──────────────────────────────────┐   64K TOP OF
        │   ROM MONITOR & BASIC            │   MEMORY
        │         INTERPRETER              │
        │   Apple II - Integer Basic       │
        │   Others - Applesoft Basic       │
BFFF    ├──────────────────────────────────┤   48K TOP OF
        │          USER RAM                │   MEMORY
7FFF    ├──────────────────────────────────┤   32K TOP OF
        │          USER RAM                │   MEMORY
4000    ├──────────────────────────────────┤   16K TOP OF
        │          USER RAM                │   MEMORY
0300    ├──────────────────────────────────┤
        │     HARDWARE STACK-              │
        │      SYSTEM VALUES               │
0000    └──────────────────────────────────┘
```

APPLE II SPECIFICATIONS

CPU (Microprocessor)   6502

TIMING CYCLE   1 MHz

RAM (Min/Max)   6K/64K (II. II+)
64K/128K (IIc,IIe)

Display   40 × 24 text, 80 × 24 (IIe, IIc)
Graphics to 280 × 192

Languages   BASIC, Pascal, assembler, others

Mass Storage   (5-1/4-inch floppy diskette)
140K/disk

5-MB hard disk available as an option

DOS   Apple ProDOS, DOS 3.3 (proprietary)

Peripheral Support   RS-232 ports, IIc
Eight card slots available; cards include Z80 and 8088 coprocessors, various I/O boards, memory expansion, etc.

The Apple IIc has 128K total RAM with the second 64K available as a contiguous block accessed by bank-switching. Bank-switched memory (64K) is available as an option on the Apple IIe.

Apple Macintosh

The Apple Macintosh is Apple's user-friendly computer. Not intended as a replacement for the Apple II families, the MAC is an extension of Apple's LISA family of workstation computers.

APPLE MACINTOSH SPECIFICATIONS

CPU (Microprocessor) 68000

RAM (Min/Max) 28K/512K

Display Graphics 512 × 342 (b/w on integral monitor)
Text varies with font sizes

Languages BASIC, Pascal, Forth

Disk Storage (3-1/2-inch microfloppy disk)
400K/disk
10-MB hard disk available as an option

DOS Macintosh Operating System (proprietary)

Peripheral Support Mouse included, 2 RS-232 serial ports

Glossary

abend   Abortive end or abnormal ending: the term refers to an early termination of a computer function or program before it has reached a natural conclusion. Abend is usually the result of an error.

abort   To cancel or end a program, procedure, or selection while it is in progress.

absolute address   An actual location in main memory for a piece of data that the control unit can interpret directly. Synonymous with machine address.

absolute maximum rating   The maximum limit to which the machine can perform, as indicated by the unit's specifications and modified by the environment in which the machine will function. This rating should not be exceeded.

AC   Alternating current. This form of electricity can be visualized as a sine wave with the positive (+) cycle above the base line and the negative (−) below the base line. There are two key measurements associated with AC, voltage (typically 117) and frequency (typically 60 Hz). Frequency refers to the number of either positive or negative peaks per second. By contrast, pure DC (direct current) is produced by a battery and can be represented by a straight line. Frequency is irrelevant. AC can be converted to DC and vice versa. AC must be converted to DC for your computer. The purpose of the computer power supply is to reduce line voltage, convert AC to DC, and regulate the newly created DC to the specific needs of the computer circuitry, which is typically 5 volts and 12 volts.

acceptance testing   The validation or burning in of the system or program to user specifications or requirements.

access   The ability to retrieve data from a storage device or peripheral and place it into memory.

access arm   The mechanical device in a disk storage unit that holds one or more reading and writing heads.

access code   An identification number or alphabetic password assigned to a user to grant him or her entry to a system.

access methods   The technique and/or program code for moving data between main storage and I/O devices.

access time   The length of time or interval required between when data is called for or requested to be stored and when delivery or storage is accomplished in a computer system.

accumulator   A holding register in the computer's arithmetic logic unit to temporarily store the results of an arithmetic or logic operation. Most computers have more than one accumulator and they are used for I/O (input/output) operations as well.

accuracy   The degree of freedom from error. Not to be confused with the concept of precision; accuracy refers to the degree of closeness to a correct value, whereas precision refers to the degree of preciseness of a measurement.

accuracy control characters   Characters that indicate whether data is valid for representation on the device being used, and whether the data is correct, incorrect, or should be disregarded.

ACIA   Asynchronous Communication Interface Adapter: a programmable integrated circuit used for data transmission. Typically, such an IC will allow the central processing unit (CPU) of the computer to communicate with a modem or other serial device.

ACK   Conventional name for a positive acknowledgment control character. Normally it means that no errors were detected in the just received data block and that transmission of the next block of data can begin. The corresponding negative response is NAK.

acknowledge (ACK)   A term for the control signal or character that is used to verify that a block of data or transmission has been accepted by the receiver.

acoustic coupler   A data communications device, usually used with a modem, that converts electrical data signals to tones for transmission over a telephone line using a conventional telephone headset.

activity ratio   A measurement of file activity computed as the relationship of records used to the total number of records in a file.

A/D converter, D/A converter   Analog-to-digital and digital-to-analog converter. Circuits which convert analog signals (like sound) to digital signals (0's and 1's) and digital signals to analog signals. A modem includes both A/D and D/A circuitry. Analog signals are characterized by a continually changing waveform, while digital signals are never anything but 0's and 1's (i.e., digits).

Ada   A high-level language developed by the Department of Defense. It was designed as a common language for all military computer projects. Ada's most unusual feature is its ability to recognize Englishlike words for easy use. The language's organization is structured around building-block modules and allows for combinations of smaller units into hierarchies and nested structures.

adapter   A device used to control or interface a piece of hardware to the computer. Typical adapters are RS-232 or Centronics interface adapters and adapters for game paddles, joysticks, lightpens, or disk drives.

adaptive   A term used to refer to the capability of a piece of software to handle a wide variation in one or more system characteristics and still perform the intended function; the adjustment is made automatically.

ADCCP   Advanced Data Communications Control Procedure. This is a bit-oriented communications protocol developed by ANSI for the purposes of standardizing data communications procedures.

add-on   The process of increasing the memory capacity, modifying the architecture, or upgrading the system's performance capabilities by attaching either circuitry or components to the system.

address   A computer system location, identified by a name, label, or number that can be referred to in a program. It can define a main memory location, a terminal, a peripheral device, or a cursor location to any other physical item in a computer system.

address register   A register holding the location of memory, peripherals, or other physical system items.

address space   The complete range of addresses that is available to a programmer.
   See also virtual address space.

address translation   The process of changing the address of an item of data or an instruction to the address in main storage at which it is to be loaded or relocated.

add-subtract time   The actual time required to perform addition or subtraction procedures. Add-subtract time does not include the time required to retrieve the operands from storage or to return the result to the storage medium after the operation.

ADP   Automatic Data Processing. See data processing.

AI   See artificial intelligence.

algebraic language   An algorithmic language whose statements are structured to resemble algebraic expressions, e.g., Algol, Fortran.

Algol   A programming language taken from algebraic language that is designed for the concise, efficient expression of arithmetic and logical processes and the control of these processes.

algorithm   A specific set of defined rules for the mathematical and/or logical processes required for the solution of a problem in a finite number of steps.
   See also heuristic.

alignment   The adjustment of tolerances within the mechanism of a device so that tension, torque, and speed are all synchronized.

allocate   To assign a resource for use in performing a specific task.

alphameric characters   Consisting of letters, punctuation marks, numbers, and special characters: in programming, usually the characters A through Z, digits 0 through 9, and #, $, and @.

alphanumeric   See alphameric characters.

alpha test   The stage during the research and development of a new product during which a prototype of the system is operated to ascertain that the system concept and design are functional and to identify areas that need further development and/or enhancement.

alternate route   In communications networks, a secondary path that is used to reach a specific destination if the primary path is unavailable.

ALU   See arithmetic and logic unit.

American National Standard control characters
Thirty-two nondisplayed control characters defined by American National Standard Fortran, ANSI X3.9-1966. Synonymous with ASCII control character, Fortran control character.
See also ASCII.

American Standard Code for Information Interchange   See ASCII.

amplitude modulation (AM)   In communications technology, a method of transmission whereby the amplitude of the carrier wave is modified in accordance with the amplitude of the signal wave.
Compare: frequency modulation (FM).

analog   In data transmission, the term is used in opposition to digital. In this context, analog transmission uses amplifiers (required due to attenuation of the signal with distance) that magnify the incoming signal. Digital transmission uses repeaters that generate completely new signals based on whether the incoming signal was mostly a one or mostly a zero during the period the incoming signal was measured.

analog computer   A computer that solves a problem by creating a physical (usually electrical) model giving continuous data simulating the behavior of the variables and their interrelationships. Used in scientific applications and in manufacturing for controlling the operation.

analog/digital converter   The changing or converting of analog (continuous) representations of a physical quality into a form suitable for digital computer processing. For example, the process of translating musical tones into a binary system of on and off electrical impulses.

analysis   The methodical study of a problem and the process of separating that problem into smaller related units for further detailed investigation.

analyst   A person who analyzes and defines problems and develops algorithms and procedures for their solution.

AND   The boolean operative or connective which gives the logical result that the output is one (or positive) only when both inputs are one (or positive).

ANSI   American National Standards Institute. The name of the standards-forming body headquartered in the United States.
See also ASCII.

answer back   A manually or automatically initiated reply message from a terminal which usually includes the terminal address to verify that the correct terminal has been reached and that it is operational.

anti-aliasing   The technique used in a graphics display to diminish the error that appears as a function of the graphics hardware.

APL   The acronym for this high-level language stands for "a programming language." APL is a problem solving language designed for use at remote terminals that uses specially developed arithmetic operations. It offers an unusually extensive set of operators and data structures for handling arrays and for performing mathematical functions and is considered a powerful language for algorithmic procedures, particularly those involving arrays.

append   To change or alter a file or program.

application generator   Software that generates an application program with information supplied by the user. Also known as a program generator.

application-oriented language   A problem-oriented language whose statements contain or resemble the terminology of the user, e.g., a report program generator.

application package   A commercially available applications program. In most cases the routines in the application packages are necessarily written in a generalized way, and will need to be modified to meet each user's own specific needs.

application study   The investigation and the determination of system or procedural requirements and the establishment of criteria for selection of suitable solutions.

application system   A collection of programs and documentation relevant to applications.

applications software   The instructions that direct the hardware to perform specific functions. Common applications include payroll, inventory control, and electronic spreadsheets.

APT   Automatically Programmed Tools. A language for programming numerically controlled machine tools.

architecture   The interrelationship between the parts of a computer.

archive   A procedure for transferring information from an on-line storage diskette or memory area to an off-line storage medium.

argument   The term for a variable within a function. The value of the function is dependent upon that of the variable and as each new argument value is substituted, the value of the function can be determined. The value of the argument can be passed from the main routine to a subroutine or function and then back again. It is possible to have more than one argument for a function or a subroutine.

arithmetic and logic unit (ALU)   An essential hardware component of a central processing unit (CPU) that executes arithmetic and logical operations such as addition, subtraction, AND, OR, NOR, etc., on data.
     See also arithmetic unit.

arithmetic expression   A meaningful combination of data, numbers, names, and arithmetic operations.

arithmetic operator   A symbol that tells the computer to perform an arithmetic operation. Operators include: + (addition), − (subtraction), × (multiplication), / (division), and   (exponentiation).

arithmetic register   A register containing the operands and the results of an arithmetic function.
     See also register.

arithmetic shift   The movement of digits to the left or right in the computer's memory, resulting in a multiplication or division of the number by two.

arithmetic unit   The section of the CPU, in a computing system, that contains the circuits that do arithmetic operations and perform logical comparisons.

ARPANET   The acronym for Advanced Research Projects Agency Network. This project was developed in 1968 by the Department of Defense to create a nationwide computer network.

ARQ   An error control technique that requires retransmission of a data block that contains detected errors. It requires positive (ACK) and negative (NAK) responses from the receiving terminal. A special form called "go-back-in" allows multiple blocks to be acknowledged with a single response.

array   A named, ordered collection of data elements, all of which have identical attributes. An array has dimensions and its individual elements are referred to by subscripts. An array can also be an ordered collection of identical structures as in the high-level languages of PL/I and Fortran.

artificial intelligence (AI)   The capability of a computer to perform functions that are normally associated with human intelligence such as reasoning, learning, and self-improvement.

artificial language   A language based on a set of rules established prior to its usage and without a precise relationship to the user applications for which the language will be used.
     Compare to natural language.

ASA   American Standards Association. Now known as the American National Standards Institute.

ascenders   The parts of some lowercase characters such as d, f, and k, that extend into the upper part of the text line.

ASCII   American (National) Standard Code for Information Interchange, X3.4-1968. This is a 7-bit plus parity code established by the American Standards Institute (formerly American Standards Association) to achieve compatibility between data services. Consists of 96 displayed characters (64 without lowercase) and 32 non-displayed control characters (also called USASCII). Various combinations of 0's and 1's represent the letters, numerals, punctuation marks, and functions like backspace, line feed, carriage return, and escape. Adopted in the early 1960s, the code now permeates all facets of data processing.

ASCII keyboard   A keyboard comprising of most or all of the ASCII character set. Most microcomputer keyboards utilize the ASCII code so that as each key is depressed, that key's appropriate code is sent to a memory location in the computer.

aspect ratio   The ratio of horizontal to vertical dimensions of a frame or image within a frame. It is used in computer graphics. The ability to maintain or control this ratio is important in the transfer and reproduction of an image on various types of display or printed material.

ASR   Automatic Send Receive. A teleprinter terminal with paper tape or magnetic tape devices, or editable internal memory. Refers to any keyboard terminal with off-line storage capabilities that permits a message to be generated off-line for later transmission.

assemble   The process of preparing a machine language program from a symbolic language program by substituting absolute operation codes and addresses for symbolic operation codes and addresses on a one-for-one basis.

assembler   A computer program that converts symbolically coded computer source programs into object-level machine code. The assembler was the first major step in the automation of software development. It permitted symbolic (i.e., named) references to storage locations rather than requiring the use of numbers, and eliminated the necessity to program in binary or other machine language.

assembler language A source language that includes symbolic machine language statements in which there is a one-to-one correspondence with computer instructions. This language lies midway between high-level language and machine language; it is closer to the latter. Programmers use assemblers to make more efficient use of the computer. Mnemonics are used by the programmer.

assembly program A computer program that takes nonmachine language instructions prepared by a programmer and converts them into a form that can be used by the computer.

assign To give a new value to a variable during the running of a program.

associative memory A high-speed memory search based upon data content rather than addresses.

associative storage A storage arrangement in which storage locations are identified by their contents, not by names or positions. Synonymous with content-addressed storage.

asynchronous communication Data transfer, the timing of which is dependent on the actual time for the transfer to take place, as opposed to synchronous communication, which is rigidly timed by an external clock signal.

asynchronous computer A computer in which each operation starts as a result of a signal generated by the completion of the previous operation, or by the availability of the parts of the computer required by the next event or operation. It contrasts with a synchronous computer, where all operations are timed to synchronize with a master clock.

asynchronous transmission A mode of data communications transmission in which time intervals between transmitted characters may be of unequal length. Transmission is independently controlled by start and stop elements at the beginning and end of each character. Also called start-stop transmission.

attenuation A diminishing. In wave forms or signals, it can result from a distortion that alters the original form and causes a diminishing of particular portion of the signal.

audio cassette recording A common serial access mass storage method using a standard home cassette tape player in combination with thin magnetic recording tapes stored in a plastic housing or cassette. To enable these standard home cassettes to be used with com-

puters, tonal frequencies are used to represent digitized 0's and 1's instead of employing a direct digital recording.

audio frequencies Frequencies which can be heard by the human ear (usually between 15 and 20,000 hertz, or cycles per second).

audio response unit (ARU) A device that links a computer system to a telephone network to provide voice responses to inquiries made from telephone-type terminals.

audio track of cassette A separate track of the cassette that allows the computer to play sound through the television speaker.

audit trail A method of following and recording data from the input stage, through any transitions, to the output stage. An audit trail can be used to trace an input or output error to its source, verify steps that have taken place during a certain process, or recover data lost during a hardware failure.

auto-answer The ability of a modem to automatically read incoming telephone messages.

auto call A machine feature that allows a transmission control unit or a station to automatically initiate a call over a switched line.

autoexecute A utility of many operating systems which allows the program to automatically negotiate many of the statements necessary for the program to run; therefore the program executes automatically.

automated audit The feature whereby steps in a program or procedure automatically cause a review of the steps previously taken or the results previously prepared.

automatic calling unit (ACU) A dialing device supplied by the communications common carrier that permits a business machine to automatically dial calls over the communications networks.
See also automatic dialing unit.

automatic data processing (ADP) See data processing.

automatic dialing unit (ADU) A device capable of automatically generating dialing digits.
See also automatic calling unit.

automatic message-switching center In a communications network, location at which messages are automatically routed according to information in them.

automatic programming The process of using a computer to perform some stages of the work involved in preparing a computer program.

automation   The implementation of processes by automatic means.

auxiliary data   Data that is related to other data but not part of it such as backup data.

auxiliary equipment   Equipment not under direct control of the central processing unit. Synonymous with ancillary equipment.

auxiliary operation   An off-line operation performed by equipment not under continuous control of the central processor.

auxiliary storage   Supplementary data storage other than main storage; for example, storage on magnetic tape or direct access devices. Synonymous with external storage, secondary storage.
Compare main storage.

availability   The degree to which a system or resource is ready when needed to process data.

available time   The number of hours the computer is available for use. Synonymous with uptime.

axes   In a two-dimensional coordinate system, axes refers to the lines used as references for horizontal (x) and vertical (y) measurement in graphic representation.

background   The environment in multiprogramming in which low-priority programs are executed.
Compare foreground.

background job   A low-priority job, usually a batched or noninteractive job.
Compare foreground job.

background noise   A term used to describe the presence of any disturbance that interferes with the operation of the microprocessor. Background noise is often introduced to the system in the form of electrical current or static.

background processing   The execution, under automatic control, of lower-priority computer programs when higher-priority programs are not using the system resources.
Compare foreground processing.

background program   When more than one program is being processed, this is the term for the program with the lowest priority. Background programs execute from batched or stacked job input.
Compare foreground program.

backplane   That area in a computer for insertion of additional circuit boards or cards. Also known as a motherboard.

backup   The process of duplicating a program or file onto a separate storage medium, such as magnetic tape, so that an original copy will be retained in the event of loss or failure of the original.

backup copy   The term used for the copy of a file or program that is kept for reference in case the original file or program is destroyed.

bandwidth   The range of frequencies assigned to a channel system. Expressed in hertz as the highest and lowest frequencies of a band.

bank switching   A software technique that allows the computer to switch to various RAM locations.

base   Refers to the number of unique or different symbolic values used in a numbering system and represented by each digit position, beginning with zero. For example, binary or base 2 has two values for each digit position, 1 and 0.
See also radix.

baseband signaling   Low-frequency, unmodulated transmission of a signal at its original frequencies across coaxial cables for short-distance local area network (LAN) transmission.
Compare broadband transmission. See also local area network.

BASIC   Beginner's All-purpose Symbolic Instruction Code. The high-level language developed at Dartmouth College for beginning programmers. BASIC is similar to Fortran II and was developed for a General Electric 225 computer system. Now the most common microcomputer language, it is algebra-like and easily learned; used for problem solving by engineers, scientists and others, who may not be professional programmers. It is now common on almost all computer systems.

basic input/output system (BIOS)   A part of the CP/M operating system that consists of drivers and other software designed to manage the peripheral devices.

basic telecommunications access method (BTAM)   An access method that permits read/write communications with remote devices.

batch mode Application programs which are run on the computer one at a time.

batch processing A processing technique in which similar transactions are gathered over a period of time and aggregated for processing as a group during a machine run. Contrasts with real-time processing, in which input is processed as it is recorded.

batch total A quantity calculated manually for comparison with a machine-produced sum. The totals must be equal to prove the accuracy of the data.

baud The measure or rate of transmission speed at which information or data is sent from one device to another. In microcomputers, baud is defined as one bit per second (bps). In asynchronous transmission, the unit of signaling speed corresponds to one unit interval per second; that is, if the duration of the unit interval is 20 milliseconds, the signaling speed is 50 baud. Common baud rates are 110, 300, 1200, 2400, and 9600. A simple translation method to determine the approximate number of English words transmitted per minute at these rates would be to divide the above numbers by 10.

Baudot code Named for Emile Baudot, a pioneer in printing telegraphy, this is a code for the transmission of data. It is usually applied to the code used in telex systems, and in it, five bits represent one character.

BCD code Decimal numbers that appear as binary numbers.
See also binary coded decimal.

benchmark A measured point of reference in the evaluation process for hardware and software from which comparisons can be made. The process usually involves the use of typical problems for comparisons of hardware performance or software execution.

benchmark problem A problem used to evaluate the performance of computers relative to each other. A flowchart that is coded for execution on various systems is often used so that the problem-solving ability of different systems can be compared under similar circumstances.

beta test The stage at which a new product is tested under actual usage conditions. The purpose of beta testing is to locate and correct potential problems before consumer marketing begins.

bibliographic database A type of reference database containing citations to published literature. Included are abstracts, and full citations to newspapers, journals, books, monographs, patents, conference proceedings, contracts, radio or television transcripts, and dissertations.
See also database, reference database.

bidirectional Refers to lines over which data can move in two directions, e.g., via a data bus or a telephone line.

bidirectional printing The ability of a printer head to move in two directions, from left to right and right to left alternately. Bidirection increases the speed at which a printer can output pages.

binary Also called base-2, binary refers to the numbering system using two as its base and consisting of only two symbols: 0 and 1. Binary numbering is based on the addition of progressive powers of two, and it is especially well adapted to computer use since 0 and 1 can be represented as on and off or negative charges and positive charges. The binary digits appear in strings of 0's and 1's. Most computers do their calculations in binary.

binary coded decimal (BCD) A system of number representation in which each decimal digit is represented by four binary digits. These digits are actually the ASCII code representations for the individual decimal numbers, minus the three digits at the extreme left of the 7-bit ASCII code. Letters and symbols are represented by using four numeric and the two zone channels.

binary digit (bit) The fundamental unit of binary notation, represented logically by 0 or 1 and electrically by 0 volts and 5 volts. The bit can take the form of a magnetized spot, an electronic impulse, a positively charged magnetic core, or a tone. A number of bits together are used to represent a character in the computer.
See also byte, word.

binary synchronous transmission (bisync) Data transmission in which synchronization of characters is controlled by timing signals generated at the sending and receiving stations.
Compare asynchronous transmission.

bipolar Literally, having two poles. An input signal is bipolar when one electrical voltage polarity represents a logically true input, and its opposite polarity represents a logically false input. Contrasts with unipolar, a situation resulting when both logical opposites are represented by the same electrical voltage polarity.

bistable Refers to a circuit that can assume one of two states. The application of an energy pulse will cause a reversal so that if the current state is 1, the pulse will cause it to become 0.

bit A binary digit. This is the most basic element of a binary number, consisting of either a 1 or a 0. Grouped bits are used as codes to represent different kinds of information to the computer. The most common group sizes are 4 and 8 bits and are called words. Bit also refers to the one unit of storage space in the computer's memory, or the most elementary representation of data: usually the presence of voltage represents a 1 while the absence of voltage represents 0.

bit-mapped   Refers to a display screen on which a character or image is generated or refreshed from a bit-map memory. The bit-map contains a bit for each point or dot on the screen and allows for very fine resolution since any point on the screen can be addressed. Movement of the scan beam is directed by software or microcode rather than by a character generator in order to create characters and/or graphics. Image resolution is usually referred to in pixels (picture elements).

bit-slice processor   A microprocessor designed to allow microcomputer organizations of variable word sizes, with processor units separated into 2-, 4-, or 8-bit slices on a single chip. These devices can be paralleled to yield an 8-, 12-, 16-, 24-, or 32-bit microcomputer when assembled with the other necessary overhead components of the system.

bit transfer rate   The number of bits transferred per unit time, usually expressed in bits per second (bps).

blinking   Refers to the flashing or pulsing of the cursor on a display screen which is designed to attract the operator's attention.

block   A group of characters, bytes, or words communicated as a unit. Also, a generic term for any kind of grouped data, such as bits, words, bytes, or records, that are handled as a single unit. The term is also associated with a contiguous group of records on a disk.
See also packet.

block diagram   A diagram in which a system or computer program is represented by annotated boxes and interconnecting lines to show its basic function and the functional relationship between the parts.
See also flowchart.

blocking   Combining two or more records into one block.

blocking factor   The number of logical records combined into one physical record or block. If the blocking factor were four, there would then be four logical records in one (physical) block.

block length   A measure of the size of a block, usually specified in units such as records, words, computer words, or characters.

block move   Moving a block of data or text as a single unit. Usually this process can be viewed on the monitor.

block sort   A sorting method that puts the data into smaller groups for further sorting.

block transfer   Moving an entire block of data, either from one memory location to another or between a memory location and an external drive.

board   The sheet on which integrated circuits are mounted.

boolean algebra   A binary system of algebra where the variables do not represent numbers but statements and logical operations, e.g., or, and, nor. This allows the computer to follow different instructions depending on the result of a comparison.

boolean logic   See boolean algebra.

booting   A technique for loading a program into a computer's memory in which the program's initial instructions direct the loading of the rest of the program. Usually a few manual instructions must be entered on a keyboard or a switch implemented to initiate the process.

bootstrap   Long for "boot." Refers to the technique whereby the program can get itself up and running, to pull itself into functionality by its own bootstraps. The bootstrap program usually resides in the system monitor ROM bridge.

bps   Bits per second. In serial data transmission, the instantaneous bit speed with which a device or channel transmits a character.

branch   An instruction in a program that will cause transfer from the current sequence of instructions to a different sequence if certain conditions are satisfied. If the condition is not satisfied, the transfer will be to the next instruction in the sequence.

breadboard   The test or experimental model of a circuit system which is roughly fastened to perforated hobby board. Such a model is generally used as a prototype for planning, design, or feasibility studies. The blank circuit board, called a perf board, is available in hobby stores.

break   An interruption to a transmission; usually a provision to allow a controlled terminal to interrupt the controlling computer.

break key   A keyboard character that is programmed to stop the existing program when pressed and to wait for further instructions.

breakpoint   A term associated with on-line debugging; refers to the stop points in the program's execution that are used to monitor the program's progress. In addition to examining the program's variables at these assigned breakpoints, the programmer can also temporarily change the variables in order to test different conditions within the program.

broadband   See wideband.

broadband exchange (BEX)   Public switched communication system of Western Union featuring various bandwidth full-duplex connections.

broadband transmission   A high frequency mode of

transmission often used with local area networks (LAN). Coaxial cables may sometimes be used which will permit longer transmission distance than is possible with baseband transmission.

broadcast   Transmission to a number of receiving locations simultaneously; normally associated with a multidrop line, where a number of terminals share the line.

BSC   An IBM designation meaning Binary Synchronous Communication. Refers to a specific communications procedure using synchronous data transmission.

BTAM   An IBM designation meaning Basic Telecommunication Access Method. Refers to the use of macro instructions to achieve date communications with specific terminals.

bubble memories   Tiny cylinders of magnetization whose axes lie perpendicular to the plane of the single-crystal sheet that contains them. Magnetic bubbles arise when two magnetic fields are applied perpendicular to the sheet. A constant field strengthens and fattens the regions of the sheet whose magnetization lies along it. A pulsed field then breaks the strengthened regions into isolated bubbles, which are free to move within the plane of the sheet. Because the presence or absence of bubbles can represent digital information, and because other external fields can manipulate this information, magnetic bubble devices will likely find uses in future data storage systems.

bubble sort   A program to sort many types of data through exchanges of pairs of numbers. Bubble sort is considered relatively easy to program, but execution may be slow.

buffer   A high-speed area of storage that is temporarily reserved for use in performing the input/output operation, into which data is read or from which data is written. Used to accumulate data into blocks of sufficient size to be handled efficiently by a processor or terminal. Synonymous with I/O area.

bug   A program defect or error. According to legend, in 1946, Grace Hopper detected a problem with an Eniac computer at the University of Pennsylvania. Investigation uncovered an insect lodged within the computer

causing the malfunction. Hopper is reported to have said, "There's a bug in the computer."

bundled   A pricing strategy in which a computer manufacturer includes all products—hardware, software, services, training, etc. in a single price.

burn-in   A testing procedure which refers to the operation of a new device off the assembly line for a specified amount of time, often at the limits of operating temperature. This process pinpoints component failures that are due to defective manufacture. Similarly, it is always a good idea to leave a newly purchased piece of computer equipment turned on for several days. In this way, problems will occur while the machine is still under warranty.

burst   In computer operations, the action of separating continuous-form paper into discrete sheets. In data transmissions, a sequence of signals counted as one unit.

bus   A path or channel for transmitting electrical signals and data, usually between a computer and peripheral equipment.

business application   An application that pertains to the functions of a business, e.g., invoicing, accounting, etc.

business data processing   Synonym for administrative data processing.
See also data processing.

business processes   The essential activities and decision areas in a business.

business systems planning (BSP)   A structured approach to assist a business in establishing an information systems plan to satisfy its near- and long-term information needs.

byte   A sequence of bits operated upon as a unit and usually shorter than a computer word. The representation of a character. Often, a sequence of eight adjacent binary digits that are operated upon as a unit and that constitute the smallest addressable unit in the system.

C   High-level programming language that can often be used in lieu of the lower-level assembler language. C was developed at Bell Laboratories for writing systems software, and the UNIX system, also developed at Bell Labs, was written using the C language.

cable connector   A device that provides the male and/or female plugs necessary for connecting industry-standard cables, such as the RS-232, together.

cache memory   A high-speed, buffer-type memory filled at medium speed from the main memory. Programs and instructions found in the cache memory can be operated at higher speeds without the necessity of loading another segment.

CAD/CAM   Computer-aided design/computer-aided manufacturing. These terms describe systems that aid in the design of products and then transfer the information to computer-controlled manufacturing equipment.

CAI   See computer-assisted instruction.

call   A request by the operating system, i.e., for display, the access of memory, confirmation, etc.

calling sequence   The set of instructions that serves as a linkage going to and returning from program subroutines.

call instruction   A type of instruction which permits a return to the program's original sequence after diverting execution to a new sequence of instructions.

CAM   Computer-aided manufacturing. The use of computerized data to control machines.

cancel   To stop or abort a command or program procedure in progress, or to perform the same action pending execution.

canned program   A software program written to meet the expected needs of a certain application.
    Compare custom software.

capacitor   A device consisting of two plates separated by insulating material and designed to store an electrical charge. Capacitors block the flow of DC and allow the flow of AC.

card   The individual circuit boards that carry the necessary electronics for particular functions, e.g., memory, disk drive control, etc. These cards or boards neatly fit into expansion slots provided by Apple, IBM, Radio Shack, and other computer manufacturers.

card cage   A frame for holding circuit cards in a microprocessor. A standard cage holds 9 cards; units with motherboards can hold up to 20 cards. Also referred to as card chassis.

card reader   A device that can transcribe punched-hole data from paper cards into electrical impulses for input into computer memory.

carriage   The assembly in a printer that moves the paper past the print mechanism or vice versa.

carriage return   The act of returning the carriage to the beginning of a line.

carrier   A continuous frequency capable of being modulated or impressed with a signal.

carrier system   A measure of obtaining a number of channels over a single path by modulating each channel on a different carrier frequency and demodulating at the receiving point to restore the signals to their original form.

cartridge   Magnetic tape loaded into a cartridge (such as the single reel IBM MT/ST cartridge or the reel-to-reel 3M Data Cartridge) that holds multiple pages of text. Used by older processing systems for text and sometimes program storage. Also, the term refers to a 2×3-inch plastic box that contains ROM software, such as BASIC for the TI 99/A.

cassette   A small, self-contained volume of magnetic tape used for data storage. Similar to a sound recording cassette.

cassette drive   A standard tape recorder.

cassette interface   The special circuitry used to control data transfer between a cassette tape recorder and a computer.

cassette recording   An audio recording of analog signals representing continuous tones.

catalogue   To place data sets permanently in a storage device for use when required. This technique avoids having to read in a deck of cards each time the program or data are required.

cathode ray tube terminal   See CRT display device.

CAV   Constant angular velocity. A disk recording method that records the same amount of information on each track—the data is more densely packed on tracks closer to the center.

CBASIC   A compiler version of the BASIC programming language, designed for use with the 8080 and Z80 family of microprocessors.

CBBS Computerized bulletin board service.

cell Storage location. The storage position of one unit of information, such as a character, a bit, or a word.

centralized (computer) network A computer network configuration in which a central node provides computing power, control, or other services.
Compare decentralized network.

centralized data processing Data processing performed at a single, central location on data obtained from several geographical locations or managerial levels. Decentralized data processing involves processing at various managerial levels or geographical points throughout the organization.

central processor Central processing unit. See CPU.

Centronics Interface An 8-bit, parallel interface that has become the de facto standard for microcomputer printers. Peripherals can be connected to the computer using the same standards as printers from the Centronics Corporation.

certification An authoritative endorsement of the correctness of a program, analogous to the certification of electrical equipment by the Underwriters Laboratories.

chained files Data files that consist of a data block series in which the blocks are chained together using forward and backward pointers.

chained list A list in which each item points to the next item and the order of retrieval does not necessarily have any relation to the storage order.

chained sector A storage method that allows one logical unit to be spread across different areas on disk instead of being stored in one contiguous area.

chaining A system of storing records in which each record belongs to a list or group of records and has a linking field for tracing the chain.

chaining search A search method in which each item that is found has information that leads to the next item in the chain. The search depends on a specific identifier and the chain continues until the end is reached or until the desired record is found.

channel In data communications, a path for electrical transmission between two or more points. Also called a circuit, facility, line, link, or path. Within a computer, the device along which data flows between the input-output units of a computer and the CPU. Devices attached to the CPU communicate electronically with it via these channels.

channel adapter A device that enables communication between data channels on different hardware.

channel capacity A term which expresses the maximum bit rate that can be handled by the channel.

character An individual letter, numeral, or special character. In computers, characters are made up of a number of bits. Synonymous with byte.

character code A code such as ASCII (American Standard Code for Information Exchange) or ISO (International Standards Organization) that assigns a special standardized group of binary digits to each printed character.

character generator The subsystem in a display unit or printer that creates characters from the codes used to represent them.

character pitch The number of characters per inch in a line of text.

character pitch display The ability of a printer to output characters in a number of different pitches or sizes as requested by the software.

character printer A device that prints a single character at a time.
Compare line printer.

character set The total number of different characters displayable, including alphabetics, numerics, and special symbols.

character size control The ability to view the full page of data at a regular size or one-half page at double size.

charge coupled device A semiconductor device for high-density memory storage with low power consumption. Sometimes called a bucket brigade device because of the way in which it transfers charges at prescribed intervals, resulting in a ripple process.

chart See flowchart.

check digit A digit added to each number in a coding system which allows for detection of errors in the recording of the code numbers. Through the use of the check digit and a predetermined mathematical formula, recording errors such as digit reversal can be noted. Synonymous with parity bit.

checkout See debug.

checkpoint/restart facility A facility for restarting

execution of a program at some point other than the beginning after the program was terminated due to a program or system failure. A restart can begin at a checkpoint or from the beginning of a job step and uses checkpoint records to reinitialize the system. In teleprocessing, a facility that records the status of the teleprocessing network at designated intervals or following certain events. Following system failure, the system can be restarted and continue without loss of message.

checksum   Short for summation check, a technique for determining whether a package of data is valid. The package, which is a string of binary digits, is added up and compared with the expected number.

chips   Microprocessors that are complete computers on a single chip of silicon. No larger than one-half-inch square, and in many cases much smaller, they contain all the essential elements of a central processor including the control logic, instruction decoding, and arithmetic processing circuitry. To be useful, the microprocessor chip or chips are combined with memory and I/O integrated circuit chips to from a microcomputer. They usually fill no more than a single printed circuit board.

CIM   Computer Input Microfilm, a system that uses microfilm technology rather than printing on paper.

circuit   In communications, the complete transmission path providing one- or two-way communication between two points comprising associated go and return channels.
   See also channel.

circuit board   A board on which are mounted integrated circuits in a microprocessor; also called circuit cards or cards. Multiple boards can be held in a card cage or motherboard.

circuit capacity   The number of channels in a circuit that can be dealt with simultaneously.

circuit grade   The information-carrying capability of a circuit, in speed or type of signal. For data use, these grades are identified with certain speed ranges.

circuit switching   A method of communications where an electrical connection between calling and called stations is established on demand for exclusive use of the circuit until the connection is released.
   See also message switching, packet switching, store and forward.

clear   To place every storage location or cell in the same state, usually zero or blank.

clear to send (CTS)   An RS-232 standard control signal used in line control sequences to indicate the availability of a data link for transmission in a particular direction.

clipping   A program procedure used to avoid unwanted shifting to the side of an image that is too large for the display. A clipping procedure determines which parts of the picture lie outside the screen's boundaries and thus eliminates those portions.

clock   A repetitive signal device used to control a synchronous computer.

clock generator   A timing device which generates periodic signals, controlling and regulating the timing of all operations in a microprocessor.

clock rate   The speed at which pulses are emitted from a clock generator. The unit of measure for a clock cycle is megahertz, or millions of cycles per second.

CLS (clear screen)   A common data processing expression instructing the operator to clear, or blank, the video display screen.

CLV   Constant linear velocity. A disk recording method that alters the rational speed of the disk as the recording heads move in and out to maintain a constant relative speed.

CMOS   Complementary metal-oxide semiconductor, a technology that makes a type of integrated circuit that consumes less power and expends less heat. This type of semiconductor will be used in more and more microcomputers, especially portables, because of its properties.

coaxial cable   A cable consisting of one conductor, usually a small copper tube or wire, within and surrounded by a shield made of a separate electrically insulated wire.

COBOL   Common Business Oriented Language. A data processing language that makes use of English language statements. It is especially adapted to business and commercial problems.

CODASYL   Conference On Data Systems Languages. The conference which developed COBOL.

code   The conventions specifying how data can be represented in a particular system.

coder   A person whose primary duty is to write (but not design) computer programs.

coding   Writing of a list of instructions which will cause a computer to perform specified operations.

cold boot   The first initialization of the computer, or booting just after the computer has been turned on.
   See also bootstrap.

cold start   The restart activity following a serious failure in a real-time system which has made the direct access storage inaccessible, and recent processing cannot be used. The system must be loaded and activity restarted in initial program load mode.

COLOR   A BASIC command that is unique to computers that have color graphics capability. This command tells the computer what color to use.

color register   The specific location in the computer's memory that stores a color for a particular program.

collating sequence   The order in which various sets of data are merged when they are combined into one set.

column   A vertical arrangement of characters.

COMAL   Common algorithmic language. An all-purpose programming language that combines the ease of BASIC with the powerful structures of PASCAL.

command   A signal or group of signals which causes a computer to execute an operation or series of operations.

command-driven   Programs that require the task to be performed be described in a special language with strict adherence to syntax.
Compare menu-driven.

command language   A source language consisting primarily of commands capable of invoking a function.

comment   A string of information in a computer program meant for people to read and not for the machine to operate; also referred to as remarks.

common carrier   A government-regulated private company that furnishes the general public with telecommunications service facilities, for example, a telephone or telegraph company.

common storage   A portion of memory for each user that holds data or parameters that are accessible to all programs.

communication   Transmission of intelligence between points of origin and reception without alteration of sequence or structure of the information content.
See also data communication.

communication control characters   In ASCII, a functional character intended to control or faciliate transmission over data networks. There are ten control characters specified in ASCII which forms the basis for character oriented communications control procedures.
See also control character.

communication line   Any medium, such as a wire or a telephone circuit, that connects a remote station with a computer for the purpose of transmitting and/or receiving information.

communications channel   See channel.

communications computer   See communications controllers.

communications controllers   Dedicated computers with special processing capabilities for organizing and checking data. Such controllers handle information traffic to and from many remote terminals or computers, including such functions as message switching. Also called front-end communications processors.

communications processor   See communications controller.

compare   To examine the relationship between two pieces of data and present the result.

compatibility   The characteristic of data processing equipment by which one machine may accept and process data prepared by another machine without conversion or code modification.

compatible software   The ability of software to run on different computers without modification. Also, a feature that enables different applications programs, such as Framework and WordStar, to share common conventions and rules so that they can be run together as one coordinated package.

compilation time   The time during which a source language is compiled or translated into a machine language object program as opposed to the time during which the program is actually being run (execution time).

compile   To prepare a machine language program from a high-level, symbolic language program by generating more than one machine instruction for each symbolic statement, as well as performing the function of an assembler.

compilers   Programs that accept instructions in high-level language and convert each instruction into a multitude of machine language instructions from which the computer can run the jobs. Also called language processors. If a programmer uses a compiler language, the compiler will, for all practical purposes, become the computer; making the register sets, flags, and other such data invisible to the programmer. But, if users want to make full use of all the ranges, flexibilities and capabilities of a computer, they will program in assembly language.

compression   See data compression.

compute (CPU) bound Generally refers to a limit upon output because operations are delayed awaiting completion of a computation operation. Synonymous with compute limited.

Compare I/O bound.

computer A device capable of solving problems or manipulating data by accepting data, performing prescribed operations on the data, and supplying the results of these operations. Various types of computers are: analog, digital, and calculator.

computer-aided design (CAD) The use of a computer plus peripherals to perform various operations according to design specifications, especially when a graphic representation is desired.

computer-assisted instruction (CAI) A data processing application in which a computing system is used to assist in the instruction of students. The application usually involves a dialog between students and a computer program which informs them of their mistakes as they make them.

computer graphics Graphs, charts, and drawings that are generated by computer. These graphics can be displayed on the video monitor or output to a dot-matrix printer or to a plotter. Some systems, such as the Macintosh, add digitized imaging techniques to the graphics representation.

computer-independent language A high-level language designed for use in any computer equipped with an appropriate compiler, and relatively independent of such characteristics as word size and code representations. COBOL, Fortran, and RPG are computer-independent.

computer language The grammar, reserved words, symbols, and techniques that constitute the communication interface with a computer system.

computer literacy General learning, knowledge, and fluency with computer terms and computer usage.

computer network An interconnection of two or more computer systems, terminals, and communications facilities.

computer network components Facilities that support the host computer, including the user communication interface, the communications subnetwork, and facilities for the network control function.

computer program A series of instructions or statements in a form acceptable to a computer prepared in order to achieve a certain result.

computer science The study of computer hardware and software.

computing system A central processing unit, with main storage, input/output channels, control units, direct access storage devices, and input/output devices connected to it.

COMSAT The Communications Satellite Corporation. A privately owned communications carrier company incorporated in 1963.

concatenation A linking together of character strings to form a single character string.

concentrator A device which makes a larger number of input channels with a fewer number of output channels. The input channels are usually low-speed, asynchronous, and the output channel is high-speed, synchronous. The low-speed channels may have the capability to be polled by a computer and may in turn poll terminals.

conceptual network models In information system planning, definition of the major systems and how they interrelate, and determination of the data flow between and among the systems.

concurrent processing The simultaneous processing of more than one program.

conditional branch A transfer of control within a program, dependent upon a certain condition being met either by a mathematical or logical operation or a combination of the two.

See also conditional transfer.

conditional transfer An instruction that may cause a departure from the sequence of instructions being followed depending upon the result of an operation, the contents of a register, or the setting of an indicator.

conditioning The addition of equipment to voice grade lines to provide specified minimum values of line characteristics, in ranges from C1 to the best, C4. The common carrier will often recommend no conditioning for lines transmitting at 1200 baud; C1 conditioning is recommended for 2400 baud, C2 for 4800 baud, and C4 for speeds over 4800 baud.

configuration A group of machines which are interconnected and are programmed to operate as a system.

connect time A measure of system usage by a user, usually the time interval during which the user terminal was on-line during a session.

See also CPU time.

console That part of a computer used for communication between the operator or maintenance engineer and the computer. A CRT terminal or typewriter console is the most common.

console debugging Debugging a program at the machine console or at a remote console by slowly stepping the machine through each instruction and observing the contents of appropriate registers and memory locations.

constant Data that does not vary in value.
Compare variable.

contention A condition on a communications channel or in a peripheral device when two or more stations try to transmit at the same time, or when access to a resource is simultaneously required by two or more users.

contention system A technique of trial and error when transmitting data on a local area network (LAN). If the data channel is free, transmission may occur. If not, the sending station must wait and try at a later time. A contention system permits multiple users without requiring central control.

continuous form A supply of paper made up of numerous individual sheets separated by perforations and folded to form a pack. Sprocket holes are punched in the margins to permit automatic feed through the printer.

continuous tone image A black and white or color image formed of combinations of separate areas made up of different color tones or gray tones.

control board A visual means of showing machine loading or project planning.
See also control chart.

control cards See job control language.

control characters A character whose occurrence in a particular context initiates, modifies, or stops a control function. In the ASCII code, any of the 32 characters in the first two columns of the standard code table.

control chart Usually a large piece of graph paper used in the same manner as a control board. Where the control board often uses strings and pegs or movable slips of paper to represent the plan and progress, the control chart typically would be filled in in pencil.
See also control board.

control information Information that is sent between devices in order to control their functions.

control key A computer key that alters the meaning of another key; usually used to generate commands.

controller Electronic circuitry, usually a microprocessor, that allows communication between a computer processing unit and a peripheral device.

control panel That part of a console that actually contains the controls and indicators.

control procedure The means to control communication of information in an orderly way between stations on a data link; sometimes known as link discipline.
See also protocol.

control program An operating system support program that monitors the flow of transactions in a computer system; for example, a date communication program.

control section That section of the CPU that interprets instructions and directs the operation of all of the other units of the computer system. It has a temporary memory called a scratch pad where contents of registers are stored.

control station The network station which supervises control procedures such as polling, selecting, and recovery. It is also responsible for establishing order on the line in the event of contention or any other abnormal situation.

control unit Intermediary device between peripheral devices and channel. May be part of the I/O device or actual hardware.

conversational A program or a system that carries on a dialog with a terminal user, alternately accepting input and then responding to the input quickly enough for the user to maintain his train of thought.
See also interactive.

conversational mode Communication between a terminal and a computer in which each entry from the terminal elicits a response from the computer and vice versa.

conversational time sharing See time sharing.

conversion The process of changing from one method of data processing to another or from one computer system to another; or the controlled transition from an old system to a new one. It involves careful planning for the various steps that have to be taken, and equally careful supervision of their execution. Also applies to the representation of data.

coordinate paper A continuous-feed graph paper that is used for printouts on a plotting device.

coordinate system A representation of measurement along axes or intersecting lines. It is used to create graphs showing computation results or comparisons.

coordination models A class of operations research models involving the relationship between the starting times of the component tasks of a project and the completion date of the project.

co-processor   An additional processor working with the main processor which does specific tasks while the main processor executes its primary tasks. Frequently, special co-processor chips are added to speed up mathematical tasks.

copy   To reproduce data in a new location without changing the original data source, although the form the new data takes may differ from the original data source.

core image library   A library of machine language versions of user programs that have been produced as output from link-editing. The programs in the core image library are in a format that is executable either directly or after processing by the relocating loader in the supervisor.

core memory   An obsolete main memory technology. It was the computer's internal information storehouse. Core memory was fast and expensive. Information in core memory is located by addresses. Physically, core memory is made up of tiny doughnut-shaped pieces of magnetizable material that can be in either an on or off state to represent either a binary 1 (on) or binary 0 (off).

counter   A device (e.g., a register) used to represent the number of occurrences of an event.

coupling   Connecting two or more computers together at one site to share the workload, the resources (e.g., disk drives, memory), and provide immediate backup for one another in case of malfunction.

courseware   Computer programs that are used in teaching environments.

CPM   See critical path method.

CP/M   Abbreviation for control program microcomputer, a family of operating systems developed by Digital Research, Inc.

CP/M-68K   A CP/M implementation for the Motorola 68000 series of microprocessors.

CP/M-80   An 8-bit generation of the CP/M operating systems, used on the 8080, Z80, and 8085 based microcomputers. CP/M-80 was the first transportable operating system.

CP/M-86   A 16-bit generation of the CP/M operating system used on the IBM Personal Computer.

cps   Characters per second.

CPU (central processing unit)   The heart of the general purpose computer that controls the interpretation and execution of instructions. Does not include interface, main memory, or peripherals. It also controls input and output units and auxiliary attachments. Synonymous with mainframe.

CPU busy time   Same as CPU time.

CPU handshaking   Interaction between a CPU and peripheral devices or between the CPU and users.

CPU time   The amount of time devoted by the central processing unit to the execution of instructions. Synonymous with CPU busy time.
   See also connect time.

crash   A breakdown resulting from software or hardware malfunction.

CRC   See cyclic redundancy check.

critical path method (CPM)   A technique that defines a project in terms of its component events. By ordering the events and showing their interdependency, this method allows the user the ability to isolate the critical events whose delay might cause eventual delay to the overall completion of the project. These events are said to lie on a critical path. Programmers generally use a diagram to map out the parallel paths along a time scale to show the critical path of those functions which, if delayed, would postpone the entire project.

CROM   Control read-only memory. The storage area in a CPU that is set aside for the instructions that form procedures such as branch, add, etc.

cross-assembler program   A program run on one computer but which was built or prepared on another computer. Small computers, especially microcomputers, generally do not have enough memory or are not equipped with the necessary peripheral devices to support many utility programs. In such a situation, another, larger computer is used to perform the assembly or compilation, and the programs used are called cross-assemblers or cross-compilers. For example, a microcomputer program might be cross-assembled on a time-sharing system or a large mainframe.

cross-compiler   A program that translates instructions from a high-level language on one computer to the machine language of another computer on which the program is to be run.

crosstalk   Voice communications in one circuit being overheard in another circuit.

CRT display device   A televisionlike picture tube used in visual display terminals on which images are produced on a cathode ray tube. The CRT enables batches or blocks of information in memory to be instantly accessed, read, and displayed on a screen. In an on-line or real-time data processing system, the device permits instant or impromptu display of any desired information. It eliminates the necessity for printing the same information where the display, in temporary form, serves the application needed.

crystal   A quartz crystal that, due to its piezoelectric properties, vibrates at a specific frequency when energy is supplied to it. The vibrations provide a highly accurate frequency by which to time the clock within a computer system.

CTRL   Abbreviation for control.

CTS   Clear to send.

CU   Control unit. A CPU hardware component which is responsible for the sequencing, interpretation, and execution of instructions.

current   The rate at which electrons move past a given point in a given amount of time. Measured in amperes. Most microcomputers are low-current devices, using no more electricity than a regular light bulb.

current loop   Transmission technique that recognizes current flows rather than voltage levels. It has traditionally been used in teletypewriter networks incorporating batteries as the transmission power source.

cursor   A position indicator frequently employed in CRT terminals to indicate a character to be corrected or a position in which data is to be entered.

cursor keys   Keys that move the cursor; usually designated with arrows.

cursor positioning   Describes the action of moving the cursor in different directions.

cursor tracking   Controlling a cursor on a graphics display by moving a stylus on a graphics tablet connected to the terminal.

curve follower   A peripheral device that will read data represented on a graph.

customer engineer (CE)   An individual responsible for field maintenance of computer hardware and software.

custom software   Programs designed by special order to serve a user's specific requirements. Usually more costly in the short run than packaged or canned software.

cut & paste   A text editing function that moves text from one place to another.

cut-sheet feeder   A device that fits on a printer and feeds individual sheets of paper (cut sheets).

cybernetics   The field of science involved in the comparative study of the automatic control of, regulation of, and communication between machine and human. These studies include comparisons between information-handling machines and the brains and nervous systems of animals and humans.

cycle stealing   Taking an occasional machine cycle from a CPU's regular activities in order to control such things as an input or output operation. Commonly used on minicomputers.

cycle time   The time it takes for a device to complete its cycle and become available again.

cyclic redundancy check (CRC)   A data transmission error detection scheme in which the check character is generated by taking the remainder after dividing all the serialized bits in a block of data by a predetermined binary number.

cylinder   A group of tracks which can be read without moving the access mechanism on a disk storage device.

D/A   Digital to analog. The act of converting digital electrical signals (individual, separate units) from the computer into analog or continuous signals, such as sound, voltage, etc. Such conversion is used to drive external devices, such as a music synthesizers, that require analog input.

daisy chain   Refers to the movement of signals from one point to another along a bus; a method of prioritizing interrupts.

daisy wheel   An interchangeable-element, electronic-impact printer, offering faster print speeds than a Selectric typewriter-printer and producing a fully formed character. The printing element is shaped like a wheel with radial spokes; each spoke has a single raised character on the end. As the wheel turns, the spokes are hit by a tiny hammer.

data   A general term used to denote any or all facts, numbers, letters, symbols, etc., which can be processed or produced by a computer; or the source data or raw data as contrasted with information obtained by the processing of data.

data access arrangement (DAA)   Data communication equipment furnished by a common carrier, permitting attachment of privately owned data terminal and data communication equipment to the common carrier network.

data acquisition   The retrieval of data from remote sites initiated by a central computer system; i.e., retrieving data during off-hours processing from a previously mounted magnetic tape at an unattended terminal, or taking periodic readings from an unattended real-time station.

data aggregate   A collection of data items within a record, which is given a name and referred to as a whole.

data bank   A comprehensive collection of libraries of data. For example, one line of an invoice may form an item, a complete invoice may form a record, a complete set of such records may form a file, the collection of inventory control files may form a library, and the libraries used by an organization are known as its data bank. Synonymous with database.

database   A nonredundant collection of interrelated data items processable by one or more applications. Nonredundant means that individual data elements appear only once (or at least less frequently than in normal file organizations) in the database. Interrelated means that the files are constructed with an ordered and planned relationship that allows data elements to be tied together, even though they may not necessarily be in the same physical record. Processable by one or more applications means simply that data is shared and used by several different subsystems.

Development of a database has some obvious benefits. By consolidating files, the user can obtain better control of data and reduce storage space and processing time. Equally important are the resultant data synchronization and timelines. Use of a single information source makes processing more accurate because all subsystems refer to the same data. A database system helps overcome some of the complexities of data management by managing data centrally. It can provide additional data relationships while minimizing storage redundancy.

While the data are stored together with as little redundancy as possible to serve one or more applications in an optimal fashion, some measure of redundancy exists in many databases in order to give improved access times or simpler addressing methods. Some records are duplicated to provide the capability to recover from accidental loss of data. There is a tradeoff between nonredundancy and other desirable criteria.

database administrator   The custodian of the corporation's data—or that part of it which that system relates to. The database administrator controls the overall structure of the data.

database management system   A systematic approach to storing, updating, and retrieval of information stored as data items, usually in the form of records in a file, where many users access common data banks.

database producer   A company or organization that collects and arranges the data for a database.

data center   This is an abbreviated term applied to a computer-equipped, central location. The center processes data and converts it to a desired form such as reports or other types of management information records.

data chaining   A technique in which parts of records are stored in areas that are not contiguous, but are referenced as a whole by each record having the ability to call the next.

data channel   A two-way link for communication between two points.

data class   A category of logically related information, e.g., customer, vendor, customer orders, parts inventory, and appropriations.

data collection   The act of bringing data from one or more points to a central point.

data communication equipment   The equipment that provides the functions required to establish, maintain, and terminate a connection, the signal conversion, and coding required for communication between data terminal and data circuit. The data communication equipment may or may not be an integral part of a computer; e.g., a modem.

data communications   The transmission and reception of data, often including operations such as coding, decoding, and validation. Much data communications is carried over ordinary telephone lines, but often it requires specially conditioned leased lines where in effect, several telephone lines are linked side by side to provide the required wide carrier bandwidth which carry a heavy and broad flow of information traffic. This is in contrast to voice-grade communication for which narrower carrier bandwidths are sufficient.

See also data transmission, telecommunications.

data compression   A technique that saves storage space by eliminating gaps, empty fields, redundancies, or unnecessary data to shorten the length of records or blocks. For data transmission a byte string of data is transmitted as a count plus a string value.

data concentration   Collection of data at an intermediate point from several low- and medium-speed lines for retransmission across high-speed lines.

data division   One of the four main component parts of a COBOL program. The data division describes the files to be used in the program and the records contained within the files. It also describes any internal working-storage records that will be needed.

data entry   Entering data into a computer.

data file   A collection of related data records organized in a specific manner. Data files are currently being replaced in information system design by a database.

data independence   Often cited as being one of the main attributes of a database, the term implies that the data and the application programs which use them are independent so that either may be changed without changing the other.

data integrity   A performance measure based on the rate of undetected errors.
See also integrity.

data item   The smallest unit of named data. It may consist of any number of bits or bytes. A data item is often referred to as a field data element.

data link   The communications lines, modems, and communication controls used in transmitting information between two or more stations.

data logging   Recording data about events in the time sequence in which they happen.

data management system   Assigns responsibility for data input and integrity, within the organization, to establish and maintain the database. Also provides necessary procedures and programs to collect, organize and maintain the data required by the information systems.

data manipulation language (DML)   The interface between the application program and the database management system, referred to as the data manipulation language, is embedded in a host language such as COBOL. It is desirable that it should have a syntax compatible with the host language because the application program has host language and data manipulation language statements intimately mixed.

data processing   The execution of a programmed sequence of operations upon data. A generic term for computing in business situations and other applications with machines such as bookkeeping machines, digital computers, etc.

data processing system   A network of machine components capable of accepting information, processing it according to a plan, and producing the desired results.

data protection   Measures to safeguard data from undesired occurrences that intentionally or unintentionally lead to modification, destruction, or disclosure of data.

dataset   Same as modem.

data sharing   The ability of users or computer processes at several nodes to access data at a single node.

data sink   Any device that can accept data signals from a data transmission device.

data storage   The preservation of data in various data media for direct use by the system.

data terminal equipment (DTE)   The source of data and the destination of data. Data communication equipment (DCE) is the hardware that does the actual communicating, the classic example of which is the modem. It can be thought of as a loop with a DTE at either end, with each end talking to a modem (DCE) and each modem talking to the other. A modem port on a computer is generally set up to a DCE device.

data transmission   The sending of data from one part of a system to another part.
See also data communications.

dating routine   A set of instructions which computes or stores the date (such as the current day's date).

DB/DC systems   Database/data communications systems.

DBMS   Database management system. Application software that is designed to organize data so that it can be quickly filled in or retrieved.

DDD   Direct-distance dialing, or the facility that is used to make long-distance calls without operator assistance. DDD is frequently used to mean the switched telephone network.

DDP   Distributed data processing. Decentralized computer power arranged by hooking two or more processors together in a network so that each CPU is not tied up with processing information not related to its specific function.

dead halt   A halt situation in which the system cannot return to the point at which it stopped. Same as drop dead halt.

deadlock   The unresolved contention for the use of a resource.

deadly embrace A state of a system in which it is logically impossible for the activity to continue. A deadly embrace may result, for example, when the existence of a response is not recognized.

deblocking Separating blocked data into individual logical records.

debug Checking the logic of a program to isolate and remove the mistakes from a computer program or other software. Synonymous with troubleshoot.

debugging The act of troubleshooting, isolating, and removing of errors or malfunctions from a computer or a computer program to improve its accuracy or to restore it to operation.

debugging suppression Suppression of printing repetitions of the same bug in a program. Only the first occurrence of a bug in a loop will be printed out for examination.

decentralized (computer) network A computer network, where some of the network control functions are distributed over several network nodes.
Compare centralized network.

decimal Numeric representation having a selection, choice, or condition in which there are ten possibilities.

decimal digit One of the characters 0 through 9.

decision table A matrix of contingencies that are to be considered with the actions to be taken. Sometimes a decision table is used in place of flowcharts for program documentation.

decision trees An approach toward identifying risks and probabilities in a problem situation involving uncertainty or chance events by sketching in the form of a tree the various courses that might be undertaken. The expected value of each alternative is the sum of the various possible outcomes weighted by their probability of occurring.

declarative statement A source program statement that specifies the format, size, and nature of data.

decode To determine the meaning of a set of signals that describe an operation or an instruction to be executed; or to apply a code that reverses a previous encoding.

decoder A device that translates a set of coded signals.

decrement To decrease a variable or a counter by a fixed quantity.

dedicated line A line permanently assigned to specific data terminals not part of a switched network. Also called a private line.

dedicated system A computer system designed for a primary application such as word processing or graphics. Additional applications may be possible with supplementary components and software.

default What is assumed by the computer if nothing else is specified.

default value The value supplied by the computer system itself when no explicit value is received from the program or user.

degradation factor A measure of the loss in performance that results from reconfiguration of a data processing system, for example, a slow down in run time due to a reduction in the number of central processing units.

degradation testing Measuring the performance of a system at its extreme limit of operation.

delay distortion Distortion resulting from nonuniform speed of transmission of the various frequency components of a signal through a transmission medium.

delete To remove data from context; to remove a record from a file of records or a file from a library of files.

delimiter In data communications, a character that separates and organizes elements of data.

demo-disk A demonstration disk or test disk.

demodulate To turn an analog signal back into a digital one.

demodulation See modem.

density The number of bits in a single linear track measured per unit of length of the recording medium.

depth queuing The technique that is used to enhance the three-dimensional appearance of a two-dimensional subject. Some examples are perspective and shading. Also known as pseudo 3-D.

descenders The parts of lowercase characters that fall below the base line. Some dot matrix printers do not form descenders below the letter base line, but rather squeeze the descendant part of the letter onto the base line.

descriptor Data that designates a record allowing it to be called, classified, sorted, etc.

desktop computer   A personal computer used for business tasks, or one that is located in a corporate environment.

destructive read   A computer memory read process that also erases the data in the source.

detail file   See transaction file.

deterministic model   A mathematical model that, given a set of input data, produces a single output or a single set of output. An example would be an equation for computing the optimum level of inventory for a given product; such a model generates a single number that, given the assumptions of the model, is considered to be the correct answer.

development time   The time used for debugging new routines or hardware. Considered part of the operating time.

device independence   The ability to request I/O operations without regard for the characteristics of specific types of input/output devices.

diagnostic   Pertaining to the detection, discovery, and further isolation of an equipment malfunction or a processing error.

dial exchange   An exchange where all subscribers can originate calls by dialing (Dial Telephone System).

dial-up line   A communications circuit that is established by a switched circuit connection.

dibit   A pair of bits treated as one information element. In modulation schemes with more than two states, multiple bits are represented by each state. The term dibit originally was used for the AT&T 201 series of modems which used four phase states to encode information; each state could therefore represent two bits.

digit   A character used to designate a quantity. The decimal system uses the digits 0-9; the binary system, 0-1; hexadecimal system, 0-F.
   See also binary digit.

digital   Pertains in general to information represented by the code consisting of a sequence of discrete elements; when associated with computers, it usually refers to electrical on/off impulses represented in binary by a 1 or a 0.

digital computer   A computer that solves problems by operating on discrete data representing variables by performing arithmetic and logical processes from a stored program on this data.
   Compare analog computer.

digital data   Information represented by a code consisting of a sequence of discrete elements.

digital reading   A technique that is used for recording information as discrete points onto magnetic recording media, such as magnetic tape or disks.

digitize   To convert a measurement into a number. A substantial amount of data that reaches the computer starts as physical quantities, pressures, temperatures, rates of flow, etc., and is converted to a voltage and then to a number. This is also called analog to digital (A to D) conversion.

digitizer   A device that converts analog measurements, such as those found in a line drawing, into digital form for input into a digital computer.

digitizer, cross-haired cursor   A device used to position each point individually, relative to a system of coordinate axes, when inputting data with a digitizer.

digitizer, three-dimensional   A digitizing device that inputs coordinate information directly from a physical three-dimensional object by means of a movable arm that measures the dimensions. In contrast to a two-dimensional digitizer, which would require scaled drawings of front, side, and top views of a three-dimensional object as input.

dimension   The maximum number and order of a series of related items.

diodes   Usually diodes are in the form of liquid crystal diodes (LCD) or light-emitting diodes (LED) and are especially applicable to portable computers.

DIP   Dual in-line package. Packaging that houses chips and connects to the board with prongs.

DIP switch   A control switch on the dual in-line packaging of chips that allows the user to alter applications or specifications on a particular piece of hardware to which the chip is attached. Examples would be to change the color of the monitor display, the pitch on a printer's output, or the communications parameters on a null modem.

direct-access storage device (DASD)   A basic type of storage medium which allows information to be accessed by positioning the medium or accessing mechanism directly to the information required, thus permitting direct addressing of data locations. The time required for such access is independent of the location of the data most recently accessed. Direct access is synonymous with random access. File organizations can be sequential, direct, or indexed sequential.

Compare sequential access, serial access.

direct distance dialing See DDD.

direct memory access (DMA) A facility that performs I/O transfers directly into or out of memory without passing through the processor's general registers; either performed independently of the processor or on a cycle-stealing basis.

direct numeral control (DNC) A system connecting a set of numerically controlled machines to a common memory for part program or machine program storage, with provision for on-demand distribution of data for the machines. Direct numerical control systems typically have additional provisions for collection, display, or editing of part programs, operator instructions, or data related to the numerical control process.

See also N/C system.

directory The list of all files, which is itself a file, on a computer storage medium such as a floppy disk. The directory is created for the user's easy access to listed files. Also called catalog by some systems.

direct statement An instruction in a program language which is not numbered and is therefore executed by the computer immediately. A direct statement cannot be stored or executed again during a program.

disable To remove a hardware or software feature.

discrete Pertaining to separate, discrete parts.

disk See magnetic disk.

disk, magnetic A flat, circular storage medium capable of storing digital information. It is organized into a hierarchy of tracks and sectors, allowing information to be read or written via random access.

disk cartridge Removable hard disk platters.

disk controller An integrated circuit designed for incorporation into a disk controller board and dedicated to the various functions required to access a disk drive, format a disk, read from and write to the disk, etc.

disk crash The failure of a disk which thereby causes the system to malfunction, usually due to destructive contact between the read/write head of the disk drive and the surface of the disk.

disk drive The device that operates the connection between the computer and the magnetic disk.

disk file A file that resides on a magnetic disk.

disk operating system (DOS) The operating system that manages the disk. An operating system that uses disks for its secondary storage medium. Typically, the disk operating system regulates space allocation, keeps track of files, saves and retrieves files, and manages other control functions associated with disk storage.

disk pack A removable direct-access storage media containing magnetic disks on which data is stored. Disk packs are mounted on a disk storage drive.

disk sector A subdivision of a tract on a magnetic disk; usually the smallest unit of storage operated on by the disk drive at one time.

See also track.

disk storage Information recording on continuously rotating magnetic platters. Handles huge amounts of storage on-line. Storage is random access, meaning the recording arms move quickly to any address (location) on any track on any disk to read or write (record) information. Much faster and more expensive than magnetic tape. However, disk storage is slower than core, but much less expensive for a given amount of information.

disk system All the components required for disk storage, including the disk, disk drive, read/write heads, control electronics, and software.

diskette Flexible or floppy disk. Magnetic-coated mylar disk enclosed in a protective envelope. A standard diskette is 5-1/4 in. in diameter, with a capacity of approximately 75 text pages or 4000 characters per single-spaced page.

display The representation of data in visible form, i.e., cathode ray tube, lights or indicators on the console of a computer, or a printed report.

display buffer memory The number of characters that can be held in storage for immediate display on the screen.

display highlighting Refers to the way that text is emphasized on the screen, using such enhancers as reverse video, underline, blinking, bold, low contrast, and high contrast.

display RAM A randam-access memory area, separate from the main memory, which is used to store the information that will be shown on the video display. This information is usually not retained in memory once the power is turned off.

distortion Any change from the original wave form or signal. Normally, distortion refers to nonpredictable changes which interfere with interpretation of the result.

distributed network A network configuration in which all node pairs are connected either directly, or through redundant paths through intermediate nodes.

distributed processing Distributed-intelligence systems differ from multiprocessing systems in the way that tasks are handled. Although both systems use multiple processors, the tasks assigned to a distributed system remain fixed. By contrast, in a multiprocessing environment, a continuous stream of assignments is fed to a single node and allowed to be distributed according to complex resource allocation algorithms across the entire network.

distributed systems Refers to various arrangements of computers within an organization in which the organization's computer complex has many separate computing facilities all working in a cooperative manner, rather than the conventional single computer at a single location.

dithering With a color display, dithering describes the process of using a combination of juxtaposed different colored dots which in combination will create the illusion of yet another single color. With a black and white display, the process of juxtaposing black and white dots in varying ratios so that groups of these dots will create the illusion of a gray scale tone.

division One of the four major portions of a COBOL program: the identification division, which names the program; the environment division, which indicates the machine equipment and equipment features to be used in the program; the data division, which defines the nature and characteristics of data to be processed; and the procedure division, which consists of statements directing the processing data in a specified manner at execution time.

DMA Direct memory access.

DNC See direct numerical control.

document A medium and the data recorded on it for human use, e.g., a report sheet, a book. By extension, any record that has permanence and that can be read by a human or machine.

documentation The process of collecting and organizing documents or the information recorded in documents. Usually refers to the development of material specifying inputs, operations, and outputs to a computer program. Consists of information that describes an application such as what it does, for whom, when, what data files it uses, etc.

documentation aids Materials that help automate the documentation process, such as flowcharts, programs, etc.

do-loop A command in Fortran and certain other high-level languages that causes a program segment to be executed repeatedly, with values substituted, until certain conditions are satisfied. It then proceeds to the sequence immediately following the loop.

DOS Abbreviation for disk operating system.

dot matrix A method of display character generation in which each character is formed by a grid or matrix pattern of dots.

dot matrix printer A printer with several tiny projecting wires or needles that combine to form dotted representations of individual characters within a matrix. Dot matrix printers have poorer image quality than letter quality printers, but they can type more quickly and are less costly.

double density Term describing the storage of information on a diskette so that the capacity is twice that of a standard diskette. This is accomplished by either doubling the number of tracks per inch, or doubling the serial bit density, or a combination of both.

double precision Pertaining to the use of two computer words to represent a number.

double-sided diskette A type of diskette that utilizes both of its sides for the storage of information. A double-sided diskette can be loaded into a floppy disk drive with dual read/write head assembly or used on a standard single-head drive, taken out, flipped and reinserted for read/record operations on both sides.

Dow Jones News Retrieval Service An information retrieval service of Dow Jones & Company which provides a variety of business information. Available as an on-line system using dumb terminals, it is also one of the personal series package programs for the IBM Personal Computer.

download The process of transferring programs and/or data files from a computer to another device or computer.

down time The period during which a computer, communications line, or other device is malfunctioning or not operating correctly because of mechanical or electronic failure. Opposed to available time, idle time, or stand-by time.

DPMA certificate A certificate given by the Data Processing Management Association which indicates that a person has a certain level of competence in the field of data processing. The certificate is obtained by passing an examination that is offered yearly throughout the United States and Canada.

driver Small programs that are used to control external devices or to run other programs. Driver software directs production, manipulation, and presentation of appropriate signals by the processor so that at the correct moment the peripheral device will perform as required.

drop A connection for a terminal unit on a transmission line.

drop dead halt A halt from which there is no recovery.

drop out In magnetic tape, a recorded signal whose strength is less than a predetermined level. In data transmission, a momentary loss in signal, usually due to the effect of noise or system malfunction.

drum storage Direct access storage that records data magnetically on a rotating cylinder. A type of addressable auxiliary storage associated with some computers. Drum storage is almost never used today.

DSK Dvorak simplified keyboard. See Dvorak keyboard.

DTE See data terminal equipment.

dual channel controller A controller that enables reading from and writing to a device to occur simultaneously.

dual density A technique of writing twice as much information on a diskette.

dual disk drive A floppy disk system with two drive mechanisms and recording heads which allows increased storage capacity and disk-to-disk data transfer and backup.

dual in-line package (DIP) The most common integrated circuit package having dual, or parallel, rows of pins at 0.1 in. intervals.

dual intensity The capability of some printers and display devices to reproduce symbols in both regular and boldface formats.

dual processors A computer that uses two processors, the second of which could be a backup either to perform additional functions or to aid in the use of an auxiliary operating system.

dumb terminal A device with a keyboard for inputting data and a display screen for the output of data but lacking processing capability. A dumb terminal provides remote access to a computer but cannot itself be programmed.

dummy argument Temporary storage that is created automatically to hold the value of an argument that is a constant, an operational expression, a variable whose attributes differ from those specified for the corresponding parameter in a known declaration, or a variable enclosed in parentheses.

dummy variable Used as an argument for a function or subroutine and whose purpose is to transfer the data from the main program to the function or subroutine.

dump To transfer all the information contained in a record into another storage medium. For example, a disk record could be dumped onto tape. However, dump usually refers to copying from an internal storage device to an external storage device for a specific purpose such as to allow other use of the storage, as a safeguard against faults or errors, or in connection with debugging. Also referred to as core dump, tape dump, or disk dump.

duplex Simultaneous two-way independent transmission in both directions. Also referred to a full duplex.

Dvorak keyboard A keyboard arrangement that is easier and faster to use than the standard QWERTY keyboard.
   See also QWERTY keyboard.

dynamic printout A situation in which a computer program directly creates its printed output. Because of the greatly disparate speeds of the computer processing unit and the printer, this situation is usually not preferred. In some computers, a buffer enables the printing to occur without limiting the CPU speed.
   See also spooling.

dynamic programming A method of sequential decision making in which the result of the decision in each stage affords the best possible position to exploit the expected range of likely (yet unpredictable) outcomes in the following decision-making stages.

dynamic RAM Random access memory that cannot be retained without continuous electrical regeneration. Faster, denser, and more expensive than static RAM.
   See also static RAM.

dynaturtle In Logo, a dynamic cursor instead of a static one. The cursor is referred to as a turtle, which is used to produce graphics. Commands to a dynaturtle specify a change in velocity and acceleration during the creation of a drawing. The path of the turtle becomes a line in the drawing.

EAROM device Electrically alterable read only memory. A specialized random access read-memory with a special, slow write cycle and a much faster read cycle, used with microprocessors and microcomputers.

EBCDIC Extended binary coded decimal interchange code. Includes all 51 COBOL characters; this code provides for 256 different bit patterns. This 6-bit code is one of the top basic codes used in the IBM System. The other is an extended version of the USASCII code, called 8-bit USASCII (USASCII-8) used especially by IBM.

echo A portion of the transmitted signal returned from the distant point to the source with sufficient magnitude and delay so as to cause unwanted interference.

echo check An error control technique wherein the receiving terminal or computer returns the original message to the sender to verify that the message was received correctly.

echoplex An echo check applied to network terminals operating in two-way simultaneous mode.

EDAC See error correcting code, error detecting code.

edge card connector A unit that connects printed circuit cards to a motherboard or to other devices such as an input/output device hooked up through cables.

edge connector The electrical socket on a motherboard which mates with the contact strip on a printed circuit board to exchange signals.

edit The insertion of constant characters such as page numbers and decimal points into the computer output to make it more recognizable and meaningful. Editing may include the modification or the addition of data, the deletion of unwanted data, format code conversion, and the application of standard processes such as zero suppression.

editor Software that permits the review and editing of a program or text.

edit run A computer run to validate that the data is within allowable parameters and/or to perform other edit functions.

EDP Electronic data processing. An all-inclusive term liberally interpreted to mean the overall science of converting data by electronic means to any desired form. See also data processing.

effective address The address used by a computer to execute an instruction. Due to a modification in the instruction, this address will differ from the original address in storage.

efficiency The relationship between the planned labor requirements for a task and the actual labor time charged to the task.

EIA Electronic Industries Association.

EIA interface A standard set of signal characteristics (time duration, voltage, and current) specified by the Electronic Industries Association for connection of terminals to modem units, and specific physical coupler dimensions specified by the Electronic Industries Association.

8-bit system Refers to the number of bits in a word that can be processed, stored, and recalled at one time in one machine cycle. Eight bits normally equal one byte.

8080 An 8-bit system developed by Intel. The 8080 was the first chip adapted for widespread use in business microcomputers.

8085 A faster version of the Intel 8080; is software compatible with the 8080.

8086 A 16-bit microprocessor produced by Intel.

8088 The chip at the heart of the IBM Personal Computer, using a 16-bit internal structure and an 8-bit external structure.

electronic bulletin board An electronic call-up service that lets users compose and store messages to be retrieved by other users.

electronic data processing See data processing.

electronic mail The electronic transmission of letters, messages, and memos from one computer to another.

electronic publishing The electronic transmission of published material.

electronic spreadsheet A software package for variable calculations. The screen display consists of an accountant's spreadsheet of up to 60 or more columns and over 250 or more rows. Any element in the display grid can be a numeric value, a formula, or an arithmetic calculation; any item can relate to and/or affect any other element.

electronic switching system (ESS) Bell System's electronic switching center for central office functions, using solid state devices and other computer-type equipment and principles.

electrosensitive printer A nonimpact printer that employs electrically charged dots to develop specially coated paper.

electrostatic printer A nonimpact printer that employs electrically charged dots to attract ink which is then embedded onto the paper by heat and pressure.

embedded command One or more characters in word processing that, when inserted into the text, do not print but rather instruct the printer or word processing program to carry out a task. Such tasks might include: go to half-spacing, indent tabs, end the page, etc.

empirical Based upon experience or experimental evidence rather than on mathematical conclusions.

emulation The use of programming techniques and special machine features to permit a computing system to execute programs written for another system. This form of imitation is primarily done via software. Emulation is generally used to minimize the impact of conversion from one computer system to another and is used to continue the use of production programs. These techniques are in contrast to simulation, which is used to study the operational characteristics of another (possibly theoretical) system.

emulator A combination of programming techniques and special machine features that permits a computing system to execute programs written for another system.

emulator, software Software that gives one computer system the ability to execute programs originally written for another system without changing the hardware or reprogramming the original programs. In execution, the computer acts on the second system in question while looking up the corresponding machine language from the first program each time an instruction appears. The resulting runs usually take longer than normal runs.

enable To restore a suppressed feature, as an interrupt.

encoder A device that substitutes one set of symbols for another.

encoding Inscribing or imprinting MICR characters on checks, deposits, and other documents to be processed by an MICR (magnetic ink character recognition) reader, or the introduction of data on a medium such as a magnetic stripe on plastic cards.

encryption The conversion of data into code form for security purposes during data communications. The data is reconverted at the receiving end.

end of file (EOF) The point at which quantity of data is complete. An EOF mark signifies this point on magnetic files.

end of page indicator A feature that halts the printer at the end of each completed page of output to allow the user to handle paper, ribbon, or font changes manually.

end of transmission (EOT) A signal indicating that the end of the data transmission has been reached.

endogenous variables Variables whose values are determined by relationships included within the model. Also called autonomous variables.

end-to-end test As used by the Bell System, a test utilizing a 900-series test equipment. It requires Bell maintenance personnel at each end of the circuit.

end value A value that is used for comparison with a count, index, etc., to see if certain conditions have been met.

ENQ Enquiry. In data communications, a request for response to obtain identification and/or an indication of station status in a transmitted message.

ENTER A command that is often used interchangeably with Carriage Return.

enter key A special function key on a terminal keyboard used to transmit a line of data on a display screen to a computer. The enter key is pressed after the message is complete.

environment The mode of operation of a computer.

environment division One of the four main component parts of a COBOL program. The environment division describes the computers upon which the source program is complied and those on which the object program is executed, and provides a linkage between the logical concept of files and their records and the physical aspects of the devices on which files are stored.

EOM End of message. Indicates the end of a message to the user.

EOT End of transmission. Indicates the end of a transmission, which may include one or more messages, and resets all stations on the line.

EPROM An acronym for erasable programmable read only memory. Usually imbedded into a chip, this component features programmable memory which can only be read, and normally not changed or written to, as contrasted with random access memory. The chips can be altered, however, with a hardware reprogramming unit called a PROM burner, which is equipped with ultraviolet light for erasing and reprogramming the chips.

equalization　In data communications, a compensation for the increase of attenuation with a frequency. Its purpose is to produce a flat frequency response.

erase　To obliterate information from a storage medium, e.g., to clear, to overwrite.

ergonomics　The study of the interaction between people and machines.

error　A difference between a computed value and the theoretically correct value.

error control　An arrangement that will detect the presence of errors. In some systems, refinements are added that will correct the detected errors, either by operations on the received data or by retransmission from the source.
　　See also error correcting code.

error correcting code　A code in which each transmission conforms to specific rules so that if certain errors occur the result will be one of its equivalents and thus the error can be corrected.

error detecting and correcting　A system employing an error detecting code and so arranged that a signal detected as being in error automatically initiates a request for retransmission.

error detecting code　A code with specific rules of construction, so that if certain errors occur, the presence of the errors is detected. Synonymous with self checking code. Such codes require more transmission data than necessary to convey the fundamental information.

error rate　The ratio of the amount of data incorrectly received to the total amount of data transmitted.

ESC key　Abbreviation for escape key. A control character whose function varies with the software or type of terminal, i.e., ESC can serve as the shift from lower to upper case characters in word processing programs.

escape character　A character that signifies that the next character is a member of a different character set.

ETB　End of transmission block.

Ethernet　Xerox, DEC, and Intel's Local Area Network office communications system which connects various electronic office machines and enables them to communicate, but uses no central computer to control traffic. Many other companies have licensed Ethernet.

ETX　End of text.

ETX/ACK protocol　End of text acknowledge. A procedure used in communications to verify transmission.

event　A processing action or occurrence that alters data files.

exception principle system　A system that reports only those results that differ from predesignated results or criteria.

exception reports　Reports which list or flag only those items that exceed a specified range of acceptable values.

exclusive OR (XOR)　A boolean operative whose definition is that the output is 1 only when either (but not both) of the two inputs is 1.

executable　Capable of being processed or executed by the computer without need for translation.

execute　To carry out an instruction or perform a routine.

execution time (E-time)　For a computer system, the time at which an object program actually performs the instructions coded in the procedure division, using the actual data provided. For the arithmetic and logic unit portion of the CPU, the time during which an instruction is decoded and performed.
　　See also instruction.

executive routine　A segment of the operating system that controls the execution of other portions of the operating system. Synonymous with supervisory routine.

expander boards　Boards that interface to the system and allow the user to add more circuitry for system expansion.

expansion card　Circuit boards or cards that can be inserted into the motherboard of the computer to increase its capacities.

expansion slot　The space into which additional cards are inserted into a motherboard.

exponential smoothing　A weighted, moving average technique in which past observations are geometrically discounted according to their age. The heaviest weight is assigned to the most recent data. The smoothing is termed exponential because data points are weighted in accordance with an exponential function of their age.

extended binary coded decimal interchange code
See EBCDIC.

extended precision arithmetic   An operation that yields an answer that is more accurate (with more significant figures) than double-precision arithmetic.

extent   A collection of physical records which are contiguous in secondary storage. The number of records in an extent depends on the physical volume and the user's request for space allocation. Associated records are not necessarily stored contiguously; this depends on the storage organization.

external function testing   The verification of the external system functions as stated in the external specifications.

external memory   Same as mass storage.

facilities control   Management of the development or acquisition of facilities to support information systems. It requires a function or activity responsible for information systems facilities planning, sequencing of facilities development or acquisition that is related to information systems development requirements, facility costs included in the funding, and accounting for major systems and operational procedures for facilities such as security and emergency procedures.

facsimile (fax)   A system of telecommunication to transmit images for reproduction on hard copy. The original image is scanned and converted to an electrical signal, and the electrical signal is subsequently converted to a replica of the original image at the receiving terminal.

facsimile transceiver   A device used to implement facsimile production and transmission.

facsimile transmission   An electronic means for transferring an image or precise reproduction from one place to another.

families of computers   Series of CPUs allegedly of the same logical design but of different speeds and configuration rules. This type of system is intended to enable the user to start with a slow, cheap CPU and grow to a fast one as his workload builds up, without having to change the rest of the computer.

fan fold paper   Continuous sheets of paper connected with perforations, folded in an accordion fold and used with a printer to provide a continuous feed without operator assistance. Also called Z-fold.

fault   A condition that causes any physical component of a system to fail to perform in its normal fashion.

fault time   Same as down time.

fault tolerance   The ability of a program or system to operate properly even if faults occur.

fax   See facsimile.

FCC   See Federal Communications Commission.

FDC   Floppy disk controller.

Federal Communications Commission (FCC)   A board of seven commissioners appointed by the President under the Communications Act of 1934, and having the power to regulate all interstate and foreign communication systems originating in the United States.

Federal Telecommunications System (FTS)   A government communications system administered by the General Services Administration and covering fifty states plus Puerto Rico and the Virgin Islands. Provides services for voice, teletypewriter, facsimile, and data transmission.

feedback   The return of part of the output of a machine, process, or system to the computer as input from another phase, especially for self-correcting or control purposes. Actual performance can thus be compared with planned performance.

fetch   To access data or instructions from a file in memory.

fiber optics   See lightwave communications.

field   A reserved area in a record that serves a similar function in all records of that group; the data contained in two or more core positions and treated as a unit.

field developed program   A licensed program product that performs a specific user application. It may interact with other program products, or it may be a stand-alone program. Designed originally for the specific needs of an existing computer system installation.

FIFO queuing   The "first in-first out" method where the next item to be retrieved is the item which has been waiting the longest.

file   An organized, named collection of records treated as a unit, or the storage media on which these records are kept.

file gap   A space at the end of the file that signifies to the system where the file ends.

file maintenance   The activity of keeping a file up to date by adding, changing, or deleting data.

file name extension   A code, very often of three letters, that forms the second part of a file name and which is separated from the file name by a period. This supplement to the name is often used to help differentiate the related files. For example, FILE.BAS might be a BASIC program for order entry; FILE.SAV might be the executable version of FILE.BAS; and FILE.DAT might be a data file that holds the order data.

file organization   The view of the data as perceived by the application programmers. The storage method that determines the method by which file contents can be accessed.

file protection   A means of protecting the disk or tape from being erased or written over. Labels can be pasted onto floppy disks and plastic rings can be inserted on tape reels. In logical file protection, software protects files on disk or tape.

file purging   Erasing the contents of old files to make room for new ones.

firmware   A term usually related to microprogramming and those specific software instructions that have been more or less permanently placed into control memory. An extension to a computer's basic command (instruction) repertoire to create a user-oriented instruction set. This extension to the basic instruction set is done in read-only memory and not in software. The read-only memory converts the extended user-specific instructions to the basic instructions of the computer.

first generation   See generation one.

first-level code   A telegraph code that utilizes five impulses for describing a character. Start and stop elements may be added for asynchronous transmission. A common five-level code is Baudot.

fixed disk   A nonremovable disk.

fixed-length record   A record having the same length as all other records with which it is logically or physically associated.
   Compare variable-length record.

fixed-partition memory management   A memory management technique in which main memory is subdivided into a number of fixed-length partitions.

fixed point   Refers to an integer number system in which the position of the radix is fixed.
   See also floating point.

flag   An indicator that an equipment or a program has reached a certain condition.

flat bed plotter   A plotter that employs plotting heads that move over a flat surface in both horizontal and vertical directions. Compare also with drum plotter, in which the heads move in one direction and the paper in another.

flat screen   A thin video display screen, as opposed to the boxy cathode ray tubes (CRTs) predominantly in use.

flexible disk   A floppy disk. See disk.

flexible membrane keyboard   See membrane keyboard.

flicker   In a raster screen display, flicker refers to the actual detection by the human eye of the repeated on-off cycle resulting from the phosphor screen image being regenerated by an electron beam thirty or more times per second.

flip-flop   A bistable circuit; or a circuit capable of storing a bit of information and of assuming two stable states (0 and 1) as long as power is supplied. Flip-flops may be grouped together to form registers.

float   In manufacturing, refers to work-in-progress. In cpm, it refers to the extra time before an activity becomes critical.

floating point   Refers to a number system in which the radix varies according to the power of the number base and the value of the mantissa or coefficient.

floating point processor   A processor utilizing floating point arithmetic.

floppy disks   Storage devices in the form of small flexible disks (about the size of 45 rpm phonograph records) used for random access requirements in controllers and CPUs and as a compact substitute for punched cards. A typical floppy disk provides capacity for about 300,000 data bytes. Floppies were originally developed for low cost, low capacity data storage, and relatively low data transfer rates. Also known as diskettes.

flow diagram   See flowchart.

flowchart   A systems analysis or programming tool to graphically present a procedure in which symbols are used to designate the logic of how a problem is solved. A flowchart represents the path of data through a problem solution. It defines the major phases of the processing as well as the various data media used. Flowcharts also enable the designer to conceptualize the procedure necessary and to visualize each step and item on a program. A completed flowchart is often a necessity to the achievement of accurate final code. A program is coded by writing down the successive steps which will cause the computer to perform the necessary logical operation for solving the problem as presented by the flowchart. Synonymous with block diagram.

flowchart symbols   Flowcharts use standardized sets of symbols to represent operations. Boxes represent order or computations, diamonds represent tests and decisions, and other shapes are used to represent input/output, connector points, etc. The symbols aid in organizing sequences of operations when writing computer programs.

flow control   A production control system that is based primarily on setting rates and feeding work to meet these planned rates. Flow control has its most successful application in repetitive production.

font   A character set in a particular style and size of type, including all alpha characters, numerics, punctuation marks, and special symbols.

footing   Adding fields of information vertically.

foreground   In multiprogramming, refers to the environment in which high-priority programs are executed.
Compare background.

foreground job   A high-priority job, usually a real-time job. A teleprocessing or graphic display job that has an indefinite running time during which communication is established with one or more users at local or remote terminals.
Compare background job.

foreground processing   High-priority processing, usually for real-time activities, automatically given precedence, by means of interrupts, over lower priority background processing.

foreground program   See foreground job.

foreign exchange (FX) line   A line offered by a common carrier in which the user is assigned a telephone number belonging to a remote location to minimize long distance charges.

form feed key   A printer control key that advances the paper in the printer to the top of the next page.

format   A contraction meaning the form of material, designating the predetermined arrangement of characters of data for input/output.

formatter   Software, usually word-processing programs, that allows the user to design the layout of text.
Compare editor.

formatting   Setting up the order of the information that is input to a computer or a peripheral device. Also, arranging the layout of the data that is output from the computer or a peripheral.

for/next loop   A looping instruction in BASIC used to repeat segments a number of times without rewriting the program. Instructions are placed between the FOR and NEXT commands.
See also do-loop.

Forth   An extremely flexible programming language for control applications used widely in industrial and now in personal computers. Forth builds the language around the application, enabling added words to become commands in the language.

Fortran   Formula Translating system. A common language primarily used to express computer programs by arithmetic formulas. It is especially adapted to mathematical, scientific, and engineering problems.

four-wire channel   Provision of two wire pairs (or logical equivalent) for simultaneous two-way transmission.

four-wire circuits   Indicates the capability of the switching system to accommodate connections to special four-wire circuits.

fragmentation   See storage fragmentation.

frame   See block.

framing bits   In data transmission, noninformation-carrying bits used to make possible the separation of characters in a bit system. Synonymous with synch bits.

free format   No restrictions are imposed on the format in which the data is entered.

frequency   An indication of how frequently a periodic (repetitive) wave form or signal repeats itself. Sometimes frequency is used as if it were an independent property of a signal, but it is not. Frequency is usually expressed in terms of Hertz (Hz) which is the same as the older expression of cycles per second.

frequency division multiplexing (FMD)   Division of the available transmission frequency range into narrower bands, each of which is used for a separate channel.

frequency modulation (FM)   A method of transmission whereby the frequency of the carrier wave is changed to correspond to changes in the signal wave.

frequency shift key (FSK)   A method of frequency modulation in which frequency is made to vary at significant instances by smooth as well as abrupt transitions.

friction feed   A paper-feeding mechanism on printers that employs rollers that hold paper against the platen, much like a typewriter.

front end processor   A dedicated communications computer at the front end of a host computer. It may perform line control, message handling, code conversion, error control, and applications functions such as control and operation of special purpose terminals.

full duplex   See duplex.

full page display   A terminal that displays at least 80 columns that are 80 characters across. In addition, the display will hold 50 lines of copy, or the average $8\frac{1}{2} \times 11$ in. page capacity.

full text database   This type of source database contains complete textual records of primary sources. These sources include newspapers, specifications, court decisions, journals, etc.

See also database, source database.

fully connected network   A network in which each node is directly connected with every other node.

function   In business, a job. In mathematics, an algebraic expression describing the relation between two or more variables.

functional design   The specifications of interrelationships between the parts of a system.

functional diagram   A diagram of the functional relationships between the parts of a system.

functional-level information systems   An MIS design that normally parallels organizational boundaries. Its vertical orientation may restrict system modularity, particularly when data needs to be shared across functional organization lines.

function codes   Codes that help contol functions of peripheral devices. For example, a line feed for a printer would be a function code.

function keys   Separate keys on a keyboard that do not produce characters but execute commands. There are two kinds: fixed or programmable (soft keys).

FX   Fixed area, or the area on a disk that is protected and that holds certain files and programs.

game control adapter   A device used to change from one game control to another, as from a game paddle to a joystick.

game port   A small computer port used to attach joysticks, game paddles, or light pens.

Gantt chart   The earliest and best known type of control chart especially designed to show graphically the relationship between planned performance and actual performance. Named after its originator, Henry L. Gantt. Synonymous with job process chart.

garbage   Unwanted or meaningless information being stored in a file or used in a process.

gate   An electronic circuit microprocessor having several input channels to determine one output channel.

general purpose computer   A computer designed to solve a large variety of problems, e.g., a stored program computer which may be adapted to any of a very large class of applications. Usable by most commercial installations.

general purpose operating system   An operating system designed to handle a wide variety of computing system applications.

generate   To produce a program from skeletal coding under the control of parameters.

generation   The designation of computers according to their lineage. Each new generation is characterized by a brand new kind of computer, utterly incompatible with all existing computers; but the dates and definitions are not universally agreed upon.

generation one (first generation)   From 1951: the first commercially produced machines. Univac 1 and 1101, Electrodata 205, IBM 701 and 650, LEO, Ferranti Pegasus, and machines derived from these; vacuum tubes, drum and delay-line memories; later, more reliable, slow core memories of 8K to 32K, 25 microsecond add times, modest magnetic tape, assembly languages, and introduction of Fortran 1, still mainly open shop, introduction of operating systems.

generation two (second generation)   From 1958: transistor technology. Philco S-2000, IBM 7080 and 7090, CDC 1604, Univac 1107, Burroughs B 5000, English Electric KDF 9, Ferranti Atlas, IBM's Stretch and Univac's LARC. Faster core, introduction of thin film, good reliability, memories of 32K and 64K, add times 5 microseconds down to 1 microsecond, substantial use of magnetic tape, introduction of disk and large drum, monitor systems become standard practice, highly closed shop. Fortran II and IV. Algol, Cobol, and general language explosion, introduction of paging and hardware stacks, introduction of data communications over telephone lines.

generation three (third generation) From 1964: integrated circuitry, IBM 360, Univac 1108, CDC 6600, Burroughs 8000, ICL Systems 4, and 1900 myriads of small computers, introduction of minicomputers. Very fast core, plated wire, good reliability, memories of several million locations, submicrosecond add times, executive systems of considerable complexity cataloging data communications entrenches, real-time, time-sharing, multiprocessing, introduction of compatible families of CPUs.

generation four (fourth generation) Computers that simulate human intelligence by learning, reasoning, adapting, or self-correcting; artificial intelligence.

generator A computer program that constructs other programs to perform a particular type of operation, e.g., a report program generator.

gigabyte One billion or one thousand million bytes.

GIGO (garbage in-garbage out) A term used to describe the data into and out of a computer system; that is, if the input data is bad (garbage in) then the output data will also be bad (garbage out).

glitch A hardware malfunction, as opposed to a software error, called a bug.

global logical data organization Concerned with the overall organization for the database from which multiple file organization may be derived. It is a logical view of the data, entirely independent of the physical storage organization. It is described in a data description language which is part of the database management software.

global search and replace The ability of a system to search for repeated occurrences of a character string (typically up to 32, 64, or 128 characters long). In some instances, the system can automatically delete all occurrences of a string or replace all occurrences of one character string with another character string. In other cases, the system merely locates the string for operator-selected deletion of replacement. A few high-powered systems can apply logical considerations to making the placement or perform multiple searches simultaneously.

global variable A variable that may be referred to throughout a main program and all of its subordinates, as compared to a local variable that may be referenced only within the specific program segment in which it has been defined.

goto A branch instruction in a high-level language.

GPIB General purpose interface bus. This is the name given to the IEEE 488 bus standard.

GPSS General purpose simulation system. See simulation language.

graceful exit The ability of the user to exit from a program without having to turn off the machine.

grandfather cycle The period during which records are retained on magnetic tape so that the data can be reconstructed in the event of loss of information stored in the main file.

grandfather tape (or disk) The first of a series of three generations of tapes that are written. The original tape is kept until another grandfather tape is prepared later, at which time the original is scratched. The process ensures backup in case latent programming and/or data errors are discovered within a reasonable period of time.

graphics The use of the computer for drawing lines under complete program control; or the attachment of a vector scope and light pen online to the computer, enabling the user and the computer to interact and jointly draw pictures on the face of the scope.

graphics, business Refers to various types of graphs and charts that represent sales, profits, losses, inventory, and similar concepts; for example, bar graphs, scatter graphs, and pie charts.

graphics, three-dimension See line drawing, three-dimensional.

graphics, two-dimension See line drawing, two-dimensional.

graphic solution The result of problem solving, put into a visual form for clarity.

graphics tablet A popular type of digitizing device that utilizes a flat tablet and stylus for graphic input. Existing drawings can be traced or new drawings created by moving the stylus across the tablet, which records the stylus position relative to an x-y coordinate system and inputs this information into the system. The image that is being created will appear simultaneously on a connected display screen. The tablet may have a menu of predefined specialized graphic symbols that can be chosen and used as an aid in creative drawings. The tablet provides an efficient method of converting object shapes into computer storable information.

See also cursor tracking, digitizer, stylus.

gray scale images A hierarchy of continuous blocks of solid color that can be combined in different sizes and shapes to form or represent an image. In its most sophisticated form, a sufficient number of gray scale tones can be combined and interpolated to form an image emulating a standard, continuous tone, black and white photograph.

group indicate The first record of a group is used to indicate information about the contents of the group.

group processing Usually a setup whereby several users jointly use, rent, or own data processing equipment. In some instances, a group form a separate data processing organization to make it economically feasible to utilize EDP techniques.

gulp A slang term for a group of bytes.

hacker Computer jargon for a person who is intensely interested in and/or very knowledgeable about computer hardware and software.

half duplex A circuit designed for transmission alternately in either direction but not both directions simultaneously.

Compare duplex.

half-height floppy disk drives A design that allows a floppy disk drive to displace approximately half the physical space required by a traditional floppy disk drive.

halt The situation in which the computer system stops processing in the middle of a program, often in response to a particular instruction.

hand-held computer A system small enough to carry in a pocket, as compared to a portable computer or a desktop computer.

handler A program with the sole function of controlling a particular input, storage device, file, or the interruption facility.

handshaking A preliminary exchange of predetermined signals performed by modems and/or terminals and computers to verify that communication has been established and can proceed.

hands on The act of physically using a computer.

hang up The period in which the computer system stops forward progress in the program, and is for all practical purposes halted even though the machine is still running. For example, an infinite loop can cause the system to become hung up even though the program is still running.

hard copy Machine output in a permanent visually readable form for human beings, for example, printed reports, listings, documents, and summaries. The term has gained greater significance compared to CRT displays which are transient or to magnetic records which cannot be read by humans and require computer processing for conversion to printed records or reports.

hard disk Rigid, random access, high-capacity magnetic storage medium. Disks may be removable (cartridges), providing off-line archival storage, or nonremovable. Capacities range from 5 Mb to well over 300 Mb (250 to 7,500,000 pages) per disk (calculated at 4000 characters per single spaced page).

hard disk cartridge A cartridge containing a rigid disk designed to be loaded and unloaded into a hard disk system.

hard disk cylinder A term that refers to the same track on all of the platters in a hard disk pack, producing a vertical stack of tracks that has been filled when, in order to minimize head movements during access, subsequent records are allocated to the same track position on the disk directly underneath or above the original track. This allocation strategy cuts down on the time needed to retrieve data.

hard disk pack A removable set of magnetic disks loaded as a unit on a disk drive.

hard disk system The hardware needed in order to interface hard disks for data and program storage. In contrast to floppy disk systems, hard disk systems have faster access times, higher capacity, and greater reliability.

hard error An error caused by some malfunction in the hardware; for example, a disk head incorrectly reading the information on the disk.

hard sectored A term used to describe a particular diskette format and a way of recording information on the diskette. Hard sectored diskettes employ a single index hole placed between any two of thirty-two equidistant sector holes. The index hole is used to designate the beginning of the disk, and the sector holes designate the location of the information on each disk. Since hard sectored diskettes are not preformatted they have more potential storage capacity than the soft sectored variety, employing up to 300 K bytes out of a possible 400 K for text storage.

hardware Physical computer equipment, for example, mechanical, magnetic, electrical, or electronic devices.
Compare software.

hardwired A processing system employing wired circuitry to implement system functions. Such equipment is generally cheaper than software programmed systems; it is also less flexible.

hash total An arithmetic total of data used for checking the accuracy of one or more corresponding fields of a file such as job numbers, invoicing serial numbers, etc., that ordinarily would not be summed, to see that all transactions have been processed. When the hash totals agree, the data are considered verified.

HDLC Bit-oriented protocol developed by ISO (International Standards Organization).

head A device that reads, writes, or erases data on a storage medium, e.g., a small electromagnet or the set of perforating, reading, or marking devices used for punching, reading, or printing on paper tape.

head crash The physical collision of the read/write head and the recording surface of the magnetic media. It usually results in the destruction of data.

header The initial portion of a message containing any information, control codes, and so on that are not part of the text (e.g., routine, priority, message type, destination addressee, and time of origination).

header record A record containing common, constant, or identifying information for a group of records which follow.

head gap The distance between the read/write head and the surface of the magnetic medium.

help Frequently, a command whose response is a menu displaying all available program choices, from which the operator can select the next action to be performed.

Hertz A unit of frequency equal to one cycle per second. Cycles are referred to as Hertz in honor of the experimenter Heinrich Hertz. Abbreviated Hz.

heterogeneous (computer) network A network of different host computers, such as those of different manufacturers.
Compare homogeneous network.

heuristic Pertaining to exploratory methods of problem solving in which solutions are arrived at by an interactive, self-learning method.

hexadecimal Pertaining to a number system with a base of 16; valid digits range from 0 through F, where F represents the highest units position (15). Synonymous with hex.

hidden line In a graphic display of a three-dimensional object in line form, the line or edge which would be obscured from the viewer's sight by the mass of the object itself is visible as a result of the projection. Additional routines must by implemented to remove these "hidden lines."

hierarchical (computer) network A computer network in which processing and control functions are performed at several levels by computers specially suited in capability for the functions performed.

high-level languages Programming methods that allow the programmer to express operations in a less direct form that is closer to the normal human language representation of the procedures the computer is to perform. Such languages are usually problem-oriented or procedure-oriented as distinguished from machine-oriented and/or mnemonic languages. Common examples are COBOL (for business applications), Fortran (for mathematical work), PL/I, and BASIC (a simple easy-to-use language). These languages were originally intended to be "machine independent," but it has not worked out that way, and variations are common.

high resolution Refers to the quality and accuracy of detail that can be represented by a graphics system such as a video display or a printer. Resolution quality depends upon the number of basic image-forming units (pixels) within a given area; the greater the number, the higher the resolution.

histogram A graph of contiguous vertical bars representing a frequency distribution in which the groups or classes of items are marked at equal intervals in ascending order on the x axis, and the number of items in each class is indicated by a horizontal line segment drawn above the x axis at a height equal to the number of items in the class.

HITS Hobbyist's interchange tape standard. A data recording format using tape cassettes; the standard format was designed to allow interchangeability of cassettes and programs.

HLL High-level language.

HOL High-order language. See high-level languages.

holding time The length of time a communications channel or facility is in use for each transmission. Includes both message time and operating time.

hold instruction An instruction that causes information to be retained in its original storage area even after it has been copied in another location due to a transfer instruction.

Hollerith code An alphanumeric punched card code, invented by Dr. Herman Hollerith in 1889, in which the top three positions in a column are called "zone" punches (12, 11, and 0, or Y, X, and 0, from the top downward), and are combined with the remaining punches, or digit punches (1 through 9) to represent alphabetic, numeric, and special characters.

home A command from a program or key on the keyboard that moves the cursor to the starting point of the screen, usually the upper lefthand corner.

homebrew A hardware configuration which the owner has purchased from a variety of sources and assembled, rather than buying a computer and all peripherals from one manufacturer. Also, one of the earliest microcomputer clubs in the United States.

home computer A microcomputer designed to be used at home. Usually costing less than a thousand dollars, it runs both games and various personal applications.

homogeneous (computer) network A network of similar computers such as those of one model by the same manufacturer.

horizontal scrolling Ability of the system to shift horizontally blocks of lines of text or data in order to view more characters than can fit on the screen at one time.

host computer The primary or controlling computer in a multiple computer network operation. This computer normally provides high-level services such as computation, database access, or special programs or programming languages for other computers in the network. A computer used to prepare programs for use on another computer or on another data processing system, for example, a computer used to compile, link edit, or test programs to be used on another system.

hostile environment The practice of applying software to a system for which it was not designed, using special utilities to make the software and the system compatible.

host interface The interface between a communications processor or network and a host computer.

housekeeping Operations or routines that do not contribute directly to the solution of the problem but do contribute directly to the operation of the computer.

HPIB Hewlett-Packard interface bus. One of a number of standards for connection of hardware. Also called the GPIB or general purpose interface bus.

human engineering The theory and application of designing in order to serve people, as opposed to designing for a machine.
See also ergonomics.

hybrid computer A data processing device using both analog and discrete data representation.

hyper-density tape One-inch magnetic tape with a density of 3200 characters per inch.

Hz See Hertz.

IBM IBM Corporation, the largest computer manufacturer.

ICES Integrated Civil Engineering System. A general system for engineering uses designed with some facilities for defining new languages. Includes such systems as COGO and STRUDL, an internal language ICETTAN, and other languages such as ROADS, BRIDGE, TRANSIT, PROJECT, and SEPOL.

identification The process of providing personal, equipment, or organizational characteristics or codes to gain access to computer resources.

identification division One of the four main component parts of a COBOL program. The identification division identifies the source program and the object program and, in addition, may include such documentation as the author's name, the installation, where written, date written, etc.

identification phase In information system design, the identification phase in which the following steps are taken: develop study action plan, study team orientation, announce study to executives, gather key business and information systems data, establish study control room, and acquire administrative support.

idle characters   Characters that are used in data communications to synchronize the transmission.

idle time   Time when hardware is not producing because of setup, maintenance, lack of material, etc.

IEEE   Institute of Electrical and Electronical Engineers, involved in the setting of standards for the computer and communications field.

if-then-else   A program statement used in high-level languages, indicating alternative responses to an initial action. If the initial statement is not true, then the else, or alternative, expression is executed.
　　See also boolean algebra.

image processing   A method of inputting two-dimensional images to a computer and then enhancing or analyzing the imagery into a form that will be more meaningful to the user. Examples include enhancement of drawings for animation, photographs, or computer-aided design models.

impact printer   A printer which forms characters by physically striking a ribbon and paper.

implement   To carry out or give physical, functional reality to a theory or plan. Various types of software are the tools for implementing usable applications of mathematical, logical, or business theory.

implementation   The act of finishing or installing a program or a system.

IMS (information management system)   An IBM program product that supports database management.

increment   As a verb, increment means to increase an integer by a specified amount. As a noun, an increment is the amount by which the integer is increased.

index   A directory of what is stored on a disk.

indexed sequential access method   See ISAM.

indexed sequential organization   A file organization used on direct access storage devices in which records are arranged in logical sequence by key. Indexes to these keys permit direct access to individual records.

index hole   A hole in a floppy disk that indicates the start of the first sector.

infinite loop   A never ending loop.
　　See also loop.

information   The meaning derived from data which has been arranged and displayed in such a way that it can be related to that which is previously known.
　　See also data.

information path   The functional route by which information is transferred in a one-way direction from point to point.

information processing   See data processing.

information retrieval system   A complete application for cataloging vast amounts of stored data so that any part or all of this data can be called out at any time.

information system   A logical group of subsystems and data required to support the information needs of one or more business processes.

information systems independence   An information system defined so that data is independent of the organizational structure of the business.

information systems network   A network of multiple operational-level information systems and one management-oriented information system (centered around planning, control and measurement processes). The network retrieves data from databases and synthesizes that data into meaningful information to support the organization.

information systems plan   A plan for managing an information systems network implementation, including definition of the major actions, schedules, and resources required. Must be integrated with the business plan and should be developed from the point of view and with the active participation of top management.

information theory   The branch of learning concerned with the likelihood of communication of messages subject to transmission failure, distortion, and noise.

information word   A word that conveys computer information rather than an instruction.

inhibiting input   Input that in some way inhibits production of output.

initialization   A process that is carried out at the beginning of a program. It sets all starting values within the system to the prescribed conditions needed for use. Initialization is also a procedure carried out when a disk is first used. The process itself creates a sort of road map on the blank disk to suit the data formats that it will receive. The disk is re-initialized only when the user desires to clear out all the old files and start with a blank, newly formatted state. Disk initialization carries out these three steps: (1) enters DOS onto the disk, (2) enters the program that runs each time the disk is booted, (3) defines the sectors, and (4) establishes the volume table of contents.

ink jet printer   A non-impact printing technique

which utilizes droplets of ink to form copy images. As the print head moves across the surface of the copy paper it shoots a stream of tiny, electrostatically charged ink drops at the page, placing them precisely to form individual print characters.

in-line subroutine A subroutine that is inserted into the main routine as many times as is needed.

input The data to be processed. Also the transfer of data to be processed from keyboard or an external storage device to an internal storage device.

input device A device such as a card reader, CRT, teletypewriter, etc., which converts data from the form in which it has been received into electronic signals that can be interpreted by the computer.

input equipment See input device.

input media Data sources for computers such as punched cards, punched tape, or MICR encoded documents. The word input used alone often includes the medium or media. Any process which transfers data from an external source to an internal storage is designated as input.

input/output The process involved in transferring information into or out of a central processing unit.

input/output control system (IOCS) A set of programs used in an operating system. It handles all input and output work such as opening files, closing files, backspacing tape, moving tape forward when a bad spot is encountered, etc. IOCS is used on all secondary storage devices. The programmer's source instructions (macro instructions) call in the IOCS instructions.

input/output processor (IOP) An auxiliary processor dedicated or used for controlling I/O transfers, which frees the central processing unit for other tasks.

inquiry A request for information from storage; for example, a request for the number of available airline seats, or a machine statement to initiate a search of library documents.

inquiry station A terminal where inquiries can be entered directly into the computer. The inquiry terminal can be geographically remote from the computer or at the computer console, and usually includes a typewriter keyboard.

inscribing To read the data recorded on a document and write the same data on the same document but in such a form that the document becomes suitable for automatic reading by a character reader. Synonymous with imprinting or encoding.

installation A particular computing system, in terms of the work it does and the people who manage to operate it, apply it to problems, service it, and use the results it produces.

installation testing The validation of each particular installation of the system with the intent of pointing out any errors made while installing the system.

installation time Time spent in installing testing and accepting equipment and/or programs.

instruction A statement to the computer that specifies an operation to be performed by the system and the values or locations of all operands. An instruction is usually made up of an operation code and one or more operands.

instruction cycle The time necessary to process a program instruction. This includes fetching, decoding, and execution.

instruction repertory The set of instructions which a computer data processing system is capable of performing.

instruction set The sequence of directions a computer follows in order to process information.

instruction time The portion of a CPU cycle during which an instruction is fetched and decoded.

INT Interrupt.

integer A numeric data item or literal that does not include any character positions to the right of the decimal point, actual or assumed, i.e., a whole number.

integrated adapter An integral part of an IBM central processing unit that provides for the direct connection of a particular type of device and uses neither a control unit, not the standard I/O interface.

integrated circuit A combination of the interconnected circuit elements inseparably associated on or within a continuous substrate.

integration The sharing of data or information among subsystems and systems.

integration testing The verification of the interfaces among system parts (modules, components, and subsystems).

integrity Preservation of data or programs for their intended purpose. The resistance of a system to breakdown; automatic backup in which the system detects a potential failure and automatically uses alternatives to the failing component. An example is a duplicated reference file employed so that the copy would be used if input errors were detected on the primary version. Another example is a permanently connected switch to provide two data paths to a storage device.

intel   Intel Corporation, a major microprocessor manufacturer of 8-, 16-, and 32-bit chips owned in part by IBM; also a computer systems manufacturer.

intelligent terminal   A terminal with some logical capability; a remote device that is capable of performing some editing or other function upon input or output data. The intelligent terminal has a flexible design for simplified user interface including custom keyboards, modularity to meet a variety of user requirements including control of other terminals and a buffering capability to simplify the communications interface and to lessen the impact of multiple systems on host computer software.

INTELSAT   The International Telecommunications Satellite Consortium, established under international agreements in 1964. With the ratification by the required 54 partner-member countries, the International Telecommunications Satellite Organization came into being in 1973. INTELSAT is the international joint venture created to establish the global communications satellite system.

interactive   Pertaining to an application in which each entry elicits a response, as in an inquiry system or an airline reservation system. An interactive system may also be conversational, implying continuous dialog between the user and the system.

interactive operation   On-line operation where there is a give-and-take between person and machine. Also called conversational mode: user presents problem to computer, gets results, asks for variation or amplification of results, gets immediate answer, etc.

interblock gap   An area on a data medium used to indicate the end of a block or record. Same as block gap.

interchange point   A location where interface signals are transmitted.

interest worlds   Areas of special interest for which the computer can serve as a tool or laboratory; for example, art, music, mathematics, physics, or language.

interface   A shared boundary between system elements defined by common physical interconnection characteristics, signal characteristics, and meanings of interchanged signals.

interface EIA Standard RS-232-C   A standardized method adopted by the Electronic Industries Association to insure uniformity of interface between

data communication equipment and data processing terminal equipment. Has been generally accepted by most manufacturers of data transmission and business equipment.

interlaced field   A technique found in raster display systems to minimize flicker on the display screen.

interleaving   A multiprogramming technique in which segments of one program are inserted into other programming so that during delays in the processing of one of the programs, the other program can be processed.

internal memory   See main memory.

internal sort   A sorting technique that creates sequences of records or keys. Usually, it is a prelude to a merge phase in which the sequences created are reduced to one by an external merge.

internal storage   Addressable main storage memory directly controlled by the central processing unit of a digital computer. Types of internal storage are core storage, monolithic integrated circuits, and thin film memory rods.

International Organization for Standardization (ISO)   An organization established to promote the development of standards to facilitate the international exchange of goods and services, and to develop mutual cooperation in areas of intellectual, scientific, technological, and economic activity.

interpret   To translate a higher level language program into a program that the machine understands.

interpreter   A computer program that translates and executes each source language statement before translating and executing the next one. Also known as incremental compiler.

interrecord gap   An area on a data medium used to indicate the end of a block or record. Same as record gap.

interrupt   A break in the normal flow of a computer routine such that the flow can be resumed from that point at a later time. An interrupt is usually caused by a signal from an external source. The availability of an interrupt feature relieves the computer of the need for time-consuming scanning to sense special conditions. Some controllers send interrupts to the processors after the receipt of each character from the line; others—the message-oriented controllers—only send interrupts at the end of the message or end of transition.

I/O   See input/output.

I/O bound Refers to programs with a large number of I/O (input/output) operations which result in much wasted CPU time.

I/O channel A piece of equipment forming part of the input-output system of a computer. Under the control of I/O commands, the channel transfers blocks of data between the main store and peripherals.

IOCS Input/output control system.

IOP Input/output processor.

ISAM Indexed sequential access method. A procedure for storing and retrieving data. It uses a set of indexes (such as the table of contents in a book) that describes where the records are on the disks. Each record has key information, such as a customer name, that is used to retrieve the whole record.

ISO See International Organization for Standardization.

item A group of related characters treated as a unit. A record is a group of related items, and a file is a group of related records.

iterative The process of repeating a series of operations until a desired result is obtained.

jcl See job control language.

job A unit of work for the computing system from the standpoint of installation accounting and/or operations system control. A job consists of one or more steps or programs. Usually includes all necessary computer programs, linkages, files, and instructions to the operating system.

job control An operating system program that is called into storage to prepare each job or job step to be run. Some of its functions are to assign I/O devices to symbolic names, set switches for program use, log (or print) job control statements, and fetch the first phase of each job step.

job control language (JCL) A programming language used to code job control statements. These statements supply information on the operating system and the operators about the program, e.g., name of user, how much memory is required, estimated run time, priority, tapes required, other programs, etc. The JCL for modern operating systems is often quite complex, and there are probably nearly as many user-prepared jobs which fail to execute due to JCL errors as due to compiler language errors.

job progress chart See Gantt chart.

job step A unit of work for a computing system presented as a request for execution of an explicitly identified program and a description of resources it requires.

job stream The tack of jobs that are to be inputted, awaiting initiation and processing. Sometimes called input job stream. It follows the same principle as batching jobs.

Josephson junction A type of circuit capable of switching at very high speeds.

joystick A game control. A stick or lever used to change the position of the cursor or other position marker on a display screen.

Julian calendar The calendar that is used in data processing. The dates are five-digit numbers—the first two digits pertain to the year and the last three to the day of the year—001 through 365 or 366.

jump A departure from sequence in executing instructions in a computer.
See also conditional transfer.

jumper selectible An option on hardware that allows the user, typically through use of a DIP switch, to change various characteristics of the hardware.

jumper tester A device that can test whether or not the assorted options of a device are functioning.

junk Garbled data, most often referring to signals received in communications.

justification The act of adjusting, arranging, or shifting digits to the left or right to fit a prescribed pattern.

justify To position characters of text so that the left or right margins are aligned. Also, to order digits so that the least significant or most significant is always at the left or right margin.

K   The symbol for 2, raised to the tenth power, equal to 1024.
See also kilobyte.

KB   See kilobyte.

key   A field or concatenation of fields within a record, utilized in identifying an item or record for access purposes. Also, an individual button of a keyboard used to generate a code to represent a character.

keyboard   An input device consisting of switches with marked keytops that, when pressed manually, generate a code representing individual characters.
See also ASCII keyboard, Dvorak keyboard, QWERTY keyboard.

keyboard processor   A processor used in the keyboard to determine the active key position, to look up a corresponding character code in memory via the keyboard ROM, or to place the appropriate code on the data bus.

keyboard ROM   A small ROM (read only memory) in the keyboard that contains standardized character code tables used by the keyboard processor so that the appropriate code can be looked up on the data bus.

keyboard terminal   A terminal through which data can be entered to a data processing system by means of a typewriter-like keyboard.

key data entry devices   A keyboard-equipped device used to prepare data so that the computer can accept it, including keypunches (card punches) plus the newer key-to-tape and key-to-disk units.

keypad   Usually a small group of keys set up for a special purpose to the right of the QWERTY keyboard.

keypunch   A device that records information by punching holes in cards to represent letters, digits, and special characters.

key stations   The number of terminals used for data input on a multiple-user system.

key switch   The actual switch part of a key—the input key on a keyboard. The most commonly used is a leaf contact-type switch, which yields high-speed operation.

keyword   One of the significant and informative words in a title or document that describes the content of that document.

keyword in context (KWIC)   An index which lists available programs in alphabetical order by each keyword in the title. A KWIC index is prepared by highlightning each keyword of the title in the context of the words on either side of it, and then aligning the keywords of all titles alphabetically in a vertical column.

kill   To eliminate or erase. Frequently a control (EC) character in a word processing program meaning to drop or purge a line of text or a blank line.

kilo   A prefix often used to represent 1000. In the context of computer use, it does not exactly equal 1000 but refers to 1024—or 2 to the tenth power—which is a convenient binary approximation of 1000. A 1K byte memory storage has 1024 bytes; a 64K byte memory has 65,536 bytes. A 4K chip is a 4096 bit chip. When not used in reference to a chip, it usually indicates the number of bytes; when used in terms of a chip, the number refers to bits.

kilobaud   One thousand bits per second.

kilobyte   One thousand twenty-four bytes.

KSR   Keyboard send and receive.

KWIC   See keyword in context.

label   One or more characters used to identify a program statement or a data item.

LAN   See local area network.

language   A set of rules and conventions used to convey information.

language processor   See processor program.

large-scale computer   A computer with the highest operating characteristics. Large-scale computers provide complex and powerful programmable logic to attack complex problems which require highly centralized computing power. Examples: CDC 7600, Cray Amdahl 470, ILLIAC IV, and others. Some operate at speeds of 100 million instructions per second (mips).

large-scale integration (LSI) A process for fabricating integrated circuits that have thousands of semiconductors such as diodes and transistors (approximately 20,000) on a single silicon chip.
See also very large-scale integration.

laser A device which transmits an extremely narrow and coherent beam of electromagnetic energy in the visible light spectrum.

laser disk An analog or digital storage medium written and read by laser.
See also video disk.

laser printers A printer technology that focuses laser beams to form images on photosensitive drums in a principle similar to that used in Xerographic office copiers. Laser printers are now used as output devices for computers. They are high speed, high quality, and have relatively high first costs compared to other printer technologies.

latency The time between an address interpretation and the start of the actual transfer. Latency includes the delay associated with access to storage devices.

LCD display A display employing liquid crystal diode technology. This technology is often used in pocket and briefcase calculators, computers, and wristwatches because of its thin profile. It features high visibility in high illumination levels, but low to no visibility in low illumination levels.

leading zeros Zeros that have no significance in the value of an arithmetic integer; all zeros to the left of the first significant integer digit of a number.

learning curve A planning technique calculation based on the premise that workers will be able to produce a new product more quickly after they get used to making it.

lease A contract whereby one party, known as the lessor, grants to another party, known as the lessee, the rights of use to property owned by the lessor. This property may be land, buildings, or equipment. The lease agreement describes the rights of the owner (lessor) and the rentor (lessee), and the terms of payment and the tenure of the lease.

leased line A communication channel leased for exclusive use from a carrier, and frequently referred to as a private line.

least significant bit The bit in the right-most position of a binary word or byte which is the bit that could be eliminated with the least effect on the precision of the word.
See also most significant bit, significant figures.

least significant character The extreme right-hand character in a group of characters.
Compare most significant character.

least squares method A method of smoothing or curve fitting which selects the fitted curve so as to minimize the sum of squares of deviations from the given points.

LED See light-emitting diode.

letter quality printer A printer that generates output that is suitable for high quality business correspondence. Term implies that output quality matches that of a standard office typewriter.

level In date management structures, the degree of subordination in a hierarchy.

library A collection of organization information. In electronic data processing, a program library is a collection of available computer programs and routines. The libraries used by an organization are known as its data bank.

library case A container, usually made of plastic, for storing and protecting floppy disks.

library routine A proven routine that is stored in a program library.

LIFO (last-in-first-out) In data processing, indicates that the newest entry in a queue or file is the first to be removed. For accounting purposes, a method of inventory evaluation. The assumption is that the most recently received (last) is the first to be used or sold (first out).

light-emitting diode (LED) A diode which glows when supplied with an electric current.

light pen A tool for CRT terminal operators that causes the computer to change or modify the display on the cathode-ray tube. The pen's response to light from the display is transmitted to the computer which, in turn, relates the computer action to the section of the image being displayed. In this way, the operator can delete or add text, maintain tighter control over the program, and choose alternative courses of action.

lightwave communications A term coined to identify the use of light as an information carrier. The term is used in place of optical communications to avoid confusion with visual information and image transmission. Fiber optic cables (light guides) are a direct replacement for conventional coaxial cables and wire pairs. The glass-based transmission facilities occupy far less physical volume for an equivalent transmission capacity.

limiting operation The operation with the least capacity in a total system with no alternative routings. The total system can be effectively scheduled by simply scheduling the limiting operation. Synonymous with bottleneck.

line   A circuit connecting two or more devices.

line (video screen)   A horizontal row of characters on a display or terminal screen. Most screens are either 40- or 80-width column displays.

linear programming   A mathematical means of finding the best possible solution to a problem that is expressed as a series of linear equations. The solution must satisfy restrictions that are imposed on the variables being considered.

line balancing   The assignment of assembly line tasks to work stations so as to minimize the number of work stations and the total amount of unassigned time at all stations. Line balancing can also mean determination of the product mix that can provide a fairly consistent flow of work through that assembly line at a planned rate.

line coordination   Determining whether devices at both ends of a communication line are ready to talk.

line discipline   See control procedure.

line drawing   Representation of an object's image by entering a solid-line outline of surfaces. The mass or shape of the form between the lines will be inferred by the viewer.
Compare continuous tone image.

line drawing, three-dimensional   A display method involving a three-dimensional display surface. Techniques of perspective projection are employed similar to the projection of a real object through a lens onto the flat viewing glass of a camera.

line drawing, two-dimensional   A method of display that represents line drawings of a flat image, such as a building floor plan or a two-axes graph. No depth is suggested.

line feed   A mechanism, control, code, or character that causes paper in a printer to advance one line, or the cursor on a CRT screen to move down one line.

line height   The height of one line of type measured by the number of lines per inch.

line hit   A disturbance causing a detectable error on a communications line.

line load control   Equipment in a telephone system that provides a means by which essential lines may be assured continuity of service under overloaded conditions. This is normally accomplished by temporarily denying originating service to some or all of the non-essential lines. Line load control does not affect calls already established and does not prevent calls to be completed on lines temporarily denied originating service.

line number   The identification number of an instruction or statement in a sequential program.

line printer   The computer output peripheral that prints an entire line of characters as a unit. This principle is largely responsible for the high printing speed.

line quality printer   See letter quality printer.

line redundancy level   The ratio of actual number of links to the minimum number of links required to connect all nodes of a network.
See also fully connected network.

line surge   A sudden high voltage condition that can damage equipment that does not have surge protection.

link   A communications path between two nodes in a network.

linkage editor   An operating system program that prepares the output of language translators for execution. It combines separately produced modules, resolves cross references among them, and in addition, it replaces, deletes, and adds control sections and produces an executable load module.

linking loader   A program designed to link separately compiled program modules together into one consecutive memory configuration for execution. Also called link editor.

liquid crystal display (LCD)   A graphic display on a terminal screen using an electroluminescent technology to form symbols or shapes.

LISP   A high-level language whose name is derived from the words "list processing." LISP is an interpretive language developed for manipulation of symbolic strings and recursive data. While the language has been developed to aid in the handling of symbolic lists, it has been used successfully in the manipulation of mathematical and arithmetic logic.

list   A data structure in which each item of data can contain pointers to other items. Any data structure can be represented in this way, which allows the structure to be independent of the storage of the items. The term also means to print data.

listing   A printout, usually prepared by a language translator, that lists the source language statements of a program.

list processing Methods for processing data that are in list form. Usually, priority is given to techniques such as chaining, altering the logical order of items without changing their physical locations in memory.

load In computer operations, the amount of scheduled work, usually expressed in terms of hours of work. In programming, to feed data or programs into the computer.

load center A group of work stations which can all be considered together for purposes of loading and scheduling.

loading The process of applying expected requirements against capacity.

local area network (LAN) A system for linking terminals, programs, storage, and graphic devices at multiple workstations over relatively small geographic areas for rapid communication.

local batch Off-line batch processing. Users send raw data by courier to service bureaus to be processed and returned.

location Part of the main memory in which an instruction or item can be stored and which is usually identified by an address.

logical date independence The capacity to change the overall logical structure of the data without changing the application programs. The changes must not, of course, remove any of the data the application programs use.

logical record A collection of items independent of their physical environment. Portions of the same logical record may be located in different physical records.

logical terminal A device addressable by its logical functions rather than its physical address. Translation from logical to physical addresses is achieved by a common routine using a table. The table can be updated during on-line operation by the network manager to alter the physical terminal assigned to a logical function. The routine can be incorporated into that used to achieve the concept of a standard terminal.

logic chart See flowchart.

logic circuit An electronic circuit that performs information processing. Usually encoded on a chip, it is composed of logic gates which are the boolean logic building blocks.
See also boolean logic and logic gates.

logic design The specification of the working relations between the parts of a system in terms of symbolic logic.

logic gate A combination of transistors that detects the presence or absence of electrical pulses, which in turn represent binary digits (1's and 0's).

logic theory The science that takes into account logical operations, which are the basis of computer operations. This simulation of simple logic uses electronic circuits to test hypotheses, which are indicated as either true or false by "on" or "off" in the electronic circuit.
See also boolean algebra.

log-in See log-on.

Logo An interactive programming language, developed by Seymour Papert at MIT, primarily for students using an on-line terminal or personal computer.

log-off The procedure by which a user ends a terminal session.

log-on The procedure by which a user begins a terminal session.

log-out See log-off.

longitudinal redundancy check (LRC) A data communications error checking technique. An LRC character is accumulated at both the sending and receiving stations during the transmission and is compared for an equal condition, which indicates a good transmission of the previous block.

Long Lines A department of AT&T that manages all interstate telephone circuits in Bell Systems.

loop In programming, a sequence of computer instructions that repeats itself until a predetermined count or other test is satisfied.

low-level language A programming language in which instructions have a one-to-one relationship with machine code.
See also computer language.

LP Line printer.

lpm Lines per minute, a reference to printer speed.

lps Lines per second, a reference to printer speed.

LSI Large-scale integration. Refers to a chip with more than 100,000 transistors.

machine   In industry vernacular, a word often used synonymously for a computer or a processing unit.

machine code   Machine language instructions.

machine cycle   The basic operating cycle of a CPU during which a single instruction is fetched, decoded, and executed.

machine-dependent   Capable of being used only on the machine for which it was originally designed.

machine-independent   Pertaining to procedures or programs created without regard for actual devices that will be used to process them. Often refers to high-level programming in COBOL, Fortran, etc.

machine-independent language   A programming language that can be used on any computer that has the appropriate compiler or interpreter. Programs written in high-level languages are theoretically machine independent. However, in practice they often need some modifications in order to operate on equipment of different manufacturers. Assembly languages are never machine independent; their instructions are designed exclusively for a specific type of processor.

machine instruction   An instruction that a particular machine can recognize and execute.

machine language   A binary language all digital computers must use. All other programming languages must be compiled or translated ultimately into binary code before entering the processor. Binary language is used directly by a machine, and is machine language.

machine-oriented language   A programming language that is more like a machine language than a human language, e.g., assembly language as opposed to COBOL.

machine-sensible   The ability of a medium and its content to be processed by computer equipment.

machine utilization   The percent of time that a machine is running production as opposed to idle time.

macro   A programming symbolic language instruction which will generate more than one absolute language instruction. In assembler programming, an as-sembler language statement that causes the assembler to process a predefined set of statements called a macro definition. The statements normally produced from the macro definition replace the macro instructions in the program. Synonymous with macro call.

macro assembler   A special assembler that recognizes key words in the assembly code and expands them into their full instruction set. The user defines the macro key words and their corresponding instruction set.

macro instruction   A source-language instruction that is equivalent to a specified number of machine-language instructions. These frequently used instructions are predefined to perform a specific operation. The function is associated with one code word that is defined by the user. Code words (macros) are inserted within the main program where needed. The code word references the predefined macro instruction set (body), which is a separate machine language routine or assembly routine. Using a macro, a user can define a recurring task just once and then, when that task is called for, the macro can be substituted. This action will shorten program length, but a special macro assembly program is necessary to expand the macro into its body and into machine code. The macro is a shared resource in that its access is not restricted to one program. A macro is different from a subroutine in that when a macro program goes through the translation (assembly) process, the code for the macro key word is actually inserted into the program. Therefore, when the program is executed, those substituted statements are read sequentially and there is no transfer of control to any other area of memory. A subroutine, on the other hand, uses a call statement that is executed in order to transfer control to a different area. In word processing, the macro can be a word or a phrase that is called up when a code word is used. The code word is sometimes called a token.

mag card   Abbreviation for magnetic card. A plastic, flexible card about 3 inches by 7 inches with a magnetized surface for data storage.

magnetic bubble memory   A main storage technology characterized by densities of 10 million bits per square inch, and with realized densities up to one billion bits per square inch conceivable. Since bubble memory is magnetized, it does not lose its charge when electricity is disabled. Therefore, it is non-volatile main memory.

magnetic core   A tiny doughnut-shaped piece of magnetic material that is used to store data in main memory.

magnetic disk   A flat circular plate with a magnetic surface on which data can be stored in the form of magnetized spots. This data is arranged in circular tracks around the disk and is accessible to reading and writing heads on an arm which can be moved to the desired tracks as the disk rotates.

magnetic disk, layout A schematic representation of common space allocations on a magnetic disk.

magnetic drum A device that stores information in the form of magnetized spots on a continuously rotating cylinder. A magnetic reading and writing head is associated with each track so that the desired track can be selected by electrical switching. Provides faster access to information than disks.

magnetic storage Any device that stores data, using magnetic properties such as magnetic cores, tapes, and films.

magnetic tape Flexible plastic tape, often 0.5 inches wide with seven or nine channels or horizontal rows that extend the length of the tape. One side is uniformly coated with magnetic material on which data is stored. It is used for registering television images, sound, or computer data. Magnetic tape is a sequential medium with a very low cost per bit, used for archival storage, sorts, etc. Magnetic tape is being suspended as a storage medium in on-line systems where immediate access is required.

magnetic tape system High-capacity hardware storage including tape drive and control circuitry. Because of the tape's serial access it is well suited for large batches of stored information that do not require frequent access, or for applications where most of the records do not need to be accessed.

mail merge A procedure for combining names and addresses from one record file with correspondence from another record file for mailing purposes. Also the term for software that accomplishes this task.

mainframe Same as central processing unit. See CPU.

main memory The primary storage facilities forming an integral physical part of the computer and directly controlled by the computer. In such internal facilities all data is automatically accessible to the computer.

main program A program unit not containing a function, subroutine, or block data statement and containing at least one executable statement. A main program is required for program execution.

main storage The general-purpose program addressable storage of a computer from which instructions may be executed and from which data can be loaded directly into registers.

maintenance time Preventive and corrective time required for hardware maintenance.
  Compare available time.

makeup time Available time used for reruns due to malfunctions or mistakes.

malfunction A failure in the operation of the hardware of a machine.

management information system (MIS) A data processing system that is designed to furnish management and supervisory personnel with current information to aid in the performance of management functions. Data is recorded and processed for operational purposes, problems are isolated and referred to upper management for decision making, and information is fed back to reflect progress in achieving major objectives.

manipulation The act of changing or arranging data or its format to ease processing or to arrive at a problem solution.

mantissa The significant digits of a number written in scientific notation.

manual input Data entered manually by the operator or programmer to modify, continue, or resume processing of a computer program.

map A listing indicating where different elements of memory are laid out, such as the operating system, libraries, etc.

mapping Transforming one set of information to another set; or the setting up of correspondence between one set of information and another set.

mark The presence of a signal equivalent to a binary one.

mask In integrated circuit technology, a template, usually etched on glass and used to define areas of the chip on the silicon wafer. Masks are used for the diffusion, oxidation, and metalizing steps in the process of manufacturing chips. In computer logic, a mask is a pattern of bits used to selectively set, ignore, or clear bits within the word or bit pattern that is to be operated upon.

mass storage Massive amounts of on-line, secondary storage, readily accessible to the CPU of a computer providing lower cost for a given amount of information stored than main memory. Includes devices such as magnetic disk, drum, data cells, etc.

master control program An operating system, especially on Burroughs machines, designed to reduce the amount of intervention required of the human operator by providing the following functions: schedules programs to be processed, initiates segments of programs, controls all input/output operations to insure efficient utilization of each system component, allocates memory dynamically, issues instructions to the human operator and verifies that his actions were correct, performs corrective action on errors in a program or system malfunction.

master file   A main reference file of information used in a computer system. It provides information to be used by the program and can be updated and maintained to reflect the results of the processing operation.

master station   See primary station.

master terminal   A terminal designated as reserved for the system manager and thus privileged to initiate conservations for network management not available to user terminals. The identity of the master terminal may be changed when necessary by entering a special network management entry, after sign-on by a user recognized to be a system manager.

match   A data processing operation used to compare items of data for identity. Sequences are matched against each other on the basis of a given key.

mathematical programming   In operations research, a procedure for locating the maximum or minimum of a function subject to constraints.

matrix   An arrangement of elements (numbers, characters, dots, diodes, wires, etc.) in perpendicular rows.
   See also: x, y coordinates.

matrix printer   A printer which forms characters by printing a pattern of dots.

MB   Megabytes.

mean time to failure (MTBF)   The average time the system or a component of the system works without faulting.

mean time to repair time (MTTR)   A specific measurement that relates to the normal repair time.

media   The vehicles by which information is stored or transmitted, or can be classified as source, input, and output.

media eraser   An electromagnetic device that can completely erase stored data from any flexible magnetic media such as tape, diskette, cassette, or data storage. Also called a degausser.

medium   Plural: media. The material on which data is recorded, for example, magnetic tape, floppy diskette, winchester disk, etc.

medium-scale integration (MSI)   Usually less than 100 circuits on a single chip of semiconductor. Widely used in third generation systems.

mega   Prefix meaning one million.

megabyte   Literally 1,000,000 bytes; usually 1024 times 1024 bytes.

megahertz   One million cycles per second, abbreviated as MHz.

membrane keyboard   A type of keyboard composed of a single sheet of semiflexible plastic material with a conductive rear surface. When flexed approximately 0.005 inch with slight finger pressure, contact results and a signal is transmitted.

memory   The circuitry and devices that accept and hold binary numbers and are capable of storing data as well as a program. Memory must allow rapid access to information. Various types are: disk, drum, semiconductor, magnetic core, charge-coupled devices, bubble domain, etc.

memory, external   See mass storage.

memory, internal   See main memory.

memory address   A coded designation for the location of a byte in memory.

memory dump   A listing of the contents of a storage device, or selected parts of it.

memory location   The smallest position in a computer memory to which the computer can refer.

memory management   The allocation of main memory space on a multiprogramming system.

memory map   The graphic representation of all of the memory locations a computer can address.

memory mapped I/O   A technique in which addresses placed in peripheral devices appear to the processor as memory locations. The processor can send data to, or receive data from, the peripheral devices using the same instructions it uses to access memory. The advantage is that existing processor instructions can serve this dual purpose. The disadvantage is that this procedure diminishes the range of memory locations used for programs and data.

memory mapped video   A system in CRT high-resolution graphics displays in which each pixel position on the screen has a unique memory location or locations assigned to it. This is for storing data describing updated display attributes for that particular pixel, such as on-off, blinking, color, etc.

memory mapping   A listing of memory addresses showing how the system memory is allocated among various devices or programs.

memory protect   A feature designed to prevent accidental modification of the operating system. It separates the operating system from the user programs.

This hardware protection of certain areas of memory inhibits unauthorized reading from, or writing to, designated areas.

memory protection   See storage protection.

menu   The list of commands in a program available to the user.

menu-driven   Programs that use menus or a list of commands available to the user. The user simply selects the desired option.

merge   An operation combining two or more files of data into one in a predetermined sequence.

message   A sequence of characters used to convey information or data. In data communication, messages are usually in an agreed format with a heading, which controls the destiny of the message, and text, which consists of the data being carried.

message switching   A method of receiving a message over communications networks, transmitting it to an intermediate point, storing it until the proper outgoing line and station are available, and then transmitting it again toward its destination. The destination of each message is indicated by an address integral to the message.

metal oxide semiconductor (MOS)   A common material and method for making integrated circuits.

MHz   Megahertz.

MICR   Magnetic ink character recognition.

MICR reader/sorter   A document handler that permits both the reading of MICR-encoded documents and the sorting of those documents on digits selected either at the unit console (off-line) or by the computer program (on-line).

micro   A prefix meaning very small.

microcomputer   A complete tiny computing system, consisting of hardware and software that usually sells for less than five thousand dollars and whose main processing blocks are made of semiconductor integrated circuits. In function and structure it is somewhat similar to a minicomputer, with the main difference being price, size, speed of execution, and computing power. The hardware of a microcomputer consists of the microprocessing unit (MPU) which is usually assembled on a PC board with memory and auxiliary circuits. Power supplies, control console, and cabinet are separate.

microcomputer, 8-bit   A computer system utilizing a central processing unit that has an 8-bit word size.

microcomputer, 8/16-bit   A computer system that utilizes a processor with a 16-bit word size, but which multiplexes data across an external 8-line data bus. The larger word size increases the amount of memory that can be addressed, and enables more precise and complex instruction sets.

microcomputer, 16-bit   A computer utilizing a central processing unit (CPU) that has a 16-bit word size.

microcomputer, 16/32-bit   A system that uses a 32-bit processor, but which multiplexes data across an external 16-line data bus. The larger word size provides for more precise calculations and complex instructions. The larger data bus enables faster transfer of data to and from storage.

microcomputer architecture   The architecture of a microcomputer is designated in terms of bits: 8-bit, 16-bit, 32-bit, etc., and indicates the size of the chunk of data that can be handled in one execution of read, write, move, etc. In addition, these bits designate the number of memory cells in which data can be stored. An 8-bit machine moves 8 bits of data in a machine instruction; a 16-bit machine moves 16 bits., etc. The higher the number of bits defined in the microcomputer architecture, the faster the machine will perform most instructions. Software that is created on an 8-bit machine will not usually run on a 16-bit machine.

microcomputer kit   Small, inexpensive microcomputers marketed in kit (unassembled) form. One of the most popular is manufactured by Sinclair.

microcomputer system   A complete small system including the central processing unit (CPU), input/output interfaces and devices, memory and power supply, alphanumeric keyboard, CRT display, and massstorage device. Generally, a microcomputer system is smaller than a minicomputer in physical size, word size, memory size, and other factors, and this kind of system is referred to as a personal or desktop computer. There is a range of storage capabilities available, and this capacity is partially dependent on word size (8-bit, 16-bit, or 32-bit).

microfiche   A rectangular transparency approximately 4 in. × 6 in. containing multiple rows of greatly reduced images of reports, catalog, rate books, etc. Data reductions range from 13 up to several hundred times smaller than the originals. Uses are consistent with those of microfilm. Multiple copies are easily made to distribute pertinent data to various levels of operations.

microfilm   A roll of photographic film, small in size, but when developed and projected onto a screen produces a legible copy of the item or form photographed.

microfloppy disk   A floppy disk characterized by a 3-in. or 3.5-in. square disk jacket.

microfloppy diskette   Storage medium developed by Sony, enclosed in a plastic case, 3-1/2 in. diameter, capacity to store 278K characters when formatted and 437.5K when unformatted.

micro instructions   A simple instruction representing one step in a process. For example, an assembly instruction might consist of micro instructions such as move data register to accumulator, move contents of a memory location to the data bus, etc. These types of instructions are internal to the specific computer.

microprocessor   The central unit of microcomputer that contains the logical elements of manipulating data and performing arithmetical or logical operations on it. A single chip may contain RAM, ROM, and PROM memories, clocks, and interfaces for memory and I/O devices.

microprocessor, 8-bit   A microprocessor that has 8-bit registers and manipulates data that is in the form of 8-bit words.

microprocessor, 16-bit   A microprocessor that has 16-bit word size. The ability to handle words that are twice as big compared to the standard 8-bit word size means that it can process twice as much data at a time. It also offers greater speed and precision and is accurate to a greater number of significant figures than an 8-bit processor. Sixteen-bit processors also have more powerful and complex instruction sets.

microprocessor unit   See microprocessor.

microprogram   A sequence written in micro instructions and stored in the control unit of the microprocessor unit. When executed, it will perform the function of various micro instructions. The microprogram references the control unit directly; it is not accessible to the user.

microprogramming   A method of operation of the CPU in which each complete instruction starts the execution of a sequence of instructions, called microinstructions, which are at a more elementary level.

microsecond   One-millionth of a second.

microwave   High radio frequencies nominally between 1000 and 300,000 megahertz.

microwinchester disk   A 3-1/2 in. winchester disk.

microworld   A well-defined but limited learning environment in which interesting happenings occur and important ideas are offered. A microworld can have other microworlds within.

millisecond   One thousandth of a second.

minicomputer   A small programmable general purpose computer typically used for dedicated applications. The term often refers only to the mainframe, which typically sells for less than $25,000. Usually it is a parallel binary system with 8-, 12-, 16-, 18-, 24-, or 36-bit word length incorporating semiconductor or magnetic core memory offering from 4 to 64K words of storage and a cycle time of 0.2 to 8 microseconds or less. A bare minicomputer (one without cabinet, console, and power supplies) consisting of a single PC card can sell for less than $1,000 in OEM quantities. Minicomputers are used nearly everywhere large computers were used in the past but with much lower prices. As minicomputer prices have dropped, performance has increased and is likely to continue increasing as faster memories and logic evolve, thereby further broadening the application base.

minidisk   A floppy disk size designation characterized by its 5-1/4 in. (13.3-cm) square protective jacket. Also called a diskette.

minifloppy diskette   A flexible storage medium, 5-1/4 in. in diameter, with a capacity of approximately 45 to 60 text pages (calculated at 4,000 characters per single-spaced page).

miniwinnie   A 5-1/4 in. winchester disk.

MIS   See management information system.

mnemonic   Assisting human memory. Thus a mnemonic term is often an abbreviation designed to help programmers remember instructions, e.g., ART for arithmetic operation or MPY for multiply.

mode   The most common or frequent value in a group of values.

model   As approximate mathematical representation that simulates the behavior of a process device or concept so that an increased understanding of the system is attained.

modem   Contraction of modulator-demodulator. A device which modulates and demodulates signals transmitted over communication facilities. A modem is also known as a dataset.

modem bypass   A special cable that allows a local device to be connected directly to a modem communication port. It is used when modem communication is not necessary but operation of the local device is. For example, the user may not wish to disconnect the modem but might have need of another terminal. The terminal could be attached to the bypass and then disconnected for later use of the modem.

modem communications   The proceess of using modems for communication between computers and peripherals. For example, data flows from a computer through a modem, where digital signals are converted to audio signals, then across telephone lines to another modem that reconverts the audio information into digital signals that can be used by the receiving data device or terminal.

modem, direct connect   A type of modem that is connected electrically (by means of a plug) to the telephone system, thus eliminating the need for an acoustic coupler connection, or telephone instrument.

modes of operation   Computers can be made to operate in many different ways to meet differing company needs. These modes of operation are a major consideration because new ones have a big impact on company operations and EDP operations. Plans to go to new modes may mean significant change and cost.

modulation   Impressing of information on a carrier signal by varying one or more of the signal's basic characteristics: frequency, amplitude, and phase. Differential modulation carries the information as the change from the immediately preceding state rather than the absolute state.

module   A program unit that is discrete and identifiable with respect to compiling, combining with other units, and loading.

module testing or unit testing   The verification of a single program module, usually in an isolated environment (i.e., isolated from all other modules). Module testing also occasionally includes mathematical proofs.

monitor   A software or hardware tool that is used to supervise, control, or verify the operations of a system.

monitor (display)   A dedicated device used to display computer generated information. Monitors may be black and white, green, or color CRT displays.

MOS   Metal oxide semiconductor. The high-density integrated circuit technology used for most large-scale integration (LSI) devices, including microprocessors.

most significant bit   The bit in the left-most position of a binary word.
 See also least significant bit, significant figures.

most significant character   The extreme left-hand character in a group of characters.
 Compare least significant character.

motherboard   The main board or chassis with female connectors into which all printed circuit boards are attached to the microprocessor.
 See also breadboard.

mouse   A hand-held device, separate from a keyboard, used to control cursor position on a display screen. As the mouse rolls along a table top, its relative position approximates the position of the cursor. Introduced by Xerox in the Star 8010 professional workstation in 1981, it is now quite popular.

moving average   An arithmetic average of the most recent observations. As each new observation is added, the oldest one is dropped.

MPU   Microprocessor unit. See microprocessor.

ms   Millisecond. One-thousandth of a second.

MS-DOS   An operating system developed by Micro-Soft, Inc. and Seattle Computer for 16-bit systems.

MSI   Medium-scale integration. A term that describes the amount or density of integrated circuitry in a given area. MSI is more complex or densely packed than small-scale integration and less dense than large-scale integration.

MTBF   Mean time between failures. The average time between failures for any device.

multiaccess   The ability for several users to communicate with the computer at the same time, each working independently on a job.

multibus   A bus developed by Intel and widely used in industrial computer systems.

multidrop line   A communication system configuration using a single channel or line to serve multiple terminals. Use of this type of line normally requires some kind of polling mechanism, addressing each terminal with a unique ID. Also called multipoint line.

multileaving   A technique for allowing simultaneous use of a communications line by two or more terminals.

multiplexer   A hardware device that allows handling of multiple low-speed signals over a single high-speed channel.

multiplexing   The division of a transmission facility into two or more channels either by horizontally splitting the frequency band transmitted by the channel into narrower bands, each of which is used to constitute a distinct channel (frequency division multiplexing), or by alloting this common channel to several different vertical information channels, one at a time (time-division multiplexing).

multiplexor   The device used for multiplexing, often a shared transmission line such as a bus or a shared memory area.

multipoint line   See multidrop line.

multiprecision arithmetic Using more than one word to define the numbers in a computation; the larger word size permits greater accuracy.

multiprocessing system A computing system employing two or more interconnected processing units each having access to a common, jointly addressable memory to execute programs simultaneously. Also, loosely refers to parallel processing.

mutliprocessor A computer network consisting of two or more central processors under a common control.

multiprogramming A technique used to balance the CPU's speed with the slower peripherals by allowing several programs to run on the computer system at the same time. The goal is to make more efficient use of the system by keeping more parts of it busy more of the time. The difficulty is that this increases greatly the complexity and cost of the operating system and the overall computer system operation. This interleaving of the execution of two or more programs results in time sharing of machine components.

multitasking An IBM term for multithreading. Used in the literature for IBM's real software package CICS. Refers to the concurrent execution of one main task and one or more subtasks in the same partition or region. Routines, memory space, and disk files are held in common and are accessible to all. The operations will appear to be simultaneous, but will be simultaneous only in a multiprocessor system.

multithread operation A program construction technique which allows more than one logical path through the program to be executed simultaneously.

multiuser A computer that can support several work stations working simultaneously.

multiviewports A display that is able to simultaneously generate two or more viewing screens that are adjacent but independent.
  See also split screen, window.

NAND A boolean operative whose definition is that the output is 1 (true) only if both inputs are 0 (false). It is the opposite of AND.

nanosecond (ns, nsec) One-thousand-millionth (billionth) of a second (10.0 second).

narrowband channels Sub-voice grade channels characterized by a speed range of 100 or 200 bits per second.

native compiler A compiler that produces code usable only for a particular processor or brand of equipment.

natural language A language reflecting the application rather than an artificial structure based upon logical principles.

N-channel MOS (NMOS) The metal oxide semiconductor technology that is used for large scale integration (LSI) devices developed after PMOS. It has a higher speed but lower density than PMOS.

N/C system (numeric control) A manufacturing machine system which uses a tape (usually) of numerical data to control a machine or process. The N/C system consists of all elements of the control system and of the machine being controlled. As most numerically controlled devices have very limited logical or arithmetic capability (to keep costs low), they rely on their input tapes for detailed and explicit guidance. It is common for a computer to prepare the control tapes, using information presented in a manageable and concise form.
  See also direct numerical control

NE A notation for NOT EQUAL TO. The other symbols of inequality are ≠, < (less than), or > (greater than).

negative acknowledgment (NAK) In data communication, indicates that the previous transmission was in error and the receiver is ready to accept a retransmission. NAK is also the "not ready" to reply to a station selection (multipoint) or to an initialization sequence (line bid).

negative true logic A system of logic where a high voltage represents the bit value 0 and a low voltage represents the bit value 1. This is the reverse of traditional logic representation.

nest To imbed subroutines or data at a different hierarchical level so that routines can be executed or accessed iteratively.

network A computer communication system consisting of one or more terminals communicating with a single host computer system which acts as the network control component through internal programming or through a front end processor. The chief characteristic of a network is the single, controlling host computer system, which may include multiple processors. The general use of the word network to mean a collection of interconnected components is no longer precise, just as the word system no longer carries the connotation of close proximity of components.

network (database)   A method of organizing a database with linkages external to the physical organization.

network, bus   A popular local area network (LAN) configuration that utilizes a long length of cable which is often coaxial) running near each station. Each station may exist on individual short branch segments connected to the common cable. A node, or controller, connects the station to the cable, monitors the network traffic, and pulls off the communications addressed to the node. The signal passes in front of each station, and it can run in two directions. One advantage to a bus network is that if one access node fails, it usually does not bring down the entire system. It is often relatively easy to add stations to the network. One such bus network is called Ethernet.

network, data communications   A service for distribution of information to subscribers, often throughout the country. Data from local sources is compressed into packets and sent in a continuous stream from point to point. At the destination, the data is routed over local lines to receiving terminals.

network, local area (LAN)   A system allowing several concentrations of computers and terminals within a local area to share resources such as peripherals, software, or data. This encourages low-cost computer-based work stations throughout an office or campus, all of which have access to expensive peripherals such as hard disk drives, printers, or databases without the cost of equipment duplication. In addition, enhanced communication between work stations avoids repetition of work. Various configurations of networks are available, as well as gateways capable of connecting several networks to each other.

network, local area, general-purpose   A local area network system that links a large community of different terminals, peripherals, and computers, and which is capable of supporting a wide range of transmission speeds.

network, local area, single-purpose   A local area network system devoted to one application; the network interconnects computers and work stations of one manufacturer.

network, ring   A local area network arrangement in which signals pass through the nodes instead of in front of them, as in a bus network. The stations form a ring, often using a coaxial cable. Each station connects to the cable through a controller that examines the messages to the network. If the message is for the station, the con-

troller holds it for processing; if the message is for another station, the controller transmits the message to the next station. Failure of one node can jeopardize the whole ring.

network, star   A local area network in which individual stations branch from a central control node. Messages from one station to another are first routed to a central controller. The advantage is that private automatic branch exchanges (PABXs) are organized as star networks, which enables some companies to utilize their existing PABX wiring. However, if the central node fails, the entire system shuts down.
    See also PABX

network control program   The interface program that communicates with the network on one side and with user programs in the host computer on the other side.

networking   Hooking geographically separated computers together over transmission lines. This allows computers to ship data to each other or ship jobs around (either in case of overload or because one of the computers has the necessary computer programs or data to do a particular job). In teleprocessing, a number of communication lines connecting a computer with remote terminals. In general communication applications, the interconnection of multiple communication channels, multiple terminals, and/or computers (nodes).
    See also multiprocessing system.

network operations center   A specialized center that assists in network operations, monitoring of network status, supervision and coordination of network maintenance, accumulation of accounting and usage data, and user support.

network planning   Techniques that are used to plan complex projects, including critical path method and PERT.

network redundancy   Describes the property of a network that has additional links beyond the minimum number necessary to connect all nodes.
    See also link redundancy level.

network security   The measures taken to protect a network from an unauthorized access, accidental or willful interference with normal operations, or destruction, including protection of physical facilities, software, and personnel security.

network topology   The geometric arrangement of links and nodes in a network.

nibble   Popular name for 4 bits, or half a byte. Also spelled nybble.

NMOS   N-channel metal oxide semiconductor.

node Any station, terminal, terminal installation, communications computer, or communications computer installation in a computer network.

noise Undesirable signals bearing no desired information, and frequently capable of introducing errors into the communication process. In operations research, the unpredictable difference between the observed data and the true process.

non-print character A control character that can invoke a special function, but which has no printed symbol.

non-switched line A communications link which is permanently installed between two points.

non-transparent mode In data communications, transmission of characters in a defined format, e.g. ASCII or EBCDIC, in which all defined control characters and control character sequences are recognized and treated as such.

non-volatile memory A memory type which holds data even if power has been disconnected.

NOR A boolean operative whose definition is that the output is 1 (true) only when neither of the inputs are 1 (true).

NOT The logical operator. It changes every 1 to 0 and every 0 to 1 in a collection of binary data.
See also boolean algebra.

null An absence of information used as a positive confirmation of no information, as opposed to a 0 or a blank.

null cycle The time required to cycle through the entire program without introducing new data.

null instruction A program instruction that has no functional significance during program execution, but which may satisfy a structural requirement such as breaking a program into segments or reserving memory space for an instruction to be inserted later.

null modem See modem bypass.

number crunching Repetitive or complex arithmetic calculation, as opposed to moving data in the computer system.

number system, base Number systems vary principally by their base. The choice of the base can be advantageous for a particular application. The base is indicated in subscript notation.

numerical analysis A method of obtaining useful quantitative solutions to problems that have been expressed mathematically and which involve complex processes or relationships, e.g., integrations, by means of trial and error.

numerical control See N/C system.

numeric character A character that belongs to one of the set of digits 0 through 9.

numeric database This type of source database typically contains numeric values from original sources and/or data that has been summarized or otherwise statistically manipulated. Most often presented in the form of time series, numeric databases range from simple balance sheet data to complex econometric models. Economic, demographic, and financial data are often depicted in numeric databases. See database, source database.

numeric keypad A set of auxiliary keys at the right of the standard alphanumeric keyboard that has numbers for use in efficient input of numeric data. It is a convenient auxiliary to the alphanumeric keyboard.
See also keypad

numeric processor chip A processor specifically designed to handle high precision arithmetic and scientific function evaluation.

object code Absolute language output from a compiler or assembler which is itself executable machine code or is fully compiled and is ready to be loaded into the computer.

object language The output of a translation process. Synonymous with target language.
Compare source language.

object program See object code.

OCR (optical character recognition) A process of light-sensitive recognition by machines of printed or written characters from an output device, such as a cash register or adding machine, that serves as direct input to a computer system. This permits capturing input data at the entry source, bypassing additional processing operations.
Compare MICR.

octal A number representation system with a radix of eight.

OEM (original equipment manufacturer)   A purveyor of a product made for assembly into a final system or larger subassembly by another manufacturer. Often OEMs make computer peripherals that are integrated into a complete system by a mainframe vendor.

off-line   Pertaining to equipment or devices not under direct control of the central processing unit. For example, the computer might generate a magnetic tape which would then be used to generate a report off-line while the computer was doing another job. May also be used to describe terminal equipment which is not connected to a transmission line.

off-the-shelf   Production items which are available from current stock and need not be either newly purchased or immediately manufactured. Also relates to computer software or equipment that can be used by customers with little or no adaptation, thereby saving time and expense of developing their own.

one-chip computer   A computer where all the elements —RAM, ROM, CPU, and input/output interfaces—are implemented on a single chip.

one-way-only-operation   A mode of data communication operation in which data is transmitted in a preassigned direction over a channel. Synonymous with simple circuit.

on-line   The operation of peripherals or terminals in direct interactive communication and under control of the central processing unit via communication channel. May also be used to describe terminal equipment connected to a transmission line. Also pertains to a user's ability to interact with a computer either via the console or a terminal.
   See also on-line processing.

on-line debugging   The act of finding and fixing program bugs while the program is loaded in the computer.

on-line processing   A general data processing term concerning access to computers. The input data enters the computer directly from the point of origin or in which output data is transmitted directly to where it is used. The process usually requires random access storage. In on-line processing, a user has direct and immediate access to the computer system via terminal devices. Information and instructions are entered via a terminal, processing by the computer is begun virtually immediately, and a response is received as soon as possible, often within seconds. Examples: stockbroker getting information on current stock price, credit card checking, factory terminals for production control information.
   Compare batch processing.

on-line services   A term referring to computer functions available to end users not in possession of a host computer. Services include: the use by many users of one computer's processing power (time sharing), access to stored files of information (reference and source database), the use of storage media for private data (archival storage), the use of prepared programs (on-line software packages), and peripheral output (printed or recorded representative of data). Two or more of these services are often combined for the convenience of the end user.
   See also: time sharing

on-line services company   Typically provides computer services to end users connected, via terminal, with the host computer. These services include access to: processing power (time-sharing), prepared programs (on-line software packages), research information (source and reference database), storage media (archival storage), and peripheral output (printed or recorded representations of data in either a raw or a processed state).
   See also service bureau.

on-line software package   A service offered by on-line services companies. On-line services companies offer the use of these up-and-running programs to end users, usually for a fee. The end user inputs his/her own data (usually via telecommunications) and utilizes the on-line services company's software to manipulate said data. Examples include payroll and database management systems. In the latter case the on-line services company provides both the software and the storage necessary to create private databases.

opcode   Operation code.

open-shop   A computer facility in which programming is performed by the user rather than by a group of computer programmers. The computer operation itself may be described as open shop if the user/programmer also serves as the operator, rather than a full-time trained operator.

operand   The part of a computer instruction that tells the computer where the data to be processed is stored.

operating system   Software that controls the operation of a data processing system and that may provide the following services: determine what jobs are running and what parts of the computer system are working on each job at any given time, impose standards and procedures on machine operation, take care of the numerous little details lumped together as housekeeping, and invoke standard troubleshooting actions in case of malfunction. These operating systems are usually very complex and require large amounts of machine and disk storage. Sometimes called Supervisor, Executive, Monitor, Master Control Program, depending on the computer manufacturer.

operating time   That part of available time during which the hardware is operating. It includes development time, production time and makeup time.
Compare idle time.

operation   The action specified by one computer instruction or the act of performing arithmetic, logical, or manipulative actions upon data.

operation code   That part of a computer instruction that tells it what function (such as addition) to perform.

operations manual   The manual which contains instructions and specifications for a given application. Typically includes components for operators as well as programmers. Sometimes also includes a log section.

operations research   Quantitative analysis of industrial and administrative operations to derive an understanding of the factors controlling operational systems with the view of supplying management and objective basis to make decisions concerning the actions of people, machines, and other resources in a system involving repeatable operations. Frequently involves representing the operation or the systems with a mathematical model.
See also linear programming, numerical analysis.

operator   A logical or mathematical symbol or character that represents a process to be performed on an operand such as +, −, AND, OR, etc. A person or machine (such as a robot) that operates a machine.

operator console   The device which enables the operator to communicate with the computer, i.e., it is used to enter data or information, to request and display stored data, to actuate various programmed command routines, etc.

optical character recognition   See OCR.

optical disks   See video disk.

optical scanning   See OCR.

optimization   Achieving the best solution to a problem from an overall point of view as opposed to optimizing the component parts of the overall problem (suboptimizing).

OR   A boolean operative whose definition is that the output is 1 (true) only if at least one of the inputs is 1 (true). This is used to logically compare two or more values.

ordering   The process of arranging groups of characters by sorting and sequencing them in some arbitrary manner; for example, ascending or descending.

original equipment manufacturer   See OEM.

OS   See operating system.

output   Data emitted from a storage device, transferred from primary to secondary storage, or which is the product of an information processing operation; reports produced by a computer peripheral device.

output device   A computer peripheral such as a card punch that converts electrical signals into the form used by the output device, such as holes punched into cards, etc.

output media   Reports, documents, and punched cards or tape generated as output from a computer.

output table   The bed, or flat surface, of a plotter.

overflow   A condition caused by an arithmetic operation that generates a number that is too big for either the hardware or software word size limitations of the machine.

overhead   Nonproductive effort, taking place when the operating system and the programs are performing administrative task, but no production work is getting done. In worst cases, overhead may eat up more machine time than data processing does.

overlapped schedule   The overlapping of successive operations, whereby the completed portion of a job lot at one work center is processed at one or more succeeding work centers before the pieces left behind are finished at the preceding work center.

overlay   A technique for bringing routines into high-speed memory from some other form of storage during processing, so that several routines will occupy the same storage locations at different times. It is used when the total memory requirements for instructions exceed the available high-speed memory. Generally the sets of information are not related, except that they are needed in the same program at different times. The overlay concept thus permits the breaking of a large program into segments which can be used as required to implement problem solution.

overprint   To print over a previously printed character or characters in order to emphasize or improve the type. Also called boldface or overstriking.

PABX   Private automatic branch exchange.

packet   A group of bits including data and control elements which is switched and transmitted as a unit. The data is arranged in a specified format.

packet switching   Conceptually similar to message switching. A packet consists of a (usually) fixed-length message segment plus all the information needed to completely identify the message (service, destination, protocol, priority, etc.). The packet thus exists within a network as an entity wholly independent of its service, destination, and message content, and is routed, stored, distributed, etc. completely under control of the network computer, which causes the packet to migrate in controlled store-and-forward leaps throughout the network from its service to is destination.

packet switching network   A network of devices that communicate by means of packets of information. Each device requires software to identify which packets to keep and which to send.

packing density   The number of units of useful information contained within a given linear dimension, usually expressed in units per inch, i.e., the number of characters stored on tape or drum per linear inch on a single track.

paddle   A cursor control device used for computer games.

page   In virtual storage systems, a fixed-length block of instruction, data, or both, that can be transferred between real storage and external page storage; typically about 4K bytes. A program will be divided into pages in order to minimize the total amount of main memory storage allocated to the program at any one time. The pages will normally be stored on a fast direct access store and can be moved into main memory by operating system or hardware whenever the instructions of that subdivision need to be performed.

page fault   In virtual storage systems, a program interruption that occurs when a page that is marked "not in real storage" is referred to by an active page.

page fixing   In virtual storage systems, marking a page as nonpageable so that it remains in real storage.

paging   In virtual storage systems, the process of transferring pages between real storage and external page storage. If a page is not transferred from auxiliary storage until it is actually needed, then paging is said to be done by demand. Look-ahead schemes have been implemented with some success.

paging rate   In virtual storage systems, the average number of page-ins and page-outs per unit of time.

paper feed   The method by which paper is pulled through a printer.
See also friction feed, tractor feed.

paper tape   An old but reliable storage medium by which data is stored in a punched hole sequence on a paper tape. The technique is considered slow but inexpensive.

paragraph   A set of one or more COBOL sentences, making up a logical processing entity and preceded by a paragraph name or a paragraph header.

parallel   Several bits traveling over separate pathways (grouped together) simultaneously.
See also serial.

parallel processing   Processing more than one program at a time on a parallel basis, where more than one processor is active at one time, as distinguished from multiprocessing where only one processor is active on one program at a time.

parallel storage   Storage in which all elements of a word are handled at the same time.

parallel transmission   Transfer of data so that all bits are transmitted simultaneously, each one over a separate path. Parallel transmission requires more equipment than serial transmission, but it is faster.

parameter   A variable whose value is set in the main program and passed along to a subroutine, and vice versa. Also, this term is used for a definable characteristic, or one of a set, whose value determines the values and limitations of the system.

parity bit   Used to check that data has been transmitted accurately; a receiving device counts the on bits of every arriving byte; if odd parity is specified, an error condition will be flagged any time an even number of on bits are detected.

parity check   An error detection technique for checking the accuracy of computer words after transmission. One extra parity bit is included with each character or byte. In an even parity convention, the parity bit is set to 0 only if the sum of digits in the original word is an even number. The reverse holds in an odd convention. If a single bit changes state because a hardware malfunction has occurred, the parity check will detect an inconsistency.

partial RAM   A RAM in which some bits do not function. In some of the newer 64K chips as many as half of the bit locations turn out to be unusable.

partition   A portion of a computer's main memory set aside to hold a single program on a fixed-partition memory management system.

Pascal   A high-level programming language known for features that promote structured programming, block structure, and data types. Invented by Niklaus Wirth, but named for the seventeenth century French mathematician and philosopher, Blaise Pascal.
See also structured programming.

pass   One cycle of processing a body of data.

password   A unique word or string of characters that a program, computer operator, or user must supply to meet security requirements, before gaining access to the system.

patch   To modify a program in a rough or expedient way, often the object version of the already compiled program. This practice generally leads to severe documentation problems.

pattern recognition   The recognition and identification by a computer of shapes, forms, signals, sequences, and configurations.
See also character recognition.

PAX   See private automatic exchange.

PBX   See private branch exchange.

PC   Printed circuit; or personal computer.

PC-DOS   IBM's version of MS-DOS for the IBM Personal Computer.

PCI/O   Program controlled input/output.

P-code   A method of translating a source code to an intermediate code, called P-code, by means of a compiler, then using a special P-code interpreter on a host machine to obtain executable object code. The advantage of this apprach is portability. Each host machine needs only its own P-code interpreter and not a separate compiler. The compiler module is standard for all machines. The disadvantage is that the execution is slower than occurs with one-step translation to object code. Many versions of Pascal use P-code.

peek   A statement in the BASIC programming language that displays the contents of a particular memory location in decimal form.

performance (computer)   One of the major factors on which the total productivity of a system depends, largely determined by a combination of three other factors: throughput, response time, and availability.

performance degradation   Any situation in which the performance of the system is not optimal; for example, when two or more programs are competing for necessary resources. Also, this term defines the hardware failure of a component.

peripheral equipment   Usually called simply peripherals. These are external to the CPU devices performing a wide variety of input, output, and other tasks. On-line peripherals are connected electronically to the CPU. Others are off-line (not connected). Examples are printers, monitors, and storage devices.

peripheral interchange program (PIP)   A short CP/M utility that allows a file(s) to transfer to another device.

peripheral processor   See input/output processor.

peripheral slots   Holding slots built into the housing of some microprocessor units so that cards can be added in order to increase capabilities without hardware modification.

perpendicular recording   A recording technology that replaces longitudinal, or end-to-end, organization of magnets along the recording track with vertically oriented magnets in order to increase potential recording capacity.

personal computer (PC)   A small, relatively inexpensive computer well suited for use in the home, office, or school.

PERT   Program evaluation and review technique. A time-event network analysis system in which the various events in a program or project are identified, with the planned time for each, and are placed in a network showing the relationships of each event to other events.

phase reviews   In information system planning and design, a method for timely evaluation of a project's progress.

phoneme   One member of the set of the smallest components of speech which distinguishes individual utterances from each other in a language.

phonetic system   A system that uses a database of voice information or phonemes to produce sounds to emulate speech.

phospor dots   The minute particles of phosphor on a CRT picture tube that are used to create the image. On a color picture tube, combinations of red, blue, and green dots are organized into a pattern of triads.

physical data independence   An arrangement where the physical layout and organization of the data may be changed without changing either the overall logical structure of the data or the application programs.

physical record   A basic unit of data which is read or written by a single input/output command to the computer. It is this data which is recorded between gaps on tape or address markers on disk. One physical record often contains multiple logical records or segments.

physical storage organization   The physical representation and layout and organization of the data on the storage units. It is concerned with the indices, pointers, chains, and other means of physically locating records and with the overflow areas and techniques used for inserting new records and deleting records.

PIC   Priority intercept controller. A special chip utilized to manage several external interrupts. It decides priority in a situation of sumultaneous interrupts, and in some cases interrupts the servicing of devices that have low priority in favor of devices that have higher priority.

See also priority interrupt.

picosecond   One trillionth of a second. One thousandth of a nanosecond.

picture element   See pixel.

piecework programming   The method of using an outside service organization to prepare a program for which payment is arranged by accomplishment rather than on a time basis.

piezoelectric   A property of some crystals which undergo mechanical stress when subjected to voltages, or which produce a voltage when subjected to mechanical stress.

Pilot   An authoring language developed by John Starkweather.

pin-compatible   Integrated circuit devices that use the same pins for the same signals.

pin feed   The pin mechanism of a printer which guides the punched holes of fanfold paper through the sprocket. Also called tractor feed or sprocket feed.

pipelining   Starting the execution of one computer instruction before a previous instruction is completely executed.

PIT   Programmable interval timer.

pixel   Short for picture element. The dots which form a television screen. Also called a pel.

PLA   Programmed logic arrays. A logic device alternative to ROM which uses a standard logic network programmed to perform a specific function. PLAs are implemented in either MOS or bipolar circuits and are particularly suited to decoding and/or logic with advantage over ROMs. As such they are likely to be used in code converters, computer instruction decoding and I/O device command decoding.

planning board   See control board.

platen   The backing that a print element strikes against to make character imprints.

PLATO   A computer-based educational system that consists of a large, high-speed central computer that can service up to one thousand terminals in a time-share mode. It is geared to individual instruction consisting of interactive lessons with the student entering the responses through the keyboard or touching answers displayed on the screen. The system is currently being implemented for use with microprocessors.

PL/I   A high-level programming language designed for use in a wide range of commercial and scientific computer applications which has features of Fortran and COBOL plus others.

PL/M   Programming language for microprocessors. Derived from PL/I and used primarily on microprocessors.

plotters   Devices that convert computer output into drawings on paper or on display-type terminals instead of a printed listing. They can produce line graphs, bar charts, maps, engineering drawings, etc.

plug compatible   The ability to interchange one device for another, usually without modifying the hardware or the software.

PMOS   P-channel metal oxide semiconductor. A relatively old MOS technology for large-scale integration (LSI) devices. It is characterized by high circuit density, but it has a relatively slow microprocessor speed when compared to NMOS.

point-to-point   A limited network configuration with communication between two terminal points only, as opposed to multipoint and multidrop.

Poisson distribution   A statistical distribution similar to normal distribution except that the standard deviation is always assumed to be equivalent to the square root of the mean.

poke A statement used in the BASIC programming language to place data directly into a specified memory location.

Polish notation An arbitrary way to state mathematical relationships in order to avoid parentheses. For example, $(A + B) \times (C + D)$ might be written as $A\, B + C\, D + \times$ which means: get A and B, then add; get C and D, then add; then multiply. This offers advantages in hardware and software design.

polling A centrally controlled method of permitting terminals on a multiterminal line to transmit without contending for the line. The polling device contacts terminals according to the order specified by the user.

port The place where another device is connected to the computer. Ports can be serial or parallel.
  See also parallel, serial

portability The ability of a program to be used on more than one system. Theoretically, programs written in high-level languages are portable. In reality, variations between manufacturers' systems require some degree of modification on most programs that are used on different systems. Only subsets of a language are, therefore, truly portable.

portable computer A microcomputer small and light enough to be easily transported, usually not weighing more than 30 pounds for a complete system.

P/OS Abbreviation for professional operating system, introduced by Digital Equipment Corp. (DEC) for its Professional 300 series microcomputers.

positive true logic A logic system where a lower voltage represents a bit value of 0 (false) and a higher voltage represents a bit value of 1 (true).

post To enter a unit of information on a record.

postprocessing The coordination and handling of materials produced.

powerful Software is considered powerful if it is efficient and provides a wide range of options. In user software, it refers to the user's ability to put these options into action without too much effort. In system software, it denotes the ability to generate complex commands with a minimum of instructions. Hardware is considered powerful if it is faster, larger, and more versatile than comperable machines.

power supply The unit, usually within the computer housing, that converts the alternating current (AC) line voltage from the wall outlet to the direct current (DC) required by the individual electrical components.

precision The exactness or accuracy associated with a number. For example, 5.1234 has 5 digits of precision; if it were to have 3 digits, it would be rounded off to 5.12.

precompiler program A program that detects and provides source program correction before the preparation of the object program.

preprocessor In emulation, a program that converts data from the format of an emulated system to the format accepted by a target system. In general programming, a preprocessor is a program that examines the source program for preprocessor statements which are then executed, resulting in the alteration of the source program.

pressure-sensitive keyboard See membrane keyboard.

preventive maintenance Precautionary measures taken on a system to forestall failures, rather than to eliminate them after they have occurred, by providing for systematic inspection, detection, and correction of incipient problems before they develop into major defects.

primary station In a network, the station which has the priority to select and transmit information to a secondary station and has the responsibility to insure information transfer. The assignment of primary status to a station is temporary and governed by standardized procedures.

printed circuit board An insulating board onto which a metal coating is applied, then etched away, leaving paths or circuits. Also called PC boards, boards, cards, PC cards.
  See also motherboard.

printer Any output device that produces printouts. Very slow compared to the CPU's electronic speed.

printer, dual mode A dot matrix printer that produces characters on paper at one rate for near-letter-quality printing for word processing (averaging 100 characters per second) and at a faster rate (averaging 160 cps) for draft quality results in data processing.

printout The paper output material, also known as a hard copy.

priority indicator In data communications, a group of characters that indicate the relative urgency of a message and thus its order of transmission.

priority interrupt A system of interrupt in which devices of a higher priority may obtain servicing by the central processing unit before lower priority devices.

priority modes The organization of the flow of work through a computer, varying from a normal noninterrupt mode to a system in which there are several depths of interrupt.

priority rules Rules that are given to the scheduler so that it can be decided which job to do next.

private automatic branch exchange (PABX) A private automatic exchange that provides for the transmission of calls to and from the public telephone network.

private automatic exchange A dial telephone exchange that provides private telephone service to an organization.

private branch exchange (PBX) A manual exchange connected to the public telephone network on the user's premises and operated by an attendant supplied by the user.

private line A communication channel for private use; a leased, owned, or otherwise dedicated channel.

problem-oriented language A source language suited to describing procedural steps that is designed for convenience of program specification in a general problem area rather than for easy conversion to machine instruction code. The components of such a language may bear little resemblance to machine instruction. POLs are generally machine independent (Fortran, BASIC, COBOL, PL/I, etc.).

problem program Any program that is executed when the central processing unit is in the problem state; that is, any program that does not contain privileged instructions. This includes language translators and service programs, as well as programs written by a user.

procedure block A collection of statements headed by a procedure statement and ended by an end statement that is a part of a program, especially PL/I.

procedure division One of the four main component parts of a COBOL program. The procedure division contains instructions for solving a problem. The procedure division may contain imperative statements, conditional statements, paragraphs, procedures, and sections.

procedure-oriented language See problem-oriented language.

process To employ a systematic sequence of operations to produce a specified result by performing operations on data.

process control Pertaining to systems whose purpose is to provide automation of continuous operations, and characterized by in-line adjustments to regulate an operation. This is contrasted with numerical control, which provides automation of discrete operations.

processing program A general term for any program that is not part of the operating system. This includes language processors, application programs, service programs, and user-written programs.

processor A computer capable of receiving data, manipulating it, and supplying results.

processor bound Pertaining to a situation in which the limits of the speed of a computation are determined by the capabilities of the processor.
See also I/O bound

processor program In software, a computer program language processor that performs functions such as compiling, assembling, and translating for a specific programming language.

program A set of instructions arranged for directing a digital computer to perform a desired operation or operations. Also to prepare a program.

program chaining A technique for allowing programs to be run that are larger than main memory by sequential loading and executing of successive modules of that program.

program counter A register in the control unit of the central processing unit that contains the address of the next instruction to be fetched from memory. The program counter is automatically incremented after each instruction is fetched.

program generator Generally, a program which permits a computer to write other programs automatically.

program library A collection of programs and routines.

programmable communications interface An interface board used for communications control in which the major features, such as baud rate, are programmable rather than being preset.
See also EPROM

programmable read only memory (PROM) Similar to read only memory (ROM) but can be programmed once by the user. A special PROM programmer is used to write in the new program.
See also EPROM

programmed learning An instructional methodology based upon alternating material with questions on book form (programmed text) or on an interactive terminal (computer-assisted instruction, CAI).

programmer   A person involved in designing, writing, and testing computer programs. Depending upon the philosophy of the particular institution, programming can include substantial amounts of analysis, etc.

programmer's template   A pattern guide on which there are flowchart, logic, and other symbols used in programming.

programming   Preparing a list of instructions for the computer to use in the solution of a problem.

programming flowchart   A chart showing the sequence of operations in a program.
　　See also flowchart.

programming language   A language other than machine language, used for expressing computer programs. The major kinds of programming languages are as follows: a) assembly or symbolic machine languages that are characterized by a one-to-one equivalence with computer instructions but with symbols and mnemonics as an aid to programming; b) macroassembly languages which are the same as assembly or symbolic machine languages but permit macroinstructions used for coding convenience; c) procedure-oriented languages for expressing methods in the same way as expressed by algorithmic languages; and d) problem-oriented languages for expressing problems. Procedure-oriented languages may be further divided into: (1) algebraic languages (numerical computation), (2) string-manipulating languages (text manipulation), (3) simulation languages (such as GPSS, DYNAMO), and (4) multipurpose languages (such as PL/I).

programming modules   A limited set of instructions handled as a unit of for development, testing, and implementation.

programming RPQ (PRPQ)   A custom alteration or addition to the operating system programming or program products. The PRPQ may be used to solve unique data processing problems.

programming support representative (PSR)   An individual responsible for field maintenance of vendor supplied software.

program product   A licensed, charged-for program provided by a mainframe vendor that performs a function for the user. A program product contains logic usable or adaptable to meet the user's specific requirements.

program sharing   In networks, the ability for several users or computers to utilize a program at another node.

program temporary fix (PTF)   A temporary solution or bypass of a problem diagnosed by vendor field engineering as the result of a defect in a current unaltered release of the program.

project evaluation and review technique   See PERT.

project planning   The preliminary activity before the commencement of the actual study in which areas to be studied and objectives desired are defined.

PROM   A control memory in which the stored information can be altered, but not as easily as in ordinary memory. In some PROMs, the contents may be erased by prolonged (minutes-long) application of ultraviolet light, and then rewritten. A core-memory version is called EAROM (electrically alterable ROM).

prompt   A symbol generated on an input/output terminal; its purpose is to make the user aware of the necessity of further input, or the location of an input.

prompting   In systems with time sharing, a function that helps a terminal user by reminding him to supply operands necessary to continue processing.

proof   An attempt to find errors in a program without regard to the program's environment. Most proof techniques involve stating assertions about the program's behavior and then deriving and proving mathematical theorems about the program's correctness.

proof copy mode   The ability of a printer to make a proof copy with notations, highlighting, or symbols to mark revisions.

propagation delay   The time between when a signal is impressed on a circuit and it is recognized at the other end; of great importance in satellite channels.

properties database   This type of source database contains dictionary or handbook-type chemical or physical data.
　　See also database, source database.

proportional spacing   The ability of a printer to allocate spaces in tiny increments in order to compensate for the varying widths of the characters. Although more complex routines are necessary, the output appears more pleasing than outputs in which the characters are given equal space regardless of width. This is essential to the production of completely justified copy, as that produced in formal typesetting.

proprietary program   A program controlled by an owner through the legal right of possession and title. Commonly, the title remains with the owner and its use is allowed with the stipulation that no disclosure of the program can be made to any other party without prior

agreement between the owner and user. This applies to privately sold programs, program products offered for sale by mainframe vendors, and no-charge software provided by mainframers.

prosthetic Sometimes used to refer to the computer's use as a versatile tool that provides access to a large variety of inaccessible spaces and activities.

protected field An area of the CRT screen containing data that cannot be altered by an operator until it is freed by a special command. Also, an area of memory that cannot be altered by a user program.

protocol A formal set of conventions governing the format and relative timing of message exchange in a communications network.

public domain software Software that is not copyrighted and that can be freely copied and exchanged. Sometimes called freeware.

pulse A signal that can be wholly described by a constant amplitude and the duration time. This signal form is typically used internally in computers, terminals, and other business machines, but is also used by some communication facilities.

pulse modulation Transmission of information by varying the basic characteristics of a sequence of pulses: width (duration), amplitude, phase, and number.

punch card A standardized stiff paper card used for storing information via strategically punched holes. The card can be handled mechanically and machine-processed; the punched holes are sensed electrically by metal fingers or photoelectrically by photo cells.

push down list A list control procedure used in memory where the next item to be retrieved and removed is the most recently stored item still in the list. This is also known as last in, first out, and is synonymous with push down stack.

push down stack A set of computer registers or memory locations that uses the push down list concept.
See also push down list.

push up list A list control procedure used in memory where the next item to be retrieved and removed is the oldest item still in the list, that is, first in, first out.

push up storage A method of storing data that retrieves the items in the same order in which they were entered; that is, the oldest piece of data is retrieved first.

QTAM Queued telecommunications access method. A method used to transfer data between main storage and remote terminals. QTAM may be employed for data collection, message switching, and many other teleprocessing uses involving queued messages or direct access storage devices. QTAM insulates the programmer from most of the details involved in programming front-end communications processors and the attached terminal devices.

quad Involving four elements.

quad capacity A floppy disk with double-density, double-sided recording characteristics in order to achieve more storage per disk.

quality assurance The actions necessary to provide suitable confidence that an item will perform satisfactorily in actual operation.

query A request for data entered while the computer system is processing.

query language A user friendly set of commands that allow a user to access information from a database.
See also user friendly.

queue A series of elements, one waiting behind the other; also, a waiting line.

queueing theory A collection of mathematical techniques and models designed to estimate the length and duration of waiting lines, given a probabilistic description of arrivals and servicing times.

quick kill A sorting technique that eliminates additional handling of documents by early identification of those items that can be dropped from the sorting sequence.

quiescing The process of bringing a multiprogrammed system to a halt by rejection of new jobs.

QWERTY keyboard A standard typewriter alphanumeric keyset. Carried over from the printing industry and named for the first six keys of the third row from the bottom.

radio frequency A frequency or wave within the range of radio transmission.

radix The base of a number system. For example, the binary system radix is 2; the decimal system radix is 10; octal is 8; etc.
See also base.

RAM Random access memory. A storage technique in which the time required to obtain data is independent of the location. There is no difference in the time required to operate to or from any address. Core memories are RAMs; however, the term is usually used with respect to semiconductor memories.

random access Pertaining to a storage device where data or blocks of data can be read in any particular order (e.g., disk). Random access devices do not have to be read from the beginning to find a specific address as is necessary with paper tape and magnetic tape.
See also direct access storage.

random access memory See RAM.

range A statistical term referring to the spread of observed values.

raster The predetermined pattern of horizontal lines on the viewing screen of the cathode ray tube. The lines are scanned by an electron beam and are spaced to aid uniform coverage.
See also raster scan.

raster scan On the cathode ray tube display, this is a display technology in which an image is built from phosphor dots of varying intensity and illuminated by the focus of an electron beam. Since the luminescent quality of the phosphor does not last long, continued regeneration by the electron beam is needed to maintain the image. This is the type of system used for most black and white, and also for most color television sets, as well as for many computer displays, including the black and white, green and white, and amber and black display monitors.
See also cathode ray tube, interlaced field, phosphor dots, raster.

raw data Data before it has been processed, which may or may not be in a form comprehensible to the machine.

read To receive data from a device and to interpret it in preparation for processing.

reading The transferring of input data into the computer system.

read only memory (ROM) A memory that cannot be altered during normal computer use. Information is permanently stored and can be read from any location at high speed, but can never be altered. Users have to be sure that their program is right before they enable it into a ROM. On most computers, once the program in ROM is enabled, the program will allow for no further flexibility. Because programming ROMs is expensive, relatively short programs are usually enabled in an ROM.

read/write head The mechanism which writes data to or reads data from a magnetic recording medium.

read/write memory See random access memory.

real storage In virtual storage systems, the storage of a computing system from which the central processing unit can directly obtain instructions and data and to which it can directly return results. Same as processor storage.

real time The processing of transactions as they occur rather than batching them. Pertaining to an application in which response to input is fast enough to affect subsequent inputs and/or guide the process, and in which records are updated immediately. On-line processing is used for real time systems; however, not all on-line processing is real time. An on-line system may be shared by many users so that response time is not always immediate.

real time clock A clock in the computer that keeps track of time (hours, minutes, and seconds) and makes this information available to programs.

record A collection of related items of data (fields) treated as a unit.

recording density The quantity of bits recorded per unit area on magnetic media; usually measured in bits per inch (bpi).

recursive routine or procedure A routine or procedure that calls itself, or calls a different procedure or routine which, in turn, calls the first one again. This type of processing develops a set of levels and is related to tree structures.
See also tree structure.

red, green, blue (RGB) monitor A color display monitor for computers; capable of outstanding clarity and resolution.

reduction, data Taking raw data and converting it to useful, understandable data.

redundancy A repetition of information or the insertion of information which is not new. Example: the use of check bits and check characters in data communication is a form of redundancy, hence the terms: cyclic redundancy, longitudinal redundancy, vertical redundancy. Also, the presence of dual processors, output devices, etc., to assure continuous operations in the event of failure in one.

redundant processor A processor that duplicates or partially duplicates the operation of another processor to substantially reduce the possibility of total system failures.

redundant recording A cassette tape recording method where each piece of information is stored twice on the tape as insurance against information loss in the event of damage to any portion of the tape.

reel-to-reel A type of ribbon or tape feed used on some printers or tape recorders.

reference database This type of database contains information that directs users to a primary source (printed or non-printed) for additional details or for the complete text. There are two types of reference databases, bibliographic and referral. Reference database contrasts with source database.
See also bibliographic database, database, referral database.

referral database This type of reference database contains citations to non-print material. Non-print materials include individual, organization, audiovisual data, radio or television programs, unpublished proceedings data, and others. Abstracts are often included with the citations.
See also database, reference database.

refresh The continuing process of regenerating a signal over and over again in a situation where it decays or fades when left idle. The cells in a dynamic memory chip and the phosphor illuminated image on a cathode ray screen are two examples.

regional (computer) network A computer network whose nodes cover a defined geographical area.

register Memory device capable of containing one or more computer bits or words.

regression analysis A technique for determining the mathematical expression that best describes the functional relationship between two or more variables.

relational database A method of organizing a database to permit association of information contained in separate records by placing data associated with each key in separate tables.

relocatability A capability whereby programs or data may be located to different places in main memory at different times without requiring modification to the program.

relocatable addresses The addresses used in a program that can be positioned at almost any place in primary storage. Usually, however, once the program is link edited, the addresses used are absolute for the remainder of that processing run. Some programs are self-relocating: they can be located at any storage position at any particular time. Addresses are assigned by the use of base address and displacement or paging.

relocatable program A module of an object, program, or routine that does not have a fixed address and that is structured so that it can be moved and executed from any location in main memory without loss of efficiency.

remote access Pertaining to communication with a computer by terminal stations that are distant from that computer.

remote batch A method of entering jobs into the computer from a remote terminal in a conversational mode, for processing later in a batch processing mode. In this mode, a plant or office geographically distant from the central computer can load in a batch of transactions, transmit them to the computer, and get back the results by mail, or via direct transmission to a printer or other output device at the remote site.

remote computing See remote access.

remote data concentration The use of communications processors for the multiplexing of data from many low-speed lines or terminals (or low-activity lines or terminals) onto one or more higher speed lines.

remote job entry (RJE) Input of a batch job from a remote site and receipt of the output via a line printer or card punch at a remote site. The technique allows various systems to share the resources of a batch-oriented computer by giving the user access to centrally located data files and access to the power necessary to process those files.

repagination An automatic routine to change page endings if text is inserted or deleted within a document, or if a new page length is desired. Text will be removed from or added to pages, as required, to maintain page length.

repeatability   The ability of a device to minimize variation each time it performs a repetitive operation that is based upon a constant input signal. It is often expressed as a percentage of error.

repeat counter   A software counter that records the number of times an event takes place in a program for later comparison.

repeat key   A key that can be held down so that it repeatedly makes contact without need for additional depression, or a key that is pressed at the same time as another key in order to make the second key repeat for the duration of the time that the repeat key is depressed. For example, it can be used in combination with the cursor movement keys in order to move rapidly across the screen.

replication   The use of a dual piece of hardware to reduce the risk of data loss in the event of a failure.
See also redundant processor, redundancy.

report generation   Production of a report as output, requiring only the specification of the arrangement and content desired and designating the existing data as output.

report generator   A program that generates a report. It takes care of formatting and other details and can do some processing of data, such as adding up columns or rows of numbers.

reprogramming   Changing a program written for one computer so that it will run on another.

rerun   A repeat of a machine run, usually because of a correction, an interrupt, or a false start.

rerun point   In a computer program, one of a set of carefully selected points designed into a computer program such that if an error is detected between two such points, the problem may be rerun by returning to the last such point instead of returning to the start of the program.

RES   Reset signal.

reserved word   A word used in a COBOL source program that has special privileged meaning to the language processor. It must not appear in a program as a user-defined operand.

reset key   Erases all programs and restores the computer to its original mode.

resident   Existing permanently in computer memory.

residual value   The value of a piece of equipment at the end of a lease term.

resolution   Refers to the visual clarity of a display screen, the result of the number of dots per square inch in a particular screen matrix.

resource   Any means available to network users such as computational power, programs, data files, storage capacity, or a combination of these.

response time   The amount of time elapsed between generation of an inquiry at a data communications terminal and receipt of a response at that same terminal. Response time, thus defined, includes: transmission time to the computer; processing time at the computer, including access time to obtain any file records needed to answer the inquiry; and transmission time back to the terminal.

retrofit   Updating of or adding to an existing system in order to improve it or to accommodate a change.

return   An instruction used at the termination of a subroutine causing control to return to the main program.
See also carriage return.

return key   The carriage return key on a terminal keyboard which when struck places the cursor at the left margin one line below its previous horizontal position.

reverse channel   Provision of a simultaneous data path in the reverse direction over a half-duplex facility. Normally it has a much lower bandwidth (transmission speed) than the main data path. Most commonly, it is used for positive/negative acknowledgments of previously received data blocks.

reverse Polish notation   The procedure used in some calculators for basic arithmetic functions. To use such a calculator, one must first learn a specialized method for entering calculations.
See also Polish notation.

reverse video   A mode of displaying selected characters in a manner that is exactly the opposite of that screen's normal display color. For example, on a screen with light characters against a dark background, reverse video would show dark characters against a light background.

rewrite   The process of putting out information to memory or to a storage device.

RF   Radio frequency.

RF modulator   Abbreviation for radio frequency modulator. A device which transfers the video display information from a video interface to a television.

RGB monitor Red, green, blue monitor. A type of color monitor with separate inputs for red, green, and blue. This type of monitor is required for high resolution color images. The red, green, and blue signals must be sent separately.

ribbon cartridge The plastic holder and feed device for a printer ribbon. These devices vary considerably from printer to printer.

ring network A computer network where each computer is connected to adjacent computers.

RJE See remote job entry.

RO Receive only. A printer terminal with no keyboard for data entry.

robot A device capable of receiving input signals consisting of commands or information about environmental conditions and then using the information as a basis for performing mechanical, repetitive tasks. Robots are used primarily in industry to increase productivity, to free workers from mundane tasks, and to repair and make other machines.

robotics A field of study that involves the use of robots to perform tasks in industrial and other environments.

rollback A programmed return to a prior checkpoint or rerun point.

roll over A keyboard encoding mechanism that eliminates error when more than one key is pressed at the same time.

ROM See read only memory.

ROMable Pertaining to code designed to be placed in ROM memory.

routine An ordered set of general-use instructions. See program.

RPG Report program generator.

RPQ Request for price quotation. See computing system RPQ, programming RPQ.

RPROM Reprogrammable read only memory.

RS-232-C A technical specification published by the Electronic Industries Association establishing the interface requirements between modems and terminals or computers.

RS-422-A An interface standard published by the Electronic Industries Association establishing the requirements for serial communications between computers. Not as popular as RS-232-C but provides increased capacities.

RST Restart.

RTC Real time clock.

run The single and continuous execution of a program by a computer or a given set of data.

running in parallel Where two central processors are used jointly for the same operation. If one central processor fails, the second central processor is used for backup.

running time The time during which a machine is actually producing. For example, the running time would include execution, but would not include set up, maintenance, waiting for the operator.

run-unit The CODASYL word for a single application program execution or task.

R/W Read/write.

S-100 bus Used as a standard bus in many personal computers. It can accept up to 20 devices, such as memory or I/O ports.

sampling A statistical process whereby generalizations regarding an entire body of phenomena are drawn from a relatively small number of observations.

satellite computer A processor connected locally or remotely to a larger central processor, and performing certain processing tasks—sometimes independent of the central processor sometimes subordinate to the central processor.

save To permanently record and store a program or data on a storage device such as a floppy disk.

SBC Single board computer.

schematic A drawing showing component interconnections of a circuit.

schematic symbols   Stylized line drawings that represent various elements and which are usually used universally.

Schottky circuits   A circuit technology that is characterized by high speed and high power consumption.

scientific notation   A technique for expressing quantities as powers of ten.

scratch pad memory   A fast internal storage area where the control section finds out what it is to do. It is reserved for intermediate results, various notations, or working areas.

scratch tape   A tape that is available for writing on. The previous contents are obsolete and thus can be scratched.

screen dump   The transfer of data or images from a terminal display to storage or to a peripheral device in order for it to be printed.

screen size   The physical viewing dimension of a cathode ray tube screen, usually expressed as a diagonal measure in inches. Screen size does not limit screen resolution.

screen type   The technology of the display. For example, there is the cathode ray tube (CRT), the liquid crystal display (LCD), and the light-emitting diode (LED).

scrolling   Moving through information on a computer display, either vertically or horizontally, to view information otherwise excluded.

SDA   See source data automation.

search and replace   The ability of a word processing program to find a specified character, word, or string each time it appears in the text and to replace it with another character, word, or string as specified by the operator.

secondary station   In a network, a station that has been selected to receive a transmission from the primary station.

secondary storage   Same as mass storage.

sectors   An organization of data storage on a magnetic disk, where data is stored and accessed in a system of tracks and sectors.

security   The general subject of making sure the computerized data and program files of the company can't be accessed, obtained, or modified by unauthorized personnel, and can't be fouled up by the computer or its programs. Security is implemented by special software, special hardware, and the computer's operating procedure.

seek   To position the access mechanism of a direct access device at a specified location.

seek time   The time that is needed to position the access mechanism of a direct access storage device at a specified position.
    See also access time.

segment   A set of data that can be placed anywhere in a memory and can be addressed relative to a common origin. A segment contains one or more data items (usually more) and is the basic quantum of data which passes to and from the application programs under control of the database management software.

selecting   A communication network technique of inviting another station or node to receive data.

selection sort   A sorting technique where one key or item of data is designated as the lowest or the highest. Then all of the remaining items in the list are compared and ordered in relation to the first key of data.

self-relocating program   A program that can be loaded into any area of main storage and that contains an initialization routine to adjust its address constants so that it can be executed at that location.
    See also relocatable program.

self-test   The ability of a device, such as a printer, to run through its entire instruction set and to test the internal circuitry to be sure that it is working properly before proceeding with a specific task.

semiconductor   A substance that can act as a conductor of electricity or an insulator of electricity depending on its charged state. It in effect acts as an on/off switch signifying binary digits (1's and 0's).

semiconductor memory   A method of storing data (binary digits) using semiconductors.
    See also semiconductor.

sensor-based system   An organization of components, including a computer, whose primary source of input is data from sensors and whose output can be used to control the related physical process.

sequencing   In numeric sequence, normally in ascending order.

sequential access   A term used to describe files such as magnetic tape which must be searched serially from the beginning to find any desired record.

sequential data set A data set whose records are organized on the basis of their successive physical positions, such as on magnetic tape.

sequential storage Secondary storage where data is arranged in ascending or descending order, usually by item number. This type of storage is usually associated with magnetic tape. Sequential storage usually is processed in a batch.

serial One bit following another over a single pathway.
See also parallel.

serial access Descriptive of a storage device or medium where there is a sequential relationship between access time and data location in storage—i.e., the access time is dependent upon the location of the data.
Compare direct access storage device, random access.

serial interface An interface which transmits data bit by bit rather than in whole bytes. Serial interfaces are much slower than parallel interfaces but they are also much cheaper.

serial transmission The transmission of data in such a way that all the bits in a byte are handled one after another.
Compare parallel transmission.

serviceability The ease with which hardware or software failures can be detected, diagnosed, and then repaired.

service bureau A company that supplies users with batch or interactive processing either on-line or off-line. This type of company does not usually provide access to database material. Typical applications satisfied by the service bureau can include payroll, billing, and bookkeeping.
See also on-line services company.

service computer See host computer.

service organizations Companies which offer and contract for field maintenance and operation of computers not owned or leased by them in exchange for charges and fees commensurate with the size and complexity of the system. This type of service is also called third-party maintenance.

session The period of time during which a user engages in a dialog with a conversation time sharing system; the time elapsed from when a terminal user logs on the system until the user logs off the system.

shift The operation of moving the binary contents of a storage register one or more bits to the left or right within the register in order to multiply or divide.

short-line seeking The action performed by a printer when the line to be printed does not span the entire page. The printer performs a carriage return at the end of the short line and begins to print a new line, speeding up printer performance.

shutdown The action of making a real time system unavailable at the end of the real time day. It includes disabling all terminals so that no more entries can be made, monitoring the completion of exchanges in progress, and upon completion, closing all files in an orderly fashion and terminating the real time job.

SIG Special interest group.

SIGGRAPH Special interest group for graphics. A non-profit organization devoted to the advancement of computer graphics.

signal-to-noise-ratio Relative power of the signal to the noise. As the ratio decreases on a line, it becomes more difficult to distinguish between information and non-information (noise).

significant digit A digit that contributes to the precision of a numeral. The number of significant digits is counted beginning with the digit contributing the most value, called the most significant digit, and ending with the one contributing the least value, called the least significant digit.

significant figures The number of digits in a number that are known to be entirely correct or meaningful for further use. For example, in computer calculations numbers are often rounded off due to the restrictions of the word size. As these rounded-off numbers are used in additional calculations and are subsequently rounded off in turn, the numbers farthest to the right become less and less accurate. Therefore, although the computer may come up with a result that has as many as nine digits (as in 1.23456789), the last five digits may be meaningless because they have become distorted by the calculation process itself. In this case, the number would have been said to have four significant figures, or 1.234.

sign-off See log-off.

sign-on See log-on.

silicon wafer A silicon ingot slice on which integrated circuits are fabricated. After fabrication and testing, the wafer is cut into individual chips which are then used as finished integrated circuit components.

simplex A communications line that carries data from one point to another in only one direction.

simplex circuit   A communication line used in one direction only, or in either direction but not at the same time. It is perhaps best not to use the term. The first case is rare and the word channel is available; in the second case, half-duplex is commonly used.

simscript   See simulation languages.

simulation   The use of programming techniques alone to duplicate the operation of one computing system on another computing system. In computer programming, the technique of setting up a routine for one computer to make it operate as nearly as possible like some other computer.
Compare emulation.

simulation languages   Programming languages, such as Simscript II or GPSS that tend to offer more comprehensive diagnostics than do the general purpose languages, such as Fortran and PL/I. If users have the facility to run these, they will find both quite suitable in representing logic or whole computer systems in functional form. Both GPSS and Simscript II provide an event monitor that keeps track of events and advances a clock to the next instant of time when a change may occur. With GPSS (General Purpose Simulation System), transactions move from point to point in the system mode, make use of facilities such as arithmetic units, and can be stored as queues such as cache buffers.

simultaneity   The facility of a computer to allow input/output on its peripherals and to continue in parallel with operations in the central processor.

single board computer   A complete computer, including ROM, RAM, central processing unit, and I/O interface, implemented on a single printed circuit board. These small computers are frequently used for industrial control applications.

single precision   Refers to the number of memory locations used for a number in a computer. Single precision indicates one location for each number. In order to store a number with decimal places, higher precision is necessary.

single-purpose local area network   See network, local area, single-purpose.

single threading   A program that completes the processing of one message before starting another message.
See also multithreading operation.

sink   The terminal node at which data is used in a network.

6502   An 8-bit word length microprocessor developed by MOS Technology and used in the Apple, Commodore PET, and Ohio Scientific computers.

68000   A 32-bit internal and 16-bit external word length microprocessor developed by Motorola. Radio Shack uses this chip in the TRS-80 Model 16.

16-bit system   Refers to the number of bits in a word that can be processed, stored, and recalled at one time in one machine cycle. Longer word lengths increase efficiency and accuracy but also increase complexity.

slave   An I/O or printer-driven module controlled by a master unit. In some low-level word processing applications, it is common to have a master unit plus a number of slaves, automatically grinding out repetitive letters.

slice architecture   A method by which a section of the register file and ALU in a computer is placed in one package. In some systems the registers are all 4 bits wide, others accommodate 2 bits. Two or more of these slices can be cascaded together to form larger word sizes.
See also bit-slice processor.

slot   A means of expanding microcomputer capabilities by adding circuit boards for specific applications. Slots are the receptacles that handle these boards.

slot bound   A situation in which the expansion of a microcomputer system becomes restricted by the number of expansion slots available to it.

small computer   A variety of computer types based on relative size and power.
See also desktop computer, microcomputer, minicomputer, personal computer, portable computer.

Smalltalk   Programming language for the Xerox Star 8010 work station.

smart peripheral   A peripheral device such as a terminal or a printer that contains its own processor and memory so that it may relieve the host system of many functions normally associated with the functioning of that peripheral. Sometimes called an intelligent peripheral.

smart terminal   A terminal having computational capability, i.e., editing commands, graphic abilities.

smash   The destruction of an area of memory or program by overwriting with another segment of memory or program.

SNOBOL   String-oriented symbolic language. A high-level programming language geared toward the manipulation of character strings.

softcard A circuit board made by MicroSoft, Inc. which enables an Apple to use the CP/M-80 operating system.

soft error A transient, unpredictable fault usually associated with software rather than hardware.

soft keys Keys that can be defined in software for any nonprinting, nondisplay character functions such as erase, block move, etc. This term is also used to describe function keys.

soft sectored A term used to describe a particular diskette format, and a way of recording on the diskette. Soft sectored disks are pre-formatted, having data fields that are changed and updated. The first track of a soft sectored diskette identifies the disk, the next four tracks store basic format information such as the track and sector location of stored material. Since soft sectored diskettes require a format, less storage capacity is available for text storage (250 out of a possible 400K) than is available with hard sectored diskettes. Soft sectored diskettes may be initialized and used with most popular microcomputers and operating systems.

software A term coined to contrast computer programs with the hardware of a computer system. Software programs are stored sets of instructions which govern the operation of a computer system and make the hardware run. Software is a key determining factor in getting more computer power per dollar. Software is used to define the processor programs, library routines, manuals, and other service programs supplied by a computer manufacturer to facilitate the use of a computer. In addition, it may refer to other programs specially developed to fit the users need. All the documents associated with a computer.

software, public domain Also known as freeware. See public domain software.

software house A company which offers software support service to users. This support can range from simply supplying manuals and other information to a complete counseling and computer part-time programming service (job shop or body shop).

software library The software tools supplied by manufacturers required for the development of user application programs.

solids modeling Geometric modeling of an object by construction of a computer model based on the measurements, properties, and relationships of points, lines, angles, and surfaces of the object.

solid state Electronic components that are known for reliability and economy and which control electrons within solid materials known as semiconductors. Their small size and suitability to mass production techniques have revolutionized electronic applications.

solid-state computer A computer that is built primarily from circuits and components that contain semiconductors.

solid-state device Any element that can control current without moving parts, heated filaments, or vacuum gaps. All semiconductors are solid-state devices, although not all solid-state devices (e.g., transformers) are semiconductors.

sort A processing run or operation to distribute data in numerical, alphabetic, or alphanumeric groups according to a given standard or rule. A key consisting of a prescribed, uniform string of characters can be used as a means of making workable size groups from a large volume of records.

sorter/reader See MICR reader/sorter.

source The terminal node at which data enters a network.

Source, The An electronic information service operated by Source Telecomputing Corp., a subsidiary of The Reader's Digest Association, Inc. It is available to the public on a subscription basis and offers access to large databases of varied information, electronic mail, shopping, software reviews, bulletin boards, etc, through use of a home computer or dumb terminal plus modem connected to a mainframe by telephone.

source data automation (SDA) The capturing of data for machine entry as a key product of producing a required document such as a purchase order, job order, or other source document. The by-product then serves as input for a computer.

source database This type of database contains a full representation of original information. This type of database provides users with quantitative answers without referencing other sources. There are four types of source database: numeric, textual-numeric, properties, and full text.

source document An original record of some type which is to be converted into machine readable form.

source language The language that is an input for statement translation.

source listing A record of the computer instructions in program language.

source program   A computer program written in symbolic language which will be converted into an absolute language object program using a processor program.

space   Binary 0, or no voltage.

SPC   See switching center, processing center.

special character   A character that is neither numeric nor alphabetic. Special characters in COBOL include the space, the period (.), as well as the following: + − * / = $; ") (.

special interest group (SIG)   People who meet to discuss and exchange information about a specific computer-oriented interest, such as computer graphics, robotics, education, business applications, word processing, etc.

specialized common carrier   A company that provides private line communications services, e.g., voice, teleprinter, data, facsimile transmission.
See also value-added service.

special-purpose computer   A computer that is designed to handle a restricted class of problems.

speech synthesizer   A device that creates representations of speech from electronic phonemes by using a set of rules that describe English pronunciations. It enables the computer to "talk" to its user.

spelling checker   Software that proofreads by comparing each word in a text file to a dictionary, and then marks or otherwise indicates misspelled words.

split screen   A cathode ray tube display in which the software divides the screen into two or more separate sectional areas for the independent viewing of portions of graphics, text, etc.

spooling   The reading and writing of input and output streams on auxiliary storage devices, concurrently with job execution, in a format convenient for later processing or output operations. Synonymous with concurrent peripheral operations.

spreadsheet, electronic   See electronic spreadsheet.

sprocket feed   See pin feed, tractor feed.

SQ   See squeezed files.

squeezed files   Normal data or program files that have been organized more efficiently using squeeze (SQ) and unsqueeze (USQ) utilities to save space and to reduce transfer time.

stack   An area in memory for the temporary storage of data. Data in a stack is not retrieved by address, but rather in chronological order, last in, first out (LIFO).

stair stepping   Refers to the discontinuous nature of a line that is drawn by a raster display at any angle other than the vertical, horizontal, or 45 degrees. The raster display must approximate the line because of the limitations of its technology and resolution.

stand alone program   A program that can be executed independently of an operating system.

star bit   In asynchronous transmission, the bit that indicates the beginning of a block of data.

star network   A computer network with peripheral nodes all connected to one or more computers at a centrally located facility.
See also centralized network.

start-stop transmission   See asynchronous transmission.

STAT   Status.

statement   In programming, an expression or generalized instruction in a source language.

state of the art   The most current research and up to date technology in a specific field of knowledge.

static RAM   Random access memory that requires continuous power but not continuous regeneration to retain its contents.
Compare dynamic RAM.

static turtle   In the Logo language, a turtle cursor with a fixed spatial position and heading that responds to such commands as FORWARD and LEFT.
See also turtle graphics.

station   A data terminal device connected to a data link. It includes sources or sinks for the messages, as well as those elements which control the message flow on the link by means of data communication control procedures.

status information   Information about the logical state of a piece of equipment. Examples are a peripheral device reporting its status to the computer or a network terminating unit reporting its status to a network switch.

step   One operation in a computer program.

stepper motor An electromagnetic device that moves or rotates by a fixed amount each time an electrical pulse is applied to it. Often, such a motor is found in printers, disk drives, and other computer equipment.

stop bit In asynchronous transmission, the bit that indicates the end of a block of data.

storage A computer-oriented medium in which data is retained. Primary (main) storage is the internal storage area where the data and program instructions are retained for active use in the system (normally core storage). Auxiliary or external storage is for less active data, and the media may include magnetic tape, disk, or drum.

storage capacity The amount of data that can be contained in a storage device or main memory, usually expressed in terms of K (1 K = 1024 bytes). If the storage capacity of a computer is 16K, the capacity is 16,384 characters (bytes).

storage fragmentation A phenomenon observed in systems using dynamic allocation or core storage which permit variability in the amount allocated.

storage media Refers to the type of medium used: disk, cassette tape, hard disk, mag cards, etc.

storage protection Methods of preventing access to storage, or the loss of stored data during power interrupts. Synonymous with memory protection.

storage tube A display technology that behaves like a cathode ray tube (CRT) screen but which has extremely long-persistence phosphors that retain their charge for hours. The picture will remain on the screen for hours rather than for the fraction of a second common to dynamic storage, thus eliminating the need for refresh or frame buffers. Storage tubes excel in high resolution that is unmatched by raster systems, although they are not as well suited as raster systems for color graphics or interactive applications.
See also raster, refresh.

store To place data or programs in the computer for later use.

store and forward The handling of messages or packets in a network by accepting the messages or packets completely into storage then sending them forward to the next center. Also, the capture of transaction data on magnetic media for subsequent batch input to a computer.

stored program computer (SPC) A computer controlled by internally stored instructions that are treated as though they were data, and that can subsequently be executed.

STRESS Structural engineering systems solver. A language useful for structural analysis problems in civil engineering. For design applications, larger problems, and more sophisticated modeling and analysis, this language has been replaced with STRUDL. Implemented on several computers, primarily small minis.

string A connected sequence of characters of bits that is treated as a single data item.

string length The numbers of characters on a string.

strobe A hardware control signal for information transfer.

structured language A computer language that fosters structured programming techniques through its use of vocabulary, syntax, and grammar.
See also structured programming.

structured programming Planning and implementing a program as a series of linked logical modules, paying special attention to documentation, testability, and program clarity so as to simplify program debug and maintenance.

structured walkthrough A formalized technique whereby one programmer describes the step-by-step functioning of the program to other programmers.

STRUDL Structured design language. A language used for the design and analysis of structures.

stylus A penlike device used with a graphics tablet for inputting position information relative to a coordinate axes system employed by the tablet.

SUB Subroutine.

subprogram See subroutine.

subroutine Program segments which perform a specific function. A major reason for using subroutines is that they reduce programming and debugging labor when a specific function is required to be executed at more than one point in a program. By creating the required function as a subroutine, the statements associated with that function may be coded once and executed at many different points in a program.

subscript A symbol that appears below and after a character.

subsystem A secondary or subordinate system which is usually capable of operating independently of, or asynchronously with, a controlling system.

superscript   A symbol that appears above and after a character.

supervisor   The part of an operating system that coordinates the use of resources and maintains the flow of CPU operations, rather than processing data to produce results.

supplier   See vendor.

support   In computer practice, the promise by vendors to offer help and guidance in using purchased or leased software and hardware.

surge   A sudden voltage or current change in an electrical circuit. It can cause a microcomputer and its peripherals to give erroneous results or to stop functioning altogether.

surge protector   A device that plugs into the wall socket to protect microcomputers from alternating current (AC) line surges. The computer plugs into the surge protector.
See also surge.

swap   In systems with time sharing, to write the main storage image of a job to auxiliary storage, and read another job's main storage image into main storage.

swapping   In systems with time sharing, a process that writes a job's main storage image to auxiliary storage, and reads another job's main storage image into main storage.

switched line   A telephone line that is connected to the switched telephone network.

switched network   A multipoint network with circuit switching capabilities. The telephone network is a switched network, as are Telex and TWX.

switching center   A location where an incoming call/message is automatically or manually directed to one or more outgoing circuits.

symbolic language   A language which is convenient for the programmer because it uses mnemonic terms that are easy to remember. Once the program has been written in symbolic language, it must be converted to absolute language using a processor program.

symbolic name   A data field identifier synonymous with symbolic address. The programmer creates symbolic names; the computer changes these symbolic names into storage addresses. Fortran and BASIC call the symbolic name as a variable.

sync character   A character of defined bit pattern that is used by the receiving terminal to adjust its clock and achieve synchronization.

synchronization   Process of adjusting a receiving terminal's clock to match the transmitting terminal's clock.

synchronous communications binary (BISYNC)   A set of operating procedures for synchronous transmission used in IBM teleprocessing networks. With BISYNC, some system batch terminals automatically perform error checking on all incoming data and request retransmission of a message whenever it is not received exactly as sent. As a transmitting terminal, the system automatically retransmits messages when they are not accurately received by the remote station. Because of the reliability of data transmissions using binary synchronous methods, it becomes economical to collect and store large amounts of data at the processor using either cassettes or a mass memory subsystem and to later transmit the data to computers or terminals, including other systems.

synchronous transmission   A mode of data communications by which the bit stream and character stream are slaved to accurately synchronized clocks at the receiving and transmitting stations. Start and stop pulses are not required with each character.

syntax   The rules governing structure in a programming language.

syntax error   A system response to a mistake in instruction, such a transposition of characters or an omission of a character or word.

SYSGEN   See system generation.

SYSLOG   See system log.

system   An organized collection of parts and procedures united by regulated interaction and interconnected to perform a function.

system approach   A general term for reviewing all implications of a condition or group of conditions rather than the narrow implications of the problem at hand.

system control programming (SCP)   Vendor supplied programming (especially IBM) that is fundamental to the operation and maintenance of the system. It serves as an interface with program products and user programs and is available without additional charge.

system design   The specification of the working relations between all the parts of a system in terms of their characteristic actions.

system flowchart   See flowchart.

system generation (SYSGEN)   The process of using an operating system to assemble and link together all of the parts that constitute another operating system.

system library A collection of data sets in which the various parts of an operating system are stored.

system log (SYSLOG) A data set in which job-related information, operational data, descriptions of unusual occurrences, commands, and messages to or from the operator may be stored.

system programmer A programmer who plans, generates, maintains, extends, and controls the use of an operating system with the aim of improving the overall productivity of an installation. Also a programmer who designs programming systems and other applications.

system resource Any facility of the computing system that may be allocated to a task.

system software See systems and support software.

systems analyst An individual who defines application problems, determines system specifications, recommends equipment changes, designs data processing procedures, and devises data verification methods. Prepares block diagrams and record layouts from which the programmer prepares flowcharts. May assist with or supervise the preparation of flowcharts.

systems and support software The variety of software including assemblers, compilers, subroutine libraries, operating systems, application programs, etc.

systems reliability The probability that a system will perform its specified task properly under stated conditions of environment.

systems test The running of the whole system against test data. A complete simulation of the actual running system for purposes of testing the adequacy of the system.

tabbing Sending a printer head or display cursor to a preset column position on the paper or screen.

table look-up The process of using a table of data stored in main memory during the running of the program to obtain a function value.

tag A unit of information with a composition that differs from that of other members of the set so that it can be used as a marker or label. This unit is given a name or a memory location to make it easier to reference.

tape, magnetic See magnetic tape.

tape cartridge Magnetic tape in a cartridge used with a tape drive, usually for the purpose of media backup for a disk. The data cartridges can be high capacity, holding as much as 20 megabytes of unformatted data, and data can be transferred quickly in a steaming mode.

tape drive A mechanism for controlling the movement of magnetic tape past a reading or writing head.

tape reel A magnetic tape wound around a spool and referred to collectively as a tape reel. These units are generally used with industry standard magnetic tape storage systems.

task A unit of work for the central processing unit.

telecommunication lines Telephone and other communication lines that are used to transmit messages from one location to another.

telecommunications Data transmission between a computing system and remotely located devices via a unit that performs the necessary format conversion and controls the rate of transmission.

teleprinter Any device employing a keyboard integrated with a printer and used for telecommunications.

teleprocessing The processing of data that is received from or sent to remote locations by way of telecommunication lines. Such systems are essential to hook up remote terminals or connect geographically separated computers.
See also telecommunications.

teletext A generic name for the broadcast of messages and graphics as part of a television signal, using the blank space or unused portion of the signal.

Teletype Trademark of the Teletype Corporation. One of the first peripheral devices used for sending and receiving messages with a computer. A Teletype is characterized by high reliability, noisy operation, and low cost. It also has relatively slow printing speeds of about ten characters per second and slow transmission rates of 110 baud.

Teletypewriter Exchange Service (TWX) A public teletypewriter exchange (switched) service in the United States and Canada formerly belonging to AT&T

but now owned by the Western Union Telegraph Company. Both Baudot- and ASCII-coded machines are used.

Telex (TLX) An automatic teleprinter exchange service provided worldwide by Western Union, similar to the teletypewriter exchange service. Telex uses the public telegraph network. Only Baudot equipment is provided; business machines may also be used.

temporary storage Main memory locations reserved for intermediate programming results.

terminal A device equipped with a keyboard (or other input device) and an output device (e.g., display or printer) that is connected to a computer system for the input and/or output of data. A terminal may be as simple as a telephone, or as complex as a small computer. Terminals are generally used for on-line systems.

terminal job In systems with time sharing, the processing done on behalf of one terminal user from log-on to log-off.

terminal session See session.

terminal user In systems with time sharing, anyone who is eligible to log on.

test data generator Software for forming test data files holding desired or randomly generated values in nominated fields of nominated records.

test generators A software aid used to help test new programs.

testing (program) The process of executing a program (or part of a program) with the intention or goal of finding errors.

testing (system) The verification and/or validation of the system to its initial objectives. System testing is a verification process when it is done in a simulated environment; it is a validation process when it is performed in a live environment.

text The information portion of a transmitted message, as contrasted with the header, check characters, and end-of-text characters.

text editing Specific flexible editing facilities which have been designed into a computer program to permit the original keyboarding of textual copy, without regard for the eventual format or medium for publication. Once the copy has been placed in computer storage, it can be edited and justified easily and quickly into any required column width and for any specified type font merely by specifying the format required.

text editor A program or set of routines in a computer system, most often used by programmers to edit a source program. It allows the user to enter, change, order, output, or delete information.

textual-numeric database This type of source database contains records made up of a combination of textual and numeric data elements.
See also database, full text database, numeric database, source database.

thermal printer A small format, nonimpact printer that forms characters by applying heat to special heat-sensitive papers. Thermal printers have slow speeds, mediocre quality reproduction, and expensive paper overhead. However, they have low initial cost and are able to easily combine graphic and alphanumeric output.

thimble print element A plastic thimble-shaped element containing flat spokes with raised characters. The thimble rotates, positioning the spokes so that the striking device can hit the spoke tip against the ribbon; this action imprints the character onto the paper.

third-party lease An arrangement by which an independent firm buys equipment from the manufacturer and in turn leases it to the end user. The middleman firm is called the third party.

third-party maintenance See service organizations.

32-bit system Refers to the number of bits in a word that can be processed, stored, and recalled at one time in one machine cycle. Longer word lengths increase efficiency and accuracy but also increase complexity.

threat One or more events that may lead to intentional or unintentional modification, destruction, or excessive paging.

three-dimensional digitizer See digitizer, three-dimensional.

throughput The total useful information processed or communicated over a given period of time.

tie line A private-line communications channel of the type provided by communications common carriers for linking two or more points together.

time division multiplexing Sharing a single facility among several data paths by dividing up the channel capacity into time slices. Transmission is in successive frames, each consisting of one bit from each path.

time out A set time period for waiting before a terminal/system performs some action. Typical uses include poll release (assumes terminal cannot transmit further or there is a line problem of some sort). It is the most convenient control technique to prevent difficulties with one terminal in a network from bringing the whole net to a stop.

time series   A sequence of quantitative data assigned to specific moments in time. These data are usually studied with regard to their distribution in time.

time sharing   A method of operation in which the resources of a computer facility are shared by several uses via terminals for different purposes at (apparently) the same time.

time slice   An interval of time on the central processing unit allocated for use in performing a task. Once the interval has expired, CPU time is allocated to another task; thus a task cannot monopolize CPU time beyond a fixed limit.

top-of-forms set   A forms handling ability that can advance paper automatically to a preset position and which is initiated by receipt of a form feed character. This can be accomplished by hardware or software.

touch sensitive   Refers to technology which enables a system to identify a point of contact on the screen by coordinates to be translated into some system action.

touch terminal   A terminal with which the user physically interacts by touching the screen with a finger in order to choose and input, instead of using traditional input devices such as keyboards, digitizers, or light pens.

tpi   Tracks per inch.

trace   A listing of all the steps that have taken place during a software procedure. The purpose is to help to locate sources of logic error.

track   A channel on a direct-access device that contains data which can be read by a single reading head without changing its position. It may refer to the track on a disk which rotates under a read head, or the track on a magnetic stripe that is passed by a fixed read head.

trackball   A device used mainly to enter data resulting from the movement of a ball which is set in a small box so that it rotates freely. The ball is manipulated by hand, and the corresponding positions are shown on the screen.

tracks   A physical organization in the form of concentric rings, used to store data on a magnetic disk. The arrangement is similar to that of a phonograph record. However, any location on a track can be accessed direct-

ly without a sequential search. Each track is divided into sectors.

See also sectors.

tracks per inch (tpi)   A unit of measurement for track density on a floppy disk.

tractor feed   A printer attachment that guides paper using advancing sprockets, or pins, that fit into holes in the paper. The method yields more precise alignment than friction feed methods. This procedure is sometimes called pin feed.

traffic   In communications, transmitted and received messages. The total information flow of a communications system.

trailer label   Information written after a file has been processed indicating how many logical records make up the file, what is the batch total, and so on.

transaction code   A code used to identify a specific type of transaction.

transaction file   A file containing update transactions to be processed against a master file. Synonymous with detail file.

transaction listing   A record of everything that has happened on a system. This record is sometimes called a system log. Also, this term refers to a listing of all transactions processed in a user program, which is sometimes called an audit trail.

transaction processing   A style of data processing in which files are updated and results generated immediately as a result of data entry.

transceiver   A device or circuit capable of both receiving and transmitting.

transfer rate   The speed at which data can be read/written into storage.

transient   Fast, temporary variations in a line voltage.

transistor   An electronic device that uses semiconductor properties to control the flow of current.

translation   In data communication, the conversion of one code to another on a character-by-character basis. In programming, a type of language processor that converts a source program from one programming language to another.

translator A program that converts a sequence of statements in one language into corresponding statements in another language. Interpreters, assemblers, and compilers are types of translators.

transmission speed The rate at which data is passed through communication lines, usually measured in bits per second (bps).

transmit To send data from one location and to receive it at another location.

transparency The property of independence from codes, media, or processing equipment. Program transparency means that any of a variety of computer equipment can be used to run the program. Transparency is the opposite of virtual in the sense that something virtual appears to exist but does not; while something transparent appears not to exist but in fact does.

trashing In virtual storage systems, a condition in which the system can do little useful work because of excessive paging.

tree structure A hierarchical method of indicating data relationships, tree structures promote efficient search and retrieval of data. In traveling down the logic tree, the user makes a series of binary choices that exclude unwanted possibilities until the object of the search is located. In most cases, the tree structure can only be entered from the top, which corresponds to the most general level. The logic moves from the general to increasingly specific queries.

troubleshoot See debug.

truncation The removal of one or more digits, characters, or bits from one end of an item of data when a string length or precision of a target variable has been exceeded. To cut off a specified spot (as contrasted with round).

truth table A mathematical table that states input values and lists all possible combinations (boolean relationships) of output values as a function of the input.
  See also AND, OR, NOR, boolean algebra.

T/S Time sharing.

TSS Time sharing system.

T switch A device that allows two peripherals to share a common third component or input/output port.

TTY Teletypewriter. Also teletype machine.

tuning The process of adjusting system control variables to make the system divide its resources most efficiently for the workload.

turnaround time The elapsed time between submission of a job to a computing center and the return of results. In communications, the actual time required to reverse the direction of transmission from send to receive nor vice-versa when using a half-duplex circuit. For most communication facilities, there will be time required by line propagation and line effects, modem timing, and machine reaction. A typical time is 200 milliseconds on a half-duplex telephone connection.

turnkey system A system in which the manufacturer takes full responsibility for complete system design and installation, and supplies all necessary hardware, software, and documentation elements.

turtle The name for a small triangular pointer on a display screen which is used with the Logo language to implement turtle graphics.
  See also turtle graphics.

turtle geometry A new mathematics based on the turtle movements in the Logo language.

turtle graphics A system of graphics commands developed by Seymour Papert and the Logo group at MIT. It is used widely for graphics and geometry, especially with children, in Logo.

tutorial Lessons, classes, demonstrations covering a subject area; or instructions about running hardware and/or software, usually in manual or program form.

two-way alternate operation See half duplex.

two-way simultaneous operation See duplex.

two-wire channel Half-duplex transmission facility, characterized by a single wire pair.

typeball A molded metal printer element shaped like a golfball with raised characters set around the surface. It is mounted on a movable axis and acts as a hammer, striking the ribbon against the paper to produce the character image.

type font See font.

UART Universal asynchronous receiver/transmitter. A large scale integration logic circuit that converts parallel input from the computer into asynchronous serial data for transmission. In the other direction (for a received transmission) UART translates received asynchronous serial data into parallel bits for use by the computer. It is normally used to connect a parallel port to a serial communication network.

UCSD Pascal University of California, San Diego, Pascal. A version of the Pascal language developed at that university.

UCSD p-System An operating system developed by the Regents of the University of California at San Diego which uses Pascal and which can be implemented on any microprocessor. Now known as Softech Microsystems p-Systems.

UDLC Universal data link control, a bit-oriented protocol developed by Sperry Univac.

UG User group.

UHF Ultra-high frequencies.

ultraviolet erasing Use of a high-intensity short-wave light to erase the contents of an EPROM chip. See also EPROM.

unattended operation The automatic features of a terminal station's operation which permit the transmission and reception of messages on an unattended basis.

unbundled The services, programs, training, etc. sold independently of the computer hardware by the computer manufacturer. Thus, a computer system that includes all products and services in a single price is said to be bundled.

unconditional branch An instruction used to transfer control to another part of the program regardless of the results of previous instructions.

unconditional transfer An instruction that always causes a branch in program control away from the normal sequence of executing instructions.

underlining To underscore part of a text for emphasis, a feature of text editing and word processing.

Universal Product Code (UPC) A bar-code, printed on a supermarket package, which uniquely identifies the product.

universe The population from which samples are drawn. Usually very large relative to the sample.

UNIX A multiuser operating system developed by Bell Laboratories.

unrecoverable error An error that results in abnormal termination of a program.

update To modify a master file with current transaction information according to a specified procedure.

up time The time during which equipment is either operating or available for operation, as opposed to down time when no productive work can be accomplished.

USART Universal synchronous/asynchronous receiver / transmitter. A peripheral device that converts parallel data from the central processing unit (CPU) into a serial stream of data for transmission. At the same time, it can receive and convert serial data into parallel bits for use by the computer. USART differs from UART and ASRT in that it can comunicate by means of both synchronous and asynchronous techniques.

USASCII (United States of America Standard Code for Information Interchange) See ASCII.

user Anyone who requires the services of a computing system.

user definable keys Special keys on the keyboard that can initiate certain operations in the program; the keys' functions can be defined by the user.

user friendly Refers to software and hardware systems that are supposedly easy for a user to learn to operate without requiring a great deal of specialized knowledge or training.

user group Any organization made up of users (as opposed to vendors) of various computing systems, software package, etc., that give the users an opportunity to share knowledge they have gained in using a particular system, to exchange programs they have developed, and to jointly influence vendor software and hardware support and policy.

user hotline Direct telephone access to a manufacturer who provides end users with answers to technical questions regarding their products.

user identification (USERID) A one-to-eight-character symbol identifying a system user.

user interaction Active communication between the computer system and the user. A user entry will cause a direct response by the system. Also called interactive systems.

user memory Central processing unit (CPU) memory that can be accessed and changed by the user. It usually refers to the portion of random access memory that is used in the application programs.

user programs Programs that have been written by the user as contrasted to those supplied by the manufacturer.

USRT   Universal synchronous receiver/transmitter. A high-speed transmission converter which differs from UART in that it is a synchronous device. When the computer sends a message through USRT for transmission, the parallel bits are converted to a serial stream. When receiving serial bits, USRT converts the serial data into parallel words. Because it is a synchronous device, USRT depends upon a timing system rather than upon the start and stop bits used in UART.

See also UART.

utility functions   Functions that are used to perform common system procedures such as printing, moving data, reading from disk, etc.

utility programs   A specialized program performing a frequently required everyday task. Examples include: sorting, report generation, file updating, file dump and backup (maintaining backup files in case a master working file is fouled up), etc. Those programs are usually supplied by the manufacturer of the equipment.

utility routine   software used to perform some frequently required process in the operation of a computer system, e.g., sorting, merging, etc.

validation   An attempt to find errors by executing a program in a given real environment.

validity check   Verification that each element of data is actually a valid character of the particular code in use.

value-added carriers   A new class of communications common carrier authorized to lease raw communication trunks from the transmission carriers, augment these facilities with computerized switching, and provide enhanced or value-added communications service. Telenet Communications Corporation and others are now employing packet switching to provide value-added data communications services.

value-added network (VAN)   See packet switching, value-added service.

value-added service   A communications service utilizing communications common carrier networks for transmission and providing added data services with separate additional equipment. Such added services features may be store and forward message switching, terminal interfacing, and host interfacing.

variable   A quantity which can assume any of a given set of values.

variable-length record   A record having a length independent of the length of other records with which it is logically or physically associated.

variance   The difference between the expected or planned and the actual.

VDT   Video display terminal. See CRT.

vectored interrupt   A technique in which each interrupting device provides an address at the time of the interrupt request, enabling the operating system to branch to the appropriate interrupt routine. This results in increased efficiency in determining which device is requesting attention, as compared to use of a polling technique.

vendor   A company that supplies material.

Venn diagram   A diagram in which sets are represented by circles or ellipses to give a graphic representation of basic logic operations.

verification   An attempt to find errors by executing a program in a test or simulated environment.

verifier   A device similar to a card punch used to check the inscribing of data by rekeying.

vertical scrolling   The ability of the system to move up and down through a page or more of data that is displayed on the terminal screen.

very large-scale integration (VLSI)   The process of fabricating integrated circuits on a silicon chip that contains up to 100,000 semiconductor devices.

video   The data displayed on the screen of a CRT.

video bandwidth   The number of dots per second that can be displayed on a television screen or computer monitor. The greater the bandwidth, the higher the number of characters that can be displayed clearly at one time.

video computer   A computer designed principally for running commercially produced cartridges that contain games and rote learning programs.

video disk   A rigid storage medium for analog or digital data written/read by laser. A main feature is random access.

video disk system   A mass storage technology that uses optical lenses to record information by burning holes in a telleurium medium. One disk can hold about 55,000 pages of information.

video display terminals (VDT)   See CRT.

video monitor   A display unit that resembles a television set but does not have a speaker or apparatus for detecting UHF/VHF frequencies. A monitor does have a direct video connection and accepts a higher bandwidth than a television, thus allowing more characters to be displayed clearly at one time. Since the monitor has no logical intelligence or control electronics, the computer must contain appropriate interfaces to control the monitor.

video signal   Refers to a video signal that conveys all the necessary information such as color, intensity, location, and synchronization about each position on the screen so that the image is placed properly on the screen.

videotex   An interactive information network that uses telephone lines, a decoder, and a television to connect a home user with a mainframe computer to display both text and graphic information.

virtual address   In virtual storage systems, an address that refers to virtual storage and must, therefore, be translated into a real storage address when it is used.

virtual address area   The area of virtual storage whose addresses are greater than the highest address of the real address area.

virtual address space   In virtual storage systems, the virtual storage assigned to a job, terminal user, or system task.

virtual circuit   A connection between a source and a sink in a network that may be realized by different circuit configurations during transmission of a message.

virtual memory   See virtual storage.

virtual mode   In IBM systems, a program that may be paged.

virtual storage   Addressable space that appears to the user as real storage, from which instructions and data are mapped into real storage locations. The size of virtual storage is limited by the addressing scheme of the computing system (or virtual machine) and by the amount of auxiliary storage available, rather than by the actual number of real storage locations. This procedure leaves the programmer free to address total storage without concern as to whether primary or secondary storage is actually being addressed, and effectively includes the large, inexpensive capacity of secondary storage in the system. Optimally, the computer should be able to operate either with or without virtual storage

without major software modification. Benefits of virtual storage operation are enhanced when it is implemented by hardware which carries out the data swapping algorithms.

VisiCalc   The first electronic spreadsheet; trademark of VisiCorp.
   See also electronic spreadsheet.

VLSI   Very large-scale integration.

VMOS   V-channel metal oxide semiconductor. A type of NMOS technology in which a V-shaped notch is used to improve density. Sometimes used for high density dynamic AM chips.

voice-grade channel   Typically a telephone circuit normally used for speech communication, and accommodating frequencies from 300 to 3,000 Hz. Up to 10,000 Hz can be transmitted.

voice-operated device   A device used on a telephone circuit to permit the presence of telephone currents to effect a desired control. Such a device is used in most echo suppressors.

voice print   A technique for verifying an individual's identity by the pattern produced by his or her voice.

voice recognition   A system of sound sensors that translate the tones of the human voice into computer commands.

voice response unit (VRU)   A device which can accept a coded request for data, compose a coded response, interpret the coded response into locations of stored vocabulary, and produce speech as output.

voice synthesis   Computer-generated sounds that simulate the human voice.

volatile memory   Memory that does not retain its information content when the power is turned off.

volatile storage   A storage medium in which information cannot be retained without continuous power dissipation (semiconductor).

volatility   The percentage of records on a file that are added or deleted in a run.

volume   A recording medium that is mounted and demounted as a unit, for example, a reel of magnetic tape, a disk pack, a data cell.

volume table of contents (VTOC)   A table or directory on a direct access volume, that describes each data set on the volume.

von Neumann, John   Usually credited with formulating the concept of a stored program computer; for example, controlling the computer by means of a program stored in its internal memory.

VRC   Vertical redundancy check; character parity.

VTOC   See volume table of contents.

W   Write.

wafer   See silicon wafer.

wait state   The condition of a central processing unit when all operations are suspended.

Wangnet   A local area network (LAN) system offered by Wang Laboratories, Inc.
See also network, local area.

warm boot   Reloading the operating system or initializing the computer after it has been on and without turning the computer off.
Compare cold boot. See also booting.

warm start   The restart activity appropriate when a temporary failure has not disturbed backup storage. Current conversations can be continued by reading in the last filed version of the conversation control records although the interrupted exchanges may be lost.

warning message   An indication during program compilation that a possible error has been detected.

WATS (Wide Area Telephone Service)   A service provided by telephone companies which permits a customer, by use of an access line, to make calls to telephones in a specific zone on a dial basis for a flat monthly charge. Monthly charges are based on the size of the area in which the calls are placed, not on the number or length of calls. Under WATS arrangement, the United States is divided into zones to be called on a full-time or measured-time basis.

weighted average   An averaging technique where the data to be averaged is multiplied by different factors. For example, a regular average is equivalent to a 50-50 weighted average. An average could be made up by taking 90% of one figure and 10% of another figure. This would then be weighted average. Note that the weights must always be equal to 100%.

Wide Area Telecommunications Service   See WATS.

wideband   A communications channel having a bandwidth characterized by data transmission speeds of 10,000 to 500,000 bits per second.

Winchester disk   Rigid, non-removable, magnetic oxide-coated, random access disk sealed in a filtered enclosure along with the read/write heads and head actuator. Heads fly only about 20 microinches from disk surface, allowing very dense data storage. Capacity ranges from 5 Mb (325 to 16,000 pages) for the 5-1/4 in. disk, and from 6.5 to 635 Mb (1625 to 158750 pages) for the 8 in. disk, calculated at 4000 characters per single-spaced page.

window   An isolated portion of a cathode ray tube screen that is used to display information independently from the rest of the screen display.

wire frame representation   A three-dimensional representation of an object with hidden lines shown, giving the impression of a transparent object with only its structure visible.
See also hidden line.

word   A group of characters occupying one storage location in a computer. It is treated by the computer circuits as an entity, by the control unit as an instruction, and by the arithmetic unit as a quantity.

word length   The number of bits in a word. Longer word lengths increase efficiency and accuracy, but add complexity and cost. Word length limits the number of memory locations which can be directly addressed using single-word addresses.

word processing   The transformation of ideas and information into a readable form of communication through the management of procedures, equipment and personnel.

word processing terminal   A device used for the preparation and dissemination of letters, memoranda, reports, and articles using office typewriters and word processing systems.

word size   See word length.

WordStar   A popular word processing software package developed by MicroPro International.

word wrap   In word processing, the automatic placement of a word on the next line if that word would otherwise extend beyond the margin.

work center   A physical area where a particular type of work is performed.

work file   In sorting, an intermediate file used for temporary storage of data.

working set   The set of a user's program pages in a virtual storage system that must be active in order to avoid excessive paging.

worksheet   See electronic spreadsheet, VisiCalc.

World Computer Citizen   A center located in Paris devoted to placing computer power in the hands of the people and expanding computer literacy to benefit every world citizen.

wp   Word processing.

wpm (words per minute)   A measure of transmission speed computed on the basis of six characters (five plus a space) per word.

wraparound   The continuation from the maximum addressable location in storage to the first addressable location. On a CRT display device, the continuation from the last character position in the display buffer to the first position in the display buffer.

write   To record data in a storage device, a data medium, or an output display.

write-enable   To allow access to a device, such as a disk drive, so that the user has the ability to put information into the device. A write-enable procedure is required in order to disable a write-protect procedure.
See also write-protect

write-protect   A procedure that prevents inadvertent writing over previously stored information on a storage medium such as a disk. With a floppy disk, a protective tab may be placed over the write-protect notch of the jacket to control this feature. With a hard disk drive, a switch would be engaged. With a tape, a plastic ring must first be removed from the tape.

X.25   A protocol developed by CCITT, the standards writing organization for international telephone carriers, for packet switching procedures.

Xenix   A multiuser operating system developed by MicroSoft, Inc.; a subset of UNIX.
See also UNIX.

xerography   A non-chemical photographic process in which light discharges a charged dielectric surface. This is dusted with a dielectric powder, which adheres to the charged areas, rendering the image visible.

XOR   Exclusive or.

x,y coordinates   The horizontal (row) and vertical (column) designation of a position or dot in a matrix.

xy recorder   A recorder that traces on a chart the relationship between two variables, neither of which is time. Sometimes the chart moves and one of the variables is controlled so that the relationship does increase in proportion to time.

Z Zero bit.

Z-80 An 8-bit microprocessor developed by Zilog, Inc.

zap Intentional use of a command found in many programs to clear the screen. Also, the term is used to define the action of overwriting a file unintentionally.

zero suppression The elimination of nonsignificant zeros in a numeral.

Zilog Manufacturers of microprocessors, including the Z-80 and the Z-80A.

Z-Net A local area network (LAN) system similar to Ethernet.
See also network, local area.

Bibliography

1
Program Design and Architecture

Bohl, Marilyn, *Flowcharting Techniques,* Chicago, IL: Science Research Associates, 1971.

Emmerichs, Jack, *How to Build a Program,* Blue Ridge Summit, PA: TAB, 1983.

Hansen, Per Brinch, *Programming a Personal Computer,* Englewood Cliffs, NJ: Prentice-Hall, 1983.

Lewin, Morton H., *Logic Design & Computer Organization,* Reading, MA: Addison-Wesley, 1983.

Sanderson, Peter C., *Introduction to Microcomputer Programming,* Woburn, MA: Focal Press, 1982.

Willis, Jerry, and William Danley, Jr., *Nailing Jelly to a Tree,* Beaverton, OR: Dilithium Press, 1981.

2
Principles of Effective Programming

Barden, William, Jr., *How to Program Microcomputers,* Indianapolis, IN: Howard W. Sams, 1977.

Downing, Douglas, *Computer Programming the Easy Way,* Woodbury, NY: Barron's Educational Series, 1983.

Drury, Donald W., *Art of Computer Programming,* Blue Ridge Summit, PA: TAB, 1981.

Faulk, Edward, *How to Write a Program II,* Chatsworth, CA: Datamost, 1983.

Gardner, Albert C., *Practical LCP: A Direct Approach to Structured Programming,* New York: McGraw-Hill, 1982.

Maisel, Herbert, *Computers: Programming & Applications,* Chicago, IL: Science Research Associates, 1976.

Marcellus, Daniel, *Systems Programming for Small Computers,* Englewood Cliffs, NJ: Prentice-Hall, 1983.

Schindler, Max, *Software Toolkit for Microcomputers,* Hasbrouck Heights, NJ: Hayden, 1983.

3
Special Applications Software

EDUCATION

Barden, William, *Microcomputer Math,* Indianapolis, IL: Howard W. Sams, 1982.

Burke, Robert L., *CAI Sourcebook,* Englewood Cliffs, NJ: Prentice-Hall, 1982.

Chambers, Jack, and Jerry Sprecher, *Computer-Assisted Instruction: Its Uses in the Classroom,* Englewood Cliffs, NJ: Prentice-Hall, 1983.

Clay, Katherine, *Microcomputers in Education: A Handbook of Resources,* Phoenix, AZ: Oryx Press, 1982.

Dickson, Wayne, and Mike Raymond, *Language Arts- Computer Book: A How To Guide for Teachers,* Reston, VA: Reston, 1983.

Hockey, Susan, *Guide to Computer Applications in the Humanities,* Baltimore, MD: Johns Hopkins University Press, 1980.

Howell, Robert, *Educators, Parents, and Micros: How to Help Your School Get and Use Computer Power,* Holmes Beach, FL: Learning Publications, 1983.

Joiner, Lee M., *Microcomputers in Education,* Holmes Beach, FL: Learning Publications, 1982.

Judd, Dorothy H., and Robert W., *Guide to Microcomputer Instructional Applications,* Glenview, IL: Scott Foresman, 1983.

Lindelow, John, *Administrator's Guide to Computers in the Classroom,* New York: ERIC, 1983.

Miller, Inabeth, *Microcomputer Directory: Applications in Educational Settings,* 2nd Edition, New York: Gutman Library, 1982.

--------------, *Microcomputers in School Media Centers,* New York: Neal-Schuman, 1983.

Orwig, Gary, *Creating Computer Programs for Learning: A Guide for Trainers, Parents and Teachers,* Reston,VA: Reston, 1983.

Tagg, D., *Microcomputers in Secondary Education,* New York: Elsevier, 1980.

GRAPHICS

Artwick, Bruce, *Applied Concepts in Microcomputer Graphics,* Englewood Cliffs, NJ: Prentice-Hall, 1984.

Curnow, Ray, and Susan Curran, *Games, Graphics, and Sound,* New York: Simon & Schuster, 1984.

Foley, James D., and Andries Van Dam, *Fundamentals of Computer Graphics,* Reading, MA: Addison-Wesley, 1980.

Harrington, Steven, *Computer Graphics: A Programming Approach,* Ed. James E. Vastyan, New York: McGraw-Hill, 1983.

Katzan, Harry, Jr., *Microcomputer Graphics and Programming Techniques,* New York: Van Nostrand Reinhold, 1982.

Marshall, Garry, *Programming with Graphics,* Englewood Cliffs, NJ: Prentice-Hall, 1983.

Myers, Roy E., *Microcomputer Graphics,* Reading, MA: Addison-Wesley, 1982.

Ryan, Daniel L., *Computer Graphics Problems Manual,* Monterey, CA: Brooks/Cole, 1983.

Wadsworth, Nat, *Introduction to Computer Animation,* Hasbrouck Heights, NJ: Hayden, 1983.

Waite, Mitchell, *Computer Graphics Primer,* Indianapolis, IN: Howard W. Sams, 1979.

ARTIFICIAL INTELLIGENCE AND EXPERT SYSTEMS

Barr, A., and E. Feigenbaum, *The Handbook of Artificial Intelligence*, Los Altos, CA: William Kaufman, 1981.

Charniak, E., C. Riesbeck, and D. McDermott, *Artificial Intelligence Programming,* Hillsdale, NJ: Lawrence Erlbaum, 1980.

Davis, R., and D. Lenat, *Knowledge-Based Systems in Artificial Intelligence*, New York: McGraw-Hill, 1982.

Hayes-Roth, F., D. Waterman, and D. Lenat, *Building Expert Systems*, Reading, MA: Addison-Wesley, 1983.

Krueger, M. W., *Artificial Reality*, Reading, MA: Addison-Wesley, 1983.

Michie, D.,ed. *Expert Systems in the Microelectronic Age*, Edinburgh, Scotland: Edinburgh University Press, 1979.

Nilsson, N., *Principles of Artificial Intelligence*, Tioga, 1984.

Schank, R., and C. Riesbeck, *Inside Computer Understanding*, Hillside, NJ: Lawrence Erlbaum, 1981.

Shapiro, S., *Techniques of Artificial Intelligence*, New York: Van Nostrand Reinhold, 1978.

Winogrod, T. *Language as a Cognitive Process*, Reading, MA: Addison-Wesley, 1983.

Winston, P., *Artificial Intelligence*, 2nd Edition, Reading, MA: Addison-Wesley, 1984.

Wos, L., Ross Overbeek, E. Lusk, and J. Boyle, *Automated Reasoning*, Englewood Cliffs, NJ: Prentice-Hall, 1984.

ROBOTICS

Albus, James, *Brains, Behavior, and Robotics,* Peterborough, NH: Byte Books, 1981.

D'Ignazio, Fred, *Working Robots,* New York: Elsevier, 1982.

Engleberger, Joseph, *Robotics in Practice,* New York: American Management Association, 1980.

Loofburrow, Todd, *How to Build a Computer-Controlled Robot,* Hasbrouck Heights, NJ: Hayden, 1978.

4
Microprocessor Basics

Buchsbaum, Walter H., and Gina Weissenberg, *Microprocessor and Microcomputer Data Digest*, Reston, VA: Reston, 1983.

Calingaert, Peter, *Assemblers, Compilers, and Program Translation*, Rockville, MD: Computer Science Press, 1979.

Carr, Joseph J., *8-Bit and 16-Bit Microprocessor Cookbook*, Blue Ridge Summit, PA: TAB, 1983.

Horowitz, Ellis, and Sartaj Sahni, *Fundamentals of Computer Algorithms*, Rockville, MD: Computer Science Press, 1979.

Kernighan, Brian W., and P.J. Plauger, *Software Tools*, Reading, MA: Addison-Wesley, 1976.

Lancaster, Don, *Don Lancaster's Micro Cookbook*, Volume 1, Indianapolis, IN: Howard W. Sams, 1982.

--------------, *Don Lancaster's Micro Cookbook*, Volume 2, Indianapolis, IN: Howard W. Sams, 1983.

Mansfield, Richard, *Machine Language for Beginners*, Greensboro, NC: Compute! Books, 1983.

Ogdin, Carol Anne, *Software Design for Microcomputers*, Englewood Cliffs, NJ: Prentice-Hall, 1978.

Poe, Elmer C., *The Microprocessor Handbook*, Indianapolis, IN: Howard W. Sams, 1983.

INTEL 8080A

Findley, Robert, *Scelbi "8080" Software Gourmet Guide and Cookbook,* Milford, CT: Scelbi Computer Consulting, Inc., 1976.

Intel Corporation, *The 8080/8085 Microprocessor Book,* New York: John Wiley & Sons, 1980.

Leventhal, Lance A., and Winthrop Saville, *8080/8085 Assembly Language Subroutines,* Berkeley, CA: Osborne/McGraw-Hill, 1983.

Titus, Christopher A., *TEA: An 8080/8085,* Indianapolis, IN: Howard W. Sams, 1979.

Titus, Christopher A., Peter R. Rony, David G.Larson, and Jonathan A. Titus, *8080/8085 Software Design,* Indianapolis, IN: Howard W. Sams, 1978.

INTEL 8085

Fernandez, Judi N., and Ruth Ashley, *Introduction to 8085 Assembly Language Programming*, New York: John Wiley & Sons, 1981.

Intel Corporation, *The 8080/8085 Microprocessor Book*, New York: John Wiley & Sons, 1980.

Leventhal, Lance A., and Winthrop Saville, *8080/8085 Assembly Language Subroutines*, Berkeley, CA: Osborne/McGraw-Hill, 1983.

Titus, Christopher A., *TEA: An 8080/8085,* Indianapolis, IN: Howard W. Sams, 1979.

Titus,Christopher A., Peter R. Rony, David G. Larson, Jonathan A. Titus, *8080/8085 Software Design,* Indianapolis, IN:Howard W. Sams, 1978.

ZILOG Z80

Carr, Joseph J., *Z80 Users Manual*, Reston, VA: Reston, 1980.

Leventhal, Lance A., *Z80 Assembly Language Programming*, Berkeley, CA: Osborne/McGraw-Hill, 1979.

Leventhal, Lance A., and Winthrop Saville, *Z80 Assembly Language Subroutines*, Berkeley, CA: Osborne/McGraw-Hill, 1983.

Spracklen, Kathe, *Z80 and 8085 Assembly Language Programming*, Hasbrouck Heights, NJ: Hayden, 1979.

Wadsworth, Nat, *Z80 Instruction Manual*, Hasbrouck Heights, NJ: Hayden, 1979.

Wadsworth, Nat, *Z80 Software Gourmet Guide and Cookbook*, Hasbrouck Heights, NJ: Hayden, 1979.

NATIONAL SEMICONDUCTOR NSC800

Alford, Roger C., *The NSC800 Microprocessor Cookbook*, Blue Ridge Summit, PA: TAB, 1982.

MOTOROLA MC6800

Bishop, Ron, *Basic Microprocessors and 6800*, Hasbrouck Heights, NJ: Hayden, 1979.

Findley, Robert, *6800 Software Gourmet Guide and Cookbook*, Hasbrouck Heights, NJ: Hayden, 1976.

Leventhal, Lance. A., *6800 Assembly Language Programming*, Berkeley, CA: Osborne/McGraw-Hill, 1978.

Poe, Elmer, *Using the 6800 Microprocessor,* Indianapolis, IN: Howard W. Sams, 1978.

Simpson, R. J. and T. J. Terrell, *Introduction to 6800, 6802 Microprocessor Systems: Hardware, Software & Experimentation,* Woburn, MA: Focal Press, 1982.

MOTOROLA MC6809

Leventhal, Lance A., *6809 Assembly Language Programming*, Berkeley, CA: Osborne/McGraw-Hill, 1976.

Warren, Carl D., *MC6809 Cookbook,* Blue Ridge Summit, PA: TAB, 1982.

MOS TECHNOLOGY 6502

Fernandez, Judi N., Donna N. Tabler, and Ruth Ashley, *6502 Assembly Language Programming: A Self-Teaching Guide,* New York: John Wiley & Sons, 1983.

Findley, Robert, *6502 Software Gourmet Guide and Cookbook,* Hasbrouck Heights, NJ: Hayden, 1979.

Leventhal, Lance A., *6502 Assembly Language Programming,* Berkeley, CA: Osborne/McGraw-Hill, 1979.

Leventhal, Lance A., and Winthrop Saville, *6502 Assembly Language Subroutines,* Berkeley, CA: Osborne/McGraw-Hill, 1982.

Scanlon, Leo J., *6502 Software Design,* Indianapolis, IN: Howard W. Sams, 1980.

Zaks, Rodnay, *6502 Applications,* Berkeley, CA: Sybex, 1979.

INTEL 8088 and INTEL 8086

Coffron, James W., *Programming the 8086 & 8088,* Berkeley, CA: Sybex, 1983.

Morgan, Christopher L., and Mitchell Waite, *8086/8088 16-Bit Microprocessor Primer,* Peterborough, NH: Byte, 1982.

Morse, Stephen P., *The 8086/8088 Primer: Introduction to Architecture, System Design & Programming,* Hasbrouck Heights, NJ: Hayden, 1982.

Rector, Russell, and George Alexy, *The 8086 Book,* Berkeley, CA: Osborne/McGraw-Hill, 1980.

ZILOG Z8000

Coffron, James, *Using and Troubleshooting the Z8000,* Reston, VA: Reston, 1982.

Fawcett, Bradly, *Z8000 Microprocessor: A Design Handbook,* Englewood Cliffs, NJ: Prentice-Hall, 1982.

Leventhal, Lance A., Adam Osborne, and Chuck Collins, *Z80000 Assembly Language Programming,* Berkeley, CA: Osborne/McGraw-Hill, 1980.

Moore, Martin L., *Z80000 Handbook,* Englewood Cliffs, NJ: Prentice-Hall, 1983.

ZILOG Z8002

Moore, Martin L., *Z8000 Handbook,* Englewood Cliffs, NJ: Prentice Hall, 1983.

MOTOROLA 68000

Coffron, James, *Using and Troubleshooting the MC 68000,* Reston, VA: Reston, 1983.

Kane, Gerry, *68000 Microprocessor Handbook,* Berkeley, CA: Osborne/McGraw-Hill, 1981.

Kane, Gerry, Doug Hawkins, and Lance A. Leventhal, *68000 Assembly Language Programming,* Berkeley, CA: Osborne/McGraw-Hill, 1981.

Scanlon, Leo J., *68000: Principles and Programming,* Indianapolis, IN: Howard W. Sams, 1981.

5
High-Level Programming Languages

ADA

Freedman, Roy, *Programming Concepts with the Ada Language,* New York: Petrocelli Books, 1982.

Ledgard, Henry F., *Ada: An Introduction and Ada Reference Manual,* New York: Springer-Verlag, 1981.

Shumate, Kenneth C., *Understanding Ada: A Gentle Introduction to Symbolic Computation,* New York: Harper & Row, 1984.

ALGOL

Gregory, Donald J., *Algol on the B6700: A Complete Primer,* Sonoma, CA: Gregory Publishing Co., 1979.

Lindsey, C.H., and G. van der Meulen, *Informal Introduction to ALGOL 68,* New York: Elsevier, 1977.

Meek, B.L., *Algol By Problems,* New York: McGraw-Hill, 1971.

APL

Gilman, L., and A. J. Rose, *APL—An Interactive Approach,* New York: John Wiley & Sons, 1974.

Iverson, K. E., *A Programming Language,* New York: John Wiley & Sons, 1962.

Katzan, Jr., Harry, *APL Programming and Computer Techniques,* New York: Van Nostrand Reinhold, 1970.

Polivka, R. P., and S. Pakin, *APL: The Language and Its Usage,* Englewood Cliffs, NJ: Prentice-Hall, 1975.

Prager, W., *An Introduction to APL,* Boston: Allyn and Bacon, 1970.

Zaks, Rodnay, *APL Microprogrammer and Computer Techniques,* New York: Van Nostrand Reinhold, 1970.

BASIC

Albrecht, Robert L., LeRoy Finkel, and Jerald R. Brown, *BASIC 2nd Edition: A Self Teaching Guide,* New York: John Wiley & Sons, 1978.

Coan, James S., *BASIC BASIC: Introduction to Computer Programming in BASIC Language,* Hasbrouck Heights, NJ: Hayden, 1978.

Dwyer, Thomas, and Critchfield, Margot, *BASIC and the Personal Computer,* Reading, MA: Addison-Wesley, 1978.

Finkel, Leroy, and Jerald R. Brown, *Data File Programming in Basic: A Self-Teaching Guide,* New York: John Wiley & Sons, 1981.

James, Mike, *The Complete Programmer: A Guide to Better Programming in BASIC,* Englewood Cliffs, NJ: Spectrum, Prentice-Hall, 1984.

Lamoitier, Jean-Pierre, *Fifty BASIC Exercises,* Berkeley, CA: Sybex, 1981.

Mau, Ernest E., *Secrets of Better BASIC,* Hasbrouck Heights, NJ: Hayden, 1983.

Nevison, John M., *The Little Book of Basic Style: How to Write A Program You Can Read,* Reading, MA: Addison-Wesley, 1978.

Porter, Kent, *Beginning BASIC: An Introduction to Computer Programming,* New York: New American Library, 1984.

Rob, Peter, *Introduction to Microcomputer Programming BASIC,* Belmont, CA: Wadsworth Publishing Company, 1984.

Swanson, Paul, *Microcomputer Disk Techniques,* Peterborough, NH: Byte Books, 1982.

Tracton, Ken, *The BASIC Cookbook,* Blue Ridge Summit, PA: TAB, 1978.

Zaks Rodnay, *Your First BASIC Program,* Berkeley, CA: Sybex, 1983.

MBASIC 86

Boisgontier, Jacques, and Suzanne Ropiequet, *Microsoft BASIC and its Files,* Beaverton, OR: Dilithium Press, 1983.

Ettlin, Walter A., and Gregory Solberg, *The MBASIC Handbook,* Berkeley, CA: Osborne/McGraw-Hill, 1983.

Knecht, Ken, *Microsoft BASIC,* Beaverton, OR: Dilithium Press 1982.

COMPILED BASIC

Osborne, Adam, Gordon Eubanks Jr., and M. McNiff, *CBASIC Users Guide,* Berkeley, CA: Osborne/ McGraw-Hill, 1981.

Weber, Jeffrey R., *CBASIC Simplified,* Chesterland, OH: Weber Systems, 1982.

APPLESOFT BASIC

Blackwood, Brian D., and George H. Blackwood, *Applesoft Language,* Indianapolis, IN: Howard W. Sams, 1983.

Carlston, Doug, *Applesoft Isn't Hard,* North Hollywood, CA: Softalk, 1983.

Cuellar, Gabriel, *Fancy Programming in Applesoft,* Reston, VA: Reston, 1983.

Morrill, Harriet, *Mini and Micro Basic: Introducing Applesoft, Microsoft & BASIC Plus,* Boston, MA: Little, Brown, 1983.

Mottola, Robert, *Assembly Language Programming for the Apple II,* Berkeley, CA: Osborne/McGraw-Hill, 1982.

Vile, Richard, *Apple II Programmers Handbook,* Englewood Cliffs, NJ: Prentice-Hall, 1982.

Wintermeyer, Larry G., *Applesoft BASIC Toolbox,* Reading, MA: Addison-Wesley, 1983.

ATARI BASIC

Berenbon, Howard, *Mostly BASIC—Applications for Your Atari/Book 1,* Indianapolis, IN: Howard W. Sams, 1983.

----------------, *Mostly BASIC—Applications for Your Atari/Book II,* Indianapolis, IN: Howard W. Sams, 1983.

Carris, Bill, *Inside Atari BASIC,* Reston, VA: Reston, 1983.

Haskell, Richard, *Atari BASIC,* Englewood Cliffs, NJ, Prentice-Hall, 1983.

Trost, Stanley R., *Atari BASIC Programs in Minutes,* Berkeley, CA: Sybex, 1984.

Wilkinson, Bill, Kathleen O'Brien, and Paul Laughton, *The Atari BASIC Source Book,* Greensboro, NC: Compute! Publications, 1983.

C LANGUAGE

Hancock, Les, and Morris Krieger, *C Primer,* New York: McGraw-Hill Book Company, 1982.

Purdum, Jack, *C Programming Guide,* Indianapolis, IN: Que, 1983.

Perdum, Jack, Timothy Leslie, and Alan Stegemoller, *C Programmer's Library,* Indianapolis, IN: Que, 1984.

Plum, Thomas, *Learning to Program in C,* Cardiff, NJ: Plum Hall, 1983.

Waite, Mitchell, Stephen Prata, and Donald Martin, *C Primer Plus,* Indianapolis, IN: Howard W. Sams, 1984.

COBOL

Ashley, Ruth, *Structured COBOL: A Self-Teaching Guide,* New York: John Wiley & Sons, 1980.

Davis, Gordon B., and Charles A. Litecky, *Elementary COBOL Programming,* New York, McGraw-Hill Book Company, 1971.

Farina, Mario V., *COBOL Simplified,* Englewood Cliffs, NJ: Prentice-Hall, 1968.

Peddicord, Richard G., *Understanding COBOL,* Sherman Oaks, CA: Alfred Publishing, 1981.

Seidel, Ken, *Microsoft COBOL,* Beaverton, OR: Dilithium Press, 1983.

COMAL

Atherton, Ray, *Structured Programming With COMAL,* Chichester, West Sussex, England: Horwood, John Wiley & Sons, 1982.

Christensen, B. R., *The Programming Language COMAL (Denmark),* International World of Computer Education, 1, No. 8, April 1975.

Osterby, Tom, *COMAL 80 (Nucleus) Definition,* Technical University of Denmark, March, 1980.

FORTH

Baker, Linda, and Mitch Derick, *Pocket Guide to FORTH,* Reading, MA: Addison-Wesley, 1983.

Brodie, Leo, *Starting FORTH: An Introduction to the FORTH Language,* Englewood Cliffs, NJ: Prentice-Hall, 1981.

Chirlian, Paul, *Beginning FORTH,* Beaverton, OR: Matrix, 1983.

McCabe, C. Kevin, *FORTH Fundamentals, Language Usage,* Beaverton, OR: Dilithium Press, 1983.

----------------, *FORTH Fundamentals, Language Glossary,* Beaverton, OR: Dilithium Press, 1983.

Oakey, Steve, *FORTH For Micros,* Woburn, MA: Focal Press, 1984.

FORTRAN

Alcock, Donald, *Illustrating FORTRAN,* New York: Cambridge University Press, 1983.

Anderson, D. M., *Basic Computer Programming: IBM 1620 FORTRAN,* New York: Appleton-Century-Crofts, 1964.

Coan, James S., *Basic FORTRAN,* Hasbrouck Heights, NJ: Hayden, 1980.

Lewis, William E., *Problem-Solving Principles for Fortran Programmers,* Hasbrouck Heights, NJ: Hayden, 1983.

Ludwig, Herbert R., *Understanding FORTRAN,* Sherman Oaks, CA: Alfred, 1981.

McCracken, D. D., *A Guide to FORTRAN Programming,* New York: John Wiley & Sons, 1961.

Ridler, Philip, *Pocket Guide to FORTRAN,* Reading, MA: Addison-Wesley, 1982.

Zwass, Vladimir, *Programming in FORTRAN,* New York: Barnes and Noble, Harper & Row, 1980.

LISP

Allen, J., *Anatomy of LISP,* New York: McGraw-Hill, 1978.

Touretzky, David S., *LISP: A Gentle Introduction to Symbolic Computation,* New York: Harper & Row, 1984.

Tracton, Ken, *Programmer's Guide to LISP,* Blue Ridge, PA: TAB, 1979.

Winston, Patrick H. and Berthold K. P. Horn, *LISP,* Reading, MA: Addison-Wesley, 1981.

LOGO

Abelson, Harold, *Apple Logo,* Manchester, MO: Byte/McGraw Hill, 1982.

Bitter, Gary, *Apple Logo Primer,* Reston, VA: Reston, 1983.

Burnett, Dale, *Logo: An Introduction,* New York: Creative Computing, 1983.

Ross, Peter, *Introducing Logo,* Reading, MA: Addison-Wesley, 1983.

Thornburg, David, *Discovering Apple Logo (An Invitation to the Art and Pattern of Nature),* Reading, MA: Addison-Wesley, 1983.

Watt, Daniel, *Learning with Logo,* Peterborough, NH: Byte Books, 1984.

MODULA-2

Ogilvie, John W. L., *Modula-2 Programming,* New York: McGraw-Hill Book Company, 1985.

Wirth, Niklaus, *Programming In Modula-2,* Second Corrected Edition, Berlin: Springer-Verlag, 1983.

PASCAL

Brown, Peter, *Pascal from BASIC,* Reading, MA: Addison-Wesley, 1982.

Cooper, Doug, *Standard Pascal User Reference Manual,* New York: W. W. Norton & Co., 1983.

Eisenbach, S., and C. Sadler, *Pascal for Programmers,* New York: Springer-Verlag, 1981.

Fox, David, and Mitchell Waite, *Pascal Primer,* Indianapolis, IN: Howard W. Sams, 1981.

Jensen, Kathleen, and Niklaus Wirth, *Pascal User Manual and Report: 2nd Edition,* New York: Springer-Verlag, 1974.

Keller, Arthur, *First Course in Computer Programming Using Pascal,* New York: McGraw-Hill Book Company, 1982.

Koffman, Elliot B., *Pascal: A Problem Solving Approach,* Reading, MA: Addison-Wesley, 1982.

Ledgard, Henry F., and Andrew Singer, *Elementary Pascal,* New York: Vintage, Random House, 1982.

Liffick, Blaise W., *The Byte Book of Pascal,* Peterborough, NH: Byte Books, 1979.

Miller, Alan R., *Pascal Programs for Scientists & Engineers,* Berkeley, CA: Sybex, 1981.

Tiberghien, Jacques, *The Pascal Handbook,* Berkeley, CA: Sybex, 1981.

PILOT

Conlan, Jim, and Tracy Deliman, *ATARI PILOT for Beginners,* Reston, VA: Reston, 1983.

Conlin, Tom, *PILOT—The Language and How To Use It,* Englewood Cliffs, NJ: Prentice-Hall, 1984.

Ledin, Victor, *Understanding PILOT,* Sherman Oaks, CA: Alfred, 1984.

Starkweather, John A., *User's Guide to PILOT,* Englewood Cliffs, NJ: Prentice-Hall, 1984.

Thornburg, David D., *Picture This Too!,* Reading, MA: Addison-Wesley, 1982.

PL/I

Barbour, Edna H., *PL/I: A Self-Instruction Manual,* Toronto: Collier-MacMillan, 1970.

Grover, Gabriel F., *PL/I Programming in Technological Applications,* New York: John Wiley & Sons, 1971.

Smedley, Dan, *Programming the PL/I Way,* Blue Ridge Summit, PA: TAB Books, 1982.

PROLOG

Clark, K. L., and F. G. McCabe, *Micro-PROLOG: Programming in Logic,* Englewood Cliffs, NJ: Prentice Hall, 1984.

Clocksin, W. F., and C. S. Mellich, *Programming in Prolog,* New York: Springer-Verlag, 1981.

Ennals, Richard, *Beginning Micro-Prolog,* New York: Harper & Row, 1983.

SMALLTALK

Goldberg, Adele, and David Robson, *Smalltalk-80: The Language and its Implementation,* Reading, MA: Addison-Wesley, 1983.

---------------, *Smalltalk-80: The Interactive Programming Environment,* Reading, MA: Addison-Wesley, 1984.

Krasner, Glenn, *Smalltalk-80: Bits of History, Words of Advice,* Reading, MA: Addison-Wesley, 1983.

SOFTWARE COMMAND LANGUAGES: DBASE II

Byers, Robert A., *dBASE II for Every Business,* Culver City, CA: Ashton-Tate, 1983.

Chirlian, Barbara S., *Simply dBASE II,* Beaverton, OR: Dilithium Press, 1984.

Dinerstein, Nelson T., *dBASE II for the Programmer: A How-To-Do-It Book,* Glenview, IL: Scott,

Freedman, Alan, *dBASE II for the First Time User,* Culver City, CA: Ashton-Tate, 1984.

Foresman, 1984.

Green, Adam B., *dBASE II User's Guide,* Englewood Cliffs, NJ: Prentice-Hall, 1983.

Heiser, Paul W., *Mastering dBASE II,* Englewood Cliffs, NJ: Prentice-Hall, 1984.

Prague, Cary N., and James E. Hammit, *Programming with dBASE II,* Blue Ridge Summit, PA: TAB, 1984.

Townsend, Carl, *Using dBASE II,* New York: McGraw-Hill, 1984.

VISICALC

Bager, Barry D., and Joseph J. Sobel, *Dynamics of VisiCalc,* Homewood, IL: Dow Jones-Irwin, 1983.

Castlewitz, David M., and Lawrence Chisausky, *VisiCalc: Home and Office Companion,* Berkeley, CA: Osborne/McGraw-Hill, 1982.

Hergert, Douglas, *Mastering VisiCalc,* Berkeley, CA: Sybex, 1983.

Klitner, Carol, and Matthew J. Plociak, *Using VisiCalc: Getting Down to Business,* New York: John Wiley & Sons, 1983.

Trost, Stanley, *Doing Business with VisiCalc,* Berkeley, CA: Sybex, 1982.

SUPERCALC

Cobb, Douglas Ford, and Gena Berg, *SuperCalc Supermodels for Business,* Indianapolis, IN: Que, 1983.

Flast, Robert H. *Fifty-four SuperCalc Models: Finance, Statistics, Mathematics,* Berkeley, CA: Osborne/McGraw-Hill, 1983.

Smithy-Willis, Deborah, and Jerry Willis, *How to Use SuperCalc,* Beaverton, OR: Dilithium Press, 1982.

Tymes, Elna, and Peter Antoniak, *SuperCalc: Home and Office Companion,* Berkeley, CA: Osborne/McGraw-Hill, 1983.

Williams, Robert, and Bruce Taylor, *Power of Supercalc,* Englewood Cliffs, NJ: Prentice-Hall, 1982.

MULTIPLAN

Alves, Jeffrey R., and Michael Selva, *Controlling Financial Performance with MultiPlan: A MultiPlan Business User's Guide,* Somerville, MA: Curtin & London, 1984.

Cobb, Douglas, and Gena and Thomas Henderson, *MultiPlan Models for Business,* Indianapolis, IN: Que, 1983.

Osgood, William R., and James F. Malloy Jr., *Business Decision Making for Higher Profits: A MultiPlan Business User's Guide,* Somerville, MA: Curtin & London, 1984.

LOTUS 1-2-3

Baras, Edward M., *Guide to Using Lotus 1-2-3,* Berkeley, CA: Osborne/McGraw-Hill, 1984.

Osgood, William R., and James F. Malloy, Jr., *Business Decisions for Higher Profits: A 1-2-3 Business User's Guide,* Somerville, MA: Curtin & London, 1984.

Schware, Robert, and Alice Trembour, *All About 1-2-3,* Beaverton, OR: Dilithium Press, 1983.

Simpson, Alan, *The Best Book of: Lotus 1-2-3,* Indianapolis, IN: Howard W. Sams, 1984.

Weber Systems, Inc. Staff, *Lotus 1-2-3 User's Handbook,* Chesterfield, OH: Weber Systems, 1984.

FRAMEWORK

Forefront Corporation, *Framework: A Programmer's Reference,* Culver City, CA: Ashton-Tate, 1984.

Harrison, Bill, *Framework: An Introduction,* Culver City, CA: Ashton-Tate, 1984.

6
Operating Systems Directory

UNIX

Brown, P. J., *Starting With Unix,* Reading, MA: Addison-Wesley, 1984.

Halamka, John D., *Real World Unix,* Berkeley, CA: Sybex, 1984.

Kernighan, Brian W., and Rob Pike, *The Unix Programming Environment,* Englewood Cliffs, NJ: Prentice-Hall, 1984.

McGilton, Henry, and Rachel Morgan, *Introducing the Unix System,* Peterborough, NH: Byte Books, 1983.

Yates, Jean L., and Sandra L. Emerson, *The Business Guide to the Unix System,* Reading, MA: Addison-Wesley, 1984.

MS-DOS

DeVoney, Chris, *MS-DOS User's Guide,* Indianapolis, IN: Que Corporation, 1984.

Hoffman, Paul, and Tamara Nicoloff, *MS-DOS User's Guide,* Berkeley, CA: Osborne/McGraw-Hill, 1984.

Townsend, Carl, *How to Get Started With MS-DOS,* Beaverton, OR: Dilithium Press, 1983.

Waite, Mitchell, *The DOS Primer,* New York: NAL, 1983.

Woverton, Van, *Running MS-DOS,* Bellevue, WA: Microsoft Press, 1984.

COMMODORE DOS

Commodore Business Machines, *Commodore 64 Programmer's Reference Guide,* Indianapolis, IN: Howard W. Sams, 1983.

Osborne, Adam, and Carroll S. Donahue, *PET/CBM Personal Computer Guide,* 2nd edition, Berkeley, CA: Osborne/McGraw-Hill, 1980.

West, Raeto Collins, *Programming the PET/CBM,* Greensboro, NC: Compute! Books, 1982.

CP/M

Fernandez, Judi N., and Ruth Ashley, *Using CP/M: A Self-Teaching Guide,* New York: John Wiley & Sons, 1980.

Hogan, Thom, *Osborne/McGraw-Hill CP/M User's Guide: Third Edition,* Berkeley, CA: Osborne/ McGraw-Hill, 1984.

Johnson-Laird, Andy, *The Programmer's CP/M Handbook,* Berkeley, CA: Osborne-McGraw-Hill, 1983.

Libes, Sol, *Programmer's Guide to CP/M,* New York: Microsystems Press, 1982.

Waite Mitchell, and Robert Lafore, *Soul of CP/M,* Indianapolis, IN: Howard W. Sams, 1983.

APPLE DOS 3.3

Miller, David, *Apple Files,* Reston, VA: Reston, 1982.

Sanders, William B., *The Elementary Apple,* Chatsworth, CA: Datamost, 1983.

Wintermeyer, Larry G., *Applesoft Basic Toolbox,* Reading, MA: Addison-Wesley, 1984.

Worth, Don, and Peter Lechner, *Beneath Apple Dos,* Reseda, CA: Quality Software, 1981.

PRODOS

Campbell, John, *Inside Apple's ProDOS,* Reston, VA: Reston, 1984.

OBrien, Bill, *The Apple IIc Book, New York: Bantam Books,* 1984.

TRS-DOS

Favour, James L., *TRSDOS 2.3 Decoded and Other Mysteries,* TRS-80 Information Series, Upland, CA: IJG, 1982.

MACINTOSH OPERATING SYSTEM

Dayton, Rick, *Understanding the Macintosh Computer,* Reston, VA: Reston, 1984.

Duff, Charles B., *Introducing the Macintosh,* Peterborough, NH: Byte Books, 1984.

Poole, Lon, *Mac Work Mac Play,* Bellevue, WA: MicroSoft Press, 1984.

7
Microcomputer Systems Hardware

Horowitz, Paul, and Winfield Hill, *The Art of Electronics,* Cambridge, MA: Cambridge University Press, 1980.

Mims, Forest M., *Understanding Digital Computers,* Ft. Worth, TX: Tandy/Radio Shack, 1978.

Osborne, Adam, *An Introduction to Microcomputers,* Berkeley, CA: Osborne/McGraw-Hill, 1979.

Pooch, Udo W., and Rahul Chattergy, *Designing Microcomputer Systems,* Hasbrouck Heights, NJ: Hayden, 1979.

Radio Shack, *Understanding Digital Electronics,* Ft. Worth, TX: Tandy Corp., 1978.

8
Major PC Products: Markets and Specifications

IBM PC AND COMPATIBLES

Abel, Peter, *Assembler for the IBM PC and PC-XT,* Reston, VA: Reston, 1984.

Bane, Michael, *The IBM PC User's Guide,* New York: MacMillan, 1983.

Derfler, Frank J., and the Editors of InfoWorld, *Infoworld's Essential Guide to the IBM PC,* New York: Harper & Row, 1984.

Enders, Bernard, and Bob Peterson, *Basic Primer for the IBM PC,* New York: Plume/NAL 1984.

Fabbri, Tony, *Animation, Games and Sound for the IBM PC,* Englewood Cliffs, NJ: Prentice-Hall, 1983.

Hildebrand, George H., *Business Program Portfolio for Your IBM PC,* Hasbrouck Heights, NJ: Hayden, 1984.

Jordan, Larry E., and Bruce Churchill, *Communications and Networking for the IBM PC,* Bowie, MD: Robert J. Brady, 1983.

Kelley, James E., Jr., *The IBM/PC Guide,* New York: Banbury, 1983.

King, Richard Allen, *The IBM PC-DOS Handbook,* Berkeley, CA: Sybex, 1983.

Lafore, Robert, *Assembly Language Primer for the IBM PC and XT,* New York: Plume/NAL, 1984.

Trost, Stanley R., *The Best of IBM PC Software,* Berkeley, CA: Sybex, 1984.

APPLE II

Banse, Timothy P., *Home Applications and Games for the Apple II+ and IIe,* Boston: Little, Brown, 1983.

Barnett, Michael P., and K. Graham, *Personal Graphics for Profit and Pleasure on Apple II+,* Boston: Little, Brown, 1983.

DeJong, Marvin L., *Apple II Assembly Language,* Indianapolis, IN: Howard W. Sams, 1982.

Hergert, Douglas, *The Apple II Basic Handbook,* Berkeley, CA: Sybex, 1983.

Kascmer, Joseph, *The Easy Guide to Your Apple II,* Berkeley, CA: Sybex, 1983.

Peckham, Herbert, *Hands-on BASIC for the Apple II,* New York: McGraw-Hill, 1983.

Phillips, Gary, and Donald Scellato, *Apple IIc User Guide,* Englewood Cliffs, NJ: Prentice-Hall, 1984.

Poole, Lon, *Apple II User's Guide: For Apple II Plus Apple IIe,* Berkeley, CA: Osborne/McGraw-Hill, 1983.

Vile, Richard C., Jr., *Apple ll Programmer's Handbook,* Englewood Cliffs, NJ: Prentice-Hall, 1982.

Winter, M. J., *Computer Playground on the Apple II, II+, IIe,* Chatsworth, CA: Datamost, 1982.

APPLE MACINTOSH

Clapp, Doug, *Macintosh! Complete,* North Hollywood, CA: Softalk, 1984.

Connolly, Edward S., and Phillip Lieberman, *Introducing the Apple Macintosh,* Indianapolis, IN: Howard W. Sams,1984.

Dayton, Rick, *Understanding the Macintosh Computer,* Reston, VA: Reston, 1984.

Holtz, Frederick, *Using and Programmming the Macintosh,* Blue Ridge Summit, PA: TAB, 1984.

Lu, Cary, *The Apple Macintosh Book,* Bellevue, WA: Microsoft Press, 1984.

Miller, Merl K., and Mary A. Myers, *Presenting the Macintosh,* Beaverton, OR: Dilithium Press, 1984.

Poole, Lon, *Mac Work Mac Play,* Bellevue, WA: Microsoft Press, 1984.

Sanders, William B., *The Apple Macintosh Primer,* Chatsworth, CA: Datamost, 1984.

TRS-80

Berlin, Howard M., *Circuit Design Programs for the TRS-80,* Indianapolis, IN: Howard W. Sams, 1980.

DaCosta, Frank, *Writing BASIC Adventure Programs for the TRS-80,* Blue Ridge Summit, PA: TAB, 1982.

Frank, Ed, *How To Write a TRS-80 Program,* Chatsworth, CA: Datamost, 1982.

Gratzner, George A., *Fast BASIC: Beyond TRS-80 Basic,* New York: John Wiley & Sons, 1982.

Heiserman, David L., *Intermediate Programming for the TRS-80 Model 1,* Indianapolis, IN: Howard W. Sams, 1982.

Kater, David A., and Susan J. Thomas, *TRS-80 Graphics: For the Model I and Model III,* Peterborough, NH: Byte Books, 1982.

Klitsz, Dennis Bathory, *Custom TRS-80 & Other Mysteries,* TRS Information System Vol. II, Upland, CA: IJG, 1982.

Lien, David A., *Learning TRS-80 Model 4/4P BASIC,* El Cajon, CA: CompuSoft Publishing, 1984.

Lien, David A., *Learning TRS-80 Model III BASIC,* El Cajon, CA: CompuSoft Publishing, 1984.

Rosenfelder, Lewis, *BASIC Faster and Better & Other Mysteries,* TRS-80 Information Series, Vol. IV, Upland, CA: IJG, 1981.

TRS-80 COLOR COMPUTER

Albrecht, Robert L., *TRS-80 Color BASIC,* New York: John Wiley & Sons, 1982.

Clark, Ron, *TRS-80 Color Computer Program Writing Workbook,* Woodboro, MD: Arcsoft, 1983.

Mosher, Doug, *Your Color Computer,* Berkeley, CA: Sybex, 1984.

Regena, C., *Programmer's Reference Guide to the Color Computer,* Greensboro, N.C.: Compute! Books, 1984.

COMMODORE PET, VIC 20, AND C64

Banse, Timothy P., *Home Applications and Games for the VIC-20,* Boston: Little, Brown, 1983.

Bush, Derek, and Peter Holmes, *Commodore 64 Assembly Language Programming,* Hasbrouck Heights, NJ: Hayden, 1984.

Coan, James S., *Basic Commodore 64 BASIC,* Hasbrouck Heights, NJ: Hayden, 1984.

Commodore Business Machines, *Commodore 64 Programmer's Reference Guide,* Indianapolis, IN: Howard W. Sams, 1982.

Commodore Business Machines, Inc., Software Group, *Commodore Software Encyclopedia: Third Edition,* Indianapolis, IN: Howard W. Sams, 1983.

COMPUTE!, *COMPUTE!'s First Book of PET/CBM,* Greensboro, NC: Compute! Books, 1981.

Davies, Russ, *Mapping the VIC,* Greensboro, NC: Compute! Books, 1984.

Foley, Matthew J., *PET for the Beginning Beginner,* San Jose, CA: Enrich, 1983.

Goldstein, Larry Joel, and Fred Mosher, *Commodore 64 BASIC Programming and Applications,* Bowie, MD: Robert J. Brady, 1984.

Hartnell, Tim, *Getting Acquainted with your VIC 20,* New York: Creative Computing, 1981.

Haskell, Richard, and Thomas Windeknecht, *Commodore 64/VIC 20 BASIC,* Englewood Cliffs, NJ: Prentice-Hall, 1984.

Klein, Mike Dean, *The Commodore 64 Experience,* Chatsworth, CA: Datamost, 1983.

Kreutner, Donald C., *Commodore 64 Favorite Programs Explained,* Indianapolis, IN: Que, 1983.

Ramshaw, Clifford, *VIC Innovative Computing,* New York: Melbourne House, 1982.

Skier, Ken, *Top-Down Assembly Language Programming: For Your VIC-20 and Commodre 64,* Peterborough, NH: Byte Books, 1984.

West, Raeto Collin, *Programming the PET/CBM,* Greensboro, NC: Compute! Book, 1983.

CP/M COMPUTERS

Dennon, Jack D., *CP/M Revealed,* Hasbrouck Heights, NJ: Hayden, 1982.

Dwyer, Thomas A., and Margo Critchfield, *CP/M & the Personal Computer,* Reading, MA: Addison-Wesley, 1983.

Miller, Alan R., *Best of CP/M Software,* Berkeley, CA: Sybex, 1983.

Murtha, Stephen M., and Mitchell Waite, *CP/M Primer,* Indianapolis, IN: Howard W. Sams, 1983.

Waite, Mitchell, *CP/M Bible: The Authoritative Reference Guide to CP/M,* Indianapolis, IN: Howard W. Sams, 1983.

Weber, Jeffrey, *CP/M Simplified,* Chesterland, OH: Weber Systems, 1982.

Zaks, Rodnay, *The CP/M Handbook with MP/M,* Berkeley, CA: Sybex, 1980.

Index of
High-Level Language
Keywords

The index to high-level language keywords is a cross-reference to some of the programming languages in the Encyclopedia. This index can be used in a variety of ways. First, it is an effective translation table between the high-level languages and between language dialects. The page references beneath each keyword indicate what language contains the keyword and on what page the definition of the word can be found for each language. Therefore, if a programmer wants to translate the DATA statement in BASIC into Fortran, he or she simply looks under the DATA citation in this index to see if DATA is also a Fortran keyword.

Programmers can also look for general occurrences of the keyword under each citation and for different instances of the keyword in neighboring citations. For example, readers who want to translate the DIM statement in BASIC or COMAL into the corresponding statement in Fortran or PL/I can look either in the Fortran or PL/I glossaries for the translation, or they can look in this index for the neighborhood citation where they will find the DIMENSION statement with page references to the Fortran and PL/I glossaries underneath.

Finally, the index to high-level languages keywords is a general page index to all of the language glossaries. If a keyword is cited in one of the glossaries, it will be listed alphabetically in this index. The index, however, does not cite APL and SAM76 symbols. Readers who are looking for symbols or special characters, specifically in APL and SAM76, should refer to the APL and SAM76 glossary.

DATA—*cont.*
    COMAL 324
    Fortran 354
    Lotus 1-2-3 445-6
    ZBASIC 286

Data Assembly Commands
    SuperCalc 438

DATA DIVISION
    COBOL 417

Data Protection Commands
    SuperCalc 438

DATE
    COBOL 417
    PL/I 383

@DATE
    FRED 452

@DATE1
    FRED 452

@DATE2
    FRED 452

@DATE3
    FRED 452

@DATE4
    FRED 452

DATE-COMPILED
    COBOL 317

@DATE-TIME
    FRED 453

DATES
    ZBASIC 286

DATE-WRITTEN
    COBOL 317

@DBASEFILTER
    FRED 453

DEBUG
    RPG 397

DECIMAL
    Forth 335
    PC Forth 343
    PL/I 364

@DECIMAL
    FRED 455

DECLARATION
    Ada 239

DECLARATIVE PART
    Ada 239

DECLARE
    PL/I 383

DEC(x,n)
    Modula-2 369

decrement operator
    C 310

DEF
    BASIC 260
    Compiled BASIC 293

DEFDBL
    BASIC 260
    ZBASIC 286

DEF FN
    Applesoft BASIC 301
    ZBASIC 286

Defining Words
    PC Forth 347-8

DEFINITION
    Modula-2 369-70

DEFINITIONS
    Forth 335
    PC Forth 346

DEFINT
    BASIC 260
    ZBASIC 287

DEFMARCO
    LISP 360

DEFSEG
    ZBASIC 287

DEFSNG
    BASIC 260

DEFSTR
    BASIC 260
    LISP 360
    ZBASIC 287

DEFUN
    LISP 360

DEF USR
    ZBASIC 287

DEG
    Atari BASIC 303
    BASIC 260

delete
    Prolog 384

DELETE
    BASIC 260-1
    dBASE II 423
    MultiPlan 440

DELETE FILE < >
    dBASE II 423

DELIMITED
    COBOL 317

DENOTE
    Ada 239

DEPENDENCE RELATION
    Ada 239

DEPENDING
    COBOL 317

DEPTH
    Forth 335
    PC Forth 341

DERIVED TYPE
    Ada 234

DESIGNATE
    Ada 234

DET
    BASIC 261

DICTIONARY
    Smalltalk 412-3

Dictionary Related Functions
    PC Forth 346

@DIFFDATE
    FRED 453

DIGIT
    PC Forth 343

DIGITS
    BASIC 261

DIM
    Applesoft BASIC 301
    BASIC 261
    Compiled BASIC 293
    COMAL 324
    ZBASIC 287

DIMENSION
    Fortran 354
    PL/I 384

ELSE—*cont.*
    Modula-2 370
    Pascal 375
    PC Forth 345

ELSE IF
    Modula-2 370

EMIT
    Forth 335
    PC Forth 344

EMPTY-BUFFERS
    PC Forth 344

END
    Algol 246
    BASIC 261
    Compiled BASIC 393
    Fortran 354
    Logo 364
    Modula-2 370
    Pascal 375
    Pilot 376
    PL/I 384
    ZBASIC 287

END?
    PC Forth 349

ENDCASE
    COMAL 334

END-CODE
    PC Forth 347

ENDFILE
    Fortran 354

ENDIF
    COMAL 324

ENDPROC
    COMAL 324

ENDSR
    RPG 397

ENDWHILE
    Fortran 354

ENTER
    Atari BASIC 303

ENTITY
    Ada 239

ENTRY
    Ada 239
    Fortran 254
    PC Forth 349
    PL/I 384

ENUMERATING TYPE
    Ada 239

ENVIRONMENT
    PL/I 384

ENVIRONMENT DIVISION
    COBOL 317

EOF
    Pilot 386
    ZBASIC 287

EOL
    Modula-2 370

EQ
    BASIC 261

EQL
    LISP 360

EQUAL
    LISP 360

equality operator
    C 310

EQUIVALENCE
    Fortran 354

EQV
    S-BASIC 298

ERASE
    BASIC 261
    dBASE II 424
    PC Forth 344
    RPG 397

ERASE(ER)
    Logo 364

ERASEFILE
    Logo 364

ERASEPICT
    Logo 346

@ERASEPROMPT
    FRED 455

ERL
    ZBASIC 287

ERR
    BASIC 261
    ZBASIC 287

ERROR
    BASIC 261

@ERROR
    VisiCalc 434

ERROR, NA
    SuperCalc 437

ESAC
    Algol 246

ESTABLISH
    PC Forth 345

EVAL
    LISP 360

EXAM
    BASIC 262

EXCEPTION
    Ada 239

EXCHANGE
    BASIC 262

EXCL (x,n)
    Modula-2 370

EXCPT
    RPG 397

EXEC
    COMAL 324

EXECUTE
    Forth 335
    PC Forth 346
    S-BASIC 299

@EXECUTE
    FRED 452

Execution Control
    PC Forth 346

EXIT
    BASIC 262
    C 310
    COBOL 318
    Forth 335
    Modula-2 370
    PC Forth 345
    RPG 397

EXP
    Applesoft BASIC 301
    BASIC 262
    Compiled BASIC 293
    COMAL 324
    Modula-2 370
    PL/I 384
    SuperCalc 437
    ZBASIC 287

/V
VisiCalc 435

VAL
Applesoft BASIC 302
Compiled BASIC 295
MBASIC 285
Modula-2 371
ZBASIC 291

VALUE
COBOL 321
MultiPlan 442

VALUE ENTRY
VisiCalc 434

VAR
Modula-2 371
S-BASIC 299

@VAR
FRED 455

VARIABLE
Ada 243
Forth 338
PC Forth 347
PL/I 386

2VARIABLE
PC Forth 347

VARIANT
Ada 243

VARIATION SET
Ada 243

VARPTR
Compiled BASIC 295
MBASIC 285
ZBASIC 291

VARPTR#n
ZBASIC 291

VARYING
COBOL 321
PL/I 386

VERIFY
PL/I 386

VIEW
PC Forth 345

Virtual Memory Disk I/O
PC Forth 344

VISIBILITY
Ada 243

VISIBLE PORT
Ada 243

@VLOOKUP
FRED 455

VOCABULARY
Forth 338
PC Forth 348

VOC-LINK
PC Forth 349

VOCS
PC Forth 346

#VOCS
PC Forth 348

VOLUME
PC Forth 349

/W
SuperCalc 438
VisiCalc 435

WAIT
Applesoft BASIC 302
dBASE II 431
Pilot 380

WAIT X...WEND
ZBASIC 291

WARM
PC Forth 348

WARNING
PC Forth 350

WEND
Compiled BASIC 295

WHEN
COBOL 321
COMAL 325

WHILE
Algol 246
Compiled BASIC 295
COMAL 325
Forth 338
MBASIC 285
Modula-2 371
Pascal 376
PC Forth 346
ZBASIC 291

while
C 314

@WHILE
FRED 456

WHILE...DO
Fortran 355

WIDTH
ZBASIC 291

WINDOW
Lotus 1-2-3 444
MultiPlan 442

WITH
Modula-2 372

WITH CLAUSE
Ada 243

WORD
Forth 338
Modula-2 371
PC Forth 348

WORDS
PC Forth 346

WORKING-STORAGE SECTION
COBOL 321

WORKSHEET
Lotus 1-2-3 444

Worksheet Adjustment Commands
SuperCalc 438

WORKSTN
RPG 399

WRAP
Logo 366

WRITE
COBOL 321
Fortran 355

Index

Abelson, Harold, turtle geometry 101
Abbreviations, SAM76 402
Abort 130
Abstraction property, Smalltalk 406, 407
ACCEPT, Pilot 377-8
Access time 130
Accumulator, microprocessor 164
ACKnowledge, Centronics 529
Active high 130
Active low 130
Ada
    advantages 235-6
    code 236
    compilers 237-8
    glossary 238-43
Ada Validation Office 235-6
Address 130, 147
Address bus 130, 509
Addressing mode 130
Addressing modes, microprocessor
    direct 144
    extended 144
    immediate 143-4
    INC 143
    indexed 144
    register or accumulator 143
    register indirect 144-5
    relative 144
Addressing modes, operating systems
    Intel 8086 202
    Intel 8088 196
    MOS Technology 6502 188
    Motorola MC6800 181
    Motorola MC6809 185
    Motorola MC68000 217
    National Semiconductor NSC800 175
    TMS 9900 191
    Zilog Z80 172

Zilog Z8001 205
Zilog Z8002 214
Addressing space 130
Advisory systems, microcomputer
    expert systems 97-8
    See also ESP/Advisor
AI (artificial intelligence)
    automatic programming 104-5
    common sense problem 108-9
    creative arts 106-7
    frames 87
    games 81-2
    heuristic search 82-3
    Japan, Fifth Generation Project 107-8
    knowledge representation 83-7
    languages 30-1, 278, 387
    machine learning 102-3
    natural language interface 233
    natural language processing 88-9
    networks 92-3
    parallel architecture 107
    pattern recognition 103
    research 102-4, 107-9
    robotics 103-4
    semantic grammar 93
    semantic primitives 93-4
    space technology 105-6
    template matching 89-92
    turtle geometry 101-2
AL, robot programming language 126
Algebraic operations order
    calculations 24
Algol 244
    glossary, 245-7
    robot programming 126
Algorithmic languages 30
Algorithms
    AI heuristic searches 82, 83
    B* tree search 83

Alphabetizing, sort routine 21-2
ALU (arithmetic/logic unit) 131, 164
Analog I/O 508
Analogy, AI machine learning 102
ANGL command, pie chart 76
Altair computer, 228
APL 248
    array (vector and matrix) operators 252
    arithmetic operators 250
    boolean operators 251
    decode and encode 254
    glossary 250
    mathematical functions 251
    permutation functions 255
    relational operators 250
    set operation functions 254
    sorting functions 253
    trigonometric and inverse
        trigonometric functions 251
Apple, company growth 539-41
Apple computers 37, 78, 458-9
    See also LISA, Macintosh
Apple DOS operating system 458
Apple DOS 3.3 and Applesoft BASIC 482-3
Apple Macintosh specifications 552
Apple II family specifications 551
Apple II series, Logo glossary 363-4
Applesoft BASIC, glossary 301-2
Applesoft DOS 3.3 and glossary 482-3
ARAMIS project, NASA Study Group 105
Architecture 131
    AI, parallel 107
    UNIX 460, 462
Arithmetic and Logical Instructions
    Intel 8080A 166-7
    Intel 8085 166-7

DATE DUE

MAY 3 '91			
DISCHARGED			

DEMCO NO. 38-298